Better communication.

Better teamwork.

Better performance.

Better planning.

Better management.

Better service.

Better profits.

Better integration.

Better productivity.

Better ideas.

Better results.

Better outlook.

A better return on information. It's what makes better companies.

SAP gives you more than better software. We give you a better return on information.

We do that with business applications that integrate your company and streamline

your processes. And that means everything from increased efficiency and

productivity to increased revenues and profits. In short, it means

a better company. And, so far, SAP has helped over 7,000

companies in 50 countries become just that. To find

out what a better return on information

can do for you, visit us at http://

www.sap.com, or call

1-800-283-

1SAP.

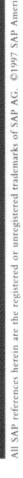

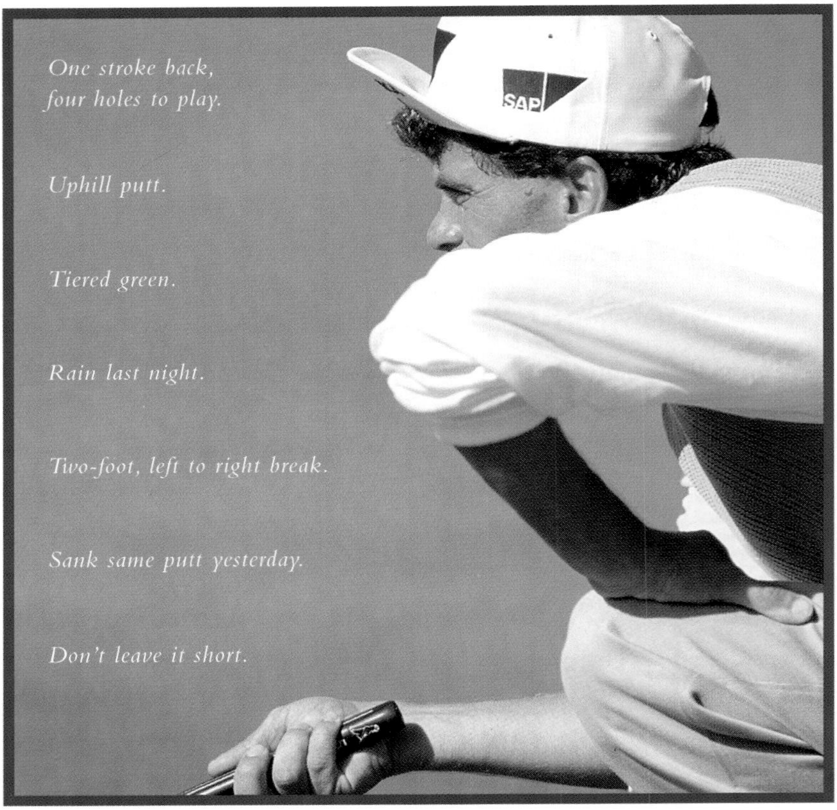
One stroke back,
four holes to play.
Uphill putt.
Tiered green.
Rain last night.
Two-foot, left to right break.
Sank same putt yesterday.
Don't leave it short.
SAP

Good results start with good information. Just ask PGA Tour golfer Jesper Parnevik.

Knowing when the par 5 is reachable in two, or if conditions have softened the greens,

can make all the difference. For Jesper, it means a career year in 1997, record

earnings and a lot of questions about his unusual hat. You can get the same

success for your company by looking at the name printed on the hat.

SAP's R/3 client/server software gives over 7,000 companies a

better return on information, making them faster,

smarter and more efficient. And just like Jesper,

that's helped take them right to the top

of the leader board. For more

information, visit us at http://

www.sap.com, or call

1-800-283-

1SAP.

Proud Sponsor of Jesper Parnevik.

DEDICATION

To Peter Dobereiner

The last of the great British writers who defined golf for the English-speaking world after World War II. He was rightfully called the most rounded, most civilized, most erudite man ever to inhabit a press tent.

A Better Return On Information.[SM]

PRESENTS

The World of Professional Golf 1997

Mark H. McCormack

An IMG PUBLISHING Book

An IMG PUBLISHING Book

All rights reserved
First published 1997
© IMG Operations, Inc. 1997

Designed and produced by Davis Design

ISBN 1-878843-17-6

Printed and bound in the United States of America.

Contents

1. The Sony Ranking

Golfers from the United States have always dominated the top 50 of the Sony Ranking, if not the top 10 positions, and in 1996 the Americans were poised to take over the leading roles as well. At the year's end there were five Americans ranked in the top 10 in contrast to just two in 1994 and 1995.

Greg Norman of Australia remained No. 1 through 1996, ending the year with a record 84 successive weeks at the fore, three weeks more than Nick Faldo held that position in 1992-94. British Open champion Tom Lehman rose from No. 11 to No. 2 during the year, following by Colin Montgomerie of Scotland and Ernie Els of South Africa.

Fred Couples, the only American ever to be ranked No. 1 (during 1992), finished the year as No. 5, then came Faldo of England, Phil Mickelson, Masashi (Jumbo) Ozaki of Japan, Davis Love III and Mark O'Meara.

Further evidence of the American surge could be seen in the U.S. PGA Tour money list, where all 10 leading positions were occupied by Americans, compared with seven in 1994 and 1995, and in the results of the four major championships. American players won six of the eight major titles in 1994 and 1995, compared to just seven of the 20 major titles from 1990 to 1994.

While Norman was able to hold onto the Sony Ranking No. 1 position despite an indifferent year by his standards, there could be a strong challenge to his lead in 1997. Norman experienced a net loss of Sony Ranking points in 1996, as did the other four in the top five of the final 1995 list, only one of whom was an American: Nick Price of Zimbabwe (No. 2 to No. 13), Els (No. 3 to No. 4), Bernhard Langer of Germany (No. 4 to No. 16) and Corey Pavin (No. 5 to No. 11).

There was an encouraging trend for the Europeans too, with a new wave of promising young players who began to make an impact in 1996, all placing in the top 15 of the PGA European Tour money list and climbing well on the Sony Ranking: Lee Westwood (No. 258 to No. 64), Andrew Coltart (No. 118 to No. 71), Padraig Harrington (unranked to No. 95), Thomas Bjorn (unranked to No. 109) and Raymond Russell (unranked to No. 146).

Whenever the Sony Ranking is brought into question, usually the high ranking of Ozaki is mentioned. But guess who was No. 1 (compared to his No. 8 position on the Sony Ranking) when the first International Money List was compiled by the PGA Tours International Federation? Ozaki, of course, with $1,944,034 from the official 1996 money lists of the U.S. PGA Tour, PGA European Tour, Australasian Tour, Japan PGA Tour and FNB Tour of Southern Africa.

Ozaki led the Japan PGA Tour money list for the third successive year, a period in which he has accumulated 20 victories. He remained the only Japanese golfer in the top 50 of the Sony Ranking. Shigeki Maruyama, ranked No. 56, was next.

As most people know by now, the Sony Ranking is a specially developed computerized method of evaluating the relative performances of the world's leading players. The Sony Ranking is sanctioned by the Championship

Committee of the Royal and Ancient Golf Club of St. Andrews, and is endorsed by the major professional tours.

Some of the most respected people in golf worldwide bring their opinions to bear on the workings of the system. The Sony Ranking Advisory Committee meets at St. Andrews each October, and its recommendations are passed on to the R&A for approval. In addition to myself, the Sony Ranking Advisory Committee consists of:

Brenda Blumberg (advisor to South African PGA), Tim Finchem (U.S. PGA Tour), Taizo Kawata (Japan Golf Association), Kosaku Shimada (PGA of Japan), Colin Phillips (Australian Golf Union), Richard Rahusen (European Golf Association), Pat Rielly (PGA of America), Ken Schofield (PGA European Tour), Frank Tatum (past president, United States Golf Association), Colin Maclaine (past captain and chairman of the Championship Committee of the R&A), and Peter Townsend (PGA European Tour Policy Board).

All tournaments from the world's golf tours are taken into account and points are awarded according to the quality of the players participating in each event. The number of points distributed to each golfer is dependent upon his finishing position.

The four major championships (Masters Tournament, U.S. Open, British Open and PGA Championship) and the flagship events of the major tours (The Players Championship (U.S.), Volvo PGA Championship (Europe), Japan Open and Australian Open) are weighted separately to reflect the greater prestige of the events and strong fields participating.

The Sony Ranking system is based on a two-year "rolling" average weighted in favor of more recent results, with the points accumulated in the most recent 52-week period doubled.

Each player is ranked according to his average points per tournament, which is determined by dividing his total number of points by the number of tournaments he has played over that two-year period. There is a minimum requirement of 20 tournaments for each 52-week period. For example, if a player were in 32 tournaments in the most recent 52 weeks and 15 tournaments in the previous 52 weeks, his divisor would be 52 (32 plus 20). A player who was in 32 tournaments in each year would have a divisor of 64 (32 plus 32).

The winners of the major championships are awarded 50 points (doubled to 100 points in the current year) and the winner of The Players Championship is awarded 40 points (80 points in the current year), which is also the most points possible to be earned from winning any other tournament in the world. The winner of a tournament with a relatively strong field would probably receive approximately 25 to 30 points (50 to 60 points in the current year).

Minimum points for the winners of official tour events have been set at six points for Asia and South Africa, eight points for Australasia and Japan, and 10 points for Europe and the United States. In addition, the Volvo PGA Championship in Europe has a minimum of 32 points for the winner, and the Open Championships of Australia and Japan have a minimum of 16 points for the winner (minimum points doubled in the current year). Points are reduced proportionately for tournaments reduced to 36 or 54 holes because of inclement weather or other reasons.

Points to be awarded above the minimum levels for these events are determined by the strength of field. This is determined by the number and ranking of players in the tournaments who are among the top 100 golfers on the Sony Ranking. Each player ranked in the top 100 of the Sony Ranking is assigned "ratings points" ranging from 50 points for the No. 1 player, then down to two points each for those ranked 81st to 100th.

The total of the ratings points is then applied to the table on pages 8 and 9 to adjust the Sony Ranking points to reflect the quality of the field.

As a by-product, the Sony Ranking system is able to identify the strongest tournaments in the world. Many tournament organizers use the Sony Ranking to determine qualifiers or as a basis for issuing invitations.

Following were the highest-rated tournaments in the world for 1996:

	Event	No. of Sony Ranked Players Participating					Sony Rating Points
		Top 5	Top 15	Top 30	Top 50	Top 100	
1	PGA Championship	5	15	30	48	81	762
2	British Open	5	13	27	43	74	699
3	The Players Championship	5	13	28	44	70	683
4	Masters Tournament	5	14	29	43	70	681
5	U.S. Open Championship	4	13	28	40	67	645
6	Bay Hill Invitational	4	11	21	31	50	525
7	Doral-Ryder Open	4	11	20	30	49	507
8	Motorola Western Open	3	9	20	30	56	505
9	Memorial Tournament	2	9	20	32	60	504
10	Sprint International	4	10	18	28	54	487
11	MasterCard Colonial	3	8	16	28	48	424
12	MCI Classic	4	8	15	27	40	421
13	Tour Championship	4	10	21	28	30	419
14	NEC World Series of Golf	4	9	16	22	35	382
15	AT&T Pebble Beach Pro-Am	1	6	16	27	44	377
16	GTE Byron Nelson Classic	2	7	13	25	41	365
17	Buick Classic	4	7	16	21	32	363
18	BellSouth Classic	4	5	13	23	33	338
19	Bell Canadian Open	2	7	13	21	37	325
20	Buick Invitational	-	5	13	23	37	311
21	Mercedes Championship	2	6	15	19	27	304
22	Buick Open	2	6	9	18	37	295
22	Honda Classic	3	5	12	18	26	295
24	Buick Challenge	-	4	12	20	42	294
25	Las Vegas Invitational	-	3	8	21	40	286
26	Phoenix Open	-	3	9	20	39	274
27	Walt Disney/Oldsmobile Classic	-	3	8	19	36	250
28	Nissan Open	-	5	8	15	33	233
29	Nedbank Million Dollar Chal.	3	9	12	12	12	220
30	Greensboro Chrysler Classic	1	3	8	12	28	210

Age Groups of Top 100 Sony Ranked Players

Under 25	25-27	23-30	31-33	34-36	37-39	40-42	43-45	Over 45
					Lehman			
					Couples			
					Faldo			
					O'Meara			
					Pavin			
					Price			
					Langer			
			Montgomerie	Elkington	Woosnam			
	Els		Love	Brooks	Jones			
	Mickelson		Singh	Faxon	Stewart			
	Duval		Maggert	Perry	Tway			
	Allenby		Janzen	Nobilo	Senior			
	Furyk	Stricker	Parnevik	Calcavecchia	Sluman			
	Maruyama	Mayfair	Austin	Waldorf	Frost	Norman	McNulty	
	Stankowski	Bradley	Jimenez	Gallagher	Cook	Hoch	McCumber	
	Coltart	Tolles	Jobe	Mediate	Minoza	Roberts	Haas	
	Tanaka	Watts	Hamilton	Westner	Morse	Rocca	Torrance	
	Campbell	Parry	Ames	Kaneko	Clements	Jacobsen	Stadler	
	Cejka	Clarke	Franco	Huston	Rose	Funk	Weibring	
Leonard	Hosokawa	Johansson	Goydos	Triplett	Mize	Simpson	Crenshaw	M. Ozaki
Woods	Harrington	McGinley	O'Malley	Riley	Mitchell	N. Ozaki	Purtzer	Watson
Westwood	Herron	Daly	Turner	Lane	Ogrin	Bryant	Zoeller	Kite

As we have been predicting for several years, and as the graph above illustrates, the Seve Ballesteros-led generation of non-American golf leaders steadily is slipping from the most prominent positions on the Sony Ranking. In fact, Ballesteros, who will reach age 40 in April 1997, has already fallen from the graph, dropping to No. 110 on the Sony Ranking during 1996. On the far left is the arriving group of under-25 golfers (Justin Leonard, Tiger Woods and Westwood) and on far right is the last of the over-45 group (Ozaki, Tom Watson and Tom Kite).

The top 200 players on the Sony Ranking as of December 31, 1996 are to be found on pages 6 and 7, and in greater detail in the Appendixes. The opposite page makes note of the trends which occurred during the year.

Mickelson, with four victories in 1996 on the U.S. PGA Tour, was the leader among six Americans who made the largest upward movements within the top 50 of the Sony Ranking. Pavin was the only American among the six players who had the largest downward movements within the top 50, a group led by Langer.

Seven Americans led the march into the top 50, topped by Mark Brooks, who won the PGA Championship, and Steve Jones, the U.S. Open champion. Spaniards Jose Maria Olazabal, whose rheumatoid arthritis kept him out for the year, and Ballesteros were most prominent among those departing the top 50, a group which also included two 1995 major champions, Ben Crenshaw (Masters) and John Daly (British Open).

Woods made the fastest rise into the top 50 in the history of the Sony Ranking, climbing to No. 33 after starting the year ranked No. 509 while an amateur. Other major upward movements included those by Paul Stankowski, Westwood and Japan's Yoshinori Kaneko.

1996 Sony Ranking Review

Major Movements Within Top 50

Name	Upward Net Points Gained	Position 1995	1996	Name	Downward Net Points Lost	Position 1995	1996
Phil Mickelson	181	24	7	Bernhard Langer	327	4	16
Mark O'Meara	161	41	10	Nick Price	231	2	13
Tom Lehman	116	11	2	Greg Norman	139	1	1
Davis Love III	112	20	9	Corey Pavin	137	5	11
David Duval	80	33	19	Sam Torrance	134	14	40
Tom Watson	58	34	17	Ernie Els	127	3	4
Mark McNulty	48	43	21	Peter Jacobsen	115	15	46
Kenny Perry	46	42	25	Lee Janzen	83	17	32
Scott Hoch	40	19	15	Steve Elkington	83	9	14
Fred Couples	35	7	5	Loren Roberts	76	12	22
Frank Nobilo	31	45	31	Jim Gallagher, Jr.	70	27	45

Major Movements Into Top 50

Name	Net Points Gained	Position 1995	1996
Mark Brooks	211	99	18
Steve Jones	186	168	28
Steve Stricker	173	73	12
Tiger Woods	148	509	33
Tommy Tolles	141	329	48
Michael Bradley	119	227	44
Justin Leonard	102	54	29
Ian Woosnam	98	56	26
Jim Furyk	56	78	49
Robert Allenby	30	57	37
Bob Tway	29	52	35
Duffy Waldorf	15	63	41
Brian Watts	5	54	50

Major Movements Out of Top 50

Name	Net Points Lost	Position 1995	1996
Jose Maria Olazabal	265	13	221
Seve Ballesteros	153	22	110
Barry Lane	127	38	100
Ben Crenshaw	126	21	58
David Frost	110	25	57
Bob Estes	105	47	127
Bill Glasson	99	36	122
Michael Campbell	95	28	78
Fuzzy Zoeller	87	35	89
John Daly	73	40	91
Miguel Angel Jimenez	67	48	72
Scott Simpson	38	46	54
Craig Parry	24	39	52

Other Major Movements

Name	Upward Net Points Gained	Position 1995	1996	Name	Downward Net Points Lost	Position 1995	1996
Paul Stankowski	123	292	59	Hale Irwin	96	53	234
Lee Westwood	119	258	64	David Gilford	85	60	144
Yoshinori Kaneko	92	224	67	Anders Forsbrand	77	61	135
Tim Herron	88	667	99	Steve Lowery	72	66	118
Clarence Rose	88	–	85	Mike Clayton	71	112	316
Padraig Harrington	84	–	95	Howard Clark	71	67	180
Rocco Mediate	82	303	61	Hal Sutton	69	72	128
Thomas Bjorn	76	–	109	Mark James	68	58	138
Paul Goydos	74	252	87	Jim McGovern	63	101	218
David Ogrin	71	283	98	Mark Roe	63	107	385
Scott McCarron	70	344	103	Brad Bryant	61	70	90
Jerry Kelly	69	667	143	Bruce Lietzke	60	59	142
Raymond Russell	60	–	146				
Stephen Ames	59	202	80				

The Sony Ranking

(As of December 31, 1996)

POS.	NAME, COUNTRY	POINTS AVERAGE	POS.	NAME, COUNTRY	POINTS AVERAGE
1	Greg Norman, Australia	10.78	51	Fred Funk, USA	3.03
2	Tom Lehman, USA	9.74	52	Craig Parry, Australia	3.03
3	Colin Montgomerie, Scotland	9.10	53	Jeff Sluman, USA	3.02
4	Ernie Els, South Africa	8.60	54	Scott Simpson, USA	2.76
5	Fred Couples, USA	8.16	55	D.A. Weibring, USA	2.75
6	Nick Faldo, England	7.98	56	Shigeki Maruyama, Japan	2.74
7	Phil Mickelson, USA	7.77	57	David Frost, South Africa	2.74
8	Masashi Ozaki, Japan	7.58	58	Ben Crenshaw, USA	2.72
9	Davis Love III, USA	7.53	59	Paul Stankowski, USA	2.69
10	Mark O'Meara, USA	7.12	60	John Cook, USA	2.56
11	Corey Pavin, USA	6.94	61	Rocco Mediate, USA	2.51
12	Steve Stricker, USA	6.19	62	Darren Clarke, N. Ireland	2.50
13	Nick Price, Zimbabwe	6.12	63	Woody Austin, USA	2.46
14	Steve Elkington, Australia	5.84	64	Lee Westwood, England	2.45
15	Scott Hoch, USA	5.44	65	Wayne Westner, South Africa	2.42
16	Bernhard Langer, Germany	5.31	66	Naomichi Ozaki, Japan	2.36
17	Tom Watson, USA	5.28	67	Yoshinori Kaneko, Japan	2.31
18	Mark Brooks, USA	5.18	68	John Huston, USA	2.28
19	David Duval, USA	5.15	69	Per-Ulrik Johansson, Sweden	2.22
20	Vijay Singh, Fiji	5.03	70	Kirk Triplett, USA	2.22
21	Mark McNulty, Zimbabwe	4.98	71	Andrew Coltart, Scotland	2.20
22	Loren Roberts, USA	4.92	72	Miguel Angel Jimenez, Spain	2.19
23	Brad Faxon, USA	4.90	73	Brandt Jobe, USA	2.08
24	Costantino Rocca, Italy	4.75	74	Frankie Minoza, Philippines	2.08
25	Kenny Perry, USA	4.74	75	Wayne Riley, Australia	2.03
26	Ian Woosnam, Wales	4.58	76	Hidemichi Tanaka, Japan	2.00
27	Jeff Maggert, USA	4.48	77	Todd Hamilton, USA	1.93
28	Steve Jones, USA	4.33	78	Michael Campbell, NZ	1.92
29	Justin Leonard, USA	4.15	79	John Morse, USA	1.91
30	Mark McCumber, USA	4.10	80	Stephen Ames, T&T	1.90
31	Frank Nobilo, NZ	4.02	81	Paul McGinley, Ireland	1.90
32	Lee Janzen, USA	3.93	82	Lennie Clements, USA	1.88
33	Tiger Woods, USA	3.88	83	Carlos Franco, Paraguay	1.88
34	Payne Stewart, USA	3.82	84	Tom Purtzer, USA	1.86
35	Bob Tway, USA	3.75	85T	Tom Kite, USA	1.83
36	Jay Haas, USA	3.57	85T	Clarence Rose, USA	1.83
37	Robert Allenby, Australia	3.56	87	Paul Goydos, USA	1.82
38	Mark Calcavecchia, USA	3.51	88	Larry Mize, USA	1.80
39	Jesper Parnevik, Sweden	3.42	89	Fuzzy Zoeller, USA	1.77
40	Sam Torrance, Scotland	3.39	90	Brad Bryant, USA	1.76
41	Duffy Waldorf, USA	3.28	91	John Daly, USA	1.75
42	Craig Stadler, USA	3.25	92	Peter O'Malley, Australia	1.74
43	Billy Mayfair, USA	3.21	93	Alexander Cejka, Germany	1.73
44	Michael Bradley, USA	3.13	94	Greg Turner, NZ	1.72
45	Jim Gallagher, Jr., USA	3.10	95T	Padraig Harrington, Ireland	1.71
46	Peter Jacobsen, USA	3.09	95T	Kazuhiko Hosokawa, Japan	1.71
47	Peter Senior, Australia	3.08	97	Peter Mitchell, England	1.70
48	Tommy Tolles, USA	3.08	98	David Ogrin, USA	1.70
49	Jim Furyk, USA	3.07	99	Tim Herron, USA	1.70
50	Brian Watts, USA	3.06	100	Barry Lane, England	1.70

POS.	NAME, COUNTRY	POINTS AVERAGE
101	Gil Morgan, USA	1.68
102	Paul Lawrie, Scotland	1.68
103T	Billy Andrade, USA	1.67
103T	Scott McCarron, USA	1.67
103T	Paul Broadhurst, England	1.67
106	Jose Coceres, Argentina	1.64
107	Eduardo Romero, Argentina	1.64
108	Nolan Henke, USA	1.61
109	Thomas Bjorn, Denmark	1.58
110	Seve Ballesteros, Spain	1.58
111	Retief Goosen, South Africa	1.56
112	Jay Don Blake, USA	1.56
113	Jean Van de Velde, France	1.52
114	Bradley Hughes, Australia	1.51
115	Andrew Oldcorn, Scotland	1.50
116	Larry Nelson, USA	1.48
117	Hajime Meshiai, Japan	1.47
118T	Steve Lowery, USA	1.46
118T	Masahiro Kuramoto, Japan	1.46
120	Tsuneyuki Nakajima, Japan	1.46
121	David Ishii, USA	1.45
122	Bill Glasson, USA	1.45
123	Robert Gamez, USA	1.42
124	Andrew Magee, USA	1.40
125	Paul Azinger USA	1.40
126	Masanobu Kimura, Japan	1.39
127	Bob Estes, USA	1.39
128	Hal Sutton, USA	1.38
129	Nobuo Serizawa, Japan	1.37
130	Hisayuki Sasaki, Japan	1.37
131	Miguel Angel Martin, Spain	1.37
132	Katsuyoshi Tomori, Japan	1.37
133T	Rick Gibson, Canada	1.36
133T	Dudley Hart, USA	1.36
135	Anders Forsbrand, Sweden	1.36
136	Satoshi Higashi, Japan	1.35
137	Joey Sindelar, USA	1.35
138	Mark James, England	1.33
139	Russ Cochran, USA	1.32
140	Emlyn Aubrey, USA	1.31
141	Curtis Strange, USA	1.31
142	Bruce Lietzke, USA	1.30
143	Jerry Kelly, USA	1.29
144	David Gilford, England	1.29
145	Grant Waite, NZ	1.28
146T	Raymond Russell, Scotland	1.28
146T	Eduardo Herrera, Colombia	1.28
148	Glen Day, USA	1.27
149	Brandel Chamblee, USA	1.27
150	Rick Fehr, USA	1.26

POS.	NAME, COUNTRY	POINTS AVERAGE
151	Anthony Painter, Australia	1.25
152	Diego Borrego, Spain	1.21
153	Peter Teravainen, USA	1.20
154	Brett Ogle, Australia	1.20
155	Ignacio Garrido, Spain	1.17
156	Mike Brisky, USA	1.17
157	Jose Rivero, Spain	1.17
158	Marco Dawson, USA	1.17
159	Jarmo Sandelin, Sweden	1.17
160	Paul Eales, England	1.15
161	Peter Lonard, Australia	1.15
162	Richard Green, Australia	1.15
163	Daniel Chopra, Sweden	1.14
164	Tony Johnstone, Zimbabwe	1.14
165	John Adams, USA	1.13
166	Toshimitsu Izawa, Japan	1.13
167	Mark Wiebe, USA	1.13
168	Peter Hedblom, Sweden	1.13
169	Patrick Burke, USA	1.10
170	Sven Struver, Germany	1.09
171	Peter Baker, England	1.09
172	David Edwards, USA	1.09
173	Sandy Lyle, Scotland	1.08
174	Philip Walton, Ireland	1.07
175	Mike Hulbert, USA	1.06
176	Peter McWhinney, Australia	1.06
177	Toru Suzuki, Japan	1.05
178	Dan Forsman, USA	1.05
179	Michael Long, NZ	1.02
180	Howard Clark, England	1.02
181	Shoichi Kuwabara, Japan	1.02
182	Scott Verplank, USA	1.02
183	Katsunori Kuwabara, Japan	1.02
184	Hideki Kase, Japan	1.00
185	Russell Claydon, England	0.98
186	Greg Kraft, USA	0.97
187	Jamie Spence, England	0.96
188	Joakim Haeggman, Sweden	0.96
189T	Paul Curry, England	0.96
189T	Jean Louis Guepy, France	0.96
191	Guy Boros, USA	0.95
192	Ed Fiori, USA	0.95
193	Andrew Sherborne, England	0.95
194	Ross McFarlane, England	0.93
195	Hideyuki Sato, Japan	0.93
196	Gary Orr, Scotland	0.93
197	Ross Drummond, Scotland	0.92
198	Gene Sauers, USA	0.92
199	Mathias Gronberg, Sweden	0.90
200	Gordon Brand, Jr., Scotland	0.88

Detailed Structure For Allocation of Sony Ranking Points

TOTAL RATING POINTS	1st	2nd	3rd	4th	5th	6th	7th	8th	9th	10th	11th	12th	13th	14th	15th	16th	17th	18th	19th
0	2	1	1	1															
2	3	2	1	1	1	1													
3	4	2	2	1	1	1	1												
4	5	3	2	2	1	1	1	1											
5 — Asia & SAF Minimum	6	4	2	2	1	1	1	1											
6-15	7	4	3	2	2	1	1	1	1										
16-25 — Austr/NZ & Japan Minimum	8	5	3	2	2	2	1	1	1										
26-35	9	5	4	3	2	2	2	1	1	1									
36-45 — Eur & USA Minimum	9	6	4	3	2	2	2	2	1	1									
46-55	11	7	4	3	3	2	2	2	2	1	1								
56-65	11	7	5	4	3	2	2	2	2	2									
66-75	13	7	5	4	3	3	2	2	2	2					1				
76-85	14	8	6	4	3	3	3	2	2	2	2	2	2	1	1				
86-95	15	9	6	5	4	3	3	3	2	2	2	2	2	1	1		1		
96-105 — Austr & Japan Opens Minimum	16	10	6	5	5	4	3	3	3	2	2	2	2	2	1	1	1		
106-115	17	10	7	5	5	4	4	3	3	3	2	2	2	2	2	1	1	1	
116-125	18	11	7	5	5	4	4	3	3	3	2	2	2	2	2	1	1	1	
126-150	19	11	8	6	6	5	4	4	3	3	3	2	2	2	2	2	1	1	1
151-175	20	12	8	6	6	5	4	4	3	3	3	3	2	2	2	2	2	1	1
176-200	21	13	8	6	5	5	4	4	3	3	3	3	2	2	2	2	2	2	1
201-225	22	13	9	6	5	5	4	4	3	3	3	3	2	2	2	2	2	2	2
226-250	23	14	9	7	7	6	5	4	4	3	3	3	3	2	2	2	2	2	2
251-275	24	14	10	7	7	6	5	4	4	3	3	3	3	2	2	2	2	2	2
276-300	25	15	10	8	6	6	5	4	4	3	3	3	3	2	2	2	2	2	2
301-325	26	16	10	8	6	5	5	4	3	3	3	3	2	2	2	2	2	2	2
326-350	27	16	11	8	6	7	5	5	4	4	3	3	3	2	2	2	2	2	2
351-375	28	17	11	8	7	6	5	4	4	4	3	3	3	2	2	2	2	2	2
376-400	29	17	12	9	6	6	5	5	4	4	3	3	3	3	2	2	2	2	2
401-425	30	18	12	9	7	6	5	5	4	4	3	3	3	3	3	2	2	2	2
426-450	31	19	12	9	8	6	6	5	5	4	4	3	3	3	3	3	2	2	2
451-475 — Europe PGA Champ. Minimum	32	19	13	10	8	6	6	5	5	5	4	4	3	3	3	3	3	3	2
476-500	33	20	13	10	8	7	6	5	5	5	4	4	4	3	3	3	3	3	2
501-525	34	20	14	10	8	6	6	6	5	5	4	4	4	3	3	3	3	3	3
526-575	35	21	14	11	9	7	6	6	6	5	5	4	4	4	3	3	3	3	3
576-625	36	22	14	11	9	7	7	6	6	5	5	4	4	4	3	3	3	3	3
626-675	37	22	15	11	9	7	7	6	6	5	5	4	4	4	3	3	3	3	3
676-725	38	23	15	11	9	8	6	6	6	5	5	4	4	4	4	3	3	3	3
726-775	39	23	16	12	9	8	7	6	6	6	5	5	5	4	4	4	3	3	3
776-825	40	24	16	12	9	8	7	6	6	6	5	5	5	4	4	4	3	3	3
Players Championship	40	24	16	12	10	8	7	6	5	5	5	4	4	4	4	3	3	3	3
MAJOR CHAMPIONSHIPS	50	30	20	15	12	10	9	8	7	7	6	6	5	5	5	4	4	4	4

RATING POINTS

Current Rank of Players	Rating Points
1st	50
2nd	34
3rd	30
4th	27
5th	24
6th	21
7th	20
8th	19
9th	18
10th	17
11th	16
12th	15
13th	14
14th	13
15th	12
16th to 30th	11
31st to 34th	10
35th to 38th	9
39th to 43rd	8
44th to 50th	7
51st to 55th	6
56th to 60th	5
61st to 70th	4
71st to 80th	3
81st to 100th	2
Total Available	825

51st plus all making 36-hole cut in major championships

World Golf Rankings 1968-1996

Year	No. 1	No. 2	No. 3	No. 4	No. 5	No. 6	No. 7	No. 8	No. 9	No. 10
1968	Nicklaus	Palmer	Casper	Player	Charles	Boros	Coles	Thomson	Beard	Nagle
1969	Nicklaus	Player	Casper	Palmer	Charles	Beard	Archer	Trevino	Barber	Sikes
1970	Nicklaus	Player	Casper	Trevino	Charles	Devlin	Coles	Jacklin	Beard	Huggett
1971	Nicklaus	Trevino	Player	Palmer	Casper	Barber	Crampton	Charles	Devlin	Weiskopf
1972	Nicklaus	Player	Trevino	Crampton	Palmer	Jacklin	Weiskopf	Oosterhuis	Heard	Devlin
1973	Nicklaus	Weiskopf	Trevino	Player	Crampton	Miller	Oosterhuis	Wadkins	Heard	Brewer
1974	Nicklaus	Miller	Player	Weiskopf	Trevino	M. Ozaki	Crampton	Irwin	Green	Heard
1975	Nicklaus	Miller	Weiskopf	Irwin	Player	Green	Trevino	Casper	Crampton	Watson
1976	Nicklaus	Irwin	Miller	Player	Green	Watson	Weiskopf	Marsh	Crenshaw	Geiberger
1977	Nicklaus	Watson	Green	Irwin	Crenshaw	Marsh	Player	Weiskopf	Floyd	Ballesteros
1978	Watson	Nicklaus	Irwin	Green	Player	Crenshaw	Marsh	Ballesteros	Trevino	Aoki
1979	Watson	Nicklaus	Irwin	Trevino	Player	Aoki	Green	Crenshaw	Ballesteros	Wadkins
1980	Watson	Trevino	Aoki	Crenshaw	Nicklaus	Pate	Ballesteros	Bean	Irwin	Player
1981	Watson	Rogers	Aoki	Pate	Trevino	Ballesteros	Graham	Crenshaw	Floyd	Lietzke
1982	Watson	Floyd	Ballesteros	Kite	Stadler	Pate	Nicklaus	Rogers	Aoki	Strange
1983	Ballesteros	Watson	Floyd	Norman	Kite	Nicklaus	Nakajima	Stadler	Aoki	Wadkins
1984	Ballesteros	Watson	Norman	Wadkins	Langer	Faldo	Nakajima	Stadler	Kite	Peete
1985	Ballesteros	Langer	Norman	Watson	Nakajima	Wadkins	O'Meara	Strange	Pavin	Sutton
1986	Norman	Langer	Ballesteros	Nakajima	Bean	Tway	Sutton	Strange	Stewart	O'Meara
1987	Norman	Ballesteros	Langer	Lyle	Strange	Woosnam	Stewart	Strange	McNulty	Crenshaw
1988	Ballesteros	Norman	Lyle	Faldo	Strange	Crenshaw	Woosnam	Wadkins	Azinger	Calcavecchia
1989	Norman	Faldo	Ballesteros	Strange	Stewart	Kite	Olazabal	Calcavecchia	Woosnam	Azinger
1990	Norman	Faldo	Olazabal	Woosnam	Stewart	Azinger	Ballesteros	Kite	McNulty	Calcavecchia
1991	Woosnam	Faldo	Olazabal	Ballesteros	Norman	Couples	Langer	Stewart	Azinger	Davis
1992	Faldo	Couples	Woosnam	Olazabal	Norman	Langer	Cook	Price	Azinger	Love
1993	Faldo	Norman	Langer	Price	Couples	Azinger	Woosnam	Kite	Love	Pavin
1994	Price	Norman	Faldo	Langer	Olazabal	Els	Couples	Montgomerie	M. Ozaki	Pavin
1995	Norman	Price	Langer	Els	Montgomerie	Pavin	Faldo	Couples	M. Ozaki	Elkington
1996	Norman	Lehman	Montgomerie	Els	Couples	Faldo	Mickelson	M. Ozaki	Love	O'Meara

(*The World of Professional Golf* 1968-1985; Sony Ranking 1986-1996)

Sony Ranking of Leading Players 1986-1996

Player	Dec 31 (1996)	Sept 1 (1996)	April 28 (1996)	1st 2-Year Ranking (1995)	August 27 (1995)	April 30 (1995)	December 25 (1994)	August 28 (1994)	May 1 (1994)	December 26 (1993)	August 29 (1993)	April 25 (1993)	December 27 (1992)	August 30 (1992)	April 27 (1992)	December 29 (1991)	August 25 (1991)	April 28 (1991)	December 30 (1990)	August 26 (1990)	April 29 (1990)	December 31 (1989)	August 27 (1989)	April 30 (1989)	December 25 (1988)	August 28 (1988)	May 1 (1988)	December 27 (1987)	August 30 (1987)	April 26 (1987)	December 28 (1986)	August 31 (1986)	1st Ranking (1986)
Norman	1	1	1	1	1	3	2	2	1	2	2	4	5	7	7	5	4	4	1	1	1	1	1	2	2	1	1	1	1	1	1	2	6
Lehman	2	3	11	11	12	19	17	14	21	48	47	57	74	115	140																		
Montgomerie	3	6	2	6	6	7	8	9	12	14	16	16	20	24	32	36	36	83	81	107	158	162											
Els	4	2	4	3	5	5	6	7	14	20	27	53	40	80	95																		
Couples	5	7	8	7	8	6	7	5	5	5	6	3	2	2	1	6	9	18	11	11	12	15	16	14	19	27	31	46	53	80	73	62	42
Faldo	6	4	5	8	3	2	3	3	2	1	1	1	1	1	2	2	3	3	2	2	2	2	3	3	4	5	12	14	22	62	48	28	24
Mickelson	7	9	13	24	25	20	22	22	28	47	68	103	145	163																			
M. Ozaki	8	5	9	10	10	9	9	12	13	12	13	13	15	20	24	30	22	16	17	12	11	12	13	13	11	18	15	18	19	22	23	35	96
Love	9	14	17	20	17	21	25	18	15	9	11	11	10	12	8	23	25	23	44	59	79	65	62	74	91	82	69	60	60	78			
O'Meara	10	10	12	41	61	79	83	82	70	28	19	17	12	13	11	14	15	21	22	30	26	27	27	23	29	30	39	26	26	12	10	5	5
Pavin	11	8	6	5	7	10	10	10	10	10	14	19	16	16	18	18	15	30	54	65	91	85	59	63	46	56	45	24	17	11	19	15	9
Stricker	12	19	66	73	71	73	133	169	193																								
Price	13	11	3	2	2	1	1	1	3	4	4	5	8	10	20	24	41	43	38	47	45	38	43	27	41	33	50	47	46	57	54	40	52
Elkington	14	13	10	9	11	29	43	40	34	19	18	18	18	27	41	44	46	47	62	80	86	142	143	138	163	175							
Hoch	15	18	16	19	26	32	30	36	61	88	87	110	116	101	54	41	42	52	39	39	29	24	24	26	41	26	21	27	24	32	33	36	37
Langer	16	12	7	4	4	4	4	4	4	3	3	2	6	4	6	7	8	9	14	17	14	16	20	18	15	9	4	3	3	3	2	3	1
Watson	17	22	32	34	35	28	23	26	23	26	28	46	30	32	23	33	29	28	43	33	24	20	18	21	17	19	18	16	25	24	18	9	4
Brooks	18	23	61	99	102	106	113	104	114	95	91	67	44	47	46	66	64	78	95	100	141	172	157	137	130	139							
Duval	19	20	27	33	40	76																											
Singh	20	17	15	16	13	18	15	19	16	16	20	26	38	37	50	77	56	62	76	64	76	87	130	175									

2. The Year In Retrospect

The year of 1996 in professional golf did not begin on Tuesday, August 27 in Milwaukee, Wisconsin. It only seemed that way as one name continued to dominate: Tiger Woods. It was a big story that kept getting bigger, and in his final public appearance Woods accepted the *Sports Illustrated* Sportsman of the Year award.

The statement Jack Nicklaus made in April didn't seem so extravagant now: "Both Arnold (Palmer) and I agree that you could take my Masters (six) and his Masters (four) and add them together, and this kid could win more than that."

First Woods made endorsement agreements with guarantees of $60 million over five years with Nike and Titleist, prompting Lee Trevino to ask, "Doesn't Nike need an old Mexican?" Hardly before anyone could question those deals, Woods proved his value with unprecedented public attention, then with his golf clubs.

His goal starting out was to make enough money in seven tournaments, about $150,000, to earn his PGA Tour player's card for 1997. He instead won two of those seven tournaments, finished with $790,668 in official prize money ($894,060 worldwide), became the first player in 14 years to have five successive top-five American finishes, and rose to No. 33 on the Sony Ranking, the fastest climb into the top 50 in history.

TIGER WOODS

Event	Position
Greater Milwaukee Open	T-60
Bell Canadian Open	11
Quad City Classic	T-5
B.C. Open	T-3
Las Vegas Invitational	1
LaCantera Texas Open	3
Walt Disney World/Oldsmobile Classic	1
The Tour Championship	T-21
Holden Australian Open	T-5
JCPenney Classic	T-2

Woods was changing the face of golf. He was one-eighth Native American, one-eighth white, one-quarter African American, one-quarter Thai and one-quarter Chinese. He was still shy of his 21st birthday (December 30) and because of him, golf was "cool" even among inner-city youth. "To understand what golf is now, don't watch Tiger Woods," said *Sports Illustrated*. "Watch who watches Tiger Woods." It was everyone, all ages, sexes, colors, backgrounds.

Nike challenged the establishment with an advertisement which included the lines: "There are still some golf courses I can't play because of the color of my skin ... Hello world. I've heard I'm not ready for you. Are you ready for me?" After that introduction, Nike took a softer, still effective approach, with children of various ages and colors proclaiming "I am Tiger Woods."

Just as Palmer was the right person for his time, so too can be Woods, whose appeal has no ethnic or geographic bounds, in the 21st century. If Woods can be half as successful as Nicklaus, the best golfer of the last 100 years, he will become as famous as Muhammad Ali, often called the most recognizable person on earth. Half as successful as Nicklaus means a career like that of Tom Watson, 33 PGA Tour victories and eight major championships.

The story of Eldrick Woods was told many times, including the cover of *Newsweek* and in two instant biographies. His father, Earl, now a retired lieutenant colonel in the U.S. Army, met his mother, Kultida, while serving in Thailand. He was nicknamed "Tiger" after a South Vietnamese soldier and friend of his father, Nguyen Phong, to whom his father had also given that nickname in combat. Raised in Cypress, California, near Los Angeles, Woods was not out of the crib before taking an interest in golf and went on to a phenomenal series of accomplishments from age two.

The weekend before becoming a professional Woods won a record third consecutive U.S. Amateur Championship. That followed three consecutive U.S. Junior Amateur titles, also a record. At age 15 Woods had been the youngest ever to win the Junior Amateur and at age 18, the youngest ever to win the Amateur. No one before him had ever won both the Junior Amateur and Amateur titles.

What's more, Woods had come from five holes down, then two down with three to play in the 1996 Amateur, holing a 35-foot putt to square the match on the 35th hole before beating Steve Scott on the 38th, "a comeback as dramatic as any in the annals of golf," said *The New York Times* in a front-page story. Comebacks and front-page headlines were nothing new for Woods, who was six down after 13 holes of his first Amateur final, and he was on page one again with his announcement in Milwaukee and press conference there the next day.

That was only the beginning of Tigermania, which brought tens of thousands of additional spectators to the PGA Tour in that usually humdrum portion of the schedule during the football season and baseball playoffs.

He was featured almost every day in *USA Today* and on ESPN's *SportsCenter*, and hundreds of media requests from around the world — including seven non-sports magazine covers, every news and interview program on American television, and several situation comedies — were declined simply because of the volume. At the year's end, there were still about 20 new requests arriving each week.

Exhaustion, however, caught up with Woods after five consecutive tournaments including the U.S. Amateur. He was criticized for withdrawing from the Buick Challenge in Pine Mountain, Georgia, the same week he was to receive the collegiate Fred Haskins Award, which was later rescheduled. He won his first PGA Tour event the next week, the Las Vegas Invitational, and won again two weeks later at the Walt Disney World/Oldsmobile Classic in Orlando, Florida, his new residence.

Along the way Woods was compared to many people, such as John Daly, whose long drives he now exceeded; Teddy Rhodes and Charles Sifford, black pioneers in golf; Jackie Robinson (baseball) and Arthur Ashe (tennis).

More than one old-timer offered this comparison, which intrigued Woods: Ty Cobb, the temperamental baseball legend, because of their strong, lean physiques and quick hands.

Woods is six feet, two inches tall and weighs 160 pounds, which will increase some as his body matures. Cobb stood at six feet, one inch and weighed 175 pounds in his prime. He was the American League batting champion for 12 out of 13 years beginning in 1907 when he was 20, the same age as Woods during his professional debut.

What makes Woods so special? Said long-time observer Larry Dorman in *The New York Times*: "... a combination of things, none of them terribly mystical or mysterious. He is a tremendously gifted athlete possessing all the requisite skills and he has worked diligently to hone those skills and combine them with the intangibles that separate him from mere mortals.

"His big shoulder turn works with what swing aficionados call a 'quiet lower body,' meaning his hips cannot turn excessively, to create a great deal of resistance. When Woods clears his hips, something he does faster than anyone in the game, he creates an action that is almost scary, in effect that is like cracking a whip. This generates the power that launches tee shots that have turned par-fives into par-fours. ...

"But Woods is not merely a monster off the tee. His iron play has improved to the point where the little knockdown shots and low wedges into the wind that once eluded him are now a key part of the arsenal. ... Around the green, Woods has touch and imagination. He pitches the ball like a young Seve Ballesteros ... If there is an Achilles heel, it is that he is a streaky putter. ... Which brings us to the two elements that dovetail to complete the package: Course management and mental toughness. Woods has both in abundance."

Woods offered this after winning at Disney: "It may be surprising to some guys, but it's not surprising to people who know me, but I haven't really played my best yet. I've hit the ball pretty good, but not the greatest. I haven't had the greatest putting round yet. But I've managed my game really well and I think that's the key to winning. If you ask Nicklaus how many majors he won when he hit the ball great all week, he would say zero. Because he never did. He managed his game really well. That's exactly what I'm doing."

Nicklaus had this observation: "I don't think we've had a whole lot happen in what, 10 years? I mean, some guys have come on and won a few tournaments, but no one has sustained and dominated. I think we might have somebody now."

For years most professional golfers have been complacent, too comfortable with their occasional victories and six- or seven-figure incomes, too willing to accept the theory that there were too many great players — in reality, just many good ones — for anyone to dominate again. At last, Tiger Woods has come along to challenge and try to prove them wrong. And they know it. Said Tom Lehman, the most successful player of the year, "Someday there will be a dominant player who wins two majors and eight tournaments in a year. Maybe it will be Tiger, or somebody motivated by Tiger."

Before introducing my top five of 1996, this from Chi Chi Rodriguez, who said, "The good thing is, I don't have to play Tiger Woods until I'm 90."

TOM LEHMAN

Event	Position
Mercedes Championships	T-12
Phoenix Open	MC
Buick Invitational	T-3
United Airlines Hawaiian Open	T-4
Nissan Open	T-6
Bay Hill Invitational	T-9
Freeport-McDermott Classic	T-10
The Players Championship	T-8
Masters Tournament	T-18
MCI Classic	T-13
Andersen Consulting World Championship (United States Qualifying)	T-5
Greater Greensboro Chrysler Classic	T-11
MasterCard Colonial	MC
Memorial Tournament	T-30
Buick Classic	T-2
U.S. Open Championship	T-2
Motorola Western Open	T-18
British Open Championship	1
PGA Championship	T-14
Sprint International	T-5
Fred Meyer Challenge	3
NEC World Series of Golf	T-10
Bell Canadian Open	T-7
Smurfit European Open	T-33
Linde German Masters	MC
Toyota World Match Play	4
Tour Championship	1
MasterCard PGA Grand Slam	1
Nedbank Million Dollar Challenge	T-9
Diners Club Matches	1

Lehman had a neat summary of his status, at age 37, towards the end of 1996. "To go from the mini-tours six years ago to the pinnacle, it's just amazing," Lehman said. "It makes all the hard work and lean times worthwhile."

It was amazing indeed, as Lehman continued his progression to No. 2 on the Sony Ranking. He nearly completed twin victories in the U.S. Open and British Open, falling one stroke short of a tie for the American title when his drive on the last hole kicked left into a bunker, so close to the edge that he could only lay up with his next shot. He won in Britain the next month, taking a six-stroke lead into the final round after a course-record 64, then winning by two with a gritty 73.

He concluded the PGA Tour season with a wire-to-wire, six-stroke victory in the Tour Championship. He finished first on the money list with $1,780,159, earned the Vardon Trophy for low adjusted scoring average (69.32), and received Player of the Year honors from the other players, the golf writers and the PGA of America.

He padded his 1996 worldwide earnings to $2,634,804 by winning the late-year MasterCard PGA Grand Slam and the Diners Club Matches, the latter with partner Duffy Waldorf.

Lehman traced his success to his 1991 performance on the Ben Hogan (now Nike) Tour, when he was Player of the Year and a three-time winner. He said he "got back on tour with a lot of confidence and had a mindset of this is where I belonged." He was 24th on the PGA Tour money list in 1992 and 33rd in 1993, then advanced to another level in 1994, when he won the Memorial Tournament, earned $1,031,144 for fourth place, and was runner-up to Jose Maria Olazabal in the Masters.

He came close again in 1995, placing third in the U.S. Open, and won the Colonial National Invitation while finishing 15th on the money list with $830,231.

"Now that I've won the British Open," Lehman said, "I realize how significant winning a major is, and how enjoyable it is, and how important it is to your career in many different ways. I definitely have, and will, continue to try to gear my game for the biggest tournaments."

MARK BROOKS

Event	Position
Nortel Open	MC
Bob Hope Chrysler Classic	1
Phoenix Open	T-26
United Airlines Hawaiian Open	T-21
Nissan Open	T-2
Doral-Ryder Open	T-50
Bay Hill Invitational	MC
Freeport-McDermott Classic	T-47
The Players Championship	MC
Masters Tournament	MC
MCI Classic	77
Greater Greensboro Chrysler Classic	T-23
Shell Houston Open	1
GTE Byron Nelson Classic	T-6
MasterCard Colonial	T-46
Memorial Tournament	T-26
U.S. Open Championship	T-16
FedEx St. Jude Classic	72
Canon Greater Hartford Open	MC
Motorola Western Open	T-8
British Open Championship	T-5
PGA Championship	1
Sprint International	T-21
NEC World Series of Golf	T-10
Bell Canadian Open	T-26
Buick Challenge	MC
Las Vegas Invitational	T-67
LaCantera Texas Open	T-36
Toyota World Match Play	3

Event	Position
Tour Championship	T-27
Sumitomo Visa Taiheiyo Masters	T-24
MasterCard PGA Grand Slam	4
Casio World Open	T-21
Nedbank Million Dollar Challenge	T-9
Diners Club Matches	T-3

Until tying for third place in the 1995 British Open, Mark Brooks had never been regarded as a contender in the major championships, but rather as another professional golfer earning a good living on the PGA Tour without doing anything of much significance. He had been subjected to the Tour's qualifying process as many times (four) as he had won tournaments.

In 1996, at age 35, Brooks had perhaps the year of his career, winning three times including the PGA Championship, and earning $1,448,692 ($1,850,296 worldwide), which was more than double his income in any of his previous 12 years. He jumped from No. 99 to No. 18 on the Sony Ranking. His other victories were in the Bob Hope Chrysler Classic and Shell Houston Open, and he was second in the Nissan Open after a final-round 64.

He got into position to win but could not deliver in two 1996 major events before the PGA, tying for 16th place in the U.S. Open and for fifth in the British Open. He began the final round of the PGA tied for second place, two strokes out of the lead, but with four holes remaining Brooks seemed to have exhausted his chance of winning. He had made three bogeys in four holes and was three strokes behind Kenny Perry, the home favorite in Louisville, Kentucky.

"It was looking more than bleak at that point," Brooks said. Then Brooks birdied two of the last four holes, got in a playoff when Perry bogeyed the 18th, and won with another birdie on the first extra hole.

So, just how bleak was the situation? "I don't know," Brooks said. "The way I do it, I just keep plodding along. I guess I've been that way for quite a while. I had enough ups and downs my first four years out here, I learned what going up and down does for you. You can go bang your head on a tree, throw up ... I don't do any of that. I do get upset at times. That's what they have a practice tee and all that other stuff for."

Brooks was less enthusiastic than most winners of major championships. "I will celebrate with my friends, my family, my close friends ... But I was taught a long time ago that if you drop your guard, then the other guy knows what's going on. So I try not to drop my guard."

PHIL MICKELSON

Event	Position
Mercedes Championship	28
Nortel Open	1
Phoenix Open	1
Buick Invitational	2
Nissan Open	MC
Doral-Ryder Open	T-38

Event	Position
Bay Hill Invitational	MC
The Players Championship	T-33
Masters Tournament	3
MCI Classic	T-66
GTE Byron Nelson Classic	1
Memorial Tournament	T-71
U.S. Open Championship	T-94
Motorola Western Open	T-26
Ernst Championship	1
British Open Championship	T-41
Buick Open	T-33
PGA Championship	T-8
Sprint International	16
NEC World Series of Golf	1
Suntory Open	3
Las Vegas Invitational	T-8
Alfred Dunhill Cup	1
Toyota World Match Play	T-9
Tour Championship	12

In his fourth full year on the PGA Tour, Phil Mickelson began to achieve the sort of success that had been predicted for him since winning the U.S. Amateur and three NCAA championships. Which was saying a lot because Mickelson had done very well in his first three years as a professional, winning five tournaments.

Mickelson, who reached age 26 in June, was the PGA Tour leader for most of the year, and it took Lehman's victory in the season-ending Tour Championship to deprive the lefthander of the title of leading money winner. Mickelson won $1,697,799 for second place, less than $100,000 behind Lehman, and had a worldwide total of $2,115,990. He advanced from No. 24 to No. 7 on the Sony Ranking.

He had four PGA Tour victories, winning twice in his first three starts, in the Nortel Open and then the Phoenix Open, where he birdied the third playoff hole against another rising star, Justin Leonard, in one of the most exciting Tour events of recent years. He later won the GTE Byron Nelson Classic and NEC World Series of Golf. He also was on the winning United States team in the Alfred Dunhill Cup and won the unofficial Ernst Championship.

In the major championships, Mickelson was a distant third in the Masters, tied for eighth in the PGA Championship, tied for 41st in the British Open and tied for 94th in the U.S. Open.

Victories in the majors should be next for Mickelson. "When you think of Phil, you think of a guy who is going to win a lot of tournaments," Curtis Strange said. "What Phil has got is a sixth sense, a touch, an instinct, a feel, a way to win."

COLIN MONTGOMERIE

Event	Position
Dubai Desert Classic	1
The Players Championship	T-2
BellSouth Classic	T-23
Masters Tournament	T-39
MCI Classic	T-8
Peugeot Open de Espana	WD
Benson and Hedges International Open	T-9
Andersen Consulting World Championship (European Qualifying)	2
Volvo PGA Championship	T-7
Deutsche Bank Open–TPC of Europe	2
Alamo English Open	T-2
U.S. Open Championship	T-10
Peugeot Open de France	MC
Murphy's Irish Open	1
Scottish Open	T-16
British Open Championship	MC
Volvo Scandinavian Masters	T-12
PGA Championship	MC
One 2 One British Masters	T-9
Canon European Masters	1
Trophee Lancome	2
Loch Lomond World Invitational	T-4
Smurfit European Open	T-24
Linde German Masters	4
Alfred Dunhill Cup (Group 2)	4
Toyota World Match Play	T-5
Volvo Masters	T-29
Alfred Dunhill Asian Masters	T-39
Johnnie Walker Super Tour	3
Nedbank Million Dollar Challenge	1

It was both a disappointing and rewarding year for Colin Montgomerie. He was disgusted by his play in the major championships, especially in missing the 36-hole cuts in both the British Open and PGA Championship. But Montgomerie led the PGA European Tour money list for the fourth successive year, winning three tournaments, and became the first to earn $3 million worldwide in one year with his victory in the Nedbank Million Dollar Challenge.

Montgomerie, age 33, improved two positions to No. 3 on the Sony Ranking while earning $3,071,442 to lead the World Money List. He did not play his first tournament until mid-March while undertaking a fitness program that resulted in a loss of 30 pounds. He then won the Dubai Desert Classic and was off to America, where he tied for second in The Players Championship. He tied for 39th in the Masters, and so went the rest of the year.

He was second three more times in Europe while winning the Murphy's Irish Open and Canon European Open, then won the Million Dollar event in South Africa in a playoff with Ernie Els, which was the first extra-holes victory of his career after five misses.

ERNIE ELS

Event	Position
Philips South African Open	1
Johnnie Walker Classic	T-6
Alfred Dunhill South African PGA	T-2
FNB Players Championship	T-10
Doral-Ryder Open	MC
Bay Hill Invitational	T-42
Freeport-McDermott Classic	T-47
The Players Championship	T-8
BellSouth Classic	T-29
Masters Tournament	T-12
GTE Byron Nelson Classic	T-18
MasterCard Colonial	T-67
Memorial Tournament	T-6
Buick Classic	1
U.S. Open Championship	T-5
Murphy's Irish Open	T-12
Scottish Open	T-16
British Open Championship	T-2
Andersen Consulting World Championship (International Qualifying)	T-5
Buick Open	T-38
PGA Championship	T-61
Sprint International	T-19
NEC World Series of Golf	T-23
Bell Canadian Open	T-20
Linde German Masters	T-5
Alfred Dunhill Cup	T-3
Toyota World Match Play	1
Tour Championship	T-6
Alfred Dunhill Asian Masters	T-6
World Cup of Golf	1
Nedbank Million Dollar Challenge	2

The two highlights of 1996 for Ernie Els were his record third successive victory in the Toyota World Match Play Championship and his 18-stroke triumph with Wayne Westner in the World Cup of Golf while being cheered on home soil by their fellow South Africans.

Els might well have had the British Open on top of that list. Starting the final round eight strokes behind Lehman, Els played his way into contention only to hit drives into fairway bunkers for bogeys on two of the last three holes and lose by two strokes with his 67. In other major events, Els tied for fifth place in the U.S. Open, tied for 12th in the Masters and tied for 61st in the PGA Championship.

It was another outstanding year for Els, age 27, who was ranked No. 4 on the Sony Ranking. He started by winning the Philips South African Open. He had a victory in the United States, by eight strokes in the Buick Classic, and took the individual title as well as the team title in the World Cup of Golf, for a total of four victories. His worldwide earnings were $2,089,428.

In the Toyota World Match Play, Els defeated Steve Stricker (after being 6 down after 18 holes), Mark Brooks and Vijay Singh. He and Westner had a 547 total to easily beat the United States team of Lehman and Steve Jones at Erinvale Golf Club near Cape Town before 20,000 spectators. "The feeling I had walking up the 18th was almost as good as when I won the U.S. Open," Els said. "It was an unbelievable week."

Others whose achievements were swept aside by Tigermania included Greg Norman, Nick Faldo, Steve Jones and Masashi (Jumbo) Ozaki. Two controversies involving Norman also lost momentum in the crush of Woods' publicity.

One incident was the forced resignation of David Graham as captain of the International team in the Presidents Cup, a Ryder Cup-style competition in September. Norman, rightly or wrongly, was at the center of that storm as the most prominent International player.

Then, during the Presidents Cup, the formation was announced of the PGA Tours International Federation, consisting of the U.S. PGA Tour, PGA European Tour, Australasian Tour, Japan PGA Tour and FNB Tour of South Africa. Their plans included at least three "World Championship" tournaments to start in 1999.

Norman felt he had been ignored by the American commissioner, Tim Finchem, who had diffused the World Tour proposal which Norman supported in November, 1994. "I've had it up to here with Tim Finchem," Norman said. "It's the end of the rope for me. He hung me out to dry. I had two meetings with him (in 1995), one at Doral and one in my office after Doral. He told me, 'Greg, I'll keep you in the loop.' That's the last communication I had with him."

Next to Woods, the second-biggest story of the year was Norman's collapse in the Masters. He had a record-equalling 63 on the first day, entered the last round with a six-stroke lead, shot 78 and lost by five strokes to Faldo's 67. The most dominant player of the past 10 years, with 37 worldwide victories, Norman also has had more near-misses in the major championships than any of his contemporaries. This was his eighth runner-up finish against two major titles.

Norman won four more tournaments in 1996, for a total of 41 in 11 years and 75 in his career, and the 41-year-old Australian remained No. 1 in the world on the Sony Ranking, extending his hold on the top position to a record 84 consecutive weeks.

His victories were in the Doral-Ryder Open on the U.S. PGA Tour and in two Australian events, the Ford South Australian Open and Holden Australian Open, where he defended his title and won for the fifth time. He also won the Andersen Consulting World Championship and repeated as champion, with Brad Faxon, in the Fred Meyer Challenge for a total of 79 career victories including team competitions.

He was merely 15th on the American money list with $891,237 but had $2,258,678 for third place worldwide while improving his record worldwide career total to $18,671,779. Also of note in 1996, Norman parted company in August with his coach, Butch Harmon, who had Woods as his new star, and went to David Leadbetter, Faldo's long-time swing instructor.

When Faldo decided to move his base from England to Florida and concentrate on the U.S. PGA Tour, the purpose was to improve his chances of winning the major championships. It's reasonable to assume that Faldo expected better results than he has had. If Norman had only finished with even-par 72 in the Masters, Faldo would be without a major title in his two years in America.

Nevertheless, Faldo had his third Masters title to match his three British Open victories, and his total of six major championships, for 38 worldwide career victories, was all that really mattered. Any year that includes a major title must be considered a success. Credit too must go to Faldo for that tremendous 67 in the Masters, which meant that he would have won even if Norman's score had been four strokes lower.

What of those other seven majors since Faldo departed the PGA European Tour? His best showing in 1995 was a tie for 24th place in the Masters. He was a distant fourth in the 1996 British Open, finishing three strokes behind after starting the last round with a six-shot deficit, tied for 16th in the U.S. Open and tied for 65th in the PGA Championship.

Otherwise in 1996, Faldo was runner-up in the Mercedes Championships and Volvo PGA Championship while earning $1,435,670 and advancing two positions to No. 6 on the Sony Ranking.

Like Faldo, Jones won a major championship but nothing else. There the similarity ended. The U.S. Open title represented an unexpected revival of Jones' career at age 37, after a dirt-bike accident in late 1991 sidelined him for nearly three years. He once was a promising player, with three victories in 1989, but no longer was mentioned among the elite.

He started the U.S. Open inconspicuously with 74, then shot 66 and two 69s for a one-stroke victory over his good friend Lehman and Davis Love III. Lehman's drive on the 18th hole took an unlucky bounce, after Love had bogeyed the 17th and 18th, three-putting the last green. That left Jones to try, and he nearly holed a seven-iron approach shot, leaving himself with two putts for the victory.

Jones won $1,573,108 worldwide and rose from No. 168 to No. 28 on the Sony Ranking.

As surprising as was Jones' victory, nothing continued to confuse golf observers outside Japan as did the play of Ozaki. The 49-year-old star, who held No. 8 on the Sony Ranking, won eight tournaments on the Japan PGA Tour, raising his total to 20 victories in the past three years, 82 official career titles and 101 overall.

Despite earning $1,944,034, nearly all on his home tour, Ozaki had his relative ability brought into question. His best finish in four starts in the United States was a tie for 29th place in The Players Championship. His worst in Japan was a tie for 30th place. Still, no one even close to Ozaki's age had ever reigned so clearly as a tour's No. 1 player as Ozaki did in Japan in 1996.

These were other highlights, starting with the U.S. PGA Tour.

Steve Stricker, Mark O'Meara, John Cook and Loren Roberts had two victories each. It was a breakthrough year for Stricker, age 29, who trailed only Els and Mickelson among professional golfers under age 30 after those first two triumphs in the Kemper Open and Motorola Western Open, which he won by eight strokes. He had joined the Tour in 1990 but did not earn enough to retain his player's card until 1994. "Throughout my career, I've struggled to get to the next step," Stricker said. "But once I've gotten there, I've stayed."

Stricker was fourth on the Tour money list with $1,383,739 and had $1,905,366 worldwide while advancing from No. 73 to No. 12 on the Sony Ranking.

Other 20-somethings of special note were David Duval, age 25, and Justin Leonard, age 24. Duval, seeking his first win, had five top-three finishes, was No. 19 on the Sony Ranking and won $1,043,079 worldwide. Leonard, a former U.S. Amateur and NCAA winner, got his first victory in the Buick Open, was runner-up to Mickelson in the Phoenix Open, was No. 29 on the Sony Ranking and won $1,004,640.

O'Meara won the Mercedes Championships and Greater Greensboro Chrysler Classic, raising his total to four victories in 14 months after going winless in 1993 and 1994. He also finished second twice, climbed 31 positions to No. 10 on the Sony Ranking and earned $1,654,149 worldwide.

"When slumps happen, you can go one of two ways," said O'Meara, age 39 with 17 worldwide career victories. "You can either go south and get in the doldrums where you just slowly dwindle away, or you can make up your mind, 'Hey, I'm going to do it.' Basically, you control your own destiny — no teacher, no sports psychologist, no one but you."

Cook, who had not won since 1992 and had only one top-10 finish in 1995, won the FedEx St. Jude Classic by seven strokes with a 26-under-par 258 total, one stroke off two Tour records, and the CVS Charity Classic. Roberts, who won at Bay Hill in 1994 and 1995 for his first victories, won the MCI Classic and Greater Milwaukee Open this year for a career total of four at age 41.

Fred Couples' only win of the year was an impressive one, by four strokes in The Players Championship. He was No. 5 on the Sony Ranking and had $1,556,613 in worldwide earnings. Scott Hoch won the Michelob Championship plus the unofficial Family House Invitational, and was runner-up to Norman in the Andersen Consulting event for fourth place in worldwide winnings with $2,155,893. He was No. 15 on the Sony Ranking.

One of the year's most celebrated victories was by Tom Watson in the Memorial Tournament, his first on the Tour since 1987. Davis Love III won the Buick Invitational, but would be remembered more for his three-putt bogey on the final hole of the U.S. Open. He also lost two playoffs, including Woods' first victory in the Las Vegas Invitational

In this Year of the Tiger, Woods was one of 13 first-time Tour winners. Of particular note, in addition to those already mentioned, Paul Stankowski won the BellSouth Classic one week after winning on the Nike Tour, and later triumphed in the unofficial Lincoln-Mercury Kapalua Invitational and the Casio World Open in Japan. Tommy Tolles did not win, but had six top-10 finishes including a tie for second in The Players Championship and a tie for third in the PGA Championship.

Brad Faxon, who won the unofficial Fred Meyer Challenge with Norman, had the highest Tour earnings without a victory, $1,055,050 ($1,198,121 worldwide) and was second four times, including twice in playoffs.

The major champions of 1995 — Ben Crenshaw, Corey Pavin, John Daly and Steve Elkington — had but two victories among them, Pavin in the MasterCard Colonial and Elkington in the Honda City Invitational in Thailand. Pavin led the 1995 World Money List with over $2.7 million, but earned $971,320 this year while falling from No. 5 to No. 11 on the Sony Ranking. Elkington went to the final hole in his defense of the PGA Championship, missed a 15-foot birdie putt and tied for third place. He won $707,287 worldwide and dropped from No. 9 to No. 14 on the Sony Ranking.

Neither Daly nor Crenshaw were among the top 100 money winners in America. Daly earned only $337,964 worldwide and Crenshaw, $191,790. They also plunged on the Sony Ranking, as Crenshaw went from No. 21 to No. 58 and Daly, from No. 40 to No. 91. More disturbing, Daly acknowledged that he was drinking beer again, after abstaining for more than two years.

Billy Mayfair, second on the U.S. money list in 1995, fell to 55th place, and promising New Zealander Michael Campbell, trying to play both the American and European circuits, did not earn enough to retain his player's card on either.

Nick Price's slump continued, and he fell from No. 2 to No. 13 on the Sony Ranking, although winning $888,882 worldwide. He was ranked No. 1 from August, 1994, through June, 1995. Price won twice in Africa late in 1995 but his last victory on the Tour was the 1994 Bell Canadian Open. He has been troubled by poor business decisions, poor putting and poor health, a deviated septum that affected his sinuses, upset his equilibrium and led to chronic fatigue.

Price was encouraged by nine top-10 finishes worldwide, including four seconds or thirds and a tie for eighth in the PGA Championship. "I'll be back — I have no reservations about that," he said.

It was a time of change on the PGA European Tour aside from Montgomerie, the leading money winner, and Ian Woosnam, who led for most of the year before placing second. Only four players — Montgomerie, Costantino Rocca, Andrew Coltart and Darren Clarke — from the top 15 on the money list in 1995 were there in 1996.

Some of the more familiar names were either in America, not playing well or injured, and their places were taken by others including first-year players Thomas Bjorn, Padraig Harrington and Raymond Russell. There were 13 first-time European winners.

Bjorn, age 25, the Danish player who led the 1995 Challenge Tour in Europe, was the top rookie on the money list, in 10th place, and won the Loch Lomond World Invitational. Harrington, age 25, won the Peugeot Open de Espana and Russell, age 24, won the Air France Cannes Open.

Woosnam had the most European victories, four, raising his career total to 40, after failing to win in 1995 for the first time in 10 years. Woosnam got back on form after participating in a video that showed him swinging bare-chested in slow motion. He could see what he was doing wrong.

Woosnam, age 38, won the first two tournaments of the year, the Johnnie Walker Classic in Singapore and Heineken Classic in Australia, and later won the Scottish Open and Volvo German Open. He earned $1,321,719 worldwide and was back to No. 26 on the Sony Ranking after falling the previous year to No. 56, a steep drop from his No. 1 perch in 1991, when he won the Masters and five other events.

The jovial Rocca, one of the best-liked players on the European Tour, was fourth on the European money list, the third time in four years that he has been among the top six. The 39-year-old Italian, ranked No. 24 in the world, won $957,397 worldwide and had his third career victory in the Volvo PGA Championship.

The players just ahead of and behind Rocca on the European money list, Robert Allenby and Mark McNulty, each won three times.

Allenby, a 25-year-old Australian, was beginning to achieve the level of success that had been predicted for him as he advanced 20 positions to No. 37 on the Sony Ranking and won $886,316 worldwide.

Before 1996 Allenby had won five times in Australia and once in Europe. He added titles in the Alamo English Open, Peugeot Open de France and One 2 One British Masters. He fractured his sternum in a car accident in September. He returned only to hit a tee shot in the final Volvo Masters to qualify for a bonus pool.

McNulty won the Dimension Data Pro-Am, a co-sanctioned event in South Africa, the Sun Dutch Open and European season-ending Volvo Masters plus his national championship, the Zimbabwe Open, later in the year. He won $838,835 worldwide and ranked No. 21 on the Sony Ranking. Now 43 years old, McNulty has 42 career triumphs.

The highest-placed of the European first-time winners was Lee Westwood, age 23, who won the Volvo Scandinavian Masters, was sixth on the European money list and won $939,104 worldwide. He had a second victory in Japan in the Sumitomo Visa Taiheiyo Masters. He advanced to No. 64 on the Sony Ranking from No. 258.

On the downside, Bernhard Langer did not win on the European Tour after 16 consecutive years with at least one victory, and he missed the 36-hole cut for the first time in 69 tournaments. His best chance to win was in the Peugeot Open de France, where Allenby birdied the last regulation hole to tie him and sank a 30-foot putt in the playoff.

The 39-year-old German, who dropped from No. 4 to No. 16 on the Sony Ranking, extended his worldwide victory string to 18 consecutive years by winning the Alfred Dunhill Asian Masters. It was his 47th career victory, including two majors in the Masters.

Langer has always battled putting woes, and won with a long-shafted putter which he was using for only the fourth tournament.

Three more of the Europeans, who — along with Faldo, Woosnam, Langer and with Norman's help from Down Under — changed the world order of golf in the late 1970s and early 1980s, appeared close to the end of their primes. One was their spiritual leader, Seve Ballesteros, age 39, and another was Sandy Lyle, age 38. And Jose Maria Olazabal, although just 30 years old, did not play any tournaments in 1996 because of rheumatoid arthritis in both feet.

Ballesteros had only two top-10 finishes, won $178,705 worldwide and tumbled from No. 22 to No. 110 on the Sony Ranking. "My game cannot get any worse," Ballesteros said. "I used to overpower the golf course, and now the golf course overpowers me." He was down to that, after 72 career victories including three British Opens and two Masters.

Lyle, whose 32 career wins included one British Open and one Masters, earned $187,637 worldwide and went down to No. 173 on the Sony Ranking.

Olazabal made a surprise visit to the Open Novotel Perrier in October, and was optimistic about playing again in 1997. "My doctors reckon that if everything goes as expected, and if I progress the way they expect, I should be close to playing early next year," said the 1994 Masters champion.

Australasia continued to have an abundance of high-ranking players. In addition to Norman and Elkington in America, and Allenby in Europe, Frank Nobilo stood out on both of those circuits. He won the Deutsche Bank Open in Europe and, for the second time, the unofficial Sarazen World Open in America, for a total of nine career victories.

The 36-year-old New Zealander, who won $1,033,737 worldwide and advanced from No. 45 to No. 31 on the Sony Ranking, also demonstrated that he could be on the verge of winning a major title. He finished fourth in the Masters, tied for eighth in the PGA Championship, tied for 13th in the U.S. Open and tied for 27th in the British Open.

There was not much difference in the performances of two other Australians, Peter Senior, age 37, and Craig Parry, age 30. Senior was No. 47 on the Sony Ranking and earned $627,781 worldwide. Parry was No. 52 and won $654,448. Playing in Australia and Japan, Senior won twice on the home circuit in the Canon Challenge and Holden Classic, and was second or third four times in Japan. Parry won the Ericsson Australian Masters and was second twice in America.

Australian Wayne Riley, age 34 and ranked No. 75 on the Sony Ranking, won for the second straight year in Europe at the Portuguese Open. He earned $435,424 worldwide. Countryman Peter McWhinney won the Tsuruya Open in Japan and $314,049 worldwide. His ranking was No. 176.

In South Africa, special mention must go to Wayne Westner, age 35, who improved on the Sony Ranking from No. 123 to No. 65 while earning $753,973. In addition to winning the World Cup of Golf with Els, Westner had three domestic victories in the San Lameer South African Masters, Nashua Wild Coast Sun Challenge and FNB Players Championship.

As noted earlier, Jumbo Ozaki dominated the Japan Tour with eight victories. Yoshinori Kaneko was second with three titles and $1,085,706, little more than half of Ozaki's earnings. Hajime Meshiai, Masanobu Kimura and Kazuhiko Hosokawa each won two tournaments. American journeyman Peter Teravainen won the Japan Open and was one of eight non-Japanese winners.

Teravainen also won on the Omega Tour in Asia. The Omega Tour consisted primarily of players from Asian countries, while the older Asia Tour continued as training ground for players from around the world. Four Americans were among the Asia Tour winners.

On other minor circuits, Stewart Cink had three victories on the Nike Tour, the stepping stone to the U.S. PGA Tour, and also won the Mexican Open. Trevor Dodds won four times on the Canadian Tour. Pedro Martinez had two triumphs in South America and kept the richest prize, the Argentina Open title, out of U.S. hands.

The U.S. Senior PGA Tour was again headed by Jim Colbert, although

Colbert had stiff competition from Hale Irwin before repeating as the leading money winner with $1,627,890, just over $12,000 more than Irwin. Colbert won five tournaments to Irwin's two.

It was a different result on the Senior World Money List. Irwin had a record total of $1,991,569 and Colbert won $1,853,140, although Colbert added another victory in the Diners Club Matches with Bob Murphy. Irwin also had an extra victory in a professional/celebrity event, the Lexus Challenge, with actor Sean Connery. Among Irwin's triumphs was a senior major title in the PGA Seniors' Championship.

Other senior majors were won by Dave Stockton in the U.S. Senior Open, Raymond Floyd in the Ford Senior Players Championship, and Jack Nicklaus in The Tradition.

Floyd was third on the Senior World Money List with $1,621,101, followed by South Africa's John Bland, who earned $1,359,987. Five other seniors won more than $1 million. Bland was second to Colbert with four official Tour victories.

Lee Trevino won three times, although only one was official. He also won the Australian Seniors title and the Liberty Mutual Legends of Golf with Mike Hill. Floyd and his son, Raymond, Jr., repeated as champions of the Office Depot Father-Son Challenge. Isao Aoki won twice in America plus the Japan Senior Open.

Other two-time winners in America were Murphy (plus the Diners Club Matches), Hill (including the Legends of Golf), Stockton, Nicklaus, Graham Marsh, Walter Morgan and Tom Weiskopf.

Tommy Horton was the leading player on the European Seniors Tour with four victories, John Morgan won twice and Brian Barnes repeated as champion of the Senior British Open.

Women's golf was invigorated by the emergence of 21-year-old Karrie Webb of Australia, who became the first player to win $1 million on the U.S. LPGA Tour, but England's Laura Davies, age 35, remained No. 1 in the world.

In her first year in America, Webb won four tournaments and $1,002,000. Davies also had four U.S. victories, including two major titles in the McDonald's LPGA Championship and du Maurier Classic, and was second on the money list with $927,302.

Davies, however, had five more victories elsewhere, three in Europe and two in Japan, for a record total of $1,383,003 on the Women's World Money List. Webb's worldwide total was $1,135,971, and Annika Sorenstam of Sweden was third with $868,483. Other leaders were America's Dottie Pepper with $730,698, Sweden's Liselotte Neumann with $707,216 and Japan's Akiko Fukushima with $666,303.

Sorenstam won four tournaments, including one in Europe, and repeated as champion in the U.S. Women's Open. Other major titles were won by Patty Sheehan in the Nabisco Dinah Shore and Emilee Klein in the Weetabix Women's British Open. Neumann and Michelle McGann also had outstanding American seasons with three victories each, and Meg Mallon won twice.

Elsewhere, Trish Johnson of England had three worldwide victories, one in America and two in Europe, Corinne Dibnah won twice in Australasia, and Aiko Hashimoto won three times in Japan. Fukushima, the leading Japanese money winner, won twice.

3. Masters Tournament

The 1996 Masters Tournament ended with Nick Faldo putting on the green jacket for a third time then saying, "I hope I'm remembered for shooting 67 on the last day, and not what happened to Greg. But obviously, this will be remembered for what happened to Greg."

What had happened was one of the greatest collapses in the history of golf.

Greg Norman led for the first three rounds, led by six strokes going into the final round, then lost it all. Everyone was trying to make sense of it. If Norman had shot 67, his average for the first three rounds, he would have beaten Faldo by six strokes. A par 72 would have been Norman's worst round of the week, but he would have beaten Faldo by one.

They say no one ever remembers who finishes second, but they will for this Masters, because Norman not only blew a six-stroke lead, he shot a final-round 78 and lost by five strokes. He suffered an 11-stroke swing.

Faldo was head-to-head against Norman in the final round, and he played beautifully, posting that one-bogey 67. He played well enough to deserve a victory. But he had assessed the situation correctly. History will say this was both a Masters Faldo won and that Norman lost.

If Faldo said it for history, *Sports Illustrated* showed it for history. The magazine's cover photo the next week didn't show a triumphant Faldo. It didn't even show the memorable, touching moment when Faldo, victorious and unbelieving, hugged the whipped Norman on the 18th green. Instead, it showed Norman bowed completely, bent over from the waist, hands on knees. You saw the crown of his black, wide-brimmed hat. You didn't see his face. You didn't need to. You knew what was on it.

Norman's crash sent the archivists scrambling through their records. This is what they found.

Norman's collapse was the greatest ever by a 54-hole leader in any of the four major championships. Five others lost five-stroke leads: Mike Brady in the 1919 U.S. Open, Macdonald Smith in the 1925 British Open, Jose Jurado in the 1931 British Open, Tom Watson in the 1978 PGA Championship and Ed Sneed in the 1979 Masters.

Afterwards, Norman came striding into the Augusta interview room with the same old vigor. He took a seat at the table, behind the microphone. "I played like (expletive deleted)," he began. "I don't know any other way to put it." He was grinning, and he had that gleam in his eye. But who could believe the grin and the gleam.

It was all the more painful for him — and for those in the gallery and watching on television — because in a cruel twist of contrasts, the fates had made him the Norman Conqueror for the first three rounds. He was awesome, beginning in the first round with 63 that tied the course record.

Norman's 63 also came within a whisper of being 62.

At the par-four 11th, his putt for a birdie did everything but drop. "The ball defied gravity," Norman said. "It went right over the edge of the hole. I don't know how it stayed out."

Maybe it was the hand of Bobby Jones, someone noted. Back in the 1986

Masters, Nick Price set the Augusta record with 63, but he nearly had 62. His putt for a birdie on the 18th hung on the lip. "Bobby Jones," Price said, with a wry grin, "put up his hand and said, 'That's enough.'"

On reflection, Norman had no complaints. The first round of the Masters had always been tough for him. In 15 previous Masters, he'd had only one first round in the 60s, and that was 69 in his first, 1981. There have been 18 63s shot in the majors, and Norman is the only player with two. He got his first in the 1986 British Open, the first of his two British Open victories. He'd had many close calls, but these were the only majors he had won.

And this was a good start after some lackluster play. He had won the Doral-Ryder Open six weeks earlier, in the first week of March, but missed the 36-hole cut in his last two events leading up to the Masters. The first signs he was back were the pars at two of the toughest holes on the course. He blasted out of a bunker to three feet at the par-three No. 4, and hit a seven iron to 10 feet and two-putted at No. 5. (No. 4 would end up being the toughest hole in the first round, No. 5 the sixth toughest.)

Norman parred the first five holes, and felt the first stirrings of impatience. "I told myself to be patient, to stick to my game plan," he said. "Otherwise, you can let it slip away." It worked. He parred No. 6 with two putts from 35 feet, then birdied the next three holes from 10, 10 and 14 feet for 33 on the first nine. "The front is much more difficult to score on," he said. "You're churning your guts out."

His back-nine 30 was a rush — four birdies from No. 12, including a miracle at the 14th, where he hit a tree with his tee shot and came down short, then fired a three iron 220 yards to three feet. Then he birdied the 17th from 10 feet, and the 18th from 24 feet. He had six one-putt greens, which takes some doing on Augusta's first line of defense, its fast, undulating greens.

"It's just one of those things where I just let it flow," Norman said. "When you get into the type of roll that I got into today, it feels very comfortable."

For a while, it seemed the Masters would have a left-hander for a leader. Phil Mickelson, that odd wonder — a natural right-hander who learned to play golf left-handed — was comfortably in the clubhouse with a seven-under-par 65. A 65 at Augusta at any time is a powerful score, but especially so in the first round, when everybody is feeling out the course. Norman came along three hours later with his 63. Mickelson shared the first-round lead with 66 in 1995. Now he was second with 65, his best-ever score in four visits to Augusta. "When I first came here," he said, "I felt I should fire at every pin. I've been trying to play smarter."

Mickelson and Norman had almost identical performances. They both hit 16 of 18 greens and 12 of 14 fairways. Mickelson needed 28 putts, Norman 27. Both shot 30 on the second nine. Norman saved par out of the sand twice in two tries, and Mickelson missed in his only try. It cost him his only bogey of the day, at the par-three No. 4.

Scott Hoch and Bob Tway tied for third at 67. Hoch, the Masters runner-up to Faldo in 1989, couldn't believe his close calls on the greens. His playing partner, Paul Stankowski, said it for him. "He said, 'Man, you could have birdied the first 13 holes,'" Hoch said. It was the tale of what the golfers call the Cellophane Bridge — you can't see it, but balls roll over it. "The ball kept going over the edge of the hole," Hoch said. "I couldn't make a birdie. It was unbelievable." Three consecutive putts lipped out, from No. 5. But he did make six birdies — five of them on the second nine — and only one bogey.

Tway also found the second nine more agreeable. He had one bogey and one birdie on the first nine, then birdied three in a row from the 11th, then the 15th and 17th. "I wasn't struggling for par, and that's important here," Tway said. Tway is famed for holing the bunker shot on the final hole to beat Norman in the 1986 PGA Championship, and then almost falling out of sight. He committed a common error. "In pursuit of getting better, I changed a few things — and got worse," he said. "I went back to my natural style, and it didn't come overnight." But it did seem to be coming. He won the MCI Classic in 1995 — his first win in five years.

Lee Janzen birdied four of the last six holes for 68 and put off thoughts of winning. "I'm more worried about tomorrow than I am of Sunday," he said.

Brad Faxon posted a no-bogey 69 and was just happy to be on board. He had been having trouble with his back and was weak on the left side. "I didn't know if I would be able to play a week ago," he said. "This is the first round I've played in five weeks. I'm happy I finished 18 holes. I walked up 18 thinking, should I be mad for not shooting 66 or happy with finishing 18?" He settled for the obvious answer.

David Gilford, the mild-mannered Englishman in his second Masters, shot 69, but had the weird round of the day. Two birdies on the first nine left him two under par through the turn. He eagled the 13th to get to four under, then double-bogeyed the par-three 16th. He over-clubbed himself, hitting a three iron off the tee, and he missed the green. He opted for his putter. He used it four times from 30 feet.

Faldo was practically a forgotten man in the first round, buried as he was in the pack with 69. It was his best opening round since his first victory in 1989. Maybe that was one sign of what was to come. And maybe there was another, a stronger one. "I hit the ball where I intended to," he said.

He made only one bogey, at the 14th. He had four birdies, none of them trials, that's how solid his game was. He had two birdies from eight feet, one from five, and one from one foot.

Faldo said he had never seen Augusta dry on Monday, Tuesday and Wednesday. "Normally, it's wet on the greens and the ball stops," he said. "It's the first time we've had them dry, so we know what we're in for with the weather." He offered some advice, in the event the course got firmer: "You're just going to have to play very safe, cagey, of whatever you want to call it. I call it smart, aggressive, defensive."

There seemed to be a contradiction there — aggressive, defensive. But Faldo knew what he meant. As he was to demonstrate.

The attack on Augusta's soft underbelly, the par-five holes, started early and in earnest. There were eight eagles by eight different players — one each at No. 2 and No. 8, and three each at the 13th and 15th. The toll at the 13th has been heavy. Gilford, Hal Sutton and Italy's Costantino Rocca made it 53 eagles at the hole in the 1990s alone.

Norman made no eagles. But he did make nine birdies in a flawless, pristine round of 63. It looked like Norman's week.

The first-round leaderboard:

Greg Norman	63	David Gilford	69
Phil Mickelson	65	Brad Faxon	69
Bob Tway	67	Nick Faldo	69
Scott Hoch	67	Scott Simpson	69
Lee Janzen	68	Vijay Singh	69

If anyone would like a fanciful name for the second round of the 1996 Masters, maybe the Ambush at Golden Bell will do. Golden Bell, taken from the beautiful flower, is the name for the treacherous 12th hole, the 155-yard par-three tucked behind Rae's Creek. It's the pivot hole of the famed Amen Corner, and it took a heavy toll in the second round. It took the biggest bite out of defending champion Ben Crenshaw. He triple-bogeyed it, shot 74–151, and missed the 36-hole cut by five strokes. The 12th is heart-stopping in the calm air. When the wind is up, it's maddening, and the wind was up for the second round.

"The hole had the worst gusts I've seen," Crenshaw said. His seven-iron tee shot fell short into the water, and so did his wedge from the drop area. He made a triple-bogey six. So did Sutton, Payne Stewart and Paul Goydos. One of the three first-time winners on the PGA Tour so far this season, Goydos got some rude treatment from the 12th. He made his six without ever hitting the water. The wind died just as he was hitting, and his ball flew over the green and into the bushes. The ball wasn't found. Goydos had to go back to the tee and hit again.

The par-three fourth again played the toughest on the course, but No. 12, third toughest, inflicted more big wounds. No. 4 took five double bogeys and no "others" — worse than double bogeys. No. 12 took eight doubles and four of the "others" — all triple bogeys — twice as many as any other hole.

Oddly enough, it spared Norman, the same way it spared Fred Couples when he won the Masters in 1992. Norman's tee shot hung on the bank, about a foot above the water. True, the grass was a bit longer now than it was for Couples, but the water still claimed 12 of the 18 balls that came down short. Norman got up-and-down for his par. "There was a lot of moisture on the bank, and it kept the ball up," he said. "I'm glad they didn't cut it real low. I just kind of tip-toed up there. I did just what Freddie did — I made my par and got away from there." Two days later, Norman would be wishing he could say the same thing.

Faldo came away thanking his lucky stars. The air was calm when he came to the 12th. He hit the green safely and left happy, with his par, on his way to 67 that would begin shaping this Masters into a Norman-Faldo battle.

Norman, bidding to become the first Australian to win the Masters, doubled his lead to four strokes. It was starting to look like a repeat of Raymond Floyd's romp in 1976 with a 17-under-par 271, which tied Jack Nicklaus' Masters record, and an eight-stroke victory. As it was, Norman shot a three-under-par 69 to post the second-lowest first 36 holes in Masters history, 132, just one stroke behind Floyd's record 131 in 1976. When Norman birdied the 18th for his 69, he became the first to shoot in the 60s in five consecutive rounds in the Masters.

It seemed he had to work the kinks out of his game this time. After a birdie at the par-five No. 2, he bogeyed the third and fourth holes, two-putting first from four feet, then from 12 feet. He picked up three birdies on the other par-fives, then holed a four-footer for the final birdie at the 18th, the 69 and the four-stroke lead.

"Greg has the potential to run away with it," said John Daly, the 1995 British Open champion, who was trailing by 13 strokes. "I don't see anybody catching him with the course the way it is." Janzen, seven strokes behind, agreed that Norman would be tough on the fast fairways and firm greens. "But I don't think anybody's invincible," Janzen said. "It will be very tough sleeping on the lead."

If Norman was nervous about the coming challenge, he gave no sign of it. "I'm looking forward to it," he said. "I'm very relaxed. I feel very comfortable within myself."

It showed in his play. In the two rounds, he had hit 24 of 28 fairways and 29 of 36 greens in regulation. He needed 27 putts in the first round, 30 in the second round.

"Obviously, Greg's not making any mistakes," Janzen said.

Playing along almost unnoticed, Faldo was making even fewer. He opened with a birdie, a two-putt from 20 feet at No. 1, and was flawless the rest of the way to a five-under-par 67. His short game was superb. He made six one-putt birdies — one from 20 feet, two from 12, two from six, and one from eight. The connoisseur's shot, though, might have been his lay-up at No. 13, where he was blocked by trees on the right. He was thinking of hitting down into the 14th fairway, but there were spectators in the area. "I had to reshape my game plan due to the crowd," he said. He hit a snap hook with a five iron around the trees and down into the fairway. Next came a pitch-and-run that got him to eight feet, then the putt for the birdie.

"I'm obviously very pleased because Greg was way ahead and going along nicely," Faldo said. "So I've taken every chance I was given today." Including, he noted, getting past the 12th again with a par. What's your strategy, someone asked. "Well," he said, "I like to breathe in and out."

Mickelson got wild with his driver but rescued himself with his wondrous short game, shooting 73. It took a miracle birdie at the 18th, though. He had driven into the woods and was probably going to put his next shot into one of the greenside bunkers. "A very difficult par," he said. Instead, he fired the ball between the bunkers, and it ran right up near the hole. The birdie tied him for third with David Frost, who shook off a double bogey at the 10th and shot 68.

The great amateur shootout never happened. It was to have been British Amateur champion Gordon Sherry against U.S. Amateur winner Tiger Woods. Sherry, all 6-foot-8 of him, playing in his first Masters, was nowhere in sight. He shot 78-77—155 and missed the cut by nine strokes. "It's been a good experience," Sherry said, "although my first impression would be to say that it's been the worst experience I've ever had on a golf course. I knew the greens were going to be tricky." It was the last chance for a Sherry-Woods amateur duel. When Sherry came through the ropes behind No. 18, he was greeted by his mother, Anne Sherry. She took his hand. "Welcome," she said, "to your professional career." He was turning professional immediately after the Masters.

Woods had come to the 1995 Masters as a young hero. He came to the

1996 Masters fresh from his sophomore year at Stanford University still a hero, but now carrying a load of expectations perhaps too heavy for a 20-year-old. "If he can handle all the attention, all the pressure from you folks," Nicklaus told a media gathering, "Tiger can be as good or better than anybody who ever played the game." As praise goes, that's the limit.

"I don't read the papers," Woods said, on hearing this, "but that's quite a compliment."

The second Masters, however, didn't go as well for Woods as the first. Where he shot a pair of 72s and made the cut in 1995, he shot a pair of 75s and missed the cut this time. Two of his five bogeys in the second round came at the tougher holes. He three-putted the 11th hole from six feet — his second putt was longer than the first — and he hit a shot into the water at the 12th. "The score didn't show it, but I played better this year than I did last year," Woods said. "I was a lot more comfortable, and I knew what to expect this time."

The cut came in at two-over-par 146. Woods and Crenshaw weren't the only two unexpected victims. Also gone were Gilford, Stewart, Fuzzy Zoeller, Curtis Strange and Tom Watson, a two-time Masters champion, missing the cut for the first time in 21 Masters. A disaster in the first round — a five-putt at the 16th, his first ever in a tournament — did him in. He shot 75-72 and missed by one stroke. And also gone was the strangest story in golf — Ian Baker-Finch. The amiable Aussie won the British Open in 1991, then mysteriously became a shadow of himself. This time, he shot 78-79 and missed his 22nd consecutive cut in the United States.

The final battle was actually joined after the second round ended. Norman and Faldo were paired in the final group for the third round — the first time they had played together since the 1990 British Open at St. Andrews. They played in the first two rounds that time. In the fateful second, Faldo shot 67, Norman 76, and Faldo went on to win. This time, things looked much different.

"It looks like Greg is in control of everything, the way he's going," Faldo said. "I'm going to play my own game tomorrow. I'll worry about little old me first."

The second-round leaderboard:

Greg Norman	69 - 132	Scott McCarron	70 - 140
Nick Faldo	67 - 136	Vijay Singh	71 - 140
David Frost	68 - 138	Scott Hoch	73 - 140
Phil Mickelson	73 - 138	Corey Pavin	66 - 141
Lee Janzen	71 - 139	Ian Woosnam	69 - 141
Bob Tway	72 - 139		

Faldo had reason to worry about himself. He got off to a shaky start, and by the end of the third round, he found himself in a hole that would be too deep to get out of — ordinarily. But then, that's the story of the 1996 Masters.

Saturday, Augusta's famed spring breezes came up strong and capricious. "The difference today was a four-letter word — wind," Norman said. "It was gusting to 20, 25 miles an hour. Sometimes you had to hit when the wind was in a lull. I'm very happy with 71. It's the equivalent of shooting in the 60s."

There was a lot of guess work, some bad breaks, some good ones. Norman made some of his own good breaks, notably at the 12th hole. There are such things as good bogeys, and he made one there — his first bogey on the second nine of the week. "I hit a good tee shot at No. 12," Norman said, "but when it got caught up in the wind I said, 'Take your medicine.' I said just try to make four. It could have been a lot worse." His eight-iron tee shot came down short in the pond. He took a drop 88 yards from the hole, flipped a wedge shot on to 10 feet, and made an excellent four.

He and Faldo, playing together, took turns opening the door to each other.

Norman bogeyed the third and fourth holes again, as he had in the second round. A birdie at No. 8, where he pitched to one foot, got him an outward 37. His lead over Faldo was down to five strokes through the turn. But he got up to speed on the second nine. After the bogey at No. 12, matching Faldo's, he fired a five iron to 10 feet at No. 13. The eagle got away, but the birdie didn't. He birdied the 15th from six feet, then birdied the 16th after a nine iron to six feet.

Faldo started so shakily there was no telling where he might end up. He picked up a stroke on Norman with a birdie at No. 2, but he followed that with a double-bogey six at No. 3. Faldo is known for his steady play, but the crash at No. 3 was just the start of one of the rockiest rounds he ever played in a major.

"Very tough pins and blustery wind," Faldo said. That explained the entire day. Of the 44 players who made the cut, only nine broke par. Duffy Waldorf and David Duval, a Masters rookie, had the low round, each shooting 69, and there were one 70 and six 71s. One of the 71s belong to Norman, which complicated things for Faldo. He was second, but he had fallen six strokes behind.

The double bogey at No. 3 set the tone. Faldo was short with a wedge, then didn't make the green with his chip. He followed that with a bogey at the mean No. 4, hitting his three-iron tee shot over the green, then chipping poorly. Then he closed out the first nine birdie-par-bogey-birdie-birdie for an outward par 36. He came home with three bogeys and two birdies for 73.

Like Norman, Faldo made an outstanding bogey at the 12th. He missed the green, then had to chip from a downhill lie to an upslope, with a downslope just over that crest and the water lying beyond. He narrowly missed his par putt.

"My play wasn't bad," Faldo said. "I could have saved the day, you know, making some putts on 12, 13, 14, 15, 16. I mean, I missed all of those, the longest being about eight or 10 feet."

Meanwhile, Norman was tightening his grip on this Masters. With just 71, Norman increased his lead over Faldo by two strokes — to six.

Mickelson played one of the steadiest rounds of the windy day, a two-birdie, two-bogey 72, to stay in third place at six-under-par 210. But he wasn't happy with his play on the par-fives. "You've got to birdie those holes," he said. He parred all four of them. He was short with a seven iron into No. 13, and he was long with a six iron at the 15th. Then he was gearing up for the final round.

"The first six holes are the toughest holes on the course," Mickelson said. "That's my mind-set right now — to play the first six holes aggressively and somewhere under par."

Mickelson had put his finger on it: the first six holes. Other dreamers saw their hopes die there. Augusta's Amen Corner — the 11th through the 13th — is famed throughout the world. Now a little-known but much-deserving stretch on the front nine was gaining a matching reputation. It was the third, fourth and fifth holes, almost anonymous because they don't have dangerous reaches over water, they're not carried on television, and because most of the gallery doesn't get out to that area. The golfers know, though. Davis Love III had built up some steam with birdies on the first two holes, then was about 100 yards from the small, hard green at No. 3, where the flag was just 12 feet from the right edge. His wedge hit the green, and he four-putted for a double bogey. Then he bogeyed No. 4 and No. 5, on his way to a destructive 74. "They're all tough holes, no matter what the conditions are," Love said.

The second nine took its toll, too. Tway, tied for fifth after the second round, was in the running through the first 15 holes in the third round. Then he bogeyed the last three holes, shot 76, and fell into a tie for 16th place. And at the 15th, which gave up 15 birdies and an eagle, Colin Montgomerie rang up a day's-worst triple-bogey eight. He laid up in front of the pond, flipped his third shot over the green, left his weak chip in the back fringe, and four-putted — after his first putt came within a foot of the hole. He shot 75.

The third round ended with Norman leading at 13-under-par 203, and Faldo second at 209, six strokes behind.

Norman led the Masters once before coming into the final round. That was in 1986, the year of Nicklaus' victory at age 46. Norman closed with a 70 that year, but he suffered one of his chronic problems at the final hole. He pushed his approach shot. It cost him a bogey and a chance to tie Nicklaus.

Norman had been the 54-hole leader in major championships six times. He won only one, the first of his two British Opens at Turnberry in 1986. He led that one by four strokes going into the final round. "I don't live in the past," Norman said. "I don't dwell on it. People made some good shots to win those tournaments."

"I'm going to enjoy tomorrow," Norman said. "Irrespective of what happens, I'm going to enjoy every step I take. It's one of those deals where I've got a chance to win the Masters. I've been there before, and there is no better feeling than having a chance of winning a major championship. I'm going to enjoy the moment. I'm going to go to the first tee tomorrow as relaxed and comfortable as I have been since the first day."

As for Faldo, what was he supposed to say? Than any man six shots behind Norman with one round to play had no chance? "It's a long way back," Faldo said, conceding the obvious, "but you know, anything's possible."

Faldo's words turned out to be true. So did those of *Charlotte (N.C.) Observer* columnist Ronald Green. Wrote Green: "Greg Norman won the Masters on Saturday. Now, if he can only keep from losing it."

The third-round leaderboard:

Greg Norman	71 - 203	David Duval	69 - 214
Nick Faldo	73 - 209	Frank Nobilo	72 - 214
Phil Mickelson	72 - 210	Ian Woosnam	73 - 214
Duffy Waldorf	69 - 212	Ernie Els	72 - 214
Scott McCarron	72 - 212	Corey Pavin	73 - 214
David Frost	74 - 212	Vijay Singh	74 - 214
John Huston	71 - 213	Lee Janzen	75 - 214
Scott Hoch	73 - 213		

Norman and Faldo were not the only two men in the field for the fourth round. It only seemed that way. So in all fairness to history, perhaps we ought to account for some of the others who left their mark, in one way or another.

Montgomerie left a mark he would like to erase. If he ever wants to win the Masters, he had better do something about the par-fives, where you're supposed to make hay. Here's how Montgomerie fared at the fives: At No. 2, he had a birdie and three pars. At No. 8, two birdies and two pars. At No. 13, two birdies and two pars. Not bad, so far. Then came the 15th. He had par, bogey and two triple bogeys. He played the hole in seven over par, was a net two over on the par-fives, totalled an eight-over 296, and finished 39th in the field of 44, which is no place for the top European to be.

Seve Ballesteros, a two-time winner whose game had fallen on hard times, left on a high note. Not the final-round 76 that left him a next-to-last 43rd, but some higher spirits. "I feel like my game is getting better," he said. "When you reach the bottom, there's only one way to go, and that's up. I think I reached bottom. Now I'm going to go up."

Last place belonged to Alexander Cejka, the new German star playing in his first Masters. He closed with a whopping 80 and totalled 302. He matched 1991 champion Ian Woosnam, whose 80 included a mortifying nine at the par-five 15th. The high round of the day belonged to Vijay Singh, who shot 82. He tied for 39th. And Nicklaus left smiling. He shot 78 and came in to a standing ovation. "I appreciate that," he said. "But I did not have a good Masters. I three-putted a half dozen times the last two days, and once I stop playing well, concentration is hard."

As for challenges, there were no serious ones. Not for the victory, anyway. Mickelson mounted the big threat for second place. Oddly enough, he started the day in third place, a stroke out of second, and finished third, a stroke out of second.

He was behind Faldo at the start, and behind Norman at the finish. Mickelson looked like he might get something going when he birdied No. 2, but it was a false alarm. His brightest moment came at No. 6, when a birdie tied him with Faldo and moved him to within five strokes of Norman. Bogeys at the seventh and eighth made Mickelson an also-ran. He closed with 72 for a six-under 282 total, and finished third, six behind Faldo and only one behind Norman. Like everyone else, he was stunned by the man's collapse. "My heart goes out to him," Mickelson said. "It just wasn't his day. I don't know what the deal was. It's hard for me to imagine that 78."

The stage that final day belonged to Norman and Faldo. Actually, Norman had it all to himself at the start. He was 13 under par and leading by six. He had drawn up his terms with himself the day before, at the end of the third round. "I've got a lot of work to do," Norman had. "I've got 18 tough holes. And everybody's even. There is no lead. I just have to shoot a score."

Norman's collapse started quietly enough, at No. 1. He drove into the trees on the left, then was short and in a bunker with his second shot, and two-putted from seven feet. It wasn't much, just a bogey, and it didn't do any great damage. He would get the stroke back quickly. But it was a tipoff that trouble was on the way. He would say that he was strong and confident and comfortable, but he just wasn't in rhythm. It seems there's a contradiction here somewhere, but he couldn't explain it.

That bogey was fast forgotten the way he played No. 2. He put his second shot into the gallery at the left, then putted from the swale and nearly holed it for an eagle. He tapped in for a birdie. Faldo also birdied, blasting out of a bunker to two feet. Norman's lead was down to five strokes.

It fell to four when he bogeyed the par-three No. 4 for the third straight day. "I just came up two feet short," he said. He bunkered his tee shot, but came out weakly, 18 feet short. He two-putted.

Norman led by five again when Faldo bogeyed No. 5 out of a bunker. It looked like a day of give-and-take. Maybe Faldo would close the gap a bit, but whoever wanted to win this Masters was going to have to take it away from Norman. Then the pace quickened. Things started happening.

First, Faldo birdied the par-three No. 6, hitting a seven iron to four feet. Norman parred. His lead was four.

Next came Norman's first crucial error. At the par-five No. 8, he hit his second shot wildly into the left trees. He had birdied No. 8 three days running. Now he couldn't birdie it again. It was an opportunity lost. He parred. Faldo birdied, two-putting from 20 feet. Norman's lead was down to three. Now the galleries at Augusta were stirring nervously. Was Norman unraveling?

Next came four of the darkest holes of Norman's career. Now it was like Chinese water torture. Drop by drop, Norman's Masters was draining away.

Nick Price, his good friend, had finished and was watching on television in the clubhouse. He turned away. "I feel sick to my stomach," he said.

At No. 9 was a shot Norman would like to have over. "Just a mis-hit, and I tried to turn it into the front right." The approach was just short enough to inflict damage. The ball came rolling down off the sloping nose of that green and back into the fairway. He bogeyed. Faldo parred. Norman was out in 38, and his six-stroke lead was down to two.

And then it was one. At No. 10, Norman missed the green just to the left, and chipped badly, 10 feet past the hole. He two-putted for a bogey. Faldo parred on two putts from 20 feet.

And then the last stroke of that once-healthy lead disappeared. At No. 11, Norman made his third straight bogey. He hit the green, but he three-putted from only 15 feet. His first putt went three feet past the hole. He had squandered a six-stroke lead in 11 holes. They were tied.

Then came a disaster.

Norman had been on fairly good terms with the 12th hole. He birdied it in the first round, got a great break in the second round and parred after his ball clung to the bank just above the water, and in the third round, he salvaged a good bogey from a watered tee shot.

This time Norman's tee shot hit the bank and didn't hang on. It rolled back into the water. He took his penalty drop, wedged on to 12 feet, and two-putted for a double bogey.

In this entire stretch, Faldo didn't make anything better than par, and he picked up five strokes. Now, through the 12th, he had a two-stroke lead on Norman. The balance had shifted completely. "That's when it was mine to lose," Faldo said.

Norman hadn't run completely out of gas. He still had enough left to birdie the 13th and 15th — at the 15th, he nearly chipped in for an eagle. But then, Faldo birdied both holes too.

At the 13th, he deliberated over a five wood and a two iron for his approach shot. He finally put the five wood back and took out the two iron. It was an inspired choice. He put the ball about 30 feet from the flag, and two-putted for the birdie.

"He hit a great second shot, considering how many times he backed off it," Norman said. "That was for the whole shooting match there, even though I was behind by two — making four there and him making four."

At the 15th, he chipped from the back to two feet. He still led by two. The clincher came at the 16th — not his, Norman's.

The 16th is a par-three, about 170 yards across a big pond to a severely undulating green protected by bunkers. This is where Nicklaus made the long "bear tracks" putt when he beat Tom Weiskopf and Johnny Miller in the 1975 Masters. Putting wasn't Norman's problem. Norman's tee shot never got near the green. "I just tried to hook a six iron in there, and it hooked all right," he said.

Norman hit the shot into the water and made a double-bogey five against Faldo's par. Norman was now four strokes behind with two holes to play. Was it over? Not yet, Faldo said. "Greg could have holed that putt on No. 17," he said. "Who knows — I could have hit a tree, I could have taken six, and he could have had three. I wasn't counting my chickens until I hit that last shot out of the bunker onto the green at the 18th."

Norman parred the last two holes. Faldo parred the 17th, bunkered his tee shot at the 18th, fired a nine iron out to 15 feet, and closed like a champion. He holed the putt for the birdie and the 67 he wants to be remembered for. Then he wrapped Norman in a hug on the green and said something to him. "I just said, I don't know what to say," Faldo said. "I just want to give you a hug."

Faldo had won his third Masters. In 1989, he caught Scott Hoch with a final-round 65, but Hoch missed an 18-inch putt in the playoff. In 1990, Raymond Floyd was tied by Faldo's 69 in the fourth round, then Floyd hit his approach shot into the water at the second playoff hole. And now there was Norman, blowing a six-stroke lead. Still, Faldo played his game and did what he had to do. Nothing of this magnitude had happened since Jack Burke, Jr. staged the biggest final-round rally in Masters history in 1956, coming from eight shots behind to beat Ken Venturi, the third-round leader, and still an amateur.

Norman was now the runner-up for the eighth time in the majors — three times in the Masters, twice in the U.S. Open, twice in the PGA Championship and once in the British Open.

4. U.S. Open Championship

The field of any tournament might be loaded with the game's leading players, but picking the winner is a risky exercise. There's no assurance any of them will make the cut. Tennis is different. The best players nearly always reach the semi-finals. For a long time during the 1980s you could write down Bjorn Borg every year for Wimbledon and assume he would beat either Jimmy Connors or John McEnroe in the championship match.

It can't be done in golf. Jack Nicklaus dominated the game during much of the 1970s, when he won one U.S. Open, two British Opens, two Masters Tournaments, and three PGA Championships, but while Borg won five Wimbledons in succession, Nicklaus didn't defend any of his championships successfully, and at one time or another finished behind Lou Graham, Jerry Pate, Hubert Green, Andy North, Tommy Aaron, Charles Coody, Dave Stockton and John Mahaffey.

The lesson was driven home once again in June of 1996 at the U.S. Open Championship which was played for the sixth time over the South Course of the Oakland Hills Country Club outside Detroit, always among the strongest and most severe tests on the Open rota. The Open's unexpected finish came after two of the game's leading players had battled through the final round at Augusta.

The Masters, which had been such a triumph for Nick Faldo and such a heartache for Greg Norman, had been over for two months by now. Understandably disheartened, Norman had played mediocre golf at the MCI Classic in Hilton Head Island, South Carolina, the following week, placing 22nd, then took six weeks off, finally surfacing in the Memorial Tournament in late May, where he played even worse and missed the cut. The following week he tied for 16th place in the Buick Classic at Westchester Country Club in New York.

Almost as inactive as Norman, Faldo, meantime, played even worse at the MCI Classic, dropping to 29th place, and finished 40th at Westchester. He did, however, return to England for two events, tying for second in the Volvo PGA Championship, two strokes behind Costantino Rocca, the Italian who nearly won the 1995 British Open.

While Norman and Faldo plodded, Tom Watson regained control of his putter well enough to win the Memorial; Phil Mickelson won the eighth tournament of his career at the GTE Byron Nelson Classic; Corey Pavin won the MasterCard Colonial, his first victory since the 1995 U.S. Open; Ernie Els, the 1994 U.S. Open champion, won at Westchester; Mark Brooks, who would win the PGA Championship later in the year, won at Houston, and other tournaments were won by Scott Hoch, Mark O'Meara, and 29-year-old Steve Stricker, who had never won before.

With the revival of Watson, along with Pavin's return to form, the continued first-class play of Els, Mickelson, O'Meara, and Brooks, and the smug assumption that both Faldo and Norman would raise their levels of play for the major championships, the outlook for the U.S. Open looked promising. Furthermore, Colin Montgomerie had been in top form throughout the year in both the United States and Europe — a winner in the Dubai

Desert Classic in the opening tournament of the PGA European Tour and in two others in Europe, second in The Players' Championship and eighth in the MCI Classic following a disappointing Masters. It seemed probable the U.S. Open would be decided by the game's leading players.

Meanwhile, Steve Jones had played six tournaments through the period between the Masters and Westchester, the week before the U.S. Open, missed four cuts, placed 61st in another, and only once broke into the first 10 by tying for sixth place at Colonial.

So then Mickelson opened with 76 and played absolute rubbish the rest of the way; neither Faldo nor Watson could break 70 even once (Faldo birdied only seven holes and Watson eight); Norman showed some spark with a second-round 66 but followed with two lifeless rounds of 74 and 70, after working himself into position by going out in 30 in the third round; Brooks played the next 27 holes in six over par, and only Hoch, Lee Janzen and Davis Love III, among those within range after 54 holes, shot under 70 in the last round.

Instead, Jones seized the opportunity, overcame a sloppy opening-round 74 with 66 the next day and added two consecutive 69s, and with 278 won by one stroke over Tom Lehman and Love. Even John Morse, who hardly anyone had ever heard of and who had fought his way through sectional qualifying, slipped in ahead of most of the game's big winners.

Still, the game's leading players didn't do badly. With the exception of Pavin, who tied for 40th place with 289, and Mickelson, who tied for 94th with 296, the others finished high. Els tied for fifth, Hoch for seventh, Janzen, Norman and Montgomerie for 13th, and Faldo, Brooks and O'Meara for 16th.

The result confounded a great many of those close to the game for two reasons. Championships played over great courses are usually won by great players. Jones wasn't among them. Besides, he had injured his left hand so badly a few years earlier he had dropped off the PGA Tour and came back only after changing to an unorthodox grip. Golfers with strange grips rarely win major championships.

Jones had given up the game because he had torn a ligament and damaged a joint of his left ring-finger when he crashed his dirt bike in the Arizona desert in November of 1991, then hurt it again repairing his backyard putting green. Unable to grip the club because of the damage, he left the PGA Tour for two and a half years. The accident might have ruined what had become a promising career. Jones had won one tournament in 1988 and three in 1989 and had tied for eighth place in the 1990 U.S. Open at Medinah.

Off the PGA Tour, Jones began chipping balls late in 1994 by using the reverse-overlap grip so common for putting. Instead of placing the little finger of the right hand over the index finger of the left, Jones lapped the index finger of the left hand over the little finger of the right, reversing the normal procedure. This method had its dangers. With all five fingers of the right hand on the club, players tend to hook the ball. Jones fought it with an especially firm left-hand grip.

Returning to competitive golf with a limited schedule late in 1994, Jones had been able to control the ball, and indeed became one of the longest drivers in the game, averaging 279 yards in 1996, a yard and a half behind John Daly. Unfortunately for him, he couldn't convert distance into high finishes. In 15 tournaments, he had placed among the 10 leaders only at Phoenix, where he lives, at Bay Hill and Colonial. With $183,000, he ranked below 50th among the money winners.

Throughout 1995 and 1996, he determined that once his hand healed he would go back to the standard grip, and perhaps he still might, but his unorthodox method worked especially well for him in the Open.

In the tensest moment of his golf career, Jones threaded his drive between fairway bunkers on the finishing hole while Lehman, who was tied with him at the time, drove into a bunker. From the middle of the fairway, Jones played a superb seven iron onto the green and made the par four that won the championship while Lehman bogeyed and tied for second place, one stroke behind, with Love, who bogeyed both the 17th and 18th holes when pars would have won him the championship.

Jones won over a course that played extremely long, even though at 6,974 yards it measured 221 yards shorter than Medinah, at 7,195 yards the longest ever. Weather conditions that softened the ground caused Oakland Hills to seem longer than its measured distance. Detroit had gone through a very wet spring, and then more rain fell the weekend before the U.S. Open was to begin. The rain that had fallen before looked mild when, at about noon Wednesday, a monsoon-like storm hit Oakland Hills.

Thunder rolled across the skies, lightning flashed, and the rain poured down. Two and a half inches fell in just two hours. Finally, the rain slackened off, the sun broke through the black clouds, and the United States Golf Association officials stepped outside to assay the damage.

They were shocked. Parts of the course lay under two or three feet of water. Aside from the collected water on the fairways, every bunker on the course was flooded, and the big bunker on the right side of the 18th green had collapsed. With the Open scheduled to begin at seven o'clock the following morning, in less than 17 hours, the chances weren't good it would begin on time.

After a quick glance at the horrors, the grounds crew set to work. First, the grounds superintendent organized a crew to begin rebuilding and reshaping the bunker at the 18th. Meantime, superintendents from neighboring clubs began arriving to help out. Soon a 60-member crew that included 25 superintendents from other clubs struggled to drain the fairways and rebuild bunkers.

Because they drain so well, the greens needed very little work. Three hours after the mid-day rain had stopped, crews were blowing away leaves, and within another hour they were mowing.

Through it all the USGA maintained two things. First, play would begin on schedule at seven o'clock Thursday morning. Second, there would be no preferred lies. Asked if the USGA might allow players to lift, clean and place the ball, Tom Meeks, the USGA's chief rules administrator, insisted, "No, no, no, no. Golf," he said, "We're going to play golf here."

The weekend of rain climaxed by the downpour on Wednesday left opinions divided on whether the players would find Oakland Hills a more difficult test than it might have been. Watson felt it would play about as it would have without the rain. "I don't think it takes that much teeth out of the course," he said. "It makes the rough more difficult, but it makes the greens softer."

Watson also felt the softer greens might not be the blessing everyone assumed. "They'll hold better," he said, "but on the other hand they'll be spongy. With the later groups, the ball will bounce close to the hole because of all the traffic, and that will make putting difficult. This course is as tough as I remember it."

Twelve men broke par and 11 shot 70s in the opening round. Payne Stewart and Woody Austin shot 67s, Janzen and Morse shot 68s and eight others shot 69s. Included among them were Bob Ford and Gary Trivisonno, both club professionals. Watson was among the 70 shooters, along with Montgomerie, who nearly won in 1992 and 1994; Scott Simpson, who actually did win in 1987; Brad Faxon, who nearly won the 1994 British Open, and seven others.

Meantime, Love and Lehman were among those at 71; Nicklaus, Faldo, Els, Daly and Steve Elkington, the 1995 PGA champion, were at 72, and Pavin and Norman at 73. At the other end of the scale, Ben Crenshaw shot 80 and Ian Baker-Finch, who had been such a promising player only a few years earlier, shot 83. At the same time, seen only by those with nowhere else to go, Jones shot 74.

The day was filled with golf that raised the spirit of many golfers but ended in despair for some others. Mickelson, for example, had tied for fourth place at Shinnecock Hills in 1995. Clearly one of the favorites, he began by butchering the opening hole and making six, committed an unpardonable sin by losing another stroke on the second, a par-five, then bogeyed both the fourth and fifth. Playing like an 18-handicapper, Mickelson stood five over par after five holes. By the time he steered himself back on course, his Open was over. He went out in 40, dropped another stroke coming home, and shot 76.

Young Tiger Woods suffered a terrible collapse after threatening to shoot one of the low scores. Three under par after 13 holes, he bogeyed the 14th, double-bogeyed the 15th, then made an eight on the 16th, hitting two shots into the willow-lined pond that had overflowed during the Wednesday storm. Four over now, he bogeyed both the 17th and 18th, played the last five holes in nine over par, came back in 43, and shot 76. He was finished as well.

The round began on schedule under a threatening overcast, but by 9:30 the sun had broken through and the temperature began to climb. It became a pleasant day, although spectators walking in the galleries churned the area just outside the restraining ropes into muck. Even though the ground was soft and wet, rules officials had very few occasions to allow relief from casual water.

It is common for someone to run off a string of birdies, but we saw nothing of the sort at Oakland Hills. Janzen reached four under par with birdies on the 12th and 13th, a par-five and a par-three, but he bogeyed the difficult 14th, at 471 yards the longest of the par-fours, and the 17th, an uphill par-three of 200 yards with a very difficult green. Paul Goydos, who had won at Bay Hill earlier in the spring, eagled the second, went four under par after six, played the rest of the way in five over and was on his way to missing the cut.

It is equally common that low rounds are scattered throughout the day, but again, not at Oakland Hills. Of the 12 men who shot under par 70, eight teed off in the morning. Only Morse, Frank Nobilo, Jumbo Ozaki and Paul Azinger began after noon, and both Stewart and Austin had teed off by 9:30.

Dressed in a white shirt and stockings and navy blue pants and cap, Stewart went off at 8:20 playing nothing like a potential leader. He went out in 36, one over par, with a bogey on the first, where he drove into a fairway bunker, and a double-bogey five on the ninth, a demanding par-three of 220 yards, where his tee shot plugged in the freshly laid sand of a greenside bunker. Misjudging the texture of the new sand, Stewart dug too deeply, failed to reach the green, buried his ball under the bunker's lip, and holed from six feet to save his five. He had played a frustrating nine, scrambling for his bogey on the first and seventh and birdieing the second and sixth.

Quickly, though, Stewart turned his game around, raced back in 31 with four birdies, and shot his 67. His par on the 14th had to be seen to be appreciated. He pulled his drive among trees in the left rough, and when he tried to reach the green with a four iron, the ball nicked a tree branch and dropped behind another tree close to a fence and a television tower. Stewart lobbed an eight iron over the tree and holed a 50-foot putt from about three feet short of the green. When the putt fell, Payne spread his arms, threw back his head, and laughed.

He finished with flair. After birdieing both the 15th and 16th with remarkable iron play — a seven iron to six inches on the 15th and a six iron that hit and stuck two feet from the cup on the 16th — he holed a six-footer to save par on the 17th, then overshot the 18th with another six iron and holed from six feet once again.

When he had finished, glowing like a man who had broken par should, Stewart grinned and said, "There was some ugly out there, and there was some pretty. It all added up to 67. I didn't feel like I drove the ball very well, but I got away with it. I hit some beautiful iron shots and I putted the ball extremely well. I had a lot of fun, and I'm going to laugh about it all day long."

Stewart had barely finished chatting about his fun day when Austin romped home with a much steadier 67 of his own. Where Stewart had scrambled, mixing seven birdies with two bogeys and a double bogey, Austin played steady, precision golf, parred 15 holes and birdied three. He was never in trouble. When he missed a green, as he did on both the eighth and ninth, he left himself simple chip shots to save his pars.

Playing in his first Open, Austin ran off 10 consecutive pars, birdied three in a row, then closed out with five more pars, finishing with difficult two-putt pars at the 17th, where he holed from 10 feet, and the 18th, when he struggled to get down in two from 45 feet.

Austin was an interesting case. Now 32 years old, he had played college golf at the University of Miami, turned professional in 1987, but long and hard practice sessions preparing for the qualifying tournament put too much strain on his left knee, which had never developed properly after a childhood injury. It buckled under the stress, tearing tendons and cartilage, and sending him back home to Tampa, where he took a job with a credit union.

Still dreaming of a golf career, he worked to build a stake by moonlighting as a bartender and took the graveyard shift at a 24-hour drugstore. After an occasional trial on the mini tours and in Japan, he went back to the qualifying tournament in 1994 and not only survived but shot the lowest score. The following August he won the Buick Open and played so well he became the Rookie of the Year.

Although he had done nothing spectacular early in 1996, placing 10th or better in only three of the 20 tournaments he had entered and missing the cut in the Masters by miles, Austin played Oakland Hills as a U.S. Open course should be played — hitting fairways and greens. Where Stewart hit nine fairways, Austin hit 11, and where Stewart hit 12 greens, Austin hit 14. And where Stewart had bogeyed two holes and double-bogeyed another, Austin hadn't a bogey on his card.

Like Stewart, Austin's birdies followed some exceptional shots. On the 11th, for example, a 399-yard par-four to an elevated green, he lofted an eight iron to four feet and holed it, played a drive and a three wood just short of the 12th, at 560 yards the longest hole on the course, and chipped within six feet, then played a five iron within five feet on the 13th and holed it.

Later in the day, Nobilo, Ozaki and Morse all worked their way to three under par and might have caught Stewart and Austin, but all three wavered on the home holes. Three under after 16, Ozaki bogeyed both the 17th and 18th; Nobilo stood three under after the 15th but bogeyed the 16th and 18th, and Morse stood three under after 12, bogeyed the 13th and 16th, but brought the gallery to its feet by holing from the greenside bunker at the 18th and saving his 68.

It had been a long and trying day, with rounds toward the end taking five and a half hours, but the course had held up remarkably well considering what it had gone through. A couple of situations affecting the leaders raised mild complaints — the fluffy sand in the ninth greenside bunker where Stewart needed two strokes to get out, and Janzen wanted relief from a wet lie on the 14th. The rules state, though, that for a player to be given relief, water must be visible either where he is standing or where the ball is lying. Denied relief, Janzen bogeyed.

The first-round leaderboard:

Payne Stewart	67	Philip Walton	69
Woody Austin	67	Gary Trivisonno	69
Lee Janzen	68	Stewart Cink	69
John Morse	68	Frank Nobilo	69
David Berganio	69	Jumbo Ozaki	69
Bob Ford	69	Paul Azinger	69

The weather continued fair the next morning, and a slight cooling breeze helped dry the ground. By then the players were learning more about how to cope with Oakland Hills. Where 11 men had broken par 70 in the first round, 20 shot under 70 in the second and eight more matched par — 28 men at par or better against 23 in the opening round.

Nevertheless, the total scores crept higher. When the long day ended, profaned by more five-and-a-half-hour rounds, only four men stood below par for 36 holes and five others had played even. Stewart led with 138 after shooting 71, but now he was threatened not only by Austin, who slipped back with 72, but also by Els and Norman, all three one stroke behind Stewart, at 139.

It was in this round that Jones began his march by shooting 66 and climbing to even-par 140, along with Love and Nobilo, who would be in the hunt until the end, and Sam Torrance and Ken Green, who wouldn't. Lehman, meanwhile, fell farther back, at 143, following a round of 72. Others who had been close after the first round played indifferent golf in the second. Morse, for example, shot 74 after his opening 68. Among those who had opened with 69, Ford, the professional at Oakmont, followed with 77; Trivisonno, three times the Northern Ohio Player of the Year, shot 75; Azinger slipped to 74; Ozaki shot 72; Philip Walton shot 73, and Stewart Cink and David Berganio shot 72.

Others played sensational golf. Jones and Norman shot 66s, Neal Lancaster shot 29 on the second nine and finished with 67, along with Els and Green, and Brooks shot 68, which thrust him back into a contending position after he had opened with a grim 76. In a tightly bunched field, Brooks was among 54 players within six strokes of Stewart.

The day ended with the USGA reconsidering one of its policies, fans asking a new trivia question, and one man suffering from a very sore head.

It had been customary since 1972 for the Open's 36-hole cut to include not only the low 60 scorers and ties but those within 10 strokes of first place as well. When Stewart bogeyed the 16th and 18th holes, along the way hitting a spectator on the head on the 16th, he brought 22 additional players into the field for the last two rounds. With scores of 148 and better eligible for the final 36 holes, 108 players qualified, 20 more than the previous record of 88 at Baltusrol three years earlier. While it is still less than the 113 who made the cut in the 1991 British Open (reeling from the extra prize money expense, the Royal and Ancient Golf Club of St. Andrews dropped the 10-stroke rule), 108 is more than the USGA wanted to deal with. For a time the USGA considered dropping the 10-stroke rule and expanding the cut to the low 70 and ties, but in the end decided to continue with it.

Now for the trivia question. In the entire history of the Open a score of 29 for nine holes had been done only twice. Who shot them? The answer is Lancaster. He shot 29 on the second nine at Shinnecock Hills in 1995 and again on the second nine at Oakland Hills in 1996.

Lancaster had been playing such uninspired golf that after he went out in 38 and obviously would miss the cut, his father reminded him, "It's only a game," wished him well, climbed into a van with four friends, and headed home to North Carolina. They left too soon.

Disheartened, Neal said to himself, "Let's get this thing over with." After pulling his drive into the rough on the 10th he holed from five feet to save his par four, and suddenly he couldn't miss. He played the next five holes in four birdies and an eagle on the 12th, six under on the second nine. With his 29 he shot 67 and made the cut easily. But he wasn't totally happy. "I wanted that 28," he said.

Although Lancaster's heroics may have been admirable, it was Norman who brought the spark to the Open's second round. Grim-faced ever since he double-bogeyed the opening hole of the championship, Greg began holing the putts that had simply grazed the edges on Thursday, and when Norman is playing like this, he draws the galleries to him. They cheered on the 16th, where he holed his approach for an eagle two, and rushed along the ropes straining to catch a glimpse of him as he played the closing holes.

Left with an approach of 140 yards, Norman knew just what he wanted to do with an eight iron. "I saw the shot, I felt the shot, I knew where I wanted to land it."

His ball soared directly at the flagstick, carried 10 or 12 feet past, drew back and topped gently into the cup. As the cheers grew, Greg doffed his wide-brimmed hat to the gallery.

While Norman had fought his way back into the chase, he still lagged behind Stewart, who had held his lead even though he continued to play erratic golf. In two rounds he had missed eight fairways and 12 greens. Where Austin had parred 31 holes in two days, Norman 27 and Els 26, Stewart had played only 17 of 36 holes in regulation figures, fewer than half, and had bogeyed seven holes and double-bogeyed one. He made up for those mistakes, though, with 11 birdies. His was not the most stable golf in the championship.

He had four of his birdies and five of the bogeys in the second round, but in spite of his occasional loose play, claimed he was satisfied with his game. He began by parring the first four holes, the longest stretch of parred holes so far, then birdied both the fifth and seventh. Four under par then, he lost a stroke at the eighth, where he pulled his drive into the rough and had to waste a shot digging it out, then lipped out the putt. Quickly, though, he rifled a stunning two iron to two feet on the ninth and birdied once more. Out in 32, he lost strokes both on the 10th, where he drove into a fairway bunker, and the 11th, where he three-putted. Even par for the day now.

A two-putt birdie from 20 feet on the 12th, where he reached the green with a three wood, brought him back to one under, but he lost one stroke on the 16th where his approach, pulled violently left, caromed off an oak tree beside the 17th tee and conked a spectator on the head. That spectator had evidently become an easy target. Earlier in the day, Steve Lowery had hit him as well.

Playing the 18th Stewart pulled still another approach, his ball hit the cart path and bounced toward the big grandstand at the left of the green, and he bogeyed once again. Still, he had survived with the lead still in hand while all around him others were falling back.

The second-round leaderboard:

Payne Stewart	71 - 138	Davis Love III	69 - 140
Greg Norman	66 - 139	Frank Nobilo	71 - 140
Ernie Els	67 - 139	Sam Torrance	69 - 140
Woody Austin	72 - 139	Ken Green	67 - 140
Steve Jones	66 - 140		

Over the years Stewart had built an impressive record as a frontrunner. When he led the field after 36 holes he had never failed to finish among the low 10 scorers, and he had won three tournaments, most notably the 1991 Open, when he beat Simpson in a playoff. He had also placed second in three, and third in three more. When he began the third round by birdieing both the first and second holes, he might have run away with the Open, but the magic had flown. He bogeyed both the third, eighth, 12th, 15th and 17th, and made seven on the 16th. He shot 76, and fell from the clear leader into a tie for 22nd.

Stewart wasn't alone. Of the 18 men who began the day within three strokes of first place, only Love, Nobilo and Jim Furyk shot 70s, and Jones shot 69. After working himself into second place with his 66, Norman played some dismal stuff, which included a missed putt from less then two feet on the 17th, shot 74, and slipped to 15th place. Both Austin and Els shot 72, along with Green, and hung close, and Lancaster fell back to his comfort zone with 74, dropping him to 28th place, along with Faldo, Pavin, Hoch and Nicklaus.

When the day ended, they all lagged behind Lehman, who played a blistering round of 65 that jumped him over 26 men into first place, with a 54-hole score of 208.

Jones, meanwhile, continued his persistent though barely noticed climb from seven strokes out of first place after the opening round to one stroke behind Lehman after the third. With 209 he stood one stroke ahead of Love, Nobilo and the surprising Morse, who shot 68, the third best score of the day. Justin Leonard shot 67, and Bob Tway, Sean Murphy and O'Meara shot 68s as well, but theirs accomplished nothing significant. Morse, on the other hand, accomplished quite a lot.

By hanging so close to the lead, Morse had become a local hero, not only because he was from Michigan — in fact the only Michigan native in the field — but also because of his struggles to make the grade as a tournament golfer.

While Morse had captured the hearts of the Michigan galleries, this was Lehman's day. He teed off a little before 12:30, paired with and tied with Jack O'Keefe, the Rookie of the Year on the 1994 Australasian Tour. After shooting 72-71 in the first two rounds, O'Keefe had nothing more to give and finished with two 76s. Lehman, on the other hand, had been warming up.

He began with a routine par four on the first and followed with birdies on both the second, perhaps the most birdieable hole on the course, and the third, which wasn't. He reached the green of the second with a four wood and got down in two from 20 feet, then hit a marvelous five iron to the second that braked perhaps a foot from the hole. Stalled by a bogey five on the fourth, he bounced back with birdies on the sixth, where he made his putt from 20 feet, and the seventh, where he nearly holed his seven-iron approach. The ball bit and stopped less than six inches from the cup.

Three under par now, he made his par on the eighth, then ran into trouble on the ninth, the long par-three. His three-iron tee shot pulled up short and sat on the edge of the rough, his pitch ran eight feet past the cup, leaving him a downhill putt that would slide perhaps a foot from left to right. He gauged the putt perfectly and saved the three. Out in 32, three under par.

Turning for home, Lehman struggled to save his par on the 10th after driving poorly, pitched a nine iron to six feet on the 11th and birdied again, and then holed from 30 feet on the 16th.

Five under par now, he still had two hard holes to play, and they nearly cost him strokes. Leaving himself 50 or 60 feet from the cup on the 17th, he left his first putt 10 feet short but made it, and after driving into a bad lie in the secondary rough close to the edge of a fairway bunker, he aimed for the front of the 18th green hoping to leave himself a chip and putt for a par if he didn't reach it. Instead he pushed the shot into the reconstructed bunker next to the green. With his ball less than three feet from the sharply rising lip he took an awkward stance, with his right foot out of the bunker, but still pitched out to eight feet and holed the putt. Back in 33, Lehman had shot into the lead.

Still reeling from his marvelous round, Lehman said, "A 65 at Oakland Hills is beyond my wildest dreams. The creativity you need around these greens is almost mind-staggering. You can make some birdies here, but it's so hard to hang onto a good round and not give strokes back."

Most of the others did indeed give strokes back. Starting an hour ahead of Lehman, Brooks climbed steadily up the leaderboard by going out in 30, the best first nine of the week, but he couldn't hold on. His round began falling apart when he three-putted both the 10th and 11th, and it collapsed totally when he four-putted the 13th, a par-three. With five fives on the home nine, he came back in 39 and shot 69.

Meantime, while Stewart struggled, Els began gaining on him. Minutes after Ernie had gone out in 33, Stewart turned in 35; Els had passed him and stood in first place, a stroke ahead of both him and Lehman, who had just birdied the 16th. Els could make up no further ground, though. Just off the 12th green with his second, he jabbed a chip when a gallery roared close by and parred instead of birdieing, and he mis-played another putt at the 15th, which cost him a bogey.

Then he stepped onto the 16th tee. Whenever Els had hit a bad shot under pressure he tended to hook the ball. He had done it twice on the closing holes at Oakmont when he won the U.S. Open in 1994, and he had done it on the 16th and 17th holes at Wentworth during the final of the 1995 Toyota World Match Play Championship. Now he did it again. Drawing his three wood, Els snapped the ball left into a stand of trees.

At first he didn't seem to be in serious trouble. His ball lay cleanly on bare ground and he had a clear line to the green. He didn't notice a branch of a young willow hanging over his head, though. As he drew back his seven iron he nicked the branch. Too late to stop, he followed through with the shot and hit the ball against the rocks at the edge of the water. Taking a penalty drop from the hazard, Ernie made a six, then bogeyed the 18th as well. Four strokes gone on the last four holes. He shot 72 and fell into a tie for sixth place.

Stewart played the 16th even worse. Two over by then after some truly shoddy golf on the 12th and 15th, and his lead long since gone, Stewart pulled his drive into heavy rough off the left side of the fairway. In spite of the dreadful lie, he went for the green and half shanked his eight iron. The ball flew with all the liveliness of a leaky balloon and plopped weakly into the water. After dropping out, Stewart hit a tentative shot that drew back off the green, took three more shots to get down, and made seven. Deflated, he bogeyed the 17th as well, shot 41 on the second nine, and with 76 for the round, tumbled out of the chase. The Open would be left to others.

The third-round leaderboard:

Tom Lehman	65 - 208		Colin Montgomerie	69 - 211
Steve Jones	69 - 209		Jim Furyk	70 - 211
Frank Nobilo	70 - 210		Sam Torrance	71 - 211
Davis Love III	70 - 210		Woody Austin	72 - 211
John Morse	68 - 210		Ernie Els	72 - 211

As the fourth round began, 10 men stood within three strokes of one another, a perfectly possible margin to overcome, but most of them either played poorly or not quite well enough. Even so, with the leaders well into the closing round, seven men could have won, and in the end five men were left. Four of those held on until the very end, and with only the closing hole to play, either Love, Lehman or Jones could have claimed the championship. Love bogeyed the last two holes and lost by one stroke, Lehman bogeyed the 18th and dropped into a tie with Love, and Jones played that final hole with precision, scored a par four, and walked away the champion.

Playing better than anyone from tee to green, Montgomerie closed within two strokes of the lead after birdieing the 12th, but a double-bogey five on the 13th killed him. Torrance, who began the day three strokes behind Lehman, could go no further; Austin went out in 34 but bungled the home nine and shot 41, and Furyk stood at one under par as late as the 16th hole, but he foundered on the last two and tied Els for fifth place. Els had worked himself into position as well, reaching even par with birdies on the sixth and seventh, but he bogeyed the next two, which finished him.

Morse, the total outsider, had a very good chance to win. Tied with Lehman, just one stroke behind Love and Jones with three holes to play and needing only another birdie, he bogeyed both the 16th and 18th but still took fourth place.

Even Norman might have won. Six strokes behind when the day began, Norman seemed to be off on one of his sizzling bursts of scoring when be birdied four of the first seven holes. Spurred on by his enthusiastic gallery, he broke their hearts with bogeys on both the eighth and ninth. Never able to recover, he shot 70 and tied Janzen and Montgomerie for 10th.

In the end, though, the Open came down to three men — Jones, Lehman and Love.

Once again the sun shone most of the day, drying the fairways and greens further and turning an already difficult course savage. Drives that had hit and stuck earlier in the week were running along the hard ground, and balls that had hit and bit into the greens earlier now bounced away. Furthermore, with slopes that reminded many players of those at Augusta, the Oakland Hills greens had become treacherous.

As the two leaders, Lehman and Jones went off last, just behind Nobilo and Morse, with Montgomerie and Love in the third-from-last pairing. Playing last was nothing new to Lehman. He had held first place going into the final round of the 1993 Masters and the 1995 U.S. Open, but had lost the Masters to Jose Maria Olazabal and the Open to Pavin. When he began the fourth round by pulling his opening drive into fairway bunker and bogeying, he looked as if he would lose still another, but he recovered quickly, birdied the second, and began playing one fine shot after another.

When he birdied the sixth he had opened a two-stroke lead over Jones, and when he pitched a nine iron to 12 feet and birdied the seventh he stood three strokes ahead of Jones, who had been making nothing but pars, over Love, who had holed a nerve-wracking downhill birdie putt on the eighth that was barely moving as it ghosted into the cup, and over Nobilo and Morse. Austin and Montgomerie stood another stroke behind at even par, but Norman had fallen five strokes behind, and Els trailed by six. It looked like a runaway for Lehman.

The complexion of the championship changed over the next four holes.

Instead of a walkover, the Open turned into another tense, tight battle.

First Jones had a stroke of luck. His four iron to the ninth barely made the green. It hit the rough-covered ridge above the right greenside bunker. Instead of becoming tangled in the grass, it hopped on, curled toward the hole, pulled up within 10 feet, and he birdied. Two under for 63 holes, he had cut Lehman's margin to two strokes.

Next, Jones' lag putt from 40 feet dived into the cup for a birdie on the 10th just as Lehman bogeyed. A swing of two strokes; Jones had caught Lehman. Now they both stood at three under par, two strokes ahead of Nobilo, who had began to fade to his incoming 41, and Love and Morse.

Both Jones and Lehman made their pars on the 11th, and then they came to the 12th. It became the critical hole of he championship.

Both men drove well, but where Jones' second shot dropped into the front bunker, Lehman's carried onto the green. He had played the same shot a day earlier and his ball held. Now, with the ground drying out, his ball raced across the green, dived into the rear bunker, and settled near the back lip. Jones played a routine pitch within a few feet of the cup and birdied, but when Lehman studied his lie he saw that from where his ball lay, he couldn't play toward the pin because the back lip of the bunker would block his backswing. Instead, he had to play about 30 feet to the right of the hole, and then three-putted. A bogey six and another two-stroke swing. Now, at four under par, Jones had climbed two strokes ahead of Lehman and of Love, who had birdied the 12th as well.

Jones lost a stroke with a bogey on the 13th, and almost at the same time Love coaxed in a 15-foot putt on the 15th. Now Love and Jones were tied at three under par with Lehman one stroke behind. It was becoming difficult to follow.

Now Love made the first of his critical mistakes. With a ridge running from front to back about halfway across, the 17th green is almost two greens. A ball sitting on the opposite side of the ridge invites three-putting. Seeing the pin about 25 feet from the left edge, Love played a five iron, but the shot got away from him and ran onto the back fringe of the wrong side of the green. He had no way of putting toward the hole and instead played a high lob that hit short of the pin but rolled perhaps 20 feet past. From there he hit a marvelous putt that ran directly at the cup but pulled up two inches short. He made a bogey. Back to two under par, he was tied with Lehman once again, a stroke behind Jones, who kept on making pars.

Now Jones made a mistake. Seeing Lehman's six iron hit the hard ground and run off the back of the green, Jones chose to play a six iron as well, but he opened the blade slightly and the ball ran off the right side into high grass. From miles away he pitched across the green to eight feet, but pulled his putt. A bogey, back to two under par.

The tension had built to unreasonable levels, for now all three men were tied, Jones and Lehman standing on the 18th tee, Love crouching over his birdie putt on the 18th. It became a matter of who would crack and who among them could play his best when it mattered most.

Love had played the 18th perfectly, a three wood to the center of the fairway and then a six iron that rolled past the hole. His approach, though, had left him with a devilish downhill putt from perhaps 20 feet. With the green slick as ice, Love felt he should do no more than start his ball rolling;

the least nervous tick might send it off the green. He tapped the ball with a feathery touch, and the gallery gasped when it pulled up short of the hole. Now he had a nasty breaking downhill putt from three feet. His second putt grazed the left lip but stayed out. Love tapped it in, pressed his lips together, shook his head, and walked away.

Back on the 18th tee, Lehman, up first, lashed into his drive. It soared on toward the center of the fairway, but now luck took a part. When the ball hit the ground it kicked left and rolled into the left fairway bunker and quite close to the front edge. Not quite as long, Jones' drive held the fairway. From there he played a brilliant seven iron that hit inches right then rolled several feet past the hole, but Lehman hadn't a chance. His ball lay so close to the rise at the bunker's front, he couldn't play the seven iron he felt he needed and had to lay up with an eight iron. He bogeyed, and when Jones got down in two, holing his second putt from little more than a foot, he had won the Open.

While his winning had been a surprise, Jones had actually played very well. After his indifferent opening 74, one of the worst opening scores by a champion since the end of the Second World War, he had played the last 54 holes in 204, one stroke more than the record Loren Roberts had set over the last three rounds at Oakmont in 1994. Jones had played those rounds in 66, 69 and 69, six under par. Furthermore, his winning score of 278 was the lowest 72-hole score ever shot in an Open at Oakland Hills.

Throughout the four rounds Jones played the kind of golf that wins major championships. He hit the fairways, he hit the greens, and he saved his pars half the times his approaches wandered into bunkers. He hit 50 of the 72 greens, which doesn't seem like a lot, but Montgomerie hit 57 greens, and he had the best record in the field. Once on the greens, Jones putted beautifully, holing everything in sight during the critical fourth round except for the eight-footer on the 17th when the tension had climbed so high.

Strangely, he had his worst day not in the opening round but in the third, where he hit just seven fairways and 10 greens. And he played his best in the last round, hitting 13 of the 14 fairways on driving holes, and 13 greens. On the other hand, he wasn't exactly a birdie machine, especially compared to Stewart. Jones birdied 11 holes; Stewart had that many in the first two rounds, and finished with 15. Ken Green birdied 17 holes. And yet they both finished behind Jones.

All of which means statistics don't prove much.

5. British Open Championship

Even though the Masters Tournament had been over for three months, memories of that shocking last round at Augusta flooded back as we reached the final round of the British Open Championship, for here we were with precisely the same situation — Nick Faldo six strokes behind with only 18 holes to play. He had made up 11 strokes on Greg Norman in April; now Tom Lehman held the lead. Could Faldo do it again?

It seemed possible. By any measure, Norman in 1996 was a better golfer than Lehman; certainly he owned a better record. The longest straight driver in the game, Norman might shoot any score at all. He had won the British Open twice and had been in playoffs for the U.S. Open, the Masters and the PGA Championship. He had lost all of them, of course, including another for the 1989 British Open. Lehman hadn't won any major titles, and had indeed thrown away strokes over the last nine holes at Shinnecock Hills a year earlier when he might have won the 1995 U.S. Open, and only three weeks earlier had bogeyed the 18th hole at Oakland Hills where a par would have tied Steve Jones for the 1996 U.S. Open. With this background Lehman looked an easier mark than Norman.

It didn't work out that way; although he had his chances, Lehman didn't shoot 78 as Norman had done at Augusta, and Faldo didn't shoot 67, although he might have with better putting. On this day Faldo shot 70 against Lehman's 73 and didn't even finish second. Both Mark McCumber, wincing from a painful shoulder that would require surgery, and Ernie Els tied for second place. Faldo placed fourth.

Lehman had shown, as Norman hadn't, that he could make his scores even without playing his best, and that he not only could hold up to the tension of playing for the oldest championship in the game, but neither give in to the fluttering heartbeats that are part of a pairing with Faldo, nor to the challenges thrown at him by others.

In the end Faldo played as shaky golf as Lehman. Nick cut two strokes off Tom's six-stroke lead after four holes, raising the hopes of his fans, but he could gain only one more over the next 14 holes. Actually he stood just three strokes behind with nine to play and picked up no ground at all over the closing holes. Meantime he was passed by McCumber, Els, Fred Couples and Mark Brooks at some stages. Both Couples and Brooks faded over the home nine, and Els threw away strokes on the 16th and the 18th where pars might have forced a playoff.

Through all the challenges, Lehman never lost sight of his goal. He simply put his head down and struggled through as best he could; it was good enough. In spite of his loose golf he won by two strokes over McCumber and Els, and by three over Faldo. Brooks and Jeff Maggert shared fifth place.

Even with his disappointing finish, Lehman shot 271, only four strokes over the record of 267 Norman had shot at Royal St. George's in 1993. He is given credit for beating par by 13 strokes, but Royal Lytham and St. Annes played more like a par 69 than its advertised 71.

Western England had been caught in a prolonged period of dry weather. Reservoirs sat half empty by mid-July, and only because of the coming golf championship was Lytham give special permission to irrigate its course. Whatever little water Lytham was allowed to pump onto the ground wasn't enough. The soil became parched and the grass withered. Balls rolled endlessly over the hard, packed ground, and when they struck ground they raised tiny puffs of dust. Walking alongside the restraining ropes, the galleries churned the soil to powder and ground the grass to chaff. When great masses of spectators followed their heroes, especially Faldo, they raised clouds of dust that hung like ground fog and clouded views of the golf. In the third round a spectator scrambled to avoid one of Faldo's shots but slipped on a slick hillside and nudged the ball back toward the seventh green.

With such benign weather — temperatures in the high 70s to low 80s throughout the week, negligible breezes occasionally clocked as low as five miles an hour — the integrity of the golf course was certainly affected. The benign climate may have been pleasant for spectators, but it wasn't so welcome for those who count on unpredictable and occasional foul weather to hold scoring in check. The conditions had become so mild that Michael Bonallack, the secretary of the Royal and Ancient Golf Club of St. Andrews, expressed the club's concern by saying, "I'm afraid of what is around the corner. The weather is incredible, really. Nick Price has just been saying he would like a little more breeze, but, sadly, we don't have any control over that."

With the combination of balls rolling indecent distances — for example, Shigeki Maruyama drove his ball 390 yards on the seventh in the third round — thinnish rough, no wind, bright sunshine and cloudless skies, and abnormally warm weather, few British Open fields have scored so low collectively.

Lehman played the first three rounds in 198, besting the record of 199 Faldo shot first at St. Andrews in 1990 and matched at Muirfield two years later. Tiger Woods equaled two records by amateurs, first by shooting 66 in the second round, which matched Frank Stranahan's 66 at Troon 1950, and then by shooting 281 for the 72 holes and tying Ian Pyman's record set at Royal St. George's in 1993.

Furthermore, the field as a whole accounted for five of the 11 lowest single rounds and six of the eight lowest 72-hole scores ever shot in the nine British Opens held at Lytham. Not only did Lehman's 271 stand as the lowest 72-hole score, but the 273s of Els and McCumber equaled Seve Ballesteros' 273 of 1988, one stroke better than Faldo's 274, and the 275s of Maggert and Brooks matched Price's score of 1988, when Ballesteros won by two strokes.

Additionally, Lehman's third-round 64 set the course record. Paul Broadhurst, Paul McGinley, Peter Hedblom and Maggert all shot 65s, seven others shot 66s, and 18 more shot 67s. Scores of 68 and over were so common they weren't worth noting.

It was a shame that a trick of weather made Lytham so vulnerable, for it is indeed a fine and testing golf course. It is known as an ugly course, but that simply is not true. Certainly it is not festooned with plants that burst into bloom every spring like Augusta National, nor does it have the natural grandeur of Pebble Beach with so many of its holes running along the shoreline of the Pacific Ocean. But then name others that do.

Lytham, on the other hand, is located in a residential setting, ringed by houses of red brick and with one side bordered by a rail line. About a mile inland from the Irish Sea, it is a solid links course nevertheless. Its fairways roll and tumble, and the ground where the seventh and 11th holes run parallel ripples like an old-fashioned washboard. Bunkers abound, deep pits with revetted faces of layered sod creating sheer faces that leave no alternative but a safe shot back to a playable position. Its fairways weave back and forth, half its holes running in a general northerly or southerly direction, the other half running either easterly or westerly. When the wind blows, half the holes will play into crosswinds, the other half either upwind or downwind.

As it was set up for the 1996 British Open, Lytham measured 6,892 yards. Its first nine, which has three par-three holes and two par-fives, measured 3,330 yards with a par of 35, and its second, much the harder of the two, stretched 3,562 yards and played to a par of 36.

Its finish is brutal — six par-fours that together measure 2,488 yards, 36 percent of its total length. Calling for shotmaking of the first order, the nerve-wracking run for home really begins with the 12th, the last and the hardest of the par-threes. In 465 rounds over the four days, the 12th gave up only 35 birdies, one by Lehman in the final round, but claimed 124 bogeys and eight fives. In relation to its par, the 12th ranked only behind the 17th as Lytham's hardest hole.

From there the course moves on to the 13th, a relatively easy 324 yards, the most birdied of all the par-fours, then to the 445-yard 14th, which runs dead straight and yet is no easy mark, to the 463-yard 15th, which swings from left to right, then the 357-yard 16th, another hole that gave up more birdies than bogeys, to the 17th, another brutal stretch of 467 yards with little room for error, and finally to the home hole, which sounds easy at 414 yards yet gave up only one more birdie than the 17th. The direct line from tee to green is pitted with bunkers that begin at 200 yards and end 285 yards out. There are some who believe the 18th is the most exacting driving hole of all because the shot must be played to a precise location; it must go so far and no farther. If a ball rolls into one of those foxholes posing as hazards, only luck and an exceptional third shot will save a par.

As the championship began, Broadhurst wasn't the man others would have expected to lead the way, but he whipped around Royal Lytham in 65 strokes. At the end of the first day Broadhurst led by two strokes over eight men clustered at 67 and eight more at 68. Altogether 42 players broke par and 20 others matched it — 62 men at par or better.

Seven Americans and one Japanese made up the group at 67. Hidemichi Tanaka, from Hiroshima, showed more enthusiasm than any of the others. Asked how he would rate his round, he said that on a scale of one to 100, he'd give it 20,000.

Tied with him were Couples, Brad Faxon, Mark O'Meara, Loren Roberts and, more significantly, Brooks, McCumber and Lehman. It was difficult to remember the last time we saw such a powerful American presence in the British Open.

Celebrating his 39th birthday, Faldo shot 68, along with Maruyama, another Japanese, the Englishman Carl Mason, the Swede Klas Erickson, Jim

Furyk, an American with a bizarre swing, the Irishman Padraig Harrington, the Zimbabwean Price and the South African Els. The British Open is clearly the most cosmopolitan of all the world's championships.

It was a fine day for Jack Nicklaus as well. Playing in his 35th consecutive British Open, Nicklaus was among the seven men who shot 69.

Others, though, played worse, especially Colin Montgomerie and Ian Woosnam. Montgomerie had come to Lytham seething because, he claimed, high winds at the Scottish Open the previous week had ruined his swing. He drove with confidence but putted with none, seldom giving his ball a chance to fall. He was short with his first putts on the first, third, sixth, eighth, ninth and 16th, holed nothing longer than six feet, double-bogeyed the home hole and shot 73, two over par.

The winner of the Scottish Open, Woosnam shot 75 that featured one eagle, one double bogey and an eight on Lytham's storied 17th. John Daly, the defending champion, went out in 31 and came back in 39; Jones, the surprise winner of the U.S. Open, shot 73, and Steve Elkington, the 1995 PGA Championship winner, shot 75. They would have to improve to survive the 36-hole cut.

Broadhurst in fact wasn't a complete surprise because he had a history of low scores. He had shot 63 in the third round of the 1990 British Open and he had won the 1995 French Open with another 63. When he had to finish second in the German Open to win a place on the 1991 Ryder Cup team, he shot 65 and made it.

At the same time he was known to score higher. Five-putting one green, he closed out the Scottish Open by shooting 80 (even so he beat Montgomerie's 81). There were no five-putts at Lytham, for his putting could hardly have been better. He needed only 11 putts over the last 10 holes and only 23 putts for the entire round.

A 30-year-old Englishman, with wavy, flame-colored hair and a complexion to match, Broadhurst teed off at 10:30; by then Lytham had already been under attack. The first man off the tee, Malcolm Mackenzie, a 5-foot-8-inch Englishman who had missed the cut in seven of the 17 tournaments he played, played the first 12 holes in three under par, and Arnaud Langenaeken, a 22-year-old Belgian, was playing almost as well. Meantime, more celebrated golfers were tearing into Lytham. Couples stood five under par after 10 holes, Tanaka four under through nine, and McCumber, Faxon, O'Meara, Lehman and Roberts stood at three under. By 12:30 Couples and McCumber had finished with 67s, and Faldo and Harrington had shot 68s.

Meantime, Broadhurst had begun making his move. Playing cautious golf on the early holes, driving with two irons on the second, third and fourth holes, he made par figures on the first five even though he had hit and held only two greens and overshot the others. Reaching the sixth tee, the first of the par-fives, he pulled out his driver for the first time, ripped a long shot that curled around the lone fairway bunker, set in the face of a mound on the left, and bounded 290 yards down the rolling, tumbling fairway. From prime position he rifled a five iron from about 200 yards to eight feet and holed the putt for an eagle three.

After parring both the seventh and eighth, Broadhurst suddenly picked up the pace, holed from 30 feet on the ninth after a nine-iron tee shot, played another nine iron to three feet on the 10th, then pitched to 12 feet on the

11th after laying up with his second to avoid bunkers pinching both sides of the fairway. The putts fell, and now Broadhurst had dipped five under par, clearly with an opening to claim the first-round lead.

Now he began a run of remarkable saves. He holed from three feet on the 12th, from two feet on the 13th, from 12 feet on the 14th, from four feet on the 15th and from three feet on the 16th, all for pars. Still five under, but unless he botched those two hard finishing holes, only Brooks, playing more than three hours behind, could catch him now.

Taking a deep breath, Paul lashed a long and straight drive down the 17th and followed with a superb seven iron to 30 feet. Still another putt dropped and Broadhurst slipped six under par with only the home hole left. Another driver missed all those bunkers, and then a fine eight iron to 15 feet set up still another birdie opening. The putt missed, though, and he had his first two-putt green since the eighth hole.

Although two others challenged Broadhurst's 65, it held up. Five under after birdieing the 11th, Brooks bogeyed the 12th and shot 67. Even later in the day, Carl Mason went out in 31, fell to five under with a birdie on the 10th, but crumbled over the pitiless finish, bogeyed three of the last four holes, and shot 68.

Stepping off the course, Broadhurst glowed.

"It's tremendous," he said. "I would definitely place this among the best rounds I've ever played, but I probably didn't play as well as I can."

The first-round leaderboard:

Paul Broadhurst	65	Mark O'Meara	67
Fred Couples	67	Tom Lehman	67
Mark McCumber	67	Loren Roberts	67
Hidemichi Tanaka	67	Mark Brooks	67
Brad Faxon	67		

Asked if he thought he could win, Broadhurst said, "I'm pretty confident I can stay up there, but whether it happens is another thing. I think I'm good enough."

Perhaps, but not this time. One of the latest to start, at 3:15 the next afternoon, Broadhurst shot an erratic 72 and slipped from a two-stroke lead into a tie for 13th place, at 137, while McGinley, a short, broad-shouldered Irishman, shot 65 and climbed into a tie for the lead at 134 with Lehman, who shot his second 67 late in the day.

With a second consecutive 68, Faldo tied six others at 136, only two strokes off the lead along with Corey Pavin, Roberts, O'Meara, Harrington and McCumber. Couples and Brooks, who had opened with 67s, slipped into a tie with Broadhurst after shooting 70s, Tanaka shot 71 and 138, and Faxon shot 73 and 140.

Never mind all that. This day belonged to Nicklaus. One round does not make a championship, but when Nicklaus shot 66 early in the day he thrust himself into second place, just one stroke behind McGinley and Lehman. Jack's effervescent round drove the gallery into a frenzy and stirred hope he might hold on for two more days and perhaps even reprise his victory in the Masters 10 years earlier. Realistically they understood that rather than a genuine threat to win, this was more likely a moment similar to Ben Hogan's great day in 1967 when, at the age of 54, he shot 66 in the second round of the Masters.

Nicklaus had reached his 56th birthday in January of 1996; only the rare golfer finishes high in national championships at that age. J.H. Taylor, who had won his first British Open in 1894 and his fifth in 1913, placed 11th in the 1926 championship at the age of 56. Winner Bobby Jones was so impressed, he sought out Taylor to congratulate him.

Others have played exceptionally well after reaching 50. Dutch Harrison tied for third place behind Arnold Palmer and Nicklaus in the 1960 U.S. Open at Cherry Hills at 50; Gene Sarazen had tied for 16th place in the 1958 British Open at 56; a month before his 51st birthday Sam Snead tied for third in the 1963 Masters, and at 62 he tied for third in the 1974 PGA Championship. Nicklaus' showing at Lytham broke no new ground, but it was remarkable nonetheless.

Once again the temperature climbed into the 80s, prompting the gallery to swap its normal dress of thick Shetland sweaters and rainsuits for shorts and sleeveless dresses, and some men cast off their shirts, propped themselves against anything handy, and savored the rays. The greens, meanwhile, had turned to rock, and players commonly had trouble finding their pitch marks. Instead of pitching to the flagsticks, they played run-up shots, especially on the longer holes.

Nevertheless, the field scored even better than in the first round. Where 42 men had broken par on Thursday, 57 shot under 71 on Friday, and where 17 men had been under 69 on Thursday, 23 shot 68 or better on Friday.

Hedblom, a blond, 26-year-old Swede struggling to make his way on the PGA European Tour matched McGinley's 65 as the best scores of the day, and in addition to Nicklaus, Pavin, Woods and Tom Kite shot 66, and Lehman, Els, Vijay Singh, David Gilford, David Duval, David Feherty and Alexander Cejka of Germany shot 67s.

Nicklaus' remarkable round blinded the gallery to one of the more sensational first nines of recent memory. Climaxed by a hole-in-one on the ninth, McGinley played Lytham's first nine in 29 strokes, the ninth 29 in British Open history and the fifth at Royal Lytham. The record, though, stands at 28 strokes, shot at Royal Birkdale in 1983. By contrast, the U.S. Open has seen only two 29s, by Neal Lancaster at Shinnecock Hills in 1995 and at Oakland Hills in 1996, and Mark Calcavecchia shot 29 at Augusta National in the 1992 Masters.

Teeing off at 7:22, in the third group of the morning, McGinley attacked from the start. He rifled a four iron to 12 feet and birdied the first, holed again from six feet on the fourth, and after missing the green with his second shot, settled for par on the sixth, a hole half the field birdied that day.

Although a birdie at the seventh couldn't make up for a lost opportunity, it dropped him to three under par nevertheless, and he followed with another at the eighth after a pitch to three feet. Then he holed his seven-iron tee shot at the ninth. Six under par now, he had played his last three holes in four under par and gone out in 29.

His second nine wasn't nearly so gripping. Struggling with his swing, he missed a birdie opportunity on the vulnerable 11th, saved par from a bunker on the 12th, and followed with two wonderful shots — a drive down the middle of the 14th fairway, and then, on a hole that measures 445 yards, a wedge to three feet. Seven under now, he had to battle the rest of the way, losing a stroke on the merciless 15th, then winning it back with a marvelous four iron into the 17th, then holing from 25 feet. Still seven under, needing a par on the home hole to shoot 64, he played a nine-iron pitch from the rough that hit the hard green and rolled over the back. After an indifferent chip to four feet, he missed the putt and settled for 65. Still, he had played the round of his life.

McGinley was well into his round when Nicklaus teed off, accompanied by Maruyama, a blocky Japanese, and Gordon Brand, Jr., a slender Scot with a bushy mustache. The gallery was about to be treated to vintage Nicklaus. Jack is at heart a conservative; he had not been driving well, and so he left his driver in his bag, pulling it out only on the very long holes — the sixth and seventh on the first nine, the 11th, 14th and 15th on the second. Only on the 15th did he hit the ball solidly, but he wasn't expecting it. He had aimed for the bunker 260 yards out in the left rough expecting his ball to fall short and kick off the rising ground back into the fairway. Instead, his ball shot straight into the sand.

While he may have spent the day struggling with his drive, Nicklaus felt he was fortunate to be playing at all. Bothered by a painful back, the result of a lifetime of hitting golf balls, he had spent a few hours on the phone the previous evening talking with Pete Egoscue, who lives in San Diego and calls himself an "anatomical functionalist." Egoscue responded with a 23-page fax describing in excruciating detail a series of exercises designed to loosen Jack's back muscles. Obviously the drills worked, for aside from the weakness in his driving, Nicklaus performed as if this was 1966 rather than 1996. He played impeccable irons, missing only three greens, played the little chips and pitches that had caused him such pain in the past, and he putted with all his old confidence.

If his round had one blemish it was his play on the three par-fives. Where once he would have gobbled them up, he hit none of them with his second shots and birdied only the seventh after a nice pitch to four feet. He had already birdied the first with a four iron to eight feet, and he followed with an eight iron to seven feet on the ninth for still another birdie.

Out in 33, he picked up two more birdies coming home, the first of these on the 10th, where he lofted a sand wedge inside four feet, and the last on the 14th, where he pulled his drive into the left rough and played a nine iron for his second. When his ball hit the green, Jack felt sure it would bounce over, but it must have hit a soft spot because it braked within 10 feet of the cup, and he holed it.

In his time the best putter of the great players, rarely missing a putt he had to hole, Nicklaus looked certain to match McGinley's 65 when he laid his approach within six feet on the 18th. With the big gallery hushed and Nicklaus crouched over his putt, he suddenly stepped back and swatted at a bug buzzing around his ball. He picked up the ball and blew the bug away, then set up to putt once again. When a man backs off from nervous putts, it says he doesn't have confidence he can hole it. Jack's ball caught the lip of the cup, then spun away. He settled for his par four and a round of 66.

Nevertheless, Jack had thrust himself into the heart of the struggle, and reminded us all that this was the most remarkable golfer of his time. Even though he had aged, he should never be underestimated. Even now, when he played the occasional shoddy round, he could hold his head high, and he never let go of his superior attitude.

Asked if he had been surprised by his exceptional round, Nicklaus misinterpreted the question. With ice in his voice he replied, "I'm never surprised when I play well. I have played well before."

So had others, but they didn't this week. Saying that he saves his worst golf for the third week in July, Montgomerie shot 39 on the home nine where he needed 35, and with 147 missed the cut by four strokes. Sam Torrance went out with 144, one stroke too many. Elkington prepared to defend his PGA Championship in three weeks by shooting 145. Less than a month after beating Lehman in the U.S. Open, Jones left with 146, the same score as Davis Love III, who played the last four holes in four over par with two double bogeys, one bogey and a birdie on the 17th. Woosnam shot 147, Paul Azinger and Lee Janzen shot 151, and while the huge gallery bordering the 18th cheered and applauded, Ballesteros left with 152.

Unable to raise his club higher than his hips, Bernhard Langer had withdrawn earlier in the day with an injury to his left shoulder, and both Michael Campbell, who had played so well at St. Andrews a year earlier, and Des Smyth were disqualified for rules violations. Then there was Ian Baker Finch, the 1991 champion, who has evidently forgotten how to play. He played the last five holes in six over par, shot 84, and with 162 finished dead last among those who turned in 36-hole scores.

The second-round leaderboard:

Tom Lehman	67 - 134		Corey Pavin	66 - 136	
Paul McGinley	65 - 134		Nick Faldo	68 - 136	
Jack Nicklaus	66 - 135		Mark McCumber	69 - 136	
Peter Hedblom	65 - 135		Padraig Harrington	68 - 136	
Ernie Els	67 - 135		Mark O'Meara	69 - 136	
Vijay Singh	67 - 136		Loren Roberts	69 - 136	

Hope dies hard, but even Nicklaus' most dedicated and loyal followers must have known he couldn't keep up his early scoring. His record showed it. Within recent years he had played himself into contention in other tournaments, most notably the 1994 U.S. Open when he opened with 69-70 and went into the third round three strokes behind Montgomerie, then shot 77 and dropped like a stone.

Only one stroke off the lead now, he shot 77 again, followed with 73 in the last round, and with 285 finished 14 strokes behind Lehman. Paired with the Irishman Eamonn Darcy in the last round, Nicklaus watched a garbage truck cross the 11th fairway and with a twisted smile said, "Eamonn, they've come to pick us up."

Now, instead of a wild Nicklaus charge, we were treated to one of the outstanding rounds in recent championship golf. Grouped with McGinley in the last pairing of the day, Lehman shot 64, the lowest score ever shot in a British Open at Lytham, and, more than that, with his record 198 he had opened a gaping six-stroke lead over Faldo, who shot a third consecutive 68. He led Brooks and Singh by seven, with Couples and Els a further stroke to the rear.

Few of us had expected much from McGinley and he quickly justified the doubts. He began the third round by missing the first green, chipping into a bunker, and walked away with a one-putt bogey. It got no better, and at the end of the day he had shot 74 and dropped to 10th place.

Others had bad days as well. Broadhurst shot 40 on the second nine, and with 74 continued to fall back. Hedblom raced to the turn in 32 and stood 10 under par, but with a seven on the 15th and a six on the 18th came back in 43, shot 75, and slid to 22nd place. Mason had fought to nine under par through the 15th, but after bogeying the 16th he hacked his way to a seven on the 17th, his second seven there, shot 71, but still climbed from 16th place into a tie for 11th.

Like Mason, others played disappointing rounds that did little damage. Out in 34, McCumber didn't birdie a hole on the homeward nine, and with 71 slipped from sixth to seventh place. Ernie Els shot 71 as well but held onto a share of fifth place with Couples, who shot 69. Usually a deadly putter, Pavin missed one from no more than two feet, and with 74 lost ground he would never make up; O'Meara and Roberts shot 72s and fell back, and Harrington's 73 ended what had been a promising start.

The day belonged to Lehman. He seized it from the opening shot, a seven iron that settled 18 feet from the cup. He holed it, then ripped through the first nine in 30, which truly could not have been much better. He scrambled for his pars on the both the fifth and eighth, and for his birdie on the sixth, where he bunkered his second shot, but except for the seventh, his play on the other six holes couldn't have been improved.

Nine under par after the first, he climbed to 10 under by holing from 14 feet on the second, nearly holed his eight-iron pitch to the fourth, holed from 15 feet on the sixth, and played a perfectly gauged nine iron to the ninth that braked hole-high about 10 feet left of the cup. Everyone assumed he would make it, and he did — he hadn't missed a holeable putt yet. Five under par for the round and 13 under for 45 holes, Lehman had slipped three strokes ahead of Faldo and Hedblom.

Coming back he pitched to eight feet and birdied the 11th, and after playing a sound par three on the dangerous 12th, he pitched to the back of the 13th and missed from about 12 feet, the first makeable putt he had missed all day.

No matter, he picked up another birdie with a six iron to six feet on the 14th, and added another, although unlikely, birdie at the 16th. All his birdies had followed shots within reasonable distance, but here he ran one in from 35 feet, startling even himself. When the putt fell, he dropped his putter, and wearing an expression of genuine amazement, raised his hands and looked heavenward in thanks.

He stood eight under par for the round, 16 under for 52 holes; two more pars and he would shoot 63. He looked as if he would birdie the 17th when he laid an eight iron within 15 feet of the cup, but as the gallery gasped, his putt brushed the edge of the cup and stayed out. Now for the bunker-pocked 18th. Here he made his biggest mistake of the day. Trying to fade his drive around a fairway bunker about 240 yards out, the shot didn't work. Hit too weakly, the ball dived into the sand pit, and Lehman bogeyed. A 64.

It had been a wonderful round to watch, filled with sparkling shotmaking and extraordinary putting. It had had one scary moment, when his drive on the second pulled up only a yard or so short of a fairway bunker on the left, and he might have birdied the seventh with a better drive. He pulled it into the left rough, which left him no opening onto the green, and with the hole set close behind a high mound on the green's left front, it was impossible to reach with a pitch.

That mistake aside, Lehman didn't miss one putt he should have made, only two he might have made, and he holed one he had no right to make.

While Lehman had holed everything he had looked at, Faldo had played marvelous shots but had missed birdie openings on the three opening holes and three-putted the fourth from less than 20 feet. Quickly, though, he thrust himself back into the race with an eagle three on the sixth and birdies on the seventh and eighth. Faldo had picked up four strokes in three holes, gone out in 32, and lost only two strokes to Lehman.

Still, with both men through the ninth, Lehman led Faldo by four strokes, and Lehman would continue his assault while Faldo would lose ground. Nick came back in 36, even par, his round ruined by bunkering his approaches to both the 14th and 16th. His bogey on the 16th was hard won. From the right rough he hit a terrible shot that squirted across the fairway and dived into a steep-faced little greenside bunker. As the ball flew off line, Faldo, his eyes widening, cried, "I don't believe it." He took two strokes to get out, then holed a nervous five-footer to save the five.

Then, as great players do, Faldo struck back, played the 17th with a one iron and a seven iron that trickled down a rise on the left within two feet of the cup. A birdie there, and then a nice putt on the 18th that rolled dead toward the center of the cup but stopped short. Another 68.

The third-round leaderboard:

Tom Lehman	64 - 198		Ernie Els	71 - 206
Nick Faldo	68 - 204		Steve Stricker	66 - 207
Mark Brooks	68 - 205		Darren Clarke	69 - 207
Vijay Singh	69 - 205		Shigeki Maruyama	69 - 207
Fred Couples	69 - 206		Mark McCumber	71 - 207

Lehman's six-stroke lead was the largest anyone had taken into the last round of a British Open since 1964, when Tony Lema led Nicklaus by seven. Nevertheless, considering what happened to Norman in the Masters, someone wondered if Lehman's six strokes would be enough.

"Like lightning striking twice?" Lehman asked. Then, with a weary smile, he said, "This is a different time and a different place."

Indeed it was. Having one of those days when his coordination wasn't what it should have been and his putter felt like a lead pipe, Lehman was indeed vulnerable, but no one within range held up to the challenge.

Several men made their runs, but every challenge died. Couples sped around the first nine in 30 and closed within two strokes, but he played absolute rubbish on the second nine and fell aside. Brooks closed to 11 under par with thee early birdies, but he had nothing in reserve, closed with two disappointing bogeys and shot 71. McCumber shot 66, but he had started nine strokes behind Lehman and had little hope of catching him.

Playing the best golf of those closest to Lehman, Els moved within two strokes of Lehman for a brief time, but needing more birdies, he bogeyed both the 16th and 18th, shot 67, and finished two strokes behind, tied with McCumber.

In the end Lehman won because he simply refused to give in. His golf wasn't the prettiest we had seen, but he played well enough. His driving was erratic at times, but he missed only three greens, not including the 14th where his ball rolled onto the collar. His putting could have been better, though. He holed only one makeable putt for a birdie, from 12 feet on the 12th, and he missed others from 15 feet on the fourth, from seven feet on the eighth and from 12 feet on the 13th. Still, his putter actually saved him. Constantly bold with his first putts, he saved himself by running in second putts of from four to six feet on three holes.

The British fans cheered Faldo on as he moved along, looking neither right nor left, taking whatever time he wanted to plan and execute his shots, and generally ignoring Lehman, who, to his credit, ignored Faldo as well.

After making par figures on the first two holes, Lehman drove into a fairway bunker and bogeyed the third, and Faldo hit a crisp six iron into the fourth and birdied from 12 feet. Lehman's lead had been cut to four strokes, and possibly to three after Nick played a gorgeous iron into the fifth that braked about six feet right of the hole. Again he missed; the ball caught the lip of the hole and spun out.

Then he missed another at the sixth, a hole where he seemed certain to gain one stroke, if not two. After Faldo split the fairway, Lehman played a terrible drive that ducked left and disappeared into a jungle of pine and plane trees and settled among dead leaves and dried twigs. Luckily, though, Lehman found an opening, punched out, left his third shot alongside a greenside bunker, pitched on, and holed from six feet for the par.

Faldo had played the hole perfectly — a daring drive over the mound at the corner of the dogleg, and then a seven iron that didn't hold the rock-like green but rolled just off the back and down a slight incline. His birdie seemed safe when he played a nice little chip to perhaps little more than three feet. With the chance to climb within three strokes, Faldo missed still another putt.

At the beginning Faldo's coach, David Leadbetter, had said, "The first six or seven holes are crucial. Nick just needs a few early putts." So far he had missed from six feet on the first, from about 10 feet on the second, from six feet on the fifth and from three feet on the sixth. Then he missed another birdie opportunity from six feet on the seventh. Now a look at the scoreboard showed that rather than challenging Lehman, Faldo had dropped to fourth place; while everyone had been watching for the ghost of Augusta, Couples had run wild and Brooks hadn't lagged far behind. With Lehman 14 under par, Couples stood 12 under, Brooks 11, and Faldo 10, tied with McCumber, who had birdied the sixth, seventh and eighth. Instead of fighting off one man, Lehman was under siege from four others, with Els about to make his move. Instead of a walkover, the last round had turned into another tense, tight struggle.

Not one of them could shake Lehman's composure. Couples played the second nine in 41, Brooks played the last 12 holes in three over par, including a disappointing pitch to the eighth, where his shot from the base of the upslope didn't quite reach level ground and rolled back almost to his feet.

Meantime, Lehman and Faldo struggled on. Nick picked up his last stroke with a birdie on the ninth, but he could gain no more ground. Lehman played the shot that won the championship on the 12th, a stunning four iron that braked about 10 feet right of the flagstick. When he holed the putt he changed the complexion of the tournament; the extra stroke not only buoyed his spirit, it set off a surge of confidence. Now he stood at even par for the day and 15 under for the 66 holes he'd played.

It would be enough to see him through. Even a three-putt bogey at the 14th did little damage. Minutes later Faldo realized his hopes had died when he drove into the fairway bunker on the left of the 15th. As the ball rolled into the sand, Nick's shoulders sagged, and he hung his head.

Els lost it all at about the same time. Playing two holes ahead of Lehman and Faldo, he had gone out in 33 and had birdied four more holes on the homeward nine, his last on the dreaded 15th, where he played an eight-iron pitch to four feet. The birdie dropped him to 13 under; had he held on it might have been good enough, but he couldn't. As he had done in the 1995 PGA, Ernie threw it away, driving into one fairway bunker on the 16th and into another on the 18th. Both cost him strokes and left Lehman nothing to do but hang on.

He very nearly didn't. A nice pitch from a bunker saved one par on the 15th, a safe one iron and wedge earned him another at the 16th, but a drive into the bunkers at the 17th where the fairway makes its turn left him no shot to the green. Standing 14 under par he had three strokes in hand; he accepted the bogey and used one of them to play safely out.

Now he had reached the 18th tee holding a two-stroke lead. With the end in sight he steered a one iron into the rough along the left to avoid all those bunkers and played an eight iron to the front of the green, leaving himself in the comfortable position of knowing he could three-putt and still win. He needed only two, shot 73, and with 271 won by two stokes and became the only American professional to have won at Royal Lytham. Jones had been an amateur.

Walking past him on the way to his ball, which once again lay closer to the hole, Faldo patted Lehman on the back and said, "Well done; you deserve to win."

Certainly the gallery agreed, cheering wildly as Lehman took off his cap, waved to them and even threw a few kisses.

Clutching the silver claret jug, the symbol of the British Open, Lehman said, "I can't describe the way I feel. I didn't play at all well, but I stuck it out, and I came through. To win this silver trophy and take it home makes all the hard work that led to this day worthwhile."

6. PGA Championship

After Mark Brooks won the PGA Championship, anyone who had been watching recently could look back and believe he had seen it coming. A fanciful notion perhaps, but like an old Ellery Queen mystery, Brooks had scattered a few clues suggesting he was ripe to win a major championship. How to interpret them had become the problem, for Brooks had given no hint he might win the PGA. He had, in fact, a dismal record. He had missed the 36-hole cut in five of the eight previous PGAs he had entered and had placed 26th, 15th and 31st in the three he had finished.

Even though he had tied for 31st in 1995, Brooks had played reasonably well, shooting three rounds in the 60s, but he had been ruined by 74 in the second. It was too much to overcome; with 279 he finished 12 strokes behind Steve Elkington and Colin Montgomerie. Elkington holed a 20-foot putt on the 18th and won the one-hole playoff.

Anyone tracking his career might have expected Brooks to break through by winning the British Open, for this had been the big tournament where he played his best. Only an unlucky break cost him a possible victory in 1995. Taking the bold route on the 16th at St. Andrews, Brooks drove straight down the middle, between an out-of-bounds fence on the right and the nest of bunkers on the left called the Principal's Nose. His ball threaded its way past the Principal's Nose but lurched left and dived into another bunker called Deacon Sime, and he double-bogeyed. With 283 he finished one stroke behind John Daly and Costantino Rocca. Daly won the playoff.

Three weeks before the 1996 PGA, Brooks had been in position to win the British Open once again, and had actually picked up four strokes on Tom Lehman, the eventual winner, over the early holes of the last round, but he seemed to wear out, lost all the strokes he had gained, shot 276, and tied Jeff Maggert for fifth place, five strokes behind.

Then, a month earlier, after 76 in the opening round of the U.S. Open, Brooks had struck back with 68 in the second round and then burned the grass off the first nine by going out in 30 the following day. Once more he had nothing more to give, came back in 39, and tied for 16th place, seven strokes behind Steve Jones.

Still, over the previous two years, Brooks had shown he had the game to threaten to win but perhaps not actually win. After he had worked himself into position in the U.S. Open and those two British Opens, he seemed to weaken, as if he hadn't the stamina for four rounds over the game's most difficult courses under the mounting pressures of national championships. At five-foot-nine and 150 pounds, there is no question he doesn't have the strength of Lehman or Nick Faldo. When the PGA Tour compiled its 1995 statistics, Brooks' drives averaged 262 yards, which put him in 100th place. When he must play a long hole, Brooks swings with everything he has, occasionally throwing himself off balance.

Nor does he have the ball-manipulating finesse of Corey Pavin, who is about his size. In fact, Brooks ranks high in none of the Tour's statistical categories, although he stood 25th in greens hit in regulation at the end of

1995. Yet, when all the figures are stirred in the pot, he comes out 16th in all-around game.

Statistics, however, didn't show his tenacity. While he may not have had the finishing kick, he fought back at St. Andrews after a third-round 73 dropped him from fourth to eighth; he fought back in the U.S. Open from an opening score that might have wrecked a player with a lesser will, and he certainly fought back in the PGA Championship.

Tied with Kenny Perry at 12 under par through 10 holes of the last round, Brooks dropped three strokes over the next four holes. Again he struck back, picking up one birdie on the 15th, a hole he had eagled the previous day, and after Perry bogeyed the 18th and fell back to 11 under par, Brooks pitched out of a bunker on the final hole, a par-five, and holed from a little more than three feet to force a playoff. He birdied the 18th once more and won.

A native of Fort Worth, Texas, Brooks had shown his fighting spirit early. Introduced to the game at the age of eight by his grandfather, he played for the University of Texas, then set out for the PGA Tour. First, though, he would have to survive the qualifying tournament. He did — four times, in 1983, 1984, 1985 and 1987. He would qualify, then play such indifferent golf he would have to try again the following season. Finally, after reinventing his swing in 1987, he stuck, and when he won the 1988 Greater Hartford Open, he was on his way.

Through the middle of 1996 he had won six tournaments in a little more than 12 years, his latest the Shell Houston Open in early May, beating Maggert in a playoff. He was indeed making a good living, but at this stage careers are measured by performances in the major events — the Masters, U.S. and British Opens and the PGA Championship. Only in the middle 1990s had he made an impression in any of those. Until his third-place finish in the 1995 British Open, his record in the big events had been grim. In addition to missing all those cuts in the PGA, he had played in nine U.S. Opens and missed the cut in five, and had had such ignoble finishes as 88th and 55th in the British Open. Nor had he ever been even visible in the Masters, and had in fact made the cut only once in five appearances.

Furthermore, except for his third place in the British Open, he had not had a good year in 1995. He had won money in only 15 of the 23 tournaments he had played and had fallen to 100th in the ranks of money winners. He had missed the cut in the PGA, and hadn't even qualified for the U.S. Open, the first he had missed since 1989.

Nevertheless, he had sprung back to life in 1996, won the Bob Hope Chrysler Classic early in the year, added the Shell Houston Open, then tied for eighth in the Motorola Western Open and for fifth in the British Open before coming to the PGA. He had indeed been playing solid golf, but whether he could handle the golf course left doubt in some minds.

The PGA of America took its championship to the Valhalla Golf Club on the outskirts of Louisville, Kentucky, a course that in its 10 years of existence had staged nothing more grand than a member-guest tournament. Named for the hall where, in Norse mythology, Viking heroes slain in battle feasted with the great Odin, Valhalla was designed by Jack Nicklaus. After looking it over and shaking his head in wonder, someone summed up the design nicely by suggesting, "Jack doesn't understate anything, does he?"

Everything about Valhalla was big. To begin with, the entire property, including tracts originally set aside for housing, spread over 400 acres. The course itself covers 260 acres, more than twice the size of Merion, a classic course of American golf, which has just 127 acres.

Valhalla covers 7,144 yards, first over open ground quite recently a flood plain, and then through forest land, over rolling, sometimes hilly ground, its fairways wider than most, and its greens not only big but tumbling with exaggerated slopes and dips.

As the week began we had the impression the weather, not the course, would become the championship's controlling element. Temperatures in the 90s and humidity you could feel pressed in and left everyone uncomfortable. Golfers slumped off the course dripping perspiration, and some wondered if the European players might wilt in these unaccustomed conditions.

While the temperature and the humidity continued miserably high as play began early Thursday morning, big black clouds began blocking out the sun toward noon. Storm warnings went up on the big scoreboards, and marshals urged spectators to find shelter. Soon thunder rumbled, lightning lit the sky, and the rain poured down. Sirens wailed at about 2:30, suspending play.

In a way the storm was a blessing. After a four-hour delay, play began once again under much cooler temperatures and low humidity, and the weather remained pleasant the remainder of the week, until another storm moved in after play had ended late Sunday afternoon.

Nevertheless, the storm cost four precious hours and left nearly half the field marooned on the golf course without enough time to finish. Some had barely started; when play ended, six players had finished only five holes. All those with holes to play would return to Valhalla at 7:30 the following morning and complete their rounds.

The siren ending play for the day caught Perry on the 18th hole. With the option of either finishing or marking his ball and coming back the next day, Perry chose to finish, holed a 15-foot birdie putt, his second of the second nine, shot 66, and moved into first place, a stroke ahead of Elkington, whose 67 had led through most of the long day.

Meantime, Brooks birdied six consecutive holes, sped home in 32, and shot 68. Russ Cochran, a left-hander and like Perry a Kentuckian, birdied the last two holes and matched Brooks, and Nick Price shot 68 as well.

At the same time, Phil Mickelson stood six under par through 12, Ian Woosnam had played 14 holes in five under, and Frank Nobilo had also played 14 holes in four under. They looked as if they were the only threats, but both Greg Norman and Lee Janzen would break loose the next day.

Elkington had teed off at 9 o'clock, along with Nicklaus and Wayne Grady, both former PGA champions, and played as impeccably as he dressed, hitting 12 of the 14 fairways on driving holes and 14 greens. With his economical swing that is hardly more than a shoulder turn back and then a shoulder turn through the ball, he constantly left himself within birdie range. Out in 34, two under par, with a four iron to 10 feet on the dangerous third, a 199-yard par-three, and a seven iron to 10 feet again on the ninth, he came back in 33 with a more erratic second nine made up of four birdies and a bogey on the 14th, another dangerous par-three of 208 yards, where he missed the green.

He holed from 20 feet on the 12th and 13th, ripped another seven iron to

10 feet on the 16th, and holed from four feet on the last after a nifty pitch from the bunker.

Elkington's score held up until Perry's late rush. With what seemed like half the population of Kentucky cheering him on, Perry played intelligent golf throughout the day, driving well and hitting especially good irons into the greens. He did indeed hit 15 greens. (Chris Tucker, who wouldn't make the cut, hit 16, and when he completed his round the next day, Norman would have hit all 18.)

Perry quickly became the gallery's choice. A Kentucky native who was born in Elizabethtown, just a few miles south of Louisville, and lived in Franklin, about 100 miles farther south, near the Tennessee border, he had played college golf for Western Kentucky before joining the PGA Tour in 1986. Although he had won three tournaments in his 10-year career, he had played with little distinction and had risen above 25th place only once in the major championships. He had tied for 12th in the 1994 Masters.

So far in 1996 he had run up an indifferent record. After tying for 50th place in the U.S. Open, he had placed third in the FedEx St. Jude Classic, missed the cut in the Canon Greater Hartford Open, tied for fourth in the CVS Charity Classic, and missed the cut in the Buick Open. He was not among the game's premier players.

Nevertheless, Perry ripped Valhalla's first nine to shreds, racing out in 31 with six birdies and a lone bogey on the sixth, where he drove into the vicious bluegrass rough and had to waste a shot to get back to the fairway. He birdied both par-fives, leaving his second shot just off the green and chipping inside two feet on both, holed from four feet on the fourth, from eight feet on the eighth, and from six feet on the ninth. He made his only sizable putt on the third, where his five-iron tee shot left him 20 feet away.

Perry came back in 35 with birdies on the 13th and 18th and a bogey on the 12th, where he pushed his drive into the trees, nicked a tree playing safely back to the fairway and struggled to save a five when his third shot pulled up short of the green. His putt from 20 feet in the gloom of the 18th tumbled into the cup on the last turn of the ball.

The first-round leaderboard:

Kenny Perry	66
Steve Elkington	67
Russ Cochran	68
Joel Edwards	68
Mark Brooks	68
Nick Price	68

Still playing:

Phil Mickelson	6 under par, 12 holes
Ian Woosnam	5 under par, 14 holes
Frank Nobilo	4 under par, 14 holes

The weather, so threatening on Thursday, had turned delightful. Friday was a day of low humidity, bright sunshine and temperatures in the low 80s. After a day of low and cloistering overcast, only a few cottony white clouds drifted in a light cooling breeze. It was a perfect day for golf, and some golfers seized the day. Perry held the first-round lead when Mickelson dropped a stroke over the last six holes of his first round and tied Elkington at 67; but when Mickelson added another 67 in the second round and Perry slipped to 72, Phil took over first place with 134. Perry fell into a tie for third at 138 with Vijay Singh, who shot another 69, and Brooks, with 70.

Fighting the early morning cobwebs, Justin Leonard came back to Valhalla to play 10 holes of the first round, shot 71, then opened the second round with a birdie on the first hole and an eagle three on the second, matched Perry's opening 66, and shot into second place with 137.

Among the other low rounds, Grady, Fuzzy Zoeller and Jesper Parnevik shot 67s, and Ernie Els, Brad Faxon and Fred Couples shot 68s. At the other end of the scale, Faldo went from 69 to 75, Joel Edwards from 68 to 76, and John Cook from 69 to 75.

Elkington shot 74 and fell seven strokes behind Mickelson; Price and Janzen both shot 71s and fell back, and Cochran followed his 68 with 72, tying at 140 with Norman, Woosnam and Watson, among others.

The cut fell at 145 and caught Nicklaus, whose 69 could not overcome his opening 77. John Daly dropped out as well, along with Steve Jones, who had shown nothing since winning the U.S. Open in June; Colin Montgomerie, who had also missed the cut in the British Open; Davis Love III, who had come so close in the U.S. Open, and Tom Kite. Daly, Love and Nicklaus missed by one stroke, Montgomerie by three, and Jones by six.

Some of the golf was not pretty. Along with three birdies, Singh had a hole-in-one on the 14th, but he also had three bogeys. On his way to his 71, Price birdied six holes, bogeyed three and double-bogeyed another, and Cook may have earned the inconsistency prize. His four birdies were offset by two bogeys, a double bogey on the 15th and a triple-bogey seven on the teasing 13th.

Norman may have been the most disappointed man of all. Caught by darkness after playing 14 holes Thursday, he had played listless golf through the first nine holes, going out in 37. But he suddenly caught fire, eagled the 10th, a reachable par-five, birdied the 11th, a par-three of 165 yards, then lost a stroke on the 14th, the most difficult of the par-threes. He stood at one under par when he began play from the 15th tee the following morning, then ran off three straight birdies. Back in 31, he had shot 68 and stood just two strokes behind Perry, who no one suspected would still be around at the finish.

Beginning his second round with birdies on the first and second, Greg had picked up five strokes in six holes, his only par on the 18th. Out in 34 and six under par, he birdied the 10th, another of the reachable par-fives, by playing a daring second shot that skipped through the rough, past a deep bunker on the right, and rolled onto the left corner of the green. His putt for an eagle three grazed the left lip of the cup, leaving him a little tap-in for the birdie. Now Norman stood seven under par, tied with Perry.

He could go no further. Bunkered on the 12th, he bogeyed, then made a major blunder on the 15th. Standing 185 yards from the hole, he played a six iron, misjudged the shot, misread the wind, and messed up the shot. His ball drifted right of the green, bounced off the rocks bracing the right side of the green, and splashed into the creek. He made six, came back in 34, and slowly drifted back into the pack, never making another move.

Perry had hung on gamely through the early holes, and stood two under for the day and eight under for the championship through the first 11 holes, but he pushed his drive into the woods and bogeyed the 12th, then was warned to speed up play on the 13th tee. He was never the same. He bogeyed the 14th and finished the day by missing a four-foot birdie putt on the 18th.

Mickelson had no real problems after the first couple of holes of the first round. Six under par for the 12 holes he had played late Thursday, he began by three-putting the 13th and missing the 14th green and bogeyed again. A birdie on the 15th saved his 67, and after a 10-minute rest he began the second round by going out in 35 with birdies on the second and ninth and a bogey on the fifth, where he drove into rough so deep he couldn't reach the green.

Out in 35, he saved his best golf for the final six holes. A pitch to the 13th drew back almost into the hole for one birdie; he played a four iron to 15 feet on the 14th for another, drove into the left fairway bunker on the 17th and recovered to 25 feet and holed the putt, played a driver and three wood into the bunker on the 18th and pitched to four feet for his final birdie. Four birdies on the last six holes and Mickelson had the lead.

Just 24 years old, two years younger than Mickelson, Leonard had been playing well over the previous month. Early in the year he had lost the Phoenix Open playoff to Mickelson, and after a series of indifferent finishes suddenly began playing better. He tied for fourth in the FedEx St. Jude Classic in June, tied for eighth in the Motorola Western Open two weeks later, missed the cut in the British Open, though. Then, back home in the United States, he won the Buick Open with two shattering opening rounds of 65 and 64 followed by 69 and 68.

Where Mickelson had only six holes to play Friday morning, Leonard had 11. One under after the first eight, he held his ground and shot 71. Then, thoroughly warmed up, he began the second round by rifling a six iron to three feet and birdieing, and followed with a drive and three wood to 10 feet on the second and holing the putt for an eagle three. After a routine par three on the fourth, Leonard played a soft eight iron to eight feet and birdied the fourth. Four under after four holes.

His march was slowed by a bogey four on the eighth, where he bunkered his eight-iron tee shot. Out in 33, he began the second nine with a series of routine pars, then birdied the 13th with a sand wedge to four feet, then played an even better six iron into the 15th that braked within two feet of the cup. He missed the putt.

Two holes later Leonard hit another six iron to 20 feet but holed this one and finished by pitching to eight feet and birdieing the 18th. His 66 had tied the course record Perry had set only a day earlier.

The second-round leaderboard:

Phil Mickelson	67 - 134	Vijay Singh	69 - 138
Justin Leonard	66 - 137	Lee Janzen	71 - 139
Mark Brooks	70 - 138	Nick Price	71 - 139
Kenny Perry	72 - 138		

Thirty-three years had passed since Bob Charles had won the 1963 British Open. After the third round of the PGA Championship, it had become clear that Mickelson would not succeed him this year as a left-handed winner of one of the game's four benchmark tournaments. Three strokes ahead after two rounds, Mickelson stumbled around Valhalla in 74 and dropped into a tie for eighth place, three strokes behind Cochran, who raced around in 65, setting the course record and leaping into a two-stroke lead at 205. Cochran, however, was a left-hander as well, so Charles wasn't exactly safe.

Nor was the Valhalla course record. In three rounds it had been broken in the first, tied in the second, and broken again in the third. Moreover, where 51 men had broken par in the first round and 44 in the second, with the field cut to 81 players, 36 men shot under par in the third round, 19 of them in the 60s.

Cochran's 65 was the lowest, of course, but then Per-Ulrik Johansson shot 66, Elkington and Rocco Mediate shot 67, and Curtis Strange, Tim Herron and David Ogrin shot 68.

Brooks and Singh, meantime, shot 69 and climbed into a tie for second place with 207, two strokes behind Cochran. Price shot 69 as well and tied Elkington and Mickelson for fourth place at 208. After matching the course record on Friday, Leonard shot 72 and drifted back into a tie for seventh place at 209 with Norman, who shot 69, and Perry with 71.

Again, those were the decent rounds. Els, on the other hand, had one of those days when everything goes wrong. He went out in 44, his entire tournament ruined by an eight on the sixth and a seven on the seventh, six strokes lost to par on two holes. Els rallied on the home nine, came back in 35, and shot 79. Even so, with 221 he finished the third round ahead of only three players, one of them Bernhard Langer, who was having a terrible year.

Cochran had started the day in a tie for eighth place, six strokes behind Mickelson, but he lofted a nine iron to six feet on the first for one birdie, reached the second green with a four-wood second and two-putted from 20 feet for another, pitched to 20 feet and holed another putt on the fourth, drove perfectly to the angle of the left-to-right dogleg on the sixth and pitched to eight feet for his fourth birdie of the first nine. Two more pars and he had gone out in 32 and stood eight under par for 45 holes.

Playing about five holes behind Cochran, Mickelson had shown no signs of the collapse that lay ahead. He had bogeyed the eighth, one of the par-threes, but he had birdied the second and seventh, both par-fives, and at that stage stood 11 under par, still holding first place. A birdie at the 10th and he went to 12 under, still in control.

His ruin began at the 11th, where he bogeyed, and peaked at the 13th. His tee shot, a two iron, drifted left into deep rough, and the grass snuffed out his pitching wedge. His ball plunged into the creek in front of the island green. On with his fourth shot, he two-putted from 25 feet, then bogeyed the 15th. Playing the last eight holes in four over par, he came back in 39 and shot 74.

Earlier, though, Cochran had pitched to 15 feet and birdied the 13th, hit a huge drive on the 15th that left him only a pitching wedge and birdied from eight feet, then barely missed the 18th green but chipped inside three feet and birdied again. Back in 33, he had shot his 65 and now stood 11 under par.

Now Brooks began making his move. He had run off six consecutive birdies in the first round and then closed with four straight in the second, but he had done nothing much so far in the third. Playing two to three holes behind Cochran, he had been putting himself in position to make some birdies, but the putts wouldn't fall. He had missed from inside five feet on the first hole, from less than four feet on the second, and gone out in 35. Starting back with a birdie on the 10th, he stumbled through the 12th making a nice putt to save his bogey, and after routine pars on the next two, drove nicely on the 15th, a little right of center fairway, leaving himself 170 yards to the hole.

Seven under par then, four strokes behind Cochran, who had finished, Brooks drew his six iron and played a daring shot. The hole was set in the right rear of the green, about 15 feet or less from the right edge, where the creek swirls past and mis-hit shots crash among the limestone rocks in the stream bed.

Brooks played his shot just right. The ball hit short of the hole, bounced once or twice, then rolled into the cup. He had made two on a par-four hole and now stood at nine under par, within two strokes of Cochran. He had a chance to move closer, but after ripping a 225-yard two iron onto the 18th green, he three-putted, missing his second, a scary downhill three-footer, then holing his third from three feet as well. He finished with 69, solidly in contention in a major championship once again.

The third-round leaderboard:

Russ Cochran	65 - 205		Mike Brisky	69 - 209
Mark Brooks	69 - 207		Jesper Parnevik	69 - 209
Vijay Singh	69 - 207		Greg Norman	69 - 209
Steve Elkington	67 - 208		Kenny Perry	71 - 209
Nick Price	69 - 208		Justin Leonard	72 - 209
Phil Mickelson	74 - 208			

Played under overcast and threatening skies, the fourth round turned into one of the most gripping and tense closing rounds of a major championship within memory. Before it ended, nine men had their chance to win or tie for first, and four of them still contended on the final hole.

Perry might have won but he threw away a crucial shot at the final hole. Elkington might have won but he couldn't make the birdie he needed on the 18th. Singh might have won, but he bogeyed four holes on the home nine, and when he needed a final birdie at the 18th that would have tied him with Perry, he bogeyed instead. Tommy Tolles might have won with his closing 67, climaxed by birdies on the 17th and 18th, but he had started too far back and missed by one. Mickelson might have won, and indeed worked into a tie with Brooks, Singh and Cochran at 10 under par after he birdied the seventh, but he bogeyed the 10th, double-bogeyed the 13th again, and bogeyed the 14th. Leonard might have won when he birdied the second and fourth to go nine under par, but where he needed to make up two more strokes on the second nine he could do no better than par.

Even Tom Watson might have won. Beginning the round more than two hours ahead of Brooks and Cochran, the last men off, and eight strokes behind, Watson birdied five holes on the first nine and went out in 31, added another birdie on the 10th and fell to nine under par, but he played shoddy golf on the home nine. Needing a few more birdies, he bogeyed three of the last seven holes, shot 69 at that, and fell into a tie for 17th.

About the only person who couldn't have won was Cochran. Beginning at 11 under par, he could have tied had he played even a par round of 72, but that likelihood died when he bogeyed the fifth and double-bogeyed the seventh. Out in 39, he came back in 38, shot 77, and dropped like one of those boulders propping up the 13th green.

In the end Brooks won because he held his composure and showed he had the will to play his best shots when he needed them most. For a time, though, he seemed hopeless.

Beginning a little more than half an hour ahead of Brooks and Cochran, Perry opened with a series of rock-solid pars while Cochran played uneasy golf, losing one stroke on the fifth and two on the seventh. By then Cochran had fallen out of first place and had been passed by Perry, Parnevik, Mickelson, Janzen, Leonard and, of course, Brooks, who had picked up three strokes when Cochran bungled the seventh.

Now Perry made his move on the eighth, rifling a seven iron to four feet for his first birdie, added another with a nine-iron pitch to 12 feet on the ninth, then made a sensational birdie on the 11th, the little 165-yard par-three. His seven iron drifted onto the green's right fringe and, instead of a putter, Perry laid back his wedge and intentionally bladed the ball with the club's leading edge. It rolled true to the hole and dived into the cup. Another birdie; now he stood 10 under par, ahead of everyone but Brooks, who had gone into another of his birdie binges, and Singh, who had picked up two strokes on par through the seventh and moved to 11 under par.

After a routine par four on the first, Brooks salvaged a birdie on the second after driving into rough so deep he had to play a pitch shot out, then from inside 100 yards lofted a pitching wedge to three feet. Ten under par now, he gave a stroke away by bunkering his tee shot to the third, and after routine pars on the next two holes, ran off three consecutive birdies, holing from 15 feet on the sixth, from inside four feet on the seventh, then from six feet on the eighth. Now Brooks stood at 12 under par, one stroke ahead of Singh and two strokes ahead of Perry and Mickelson.

Elkington, meanwhile, had made no progress and stood at eight under par through nine, just where he had started.

Perry wasn't through just yet. He picked up another birdie on the little 13th and still another on the 14th, the difficult par-three, where he holed from 12 feet after a five iron that hit left of the flag and curled down a slope toward the hole.

By then the gallery was going wild, cheering on their local hero. Perry stood at 12 under now, just when Brooks looked as if he was falling apart. After a safe par five on the 10th, Brooks blocked a six-iron tee shot into a bunker on the 11th, pitched over the green, chipped back to two feet, and one-putted for a bogey. He botched the 12th by driving into the rough, left his second short of a greenside bunker, dumped his third into the bunker, then holed from four feet to save still another bogey. He squeezed past the 13th, but lost another stroke when he missed the 14th green.

Nine under now, Brooks had squandered three strokes in four holes, and dropped three strokes behind Perry and one behind both Elkington and Singh, playing ahead of him. Making his position even worse, he had only four holes to make up those three strokes.

Making Brooks' position look even more hopeless, while he had tossed strokes to the wind, Perry had kept right on making his pars. He saved one with a marvelous chip-and-run from bare dirt alongside a tree to the left of the 15th green that coasted less than two feet from the hole, and after a routine par on the 16th, putted within a foot of the hole from the fringe of the 17th. He was still 12 under par, solidly in command, with only the 18th to play.

The crowd had continued to grow as Perry closed in on the home hole, and now the spectators stood five and six deep from tee to green along the left of the fairway and beside and behind the green. They cheered every step and every shot, no matter how pedestrian it might have been; this was a Kentucky boy about to win the PGA Championship in Kentucky, and they all wanted to share the glory.

Strangely, though, Perry hadn't looked at a scoreboard; he had no idea how close anyone else might be, wasn't aware that Brooks had fallen back, or that Elkington lay only one stroke behind, with Singh just behind him. He did know that he was feeling pressure he had never known, and perhaps that caused him to come over the top on his drive and pull it into the left rough. It was a damaging mistake. His ball lay deep in the dense bluegrass, the toughest kind of rough.

Not taking any chances with an overly ambitious shot, Perry dug into the grass with his eight iron, but the coarse blades twisted the clubhead and the ball shot off left, still in the rough. He reached the fairway with a seven iron for his third and ran a shot within seven or eight feet of the cup. Needing the putt for a par five, he missed. Instead of the 67 that seemed likely only minutes earlier, he had shot 68, still an excellent round, but now he stood at 11-under-par 277, hanging by a thread, for Brooks had birdied the 15th to climb back to 10 under, along with Elkington, who had played through 16. Next Elkington, bunkered on the 17th, holed a clutch eight-footer to save par and Singh birdied. Now Brooks, Elkington and Singh stood 10 under par.

Then Perry did something strange. He climbed the television tower and sat with CBS commentators Jim Nantz and Ken Venturi, helping describe his day and commenting on the play going on behind him. With three men needing only a birdie on the 18th hole to force a playoff, Nantz and Venturi suggested after a time that perhaps Perry should leave for the practice range and warm up. Perry decided to wait; he would rather be on television.

Singh and Elkington were playing together, just ahead of Brooks. Instead of birdieing, Singh bogeyed. Elkington went for the green with his second, but his ball didn't carry far enough, hit the slope above the bunker and rolled back into the sand. He pitched out nicely but missed the putt. Singh finished at nine under, Elkington at 10 under. Only Brooks was left now.

Throwing himself into his drive, Brooks hit the fairway and went for the pin as well, which had been set in the right rear corner. Like Elkington's, his four wood caught the bunker, and when he pitched out he faced a curling downhill putt from a bit less than four feet. It was the kind of putt that causes the knees to shake a bit and the hands to tremble. He had missed from about the same distance the previous day, and now he needed this testing little putt to give himself a chance at glory.

Setting himself, Brooks tapped the ball lightly; it ghosted down the slope and tumbled into the cup. Brooks had shot 70, and with 277 had caught Perry. There would be a playoff on the 18th hole.

Now Perry clambered down the ladder and asked a PGA official if he would have time to hit a few warm-up shots. He was told he could, but before he could take two steps toward the range, he was told he didn't have time; he would have to go to the 18th tee right then.

We'll never know if missing a warm-up had any effect, but we do know that Perry played the 18th hole about as badly as it could be played. As he had earlier, he drove into the left rough, then continued chopping his way through the heavy grass until he finally reached the green with his fifth shot.

Brooks, meantime, drove nicely into the fairway, and with the hole set directly behind the bunker, he figured he had to fly his shot a little more than 215 yards uphill to carry the bunker. After discussing the shot with his caddie, they agreed anything over the green might ruin him; to hold the green he would have to play a high fade with his four wood.

The decision made, he wiped his grip dry, set himself, and moved into the ball. But he had started the shot too far right; instead of working toward the flagstick, the ball soared right of the bunker and away from the flagstick, apparently headed for trouble. Now he had a bit of luck. His ball flew so far right it missed the rough and somehow caught the right corner of the big, curving green. From there he lagged to about four feet and holed the putt for a birdie four.

It was strange in a way, but except for his putting, which really wasn't bad at all, Perry had played better tee-to-green golf than Brooks. He had hit 45 of the 56 fairways on driving holes while Brooks had hit just 41, and he had hit 50 greens, one more than Brooks. But Brooks had used only 104 putts, a remarkable figure, while Perry had used 110.

The PGA Championship acted as a vindication for Brooks' persistence early in his career when it wasn't at all certain he had the game to prosper at this level. He had fought off any doubts, and even when his position seemed bleak after dropping three strokes in four holes, he still felt he could win. Stepping onto the 17th tee, with Perry finished, he told his caddie he had to finish three-three. Obviously not a math major, Brooks had it slightly wrong; a three-three finish would have won even if Perry hadn't bogeyed the final hole. But who's counting?

7. The Players Championship

"I couldn't care less about $630,000, and I couldn't care less about a 10-year exemption." Now there was someone so wonderfully fixed in his career that a huge first prize and a 10-year free pass on the PGA Tour were not worth his attention.

The comment came from Fred Couples at The Players Championship, and veteran Couples-watchers were not taken aback. They knew exactly what he meant, and they held him completely innocent of all charges. Of course, a full translation is in order.

This was after the third round. Couples had just shot 68 and was four strokes off the lead. Four of the top 11 had not yet won on the PGA Tour, and the first-time winner was now the rage on the Tour. The past three tournaments had been won by first-timers, and now, here in The Players Championship, chances seemed excellent for a fourth. There was one with his foot in the door, and three others on the threshold: Tommy Tolles was the leader at 14 under par. David Duval was second, two strokes behind. Michael Bradley trailed by only three, and Scott Gump, by four.

Thus the question to Couples, who was also four behind: Considering all that was at stake here in golf's "fifth major," could these players hold up under the pressure? When he answered that he couldn't care less about $630,000 and a 10-year exemption, he was saying, in Couples-speak, that at the age of 36, after 16 years, 11 victories and $7 million in Tour winnings, he was not about to choke at the thought of such prizes.

Couples didn't. Tolles stumbled down the stretch, and so did Duval, and so did Colin Montgomerie. But Couples, who never led, zipped around the Tournament Players Club at Sawgrass in Ponte Vedra Beach, Florida, in a bogey-free 64 capped by an eagle-birdie-par spurt to the finish to win by four strokes.

Were you thinking about the $630,000 first prize?

"It never crossed my mind," Couples said.

How about the 10-year exemption?

"I wasn't planning on playing until I'm 46," he said.

All the riches were welcome, of course. But there was another prize that wasn't mentioned in the warm glow of victory that Sunday evening: His back. It had held up. His season was looking bright.

If Couples gave a hint to what kind of week this would be, it was in a fragmented first round, spread over two days because of a storm. He had to come back Friday morning to complete his first round, and started by holing a 25-foot birdie putt at the 14th. He then birdied the 16th and 17th for a six-under-par 66, one stroke off the lead.

When the first round was finally wrapped up on Friday morning, Kenny Perry, a career three-time winner, and Justin Leonard were tied for the lead at 65, an ominously low figure for the once-feared TPC at Sawgrass. The tie notwithstanding, the pundits said Leonard was the man to watch. That was because Leonard, in his second year on the PGA Tour, hadn't won yet, and this already was the year of the first-timer. There were three first-time winners in the three weeks leading up to this Players Championship: Tim

Herron won the Honda Classic in March, followed by Paul Goydos at the Bay Hill Invitational, followed by Scott McCarron in the Freeport-McDermott Classic. Some observers — moved by sentiment, not logic — believed that a first-timer also would win The Players.

What were the chances of someone breaking through here? Fairly good, if numbers meant anything. Nearly one-third of the field hadn't won yet. Of the 147 starters, 44 had not won on the Tour, and 38 of these had not won anywhere.

These figures offered some academic interest, but beyond that they meant nothing. Leonard himself was the first to reject the notion that someone else's performance had any bearing on his own. When someone asked whether the success of the three first-timers made him realize he also could also win, he said, "That hasn't made me realize anything. I've felt I could really do it since the end of last year." Leonard was drawing confidence from two second-place finishes as a rookie in 1995, and he had started 1996 strong, as runner-up to Phil Mickelson in a playoff at the Phoenix Open in January.

A number of things argued against a first-time winner here. There was the pressure of the Tour's richest purse, $3.5 million. Then the tough TPC course, which favored the veteran with his local knowledge (Leonard played in only one other Players, in 1995, and he tied for 34th). Then there was the strength of the field itself — 45 of the top 50 from the Sony Ranking. Thus chances were that the 44 who hadn't yet won, wouldn't win here.

When the tournament started, Leonard, a two-time All-American at the University of Texas, wasn't indulging himself in academic notions. He was hitting the golf ball. He had a one-birdie front nine, then exploded for six on the second nine, including a 40-foot putt at the par-three 13th and a three-footer at the dangerous island-green 17th. He one-putted eight times in a course-record 30 on the back, and he needed just 24 putts for the round.

"I haven't been able to say 'made it' that often for a long time," the encouraged Leonard said. He had missed the cut in three of his last four tournaments and had shot 75 or worse in three of his last four rounds. Perry made six birdies on the first nine, starting with the first three holes. "That got me in a good frame of mind," Perry allowed. So did the good break at the 14th. His approach got away from him, but hit a palm tree and caromed back onto the green and stopped 10 feet past the hole. He two-putted for his par.

The first round wasn't going to go this smoothly, though. A storm moved in and play had to be suspended, leaving 69 players to complete their first round before teeing off for the second round the next day.

Fuzzy Zoeller, playing with a sore finger, came back on Friday morning, birdied three holes in succession in his 66, and had three tap-in birdies and one from three feet. "I guess I like this place," he said. Kirk Triplett birdied four holes in a row and five out of six on his second nine and shot 67. Mark Calcavecchia holed a wedge from 90 yards for an eagle two at the 12th and also shot 67.

Seve Ballesteros, trying to nurse his once-awesome game back to health, would have to wait for another time. He shot 41 on the first nine, and withdrew after 10 holes, citing a sore back. Robert Gamez, his playing companion, said he didn't see where Ballesteros hurt his back. "The way he was hitting it," Gamez said, "I didn't want to watch."

When it came to first-timers, no one had mentioned Tolles. So in the second round, Tolles introduced himself: He was 29, living in Flat Rock, North Carolina, a town of about 1,000 to where he fled after Cape Coral, Florida, grew too big and busy for his tastes. He was a second-year man after some success on the Nike Tour, a shy guy with a willing smile. He was also, by the way, the leader of this Players Championship after a sparkling eight-under-par 64, one stroke off the course record, in the second round.

"It was almost a perfect round of golf," Tolles said. Just that three-putt bogey at No. 14 kept him from tying or even beating the course record of 63. The 64 put him at 11-under-par 133, for a two-stroke edge on first-round leader Justin Leonard (70) and Mark Calcavecchia (68). With Duval (66) just three strokes behind, it meant three of the top six on the board were looking for that first win.

"There are a lot of really good young players out here who haven't gotten the exposure of the veterans," Tolles said, "but they have played without any fear." Which was precisely the point some veterans were making. "I don't know if they have less fear than we had, but I wish they were a little more scared," cracked Jay Haas, who was three strokes behind Tolles after 68.

Tolles' short game was remarkably sharp. He chipped to one foot at No. 2 to set up the first of his four outward birdies. Then came a six-footer, a 30-incher and a chip-in from 25 feet. Coming in — except for the 14th — it was his putter. He got two of his five birdies from 30 feet, another from 20.

Leonard had picked up where he left off, getting to 10 under par with three straight birdies from No. 4, then cooled coming home with a birdie and his first two bogeys of the tournament. His former co-leader, Kenny Perry, lost his touch. "I couldn't hit it solid," he said. He shot a three-bogey 71 and slipped three strokes off the lead, tying with Duval, whose aching shoulder clearly was feeling better. "I'm a little further along than I thought I might be," Duval said. In a one-bogey 66, he hit 16 of 18 greens, birdied No. 8 from 50 feet and eagled No. 16 from 20.

Couples, meanwhile, just one off the lead in the first round, slid back into the pack with a par 72 for a 138 total, five off the lead. The spectators, meanwhile, must have thought the usually placid Couples had become a bundle of nerves the way he had been twisting and turning while waiting to hit. But it was for his chronic back problem. "The doctors want me to to that," he said. "They want me to fidget."

The sharp scoring brought the 36-hole cut at one-under-par 143, and sent some surprising names packing. Paul Azinger and Ian Woosnam missed by one stroke, Nick Faldo by two, and Naomichi (Joe) Ozaki, Sandy Lyle and Greg Norman by three. Here was some strange stuff: Lyle had now made just two cuts in his 11 Players Championships. He won one, in 1987, and was 74th in 1994. Norman, who won with a record 24-under-par score in 1994, had shared the record of 11 straight cuts made. This was his second straight miss on Tour this year, and he had never done that before. "As long as I don't make it three in a row," he said.

The second round had its diversions. Tom Watson, for example, en route to a 68, holed a bunker shot for a birdie at the par-five ninth, then holed his approach for an eagle at the par-four 10th. "I would have been happy with a birdie," he said. New Zealand's Frank Nobilo would have been happy to be dry. Only nine players watered shots at the island 17th, and his was costly. He suffered a double bogey, shot 72, and finished seven shots off the lead.

This was lost on the residents of a town in North Carolina. Flat Rock is small, and it's so private that Tolles said only a few of the folks knew who he was or what he did. "Which is the way I like to keep it," he said. But making a splash in a big golf tournament is no way to remain anonymous. Tolles didn't know it, but the folks down at the combination gas station and convenience store were already watching him on television, and they were rooting for the hometown boy.

The third round was played in a fairly steady rain that got heavier as the day wore on. Rain or no rain, you could have found generous odds that Tolles was going to fold. The Tolles watch came empty. The question was whether he would make another bogey and give someone a chance to catch up. His last was at the 14th hole in the second round. He finally made another in this third round, at the 18th, when he and Jay Haas were finishing as the final group.

He posted 69, moved to 14-under-par 202 and kept his two-stroke lead, this time over Duval, who shot 68. "It was a little miserable out there," said Tolles, "but I was always in the fairway and I was always on the green. I was taking my two-putts. Par was a very good score."

Tolles hadn't planned on this kind of day. He woke up with a strategy in mind — protect that lead.

"But when Justin hit his first drive right down the middle, and his first iron shot three feet from the pin, that was an eye-opener," he said. "That got my motor running."

He didn't need it against Leonard. Scratch one potential first-timer. Leonard, co-leader in the first round, blew to 80, the highest score in a day when the soft and vulnerable Sawgrass took an awful beating. Of the 77 players remaining in the field, 50 broke par and 36 shot in the 60s. The rain would still be a factor in the final round, with the greens soft and agreeable. "There's no way they can firm them up," said Bradley, another potential first-time winner. "They can roll them or cut them or do what they want, they're still going to be pretty receptive." Bradley crowded into the picture with a 66 to join Haas at 11 under, a stroke behind Duval and three off Tolles' lead. That meant three non-winners were atop the leaderboard going into the final round — Tolles, Duval and Bradley.

Ernie Els, Montgomerie and Couples were right behind, in a crowd of seven just four off the pace. Els, who shot 65, none too subtly reminded the three winless hopefuls of the pressure of the final round. "There are a lot of youngsters, so to speak, out there," Els said, "so it's an even bigger test for them."

Couples, meanwhile, was still the quietest of the bunch. He had a workman-like 68, with five birdies and one bogey. It was one of 13 in the day.

The third round had its interesting off-spotlight moments. The 17th hole, for example, claimed only one ball, making that a mere 17 for the tournament. Jay Don Blake aced the par-three 13th, 187 yards, with a six iron, becoming the 11th in tournament history to score a hole-in-one. He shot 68. And Mark O'Meara shot 69 with the help of a crazy save at the par-four 10th. His wide-right tee shot lodged in the wheel well of a golf cart. His free drop rolled into a tough lie in a patch of sand. His seven-iron shot then hit a tree branch and dropped into the rough at the green. He chipped to two feet and holed the putt. "It was like a television commercial," O'Meara said.

Phil Mickelson, who shot the day's low round, 64, to move within five strokes of the lead, said it would take another 64 to win. He was right. But it wasn't his.

And Tolles was reminded of that first prize. What would $630,000 do back at Flat Rock? "I could probably buy the place," Tolles said.

In the final round, the field would shake itself down for the closing rush, but not before some fleeting tremors.

Australian Wayne Grady, who won the 1990 PGA Championship but nothing since, suddenly caught fire. He went through the first nine in 31, and was tied for the lead through the 13th hole. Then came a horrendous crash. Starting at the 14th, he went double bogey, bogey, double bogey. "The most expensive few holes I've ever had," Grady said. "It would be nice to say I choked, but I didn't." He shot 70 and tied for 19th.

Duval, playing at home in Jacksonville, was in fairly good position to become one of the first-time winners people were watching for. He had started the final round alone in second place, two strokes behind Tolles. He got ambushed at the 11th. What he thought was a routine fairway three iron ended up in the water behind the green. Maybe it was water in the fairway, maybe some mud. No matter. He double-bogeyed, and needed birdies at the 16th and 17th for 71 and a share of fourth place.

Tolles made a stir, but couldn't really get going. "I never could get really excited about today," he said. "Just one of those days. I just wasn't ready to play golf. I was just kind of in a fog, watching myself play stupid and everything else."

Tolles had started with that two-stroke lead, and was still leading by two coming to No. 9. There, he caught a bunker and trees, and bogeyed. He was about done for. He bogeyed twice coming in, shot 72 — his first round out of the 60s — and tied Montgomerie for second at 14-under-par 274.

Couples was to say in his championship interview at the end of the day that he didn't plan to play until he was 46, but in this final round, he was vintage Couples and playing as though he wouldn't reach 37. He raced through Sawgrass without a bogey. In fact, with only a hint of one. At the par-five No. 2, he escaped from trees and bushes to save his par. He made four birdies on the first nine that stamped him a winner even that early. Two came from strong putting, a 20-footer at No. 3 and a 25-footer at No. 6. The other two came from great iron shots, having only three-foot putts at No. 5 and No. 8.

He missed a two-foot birdie putt at No. 11, and gave an embarrassed grin. "You want to crawl into a hole and not let anyone see you," he said. He got even at the 12th, dropping a six-footer for the birdie that tied him with Tolles and Montgomerie at 15 under par. Then he put them away with a miracle shot at the 16th, almost the equal of that hanging lie on the bank at Augusta's 12th that spared him and sent him on to the 1992 Masters title.

Sawgrass' 16th, a par-five of 497 yards, which played the easiest in the fourth round, claimed more than its share of unwary victims. It almost got Couples. He had 220 yards for his second shot. He was trying to cut a two iron into the green.

"It hung out there, and I thought it was in the water," Couples said.

But it caught the green and stopped 25 feet from the flag. Couples drilled the putt for an eagle three.

Tolles was back at the 15th fairway at the time. The thunder from the gallery rocked him. "You thought 20,000 people won the state lottery," he said.

Montgomerie was two groups behind. "No one had to tell me what that meant," he said.

Couples was asked to grade his miracles. The one at Augusta? "That one was really, really, really, really lucky," he said.

This one? Just one "really."

Montgomerie came to the 16th then, needing a miracle of his own. He tried a three wood from 230 yards. Like Couples' shot, it hung out there. But it didn't cut back. It was Montgomerie's only watered shot on the watery course all week. He bogeyed.

Couples birdied the 17th as well, with a nine iron to 30 feet, and Montgomerie bogeyed the 18th for 68. He still hadn't won in the United States. This was his third runner-up finish, after the 1994 U.S. Open and the 1995 PGA Championship. He managed a chuckle. "Thank you for reminding me," he said. "It beats third."

And so it came down to Couples standing up to the pressure, manufacturing some of his own, and cruising home in championship fashion. Couples-watchers were accustomed to such performances.

"I felt great today," Couples said. "I was so far behind. Kind of like — pardon the pun — the Bob Hope Classic."

What pun? Even veteran Couples-watchers didn't know what to make of that one.

8. Alfred Dunhill Cup

At some point every serious golfer should play the Old Course at St. Andrews. Steve Stricker certainly had the right credentials when he came to the Old Grey Toon on the east coast of Scotland. Stricker had made his way through the Canadian Tour and onto the United States PGA Tour in 1994, when he was the fourth leading rookie in earnings. Quietly, Stricker, with his wife Nicki as his caddie, was earning a growing reputation. In 1996, he enhanced that renown by first winning the Kemper Open, and then adding the Motorola Western Open by the little matter of eight strokes.

Stricker was then named to the three-man American team with Phil Mickelson and Mark O'Meara for the Alfred Dunhill Cup. On the basis of their Sony Ranking, the trio was seeded No. 1 and, indeed, came through to lift the trophy for a record third time. They left Australia, England and Ireland as two-time winners after the 12th playing of the 16-nation team event.

Mickelson, fulfilling his potential, was riding high at the top of the U.S. money list. O'Meara, at 39 the veteran of the team, was enjoying one of his best-ever seasons. Stricker had never played in an event at the Old Course previously, yet in his five competitive rounds over golf's original layout he was 10 under par. More importantly, given the medal-match play format of the competition, Stricker won all of his five matches.

"I did not know what to expect coming here and it was a bit of a surprise to win all my matches," Stricker said modestly. "I got to know Mark and Phil a lot better and we got on well off the course. We had a good time. It was an honor to be a part of the U.S. team."

As many before him, Stricker had to contend with the fickle nature of the St. Andrews winds, and the huge double greens on the Old Course. "I went to the University of Illinois so I learned how to play in the wind, but I never considered myself a great wind player," the 29-year-old said. "I don't think you can know enough about the Old Course, with the wind and all those long putts. I felt that I was a key to the whole week in a way because if I won my match, that would force the other team to win both of the other matches against Mark and Phil, which would be hard to do."

Before getting through to Sunday's semi-finals and final, the Americans had to qualify by topping Group 1, where they were drawn with Spain, the other seeded team of the quartet, England and Italy. The group matches took place over the first three days, but O'Meara ensured the Americans were center of attention from the opening round by shooting a nine-under-par 63. The conditions were benign, as when Curtis Strange shot his course-record 62 in the 1987 Dunhill, and it was certainly a pleasant golfing day on the ancient links.

O'Meara parred the first hole, but then birdied the next eight in a row to set an Old Course record of 28 to the turn. Birdies at the 11th and 12th followed, but then he could get no further. First the birdies dried up, and then disaster struck.

The reason the medal-match play format works so well in this event is that it forces everyone to play the 17th or Road Hole. O'Meara, on the stony path over the green in two, failed to clear the slope with his first putt and took four putts to hole out for a double-bogey six. A birdie three at the 18th gave him a seven-shot win over Costantino Rocca of Italy.

"Costa was going, 'I concede, you're the man'," O'Meara said. "I know I threw away a chance to break Curtis' record. Needless to say, I holed my share of putts. But the 17th has got me a few times, although once I went in there two behind Richard Zokol, took a bogey and came out one ahead. It is a great hole."

The Americans beat Italy comfortably enough 2-1, although Mickelson lost to Emanuele Canonica in extra holes, while England beat Spain 3-0. The two winners met the next day and, with O'Meara slumping to 75 as the weather deteriorated, Mickelson finished birdie-par-birdie to beat Lee Westwood by a shot and give America a crucial 2-1 win.

That meant they just had to beat Spain on the third day to go through as winner of their group and they did so 3-0. In the only tight game, O'Meara beat Miguel Angel Jimenez 67-68, while Stricker won 70-74 against Diego Borrego, and Mickelson's 66 was 11 shots too good for Ignacio Garrido. England lost 2-1 to Italy, but Barry Lane survived with an unbeaten record.

Group 2 featured both the defending champions, Scotland, and the previous year's runners-up, Zimbabwe. Neither of those sides was to qualify, and although Sweden topped the group, it was India which was the hero of the early stages.

This was the first time the Indians had been invited to St. Andrews and they arrived with two players, Jeev Milkha Singh and Gaurav Ghei, jointly ranked 696th in the world, and another who was unlisted, Ali Sher. But Indian golf has been given a boost by performances on Asia's new Omega Tour and in their manager, Vikramjit Singh, they had a secret weapon. He is a member of the Royal and Ancient Golf Club of St. Andrews.

On the first day, India almost caused a major upset by losing only 2-1 to Zimbabwe, Sher beating Tony Johnstone 72-73. A day later, they did cause a major upset by beating Scotland. The Home of Golf had seen it all before when the Scots lost to Paraguay in 1993, but that did not ease a proud nation's reaction to another chapter of calamity.

Sher was always behind Raymond Russell, losing by 13 shots, but Colin Montgomerie, who was assured of being No. 1 in Europe for the fourth consecutive year, had to birdie the 18th to break 80 and finish one stroke behind Ghei, the pro at Delhi Golf Club. When Singh beat Andrew Coltart at the first extra hole, the greatest day in Indian golf was sealed.

"This is the first time we have played in major international team competition and we wanted to make an impact," said Ghei. "We have done that now. The whole experience of St. Andrews has been wonderful, although it is a little cold for us."

The magic could not continue and the following day India lost 3-0 to Sweden, which was no disgrace since they had done the same to Zimbabwe. The Swedes may have been without their top names — Parnevik, Haeggman, Johansson and Forsbrand — but in Jarmo Sandelin, Peter Hedblom and Patrik Sjoland they had three players in top form and overdosing on team spirit.

They beat Scotland 2-1 on the first day, with a little help from a 110-foot putt from the edge of the 16th green during Sandelin's 68-69 win over Montgomerie. Only moments before, the Swede's second shot had looked to be going out of bounds. "I think Monty was more shocked than I was," Sandelin said.

Sandelin was at it again the following day, holing from 65 feet on the playoff hole to beat Nick Price and give Sweden a sweep that meant they only had to win one game against India on the third day.

What should have been the group decider, Scotland against Zimbabwe, was made irrelevant. For the record the Zimbabweans won 2-1 and Montgomerie suffered his third defeat in his three matches.

The two seeded in Group 3, South Africa and Ireland, were involved in the expected third-day showdown. Both had won their first two matches, South Africa beating both Canada and Wales 2-1, Ernie Els and Wayne Westner seeing them through on each occasion, while Ireland managed a 3-0 result against the Canadians on the second day.

This was an Irish team that represented the new era in European golf. Paul McGinley, the oldest of the trio at 29, had won his first tournament during the year, Darren Clarke had won his second title the week before in Germany, and Padraig Harrington was challenging for Rookie of the Year honors.

McGinley led the way and such was his confidence that he was picked to take on Els on Saturday. He won, too, with 69 to 70 that gave him an unbeaten record over the three days. Retief Goosen had not won a match yet for the South Africans, but he discarded his driver, stuck to his long irons and outlasted Clarke at the first playoff hole. Clarke was first to putt, his 20-footer swinging off line at the last moment. "The ball looked as if it could not miss two feet from the hole," he said. Goosen, with almost the identical putt, holed his.

About the same time, Westner, having birdied the 16th to square his match with Harrington, faced his second shot from the rough at the 17th. He had 192 yards to the green, needing to avoid the Road Hole bunker, and played a sublime low runner with draw, which took the contours of the green and finished three feet from the flag.

"It was one of those Scottish shots, keeping it low and letting it run up," Westner said of his five-iron approach. "There was quite a lot of luck involved." One behind playing the 18th, Harrington could have forced a playoff but his birdie putt stayed three inches outside the cup. "Wayne's shot at the 17th won us the match," said Els. "He is a little modest about those two great shots at 16 and 17."

The Irish players could not hide their disappointment. "You are either destined to win in this tournament or not. We played well and it took very good golf to beat us," said McGinley. Added Clarke, "We had the team to win it this year, but they had a bit more luck."

Luck is something that seems to desert the Australians when it comes to getting through the qualifying scramble. After dominating Group 4 for two days, the No. 2 seeds lost on the third day for the third year running. Greg Norman, captain of the team that won the trophy in its first two years in 1985 and 1986, had earlier said, "Australia has not done the job in the last couple of years and this time we are a little more keyed up."

They started well enough, with a 2-1 win over Japan, only Wayne Riley going down to 67 from Naomichi Ozaki. The Japanese caused a minor upset the following day by beating the other seeded team in the group, New Zealand.

Ozaki won again and Kazuhiro Takami beat Greg Turner by three strokes with 70.

The Aussies beat Germany, who had lost to the Kiwis 2-1 on the opening day, 3-0. This led to a whole host of possibilities for the final day's qualifying, but by far the simplest was that Australia just had to win one point against the Kiwis to go through. If they could not do that, then either New Zealand or Japan could progress, but the Japanese lost their opportunity by going down 2-1 to Germany.

It never looked good for the Australians. Riley shot 76 and was beaten by seven strokes by Grant Waite. Turner, winning his first match, finished four ahead of Steve Elkington with 69. A win from Norman would have been enough, but he was up against an in-form Frank Nobilo.

The bearded Nobilo had beaten Norman by nine shots in 1990, and despite visiting the burn at the first, he set off to try and do it again, marching to the turn in 31. He survived a scare at the 10th, when he drove wildly and ended up taking a drop on the New Course, leaving himself a third shot of 160 yards. He got away with a bogey, but Norman birdied the 15th, then hit a five iron to three feet at the 17th.

With Nobilo bogeying the 17th, the Australian had made up three shots in three holes to be only one behind. But Nobilo wedged perfectly to a foot at the 18th to clinch the match. "I had 76 yards to the green and I hate those shots," Nobilo said. "Greg Turner plans those shots really well, and I just imagined I was him and flipped it in to a foot. Any time you shoot 66 with two penalty shots, you know you have had an exciting day."

The semi-finals, drawing four countries from the furthest corners of the globe, pitched America against Sweden in the northern hemisphere, and South Africa versus New Zealand from the southern hemisphere. The top two games of the first semi-final seemed to leave little doubt about the result. O'Meara was never over par and Hedblom was never under par as the American won 68-74. But for bogeys at the 16th and 17th, Stricker would have beaten Sjoland by more than the three strokes of the final margin.

That was enough for the Americans, but some friction developed in the bottom match where Mickelson was playing Sandelin, who has an excitable nature. Mickelson thought he had gone overboard in his celebration after beating Price on the second day, and he was not too happy with being two behind after 11 holes either.

On the 12th tee, according to Sandelin, Mickelson said, "You should show me some respect, and don't behave like that." Sandelin added, "I said, what's the problem. He said this is a friendly game and I said I know it is a friendly game but I want to win. He then said, 'You have been playing (expletive) in the States.'

"I know I have been playing badly there and that's true, but just because he's in the top 10 in the Sony Ranking doesn't mean he can say things like that. I can't understand why he said them. I just showed I was pleased when I holed putts. We shook hands at the end. I think I was overreacting."

Mickelson commented, "I don't want to comment directly on what happened. The Alfred Dunhill Cup and the Ryder Cup and the Presidents Cup promote the game of golf and sportsmanship. I felt the match could have been handled with more sportsmanship." It was a curious affair, the Swede ultimately winning 68-71.

The other semi-final was closer. Turner sneaked home one shot in front of Goosen 71-72, while Els could afford a double-bogey six at the 17th hole and still beat Nobilo 69-72.

That meant everything rested on the top match which had been tied at 74. Both Waite and Westner parred the first extra hole, then Westner drove the green at the second. But the South African faced a tough 55-foot putt and Waite wedged in to three feet to put the pressure on. The South African holed his second putt from five feet and the hole was halved in birdies.

Both drove poorly at the 17th, the third playoff hole, and could not reach the green in two, but Waite, undefeated so far this week, again produced a superb sand-wedge shot to a foot. "The match could have gone either way and fortunately it fell on our side," Waite said.

Waite was at it again in the final, pitching in with a nine iron from 155 yards for an eagle two at the fourth hole to cancel out Stricker's birdies at the first two holes. But Stricker was not to be denied. A five-under-par round of 67, his best of the week, did not contain a bogey, and Waite's demise was confirmed when he found the Road Hole bunker and took a double-bogey six.

Although O'Meara lost to Nobilo — the latter rolling in three birdies in a row around the turn during a 69-72 win — Mickelson made sure of victory in a tight match with Turner. There was never more than one hole in it and the American was one ahead as they went to the 16th. While Mickelson's approach rolled sweetly off a bank to four feet, Turner was over the green and his par putt lipped out for a two-shot swing. Mickelson played the 17th conservatively, taking a bogey five, but birdied the 18th for a 69-72 win.

"We are very excited and thrilled to have won the Alfred Dunhill Cup," O'Meara said. "I have been on two teams in the past and it is very gratifying to be on a winning team. We knew if we played up to our ability we could get to the final. After the first day, we decided to put me out against their best guy. I felt if I won it would be a bonus, and if I didn't then I knew I had two players who would back me up. Steve had an outstanding week winning five times and Phil was solid when we needed him."

America had previously won in 1989 and 1993, but for New Zealand, it was their first appearance on the final day of this tournament. "The way we have played this week, we can't be too disappointed," said Nobilo. "It is a great week for New Zealand golf and we can feel proud of ourselves getting to the final."

9. Toyota World Match Play

While Ernie Els was rewriting the record book at the Toyota World Match Play Championship, the man who made the original entries was playing nearby. Gary Player was inaugurating the Player Championship, an end-of-season event on the European Seniors Tour not far away from Wentworth at The Buckinghamshire course.

Els has spent most of his short career making giant strides along a path Player first trod. They remain the only two men to have won the triple crown of South African golf — Open, PGA and Masters — in the same season and now we can report that the South African connection at the World Match Play is as strong as ever.

As Els, in his amiable way, went about his business beating everyone in sight at Wentworth, he was asked if he had been in contact with his great predecessor. "No, I haven't spoken to Gary this week," Els said. "I don't know all the details about Gary in the World Match Play, but I know he has won it five times and has a great record here. He and Seve (Ballesteros) have almost owned this tournament for a long time.

"Gary will go down in the books as one of the great players in the game. He's a great match player and this competition was right down his alley. He was a real grinder, a positive kind of golfer. I love this Match Play event myself. I don't want to get ahead of myself but I'd love to win it a couple more times."

A day later, Els had achieved something not Player, nor anyone else, had done. He had won the World Match Play for the third straight year. His three titles since his debut in 1994 put him equal with Greg Norman and two behind Player and Ballesteros' five titles. Player won back-to-back titles in 1965 and 1966; Ballesteros did it twice in 1981-82 and 1984-85. But the man who had previously come closest to winning three in a row was Hale Irwin, who won in 1974 and 1975, but lost to David Graham at the 38th hole of the 1976 final.

"It hasn't sunk in yet, but I'm really going to enjoy this," Els said after beating Vijay Singh 3 and 2 in the final. He earned a prize of £170,000, which took his tally from three years at the event to £500,000. "The first thing I should do is buy a couple of rounds in the clubhouse," Els added. "It is a lot of rand. Thank goodness we have such good sponsors like Toyota."

"It wasn't intimidating playing against Ernie by any means," said Singh, trying to explain what it is that makes the South African such a dominant force over 36 holes of match play. "But if you give away shots to Ernie, he is a very hard person to win holes from." The Fijian had a fine run in the tournament but finally had to be added to a pretty impressive list of those who have fallen to Els.

In 1994, Els overcame Ballesteros, Jose Maria Olazabal and Colin Montgomerie. A year later, Lee Janzen, Bernhard Langer and Steve Elkington were his victims. The run almost ended when Els was 6 down to Steve Stricker at lunch in the second round but he survived by mounting one of the greatest ever comebacks in the competition. Then Mark Brooks was dispatched in one of the quickest matches ever, and finally Singh had to succumb. "I have played some good golf, beaten some good players and had some memorable matches over the last three years," said Els.

There are two questions. Firstly, why is he so suited to match play golf? Els said, "I think when you play stroke play you look after your score. If you start making birdies and find yourself a couple under par, you start protecting your score sometimes. You look at the scoreboards and try not to lose your position in the field.

"In match play you are only as good as the last hole you have played. At other times you might be making doubles or triples, but in match play you have only lost one hole. That's the difference. You have to be a lot more aggressive in match play. The normal thing is to go for as many birdies as you can, although if your opponent is in trouble you can play safe."

Secondly, what is it Els loves about the 6,957-yard West Course at Wentworth? "It goes back to when I was second to Jose Maria in the Volvo PGA Championship in 1994. I really learned how to play the course. It suits my game. There are a lot of holes where you can hit three wood or two iron and then have a go at the flag. And at this time of year the course is always in such good condition and it is hard not to enjoy playing it."

This was the 33rd annual World Match Play, the sixth under the sponsorship of Toyota, to be played at the Wentworth Club, outside London. The field was one of the strongest ever — three of the 1996 major champions, the top five from the United States money list and the top two from Europe.

As the No. 1 seed, Els was not in action on a sunny autumn's day for the first round. In addition to Els, the seeded players who received byes in the first round were 1996 major champions Steve Jones (U.S. Open), Tom Lehman (British Open) and Brooks (PGA Championship). Masters champion Nick Faldo was not entered this year because of a commitment in Japan.

"It is a big advantage not playing until Friday," Els said. Said Montgomerie: "I don't agree with four of the 12 players having the day off. But then I have never been seeded in the top four here." The Scot was involved in the feature match, as far as the home gallery was concerned, of the first round as he played his Welsh rival for the European money list, Ian Woosnam.

Montgomerie had won that battle, winning the Vardon Trophy for the fourth consecutive year, and he won here again. Throughout the morning, the match was close, Montgomerie winning the last two holes to take a 1-up lead into the afternoon. Woosnam had thought he would spend the lunch break having treatment on his fragile back. Instead, it was his putting that needed attention, but a session on the practice green did not help.

Montgomerie birdied the third and sixth holes and then won the ninth with a par to go 4 up. After that the Scot was firmly in control, Woosnam even starting to offer his hand, thinking he had lost 3 and 2 at the 15th. A hole later it was all over. "I feel it was unfortunate that we were paired together," Montgomerie said. "Ian may have won in another match and then we would have two Britons playing tomorrow. But you take the draw as it comes. You have to beat everyone in the end."

By far the closest match of the first day, although it did not appear so early on, was between Singh and Phil Mickelson. The American was 5 down after seven holes. "I don't know what it was," Mickelson admitted. But in a brave fight he was only 1 down at lunch and Mickelson had squared the match by the second hole. Yet he could never edge in front of the Fijian, who soon regained a couple of holes advantage. But at the par-five 17th, a sweeping dogleg-left, Singh hit his three-wood second shot out of bounds to give a hole back.

One down, Mickelson found the front left bunker at the 18th and, with Singh just off the green in two, the American almost produced the sort of short game miracle for which he is rightly renowned. His bunker shot pitched into the hole — and then bounced out. It was close enough to be conceded and put the pressure on Singh to get up and down for a half, but only if Mickelson's ball had stayed in the cup would they have gone to extra holes. "I can't believe it came out of the hole," Mickelson said. "Obviously there was a lot of luck involved in the first place, but for it to pop out again was quite surprising."

Nobuo Serizawa of Japan had played in the Match Play once before, losing 6 and 5 to Jeff Sluman in 1988. His visit this time was no longer. Mark O'Meara, himself only playing in the event for the second time, won four of the last six holes to record a 7-and-5 win.

The remaining first-round match was between the previous year's losing finalist, Steve Elkington, and Stricker. The 29-year-old American had been a member of the winning United States team at the Alfred Dunhill Cup along with Mickelson and O'Meara, but Stricker had been the star of the show, winning all five of his matches.

Taking into account his 6-and-5 victory over Robert Allenby in the singles of the Presidents Cup, Stricker was on quite a roll in head-to-head golf. However, he was 2 down at lunch and only got level at the 26th hole, but from then on he dominated. Elkington double-bogeyed the ninth and could not match Stricker's birdies at the 12th and 14th. At the latter, the uphill short hole, Stricker struck a five iron to 12 feet and holed the putt. He won 3 and 2.

"I think I have reinforced some things that I thought about myself," Stricker reflected afterwards. "A never-give-up attitude. I was down in a couple of my matches last week and came through, and I did the same today. I didn't make a lot of putts, but I made the ones I had to."

With Stricker in such a winning vein, and the way the draw was arranged, it was hard not to draw the conclusion that he was about to give the defending champion his hardest match in the second round. Nobody was quite ready for what happened, however. When Stricker holed from six feet at the ninth, it put him 3 up. With birdies at the 12th and 13th, the margin became 5 up. And another at the 17th put Stricker 6 up. Els' first birdie of the day came at the 18th, but it was only good enough for a half. His round of approximately 73 was the first time he had been over par in the event.

It was wet and cold, and there had been a delay when the greens had flooded early on, but that could not explain it. What happened over lunch we don't know. But Els later said, "Maybe I should become a very religious person because I was really praying just to get to the second nine in the afternoon." He was certainly not thinking about winning the championship three times in a row.

But there were precedents. Player had been 6 down to Tony Lema at lunch in 1965, lost the 19th and won, exhausted, at the 37th. In 1982, Sandy Lyle had been 6 down to Nick Faldo and won 2 and 1. Just the day before, in a friendly game at Sunningdale, Els and Sean Connery had scored a fight-back victory over Els' father, Nils, and Jackie Stewart. The occasion had been Ernie's 27th birthday. "Honestly, I didn't have a beer all day," he said, "although I played like I had a hangover this morning."

In the afternoon, the tide started to turn when Els chipped in at the third. Then he did it again at the eighth to get back to 2 down. At the ninth, he holed from 40 feet for par and saw Stricker miss from 18 feet for birdie. "That's when I started to wonder what was going on," Stricker said.

Els missed the green at the 10th and, with a smile, the American mischievously said, "Shall I give you that, or do you want to go ahead and hole it?" Instead, Stricker's birdie won the hole, but it was his last.

Els drew level at the 15th, with a sumptuous six iron to four feet, and they were still tied at the 18th. Stricker drove into a bunker, only just got out with his second and then, with an awkward stance, rifled a three wood right at the flag. It stopped at the back of the green, but closer than Els' eagle effort. Both two-putted to give the South African a one-hole victory.

"I feel for Steve," Els said. "He was all over me this morning. I didn't know where it was going. But on the back nine this afternoon, I hit some great shots when I needed to. It is very satisfying."

Stricker was stunned at his exit. "With a six-hole lead I didn't try to change my game plan," he said. "I stayed aggressive but didn't make any birdies. Every time he stepped up, he was doing something great."

Inevitably, the match overshadowed all others that day, but in the rain and gloaming, Brooks and Montgomerie went to the last hole, too. Brooks' putter was in mighty form and helped him to seven birdies in the last 11 holes to turn a 2-down score line into a 1-up win. All square with two to play, he got up and down for birdies each time to go 1 up and then to save going into extra holes. "He holed a number of putts. That's the strength of his game and he proved it today," Montgomerie said.

The two matches in the lower half of the draw were more one-sided. Lehman, the Open champion, returned to Britain with a 6-and-5 win over O'Meara, while Singh swept aside U.S. Open champion Steve Jones 9 and 8. To his excellent driving of the day before, Singh had added the unbeatable combination of hitting his irons close and finishing off the putts, and a four-hole winning spell on the front nine in the afternoon put matters beyond doubt. Earlier, at the 17th, Jones had driven out of bounds and conceded the hole. "I wanted to watch the match in front," he said. "It was more interesting."

Saturday's semi-finals, the weather back to pleasant sunshine, were an extreme contrast. One was over in the blink of an eye, the other went the full distance and more. Els made short work of Brooks, winning 10 and 8, and earning a place in the list of biggest wins. It is led by Tom Watson's 11-and-9 thrashing of Dale Hayes in 1978 — Hayes went on to win the first-round losers competition and earn more than Watson in the main event — and then comes Player's 10-and-9 win over Jean Garaialde in 1969, and Arnold Palmer's 10-and-8 victory over Roberto de Vicenzo in 1966. Brooks joined de Vicenzo as being the only men not to win a hole in a match.

Els found himself 6 up at lunch this time, without particularly exerting himself, and won the first two holes afterwards with pars. Brooks had spent the break on the practice range. "I had the right ball going," Brooks said. "The harder I tried not to hit it right, the further it went. I went to the range, but the tee shot on the first in the afternoon was probably my worst shot of the day. I never threatened him. If I had not chipped and putted decently, I would have shot 15 or 20 over." Said Els, "I don't know what happened to Mark. His wheels came off. It was a bit of a cruise."

Meanwhile, a couple of grinders who do not know when they are beaten were slugging it out in the other semi-final. Two holes was the biggest lead either player had in the morning, which finished all square, and there was not more than a hole in it after lunch. Lehman hit his pitching wedge approach at the 16th to five feet and a birdie there put him back to 1 up. Singh's eagle chance at the 17th pulled up just in front, but at the 18th Lehman left himself with an 80-foot approach putt. He put it 10 feet past and missed the return. Back to the first. From a huge drive, Singh hit a five iron to 10 feet and holed for his third successive birdie and the match.

"Win or lose, that was a tremendous match and a lot of fun to be a part of it," Lehman said. The next day, he would lose the last two holes to fall 1 down to Brooks in their 18-hole playoff for third place.

"The key to my week is to not make bogeys and give holes to the other guy. You have to make him earn the hole with birdies," Singh said. It had been a policy which had served him well in making him the first unseeded player to make the final since 1979. He was also trying to achieve the rare feat of winning the tournament from the first round, last done by Corey Pavin in 1993. But he was up against Els.

Singh's early two-hole advantage was nullified by the fifth and Singh was never up again. When Els was bunkered at the 18th, the deficit did come down to one hole at lunch. Els was still slightly unsettled after hitting an observer full on the forehead with his drive at the 17th, although the gentleman was not hurt.

Singh also won the first in the afternoon when Els was bunkered again, but when the Fijian went out of bounds with his recovery from the trees at the fourth, Els was sparked into form. By then it was raining heavily, and clearly the South African decided to take command. He played a beautiful chip for a half at the short fifth, hit an eight iron to 10 feet at the next and holed for birdie, won the seventh with a par, and hit another close eight iron at the eighth for another birdie.

Then at the ninth, Els sent his five iron to within a foot of the hole. Extraordinary. But Singh matched him by hitting his five iron to five feet and holing the putt. A birdie from Singh at the 11th got him back to 3 down, but he let a chance to capitalize on Els' visit to the trees on the 12th slip and from there the game, too, slipped away. The next four holes were halved in pars to bring the match to an end at the 16th.

"I made too many mistakes," Singh said. "I made more bogeys today than in the rest of the week. Five holes is too many to give Ernie. I wish I could play the game over. If I had played the golf I did yesterday, I would have had a chance to beat him."

"I played steady all week," Els said. "No heroics. I don't think I played as well as in the past, but the weather was not as good as in the last two years." For the record, in winning nine out of nine matches in the three years, Els has averaged seven under par for each encounter. Who will take him on next?

10. American Tours

If the signs prove out, the year 1996 will go down as a benchmark year not only in the history of the U.S. PGA Tour, but in the history of golf. These were the key developments:

• Greg Norman had his first Masters Tournament victory well in hand, leading by six strokes going into the final round. Then he collapsed and handed Nick Faldo his third green jacket. This was one of the greatest collapses ever in the game.

• The sound of that crash could only be drowned out by something louder, and that was the arrival of amateur phenomenon Tiger Woods, age 20, who won an unprecedented third consecutive U.S. Amateur in August, then became a professional golfer the next week at the Greater Milwaukee Open. He went on a rampage. In eight events as a pro, Woods won twice — Las Vegas Invitational and Walt Disney World/Oldsmobile Classic — had three other top-10 finishes, and earned $790,594 for 24th place on the money list.

• Big, pleasant Tom Lehman, age 37, who doesn't have the flash of either Norman or Woods, continued to grow as a force on the PGA Tour. He won the British Open, Tour Championship and the MasterCard PGA Grand Slam, was runner-up in the U.S. Open, led the PGA Tour money list with a record $1.78 million, and won the Vardon Trophy with a stroke average of 69.32. He won the PGA of America's Player of the Year Award on performance points, and was voted Player of the Year by the Golf Writers Association of America.

"I feel," said Lehman, "that I'm not real far away from having a super year."

Mark Brooks had almost as good a year. He won three times, including his first major title, the PGA Championship, in a playoff against Kenny Perry.

It was Phil Mickelson's year much of the way. The amiable left-hander, growing into his considerable promise, led the PGA Tour with four victories. These included a third Nortel Open in Tucson, Arizona, and his first win east of the Mississippi, the NEC World Series of Golf in Akron, Ohio.

Other multiple winners were Mark O'Meara, Steve Stricker, John Cook and Loren Roberts, all with two victories each. Steve Jones' long comeback from a hand injury was rewarded with the U.S. Open Championship, in which he edged out Lehman, his good friend.

Other high points and oddities: The AT&T Pebble Beach National Pro-Am was cancelled for the first time in its 50 years, because of rain. Tom Watson took the Memorial Tournament, his first PGA Tour victory in nine years. This came after John Huston flirted with a sub-60 score in the second round, then settled for 61.

The PGA Tour had 13 first-time winners, none more unlikely than Paul Stankowski. In fact, he scored back-to-back first-time victories. First, he won the Nike Tour's Louisiana Open, and thus inspired, changed his plans and headed for Atlanta and the BellSouth Classic, where as sixth alternate he would have practically no chance to play. But he did get in, and he won.

Taylor Smith, a rookie, wrote the year's oddest failure story at the Walt

Disney World/Oldsmobile Classic. Smith birdied the final hole to tie Woods. It it turned out that the split grip on his putter was non-conforming to U.S. Golf Association rules. He was disqualified.

Most of all, though, 1996 would be remembered because of Woods. There was no denying his impact. Lehman put it as well as anyone. "Tiger may be pushing us," Lehman said. "He makes us work harder. He gives us a new challenge. I feel someday there will be a dominant player who wins two majors and eight tournaments in a year. Maybe it will be Tiger, or somebody motivated by Tiger."

U.S. PGA Tour

Mercedes Championships—$1,000,000
Winner: Mark O'Meara

Mark O'Meara seemed out of place. The King of Northern California — he had won four AT&T Pebble Beach National Pro-Ams — found himself at La Costa Resort, not far from San Diego. Very well, O'Meara would stake a claim to Southern California, too, in the Mercedes Championships. That would take some doing, however. Nick Faldo was in the way.

It was a battle of accurate drivers. O'Meara hit 48 of 56 fairways. Faldo was even better. He hit 51 of 56. But of the mere five he missed, there was one in particular he shouldn't have. He had pulled to within two strokes of O'Meara in the final round when his tee shot at the 16th hole ended up in a predicament more typical of Seve Ballesteros, behind a tree. "I tried to hit a big Seve hook," Faldo said, "but there wasn't enough Seve on it." His seven iron missed the green to the right, and he bogeyed.

O'Meara was not about to squander a three-stroke lead over the final two holes, and gained his third PGA Tour victory in 10 months. He played the par-72 La Costa course in 68, 69, 66 and 68 for a 271 total, 17 under par. He won by three strokes over Faldo (67) and Scott Hoch, who birdied seven of the first 13 holes on his way to a closing 66. Greg Norman thrilled the fans with seven straight birdies for 67, but three 73s had put him out of contention. He finished 18th out of the 30 in the champions-only field. The season opened ominously for British Open champion John Daly. He placed last, 11 over par and 28 strokes behind O'Meara.

O'Meara was second by one stroke in the first two rounds, behind Corey Pavin (67), then Lee Janzen (65–136), then took a four-stroke lead on Faldo going into the final round, 203-207. Faldo opened the last round with a par-eagle-birdie start, but that failed to rattle O'Meara. "The key was that I drove the ball well and made good solid birdies on No. 2 and No. 3 and kept the ball in play off the tee," O'Meara said. And at the par-three 11th, O'Meara dropped a 25-footer for a birdie and Faldo missed from five.

"I thought a 67 the last day would give him something to think about," Faldo said. "But it didn't."

Nortel Open—$1,250,000
Winner: Phil Mickelson

Bob Tway was speaking for everybody. "I guess you can say Phil owns this tournament," Tway said, after Phil Mickelson beat him in the Nortel Open, the first full-field stop on the 1996 PGA Tour, in Tucson, Arizona. Mickelson won in 1991, when he was still an amateur out of Arizona State University, again in 1995, and again in 1996, for the second time in a row and the third overall.

"I won't say I own it, but I sure do like it," Mickelson said with that dimpled smile. Now 25 years old, he had his sixth PGA Tour victory, his fifth as a professional since 1991. He was picking up where Johnny Miller left off in the mid-1970s as the Desert Fox. Familiarity bred confidence in this case.

"I had a lot of positive thoughts coming in here because of what I've done here in the past," Mickelson said. That helped down the stretch, when he had to fight off Tway and Lee Janzen. He chipped in for a birdie from 30 feet on the last hole to wrap up a two-stroke victory on rounds of 69, 66, 71 and 67 for a 273 total, 14 under par at the Tucson National Resort (par 72) and Starr Pass (par 71). Tway matched his closing 67 for 275, and Janzen slipped to a tie for third with 69.

Mickelson, who didn't lead after any of the first three rounds, was in the middle of a dogfight in the fourth round. Tway started the final round four strokes behind leader David Toms, a Nike Tour graduate, shot 31 on the first nine to tie for the lead, and took the lead with a birdie at No. 10. He birdied the 14th to get to 14 under par, then stumbled. An out-of-bounds tee shot cost him a bogey at the 15th, and he three-putted the 17th for another bogey. Janzen birdied the 15th and got within one stroke, but missed the green at the 18th and bogeyed.

While Toms was fading out with 74, Mickelson shook off a bogey and staked another claim in the desert with six birdies. "It's been a year since I've won," Mickelson said, "and I haven't played with this much intensity since the Ryder Cup. I went from playing, to playing with a purpose."

Bob Hope Chrysler Classic—$1,300,000
Winner: Mark Brooks

There are two kinds of golfers. One thinks scoreboards are the enemy. They won't look. They prefer to play in the dark. The others — and they seem to be in the minority — watch the scoreboards like a cook watching the soup. Mark Brooks is in the second group. And in the fifth and final round of the Bob Hope Chrysler Classic, he was watching like a hawk.

"I like to know what's going on," Brooks said. "What was going on in our group told me what I needed to do."

What golfers need to do is make birdies, of course, but sometimes more so than others. This was one of those times. Brooks led or was near the lead through the first four rounds, and he was tied for the lead going into the final round at Indian Ridge, the last of the four courses. He had got his share of the lead with 67, but others had made up even more ground. Payne Stewart shot 63, Jeff Maggert 64, and John Huston 65.

"I think it was good for me that it was close," Brooks said. "I felt like I needed to make birdies." And that's what he did. The clincher came at the par-five 15th, where he dropped a six-foot putt for his birdie. That was the turning point. "John should have made four, and Payne could have," Brooks said. "Instead, they made fives and I made the four."

The birdie gave Brooks a two-stroke lead, and he needed it. Houston birdied the 18th and finished second by one stroke. "Any time you have that good a chance to win and you don't, I think it's a little disappointing," Huston said.

Brooks parred the last three holes, including a beauty out of the rough at the 18th. He fired a six iron to 12 feet, and trying to lag the putt, nearly holed it. The tap-in par gave him his second consecutive five-under 67 and a 23-under total of 337 on rounds of 66, 68, 69, 67 and 67.

Scott Hoch jumped into third place with a 65. Payne Stewart (70) slipped to fourth and Maggert (71) to seventh.

Phoenix Open—$1,300,000
Winner: Phil Mickelson

To rephrase a tired line: If this is a golf tournament in the desert, that must be Phil Mickelson. And that's who it was, making the Phoenix Open his second victory of the season, the seventh of his career and — more to the point — his fourth in the Arizona desert. If he wasn't already the new Johnny Miller, he was now. Not so, Mickelson protested. "Johnny won tournaments by 10 or 12 shots," Mickelson said. "I'm grinding them out in playoffs." Mickelson just ducked under the wire at the Nortel Open and this time he had to go three extra holes, but a win is a win.

Justin Leonard, another member of the new generation — he was starting his second full year on the PGA Tour and was looking for his first victory — would have settled for that. He was leading Mickelson by two strokes going into the final round, and shot a two-under-par 69. But Mickelson shot 67. Maybe Leonard deserved better for four rounds in 60s — 67, 67, 66 and 69 — for a 15-under-par total of 269 at the TPC of Scottsdale. Low scores were the rage. Apart from Mickelson (69, 67, 66 and 67), Blaine McAllister, Kenny Perry and Andrew Magee all had four rounds in the 60s, and three men had jewels in the final round. New Zealand's Grant Waite became the 10th player to shoot 60 on the PGA Tour, and Mark Calcavecchia and Curt Byrum shot 62s.

The playoff was a classic. Mickelson birdied the first extra hole from eight feet, and Leonard followed him in from six. At the next, Mickelson bunkered his drive and his approach shot, and came out poorly, 20 feet from the hole. Leonard had a 20-foot putt for a winning birdie. But Leonard two-putted, and Mickelson holed his to stay alive. At the third hole, Leonard missed a birdie from eight feet, and Mickelson tapped in from 30 inches for the win.

"Today was a really difficult day for everybody," Mickelson said. "Nobody was more than two shots apart at any time, and on the back nine, I felt out of control, then in control, then out of control."

AT&T Pebble Beach National Pro-Am—$1,500,000
Winner: Cancelled

From its beginning, when it was the beloved Crosby Clambake to its current incarnation as the AT&T Pebble Beach National Pro-Am, the jewel on California's Monterey Peninsula has known tough weather — rain, wind, fog, cold. This year, for the first time in its 50 years, the tournament was canceled because of heavy rains. All because of one hole. All three courses — Pebble Beach, Spyglass and Poppy Hills — were soaked, but the par-four 16th at Spyglass was the cause of the problem. This was the first cancellation on the PGA Tour since the washout of the 1949 Colonial National Invitation.

The field played under the lift-clean-and-place rule through the first two rounds. Then more heavy rain caused officials to suspend play on Saturday. By Sunday, relief was not available from the casual water down part of the left side of Spyglass's 16th hole. Since all players had to play all three courses — many had already played all 18 holes at Spyglass — officials couldn't eliminate either the 16th or Spyglass from the tournament. "We couldn't play under the casual water rule strictly," said PGA Tour official David Egar. "The Tour has stayed firm about playing under the Rules of Golf."

Jeff Maggert, at eight-under-par 136, was the leader when the tournament was cancelled. All 180 contestants received unofficial prizes of $5,000 each.

Buick Invitational—$1,200,000
Winner: Davis Love III

The setting was ideal for Phil Mickelson. He was playing in his hometown, San Diego; he had won his last two starts, the Nortel and Phoenix Opens, and he was about to make the Buick Invitational his third win in a row. But there's always someone to spoil the party. This time, it was Davis Love III.

After trailing by three strokes in the first round, seven in the second and four in the third, Love had the tournament just where he wanted it. "Every time I get three or four back on the last day, I always say it shouldn't be that hard to win," Love said. That's a tall order, but he filled it.

Love played the last 35 holes without a bogey, and he got away from the crowd in a hurry with a final-round 64. He made three birdies on the first nine, then five on the second nine — one at the 10th, three straight from the 13th (all on putts from 12 feet or less), and finally a five-foot side-hiller for the fifth at the 18th. Love's rounds were 66, 70, 69 and 64 for a 269 total, 19 under par, and a two-stroke victory over a frustrated Mickelson.

"I lost it on the greens," Mickelson said. "I feel I gave three shots back in the last three holes. After I birdied 10 and 11, I really expected to win." He birdied the 15th from eight feet to tie at 18 under par with Love, three groups ahead. Then the fine touch left him. He bogeyed the 16th on three putts, lipped out a birdie putt at the 17th, and lost any chance for a tying eagle when he missed the green at the 18th hole.

Lennie Clements started with a tournament record 64-65–129 score and led by two strokes. He finished strong, 72 and 71, but dropped to a tie for third place.

United Airlines Hawaiian Open—$1,200,000
Winner: Jim Furyk

There are odd golf swings, and there are odd golf swings, and then there's Jim Furyk's. It looks like ... well, it gets the job done, as Furyk showed in the United Airlines Hawaiian Open. It came the hard way, in a playoff against Brad Faxon. Things ended at what had become Furyk's adopted home, Waialae Country Club's 551-yard par-five 18th hole. In five visits, including the playoff, Furyk logged one par, two birdies and two eagles. He made his fifth visit the last, with a two-putt playoff birdie from long range that gave him his second victory in three years on the PGA Tour. He got the first only five months earlier in the 1995 Las Vegas Invitational.

"I really put it in there on the second putt," Furyk said. "A three-and-a-half-footer to win is pretty much what you want."

Poor Faxon. He had come so far and so fast, only to be turned back. He trailed by seven strokes in the first round with two-over-par 74 to Wayne Levi's 67. Faxon climbed with 67 in the second round. Then 66 tied him with Steve Stricker for the third-round lead. Furyk, meanwhile, was also climbing the ladder. Shooting 68, 71, 69 and 69 for an 11-under-277 total, Furyk was in or near the lead, then a stroke out coming into the final round.

Then Faxon forced the issue. "At the 18th, I was assuming Jim would two-putt, so I was aggressive," Faxon said. He eagled. Furyk wasn't surprised. "You know things can happen," he said. "I knew a birdie would at least get me a playoff."

He got both with that three-and-a-half-footer at the final hole. But getting there had been an adventure. Scott Simpson, Tom Lehman, Larry Mize, David Ogrin and Stricker all took a shot at the lead. Faxon and Stricker were up by a stroke through the turn. Then both bogeyed and were tied with Furyk through the 11th hole. Furyk and Stricker took the lead with birdies at the 13th against Faxon's bogey-birdie exchange. And that's the way it went until the explosive 18th — and then the 18th once again.

Nissan Open—$1,200,000
Winner: Craig Stadler

Golfers have been known to fling their putters into the nearest lake, break them over their knees, but they rarely forget them. After the pro-am on Wednesday, Craig Stadler put down his putter near the scorer's tent. The next morning, in Thursday's first round of the Nissan Open, when Stadler was about to tee off, he discovered that his putter was no longer with him. He hastily grabbed another one, then achieved what Stadler, a San Diego native, called his "hometown sweep."

"I said nearly 10 years ago that I want to win in Los Angeles and San Diego because it's home," Stadler said. "I won San Diego two years ago, and now Los Angeles. It's special to win in front of family and friends."

Apart from revealing a soft streak, Stadler — who seems to enjoy his grumpy Walrus character — was faithful to his dream. It took some doing at the tough, par-71 Riviera Country Club course. Stadler shared the first-round lead with 67, and was tied for second in the second round with 70—

137, one stroke behind Robert Wrenn. A 73 left him four strokes behind going into the final round.

Stadler took the lead with a five-under 30 on the first nine, bogeyed the 16th and 17th, but held on for 68 and a six-under total of 278. It was a one-stroke victory over Mark Brooks (64), Scott Simpson (71) and Fred Couples (69).

Doral-Ryder Open—$1,800,000
Winner: Greg Norman

"I want to win every tournament I play in," Greg Norman was saying. "It's impossible, but you can try." In the Doral-Ryder Open, Norman did it again, winning for the third time and doing better there than some players do in an entire career. He has won $1,015,843 and shot 23 sub-par scores in 32 rounds on Doral's Blue Monster course.

This time, he did it in the final round, blasting from a tie for the lead to a six-under-par 66 and a two-stroke victory over Vijay Singh and Michael Bradley. His rounds were 67, 69, 67 and 66 for a 269 total, 19 under par.

"I think he's a great player. That's why he's No. 1 in the world," said Singh, who knew the frustration of closing with an outstanding round on a tough course, 68, and still falling short.

If Singh was frustrated, what was Bradley feeling? Bradley, 29, joined the PGA Tour in 1993 and was looking for his first victory. Another time, another place, and this might have been it. He closed with 66. But then, so did Norman. "Every time I looked up, he was making birdies," Bradley said. At the 14th hole, for example, Norman dropped a 20-foot putt for the lead shortly after Bradley holed his own 20-footer for a par up at the 15th. Norman locked up the win at the 17th, holing a 30-foot chip shot for his seventh birdie in 11 holes and a three-stroke lead.

"He's the best player in the world," Bradley said. "To hang with him that long, I feel pretty proud."

Norman was in command. He hit 46 of 72 greens in regulation, and averaged about 25 putts per round, needed only 23 in the fourth, and made only three bogeys all week. He seemed to be getting up a head of steam. "I know April is five weeks away," said Norman, pointing towards the Masters Tournament. "So I know that I've got to start getting ready now, because it takes a good two or three weeks to get to where I would like to be."

Honda Classic—$1,300,000
Winner. Tim Herron

When Tim Herron came to the Honda Classic in early March he was a 26-year-old rookie, but a battered veteran of the Australasian, Canadian and Nike Tours, and was ranked 115th on the money list with $16,924. In the first round he started to make a name for himself, shooting 62, 10 under par.

Then Herron did a rare thing for a newcomer. Against a field that promised the hottest pressure in the game, what with such as Nick Price, Mark O'Meara, Nick Faldo and Greg Norman in pursuit, he refused to fold. He led by two strokes in the first round, by six strokes after the second round, and by three strokes after the third round. Then Herron won by four strokes, adding rounds of 68, 72 and 69 for a 17-under-par 271 total. He did it like a seasoned pro. He was the first rookie to score a wire-to-wire victory since Nick Price in 1983.

"He had a lot of curveballs thrown at him and he just didn't buckle," said runner-up Mark McCumber.

"Everyone told me that I have unbelievable talent," Herron said. "When it doesn't come, you get frustrated. The last few years, I started to believe in myself." He demonstrated that confidence in the final round, at the par-three 17th hole, with his lead in danger. He hit his tee shot in the water, but holed a 20-foot putt, holding the damage to a bogey, one of seven for the week.

Herron fast became noted for his long drives, averaging 284.5 yards before the Honda Classic. But his putting did the job. He was 115th on the PGA Tour in putting coming in, but needed just 108 putts in the Honda Classic, an average of 27 putts per round. "I was rolling the ball awesome this week — the best ever," he said. It added up to an eagle, 22 birdies and a new outlook.

Bay Hill Invitational—$1,200,000
Winner: Paul Goydos

The highest compliment to Paul Goydos — apart from the cheers that greet a champion — came from Jeff Maggert, the man he beat in the Bay Hill Invitational. "He didn't look like a first-time winner," Maggert said. "He never got rattled, and he holed some 15- to 18-footers when he needed them. If a guy deserved to win, it was Paul."

For Goydos, it came down to the short putt at the 18th. "I wasn't concerned with winning or losing until I had that one-footer," he said. "I was thinking fairways and greens, and let's see what happens."

Goydos, 31, became the PGA Tour's second consecutive first-time winner. It was a masterful performance by the former school teacher. With rounds of 67, 74 and 67, he shared the lead in the first round, dropped four strokes behind in the second, and trailed by two going into the last round.

Then he surged ahead of the sliding field. He was leading by three strokes midway through the final nine, and played the last five holes in one under par. He locked up the victory with a strong par, getting down in two from 50 feet for 67 and a 13-under-par total of 275 at Arnold Palmer's Bay Hill Club in Orlando, Florida.

Tom Purtzer finished third, two strokes behind Goydos — the same two strokes he was penalized for hitting the wrong ball in the second round. Maybe it was just Goydos' time. Golf turned out to be a good career choice for the teacher who became a substitute in order to find time to work on his golf game. "Winning was always my goal," Goydos said. "Not keeping my card."

Freeport-McDermott Classic—$1,200,000
Winner: Scott McCarron

The Masters Tournament was on Scott McCarron's mind as he rolled towards the end of the Freeport-McDermott Classic in New Orleans and his first victory in two years on the PGA Tour. The $216,000 first prize was great, but there were those rolling acres at Augusta National.

"That's what I was thinking about all the way up 18," McCarron said. "I was glad about the money and the first win, but I was really thinking about playing in the Masters." McCarron, 30, a third-year man out of Rancho Murieta, California, got both kinds of green.

McCarron could afford to daydream about the Masters, just three weeks away. He was breezing to a five-stroke victory over a faltering Tom Watson. He played the par-72 English Turn course in rounds of 68, 67, 69 and 71 for a 275 total, 13 under par, to become the third straight first-time winner of the year.

Watson was the crowd's sentimental favorite. He hadn't won in nine years but challenged all week. He trailed McCarron by just two strokes going into the fourth round, and had moved to within one — then crashed on the second nine. He bogeyed the 10th from a bunkered tee shot and fell three behind. He birdied the 11th, then bunkered his tee shot at the 12th and made the second of his four bogeys on the back nine.

The final round was a test in winds gusting to 40 miles an hour. The average score was 76. McCarron, playing like a veteran, shot 71. He bogeyed No. 5, came back with a birdie at No. 6. There was perhaps a touch of bittersweet to the win. McCarron said he felt bad about Watson not getting that first win after nine years. "But he can do that next week," McCarron said.

The Players Championship—$3,000,000
Winner: Fred Couples

See Chapter 7.

BellSouth Classic—$1,300,000
Winner: Paul Stankowski

Paul Stankowski, 26, a fringe player in his two previous years on the PGA Tour, had to change his travel plans twice. First, he won the Nike Louisiana Open — his first Nike Tour victory. Thus encouraged, he switched plans and decided to try for the BellSouth Classic at Atlanta Country Club. As the sixth alternate, he had practically no chance of getting in the tournament, but suddenly he was in. And then he won it. This was his first PGA Tour victory. And now he had to change his schedule again.

"Wow!" he said. "I'm going to Augusta!"

Stankowski had grabbed the final berth in the last tournament before the Masters Tournament, and now the final spot in the Masters, too, and he won it the hard way. He had hovered near the lead the first three rounds, and was three behind leader David Duval going into the fourth round. Then while Duval and Davis Love III were blowing to 76s and Tommy Tolles to 75, Stankowski saved par from a bunker at the 18th for a one-under-par 71.

That tied Stankowski with Brandel Chamblee, another player looking for his first win, who came from seven strokes behind and grabbed the lead with 67. Stankowski shot rounds of 68, 71, 70 and 71, and Chamblee 72, 70, 71 and 67 to tie at eight-under 280. The playoff, at the par-five 18th, came down to two gambles. Only one paid off.

Chamblee decided to go for the green in two, to put the pressure on Stankowski. He had been long with his one-iron shot in regulation, and this time he was short. He caught the water in front of the green. Stankowski laid up, hit a wedge to 12 feet, and holed the putt for a birdie. It was another detour well taken. "It cost me an extra $500 to change my ticket," Stankowski said. "But I guess it paid off."

Masters Tournament—$2,200,000
Winner: Nick Faldo

See Chapter 3.

MCI Classic—$1,400,000
Winner: Loren Roberts

Big leads were the talk of Harbour Town at the MCI Classic, the point being that Loren Roberts was holding a four-stroke edge going into the final round just a week after Greg Norman led by six going into the finale at the Masters, and look what happened to him. The Norman disaster, Roberts said, never entered his mind. It was simply a matter of being in one's comfort zone. Roberts was practically in a rocking chair. He breezed to his third PGA Tour title by three strokes over Mark O'Meara.

"I like this course, and I feel comfortable here," Roberts said. "At Augusta, that's a totally different thing."

"He held his composure well," O'Meara said. "I've had four- or five-shot leads. It's not that easy."

This late-April week at Hilton Head Island, South Carolina, was an odd one. Norman had left Augusta and stepped right back out before the public. He attracted sympathetic galleries, along with a heckler who eventually was removed from the course. Norman never challenged but tied for 22nd place at six under par.

Roberts, meanwhile, was crafting an outstanding tournament on rounds of 66, 69, 63 and 67 for a tournament-record 19-under-par 265 total. Roberts, known as "The Boss of the Moss" for his putting, took command with that third-round 63. He needed only 21 putts. He needed only 25 putts in the last round, getting birdies from increasingly long range — three feet, then eight feet, then 20 feet at the 14th, 23 feet at the 17th, and finally 45 feet the 18th.

"I've spent more time on my putting than anything else," he said. "If you knock off one putt a round, that's huge."

Greater Greensboro Chrysler Classic—$1,800,000
Winner: Mark O'Meara

Mark O'Meara didn't lack for things to do over the weekend. He could always watch his hometown favorites, the Orlando Magic, in the NBA play-offs. It seemed he was headed that way when he opened the Greater Greensboro Chrysler Classic with 75, eight strokes off the lead. But O'Meara revived in time to make the cut, then shot 10-under-par 62 in the third round. That masterpiece, which tied the course record at Forest Oaks Country Club in Greensboro, North Carolina, vaulted him into a tie for the lead with Duffy Waldorf going into the final round.

A closing flurry for 69 and a 14-under-par 274 total gave him a two-stroke victory over Waldorf, who closed with 71. It was O'Meara's second victory of the year, his fourth in 13 months, and the 12th of his PGA Tour career.

The final round was almost match play. Waldorf bogeyed No. 1, and O'Meara eagled at No. 2, and O'Meara led by three strokes with only two holes played. Things looked bleak for Waldorf, especially when Waldorf bogeyed No. 8 and O'Meara birdied No. 9 despite a poor drive and went four strokes ahead.

"I still had something to show," Waldorf said. This he did, with birdies at the 14th and 16th holes. He was two strokes behind with two holes to play — then two behind with one to play when they both parred the 17th. On the 18th, O'Meara drove to the left, Waldorf to the right. Waldorf could have used some of the luck from earlier in the week that got him two eagles from the fairway at par-four holes.

But Waldorf's luck had run out. This time he put his approach shot over the back of the green, and he would chip past the hole. O'Meara was on the green in two, but 45 feet from the hole. He left his par putt eight feet short, then rolled in that putt for the win.

Shell Houston Open—$1,500,000
Winner: Mark Brooks

Mark Brooks found the secret to putting — well, for the moment, anyway — and went on to become the first native Texan to win the Shell Houston Open since Lee Elder in 1976.

"Putting was the difference," said Brooks, of Fort Worth, after coming from behind in the final round to catch Jeff Maggert, a Houston resident, and beat him in a playoff. "I started the day with the mind-set to be aggressive with the putter. On the back nine, I know that if I got it five or six feet, I was going to make it. It's been awhile since I've felt that way."

Maggert was disappointed but unbowed. "I don't have any regrets, the way I played," he said. "I just wish I could have had a few more birdie putts fall."

Brooks, apart from this bold approach, he had his secret. He simply quit taking a practice stroke. Whatever effect that had, it paid off in the final round when he made up a two-stroke deficit on Maggert, who led going into the final round, and it paid off again on the first playoff hole. He dropped a 30-foot putt for a birdie. When Maggert missed from 18 feet, Brooks had his second victory of the year and the sixth of his 13-year career.

"More goes into winning than just playing well," said Brooks, who posted rounds of 66, 68, 70 and 70 to tie Maggert (67, 69, 66, 72) at 14-under-par 274. "The cards have to play out right, and they did for me this week." For example, there was Maggert's double bogey at the par-five 13th, where he put his third shot into the water behind the green.

And then there was David Duval, who lost a share of the lead when he bogeyed the par-three 16th from just off the green. And when he missed a 12-footer for a birdie at the 18th, he also missed the playoff by one stroke. "I'm going to have to do some things better if I expect to end up on top." he said.

GTE Byron Nelson Classic—$1,500,000
Winner: Phil Mickelson

The Fort Worth area is hardly the desert, but it's far enough west of the Mississippi to qualify as fertile ground for the Phil Mickelson, the Desert Fox. Actually, it was an invitation from Byron Nelson that induced Mickelson to cut short a vacation and play in the GTE Byron Nelson Classic in Irving, Texas. It was a good decision. Mickelson took the lead in the second round, held off numerous challengers and scored his third victory of the season.

Mickelson, shooting 15-under-par 265 on rounds of 67, 65, 67 and 66, wasn't really tested. Craig Parry closed with a pair of 65s and was the runner-up by two strokes. He birdied the 16th hole to tie Mickelson for the lead at 13 under par. Mickelson promptly chipped in from 30 feet at the 16th for an eagle and a two-stroke lead.

Charlie Rymer tied the course record with 61 in the third round to close within one shot of Mickelson going into the last day. Then, still in the hunt, Rymer had a wild ride. He birdied No. 9, bogeyed No. 10, triple-bogeyed No. 14, bogeyed No. 15 and eagled No. 16 for 72 and tied for 18th place. David Duval double-bogeyed No. 1, then rebounded for seven birdies over the last 15 holes for 65 and his third third-place finish in four starts.

MasterCard Colonial—$1,500,000
Winner: Corey Pavin

As Corey Pavin was to note, "Strange things were happening ..." He was speaking about the homestretch, but he might well have meant the entire MasterCard Colonial. For example, the wild extremes: Mark Calcavecchia made a 10 in the first round, Lee Rinker made a 10 in the second round, and Omar Uresti eagled both of Colonial's par-five holes in the second round. Nick Price made his 16th consecutive cut while slumping Ian Baker-Finch didn't make it past the first nine. He withdrew. It was hot for mid-May, with the temperature in the 90s, and the wind was blowing at 30 to 40 miles an hour. One thing you could depend on, though, was Pavin himself.

Tough as ever, Pavin charged from behind with two late birdies, passing Jeff Sluman and Rocco Mediate to take his first victory since the 1995 U.S.

Open, and his second at Colonial Country Club in Fort Worth, Texas. Never more than three strokes off the lead, Pavin shot rounds of 69, 67, 67 and 69 for a 272 total, eight under par, for a two-stroke win over Sluman, who finished with 68 and a 274 total. Mediate was third at 73–275. But it was anybody's tournament to win down the stretch.

"There were a lot of momentum shifts," Pavin said. Sluman agreed, having come from four strokes behind to take the lead briefly. "What was it, for about 10 seconds?" he said.

Sluman was tied with Pavin until the 17th hole, where Sluman drove behind a tree and scored a bogey. Mediate led by one stroke going into the final round, and by two strokes on occasion. A bogey at the 17th sank him, too. Pavin took the lead for the first time at the par-four No. 9, with a birdie against Mediate's bogey, and clinched the victory with birdies at the 15th and 18th holes.

The final chase narrowly missed being a stampede. Davis Love III made a move, then bogeyed the 15th and 16th. David Duval birdied the first two holes, then self-destructed with an eight at No. 9. As Pavin said, strange things were happening.

Kemper Open—$1,500,000
Winner: Steve Stricker

Steve Stricker joined the PGA Tour in 1994 and stamped himself as a player to watch with a second, two thirds and a fourth place. And now at the Kemper Open in Potomac, Maryland, he had arrived. He stayed close for three rounds, then emerged as the fifth first-time winner of the year by late May.

Stricker had some key help this time. It came from his wife, Nicki, who also happens to be his caddie. Stricker had taken the lead with a birdie at No. 4. Now, at the par-five No. 6 at the TPC at Avenel, she urged him to go for the green with his second shot. He thought about it. The 520-yard hole had a tree on the right side to discourage players from going for the green in two shots.

"It was almost identical to the shot I had Saturday," Stricker said. "But we were a little closer, and the pin was a little closer. I felt if I made a birdie, it would get me going." He went for it. His ball cleared the tree and ended up four feet from the flagstick. He eagled the hole, and took a three-shot lead. Does he always follow Nicki's advice? "I'm more aggressive than he is," she said, "but he's the one hitting the shots."

Stricker made some other crucial shots. At No. 7, he hit a cart path, but had a good enough lie to save par. He took his only bogey at No. 9, and then escaped disaster at the par-three 11th hole when he pulled his tee shot almost into a creek near the green. He saved that par, too, and was on his way to the win. He shot rounds of 69, 68, 65 and 68 for a 270 total, 14 under par, and won by three strokes over Grant Waite, Brad Faxon, Mark O'Meara and Scott Hoch.

Memorial Tournament—$1,800,000

Winner: Tom Watson

The statement was simple: Tom Watson won the Memorial Tournament. But it almost slipped away.

Watson had gone an incredible nine long years and 141 PGA Tour events without a victory, and the Memorial in Dublin, Ohio, was at his fingertips when out of nowhere came David Duval.

While Watson was shooting rounds of 70, 68, 66 and 70 for a 274 total, 14 under par at Muirfield Village, the other challengers had obligingly got out of his way. Steve Lowery, who had missed seven cuts in 15 events, led the first round with 67. He drifted away. In the second round, John Huston was flirting with 59 or 60 until he bogeyed the 17th hole. He shot 61. "That's like playing with the bank's money in Vegas," he said. But he couldn't capitalize on it. Then Watson took the lead in the third round. One stroke wasn't much to some one whose game, especially the putting, had gone dry. But fate had set this stage.

Ernie Els, one behind at the start of the last round, hit a shot into the water at the 11th hole and shot 75. Huston put his tee shot in the water at the par-three 12th, and shot 73. The path was clear.

But then came Duval, looking for his first win. He was five behind to start the round and seven behind when Watson birdied the 13th. Duval caught fire over the last five holes. He went birdie-eagle-birdie-par-birdie for a 67–276 total and the early lead. "If Tom Watson's going to win, and I have to wait another week, another month, that's fine," Duval said.

Meanwhile, Watson bogeyed the 15th hole, missing one of those five-footers, the bane of his game. But he parred the 16th and the 17th on short putts. Then holding a one-stroke lead, he hit his drive over the right corner of the dogleg, and fired a six iron to 15 feet above the hole. Trying to two-putt for his winning par, he holed it for a birdie and a two-stroke win.

"It feels good," Watson said. "It feels so good to win again."

Buick Classic—$1,200,000

Winner: Ernie Els

There should have been a playoff in the Buick Classic in Rye, New York. Four men ended up in a tie — Tom Lehman, Jeff Maggert, Steve Elkington and Craig Parry. A playoff for second place, that is.

Ernie Els was playing by himself. He led wire-to-wire and won by eight strokes. "He made us all look like fools out there," Parry said.

Westchester Country Club's West Course, 6,779 yards and a par of 71, is hardly a weak course. And the field was not weak, not with Greg Norman, Vijay Singh and Nick Faldo in the final tournament before the U.S. Open. But Els simply dominated. His toughest time was in the first round, when he led by only one stroke. He led by five strokes in the second round, and six strokes in the third round. He shot scores of 65, 66, 69 and 71 for a 271 total, 13 under par. Lehman, Maggert, Elkington and Parry were at 279. Maggert took a run at him, shooting 68, 68 and 69, but Maggert's 74 in the first round was too much to overcome. The 66s by Elkington and Parry were the lowest by the four runners-up.

"It's quite surprising," Els said. "I thought the guys would have come after me a little more."

His eight-stroke margin tied the largest in the Buick Classic, set in 1992 by David Frost, and it was the largest on the PGA Tour since Davis Love III in the 1993 Las Vegas Invitational.

Els, ever cautious in his thinking, didn't even think about the tournament being his until early in the final nine. And at the dogleg 15th, he decided to take a shortcut over the trees. Ordinarily, that's a risky shot. "With a seven-shot lead, you can afford to hit a tree," Els said. Then he thought a moment. "Actually," he added, with a hint of a smile, "it was a 10-shot lead at that point."

U.S. Open Championship—$2,000,000
Winner: Steve Jones

See Chapter 4.

FedEx St. Jude Classic—$1,350,000
Winner: John Cook

It's scary to think what might have been but for the ones that got away. John Cook was on a roll like few have seen, and only a handful of near-misses, a spike mark here or there, and one bogey in 72 holes kept him from turning the record book into a shambles at the FedEx St. Jude Classic in Memphis, Tennessee.

Cook had to settle for a seven-stroke victory. It wasn't the season's best — Ernie Els won by eight in the Buick Classic — but it would do. Cook, on rounds of 64, 62, 63 and 69, played the TPC at Southwind in 26-under-par 258 for his first victory since 1992. John Adams finished second.

Cook threatened two of the most venerable PGA Tour records. In the second round, he was within reach of the 59 shot by Al Geiberger in the forerunner of this same tournament, the Danny Thomas Memphis Classic in 1977 (then at Colonial Country Club), and matched by Chip Beck in the 1991 Las Vegas Invitational. Cook ran off six straight birdies and was nine under par with five holes to play. A drive that ended up in a hole cooled him off, and he parred in for the 62. "I ran off the green and wanted to sign my card as quick as I could," Cook said.

Cook also had a shot at the record 257 total posted by Mike Souchak in the 1955 Texas Open. He just missed a birdie at the 12th, and left a 25-footer a tad short at the 15th. And at the 16th, he pitched on to four feet from the rough, then found a high spike mark in his line. But he couldn't complain. "This week has been too good," he said. "So I tried to hit through the spike mark, and it almost went in." At the 17th, a 15-footer came up an inch short. At the 18th, his last chance to tie the 257 died when he drove into the rough. "At that point in time, it didn't matter," he said. "I wanted to get done."

He did set one record. His 189 through 54 holes was two strokes better than Johnny Palmer's 191 in the 1954 Texas Open. Lost in all the excitement was the fact that the 7,000-yard, par-71 Southwind course took a general beating. Of the 72 finishers, only one was over par.

Canon Greater Hartford Open—$1,500,000
Winner: D.A. Weibring

D.A. Weibring had missed nearly three months of the season, first stricken with pneumonia, then by the mysterious Bell's Palsy, a viral illness that paralyzed part of his face. The Canon Greater Hartford Open, late in June, was only his eighth tournament of the year. And he hadn't played a competitive round since the Memorial Tournament a month earlier, where he missed the cut.

Weibring summed it up best at Hartford, Connecticut. "I didn't expect this to happen so soon," he said. "I didn't expect to win. This was really a trial. I just wanted to see how I would do."

He couldn't have done much better. Shooting rounds of 68, 65, 70 and 67, and taking the lead in the third round, Weibring scored a four-stroke victory over Tom Kite on a 10-under-par 270 total at the TPC at River Highlands. That final day was a test, a cold, rainy day. Weibring bogeyed No. 1 and fell behind. Eight pars saw him through the turn with a one-stroke lead, and four birdies coming home did the trick. He closed like a champion. He birdied the par-three 16th, holing a 12-foot putt. He saved par from a fairway bunker at the 17th, firing a brilliant seven iron to the green and two-putting. Then he birdied the 18th from 10 feet.

Meanwhile, if Greg Norman wondered whether anything else could go wrong after his crash at the Masters, he found out at Hartford. He was five strokes off the lead after the second round, and then learned that one of the golf balls he was playing was actually a test ball that had accidentally been included in the group the company sent to him. It was nonconforming under U.S. Golf Association rules, and he was disqualified.

Motorola Western Open—$2,000,000
Winner: Steve Stricker

By the time Steve Stricker had finished dismantling Cog Hill's Dubsdread Course in Lemont, Illinois, and the Motorola Western Open along with it, the other players were saying he was the next star. Maybe it seemed premature. Stricker was only in his third year on the PGA Tour, and he had scored his first victory just six weeks earlier. But when you notch your second so soon, against a tough field and on a good course — and do it by eight strokes — people tend to talk.

"He can be the No. 1 player in the world," said Lee Janzen. Billy Andrade added his endorsement. "People would ask who I thought was the next superstar," he said, "and I said Steve Stricker. He's just got natural ability. He's in a category with Davis Love, Fred Couples — guys who make it look so easy."

Six weeks earlier, Stricker had to fight his way to the Kemper Open title. This time, after trailing Brad Bryant by a stroke in the first round, he turned the tournament into a no-contest in a hurry. Stricker was the first ever to shoot all four rounds in the 60s (65, 69, 67 and 69 for a 270 total) since the tournament moved to Cog Hill in 1991. His eight-stroke margin over Andrade and Jay Don Blake was the biggest in the tournament in 44 years, and tied the biggest margin of the season, by Ernie Els at Westchester.

It wasn't quite as easy as it may have looked, not after the ghost of the Masters visited him. Stricker said he spent a restless night before the final round, despite a five-stroke lead. He couldn't get Greg Norman's collapse in the Masters out of his mind. If he still suffered doubts the next day, it didn't show.

"I don't know what I got into, to tell the truth," Stricker said. "I wouldn't mind if I was the next superstar. A lot of demands on your time then, but I think I can put up with that."

Michelob Championship at Kingsmill—$1,250,000
Winner: Scott Hoch

Scott Hoch, who likes it hot and humid, kept things that way for the wilting souls in the Michelob Championship at Kingsmill in Williamsburg, Virginia. And in case anybody had any lingering hopes of catching him, he doused them with a birdie-birdie-birdie start in the fourth round.

"I wanted to start off pretty quick," said Hoch, a wire-to-wire winner, "and you can't ask for more than that — birdieing the first three holes." He got the first from five feet, the second from 15 feet and the third from one foot. The start was especially tough on the hopeful Tom Purtzer, who started the fourth round tied for third place, five strokes back. "I knew he wasn't going to backtrack," Purtzer said. "I was just hoping to get off to a fast start and improve my position." He did all right, making birdies at the third and fourth holes. But against Hoch's three-birdie start, he lost ground.

Hoch, winning his seventh PGA Tour title, set the tournament record with his 19-under-par 265 total (64, 68, 66 and 67). Purtzer closed with 66 and finished second, his best since winning the 1991 World Series of Golf.

The fast start expanded Hoch's lead to six strokes, and the cushion came in handy. Going through the turn, he bogeyed the 10th hole and Purtzer birdied it. Hoch got back to 18 under par with a birdie at the 11th, then birdied the 15th as well, from 12 feet. "I can't remember making as many putts of 12 to 15 feet as I did here," Hoch said. He had a nice word for the weather, too. "I would rather have it hot," he said, "because it eliminates a lot more people. Especially those California and Phoenix guys who don't like the humidity."

Deposit Guaranty Golf Classic—$1,000,000
Winner: Willie Wood

While Tom Lehman was having the time of his life at the British Open, Willie Wood was having the time of his at the Deposit Guaranty Golf Classic. Lehman was winning his first major title, and in a way, Wood was winning one of his own.

"I've waited 13 years — 13 long years for this," said Wood, who at age 35 had already known more heartbreak than practically anyone on the PGA Tour. His wife, Holly, died of cancer in 1989, leaving him with two sons, then ages three and one. He fought hard, but the effects of the tragedy showed in his game. He made his way back slowly, and he eventually remarried. She's Wendi, and she was at the Annandale Golf Club at Madison, Mississippi, to celebrate with him when he posted that first victory. With rounds of 68, 67, 66 and 67 for a 268 total, 20 under par, he became the sixth first-time winner this year.

There was irony here. Wood was a Nike Tour player. He suddenly changed his schedule and entered the Deposit Guaranty. Back in April, Paul Stankowski, also a Nike player at the time, abruptly changed his schedule and entered the BellSouth Classic, and made it his first victory.

Wood, who trailed through the first three rounds, won this one down the final stretch in a shootout with Greg Kraft, Kirk Triplett, David Edwards and Scott Hoch. Wood holed out his approach for an eagle at the par-four 13th, took a three-stroke lead with a birdie at the 14th, and flipped a wedge to two feet for another birdie at the 17th. He parred the par-five 18th, where Triplett chipped in to cut his margin to a stroke.

"I knew if I kept plugging," Wood said, "my time would come."

CVS Charity Classic—$1,200,000
Winner: John Cook

In the event anyone thought John Cook won the FedEx St. Jude Classic on a fluke, he had a message for them. For a man who had marched to the brink of quitting in March, Cook was doing all right by July.

Cook, who hadn't won since 1992, achieved his second victory of 1996 at the CVS Charity Classic in Sutton, Massachusetts, in the last week of July, just some five weeks after he won in Memphis. This was another wire-to-wire win, but not as impressive. Earlier, he was 26 under par and won by seven strokes. Here, he was merely 16 under par and won by three strokes. If he was in any real danger, it was only briefly, early in the final round, when hard-charging Russ Cochran birdied the first three holes and eagled the fourth to catch him at 15 under par. Then Cook pulled away, not to be troubled again. Even he, bouncing back after bad times, was surprised by a second win.

"I could see somewhere in the distance, maybe, a win," Cook said. "But to win two times in the last three weeks that I've played is maybe a little more than I could see coming."

This was the amazing transformation of Cook after his visit with Ken Venturi, better known as a television commentator, but a good friend and an astute teacher. Venturi worked with Cook, and suddenly things clicked. And clicked again. He played the par-71 Pleasant Valley course in 65, 67, 67 and 69 for a 268 total. Tied for the lead in the first two rounds, he pulled ahead by three with a 67 in the windy third round. He won by three over Cochran, whose five-under start of the final round carried him over Bruce Fleisher, who had dogged Cook all the way. Cook birdied Nos. 4 and 5 to go 17 under par, made his first bogey in 34 holes at the 12th and only his fourth of the tournament at the 14th.

Buick Open—$1,200,000
Winner: Justin Leonard

There was the $216,000 first prize and the two-year exemption, but the silence would be almost as sweet to Justin Leonard.

"I'm not sure what I feel, but I'm sure some of it is relief," Leonard said. "You get tired of answering the question. Everyone wants to know — 'Why haven't you done it yet?' I don't have to hear that anymore."

In a year of both first-time winners and big victory margins, Leonard combined both at the Buick Open in Grand Blanc, Michigan. His rounds of 65, 64, 69 and 68 for a 266 total, 22 under par, gave him a five-stroke win over Chip Beck. It also led a terrific assault on Warwick Hills, an easy course, despite its 7,100 yards. Of the 88 finishers, 82 were under par and three over par was the worst score.

Leonard was the seventh first-time winner of the year. A number of things combined to send Leonard on his way. It helped that he aced the 11th in the first round and holed a bunker shot for a birdie in the third round. Then in the final round, Bob Tway, who trailed him by a stroke at the start, double-bogeyed the first hole after hitting his tee shot out of bounds. Dave Stockton, Jr. and Rick Fehr, tied for third, three behind to start, managed only par 72s. And finally, Leonard himself wasn't just standing around.

He birdied the second and third holes, and after a bogey at No. 5, birdied the next three holes for a 32 on the first nine. "After that," he said, "I really just didn't have a whole lot of pressure." But he didn't become complacent, only cautious. "After the 14th," he said, "I was just going at the center of the greens. I didn't want to do anything stupid."

PGA Championship—$2,400,000
Winner: Mark Brooks

See Chapter 6.

Sprint International—$1,600,000
Winner: Clarence Rose

"To have any chance, I knew I had to eagle 17," Clarence Rose said.

Right. But twice?

A tall order, but that's precisely what the long-troubled Rose did in the Sprint International, the bookkeeper's dream under a modified Stableford scoring system at Castle Pines, near Denver, Colorado. He eagled the par-five 17th in regulation, but Brad Faxon tied him with a two-putt birdie to force a playoff. Then Rose eagled the 17th again in the playoff, becoming the eighth first-time winner of the year, and frustrating Faxon, whose last victory was in this event in 1992.

Rose and Faxon were tied after 72 holes with 31 points each. (In Stableford, scoring is by points, not strokes. A double eagle was worth eight points, an eagle five, a birdie two, and a par none. A bogey cost one point, double bogeys and higher, three.) Two players fell just short of the playoff. Michael

Bradley birdied the last two holes and Bob Tway eagled the 17th to tie for third with 30 points each.

Rose got his first eagle at the 17th in regulation on a 15-foot putt. Faxon met the challenge with a two-putt birdie to tie him. Then at the 17th again, the third playoff hole, Faxon left a long eagle putt just short. Rose was in the fringe in two, 25 feet from the flag. He holed the putt for the eagle and the victory.

And a long-overdue win it was for Rose, 38, a resident of Goldsboro, North Carolina. Back in the late 1980s, Rose's career was just starting to bubble when his infant son developed cancer. Rose all but quit the game. "I wasn't playing well anyway," he said. "That sort of thing puts your priorities in order." Happily, his son recovered, and Rose came back out, but it was tough going, until now. "To win the second time around is really nice," he said. "Sometimes you don't know if you can come back."

NEC World Series of Golf—$2,100,000
Winner: Phil Mickelson

Phil Mickelson finally crossed the Mississippi. Oddly enough, at Akron, Ohio. After eight victories out west in his five years on the PGA Tour, Mickelson finally won east of the Mississippi, taking the rich NEC World Series of Golf on the gruelling Firestone South course.

Mickelson became the first four-time winner on the PGA Tour this year, but it looked "iffy" for a while. His tendency to misfire under pressure cost him an outbreak of poor drives on the last nine, and he squandered a three-stroke lead.

"I was kind of slipping around out there," Mickelson said. "I'm not sure what I was thinking." He saved par out of the rough at the 11th hole, bogeyed the 12th and 13th, then bunkered his approach shot at the 14th. "I had to get up-and-down to end that slide," he said. And he splashed his bunker shot to about 18 inches and got the par. By then, Duffy Waldorf and Billy Mayfair had caught him.

The monster 16th hole, a 625-yarder with a pond in front, proved decisive. Waldorf missed the green, chipped poorly to 15 feet, and two-putted for a bogey. Mayfair, cautiously going for the center on the greens all day, had a birdie try from 20 feet. He two-putted. Mickelson, 88 yards from the green, lobbed a wedge shot over the dangerous pond. The ball hit 20 feet past the flag and spun back down the slope to about two feet. He got the birdie and was back in the lead. "He took a risk," Mayfair marveled. "If he hits it short, it could spin back into the lake. He hit a great shot."

Mickelson locked up the victory at the 17th. Not risking his driver, he teed off with an iron, then hit a six iron 162 yards to six feet, and dropped that birdie, too. He finished with rounds of 70, 66, 68 and 70 for a 274 total, six under par, and won by three strokes over Waldorf (66), Steve Stricker (68) and Mayfair (70).

Greater Vancouver Open—$1,000,000
Winner: Guy Boros

As the saying goes, there's a first time for everything. And so it was for both the Greater Vancouver Open and Guy Boros — first time for the tournament, first win for Boros (the ninth first-timer of the year).

"This is the best feeling I've ever had," said Boros, 31, son of the late Julius Boros. "Yeah, coming up the last hole, I thought of him. Hopefully, he was watching. He'd have been proud of me." Yes, he would have.

At the final hole, Boros, 162 yards out, fired a six-iron shot to eight feet. "It was probably the best shot I've ever hit," he said. Taylor Smith needed a birdie to tie him. But Smith put his approach 30 feet from the pin, and tied instead with Lee Janzen and Emlyn Aubrey for second place, one shot behind. Boros two-putted for his par, completing a card of 71, 65, 65 and 71 for a 12-under-par 272 total.

Along with the $180,000 first prize and the two-year exemption, Boros seemed to have gained his own identity. Earlier, he seemed irked at mentions of his dad, and spoke of "playing in my father's shadow." Boros had caddied for his dad, then labored for four years on the Canadian Tour and two years in Australia.

This was his second victory as a professional. His first came when he was on the Canadian Tour, in the 1991 B.C. Open in Vancouver. "I might start looking for property up here," Boros cracked.

Greater Milwaukee Open—$1,200,000
Winner: Loren Roberts

It's said no one remembers who finished second. In this case, no one would even remember who finished first. This was strictly the Tiger Woods Show.

Woods finally answered the question that had been asked for two years. He had wrapped up an unprecedented third consecutive United States Amateur Championship on Sunday, August 25, in Portland, Oregon, then headed for the Greater Milwaukee Open with the sponsor's exemption he had been given months earlier. But when he stepped out in front of the media corps, it wasn't as the Amateur champion. It was as a professional golfer.

For the record, in the first two rounds Woods was paired with Jeff Hart and John Elliott. His first shot as a professional, his drive on No. 1, came in the 2:36 p.m. grouping on Thursday, August 29, and it traveled 326 yards. He birdied No. 3 with a 15-foot putt, birdied the par-five No. 4 — three iron, six iron, two putts from 35 feet, and eagled No. 6 with a putt from 12 feet. He showed his power at the 557-yard 18th, reaching the green with a driver and a four iron. He two-putted for a birdie. All told, he had an eagle, three birdies and one bogey in a four-under-par 67 at the 6,716-yard Brown Deer Park, a public golf course.

"I expected it to be crazy, but I didn't expect it to be as draining as it was," Woods said.

The 67 left him five strokes behind the leader, Nolan Henke, who shot 62. Woods was drawing the huge bulk of the galleries. So much so, in fact, that when Henke shot 66 in the second round, and kept his two-stroke lead, he was just about alone. "It makes it easier for me," Henke said. "Everybody's out there following Tiger. I like to hide a little."

The winner, by the way, was Loren Roberts, with a birdie on the first playoff hole to beat homestate favorite Jerry Kelly. The quiet, likeable Roberts, known as "The Boss of the Moss" for his skill on the greens, went into the final round three strokes behind Jesper Parnevik, the third-round leader, and fell four behind midway through the final round. Then he birdied four of the last six holes (completing rounds of 66, 65, 66 and 68) and was tied by Kelly (67, 66, 68 and 64) at 19-under-par 265. Parnevik missed the tie when he bogeyed the par-five 18th. Roberts then birdied from six feet to beat Kelly in the playoff, and chalk up his fourth PGA Tour victory.

"I take pride in the fact that I can make some putts when I have to make them," Roberts said. And he said that's what he admired about Woods. Woods got a lesson in pro golf in the second round. "It's weird," he said, "to be eight behind after a 69." His debut card: 67, 69, 73 and 68 for a 277 total, seven under par, 12 off the lead and tied for 60th place out of 76 finishers. His first paycheck was $2,544.

Bell Canadian Open—$1,500,000
Winner: Dudley Hart

Dudley Hart and Hurricane Fran arrived at the Bell Canadian Open together, in a manner of speaking. The remnants of Fran swept in with a windy Friday and heavy rains that washed out Saturday's play, leaving the tournament to be decided over 54 holes. Hart, a stormy guy himself, kept his cool and became the 10th first-time PGA Tour winner of the year. It looked for a while as though Scott Dunlap, 33, who had made nine trips to the PGA Tour qualifying tournament, was going to be this week's first-time winner. A 64-68 start gave him leads of two and three strokes. But he blew to 76 in the third and final round, and Hart, after starting with 68 and 64, closed with 70 for a 14-under-par 202 total and a one-stroke win over David Duval, who again came oh-so-close.

In his second tournament, Tiger Woods again attracted most of the attention and placed 11th with rounds of 70, 70 and 68 for a 208 total.

The victory was extra sweet for Hart. For one thing, he had kept his temper under control. "I'm really proud of myself for not getting bent out of shape when I didn't hit it to eight feet on every hole," he said. But maybe more importantly, he had overcome an injured right wrist that he once thought might end his career. Surgery kept him off the Tour until June. The cool, damp weather was no friend. He had to hit some 30 extra pitch shots to warm up before the final round.

He started the round three strokes behind Dunlap, and was still two behind after seven straight pars. They tied on a two-shot swing at the 433-yard No. 8. Hitting into a brisk wind, Hart put a two iron within two feet for a birdie, and Dunlap hit a three wood over the green and bogeyed. When Dunlap bogeyed the 13th, Hart was the leader alone, and in effect won the tournament with a two-putt birdie from 60 feet at the par-five 16th. That was the stroke that held up under Duval's closing 69.

Said a disappointed Dunlap: "I played an iffy round of golf, brought on by not being ready to win a tournament." Said a not-disappointed Duval: "What's wrong with shooting 69, 65, 69? It's hard for me to be disappointed when I performed well."

Quad City Classic—$1,000,000
Winner: Ed Fiori

It was Tiger Woods' tournament again, but it was Ed Fiori's victory, and Fiori, age 43, will take the victory any time. Especially since his last one was the 1982 Bob Hope Desert Classic, which was a host of problems ago, including a foot injury in 1994, shoulder surgery in 1995, and back surgery this year.

"I never thought I would be in this position again after 14 years," Fiori said. "My mind is numb. It hasn't really sunk in." But his tournament-tough mind wasn't numb at Oakwood Country Club in Coal Valley, Illinois. The first thing the short, chunky Fiori did was refuse to be awed by Woods' power. Fiori was forever 80 yards behind. And he didn't let the swarming crowds bother him. "Fighting all those crowds will wear you out," Fiori said. "I had to play my game. I never watched him hit a shot. But playing with Tiger raised my intensity and brought my game up a bit."

It was Woods' tournament to win. He took the lead in the second round and led through the third, by one stroke over Fiori. Then he went three strokes ahead in the final round, with a birdie at No. 3 after Fiori's bogey at No. 1. Then came the crash. At No. 4, Woods, trying to cut his tee shot, hooked it instead and found the pond. He took a penalty drop, then tried to thread the needle through some trees. The ball caromed into the water. He ended up with a quadruple-bogey eight. His lead was gone. Fiori was up by one stroke.

"There were a lot of birdie holes left," Woods said. Among them the par-four No. 7, a mere — to him — 344 yards. He had only a little flop shot left to the green, then four-putted for six. Fiori plugged away, still 80 yards behind, but he fired his approach to three feet and birdied. He was up by three. Woods couldn't catch him. Fiori shot 66-68-67-67–268, 12 under par, and won by two over Andrew Magee. Woods tied for fifth.

"It's kind of hard to tell you exactly what I'm going to learn from it," Woods said, "but I will tell you one thing — I am going to learn a lot."

Fiori saw no reason for concern. He even had a prediction: "He'll do it — he'll do it real quickly."

Presidents Cup
Winner: United States

Davis Love III had done his bit in the singles on the last day of the Presidents Cup, beating Jumbo Ozaki, and then he went out on the course to root his teammates home. It turned into a long, hard day. Then he was speaking for everyone.

"I have a huge headache," Love said. "It's nerves and tension, and I got it watching the matches. Watching Freddie on that putt at 17 — I thought my head was going to explode." His wasn't the only one. What had started as another American runaway in this second Presidents Cup match had turned into a cliffhanger in the singles that final day. In fact, it came down to the last match, with Fred Couples, leading Vijay Singh by 1-up, facing a decisive 30-foot birdie putt on the 17th green.

"I never really thought it would come down to that last match," Couples said. "The one thing I didn't want to have was for the match to go to 18 and him winning two straight holes." Couples holed that 30-footer, and when Singh missed his birdie from 15 feet, the United States had a 16½-15½ victory over the International team.

The Presidents Cup was created to provide a Ryder Cup-style competition for golfers from the rest of the world, outside Europe, against the Americans. The inaugural in 1994 was a 20-12 American victory. The event was held in mid-September at the Robert Trent Jones Golf Club in Gainsville, Virginia.

The Americans took a 7½-2½ lead the first day. Love cautioned against optimism. "All of us know that this thing is far from being over," he said. The Internationals made a prophet out of Love the second day. First, they won three of the five four-ball matches in the morning. Then, gaining momentum, they took four of the five afternoon foursomes, three of them almost one-sided, led by the Nick Price and Mark McNulty 3-and-1 win over Kenny Perry and Justin Leonard. The Internationals had cut the American lead to one, at 10½-9½.

Then came the singles on Sunday. There was some heavy hitting on both sides. Craig Parry walloped Mark Brooks 5 and 4, and David Frost demolished Kenny Perry, 7 and 6, for two big International points. The Americans countered — Steve Stricker thumped Robert Allenby, 6 and 5, and Love whipped Ozaki, 5 and 4. Soon Love was watching Couples bring home that winning point against Singh.

B.C. Open—$1,000,000
Winner: Fred Funk

The folksy B.C. Open, at Endicott, New York, took its place as the fourth stop on the Tiger Woods Tour. Would he score his first victory here? The answer was no. But he did guarantee that he could play in any PGA Tour event in 1997. He tied for third place and won $58,400 for a four-tournament total of $140,194, which put him 128th on the 1996 money list. More to the point, it guaranteed him a spot in the top 150 for 1997, and anyone in the top 150 can receive an unlimited number of sponsor's exemptions.

But it was Fred Funk's week. He started the final round from a tie for second place with Woods and Brian Claar, three strokes behind little-known Pete Jordan, who was having himself a time. Jordan, who made the cut in only nine of 24 events, birdied five straight holes en route to 64 in the second round. He cooled to 66 in the third round and was tied by Funk, who shot 63.

Then Funk was turning the tournament into a rout in the final round. He had birdied four of the first six holes and was 20 under par, four ahead of Jordan and six ahead of Woods, when rain washed out the round. Scores reverted to the third round, which found Funk (68, 66 and 63) and Jordan (67, 64 and 66) tied at 16-under-par 197. "It's disappointing," Funk said. "I got off to such a good start, and I was on cruise control. I wanted to keep going."

He did keep going, but in the playoff. On the first extra hole, the par-four 18th, he hit a 148-yard seven-iron shot to within 10 inches of the flag. "I wasn't nervous over that putt," he said. He tapped in for the fourth victory of his career and his fourth top-10 finish in his last six starts.

Buick Challenge—$1,000,000
Winner: Michael Bradley

Michael Bradley, age 30 and a fourth-year man, joined the PGA Tour's parade of first-time winners — he was No. 11 — in the Buick Challenge late in September. Like others before him the previous few weeks, he was overshadowed by Tiger Woods, but for a different reason this time. Woods withdrew, saying he was exhausted, before the tournament started.

Bradley's breakthrough may carry an asterisk. Torrents of rain forced officials to reduce the tournament to 36 holes. When Sunday's play was washed out, scores reverted to the second round, leaving a five-way tie for the lead at 10-under-par 134. Workers had to pump and mop the par-four 18th hole for the playoff, and the tee was moved up 35 yards for a better landing area.

Bradley missed the fairway but his hooked tee shot ended up in a good lie in the left rough. From there, he hit a wedge to 12 feet. Davis Love III missed the green, and Len Mattiace, John Maginnes and defending champion Fred Funk all missed their birdie putts. Then Bradley, runner-up at the Doral-Ryder Open in February, faced the putt of his career. "I was nervous — my hands were shaking," Bradley said. "And somehow it went in. I don't know how it did."

Las Vegas Invitational—$1,650,000
Winner: Tiger Woods

Everyone knew it would happen sooner or later, and probably sooner. But this soon? This was the first week of October, and Tiger Woods, just six weeks after turning pro and making only his fifth start, won his first tournament, the Las Vegas Invitational. He shot 27-under-par 332 to tie Davis Love III, then beat him with a par on the first playoff hole.

"It's been an unbelievable experience," Woods said. "It's just like winning the Amateur, though. I really can't say what it means until I think about it more." He won the Amateur three consecutive times, but this wasn't the same. Woods could think about this difference: $297,000, a two-year exemption on the PGA Tour, and a berth in the 1997 Masters. The first prize brought his five weeks' earnings to $437,194.

Woods shot a final-round 64 at the TPC of Summerlin, one of three courses used, playing the par-fives in five under par with impressive power. At the 563-yard ninth, for example, where his playing companion Keith Fergus hit his driver twice and was short of the green, Woods hit a three wood, then a six iron to within 15 feet. He wrapped up a card of 70, 63, 68, 67 and 64, leapfrogging over six players, including Love, who had double-bogeyed No. 10. Love caught him with a late charge for 67. Love drove the green at the par-four 15th, and dropped a 25-footer for an eagle, then birdied the 16th to tie Woods. Then he cooled off. He missed a 12-foot putt at the 17th and two-putted the 18th from 35 feet for a par and the tie.

They went to the 18th for the playoff. Woods had used a two iron off the tee there in regulation, but this time switched to a three wood. Both players drove into the fairway. Woods was just slightly behind, and hitting first, he put a nine-iron approach about 20 feet from the flag. Love, no stranger to match play, went for the pin, cut to the back left. He came over his eight iron slightly and pulled it into the back-left bunker. He came out to six feet. He missed his par, and Woods two-putted for his par and the victory.

"It was just like the Amateur," Woods said. "I didn't play match play that long ago. Now it's match play and you've got to try to make a three. I was fortunate I could hit first and put some pressure on him. He would know I was in position for a birdie, and I did that."

"As disappointed as I am, I'm that much happy for him," Love said. "He's a great, great player, and he's great for the Tour."

LaCantera Texas Open—$1,200,000
Winner: David Ogrin

David Ogrin, at age 38, scored his first victory after 14 years on the PGA Tour, and it came the hard way, or at least the breathtaking way. "I wouldn't think that the mess I threw out there today would win a golf tournament," said Ogrin, the PGA Tour's 13th first-time winner of the year. But, as he observed, it was enough for the low score of the week, a 13-under-par 275 on rounds of 70, 65, 68 and 72 at a course he had played often, LaCantera, not far from his San Antonio-area home. And it also was enough for a one-stroke win over Jay Haas.

Tiger Woods, fresh from winning the Las Vegas Invitational the week before, closed with 67 to finish third. Once again, he drew the galleries and the cheers.

The mess, as Ogrin called it, was some erratic play in the final round, and it very nearly cost him the tournament. The big damage was a triple bogey at the par-three No. 6, where his tee shot ended up in a little creek to the left of the green. He finally reached the green and three-putted for six. "My most interesting hole of the year," Ogrin said. "Lost my three-shot lead in one fell swoop." The crash tied him with Haas, who had birdied No. 5. But Ogrin birdied the next four holes and was on his way.

John Huston, who eagled twice on the first nine, and Mike Heinen shared the first-round lead on 66s, then fell back. Ogrin took the lead with his second-round 65 highlighted by bursts of birdies on both nines, but he bogeyed the 18th after hooking his drive under some trees. "I was going for the kill," he cracked. "I had illusions of grandeur for a second." He expanded his lead to three strokes in the third round, with some strong play. He birdied the fifth, 10th and 12th holes, and after a bogey at the 13th, he birdied the 14th on two putts from 50 feet, then holed a seven-footer for another birdie at the 18th. In the fourth round, he shook off that triple bogey, and finally victory was no illusion.

Walt Disney World/Oldsmobile Classic—$1,200,000
Winner: Tiger Woods

A little luck can't hurt — especially if it's someone else's bad luck, Tiger Woods learned. At the Walt Disney World/Oldsmobile Classic, the bad luck belonged to Taylor Smith, a winless rookie on the PGA Tour who uses a semi-long putter with a split grip. Midway through the final round, Lennie Clements, his playing companion, reported to PGA Tour officials that the lower of the two grips had a flat side. This made the putter non-conforming under U.S. Golf Association rules. Smith was disqualified. He finished the round pending an appeal, and in fact birdied the last hole to tie Woods.

But there was no need for a playoff. Officials took one look at the putter and Taylor was disqualified again. So Wood, who had started the last round one stroke behind a four-way tie for the lead — which included Smith and Clements — had a one-stroke margin over Payne Stewart for the second victory of his young career.

But the win didn't sit completely well with Woods. "Very gratifying, very satisfying," he said, "but I also have mixed emotions about it. I feel there should have been a playoff with Taylor. He birdied 18 to get into it." Smith had closed with style. At the 18th, with his appeal still pending, he dropped an eight-foot birdie putt with that controversial putter.

Woods, battling the miseries of a cold, played outstanding golf, shooting 69, 63, 69 and 66 for a 21-under-par 267 total over three courses. He also was the beneficiary of the spell of bad luck — or balky putting — that befell Stewart. On the final nine, Stewart had eight birdie chances from 15 feet or so, and made only one. He missed a four-footer at No. 15. He had one last chance at the 18th. Woods had just a tap-in left for his par. Stewart had an eight-footer left for a birdie and a tie, but he missed.

Woods made his move in the final round. He eagled No. 4, then birdied No. 5 to tie Nolan Henke, the leader in the clubhouse. He took the lead with a birdie at No. 7, and when it was over, he was the first player since Curtis Strange in 1982 to finish in the top five at five consecutive tournaments. His numbers also were impressive: He scored in the 60s in 18 of his previous 21 rounds, and 11 of the last 12.

Tour Championship—$3,000,000
Winner: Tom Lehman

As the 1996 PGA Tour season came to a finish with the Tour Championship the last week of October, Tom Lehman wrote "The End" with a bang.

In a showdown of the top 30 money winners at the tough, par-70 Southern Hills in Tulsa, Oklahoma, Lehman made it a wire-to-wire victory. He shared a one-stroke lead with Vijay Singh in the first round, led Singh by four strokes through the second round, led Singh and Brad Faxon by nine through the third, and won by six over Faxon on a card of 66, 67, 64 and 71 for a

268 total, 12 under par.

"That's some kind of golf," Faxon said. In fact, it was some kind of golf all season for Lehman, who had struggled for so long before blossoming. He won the British Open in July, then the Tour Championship, was runner-up in the U.S. Open, and had 10 other top-10 finishes in 22 PGA Tour starts. He was out of the top 20 finishers only three times. With this victory and the $540,000 prize, he finished on top of the money list with a record $1.78 million, won the Vardon Trophy with a 69.30 stroke average, and the PGA of America's Player of the Year Award, leaping over Phil Mickelson (who had four wins) and PGA Champion Mark Brooks (three).

Mickelson's chance to salvage at least the money title disappeared with a watery triple bogey at the par-five 13th in the final round. He was second in money with $1.71 million.

Lehman had gone in trying to forget what all was at stake. "That's kind of choke time when you think about stuff like that," he said. "So you push that out of your mind." He proved his point in the second round, pulling away against Oklahoma winds that gusted to 30 miles an hour. He went out in one over, then ran off four straight birdies starting back, and came home in 31 for the 67. No one would come close after that.

The tournament was marked by three incidents. Tiger Woods' dad, Earl, 64, was hospitalized early the day of the second round (he would be all right). Woods, distracted, shot a 78. He tied for 21st place. The other two were Greg Norman's. He arrived late and passed up the Pro-Am on Tuesday, and when a downpour Sunday forced the final round over into Monday, he withdrew. He wasn't in the running at any time.

Special Events

Treasure Coast Classic—$200,000
Winners: Bruce Devlin and Larry Ziegler

Bruce Devlin and Larry Ziegler combined for a best-ball, 12-under-par 60 to win by one stroke over Harold Henning and Tony Jacklin with a 124 total, 20 under par, in the Treasure Coast Classic in late January at Grand Harbor Golf & Beach Club in Vero Beach, Florida. The winners took $35,000 each from the $200,000 purse. A first-round 64 left Devlin and Ziegler five strokes behind the team of Jay Sigel and Buddy Allen, who went from 59 to 69 in the 36-hole event.

Family House Invitational—$850,000
Winner: Scott Hoch

Scott Hoch said that he had been doing everything badly. But once he got to the two-day Family House Invitational, he was doing everything right. Against 30 fellow PGA Tour pros at Laurel Valley Golf Club in Ligonier, Pennsylvania, site of the 1965 PGA Championship and the 1989 U.S. Senior Open, Hoch had a picnic. He rang up four straight birdies one time, then three birdies and an eagle the next. He breezed to the $170,000 first prize by eight strokes with rounds of 64 and 64 for a 128 total.

"I don't know how I did it," Hoch said. Runner-up Steve Stricker was hoping to get to 10 under par. "And then when I got to No. 12, I saw I was seven shots back," he said. Added 1996 champion Ernie Els: "It's a pretty helpless feeling."

Ernst Championship—$660,000
Winner: Phil Mickelson

Fred Couples was the host, but not exactly a gracious one, at the third annual Ernst Championship at Inglewood Country Club, near Seattle, Washington. Phil Mickelson, after trailing Couples by four strokes with a first-round 68, charged to 65 in the second and final round and tied Couples at 133. Couples fired back with a birdie on the first playoff hole, the par-five 18th, putting the pressure on Mickelson. To which Mickelson responded with an eagle to take the $130,000 first prize from the $660,000 purse. Scott Simpson and Brad Faxon each closed with 65s and tied for third place at 134 in the 29-man field.

Jerry Ford Invitational—$300,000
Winner: Dillard Pruitt

Dillard Pruitt, a Harley-Davidson fan, cranked up his game and raced through the second round to win the Jerry Ford Invitational in Vail, Colorado. This was after the first round belonged to Bob Lohr and Jim Thorpe, both shooting 63s to share a two-stroke lead. Both shot 72s in the second round, and Pruitt, after opening with 68, zipped to the 64 for a 132 total and a one-stroke win over Keith Fergus and Jay Don Blake. The tournament was played at the Vail Golf Club and the Country Club of the Rockies.

Fred Meyer Challenge—$700,000
Winners: Greg Norman and Brad Faxon

Billy Mayfair and Mark Calcavecchia had the last chance to head off Brad Faxon and Greg Norman. They needed a birdie to win or a par to tie at the final hole. But Mayfair missed the green and Calcavecchia missed a three-foot putt, and so Norman and Faxon won their second consecutive Fred Meyer Challenge, the 12-team, better-ball charity event hosted by Peter Jacobsen at the Oregon Golf Club at West Linn, Oregon. Norman and Faxon split the $100,000 first prize from the $700,000 purse with a tournament-record 63-61–124 total.

"I feel for Calc — we all do," Norman said. "He had the same pressure on that putt that he would have had in a major." Calcavecchia wouldn't go that far. "I wasn't shaking or anything," he said. "I just missed it. I've been having a hard time with my putting this year, and that was a prime example."

Sarazen World Open Championship—$1,900,000
Winner: Frank Nobilo

They were getting to be old pals. Once again, Frank Nobilo, the personable New Zealander, was being congratulated by Gene Sarazen. Nobilo had just won the Sarazen World Open Championship for the second year in a row. "Unbelieveable," Nobilo said. "This is the first time I've ever defended a title." Nobilo's joy was Scott Hoch's frustration. Hoch, after a course-record 64 in the second round at the Legends course in Braselton, Georgia, led Nobilo by four strokes going into the final round, then shot 74. Nobilo closed in with three near tap-in birdies on the first nine. He birdied the 10th hole from 10 feet, then drew even when Hoch bogeyed the par-three 12th after a poor bunker shot.

Nobilo birdied the 13th from eight feet to take the lead, went up by two with a birdie at the 14th, then by the final four when Hoch double-bogeyed the 17th. "I just played great today," said Nobilo, who finished with a bogey-free 66 for 272 total, 16 under par. Said Hoch, "I'm glad it doesn't go another day. There's no telling what I would shoot."

Lincoln-Mercury Kapalua International—$1,200,000
Winner: Paul Stankowski

Paul Stankowski, who went directly from winning the Nike Tour's Louisiana Open to taking the PGA Tour's BellSouth Classic back-to-back early in the season, threw another surprise party at the Lincoln-Mercury Kapalua International in Maui, Hawaii, but only after standing off a strong field. For one, U.S. Open champion Steve Jones bogeyed No. 10, bounced back with birdies at the 13th and 17th, and needed an eagle at the 18th. But his 60-foot putt was short. He tied for third with Davis Love III at 271.

The final pressure came from Fred Couples. He tied Stankowski with an eagle at the par-five 15th at the Plantation course. But Stankowski, playing just behind him, moved back in front for good with a birdie at the hole. The 18th became decisive. Couples needed an eagle to tie, but his 20-foot putt just missed. He birdied for 67 and a 270 total. Stankowski then needed a three-footer for a birdie and the win. He calmly rolled it in for 68 and a 269 total for a one-stroke victory. "I'm tired," Stankowski said, "but this is exciting. It's all kind of a blur."

MasterCard PGA Grand Slam—$1,000,000
Winner: Tom Lehman

"I'm not sure I've surpassed my goals, but I've achieved my goals for the year," Tom Lehman said. The record speaks for itself. Lehman won the British Open in July, the Tour Championship late in October, and now — still in mid-season form as the year was coming to a close — the MasterCard PGA Grand Slam in mid-November. This 36-hole shootout for the winners of the four major championships at Poipu Bay, Hawaii, turned into an awkward outing. Because of heavy rains, they played 27 holes on Wednesday and nine holes on Thursday. It didn't matter to Lehman. "Golf's golf," he said.

And no matter how you logged in his score, 100-34 or 68-66, it added up to a 10-under-par 134 total, a Grand Slam record by two strokes. Lehman beat U.S. Open champion Steve Jones by two (70-66-136) and Masters champion Nick Faldo by five (67-72–139). PGA champion Mark Brooks (74-73–147) was never in the hunt. In the first round, Faldo scored his sixth birdie at the 12th and led by four, then bogeyed the 13th and 16th. Lehman birdied the 13th and 14th, leaving Faldo with a one-stroke lead after the first round.

Lehman took a one-stroke lead over Jones and Faldo through 27 holes, then started the final nine holes the next day with a birdie at No. 10 to go up by two. He came home unchallenged. "I feel," Lehman said, "that I'm not real far away from having a super year." If this wasn't a super year, it would do until he came up with one.

Franklin Templeton Shark Shootout—$1,100,000
Winners: Jay Haas and Tom Kite

Hale Irwin summed up the Franklin Templeton Shark Shootout quite nicely: "Nine straight birdies on the back nine — that'll win most of 'em." He didn't mean himself and teammate Lee Janzen. They tied for second with Craig Stadler and Lanny Wadkins. He meant Jay Haas and Tom Kite, who combined in the scramble format for the nine birdies, a final-round 60, a three-round 187 total, and a two-stroke victory at Sherwood Country Club in Thousand Oaks, California. The victory was a huge relief. "Neither of us has been there for a long time," Kite said. "Granted, this isn't an official event, but a win is a win."

Kite was the big gun in the second-round better-ball, with seven birdies and an eagle to Haas' three birdies for 60. That got them to within one stroke going into the final round. Haas triggered the birdie binge with an eight-footer at the 10th. Kite holed from 25 and 30 feet at the next two. But the key was the escape from under a tree at the dogleg 14th. "We needed a shot out, under, up, over, around, and hooking," Haas said. And he did it, planting a 173-yard seven-iron shot five feet from the cup. Kite had no trouble finishing it off.

Mexican Open—$250,000
Winner: Stewart Cink

This may have been the Mexican Open at Club de Golf in Mexico City late in November, but it looked like the Nike Tour South. Stewart Cink, who dominated the Nike Tour that ended a month earlier, picked up right where he left off. He broke out of a one-stroke deficit in the first round and streaked to a two-stroke victory with rounds of 67, 69, 68 and 68 for a 16-under-par 272 total. Bob Tway finished second at 274. A distant five strokes off the lead, Kawika Cotner and Lee Rinker tied for third at 277. The $50,000 first prize was a nice addition to the record $251,699 and three victories Cink won on the Nike Tour.

Merrill Lynch Pebble Beach Invitational Pro-Am—$250,000
Winner: Kirk Triplett

"Man, I'm relieved," Kirk Triplett was saying after surviving the curse of the big lead. "It's tough — you start that far ahead and everybody expects you to win." Which was no less than he expected of himself in the Merrill Lynch Pebble Beach Invitational Pro-Am, but for a guy who hadn't won in seven years on the PGA Tour, a six-stroke lead going into the last round may not sit easily.

The mid-November tournament was played at Spyglass Hill, Del Monte and Pebble Beach, the last where he started with that huge lead. Then he lost all six strokes and had to sweat to win by three over David Ogrin. The big damage was a double bogey at the par-four 13th. A bogey at the par-five 14th dropped him into a tie with Ogrin. Then Triplett pulled it out. At the par-three 17th, he fired a five iron to 15 feet and made the birdie to lead by one, and he hung on. No, he said, he wasn't trying to protect that lead. "I played hard," he said. "David just out-played me for a while."

JCPenney Classic—$1,500,000
Winners: Mike Hulbert and Donna Andrews

In the JCPenney Classic early in December, all eyes were on the power pairings of John Daly and Laura Davies, and two young sensations, Tiger Woods and Kelli Kuehne, making her pro debut. But it was "average" Mike Hulbert and Donna Andrews who won. The tournament, which pairs PGA Tour and LPGA Tour players in modified alternate-shot play, was reduced to three rounds because of rain.

Hulbert and Andrews did not reach a par-five hole in two, yet they combined for a 16-under-par 197 and a one-stroke victory over Woods and Kuehne, and Joel Edwards and Missie McGeorge. "The favorites coming in here were the long-ball hitters," Andrews said. "We're just average. We hit it down the middle, then knock it on the green."

In the final round, Hulbert and Andrews birdied three of their first six holes and led by three strokes through the 12th. Woods and Kuehne tripped at the 14th, three-putting from five feet for a bogey. Hulbert and Andrews locked it up at the 18th. Andrews drove perfectly, and Hulbert, from 112 yards, lobbed the approach shot to 15 feet. Andrews' first putt left Hulbert a tap-in for the win. Thus the supporting cast walked off with the prize.

Office Depot Father-Son Challenge—$800,000
Winners: Raymond Floyd and Raymond Floyd, Jr.

Raymond Floyd and son, Raymond Jr., won their second straight Office Depot Father-Son Challenge early in December at the par-72 Windsor Club in Vero Beach, Florida. The Floyds won the 1995 tournament by six strokes. This time, it was only by two strokes. They combined for a better-ball 61 and a two-stroke lead over Larry and Drew Nelson in the first round. The Floyds shot 63 in the second-round scramble for a 20-under 124 total, and while the Nelsons slipped, Dave and Ron Stockton shot 61 to close the gap, but still fell two strokes short at 126.

Diners Club Matches—$2,100,000
Winners: Tom Lehman and Duffy Waldorf
Jim Colbert and Bob Murphy
Dottie Pepper and Juli Inkster

Tom Lehman sank the winning putt on the 17th hole, but he gave all the credit to Duffy Waldorf for their second consecutive title in the PGA Tour competition in the Diners Club Matches. "Duffy played great all week," Lehman said. "We wouldn't have been in the final without his play." After struggling with his putter earlier, Lehman came to life in the final round and made seven birdies over 17 holes. The last was on a nine-foot putt that closed out Kenny Perry and Scott Hoch, 2 and 1, at the Nicklaus Resort course at PGA West.

In the PGA Senior Tour event, Bob Murphy and Jim Colbert won their second consecutive title with a 3-and-1 victory over Vicente Fernandez and

Jay Sigel. They took command with four straight birdies down the final stretch, with Murphy squaring the match on a 10-footer at the 12th, and Colbert following with putts of 22, 20 and 25 feet. In the LPGA division, Juli Inkster and Dottie Pepper birdied two of the last three holes to end the two-year reign of Kelly Robbins and Tammie Green. They took the lead on Inkster's 18-foot putt at the 16th, and won by 1 up on Pepper's eight-footer at the 18th.

Lexus Challenge—$1,000,000
Winners: Hale Irwin and Sean Connery

Hale Irwin and his celebrity partner, Sean Connery, combined for 22 birdies against a single bogey over two rounds to win the Lexus Challenge in La Quinta, California, by four strokes with a 123 total. Irwin and Connery had scores of 61 and 62, as Irwin produced nine birdies and Connery, 13, including his handicap strokes. Three teams tied for second place: Lee Trevino and Kevin Costner, John Brodie and Ken Griffey, Jr., and Chi Chi Rodriguez and Robert Wuhl.

Raymond Floyd, the tournament host and defending champion with Michael Chiklis, tied for fifth place at 130 with Gary Player and Glenn Fry.

Andersen Consulting World Championship—$3,650,000
Winner: Greg Norman

It took five days into the New Year, but Greg Norman won over $2 million for the fourth successive year with his victory in the Andersen Consulting World Championship. The semi-finals and final were not held until the first week of January, 1997, when Norman defeated Hisayuki Sasaki and Scott Hoch to secure the $1 million prize to raise his 1996 earnings to $2,258,678 with his fifth victory of the year.

Norman holed a 15-foot birdie putt on the 36th hole for a 1-up victory over Hoch in the final at the Talon course of the Grayhawk Golf Club in Scottsdale, Arizona. Norman was 3 up after the first 18 holes, then bogeyed the first three holes of the afternoon round and it was nip-and-tuck until the finish. Hoch received $500,000 for second place and also crossed the $2 million mark with $2,155,893.

In the semi-finals, Norman defeated Sasaki, 5 and 4, and Hoch beat Sam Torrance, 4 and 2. Sasaki won the third-place match, 2 and 1, earning $350,000 to Torrance's $300,000.

There were 32 qualifiers, the top seven available players on the Sony Ranking and one invitee from each of four regions. Norman came through to the semi-finals from the International section along with Hoch (United States), Sasaki (Japan) and Torrance (Europe). The preliminary matches were held between March and July in the United States, England and Japan.

Nike Tour

As golf circuits go, the 1996 Nike Tour was looking like one grand case of parity. It was one-for-me, one-for-you, a different winner week after week. This was either very good or not so good, depending on one's point of view. Did this mean the talent was so strong and so evenly distributed that no one player could take command? Or that no one was good enough to take command?

The record for a string of different weekly winners was 20, rung up in 1994. Rocky Walcher broke it when he won the Omaha Classic early in August, and Rick Cramer made it 22 at the Wichita Open the next week. And that's where it stopped when Michael Christie took the Permian Basin Open, his second win of the year. And the very next week, the first week of September, Stewart Cink won his second, the Colorado Classic. These two would end up as the principal players of 1996, each winning three times. For the other 25 winners, one victory each was the limit.

At the end, it was Cink who would answer the question whether anyone was good enough to stamp the tour as his own. The big (6-foot-4), rangy guy from Atlanta, Georgia, became the first player in Nike Tour history to top $200,000 in winnings in a single season. He earned $251,699, more than $60,000 over the previous record and $57,000 more than Christie.

Cink won the Ozarks Open in a playoff in mid-June, the Colorado Classic by one stroke in September, and the season-ending Nike Tour Championship by four in mid-October. Christie, who won $193,971, actually reached three victories before Cink, with the Greater Greenville Classic in mid-May by six strokes, the Permian Basin by two in late August, and the Utah Classic by four the second week of September.

The victories meant more than just money. They opened an important door. It was graduation day. The top 10 Nike money winners qualified for the PGA Tour. With Cink and Christie were Joe Durant, David Berganio, Jr., Brett Quigley, Dave Rummells, P.J. Horgan III, Lee Porter, Skip Kendall and Eric Johnson. That was the good news. The bad news befell Brent Geiberger. He was 11th by a pittance. "It's a shame you go all year and miss by $112," Geiberger said. "It's hard to believe it can come down to one shot, but that's the way it goes."

Berganio began his bid spectacularly. He overcame a six-stroke deficit going into the final round and won the Monterrey Open by one stroke. Christie made up four strokes in the final round to win the Greater Greenville Classic.

Paul Stankowski also wrote a spectacular chapter. Stankowski took the Nike Louisiana Open by four strokes, and thus encouraged, changed his plans and headed the next week for the PGA Tour's BellSouth Classic. He won that, too, regaining the Tour card he had lost the year before and taking the final berth in the Masters.

P.J. Horgan was having one of the hottest springs on record. It went this way in a four-week span starting in early April: He was a playoff runner-up in the Tallahassee Open, tied for second in the South Carolina Classic, won the Alabama Classic, and was in position to win the Shreveport Open, but got disqualified by a freak accident. He had dropped his ball on the eighth green and it hit his ball marker, moving it. He and his playing companion, Steve Gotsche, agreed that this was not a rules violation. In fact, it was, as Horgan learned the next day when he asked an official. Since he failed to assess himself a penalty stroke, he had signed an incorrect scorecard.

Maybe the most reassuring win was Gary Webb's playoff victory in the Dakota Dunes Open. "This win," said Webb, who spent the last four years playing in Europe and Asia, "means I'll get to play in the States for two years — with some food that I can identify."

Canadian Tour

Globe-trotting Trevor Dodds hails from the African nation of Namibia, lives in St. Louis, Missouri, and has found a home in Canada. A summer home, at any rate. For the second straight year, he dominated the Canadian Tour, this time in spades. He won four of the 12 events — one more victory than in 1995 — and was only the second to win four times in one season (Moe Norman was the first, in 1966). Dodds won a record $129,158, more than $50,000 ahead of runner-up Arden Knoll.

Dodds did it with two sets of back-to-back wins. In the Henry Singer Alberta Open, he raced to six birdies over 10 holes in the final round for a one-stroke victory over Ian Leggatt, who had blistered Wolf Creek with a nine-under-par 61 in the third round. Dodds then took the ED TEL PLAnet Open by four strokes. After a one-week interruption, Dodds locked up a two-stroke win in the Infiniti Championship with a three-foot birdie putt on the last hole, then the next week he made only one birdie in the final round of the Canadian Masters, but that's all he needed for a one-stroke win.

The Canadian Tour didn't lack for other bright spots. For one, there was Rob McMillan, age 20, a University of New Mexico player from Winnipeg and the first amateur to win a Canadian Tour event in 20 years, the Xerox Manitoba Open. Home cooking didn't hurt. McMillan won by four strokes at Pine Ridge, his home course. It also helped that third-round leader Mike Grob closed with 75. His consolation was the first-place money of $18,888.

Canadian pro Arden Knoll, 34, one of golf's true rarities — an ex-school teacher and a left-hander all in one — took his first win, the Payless Open at Royal Colwood. He led wire-to-wire and won by four strokes through a balance of boldness and caution. "If I had an opportunity to go for the pin, I did," Knoll said. "But I just tried to keep the ball away from difficulty." He could say that of the entire season. He also had four second-place finishes, an eighth and a ninth to finish second in winnings with $78,534.

The largest margin of victory was posted by former University of Florida star Guy Hill — seven strokes in the BC TEL Pacific Open. Canadian rookie Bryan DeCorso picked off the Morningstar Classic, much to his surprise. "I didn't expect to win so soon," he said. And American Chris DiMarco, 28, another University of Florida player, blew a three-shot lead in the final round, but rallied with four birdies in five holes on the second nine to take the Montclair Quebec Open. Veteran Frank Edmonds, 37, chalked up his sixth win in the Montclair PEI Classic. Toronto pro Ashley Chinner, 38, was another first-time winner. He dropped a four-foot putt on the final hole to take the Canadian PGA Championship at Mandarin, shortened to three rounds by rain.

Martin Price, 33, made a success of his rookie year in the Export "A" Inc. Ontario Open. But he never saw the best part — his winning putt on the first playoff hole. He had told his caddie he was going to make it. "When it was three feet from the cup, I knew it was in," he said. "I didn't even see it drop. I was already jumping." Pretty fair confidence — from 35 feet.

South American Tour

Strengthened by the addition of the Argentina Open and the Volvo Masters of Latin America, the South American Tour consisted of 10 tournaments worth $1.3 million spread over seven countries from early October through the middle of December.

Pedro Martinez of Paraguay led the money list with $116,993 and was the only player with two victories, including the continent's richest, the $310,000 Argentina Open, which previously had not been part of the South American Tour. Five tournament winners were from Argentina, two were from Canada and one from the United States.

The South American Tour began with two events in Bogota, the Colombia Open, won in a playoff by Arden Knoll of Canada, and the La Sabana Open, won by Martinez. Next was the TC Ecuadorian Open, won by Gustavo Rojas of Argentina, then Philip Jonas of Canada won the Los Inkas-Peru Open, and Scott Dunlap of the United States won the Litoral Open in Argentina.

After an open week in early November, the Tour resumed with a victory by Miguel Fernandez of Argentina in the Uruguay Open. The next two tournaments were in Santiago, with Roberto Coceres of Argentina winning the Los Leones Open and Ricardo Gonzalez of Argentina winning the Prince of Wales Open. Then came Martinez' victory over American Tim Herron in the Argentina Open and, finally, the Volvo Masters in Sao Paulo, won by Angel Cabrera of Argentina.

11. European Tours

Who can stop Colin Montgomerie in Europe? Many have tried. In 1993, it was Nick Faldo. A year later, Seve Ballesteros and Bernhard Langer. In 1995, Sam Torrance pushed his fellow Scot all the way to the last day of the season; in 1996 Ian Woosnam was the challenger. "There is always someone," Montgomerie said, "but at least I'm always there, too."

While Montgomerie has been ranked as high as No. 2 on the Sony Ranking, a major championship has so far eluded him, although he has twice lost in playoffs. In 1996, the Scot missed the cut in both the British Open and the U.S. PGA Championship.

The disappointment spurred him on and in a five-week spell in September and October, he outplayed then-leader Woosnam to overtake the Welshman. Montgomerie had already secured his fourth Vardon Trophy by the time he arrived for the season-ending Volvo Masters at Valderrama. In doing so Montgomerie equalled Peter Oosterhuis' record of winning the money list for four straight years. Oosterhuis did it between 1971 and 1974, winning around £70,000 in the process. In his four years, Montgomerie won over £3 million. Like Faldo and Langer during the season, he passed £5 million in career earnings in Europe, but in considerably shorter time.

During those four years, Montgomerie played 83 PGA European Tour events, winning 10 times, finishing second 10 times, in the top 10 44 times, and outside the top 20 only eight times, apart from the 12 times he missed the cut. In 306 rounds of golf, he was 458 under par.

Montgomerie made a late start to the season, spending time on fitness training and dieting early in the year, but then won his first tournament at the Dubai Desert Classic. Two more victories followed at the Murphy's Irish Open and the Canon European Masters. Other tournaments slipped away in a range of circumstances, from Frank Nobilo's 64 at the Deutsche Bank Open, to the high winds of The Oxfordshire and Carnoustie.

But from the fewest number of events that he has played on the European Tour (18), Montgomerie again broke his own record for a season's earnings with £875,146. Whereas in 1993 he averaged just over £25,000 per tournament, he almost doubled that figure in 1996. His progression on the money list remains intact. From 1988, he has been 52nd, 14th, fourth, third and now first four times.

"I have maintained my record of improving every year on tour," Montgomerie said. "If I can keep improving, then a major might come around. I have done this by being happy at home, having a very good caddie whom I work well with, by playing better and hitting the ball further, which produces greater confidence, and by putting better than ever."

Woosnam bounced back from his drop to 65th on the money list in 1995 by winning the opening two events of the year, the Johnnie Walker Classic and the Heineken Classic. Two more wins in the Scottish Open and Volvo German Open meant he was leading the money list for most of the year. "Someone has to stop Monty," he said. Unfortunately, Woosnam was rarely fit in the closing weeks due to spondylosis in his back.

Otherwise, the familiar elite of European golf was not to the fore. Faldo returned a hero after winning the Masters for the third time, but played only five times in Europe, in which he could have won the Volvo PGA Championship and the British Open. Seve Ballesteros was chosen to be the Ryder Cup captain but made a slow return from a five-month sabbatical. He had two top-10 finishes all season. Langer battled the yips again and saw two great records ended. He missed the cut for the first time in 69 tournaments at the Volvo PGA, and he failed to continue his run winning every year since 1980. Jose Maria Olazabal, suffering from rheumatoid arthritis, did not play in any tournaments.

A new era was showing signs of beginning to come through. Excluding British Open champion Tom Lehman, there were 12 new winners, the majority young players. Lee Westwood, at 23, won the Scandinavian Masters and was sixth on the money list, while three rookies finished in the top 15 to earn places at the U.S and British Opens in 1997.

Raymond Russell won the Air France Cannes Open and Padraig Harrington the Peugeot Spanish Open. But it was a late charge from Thomas Bjorn, who had won the Challenge Tour the year before and who won the Loch Lomond World Invitational against a quality field on a quality golf course, that meant the Dane led the rookies on the money list by finishing 10th.

Although not European, Robert Allenby, for a some time paraded as a new star in his homeland of Australia, won three times at the Alamo English Open, Peugeot French Open and the One 2 One British Masters to finish third on the money list. He might have gone higher, but for a car crash in which he fractured his sternum at the end of September.

PGA European Tour

Johnnie Walker Classic—£600,000
Winner: Ian Woosnam

What Ian Woosnam can do once, he can do again. That was true in a double sense at the Johnnie Walker Classic at the Tanah Merah course in Singapore. Woosnam clinched his first win for 16 months, after a 1995 season which saw him fail to win a tournament for the first time in 10 years. The former Masters champion had to work doubly hard for it. He came to the 18th needing to hole a 25-foot birdie putt for a round of 65 to match Andrew Coltart's 16-under-par total of 272. He did.

At the second extra hole, Coltart had to hole from 20 feet to prolong the playoff and then looked in control back at the 18th. Woosnam had hooked his tee shot into trees, but spotted a tiny gap through which he threaded a five iron that turned 15 yards from right to left. The brilliant recovery left the Welshman with an identical putt to the one he had already holed in regulation. "I was fortunate to have the same line," Woosnam said. He holed it again.

Coltart, 25, a member of Scotland's victorious Alfred Dunhill Cup team in 1995, had equalled the course record with a final-round 65 that included five birdies in a row and seven in nine holes. "You will soon win on tour," Woosnam told Coltart. "If it's any consolation, I hope you beat me next time we meet in a playoff." Olle Karlsson, Paul Curry and Wayne Riley shared third place three shots back.

Woosnam's rehabilitation was helped by taking part in a documentary that featured him swinging barechested, in slow motion and close up. "Doing the program was crucial because I could see what I was doing wrong," he said. Back problems led to improper weight transfer which lost him up to 50 yards in length. He had hired Bill Ferguson, Colin Montgomerie's coach, and with little practice and ice treatment to protect his back, Woosnam admitted, "I'm enjoying playing again. I hit my irons brilliantly. The rhythm is better and my swing feels like it is back to what it was a few years ago."

Open Catalonia—£300,000
Winner: Paul Lawrie

The PGA European Tour's arrival in mainland Europe was not a good omen for some of the weather problems to come. At the Open Catalonia it was a wind called the "Cierzo," which meant that Friday's play had to be abandoned and a further delay on Saturday caused the tournament to be cut to 36 holes.

This was good news for Paul Lawrie. The 27-year-old from Aberdeen, where the wind can blow, too, had shot 65 on Thursday and 70 on Saturday despite a double bogey after finding water at his 17th hole. He then had to wait and see whether anyone would beat his nine-under-par 135 total. In the end two Spaniards came closest, Fernando Roca, with six birdies in a row around the turn, shot 70 to be one stroke back, and Domingo Hospital had 71 for 137.

A former UAP Under-25 champion, Lawrie shed 28 pounds through a fitness program and had gone to see golf coach David Leadbetter the previous July and again during the winter. "The man's a genius," he said. "He worked on my posture and takeaway. I was getting desperate before I met him."

Sweden's Anders Forsbrand hit the shot of the week when he holed a five iron from 220 yards at the 569-yard 17th hole for the first double eagle of the 1996 season. Emanuele Canonica of Italy took advantage of the wind to record a 490-yard drive at the hole which set up a pitch-and-putt eagle. But two Englishmen, Russell Claydon and Steve Webster, were not so lucky at the 17th, playing the hole in 11. Webster, winner of the Tour's qualifying tournament, was on to make his first check a healthy one, but tangling with a bush meant he finished out of the prize money.

Moroccan Open—£350,000
Winner: Peter Hedblom

Peter Hedblom likes adventure and he added an African chapter to his tales with his first PGA European Tour victory in the Moroccan Open at the Royal

Dar-es-Salam course in Rabat. Golf is part of the Hedblom family. Father Olle is the golf professional in Gavle, about 100 miles north of Stockholm, where his mother helps out in the pro shop, and sister Marlene is a professional on the women's tour.

That does not mean Hedblom's life is all golf. His friends' idea for a treat for his 25th birthday celebration was to blindfold him, take him to a fair and put him in the boxing ring with the 130-pound Swedish amateur champion. "I was bigger than he was, but he was quicker," Hedblom said. A while later Hedblom, twice a runner-up on the PGA European Tour in 1994, noticed breathing difficulties, and pneumonia and a bruised rib were diagnosed.

A little over a year later, Hedblom found himself leading the Moroccan Open — moved to Rabat due to monsoon rains in Agadir, where the tournament was due to be played — by four strokes after 36 holes with rounds of 68 and 67.

Some 22 strokes behind was Seve Ballesteros, playing his first tournament since the Ryder Cup six months previously. After 21 years as a professional, Ballesteros spent the time "doing everything but think about golf." He had only one birdie in an opening 78 and added 79 the following day. "After such a long break, I need to be patient, and I ask everyone to be patient," Ballesteros said. "I have no confidence. The ball is always coming out of the toe, or the heel, or the top or the bottom of the club. But never the middle."

In difficult conditions over the weekend, Hedblom shot a third-round 74 to maintain his four-shot advantage, and a closing 72 for a seven-under-par total of 281. Eduardo Romero, with a last-round 69, finished one stroke back as Hedblom bogeyed the last hole, and Wayne Westner and Santiago Luna shot 68 and 69 respectively to tie for third place. It was a confident two-putt from 60 feet at the short 17th which meant the Swede could go to the last hole two strokes in front.

Dubai Desert Classic—£650,000
Winner: Colin Montgomerie

Same old Colin Montgomerie, same old story. Well, not quite. Montgomerie returned to the PGA European Tour for the first time in 1996 and carried off the honors in the Dubai Desert Classic as if he had never been away. But during the winter after his second daughter Venetia was born, Montgomerie had been hard at work in his garage-turned-gym. Daily sessions on an exercise bike, a running machine, a rowing machine and a multi-gym, combined with a non-fat diet, meant he had lost 30 pounds.

"I feel fitter and stronger and I feel happier about myself," Montgomerie said. "I haven't done it for golf, but for myself." It certainly had not done any harm for what the Scot does on the golf course. After finishing runner-up to Fred Couples at the Emirates Golf Club in 1995, Montgomerie overhauled Spain's Miguel Angel Jimenez to win the 1996 tournament.

Jimenez opened with a blistering 63 and led by four strokes after 36 holes over Montgomerie and American Jay Townsend. Montgomerie started 67, 68 and was to repeat that sequence over the weekend, while Jimenez could manage only a pair of 70s.

The Spaniard lost the lead with a bogey at the seventh, where there was a two-shot swing, and fell two behind after 13 holes. A reverse two-shot swing occurred at the 14th, but Jimenez failed to get up and down at No. 16 after his chip stayed out of the hole.

At the par-five last hole, where water guarded the front of the green, Jimenez hit a perfect drive and there was no doubt he could reach the green. Montgomerie pushed his drive and faced a 222-yard carry. Out came the driver and he hit a magnificent shot to 15 feet. Two putts were all that was needed for a one-stroke win. "It was 80/20 whether to go for it on the second shot. I play percentage golf 99 percent of the time, but that was the play to win the tournament," Montgomerie said. "To say I'm delighted to win my first tournament after a long break is an understatement."

Jimenez added, "I felt I played like a winner. But Colin is a fantastic player. The top players don't forget how to win. It is like learning to swim for them."

Portuguese Open—£325,000
Winner: Wayne Riley

After finally getting his first PGA European Tour victory at the Scottish Open at Carnoustie in 1995, Wayne Riley, age 33, added another title at the 1996 Portuguese Open.

"This is now my sixth win overall," Riley said. "Everything is starting to happen for me at a nice time. My goal in golf is to become a prolific winner so that I can say at the end of my days that I won 20-30 tournaments, and thank you very much. I really do like putting those trophies up on the mantelpiece.

"When I was young I wanted to see the world and have fun. I was what you might call a colorful character. But everyone grows up and having children is part of that. I am serious about my golf now. I'm more professional. You can come and watch me play and I'll be pretty boring."

More importantly, Riley hit shot after shot between the closely positioned lines of trees on the Aroeira course, a new venue for the tournament. Atrocious winter weather had left its toll on the greens, but it was possible to hole putts as Riley proved with an opening round 65, two behind Klas Eriksson's 63. The Swede faded, and at one point on Saturday the Australian was ahead by seven strokes.

Riley's lead was down to two strokes going into the final round. First Martin Gates, with a third-round 65, and then Mark Davis, with 67 on Sunday, put on the pressure. The Englishmen tied for second, two behind Riley's 13-under-par 271 total.

Davis, with a birdie at the 17th, got closest, but he bogeyed the last hole when pressing for a birdie. "They kept coming at me and I felt I needed to keep attacking. I couldn't put the shutters up," said Riley.

A severe thunderstorm caused a three-hour delay on Sunday but could not wash out the tournament. "So many guys were coming up to me and shaking me by the hand, but that's not how I wanted to win it," Riley said. "In our profession, national championships are decided over 72 holes."

Madeira Island Open—£300,000
Winner: Jarmo Sandelin

Jarmo Sandelin hits big and thinks big. After being Rookie of the Year on the PGA European Tour in 1995, he went and won his U.S. PGA Tour card. But after making just one cut in six events early in 1996, Sandelin returned to Europe and won the Madeira Island Open.

Sandelin did it by doing the one thing you would not expect him to do. He kept his 50-inch driver in his bag and threaded his way around the side of the mountain. The Finnish-born Swede also mastered the dastardly 18th green on Sunday, which was the biggest key to his win. The final green has a severe ridge and the pin position for the last round was cut very close to it. Too close, some said.

First another Swede, Patrik Sjoland, needed to birdie the last hole to match what was Sandelin's eventual winning score of nine under par. He ended up five-putting. Then Des Smyth, the 43-year-old Irishman, had a front-nine 30 to take the lead. He had a 12-footer on the 18th to get to 10 under par. He putted off the front edge and took three more to get down. "I played the hole great, hitting a nine iron right over the flag, and then just ripped the putt and it finished 40 feet away," Smyth said.

David J. Russell also arrived at the 18th hole nine under and also four-putted. His first was from the back fringe and ended eight feet short. "Then what was I supposed to do?" he said. "I knew it was like lightning. I thought I had holed my second putt and it ended off the green."

Sandelin had the advantage of watching playing companion Stephen McAllister. Sandelin's 15-footer from right of the pin somehow stayed within tap-in range. "I hit it so slowly and was praying for it to stop. The pin position was way too hard, especially for the final day," Sandelin said.

Paul Affleck, a 29-year-old Welshman with a last-round 66, ended up in second place, his best finish, with five players sharing third, including Russell and Smyth and Daniel Chopra, an Indian-Swede who had led by three going into the final round.

Air France Cannes Open—£400,000
Winner: Raymond Russell

Europe's new breed showed up in force at Royal Mougins in the Air France Cannes Open and the last round turned into a battle of two 23-year-olds, Raymond Russell and David Carter. A birdie-birdie finish gave Russell his first title in only his ninth-ever PGA European Tour event.

Carter, South African-born of English parents — his father, Bryan, plays on the European Seniors Tour — showed his liking for low scores when he shot a course-record 62 in the second round. The round included four twos and six other birdies, but it only put him one shot ahead of Padraig Harrington, 24, a three-time member of Great Britain and Ireland's Walker Cup team. Harrington had shot 68 and 65, but closed with 72 and 74, an experience that would stand him in good stead a few weeks later.

Russell shot a third-round 67, with five birdies in the last 13 holes, to catch Carter and then survived a mid-round wobble on Sunday. He found water at the 16th, but the ball had hit the bank on the far side. Dropping on the edge of the green meant he got away with a bogey. "Then I played the last two holes perfectly," said Russell, also a former Walker Cup man.

Russell shot a final-round 71 to Carter's 73 to win by two with a 272 total, with Spain's Ignacio Garrido, 24, and Scotland's Gordon Brand, Jr., a comparative veteran at 37, two strokes further back. Brand had shot 63 on Saturday, but went to the turn on Sunday with two three-putts and a four-putt.

"I'm a bit surprised to have broken through so soon, but one win doesn't make you a superstar," Russell said "It's no use going into a tournament thinking about the cut. When you stand on the first tee, you are level with Monty, Norman, Faldo, everybody."

Turespana Masters Open—£500,000
Winner: Diego Borrego

Diego Borrego became the fifth first-time winner on the PGA European Tour of 1996 and at 24 continued the youthful theme. To do it, he had to beat Tony Johnstone on the third playoff hole of the Turespana Masters Open on the sand dunes of El Saler, just outside Valencia.

The Spaniard, who graduated from the 1995 Challenge Tour after a miserable first season on the main tour, and who marks his ball on the greens with a 100 pesera coin with the head of King Juan Carlos upturned, had led by two shots during the final round, as had Johnstone. The Zimbabwean, just short of his 40th birthday, and who had suffered a mysterious, energy-sapping tropical disease during the latter half of the 1995 season, had birdied the last hole by holing from eight feet to match Borrego's 69 and 271 total.

At the first two playoff holes, Borrego had to hole short putts to continue the playoff, and then missed the green at the short 17th. But while he chipped to two feet, Johnstone, who had holed from 50 feet on the green in the third round, put his long approach putt six feet past and missed the one back. "I can't believe what I have done," said Borrego, the son of the greenskeeper at Aloha on the Costa del Sol.

Peter Baker finished in third place, four strokes outside the playoff. Baker was in the last week of a special diet of no alcohol and no fatty foods imposed by doctors after he suffered hepatitis and pneumonia. Baker described keeping the diet as "the greatest achievement of my life."

There was relief for Steve Webster, the 21-year-old from Atherstone who was low amateur at the 1995 British Open, and went on to win the qualifying tournament. In his 10th attempt, he made his first cut of the season. "It's a relief," Webster said before going on to finish in 30th place.

Conte of Florence Italian Open—£511,000
Winner: Jim Payne

When Jim Payne completed his final-round 67, his second 67 of the day after rain caused 36 holes to be played on the last day, he was just happy to have recorded his best finish since undergoing back surgery in September 1994. "This performance should at least help to get me invitations," Payne said, knowing that his medical exemptions were about to run out.

About an hour and a half later, such thoughts could be forgotten as Payne's nine-under 275 total proved good enough for his second PGA European Tour victory in the Conte of Florence Italian Open.

As Payne finished, Lee Westwood led at 12 under par. Westwood had shot 65 in the morning and had collected 22 birdies in his first 56 holes. But at the 12th, he took an eight, which included two hacks in a grassy bank and a duffed pitch from the fairway. Westwood recovered and both he and Sweden's Patrik Sjoland arrived at the final hole needing pars to get into a playoff with Payne.

Sjoland pushed his four-iron approach into a bunker and took a bogey to finish second. Westwood pushed his drive, put his third shot into another bunker and took six to finish tied for third with Jonathan Lomas and Miguel Angel Jimenez.

For Payne, the 26-year-old Lincolnshire man, victory was a big relief. A deformity at birth led to two vertebrae slipping out of alignment, causing him increasing discomfort during the 1994 season. He underwent a spinal fusion operation and made a tentative comeback in March, 1995. "When I had the operation, I did not know if I would ever be able to play at this level again," Payne said. "My back is now stronger than most people's and this win will give me a lot of confidence."

Local hero Costantino Rocca was let down by his putting and finished tied for 20th on the Bergamo course where he started playing golf by sneaking on in the evenings on the holes away from the clubhouse. A Ryder Cup player, he is now an honorary member, and banners such as "Costantino la leggenda" and "Rocca the best" adorned nearby houses. "I am the best in the village," joked Rocca, who lives half a mile from the course.

Peugeot Open de Espana—£550,000
Winner: Padraig Harrington

For the second tournament running, 36 holes were required to complete the tournament on schedule, but the final day of the Peugeot Open de Espana was very different to the anything-can-happen events in Italy the week before.

Showing maturity beyond his 24 years, Irishman Padraig Harrington extended his three-shot halfway lead and turned it into a four-stroke victory margin over a late-charging Gordon Brand, Jr., making four birdies on the back nine late on Sunday afternoon. Rolf Muntz of Holland finished third, six strokes back.

Harrington, who won his PGA European Tour card at the 1995 qualifying tournament after playing on a winning Great Britain and Ireland Walker Cup team, opened up his advantage with a second 64. Then Saturday's play was rained out and fog delayed Sunday's activities.

A third-round 67 pretty much sealed things for Harrington, and a six-shot cushion required no better than a closing 71 for a 16-under-par 272 total. On greens described by one player as "having a mind of their own" due to torrential rain before and during the tournament, Harrington's only three-putt came at the 72nd hole. During his second round, he required only 25 putts. To do so, he grips the putter conventionally for all right-to-left putts, and with his left hand below his right for all left-to-right putts.

"I am surprised at the standard on tour, it is so tough just to make the cut each week," said Harrington, who had made all the nine cuts in his rookie season. "But once you do make a cut, two good rounds on the weekend and you can be right in contention."

Colin Montgomerie, in only his second PGA European Tour start of the season, had to withdraw after a first-round 74 due to the hospitalization of his baby daughter Venetia. Amateur Sergio Garcia, age 16, shot a first-round 68, made the cut and finished tied for 49th, alongside his hero, Seve Ballesteros.

Benson and Hedges International Open—£700,000
Winner: Stephen Ames

Grim weather had followed the PGA European Tour throughout 1996 when the Tour arrived for the first time in Britain. For the first three days it was merely cold. For the final day, the wind switched direction, warmed up and decided to really blow, scattering golf balls and golfers alike all over the exposed Rees Jones-designed Oxfordshire course in the Benson and Hedges International Open.

One of those worst affected was Colin Montgomerie, who closed with 84 after he had held a three-stroke lead after 54 holes. The man least affected was Stephen Ames from Trinidad and Tobago, who has based himself on the PGA European Tour for four years. He made the Benson and Hedges International his second Tour win with a five-under-par 283 total that was one better than Jon Robson and two in front of Derrick Cooper.

Ames was the only man to match par on the final day. Robson shot 73 and Cooper 74. Only 31 players broke 80 and the average for the day was 79.49. Ames' score included two double bogeys, which were almost unavoidable in the conditions. The first came at the par-three second hole and the next at the par-five 17th.

On Friday, Padraig Harrington scored 13 at the 17th hole after finding the water four times, once with a three wood, twice with a three iron, and lastly trying to lay up with a six iron. On Sunday, Ames pushed a one iron into the water, but two-putted from 80 feet, holing from 15 feet, at the last hole for the title.

It had been the second hole, however, which had got him going. "I was annoyed and that woke me up," the 32-year-old Ames said. "Then I decided we were out here to play golf. I thought, let's forget the fact that they didn't call it off — let's play. Playing on the European Tour has made me learn how to play in the wind. It has taken me four years to learn all the shots you need. I was dealing with the situation when some quality golfers were not."

Seve Ballesteros shot 77; Bernhard Langer 79; Nick Faldo, on his first home appearance after becoming Masters champion again, 80, and Ian Woosnam, only three strokes behind Montgomerie after three rounds, 82. Montgomerie led by four strokes after six holes, before disaster after disaster set in. His afternoon culminated in being handed a two-stroke penalty for testing the surface of a hazard when he found his ball buried in a bunker at the 13th.

Volvo PGA Championship—£1,000,000
Winner: Costantino Rocca

With two holes to play, which happen to be two par-fives on Wentworth's famous West Course, Nick Faldo was tied for the lead with Costantino Rocca. With Faldo playing a group in front, it seemed exactly the sort of situation the Englishman relishes, and that in which the Italian does not always shine. This time was different.

Faldo is still seeking a record fifth Volvo PGA Championship title after he parred those last two holes. His pitch at the 17th came up in the front fringe, 18 feet from the pin, and at the last hole, he put his second shot approach into a bunker and took three to get down. In Europe's first £1 million Tour event, it was Rocca who finished birdie-birdie to take the record £166,660 first prize.

Faldo had shot a final-round 68 to tie for second with Paul Lawrie, whose game had been transformed by going to see Faldo's coach, David Leadbetter. Rocca's 69, his third in addition to a second-round 67, gave him all four rounds under 70 and a 14-under total of 274.

Rocca, age 39, had become increasingly consistent, culminating in his runner-up finish at the 1995 British Open at St. Andrews and his Ryder Cup performance at Oak Hill, but he had not won since 1993. "This is not a consolation for the Open," Rocca said. "But it is a big goal for me — one of my proudest moments. I had a lot of pressure not having won for three years. That is a long time.

"This morning my blood pressure was 200, and at the last it was over 300. In a newspaper in Italy, Nick Faldo gave an interview in which he said if he finished second in a major championship to me he would not mind. This came into my mind when Faldo was 12 under. I tried to make him second."

Defending champion Bernhard Langer had broken Neil Coles' record of consecutive cuts made in PGA European Tour events at the championship the year before. The run had started at Wentworth in 1991. It came to an end there in 1996 at 68 as the German posted rounds of 73 and 74. "It had to happen sooner or later," Langer said. "It is sad that it happened here because this is one of our greatest tournaments and a course I like very much. It is going to take a long time to break the record again, maybe four or five years."

Deutsche Bank Open–TPC of Europe—£725,000
Winner: Frank Nobilo

When Frank Nobilo opened with a seven-under-par 65 at Gut Kaden and Colin Montgomerie shot a first-round 71, it was hard to imagine the dramatics that the New Zealander would need on Sunday to win the Deutsche Bank Open–TPC of Europe. It took an eight-under 64 for Nobilo to win his fifth European title. That meant it was the second time in the season — following Fred Couples at The Players Championship — that Montgomerie, who himself shot a last-round 66, had been beaten by such a low closing score.

The details in between were that after "a serious talking to" in his hotel room the night before, Montgomerie came out and shot 65 in the second round and added 69 on the third day. Nobilo shot rounds of 69 and 72 to fall out of the final groups. He was, therefore, in a position to dictate when he opened up with five successive threes on Sunday. Montgomerie was out in 32, but a bogey at the par-three 14th coincided with birdies from Nobilo at the 15th, 16th and 17th.

Montgomerie also birdied the par-five 15th, but his usually reliable driver from the fairway failed to bring another at the par-five 17th, which left him trying to hole his eight-iron second shot, from 172 yards, at the last hole to tie. The ball pulled up 10 feet short and Nobilo's 18-under 270 total was good for a one-shot win, with Irishman Darren Clarke three strokes further back.

"It's a lovely feeling to have whacked Monty," said Nobilo, the 36-year-old London-based Aucklander. "He's a good friend, but he's the last man you want breathing down your neck in a tight situation. When he gets the bit between his teeth, he is hard to beat. But I proved with my fourth place at the U.S. Masters that I thrive on the big occasions."

"I'm still smiling," Montgomerie said. "If someone shoots 64 to beat you, good luck to them. It's unfortunate to shoot 66 and not win."

Seve Ballesteros showed signs of a return to form with a third-round 66, his first score under 70 since returning from his winter sabbatical. It was created in typical Ballesteros fashion, with two of his six birdies coming after drives that ended in bunkers. But on Sunday, he had a triple-bogey seven at the third hole after driving out of bounds. He later complained of amateur photographers in the gallery clicking at the wrong moment.

Alamo English Open—£650,000
Winner: Robert Allenby

Colin Montgomerie wanted a victory before going off to the U.S. Open the following week and had a hand in giving himself the best possible chance — one that he could not take. In two previous visits to the Forest of Arden, Montgomerie had won the English Open in 1994 and lost a playoff to Philip Walton in 1995. During the winter he had advised on how the course could be set up so as to provide an appetizer for what those who were playing in the U.S. Open could expect.

This is the Scot's favorite form of golf, owing to his great ability to hit his driver straight. "What can be more complete about a golf tournament if you have to hit the fairway, hit the green and hole the putt," Montgomerie said. "I prefer it when people are punished for missing a fairway. This course has been set up for tournament professionals. We go to too many courses where the members have just finished playing when we turn up."

The Forest of Arden course was surrounded in heavy rough, both off the fairways and around the greens, and what it did was show up a flaw in Montgomerie's short game. In five attempts to save par during the first round, he dropped seven shots. After his first-round 75, Montgomerie said he needed three 67s or 68s. Three of the latter got him to 279, nine under par, but it could have been better.

Having fought his way from 91st place to first with two holes to play, Montgomerie failed to get up and down at the 17th for a birdie that would have taken him to 11 under, and then saw his chip at the par-three last hole barely make the green and he two-putted for a bogey. Englishman Ross McFarlane also failed to save par at the last to fall into a tie for second with Montgomerie and hand victory to Australian Robert Allenby.

Allenby, 24, from Melbourne, had won once in five years on the PGA European Tour and lost his third-round lead when he went to the turn in 37. But he birdied the par-five 12th, holed from six feet at the 15th, from 15 feet at the 16th, two-putted for another birdie at the 17th, and calmly two-putted from 40 feet for a par at the 18th. "This game is all about patience and I was patient today," Allenby said.

Slaley Hall Northumberland Challenge—£300,000
Winner: Retief Goosen

Relief Goosen seemed to be in command at the Slaley Hall Northumberland Challenge. The 27-year-old South African opened with 66 on the Slaley Hall course and led by five at the halfway mark and by four after 54 holes. When a closing 65 from Scot Ross Drummond came from out of the blue, Goosen had some work to do. A closing 72 gave him a two-shot victory at 11-under-par 277, his first victory in Europe to add to six on his home tour.

Drummond, having worked closely with a Dutch sports psychologist, belied his 19 years without a win in going to the turn in 31. That included a 25-foot eagle putt at the fourth hole followed by four birdies in a row. Two more came at the 10th and 12th holes, and the course-record 65 hauled Drummond up from nine back to one behind.

Goosen had briefly been tied for the lead during the final round of the English Open, before succumbing to five bogeys in a row. He had a slight wobble when he bogeyed the 10th, 12th and 13th holes, but he holed a double-breaking 12-footer for a birdie at the 16th to re-establish a two-shot advantage. "I tried to make it difficult for myself," Goosen said. "But I knew what I had to do after Ross had finished, the tournament was mine to win or lose. This is a very important milestone for me."

Mark and Stephen Pullan, 24-year-olds from the Sand Moor club in Leeds, became the first set of identical twins to play in the same PGA European Tour event, but both missed the cut.

BMW International Open—£525,000
Winner: Marc Farry

The latest beneficiary of the PGA European Tour's foul weather was Frenchman Marc Farry, who became the eighth first-time winner of the season when the final two days of the BMW International Open were washed out. This was the eighth out of 20 tournaments to be disrupted by the weather.

Farry, who had missed the cut in seven of his nine previous tournaments in the year, had shot rounds of 65 and 67 for a 132 total that was one better than Australian left-hander Richard Green's 67 and 66. Russell Claydon, Padraig Harrington and David Higgins were one stroke further back.

The 36-year-old Parisian holed a wedge shot for an eagle two at the 12th on Friday, a shot that proved to be the winning stroke. "I had led after two rounds last year and slipped to seventh on the weekend, so it would have been nice to prove to my peers that I have improved," said Farry, who had won 15 times on the French tour, but had had eight fruitless years on the main tour.

"I must thank my wife Isobel for my victory. I was having a nice life on the French tour, but she told me, 'You must go out and play with the big boys.'"

Peugeot Open de France—£600,000
Winner: Robert Allenby

Robert Allenby completed a cross-Channel June double by adding the French title to the English crown he won three weeks earlier. This time it took him 73 holes as he sank a putt from 30 feet at the first extra hole to beat Bernhard Langer in a playoff at the Peugeot Open de France.

Langer had shot 67 and 66 over the weekend compared to Allenby's 68 and 69 to tie at 16-under-par 272. The German had made a remarkable recovery after being disqualified after missing the cut at the U.S. Open two weeks earlier. He had admitted he was suffering a fourth bout of the yips and there had been much speculation about him retiring if he could not find a solution.

By switching to an old putter, and adding some loft to the blade, he was able to push his left elbow forward into a more natural position in his "Langer lock" putting method. On Sunday, he opened with six birdies in seven holes, but a double bogey at the 12th halted his momentum. But having set the target, Allenby, despite pushing his drive onto a bank, had to hit a wedge over the water to the last green to three feet to secure the birdie he needed to get into the playoff.

"For the first 11 holes I played some of my best golf ever," Langer said. "But I was coming from way behind and it was just one mistake."

Allenby said, "This was my third playoff and I haven't lost one yet. I felt mentally strong all week. The putt in the playoff was straight and as soon as it got over the brow of the hill it never looked like missing. Maybe it was lucky, but things happen like that in playoffs. I am happy to see Bernhard play well again. He is an inspiration for young players like myself."

The calm and sunny conditions for the first two days meant the National course played as easily as it ever will and the cut fell at a season's best three under par, one too few for Colin Montgomerie. Steve Richardson equalled Paul Broadhurst's course-record 63 on Friday, as did Paul McGinley and Miles Tunnicliff on Sunday.

Murphy's Irish Open—£765,306
Winner: Colin Montgomerie

"This is my 11th victory on the European Tour," Colin Montgomerie admitted, "and this is the most fortunate." Montgomerie was in the Druids Glen clubhouse with a final-round 69 and a five-under-par total of 279 in the

Murphy's Irish Open, one ahead of Australian Wayne Riley, who broke the course record with a last-day 66, when Andrew Oldcorn came to the 18th tee.

Oldcorn was one stroke ahead on another course set up in ferocious U.S. Open style. The 36-year-old English-born Scot pulled his drive into some thick rough on the left and could only hack out onto the fairway. His third shot did not quite make it up onto the middle tier and his approach putt rolled three feet past the hole. A bogey five would still have got Oldcorn into a playoff, but he missed.

Oldcorn, who shot a final-round 66, said, "I don't feel I bottled it. I'm proud of the way I played. I just hit one bad shot and got a terrible lie."

Montgomerie had worked on his putting since missing the cut at the French Open the week before, and after two three-putts to close out the front nine, he holed from 30 feet at the 14th and 35 feet at the 17th for his final-round 68.

Montgomerie agreed he was lucky to record his second victory of the year and one that extended his lead at the top of the European money list. "My heart goes out to Andrew as a fellow Scot," said the three-time European money leader. "We all saw what happened and it was a shame. He had it in the bag and I was playing for second. You just have to keep plodding on. I had triples and doubles out there as well, but I had time to recover."

On only his fourth hole in the first round, actually the 13th hole, Montgomerie hit his drive onto the bank of a ditch. His foot slipped as he tried to play his recovery and he played what was his first air shot on the Tour. His next shot was thinned into a ditch and he eventually took a triple-bogey seven. "This'll be a good one to win from here," said Montgomerie's caddie, Alastair McLean.

Scottish Open—£480,000
Winner: Ian Woosnam

A "wee breeze" is what the locals call the ever-present wind at Carnoustie, but on a course restored to its former glory, and tough enough on a calm day, the high winds during the four days of the Scottish Open were too much for all but Ian Woosnam. The wee Welshman shot a final-round 75 but still won by four shots over Scotland's Andrew Coltart. His one-over-par 289 total was the first over-par winning score on the PGA European Tour since the 1985 British Open at Royal St. George's.

In an eerie repeat of the Benson and Hedges International at The Oxfordshire, all Woosnam's closest challengers fell away. He led by three strokes into the final round over Russell Claydon, who shot 80, and by four over Rolf Muntz, who shot 81. Colin Montgomerie had worked his way up to second place with eight straight pars in the final round, but he had to tangle with the rough sooner or later, and from the ninth hole he went double bogey, bogey, triple bogey. He ended with 81.

"Conditions were very, very difficult," Montgomerie said. "It was almost too windy because the course was so hard and bouncy. I don't know where I am hitting the ball and I have no confidence." A week earlier he had won the Irish Open, and a week later he missed the cut in the British Open.

Woosnam had a run of five bogeys in eight holes before an eagle at the 12th eased him in front of Sweden's Mats Hallberg, who had briefly drawn even. Hallberg finished with 75, five shots back in third place, and claimed a late exemption for the British Open along with Diego Borrego, Lee Westwood, Malcolm Mackenzie and Andrew Sherborne. Said Hallberg, who bogeyed the last four holes, "This is possibly the most beautiful golf course I have ever played, but it got me in the end."

Quality ball-striking saw Woosnam through to his third win of the season and put him £60,000 behind Montgomerie at the top of the money list, which Woosnam had won in 1987 and 1990. "That wasn't a goal at the beginning of the season, I just wanted to win again, but it is now," Woosnam said. "I was hitting the ball so low out there that I topped it three times in row. It was a game of patience."

British Open Championship—£1,419,800
Winner: Tom Lehman

See Chapter 5.

Sun Dutch Open—£650,000
Winner: Mark McNulty

Scott Hoch found out what makes Mark McNulty so hard to beat at the Sun Dutch Open. "Mark is one of the best putters in the world," Hoch said after having to settle for second place at Hilversum.

Hoch collected six birdies and a chip-in eagle for 66, but it was a missed six-foot birdie chance on the last hole that the 40-year-old American rued most. McNulty started the final round three strokes ahead and his final-round 68 was good enough for a one-stroke victory at 18-under-par 266.

Hoch, playing two weeks after winning the Michelob Championship but a week after missing the British Open at Royal Lytham, for which he was heavily criticized, added, "I feel I played well enough to win and I should have won. I expected to make the putt at the last hole, but it veered off line."

"Scott made a hell of a fight of it. He's a competitor who came here on the top of his game," said McNulty, 42, from Zimbabwe, who claimed his second PGA European Tour title of the season "This is a straight hitters course and I fancied my chances from the word go." McNulty shot a front-nine 31 in the first round and a back-nine 29 on the second day.

John Daly missed the cut by 23 strokes after a second-round 89. He went to the turn in 51 with two double bogeys, a triple bogey, and a quadruple-bogey nine at the fourth where he hit two zero irons out of bounds. He was 33 strokes behind 36-hole leader Des Smyth. His manager issued a statement expressing Daly's regret at not being around for the weekend but saying he had tried on every shot.

Volvo Scandinavian Masters—£700,000
Winner: Lee Westwood

In Goteborg, Sweden, customers of the city's bars have to be 22 years old to gain entry. Lee Westwood is 23, but he didn't look it to one bar owner and was promptly turned away from his establishment. He may not look old enough to drink, but down at the Forsgarden course, Westwood was plenty old enough to make the Volvo Scandinavian Masters his first title on the PGA European Tour.

After faltering at the end of the Italian Open, but posting seven top-12 finishes, the third-year professional deserved his reward. "I was starting to think I was never going to win, but I really played well when the pressure came on over the last nine holes," Westwood said. And it was not just the last nine, there was a playoff, too.

Russell Claydon saved par from 20 feet to set the clubhouse target at seven-under-par 281. Then Paul Broadhurst birdied three of the last five holes to tie, and finally Westwood came home in 33, to make a third final-round 68, and join the playoff. Westwood holed from 40 feet for the victory on the second extra hole.

"I have to thank my coach, Peter Cowan," Westwood said. "I switched to Peter in April and he has got me hitting the ball harder and being more aggressive generally and I'm making a lot more birdies."

Hohe Brucke Open—£250,000
Winner: Paul McGinley

After four second places on the PGA European Tour, including to Ian Woosnam at the Heineken Classic earlier in the season, Paul McGinley had to do something really dramatic to win his first title. He did. The 29-year-old Dubliner shot a last-round, 11-birdie 62 to claim the Hohe Brucke Open at Waldviertel.

McGinley, who had not played since he had led the British Open at Royal Lytham at the halfway stage, started the final round eight behind Juan Carlos Pinero, the younger brother of Manuel. McGinley birdied seven of the first eight holes and his only blemish came at the ninth when he three-putted. He added more birdies at Nos. 11, 13 and 16, saved par with a 20-footer at the 17th and then wedged in to three feet at the 18th.

After opening with 73, the Irishman had gone 66, 68, 62 for a 19-under-par total of 269. Pinero, who shot a final-round 71, was still even with McGinley when the Spaniard came to the 17th, but a three-putt there left him one stroke back and tied for second with David Lynn, a 22-year-old Englishman who spent the year mainly on the Challenge Tour.

McGinley said of Pinero, "He did not lose the tournament, I won it. But I know how he feels. I've been there. My near-misses have been shattering but they have made me mentally stronger. I knew by the law of percentages that my turn would come."

It came in an event scheduled opposite the U.S. PGA Championship and in which McGinley was the only player from the top 30 of the money list playing. But he insisted, "There's no such thing as a weak field in Europe.

The standard of play in Europe right now is sky high. The cut was at three under and I had to shoot 20 under for the last 54 holes to win by one. There are a lot of terrific players out there and that speaks volumes for the future of European golf."

Chemapol Trophy Czech Open—£750,000
Winner: Jonathan Lomas

Make that a round dozen. Jonathan Lomas became the 12th first-time winner on the PGA European Tour and his victory lifted him past 26 other countrymen onto the England team, alongside Barry Lane and Lee Westwood, for the Alfred Dunhill Cup in October. It also ended a frustrating and disappointing couple of years after Lomas was the 1994 Rookie of the Year.

Lomas saw his putting deteriorate and then felt pains in both his legs. "It was a complete mystery," Lomas said. "I saw specialists and had tests, but nothing showed up. The doctors said I should keep my legs moving and the best way was to carry on playing. After two years the pain disappeared. It was a terrific relief."

He sorted out his putting by switching to a long-handled putter, something he admitted to being "a bit embarrassed" about. "I didn't have the yips, but I was three-putting and wasting birdie chances. I immediately felt comfortable and relaxed. It is a very consistent way of putting."

A last-round 66 for a 12-under-par 272 total gave Lomas a one-stroke victory over Sweden's Daniel Chopra, with Domingo Hospital one further back. Lee Westwood, attempting to win his second consecutive tournament, made six threes in a row to take the lead before back-to-back double bogeys at the 16th and 17th holes.

Czech-born tennis star Ivan Lendl, who plays golf left-handed although he plays tennis right-handed, was given an invitation but missed the cut after rounds of 82 and 76. A seven-handicapper before turning professional in order to endorse a manufacturer's products, Lendl said, "It was five times worse than a Wimbledon final. I knew what I was doing there, here I didn't have the skill, experience and confidence in my ability. I have no idea about being a top golfer. My ambition is just to get around a course without having to look for a ball."

Volvo German Open—£700,000
Winner: Ian Woosnam

When Ian Woosnam is in the sort of record-breaking streak in which the Welshman found himself at the Nippenburg course in Stuttgart, not much can stop him. Woosnam did not even get to play in the final round of the Volvo German Open, but his fourth victory of the year catapulted him above Colin Montgomerie and back to the top of the money list.

Rain flooded the greens and bunkers on the last day leaving Woosnam to be declared the winner after three rounds in which he had a 20-under-par total of 193. That equalled the PGA European Tour record for 54 holes, but he was denied a chance to establish a whole host of new ones.

Woosnam needed a final-round 65 to break Mark McNulty's German Open record of 259 in 1987; 64 to beat his own (and David Llewellyn's) record of 258 for 72 holes of a PGA European Tour event; 63 to beat the Tour's under-par record of minus-27 by Jerry Anderson in the 1984 European Masters; 62 to equal Peter Tupling's lowest national Open winning score of 255 in the 1981 Nigerian Open, and 61 to break the course record and just about everything else.

"I'm a bit disappointed at not getting the chance to break my record score of 258," Woosnam said. "The way I was playing it was definitely on. But a win is a win." The 38-year-old was keen to regain the No. 1 spot on the money list and hold on to it by the end of the following week's British Masters to earn a place in the Toyota World Match Play Championship, which he had won twice before.

Rounds of 64, 64 and 65 had given Woosnam a six-shot lead over England's Iain Pyman, Germany's Thomas Gogele, Spain's Fernando Roca and Sweden's Robert Karlsson. The young Swede had been only one stroke behind Woosnam after equalling the course record of 62 (set by Paul Broadhurst on the opening day) in the second round. Roger Chapman also scored 62 on a course where all the par-fives where reachable, there was little rough and soft greens.

Montgomerie, winner of the title for the previous two years, missed the event after his father, James, the secretary at Royal Troon, suffered a heart attack. Of the few who did get to complete their final rounds, Andrew Coltart and Frank Nobilo, playing together, both shot 63s to jump from a tie for 53rd place to second, until their scores were washed out.

One 2 One British Masters—£700,000
Winner: Robert Allenby

A new name was on everyone's lips at the Collingtree Park, but it was not the latest first-time winner. Annual meadow grass decline was what caused the greens at Collingtree to become diseased and putting on them was like trying to do so on the motorway.

The problem only came to light in the previous three weeks, too late for the event to be moved. While tournament officials and organizers apologized to everyone involved, players, spectators, media and, most importantly, the new sponsors, and though 13 players walked out with various back, shoulder and wrist injuries, one man soldiered on unperturbed.

Robert Allenby, wearing his trademark sunglasses which were maybe rose-tinted, won for the third time in the season by beating Spain's Miguel Angel Martin on the first extra hole. Allenby had just returned from a week's trip to Melbourne, during which he attended the funeral of a hemophiliac who died of AIDS and whom he had gone to visit in the hospital.

The experience helped Allenby stay patient throughout the week. "I felt relaxed and didn't even have jetlag," Allenby said. "I saw the greens and thought 'You are going to make some putts and you are going to miss some. Just be patient and you will come through.'

"I knew there would be a lot of whining. You just have to look on the bright side. We are playing for so much money and they made the course into the best condition possible. I'm not bagging the other players, I have no need to do that, but we all have to play in the same conditions."

Allenby led from the second day, but after rounds of 69, 71 and 71 he slipped to 73 on the final day. He bogeyed four holes out of five from the 11th, but still had an eight-footer for birdie at the last to win. Instead, he tied with Martin, who shot 68, at 284, four under par, before extending his playoff record to 4-0.

Playing the par-five 18th again, Martin drove into the rough, had to lay up, and missed the green with his third shot. Allenby was just short of the green in two. After the Spaniard had chipped and putted twice without holing out, he conceded with Allenby two feet away from the hole.

Costantino Rocca finished one shot out of the playoff, with Miguel Angel Jimenez a further stroke back after a last-round 67. Ian Woosnam came to the 18th needing an eagle to match the leaders, but putted off the green and took three more to get down. All in all, it was an inauspicious start to the year-long qualifying for the 1997 European Ryder Cup team.

Canon European Masters—£768,000
Winner: Colin Montgomerie

After missing the cut in two successive majors at the British Open and the PGA Championship, a little mountain air seemed to do Colin Montgomerie the world of good. The views from the Crans-sur-Sierre course, 5,000 feet above the Rhone Valley, are stunning, but the Scot's play over the weekend in the Canon European Masters was equally spectacular.

After two rounds Sam Torrance, so narrowly defeated for the money list title in 1995 by his countryman, led by six strokes after rounds of 65 and 63. Montgomerie had shot 65 and 71 to be eight strokes back.

But after a 36-hole PGA European Tour record of 124, 18 under par, for the weekend, Montgomerie had won by four strokes. His third win of the year lifted him back to the top of the money list over Ian Woosnam. "I had enough of him last year," sighed Torrance. "Nothing personal, but he's like a rash that won't go away. Monty is a hell of a player. When you lead by six and shoot two 68s you expect to win."

Montgomerie birdied 10 of the first 14 holes on Saturday in a 61 that could have been the first ever round under 60 in Europe. "I feel unfortunate not to have birdied at least one of the last four holes," Montgomerie said. "I proved 59 was on and that I could do it."

Then on the Sunday, which started with him still one behind, he shot 63 which included five birdies in a row in a back nine of 30. "If I had finished yesterday like I did today, then I would have shot 58, never mind 59," he said.

At the 325-yard seventh hole, Montgomerie drove the green and holed from 25 feet for an eagle, while Torrance took five to go from one in front to two behind. An eagle at the 14th got him back to one behind, but he failed to hole from 10 feet at the 16th when Montgomerie had already secured a birdie from 15 feet. Montgomerie's 260 total (24 under par) was one better than Jerry Anderson's 1984 record (when the course was a par 72).

"I have never played better in my life," Montgomerie said. "It's the best

I have ever driven the ball and I've never felt so relaxed."

Trophee Lancome—£650,000
Winner: Jesper Parnevik

After a hot spell on the U.S. PGA Tour with three top-10 finishes in four events, including fourth place at the PGA Championship, Jesper Parnevik returned to Europe to light a celebratory cigar. The Swede does not indulge in the weed, but at the beginning of the year a friend had given him the cigar to puff should he find himself in the comfortable position of walking down the 72nd hole assured of victory.

Parnevik thought he was about to light up at the Greater Milwaukee Open, but then he bogeyed the last hole to miss a playoff by one stroke. Instead, the cigar was unwrapped after stepping off the tee at the par-three finishing hole at St. Nom la Breteche. His third victory shared the same characteristic of the previous two of having been achieved by a five-shot margin.

And for the second time in just over a year, the man he beat was European No. 1 Colin Montgomerie. One behind at the start of the final day, and looking for a second successive win both this season and in the tournament, Montgomerie birdied the first five holes. Parnevik, however, weathered the storm and birdied the fourth and fifth holes himself to limit the Scot's advantage to two.

Then, he could only watch as Montgomerie self-destructed. Montgomerie found sand at the sixth and then water at the next for two bogeys which set in motion a seven-shot swing in 10 holes. Montgomerie bogeyed three holes in a row from the 13th and when Parnevik holed from four feet at the 14th, he could start thinking about getting out the cigar.

"For the first five holes, I was very good," Montgomerie said after his 71. "For the last 13, I was embarrassingly bad. I left the door wide open for Jesper and he walked straight through. But all credit to him. The start I gave him would have finished off most people, but not him."

Parnevik completed rounds of 66, 69, 66 and 67 for a 12-under score of 268. "I was just trying to hang on for the first five holes," Parnevik said. "It did not look like he was going to make a mistake. But winning is a nice way to end my season. Playing on both the European and U.S. Tours for the last three years has been very tough and I need a rest."

Since he cannot commit to playing 11 events in Europe, Parnevik is not a full member of the PGA European Tour and, after a new rule change, cannot earn Ryder Cup points in the qualifying process, although he may be picked as a wild card. Montgomerie was adamant when he said, "We cannot go to Valderrama, cannot go to Valderrama next year without him. He is definitely among the top 12 players in Europe."

Loch Lomond World Invitational—£750,000
Winner: Thomas Bjorn

The Loch Lomond World Invitational provided a new tournament, a new venue — the highly praised Tom Weiskopf-designed Loch Lomond — a new winner and a new country that can claim success on the PGA European Tour.

While the likes of Colin Montgomerie, Ian Woosnam and Nick Faldo failed to make an impression on the final day, Thomas Bjorn, 25, became the first player from Denmark to win and the 13th first-timer of the year. As a four-time winner on the European Challenge Tour in 1995, when he topped the junior circuit's money list, his pedigree was not in doubt.

Bjorn, who started the final round tied with France's Jean Van de Velde, received a good luck note from Danish soccer star, Brian Laudrup, who plays for the Glasgow Rangers, on the Sunday morning. "It made me feel really good," Bjorn said. "I went out there and felt like a winner."

Birdies at the 14th and 15th holes allowed Bjorn to break free from the Frenchman, who had shot 65 on Friday, although the ultimate difference was only one shot. The consistent Bjorn shot 70, 69, 68 and 70 for an 11-under-par 277 total. Robert Allenby was third, four strokes behind Bjorn, but fell and twisted his ankle as he was leaving the course.

Having led the Scandinavian Masters for three rounds, Bjorn was determined not to fade on the last day as he had then. "I said that if I got into the same position, I'd make sure I would not let it slip," Bjorn said. "But I've got to admit that even though I thought I could win, I expected it to be in a smaller event. This is big and I beat some of the best players in the world. The tournament is going to be one of the best in the world, too."

Smurfit European Open—£750,000
Winner: Per-Ulrik Johansson

It had not been a good season for Per-Ulrik Johansson. The Swedish Ryder Cup player had finished fourth in the Alamo English Open and eighth in the U.S. PGA Championship, but otherwise he was used to finishing anywhere but in the top 10.

Having missed the cut in his previous two tournaments, Johansson had almost decided to go home to Marbella, on Spain's Costa del Sol, and set about a practice regime that would see him restored to form for 1997. Instead, he entered the Smurfit European Open at the K Club, just outside Dublin, Ireland, and won.

To do so, he needed to birdie the last two holes to go from one behind Costantino Rocca to one ahead. He hit a nine iron to 10 feet at the par-three 17th and then two-putted from 40 feet at the par-five 18th. Rocca came to the 18th needing a birdie to tie, but drove into the rough and had to lay up with his second shot. He pitched to 15 feet but could not hole the putt.

"I almost did not come here because my game was so bad," Johansson said after collecting this third career title. "It was the same with the Czech Open in 1994. When I came here, I did not expect to make the cut. It is tough, this sport. Sometimes you feel you want to go home and do something else.

"But I wanted to win so badly to get to the Volvo Masters. I have not missed the tournament since I turned pro in 1991 and I didn't see why I should miss out this time. At the start of the week, I thought I needed another £60,000 from the last three events to get there."

Roger Chapman, who played the back nine in 13 under par for the week, came home in 31 to share third place with Andrew Coltart. Colin Montgomerie, although only making the cut with a birdie at the 18th in the second round, again just shaded Ian Woosnam to extend his lead at the top of the money list. And a sixth place by Thomas Bjorn brought him into contention with Padraig Harrington and Raymond Russell for the rookie honors.

Linde German Masters—£650,000
Winner: Darren Clarke

The important action on Sunday led to Darren Clarke winning his second PGA European Tour title three years after his first. But an incident on Friday was equally significant. After scoring a second-round 75, Ian Woosnam missed the cut. "It is all over now. I can go home," the Welshman said. It meant that Colin Montgomerie had only to finish in the top 40 to win the European money title for the fourth consecutive year. Two rounds of 65 over the weekend gave Montgomerie a fourth-place finish and, although three strokes behind Clarke, Montgomerie was pleased, too. He had matched Peter Oosterhuis' record of winning the Vardon Trophy four years in a row.

Montgomerie did so with a five-week spell dating back to his victory at the Canon European Masters. First, he overcame Woosnam's advantage and then made it impossible for the Welshman, whose troublesome back did not allow him to sustain his challenge, to catch Montgomerie even by winning the last event, the Volvo Masters.

"My golf over the last five weeks has been decisive," Montgomerie said. "It's been hard. I've been playing two tournaments each week, one against Woosie and one against everyone else. I won't be celebrating until it is done and dusted at Valderrama, but it is nice to be able to enjoy the last few weeks of the season. Getting to seven figures for the season is definitely on and that's my new goal."

Clarke also had his sights on Valderrama, but for the 1997 Ryder Cup. Having won £108,330, he was secure in the top 10 of the European money list, which brings such exemptions as to the U.S. Open. "More important than the money are the Ryder Cup points," said the Northern Irishman. "I've set my heart on making the team next year."

Clarke closed with a final-round 63, going to the turn in 30, including holing a pitching wedge at the fourth for an eagle two. He then holed from 25 feet at the 17th hole on the Motzener See course to give himself a two-shot advantage. That was finally cut to one by Mark Davis, who shot a career-best 62 to finish second.

Alfred Dunhill Cup—£1,000,000
Winners: United States

See Chapter 8.

Oki Pro-Am—£447,000
Winner: Tom Kite

While Mark O'Meara, Steve Stricker and Phil Mickelson were winning the Alfred Dunhill Cup at St. Andrews, Tom Kite made it an American double by claiming the new Oki Pro-Am in Madrid. Kite had not visited Spain since 1970, but will return in 1997 as captain of the U.S. Ryder Cup team. Although Angel Cabrera did his best to get in the way, Kite battled his opposite number Seve Ballesteros and both showed welcome signs of regaining their games.

For Kite, 46, it was his first victory for three years. The highlight was his third-round 64, during which he chipped in five times, and he closed with 70 to finish one shot ahead of Cabrera, the Argentinean who recorded his best finish in Europe.

"No matter how good you have been," Kite said, "when you haven't won for a while the doubts set in. There's a point when you realize the time is coming when your last win really was your last win. The fact that Seve and I both played well here indicates that we both want to make the Ryder Cup as playing captains. This has given me the impetus. I've been looking forward to going on and trying to make the team as a player."

Ballesteros, who holed two pitch shots on the third day, shot a final-round 69, equalling the best score of the day, to finish third, his best finish of the season, three strokes behind Kite's 15-under-par 273 total.

As the last full-field event of the European season, the event decided who regained their Tour cards for 1997; Klas Eriksson, by finishing fifth, was the biggest beneficiary as he earned £18,943 and moved up into the top 117 on the money list by £5,000. Countryman Niclas Fasth's 11th-place finish meant he missed out by one place, while New Zealand's Michael Campbell, who gave up a place in the Alfred Dunhill Cup to try to earn his card, finished 35th with a last-round 76 to be 120th on the money list.

Toyota World Match Play—£650,000
Winner: Ernie Els

See Chapter 9.

Open Novotel Perrier—£350,000
Winners: Jonathan Lomas and Steven Bottomley

After four days and four different formats, four players (in two teams) came down the last hole at the Golf du Medoc course in Bordeaux tied for the lead in the Open Novotel Perrier. In a thrilling finale to the PGA European Tour's unofficial team championship, Derrick Cooper three-putted the 18th hole to leave himself and partner Richard Boxall one stroke behind Jonathan Lomas and Steven Bottomley's 23-under-par total of 332.

Lomas and Bottomley had opened with a better-ball score of 63, three strokes behind first-day leaders Christian Cevaer and Antoine Lebouc, and then moved into the lead with a foursomes score of 62 on the second day. A 68 in the greensomes left Lomas and Bottomley two ahead of Boxall and Cooper, former winners of the Sunningdale Foursomes, going into the last day when both players on each team played their own ball.

That meant a rapidly changing scoreboard during the final round. Although Lomas and Bottomley were five strokes ahead after the second hole, the two teams were tied after 12 holes. Bottomley followed in Boxall's birdie putt at the 15th and got up and down at a bunker to ensure his team was tied going to the 18th.

"It was tight all the way," Bottomley said. "Richard and Derrick made it tough for us."

Volvo Masters—£900,000
Winner: Mark McNulty

The last staging of the Volvo Masters at Valderrama prior to the 1997 Ryder Cup brought victory for Mark McNulty. The Zimbabwean was in a class of his own and his seven-stroke margin was fully deserved on the strongest test of golf on the PGA European Tour.

After 36 holes, McNulty was four strokes behind leader Paul Curry. But Valderrama can destroy any golf game which is just a fraction off and Curry fell to 81 on the third day. That was when McNulty took a four-shot lead with a bogey-free 67. "Any time you do not have a bogey in a round at Valderrama, you have played great golf," he said.

On the final day, McNulty was never troubled. A closing 68 gave him an eight-under total of 276. Four players shared second place at 283 — Jose Coceres, Sam Torrance, Wayne Westner and Lee Westwood. Once McNulty had hit a seven iron to eight feet at the par-three third hole, and holed the putt, he was off and running. Two birdies at the 10th and 11th meant he could slip into cruise control, and he polished off the performance by holing from 20 feet for a birdie at the 18th.

"I'm very pleased to have only one bogey in the last two rounds," McNulty said. "It shows my course management was in good shape. In nine years of coming to Valderrama, I always felt that I would be able to sneak a win. During my practice round, I said to my caddie, Basil, that this could be my best chance. I was in a good frame of mind. This course presents a good examination paper. You can get guys moaning here, because if you are slightly off in your game and you get out of position, you are struggling to make par. It can be very frustrating."

McNulty's £150,000 first prize was supplemented by a bonus of £39,000 for finishing fifth on the money list. The rules stipulate that a player must compete in the Volvo Masters to receive a bonus, which counts as official money, for finishing in the top 15 on the money list. This led to Robert Allenby playing just one shot — a three wood with minimal backlift which went 40 yards — in an attempt to maintain his third place on the money list. He had a fractured sternum from a car crash a month before and was not well enough to complete the tournament.

Challenge Tour

Ian Garbutt was 12th on the European Challenge Tour money list when he teed off in the UAP Grand Final at Quinta do Peru, near Lisbon. The 24-year-old from Yorkshire was not quite satisfied with his season. "It would be nice to say goodbye to the Challenge Tour with a big win," Garbutt said.

That is just what Garbutt did, as he won the final event of the year by two strokes over fellow Englishman Vanslow Phillips and Denmark's Ben Tinning. And what's more, his £10,880 first prize took him to the top of the money list with £37,661, overtaking leader Dennis Edlund of Sweden.

The former English Amateur champion, who played for a year on the PGA European Tour after turning professional before dropping back to the Challenge Tour, started the final round tied with Phillips and they were still tied with two holes to play. Then Garbutt birdied the short 17th and Phillips, trying to force a playoff, three-putted at the 18th. "I've enjoyed my two years on the Challenge Tour and it is a big thrill to win such a big tournament and be No. 1 on the ranking," Garbutt said.

The Challenge Tour has grown in stature as its graduates have found success on the PGA European Tour. Eight of the 10 graduates from 1994 retained their cards on the major circuit the following year, and though only four of the 1995 graduates did so in 1996, Thomas Bjorn, Garbutt's predecessor as No. 1, did win the Loch Lomond World Invitational and Diego Borrego won the Turespana Masters Open.

To reflect the Challenge Tour's importance as a training ground, the top 15 spots on the money list were given player's cards for the 1997 PGA European Tour. They included Garbutt and three two-time winners, Edlund, Swede Adam Mednick and Ignacio Feliu of Spain. Phillips, a former Great Britain and Ireland Walker Cup player, also qualified, as did New Zealander Stephen Scahill, who finished tied for fourth in the UAP Grand Final to jump into the top 15. The other graduates were Robert Lee, Andrew Sandywell, Massimo Florioli, Fredrik Jacobsen, Joakim Rask, John Mellor, Carl Watts, Marten Olander and Kalle Vainola.

Those 15 include six Englishmen, five Swedes, an Italian, a Spaniard, a Kiwi and a Finn. Running from the Kenyan Open in February to the final event in Portugal in October, the Challenge Tour covered 45 tournaments, with 42 winners, in 18 countries. For the first time it included a Russian Open at the Moscow Country Club and a Polish Open in Warsaw.

12. Asia/Japan Tours

Masashi (Jumbo) Ozaki was approaching age 50. Hong Chia-Yuh was barely 22. Both had unprecedented achievements in 1996 during the busiest golf season ever in Asia, where the game continues its booming growth.

Their accomplishments begged questions. In Ozaki's case: How long can this remarkable player continue to dominate the Japan PGA Tour and stand out as one of the leading performers in the world? The question regarding Hong: From a single overwhelming but little-noticed victory among the plethora of tournaments all over the Pacific Rim, do we sense the coming of a new young star?

The only knock against Ozaki and his awesome record has been his failure to win when he ventures abroad, but one can only admire what he did in Japan in 1996. Winning far more than anyone else on a single tour, Ozaki piled up the equivalent of $1.9 million in just 17 starts on the Japan PGA Tour. He won eight tournaments.

Again, though, Ozaki fared poorly when he traveled to America. He missed cuts badly at the Masters and PGA Championship, tied for 29th place in The Players Championship, and tied for 67th place in the U.S. Open.

Ozaki's home tour victories, which came in such important tournaments as the Dunlop Phoenix, Japan PGA Championship, Chunichi Crowns and Japan Series, in which he was 26 under par, one off the world's record, ran his overall total over 100 victories, including his lone overseas win in 1972 in New Zealand.

Questionable records-keeping in Japan in earlier years makes this difficult to verify. Since a number of these victories were in regional and not in scheduled 72-hole events, his official total in Japan is considered to be 82 titles, still unprecedented on any of the world's tours.

So is what Hong Chia-Yuh did in Taiwan in October in the Chinfon Chinese Taipei Open. The 22-year-old amateur won the full-field tournament on the Asia Tour by 12 strokes. An amateur victory on the professional circuits has always been rare, but no one can recall a time in modern golf history when an amateur did it twice. Hong won the same tournament when he was a 20-year-old college student in Taipei. Of course, it remains to be seen if Hong elects to turn professional and pursue a career on the world scene.

Ozaki, who has won 20 tournaments in the last three years in Japan, was so monopolistic in 1996 that his earnings were nearly double those of runner-up Yoshinori Kaneko, who won three times during the first four months of the Japanese season but did not do much the rest of the year. The circuit had just five multiple victors — Hajime Meshiai, Masanobu Kimura, Kazuhiko Hosokawa, Kaneko and Ozaki — and only the latter two won more than twice.

Overseas players took eight titles, most notably American journeyman Peter Teravainen the Japan Open Championship and U.S. Tour winner Paul Stankowski the rich, late-season Casio World Open. Satoshi Higashi, the 1995 runner-up in earnings and four-time winner, was rarely heard from in 1996.

The other tours in Asia continued to shift like desert sand. The venerable

Asia Tour remained aloof of the upstart and growing Omega Tour and the less-extensive Australasian Tour, who reached a basic accord during the year.

The Omega circuit, a more commercial entity than the Asia Tour and supported by PGAs from most of the Far East's golfing nations, had 23 tournaments in 1996 for its mostly Asian — by intent and structure — entourage of professionals. The first three completed its 1995-1996 season in January as Taiwan's Lin Keng-Chi clinched the money title. Wook-Soon Kang of Korea, one of only two men to win twice during the 19 events that made up the Omega Tour's full second season in 1996, took the second title.

Of note, Australian star Steve Elkington came in for one tournament and won the Honda City Invitational in Thailand, his only victory in 1996. By contrast, total prize money on that circuit was $7 million and, by comparison to Ozaki's huge winnings, Kang easily headed the Omega money list with $173,056.

Although others with adequate credentials can and some do play on the new tour, only five non-Asians earned playing privileges at the pre-season qualifying tournament, so professionals from the nations of the Far East scored the majority of the victories and took five of the top 10 spots on the final money list.

On the other hand, the Asia Tour continued to be a haven and training ground for many players from other parts of the world. Only seven Asians, including Hong in Taiwan and Kaneko in the Kirin Open at Tokyo that doubles as an Asia and Japan PGA Tour event, scored victories in the 14 tournaments that comprised the completion of the 1995-1996 and start of the 1996-1997 seasons.

Four Americans — Steve Flesch, Todd Barranger, Christian Pena and veteran Mike Cunning — were among the 12 different first-time winners, along with Manny Zerman, the U.S. collegian from South Africa who was twice a U.S. Amateur runner-up. However, the overall money title and its prized exemption onto the Japan PGA Tour, went to Canadian Rick Todd, whose closest brush with victory came in his playoff loss in the Matoa International.

Asia Tour

Benson & Hedges Malaysian Open—US$300,000
Winner: Steve Flesch

American Steve Flesch launched the 1996 continuation of the Asia Tour season in exciting fashion, going two extra holes before capturing the Benson & Hedges Malaysian Open at Templer Park Country Club in Kuala Lumpur. His victim was Craig Jones of Australia. They tied with six-under-par 282s to force the playoff.

Flesch had opened the tournament with 66, the lowest round of the week, as it turned out, but led countryman Christian Pena by just one stroke. Yet another American, Lee Porter, went in front Friday with 72-68–140 as Flesch and Pena took 75s. Porter shared the lead at 210 Saturday with Pena. At that point, Flesch was at 212, Jones at 213, and they pushed past the others Sunday, Flesch with 70 and Jones with 69, although Northern Ireland's Darren Clarke, who started at 211, had a three-stroke lead on the first nine before taking a double bogey at the ninth. He missed the playoff by one stroke.

Flesch took the title when he holed an eight-foot par putt on the second extra hole as Jones three-putted for bogey.

Mitsubishi Manila Southwoods Open—US$250,000
Winner: Manny Zerman

Internationalist Manny Zerman, a man with significant ties to Italy (nationality), South Africa (residence) and the United States (college), went to the Philippines to acquire his first professional title. The 26-year-old Zerman, an All-American golfer at the University of Arizona who twice was runner-up in the U.S. Amateur, won the Mitsubishi Manila Southwoods Open, second stop on the 1996 Asia Tour when he prevailed in a three-man playoff that ended on a rather bizarre note at Manila Southwoods Golf and Country Club.

Zerman and the other two playoff participants — Canadian Jim Rutledge and American Don Walsworth — all made up considerable ground in the wind-blown final round when 70 was the best score of the day. Five behind Carlos Larrain of Venezuela and Todd Hamilton, the former Asia Tour champion and successful campaigner on the upper-scale Japan PGA Tour, who led with 217s, Rutledge shot one of the two 70s, while Zerman and Walsworth had 71s to post four-over-par 292s and bring about the playoff.

Walsworth went out when he bogeyed the first hole, missing a two-footer, and Zerman, who made an eight-foot par putt at the 18th to join the playoff, won with a regulation par at the next hole when Rutledge drove into the heavy rough and had to take a "lost ball" penalty when the ball couldn't be found in the five-minute search.

Thai Airways International Thailand Open—US$300,000
Winner: Todd Barranger

The precedent was there and Todd Barranger followed it to victory in the Thai Airways International Thailand Open. Americans have always fared well in Thailand. Brandt Jobe and Todd Hamilton — two who have enjoyed considerable success in Asia — won the tournament the two preceding years.

Barranger, a Knoxville, Tennessee, resident who had poor fortune in his 1994 season in the United States and his 1995 campaign in Asia, made it three in a row for America with a runaway triumph at Sriracha International Golf Club near Pattaya, recording a 17-under-par 271 total for a five-stroke victory.

Barranger broke it open in the third round after his 69-69 start gave him a share of the halfway lead with Korean Yong-Jin Shin. He moved three strokes in front with a bogey-free 65 Saturday and widened it to the final five shots with 68 Sunday. American left-hander Rob Moss, a strong contender the previous week in the Philippines, closed with 69 for 276 and second place, two in front of a five-man logjam at 278 for third, that group including Shin, Hamilton and Jim Rutledge, a playoff loser at Southwoods. In a week, Barranger improved 36 strokes.

Classic India Open—US$300,000
Winner: Hidezumi Shirakata

Other than in the season-ending tournament in their homeland, Japanese golfers have made little impact on the Asia Tour in recent years. No Japanese pro had posted a victory on the circuit outside of Japan in 10 years when Hidezumi Shirakata achieved that accomplishment in the Classic India Open at Royal Calcutta Golf Club in mid-February.

The 29-year-old Shirakata, who had never won outside of Japan, became the fourth consecutive player to land an Asia Tour title for the first time with his three-stroke victory. He was 11 under par at 277. The last previous Japanese winner overseas on the Asia Tour was Seiichi Kanai at Hong Kong in 1986, and the India Open had not had a Japanese champion since Junichi Takahashi in 1981.

Shirakata was in the thick of things from the start. He shared the first-round lead at 66 with India's Firoz Ali and was just a stroke back of Basad Ali and American Bob Mattiace after his second-round 72 for 138. Shirakata jumped three strokes in front with a 69 Saturday for 207.

Daniel Chopra, the talented, India-born pro from Sweden who was headed for a season on the European Tour, moved into second place at 210 and, playing in the final threesome with Shirakata, provided the only real challenge Sunday. He got within two shots at the 11th hole, but Shirakata established his three-stroke lead with a 15-foot birdie putt at the 16th and finished with 70 and that margin over Chopra, Basad Ali and Jyoti Randhawa, also of India.

Matoa International Invitational—US$250,000
Winner: Christian Pena

Christian Pena became the third American winner on the 1996 Asia Tour when he defeated Canadian Rick Todd, the eventual season champion, in a playoff in the Matoa International Invitational when the circuit made a two-week stop in Indonesia in early March. The Matoa International replaced the cancelled Sempati Bali Open on the schedule and was played opposite the Sabah Masters in Malaysia on the Omega Tour.

A host of players jammed the top of the standings for two days, with Todd and Olle Nordberg of Sweden emerging as one-stroke leaders after Friday's round with 136s. Todd remained on top with 68 for 204 Saturday but was joined by Todd Barranger, the Thailand Open winner. Pena shot 68 Saturday and, along with Nordberg, trailed by two going into the final round. He caught Todd Sunday when he had 69 to Todd's 71, forcing the playoff. Barranger (72), Nordberg (70) and American Dennis Paulson, who shot 64, missed the playoff by one shot.

Indonesia Open—US$250,000
Winner: Edward Fryatt

Another first occurred on the Asia Tour when Edward Fryatt landed the Indonesia Open title. Fryatt, an Englishman who honed his golfing skills in America at the University of Nevada-Las Vegas, became the tournament's first winner from the British Isles. He led most of the way and won with a 271 total, 17 under par, at Jagorawi Golf and Country Club in West Java.

Fryatt broke the course record with his second-round 65 for 132, 12 under par, which propelled him to a four-stroke lead over Australia's Anthony Painter. Fryatt added 68 Saturday and doubled his lead to six, then over Daniel Chopra. His 71 Sunday never left him in serious trouble, although Chopra, the India Open runner-up, cut the lead in half with 68 and Canadian Jim Rutledge, the Southwoods playoff loser, joined him at 274 when he broke the three-day-old course record with 64.

Rolex Masters–Singapore—US$262,500
Winner: Mike Cunning

A long vigil ended in Singapore for 37-year-old Mike Cunning, an American journeyman who had campaigned in the Far East for a decade without achieving a victory. Cunning, who had played briefly and inconspicuously on the PGA Tour in America in years past, experienced great satisfaction when he birdied the 71st hole of the Rolex Masters–Singapore and parred the 72nd to register a one-stroke victory with a nine-under-par 204 total on the Bukit course at Singapore Island Country Club. "This ends 15 frustrating years of waiting," said Cunning, a frequent runner-up in Asian events in earlier years.

Cunning headed toward the victory with a sparkling, seven-under-par 64 in Friday's second round, advancing into a first-place tie with fellow American Greg Lesher at 135. Heavy rains forced cancellation of the Saturday round. Singapore-based Peter Teravainen and Don Walsworth set out in hot pursuit Sunday and appeared to have at least playoff chances when they both finished at 205, but Cunning birdied the short 17th to go nine under par and he parred the 18th to insure the long-sought victory. Teravainen, who taken a good run in the Singapore Open four months earlier, missed a birdie putt from six feet at the last hole that would have put him in a playoff against Cunning.

UBX Philippine Open—US$300,000
Winner: Rob Whitlock

Asia's oldest golf tournament had one of its most dramatic finishes amid a bit of nationalistic controversy when the Asia Tour returned to the Manila Southwoods Golf and Country Club for the second time in 1996. Australian Rob Whitlock, who came within minutes of not even being on hand Sunday, captured the venerable UBX Philippine Open in a tense, three-hole playoff against American Tim Straub.

The 29-year-old Straub, playing in Asia for the first time, took a three-stroke lead over Whitlock into the final round, but slipped to 73 Sunday for 278, missing a short putt at the final green. The Aussie, who became the first Australian winner of the Philippine Open since Hall of Famer Peter Thomson in 1964, shot 70. Straub had taken the lead at 205 Saturday after Brian Wilson, in front after 36 holes with 136 following a second-round 63, faded with 74.

Whitlock, traveling to the course by taxi that became imbedded in highway traffic, barely made his tee time Saturday, but still shot 69. The two were still even after a two-hole playoff and went to a third hole before Straub missed a needed three-foot par putt. Manny Zerman, who won the Mitsubishi Manila Southwoods Open two months earlier, finished 11th.

Maekyung LG Fashion Open—US$400,000
Winner: Nam-Sin Park

Nam-Sin Park accomplished a 1996 first on the Asia Tour when he won the Maekyung LG Fashion Open, the national championship of Korea, in mid-April at Nam Seoul Country Club in the capital city. He was the first and only player all season to capture a tournament title on the circuit for a second time when he rolled to a five-stroke victory three years after landing his country's championship for the first time.

Scores were unusually high the first two days at Nam Seoul, but Park still had a lot of ground to make up when he started with a pair of three-over-par 75s. Rick Todd and Canadian Clay Devers led the first day with 70s and Devers edged a stroke ahead of Todd Friday with 74–144. Park made his big move Saturday when he drilled a 67 that boosted him into a three-way tie for first place with Rob Moss and Chul-Sang Cho at 217. Then he broke it wide open Sunday.

With 67, Park had no serious challenges, breezing to the five-stroke victory over Moss and countryman Sung-Ho Kim. He shot 68 for a 285 total and was the only player under par at the end. Moss and Sung-Ho Kim tied for second at 290. Todd, who had skied to 75 and 77 in the middle rounds, bounced back with 69 Sunday to take fourth place at 291 and the lead on the money list.

(Editor's note: The Kirin Open, final Asia Tour event of the 1995-96 season, is included in the Japan PGA Tour section of this chapter. It notes that Rick Todd became the Asia Tour champion there.)

Elord Cup–Korea Open—US$400,000
Winner: Kyung-Joo Choi

The Asia Tour launched its 1996-1997 season in September with two tournaments in Seoul, Korea, although both were designated as "specially approved events" that would not be considered for the money list.

The Elord Cup–Korea Open went to Kyung-Joo Choi, who scored a one-stroke victory at Han Young Country Club in a final-round battle against countryman Jong-Duck Kim. Choi had entered the Sunday finale at 211, one stroke ahead of Kim, Gerry Norquist and John Senden. He and Kim moved ahead of the rest and both wound up shooting 68s, Choi's giving him a seven-under-par 279 total. Jeev Milkha Singh closed with 67 to take third place, his 284 four strokes behind Kim.

Shinhan Donghae Open—US$400,000
Winner: Chung Joon

The home professionals monopolized the top of the standings in the next week's Shinhan Donghae Open at Jaeil Country Club. The victory went to Chung Joon, who shot Sunday's best score — 66 — to win by one stroke with his 11-under-par 277 total. Once again, Jong-Duck Kim came up one shot shy, finishing in second place for the second week in a row.

Kim, one of four 66 shooters in the opening round, moved into a two-stroke lead Friday with his 70–136, then widened it to three Saturday with 69–205. At that point, Chung Joon trailed by six and was behind eight other players. Kim could manage only 73 Sunday to lose by one stroke with his 278.

Chinfon Chinese Taipei Open—US$275,000
Winner: Hong Chia-Yuh

Because it proceeds in relative obscurity from an international standpoint, the Asia Tour showcased its own version of Tiger Woods almost without notice in the opening event on the 1996-1997 circuit schedule — the Chinfon Chinese Taipei Open.

Amateur Hong Chia-Yuh, who won Taiwan's national championship, a 30-year fixture on the Asia Tour, in 1994 while still a 20-year-old college student in Taipei, repeated the feat in overwhelming fashion in October, the same time as Woods was dominating golf headlines with his brilliance in America.

Hong vastly altered the record book when he romped to a 12-stroke victory at Ton Hwa Golf Club with his 10-under-par 278 total. With this unprecedented performance, the 22-year-old amateur won by the biggest margin in the 35-year history of the circuit and, just the fifth amateur winner in Asia Tour history, the first to beat the professionals twice.

Another amateur — Su Chin-Jung — led the first day at Ton Hwa with 68. Then Hong, with 70-68–138, moved into a 36-hole tie for the lead with Japan's Hidezumi Shirakata, the India Open champion earlier in the year. Even with bogeys on two of the last four holes, Hong fashioned a 71 Saturday and his 209 gave him a five-stroke margin over New Zealand's Stuart Holmes. The only hitch in his title run Sunday was a double bogey at the sixth hole and Hong covered that slip with a subsequent eagle and three birdies for 69 that ballooned the final edge to 12 over Holmes and countryman Yu Chin-Han.

Johnnie Walker Super Tour—US$350,000
Winner: Ernie Els

The most unusual and far-flung of all the world's special events was the Johnnie Walker Super Tour, played over four Asian countries in six days in early November, featuring four international stars and four professionals from the region. Ernie Els won in a one-hole playoff against Ian Woosnam after they tied with 274 totals, 14 under par. Woosnam shot a final-round 63 to catch Els, who finished with 65. Colin Montgomerie placed third, six strokes behind. The venues were in Taiwan, Korea, the Philippines and Thailand, with the contestants travelling on a chartered jet.

Andersen Consulting Hong Kong Open—US$350,000
Winner: Rodrigo Cuello

Rodrigo Cuello of the Philippines had established his credibility with several respectable showings on the Omega Tour, but his decisive victory in December in the Andersen Consulting Hong Kong Open still came as a surprise to most observers. This was particularly true because an Asian had not won at Royal Hong Kong since Hsieh Chin-Sheng in 1988 and the tournament had a fairly large complement of international players over and above those who campaign regularly in Asia.

The 36-year-old Cuello, who had never won outside of the Philippines, was unflappable after taking a one-stroke lead over Americans Brandel Chamblee and Don Walsworth, the first-round leader (66) with his 36-hole 68-70—138. When Cuello followed with 67 Saturday, he moved three strokes ahead of Walsworth, and his closing par 70 over Royal Hong Kong's Composite course created his four-stroke victory margin at five-under-par 275. American star Scott Hoch and Britain's Bill Longmuir both closed with 67s and shared the 279 runner-up slot.

China Tour

As in its inaugural year, the Volvo China Tour produced an international cast of winners to go with the country's No. 1 player in its second season. Zhang Lian-Wei, who won the 1995 Volvo Open which launched the circuit, captured the 1996 Blue Ribbon Open, the third event on the four-tournament, 12-day tour of 36-hole events that preceded the Volvo China Open.

The other three titles were claimed by Scotsman John Wither (Coca-Cola Open), Australian Glenn Joyner (Volvo Open) and Malaysian Ali Kadir (Hugo

Boss Open). A Scotsman, an Aussie and an Ecuadorean joined Zhang in the winner's circle in 1995.

Joyner sank a 10-foot birdie putt on the final green for 70-68–138 and a one-stroke victory over Wither in the opening Volvo Open at Shenzhen Golf Club. The entourage then moved to another Shenzhen club — Mission Hills — for the Coca Cola Open three days later. Wither jumped one shot in front of American Greg Hanrahan with an opening 65, but needed a late rally to defeat him in the final round. He birdied the 17th hole and finished with 69 for 134, 10 under par, and a three-stroke win over Hanrahan.

It was Zhang Lian-Wei's turn when the circuit traveled to the Guangz-hou area for the other two tournaments. Zhang shot a course-record 67 the first day at the Zhaoqing Resort and Golf Club and followed with a par 73 in intense heat over the 7,206-yard layout designed by Gary Player. The 140 total gave him a three-stroke victory over seven players.

Rain stretched the Hugo Boss Open to three days, but the interruption didn't seem to bother Ali Kadir. The Malaysian pro took the first-round lead with a course-record 66 at the par-72 Luhu Golf Club and was still in front after 11 holes when play was halted for the day because of course flooding. Kadir racked up two more birdies when he finished the round Sunday and his 70 for 136 gave him a three-stroke victory.

Japan Tour

Token Corporation Cup—¥100,000,000
Winner: Yoshinori Kaneko

Yoshinori Kaneko broke a four-year drought on the Japan PGA Tour in stirring fashion in the season-opening Token Corporation Cup, coming from four strokes off the pace to edge America's Brandt Jobe by one shot with his 13-under-par 275 total. The 35-year-old Kaneko rang up eight birdies en route to his winning 65, picking up his third career title and first since the 1992 Munsingwear Descente Classic.

Jobe, a four-time winner on the Asia and Japan circuits in 1995, led Zaw Moe by two strokes after 54 holes at Kedoin Golf Club with 69-70-67–206, trying to become the third straight foreign winner of the Token Cup. But Jobe managed birdies only on the par-five first and 18th holes and fell one stroke short with his 70. Australian Peter Senior, the 1995 Token runner-up, shared the 36-hole lead at 137 with David Ishii, but both fell away over the weekend.

Daido Drinko Shizuoka Open—¥75,000,000
Winner: Yoshikazu Sakamoto

After 13 years, Yoshikazu Sakamoto would take a victory no matter how he could get it, but he never expected it to come under such unusual circumstances as it did in the Daido Drinko Shizuoka Open. Poised for a final-round battle against veteran Nobuo Serizawa and Paraguay's Carlos Franco, Sakamoto instead went against the two in a playoff on a drenched Hamaoka course at Shizuoka when torrential rains, which had interrupted the second round, forced cancellation of Sunday's round.

Rain continued as the three men, who had shared the lead Saturday night at 211, played Hamaoka's 18th as the first playoff hole. Serizawa's approach from a fairway bunker struck a tree and bounced out of bounds. Sakamoto and Franco took three to get on the green at the short par-four hole, but the 35-year-old Sakamoto pitched to three feet and holed it for par and the win after Franco missed from eight feet. Franco had shared the first-round lead with Hideki Kase at 68 and was in a second-place tie at 140 with Serizawa and Kase, a stroke behind Eduardo Herrera, after the rain-interrupted second round.

Novell KSB Open—¥70,000,000
Winner: Toru Suzuki

For the third week in a row, an experienced Japanese golfer kept the strong foreign contingent at bay on the Japan PGA Tour. Colombia's Eduardo Herrera, making a strong run for the second straight week, succumbed to a final-round charge of Toru Suzuki in the Novel KSB Open at Kinojo Golf Club at Soja. The 29-year-old Suzuki birdied the last two holes for a five-under-par 67 and a one-stroke victory over Herrera and American Brian Watts, a six-time winner in Japan. It was Suzuki's fourth win on the Japan PGA Tour. He was 13 under par at 275.

Another overseas pro, Stewart Ginn of Australia, was in front the first day with 67 and shared the midway lead at 137 with Herrera, Watts, Masanobu Kimura and Shintaro Iizuka. The South American moved a stroke ahead with a 69–206 Saturday. Shinichi Yokota was at 207 and Suzuki, with rounds of 68, 72 and 68, was in position for his Sunday move. Herrera led by four after nine holes, but a bogey at the par-three 15th, his only one of the last two rounds, proved the difference.

Descente Classic—¥100,000,000
Winner: Masanobu Kimura

Masanobu Kimura, taking his cue from the season-opening performance of Yoshinori Kaneko, who had gone through a dry spell of equal length, scored his first Japan PGA Tour victory in four years at Edosaki Country Club in the Descente Classic. Outfighting Hideyuki Sato Sunday, Kimura posted 69 for an 11-under-par 273 total and a two-stroke victory. It was the fourth straight win for a Japanese pro at the start of the season, a rarity in recent years.

Kimura, the only player in the Descente to break 70 all four days, surged into contention Friday, shooting 66 and taking a share of third place with Keiichiro Fukabori and Akio Nishizawa at 135, two behind Sato, the leader. A 69 Saturday moved Kimura into a first-place tie at 204 with Sato, who shot 71. Kimura climbed two strokes in front on the outgoing nine Sunday, then hung on despite two bogeys until Sato absorbed a double bogey at the 16th after going a stroke ahead with a birdie on the preceding hole.

Tsuruya Open—¥100,000,000
Winner: Peter McWhinney

Peter McWhinney had been campaigning in Japan with little success since 1992 and with no victories anywhere since 1983 in his native Australia. Abruptly, he ended the frustration in the Tsuruya Open at the Sport Shinko Country Club's Yamanohara course in Hyogo in a stretch duel with Peter Senior, his more-accomplished countryman. McWhinney holed from a greenside bunker at the 71st hole for an eagle, gaining a one-stroke lead which he protected with a final par for a 66–276 total and the one-shot triumph over Senior.

Senior was the first-round leader with 67, then veteran Katsunari Takahashi took over for two days with 138 and 208, at which point he led McWhinney and Senior by two strokes. The victory had an added bonus for McWhinney, assuring him entry as a tournament winner into the circuit's richest events later in the season.

Kirin Open—¥100,000,000
Winner: Yoshinori Kaneko

A new sponsor took over an old tournament on the Japan PGA Tour that has long served jointly as the concluding event on the traditional Asia Tour and Yoshinori Kaneko became the first winner under the Kirin Open banner. With that victory, Kaneko also became the first double winner of the 1996 season and took over first place on the Japan money list.

Kaneko's win was quite similar in style to his opening-week triumph in the Token Corporation Cup. Again he staged a final-round rally, this time at Ibaraki Golf Club's East course from three strokes to the rear of third-round leader Shigeki Maruyama. He shot 70 with six birdies for his 10-under-par 278, just enough to edge Tsuneyuki (Tommy) Nakajima and Nobuo Serizawa by a stroke. Maruyama faltered with 75 and tied for fourth place.

Canadian Rick Todd won the Asia money list title and its 12-month exemption benefit for the Japan circuit in rather undistinguished fashion. He missed the cut at Ibaraki, but his point lead going into the Kirin Open held up when no one else from the Asia Tour performed well that week. Todd captured the title even though he didn't win any of the circuit's 13 events.

Chunichi Crowns—¥120,000,000
Winner: Masashi Ozaki

While the cat's away, the mice will play. The cat — Masashi (Jumbo) Ozaki — hadn't played on the Japan PGA Tour since the opening event six weeks earlier. He returned to action to defend his title in the Chunichi Crowns in late April and sent the rest of the circuit regulars and several prominent American visitors scurrying for other positions in the standings by week's end.

The domineering Ozaki, back from a disappointing showing in the U.S. Masters, struck immediately at Nagoya Golf Club's Wago course with a six-under-par 64 on opening day and was never caught. He registered a 268 total, 12 under par, to win his second consecutive Crowns championship and his fourth in the event's 37-year history. It was his 75th Japan PGA Tour title.

Ozaki started the tournament birdie-eagle-birdie en route to the 64 and a one-stroke lead over Katsuyoshi Tomori and Todd Hamilton, a U.S. regular on the Japan PGA Tour. He widened the margin to two over Peter Senior, Hirofumi Miyase and Masayuki Kawamura with 68–132 Friday and maintained the margin with 69–201 Saturday. Miyase and Tsuyoshi Yoneyama were at 203 with only Craig Stadler and Fred Couples among the U.S. visitors in sight of contention at that point.

The great Japanese pro polished it off with a five-birdie 67 Sunday, finishing four ahead of Tomori (67) and seven in front of Yoshinori Kaneko (71), who was coming off his second 1996 win in the Kirin Open.

Fuji Sankei Classic—¥120,000,000
Winner: Brian Watts

Brian Watts and Todd Hamilton, two Americans who have found considerable success on the Japan PGA Tour on the heels of Asia Tour seasonal championships, wound up head to head in a playoff for the title in the Fuji Sankei Classic, one of the rich events in the early months of the circuit. Watts, the 1993 Asia winner, prevailed in the playoff to annex his eighth victory in Japan.

The 30-year-old Watts, who won five times and challenged Jumbo Ozaki for the money title in 1994, took the tournament lead Friday and held it until Hamilton caught him at the end. Watts finished off his rain-delayed first round at the crack of dawn Friday for 66, two strokes off the pace, and shot 67 for 133 in the scheduled round to go one in front of Hideki Kase and Toshimitsu Izawa. Ozaki, who has won the Fuji Sankei six times, crowded the Oklahoman, shooting 67 for 205 to move within a stroke as Watts took par 71 for 204.

Uncharacteristicly, Ozaki stumbled to 73 Sunday and Hamilton, who started the day in a five-player tie two strokes off the lead, overtook Watts with a 66 off four birdies and an eagle as Watts shot 68 on the Kawana Hotel's Fuji course for his 272. A routine par at the first playoff hole won it for Watts as Hamilton dumped his wedge approach in a bunker and failed to save par.

Japan PGA Championship—¥100,000,000
Winner: Masashi Ozaki

Stung by his poor finish the previous Sunday in the Fuji Sankei, Jumbo Ozaki responded with one of the finest performances of his career, especially in a major championship. Never out of the lead, Ozaki rolled to an eight-stroke victory in the Japan PGA Championship, winning the important title for a record sixth time since 1971. He made only one meaningless bogey in the final round as he ran up scores of 68, 66, 67 and 69 for an 18-under-par 270 total over the Sanyo Golf Club's Yoshii course. Ozaki, at 49, is the oldest man ever to win the Japan PGA, which dates back to 1926.

Ozaki shared the first-round lead with Todd Hamilton, who had just lost the Fuji Sankei the preceding Sunday in a playoff, then moved two strokes ahead of tour rookie Kaname Yokoo, 23, and four in front of the rest of the field Friday. Hamilton shot 70. Ozaki expanded his lead to three Saturday as Shigeki Maruyama shot 65, the week's best score, to grab the No. 2 spot. Yokoo had a 71 and slipped into a tie for third with Masanobu Kimura, the Descente Classic winner, at 207, six strokes off the pace. Ozaki had a slight scare Sunday when he hit his tee shot out of bounds at the par-three third hole and took the lone bogey, but Maruyama, who closed to within two there, double-bogeyed the next hole and Ozaki breezed to his 76th victory.

Pepsi Ube Kosan Tournament—¥80,000,000
Winner: Hidemichi Tanaka

Maybe Tsuneyuki Nakajima shouldn't be so generous with his advice. Early in the week at Ube Country Club, Nakajima gave Hidemichi Tanaka a tip on the putting green and it came back to haunt him at the end of the week. Tanaka, one of the Japan PGA Tour's biggest hitters, putted so well thereafter that he posted the year's lowest 72-hole score to date — 264, 20 under par — and won the Pepsi Ube Kosan Tournament by two strokes over Nakajima and Brian Watts.

Tied for 13th, four strokes behind first-round leader Kazuhiro Fukunaga, Tanaka joined him at the top Friday when he matched Fukunaga's opening 64 and Fukunaga shot 68. Low scores abounded Saturday, but Tanaka's 65 for 197 jumped him three strokes ahead of Nakajima and Ikuo Shirahama, who both fired 63s, and four in front of Watts. The American, gunning for his second 1996 victory in Japan, caught the leader on the windy Sunday when Tanaka double-bogeyed the 10th hole, but Tanaka birdied the 15th and 16th holes, shot 67 and won for the second time in his four-year pro career. Watts closed with 65, Nakajima with 66.

Mitsubishi Galant Tournament—¥120,000,000
Winner: Masashi Ozaki

He took a different route, but the result was the same — a victory for Jumbo Ozaki in the Mitsubishi Galant Tournament, his third in his last four starts on the Japan PGA Tour.

It didn't look promising for Japan's greatest player after 54 holes. After mediocre rounds of 72, 70 and 73 at Oarai Golf Club, Ozaki sat in an 18th-place tie, eight strokes behind leader Brian Watts, who, in turn, was sitting in exactly the same position as he was a week earlier. He again led countryman Todd Hamilton by two strokes going into the final round after both had shot 66s Saturday, Watts for 207, Hamilton for 209.

Ozaki turned it on Sunday, racing up the leaderboard with a course-record 64, then waiting as Watts and Hamilton finished. Watts had fallen slightly off the pace, but Hamilton had a two-stroke lead until he bogeyed the last two holes for 70. That put him into a playoff, which Watts, with 73, missed by a stroke. Ozaki then took his third win of the season and tour career 77th with a par on the first extra hole as Hamilton lost in extra holes for the second time in 22 days.

JCB Classic Sendai—¥100,000,000
Winner: Masashi Ozaki

Bad news for the other players on the Japan PGA Tour. Jumbo Ozaki can win tournaments without much help from his putter. At least, that's what Ozaki was saying after he made the JCB Classic Sendai tournament his fourth victory in six starts on the 1996 circuit. "That is the worst I've putted this year," Ozaki said after besting David Ishii in a playoff at Omotezao Kokusai Golf Club at Shibata. Of course, his worst is better than most.

Both playoff participants lingered off the pace through the first three rounds. Hajime Meshiai led the first day with 66, then yielded the top spot to Ryoken Kawagishi, Nobuo Serizawa and Masayuki Okano Friday. They were at 136, Ozaki at 138 and Ishii at 139. Okano shot his third straight round in the 60s Saturday for 204, a shot in front of Ozaki and Hideyuki Sato. Ishii, five back at 209, came up with a 68 Sunday. That put him into the playoff as Ozaki merely matched par for his seven-under-par 277. The two men replayed the 18th and Ozaki won with a par as Ishii, seeking his first victory in two years, couldn't save par from a greenside bunker.

Sapporo Tokyu Open—¥100,000,000
Winner: Hajime Meshiai

Hajime Meshiai had fallen back into the ranks after reigning supreme as the No. 1 money winner on the Japan PGA Tour in 1993. Meshiai, then 39, won four times that year as he outlasted Jumbo Ozaki for the title. He went without a victory in 1994 and 1995, finally finishing first again in a down-to-the-wire battle against a host contenders in the Sapporo Tokyu Open at Kokusai Country Club's Shimamatsu course in early June. He shot a one-over-par 73 in the final round for a 279 total, nine under par, and a one-stroke victory over Harumitsu Hamano, Yoshimitsu Fukuzawa and Yasunori Ida.

A second-round 64 was the key to Meshiai's 11th tour victory. It carried him from 12th place into a three-stroke lead at 134. Although he had just a par round Saturday, Meshiai gained his three-shot lead at 206 over Masanobu

Kimura and Toru Suzuki, both winners early in the season. Meshiai was erratic Sunday, carding just nine pars to go with five birdies and four bogeys in shooting the 73.

Pocari Sweat Yomiuri Open—¥100,000,000
Winner: Kazuhiro Fukunaga

Don't mention playoffs to Todd Hamilton. It's an unpleasant subject for the 30-year-old American, who, in the Pocari Sweat Yomiuri Open, lost in overtime on the Japan PGA Tour for the third time in seven weeks. First, he lost to fellow American Brian Watts in the Fuji Sankei, then to Jumbo Ozaki in the Mitsubishi Galant. Probably a bigger disappointment was the loss in the Yomiuri because he fell to Kazuhiro Fukunaga, who had never won in his five years on the circuit.

The tournament at Tokyo's Wakasu Golf Links pretty much revolved around Fukunaga, Hamilton and Hajime Meshiai, who made a strong bid to score back-to-back victories after his win at Sapporo. Hamilton, the 1992 Asian champion, opened with an eight-under-par 63 and Meshiai was among six players who shot 64. Meshiai followed with 65 for 129 and a three-stroke lead as Hamilton slipped to 72.

On Saturday, Hamilton and Fukunaga caught fire with 64s and moved within a stroke of Meshiai (69-198) along with Roger Mackay and Tsukasa Watanabe. Meshiai couldn't hold on Sunday, Hamilton edged in front of Fukunaga and stayed there until Fukunaga birdied the 18th to match Hamilton's 67 and forge a tie at 266. Peter Senior just missed joining them with his closing 63 for 267

With Hamilton six feet from the hole with a birdie putt at the first playoff hole, Fukunaga chipped in to stay alive. Fukunaga birdied again with an eight-footer at the second extra hole for the victory.

Mizuno Open—¥100,000,000
Winner: Yoshinori Kaneko

Yoshinori Kaneko added another laurel to his finest season when he steamed to a four-stroke victory in the Mizuno Open at Tokinodai Country Club. Not only did it put him right on the heels of Jumbo Ozaki on the Japan PGA Tour money list but it also secured him an invitation to the British Open, a first for him.

Kaneko was in the thick of things all the way at Tokinodai. He shared the first-round lead — 66 — with Chen Tze-Chung, Nobuhito Sato and Peter McWhinney, the Tsuruya Open victor. Todd Hamilton, the luckless American loser of three playoffs, took over first place Friday with 71-65—136, a shot ahead of Kaneko, who reclaimed the lead Saturday with 65 for 202. Ryoken Kawagishi was at 203, but tumbled badly Sunday as Kaneko wrapped up his third 1996 title and fifth of his career with a closing 68 for 270, 18 under par. Shinichi Yokota was second at 274. Brian Watts, who won the Mizuno in 1994 and 1995, tied for fifth with a closing 66.

PGA Philanthropy—¥100,000,000
Winner: Todd Hamilton

Todd Hamilton's bizarre frustrations ended at the PGA Philanthropy tournament. After three earlier 1996 victory bids on the Japan PGA Tour had died in playoffs over a seven-week period, Hamilton finally nailed a two-stroke, come-from-behind win, his sixth since gaining full-time privileges in Japan with his 1992 Asian championship. The 30-year-old American closed with a rain-interrupted 69 for the winning, 13-under-par 275 total.

Hamilton was never far off the pace at the Oakmont Golf Club course in Nara Prefecture. He was three back after Taiwan's Hsieh Chin-Sheng opened with 66, then five behind, but in fourth place as Tsuyoshi Yoneyama took over the lead with a dazzling 64 for 133, which put him two in front of Katsunori Kuwabara. Yoneyama retained the lead with a 71–204 Saturday as Hamilton moved into the runner-up position with 68–206.

Yoneyama fell from contention with 76 Sunday and Hamilton took over despite a bogey at the par-five fourth. He birdied No. 9 and three more holes coming in, feeling he had escaped the playoff danger when the last one from 18 feet at the 17th gave him the two-stroke cushion he wanted for the final hole. He parred there for his second victory in three years in the PGA Philanthropy.

Yonex Open—¥80,000,000
Winner: Hideyuki Sato

Hideyuki Sato took advantage when he got his second good chance for victory on the 1996 Japan PGA Tour. Three months after he failed to hold the lead in the final round of the Descente Classic and finished second to Masanobu Kimura, Sato turned the tables on him in the Yonex Open at Hiroshima Country Club.

Sato overcame Kimura's two-stroke, 54-hole lead and went on to a two-stroke victory over three-time winner Yoshinori Kaneko. He did it with a closing 66 for a 273 total, 15 under par. Kimura slipped to 73 and dropped into a third-place tie with Shoichi Kuwabara, who led the first day with 65, two ahead of Sato and five others. Kimura took over Friday with 66–134 and held onto first place Saturday with 71-205 as Sato shot 71-69 in the middle rounds to move into second place.

Kaneko had 68 Sunday to grab the runner-up position and, with that prize money, supplanted Jumbo Ozaki as the leader on the Tour's money list. Ozaki had not played in Japan in five weeks while campaigning overseas and playing in the U.S. Open. The second-place check of ¥7,200,000 jumped Kaneko almost that far ahead of Ozaki.

Nikkei Cup—¥100,000,000
Winner: Hideki Kase

Victories on the Japan PGA Tour have been few and far between for Hideki Kase. The 36-year-old pro has won just three times in his career, breaking the ice in high fashion when he took the Japan PGA Championship in 1990. Kase didn't win again until the 1994 Daikyo Open, the final event of the season, then captured his third in mid-July with a brilliant finish in the Nikkei Cup tournament on the Fuji course of the Dejima Club in Ibaraki Prefecture. He fired a nine-under-par 63 and came from six strokes off the lead to claim the title by two shots with his 271 total.

Different men had possession of the lead throughout the tournament. Taiwan's Lin Keng-Chi had it first with 65 Thursday, then slipped one stroke behind Wayne Smith, Koichi Suzuki and Samson Gimson Friday as that trio posted 135s. Toshimitsu Izawa shot 66 Saturday and bored three strokes in front with 202, but he was no match for Kase Sunday, fading into a tie for third at 275 with Mitsuhiro Watanabe and Tsuneyuki (Tommy) Nakajima, the prominent Japanese star who had not won in more than a year. Lin shot 68 Sunday to take the runner-up slot. Jumbo Ozaki, playing his first tour event in six weeks, tied for 10th place.

NST Niigata Open—¥60,000,000
Winner: Masatoshi Horikawa

The Japan PGA Tour got its fourth first-time winner of the 1996 season at the NST Niigata Open. Joining Yoshikazu Sakamoto (Shizuoka), Peter McWhinney (Tsuruya) and Kazuhiro Fukunaga (Yomiuri) was Masatoshi Horikawa, who captured the Niigata Open almost without warning.

Winless during his five years on the circuit, Horikawa had given little hint at Nihonkai Country Club during the first two rounds that he was on the verge of victory. With his 70-67–137, he trailed leader Tsutomu Higa by six strokes halfway through the tournament. Then, Horikawa burst forth with 64 Saturday and climbed within a stroke of the lead, then held by Higa and Masayuki Kawamura with 200s. He continued the birdie barrage Sunday, running off seven of them as he shot 67 for a 268 total, 20 under par, and beat Kawamura (69) by one stroke, Higa (70) by two.

Sanko Grand Summer—¥100,000,000
Winner: Kazuhiko Hosokawa

Kazuhiko Hosokawa's performance in the Sanko Grand Summer tournament in early August was that of a seasoned veteran, which he is not. Playing in just his third year on the Japan PGA Tour and with a lone victory on his record, Hosokawa forged into the lead with a second-round 66 and was never headed as he rolled to a five-stroke victory with a 16-under-par 272 total at Sanko 72 Country Club in Gunma Prefecture.

Hosokawa opened with 68, just one shot off the lead shared by Katsumi

Kubo, Yasunobu Kuramoto and Masayuki Okano. His second-day 66 advanced Hosokawa into first place, one stroke in front of Eduardo Herrera and Hiroyuki Fujita. He widened the margin to two over Herrera Saturday when he shot a second 68 and the Colombian had 69, and his 70 Sunday was all he needed to coast home. Herrera fell to 73, but retained second place at 277, a stroke ahead of Kuramoto.

Acom International—¥100,000,000
Winner: Kazuhiko Hosokawa

The Japan PGA Tour shifted gears for its offbeat Acom International tournament in mid-August, but Kazuhiro Hosokawa never slowed down. Coming off his decisive victory in the Sanko Grand Summer, the third-year pro dominated the modified Stableford event and won again with a tournament-record 51 points. He finished four points ahead of Frankie Minoza of the Philippines in picking up his third title on the tour. American star Payne Stewart, a special invitee, placed third with 43 points, piling up 19, the week's biggest single collection, in the final round at the Seve Ballesteros Golf Club at Iwaki.

Hosokawa started the tournament in the hole, nine points behind first-round leader Masatoshi Horikawa and his 17. Then, Hosokawa surged into a first-place tie with Tsukasa Watanabe at 26 with 18 points Friday and built a five-point lead over Minoza with 14 more Saturday for a 40 total. Six birdies and a bogey added up to 11 points for the victor Sunday.

KBC Augusta—¥100,000,000
Winner: Masashi Ozaki

Jumbo Ozaki returned to action on the Japan PGA Tour after a three-week absence and the result was predictable — his fifth victory of the year — but precarious. A new challenger emerged in the person of Taichi Teshima, who forced Ozaki to pull out all stops at the end of the final round and survive a two-hole playoff to win his 79th official Japan PGA title in the KBC Augusta tournament at Keya Golf Club in Shima.

Actually, Jumbo's presence in the KBC Augusta was a bit of a surprise. He was eligible for the rich and prestigious NEC World Series of Golf in America that week, but, obviously discouraged by his third feeble performance of the year in a U.S. major event two weeks earlier in the PGA Championship, he passed it up and returned home.

Back on familiar ground, Ozaki fired an opening 64 at Keya and was never headed. He followed with a pair of 70s, leading Hideki Kase, the Nikkei Cup winner, by two after each of those rounds. However, the 27-year-old Teshima came from nowhere Sunday with his own 64 and Ozaki, with the poise of a champion, birdied his last two holes for 69 to tie Teshima at 273.

After both players parred the first extra hole, Ozaki ran in an 18-footer for a birdie at the second to win the KBC Augusta for the second time.

Japan Match Play Championship—¥80,000,000
Winner: Nobuo Serizawa

Experience stood the test as Nobuo Serizawa, a 14-year veteran on the Japan PGA Tour with just three wins on his record, held off a late charge by Brandt Jobe, an up-and-coming American who won four times in Asia in 1995 alone, and walked off with the Japan Match Play Championship at the Nidom Classic Golf Course on Hokkaido.

Jobe, the 1995 Asia Tour champion, rallied from a four-hole deficit after 27 holes of the title match with birdies at the 32nd, 33rd and 35th. But the 36-year-old Serizawa matched Jobe's par at the final hole for a 1-up victory, his first since 1993.

Both had equally tough matches in reaching the finals, scoring 1-up triumphs in the semis, Jobe over Shigeki Maruyama and Serizawa in 40 holes over Hisayuki Sasaki, back from America where he played with minimal success after a strong 1995 season in Japan. In the earlier rounds, Serizawa defeated Nobumitsu Yuhara and Hidemichi Tanaka in 3-and-2 decisions, then Shigenori Mori, 2 and 1, in the quarter-finals. Jobe's advance was with a 1-up victory in 19 holes against Masahiro Kuramoto, a 2-and-1 win over Rick Gibson of Canada and a 4-and-3 triumph against Hajime Meshiai.

Suntory Open—¥100,000,000
Winner: Hajime Meshiai

Hajime Meshiai achieved what just three others had done on the 1996 Japan PGA Tour when he won the Suntory Open in early September at Narashino Country Club at Chiba. Meshiai became the fourth player to win more than once during the season, joining Jumbo Ozaki (five), Yoshinori Kaneko (three) and Kazuhiko Hosokawa (two), when he added the Suntory to his June victory in the Sapporo Tokyu Open for his 12th career win.

Meshiai, 42, the 1993 Japan Tour money leader, broke from a first-place tie at 203 with Hidemichi Tanaka, the Pepsi Ube winner, shooting 69 for a 16-under-par 272 total and a three-stroke victory. He was never out of the 60s all week, opening with 68 to trail one-day wonder Kevin Wentworth by four.

American star Phil Mickelson, on a one-stop visit to Japan, entered the picture Friday. The left-hander, who won four tournaments and almost $1.7 million on the U.S. circuit, shot 69 for 135 to join Tanaka (65-70) at the top of the standings. Then, Meshiai, two back in a five-way tie for third, put them all away Sunday. Tanaka managed only a 72, just enough to edge Mickelson by one stroke for the runner-up spot.

ANA Open—¥100,000,000
Winner: Carlos Franco

Carlos Franco ended a run of victories by Japanese pros on their home tour when he came from five strokes off the pace to win the ANA Open at Sapporo Golf Club in mid-September. The 31-year-old Paraguayan pro picked up his third victory on the Japan PGA Tour since gaining an exemption as the 1994 Asia Tour champion, posting a six-under-par 282 for a one-stroke triumph over Masahiro Kuramoto, one of the circuit's leading lights in earlier years with 28 victories on his record. Franco was the first overseas player to win on the circuit since Todd Hamilton took the PGA Philanthropy tournament in June.

Franco fell behind in the third round after leading the field the first day with 67 and trailing by just a stroke when he followed Friday with 73–140. Koichi Nogami and Tatsuo Takasaki were on top with 139s. Kiyoshi Maita entered the picture Saturday, shooting 68 and taking a two-stroke lead at 209 over Kazuhiko Hosokawa, a two-time 1996 winner, and Kazuhiro Takami. Franco fell five behind with his 74–214. Kuramoto, who had 75 Friday, came back with 71 for 215. Maita, a stranger to the lead, faded to 75 Sunday and 68s by Franco and Kuramoto produced the one-two finish.

Jun Classic—¥82,500,000
Winner: Masashi Ozaki

It only took Jumbo Ozaki 54 holes to demolish the field in the Jun Classic and chalk up his sixth victory of the season on the Japan PGA Tour. Even though he had traveled halfway around the world and back to play on the International team in the Presidents Cup matches in Washington, D.C., the previous week, Ozaki showed no signs of fatigue in his domineering performance at Jun Classic Country Club at Nasu despite his 49 years.

After trailing Toru Nakamura, another aging warrior, by one shot with his 68 Thursday, Ozaki surged into a five-stroke lead Friday. His 64 and 132 total jumped him five strokes ahead of Gohei Sato, Kazuhiro Takami and Chen Tze-Chung. When he followed with a 65 Saturday for 197, 19 under par, Ozaki had a six-stroke lead over Takaaki Fukuzawa and a blowout on tap. Instead, the weatherman produced the blowout in the form of a typhoon that forced cancellation of the final round Sunday. It was Ozaki's fifth Jun victory in the tournament's 20-year history.

Japan Open Golf Championship—¥120,000,000
Winner: Peter Teravainen

Not since 1979 had the Japan Open Golf Championship fallen into the hands of a player from abroad and never had the title been claimed by an American. Thus, it was clearly the surprise of the 1996 Japan PGA Tour season when the national championship was captured by Peter Teravainen, an American who has played since 1982 primarily in Europe and scored his only win in the 1995 Czech Open.

Teravainen broke a string of Japanese victories in the Japan Open dating back to Kuo Chie-Hsiung's win in 1979 that followed back-to-back triumphs by Seve Ballesteros the two preceding years. Teravainen's two-under-par 282 total gave him a two-stroke victory over Frankie Minoza, who also had finished second six weeks earlier in the Acom International.

The 38-year-old Teravainen, a Yale graduate, was not a factor the first two rounds at Ibaraki Country Club. His rounds of 71 and 72 left him five strokes behind Minoza and he still trailed Minoza by four after his third-round 71. Teravainen equalled the day's best score — 68 — to make up all of the ground plus two as the veteran pro from the Philippines slumped to 74 and 284. Minoza bogeyed the 16th and 17th holes and, needing a birdie to tie at the 18th, put his approach in the water. The win gave the Singapore-based Teravainen a 10-year exemption for the Japan PGA Tour. Jumbo Ozaki was on the road to a sixth Japan Open Championship until untracked by a third-round 77.

Tokai Classic—¥110,000,000
Winner: Masanobu Kimura

Masanobu Kimura became the season's fifth multiple winner on the Japan PGA Tour when he nosed out three players, including U.S. Open champion Steve Jones, to win the Tokai Classic on Miyoshi Country Club's West course the first week of October. The earlier win, his first in four years and fifth of his career, came in the Descente Classic in April.

The 36-year-old Kimura nursed a one-stroke lead through the final round after moving in front Saturday with 71 for a 210 total, one shot ahead of Hsieh Chin-Sheng, the first-round leader with 67. Kimura supplanted Masahiro Kuramoto, who had taken a three-stroke lead Friday with a pair of 68s. Jones stayed within striking distance for three days, starting the Sunday round two off the pace with Kazuhiko Hosokawa and one behind Hsieh. Jones got within a stroke but had to settle for second place with Hosokawa and Shigeki Maruyama at 281 when Kimura dropped a 12-foot par putt on the last green for 70 and an eight-under-par 280.

Golf Digest Open—¥100,000,000
Winner: Yoshinori Mizumaki

The predominance of veteran players in the winners' circle of the 1996 Japan PGA Tour continued in the Golf Digest Open. Yoshinori Mizumaki, 38, scored the fifth victory of his career and first in two years in front-runner fashion, never out of first place at the end of each round and one in front of Satoshi Higashi and Shoichi Kuwabara at the end of the tournament at Tomei Country Club at the foot of Mount Fuji. He was 11 under par at 273.

Mizumaki opened with 66, sharing the first-round lead with Harumitsu Hamano and Toru Taniguchi. When he followed with 67 for 133 Friday, Mizumaki established a two-stroke margin over Taniguchi. He widened it to three Saturday when he shot 68 for 201.

Keiichiro Fukabori was at 204, but it was Brandt Jobe who first challenged Mizumaki Sunday. He had caught him by the turn, and went a shot in front when Mizumaki bogeyed the 13th. Jobe gave the lead right back when he went bogey and double bogey on the next two holes and Mizumaki carried a one-stroke lead to victory, carding 72 for the final round. Higashi and Kuwabara took second with 68s for 274.

Bridgestone Open—¥120,000,000
Winner: Shigeki Maruyama

Shigeki Maruyama polished his credentials as a major player of the future on the Japan PGA Tour with his repeat victory in the Bridgestone Open. The two-stroke win, his third in five years on the circuit, elevated the 27-year-old Maruyama to eighth place on the money list, justifying the expectations he brought with him when he turned professional after running up 37 victories as an amateur.

Maruyama put three consecutive 67s on the scoreboard at Sodegaura Country Club, the third one giving him a one-stroke lead over American Brian Watts, the second-round leader at 68-64—132. Watts, the Fuji Sankei winner, shot 70 Saturday.

Nick Price, the international star and leading visitor in the strong field, who was just two shots off the pace after two rounds, had a par 72 Saturday to drop to five back, but he, Watts and Canadian Rick Gibson all had a shot Sunday. They found themselves in a four-way tie for the lead when Maruyama bogeyed the 14th and 15th holes. Maruyama bounced back with birdies on the last three holes for 71 and a 16-under-par 272 total. He won by two over Watts, three over Gibson and four ahead of Price and Nobumitsu Yuhara.

Philip Morris Championship—¥200,000,000
Winner: Naomichi Ozaki

Naomichi (Joe) Ozaki found familiar surroundings a tonic for his game. Back in Japan after attaining mediocre results in 22 starts on the U.S. PGA Tour, Ozaki hit it big in late October with a four-stroke victory in the ¥200,000,000 Philip Morris Championship, richest of the season, at the ABC Golf Club at Hyogo. His first-place check of ¥36,000,000 exceeded his total winnings in America for the year.

Ozaki and brother Jumbo, the runaway No. 1 man again in Japan, sat eight strokes off the fast pace set the first two days by Masanobu Kimura, who already had two 1996 tour victories. Kimura stacked up rounds of 66 and 67 for a 133 total and a four-stroke lead over Yoshinori Kaneko and U.S. southpaw Russ Cochran as the Ozakis began with matching 71-70s.

Joe Ozaki, with 67—208, tied Kimura for the lead when Kimura took his first of two 75s. Jumbo Ozaki, along with David Ishii, Brian Watts, Cochran and Kaneko, remained in contention at 211. But when Kimura continued his tumble, Joe Ozaki breezed home with 70-278, recording his 23rd victory on the Japan PGA Tour but his first in two years. Brother Jumbo, Ishii and Cochran tied for second at 282.

Sumitomo Visa Taiheiyo Masters—¥112,500,000
Winner: Lee Westwood

It had been 12 years since a British pro had won on the Japan PGA Tour when young Englishman Lee Westwood took the Sumitomo Visa Taiheiyo Masters title and he had tough time accomplishing what Sandy Lyle did in the 1984 Casio World Open. The 23-year-old Westwood, who had won the Volvo Scandinavian Masters earlier in the year on the PGA European Tour, went four extra holes on the Taiheiyo Club course against Ryder Cupper Costantino Rocca and former U.S. PGA champion Jeff Sluman before putting the important Japanese title on his record.

Hisayuki Sasaki, the 1995 Japan PGA champion who did not fare well in his extended sortie in America earlier in 1996, led the Taiheiyo Masters for two days. His first-round 67 led eight others, including Westwood, by one stroke. He stretched his margin to three Friday when he followed with 67.

The three ultimate playoff opponents, along with Hideyuki Sato and American Larry Mize, a three-time winner in Japan, were clustered at 138. Dense fog obliterated the course and forced cancellation of Saturday's round. Sasaki slipped to 72 when play resumed Sunday and Westwood, Rocca and Sluman edged ahead of him with four-under-par 68s to set up the playoff.

Sluman bowed out at the first extra hole when both Westwood and Rocca birdied the par-five 18th, Rocca with a 45-footer reminiscent of his monstrous putt that forced the playoff in the 1995 British Open. Rocca missed a four-footer for the win at the next hole, both parred the third and Westwood became the champion when the Italian put his second shot in the water and bogeyed the 18th when they played it once again.

Dunlop Phoenix Tournament—¥200,000,000
Winner: Masashi Ozaki

Twenty-five years earlier, Jumbo Ozaki, who had just turned from baseball to golf, won the first tournament of his rookie season — the Japan PGA Championship — at Phoenix Country Club, site of the present-day Dunlop Phoenix Tournament. So Ozaki took special pride in winning the Dunlop Phoenix there for the third straight year in 1996 because it represented the 100th overall victory of his career. It was his seventh win of the season, making his total of official victories 81 on the Japan PGA Tour.

As usual, the Dunlop Phoenix had a sizeable contingent of leading players from overseas, but only Tom Watson, rejuvenated by his victory in the Memorial Tournament six months earlier in America, challenged Ozaki's run to the title. Watson, in fact, shot 66 the first day and led the tournament, which shared the distinction of having the year's largest purse — ¥200,000,000 — with the Philip Morris event.

Joe Ozaki and Lee Westwood, the Taiheiyo Masters winner the previous Sunday, opened with 67s and Jumbo Ozaki was fourth at 68. The leaders shuffled Friday, Jumbo Ozaki (67) and Westwood (68) sharing first place with 135s. Watson's one-under 70 put him at 136 and Joe Ozaki (71) was at 138 with Hajime Meshiai.

Jumbo moved three strokes in front of Watson and brother Joe with a 69–204 Saturday and finished with the same margin over the same two men when all three shot 73s in the final round. The ¥36,000,000 prize insured his third straight and 10th Japan PGA money title.

Casio World Open—¥150,000,000
Winner: Paul Stankowski

Paul Stankowski completed a storybook golfing year when he laid claim to the Casio World Open title in late November at Ibusuki Golf Club at Kaimon. It put an exclamation point to an unprecedented run of four victories for the 26-year-old pro from Texas, who had been an obscure player dividing his time between the U.S PGA and Nike Tours until his fortunes made a drastic turn for the better in the early spring. On consecutive Sundays Stankowski won the Louisiana Open on the Nike Tour and, squeezing into the field as sixth and last alternate, the BellSouth Classic in a playoff on the PGA Tour. Then, two weeks before the Casio triumph, he won the unofficial Kapalua International in Hawaii.

The win in Japan also required Stankowski to work overtime. He defeated Hawaiian David Ishii, the leading Japan PGA money winner in 1987, with a birdie on the first playoff hole, the par-five 18th, which Ishii had birdied earlier for 66 that was to put him in a first-place tie at 11-under-par 277 with Stankowski when Paul posted a 68 moments later.

Stankowski was one of six men who entered the final round at 209, a shot behind leader Carlos Franco, the ANA Open winner. Stankowski and Ishii were among eight players whose 69s led the first day and Stankowski headed the field Friday after another 69. Jumbo Ozaki, bidding for his eighth win of the year, fell a stroke short with 69–278, tying for third with brother Tateo (Jet). Franco, with 70–279, finished fifth.

Japan Series Hitachi Cup—¥100,000,000
Winner: Masashi Ozaki

Appropriately, when the most successful players of the year on the Japan PGA Tour assembled at Tokyo's Yomiuri Country Club for the exclusive Japan Series Hitachi Cup, the most successful of them all won the tournament. Jumbo Ozaki not only won the Japan Series for the seventh time but he came within a seven-foot birdie putt on the last hole of matching the world record for low 72-hole score against par — 27. At 26 under par with his 262 total, Ozaki equalled the Japan PGA Tour mark set in 1995 by American Brandt Jobe in the Mitsubishi Galant. Ozaki finished his season with eight victories and 82 official and 101 overall wins for his marvelous career.

Ozaki was on track from the start at Yomiuri against the 24-player field comprised of the season's tournament victors and 20 leading money winners. He blistered the course with a 10-under-par 62 to begin with a three-stroke lead over Frankie Minoza, who was his only serious challenger all week.

Minoza followed with another 65 Friday and tied Ozaki for the lead when Jumbo shot 68. They were five ahead of everybody else. By Saturday night, Ozaki was five ahead of everybody else after firing 65. Minoza, with 70, dropped into a second-place tie with Shigeki Maruyama. Ozaki freewheeled to a four-shot victory with 67 Sunday, Maruyama taking second place with his closing 66. Minoza shot 72, tying for fourth, a stroke behind Joe Ozaki.

Daikyo Open—¥120,000,000
Winner: Eduardo Herrera

Eduardo Herrera, a regular on the Japan PGA Tour since 1993, capped his best season with a decisive victory in the year-ending Daikyo Open at Onna in Okinawa. The ¥21.6 million winner's check pumped his earnings to nearly ¥50 million and jumped him to 14th place on the final Japan PGA money list. The 31-year-old Colombian seized the lead the second day at Daikyo Country Club and carried it to a five-stroke victory. His only previous win in Japan came in the 1995 Pocari Sweat Yomiuri Open.

Toru Suzuki, who shot 65 with a back-nine 29, led Thursday, then yielded first place to Herrera and his 67-69–136 Friday. Suzuki had a one-over-par 72. Herrera followed with 68 Saturday to open a five-stroke lead over Toru Nakamura, Akihito Yokoyama and Katsunori Kuwabara, who shot 66, the day's best round. Another 68 Sunday put the money in the bank for Herrera, who finished with a 12-under-par 272 total. Kuwabara also shot 68 to take the runner-up slot, a stroke in front of Nakamura and Yokoyama.

Omega Tour

Myanmar Open—US$150,000
Winner: Boonchu Ruangkit

Boonchu Ruangkit started the new year on the right foot, keeping alive his hopes for the seasonal championship of the Omega Tour with a playoff victory in the first-ever international tournament in Myanmar. The 40-year-old Ruangkit, Thailand's No. 1 player who won the Langkawi Open in Malaysia the previous September and his national championship in 1992, barely held on in regulation after building a four-stroke lead the first two days.

Ruangkit had a 68-72 start and led by four strokes on a Yangon Golf Club course that yielded only a handful of sub-par rounds all week and forced up the scores with miserable rough. He then shot closing rounds of 76 and 77 for a 293 total and got into the playoff only when Australian Jeff Senior missed a four-foot putt at the 72nd hole, shot 76 and matched the 293, the highest first-place score of the circuit's inaugural season. Local favorite Myint Thaung bounced back from an opening 78, shot 73 Sunday and missed the playoff by a single stroke.

Ruangkit dropped a four-foot par putt for the win on the first extra hole after Senior again failed to convert a short putt on the 18th green, this time from six feet.

Omega PGA Championship—US$500,000
Winner: Yeh Chang-Ting

Yeh Chang-Ting was on top of his game — and the standings — all week in the Omega PGA Championship, the final-stroke play tournament of the Omega Tour season. Yeh started and finished with 67s at Hong Kong's Clearwater Bay Golf and Country Club and rolled to a five-stroke victory over Mark Mouland of Wales with his nine-under-par 271. Ironically, the 29-year-old pro from Taiwan had the third-round lead two months earlier in the Hong Kong Open on the long-standing Asia Tour but couldn't hang on and lost to American Gary Webb.

Yeh's 67-68-69–204 performance created a four-stroke lead over Mouland, the 1988 Dutch Open winner on the PGA European Tour, and he carried it home comfortably Sunday. The Welshman's chances dimmed when he double-bogeyed the fourth hole and Yeh created a rather secure, six-stroke margin when he drove the ninth green for an easy birdie. Mouland shot 68 for his 276 as he edged South Africa's Richard Kaplan for second place by a stroke. Kaplan closed with 65.

Asian Match Play Championship—US$200,000
Winner: Jeev Milkha Singh

It was horses for courses once again in the Asian Match Play Championship. Just a month after Jeev Milkha Singh won the Philippine Classic, his first career victory, at the Sta Elena Golf Club, he returned to the scene for the season-ending Asian Match Play Championship and added that title and its $45,000 first prize. The 24-year-old Indian pro defeated Thailand's Boonchu Ruangkit in the 36-hole final, 3 and 1, capping a gruelling 99 holes of head-to-head competition over four days.

After eking out a 1-up win over Scott Taylor, Singh scored decisive victories over Nico Van Rensburg, 4 and 3, and Yeh Chang-Ting, 6 and 5, to reach the title match. Ruangkit advanced with wins over Young-Suk Kwon, 4 and 3; Zaw Moe, 1 up, and Mike Cunning, 8 and 7. The two were deadlocked after 18 holes, but consecutive bogeys starting the afternoon round put Ruangkit, who finished second on the 1995-96 Omega Tour, two behind and he never got closer than that the rest of the way. Singh went four up at the 10th, but the 39-year-old Thai player made a fight of it with birdies at the 31st and 33rd holes to take the decision to the 17th green.

Sabah Masters—US$200,000
Winner: Thaworn Wiratchant

The Sabah Masters, a logical defector from the established Asia Tour, launched the second season of the Omega Tour in mid-March in Malaysia and Thailand's Thaworn Wiratchant staged a late rally to capture the first title of the new campaign. The Sabah Masters, a stop on the Asia Tour in 1994 and 1995, was founded by Ramlan Harun, the executive director of the Asia PGA, in the early 1980s and operated as a small event for many years.

Wiratchant obviously was pleased with the switchover. He overtook Australia's Jeff Wagner on the final holes at the Sabah Golf and Country Club in Kota Kinabalu, posted 69 for a 282 total, six under par, and won by two over Wagner and Taiwan's Lin Chih-Chen. Wagner had taken the lead Friday with 66–139, tying the course record, and had a three-stroke margin over Wiratchant after 54 holes. The issue was decided when the 28-year-old Thai picked up three shots with birdies at the 15th and 16th holes and Wagner's bogey at the 16th. The Aussie finished with 74 and Lin caught him at 284 with a closing 68.

Singha-Thai Prasit Bangkok Open—US$175,000
Winner: Thammanoon Sriroj

The growing strength of Thailand's contingent was displayed for the home country followers at the Singha-Thai Prasit Bangkok Open, second event of the new season on the Omega Tour.

Thammanoon Sriroj made it two in a row for Thai golfers when he joined countryman Thaworn Wiratchant as a first-time winner on the circuit, on which the acknowledged No. 1 player, Boonchu Ruangkit, made a major impact the previous season. Wiratchant won the Sabah Masters, the initial 1996-1997 tournament, two weeks earlier, and finished third at Bangkok as three other Thais finished in the top 10 at the Royal Gems Golf and Country Club.

Sriroj was coming off a domestic victory in the Thailand PGA Championship at Royal Gems and his strong play continued. With rounds of 67-71-68, Sriroj shared the 54-hole lead with New Zealand's Stephen Scahill (71-67-68) and Wiratchant (66-71-69) at 206 and eventually held off Scahill in the stretch. He birdied the final hole for 68 and a 274 total, 14 under par, then watched as Scahill's bid for a tie and playoff lipped out. He shot 69 for 275 and Wiratchant took a 72 for 278, tying with America's Gerry Norquist for third.

Canlubang Classic—US$175,000
Winner: Craig Kamps

South African Craig Kamps turned what appeared to be a hopeless case into his first victory on the Omega Tour at the Canlubang Classic in mid-April in the Philippines, although it required a playoff. Kamps, eight strokes off the pace after 54 holes at Laguna's Canlubang Golf and Country Club, shot a closing, four-under-par 68 for 281. That tied Craig with Korea's Wook-Soon Kang, who made up six strokes in Sunday's round as David Bransdon, who led after 36 and 54 holes, folded with 78.

Native son Rodrigo Cuello and Susumu Mori of Japan had led after the first round with 68s before Australian Bransdon took charge with middle rounds of 67 and 68 for 205, four in front of Cuello and New Zealand veteran Simon Owen. Kang was at 211, Kamps at 213 before their Sunday moves. Owen appeared headed for victory Sunday. He had a two-stroke lead until he finished bogey, double bogey. He tied for third with Cuello, who also shot 73.

The playoff ended quickly when Kang put his approach shot into the water at the first extra hole.

Tournament Players Championship—US$175,000
Winner: Wook-Soon Kang

Opportunity knocked again quickly for Wook-Soon Kang. Although disconsolate over his playoff defeat in the Canlubang Classic, the Korean pro kept his wits and game about him when the Omega Tour moved to Johor Bahru, Malaysia, for the Tournament Players Championship. He worked his way into another playoff at the Tanjong Puteri Golf Resort and didn't let the second chance get away. "It's the biggest victory of my career," said the 31-year-old Kang.

Kang's strongest challenge came from Jeev Milkha Singh, the Asian Match Play champion. The Indian pro, who began the tournament with a six-under-par 66, and shared first place with Kang and four others at 138, trailed him by one stroke — 205 vs. 206 — going into the final round.

Singh was in the battle to the end, missing a 15-foot putt on the 18th green that would have put him in the playoff. Instead, 20-year-old Go Higaki, the youngest player in the field, overtook Kang with a 66 and the Korean shot 70 for 275. Singh tied for third at 276 with John Senden of Australia (66).

Kang parred the first extra hole routinely and won when Higaki missed the green and bogeyed.

Honda City Invitational—US$300,000
Winner: Steve Elkington

The Omega Tour got a touch of star power at its Honda City Invitational with the appearance of Steve Elkington and the world-class Australian lived up to his reputation with his performance at Blue Canyon Country Club on the Thailand island of Phuket. Elkington fought off the challenge of Felix Casas of the Philippines and claimed a one-stroke victory with his seven-under-par 281 total, his first win since the 1995 U.S. PGA Championship.

Casas entered the final round with a 210 score (70-71-69) and a two-stroke lead over Elkington (71-73-68) and Andrew Bonhomme of Australia (70-70-72), the second-round leader. Elkington overtook Casas on the first nine Sunday with a one-under 35 to a 37 of Casas, but three-putted the ninth and 10th greens. However, Elkington holed sizeable putts at the 14th and 15th for balancing birdies and moved ahead to stay with a par at the short 17th, where Casas took a bogey. Peter Fowler of Australia, who fired and fell back during Sunday's round, and countryman Robert Willis shot 69s for 283 and tied for third place.

Guam Open—US$175,000
Winner: Joong-Kyung Mo

The Omega Tour took international tournament golf to the Pacific island of Guam for the first time and a young Korean, who reached the circuit via the United States and Canada, captured the championship. Joong-Kyung Mo, 25, who has lived in America since he was 15, came from five strokes off the pace to score a three-stroke victory with his one-under-par 287 total at Leo Palace Resort in mid-May.

Mo got a big assist toward his first professional victory from Jeff Senior, the Aussie playoff loser earlier in the year at Myanmar. Senior appeared on his way to victory in Guam as he led the tournament the first three days — by one with a 70 Thursday and with 143 Friday and by four over Don Fardon and Masakazu Noritake with his 215 Saturday. However, a bogey at the second and a triple bogey at the fourth wiped out his lead and opened the door, particularly to Mo.

Driving long and straight, the Korean birdied two of the par-fives and created the turning point when he hit the sixth green in two and holed the 40-foot eagle putt. He went on to 67 and finished three strokes in front of runners-up Fardon and Jeff Wagner of Australia and Aaron Meeks of the United States. Senior shot 79 and wound up in a 10th-place tie.

Volvo China Open—US$400,000
Winner: Prayad Marksaeng

Thailand struck again — and with great impact — when the Omega Tour went to Beijing for the Volvo China Open in early June. Yet another of the country's up-and-coming pros — Prayad Marksaeng — rose to the fore at Beijing International Golf Club and produced a record-breaking victory, the third of the current season for the Thais in seven tournaments.

The stocky, 30-year-old Marksaeng took command of the field the second day with his 70-66–136 and blew away all opposition over the weekend with a 67-66 finish for a 269 total, 19 under par. The 67 opened a four-stroke gap and the 66 gave him a nine-stroke victory margin over Taiwan's Hsieh Yu-Shu. Marksaeng had seven birdies and a bogey Sunday.

The nine-shot gap was the largest margin in the tour's two seasons, eclipsing the seven-shot win in the 1995 Langkawi Open by inspiring countryman Boonchu Ruangkit. The 269 was the lowest score on the Omega Tour books and eight better than Raul Fretes' winning score at Beijing in 1995. It was Marksaeng's first victory outside of Thailand.

Canon Singapore Open—US$500,000
Winner: John Kernohan

It was only for one tournament, but the three circuits in the Pacific Rim came together for a week under the banner of the Omega Tour for the Canon Singapore Open and its US$500,000 purse, largest of the year to date.

John Kernohan, a British-born American from Kentucky, was the benefi-
ciary, finding his game in time to wring out a one-stroke victory at Singapore's
Laguna National Golf and Country Club in a rain-drenched final round.
Kernohan, 32, matched his age on the back nine with four birdies for 69 and
a 285 total, and survived without a playoff as five men — Aussies Bradley
King, Peter Lonard, Darren Cole and Robert Willis and South African Craig
Kamps, the Canlubang winner — came up one stroke short.

Lin Keng-Chi, the 1995-1996 Omega Tour champion who was playing on
the Japan PGA Tour, joined the field, as the Omega circuit welcomed the
Singapore Open to its fold after its three years on the Australasian Tour, and
showed some of his old style.

Lin shared the 36-hole lead with Japan's Yoshiaki Daijo at 139 before
falling away. Daijo shot 72 Saturday to lead by one going into the rainy
Sunday and remained ahead to the turn before his game faltered and Kernohan
launched his finishing kick. He was the first American winner of 1996 as
the circuit resumed action at Singapore after a two-month break.

Kuala Lumpur Open—US$200,000
Winner: Wook-Soon Kang

Wook-Soon Kang became the first two-time winner of the season on the
Omega Tour and he was as surprised as anybody when he wound up on top
at the conclusion of the Kuala Lumpur Open at the Staffield Country Resort.
Kang, whose earlier win also came in Malaysia in the Tournament Players
Championship, shot a final-round 70, but received some unwilling help from
Scotland's Kenny Walker to acquire his one-stroke victory.

Kang began Sunday's play tied for the lead at 205 with Japan's Nobuhito
Sato and Aussie Brad Andrews, who had shared first place with China's
Zhang Lian-Wei at 135. However, Walker, starting the final day one stroke
back, went out in 32 and had a two-stroke lead with three to play when his
putting went sour. He missed three-foot par putts on each of those holes.
Kang birdied the 16th, then gave the stroke back but made a clutch bogey
after putting his tee shot in the water at the par-three 17th. His par at the
18th gave him the winning 275, 13 under par. Andrews tied Walker for
second place, barely missing a chip at the last green to force a playoff with
the 30-year-old Korean.

Fila Open—US$300,000
Winner: Oh-Chul Kwon

Oh-Chul Kwon followed two of his Korean compatriots into the winner's
circle on the Omega Tour, but he did it in front of homefolks when the
circuit traveled to Seoul for the Fila Open on the 7,415-yard West course
of Kwan Ak Golf and Country Club. The 40-year-old Kwon, winning the
most important title of his long career, headed a list of six countrymen who
placed in the top 10 in the late-August tournament. He blistered the long
course with a six-under-par 66 Sunday for a 279 total and a one-stroke
victory over Kyung-Joo Choi.

Kwon, whose only previous success came in domestic events in Korea in the early 1990s, started the final round one stroke behind Choi and Yong-Jin Shin, birdied the first hole and never trailed after that. When he dropped his sixth birdie putt at the 14th hole, Kwon had a four-stroke lead. Choi made a game bid to catch him with birdies at the 13th and 15th, but his final one at the 18th for 68 left him a stroke shy of a tie.

Philip Morris Asia Cup—US$300,000
Winner: Jeev Milkha Singh

Jeev Milkha Singh, considered by most Asian observers as India's finest pro, provided solid backing for such opinion with a devastating performance in the Philip Morris Asia Cup, a limited-field tournament on the Omega Tour schedule. Singh rocketed to a 26-under-par 262 total and a six-stroke victory at Cheung-Gu Country Club, where only one of the 42 starters finished over par. Singh set Omega Tour records with the 262 and the 26-under-par figure, seven better in both departments than Prayad Marksaeng's winning score at the Volvo China Open.

The 24-year-old Singh had hinted at the explosion with a fifth-place finish the week before in the Fila Open at Seoul after injuries and illnesses had hampered his performances following his January victory in the Asian Match Play Championship.

Singh strung together rounds of 66-66-65-65, yet surprisingly was locked in a tight battle with Koreans Jong-Duck Kim and Wook-Soon Kang, the circuit's only two-time winner in the current season. Singh was tied with Kim and a stroke ahead of Kang, but neither could cope with Singh's fourth consecutive potent round. Kang shot 70 to finish second at 268 and Kim stumbled to 73 for 270.

Lexus International—US$200,000
Winner: Boonchu Ruangkit

Never since he turned pro in 1986 had Thailand ace Boonchu Ruangkit gone through a season without a victory. When he teed it up in the Lexus International in late September, he hadn't taken care of that accomplishment for the current Omega Tour season.

The way things started for him at Bangpoo Country Club, it looked like he would have wait at least another week. Ruangkit began with 75 and didn't seem likely to even make the cut. Some serious practice on the putting green brought definite improvement, but he was still five strokes off the pace and behind 14 players with 211 entering the final round.

American Mike Cunning, 37, who had scored his first pro victory in 15 years six months earlier in the Asia Tour's Singapore Rolex Masters, led with 69-68-69—206. But Cunning couldn't stave off the 40-year-old Ruangkit Sunday, not when Ruangkit fired a course-record 65. Cunning shot 70 for a tie at 276 and the Thai veteran settled things quickly with a 12-foot birdie putt on the first playoff hole, picking up his third Omega victory. Felix Casas also had 65 Sunday and tied for third at 277 with Nico Van Rensburg.

Yokohama Singapore PGA Championship—US$200,000
Winner: Yeh Chang-Ting

Experience surely was a major factor when Yeh Chang-Ting prevailed in a final-round battle with 24-year-old Australian Andrew Bonhomme and American Fran Quinn in the Yokohama Singapore PGA Championship. The Taiwanese pro, seasoned with victories in important events on both the Omega and Asia Tours, pushed past a faltering Bonhomme midway through the final round at Jurong Country Club and scored a one-stroke victory over Quinn with his 13-under-par 275 total.

The loss was particularly disappointing for Bonhomme, who had led from the start with a dazzling 63 Thursday and a following pair of 70s for 203 after 54 holes. Quinn was at 205 and Yeh at 206 with Preecha Senaprom of Thailand. Yeh caught Bonhomme with a birdie at the eighth hole Sunday and had a one-stroke lead over Bonhomme and Quinn when Bonhomme bogeyed the ninth. The 29-year-old Taiwanese pro birdied the 18th for 69 and the winning 275. Quinn shot 71 and Bonhomme 75, dropping to fourth place.

Dubai Creek Open—US$350,000
Winner: Paul Friedlander

No one really would have expected Paul Friedlander to win the Dubai Creek Open, least of all Friedlander himself. By his own admission, the second-year pro from South Africa's Swaziland went to Dubai "to earn enough money to keep my card for the Omega Tour."

Friedlander had not finished higher than 13th in his earlier starts; hence his lack of title expectations, particularly knowing the field was tackling a Dubai Creek Golf and Yacht Club that many of the players consider the tour's most difficult test. So, Friedlander fooled himself and everybody else with a come-from-behind, four-stroke victory with an eight-under-par 280. He became the first Swazilander ever to win an international title

Friedlander was in the thick of things from the start, tied for the lead at 139 after two rounds, then two behind Korea's Kyung-Joo Choi, the Fila Open runner-up, after 54 holes. Choi was at 206, Friedlander at 208 and nobody else was close. The Korean came out flat Sunday. He shot 40 on the front nine and Friedlander, with a 35, took a three-stroke lead, which he protected with pars on the back nine. A safe bogey at the long 18th produced Friedlander's final 72. Choi wound up shooting 79, dropping into a tie for fourth behind Myanmar's veteran Kyi-Hla Han and Craig Kamps.

Merlion Masters—US$175,000
Winner: Peter Teravainen

Peter Teravainen, the American who plays out of Singapore, capped his best season with a playoff victory in the Merlion Masters. Teravainen, who campaigns in Europe and Japan, where he captured the venerable Japan Open earlier in the year, scored his second 1996 victory in Singapore, where he had finished second in March in the Singapore Rolex Masters on the Asia Tour. His last previous win there came in the 1991 Singapore PGA Championship, a domestic event.

The 38-year-old Yale graduate put together three rounds of 70 to take a two-stroke lead into the final round at the SAFRA Resort and Country Club. Six players were in hot pursuit at 212, but Zaw Moe, the Myanmar pro, overtook Teravainen from four back with a course-record 64 for 278. Aware of what Moe was doing ahead of him, Teravainen birdied the 14th and 18th holes for 68 and the tie.

A yardage error on the first playoff hole — the par-five 18th — proved a killer for Moe. Coming up 25 yards off in his calculations, he overclubbed and flew the green into a bunker. He took three to get down from there. Teravainen played just short of the green in two and chipped close to set up the winning putt.

Pakistan Steel Masters—US$225,000
Winner: Eric Rustand

Eric Rustand had a much easier time of it than his two countrymen as he became the third American winner on the Omega Tour in mid-November. Rustand, one of the seven non-Asian qualifiers for the season's tour, came alive after a mediocre year and rolled to a six-stroke victory in the Pakistan Steel Masters at Karachi Golf Club. He recorded a 276 total, 12 under par.

Thammanoon Sriroj, the Bangkok Open winner in March, shared the first-round lead at 68 with Korea's Young-Wu Nam. Then Rustand joined Nam on top at 139 before shooting a course-record 65 Saturday to go seven strokes ahead of Sriroj (70) and American Jerry Smith (71). The 28-year-old Rustand breezed home with a par round Sunday for the six-stroke win over Sriroj. Pakistan's Muhammed Sajid brought a element of national pride with his 70-72-71-70 performance and third-place finish.

Tugu Pratama PGA Championship—US$250,000
Winner: Thammanoon Sriroj

Thailand's Thammanoon Sriroj turned his game up a notch when the Omega Tour moved from Pakistan to Indonesia for the Tugu Pratama PGA Championship, a late addition to the schedule. A distant second to Eric Rustand in the Pakistan Steel Masters, Sriroj squeezed out a one-stroke victory at Damai Indah Golf and Country Club and became the second double winner of the season. He won in similar fashion in the Singha-Thai Prasit Bangkok Open in March, holing a birdie putt on the final green.

Thammanoon emerged from a group of 67 shooters with 66 Friday to lead Daniel Chopra by one stroke with his 134. American John Kernohan, the Canon Singapore Open champion, took over first place with a 69 for 204 as Sriroj slipped three behind with a 74 Saturday. However, Kernohan's game fizzled Sunday and he was quickly out of contention on his way to 79 and a tie for 17th place.

The Thai pro instead faced Singapore's Chua Guan-Soon in the stretch.

Chua cut Sriroj's lead to a single stroke with a birdie at the 17th hole and made a tough par putt on the final green, forcing Sriroj to drop a five-footer to avoid a playoff. He made it just as he did a similar putt in Bangkok.

Royal Classic—US$325,000
Winner: Richard Kaplan

Richard Kaplan prevailed in an all-South African finish to the new Royal Classic, the fourth tournament of the Omega Tour season in Thailand. Kaplan defeated countryman Nico Van Rensburg on the first hole of a playoff at Burapha Golf Club near Pattaya, a venue switch from the Thai Army course. The two high-ranking players on the money list had tied at the end of regulation with 17-under-par totals of 271, Van Rensburg shooting 66 and Kaplan 67 in the final round.

The win, his first in Asia and second of the year, gave Kaplan particular pleasure because, despite eight three-putt greens during the week, he was in contention from day one for the first time all season. Kaplan, who won the Swaziland Open in March, and Australia's Paul Foley shot leading 65s Thursday at Burapha. Both added 70s Friday and, with Van Rensburg and Korea's Joong-Kyung Mo (69-66s), trailed U.S. pro Jerry Smith (67-67) by a stroke.

Kaplan inched in front of a pack of contenders Saturday with a 69–204. Van Rensburg was next at 70–205. Boonchu Ruangkit made an early run Sunday with birdies on four of the first five holes, but eventually finished in fourth place. Kaplan held a two-stroke lead over Van Rensburg when the two men reached the 17th, but Kaplan three-putted there for a bogey and his eighth three-putt for par at the 18th brought about the tie and playoff. Kaplan birdied the 18th in the playoff for the win after Van Rensburg missed from eight feet.

Omega PGA Championship—US$500,000
Winner: Gerry Norquist

Gerry Norquist became the only American with victories in each of the first two seasons of the Omega Tour when he won the finale Omega PGA Championship with an eight-foot birdie on the last green at Hong Kong's Clearwater Bay Golf and Country Club. Norquist, who won the Royal Perak Classic on the circuit in 1995, scored a 71 that Sunday for a 12-under-par 268 total and a one-stroke victory over Australians John Senden and Jeff Wagner.

Korea's Wook-Soon Kang also had cause for celebration at Clearwater Bay, even though he finished in a tie for 17th. The two-time winner on the 1996 circuit clinched the money title with earnings of nearly US$184,000.

Norquist never trailed in the Omega PGA Championship. He and Australian Robert Stephens, who led the qualifying tournament early in the year, posted identical 63-66s the first two days. Then Norquist fashioned 68 Saturday to take a three-stroke lead over Aussie Brad Andrews and Yankee Clay Devers, who won twice in Asia in 1995.

Norquist faltered on the front nine Sunday, going out in 38 and opening the door to the other contenders. Playing well ahead of him on the course,

Senden came from nine strokes off the pace with a 63 and Wagner from seven with a 65 for 269s. Norquist also was 11 under par as he went to the par-five 18th. Despite a big drive, he laid up with a four iron, pitched eight feet above the cup and ran in the winning putt.

Volvo Asian Match Play Championship—US$200,000
Winner: Zhang Lian-Wei

If Volvo is the sponsor, look for Zhang Lian-Wei, China's first pro of star magnitude, to be a contender and likely a winner when he is in the field. He was ... in the Volvo Asian Match Play Championship at Jakarta's Emeralda Golf and Country Club ... and he captured the title in a thrilling 36-hole final match against Korea's Wook-Soon Kang, the 1996 leader of the Omega Tour. Zhang sank an eight-foot birdie putt on the last hole for a 1-up victory.

The two staged an exciting back-and-forth finish. Zhang was two up with five to play after 13 holes in the afternoon round, but Kang won the next two holes when his opponent drove out of bounds at the 14th and he birdied the 15th. They then traded birdies on the next two holes before Kang missed a 12-foot birdie putt at the 18th and Zhang dropped his eight-footer.

In reaching the finals, the Chinese star eliminated Richard Kaplan, 2 and 1; Jeev Milkha Singh, the defending champion, 4 and 2, and Thaworn Wiratchant, 4 and 3. Kang had a tougher time of it, taking out John Kernohan, 20 holes; Robert Stephens, 2 and 1, and Prayad Marksaeng, 1 up, in the earlier matches.

In the accompanying Hugo Boss Foursomes, Paul Foley and Kernohan defeated Marksaeng and Wiratchant, 2 and 1.

13. Australasian Tour

In contrast to recent years, there were fewer candidates for Australia's best player of the year. Greg Norman was never really threatened by anyone, apart from Tom Lehman, for his perch at the top of the Sony Ranking. Steve Elkington was knocked off his stride by having his golf clubs stolen, the ones he had used for years before winning the 1995 U.S. PGA Championship. He won in Thailand but not in America.

Instead, Robert Allenby was the golfer who brought international success to Australia. Allenby first arrived on the PGA European Tour at the same time as another young prodigy who was already dominating his home circuit. Ernie Els swiftly progressed to America and became a major champion. It is taking Allenby a little longer.

Despite his success at home, Allenby's first win in Europe came at the Honda Open in Germany in 1994. The following year was one of regression rather than progression. One thing particularly hurt the Melbourne native. He was not playing in major championships. At the 1995 U.S. Open, he waited around as the first alternate — having been refused permission to practice — until it became clear he was not going to be able to play.

Allenby is a man of ambition. He showed that by accepting a last-minute invitation to The Players Championship. The telephone call at home came only hours after he had just returned from America. He immediately jumped back on another series of planes and arrived just in time to play.

Returning to Europe for the 1996 season, Allenby had a very definite goal. By playing consistently, he aimed to finish in the top 15 of the money list. By doing that he could start to guarantee automatic starts in the major championships. He did even better. Allenby won the Alamo English Open, against Colin Montgomerie, who had advised the Forest of Arden in their U.S. Open-style course preparation; Peugeot French Open, by holing a 30-foot putt in a playoff against Bernhard Langer, and the One 2 One British Masters, when he was about the only player to concentrate on his golf rather than the poor state of the golf course.

Allenby, age 25, finished third on the PGA European Tour, which should guarantee him places in all the 1997 major championships. It will be a relief when he is able to play again, after surviving a car crash in southern Spain in September. Allenby suffered a broken sternum, but returned to Valderrama to tee off in the Volvo Masters to collect a bonus that ensured his position. He gave the money to charity.

While an Australian did so well in Europe, it was a Welshman, Ian Woosnam, with a return to fitness and form after a poor 1995, who dominated Down Under. The Johnnie Walker Classic in Singapore and the Heineken Classic in Perth were both co-sanctioned events between the Australasian and PGA European PGA Tours. Woosnam won both.

Norman won twice, in the Ford South Australian Open and the Holden Australian Open, in what was a strange year for him. His fifth national title at the end of the year was his first victory since that shocking defeat to Nick Faldo at the Masters. Peter Senior, the veteran battler, also scored two wins, in the Canon Challenge and Greg Norman's Holden Classic.

In Europe, aside from Allenby's success, Wayne Riley won the Portuguese Open and New Zealand's Frank Nobilo won Deutsche Bank Open. Nobilo also continued his fine form in major championships with fourth place at the Masters. Sadly, however, Ian Baker-Finch, the 1991 British Open champion, almost faded away from the scene and it can only be hoped such a fine talent is not lost forever.

Heineken Classic—A$1,000,000
Winner: Ian Woosnam

Once Ian Woosnam gets his confidence back, he is a hard man to beat. Even by John Daly. The two were paired in the last group of the final round of the Heineken Classic. Daly was out to set a very personal sort of record. He did not hit his driver once on any of the 72 holes.

"That's the first time I've ever done that," said the 1995 British Open champion. "I didn't need to use my driver. I was hitting my long irons so well." But it did not help him to win the tournament. That was Woosnam's. Daly was affected by the windy conditions on The Vines course to such an extent that he slumped to a final-round 76, four strokes adrift of the Welshman's 72 and 11-under-par 277 total.

Instead, the challenge came from elsewhere. Frenchman Jean Van de Velde got up and down from a bunker at the par-five last hole for a birdie to join Woosnam and Paul McGinley at 10 under. McGinley, the 29-year-old Irishman, was trying to succeed where Andrew Coltart failed the week before, but he pulled his drive at No. 18, found a poor lie in a greenside bunker with his second, and took three to get down. Woosnam hit a five-iron second shot to 10 feet and almost holed his eagle attempt.

It was McGinley's fourth second place on the PGA European Tour. "I've done enough to win," he said. "I just need some luck. I've had some blows, but you have to take them on the chin."

For Woosnam, it was a double celebration. "I feel I am back in the groove," he said after his 33rd career victory. "This win means a lot because I have now won everywhere in the world except Japan. The way I was playing in 1995, this is brilliant to win back-to-back. I tried doing everything the right way, but the formula for me is relaxation. That's what I did over the winter and it worked.

"I became the best in the world and I thought I had to change everything to stay the best. I tried to change my swing and that was a load of rubbish. I went to a sports psychologist and that was a load of crap. I'm a natural."

Ford South Australian Open—A$300,000
Winner: Greg Norman

How long has Greg Norman been hogging the headlines? All the way back to the 1976 West Lakes Classic when the young Australian, yet to be given his Great White Shark nickname, won his first professional tournament. Twenty years later, Norman returned for a ceremony in which the first hole on The Grange's East course was named after him.

Norman had not been back to Adelaide since he won the South Australian Open at Kooyonga in 1986. At Kooyonga again, he won the 1996 Ford South Australian Open with a last-round 69 by one stroke over Frenchman Jean Louis Guepy.

Norman's appearance caused controversy because of the reported A$300,000 fee he was paid by the South Australian government, a sum equal to the total purse, although 59,000 people, a huge increase on the previous year, turned out to watch in wet and windy conditions. "It does not make any difference whether I am paid or not," Norman said. "I have felt like an adopted son here in Adelaide this week. When people ask you to come and play, you have to perform.

"I put a lot of expectation on myself and there were a lot of people who had placed a lot of hope in me to play well this week. I was more nervous out there playing the last three holes than I have been under for a long time."

After gradually improving after a first-round 74 with scores of 72 and 69, Norman moved into position to attack by eagling the ninth hole, but he needed to make recoveries at the last two holes to set the target of 284, four under par. At the 17th, he punched a five iron off a bare lie from under a tree from 114 yards onto the green. "That was the shot of my week," Norman said.

Guepy, 28, from New Caledonia, was seeking his first main tour title and faced an 18-foot putt on the last for a birdie to tie Norman. The putt pulled up just short. "I never felt like I was going to win this week," said Norman. "All I set out to do was remain patient, stay near the lead, and pose a few problems for the guys around me."

Ericsson Australian Masters—A$750,000
Winner: Craig Parry

Craig Parry slipped on the yellow winner's jacket for the third time at the Ericsson Australian Masters. Only three more and he will tie Greg Norman's record of six, but the mark is in the diminutive Australian's vision. "I'm good enough to beat the best, but you have to get the golf course to suit you," he said.

Huntingdale, the par-73 layout near Melbourne, seems to suit Parry as snugly as that jacket, and rounds of 71, 66, 71 and another 71 for a 13-under-par total of 279 edged Bradley Hughes into second place by one shot.

Though outsider Jeff Wagner closed strongly for third place, and as third-round leader Rick Gibson from Canada slipped to 76, the lead switched between Parry and Hughes, the long-handled putter who won the title in 1993. At the last hole, Hughes sliced his tee shot into the trees on the right and had to chip out sideways. Parry neatly got up and down for his par and the victory.

Parry credited a putter made from the same metal as the propellers of the QE2; his psychologist, Noel Blundell, who told him "to think in the present," and to teaching pro Richard Flood, who suggested Parry was opening his hips causing a slice. "I'm not the prettiest golfer in the world, but when it counts I knuckle down and try and get the job done," Parry added. "I've got flaws in my swing but I just try to get by with what I've got." The win left

Parry in the unfortunate position of being the highest ranked player in the Sony Ranking, No. 33, not to be invited to the Masters Tournament in America.

Canon Challenge—A$400,000
Winner: Peter Senior

Peter Senior won his 15th Australasian Tour title at the Canon Challenge, but Ian Baker-Finch may have won a greater battle. The former British Open champion made his first 36-hole cut for 16 months and received a generous share of the cheers from the gallery at Terrey Hills Golf Club in Sydney. Baker-Finch opened with an unencouraging 78, but a two-under-par 70 the following day meant he was sure to receive his first weekend check for over a year. He even finished with a 69, the same score as his playing partner, Jeff Woodland. Not only was Baker-Finch the best man at Woodland's wedding, but the two Queenslanders both share the unwelcome feat of playing an entire season on the U.S. PGA Tour without earning any remuneration.

After finishing in 33rd place, Baker-Finch declared, "I think I have turned the corner. No, I know I've turned the corner."

Further up a crowded leaderboard, Senior jumped out in front by making three birdies on the back nine of the final round. At one point five players shared the lead at seven under par: Senior, Rob Willis, Robert Allenby, Brad King and Phil Tataurangi, who got to that score thanks to a course record 64.

Senior, who started the day three strokes behind King, went into the lead with birdies at the 14th, 15th and 16th holes before securing solid pars at the final two holes. Senior, whose long-handled putter helped him to 67 in the third round, closed with 69 for a 10-under-par total of 278. Willis, with a final-round 66, and Allenby, with 69, finished two shots behind, along with King, who had arrived at the final hole needing a birdie to tie Senior, but bunkered his approach and dropped a shot.

Australian Seniors Championship—A$50,000
Winner: Lee Trevino

Lee Trevino traveled halfway around the world to notch his first victory of the 1996 season. Trevino, the winningest senior in America with 26 individual victories at that time in early March, had the situation well in hand at Canberra's Gold Creek Country Club over the weekend and rolled to a five-stroke victory in the Australian Seniors Championship with his six-under-par 282. The colorful American took the lead Friday with 69 for a 141 total, widened the margin to four strokes over Australian Terry Gale, the first-round leader, with 70 for a 211 total Saturday and beat his target score by one stroke with 71 on a windy Sunday.

Gale, who later in the year won The Belfry PGA Seniors on the European Seniors Tour, closed with 72 for 287 and was the only man within 10 strokes of Trevino. Noel Ratcliffe, who also played well in Europe in subsequent months, was third at 292. Bruce Devlin, who designed the course in the

Australian capital, was far back at 300. Devlin, who has lived in America for years, was the only other U.S. Senior PGA Tour player in the field.

Foodlink Queensland Open—A$400,000
Winner: Steve Alker

The Australasian Tour resumed after its southern hemisphere winter break with the Foodlink Queensland Open which so nearly offered consolation to lefthander Greg Chalmers, who had just returned from his first season in Europe after losing his tour card. Although the former Australian Amateur champion managed to draw even almost halfway through his final-round battle with Steve Alker, the New Zealander was never headed and held on for a one-stroke victory.

Alker responded to Chalmers' challenge by birdieing three holes in a row before immediately dropping four shots from the 11th to the 13th. Wind caused both players problems over the closing stages, but at the 18th Chalmers missed from 12 feet when trying to force a playoff. Both shot final rounds of 72 as Alker recorded a 275 total, three strokes ahead of Stephen Leaney and Bradley Hughes, who tied for third place.

Players Championship—A$500,000
Winner: Bradley Hughes

Given that a member of the catering staff managed to drop a bucket of beer bottles just as Bradley Hughes was making his backstroke over the tiny putt he had on the final green, it was no surprise that his long putter failed to do the trick for once. It did not matter. Hughes could still afford to smile given that he had just won the Players Championship by no less than 12 strokes.

Peter Lonard and Robert Stephens tied for second place, but they were never challengers to Hughes, who left everyone else behind by playing the Robina Woods course on Queensland's Gold Coast in rounds of 70, 65, 66 and 69 for a 270 total.

Hughes made three birdies in a row starting at the third hole and such was his confidence, and his lead, he was happy to be interviewed on television as he walked to the 13th tee. "It's great to win but it's not the most enjoyable round I ever played," said the 29-year-old Hughes. "With no one coming at me, I lost concentration and made some bogeys. Emotionally there were no worries, which was a strange feeling."

Alfred Dunhill Asian Masters—A$705,412
Winner: Bernhard Langer

Only the previous week the first PGA European Tour season since 1979 had ended without an official victory from the pioneering German golfer Bernhard Langer. We should have known Langer would be a challenger for the Alfred Dunhill Asian Masters. The event, at the Fanling course in Hong Kong, was a co-sanctioned event by the Australasian and Asian PGA Tours, but also contained a few European players, and it was Langer, with a final-round 65, who claimed his first victory for 13 months.

It was also his first with a long putter, which he had turned to during the season after suffering an attack of the yips for the fourth time in his career. "I don't care what it looks like," Langer said. "We don't get paid for looking good. We get paid for getting the job done.

"It's been a long time for me since winning and it's nice to know that I can win with the long putter. They weren't the easiest greens to putt on, so I think there might be a future in the long stick. I don't think I could have putted much better."

Langer was in control until he reached the 15th hole, a par-three hole which had cost him a triple bogey in the third round. This time his approach went through the green, he fluffed his chip back and took five. That left the German in a tie with Asian PGA money leader Wook-Soon Kang. But Langer immediately holed from 15 feet for a birdie at the 16th and eventually won by two over the Korean with a 21-under-par total of 267.

MasterCard Australian PGA Championship—A$400,000
Winner: Phillip Tataurangi

Holding a six-stroke lead going into the final round of a tournament was never the safest of propositions in 1996, especially it seemed for Australians. Chris Gray, who had shot a superb 66 in the winds of the third round at the New South Wales Club in Sydney, crashed to 78 in the final round of the MasterCard Australian PGA Championship.

New Zealander Phillip Tataurangi made up nine shots to beat veteran Aussie Rodger Davis by one stroke. Davis, who had been on a lengthy sabbatical from the game before returning halfway through the European season, looked like he might claim the title until a club selection error meant he dropped a shot at the par-three 17th.

Tataurangi, at 25 some 20 years Davis' junior, showed his composure to match Davis' final-round 67 and sneak home with a 279 total. Davis shared second place with Peter Lonard, with Gray tying for fourth place a further two strokes back, after play was suspended on the final day for 45 minutes due to the high winds moving balls on the greens.

"Today I had the time of my life," said Tataurangi, a Maori who has played on the U.S. PGA and Nike Tours. "Frankly, I went out there playing for second place. It is amazing what can happen in 18 holes of golf. I did not consider myself a contender when I started so far behind. But I had a good gallery. My wife, Melanie, came across from New Zealand to caddie for me and members of her family turned up to watch me play today. I would like to thank them for their vocal support, but remind them that golf is a bit different than a game of rugby. They applauded everything, birdies, bogeys and pars."

Davis, a regular winner in Europe until recently, was just pleased to have solved his putting problems by ditching his long putter. "I'm back," he said. "I'm elated. You don't know how soul-destroying it is to walk onto a green and know you can't hole a putt from any distance."

Holden Australian Open—A$1,000,000
Winner: Greg Norman

Greg Norman lose a last-round lead? Perish the thought. Norman, who had changed coaches since his defeat in the Masters Tournament, when Nick Faldo came from six shots behind, led by four strokes going into the last round of the Holden Australian Open at the Australian Club course in Sydney and eventually won by eight over Wayne Grady.

Norman's final round consisted of three birdies and 15 pars as he completed scores of 67, 73, 71 and 69 for an eight-under-par 280. "It is nice to get results so quickly," Norman said of his switch from Butch Harmon to David Leadbetter, guru to Faldo and Nick Price. Grady who also finished with 69 to overtake New Zealand's David Smail by two strokes, wished he could have taken his putting back to the U.S. PGA Tour where he has not won since the 1990 PGA Championship.

It was Norman's fifth Australian Open title — Gary Player won seven and Jack Nicklaus six — and came in front of what the Australian Golf Union estimated to be the biggest gallery ever seen in the country. "It makes me feel great to be an Australian," said Norman, who played golf with U.S. President Clinton at a nearby club after his opening round. "I don't get all that many chances to play at home so when I do win here, it is special. To see whether a championship has credibility, you look at the past champions and the difficulty of the courses. On this trophy we have the names of Nicklaus, Player, Thomson, Nagle, Elkington. That says a lot."

After slipping to his worst round as a professional in his first tournament outside America since leaving the amateur ranks, Tiger Woods recovered from an opening 79 to finish tied for fifth after adding rounds of 72, 71, 70. "At least he got the flavor of Australian courses," Norman said of Woods. "We play very difficult courses here. He got a shock when he shot 79. Perhaps he will appreciate why Australians play so well when they leave home. The first time you play here, you get a deep appreciation of how difficult they can be. But after the first round he came back with a creditable performance. He should find it easier the next time."

Greg Norman's Holden Classic—A$700,000
Winner: Peter Senior

For the third time in his career, all the occasions in Melbourne, Peter Senior was interrupted as he stood over a putt for victory by a photographer's flash going off. Senior, one of the grittiest of characters, simply backed away, told the snapper what he thought of being inconvenienced, and then let his putter do the rest. His record in such situations is now won two, lost one.

It gave the 37-year-old Senior a one-stroke victory over Greg Norman, who made a determined bid to win his own Holden Classic for the first time. Senior had started a rain-soaked final day tied with New Zealand's Michael Long and American Jerry Kelly but immediately birdied the first three holes to pull ahead. Long and Kelly closed with rounds of 72 and 74 to finish third and fourth respectively.

Norman seemed to have blown his chance of becoming the first player to win successive tournaments in Australia for four years with a second-round 75, but when he eagled the 14th on the final day with a 20-foot putt, he was only one shot behind Senior. Both men then finished with four pars, Norman shooting 69 to Senior's 70 and a total of 281, seven under par.

"It was so cold, so wet and so windy it felt like we were playing the British Open," Norman said. "I had my chances but Peter played some tremendous golf in difficult conditions and was the better man on the day."

Senior said of this 23rd career win, "After the rain set in, I knew I only had to shoot a couple under par to win. It meant that Greg had to make a big start. He's a great player but he is not infallible. He can be beaten. Even the best golfer in the world can't win everything. I feel I have what it takes coming down the stretch. My main problem seems to be that I can't get into contention often enough."

Norman announced before the tournament that he would be taking a three-month break from tournaments after the event to rest his back, which he said was injured while he was playing football when he was young, an inherited spinal condition and a continuous worldwide playing schedule over the last 20 years.

AMP-Air New Zealand Open—A$437,484
Winner: Michael Long

Boosted by his third-place finish the week before in Melbourne, Michael Long took his first Australasian Tour victory to complete his set of New Zealand under-18, under-21, national amateur and national Open Championship titles.

The 26-year-old was content to take the birdies when they came as long as he could limit the bogeys. He only had six bogeys for the week, three of them in the third round. A four-under-par 67 on the final day at the Paraparaumu Beach course in Wellington was enough to give him a four-shot margin over defending champion Peter O'Malley.

O'Malley finished with four birdies in his last 10 holes but needed something more dramatic to challenge Long. O'Malley was pleased to break his run of missing the cut the year after winning a tournament and has now finished in the top-10 in each of his five New Zealand Opens.

"When I am practicing, I think about coming down the stretch for a big title," Long said. "But until you actually do it, you don't really know. The atmosphere this afternoon was fantastic. I have never played in front of galleries like that before. The emotion when I finally walked down 18 was overwhelming. Driving it into the right place was what I tried to do. When I got into trouble today, I struggled to make par. You know you are going to make birdies around here, but not when you want them. So I did not mind leaving myself with 40-foot putts to be sure of my pars."

Schweppes Coolum Classic—A$200,000

Winner: Anthony Painter

Having failed to secure a place on the U.S. PGA Tour at the qualifying tournament week before, Anthony Painter returned home to Australia and collected his first victory in three years.

The 31-year-old Painter has a home practice range (a few sheep keep the grass short) at his farm at Tamworth, northwest of Sydney. But it was his steady performance in the final round on the Robert Trent Jones-designed Hyatt Coolum course, a one-over-par 73, that kept him two strokes ahead of hard-charging Matthew Ecob.

Ecob, whose brother David finished 12th in the event, set a course record of 65, but Painter had been impressive from the start with rounds of 71, 68 and 68 before completing his eight-under-par 280 total.

"When I missed out on the U.S., Bradley Hughes (who got his card) told me to go back and win at Coolum," Painter said. "So I decided to play to win instead of just going out and trying to play nicely. I felt I was in control of the mental side of things after having problems in the past. I have been working hard on that aspect of my game."

14. African Tours

As one of the proudest of sporting nations, South Africa has not taken long to reestablish itself at the pinnacle of success after years of isolation. The Rainbow Nation's cricketers travel the world leaving defeats as calling cards on their hosts. And amid carnival scenes, their rugby union players rose to the occasion to win the World Cup they hosted in 1995.

In 1996, there was a similar atmosphere as South Africa staged the World Cup of Golf for the first time. Around 20,000 spectators, all vocal in their encouragement of the home team, turned up for four days at the Erinvale Club near Cape Town. Their heroes, Ernie Els and Wayne Westner, did not let them down.

"Obviously, we had an advantage as the only guys who had ever played the course, but it was having all these people cheering us every day that inspired us," Els said. "The feeling I had walking up the 18th was almost as good as when I won the U.S. Open. It was an unbelievable week."

Said Westner, "We just couldn't let the people down. The crowds were amazing. We're both so proud of what we did for the South African people." Els and Westner dominated South African golf during the year and Erinvale was their due honor. They produced a record 18-stroke winning margin, with Els winning the individual trophy by three strokes over his countryman. "Ernie was fantastic," said Westner. "He hasn't a flaw in his game. He is so relaxed and has such an ambience about him. He's a very special player."

There are times when Els plays with such brilliance, so sublimely, that it can be a disappointment when he does not retain such peaks. But that might be asking too much. When he is good, he is very, very good.

In addition to his performance at Erinvale, Els won the Philips South African Open for the second time. On the U.S. PGA Tour, Els won the Buick Classic at Westchester by the little matter of eight shots. And at Wentworth in the autumn, the 27-year-old from Johannesburg recorded his third successive victory in the Toyota World Match Play Championship, something not even the likes of Gary Player and Seve Ballesteros had managed.

On the Southern African Tour, Els was no match for Westner. Bringing Mark McNulty's long stranglehold on the money list to an end, the 35-year-old Westner took the title for the first time. He won the San Lameer South African Masters by three shots and the Nashua Wild Coast Sun Challenge by four but was denied a hat trick by getting himself disqualified at the Dimension Data Pro-Am.

During the Nedbank Million Dollar Challenge at Sun City, the 10th tee doubles as a practice tee for the 12-man field. The Pro-Am featured a full field and play on both the Player and Lost City courses, with the official practice range sited at the latter. When Westner went to hit a few balls late on the first day on the Player course's 10th hole, he was disqualified for practicing on the course. But Westner had worked too hard to throw away the best golf of his life, and two weeks later he clinched the FNB Players Championship with a birdie at the last hole.

McNulty won the Dimension Data Pro-Am, another co-sanctioned event, and then headed to the northern hemisphere to add the Sun Dutch Open and an impressive seven-stroke victory in the Volvo Masters. McNulty, age 43, returned home late in the year to take the Zimbabwe Open to seal a near-perfect year. His countryman Nick Price struggled all year and failed to record a victory anywhere for the first time since 1990.

Philips South African Open—R750,000
Winner: Ernie Els

The worst news any opponent of Ernie Els can hear is that the young South African has just been on vacation. Els enjoys playing beach cricket, gathering around the barbie, and cracking open a few bottles of beer. But he also likes getting back to work. For the second year running, Els came off his vacation to win his first tournament of the season.

An opening-round 65 at Royal Cape in the Philips South African Open was a nice way to start a new season, but he still had to work hard for his second national title. Els was up to it with three birdies in the last three holes to beat Brenden Pappas by just one stroke.

Els had let things slip with a third-round 74, but maintained the lead until three-putting the 11th hole in the final round. Pappas, one of four golfing brothers, had showed his intent with an eagle at the seventh, but dropped back into a tie with Els when he himself three-putted the 15th.

When the 25-year-old Pappas birdied the par-five 16th, Els, in the group behind, responded by playing a brilliant pitch from a sandy lie for a tap-in birdie. Both holed 10-footers at the 17th, but while Pappas could only par the last, Els put his approach close and holed the putt. Mark McNulty, thanks to a back-nine 31, finished two shots behind Els. A 20-year-old Englishman, David Howell, playing with Els and McNulty in the final group, held on to a creditable fourth place in his first tournament on one of the main tours.

San Lameer South African Masters—R750,000
Winner: Wayne Westner

Patience and accurate ball-striking were Wayne Westner's allies in a week of wet weather and saturated fairways at San Lameer on the coast of the Indian Ocean. It was a long week, too. Westner did not clinch his three-stroke South African Masters victory until Monday morning.

The 34-year-old had not won for three years, since the 1993 Dubai Desert Classic. "This is a great way to start the year," Westner said. "I haven't won for a long time and I missed the cut in the South African Open last week."

While the expected challenge of Zimbabwean Mark McNulty failed to materialize — he slumped to an uncharacteristic final-round 76 — Westner closed with 73 for an eight-under-par total, with American Patrick Moore, England's Chris Williams and Warren Schutte sharing second place.

A noted long hitter, Westner said he was searching for improvement in his short game. "I've now started to study putting very closely," he said. "This week I've shortened the stroke and I'm trying to accelerate through the putt a lot more. Recently, I've been paying attention to the likes of Colin Montgomerie, Ben Crenshaw and Mark McNulty. Monty is one of the best putters on the European Tour and Mark has a magnificent putting stroke. He hits it like silk."

Nashua Wild Coast Sun Challenge—R750,000
Winner: Wayne Westner

When Wayne Westner gets going, the rest had better look out. Westner went one better when making it two out of two at the Wild Coast Sun Challenge. Three birdies in the last three holes gave him a four-stroke victory.

Westner's final-round 65, in addition to earlier scores of 66, 68 and 69, gave him a 12-under-par total of 268. It was the second time Westner had won tournaments back-to-back. On the 1991 Tour, he won the AECI Classic and the South African Open.

Until Westner's blistering finish, his two closest pursuers were the Americans Mike Christie and Greg Petersen, who posted final rounds of 66 and 68, respectively, to share second place at 272.

Dimension Data Pro-Am—R2,400,000
Winner: Mark McNulty

The transfer of the PGA European Tour's co-sanctioned events from Australasia to South Africa brought together two men in search of a hat-trick of victories at the Dimension Data Pro-Am: Ian Woosnam and Wayne Westner had both won in the previous two weeks. While Woosnam opened with 74 and, though never in contention, finished 14th, Westner's bid was brought to an early conclusion as one of five men to be disqualified during the week.

A pro-am format meant play over two courses at Sun City: Gary Player Country Club and the Lost City course. Westner shot a first-round 72 at the latter, but is more used to playing at the former, home of the Million Dollar Challenge. It has no practice range and the 10th tee is used as such during the annual end-of-season extravaganza.

Instead of going back to the practice range at the Lost City late in the afternoon, Westner went to hit some balls from the Player course's 10th tee and was disqualified for practicing on the course. "I had no idea they had decreed it part of the course," Westner said. "But the rule is clear. It's a shame because this is my favorite course." Mark McNulty is fond of the Player course, too. A former winner over the 7,441-yard layout, McNulty had built a four-shot lead by halfway point, and despite two 73s over the rain-lashed weekend, maintained that advantage over Nick Price, Brenden Pappas and Ricky Willison. The tough conditions, requiring fairways to be hit and a deft short game, could have been made for the veteran Zimbabwean. He sealed the win with a chip-in on the 15th hole.

It was McNulty's 24th home win, his 13th PGA European Tour win and the 39th of his career. "If I can catch up my age with my career wins, then I'll have had a good year," McNulty, 42, said. "It was a day for hanging on. It was such hard work, you almost forgot there was a tournament to win." Willison's last-round 68 was the only sub-70 score of the final day.

Before the rain arrived, on Saturday morning, Pappas, a 25-year-old of

Greek descent, teed off at 6:41 a.m. and returned with 64 that equalled Nick Faldo's course record. A front nine of 28, which he played second, included only nine putts and a hole-in-one with a four iron at the 177-yard seventh. Said Pappas, "It is my first hole-in-one in competition, but I did have one before, on New Year's Eve 1984, when I was playing with my brothers, Craig, Deane and Sean, who are all professionals."

Alfred Dunhill South African PGA Championship—R2,000,000
Winner: Sven Struver

Some tournaments are blessed with fine weather, some are hampered by inclement conditions, and some are dominated by the nasty stuff. The Alfred Dunhill South African PGA Championship was one such tournament, having the misfortune to be located in the worst summer of recent Johannesburg history.

The Houghton course was closed at midday on Monday, the shootout was washed out on Tuesday, the pro-am was cancelled on Wednesday, and Thursday's first round could not take place until Friday. Ernie Els, a winner in his only previous appearance in South Africa earlier in the year, spent his time being fitted for contact lenses and watching movies, then shot a first-round 64, on a course where he achieved his first win in 1992.

As Saturday's second round continued into Sunday, and Sunday's third round slipped over into Monday, making it truly a long week, Els could not hold on. Instead, Germany's Sven Struver shot past everybody with a final-round 63. If he was lucky, it was in being able to complete his round on Sunday, before thunderstorms and fading light halted play. After that he made his own good fortune. He needed only 26 putts and had seven birdies in a row from the fourth hole. It meant he went to sleep with a three-shot lead, denied having a sleepless night, then watched as 42 players tried to match his 14-under-par 202 total. Els resumed with a double bogey, but got back to within three strokes, tying for second place with David Feherty, in his second tournament since his brief retirement.

The son of a golf professional, Struver became his country's third PGA European Tour winner, after Bernhard Langer and Alexander Cejka. The 28-year-old had risen at 5 a.m. all but one day. "It was a tiring week," Struver said. "I didn't have a practice round before the tournament, and last night I was just praying it didn't rain again this morning and the whole would be washed out."

FNB Players Championship—R2,400,000
Winner: Wayne Westner

It did not take Wayne Westner long to return to winning ways at the FNB Players Championship, which was not only his third win of the year, but his third in the province of Kwazulu Natal and enough to secure first place on the South African money list. It was also his second PGA European Tour win, after his first at the 1993 Dubai Desert Classic. The 34-year-old is a fan of the co-sanctioned tournaments. "It is a great thing that Ken Schofield has done in bringing the European Tour here," he said. "It is nice to play in your own backyard after playing in everyone else's backyard. It helps our Tour with increased money and better competition. Winning on the European Tour is more important than on the South African Tour, with the exemptions and everything."

Having won two South African Opens at the Durban Country Club, set on sand dunes close to the Indian Ocean, Westner likes the course. With thick vegetation nestling close to the fairways, there is little margin for error, and Westner's expertise with the long irons took him into a four-shot lead after three rounds of 66, 67 and 67. "I can hit my irons to where other people are hitting drivers," he said. "I can play safe, but still be aggressive."

His driving let him down during the final round, and his lead was down to one at the turn and, having built it back to three, a two-shot swing occurred at the 16th when Jose Coceres hit a six-iron shot to a foot. The Argentinean was to complete a final round of seven-under 65. Although Coceres drove into a greenside bunker at the short par-four finishing hole, he got up and down for a birdie, which meant Westner had to hole his birdie putt of five feet. He did so for a round of 70 and an 18-under total of 270.

Coceres, five of whose 10 brothers and sisters are professionals, finished one stroke back, and England's Paul Eales, after a final-round 70, was four back in third place. "It was not as easy as I thought it would be," admitted Westner. "I was shaking at the end. I wasn't playing well, but Jose was, and I had to knuckle down on the back nine. I had to go out and win it again."

Hollard Insurance Royal Swazi Classic—R500,000
Winner: Richard Kaplan

Wayne Westner was assured of first place on the money list when he teed up in the Hollard Insurance Royal Swazi Classic, but the fact was not about to end his hot streak.

Leading by two strokes with three holes to play, things were still unfolding very nicely for Westner. But then, as it has a tendency to do, golf folded in on him. At the 16th, Westner's ball plugged in a greenside bunker and it cost him a double bogey. That brought him level with Richard Kaplan, a nine-year professional from Johannesburg. Kaplan seized the moment by making a routine birdie at the par-five 17th.

Westner was again in trouble. He sliced his second shot and it finished embedded two inches above the waterline of the pond beside the green. Having taken a penalty drop, Westner then pitched poorly to 50 feet, but holed the double-break putt to be only one behind. Kaplan parred the par-three last hole for a final-round 68, but Westner hit back by hitting a superb eight iron to five feet and holing for the tying birdie.

The playoff returned to the 18th tee and this time it was Kaplan who prevailed. The 33-year-old hit his tee shot to 12 feet and holed the putt for his first title. "It was really weird what happened, but I was just happy to be in a playoff," Westner said. Des Terblanche and Chris Davison both birdied the last to tie for third, one shot outside the playoff at 16 under par. A shot further back was Bradley Vaughan, who narrowly missed out on the Rookie of the Year award, which went to Alan McLean.

Hassan II Trophy—US$393,100
Winner: Ignacio Garrido

Only two men can claim to be double winners of the Hassan II Trophy in Morocco. Billy Casper, who taught the King of Morocco to play golf, won in 1973 and 1975. Payne Stewart took the trophy in 1992 and 1993. Nick Price looked like turning that into a trio when he led Ignacio Garrido by two strokes going into the final round at Royal Dar-es-Salam.

An uncharacteristic wayward final round from the Zimbabwean, in which he bogeyed three of the last four holes, handed the victory to the 24-year-old Spaniard. Garrido, whose first victory on the PGA European Tour has yet to arrive, holed from 15 feet for a birdie at the 18th to win by two strokes with rounds of 69, 68, 72 and 70 for a 279 total.

"You cannot expect to shoot 74 in the last round and win," said Price, who had not claimed a victory anywhere in 1996. "I was pathetic. About the only thing I did right was to drive the ball straight." Price shared second place with South African Wayne Westner, who closed with 69 on the course where he was third in the Moroccan Open earlier in the year.

Garrido, who earned $93,000 for the win, said, "There can be nothing better than to play with a great player like Nick Price. I felt nervous with Nick watching me on the first tee but he made me feel relaxed. Nick was offering me encouragement from the start, which helped calm my nerves."

World Cup of Golf—US$1,500,000
Winners: South Africa/Ernie Els

The battle for individual honors in the International Trophy turned out to be more of a competitive contest than that for the World Cup itself. Being played for the first time in South Africa, at the new Erinvale club outside Cape Town, the home duo of Ernie Els and Wayne Westner provided the host nation's third World Cup victory.

Each time South Africa had won the trophy, once known as the Canada Cup, they also took the individual award. Gary Player did so when playing with Harold Henning in 1965, and Bobby Cole did so when playing with Dale Hayes in 1974. This time the two South Africans filled the first two spots as they cruised to a record 18-stroke winning margin, four strokes better than the former mark.

Els was 16 under par for his four rounds and Westner was 13 under par as they left the rest of the field behind. The South Africans led from the first round, except for a time on the second day when Scotland briefly went ahead. But the Scots one-shot deficit after two rounds suddenly stretched to 13 strokes by Saturday night. Els shot rounds of 68, 72, 65 and 67 for a 272 total, and Westner 68, 72, 65 and 70 for his 275 total.

"The feeling walking up to 18 was really great in front of the home crowd," Els said. "I'll remember this for a long time. I'll never forget it. When we played the practice round we felt we could score well. We felt we had an advantage here."

"It's an incredible feeling," Westner said. "I was delighted to play with a great player such as Ernie. Early in the week we knew how well we could play. We said, 'This is for South Africa.'"

To the huge and ecstatic crowd at the presentations, Westner said before holding up one of golf's biggest trophies with Els, "The checks are mine and Ernie's, this is yours."

The United States, with Fred Couples and Davis Love III, had won for the four previous years, and finished second this time. It was the first time that the British Open champion (Tom Lehman) and the U.S. Open champion (Steve Jones) had been paired together and they held off the Scottish duo of Paul Lawrie and Andrew Coltart by one stroke. Germany's Bernhard Langer and Alexander Cejka were five shots further back.

Nedbank Million Dollar Challenge—US$2,510,000
Winner: Colin Montgomerie

In 1994, Colin Montgomerie twice lost out to Ernie Els in important events. Els beat the Scot and Loren Roberts in a playoff for the U.S. Open and the South African also defeated Montgomerie in the final of the Toyota World Match Play Championship.

In another head-to-head encounter, Montgomerie beat Els at the third extra hole of a playoff to win the huge first prize at the Nedbank Million Dollar Challenge. Neither man had a bogey in their final rounds as Montgomerie shot 68 and Els 66 to tie at 274, 14 under par. Each of the first two playoff holes was then halved in pars before Montgomerie, aided by the bank of the right-hand greenside bunker, hit his approach to five feet at the 18th. Els missed the green on the left and had no answer when Montgomerie holed his birdie putt.

"I was a little fortunate, but what the hell," Montgomerie said. It was his first playoff win in professional golf on his sixth attempt and he dedicated the win to his father James, the secretary at Royal Troon, who accompanied his son to Sun City as part of his recuperation from a heart bypass operation. "It is great to finally win a playoff. They say if you knock on the door enough times it will open. I am delighted to get one over on Ernie, but he still leads me 2-1. I always knew he was the main danger."

Els had come close to winning the exclusive 12-man event in 1994 only to be beaten by Nick Faldo. "That was my best total here and I'm now starting to learn how to play this course," Els said. "But hats off to Colin. He's had an excellent year and capped it off here. He's one of the straightest players in world golf and that's the way you've got to play at Sun City. I've been all over him in the last couple of encounters but I guess he got one back today."

The local crowd had chanted "Ernie, Ernie" as the South African, a week after winning the World Cup with Wayne Westner, birdied the last two holes to get into the playoff. U.S. Open champion Steve Jones chipped in from a bunker for an eagle at the 14th and birdied the 15th to briefly take the lead. But the American bogeyed the 16th and 17th and missed from seven feet at the 18th. The third-round leaders, Nick Price and Ian Woosnam, fell back with last rounds of 71 and 73 respectively, while defending champion Corey Pavin trailed in 12th, or last place.

Zimbabwe Open—R400,000
Winner: Mark McNulty

Mark McNulty marked his fourth win of the year with a four-shot victory in the Zimbabwe Open at the Chapman Club in Harare. A last-round 69 preserved his lead and for much of the last day, the 43-year-old Zimbabwean was ahead by five strokes. Nick Price and Justin Hobday could not close the gap and tied for second place. McNulty, who had earlier won the Dimension Data Pro-Am, Sun Dutch Open and Volvo Masters, was behind after an opening-round 72. He put that right with a course-record 61 on the second day.

McNulty needed only 25 putts and bagged eight birdies in a row from the ninth hole, a Southern African Tour record, as was his second-nine 28. The only hole on the back nine he did not birdie was the 17th. That put him one stroke behind halfway leader Des Terblanche, but rounds of 68 and 69 left him at 18 under and seven strokes clear of Terblanche, who finished fourth.

"It's always nice to win four in a year, and obviously it is a great feeling to win in Zimbabwe," said McNulty, also winner of his national Open in 1992, but whose 1995 season was curtailed by injuries. Price, who struggled with his putter, said of McNulty, "He's tough to beat on a course like this where you have to use a lot of seven, eight and nine irons, and that's the strength of his game."

Zambia Open—R150,000
Winner: Desvonde Botes

Desvonde Botes overtook playing companion Neil Homann to win a Zambia Open dominated by South Africans. Homann led for the first two rounds after an opening 66, but it was his closing 72 which allowed Botes to claim his first victory in three years.

Botes shot 68, 70 and 70 for a 208 total, eight under par and a one-stroke victory. Countrymen Glen Hutcheson and Alan Michell tied for third place at 211. The 22-year-old from Pretoria claimed two birdies on each nine of 35.

"I played pretty consistently for all three rounds without making too many mistakes and that was crucial," Botes said. "It makes all the work I've put in on my driving and my putting over the past month really worthwhile. I holed a few key putts at the right time. Sometimes it was a five-footer for par and sometimes it was a six-footer for birdie, but they all counted in the end."

15. Senior Tours

Things continue to go as planned with the season-ending Energizer Senior Tour Championship in the United States. The big-money, limited-field finale was created to maintain interest in the Senior PGA Tour to its drawn-out conclusion in the late autumn. The hope was that the year-long race to finish first on the money list would not be decided before the last weekend of the protracted season. That is what has happened most of the time since the idea took form in 1990 and was the case for the third year in a row at the climax event of the 1996 season. In fact, this time it came down to the final putts of the last round before Jim Colbert clinched the money title for the second consecutive year, as well as, in the minds of most observers, earning the distinction as the Tour's Player of the Year.

There was considerable room for argument, though. This was especially true before Colbert, who trailed Hale Irwin in the money race almost all season and was still behind entering the Energizer Senior Tour Championship, squeezed into the No. 1 spot ahead of him by a mere $12,121 at the season's conclusion. Irwin obviously doesn't put the same weight on the money title and its Arnold Palmer Award as Colbert has for two years. He played in nine fewer events than Colbert in 1996 and skipped two late-season events when the heat was on.

Even though Colbert won five tournaments and Irwin only two, a strong case could be made by citing Irwin's record. One of his wins was the PGA Seniors' Championship and among his seven second-place finishes were three in the other Senior PGA Tour majors. In fact, in his 23 starts, Irwin was fifth or better 16 times. As they say on television on election days, it was almost too close to call.

The other three major titles went to Dave Stockton, the leading money winner in 1993 and 1994, who won the U.S. Senior Open at Canterbury; Raymond Floyd, who captured the Ford Senior Players Championship, and Jack Nicklaus, who took The Tradition title for the fourth time in seven years. Each picked up another victory during the season — among 11 multiple winners — and Floyd had two other unofficial wins, worth nearly a half-million dollars — the Senior Skins and the Senior Slam.

John Bland, who came, seemingly to Americans, from nowhere to win in his second start in late 1995, had a brilliant season in 1996. The South African launched it with victory in the Senior Tournament of Champions in the January opener in Puerto Rico and scored three more wins during the year. The other two-time winners were Bob Murphy, Graham Marsh, Walter Morgan, Tom Weiskopf and Isao Aoki, a consistent contender who also won the Japanese Senior Open Championship when he returned home after finishing fourth on the money list, one of the circuit's nine $1 million winners.

Lee Trevino went until the Emerald Coast Classic, the next-to-last event, before extending to seven his string of seasons with at least one victory, but he won the Australian Seniors and, with Mike Hill, the Legends of Golf in March. Argentina's Vicente Fernandez and Gil Morgan, both 50-year-olds, were the season's only first-time winners, down from five in 1995, seven in 1994. PGA Tour veteran Morgan won in his second start.

No question about who was No. 1 on the European Seniors Tour. Tommy Horton, the former Ryder Cup player, won four times on the 13-tournament circuit, was second in five events and out of the top five just twice. John Morgan, the European Tour's leading player in 1994 who later qualified for the 1997 Senior PGA Tour in America, was the only other multiple winner with two late-season victories. Brian Barnes, who campaigned successfully much of the year in America, repeated as the Senior British Open champion in the circuit's top event at Royal Portrush in Northern Ireland.

The Japan Senior PGA Tour regressed in 1996, staging just six events.

U.S. Senior PGA Tour

Puerto Rico Senior Tournament of Champions—$800,000
Winner: John Bland

Less than three months earlier, John Bland was just a name among a host of players competing in a Monday qualifier for the Ralphs Senior Classic in Los Angeles, not exactly one who would be expected to become a member of the elite field that would play in the 1996 season-opening Puerto Rico Senior Tournament of Champions.

Even when Bland qualified for that exclusive event with his surprise victory in the Ralphs, the 50-year-old South African certainly did not rank among the favorites as he played in just his fourth tournament on the Senior PGA Tour. That Sunday evening in January, the soft-spoken Bland had the important title in tow and had launched a season that was to surpass what had been a moderately successful earlier career in South Africa and Europe.

Heavy rains forced an overnight delay in the completion of the first round at Dorado Beach until Saturday morning and when that long day was over, Bland, with 69-68–137, shared first place with Jim Colbert, the first-round leader who posted 67 and 70 for his 137. A handful of other players, particularly Raymond Floyd, Lee Trevino and Graham Marsh, were in the hunt until the end — seven men finished within three shots of the winner — but it turned into a duel between Colbert and Bland Sunday.

Colbert went two strokes in front with birdies at the seventh and eighth holes and retained that margin until, after missing several fairly short birdie putts, he drove behind a tree and bogeyed the 15th. Bland then snatched the victory with birdies at the last two holes, hitting a seven iron to three feet at the 18th, for his 70–207 total, nine under par.

Royal Caribbean Classic—$850,000
Winner: Bob Murphy

Bob Murphy has always felt particularly comfortable on Florida golf courses and in the winds that often buffet the Sunshine State. He illustrated that very clearly in the Royal Caribbean Classic at The Links at Key Biscayne, an excellently designed municipal course in the Miami area, zipping away from the contenders to a four-stroke victory with a 67 finish in winds whipping up to 35 miles an hour.

Hale Irwin, who was to provide what challenge there was to Murphy's Sunday march to the title, started out fast with a six-under-par 65, leading Dick Rhyan by two strokes, Rick Acton and Bob Charles by three and Murphy and three others by four.

Acton, one of the eight players who topped the qualifying tournament for the 1996 Senior PGA Tour, shot 67 Saturday to take a one-stroke lead over Irwin and Murphy into the final round. Murphy, beginning his fourth Senior PGA Tour season, started the move toward his ninth title right off the bat, dropping a five-foot birdie putt while both Acton and Irwin were taking bogeys.

By the turn, Murphy had two shots in hand and he went three in front with another birdie at the 10th. He bogeyed the 12th, held his own against pursuer Irwin with a match of birdies at the par-five 14th and secured the victory when he rolled in a 10-foot par putt at the 15th after Irwin, unable to deal with the Bermuda green surfaces, missed a 12-foot birdie putt. Murphy parred in for another 67, the day's best round and one of only two sub-par scores Sunday, and a 10-under-par 203 total. Irwin shot 71 for 207, Acton 73 for 208 and $61,200, $58,000 more than he had ever won before.

Greater Naples IntelliNet Challenge—$600,000
Winner: Al Geiberger

At age 58, Al Geiberger had been wondering if he would ever win again on the Senior PGA Tour. He had scored nine victories, but the last one had come in the GTE West Classic three years earlier. He answered that uncertainty in early February when, in his first 1996 start after foot surgery the previous December, he fought off the bids of Isao Aoki and several others and posted a one-stroke victory in the IntelliNet Challenge at The Classics at Lely Resort in Naples, second stop on the circuit's four-tournament, early-season Florida swing.

The victory even stirred thoughts of his memorable record 59 at Memphis in 1977, one of the bright spots in the life of the genial Californian who has endured a brutal string of physical problems and family tragedies. Two shots behind leaders Bruce Crampton and Jim Dent (66s) after the first round, Geiberger roared in front by three strokes when he shot a nine-under-par 63 Saturday. He ran off six birdies for a 30 on the front nine and thought: "That's what I did when I shot 59."

Raymond Floyd, his closest adversary at 134, was playing well but not having much putting luck. He got as close as one stroke at the eighth hole and had a chance to tie for the lead when Geiberger three-putted the 16th. Floyd missed a five-foot birdie putt and finished three back after Geiberger birdied the par-five 17th. Aoki started the final round five shots off the pace and ran off five birdies on the first 13 holes. He failed to gather another, although he was tied for the lead when Geiberger three-putted the 16th. Geiberger's birdie at the 17th led to a 71 and his 14-under-par 202 total, one better than Aoki's 67-203.

GTE Suncoast Classic—$750,000
Winner: Jack Nicklaus

It was a bit out of character for Jack Nicklaus to be playing in the GTE Suncoast Classic. Nicklaus rarely plays in the weekly stops that surround the major championships on the Senior PGA Tour. It was also atypical Nicklaus when he began the tournament with a five-over-par 76. But, most importantly, the weekend of action at the TPC of Tampa Bay was vintage Nicklaus as he came back with a 68-67 finish to capture the title by one stroke with his two-under-par 211 total.

Some unintended help from three of Nicklaus' main opponents helped him in scoring his ninth victory as a senior. His start wasn't as bad as it appears, since the opening round was played in 40-degree weather with winds whipping up to 40 miles an hour. Al Geiberger, coming off his victory at Naples, had the day's best round — par 71. Isao Aoki, runner-up to Geiberger the previous Sunday, shot 66 in improving weather Saturday and soared into a five-stroke lead with his 139 total. Nicklaus had 68 and shared the runner-up spot with Bob Murphy and Terry Dill.

Nicklaus got himself into a contending position early on a beautiful Sunday afternoon with four first-nine birdies. Murphy fell out of contention when a rebounding bunker shot nipped his hat at the par-five seventh and, with the two-stroke penalty, he took an eight. After bogeys at nine, 10 and 12 slashed Aoki's lead to one over Nicklaus, the Japanese ace duck-hooked his tee shot into the water at the 13th, chipped back and forth across the green three times and wound up with a nine.

Nicklaus had the lead and went to three under par when he ran in a 35-foot eagle putt at the par-five 14th. He got one more assist when J.C. Snead, seven under par for the day, double-bogeyed the 16th. Snead bounced back with a birdie at the 17th and finished with 65, but Nicklaus secured the victory after a bogey at the 15th with three pars, the final one with a five-foot putt after he overshot the 18th green.

American Express Invitational—$900,000
Winner: Hale Irwin

It is certainly not a case of "crying all the way to the bank," but Hale Irwin's protests about the easy setups of the courses on the Senior PGA Tour have a bit of an incongruous ring when he is making a shambles of some of them. Take the new American Express Invitational at Sarasota's TPC at Prestancia.

Irwin scored a five-stroke victory and was 19 under par with his 197 total, yet he reiterated his oft-mentioned feeling that, with the senior courses playing short with benign pin positions, not enough emphasis is being placed on shotmaking skills. He calls it "Birdie Ball."

Like it or not, the three-time U.S. Open champion, whose brilliant record is replete with victories on demanding courses that are usually too difficult for the pedestrian players in the fields, has taken the Senior PGA Tour by storm. With the victory, his third in 16 starts, Irwin topped the $1 million mark — $1,066,100 — more quickly than anyone ever has on the circuit. "I'm not complaining," Irwin emphasized afterward. "I'm having fun. But golf to me is more than that. I just like to play courses where par is a meaningful score."

Irwin's golf Sunday was virtually flawless — an eagle, seven birdies and no bogeys — yet he didn't shake off the final pursuer, Bob Murphy, until he ran off three of the birdies in a row in the middle of the back nine. Dave Stockton, with 65, led Irwin, Graham Marsh and Isao Aoki by one stroke the first day. Irwin, Stockton and Marsh shared the 36-hole lead with 133s, then Irwin obliterated the opposition Sunday with 64, one stroke off the Prestancia course record, held by George Archer. His 197 was a 54-hole course record by six strokes. Murphy finished second with a 68–202 total.

FHP Health Care Classic—$800,000
Winner: Walter Morgan

An old bugaboo frustrated Gary Player once again at the close of the FHP Health Care Classic. A playoff. Player, with 159 international titles of varying importance in his 40-plus years of professional golf, faced Walter Morgan after the two had tied in regulation with 11-under-par 199 totals.

For the 11th time in the 16 playoffs of his career, Player was the loser as Morgan rolled in an eight-footer on the first extra hole before Player, who had putted well with just one exception all week, missed from seven feet. "I will go to my grave being against sudden-death playoffs," muttered Player, who was after his 22nd win as a senior.

Morgan, a 54-year-old Vietnam War veteran and former club pro who won the 1995 GTE Northwest Classic, broke fast from the gate Friday after miserable early-week weather gave way to sunshine at the Ojai Valley Inn east of Santa Barbara in Southern California. The cigar-smoking pro fired an eight-under-par 62 with four birdies on the last five holes to take a two-stroke lead over Player and Jack Kiefer.

When Morgan slipped to 71 Saturday, Player jumped in front with 67–131, one shot ahead of Kiefer and Tom Shaw, two ahead of Morgan. Morgan came out blazing Sunday. He birdied the first two holes and, when he turned in 31, he had a three-shot lead over the Hall of Famer. But a two-stroke swing at the 10th and another Player birdie at the 13th after missing a promising eight-footer at the 12th locked the two men in a deadlock that carried to the end. Both birdied the 18th, Morgan for 66 and Player for 68. Kiefer shot 69 for 201 and third place.

Senior Slam—$500,000
Winner: Raymond Floyd

Raymond Floyd fashioned a successful defense of his Senior Slam championship the hard way. Floyd put himself in a hole — and last place — in Monday's first round of the two-day, four-champion tournament at Mexico's Cabo Real Golf Club, at least partially because he flew in from Florida Sunday after completing play in the Doral-Ryder Open. By Tuesday, he had settled down and, as promised, played better — 10 strokes better, in fact — and won the title again by three strokes with a four-under-par 140 total.

Tom Weiskopf, the U.S. Senior Open champion, held sway the first day as Floyd, the PGA Seniors' champion, and Jack Nicklaus, the Tradition victor in 1995 who also played at Doral but just two rounds, suffered shaky first rounds of 75 and 72, respectively. Weiskopf shot 70 and J.C. Snead, the other competitor who won the Senior Players Championship to make the elite field, had 71.

Weiskopf remained in front Tuesday until a double bogey off a shot into the water at the ninth dropped him back to even par, tied with Nicklaus and just a stroke ahead of Floyd. Floyd birdied the 10th, matched a Nicklaus birdie at the 11th and went ahead with a third consecutive birdie at the 12th. Nicklaus remained in the hunt until yet another Floyd birdie and his bogey at the 16th dropped him two strokes behind. Floyd wrapped up the 65 with a final two-putt birdie at the par-five 18th. Nicklaus posted 71–143, Weiskopf 74–144 and Snead 75–146.

Toshiba Senior Classic—$1,000,000
Winner: Jim Colbert

It took awhile, but Jim Colbert made it clear at the Toshiba Senior Classic that he would be a major player on the 1996 Senior PGA Tour just as he had been since joining in 1991. Colbert had not been a factor in any of his starts since finishing second to John Bland in the season-opening Senior Tournament of Champions. He turned it around at Newport Beach Country Club in Southern California.

"I can't play much better," observed Colbert after his 12-under-par 201 accounted for a two-stroke victory that really wasn't as tight as it would seem. He took only two bogeys over the 54 holes, both in the final round, and led by as many as seven shots that Sunday in the season's first million-dollar tournament.

The 55-year-old Las Vegas resident jumped from a five-way tie at 68 in the first round into a five-stroke lead Saturday when he birdied four of the first five holes and shot a six-under-par 65 for a 133 total. George Archer and Lee Trevino, one of the others along with Bob Murphy, John Schroeder and Homero Blancas who shared the Friday front with Colbert, settled into second place at 138 Saturday.

What challenge there was to the winner Sunday came from farther back as Colbert built his seven-shot margin on the first nine, noting that he birdied the 455-yard, par-four fifth for the third day in a row. "I lapped the field there." A par 36 on the second nine secured the victory as Bob Eastwood, playing in just his third senior event, came from far back with a course record-tying 64 to take second place at 203. He had an eagle and four birdies on the last eight holes.

Liberty Mutual Legends of Golf—$1,100,000
Winners: Lee Trevino and Mike Hill

Lee Trevino and Mike Hill might as well do their financial planning every year with at least one "given" — first-place checks from the Liberty Mutual

Legends of Golf. Trevino and Hill have been almost unbeatable since teaming up for the first time in 1991 in the unique event that fostered senior golf through its television popularity in the late 1970s. They made it four victories in their five Legends appearances together, coming from four strokes off the pace with a final-round 63 — an impressive feat in that type of competition on as nasty a place as PGA West's Stadium course at La Quinta, California. They won by two strokes with an 18-under-par score of 198.

The defenders had to share much of the pre-tournament attention at PGA West with the initial appearance in the event of Jack Nicklaus and his first-ever pairing with fellow Big Three great Gary Player. That Hall of Fame team was in contention throughout and eventually finished in a three-way tie for second place behind Trevino and Hill.

The over-60 team of Orville Moody and Jimmy Powell, who eventually shared the runner-up spot with Nicklaus/Player and Chi Chi Rodriguez/Harold Henning, were the leaders for two days. Powell spurred their first-round 65 with birdies at the first four holes, starting with a 65-footer at No. 1. Nicklaus and Player were second at 66, but slipped to 69 and a deadlock with Trevino and Hill (68-67) at 135. Moody and Powell retained first place with 66–131, one shot in front of Simon Hobday and George Archer.

Nothing happened favorably for the leaders Sunday en route to a 69 and they yielded the front to Hobday and Archer. Trevino and Hill forged in front by two strokes with birdies at the 11th, 12th and 14th and parred in for the 63.

SBC Dominion Seniors—$650,000
Winner: Tom Weiskopf

Tom Weiskopf found a little time for his hobby — golf — the last week of March and the last-hour decision to play in the SBC Dominion Seniors proved a rewarding one. Weiskopf, who entered within an hour of the Senior PGA Tour deadline, went on to win the tournament in San Antonio, his first victory since the 1995 U.S. Senior Open.

"Playing golf these days is pretty much a hobby for me," said the 53-year-old who won 15 PGA Tour events and the 1973 British Open. His main interest for years has been course design and his frequent visits to San Antonio while building the LaCantera Golf Club course there led to his decision to play at the Dominion Country Club instead of staying home and preparing for the following week's prestigious Tradition tournament in his home area.

Weiskopf didn't get his game fully geared until midway through the second round. By then, first-round co-leaders Raymond Floyd and Monday qualifier Charlie Epps (66s) had fallen back, Floyd finishing the day with an uncharacteristic 76. Weiskopf, three over par for the day after a bogey and double bogey early, birdied six of the last 11 holes for 69, tying Bob Dickson, Larry Mowry and Graham Marsh for the lead at 138.

Weiskopf ran off a string of pars Sunday before scoring his first birdie at the par-five ninth. He followed with two more at the 10th and 13th and was basically home free, although he went bogey-birdie on the next two holes. He posted his third straight 69 for a nine-under-par 207 total and a two-shot victory, his third as a senior, over Dickson, Marsh and Gary Player, who finished a runner-up for the third time in the year.

The Tradition—$1,000,000
Winner: Jack Nicklaus

Jack Nicklaus picks his spots on the Senior PGA Tour sparingly. Of one thing you can be sure until he is no longer playing tournament golf anywhere: The Tradition will be one of those choices. How would he ever explain not playing in one of the Tour's majors that he has won four times in his seven starts ... in the event at which he recorded his 100th professional victory ... on the Cochise course that he designed at Desert Mountain in Scottsdale, Arizona.

In becoming the first man to win a particular tournament on the Senior Tour four times, the 56-year-old Nicklaus outdueled Hale Irwin in the final round of the early April championship with a brilliant 65 to score a three-stroke victory. He shot 272, the lowest total of his Tradition wins.

The final round was set up by these earlier highlights: Irwin shared the opening-day lead at 65 with Ed Sneed as Nicklaus began with 68. Another Snead, J.C., went ahead on a windy Friday with 69-69–138 as Ed Sneed shot 75, Irwin 76 and Nicklaus 74. Raymond Floyd was at 139, had 69 for 208 Saturday to place third and join leader Irwin, 65 again for 206, and Nicklaus, also 65 for 207, in Sunday's final threesome.

Floyd fell away early and Irwin carried a two-stroke lead to the 12th hole, where Nicklaus truly won the tournament. Nicklaus chipped in on that par-five hole for a birdie Friday and holed a 159-yard eight-iron shot for a double eagle (third of his career) on Saturday. With Irwin facing a six-foot par putt after misplaying the hole, Nicklaus chipped in again from 25 feet for an eagle. When Irwin missed his putt, Nicklaus had the lead. The margin went to two when Irwin bogeyed the 13th and to the final three when Nicklaus birdied the 16th and parred in.

PGA Seniors' Championship—$1,100,000
Winner: Hale Irwin

Hale Irwin added the final missing ingredient to his first calendar year on the Senior PGA Tour, one that he had let slip from his grasp two weeks earlier. Irwin won his first major title on the over-50 circuit when he captured the PGA Seniors' Championship, making up for his shaky finish that opened the door for Jack Nicklaus to win The Tradition, the season's first major.

Because he was playing in a high-profile tournament for the fourth week in a row — The Players Championship, Tradition, Masters and PGA Seniors', all 72-hole events, of course — Irwin would figure to be wrung out. Instead, he launched his bid on PGA National's Champions course at Palm Beach Gardens, Florida, with 66, just ahead of Larry Gilbert (67) and Vicente Fernandez (68).

The grind and extra caution caught up to Irwin Friday when he shot 74, but it only dropped him a stroke off the lead, which was assumed by Bud Allin (67–139). Irwin was tied at 140 with Isao Aoki. He came back with 69 Saturday to take a two-stroke lead over Aoki and Fernandez with his 209, forfeiting a bigger margin when he bogeyed the tough 15th and 17th holes.

Irwin made three early birdies Sunday that cushioned two bogeys and he still led his playing partners by two after both men eagled the par-five 10th. Irwin birdied there and played a calculated conservative game the rest of the way in, holing a 35-footer for a two at the 15th. Bogeys at the last two holes produced 71 and eight-under-par 280 total, reducing his victory margin to two over Aoki, who always seems to be near the top on Sundays.

Las Vegas Senior Classic—$1,000,000
Winner: Jim Colbert

After going through the first three months of the season without a multiple winner, the Senior PGA Tour produced three in a row in April as Jim Colbert followed Jack Nicklaus and Hale Irwin as a two-time winner with his triumph in the Las Vegas Senior Classic. However, Colbert, the defending champion playing in his hometown, had to do it the hard way, going four holes in a playoff while putting away Dave Stockton and Bob Charles for his 15th seniors victory.

Early on, Colbert thrilled his Las Vegas fans with a 63 that is a course record at the host TPC at Summerlin. He led Charles and Tommy Aaron by two, then came back with 74 on a windy Saturday as Charles and Aaron, with 70s, took the lead with 135s. Hale Irwin, coming off his big victory in the PGA Seniors', shot 68 for 136 and Colbert was at 137.

Yet, it all came down to the final holes Sunday. Colbert wrote himself off, he admitted, when he fell two behind Charles with a bogey at the 17th. Then, he made an 80-foot birdie putt at the 18th to stay alive with a 70–207 total, nine under par. Stockton, seeking his first 1996 victory, ran off nine pars on the back for 68 and his 207, leaving a 12-foot birdie putt just short at the 18th.

Charles let both men back in when his putting stroke deserted him at the 18th green. On in regulation, he left a 30-footer 10 feet short and didn't come close with the next one. Obviously shaken, the New Zealander, a 22-tournament victor on the Senior PGA Tour who had won only once since 1993, three-putted again on the same green at the start of the playoff and was eliminated. Colbert and Stockton matched pars on the next two holes, then Colbert won with a one-putt par at the short 17th when Stockton bunkered his tee shot and left his blast in the sand.

PaineWebber Invitational—$800,000
Winner: Graham Marsh

Graham Marsh has been showing American golf fans on the Senior PGA Tour how he established such an outstanding record in the earlier years in other parts of the world. The Australian, winner of 55 tournaments in Australia, Japan and Europe over a two-decade period in the 1970s and 1980s, decided against following the paths of contemporary countrymen Bruce Crampton and Bruce Devlin who elected to move to America and play the PGA Tour during that period.

As a result, U.S. galleries saw Marsh only briefly in the late 1970s, when he won the Heritage Classic, and since 1994, when he turned 50 and joined the U.S. Senior PGA Tour. He has been a frequent contender, particularly in 1995, when he scored his first senior victory in the Bruno's Memorial Classic and had 14 top-10 finishes.

Graham notched his second victory in early May at Charlotte, North Carolina, winning the PaineWebber Invitational in a tight battle at the TPC at Piper Glen. He was never out of the lead in one of the Senior PGA Tour's founding tournaments, but never in command until the final hole. He opened with a six-under-par 66 and shared the top spot with Brian Barnes, then followed with 71 that kept him in first place, then with Larry Gilbert, as Barnes, the Senior British Open champion, slipped to 74. The nearest pursuers then were Jack Kiefer and Dick Hendrickson, one behind at 138.

It was a tight battle most of the way Sunday. At one point, Marsh, Gilbert, Barnes and Tom Wargo were tied for the lead. Gilbert moved ahead with birdies on the testing 13th and 14th holes, but Marsh pulled even with a birdie at the 15th and moved in front to stay when Gilbert drove out of bounds at the par-five 16th. He birdied again there as Larry was taking a double bogey, but gave one back with a ball in the water at the short 17th. Barnes had also bogeyed the 17th ahead of him, so Marsh's careful par at the 18th converted a 69 for 206, 10 under par. Barnes, with a closing 67, and Wargo, with 66, tied for second.

Nationwide Championship—$1,200,000
Winner: Jim Colbert

Jim Colbert continued on a pace that brought him the money title and Player of the Year honors in 1995 when he won the Nationwide Championship in Atlanta in mid-May. The victory, his third of the season, came at virtually the same point in the schedule as he picked up No. 3 the year before and the $180,000 first-place check moved him into position to challenge Hale Irwin for the money lead on the Senior PGA Tour.

Colbert again victimized Bob Charles as he won at the Golf Club of Georgia. He took the Las Vegas Classic title away from Charles — and Dave Stockton — after an unbelievable putt and a playoff two weeks earlier. At Atlanta, he swept past Charles early in the windswept final round when the New Zealander dumped a shot in a creek and double-bogeyed the second hole and went on to 69, a 10-under-par 206 total and a three-stroke victory over the ever-present Isao Aoki, the 1992 Nationwide champion. Irwin protected his money lead with a closing 68 for 210 and third place.

Charles jumped in front Friday with 65 that gave him a three-stroke lead over John Jacobs, Don Bies, Bruce Crampton, defending champion Bob Murphy and Graham Marsh, who was coming off a win the previous Sunday in Charlotte. Although he shot 71 Saturday, Charles retained a one-shot margin over Colbert (71-66) and first-year qualifier Bobby Stroble (69-68), who was never a factor Sunday en route to 79–216. After slipping past

Charles at No. 2 with a birdie, Colbert took his only bogey at the par-three third and added three more birdies on his way to his 16th Senior Tour title.

Cadillac NFL Golf Classic—$950,000
Winner: Bob Murphy

Bob Murphy was due. For two years running, he had finished second in the Cadillac NFL Golf Classic at Upper Montclair Country Club in New Jersey on a course where 28 years ago he won the Thunderbird Classic, one of the richest events on the PGA Tour at that time. Murphy did not become over-due, working up a two-stroke victory amid the sideshow pro-am rounds involving a host of NFL quarterbacks and kickers.

The victory came harder than it seemed since Murphy began the tourna-ment with a 10-under-par 62, an Upper Montclair record, and a five-stroke lead over Lee Trevino and Tommy Aaron. He had nine birdies and followed a one-putt (15 feet) bogey at the par-three 15th with an eagle two at the 16th when he holed a 138-yard eight-iron shot. The comfort zone disappeared on a dreary Saturday, though. He struggled to 71, offsetting five birdies with four bogeys, and finished the day in a first-place tie at 133 with Jay Sigel, who shot 64, and just a stroke in front of Dave Stockton, who matched his 62.

Murphy figured he needed 68 to win Sunday, but 69 was enough for a two-stroke victory, his 10th on the Senior PGA Tour. Although outdriven by Sigel, Murphy kept his ball in the fairways and relied on his putter, pointing out that the successful round turned on consecutive, par-saving six-footers at the ninth and 10th, the latter to remain in a first-place tie with Sigel. Murphy birdied the 14th and 16th off tight approaches and Sigel bogeyed the 12th to establish a three-stroke lead that dropped to the final margin of two when Murphy bogeyed the par-three 17th. With his second 1996 win, Murphy rejoined Hale Irwin and Jim Colbert in the money race.

BellSouth Senior Classic at Opryland—$1,200,000
Winner: Isao Aoki

One had to think a victory was in store for Isao Aoki. The brilliant Japanese shotmaker had been hanging around the top of the standings on the Senior PGA Tour almost all year, finishing 12th or better in all but one of his 10 starts, placing second three times, including his last previous tournament.

Aoki, Japan's only true international star, fulfilled the expectations in the BellSouth Senior Classic at Opryland at Nashville's Springhouse Golf Club with a 14-under-par 202 total, the first wire-to-wire winner of the season. Yet he had to hole a 30-foot birdie putt on the final green to escape a three-way playoff with a one-stroke victory.

An opening 64 stoked Aoki's momentum. Aoki ran off eight birdies on the first 14 holes and parred in, taking a two-stroke lead over Dick Rhyan and Jay Sigel, who was coming off a runner-up finish the previous Sunday in the Cadillac NFL Golf Classic. Aoki led by only one stroke after 68 Satur-day and his closest pursuer was leading money winner Hale Irwin, who shot

66. John Jacobs was at 134 and a classy group of five — Bob Murphy, Simon Hobday, Gary Player, Lee Trevino and Sigel — were just three strokes off the pace.

The 54-year-old Aoki built a four-stroke lead Sunday on the first 12 holes, then gave them all back coming in with three-putt bogeys on the 13th and 15th and, shades of Tampa, double-bogeyed the 16th by chipping over the green. Meanwhile, Sigel and Graham Marsh were finishing ahead of him with 203, Sigel off 68 and Graham off 67 when a missed green and poor chip led to a costly bogey at the 18th. He waited and watched as Aoki, after gauging the speed by watching Jacobs' longer effort, rolled in the 30-footer — "a perfect putt ... the only one all day" — for 70 and the victory, his fifth on the Senior PGA Tour, one of six circuits on which he has won during his brilliant career.

Bruno's Memorial Classic—$1,050,000
Winner: John Bland

It was a strange way for John Bland to win his third title on the Senior PGA Tour, but he'll take them any way he can get them. After battling Bruce Summerhays for possession of first place in the first two rounds of the Bruno's Memorial Classic, Bland found himself in a playoff with two other players — Kermit Zarley and John Paul Cain — that accentuated the negative, even when he prevailed at the third extra hole.

Bland and Summerhays shot five-under-par 67s in the opening round at Birmingham, Alabama's Greystone Golf Club. Neither made a bogey and Summerhays came within a foot of a double eagle at the par-five 13th, as they led five players, including Cain, who shot 69s. Summerhays inched a stroke ahead of the 50-year-old South African Saturday with 69 for 136 as Bland had 70. (Summerhays had the same score in 1995 at Greystone, but then was in second place and five strokes behind eventual winner Graham Marsh.) Cain also shot 70 and shared third place at 139 with Marsh and Isao Aoki, the previous week's winner at Nashville.

It rained steadily Sunday and Summerhays was affected the most. He shot 77. But Bland holed a 10-foot birdie putt at the 18th for 71–208 and tied Zarley, who closed with 68, and Cain, who finished with 69, for their 208s. Zarley, whose only Senior PGA Tour victory came in the 1994 Transamerica, was all over the lot at the second extra hole and bowed out with a double bogey after he and Bland got a reprieve at the first extra hole when Cain missed a four-foot birdie putt. Bland had escaped a creek by inches there with an errant tee shot. At the third, Cain, a two-time winner in his eight years of senior golf, found rough and rocks and took a double bogey, too. Bland won with a bogey when he three-putted. Not glorious but rewarding.

Pittsburgh Senior Classic—$1,100,000
Winner: Tom Weiskopf

Tom Weiskopf found some time for tournament golf, experimented with and discarded a new set of clubs with unsuitable shafts while playing at Nashville and Birmingham, then went to Pittsburgh and put on a vintage Weiskopf performance. He dominated the Pittsburgh Senior Classic at Quicksilver Golf Club in the city's rural suburbs, leading from start to finish and posting a three-stroke victory with a tournament-record, 11-under-par 205 total, two better than Bob Charles' winning score in 1993.

Arnold Palmer stirred his home area fans when he shot 69 in Friday's first round and shared second place with Bob Eastwood, one stroke behind leader Weiskopf. It was his best start of the year. However, the 66-year-old master, who regularly commutes to Quicksilver from his Latrobe home some 60 miles away by helicopter, couldn't maintain the pace and eventually finished 19th after a pair of 74s. Weiskopf widened his margin over Eastwood Saturday when he shot 67 for 135 while Eastwood was carding a second 69 for 138.

Weiskopf played an uncomfortably defensive game Sunday and was never threatened. He parred the first six holes, hit the par-five seventh green in two and made his first birdie, then added another at the ninth. He was breezing, hit 16 greens in regulation and shot 70 with a bogey at the last hole. Brian Barnes, the Senior British Open champion, took another big step toward his money-list exemption (top 31) for the 1997 season. The burly Scot closed with 66, the week's best round, and tied for second at 208 with J.C. Snead, who shot 67 Sunday. Eastwood finished fourth and Hale Irwin, the money leader who started the final round four back, shot 72 for 211 and placed fifth.

du Maurier Champions—$1,100,000
Winner: Charles Coody

"When I said I was going to have to turn things around," remarked Charles Coody, "I wasn't thinking of something so dramatic." The 58-year-old Texan hadn't won anything on his own on the Senior PGA Tour since 1991 and things seemed to be going from bad to worse in 1996. In his first 13 starts, he finished in the top 25 just once and had only two rounds in the 60s. He shelved any thoughts of hanging it up though when he fired a rousing, five-under-par 65 in the final round of the new du Maurier Champions (conversationally, the Canadian Seniors) that carried him from four strokes off the pace to a one-stroke victory at Hamilton Golf and Country Club at Ancaster.

Coody had sensed some improvement in his game at Birmingham and while practicing at home in Abilene, Texas, and felt comfortable at Hamilton, but he wasn't a serious factor during the first three rounds. Instead, Larry Mowry, 59, another man suffering through a long dry spell and for three years a nagging vertigo problem, topped the standings for three days, shooting for his first win in seven years. He put together rounds of 66, 67 and 69 and had a one-stroke lead over Kermit Zarley.

John Bland, who had beaten Zarley in a playoff two weeks earlier at the Bruno's Memorial, came up with 65 and shared the second-round lead with Mowry, but 72 Saturday left him three behind. Meanwhile, Coody had quietly shot 69, 70 and 67, in position for a high finish but virtually ignored as a potential winner.

Mowry, experiencing some wildness in his game, made nothing but pars after a bogey-par-birdie start and his 70–272 total proved one stroke too many. Coody gradually crept up the leaderboard and took the lead when he rapped in a three-footer at the 14th hole. Mowry had a final chance at the 18th, but left a 25-foot birdie putt just short. The victory was Coody's fifth individual title on the Senior PGA Tour. He won the Legends for a second time in 1994 with Dale Douglass, his last victory.

Bell Atlantic Classic—$900,000
Winner: Dale Douglass

Dale Douglass was inspired when Charles Coody, his old buddy and Legends playing partner, ended a long winless streak in the du Maurier Champions tournament. Douglass had gone almost as long as Coody without an individual victory — the 1993 Ralphs Classic — when he arrived in Philadelphia for the Bell Atlantic Classic on the heels of Coody's win in Canada. Besides, he had a good track record at Chester Valley Golf Club and a playoff victory over Gary Player there in 1990.

It added up to a dominating week for Douglass, who performed the unprecedented feat of successfully defending his Merrill Lynch Shoot-Out title that Tuesday and winning not only his second Bell Atlantic title but also the concurrent, 36-hole Grand Masters competition for the 60-and-over set in the field. Douglass turned 60 in March and became the fourth oldest winner on the Senior PGA Tour with his playoff triumph, his 11th in 10 seasons on the circuit.

Douglass trailed for two days at Chester Valley but was well-positioned just three strokes off the pace going into the final round on the rolling, par-70 course at Malvern. Bobby Stroble, Rick Acton and Tom Wargo were on top with 67s Friday, then Jay Sigel and John Schroeder came to the fore Saturday, Sigel with 69 and 66 and Schroeder, playing his first full senior season, with 68 and 67 for his 135 total. Wargo (69) was at 136, Stroble (70) at 137 and Douglass, with a pair of 69s, at 138.

Douglass joined the serious contenders with a birdie at the fourth hole Sunday and got to four under par with his last two birdies at the 11th and 12th after a bogey at No. 9. That put him in a four-way tie for the lead and he parred in, despite missing the last three greens, for a 68–206 total, deadlocked with Wargo (70) and Schroeder (71), who bogeyed the 18th. Sigel, the hometown favorite, faded badly with a back-nine 41 for 76. The trio parred the first two extra holes before Douglass put his approach five feet from the cup and sank the winning birdie putt.

Kroger Senior Classic—$900,000
Winner: Isao Aoki

You could call Isao Aoki the amusement park champion of 1996, although you can be sure he paid little attention to the fun and games available at Opryland and Kings Island, where he won the Senior PGA Tour tournaments staged on the courses tied into those attractions in Tennessee and Ohio.

The latter victory came at the end of June in the Kroger Senior Classic and avenged a one-stroke defeat he had suffered at Kings Island in 1995. Mike Hill, the culprit, was the victim in 1996, though he and Rocky Thompson trailed Aoki by five strokes in the runner-up slot. Aoki became the year's seventh multiple winner and moved into the No. 2 position on the money list behind Hale Irwin with $828,008, less than $100,000 behind.

Kings Island's Grizzly course yielded its usual bevy of low scores, starting with J.C. Snead's 62 and Aoki's 63 Friday. Aoki, encumbered with a touch of flu, followed with 69 Saturday and took a one-stroke lead over Hill and Bob E. Smith with his 132. Then, on Sunday, he established his winning position on the first nine. With threatening weather moving in, Aoki birdied the fourth, fifth and sixth holes and sank a 30-foot eagle putt at the ninth to go four strokes in front. He three-putted No. 10 for his only bogey just before a 55-minute rain delay. Hill bogeyed the 13th and Aoki parred to the 18th, where he made a final birdie for 66 and 198, 15 under par. Hill shot 70 and Thompson caught him with a closing 66 for his 203 and his third straight top-four finish in the Kroger. It was Aoki's sixth win on the Senior PGA Tour.

U.S. Senior Open—$1,200,000
Winner: Dave Stockton

The success Dave Stockton has enjoyed in tournament golf over the years has generally been credited to his special proficiency on and around the greens. So he got particular satisfaction from his solid performance in capturing his first-ever USGA title — the U.S. Senior Open on the highly regarded Canterbury Country Club course in Cleveland. "This was tee-to-green as flawless as I have ever played in a major," said Stockton, who survived a late charge by Hale Irwin to score a two-stroke victory with his 11-under-par 277 total.

The win came somewhat unexpectedly, since Stockton had been enduring a sub-par season and had his wife's impending knee surgery on his mind. In fact, he had skipped two tournaments right before the Senior Open because of that. Two weeks out of the weekly pressure cooker trying to gain his first victory in 14 months at least gave him some rest.

Stockton opened with 70 as playing companion Bob Charles took the lead with a course record-tying 66. Then he took charge of things with 67s the next two days to build a seven-stroke lead with his 12-under-par 204 total. Charles remained in second place, one back after a 72 Friday and seven back after a 73 Saturday.

The challenge Sunday came not surprisingly from Irwin. Starting the round eight strokes behind, Irwin birdied seven of the first 16 holes to close within one stroke as Stockton methodically crafted 17 consecutive pars. Then Irwin cracked with bogeys at the last two holes for 67–279. Stockton took a meaningless bogey at the 18th for 73 and his 277, securing his 12th Senior PGA Tour victory and third senior major to go with his two PGA Championships in his earlier years.

Ford Senior Players Championship—$1,500,000
Winner: Raymond Floyd

As far as Raymond Floyd was concerned, the year had been pretty much a washout, even though his record really didn't show it. Out of the top 10 only four times ... more than $400,000 in earnings ... third-place finishes in The Tradition and U.S. Senior Open ... unofficial victories worth a half-million dollars in the Senior Skins and Senior Slam. But Floyd had no victories that counted.

In the weeks just before the Senior Open and Ford Senior Players Championship, Floyd decided "I was either going to stop or do the things that are necessary to make me a good player." He carved more practice time out of his business schedule, noticed improvement and sensed victory in the year's final senior major at the TPC of Michigan "if my putting is good."

It was fine, thank you, and Floyd's forecast was true to the tune of a two-stroke victory over leading money winner Hale Irwin, whose astonishing record in the 1996 senior majors was winning the PGA Seniors' Championship and runner-up finishes in the other three. Floyd won the tournament in the middle rounds, finishing with a 13-under-par 275 total. After starting with 71, five strokes behind leader Tom Weiskopf, Floyd shot 66 himself Friday and moved into a three-way tie for first with Irwin (70-67) and John Bland (68-69). When he followed with 65, the week's best score, Floyd jumped four strokes in front of Irwin.

Irwin provided the only pursuit Sunday and that came too little too late to threaten Floyd, who took a conservative approach to nurse the lead. Irwin bogeyed the first hole to fall five strokes back, was seven back after 11 holes, then got back to a four-stroke deficit when Floyd three-putted the 14th green. Irwin then followed with a par-birdie-birdie sequence to get to 11 under before Floyd bogeyed the last hole for 73 and 275.

Burnet Senior Classic—$1,250,000
Winner: Vicente Fernandez

Finally, there was a new winner on the Senior PGA Tour. Never in recent years had it taken so long in the year for a non-winner to achieve a victory. The honors this time went to Vicente Fernandez, an Argentinean who campaigned successfully in his younger days in South America and Europe for a combined total of 15 victories.

Fernandez emerged from a pack of contenders to win the Burnet Senior Classic in suburban Minneapolis in July, completing a week that started with 67 in the Monday qualifier, which puts the last four players into the field. He was the fifth player — Larry Mowry, John Paul Cain, Rives McBee and John Bland the others — to win a tournament after playing his way in through the qualifier.

The little Latin, who once caddied for Chi Chi Rodriguez, had come to America to try his hand at the Senior PGA Tour in the spring after turning age 50, but with the weekly qualifier and sponsor invitations his only entry route, Fernandez had played in only eight tournaments before the Burnet Senior Classic, finishing third in his first start in the PGA Seniors' in April.

Fernandez put together rounds of 69 and 68 for a 137 total, sharing second place with Al Geiberger, Tom Wargo and J.C. Snead, one stroke behind leader Jim Dent after 36 holes. It was a blanket finish Sunday. At one point, eight players were tied for the lead and Fernandez held or shared the lead four times before he holed a 15-foot birdie putt at the 16th to go in front for good. He parred in for 68 and an 11-under-par 205 total. Bruce Crampton, a senior star of the past who had only one top-10 finish up to then, also closed with 68 and tied Snead for second place.

The big bonus for Fernandez, in addition to the $187,500 check, was the one-year exemption on the Senior Tour he received as a tournament winner. The purse also enhanced his chance of finishing in the top 31 on the money list to stretch that exemption to the end of the 1997 season.

Ameritech Senior Open—$1,100,000
Winner: Walter Morgan

It took him four years to get comfortable on the Senior PGA Tour, but Walter Morgan has found that nothing does more for one's confidence than meeting and beating the best of the game's older players. "It gets easier every week," said the former career Army sergeant and club pro after winning the Ameritech Senior Open in Chicago, his third victory in 11 months. "I shoot for the pins now."

Morgan shot for a lot of pins in the opening round at Kemper Lakes Golf Course, the new venue for the Ameritech after five years at Stonebridge. He raced to the first-round lead with a nine-under-par 63 that broke the course-record 64 set by Craig Stadler there in the 1989 PGA Championship. It was a flawless nine-birdie effort with month-old clubs that replaced a set he lost and gave him a five-stroke lead over Rives McBee, Gibby Gilbert and Bob Murphy. "But, it's too early to celebrate," he cautioned. Raymond Floyd made that apparent Saturday, when he birdied four of the last five holes for 65 and, as Morgan shot 70 for 133, moved within a stroke of the leader, who is getting used to star pressure. He beat Gary Player in a playoff in his earlier 1996 win.

As it turned out, what pressure there was on the 55-year-old Morgan Sunday did not come from Floyd, whose putter turned cold. He shot 75 and tied for fourth with David Graham, who, along with John Bland, got within two strokes of Morgan on the back nine. However, Bland ran out of birdies at the 11th hole and Graham bogeyed the 15th and double-bogeyed the 18th, where he drove into the water. Bland's 68 gave him 207 and second place as Morgan's 72 finish essayed a winning, 11-under-par 205 total. On a rain-softened course playing 300 yards longer, Payne Stewart was 12 under par in winning the PGA Championship at Kemper Lakes.

VFW Senior Championship—$900,000
Winner: Dave Eichelberger

Dave Eichelberger's career has been a series of peaks and valleys and he couldn't have been down much lower during the first seven months of the

1996 season on the Senior PGA Tour. He finished better than 21st just once in 23 starts — sixth at Pittsburgh where he won his only Senior Tour title in 1995 — and knew why that was. His tee shots. He ranked dead last on the Tour's driving accuracy chart.

Eichelberger turned to his one iron and used it almost exclusively off the tee in the last two rounds of the VFW Senior Championship in Kansas City the first week of August. With that adjustment, he eked out a two-stroke victory over local favorite Jim Colbert, who grew up in the neighborhood.

"I literally couldn't keep the ball on the golf course," Eichelberger explained about his earlier-season driving woes. "I was hitting the ball out-of-bounds twice a round and hitting it in the water twice a round. I tried something different every shot."

The one-iron solution paid off early at Kansas City's Loch Lloyd Country Club, where he launched his bid with driver in hand. He shot a six-under-par 64 for the lead but had given up on the driver after hooking a tee shot badly at the 15th hole. Frank Conner, doing well in his first senior season, flashed two consecutive 65s and took a two-stroke lead over Eichelberger, four over Colbert into the final round. Conner's game deserted him Sunday, though. He had two double bogeys and shot 78, tying for 12th place.

It turned into an Eichelberger/Colbert shootout. Colbert, whose hot early-year game had cooled off a bit of late, forged into the lead with a birdie at the 12th. Eichelberger bounced back with birdies at the 13th and 15th and led by two when Colbert bogeyed the 16th. Colbert kept his chances alive when he birdied the 17th but Eichelberger, dead straight with his one-iron tee at the 18th, iced the victory when lashed an eight-iron approach shot three feet from the cup. The final birdie gave him 68 for a 10-under-par 200 total.

First of America Classic—$850,000
Winner: Dave Stockton

Normally a late-bloomer each year on the Senior PGA Tour, Dave Stockton was following that script once again in 1996 after deviating a bit the previous season. Five weeks after capturing the U.S. Senior Open Championship, Stockton scored again in the First of America Classic at Grand Rapids, Michigan, becoming the eighth multiple winner of the season.

The victory, the 13th in his four-plus years on the circuit, came with a final-round 69 that spurted him from a four-stroke deficit to a one-stroke final margin over Bob Murphy, another of a half-dozen players trying to catch Hale Irwin on the money list. Stockton, who won without his usual deadly putting, was 10 under par for the distance at the testing Egypt Valley Country Club.

Both Stockton and Murphy bided their time during the first two rounds. Tommy Aaron, age 59, whose only Senior PGA Tour win was in 1992 at Kaanapali, was the opening-day leader with 66, one shot in front of Bruce Summerhays and Tom Wargo, as Stockton shot 68 and Murphy started with 73. Bobby Stroble, one of the 1995 qualifying tournament exemptees who had popped into contention fairly often, surged three strokes into the lead Saturday with 65 for 133, as Summerhays, another lesser-known pro having a good year, shot 69 for 136 and Stockton joined Jimmy Powell at 137. Murphy began his move with 66 for 139.

"It was my tournament to win," said Stroble. He got through "some of the critical holes" on the front nine and was tied for the lead with Powell at nine-under after 10 holes despite three bogeys. He double-bogeyed the 11th and was out of it. Powell lost one stroke coming in to finish third with Wargo, leaving the title battle to Stockton and Murphy. Stockton birdied the 13th to take the lead, topped a Murphy birdie at the 15th, then opened his margin to two with a wedge third shot to two feet at the par-five 17th. That gave him a cushion when he came up short at 18. He chipped to six feet. Murphy had a 15-footer for a winning birdie. They both missed the putts.

Northville Long Island Classic—$800,000
Winner: John Bland

John Bland is obviously not a golfer to rest on his laurels. Virtually unknown in America when he came to California in the autumn of 1995, the South African promptly qualified and won the Ralphs Classic. Two more victories followed in the Senior Tournament of Champions and Bruno's Memorial in the early months of 1996 and he never let up.

Yet another victory came in the Northville Long Island Classic in mid-August, an impressive, come-from-behind triumph in which Bland bested the likes of Raymond Floyd and Jim Colbert, the other only player who also had three 1996 wins on his record.

Bland started with a two-under-par 70 at the Meadow Brook Club at Jericho, Long Island, trailing Floyd, Larry Gilbert and Mike McCullough by four strokes. Floyd, a noted frontrunner who had won the Senior Players a month earlier, had his eye on another victory as he took sole possession of the lead with a 67 Saturday and professed that "I'm excited about the way I'm playing." At 133, which was a tournament record, he had just a one-stroke lead on Colbert and Jay Sigel, and Bland, who had shot 66, was fourth at 136. "It's incredible for me to be playing the way I'm playing and only have a one-stroke lead," Floyd pointed out.

None of the others were any match for Bland Sunday. Bland rolled in a 12-foot eagle putt at the third hole, followed with birdies at the fourth and fifth, and took the lead. He didn't know it at the time because he was playing ahead of Floyd, who was struggling after a lower-back ailment that he had been nursing all week flared up at the second hole. Floyd did very well to get in with 73 and finish third. Bland birdied the 10th and 12th, then parred in for another 66 and 202. Colbert, in hot pursuit of Hale Irwin in the money race, shot 71 and finished second at 205. Lee Trevino, winless in 1996 and trying to make it three in a row at Northville, tied for 31st.

Bank of Boston Senior Classic—$800,000
Winner: Jim Dent

Jim Dent won his first Senior PGA Tour tournament in more than a year on the 18th green of the Nashawtuc Country Club course in the Bank of Boston

Senior Classic, but the 13th green played an even more important role in its own way. The birdie Dent made at the final hole might have been meaningless if he hadn't holed a 30-foot chip shot at the par-three 13th for a par. He still needed the birdie to edge Tom Wargo and Jay Sigel by a stroke, both missing makeable putts there, Wargo from four feet.

"Sometimes you've got to have some luck and I was fortunate today," said the 57-year-old native Georgian after registering his 10th win as a senior and first since the 1995 BellSouth at Nashville.

While the 13th was salvation for Dent, it turned out to be the undoing of Wargo, who also was without a victory in more than a year. Wargo, who had started the round at 135 with a one-stroke lead on Raymond Floyd, two on Dent, Sigel and Terry Dill, caught trees with his tee shot at the 13th, too, and eventually had to make a 10-footer for four. That bogey dropped him into a three-way tie with Dent and Sigel.

Dent parred to the par-five 18th, where he knocked a 225-yard three-wood shot over the green, chipped to five feet, made the putt for a 67–204 total and watched as Sigel missed a birdie putt from 12 feet and Wargo three-putted from 60 feet, missing the second from four feet. Defending champion Isao Aoki, who led the first day with 67, then fell back with 72 Saturday, returned another 67 Sunday to finish fourth at 206. Floyd was never far out of it until he found water and took a double bogey at the 16th.

Franklin Quest Championship—$800,000
Winner: Graham Marsh

Graham Marsh has found the area around Salt Lake City a great place to work and play. In January, he — and his family — played on the ski slopes of the Wasatch Mountains. At the end of August, he returned to Utah to work on the fairways of Park Meadows Golf Club and won the Franklin Quest Championship. Sure, you play golf, but Marsh had to work hard to emerge from a flock of contenders in strong winds that raked the 7,026-yard course and capture his second Senior PGA Tour title of the season, his third since joining the circuit in 1994 — the Bruno's Memorial in 1995 and the PaineWebber Invitational in May. He also became the ninth multiple winner of 1996 with the Franklin Quest win.

Things did not look overly promising for the globe-trotting Australian after Friday's round. Gary Player, who has done his share of traveling during his career, opened with a sparkling, eight-under-par 64 and had Marsh by six strokes. Another internationalist, John Jacobs, trailed by one, then took over first place Saturday with 69–134, as Player took a 74 and fell four strokes off the pace. Marsh made his move that day, fashioning a 65 to advance within one of Jacobs and set himself up for the final 18 Sunday.

Graham was pleased when Sunday dawned breezy. "I enjoy the wind," he said. Still, he didn't handle it all that well on the first nine — "It was more survival than anything" — but scrambled well, five times saving pars from bunkers. Jacobs fell back at once when he bogeyed the first hole and eventually shot 76 and tied for 16th place. On the other hand, Marsh sharpened his game on the second nine, birdied three of the last five holes for a 67–202 total, and won by two over Kermit Zarley, who closed with 68. Graham clinched the victory when he birdied the par-five 17th to establish the two-stroke margin.

Boone Valley Classic—$1,200,000
Winner: Gibby Gilbert

How would you figure this finish? Hale Irwin, the Senior PGA Tour's leading money winner, is coming off a course-record 63, is just two strokes off the lead and is playing in front of a huge gallery of supporters in the inaugural Boone Valley Classic in his home area just outside St. Louis, Missouri. Bunky Henry, in front with his 66-65—131 total, 11 under par at Boone Valley Golf Club, had never led a tournament going into a final round. Then Gibby Gilbert, age 55, who started the day just a stroke behind Irwin and hadn't won in more than three years, put two balls in the water at the second hole and took a quadruple-bogey eight. Piece of cake for the highly talented Irwin, right? Wrong.

Henry did stumble on the front nine with four bogeys and relinquished the lead to Irwin when Irwin birdied No. 6. But Irwin's putter went cold and Gilbert didn't quit after the shock of the eight. Tom Wargo shot 31 on the first nine to catch Irwin, then fell back to a 69. Irwin missed birdie putts inside 15 feet at Nos. 11, 12 and 13, then birdied the par-five 14th after a 50-minute lightning delay. Gilbert had recovered to a two-stroke deficit through 15, gained one when Irwin bogeyed No. 16 and forced a playoff when he holed a six-foot birdie putt at the 18th for 69—203. Irwin shot 70 for his 203 total. Henry, who got his game going on the back nine, missed the playoff by one stroke when he failed on a 20-foot birdie try on the last green.

Finally, who would expect Irwin, with a six iron to the green from a perfect fairway lie, to put the ball in the water and give the playoff and title to Gilbert with his routine par. Gibby, whose non-related namesake Larry had attracted more attention in the interim, last won in the 1993 Las Vegas Seniors, his fourth victory on the circuit.

Bank One Classic—$600,000
Winner: Mike Hill

Little had been heard from Mike Hill after he started the 1996 Senior PGA Tour season with some distinction and won the Legends of Golf with Lee Trevino for a fourth time in March. No wonder. He hadn't played much. Tired of the travel and monotonies of the road and dedicated to helping his wife regain her health and mobility after hip-placement surgery, the 57-year-old Hill, one of the Senior PGA Tour's most successful players, played only eight times through the spring and summer before starting a four-tournament run the first week of September at Boone Valley.

Remarkably, Hill doesn't get rusty with the inactivity. He finished Boone Valley with 66, then won the Bank One Classic at Kearney Hill Links in Lexington, Kentucky, the following week, breaking away from a pack with a closing 68 for a one-stroke victory over Gibby Gilbert, the Boone Valley winner, and Isao Aoki, who had been fourth and third the two previous weeks. He was nine under par at 207.

Aoki, who won the Bank One in 1994, and Jim Wilkinson, one of the eight qualifiers for the season, secured the first-round lead with 66s. Gilbert shot 69 and 11 men, including Hill, had 70s. Hill followed with 69 Saturday and moved into a four-way tie for first with Wilkinson and two of the other preseason qualifiers — Mike McCullough and Bobby Stroble.

Hill established a two-stroke lead in the middle of the final round when he had four birdies in a five-hole stretch, beginning at the eighth. Jim Albus also was hot early, six under par after eight holes, but he faded to a sixth-place finish. Hill saved par at the 14th with an improvised five-wood "chip," three-putted the 16th and parred in for the 68. Both Aoki and Gilbert birdied the 18th to make it close. The victory was Hill's 18th individual one, tying him for seventh place on the all-time victory list on the circuit with Gary Player. Hill, who was the leading money winner in 1991 when he won five times, has triumphed at least once every year since joining the Senior Tour in 1991.

Brickyard Crossing Championship—$750,000
Winner: Jimmy Powell

The record says otherwise, but don't try to tell Jimmy Powell that you are not supposed to win on the Senior PGA Tour after you turn 60. Only five players in their 60s have done so — and Powell is two of them. He won in 1995 in the First of America tournament when he was 60 and did it again in 1996 when he was 61 years, eight months and five days old in the rain-abbreviated Brickyard Crossing Championship in Indianapolis. Only Mike Fetchick, who won at Hilton Head on his 63rd birthday back in 1985, was an older Senior Tour victor. Dale Douglass was just a few months past his 60th birthday when he won the Bell Atlantic Classic in June.

Once again the Indianapolis tournament ran into weather problems. For the fourth time in nine years and third time in the last four, rains washed out a round at the old Speedway course and its upgraded Brickyard Crossing layout. An all-day rain forced cancellation of Saturday's activities after Simon Hobday, the defending champion but in the midst of an "off" season, shot "my most solid round of the season" — a seven-under-par 65 with birdies at three of the last four holes that staked him to the first-round lead. "I can't play at all until I get here," Hobday noted. He was a stroke ahead of Bob Betley and Tom Wargo, who birdied the first four holes en route to his 66. Powell was in a five-player group at 68, one behind Bud Allin and Bobby Stroble, in contention once again.

A long-putter fancier, Powell had the touch when play resumed Sunday after the postponement. He made putts of 20 and 25 feet for birdies on the first two holes and when he birdied the fifth and sixth, "I knew I was in the game." He birdied the ninth for 31. A bad tee shot cost him a stroke at the 10th, but he birdied three more times, then bogeyed the last hole for 66 and the winning 134 total. John Jacobs, who had just gotten a tip from his brother, Tommy, the former PGA Tour regular, birdied three of the last four holes to finish second, one back at 135.

Vantage Championship—$1,500,000
Winner: Jim Colbert

Jim Colbert took a big step toward a repeat of his No. 1 finish on the Senior PGA Tour money list when he won the rich Vantage Championship for a third time at the end of September. The victory — Colbert's fourth of the year, matching his 1995 total — gave him a $225,000 check and moved him within $200,000 of Hale Irwin. However, Irwin prevented his closest rival from getting even closer by finishing second for the sixth time and picking up $110,000 himself.

The players had their hands full with unpredictable greens at Tanglewood Park outside of Winston-Salem, North Carolina, leading to higher-than-normal scoring, particularly after the first round, when Colbert began his march toward the title he claimed in 1991 and 1992, his first two years on the Senior PGA Tour.

Colbert shot 65 with seven birdies and a bogey to take a one-stroke lead over Kermit Zarley, J.C. Snead, Bruce Devlin, DeWitt Weaver, Rick Acton and 66-year-old Don January, returning to action as a sponsor invitee after recovering from a separated shoulder injury he suffered in a household accident. January, one of the Senior PGA Tour's biggest stars in its early years, stayed close all week and tied for eighth, his best finish in three years.

Snead squeezed into first place by a stroke with a 68-134 total as Colbert shot 70 and Gary Player moved into contention with 65. Both stood at 135 with Irwin and Raymond Floyd challenging at 136. Colbert was spinning his wheels as Player established a two-stroke lead early in the final round. Then came the turning point. Colbert chipped in from 20 feet at the 14th, followed with two more birdies at 15 and 16, saved par from the sand with a 12-foot putt at the 17th and parred the 18th for 69–204, nine under par. Irwin, already in, had birdied the 18th for 205, joining Zarley at that score. Player, in trouble off the tee, failed to convert a 40-footer at the 18th and also finished with 205.

Ralphs Senior Classic—$800,000
Winner: Gil Morgan

Only Chi Chi Rodriguez could have handled his disappointment with such good humor. Gil Morgan, just 11 days past his 50th birthday, had just nipped him — and Jim Colbert — by a stroke to win the Ralphs Senior Classic on the Senior PGA Tour. Minutes after his fatal three-putt at the 18th green, the Latin-American quipster proclaimed: "The trouble is Dr. Morgan was born two weeks too early."

The non-practicing optometrist, playing in just his second senior tournament, became the Senior PGA Tour's youngest victory ever — winning three days quicker than George Archer did in 1989 at Abilene, Texas. Morgan posted rounds of 68, 68 and 66 for the winning 202 total, 11 under par in the event's second staging at Wilshire Country Club. It gave the Oklahoman, a seven-time winner on the regular PGA Tour, three victories on three different Los Angeles courses. He had won the Los Angeles Open at Riviera in 1978 and at Rancho Park in 1983.

Rodriguez, 61, without a victory since the summer of 1993, had inched ahead of the field Saturday, firing 66 for 133 to go one stroke in front of Colbert (66-68), already a four-time winner in the season, who had shared the first-round lead with Raymond Floyd, Bunky Henry and Harold Henning. Morgan, starting three back Sunday, came out blazing with birdies on the first five holes to take the lead. Rodriguez fought back on the incoming nine. Birdies at the 12th and 14th pulled him within one stroke of the lead.

Playing ahead of Rodriguez and Colbert, Morgan bogeyed the last hole when he missed the green and a seven-foot par putt and, expecting a playoff, watched the others finish. After Rodriguez rolled his 25-foot birdie putt from the back fringe for the win five feet past the hole, Colbert missed his 15-footer for a tie, just as he had done a year earlier to lose by one stroke to John Bland in the 1995 Ralphs Classic. Then Rodriguez failed with his short one and it was over.

The Transamerica—$700,000
Winner: John Bland

Jim Colbert figured out how to deal with his nemesis — John Bland. "We've got to get him deported back to South Africa," said Colbert kiddingly after finishing second to the surprising Bland for a fourth time among his five victories since joining the Senior PGA Tour in October of 1995. The latest victory — in The Transamerica at Silverado Country Club — was Bland's fourth of the year, matching Colbert's total for the year and projecting him into the race for Player of the Year honors and, remotely, the money title.

The last two rounds at Napa, California, revolved around those two men and the Saturday leaders, Lee Trevino and Bobby Stroble. Trevino, still winless on the Tour in 1996 except for his Legends of Golf victory with partner Mike Hill, shot 64, his best round of the year, to tie Stroble (68-67) at 135. Trevino's putting deserted him Sunday and Stroble, a contender in almost every tournament since the first of August, raced to a four-stroke lead at one point Sunday and still was ahead by two when he hooked a three-wood tee shot out of bounds at the 16th and took a triple bogey.

Just before that disaster, Stroble had heard the crowd roar when Colbert, who had started the day four strokes behind after rounds of 71 and 68, made a hole-in-one with a five-iron shot at the 185-yard No. 15. That two-stroke gain revived his chances and he felt he had given himself a shot at a playoff against Bland when he birdied the par-five 18th for 66 and 205, 11 under par. The South African refused to oblige. After watching Colbert make the birdie, Bland put his second shot in the front bunker, came out 18 feet long and sank the putt for 66 and the victory with his 204.

With money leader Hale Irwin absent for the second week in a row, Colbert moved to within $70,000 of him with the $61,600 second-place check. Bland trailed Colbert by nearly $200,000.

Raley's Gold Rush Classic—$800,000
Winner: Jim Colbert

Hale Irwin returned to the Senior PGA Tour after a two-week absence hoping to protect and extend his dwindling advantage in the race for the money title and its coveted Arnold Palmer Award and played well enough to finish fifth. However, neither he nor anyone else in the field of the Raley's Gold Rush Classic, the final event of the three-tournament fall swing through California, was any match for the streaking Jim Colbert.

The confident 55-year-old Colbert, who won and finished second twice in his last three starts, rolled to a five-stroke victory at Serrano Country Club near Sacramento and swept ahead of Irwin into the No. 1 spot by some $11,000. The $120,000 victory, his fifth of the year, boosted Colbert's earnings to a record $1,490,995. Irwin had held the top position since mid-March.

Colbert, who had been at Serrano from Tuesday on, began the tournament with 67 to join Bud Allin and Harold Henning one shot behind leader Jack Kiefer in the rain-interrupted first round. Irwin, who didn't arrive until Wednesday night, opened with 69. He remained within three strokes of the front with another 69 Saturday as Colbert took over with 68 for 135, nine under par and two ahead of Butch Baird.

Irwin showed his mettle on the front nine Sunday. He made a spectacular eagle deuce with a four-wood shot over trees and water, went out in 32 and had a stroke on Colbert. Disaster struck Irwin at the par-five 13th. He reached a greenside bunker in two, blasted 40 feet long and four-putted for a double bogey. Colbert was brilliant on the incoming nine, making five birdies on the last seven holes after saving bogey from seven feet following a watered tee shot at the par-three 11th. His 67 gave him a 14-under-par 202 and the five-stroke victory over Dave Stockton. Irwin closed with 71-209.

Hyatt Regency Maui Kaanapali Classic—$650,000
Winner: Bob Charles

This time the hot player who added to Hale Irwin's frustrations was Bob Charles, who found his storied putting stroke in time to win the Hyatt Regency Maui Kaanapali Classic and relegate Irwin to a second-place finish for the fifth time since scoring his second and last 1996 victory in the PGA Seniors' Championship in April

Charles, on the other hand, picked up his first win of the season. The 60-year-old New Zealander successfully defended his Kaanapali title, scoring his third victory on Kaanapali Golf Club's North course. He was the third player beyond his 60th birthday to win in 1996 and, with 23 victories, moved into sole third place behind Lee Trevino (26) and Miller Barber (24) in career totals.

It was a Charles/Irwin duel right from the start. Irwin shot 63, eight under par, the first day, but led Charles by only a shot. Irwin had nine birdies and a bogey, Charles six birdies, a bogey and his first of four eagles during the week. The two men then shared first place with 129s after 36 holes. The left-hander had two more eagles, one when he holed a 140-yard nine-iron shot, en route to his 65 while Irwin had six birdies and a bogey in his 66.

The putter betrayed Irwin Sunday. He three-putted three times, but, through 13 holes, had a one-stroke lead over Charles, who wasn't making anything on the greens either. Then Charles rolled in a 15-footer at the 14th to tie Irwin, got the fourth eagle with a 17-footer at the 15th and clinched victory when he ran in a 55-footer at the par-three 17th. He bogeyed 18 for 69 and the winning 198 total. Irwin finished with 70–199 and the $57,200 check enabled him to slip back to No. 1 on the money list as Jim Colbert, who had just taken over the previous week, had his poorest finish since early September, tying for 27th place. Steve Veriato, a Monday qualifier, closed with 66 to grab third place at 200.

Emerald Coast Classic—$1,050,000
Winner: Lee Trevino

It hadn't been much of a year by Lee Trevino's standards. No official wins on the Senior PGA Tour, just victories in the Legends of Golf with partner Mike Hill and the Australian Seniors in March, only nine top-10 finishes. With only the Senior Tour Championship to go, it appeared that Trevino's string of winning years was about to end at six when he finished his final round in the Emerald Coast Classic three under par with 68 for a 207 total.

Dave Stockton was still on the course, five under with two holes to play. Before Trevino, notoriously fast on his exits, could get away, Stockton bogeyed those last two holes and dropped into a five-way tie at 207 with Trevino, Hill, Bob Eastwood and David Graham. Trevino then made quick work of the Pensacola tournament's second playoff in its two-year existence, making a 35-foot birdie on the first extra hole — the 18th. So Trevino had won at least once in all seven of his full seasons on the Senior PGA Tour and leads everybody with 27 titles.

None of the playoff participants was a major factor at The Moors Golf Club, a new, Scottish-style layout on the Gulf Coast. Instead, Walter Morgan and Jimmy Powell, each with 1996 wins under their belts, led four others with their opening 65s. They fell back on a windy Saturday and Dave Eichelberger and Larry Gilbert took over first place with 136s. Stockton, the Senior Open champion who was fifth on the money list, then took the lead — and lost it at the end Sunday.

Hale Irwin missed the playoff by one shot with 69–208 but increased his money-race lead to $66,000 over runner-up Jim Colbert, who tied for 24th.

Energizer Senior Tour Championship—$1,600,000
Winner: Jay Sigel

At a time when Tiger Woods was dominating the sports pages in his early weeks as a professional golfer, another man who had a great amateur record before joining the play-for-pay ranks came up very big on the Senior PGA Tour. Jay Sigel, who turned pro when he reached 50 in late 1993 after a distinguished career that included two U.S. Amateurs and a British Amateur among a horde of victories, captured the season-ending Energizer Senior

Tour Championship and its record, first-place check of $280,000, jumping his 1996 earnings over $1 million. He shot a closing, par 72 for 279 and a two-stroke victory over Kermit Zarley, his first since his initial season in the 1994 GTE West Classic.

Although his standout performance was fully recognized, Sigel had to share the stage Sunday with the hairbreadth finish of the Senior Tour season's competition for the money title and Player of the Year honors. It came down to Jim Colbert's 12-foot birdie putt at the last hole of the demanding Dunes Golf and Beach Club course at Myrtle Beach, South Carolina. He made it, then had to wait out John Bland's third-place tie with him, a missed birdie putt by Jim Dent and Bob Charles' shot into the water at the last hole before knowing that he had finished his 32-tournament season with a $12,121 margin over Hale Irwin, who played in nine fewer events. Irwin tied for 10th at 288, five shots behind Colbert.

Irwin had started the final event, with its select field of 31 leading money winners of the year, three ahead of Colbert, shooting a five-under-par 67 for the first-round lead. Middle rounds of 75 and 76 put Irwin back in the pack as Sigel came to the fore. With a starting pair of 69s, Sigel shared the 36-hole lead with Vicente Fernandez and Frank Conner. Yet another 69 that included a hole-in-one at No. 5 moved Sigel three strokes ahead of Bob Charles and five in front of Zarley in third place. The long-hitting Philadelphian, who was six under on the par-fives, was never threatened Sunday.

European Seniors Tour

Beko/Oger Tours Turkish Seniors Open—£100,000
Winner: Bobby Verwey

The European Seniors Tour broke new ground in 1996 with its season opener, the entourage traveling to Turkey for the new Beko/Oger Tours Turkish Seniors Open. Bobby Verwey was the major beneficiary of professional golf's introductory event to the Middle Eastern nation, scoring a three-stroke victory at the National Golf Club resort course on the Mediterranean. The 55-year-old South African came from three shots off the pace in the final round to post his first victory on the circuit since the 1991 Senior British Open in his rookie season.

The National course, a David Feherty/David Jones design, and torrid weather tested the seniors throughout the tournament. Par 72s gave shares of the first-round lead to Englishmen Brian Waites and Jim Rhodes and Americans Chick Evans and Walt Sauer. Verwey, who opened with 74, still trailed by three after shooting another 74 Saturday. Snell Lancaster, a little-known U.S. player, was in front with 73-72–145, one stroke ahead of Australian Noel

Ratcliffe and two ahead of Evans.

Verwey's putting brought the victory Sunday. He sank seven straight par putts of between six and 10 feet starting at the eighth hole, then ran in a 45-footer for one of his four birdies, registering a two-under-par 70 for a two-over-par 218 total. Tommy Horton was one of only two others to break par Sunday, his 71–221 jumping him into second place. Lancaster folded with 83, Evans shot 75 and Ratcliffe 76.

De Vere Hotels Seniors Classic—£75,000
Winner: Renato Campagnoli

Renato Campagnoli produced a replica of his initial European Seniors Tour victory in 1995 when he claimed a five-stroke win in the De Vere Hotels Seniors Classic in early June at Belton Woods, near Grantham, England. The former Italian World Cup player from Florence put together three sub-par rounds for a nine-under-par 207 total, one stroke better than the three sub-par scores he strung up in winning the International German PGA Seniors in his first season on the circuit.

Campagnoli and Bill Hardwick, a Canadian resident of Florida, were the only men to break par on a windy Friday at Belton Woods, Hardwick leading with 69 and Renato shooting 70. The Italian moved in front with 69–139 Saturday. Hardwick stayed close with 72–141, then faded badly with 78 Sunday.

Instead, Antonio Garrido of Spain and especially Tommy Horton, the defending champion, challenged Campagnoli in the final round. In fact, after Campagnoli dropped a shot at the 10th and Horton birdied the 13th and 14th, the margin had constricted to one. But Campagnoli was more than equal to the challenge and rolled to his five-stroke margin with four birdies on the final six holes for a 68. Horton, with 67, and Garrido, with 68, tied for second at 212. Roberto Bernardini, the only other player to break par, shot 71 for 214.

Hippo Jersey Open—£100,000
Winner: Maurice Bembridge

It was a long time between victories for Maurice Bembridge. One of Britain's leading players in the 1960s and 1970s, Bembridge had not won a tournament since 1979. It happened finally three tournaments into his second season on the European Seniors Tour at the Hippo Jersey Open, one of the five new events on the circuit, and it was a convincing triumph — by seven strokes with a 14-under-par 202 total.

Even more impressive, Bembridge started the tournament at Jersey's La Moye Golf Club three strokes off the lead as South Africa's Vincent Tshabalala shot a seven-under-par 65, two in front of Alberto Croce, the 1995 Lawrence Batley victor, and John Morgan, the 1994 money leader. Bembridge shared the 68 slot with four others, including local favorite Tommy Horton, head pro at Royal Jersey.

Bembridge's putter went to work Saturday. He holed five putts longer than

Year of the Tiger

Michael C. Cohen

Tiger Woods dominated the PGA Tour after becoming a professional in August.

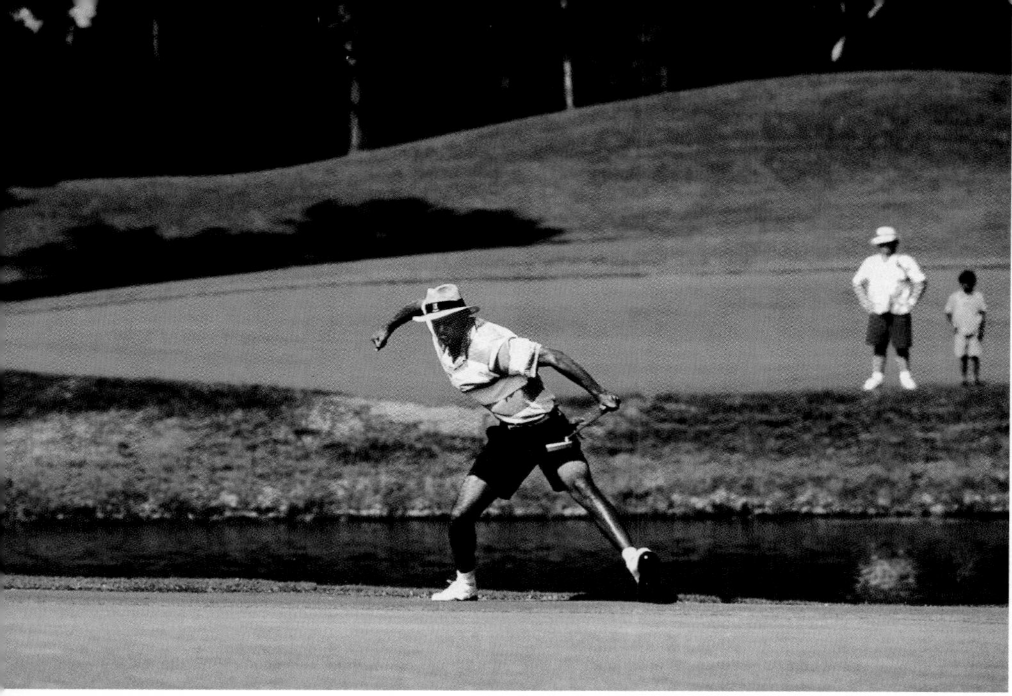

Allsport/Rusty Jarrett

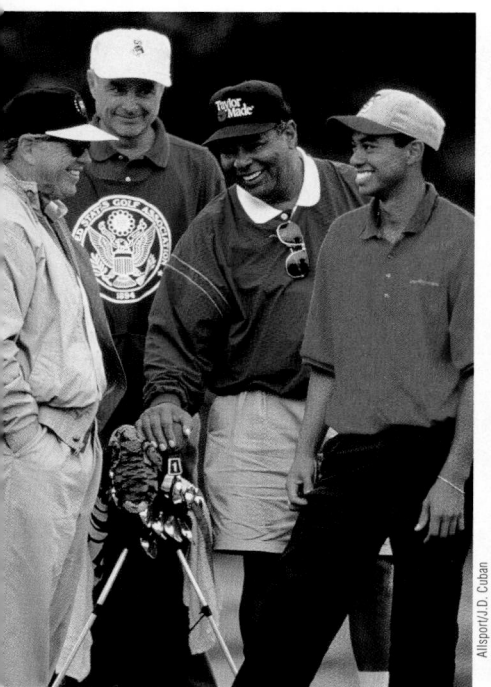

Woods won the first of a record three consecutive U.S. Amateur titles in 1994.

Allsport/J.D. Cuban

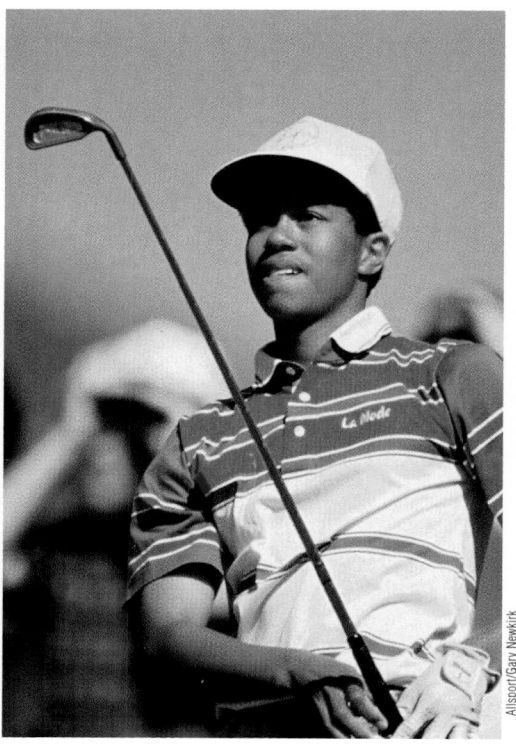

Woods' support group includes (from left): coach Butch Harmon, sports psychologist Jay Brunza, and his father, Earl.

Allsport/Gary Newkirk

At age 16, in 1992, Woods played his first PGA Tour event in Los Angeles.

Allsport/J.D. Cuban

Allsport/J.D. Cuban

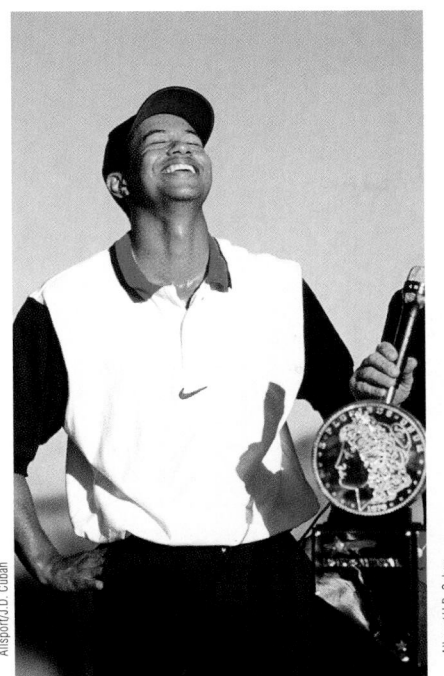

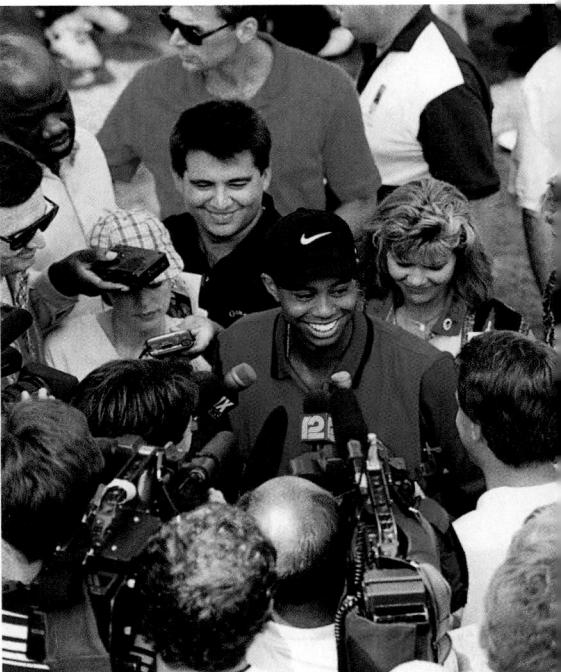

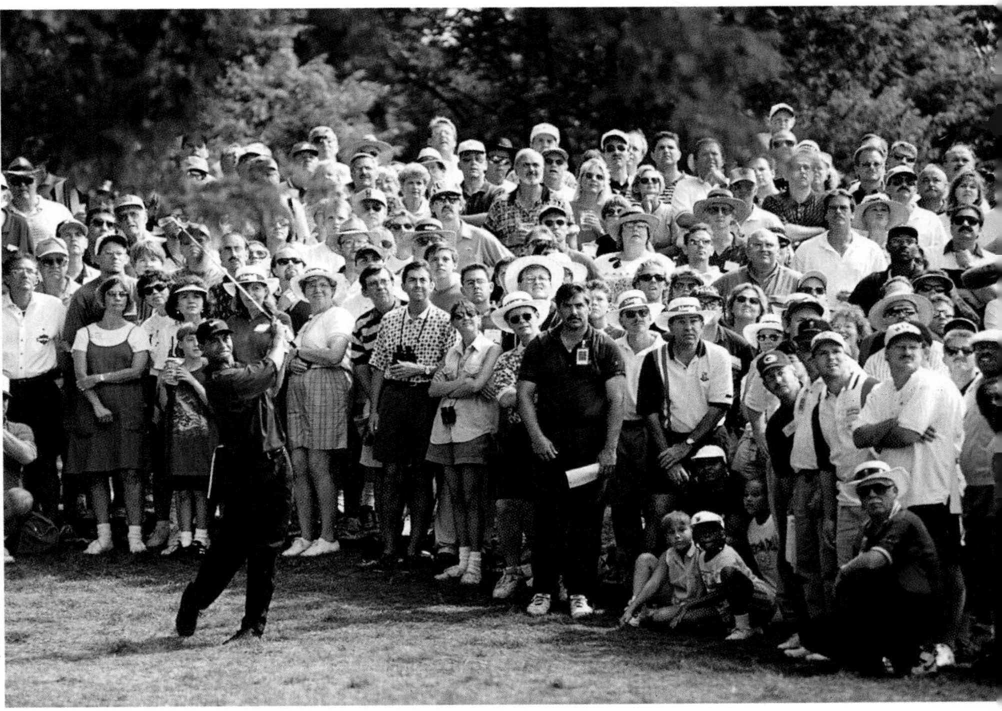

Allsport/J.D. Cuban

Surrounded by media throngs and huge galleries, Woods won twice in his first seven professional events and had $790,668 in official prize money.

Masters Tournament

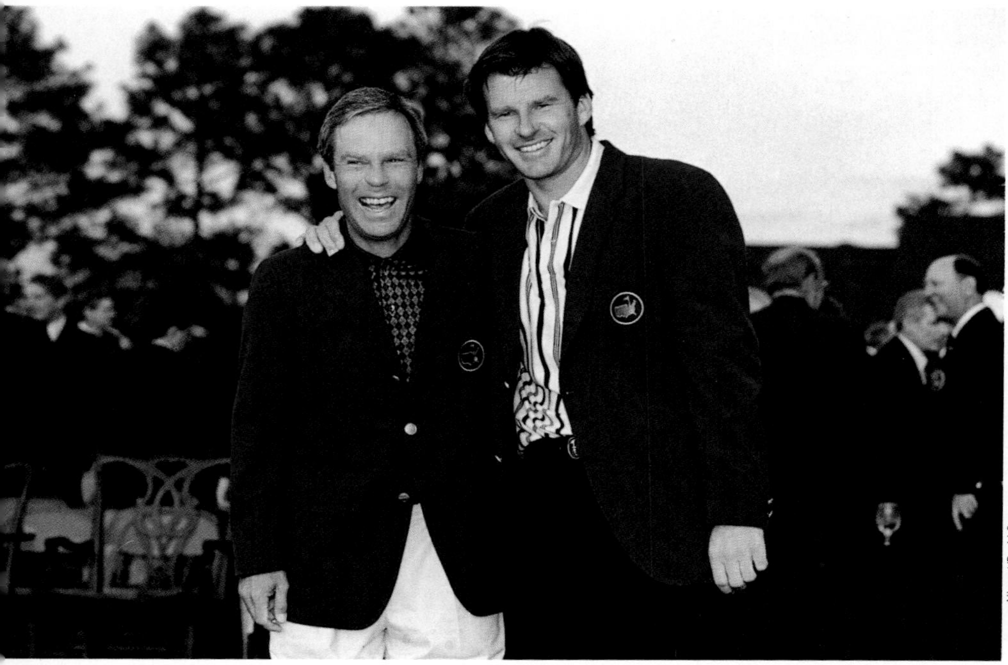

Allsport/David Cannon

Ben Crenshaw presented Nick Faldo with his third green jacket.

Allsport/David Cannon

Allsport/Stephen Munday

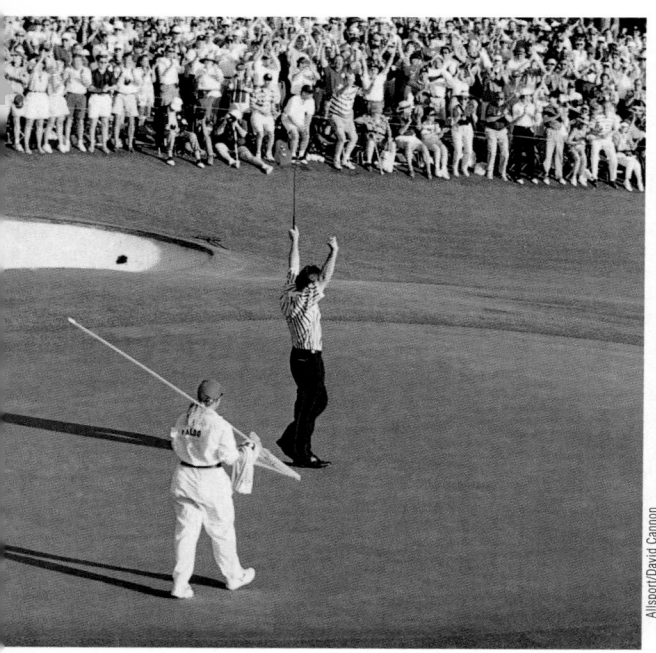

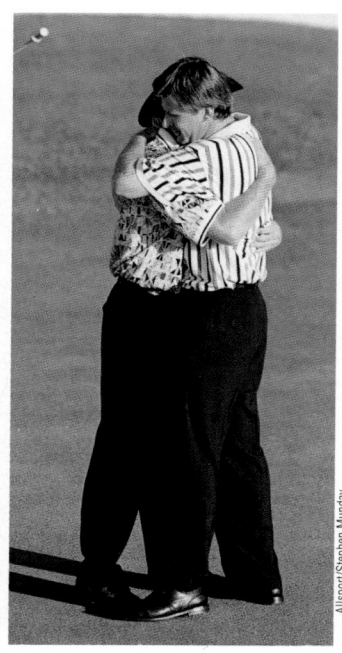

Faldo wrapped up his final-round 67 then consoled runner-up Greg Norman.

Allsport/Stephen Munday

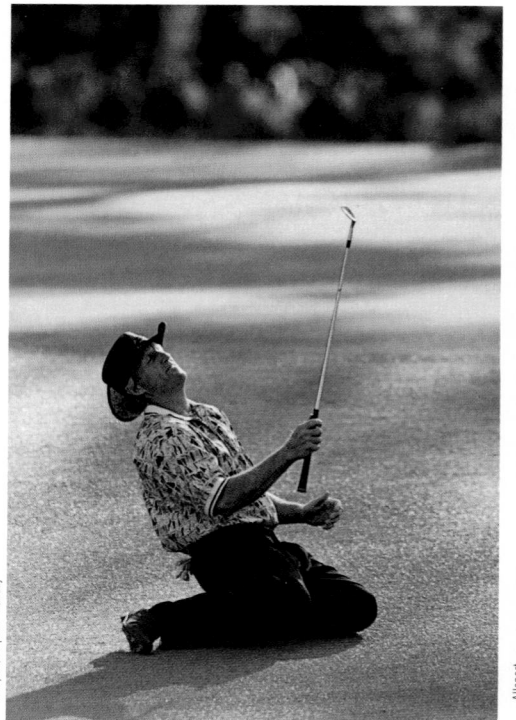

Norman's collapse was painful to watch.

Allsport

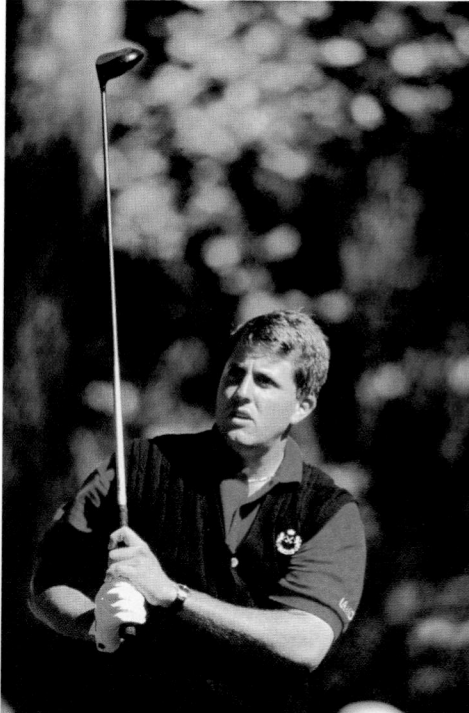

Phil Mickelson took third place.

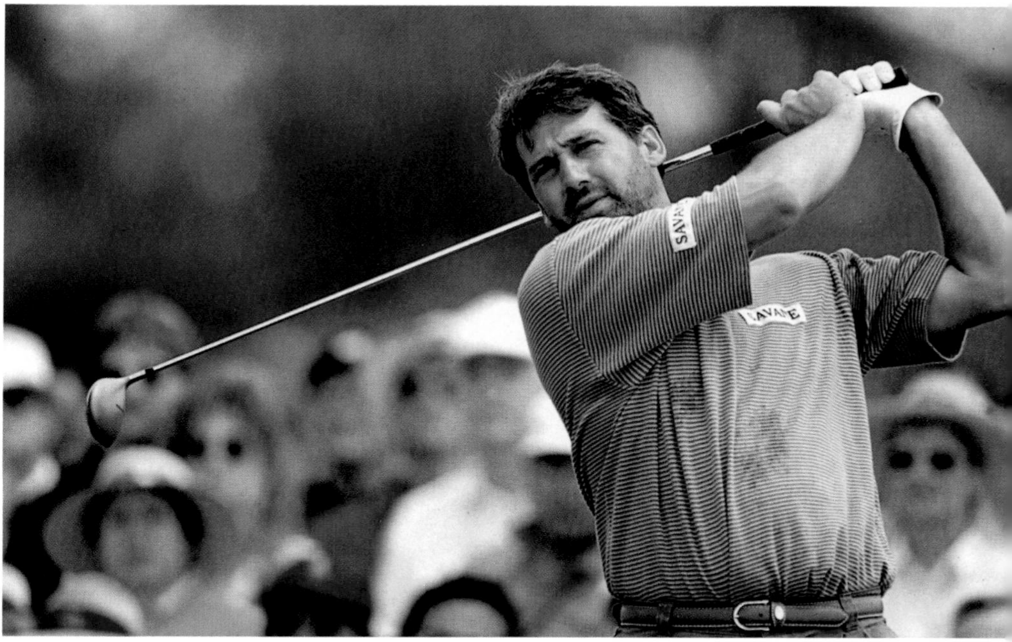

Allsport/David Cannon

New Zealand's Frank Nobilo shot 69 in the last round to take fourth place.

U.S. Open

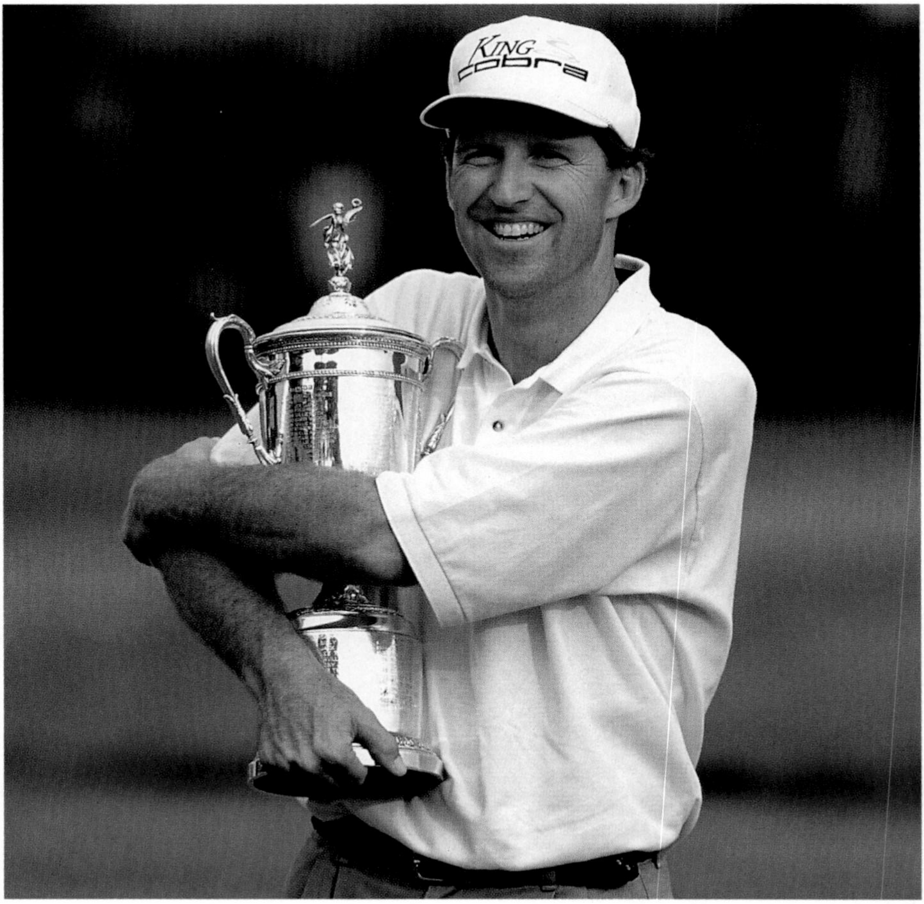

Michael C. Cohen

Steve Jones wrapped his arms around the U.S. Open trophy after being congratulated by his friend Tom Lehman (right), who tied for second place.

Fred Vuich

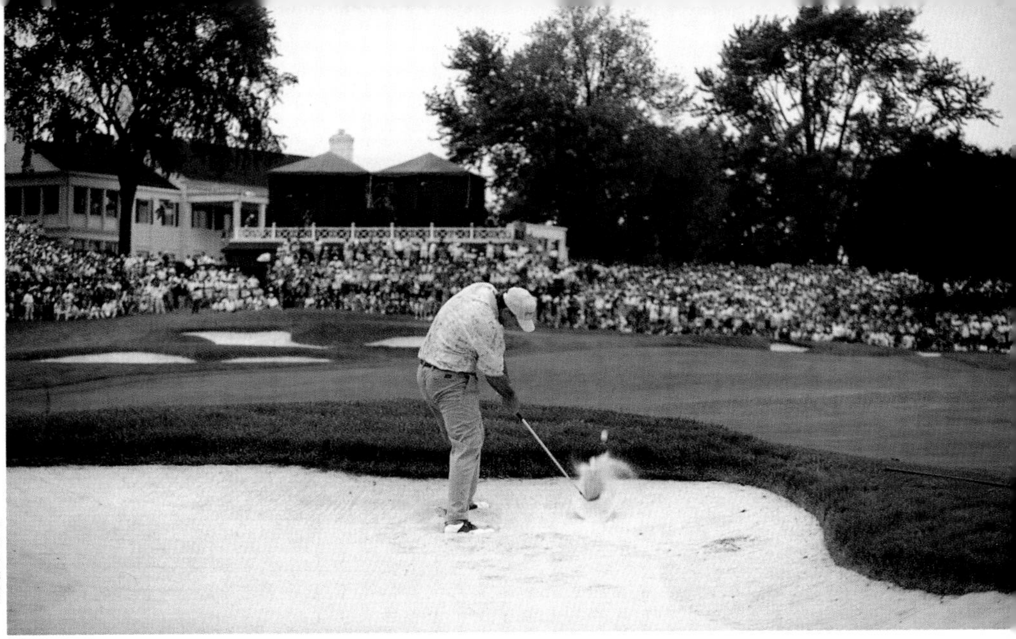
Michael C. Cohen

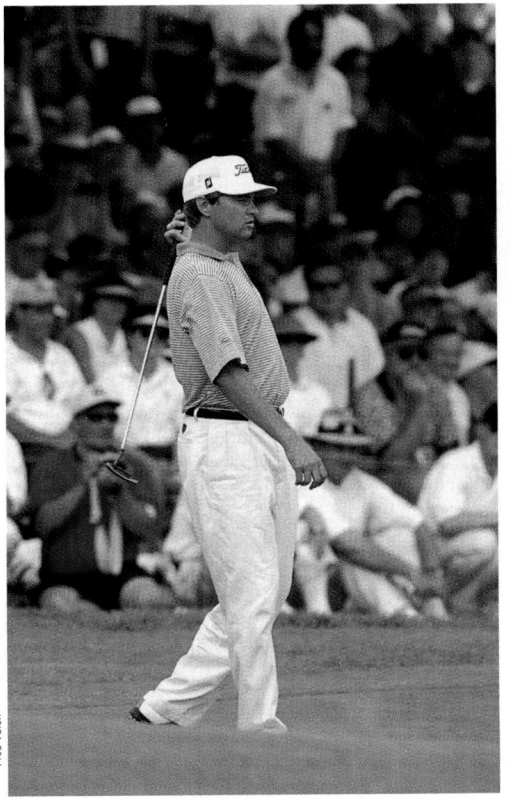

Lehman's drive on the last hole kicked left into a bunker and he could only lay up with his next shot. He tied for second place, one stroke behind.

Fred Vuich

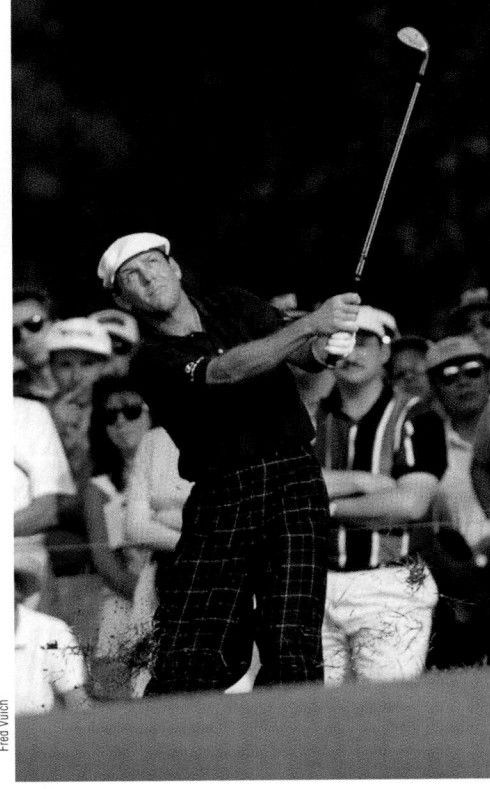

Davis Love III bogeyed the 17th and 18th.

Fred Vuich

Payne Stewart led after 36 holes.

British Open

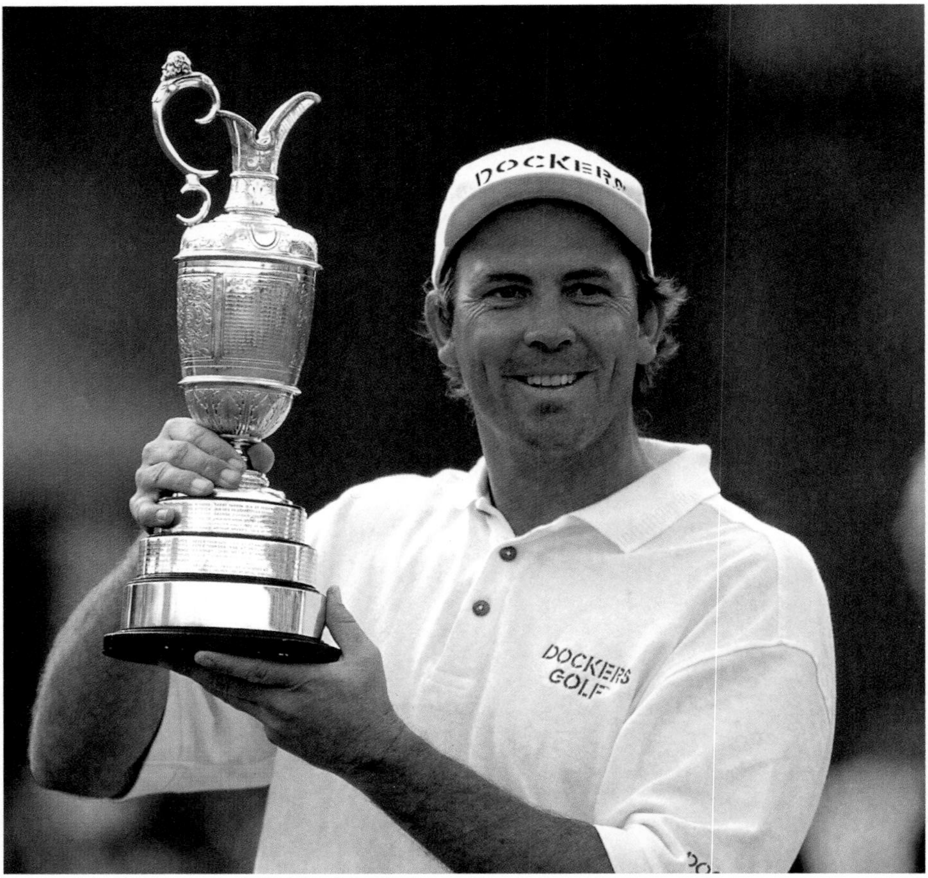

Michael C. Cohen

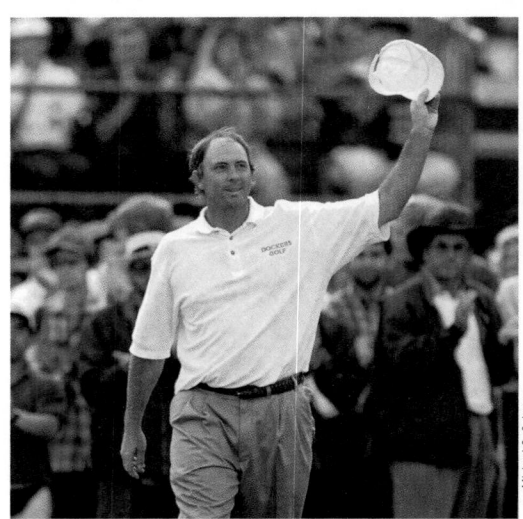

A gritty 73 in the final round enabled Tom Lehman to win the British Open by two strokes.

Michael C. Cohen

Ernie Els bogeyed two of the last three holes.

Nick Faldo's putting frustrated him.

Mark McCumber tied for second place.

Jack Nicklaus was a contender.

PGA Championship

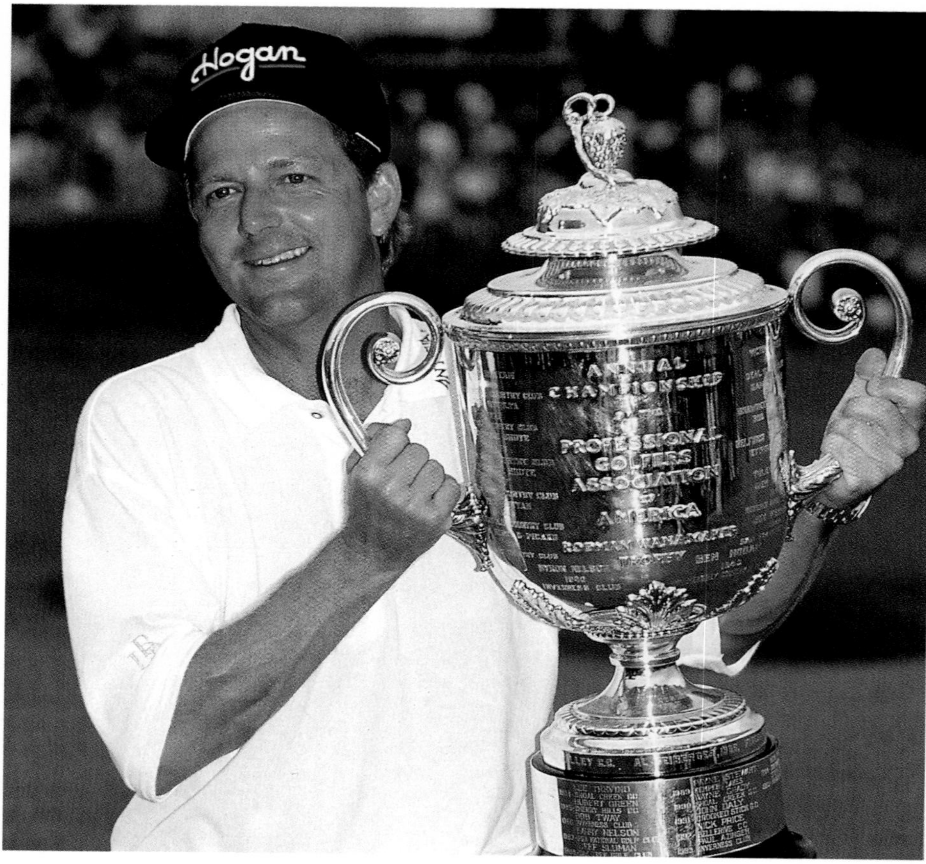

Michael C. Cohen

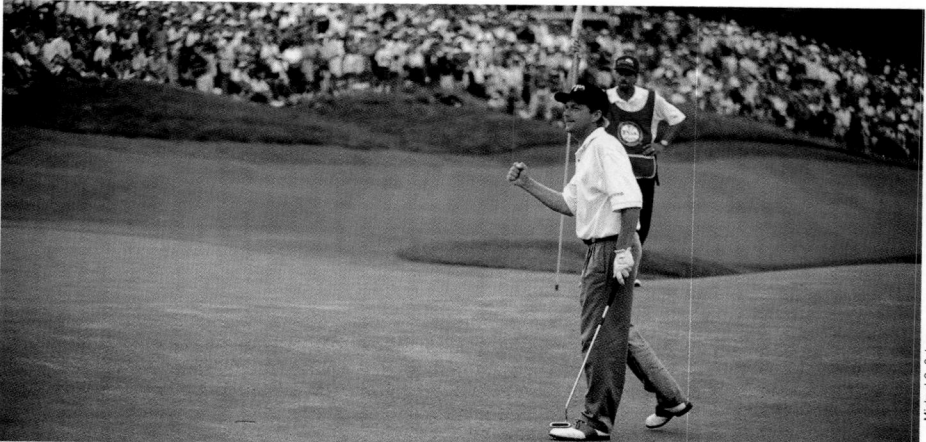

Michael C. Cohen

Mark Brooks birdied two of the last four holes, then birdied again in the playoff to win the PGA Championship over Kenny Perry (bottom right).

Kentuckian Perry was the crowd favorite.

Russ Cochran led after 54 holes.

Vijay Singh bogeyed the last hole.

Steve Elkington missed by one stroke.

Phil Mickelson faded after 36 holes.

Alfred Dunhill Cup

The United States team of Mark O'Meara, Steve Stricker and Phil Mickelson secured the Alfred Dunhill Cup over New Zealand in the final.

Frank Nobilo led New Zealand to the final and won his match against O'Meara.

Stricker won all five of his matches.

O'Meara was hugged by Costantino Rocca of Italy after his 63.

India's team upset Scotland.

Toyota World Match Play

Ernie Els won a record third consecutive Toyota World Match Play title.

Mark Brooks lost in the semi-finals.

Vijay Singh won three matches.

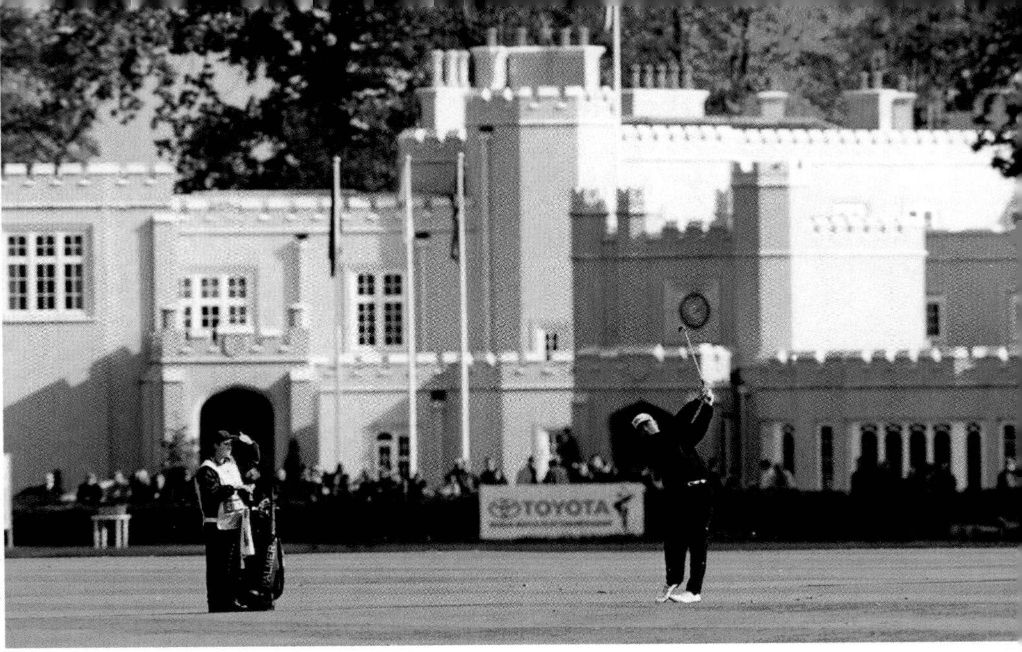

Allsport/Stephen Munday

Steve Stricker was 6 up before Els came back for a 1-up triumph.

Allsport/Stephen Munday

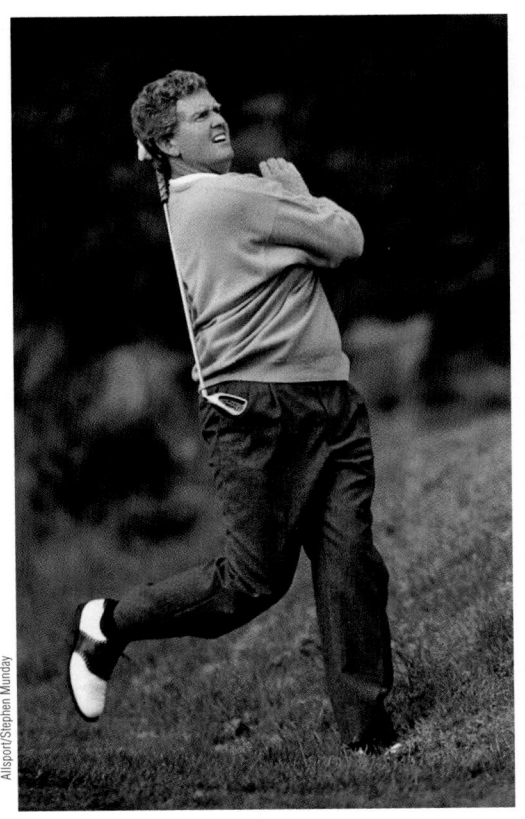

Colin Montgomerie went out after two days.

Allsport/Tim Matthews

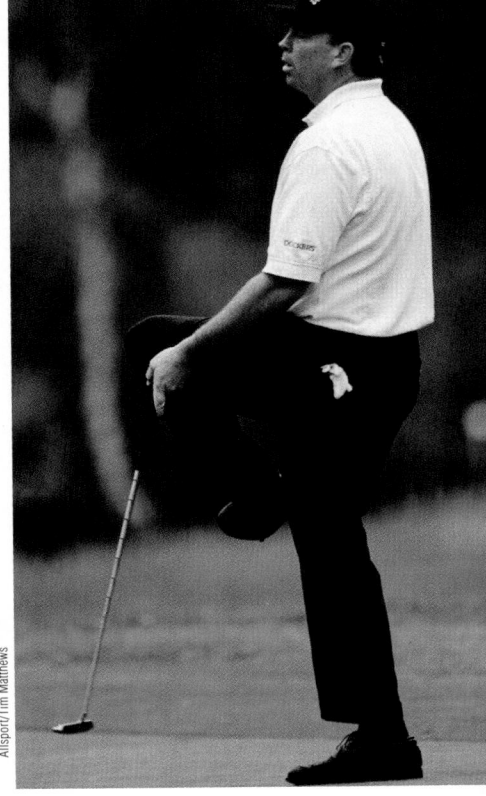

Tom Lehman lost to Singh in 37 holes.

The Players Championship

Colin Montgomerie was runner-up.

Fred Couples had a trophy and $630,000.

Couples charged through in the last round with 64 to win by four strokes over Montgomerie and Tommy Tolles.

20 feet, shot 67 and moved into the lead, a shot ahead of Croce — 67-69–136 — as Tshabalala slipped to 138 with a 73. Bembridge made a shambles of the competition Sunday, throwing two eagles and four birdies at the field en route to another 67 and the 202. Tshabalala and Croce tied for second with David Huish and Roberto Bernardini at 209.

Castle Royle European Seniors Classic—£75,000
Winner: Tommy Horton

Tommy Horton took the first big step in his season of domination on the European Seniors Tour with a playoff victory in the Castle Royle European Classic in mid-June. Horton, who turned age 55 that Sunday, rebounded from a disappointing showing in front of his home area fans at the Hippo Jersey Open after runner-up finishes in the first two events. He scored his eighth victory on the circuit at Castle Royle Golf and Country Club near Maidenhead, Berkshire, England.

Neither Horton nor Brian Huggett, his old adversary and Ryder Cup compatriot, had the lead in the tournament until they wound up tied at 11-under-par 205 Sunday afternoon and went into a playoff.

Most of the attention the first two days went to England's John Morgan and Scotland's David Huish. Morgan led after the first round with 66, one stroke ahead of Huish and Helmuth Schumacher of Switzerland. Morgan shared the 36-hole lead with Huish at 134. A two-stroke swing at the 18th forged the deadlock Sunday. Huggett, with 69-69–138 earlier, birdied there for his 67 and 205 total after going out in 32 and running off eight back-nine pars before that finish. Horton, unaware of Huggett's finish and thinking he had a two-stroke lead as he played the last hole, pitched into a bunker and bogeyed for 69 and the tie. He began the day at 68-68–136, tied with Schumacher. Morgan shot 72, missing the playoff by one stroke. Horton birdied the first playoff hole — No. 8 — for the victory as Huggett caught a bunker with his approach shot.

Ryder Collingtree Seniors Classic—£60,000
Winner: David Huish

In the early weeks of the European Seniors Tour, Scotland's David Huish proved that he belonged in that company. Huish, who has a firm reputation as one of Britain's finest players among club professionals, made strong showings at La Moye and Castle Royle, then prevailed in a three-man play-off for the Ryder Collingtree Seniors Classic title. His victims were Malcolm Gregson and Noel Ratcliffe after all three men, battling crosswind conditions all three days at Collingtree Park, Northampton, posted three-over-par 219 totals.

Huish, whose club post is at North Berwick, where breezes off the North Sea are common, shot three 73s for his 219 total. Gregson had rounds of 71-74-74 and missed an outright victory at the 54th hole when he missed a three-footer. Ratcliffe also opened with 71, one stroke off the lead of Neil Coles, John Morgan and Chick Evans, then seemingly shot himself out of contention with 79 Saturday. However, Ratcliffe rebounded with Sunday's best round — 69 — to reach the playoff, as Brian Waites and Paul Leonard, the second-round leaders at 144, went the other way, Waites with 81 and Leonard with 83.

On the par-five 18th in the playoff, Huish put up a near-routine five — drive and four-iron lay-up into the wind, pitch just over the green and near chip-in — to sixes by the others. Ratcliffe drove into the water and Gregson three-putted. Coles, the defender, recovered from a second-round 81 with a closing 70 and tied for sixth.

Stella Senior Open—£100,000
Winner: Tommy Horton

Tommy Horton shifted into high gear and captured his second victory of the European Seniors Tour season in near-record fashion in the Stella Senior Open in Frankfurt, Germany. Although his winning margin was just two strokes and he needed a couple of birdies at the end to secure the title, Horton laced together three of the finest rounds of his senior career, shooting 66-67-68 for a 201 total. At 15 under par at Idstein Golf Club, he was just one stroke shy of matching the Tour's 54-hole record.

Horton never trailed in the tournament. The first-round 66 put him one stroke in front of America's DeRay Simon, and two ahead of three others. When Horton followed with 67 Saturday, he opened a three-stroke lead over Brian Huggett, whom he defeated in a playoff a month earlier at Castle Royle. He made his only bogey of the week at the par-three 12th Sunday and Noel Ratcliffe, coming off a playoff loss in the last tournament, had the only shot at the eventual winner.

Ratcliffe, who birdied three of the last four holes for 66, closed the gap to one stroke momentarily, but Horton responded with birdies at the 16th and 17th holes to establish the final two-stroke margin. Huggett shot 70 for third place at 206. The win was Horton's ninth on the senior circuit and the 201 the lowest score of the season.

Senior British Open—£350,000
Winner: Brian Barnes

Brian Barnes had put a lot of money into his bank account during the first six months of his first full season on the Senior PGA Tour in America, but victory had eluded him there during the first six months of 1996. His solution to that deficiency was to return to Europe and successfully defend his 1995 triumph in the Senior British Open. In so doing, Barnes became the first player to win successive Senior Opens in its 10-year history.

His victory came much easier in 1996. The burly Scot, who needed a playoff eagle in 1995 to beat American Bob Murphy, built a three-stroke lead over Bob Charles, a two-time former champion, in the middle two rounds and finished with that margin and an 11-under-par 277 total on a blustery, rainy Sunday despite a two-over-par 74. Charles had the same final-day score and shared second place with American David Oakley at

280. Tommy Horton finished next at 281.

Barnes trailed by five strokes after Neil Coles, Malcolm Gregson and amateur Roy Smethurst opened the championship with 67s at Royal Portrush in Northern Ireland, then took charge the next two days. He shot a course-record 65 Friday, climbed into a first-place tie with Charles and Coles, then grabbed the three-shot margin at 13-under-par 203 with 66 Saturday. Even par Sunday after three birdies and three bogeys on the first 12 holes, Barnes double-bogeyed the 13th. That shaved his margin to a single shot over Oakley, another 51-year-old who had returned to tournament golf after 20 years in the furniture business. Oakley had moved to 10 under with birdies at the 10th and 11th. However, Barnes finished firmly with five pars and reestablished the three-shot margin as Oakley bogeyed the 14th and 17th.

Lawrence Batley Seniors—£75,000
Winner: Malcolm Gregson

"Something always stopped me from finishing off," observed Malcolm Gregson after he had solved the problem by shooting a final-round 65 that gave him a two-stroke victory in the Lawrence Batley Seniors at Fixby Golf Club in Yorkshire. Gregson had been a solid performer and frequent contender since winning the 1994 Tandem Open in his first full senior season, but had come up short of victory ever since, most recently in a playoff loss at the Ryder Collingtree Seniors in June.

Gregson appeared to have blown his chances when, after leading on a miserably wet first day with 69, he skied to 75 Saturday and dropped four strokes off the pace. He was then in a tie for 11th, as Tommy Horton, the leading money winner, moved in front with a 71-69—140 total. A terrible start Sunday — three bogeys on the first four holes — doomed Horton's bid for a third 1996 title and Gregson took command with a three-birdie string starting at the fourth.

Gregson faltered with a bogey at the 13th, then finished with a rush — holing a 15-foot eagle putt at the 14th and following with birdies at the 16th and 18th for an incoming 32 and 65 and his four-under-par total of 209, two better than runners-up Neil Coles and Alberto Croce. Horton dropped into a five-way tie for fifth at 213, one behind Maurice Bembridge.

Northern Electric Seniors—£60,000
Winner: Tommy Horton

Tommy Horton renewed his domination of the European Seniors Tour when the circuit moved to Slaley Hall at Northumberland in mid-August for the Northern Electric Seniors. Overcoming a poor start in the final round, Horton marched to a four-stroke win with a seven-under-par 209 total despite a final-round 75.

Horton, who had second- and third-place finishes in previous Northern Electric tournaments, seized control of the competition the first two days with a pair of 67s. His 134 total staked him to a five-stroke lead over Noel Ratcliffe and seven over the rest of the field. Horton struggled on the front nine Sunday. He took three bogeys and a double bogey from a flower bed for an outgoing 41 which left him just a stroke ahead of Antonio Garrido of Spain.

Horton finally nailed his first birdie with a 25-foot putt at the 14th and followed big drives on the next two holes with crisp wedge shots to eight feet and successful putts to pull away to the four-shot win, his 10th title on the senior tour. Garrido, with 71, and Ratcliffe, with 74, tied for second at 213. It was Ratcliffe's third runner-up finish of the season. The £9,700 first prize ran Horton's total 1996 earnings to a record £79,505.

Belfry PGA Seniors Championship—£150,000
Winner: Terry Gale

Terry Gale wasted little time joining the ranks of the winners on the European Seniors Tour. Less than three months after reaching his 50th birthday and seeing his first action on the senior circuit, the Australian won the Belfry PGA Seniors Championship. He did so against the best, winning a stretch duel against Tommy Horton, the tour's No. 1 player, by a single stroke on the demanding Belfry course, three times the Ryder Cup venue.

The Belfry showed its reputed teeth all week. Only four players, including leader Hugh Inggs' 69, broke par in the opening round before Gale and Horton went to the fore Friday for the duration. Horton shot 68 for a 139 total and a three-stroke lead over Gale (72-70), then the two men went back and forth, depending on their putters, the rest of the way. Horton raced to a six-stroke lead over the first eight holes Saturday, then had to birdie the 16th and 18th after a series of missed putts to salvage a one-shot advantage over Gale (72) at the end of the day.

Gale's putter blazed Sunday as he one-putted eight of the first 10 holes to assume a four-stroke margin. Though still three back when the two men, far ahead of the rest, reached the 18th, Horton put the Aussie to a final test at that difficult finishing hole. He almost holed his seven-iron approach with Gale, who had bunkered his tee shot, lying off the green in three. Gale got down in two from 25 feet for 70 and the winning, four-under-par 284 total. Horton posted 72 for 285. South African Hugh Baiocchi, who won at The Belfry on the regular tour in 1983, finished third at 289 in his senior debut.

Scottish Seniors Open—£100,000
Winner: John Morgan

Little had been heard from John Morgan during the first four months of the European Seniors Tour. Coming off first- and second-place money list finishes the previous two seasons, Morgan had only a third-place showing in the Castle Royle and three other top-10 performances on his 1996 record when the circuit made its only stop in Scotland for the Scottish Seniors Open in September at Newmachar in Aberdeen. Hard work on his game finally paid off there, as the 53-year-old West Kirby professional nailed a four-stroke victory over the ever-present Tommy Horton. Morgan closed with a two-under-par 70 for a 209 total.

Those two men started the final round in a three-way tie for the lead at 139 with 63-year-old David Snell, who had shared first place after Friday's round with Brian Barnes and David Huish. Snell got to six under par and moved ahead when he birdied the seventh, but he drove out of bounds at the next hole. Morgan went in front and rolled to his fifth title on the seniors tour, clinching it when he rifled a two-iron approach across the water at the 17th and tapped in the two-footer for a final birdie while Horton and Snell were three-putting the green.

Horton's 74–213 total produced a £11,100 check and he became the first player on the circuit to top £100,000 in earnings in a single season. Snell shot 75 and finished in a four-way tie for third with Bobby Verwey, Hugh Baiocchi and American Jim Mitchell. Baiocchi, playing in just his second senior event, was in contention until he triple-bogeyed the 17th with a ball in the water.

Motor City Seniors Classic—£80,000
Winner: John Morgan

Although he finished "with a bit of a stutter instead of a blaze of glory," John Morgan continued his late-season surge when the European Seniors Tour resumed after a one-month hiatus with the Motor City Seniors Classic at the Warwickshire Golf Club at West Midlands. He made it two in a row and became the circuit's second multiple winner, putting a two-stroke victory right behind his September triumph in the Scottish Seniors Open. His three-under-par 213 total testified to the difficulty of the Warwickshire course and the windy playing conditions.

Only three players — Canadians Ken Fulton (69) and Bill Hardwick (71) and Jose Cabo of Spain (70) — broke par in the gales Friday. Morgan and four others had 72s. Morgan moved in front by one with 69–141 Saturday, extending his string of holes without a bogey to 25. Surprising runners-up then were Siegfried Vollrath of Germany and Volker Krajewski of the United States. Morgan was breezing Sunday, having built a four-stroke lead, until he missed an 18-inch par putt at the 16th, ending the bogey-less run at 40 holes. He holed a six-foot par putt at the 17th and bogeyed again at the 18th for 72 and the three-shot win.

The £13,350 check jumped Morgan into second place on the money list behind Tommy Horton, who tied for second with Hardwick and Australia's Randall Vines. Horton, who clinched the money title, took a shot at Morgan with three birdies on the first seven holes Sunday, but two three-putt greens nipped the challenge.

The Player Championship—£120,000
Winner: Tommy Horton

What an appropriate finish to the European Seniors Tour season! On the final hole of The Player Championship, the last tournament of the year, Tommy Horton dropped a birdie putt for 69, clinching the fourth victory of his magnificent season and his second consecutive year atop the money list.

Horton's third consecutive round in the 60s gave him a 10-under-par 206 total and a two-stroke victory over Malcolm Gregson and tournament namesake Gary Player, both of whom also birdied the final hole for their 208s.

Gregson, seeking a second 1996 win, led the first day with 67, one shot ahead of Horton, Player, American Wally Armstrong and Bill Hardwick of Canada. This mix changed slightly Saturday as Horton (68-69) joined Gregson (67-70) in front, one stroke ahead of Player, Armstrong and Hardwick (all 68-70). Gregson led Horton by a stroke at the turn Sunday, but Horton went in front to stay when he birdied the par-five 10th and Gregson bogeyed the 12th and 13th. Player remained close, running in a 35-foot birdie putt at the 16th before driving into a bunker at the 17th and taking a fatal bogey there.

Noel Ratcliffe, who had the best season by far among the non-winners, finished fourth at 210. Armstrong shot 75 and tied Neil Coles for sixth, while Hardwick, who had snared the last spot in the select 30-player field with his second-place finish at the preceding Motor City Classic, collapsed to 80.

Japan Senior Tour

Daiichi Seimei Cup—¥50,000,000
Winner: Seiichi Kanai

Seiichi Kanai, by far the most successful player on the Japan Senior Tour, launched the sparse 1996 season in May with a repeat victory in the Daiichi Seimei Cup. The win, at Tomigato Golf Club in Chiba Prefecture, was his ninth in no more than 30 starts over the previous three seasons. Kanai won more handily in 1996, posting a three-stroke victory with his six-under-par 210 total.

Ichiro Ino led the first day with 68, the day's only round in the 60s. Mitoshi Tomita and Hiroshi Ishii were at 70 and Kanai had 72. Kanai moved within a stroke of the lead with 69–141 Saturday. Ryosuke Ota led with 71-69–140, but could not cope with Kanai's 69 Sunday. He shot 73 and finished in the runner-up slot for the second year in a row, this time tied with Tomita at 213.

TPC Starts—¥50,000,000
Winner: Haruo Yasuda

Haruo Yasuda, one of the early stars in Japanese tournament golf, has maintained his skills as a senior. Yasuda parlayed a five-under-par 67, the best second-round score, into a three-stroke triumph in the TPC Starts tournament at

Narita Golf Club. Yasuda has scored a victory in each of the last three seasons on the Japan Senior Tour.

He started and finished with 72s, the first one leaving him six strokes off the pace as Hiroshi Ishii opened strongly with a six-under-par 66. Yasuda's 67 brought about an eight-stroke swing with Ishii, whose 75 dropped him a shot behind Yasuda and Seiichi Kanai, the Daiichi Seimei Cup winner two weeks earlier. His 69 Saturday moved Yasuda five strokes ahead of Kanai (74) and Ishii (72), and he coasted to victory Sunday with the final 72 for his eight-under-par 280. Kanai shot 70 for 283 and Ishii finished third with 73 for 286.

HTB Classic—¥30,000,000
Winner: Fujio Kobayashi

Hsieh Min-Nan, one of Taiwan's all-time greats, made a game defense of his 1995 title in the HTB Classic at Mitsui Kanko, but yielded the championship to Fujio Kobayashi in the end. Kobayashi, picking up his second win on the Japan Senior Tour, shot rounds of 72, 70 and 71 for a three-under-par 213 total and a two-stroke margin over Hsieh and Ichiro Teramoto.

The Taiwanese star launched his defense with 68, taking a one-stroke lead over Kenichi Tsurumoto, Koji Nakajima and Manoru Onodera. Hsieh stumbled Saturday with 74–142, opening the door to Sadao Ogawa, who went in front with 70-71–141. Kobayashi shared second place with Hsieh, who shot 73 Sunday and shared the runner-up spot with Teramoto.

Komatsu Nagoya TV Cup—¥40,000,000
Winner: Masaji Kusakabe

The list of 1996 winners added a fourth champion from regular tour days when play on the Japan Senior Tour resumed in mid-September after a two-month hiatus with the Komatsu Nagoya TV Cup at Hananoki Golf Club. Masaji Kusakabe frustrated Haruo Yasuda's bid for a second 1996 victory with a come-from-behind, one-stroke triumph, his first on the circuit.

Yasuda led for two days, taking a two-stroke lead over Mitoshi Tomita, Takuo Terashima and amateur Yanei Goto with his opening, five-under-par 67. His margin dwindled to one stroke Saturday when he shot 70–137. Kusakabe (70-68), Tomita (69-69) and Seiichi Kanai (70-68) were bunched at 138. Shockingly, Kanai, the Japan Senior Tour's most successful pro, skied to 80 Sunday. Yasuda and Tomita had 71s as Kusakabe scored his victory with a 69 for 207, nine under par.

Japan PGA Senior Championship—¥50,000,000
Winner: Koji Nakajima

The players on the Japan Senior Tour had their hands full with Shimoakima Country Club's golf course in the Japan PGA Senior Championship in early October. Only Koji Nakajima, the winner, remained under par at week's end and by just one stroke with his 287 total. He needed that single shot to edge Australian visitor Terry Gale, the third-round leader.

Nakajima, who scored his first senior win in the 1995 Noboru Gotah Memorial Tokyu Cup, was in a tie for 48th place after the first round. He shot 76. Haruo Yasuda, who was in contention in virtually all of the 1996 events, led with 69, a shot ahead of the quintet of Seiichi Kanai, Wataru Horiguchi, Teruo Suzumura, Ichiro Ino and Osamu Watanabe.

Kanai, seeking his 10th tour victory, seized the lead Friday with another 70. His 140 gave him a two-stroke lead over Horiguchi. Nakajima was then nine back at 149, but he made up some of the ground Saturday with 67 for 216. Gale also shot 67 for 212, moving in front of Horiguchi (73) at 213 and Kanai (76) at 214. Nakajima's one-under 71 secured the title Sunday as the Aussie tailed to 76 for his 288. Kanai (73) and Horiguchi (74) tied for third at 289.

Japan Senior Open Championship—¥50,000,000
Winner: Isao Aoki

It's like going to see the same movie twice. It still ends the same way. We are talking about the Japan Senior Open Championship, the final event of the Japan Senior Tour season. For the third year in a row, Isao Aoki wound up holding the winner's trophy on Sunday afternoon.

Just back from the United States, where he enjoyed another highly successful season with two victories and more than $1 million in earnings, the 54-year-old Aoki put his 70th career win onto his record at Fuji Country Club in late November. He won by five strokes over Gary Player and Graham Marsh, who also had spent most of the year on the American senior circuit.

Player and Marsh challenged Aoki in the early rounds. The South African great had a first-round 66 and Marsh 68 as Aoki opened with 70. He pulled within one stroke of the lead with a 67 Friday as Player shot 70–136 and Marsh took a 71 for 139. Aoki took charge Saturday when he fired another 67 to go three strokes in front of Player (71).

The world-renowned Japanese star had an easy time of it Sunday, his 71 for a 13-under-par 275 total established the five-stroke margin over Player, who closed with 73, and Marsh, who came back with 68. The win was Aoki's fourth on Japan's senior circuit, which he plays only once or twice a year.

16. Women's Tours

"If you can't find someone to love on the LPGA Tour," commissioner Jim Ritts said, "then you just aren't paying attention."

So it seemed in 1996, in the United States and throughout the world. Already invigorated by the arrival of Annika Sorenstam the previous year, women's golf found another emerging star in the early weeks of 1996, 21-year-old Karrie Webb of Australia, who would become the first LPGA player — and the first rookie on any tour — to win $1 million in a year. Webb finished with four LPGA victories and $1,002,000 in official earnings.

Although Laura Davies, who also won four times on the LPGA Tour, earned $927,302 and was eclipsed by Webb in America, the 35-year-old Englishwoman sustained her worldwide dominance by winning three times in Europe, twice in Japan and earning a total of $1,383,003, a record in women's golf. Not included in Davies' total were nearly $350,000 from two skins games. The nine victories raised Davies' career total to 49.

Webb was second in worldwide earnings with $1,135,971, followed by Sweden's Sorenstam with $868,483, then Dottie Pepper of the United States with $730,698, Liselotte Neumann of Sweden with $707,216, and Akiko Fukushima of Japan with $666,303.

Davies was the first woman to earn over $1 million with her $1,006,143 in 1994, then Sorenstam won $1,043,121 in 1995.

While the extent of Webb's success was a surprise, she had been a player to watch for more than a year, since placing second to Davies in her second-ever professional tournament in Australia in December, 1994. She won the 1995 Weetabix Women's British Open, was Rookie of the Year in Europe, and qualified for the LPGA Tour in October.

Webb burst into prominence in America by placing second, first and second in her first three tournaments of 1996, taking her initial victory in a playoff at the HEALTHSOUTH Inaugural. She also won the Sprint Title-holders Championship, SAFECO Classic and the season-ending ITT LPGA Tour Championship, where she secured the money title as Davies tied for fifth place.

She placed sixth or better in 15 of her 25 LPGA starts, including five seconds, and was a contender in two major events.

Two of Davies' American victories were in major championships, the McDonald's LPGA Championship and du Maurier Classic. She also won the Standard Register PING and Star Bank LPGA Classic. Davies led the Women's European Tour, also known as the American Express Tour, with £110,880, having victories in the Evian Masters, Wilkinson Sword Ladies' English Open and Italian Open di Sicilia. In Japan, Davies won the Satake Classic and Itoen Classic.

Sorenstam recorded three victories in the United States, including a repeat in the U.S. Women's Open by a six-stroke margin, and back-to-back, late-year wins in the CoreStates Betsy King Classic and Samsung World Championship of Women's Golf. Sorenstam also had a fourth victory in Europe. Other major titles were won by Patty Sheehan in the Nabisco Dinah Shore and Emilee Klein, just six months older than Webb, in the Weetabix Women's

British Open. The week before, Klein won the PING Welch's Championship.

Other multiple winners in the United States included Pepper (known as Mochrie before her 1995 divorce), whose five wins included three in five weeks in the summer. Neumann and Michelle McGann each won three times and Meg Mallon won twice.

Trish Johnson of England had three worldwide victories, one in America and two in Europe, Corinne Dibnah won twice in Australasia, and Aiko Hashimoto won three times in Japan. Including Davies, there were eight two-time winners in Japan, and Fukushima led the money list with over ¥70 million.

U.S. LPGA Tour

Chrysler-Plymouth Tournament of Champions—$725,000
Winner: Liselotte Neumann

With 1995 Player of the Year Annika Sorenstam delaying her start in 1996 competition, her compatriot Liselotte Neumann was more than happy to continue Sweden's winning tradition on the LPGA Tour. Neumann won the Chysler-Plymouth Tournament of Champions by 11 strokes on rounds of 67, 66, 72 and 70 for a 275 total, 13 under par at the Grand Cypress Resort in Orlando, Florida.

Neumann's blitz left those in her wake wishing she, too, had taken the week off. She led Martha Nause by one stroke after the first round, was ahead by nine strokes going into the weekend and by eight heading into the final round. She never flinched on Sunday. Rookie Karrie Webb of Australia was second after a final-round 68.

"Getting off to such a fast start was the key for me this week," Neumann said. "To play so well in the first tournament of the year surprised me a little bit."

The 29-year-old Neumann was first recognized as a rising star in Europe, winning the 1985 European Open at age 19, and the German Open and European Order of Merit titles the next year. It wasn't until two years later, at the 1988 U.S. Women's Open that Neumann truly established herself, beating Patty Sheehan by three strokes. "In retrospect, winning a major championship so early in my career might have been more of a hindrance than a boost," Neumann said. "I had nothing else to look forward to. I wish I had won a smaller one first."

HEALTHSOUTH Inaugural—$450,000
Winner: Karrie Webb

Rookie Karrie Webb of Australia issued a warning in the season-opening tournament with her second-place finish. She wasted no time in backing it up a week later by winning the HEALTHSOUTH Inaugural, the LPGA's second consecutive event in Orlando, Florida, at Walt Disney World's Lake Buena Vista Club. Webb won in impressive style, outlasting veterans Jane Geddes and Martha Nause in a four-hole playoff.

Although it was her first victory as an LPGA member, it was her second as a professional, following the Weetabix Women's British Open in August, 1995, which was a springboard to qualifying to play in the United States. "I really can't believe it," Webb said of her victory on rounds of 70, 70 and 69 for a 209 total. "I knew I had a chance if I started out well, and I did."

Nause had a final-round 68 and Geddes shot 70.

Patty Sheehan put together rounds of 66 and 71 for a two-stroke lead over Geddes after 36 holes. Then Sheehan opened the door with uncharacteristic poor play on Sunday, shooting 73 to finish tied for fourth place at 210 with Michelle McGann.

Geddes could have wrapped up the victory in regulation if she had been able to save par from just behind the 18th green. Just before that, she missed an eight-foot putt for birdie at No. 17 that would have given her a two-stroke cushion. "I had a bad feeling about that putt," Geddes said. "I thought it would cost me."

Nause was eliminated on the first playoff hole with a bogey. Webb and Geddes played No. 18 three more times before Webb won when Geddes three-putted for bogey. Webb was in position to win the first three extra holes, but missed putts of 15, six and 14 feet. "In the playoff, I think I was more nervous than in the British Open," Webb said. "I can't believe this is happening so soon."

Cup Noodles Hawaiian Ladies Open—$600,000
Winner: Meg Mallon

Veteran Meg Mallon took her cue from rookie Karrie Webb and credited her caddie for her victory in the Cup Noodles Hawaiian Ladies Open with a birdie on the final hole at Kopolei Golf Club in Oahu, Hawaii. The final shot, which gave her a four-under-par 212 total for the 54-hole event, was the only time Mallon led. It came at the expense of Webb, who appeared on the brink of winning her second consecutive LPGA event. Mallon had rounds of 74, 70 and 68 to hold off Webb by one stroke.

During the final round, Mallon said Webb, her playing companion, kept her focused with patience not usually found in a rookie. Webb was acting more like a veteran and Mallon, the rookie. "I would follow birdies with bogeys," Mallon said. "After watching Karrie, I said, 'I don't need to get upset anymore. Just hang in there.' It worked. It's odd, but Karrie's patience rubbed off on me and calmed me down."

The winning shot was set up by Mallon's caddie John Dormann. Facing a 137-yard shot on the final hole, Mallon wavered between a six iron and seven iron on the 345-yard hole. "John told me to go with what I felt comfortable with and hit the shot without any doubts," Mallon said. "I nailed it two feet from the hole. I won't forget that for a long time."

Mallon and Webb started the final round two strokes behind co-leaders Jane Geddes and Sherrin Smyers. Webb raced off to a three-stroke lead at the turn with birdies on four of the first seven holes, while Mallon had three birdies and a bogey. Webb leveled off, and Mallon caught her with a birdie at No. 17 and closed the door with the birdie at No. 18 after Webb's birdie try from 20 feet grazed the hole. "I thought it was in all the way," Webb said. "I thought it was in."

PING/Welch's Championship—$450,000
Winner: Liselotte Neumann

Liselotte Neumann came to the PING/Welch's Championship with her bag of new tricks, and for the second time this year displayed to her LPGA opponents that she would be one to contend with all season. Neumann, who won the Tournament of Champions in January, shot a final-round 68 and zipped past stumbling third-round leader Danielle Ammaccapane to win by one stroke over Cathy Johnston-Forbes.

Since replacing her four and five irons with seven and nine woods, Neumann had honed her game to a razor edge as evidenced by her rounds of 68, 71, 69 and 68 for a 276 total. "It's such a great feeling right now because I've had to rely on my short game too much," she said. "Now I'm hitting it much farther. It really helped me this week on these greens."

Neumann wasn't giving much thought to winning when the final round began. In her mind, Ammaccapane was the one to beat. She had followed an opening 72 with a couple of 66s and led by two strokes over Johnston-Forbes. There was no reason to believe otherwise through the first five holes, which Ammaccapane parred. Then there was every reason to believe otherwise when she played the next four holes in bogey, bogey, bogey and double bogey. On the second nine, she made two more bogeys and a double bogey for 81 and a tie for 28th place.

"You don't expect those things to happen at this level, but obviously they do," said Neumann, who played the first 13 holes in four under par and the last five in even par to win by one stroke. Johnston-Forbes had a chance to tie Neumann with a birdie on the closing par-five, but she played safe, laid up short, then was long on her 115-yard wedge shot and two-putted for par.

Standard Register PING—$700,000
Winner: Laura Davies

Laura Davies found herself battling mixed emotions as she walked to the 18th green at Moon Valley Country Club in Phoenix, Arizona, in the final round of the Standard Register PING. She was tied for the lead with Kristal Parker-Gregory, which was good, but looking at a playoff, which was not. "I've lost so many playoffs in the U.S., I thought, 'here it comes again.' I had no confidence," Davies said. "But I got lucky."

Luck came wrapped in Parker-Gregory's three-putt, handing Davies a third straight Standard Register PING title. Davies never led until Parker-Gregory's slip-up. She opened with 71 and trailed Barb Mucha and Marianne Morris by three strokes. A second-round 73 left her four behind Morris and complaining about blisters on her feet and wondering why she was there.

Davies considered herself out of contention when Parker-Gregory shot 69 in the third round to lead by three strokes. But Parker-Gregory couldn't hold on, shooting 75, the three-putt at 18 a killer. "I thought she would hole her putt at 18. She had putted so well all day, I couldn't imagine her three-putting," Davies said. "I was playing well, but I wasn't making any putts, nothing very long."

It was Parker-Gregory's second runner-up finish of her career. She was second in the 1995 Youngstown-Warren Classic, losing to Michelle McGann on the third playoff hole.

Nabisco Dinah Shore—$900,000
Winner: Patty Sheehan

For Patty Sheehan, nothing could be finer than to win the Dinah; that is the Nabisco Dinah Shore event. It had been the major championship void in her golf career she hadn't filled. Yes, the du Maurier title wasn't in her resume either, but that one she could live without. But not the Dinah. "This is the tournament that introduced me to women's golf," Sheehan said. "This is the one I watched in junior high. This is the tournament I used to drive to during spring break when I was in college. This is the most prestigious as far as I am concerned."

Five strokes behind after 36 holes, the 39-year-old Hall-of-Famer pulled into a 54-hole tie with 67, the tournament's low round, then shot 71 on Sunday to win by one stroke over Kelly Robbins, Meg Mallon and Annika Sorenstam, all of whom missed makeable putts on the 18th green.

Robbins began the day four strokes off the lead of Sheehan and Brandie Burton. She came up short with her Sunday-best 68 because of two costly errors — a hook into the trees for a double bogey at No. 15, and a pushed drive into the fairway bunker at No. 18 and a missed 10-footer for par. "I knew I would have the opportunities coming in," Robbins said. "I just didn't take advantage of them."

Sorenstam can look back at the cozy, par-five 18th hole as her nemesis. She double-bogeyed it ending the third round. After taking the lead with a birdie at No. 16 on Sunday, she three-putted No. 18, missing a five-footer that would have put her in the playoff. "It was a straight putt, nothing to it," Sorenstam said. "I just missed it."

Mallon easily was the most frustrated contestant. She was the only player to shoot under par — scores of 71, 70, 71 and 70 — in all four rounds. On Sunday, there was a missed six-footer at No. 16, a missed 10-footer at No. 17 and a missed 12-footer at No. 18. "I played my best golf and still didn't win," Mallon said. "I hit 16 greens. I had one chip all day and I made bogey."

Sheehan was less than perfect, missing six fairways and three-putting four times, but she did the little things. Her two-putt par at No. 16 came from 50 feet; she birdied the par-three 17th, punching a five iron to within three feet to take the lead for the first time; and she played the 18th like a hacker — a drive to the rough, a thin three iron into the bunker, a fat sand wedge 100 feet short. But she got down in two putts. Her victory howl broke the silence at least two feet before the putt disappeared. The victory was her sixth major overall, tying her with Pat Bradley for the most among active players, pushing her one ahead of Amy Alcott and Betsy King. "This is so great," she said. "The Dinah at last."

Twelve Bridges LPGA Classic—$500,000
Winner: Kelly Robbins

Kelly Robbins found the perfect antidote for the misery which befell her at the Nabisco Dinah Shore a week earlier — a five-hole playoff victory over Val Skinner in the inaugural Twelve Bridges LPGA Classic. Robbins shot rounds of 73, 68, 68 and 64 for a 273 total and her fourth career victory. She was the beneficiary of some lax play by Skinner, who bogeyed the par-five 17th, setting up the playoff.

Robbins closed it out with a birdie, her ninth of the day, on the fifth playoff hole. But after Robbins shot a final-round 64 and Skinner, 65, the two proceeded to miss seven of 10 playoff greens in regulation and each made two bogeys. "You take more chances in a playoff; you're trying to close it out," Skinner said. Robbins added, "We both left the door open a few times. The sun was going down and we got a little tired."

Robbins appeared to have lost in regulation play when she missed a seven-foot birdie putt at No. 18 and trailed Skinner by one stroke. But Skinner, who had four consecutive birdies on Nos. 12 through 15, bogeyed the 17th after her third shot rolled into a gallery stake that had been dropped onto the course and stopped her ball from reaching the fairway. "I hit a bad shot at 17 and got a bad break and didn't convert," Skinner said in describing her bogey.

When Skinner parred No. 18, Robbins had her chance. The playoff was held over No. 1 and No. 18. They began with pars on both holes, then bogeys on both, with Skinner missing a six-footer that would have given her the victory. Finally, they went back to No. 18 once more, where Robbins won.

Chick-fil-A Charity Championship—$550,000
Winner: Barb Mucha

Barb Mucha had a strange way of preparing for the Chick-fil-A Charity Championship at Eagles Landing Golf Club just south of Atlanta. She went bowling. Mucha proceeded to shoot rounds of 68, 70 and 70 for a 208 total and beat Liselotte Neumann and Dottie Pepper by two strokes.

What does bowling have to do with it? Mucha said golf and bowling both involve hand-eye coordination, are target-oriented sports and require detailed focus during play. She even toyed with the idea of joining the professional bowlers tour. But not anymore.

Mucha's victory was a signal of her increased level of intensity and commitment to the game. She said, "In previous tournaments, I was always worrying whether my friends had tickets, and when my friends and family were around, I always made sure they had water to drink. But, no more. They can handle that on their own."

Karen Weiss led the first round with 66, two strokes in front of Mucha, Maggie Will and Val Skinner. Mucha added a second-round 70 to lead Pepper by one stroke, then fought off Neumann and Pepper on Sunday. It was her first victory of the year, but in four previous tournaments she had played in the final group three times. "That tells me I'm going to the next level," said Mucha, who won for the fourth time in her 10-year career.

Sara Lee Classic—$600,000
Winner: Meg Mallon

The last time Meg Mallon won the Sara Lee Classic, she went more than two years without a victory. But this is a different Meg Mallon, more mature, more determined and more talented.

Mallon won the Sara Lee Classic in 1993 and didn't win again until this February when she birdied the final hole to win the Hawaiian Open with a birdie on the final hole. "I didn't end up playing well in the summer after the Sara Lee," said Mallon, who over the last three events has tied for second, tied for third and now first. "My goal now is to maintain play like this and have a good summer."

It was a more confident Mallon who took on the Hermitage Golf Club in Old Hickory, Tennessee, with rounds of 70, 71 and 69 for a 210 total and a two-stroke victory over Stephanie Farwig and Pam Wright. She played almost mistake-free in the final round with two birdies and 14 consecutive pars before she made an eight-footer for birdie on No. 17 that broke the tie with Pam Wright and gave her the lead. She made par at No. 18 to complete the victory.

The wind was gusting at more than 25 miles an hour and club selection was a guessing game at best. She started the final round one stroke off the lead held by Caroline Pierce and quickly moved in front with back-to-back birdies. "I was so focused on not hitting bad shots," Mallon said. "When you hit bad shots, the wind just accentuates it even more. I knew par was a good score, and I would take a birdie when it came. Starting birdie, birdie definitely had me fired up."

After making the two birdies, Mallon hit her 14-par spurt with what she called "my two-putt barrage." Wright caught her with a birdie at No. 5 and took the lead briefly with another one at No. 13. She then bogeyed Nos. 14 and 17. Mallon said her string of 8-to-10-foot putts to save par prepared her for the birdie at No. 17. Facing a swirling wind on the 153-yard hole, she hit a five iron to eight feet and made the putt.

Sprint Titleholders Championship—$1,200,000
Winner: Karrie Webb

Few in the United States had heard of Australia's Karrie Webb before she won the 1995 Weetabix Women's British Open. After Webb won the Sprint Titleholders Championship, there was hardly anyone who knows much about golf who doesn't know who she is. The 21-year-old rookie now had two victories, two seconds and three other top-10 finishes in eight events.

"This year has been such a shock," Webb said. "I have not looked at long-term goals. I would like to win some majors and become a known player." Four days in not, humid Daytona Beach, Florida, at the LPGA International brought her closer to her wishes. With rounds of 71, 65, 70 and 66 for a 272 total, she beat Kelly Robbins with a birdie on the final hole.

Val Skinner led the first two rounds with a pair of 67s before turning the lead over to Catrin Nilsmark after 54 holes. It was mostly a Webb-Robbins show on Sunday, especially over the second nine. Webb broke a five-way tie for the lead with a birdie at No. 14, then nailed the title down at No. 18. After watching Robbins move into a tie with an eagle at the 452-yard 18th, Webb hit her three-iron second shot to the back fringe, then got her birdie, completing a bogey-free round for the victory.

"I was nervous most of the back nine and tried to focus and not get too far ahead of myself," Webb said. "It's always good to be put under that pressure and produce if you need to."

Webb enjoyed this victory more than her first, which she won in a three-way playoff when Jane Geddes three-putted. "I won this one," she said. Robbins, though impressed, had this bit of warning for Webb: "If she goes through any lulls, I hope she can keep it in perspective and go on from there. It's tough to play well week in and week out. It's draining on you, and that's something she hasn't yet faced."

McDonald's LPGA Championship—$1,200,000
Winner: Laura Davies

Maybe the LPGA and McDonald's should consider a new name for their major championship at DuPont Country Club in Wilmington, Delaware. The Laura Davies Benefit? And why not? As Julie Piers, who finished second, said, "She's got great memories of this course. I don't think anybody has dominated a tournament like this. She's finished first, first, second and first. How good is that?"

The week was rainy, windy, cold and miserable, just like so many other days in Davies' native England. The tournament was reduced from 72 to 54 holes because of the weather. Davies' rounds of 72, 71 and 70 for a 213 total came on a course shortened considerably from its original 6,386 yards. Almost every hole was played from a forward tee. The 400-yard second hole was shortened to 340 yards, for example.

The long-hitting Davies figured to have an advantage with a longer course. "It's like pitch and putt," she said. "This is a major championship. The tees were fine where they were."

The McDonald's LPGA Championship was worth $180,000 and raised Davies' DuPont Country Club earnings to $591,711. It was her third major championship victory, and her second LPGA title of the year. Davies' winning score was the second highest in the event, dating to 1972 when Kathy Ahern won at one over par. It also was the highest winning score in an LPGA major event since Hollis Stacy won the 1984 U.S. Women's Open at two over par. It had been four years since even par won an LPGA event.

Only four of the 79 players broke par in the final round —Davies, Piers, Michelle Dobek and Penny Hammel. All shot 70. The final-round scoring average was 76.1 on a day when the temperature never climbed out of the 50s, with a wind chill of high 30s and low 40s. The outcome was in doubt until Davies birdied the 16th hole from 18 feet to take a lead held or shared by as many as nine players on the final day. "We've played in colder weather in St. Louis, windier weather in Hawaii, but never this combination," Piers said. "But none of it seems to faze Laura. She just kept plowing ahead."

LPGA Corning Classic—$600,000
Winner: Rosie Jones

Rosie Jones came to the first round of the LPGA Corning Classic without benefit of a practice round, but it did not matter. Jones thrives on courses where accuracy, not length, and pin-point iron shots pay off. And in this case, the payoff was $90,000 after Jones went around the 6,062-yard Corning Country Club course in 67, 69, 71 and 69 for a 276 total, 12 under par and two strokes better than Val Skinner.

Jones didn't arrive in Corning, New York, until late Wednesday afternoon, delayed by a court appearance, the result of her dog biting a handyman working at her house. "After all that, the guy didn't show up in court," Jones said.

It obviously didn't affect her concentration. Her 67-69 start opened a three-stroke lead, and she never trailed over the weekend. She led by one stroke after the first round, needed only 19 putts in stretching her lead to three strokes in the second round, then did just enough on the weekend to hold off Skinner's 66-70 finish.

While Skinner was blasting her tee shots past Jones on every hole, Jones was beating her with deft iron play. Clinging to a one-stroke lead when they reached the par-five 12th hole, Jones split the fairway and made par while Skinner drove into a fence and bogeyed. At the 14th, Skinner hooked her tee shot into another fence and made bogey, while Jones made a 13-footer for birdie and a four-stroke lead.

"It wasn't over then, but it shifted the whole tournament in my favor," said Jones, who needed the cushion after Skinner birdied No. 15 and Jones bogeyed No. 16. Joan Pitcock and Nancy Ramsbottom, playing a group ahead of Jones, were only one stroke back after birdies at No. 17. Both bogeyed the 18th.

U.S. Women's Open—$1,200,000
Winner: Annika Sorenstam

If there was any reason to question Annika Sorenstam's inner fire in 1996, she torched all comers in the U.S. Women's Open. In doing so, she made a resounding statement in becoming the sixth woman — the first foreign player — to win back-to-back national championships. Sorenstam's 272 total, eight under par at Pine Needles Golf Club in Southern Pines, North Carolina, provided a six-stroke margin over Kris Tschetter. It was the largest victory margin since Amy Alcott won the Open by nine in 1980.

Sorenstam started with even-par 70, one behind Beth Daniel and Kim

Williams, and eventually beat them by 16 strokes on the way to a 67, 69 and 66 finish. She missed only five fairways all week and made 16 birdies and one eagle. She averaged hitting 13 greens per round.

"I will never forget this golf course," Sorenstam said. "I had a little stomach ache, some butterflies before the final round, but I knew I was playing well and I know this golf course." The only question she had was, "Can I play today? I won last year because Meg (Mallon) made some mistakes. I won this year because I played well."

Only once over the final 36 holes did Sorenstam not lead. That was after the 14th hole Saturday, when she made her only double bogey, three-putting from 10 feet and allowing Brandie Burton a share of the lead at three under par. Burton had come from five strokes behind with birdies at the ninth, 10th and 11th holes, then saved par from a bunker at the 14th, while Sorenstam missed her three-footer for bogey. Burton got no closer. She bogeyed Nos. 16 and 17, and Sorenstam's lead grew to three strokes again with her birdie at No. 17.

The championship's defining moment for Sorenstam came Sunday at No. 3, where she dropped a nine-iron shot three feet below the hole and matched Burton's birdie with one of her own. She added an exclamation point at No. 10 with a 25-foot eagle putt. At one point Tschetter said, "What golf course is she playing, anyway? She's the defending champion up there at the top every day. That's a lot of pressure."

Oldsmobile Classic—$600,000
Winner: Michelle McGann

A week after finishing 42nd in the U.S. Women's Open — her fifth straight finish out of the top 10 — Michelle McGann parlayed a charity event for a children's hospital, a conversation with Tom Watson and a new driver into a playoff victory over Liselotte Neumann in the Oldsmobile Classic in East Lansing, Michigan. It was McGann's third victory in 13 months.

The hospital visit and the talk with Watson improved McGann's outlook, and a new Callaway driver, courtesy of Bob Murphy, straightened out her game, leading to rounds of 71, 66, 70 and 65 for a 272 total. She won on the fourth playoff hole with a birdie.

"We all have times when we feel everyone is against us," McGann said. "We get that 'Why me' feeling. But after playing in the hospital benefit and talking to Tom, who's had his share of ups-and-downs lately, it puts things into perspective."

Neumann had to scramble to gain the playoff. She hit her tee shot right on the final hole, was given a free drop away from casual water, and made an up-and-down par. She self-destructed in the playoff on the fourth hole with a drive into the rough and a six iron short of the green.

Both players started the last round three strokes behind Tracy Hanson, whose nine-under-par 63 Saturday tied the course record. The two previous 63 shooters, Beth Daniel and Dale Eggeling, went on to win. This year, neither Hanson nor Meg Mallon, who shot 63 in the final round, could make the playoff.

Edina Realty LPGA Classic—$550,000
Winner: Liselotte Neumann

One week you can't get out of your own way, and the next week you win despite yourself. Such was the case the last two weeks for Liselotte Neumann.

A week ago, Neumann stumbled in a playoff and lost the Oldsmobile Classic to Michelle McGann. This week she played herself out of the Edina Realty LPGA Classic with a triple bogey, bogey finish Saturday, then shot 67 Sunday and beat Brandie Burton, Carin Koch and Suzanne Strudwick in a playoff. The playoff went three holes before Neumann won with a 45-foot birdie putt. She had rounds of 67, 73 and 67 for a 207 total for her third victory of the year at Brooklyn Park, Minnesota.

"I made a stupid mistake and all night (Saturday) I kept thinking it had cost me the tournament," Neumann said. "But, you put it behind you, go play and sometimes good things happen."

The winning putt was hardly a straight-in stroke. It rolled over a hump, along a ridge and down a slope. Neumann had been on the same side of the green earlier in the week and knew where the putt would go. Burton wasn't so fortunate. She had a similar line from 30 feet to extend the playoff, but it missed on the left edge of the hole.

Everything worked out for Neumann, though the day showed little promise starting out. Not only was she five strokes behind, but there were eight players ahead of her — Koch by five, Nancy Lopez by four and six others by three. "With that many, you don't expect all of them to have bad days," Neumann said. But they did. Koch shot even par; Lopez slipped away with 74, and none of the other six made a move.

Rochester International—$600,000
Winner: Dottie Pepper

There's a saying that applies to every successful person, from the business world to sports: "Remember what got you there." Dottie Pepper didn't do that. She found herself missing one cut after another, and hitting shots she didn't recognize.

She remembered what got her to the top of her game, and it wasn't in her bag. So out came the perimeter-weighted Titleist irons and into her bag went her old circa-1972 forged Titleist irons.

And she became a winner again.

Pepper put together rounds of 69, 66 and 71 for a 206 total over the drenched Locust Hill Country Club and won for the first time in 1996 in the Rochester International. "I'm not one to miss a lot of cuts, but I really had it going there for a few weeks," Pepper said. "I had to give myself a good, swift kick in the back end over the last couple of weeks and it worked."

Still, she had to wait. The first round was rained out, but Pepper was still there Friday with 69, one stroke behind Amy Fruhwirth. She followed that with a marathon. After playing only one hole of her second round because of inclement weather Saturday, she peppered the course with birdies Sunday, shooting 66 and 71. That put her at 206, good for a two-stroke victory over Annika Sorenstam.

Pepper had one bogey over the final 36 holes and only three for the tournament. "I think I'm a victim of success," she said. "You keep trying to get better, and the end result is you get away from what got you there. I'm back to square one and I won't forget it."

ShopRite LPGA Classic—$750,000
Winner: Dottie Pepper

Some things just aren't meant to be. Ask Amy Benz. Poised to win for the first time in 320 events, Benz had the misfortune of going head-to-head with Dottie Pepper in the final round of the ShopRite LPGA Classic, a week after Pepper broke a drought of her own.

This was Benz' tournament to lose, and she did after taking a three-stroke lead over Pepper into Sunday's final round. She got there with rounds of 64 and 66, then self-destructed with a closing 76 to Pepper's 69 and winning 11-under-par 202 total. "I'm excited to win, but disappointed for Amy," said the gracious Pepper, who opened with 67 and 66. "Her day is going to come. She hits the ball too solid not to win."

Benz had 13 birdies and only one bogey in the first two rounds at Greate Bay Resort in Somers Point, New Jersey. In the final round, she had just one birdie and six bogeys on a day when play was interrupted twice for five hours because of the weather. "I'm just going to keep putting myself there," Benz said. "That's it. Eventually, I won't get a bad break where we have two suspensions and I can just go out and play. I know I'll be there again. Eventually, it's going to happen."

Once Pepper got the lead with a birdie at No. 5, Benz hooked three consecutive drives, and never got close again. After the second rain delay, Pepper birdied the 11th and 12th holes, stretching her lead to four strokes and breezed in.

Jamie Farr Kroger Classic—$575,000
Winner: Joan Pitcock

After nine years on the LPGA Tour, Joan Pitcock doesn't have to worry about being someone who never won. She took care of that with a tap-in par on the 54th hole of the Jamie Farr Kroger Classic at Highland Meadows Golf Club, near Toledo, Ohio.

"You get a lot of neat stuff when you win," said the 29-year-old Pitcock, who became the fourth player in 12 years to make this tournament her first LPGA victory, joining Penny Hammel (1985), Tina Tombs (1990) and Kathryn Marshall (1995).

Her spoils of victory included an automobile, a Rolex watch, $86,250 and an assist of sorts from Meg Mallon, who shot an opening round-leading 65 and then was disqualified the next day for failing to call a penalty stroke on herself. It came on the 17th green where her birdie putt hung on the lip of the cup for 18-20 seconds before falling. She reported the violation the following day.

Other than a second-place finish at the 1988 Ocean City Open, in her rookie year, Pitcock's only other flirtation with success had been a share of the third-round lead at the 1991 U.S. Women's Open. Playing in the final group with Pat Bradley, Pitcock collapsed with 75 and finished seventh.

There was no collapse this time. She opened with 68 and fired 66 Saturday to lead by three strokes. A closing 70 was good for a one-stroke victory over Marianne Morris. "This is my ninth year and I hadn't been in the thick of things much," Pitcock said. "The more I went on, the more I realized I didn't want to be someone who never won. All the pressure I put on myself was to win."

Pitcock had to come from behind to do it after falling one stroke behind at the 11th hole. A birdie at No. 13 got her into a tie and Morris' bogey at No. 16 gave her the lead. Morris had a chance, but birdied neither of the closing two par-fives. "I never looked at a scoreboard, didn't know I had lost the lead," Pitcock said. "If somebody beat me, fine. If somebody put up a great number, fine. But I didn't want to hand it to anybody."

Youngstown-Warren LPGA Classic—$600,000
Winner: Michelle McGann

Early in Michelle McGann's career it was her clothes, her hats in particular, that drew attention. She could play, as evidenced by many top-10 finishes, but she wasn't winning. McGann remains a vision of bright colors on the fairways, but now fans, media and competitors talk more about her game than glamour.

Another of those occasions arose in the Youngstown-Warren LPGA Classic, where she was simply dazzling, defending her title in record-breaking fashion with rounds of 71, 64 and 65 for a 200 total, three strokes ahead of Kim Saiki. It was her second victory of the year and her fourth in the last two years. "I just tried to make as many birdies as I could," said McGann, who won the Oldsmobile Classic in June. "Everybody was making them."

McGann wasn't making birdies from the start, however, and her opening 71 left her four strokes off the lead held by Barb Mucha, Kelly Robbins and Amy Fruhwirth. Four others were at 68 and another 10 at 69. McGann made up for the slow start with 15 birdies over the final two rounds, not to mention an eagle at No. 18 in the first round that sent her positively into the final two days.

McGann and Saiki trailed Deb Richard by one stroke going into the final round, then quickly moved ahead, going out in 33 to Richard's 36. McGann took the lead with a 25-foot putt for birdie at No. 10 and sealed the victory with birdies at Nos. 16 and 18. "I think my game is maturing a little bit," McGann said. "But this is a crazy game. You take whatever it gives you."

Friendly's Classic—$500,000
Winner: Dottie Pepper

You have to hand it to Dottie Pepper. Though she's a Pepper now, when she says she's playing like the Dottie Mochrie of old, believe it. By any name, this Pepper had been hot since bringing her old Titleist irons out of the closet a month earlier.

She won the Rochester International and ShopRite Classic back-to-back and made it three wins in five weeks with a pulsating victory over Brandie Burton in the Friendly's Classic in Agawam, Massachusetts.

This latest victory came from old-fashioned grit. Fighting a virus all week, Pepper shot rounds of 68, 69, 73 and 69 for a 279 total and a one-stroke victory over Burton after starting the round five strokes behind.

It came down to the closing hole, a 379-yard par-three hole. Pepper, playing in the group ahead of Burton and Mardi Lunn, hit her approach shot to within three feet of the hole and made birdie, moving into a tie with Burton. She needed some help to win, and she got it when Burton missed a six-foot putt for par. "I couldn't believe she missed it," Pepper said. "My heart was sinking when I made my putt. I needed some help to win and my old Solheim Cup partner gave it to me. I'm sorry for her, but very happy for me."

Burton's collapse began in the middle of the round. She hooked her drive and made bogey at No. 10 and double-bogeyed the 11th. Pepper started raggedly with bogeys on three of the first seven holes, but offset that with birdies on Nos. 4, 5, 9, 11 and 13 before her three-footer at No. 18. "I had no idea I was a stroke behind Brandie until the 17th hole," Pepper said. "I just figured the worst I could finish was third."

Michelob Light Heartland Classic—$550,000
Winner: Vicki Fergon

"You can't lose 'em all," somebody once said to Vicki Fergon in a moment of compassion after the LPGA veteran came up short in a tournament several years ago. And that person was right. After 12 years of beating on the door, she finally knocked it down in the Michelob Light Heartland Classic at Forest Hills Country Club in St. Louis, winning her first tournament since 1984.

With the victory came a champagne story, dispensed by fellow players, many of whom weren't around when last she won. "Relieved? You bet," Fergon said. "When you go that long, you think you may never win again, especially with the talent out here these days."

Fergon put herself in position to win with rounds of 71, 63 and 68, giving her a six-stroke lead over Pat Hurst. The cushion was enough that she could afford a final-round 74 and secure a four-stroke victory over Hurst and Patti Liscio.

Fergon's opening 71 left her four strokes behind leader Danielle Ammaccapane, but her second-round 63 opened that six-stroke lead and the third-round 68 maintained it. Liscio applied some pressure with five birdies on the first nine and was only two strokes back following a birdie on No. 13, but there would be no more.

"It's good I had a healthy lead the way I played No. 5, a par-five, a birdie hole," said Fergon, who hit into two bunkers, blasted over the green and made double bogey. "That's when everybody had to be thinking, 'Oh, here she comes again. The wheels are falling off.' It did unnerve me for a moment, but I didn't fall off the deep end."

du Maurier Classic—$1,000,000
Winner: Laura Davies

Laura Davies is good when there's nothing more than a purse at the end of each tournament. Give her a reason to be the best she can be, and Davies is almost unstoppable.

That was Davies in the season's final major championship, the du Maurier Classic in Edmonton, Alberta, where she unleashed a six-under-par 66 on a blustery autumnlike day and won her second major title of the year by two strokes over Nancy Lopez and Karrie Webb.

This one wasn't for Laura. It was for Colin Lunn, father of LPGA players Karen and Mardi, who died of a heart attack at age 56. Davies wanted to go to the funeral, but Lunn's daughters said, "Go play and win."

"He was like a second father to me," said Davies, who shot rounds of 71, 70, 70 and 66 for a 277 total, 11 under par over the Edmonton Country Club course. "I was with him two weeks ago and he was absolutely fine. I was glad I could win for him."

Davies struggled over the first three rounds with her putter. Webb shot 65 in the first round to lead by three strokes over Barb Mucha and Lopez. Webb added 68 and led by four strokes over Meg Mallon, who then shot 69 to take over after 54 holes, one stroke in front of Webb and Pat Hurst.

The final round was windy and blustery, a day when the field averaged 74.3 strokes, and Davies made her move, shooting 66 with seven birdies and one bogey. "I thought if I could shoot 69, something would happen," Davies said. "When I got to three under par early (after eight holes), I knew I had something. People were not making many birdies on a day like this."

PING Welch's Championship—$500,000
Winner: Emilee Klein

Emilee Klein's first stop after walking out of the scorer's tent is a telephone where she calls her parents. Good round or bad, it doesn't matter. And the conversation usually goes the same.

"I said, 'Oh, I did okay,'" after shooting a final-round 65 to win her first LPGA tournament, the PING Welch's Championship at Blue Hill Country Club in Canton, Massachusetts.

"My dad said, 'You did?' I said, 'Yeah, I made everything. I shot 65. I won.' I had to call them back later. They couldn't talk because they were crying."

The 22-year-old former NCAA champion from Arizona State won with each of her rounds better than the last — 71, 69, 68 and 65 for a 273 total. She won by two strokes in a battle with rookie sensation Karrie Webb, who carried a two-stroke lead into the final round and shot 69.

Klein trailed Webb's 65 by six strokes after the first round. She was three strokes behind Janet Anderson at the halfway point and moved to two behind Webb after 54 holes. "I've been waiting for this, dreaming of it," said Klein, who won the NCAA title in 1994. "I wanted it badly, and now I have it. To win against a field like this makes it more special."

Webb was no hacker during the week, with rounds of 65, 73, 68 and 69 for a 275 total, which would be good enough to win on most weeks. Klein just played better. There was some consolation for Webb in defeat. She earned $46,564 and moved atop the money list with $643,591.

Klein wasted little time in moving to the front in the final round. She birdied the first hole and Webb bogeyed it, creating a tie. That was Webb's only bogey, but she never again led. How strong was Klein? After a bogey at No. 5, she birdied Nos. 8, 9 and 10 to establish a two-stroke lead. Her only slip after that was a three-putt bogey at No. 16, trimming her lead to one. "I got rid of all the nervousness with that bogey," Klein said. "I caught myself looking ahead. I hadn't won yet. As soon as I three-putted, I told myself, 'Get your head back in it.'"

Star Bank LPGA Classic—$550,000
Winner: Laura Davies

Laura Davies smiled when she walked onto the Country Club of the North in Dayton, Ohio, for the first time. What she saw was a Jack Nicklaus-designed course and its big, wide fairways. "I knew the minute I saw it, I was going to like it," said Davies, who knew she could attack the course with her driver and take advantage of her dominating length.

With a $100,000 bonus available to any of the 1996 tournament winners who won here in the Star Bank LPGA Classic, the incentive to be aggressive was right up Davies' alley. It all added up to a three-stroke victory on rounds of 68, 66 and 70 for a 204 total, three strokes better than runners-up Maggie Will and Pat Hurst. She earned $182,500 including the bonus for her fourth LPGA victory of the year, the most since Beth Daniel's four in 1994.

"I think they should do this every week," Davies said, jokingly. "I didn't play a great final round. I think I let the bonus affect me a little bit."

Despite that, she appeared to be in trouble only once. Her lead dwindled to one over Daniel and Hurst when she bogeyed No. 5, botching a three-foot putt for par. Birdies at Nos. 7, 8 and 9 restored her advantage and she made pars the rest of the way.

Said Juli Inkster, "Laura is a good anything player. Yes, she has great length, but the whole game is there. She's also a great frontrunner, forcing those close enough to contend to play the rounds of their lives."

State Farm Rail Classic—$575,000
Winner: Michelle McGann

There's nothing like having been there when you have to do it again.

Take Michelle McGann, for instance. Three months before, she won the Oldsmobile Classic on the third playoff hole. And then she did it again, making a 10-footer on the third playoff hole to win the State Farm Rail Classic in Springfield, Illinois. McGann's playoff victory, her third victory of the season, came against Barb Whitehead and Laura Davies, all tied at 14-under-par 202.

McGann, who had rounds of 69, 65 and 68, was six strokes behind Kris Tschetter's 63 in the first round and went to the final round tied with Alice Miller. Tschetter faded to a tie for 13th place due to a middle-round 75, and

Miller collapsed with a final-round 75 and tied for 23rd place.

"It's kind of funny and somewhat ironic," McGann said. "Donna Harley caddied for me at the Oldsmobile, and I had to make birdie on the last hole to get in the playoff. Here, my last putt in the playoff, I had almost the same putt as then, a right-to-left breaker. Coming to the third playoff hole, I said to Donna, 'I had a nine iron in Lansing and I ended up making birdie. So I can do it again.' You go back to those good positive thoughts. It was good, positive energy."

McGann held a one-stroke lead going to the 16th tee after making an eagle at the par-five 15th, but she bogeyed the 17th and fell into a tie with Whitehead and Davies, who gained a spot in the playoff when she holed a bunker shot for birdie at No. 18.

The three players parred the first two playoff holes, Nos. 18 and 17 in that order, sending them back to the 18th tee. Davies eliminated herself, driving into a fairway bunker and taking two shots to get out. Whitehead left her birdie putt two feet short. McGann hit a nine iron within 10 feet and the winning putt added $86,250 to her bulging bank account.

Safeway LPGA Golf Championship—$550,000
Winner: Dottie Pepper

During the LPGA's spring fling in California, Hawaii and parts of the South, Dottie Mochrie was conspicuous by her absence on the weekends. While Liselotte Neumann, Annika Sorenstam and Karrie Webb were winning tournaments, Pepper was looking for her game.

Then, one day, she packed away her new clubs, brought out her old ones, gave up some new swing mechanics and went back to what worked before. Her victory in the Safeway LPGA Golf Championship in Portland, Oregon, was her fourth since mid-June.

Pepper was never more than a stroke off the lead in rounds of 65, 70 and 67 for a 14-under-par 202 total to hold off Chris Johnson by two strokes. Out of this victory came the Pepper of several years ago, the one who wasn't satisfied with merely winning. "Believe it or not, I'm not very happy with the way I hit it this week," she said. "I'm going back to work on it early next week. It's just not 100 percent there. My mechanics weren't there, and that kept me on my toes."

Maybe Pepper was referring to her inability to put Johnson away, or the fact that she was still suffering from a virus. Whatever, it made for a struggle. The two were tied at 14-under after 16 holes, but Johnson's short game suddenly went sour as she bogeyed the final two holes. Pepper made pars on both holes, the last from 10 feet.

"That was a wild day," Johnson said. "That's what golf is all about. It doesn't happen all that many times, and I think it made it a good event for the gallery. Dottie just played better than I did there at the end."

Pepper broke the 54-hole course record by five strokes. Her 202 also tied for the second lowest score on the LPGA Tour this year. "All this makes you wonder where I'd be in the Player of the Year standings if I had played this well early in the year," Pepper said. Johnson, who led Pepper by one stroke entering the final round, shot 70 to finish at 204.

SAFECO Classic—$550,000
Winner: Karrie Webb

Two years ago, Karrie Webb had to borrow $200 from her mother in order to join the Australian women's golf tour. That might have been the best investment ever made by the Webb family.

Webb made the SAFECO Classic her third LPGA victory of the year and the $82,500 that went with it vaulted her over Laura Davies to No. 1 on the money list with $769,532.

Not bad for a 21-year-old, who in 1993 was making $10 an hour working at her mother's cafe. A year later, she worked at a pro shop, then convinced her mother to support her professional ambitions. Her mother has since been repaid, and then some. "I've bought a house and a car," Webb said. "I don't have anything else to do with it. The money's just sitting in the bank. But I'm sure I'll find something to do with it."

In winning for the first time since early May, Webb was hardly the picture of consistency over the 6,251-yard Meridian Valley course in Kent, Washington. She opened with 66, one stroke behind Patty Sheehan, then added a pair of 71s to fall four strokes off the lead of Tammie Green going into the final round. She closed with 69 for a two-stroke victory over Sheehan.

"I really don't have any secrets," Webb said of her rookie success. "My game got out of kilter a bit earlier this year, but now I'm confident again, and that has a lot to do with it. Obviously, I feel I can win out here."

Green struggled to a final-round 76 and tied for third place with Barb Mucha. Sheehan, who was looking to become the first four-time winner in the event's 15-year history, slumped to a final-round 72. "Karrie winning is no surprise," Sheehan said. "She's no one-year wonder. She's solid. You don't win four times against the competition we have out here by being lucky."

Fieldcrest Cannon Classic—$500,000
Winner: Trish Johnson

Call it turn-about-fair-play twice, Trish Johnson's comeback victory over Dottie Pepper in the Fieldcrest Cannon Classic in Charlotte, North Carolina.

This one goes back a few weeks, first to the Safeway Championship where Johnson led Pepper by one stroke going to the final round, and lost. Then, there was the Solheim Cup, where Johnson led Pepper 1 up at the turn only to lose 3 and 2.

Where did Johnson stand after the Fieldcrest victory?

"I'd swap it in a heartbeat to have won at the Solheim," she said. "But, it's very nice, very satisfying to say the least. Winning is winning. It feels good no matter the tournament."

This was even more satisfying considering that Johnson started the final round in fourth place, three strokes behind Pepper, then played the round of her life, a career-best 64. That was three shots better than runner-up Kim Saiki, a winless 30-year-old pro, and four over Pepper, who began Sunday's play two strokes ahead of Dale Eggeling, Saiki and Gail Graham.

"I don't know where it came from, really," said Johnson, who birdied two of her first three holes on the way to a bogey-free round that was two strokes lower than her previous best in nine years on the LPGA Tour. Johnson opened with 67, one stroke behind leader Robin Hood, then added rounds of 71, 68 and 64 for a 270 total. Her 64 broke the Peninsula Club record by one stroke, and her 270 was three strokes better than that posted by defending champion Gail Graham on the 6,318-yard, two-year-old course.

Pepper, bidding for a fifth victory in her last nine LPGA Tour events, played brilliantly the first three rounds with 68, 67 and 68, but wasn't on her game in the last round. She offset three birdies with two bogeys for 71. "I'm happy for Trish. We've been going at it, against each other the last three times out, and we've played some good golf, but not today for me," Pepper said. "It started on the very first hole. I was in between clubs it seemed all day, and I didn't make the right choice too often."

JAL Big Apple Classic—$725,000
Winner: Caroline Pierce

Caroline Pierce had toiled nine years on the LPGA Tour with not much to show for it until she arrived at the JAL Big Apple Classic in New Rochelle, New York. Three grinding days later at Wykagyl Country Club, she had removed the yoke of non-winner. Pierce's first victory came in her 224th career start and in a tournament usually played in heat and humidity, but which was moved to autumn so NBC, which televised the Olympic Games, could fulfill its sponsor commitment.

The tournament was a Pierce celebration, but a competitive disaster. The weather played a part — heavy winds in the first round, followed by 50 degree temperatures in the second round, then almost perfect conditions, clear and cool, on the final day. Pierce frolicked. Her rounds of 72, 67 and 72 for a 211 total made her the only player under par, five strokes ahead of Tina Barrett and Karrie Webb. It wasn't pretty, but as Pierce noted, "It worked." It also paid well; her $108,750 share of the $725,000 purse more than doubled her season earnings.

All of which was more than fine with Pierce, who came to the United States from England in 1983 and graduated from Houston Baptist University with a degree in political science. After turning pro in 1987, she didn't have a top-10 finish until 1991. Until winning, her strongest challenge came in 1995 when she tied for second here behind Tracy Kerdyk.

Dottie Pepper and Vicki Goetze led the first round with even-par 71s before Pierce took control with her 67 and sprinted away Sunday as only four players broke par in the week's best weather. Barrett started the day 10 strokes back and with 67 moved ahead of 20 golfers for a share of second place with Webb. It was her 11th top-five finish.

The cumulative stroke average of 76.6 was the highest of any tournament this year and the 11-over-par cut score was three strokes higher than at the U.S. Women's Open. Pierce's seven-birdie second round was the driving force in her victory, although the lead had dwindled to a single stroke over Pepper as they moved to the third tee. Then a funny thing happened. It was Pepper and Michelle McGann who fell back. Pepper dropped five strokes on the last six holes of the first nine and McGann fell away with a double bogey at No. 4.

Webb's chances of catching Pierce dissolved with a double bogey at the sixth. In all, the top eight finishers behind Pierce played Wykagyl in 16 over par Saturday. It was so bad that even after making double bogey at No. 11, Pierce led by four strokes.

CoreStates Betsy King Classic—$600,000
Winner: Annika Sorenstam

They named a golf tournament for Hall of Famer Betsy King this year and Annika Sorenstam stole her thunder, which isn't exactly what the good folks of Kutztown, Pennsylvania, had in mind when they convinced the LPGA to bring a tournament to the area where King grew up.

It's difficult to beat Sorenstam anywhere, and the large crowds over the weekend — after King had missed the cut — were as appreciative as if Sorenstam was one of their own. Unfortunately for King and the hometown fans, King's year-long struggle continued. Rounds of 79 and 75 were indicative of her year's play, which showed only three top-10 finishes.

Sorenstam's play was magical in her second victory of the year. She shot 66, 69, 67 and 68 for a 270 total over the 6,075-yard Berkleigh course, proving once again that she is one of the best frontrunners on the LPGA Tour.

She began the final round three strokes ahead of Laura Davies and strolled to an eight-stroke victory at 18 under par, tying the lowest 72-hole score on the LPGA Tour in 1996. Sorenstam ended the suspense by the par-five fifth hole with a birdie to Davies' bogey, and her lead was six strokes. It increased to as many as 11 strokes through the 12th hole before Davies reduced the margin with three birdies over the final four holes. "I've got a sneaking feeling that if I had made more birdies today, so would Annika," Davies said. "It was a losing battle almost from the start."

It was Sorenstam's first victory since the U.S. Women's Open in June and was just as precise as that one. She provided a hint in the first round of what was to come in the last round. Her eight birdie putts, in a round of 66, totalled 30 feet, six inches.

Her performance reminded some of King in her glory days, said Meg Mallon. "When I first came out 10 years ago, whenever Betsy had the lead on Saturday, she always won on Sunday," Mallon said. "That's how Annika plays. She plays to win the tournament. When she gets in position, and her competition isn't playing well, she's not going to bring her game down. It's just Annika's game."

Samsung World Championship of Women's Golf—$500,000
Winner: Annika Sorenstam

As we were saying, there aren't many better frontrunners in women's golf than Annika Sorenstam. A week later and thousands of miles from Kutztown, Pennsylvania, the reigning U.S. Women's Open champion won the Samsung World Championship of Women's Golf on the Ildong Lakes course in Seoul, South Korea, by one stroke over Helen Alfredsson.

This is the same Sorenstam who three weeks earlier in the JAL Big Apple

Classic was about as uninspired as any golfer can be in tying for 30th place, and then put an awesome whipping on Laura Davies in Pennsylvania.

It wasn't so easy this time, however, despite Sorenstam's shooting 14 under par on rounds of 66, 69, 69 and 70 for a 274 total. Sorenstam shared the first-round lead with Emilee Klein, the second-round lead with Seri Park, led Park by one stroke after three rounds, and won with back-to-back birdies at Nos. 14 and 15, just enough cushion to hold off Alfredsson, who closed with 66.

"I had a little slump this year," Sorenstam said. "I've played well, but I just wasn't finishing it off. The win last week made me feel nice. I got my game back."

Although the Swedish duo dominated the headlines, teenager Park and rookie Karrie Webb provided their own headlines. The 18-year-old Park, just a year out of the amateur ranks, was just one stroke behind going into the final round and finished with 72 for third place. Webb tied for sixth place and pulled $20,000 ahead of Laura Davies for the money title with two events remaining.

Davies skipped the Samsung World Championship in favor of the Italian Open, which she won, enabling her to clinch the top spot in Europe.

ITT LPGA Tour Championship—$700,000
Winner: Karrie Webb

Talk about being all you can be, how about Karrie Webb. She arrived on the LPGA Tour in 1996 from the qualifying tournament, won the second event of the year, the HEALTHSOUTH Inaugural, and put the topping on her season by becoming the first rookie on any golf tour to surpass $1 million in earnings.

Webb ascended to the height of her profession by winning the ITT LPGA Tour Championship at Desert Inn Golf Club in Las Vegas, Nevada, with a final-round 65 and four-stroke victory over Kelly Robbins, Nancy Lopez and Emilee Klein. The spoils of her victory were $150,000, the LPGA money title and runaway Rolex Rookie of the Year honors. "It feels great because no one can ever say she was the first to win a million dollars except me," said Webb, who shot 69, 70, 68 and 65 for a 272 total. "It's always going to be in the record books. No one can change that."

While Webb made it look easy on the last day, it was anything but that for the first three rounds. She was two strokes behind Japan's Mayumi Hirase's 67 after the first round and one stroke behind Michelle McGann, Juli Inkster, Penny Hammel and Jane Geddes.

It became the Webb and Klein show with the two youngsters tied at nine-under-par 207 with one round to play. Then it became Webb's show alone early Sunday. No one came within three strokes of Webb over the last nine holes, mainly because of the way she overpowered the 6,324-yard Desert Inn layout. She led by two strokes after nine holes, then birdied the 10th and 13th and put the victory away with an eagle on the short 453-yard, par-five 15th. "It was a dream round," Webb said. "I was nervous Saturday night, didn't sleep well, but Sunday everything was strong. I was a little worried when Laura eagled the first, but my birdie at No. 3 got me going. And after the eagle at No. 15, I felt very comfortable and could take a breather."

Women's European Tour

Women's Welsh Open—£75,000
Winner: Lisa Hackney

A winner in Asia the year before, Lisa Hackney got her 1996 American Express Tour season off to the perfect start by winning her first European title at the Women's Welsh Open. At the St. Pierre course that would host the Solheim Cup later in the year, the 28-year-old from Stoke jumped from 18th place in the points standings into the top seven, out of which she never drifted during the season.

A final round of one-under-par 72, mixing five birdies with four bogeys, at one point gave Hackney a four-stroke lead. Two strokes in front playing the par-three 18th, she could afford not to get up and down from a bunker. Her winning total was 289, three under par. Her third-round 69 was one of only three sub-70 rounds during the week, the others coming from Laura Navarro with a 69 to finish one stroke behind in second place, and from Kristel Mourgue d'Algue, whose 67 brought her up to third despite an opening 79.

Costa Azul Ladies' Open—£60,000
Winner: Shani Waugh

Inspired by seeing Lisa Hackney win the week before, Australian Shani Waugh, 26, collected her first victory in the Costa Azul Ladies' Open with a last-round 71 for a two-under-par 214 total.

Waugh came from behind to win by two strokes over Swede Helene Koch, Mary Grace Estuesta of the Philippines, Ireland's Aideen Rogers and France's Marie Laure de Lorenzi, the defending champion, who shot a Troia course-record 67 in the final round. "Lisa was my inspiration," Waugh said. "Her win in Wales made me believe in my own ability to win."

Ford-Stimorol Danish Open—£80,000
Winner: Nadene Gole

Another Australian, and another first-time winner. On this occasion it was 27-year-old Nadene Gole, from Melbourne. Gole made the perfect start to her final round of the Ford-Stimorol Danish Open at Vejle by birdieing four of the first five holes, but double bogeys at the seventh and 11th meant she had to hang on for a two-shot win over two fellow Aussies Rachel Hetherington and Anne-Marie Knight and Scotland's Gillian Stewart.

"Maybe I started to think too much about my round. I knew I could still win if I started to attack and when I recovered from a bunker for a par at the 13th, that was the crisis over," said Gole, who shot 73 for a seven-under-par 209.

Deesse Ladies' Swiss Open—£80,000
Winner: Sophie Gustafson

A Swede won the Deesse Ladies' Swiss Open played in France. But the fact that the Golf & Country Club de Maison Blanche, near Geneva, is situated four miles inside the French border did not stop Sophie Gustafson, 22, from continuing the run of first-time victories. She made eagles at the first and fourth holes of her final round and eventually had to hole a three-footer on the last green for a round of 69, a 12-under-par 280 total, and a one-shot win over Lisa Hackney.

Hackney, the Welsh Open champion, broke the course record with 66 on Saturday and birdied the last two holes in her final-round 69 to take second place by two over Patricia Meunier Lebouc and Charlotta Eliasson Wharton. Another Swede, Sara Melin, was penalized four shots in her opening 78 for carrying 15 clubs for the first two holes she played (the 10th and 11th), but then holed her seven iron at the 417-yard par-five first hole for a double eagle.

Evian Masters—£375,000
Winner: Laura Davies

Returning for the first time of 1996 to Europe, Laura Davies completed her 23rd European victory and her fourth of the year in the Evian Masters. Davies began the final round, delayed by four hours by heavy rain which flooded the Royal Evian course, with a two-shot lead, was never really threatened, and birdied the last two holes to win by four strokes over Swede Carin Koch. Her 14-under-par 274 total was made up with rounds of 72, 69, 65 and 68. Helen Alfredsson was third, five shots back.

Despite the brilliance of her play, Davies sparked controversy by taking a handheld television onto the course at which she sneaked occasional glances in idle moments of an England soccer match in the European Championship. "I never imagined that anyone would be offended," Davies said. "I hope I have not upset the sponsors. So many of the players were following what was happening with their teams."

Glashutte Ladies' Austrian Open—£60,000
Winner: Martina Koch

Austrian-born German Martina Koch returned to the land of her birth to win the Glashutte Ladies' Austrian Open, her first professional title in only her second year. The 30-year-old turned pro late after a distinguished amateur career in which she won the European Amateur title twice.

Rounds of 74, 68 and 71 gave Koch a six-under-par score of 213 and a two-stroke victory over New Zealander Lynnette Brooky. "I feel very much at home here," Koch said.

Hennessy Cup—£300,000
Winner: Helen Alfredsson

After victories in 1991 and 1992, Helen Alfredsson collected her third Hennessy Cup win, and her 14th worldwide, with a little unintentional help from a spectator.

Alfredsson, playing despite discomfort from a broken bone in her pelvis that went back to a cycling accident 11 years before, had started the final round with a three-stroke lead, but needed to hole an eight-foot birdie putt at the 18th to get into a playoff with countrywoman Liselotte Neumann and England's Trish Johnson.

Neumann had shot 67 to set the eight-under-par 280 target, which Johnson tied with 68 and Alfredsson with 71. Despite a final-round 68, Annika Sorenstam finished in fourth, three shots outside the playoff.

While Neumann drove poorly to put herself out of the playoff at the first extra hole, Alfredsson got lucky when her second shot hit a spectator and her ball bounced back onto the fairway. She halved the hole with Johnson and then rolled in a 30-foot birdie putt at the second playoff hole. "I was so lucky at the first extra hole," said the 31-year-old Swede. "I gave the ball to the lady and said thank you very much."

Guardian Irish Open—£110,000
Winner: Alison Nicholas

"You can never have a big enough lead," said Alison Nicholas, but the Gibraltar-born Yorkshirewoman need not have worried as she came in eight shots ahead of the field in the Guardian Irish Open for her 16th career victory. Nicholas, age 34, was never headed after a first-round 69, but a Citywest course record of 65 left the rest behind, and a last-day 70 gave her an 11-under total of 277.

Trish Johnson finished runner-up for the second consecutive tournament at 285, while two-time defending champion Laura Davies tied for third a further shot behind with Austria's Natascha Fink. "I was a little nervous when Laura made a couple of early birdies," Nicholas said. "I settled down when I birdied the fifth, and after the turn it was just a case of churning out the pars. I probably wasn't as aggressive as when I shot my 65, but I stuck to my game plan of keeping out of trouble."

McDonald's WPGA Championship—£150,000
Winner: Tina Fischer

A new tournament and another new winner. Tina Fischer could not have picked a more spectacular location than the King's Course at Gleneagles for her first victory in the McDonald's WPGA Championship. The 25-year-old in her second year on the Tour did not falter down the stretch, holing par putts of between three and seven feet at the 15th, 16th and 17th holes, and then two-putted from 10 feet for a birdie at the 18th for a one-shot win. "I mis-hit my seven-iron second shot but it was the best mis-hit I've ever had," she said.

Fischer's rounds of 68, 69, 72 and 69 gave her a 10-under-par total of 278, with four players tying for second: Trish Johnson, for the third consecutive European event, Loraine Lambert, Charlotta Sorenstam, the younger sister of Annika, and Wales' Helen Wadsworth. Wadsworth needed a birdie at the 18th to win, but left her approach 35 yards from the hole on the front edge and three-putted.

Weetabix Women's British Open Championship—£500,000
Winner: Emilee Klein

For Karrie Webb, read Emilee Klein. The 1996 version of the Weetabix Women's British Open Championship turned out to have similarities with the 1995 edition as a sweet-swinging, fresh-faced young champion-to-be sauntered around the fairways of the Duke's Course at Woburn with a commanding lead and was duly doused with champagne on the 18th green.

Klein, 22, who had beaten Webb the previous week for her first LPGA title at the PING Welch's Championship, brought over her winning confidence to land the £80,000 first prize with rounds of 68, 66, 71 and 72 for a 15-under-par total of 277 and a seven-shot victory. With much of Sunday about who finished second, Amy Alcott and Penny Hammel shared the honors at 284.

In what was the highest purse ever (£500,000) and the best quality and most cosmopolitan field for a Women's European Tour event, Americans filled 10 of the leading 13 places, with only Lisa Hackney and Alison Nicholas tied for fourth and Marie Laure de Lorenzi in seventh carrying the flag for Europe.

Klein's straight hitting on the tight, treelined fairways and steady putting boosted her late run. The previous Sunday she had had no time to celebrate as she dashed for a trans-Atlantic flight and her parents, Bobby and Randee, missed the moment because they had flown to London early to do some sightseeing. "I am thrilled my parents could be here to see me win this time," Klein said. "This is such a prestigious tournament and such a big win for me. I am so excited I am in a state of shock. We will definitely be celebrating tonight."

Trygg-Hansa Ladies' Open—£125,000
Winner: Annika Sorenstam

After 36 holes, it looked as if the Trygg-Hansa Ladies' Open would be guaranteed a home winner with defending champion Liselotte Neumann leading by six shots. It did, but it was Annika Sorenstam, who won for the first time in Sweden.

Sorenstam birdied the 16th hole when she holed from 30 feet, and then hit an eight iron to eight feet for another at the 18th. That gave her a 13-under-par total of 279, one better than England's Alison Nicholas and Joanne Morley, while Neumann bogeyed the last three holes to fall two behind.

"I thought I was playing for third place when I set out," Sorenstam said. "It means a lot to me winning in Sweden, and getting the better of Lotta also feels good."

Compaq Open—£100,000
Winner: Federica Dassu

It took four extra holes to decide the winner of the inaugural Compaq Open, with 37-year-old Italian Federica Dassu gaining her fifth career win. Dassu out-lasted her opponents as first Helen Alfredsson three-putted at the third playoff hole, and then Scotland's Kathryn Marshall did the same at the next hole.

Dassu, the third-round leader, had to hit a nine iron to four feet at the 18th to birdie the hole and get into the playoff at eight-under 280. Alfredsson had set the clubhouse target with a last-round 68. After going to the turn in 32, the Swede was two ahead, but only painkillers and a massage had allowed her to play on the final day after waking up in the middle of the night with back trouble.

Marshall's consolation was to be selected as one of five wild cards for the Solheim Cup by European captain Mickey Walker.

Marks & Spencer European Open—£100,000
Winner: Trish Johnson

It had been four years since Trish Johnson had won in Europe, and almost three and a half since the 30-year-old from Bristol had done so in America. At Hanbury Manor she rediscovered her winning form in style, with rounds of 64 and 70 over the weekend giving her a five-shot advantage over Sweden's Pernilla Sterner and Australia's Anne-Marie Knight.

"I was never a great ball-striker and I am definitely a better player than when I last won, but sometimes you forget the main thing is to get the ball in the hole," Johnson said.

In the first round, Johnson had been so upset with her game that she played the last eight holes without bothering with a yardage chart. That seemed to help as she was two under par for those holes which limited her first-round damage to 74. The next morning she changed putters and shot 66, which still left her seven behind Laura Davies.

Davies, having just returned from the LPGA Tour, shot 63 in the second round, including driving the green at the par-four first, but then slumped to 76 and 75 over the weekend.

Wilkinson Sword Ladies' English Open—£100,000
Winner: Laura Davies

Laura Davies was not out of winning form for long, her success at the Wilkinson Sword Ladies' English Open being her seventh victory of the year, the 47th of her career and a more than satisfactory outcome to the defense of her title. While Davies won by four shots, her desire to be No. 1 in the money lists on both sides of the Atlantic took a knock as Helen Alfredsson took second place to maintain a £2,000 advantage on the European ranking, and Karrie Webb won the Safeco Classic in America to regain the lead on the LPGA list.

Davies started slowly with 72, but then got going with rounds of 66 and 68 to take the lead and closed with 67. Laura Navarro of Spain was eight shots back in third place, while Marie Laure de Lorenzi broke the Oxfordshire course record with 64 in the second round but finished tied for sixth.

Solheim Cup
Winners: United States

In a Sunday all too familiar to those European supporters from the Greenbrier two years before, America virtually swept the board in the singles to retain the Solheim Cup and become the first team to win away from home. At the Greenbrier, the two sides had been tied going into the last-day singles, which the Americans won 8-2.

At the Marriott St. Pierre Hotel & Country Club, near Chepstow, Wales, Europe led after two days by two points, the match having been extended to a Ryder Cup format with 28 points at stake. But on Sunday, America won the singles 10-2 for an overall 17-11 victory.

Annika Sorenstam, sent out to lead the way for a European team that needed five and half points to regain the trophy, was the home side's only winner. Liselotte Neumann and Alison Nicholas claimed half points, but otherwise the scoreboard was awash with red. Psychologically, Michelle McGann's 3-and-2 victory over Laura Davies, who did not make a birdie in the match, signaled the swing in fortunes. The visitors reached the 14 points they needed to ensure they held onto the trophy when Kelly Robbins holed from three feet at the 18th to halve her match with Nicholas.

America had opened with a 3½-½ win in the first morning foursomes, but then suffered a European backlash. Davies and Trish Johnson made nine birdies in 13 holes in winning their fourball in the afternoon 6 and 5. In all on the first afternoon, there were 55 birdies and only five bogeys in the four fourballs as the competition was raised to a new level.

Europe took the second-day foursomes 3½-½ and also shaded the afternoon fourballs again to take a 9-7 lead. "Apart from the opening foursomes, the way we played was fantastic," said the European captain Mickey Walker. "I thought we would win, but the Americans outplayed us on the Sunday."

The Americans were led by Judy Rankin, who said, "When we came over here, we didn't anticipate being down on Saturday night. We were a little bit shocked. Our pride was not hurt because people had played very well against us. From Friday lunchtime until last night, we got whipped. Today the 12 players on the American side gave everything they had."

Sorenstam was the highest point scorer with three wins and two halves, while Dottie Pepper (three wins, one loss) and Betsy King (three wins out of three) led the way for the Americans.

Ladies' German Open—£75,000
Winner: Joanne Morley

Only a week after the disappointment of making her Solheim Cup debut on a losing European team, Joanne Morley bounced back to take her first title at the Ladies' German Open in Treudelberg. Morley, 29, from Cheshire, England, took the lead with three birdies at the start of her final-round 68 and was never headed again.

Her 11-under-par 281 total was four shots better than Sweden's Maria Hjorth and five better than Solheim colleague Lisa Hackney. Morley made six birdies in all on a final day of strong winds and driving rain. "I've never played better in weather like this," Morley said.

Ladies' French Open—£60,000
Winner: Trish Johnson

The moment Trish Johnson opened with 62 she was set for a record-breaking week at the Ladies' French Open in Arras. Her round included a hole-in-one and was the lowest ever on the European Tour, beating 63s by Anne Jones, Cathy Panton-Lewis, Penny Grice-Whittaker and Laura Davies (more than once).

Johnson then added 68 to set the Tour's 36-hole record at 130, and in closing with 70 she set a record score in a 54-hole event of 19-under-par 200. It was the third victory for the Englishwoman in six weeks, having already won the Marks & Spencer European Open and the LPGA Fieldcrest Cannon Classic. About the only thing that was not a record for Johnson was her 10-shot winning margin over Spain's Raquel Carriedo-Tomas. Johnson herself had won by 11 in the past.

"I should have scored better in the final round, but it is so difficult to keep going on the greens. You can't do it every day," Johnson said. She gave credit for her scoring to putting specialist Harold Swash. "He changed my set-up to the ball, my grip and adjusted my shoulders into a more square position," she said.

Italian Open di Sicilia—£100,000
Winner: Laura Davies

Prior to the penultimate event of the season, Helen Alfredsson led the money list by £1,924 over Laura Davies. The Swede did not play in the Italian Open at Il Picciolo in Sicily, where Davies won her eighth tournament of the year, her third in Europe, and the £15,000 first prize which secured first place on the money list for 1996.

With earnings of £110,880, Davies topped the European money list for the fourth time, having done so in 1985, 1986 and 1992. This was perhaps her finest achievement because it was performed while making many a mad dash in an effort to be the leading money earner on both the European and LPGA Tours.

After earlier rounds of 68, 70 and 68, Davies could afford a last-round, wind-strewn 76 and still win by three shots over Tina Fischer of Germany and Australia's Fiona Pike with a 10-under-par total of 282. That left her free to return to the LPGA Tour in an effort to complete part two of her plan.

Ladies' Spanish Open—£60,000
Winner: Caryn Louw

Caryn Louw, a former South African Women's Amateur champion, had just one thing on her mind when teeing up for the last event, the Ladies' Spanish Open. She wanted to finish in the top 80 on the money list to avoid having to return to La Manga for the qualifying tournament. Louw was 79th going into the event, but her wire-to-wire victory safely ensured her exempt status.

Louw opened with rounds of 69 and 70, then closed with 67 to win by four strokes over Spain's Amaia Arruti, with England's Lora Fairclough, who went to the turn in 31 during a last-round 67, one stroke further back. Her 10-under-par 206 total meant Louw became the eighth first-time winner of the season. Neither of the top two players on the money list played in the event, Laura Davies finishing with £110,880 to Helen Alfredsson's £97,804. Trish Johnson took third place with £80,333.

Princess Lalla Meriem Cup—£65,000
Winner: Lora Fairclough

The Princess Lalla Meriem Cup was an event for 15 women professionals alongside the Hassan II Trophy. Lora Fairclough led by four strokes after the first two rounds in a pro-am format over the Blue course at Royal Dar-es-Salam in Rabat, Morocco. After 77 when play switched to the Robert Trent Jones-designed Red course, Fairclough produced a last-round 70 to complete a four-stroke victory over fellow Englishwoman Sally Prosser. The win and $15,000 first prize may have made up slightly for missing out on a victory during the European season and failing to gain a place on the Solheim Cup team.

Women's Australasian Tours

Republic of China Open—US$120,000
Winner: Shoko Asano

Second-year professional Shoko Asano from Japan held off more experienced players to win the Republic of China Open in cold, windy weather at Chang Gung Golf Club in Taipei, Taiwan. Her surprise victory was based on starting the final round with three consecutive birdies. Her 73 for a two-over-par total of 218 beat four local players, Huang Bie-Shyun, Li Wen-Lin, Tseng Hsiu-Feng and Huang Yu-Chen, and Sweden's Sophie Gustafson by two shots.

Singapore Open—US$80,000
Winner: Debbie Dowling

It took a four-hole playoff to do it, but Debbie Dowling finally won for the first time since 1989 when the 33-year-old Englishwoman beat Korea's Young-Me Lee in the Singapore Open at Tanah Merah. The pair had tied at one-under-par 215 after Lee caught Dowling with 70 to 71 in the final round, before a par at the fourth extra hole gave Dowling, who has won six times in Europe, her second Asian victory and a check of $11,250, the biggest of her career.

Indonesian Open—US$100,000
Winner: Corinne Dibnah

Lisa Hackney made an attempt to successfully defend her Indonesian Open title at the Peter Thomson-designed Finna course, but the battling spirit of Australian Corinne Dibnah proved unbeatable. Dibnah, who caught the Englishwoman with 73 to 74 in the third round, won the playoff at the third extra hole for her 16th career victory.

Thailand Open—US$110,000
Winner: Shelly Rule

Where Corinne Dibnah succeeded a week previously, the Australian could not quite win her second successive playoff in the Thailand Open at President Country Club in Bangkok. Mind you, it took a curling 60-foot putt on the first extra hole by American Shelly Rule, accompanied by a shriek of delight, to foil Dibnah, who had hit her approach to 30 feet but could not hole the putt. Rule had taken advantage of misfortunes to second-round leaders Sophie Gustafson and Sarah Bennett of England to post a even-par total of 216, which Dibnah then matched.

Malaysian JAL Open—US$90,000
Winner: Corinne Dibnah

There were no playoffs this time. Corinne Dibnah made sure of that at the Malaysian JAL Open despite stumbling to 80 in the windswept final round. The 33-year-old Queenslander had built a substantial advantage with rounds of 67 and 70, and with a one-over-par 217 total held on for a two-stroke victory over England's Caroline Hall, who closed with 74, equalling the best score of the day. Dibnah's run of two wins and a second ensured her of top place on the money list with $38,036, with England's Debbie Dowling second at $24,143, and Hall third at $18,172.

Holden Women's Australian Open—A$300,000
Winner: Catriona Matthew

Had Catriona Matthew been on vacation she might have been annoyed to have gone all the way to the other side of the world only to wake up and find a day like those of her homeland of Scotland. But Matthew was all the happier going about her business in chilly winds and rain squalls in the Holden Women's Australian Open at the Yarra Yarra course in Melbourne.

On a day when disaster was never far away — third-round leader Corinne Dibnah began with five bogeys in her closing 80 — Matthew did not drop a shot during her four-under-par 69. A nine-under-par total of 283 gave her a first win for three years and a three-stroke margin over Karrie Webb.

Birdies at the 14th and 15th holes gave the 27-year-old Scot an unassailable lead. Matthew said, "As soon as I got out of bed this morning I knew the weather was to my advantage. It was the sort of day I grew up with."

Alpine Australian Ladies Masters—A$350,000
Winner: Jane Crafter

With thunder and lightning closing in on Queensland's Gold Coast, Jane Crafter eagled the final hole to beat Jane Geddes and Laura Davies in the Alpine Australian Ladies Masters.

Geddes, despite missing her birdie putt at the last hole, set the target at 18 under par. All three in the final group had chances of eagling the hole, and Liselotte Neumann's birdie gave her fourth place. Crafter reached the last green with a five wood, and Davies came in with an eight iron. The Australian capitalized by holing from 42 feet and then seeing Davies push her 16-footer wide of the hole.

"It was a bad putt, but Crafty showed loads of nerve to hole her putt," Davies said. By sharing second place with Geddes, the Englishwoman continued a run of finishing in the top two for her fifth tournament in a row on three different continents.

"You dream of making putts like that to win a tournament," said Crafter, who shot rounds of 69, 65, 71 and 68 for a 273 total. "It was a dead straight putt. I just wanted to make sure it got there."

Japan LPGA Tour

Daikin Orchid—¥60,000,000
Winner: Li Wen-Lin

Li Wen-Lin used the final day's best round as a springboard to her first victory on the Japan LPGA Tour in the Daikin Orchid tournament, the opening event of the season in early March. The 30-year-old Taiwanese golfer, a professional for three years, shot five-under-par 67 at Okinawa's Ryukyu Golf Club to win the title by two strokes with her 212 total.

Li trailed compatriot Huang Bie-Shyun (72-68–140) by five strokes after 36 holes, with five other players in between. She surged into contention with four consecutive birdies early in the round and clinched the victory with another on the final green. Huang tumbled from contention with 78 and the runner-up slot at 214 went to Miyuki Shimabukuro (70) and Yuko Moriguchi (72).

Saishunkan Ladies—¥45,000,000
Winner: Young-Me Lee

Weather took a heavy toll on the Saishunkan Ladies tournament, but one person who wasn't complaining was Young-Me Lee, the experienced Korean player, who wound up with the title after 27 holes of regular action and one playoff hole. "I'm just happy to win after so long," said the 33-year-old Lee, who hadn't been victorious in Japan in 21 months. It was her fourth title on the Japan LPGA Tour.

After the opening round at Kumamoto Kuko Country Club was washed out, Lee shot a three-under-par 69 and shared the Saturday lead with Shin Sora of Korea and Toshimi Kimura of Japan. When rains resumed Sunday, officials cut the final round to nine holes. Lee shot 39 and Japan's Chie Yoshida 37 to tie for first place at par 108. Lee missed a three-footer for the win at the last regulation hole, but dropped a four-footer for a winning birdie on the first extra hole.

Yellow Hat Tokyo Open—¥50,000,000
Winner: Aki Takamura

Aki Takamura turned a tight fight into a rout in the Yellow Hat Tokyo Open when she came up with a record-tying final round at the Wakasa Golf Links. The 23-year-old Takamura, the 1995 Japan LPGA champion, fired an eight-under-par 64 Sunday and raced to a nine-stroke victory with her 207 total. She had 10 one-putt greens in the final round that matched 13 other 64s as the lowest 18-hole scores posted in Japan LPGA history.

Takamura had started the tournament three strokes atop the field with 67, but dropped back into a first-place tie with Korea's Ae-Sook Kim at 143 Saturday when she slipped to 76, bringing several other players within range. She bogeyed the first hole Sunday, but was flawless after that, running off nine birdies to leave Kim and Toshimi Kimura in second place at 216.

Kenshoen Ladies—¥50,000,000
Winner: Aiko Hashimoto

It was another tearful victory for Aiko Hashimoto, who had cried when she ended a seven-year win drought at the 1995 Mitsubishi Electric tournament. The 28-year-old Hashimoto greeted her second victory — in the Kenshoen Ladies tournament at Dohgo Golf Club — the same way after coming from two strokes off the pace with a final-round 70 and a four-under-par 212 total, finishing one shot ahead of Kaori Higo, two in front of Michiko Hattori.

The veteran Korean Ok-Hee Ku had led for two days with a pair of 70s, but slumped to 76 Sunday. Hashimoto had started 72-70 and was third behind Hattori at 141 going into the final round.

Mitsukoshi Cup—¥60,000,000
Winner: Marnie McGuire

Dealing better than the rest with harsh, windy conditions, New Zealand's Marnie McGuire captured the Mitsukoshi Cup title in the first four-round event on the Japan LPGA season. In winning her fourth event in Japan, McGuire closed with a two-over-par 74 that she called "a good round in view of the difficult conditions." It gave her a 293 total, an abnormally high score for the circuit, and a one-stroke victory over Kaori Harada, the first-round leader (70) who also had a closing 74.

McGuire had shared first place at 145 after Friday's round with Ikuyo Shiotani, the Japan LPGA Tour leader with five victories in 1995, and Kaori Higo. With 74 Saturday, McGuire slipped one stroke in front of Harada, Higo, Akiko Fukushima and Tseng Hsiu-Feng of Taiwan.

Nasu Ogawa—¥50,000,000
Winner: Aki Nakano

Aki Nakano focused on her own game as others faltered, the result being a come-from-behind victory in the Nasu Ogawa tournament at Tochigi's Nasu Ogawa Golf Club. Her closing, two-under-par 70 turned a three-stroke deficit into a three-stroke win, the fifth of her career. She finished at par 216. Aiko Hashimoto, the Kenshoen winner two weeks earlier, was second at 219.

The 33-year-old Nakano had shot 73s the first two days. Woo-Soon Ku, with the week's only sub-70 round, led the first day with 69, but fell two behind Miyuki Shimabukuro Saturday when she followed with 76–145.

Shimabukuro shot 72-71–143 and Tseng Hsiu-Feng 75-70 to share second place with Ku. None of the three held up Sunday.

Satake Classic—¥50,000,000
Winner: Laura Davies

Laura Davies, the talented and powerful British star who again reigned as No. 1 in women's golf worldwide in 1996, picked up one of her nine victories in the Satake Classic in a one-stop visit to the Japan LPGA Tour in late April. Despite a sterling, second-round 66 that included a hole-in-one, Davies had to go an extra hole before putting down the challenge of Suzuko Maeda at Hiroshima Country Club.

The six-under-par 66, the product of five birdies, a bogey and her third career hole-in-one, had given Davies a 138 total and two-stroke lead over Hiromi Takamura. Maeda, four strokes back at 142, charged with 68, taking a bogey at the last hole while Davies, playing behind her, was shooting 72 that resulted in the deadlock at 210. Davies birdied the 18th when they played it again to start the playoff. Suzuko managed only a par.

Gunze Cup World Ladies—¥60,000,000
Winner: Yukiyo Haga

Yukiyo Haga came from nowhere, literally and figuratively, to win the rain-soaked Gunze Cup World Ladies tournament, the second 72-hole event on the Japan LPGA Tour season. Four strokes off the pace after 54 holes and 149th on the money list, Haga made matters worse with a double bogey on the first hole.

She bounced back with four birdies and an eagle at the 17th hole to shoot 71 for an even-par 288 total, which proved to be enough to pass the five players who started the day ahead of her. The one-stroke victory was the first of her career.

The principal victims were Man-Soo Kim of Korea and Mayumi Murai, who had gone three years without adding to her five-victory total. Kim, the third-round leader, shot 77 and Murai, who began the day in second place, had 75 to finish second.

Yakult Ladies—¥60,000,000
Winner: Kaori Harada

Kaori Harada had waited a long time to acquire her fourth title in the Japan LPGA Tour and she didn't let the opportunity slip away when she put herself among the top contenders after two rounds of the Yakult Ladies tournament at Fukuoka International Country Club. Two strokes back going into Sunday's play, Harada came up with six birdies, shot a five-under-par 67 while everyone else was in the 70s and won by five strokes with her 210 total. The eight-year veteran had gone three seasons without a victory.

Mayumi Murai, another experienced player amid a victory drought, finished as runner-up for the second week in a row. Murai who began the final round a stroke behind leader Aki Takamura (141), shot 73–215 to finish one stroke in front of Takamura, Ok-Hee Ku and Chieko Nishida.

Chukyo TV Bridgestone—¥50,000,000
Winner: Mayumi Murai

After finishing second two weeks in a row on the Japan LPGA Tour, Mayumi Murai cracked the winner's circle for the first time in three years. Though struggling with a final-round, one-over-par 73, the veteran Mural, 31, scored a one-stroke victory in the Chukyo TV Bridgestone tournament at Kasugai Country Club in Aichi. She finished at 211, one stroke in front of Kumiko Hiyoshi.

Hiyoshi, with 68-69–137, led Murai, 67-71–138, going into the final round and clung to that one-stroke margin as the two players went to the final tee. Hiyoshi pushed her drive into a water hazard and took a double bogey for 75. Murai took her sixth career victory with a routine par and the 73.

Toto Motors—¥50,000,000
Winner: Shin Sora

Convinced on the telephone by her father that it would only be just beginning, Korea's Shin Sora won the Toto Motors title with a final-round, come-from-behind victory at Toto Hanno Country Club in Saitama. Down four strokes to leader Huang Bie-Shyun after 36 holes, Shin took her father's advice to play as if Sunday was the opening round. She came up with a five-under-par 67 for a 209 total and a one-stroke victory over Miyuki Shimabukuro and Ayako Okamoto.

Taiwan's Huang, a two-time winner on the circuit in 1995, led the first two rounds with 66-72–138, but slipped to 73 Sunday to tie for fourth at 211. Starting at 71-71–142, Sora made her move on the back nine after an outgoing 36. Four birdies thrust her into a first-place tie with Shimabukuro and Okamoto after 17 holes and she won with a birdie at the 18th.

Mitsubishi Denki—¥50,000,000
Winner: Cheng Mei-Chi

She had to work overtime to accomplish it, but Taiwan's Cheng Mei-Chi finally won on the Japan LPGA Tour after 11 years of trying. The 37-year-old player scored the elusive first victory in the Mitsubishi Denki tournament at Kitarokkoh Country Club in Hyogo on the second playoff hole.

The stumbling block Cheng had to overcome was Norimi Terasawa, who led her and Yuka Shiroto by three strokes after 36 holes. Terasawa was at 69-70–139; Cheng (72-70) and Shiroto (71-71) were at 142. Crippled by a double bogey on the back nine, Terasawa shot 76 Sunday and Cheng caught her at four-under-par 215, creating the playoff. After both players parred the first extra hole, the Taiwan veteran parred from the sand at the second and Terasawa then missed a three-foot par putt.

Suntory Ladies—¥50,000,000
Winner: Jae-Sook Won

Jae-Sook Won broke out of a prolonged slump on the Japan LPGA Tour as the circuit staged one of the first sporting events in the earthquake-ravaged Kobe area since the disaster. Won, who qualified for the Tour in 1992 with promising credentials and won three times in 1994, scored her first victory since then in the Suntory Ladies, which was dubbed the "We Love Kobe" tournament in honor of the 6,000 victims of the earthquake.

The 26-year-old Korean and Kaori Harada, the Yakult Ladies winner a month earlier, took command of the standings with eight-under-par 64s Saturday. Won led with 68-71-64–203 and Harada was two strokes back with 70-71-64–205. Neither was particularly sharp Sunday, but, after taking bogeys on the first three holes, Won shifted gears and recovered to a par-72 round for 275 and won by five when Harada struggled to a 75.

Dunlop Twin Lakes—¥50,000,000
Winner: Aiko Hashimoto

Nearly four months into its season, the Japan LPGA Tour finally crowned its first double winner of the year. Aiko Hashimoto, whose victory in the Kenshoen Ladies in early April was just her second in seven seasons, moved ahead to stay in the second round and went on to a two-stroke win in the Dunlop Twin Lakes tournament at Gunma's Twin Lakes Country Club.

The 28-year-old Hashimoto had to overcome one glitch. With her rounds of 71-69-69 for 209, she carried a three-stroke lead over Tseng Hsiu-Feng into the final round. Then she double-bogeyed the first hole Sunday. Unshaken, Hashimoto came right back with a birdie at the second hole and was never seriously threatened. She shot 72 for a seven-under-par 281 total.

Japan Women's Open Championship—¥70,000,000
Winner: Aki Takamura

Youth was served at the Japan Women's Open Championship. At 23 years of age, Aki Takamura added the national crown to the Japan LPGA Championship she won less than a year earlier, clearly establishing herself among the cream of the crop in her country. She went to the top of the Japan LPGA money list with the ¥14,000,000 winner's check she received at Ryugasaki Country Club in Ibaraki Prefecture.

The decision came down to Takamura and Kaori Harada, the Yakult Ladies winner, in the final round. They went into Sunday's play tied for the lead at 220, Takamura after rounds of 75-73-72 and Harada with 74-75-71, and battled to the final hole. Takamura one-putted from three feet for par there to take the championship and her fourth win in two years when Harada was unable to save par from a bunker. The winning score was 291.

Tohato Ladies—¥50,000,000
Winner: Toshimi Kimura

Toshimi Kimura made the best of a bad situation and won the Tohato Ladies tournament. Strong winds and heavy rains bedeviled the players in the late June event at Ichihara's Oak Village Golf Club, pushing scores to a seasonal high. Best illustrating this was Kimura's final-round score of 75. No one did any better in the stormy weather and she won with a seven-over-par 223 total.

Another example of the weather woes: Suzuko Maeda and Kayoko Motoki, the first-round co-leaders at 70, shot 79-86 and 83-87 respectively the next two days. Fumiko Muraguchi, with 73-74–147, led Kimura (74-74), Chieko Nishida (75-73) and Shin Sora (73-75) by one stroke after 36 holes and she finished in second place after shooting 78 for 225 Sunday.

Toyo Suisan—¥50,000,000
Winner: Ok-Hee Ku

Ok-Hee Ku displayed the form that earned her the reputation as Korea's No. 1 female golfer with her wire-to-wire victory in the Toyo Suisan tournament at Kosaido Sapporo Country Club in Hokkaido. Ku grabbed a two-stroke lead the first day with an eight-under-par 64 and never trailed en route to her six-under-par 210 and a two-stroke victory.

She slipped to 73 Saturday, but still led by one over Man-Soo Kim. Another 73 Sunday provided the two-stroke triumph over Nasu Ogawa winner Aki Nakano, Akane Ohshiro, and Ikuyo Shiotani and Akiko Fukushima, two of the Japan LPGA major stars who had yet to win in 1996.

Resort Trust Ladies—¥50,000,000
Winner: Aiko Hashimoto

Aiko Hashimoto rode her third victory of the season into first place on the Japan LPGA Tour money list at the Resort Trust Ladies tournament in mid-July at Maple Point Country Club at Uenohara. Hashimoto, the first (and, as it turned out, only) player to win three times on the 1996 circuit, scored the triumph in a playoff against Akiko Fukushima, who was seeking her first title of the year to go with three earlier victories.

Hashimoto had carried a one-stroke lead into the final round after scoring 70-68–138 the first two days. She shot 71 Sunday, but 22-year-old Fukushima caught her at seven-under-par 209 with a 67 to bring about the playoff.

Katokichi Queen's Cup—¥50,000,000
Winner: Suzuko Maeda

Perhaps haunted by her collapse three weeks earlier in the weather-plagued Tohato Ladies, Suzuko Maeda struggled in the last round of the Katokichi Queen's Cup tournament, but she made her lead hold up for a one-stroke victory at Naie Country Club in Hokkaido. Her final-round 76, still a far cry from her Sunday 86 in the Tohato, gave her a six-under-par 210 total and the one-shot triumph over Akiko Fukushima, runner-up for the second week in a row. She finished with 71 for 211.

Maeda established her 36-hole lead with rounds of 66 and 68 en route to her start-to-finish victory.

Golf 5 Ladies—¥50,000,000
Winner: Yuka Irie

Yuka Irie nearly let the second victory of her Japan LPGA Tour career get away from her at the last minute. As it was, she gave away a three-stroke lead on the last two holes of regulation and had to beat New Zealand's Marnie McGuire in a playoff to lay claim to the first Golf 5 Ladies tournament title.

Irie took the lead in the first round at Mizunami Country Club at Gifu with 67, the only sub-70 score that day, and remained in front with her second-round 71 for 138, two ahead of Michie Ohba and Yuko Motoyama. Sailing along with a three-stroke lead after 16 holes Sunday, Irie drove into the trees at the 17th, took a double bogey, then bogeyed the 18th for 73 and 211. McGuire was already in with that total after a closing 68, the day's best round. Irie won with a par on the first extra hole as McGuire, who won the Mitsukoshi Cup early in the season, missed a six-footer to keep it alive.

Mizuno Ladies—¥60,000,000
Winner: Young-Me Lee

It was as unlikely a finish as one could imagine. Here comes the famous Ayako Okamoto charging down the stretch of the Mizuno Ladies tournament, aiming for the 60th victory of her illustrious career with a four-stroke lead. First, a bogey, then at the par-five 17th another bogey on a three-putt and finally, at the 18th, a double bogey after putting a five-iron approach shot into the water. Instead of the win, Okamoto, with 77, falls into a four-way tie for second at 213.

The winning beneficiary was Korea's Young-Me Lee, picking up her second title of the season and fifth of her career. The 33-year-old Lee started the final round six strokes behind Okamoto, who had shot 65-71 the first two days at Asahi Kokusai Golf Club in Tottori. Lee took 71 Sunday for the winning four-under-par 212 total, one stroke ahead of Natsuko Noro, Akane Ohshiro, Yuko Saito and Okamoto. She had won the Saishunkan Ladies, the season's second tournament.

NEC Karuizawa 72—¥60,000,000
Winner: Akiko Fukushima

Akiko Fukushima, frustrated twice in preceding weeks with second-place finishes, came up with an excellent solution to her quest for the elusive first win of 1996. Shoot the lowest round in the history of the Japan LPGA Tour — nine-under-par 63. The 23-year-old Japanese standout fired that round on the Saturday of the NEC Karuizawa 72 tournament and went on to a five-stroke victory with her 10-under-par 206 total at Karuizawa Country Club. It was the fourth triumph of her brief career.

Fukushima had opened the tournament with 71, then bolted into a four-stroke lead over Natsuko Noro with the 63, the product of two eagles, six birdies, nine pars and a bogey. The record, held by 11 players, was 64. Fukushima's closing 72 widened the final gap to five over Ayako Okamoto, runner-up for the second week in a row. Noro tied for third with Kaori Higo and Yuka Irie, the Golf 5 Ladies champion.

Goyo Kensetsu Ladies—¥60,000,000
Winner: Chikayo Yamazaki

An unexpected player accepted winning plaudits at the end of the Goyo Kensetsu Ladies tournament. Chikayo Yamazaki won the title with a rare, even-par score of 216, the first victory of her Japan LPGA Tour career. She moved from three strokes off the pace Sunday and registered a one-shot victory over Yukiyo Haga, Kaori Higo and Yuko Saito.

Natsuko Noro set the pace the first two days. She opened with 68, sharing the lead with Akane Ohshiro and Keiko Arai, then went three strokes in front with a 72 Saturday. Chie Yoshida, Tatsuko Morimoto and Yamazaki were at 143. Yamazaki made her winning move from there.

Fuji Sankei Classic—¥60,000,000
Winner: Ayako Okamoto

Ayako Okamoto wasn't about to let No. 60 get away again. Three weeks earlier in the Mizuno Ladies, the 45-year-old Okamoto blew a victory she had all but wrapped up as she sought to end a 23-month victory drought. In the Fuji Sankei Classic at Fujizakura Country Club, she didn't have the luxury of a comfortable lead Sunday afternoon, but she outfought Akane Ohshiro and Marnie McGuire on the second nine to post a one-stroke victory over Ohshiro with her 71 for a 210 total, six under par.

The storied Japanese player had entered Sunday's round with a one-stroke lead over McGuire, two over Ohshiro. She made four birdies and three bogeys, but needed birdies at the 11th and 12th to move ahead of Ohshiro and Aiko Hashimoto, the year's only three-time winner, to stay. It was Okamoto's 42nd victory in Japan and first since the 1994 Kosaido Ladies Golf Cup. She had won 17 times on the U.S. LPGA Tour and once in Europe.

Japan LPGA Championship—¥65,000,000
Winner: Ikuyo Shiotani

Perhaps it was the challenge of a major championship, as Ikuyo Shiotani, the No. 1 player in Japan in 1995, finally took her first 1996 victory in the Japan LPGA Championship. The five-time winner of 1995 staged an excellent rally in Sunday's final round at Nagaoka Country Club in Niigata, shooting 68 that gave her a five-under-par 283 total and a one-stroke victory over Kaori Higo, who was going through a numbing season of near-misses. The victory was the 15th of Shiotani's 14-year career and made her just the fourth player in Japan LPGA history to win the Japan Open and LPGA and the Meiji Nyugyo Cup, the circuit's three major titles.

Suzuko Maeda, the Katokichi Queen's Cup winner, seized the first-round lead at Nagaoka with 69, then yielded to Michiko Hattori (73-67–140) Friday. Akiko Fukushima, who scored her first 1996 win three weeks earlier in the Karuizawa 72, took her turn at the top Saturday, shooting 69 for 210. That put her three strokes ahead of Hattori and Keiko Arai, five in front of Shiotani, Kaori Harada and Higo. Higo made an early run at the title with birdies on the first three holes Sunday, but her 69 left her one stroke shy of Shiotani, who had six birdies and two bogeys in shooting the 68. Fukushima came apart Sunday, shooting 77 and falling into a fourth-place tie with Arai.

Yukijirushi Ladies Tokai Classic—¥60,000,000
Winner: Suzuko Maeda

Ayako Okamoto's up-and-down year continued when the Japan LPGA Tour went to Mie Prefecture for the Yukijirushi Ladies Tokai Classic at Ryosen Golf Club. With a virtual giveaway and a 60th career victory on her record of the previous five weeks, Okamoto fumbled away another potential win at Ryosen. Leading by three strokes after a pair of 69s, Okamoto stumbled to 76 Sunday and Suzuko Maeda was the one who took the biggest advantage of it.

Maeda, six strokes back going into the final round, fired a brilliant 66 for 210, just enough to beat Aiko Hashimoto, the leading money winner, who finished at 211, and Akiko Fukushima, who shot 71 for 212. She became the season's fourth multiple winner, having won the Katokichi Queen's Cup two months earlier.

Miyagi TV Cup Ladies Open—¥50,000,000
Winner: Mikino Kubo

The Japan LPGA Tour got another first-time winner at the Miyagi TV Cup Ladies Open as Kaori Higo's frustrating season continued. With winds ahead of an approaching typhoon raking the course Sunday, Mikino Kubo shot one of the day's three best scores — 71s — and came from six strokes off the pace to score a one-shot victory at Yashiro Golf Club in Miyagi Prefecture.

Kubo finished two under par at 214, a stroke ahead of Michie Ohba and Michiko Hattori.

Kubo's glee contrasted with the gloom of Higo. A four-time winner on the circuit including two in 1995, Higo had come close to victory time and again during the 1996 season — 10 top-10 finishes, among them three seconds, a third and a fourth — yet hadn't won. It was there for her taking at Yashiro. She had a three-stroke lead on the field with her 70-67, but the 27-year-old fell victim to the gales, shooting 79 to drop into a tie for fourth place. Kubo had earlier rounds of 68-75 before making her winning surge ahead of the storm.

Kosaido Ladies Golf Cup—¥60,000,000
Winner: Tseng Hsiu-Feng

Taiwan's Tseng Hsiu-Feng prevailed in a stretch duel in the Kosaido Ladies Golf Cup tournament at Kosaido Country Club in Chiba Prefecture, posting a three-under-par 213 total, for a two-stroke victory. Her only other win on the Japan LPGA Tour had come two years earlier in the Resort Trust event.

After Mariko Ohtani led the first day with 69, Tseng and Young-Me Lee, already a two-time winner during the season, went to the front. Tseng paired 70-71 and Lee 72-69 for their leading 141s. Both stumbled a bit midway through Sunday's round, then Tseng went ahead to stay with birdies at the 13th and 14th and finished with a par round for the 213. Lee never recovered from a double bogey at the 11th and wound up in a tie for second place with Kaori Harada, who closed with 69 for her 215.

Takara World Invitational—¥80,000,000
Winner: Ikuyo Shiotani

The biggest purse of the Japan LPGA season — ¥80,000,000 — attracted some overseas attention, notably Laura Davies, but Ikuyo Shiotani, the most highly regarded of the home players, made off with the winner's prize. That victory, coupled with her triumph in the Japan LPGA Championship a month earlier, made up for her lackluster, winless performances over the first five months of the season.

Davies, who has won four times in Japan, including the Satake Classic earlier in the current season, went gunning for the Takara title, taking the second-round lead with 70-70—140. Shiotani (71-71) was two back, tied for second with Akio Takasu (73-69). The British star had 74s the last two days and tied for seventh. Meanwhile, the Japanese ace shot 69 Saturday to take a one-stroke lead and held off a closing press by Kris Tschetter to capture her 16th career victory. She shot 71 and beat the visiting American by two strokes with a six-under-par 282. The ¥14,400,000 check boosted Shiotani, 1995's top money earner, into third place in the standings.

Fujitsu Ladies—¥60,000,000
Winner: Akiko Fukushima

The Fujitsu Ladies tournament turned into the longest of the scheduled 54-hole events on the 1996 Japan LPGA Tour when Akiko Fukushima and Korea's Jae-Sook Won went through three playoff holes before the 23-year-old Japanese player secured her second victory of the season. Fukushima birdied the third extra hole for the win.

The two players dominated the Fujitsu Ladies from the start at Hamano Golf Club in Chiba. Won shared the first-round lead with Tsuyako Taido at 68 and Fukushima shot 69. Then the two went jointly four strokes in front Saturday with 137s. Fukushima had the better of it through much of the final round, taking a two-stroke lead to the 15th tee. But the 27-year-old Korean, a three-time winner in women's golf in 1994, fought back with birdies at the 15th and 18th for the matching 68 that brought about the playoff.

Kibun Ladies Classic—¥50,000,000
Winner: Akane Ohshiro

Normally, a score of 75 is a killer for the leader of a professional tournament. Not in the Kibun Ladies Classic, the late-season tournament on the Japan LPGA Tour. Amid generally high scores on a tough-playing day on the Ranzan course at Arashiyama Country Club, the experienced Akane Ohshiro turned her 75 into the fifth victory of her 13-year career. It gave her a four-under-par 215 total and a one-stroke win over Young-Me Lee, Korea's most successful player in 1996.

Ohshiro led by one stroke after 36 holes with her 70-70–140 total. Lee was at 141 with Japan's Toshiko Fujisaki and compatriot Koreans Ok-Hee Ku and Jae-Sook Won, loser a few days earlier in the Fujitsu playoff. Lee matched Ohshiro's 75 to pick off the runner-up slot. Mikino Kubo, the Miyagi TV Cup winner, grabbed a share of third place with 69.

Nichirei International—US$675,000
Winners: United States

Some things never change. Take the annual Nichirei International, for instance. The United States LPGA won for the 12th consecutive year and ran its overall record against the Japanese to 16 wins and two losses. The star of the show was Australian rookie Karrie Webb. Playing in her first team competition as a member of the LPGA, Webb won three matches in leading the LPGA to a 21½-14½ victory.

Ok-Hee Ku and Natsuko Noro shot a better-ball 64 in the first round as Japan held its own with 4½ points to tie the LPGA. It was uphill from there for the Japanese. The LPGA took a commanding lead in the second round, winning seven of nine matches to take a 11½-6½ lead. The team of Pat Hurst and Barb Mucha had the day's low round, 62, while Webb made it two straight victories, teaming with Joan Pitcock for a best-ball 64.

In Sunday's singles, Webb faced Ayako Okamoto, and it was no contest. While the round was filled with friendly banter, the golf was anything but cordial. Webb won easily, dissecting the Ami Golf Club course with 68 to Okamoto's 73. It was one of three lopsided wins, as Brandie Burton and Val Skinner each won by seven strokes.

Toray Japan Queens Cup—US$750,000
Winner: Mayumi Hirase

What the Japanese LPGA as a team couldn't do a week before, Mayumi Hirase made up for a week later, winning the Toray Japan Queens Cup in spectacular fashion, in a playoff over Laura Davies. Hirase won when Davies missed a three-feet putt for par on the third playoff hole at Tone Golf Club in Inashiki.

Even in losing, Davies still won. Her runner-up check of $69,819 raised her season earnings to an LPGA record of $897,302, surpassing Beth Daniel's mark of $863,578. It gave Davies a $45,00 lead on Karrie Webb, who had been No. 1 for the year. Webb had a horrible week, finishing in a tie for 35th place and a payday of $4,097.

Davies started the final round four strokes behind co-leaders Hirase and Maggie Will. She rallied with 68 in the cold wind and rain. An eagle at the closing hole gave her the outright lead, but only until Hirase birdied that hole to tie. After both made birdies at the 18th on the first playoff hole, they halved the 16th with pars, then Davies lost with her three-putt at the 17th.

Itoen Ladies—¥60,000,000
Winner: Laura Davies

It was, without a doubt, the most dominating golf performance of 1996 anywhere — and who knows how many other seasons. Lopsided victories were recorded around the world during the year, but nothing stacked up to the 15-stroke win of Laura Davies in the Itoen Ladies tournament, her third consecutive triumph in the November event at the Great Island Club in Chiba Prefecture. Davies' 17-under-par 199 total was the lowest 54-hole score in Japan LPGA Tour history, as was her 15-stroke margin. It was Davies' second 1996 victory in Japan — she won the Satake Classic in April — and career fifth title on the circuit, among them three straight in the Itoen. She was the season's only successful defending champion.

Davies had the tournament in the palm of her hand from the first day, when she opened on top with 68 amid heavy rains. She vaulted nine strokes in front with a seven-under-par 65 for 133. Four players were at 142 and none of them mustered any sort of challenge to the powerful Davies Sunday. Davies capped the magnificent weekend with a 66 Sunday for the 199 total, the crowning touch a 25-foot birdie putt on the 18th green. Akiko Fukushima and Kaori Harada were the runners-up at 214.

Daio Seishi Elleair Open—¥65,000,000
Winner: Ok-Hee Ku

Ok-Hee Ku, one of Korea's finest players over the preceding decade, completed another successful season on the Japan LPGA Tour, picking up her second 1996 title in convincing fashion in the Daio Seishi Elleair Open at the Elleair Golf Club at Matsuyama. Ku fired a course-record 66 Sunday and recorded a five-stroke victory with her 10-under-par 206 total.

The Korean veteran, scoring her 11th Japan LPGA victory, broke from a three-way, first-place tie at the 36-hole mark. She was deadlocked with Michiko Hattori and Ai-Yu Tu at 140 after rounds of 71 and 69. Hattori, the 1994 Japan Women's Open champion and five-time winner in her first three seasons, was subverted again in her bid to end a two-year victory drought. She shot 71 and finished second at 211.

Meiji Nyugyo Cup—¥60,000,000
Winner: Yoko Inoue

Yoko Inoue ended the 1996 Japan LPGA Tour season with a bang. The 24-year-old player picked an excellent spot to score the first victory of her professional career — the rich, limited-field Meiji Nyugyo Cup, considered one of the circuit's major championships. Inoue shot a final-round 69 at Aoshima Golf Club at Miyazaki to edge out a one-stroke victory with her seven-under-par 281 total.

Inoue shared the headlines with the runner-up. Akiko Fukushima came from six strokes off the pace Sunday with a course-record 65 and the second-place check gave her the Japan LPGA Tour money title for the first time. At 23, she is the youngest No. 1 ever on the circuit.

Kaori Harada had her title prospects slip away Sunday. Harada, who had shared the second-round lead with Inoue and Marnie McGuire at 140, still had a share of first place with Ok-Hee Ku at 211 going into Sunday's round. A win would have given her the No. 1 spot, but she stumbled with 75 and dropped into a seventh-place tie. Inoue, one behind her after 54 holes, ran off five birdies in gaining her first victory.

APPENDIXES

The Sony Ranking
(As of December 31, 1996)

Pos.		Player	Country	Points Average	Total Points	No. of Events	94/95 Total	94/95 Minus	1996 Plus
1	(1)	Greg Norman	Aus	10.78	485	45	624	-409	270
2	(11)	Tom Lehman	USA	9.74	487	50	371	-254	370
3	(6)	Colin Montgomerie	Sco	9.10	528	58	579	-389	338
4	(3)	Ernie Els	SAf	8.60	490	57	617	-447	320
5	(7)	Fred Couples	USA	8.16	351	43	316	-211	246
6	(8)	Nick Faldo	Eng	7.98	359	45	367	-254	246
7	(24)	Phil Mickelson	USA	7.77	404	52	223	-153	334
8	(10)	Masashi Ozaki	Jpn	7.58	341	45	351	-238	228
9	(20)	Davis Love III	USA	7.53	384	51	272	-160	272
10	(41)	Mark O'Meara	USA	7.12	363	51	202	-109	270
11	(5)	Corey Pavin	USA	6.94	347	50	484	-309	172
12	(73)	Steve Stricker	USA	6.19	297	48	124	-77	250
13	(2)	Nick Price	Zim	6.12	263	43	494	-385	154
14	(9)	Steve Elkington	Aus	5.84	263	45	346	-187	104
15	(19)	Scott Hoch	USA	5.44	332	61	292	-190	230
16	(4)	Bernhard Langer	Ger	5.31	260	49	487	-319	92
17	(34)	Tom Watson	USA	5.28	211	40	153	-108	166
18	(99)	Mark Brooks	USA	5.18	337	65	126	-81	292
19	(33)	David Duval	USA	5.15	268	52	188	-96	176
20	(16)	Vijay Singh	Fij	5.03	317	63	384	-255	188
21	(43)	Mark McNulty	Zim	4.98	204	41	156	-118	166
22	(12)	Loren Roberts	USA	4.92	241	49	317	-220	144
23	(31)	Brad Faxon	USA	4.90	250	51	234	-162	178
24	(23)	Costantino Rocca	Ity	4.75	285	60	270	-153	168
25	(42)	Kenny Perry	USA	4.74	237	50	191	-116	162
26	(56)	Ian Woosnam	Wal	4.58	238	52	140	-110	208
27	(32)	Jeff Maggert	USA	4.48	224	50	203	-143	164
28	(168)	Steve Jones	USA	4.33	234	54	48	-24	210
29	(54T)	Justin Leonard	USA	4.15	253	61	151	-80	182
30	(18)	Mark McCumber	USA	4.10	164	40	209	-155	110
31	(45)	Frank Nobilo	NZl	4.02	229	57	198	-133	164
32	(17)	Lee Janzen	USA	3.93	236	60	319	-187	104
33	(509T)	Tiger Woods	USA	3.88	155	40	7	-4	152
34	(44)	Payne Stewart	USA	3.82	210	55	181	-97	126
35	(52)	Bob Tway	USA	3.75	195	52	166	-87	116
36	(26)	Jay Haas	USA	3.57	189	53	244	-151	96
37	(57)	Robert Allenby	Aus	3.56	210	59	180	-130	160
38	(29)	Mark Calcavecchia	USA	3.51	221	63	262	-167	126
39	(37)	Jesper Parnevik	Swe	3.42	178	52	190	-126	114
40	(14)	Sam Torrance	Sco	3.39	200	59	334	-198	64
41	(63)	Duffy Waldorf	USA	3.28	164	50	149	-93	108
42	(49)	Craig Stadler	USA	3.25	143	44	155	-102	90
43	(30)	Billy Mayfair	USA	3.21	186	58	244	-128	70
44	(227)	Michael Bradley	USA	3.13	163	52	44	-27	146
45	(27)	Jim Gallagher, Jr.	USA	3.10	158	51	228	-130	60
46	(15)	Peter Jacobsen	USA	3.09	142	46	257	-141	26
47	(50)	Peter Senior	Aus	3.08	188	61	189	-115	114
48	(329)	Tommy Tolles	USA	3.08	163	53	22	-11	152
49	(78)	Jim Furyk	USA	3.07	206	67	150	-84	140
50	(54T)	Brian Watts	USA	3.06	156	51	151	-107	112

( ) : Figures in brackets indicate 94/95 positions

Pos.		Player	Country	Points Average	Total Points	No. of Events	94/95 Total	94/95 Minus	1996 Plus
51	(65)	Fred Funk	USA	3.03	200	66	167	-101	134
52	(39)	Craig Parry	Aus	3.03	212	70	236	-154	130
53	(68T)	Jeff Sluman	USA	3.02	193	64	161	-96	128
54	(46)	Scott Simpson	USA	2.76	138	50	176	-106	68
55	(68T)	D.A. Weibring	USA	2.75	121	44	115	-68	74
56	(82)	Shigeki Maruyama	Jpn	2.74	159	58	123	-70	106
57	(25)	David Frost	SAf	2.74	156	57	266	-198	88
58	(21)	Ben Crenshaw	USA	2.72	128	47	254	-162	36
59	(292T)	Paul Stankowski	USA	2.69	156	58	33	-23	146
60	(110)	John Cook	USA	2.56	141	55	87	-72	126
61	(303T)	Rocco Mediate	USA	2.51	103	41	21	-12	94
62	(88)	Darren Clarke	NIr	2.50	150	60	110	-70	110
63	(64)	Woody Austin	USA	2.46	175	71	146	-73	102
64	(258)	Lee Westwood	Eng	2.45	159	65	40	-29	148
65	(123)	Wayne Westner	SAf	2.42	121	50	71	-52	102
66	(87)	Naomichi Ozaki	Jpn	2.36	151	64	141	-98	108
67	(224)	Yoshinori Kaneko	Jpn	2.31	136	59	44	-32	124
68	(75)	John Huston	USA	2.28	123	54	135	-106	94
69	(62)	Per-Ulrik Johansson	Swe	2.22	109	49	131	-92	70
70	(51)	Kirk Triplett	USA	2.22	113	51	167	-106	52
71	(118T)	Andrew Coltart	Sco	2.20	130	59	87	-61	104
72	(48)	Miguel Angel Jimenez	Spn	2.19	125	57	192	-141	74
73	(71)	Brandt Jobe	USA	2.08	100	48	117	-65	48
74	(103)	Frankie Minoza	Phi	2.08	104	50	82	-52	74
75	(84)	Wayne Riley	Aus	2.03	132	65	134	-78	76
76	(94T)	Hidemichi Tanaka	Jpn	2.00	104	52	76	-38	66
77	(96)	Todd Hamilton	USA	1.93	112	58	115	-79	76
78	(28)	Michael Campbell	NZl	1.92	121	63	216	-113	18
79	(106)	John Morse	USA	1.91	107	56	91	-50	66
80	(202T)	Stephen Ames	T&T	1.90	97	51	38	-27	86
81	(161)	Paul McGinley	Ire	1.90	112	59	60	-40	92
82	(85)	Lennie Clements	USA	1.88	92	49	110	-78	60
83	(102)	Carlos Franco	Par	1.88	75	40	77	-56	54
84	(202T)	Tom Purtzer	USA	1.86	82	44	38	-28	72
85T	(81)	Tom Kite	USA	1.83	88	48	113	-97	72
85T	(754T)	Clarence Rose	USA	1.83	88	48	0	0	88
87	(252)	Paul Goydos	USA	1.82	118	65	44	-32	106
88	(77)	Larry Mize	USA	1.80	90	50	118	-88	60
89	(35)	Fuzzy Zoeller	USA	1.77	71	40	158	-139	52
90	(70)	Brad Bryant	USA	1.76	102	58	163	-107	46
91	(40)	John Daly	USA	1.75	112	64	185	-115	42
92	(80)	Peter O'Malley	Aus	1.74	106	61	134	-76	48
93	(76)	Alexander Cejka	Ger	1.73	90	52	120	-64	34
94	(94T)	Greg Turner	NZl	1.72	86	50	95	-65	56
95T	(754T)	Padraig Harrington	Ire	1.71	84	49	0	0	84
95T	(131)	Kazuhiko Hosokawa	Jpn	1.71	96	56	52	-26	70
97	(133)	Peter Mitchell	Eng	1.70	102	60	83	-63	82
98	(283)	David Ogrin	USA	1.70	107	63	36	-25	96
99	(667T)	Tim Herron	USA	1.70	90	53	2	-2	90
100	(38)	Barry Lane	Eng	1.70	95	56	222	-147	20

( ) : Figures in brackets indicate 94/95 positions

Pos.		Player	Country	Points Average	Total Points	No. of Events	94/95 Total	94/95 Minus	1996 Plus
101	(92)	Gil Morgan	USA	1.68	69	41	80	-55	44
102	(290T)	Paul Lawrie	Sco	1.68	79	47	28	-21	72
103T	(124)	Billy Andrade	USA	1.67	100	60	84	-60	76
103T	(344T)	Scott McCarron	USA	1.67	90	54	20	-10	80
103T	(143)	Paul Broadhurst	Eng	1.67	105	63	65	-36	76
106	(151)	Jose Coceres	Arg	1.64	82	50	57	-35	60
107	(93)	Eduardo Romero	Arg	1.64	77	47	95	-74	56
108	(121)	Nolan Henke	USA	1.61	82	51	76	-50	56
109	(754T)	Thomas Bjorn	Den	1.58	76	48	0	0	76
110	(22)	Seve Ballesteros	Spn	1.58	68	43	221	-179	26
111	(139)	Retief Goosen	SAf	1.56	103	66	82	-55	76
112	(100)	Jay Don Blake	USA	1.56	84	54	94	-62	52
113	(231)	Jean Van de Velde	Frn	1.52	85	56	46	-35	74
114	(334)	Bradley Hughes	Aus	1.51	65	43	20	-17	62
115	(127)	Andrew Oldcorn	Sco	1.50	69	46	59	-34	44
116	(352)	Larry Nelson	USA	1.48	68	46	18	-12	62
117	(232T)	Hajime Meshiai	Jpn	1.47	78	53	39	-23	62
118T	(66)	Steve Lowery	USA	1.46	92	63	164	-118	46
118T	(90)	Masahiro Kuramoto	Jpn	1.46	92	63	123	-73	42
120	(86)	Tsuneyuki Nakajima	Jpn	1.46	83	57	123	-92	52
121	(152)	David Ishii	USA	1.45	77	53	65	-54	66
122	(36)	Bill Glasson	USA	1.45	61	42	160	-113	14
123	(98)	Robert Gamez	USA	1.42	85	60	108	-77	54
124	(109)	Andrew Magee	USA	1.40	81	58	92	-69	58
125	(145)	Paul Azinger	USA	1.40	67	48	57	-32	42
126	(335)	Masanobu Kimura	Jpn	1.39	78	56	23	-17	72
127	(47)	Bob Estes	USA	1.39	71	51	176	-133	28
128	(72)	Hal Sutton	USA	1.38	83	60	152	-99	30
129	(118T)	Nobuo Serizawa	Jpn	1.37	85	62	87	-58	56
130	(114)	Hisayuki Sasaki	Jpn	1.37	89	65	88	-57	58
131	(313T)	Miguel Angel Martin	Spn	1.37	71	52	28	-25	68
132	(105)	Katsuyoshi Tomori	Jpn	1.37	86	63	115	-73	44
133T	(130)	Rick Gibson	Can	1.36	68	50	68	-40	40
133T	(381)	Dudley Hart	USA	1.36	68	50	22	-16	62
135	(61)	Anders Forsbrand	Swe	1.36	61	45	138	-87	10
136	(79)	Satoshi Higashi	Jpn	1.35	96	71	151	-81	26
137	(175T)	Joey Sindelar	USA	1.35	70	52	47	-27	50
138	(58)	Mark James	Eng	1.33	64	48	132	-82	14
139	(195T)	Russ Cochran	USA	1.32	75	57	50	-35	60
140	(199)	Emlyn Aubrey	USA	1.31	67	51	45	-28	50
141	(74)	Curtis Strange	USA	1.31	64	49	121	-85	28
142	(59)	Bruce Lietzke	USA	1.30	52	40	112	-80	20
143	(667T)	Jerry Kelly	USA	1.29	71	55	2	-1	70
144	(60)	David Gilford	Eng	1.29	67	52	152	-111	26
145	(162)	Grant Waite	NZl	1.28	78	61	65	-35	48
146T	(754T)	Raymond Russell	Sco	1.28	60	47	0	0	60
146T	(154)	Eduardo Herrera	Col	1.28	60	47	55	-37	42
148	(192)	Glen Day	USA	1.27	80	63	60	-44	64
149	(197)	Brandel Chamblee	USA	1.27	66	52	49	-31	48
150	(111)	Rick Fehr	USA	1.26	58	46	77	-65	46

( ) : Figures in brackets indicate 94/95 positions

Pos.		Player	Country	Points Average	Total Points	No. of Events	94/95 Total	94/95 Minus	1996 Plus
151	(421T)	Anthony Painter	Aus	1.25	50	40	12	-6	44
152	(481T)	Diego Borrego	Spn	1.21	52	43	8	-6	50
153	(238)	Peter Teravainen	USA	1.20	67	56	48	-31	50
154	(83)	Brett Ogle	Aus	1.20	55	46	113	-78	20
155	(150)	Ignacio Garrido	Spn	1.17	61	52	60	-37	38
156	(229)	Mike Brisky	USA	1.17	68	58	38	-20	50
157	(91)	Jose Rivero	Spn	1.17	48	41	86	-52	14
158	(171)	Marco Dawson	USA	1.17	62	53	59	-33	36
159	(141)	Jarmo Sandelin	Swe	1.17	70	60	64	-32	38
160	(137)	Paul Eales	Eng	1.15	61	53	72	-49	38
161	(421T)	Peter Lonard	Aus	1.15	46	40	12	-6	40
162	(388T)	Richard Green	Aus	1.15	47	41	14	-9	42
163	(232T)	Daniel Chopra	Swe	1.14	57	50	30	-15	42
164	(147)	Tony Johnstone	Zim	1.14	58	51	69	-51	40
165	(201)	John Adams	USA	1.13	59	52	51	-30	38
166	(116)	Toshimitsu Izawa	Jpn	1.13	52	46	59	-31	24
167	(241)	Mark Wiebe	USA	1.13	53	47	30	-15	38
168	(169)	Peter Hedblom	Swe	1.13	62	55	54	-40	48
169	(126)	Patrick Burke	USA	1.10	56	51	62	-48	42
170	(134)	Sven Struver	Ger	1.09	58	53	70	-48	36
171	(120)	Peter Baker	Eng	1.09	63	58	82	-55	36
172	(89)	David Edwards	USA	1.09	51	47	93	-70	28
173	(138)	Sandy Lyle	Sco	1.08	56	52	68	-44	32
174	(97)	Philip Walton	Ire	1.07	60	56	101	-61	20
175	(160)	Mike Hulbert	USA	1.06	68	64	72	-44	40
176	(180)	Peter McWhinney	Aus	1.06	54	51	43	-25	36
177	(129)	Toru Suzuki	Jpn	1.05	64	61	66	-38	36
178	(175T)	Dan Forsman	USA	1.05	46	44	47	-31	30
179	(643T)	Michael Long	NZl	1.02	41	40	3	-2	40
180	(67)	Howard Clark	Eng	1.02	43	42	114	-79	8
181	(526T)	Shoichi Kuwabara	Jpn	1.02	44	43	6	-4	42
182	(108)	Scott Verplank	USA	1.02	46	45	74	-44	16
183	(198)	Katsunori Kuwabara	Jpn	1.02	59	58	43	-22	38
184	(117)	Hideki Kase	Jpn	1.00	65	65	89	-58	34
185	(155)	Russell Claydon	Eng	0.98	54	55	67	-49	36
186	(259)	Greg Kraft	USA	0.97	60	62	45	-37	52
187	(218T)	Jamie Spence	Eng	0.96	51	53	45	-26	32
188	(113)	Joakim Haeggman	Swe	0.96	49	51	85	-66	30
189T	(189)	Paul Curry	Eng	0.96	44	46	44	-34	34
189T	(165)	Jean Louis Guepy	Frn	0.96	44	46	54	-30	20
191	(157)	Guy Boros	USA	0.95	63	66	76	-47	34
192	(375T)	Ed Fiori	USA	0.95	40	42	15	-11	36
193	(267)	Andrew Sherborne	Eng	0.95	56	59	38	-24	42
194	(245T)	Ross McFarlane	Eng	0.93	53	57	40	-27	40
195	(526T)	Hideyuki Sato	Jpn	0.93	39	42	6	-5	38
196	(220)	Gary Orr	Sco	0.93	51	55	49	-36	38
197	(436)	Ross Drummond	Sco	0.92	48	52	15	-11	44
198	(115)	Gene Sauers	USA	0.92	44	48	73	-45	16
199	(166)	Mathias Gronberg	Swe	0.90	56	62	59	-33	30
200	(170)	Gordon Brand, Jr.	Sco	0.88	46	52	55	-45	36

( ) : Figures in brackets indicate 94/95 positions

World's Winners of 1996

U.S. PGA TOUR

Mercedes Championships	Mark O'Meara
Nortel Open	Phil Mickelson
Bob Hope Chrysler Classic	Mark Brooks
Phoenix Open	Phil Mickelson (2)
AT&T Pebble Beach National Pro-Am	Cancelled
Buick Invitational	Davis Love III
United Airlines Hawaiian Open	Jim Furyk
Nissan Open	Craig Stadler
Doral-Ryder Open	Greg Norman (2)
Honda Classic	Tim Herron
Bay Hill Invitational	Paul Goydos
Freeport-McDermott Classic	Scott McCarron
The Players Championship	Fred Couples
BellSouth Classic	Paul Stankowski (2)
Masters Tournament	Nick Faldo
MCI Classic	Loren Roberts
Greater Greensboro Chrysler Classic	Mark O'Meara (2)
Shell Houston Open	Mark Brooks (2)
GTE Byron Nelson Classic	Phil Mickelson (3)
MasterCard Colonial	Corey Pavin
Kemper Open	Steve Stricker
Memorial Tournament	Tom Watson
Buick Classic	Ernie Els (2)
U.S. Open Championship	Steve Jones
FedEx St. Jude Classic	John Cook
Canon Greater Hartford Open	D.A. Weibring
Motorola Western Open	Steve Stricker (2)
Michelob Championship at Kingsmill	Scott Hoch (2)
Deposit Guaranty Golf Classic	Willie Wood
CVS Charity Classic	John Cook (2)
Buick Open	Justin Leonard
PGA Championship	Mark Brooks (3)
Sprint International	Clarence Rose
NEC World Series of Golf	Phil Mickelson (4)
Greater Vancouver Open	Guy Boros
Greater Milwaukee Open	Loren Roberts (2)
Bell Canadian Open	Dudley Hart
Quad City Classic	Ed Fiori
Presidents Cup	United States
B.C. Open	Fred Funk
Buick Challenge	Michael Bradley
Las Vegas Invitational	Tiger Woods
LaCantera Texas Open	David Ogrin
Walt Disney World/Oldsmobile Classic	Tiger Woods (2)
Tour Championship	Tom Lehman (2)

SPECIAL EVENTS

Treasure Coast Classic	Bruce Devlin/Larry Ziegler
Family House Invitational	Scott Hoch
Ernst Championship	Phil Mickelson (5)
Jerry Ford Invitational	Dillard Pruitt
Fred Meyer Challenge	Greg Norman (3)/Brad Faxon
Sarazen World Open Championship	Frank Nobilo (2)
Lincoln-Mercury Kapalua International	Paul Stankowski (3)
MasterCard PGA Grand Slam	Tom Lehman (3)

Franklin Templeton Shark Shootout	Jay Haas/Tom Kite (2)
Mexican Open	Stewart Cink (4)
Merrill Lynch Pebble Beach Invitational Pro-Am	Kirk Triplett
JCPenney Classic	Mike Hulbert/Donna Andrews
Office Depot Father-Son Challenge	Raymond Floyd (3)/ Raymond Floyd, Jr.
Diners Club Matches	Tom Lehman (4)/Duffy Waldorf
Lexus Challenge	Hale Irwin (3)/Sean Connery
Andersen Consulting World Championship	Greg Norman (5)

NIKE TOUR

San Jose Open	Larry Silveira
Inland Empire Open	Jim Estes
Monterrey Open	David Berganio, Jr.
Louisiana Open	Paul Stankowski
Tallahassee Open	P.J. Cowan
South Carolina Classic	Dave Rummells
Alabama Classic	P.H. Horgan III
Shreveport Open	Tim Loustalot
Mississippi Gulf Coast Classic	Joe Durant
Carolina Classic	Glen Hnatiuk
Greater Greenville Classic	Michael Christie
Dominion Open	Olin Browne
Cleveland Open	Greg Twiggs
Knoxville Open	Eric Johnson
Ozarks Open	Stewart Cink
Dakota Dunes Open	Gary Webb
Buffalo Open	Jimmy Green
Philadelphia Classic	Brett Quigley
Miami Valley Open	J.P. Hayes
Gateway Classic	Tim Conley
Omaha Classic	Rocky Walcher
Wichita Open	Rick Cramer
Permian Basin Open	Michael Christie (2)
Colorado Classic	Stewart Cink (2)
Utah Classic	Michael Christie (3)
Boise Open	Matt Gogel
Tri-Cities Open	Phil Tataurangi
Olympia Open	Michael Clark
Nike Tour Championship	Stewart Cink (3)

CANADIAN TOUR

Payless Open	Arden Knoll
BC TEL Pacific Open	Guy Hill
Morningstar Classic	Bryan DeCorso
Henry Singer Alberta Open	Trevor Dodds
ED TEL PLAnet Open	Trevor Dodds (2)
Xerox Manitoba Open	*Rob McMillan
Infiniti Championship	Trevor Dodds (3)
Canadian Masters	Trevor Dodds (4)
Export "A" Inc. Ontario Open	Martin Price
Montclair Quebec Open	Chris DiMarco
Montclair PEI Classic	Frank Edmonds
CPGA Championship	Ashley Chinner

SOUTH AMERICAN TOUR

Colombia Open	Arden Knoll (2)
La Sabana Open	Pedro Martinez
TC Ecuadorian Open	Gustavo Rojas
Los Inkas–Peru Open	Philip Jonas
Litoral Open	Scott Dunlap

Uruguay Open	Miguel Fernandez
Los Leones Open	Roberto Coceres
Prince of Wales Open	Ricardo Gonzalez
Argentina Open	Pedro Martinez (2)
Volvo Masters of Latin America	Angel Cabrera

PGA EUROPEAN TOUR

Johnnie Walker Classic	Ian Woosnam
Open Catalonia	Paul Lawrie
Moroccan Open	Peter Hedblom
Dubai Desert Classic	Colin Montgomerie
Portuguese Open	Wayne Riley
Madeira Island Open	Jarmo Sandelin
Air France Cannes Open	Raymond Russell
Turespana Masters Open	Diego Borrego
Conte of Florence Italian Open	Jim Payne
Peugeot Open de Espana	Padraig Harrington
Benson and Hedges International Open	Stephen Ames
Volvo PGA Championship	Costantino Rocca
Deutsche Bank Open-TPC of Europe	Frank Nobilo
Alamo English Open	Robert Allenby
Slaley Hall Northumberland Challenge	Retief Goosen
BMW International Open	Marc Farry
Peugeot Open de France	Robert Allenby (2)
Murphy's Irish Open	Colin Montgomerie (2)
Scottish Open	Ian Woosnam (3)
British Open Championship	Tom Lehman
Sun Dutch Open	Mark McNulty (2)
Volvo Scandinavian Masters	Lee Westwood
Hohe Brucke Open	Paul McGinley
Chemapol Trophy Czech Open	Jonathan Lomas
Volvo German Open	Ian Woosnam (4)
One 2 One British Masters	Robert Allenby (3)
Canon European Masters	Colin Montgomerie (3)
Trophee Lancome	Jesper Parnevik
Loch Lomond World Invitational	Thomas Bjorn
Smurfit European Open	Per-Ulrik Johansson
Linde German Masters	Darren Clarke
Alfred Dunhill Cup	United States
Oki Pro-Am	Tom Kite
Toyota World Match Play	Ernie Els (3)
Open Novotel Perrier	Jonathan Lomas (2)/
	Steven Bottomley
Volvo Masters	Mark McNulty (3)

CHALLENGE TOUR

Kenya Open	Mike Miller
Open de Cote D'Ivoire	Massimo Florioli
Is Molas Challenge	Simon Burnell
Le Pavoniere Superal Challenge	Kalle Vainola
Alianca UAP Challenger	Gary Marks
Canarias–Challenge Tour	Robert Lee
Open de Dijon	Francisco Cea
Club Med Open	Ignacio Feliu
Siab Open	Kalle Vainola (2)
KB Golf Challenge	Joakim Rask
Himmerland Open	Niklas Diethelm
Italian Native Open	Marcello Santi
Nedcar National Open	*Neils Boysen
Cepsa APG	Ignacio Garrido
France Pro	Nicolas Kalouguine

Vasteras Open	Johan Axgren
German Closed	Simon Brown
Radegast Closed Championship	Jiri Janda
Team Erhverv Danish Open	Robert Jonsson
Open dei Tessali	Stephen Scahill
Audi Quattro Trophy	Erol Simsek
Memorial Olivier Barras	Juan Quiros
Open des Volcans	Andrew Sandywell
Neuchatel Open Golf Trophy	Federico Bisazza
Gosen Challenge	Gary Owen
Volvo Finnish Open	Bjorn Back
Interlaken Open	Vanslow Phillips
English Challenge Tour Championship	Dennis Edlund
Rolex Trophy Pro-Am	Dennis Edlund (2)
Esbjerg Danish Closed	Ben Tinning
Championnat Suisse ASG	Carlos Duran
Finnish Closed Championship	Mikko Rantenen
Grade Premio Andersen Consulting	Antonio Sobrinho
Karsten Ping Norwegian Open	Ignacio Feliu (2)
Dutch Challenge	Matthew Goggin
Toyota PGA Championship	Adam Mednick
Kentab/RBG Open	Max Anglert
Sovereign Russian Open	Carl Watts
Swedish Match Play	Adam Mednick (2)
Perrier European Pro-Am	Kevin Carissimi
Eulen Open Galea III	Jose Sota
Telia InfoMedia Grand Prix	Scott Watson
First Modena Classic Open	Lee James
Bank Pekao Polish Open	Erol Simsek (2)
UAP Grand Final	Ian Garbutt

ASIA TOUR

Benson & Hedges Malaysian Open	Steve Flesch
Mitsubishi Manila Southwoods Open	Manny Zerman
Thai Airways International Thailand Open	Todd Barranger
Classic India Open	Hidezumi Shirakata
Matoa International Invitational	Christian Pena
Indonesia Open	Edward Fryatt
Rolex Masters–Singapore	Mike Cunning
UBX Philippine Open	Rob Whitlock
Maekyung LG Fashion Open	Nam-Sin Park
Elord Cup–Korea Open	Kyung-Joo Choi
Shinhan Donghae Open	Chung Joon
Chinfon Chinese Taipei Open	*Hong Chia-Yuh
Johnnie Walker Super Tour	Ernie Els (4)
Andersen Consulting Hong Kong Open	Rodrigo Cuello

CHINA TOUR

Volvo Open	Glenn Joyner
Coca-Cola Open	John Wither
Blue Ribbon Open	Zhang Lian-Wei
Hugo Boss Open	Mohd. Ali Kadir

JAPAN TOUR

Token Corporation Cup	Yoshinori Kaneko
Daido Drinko Shizuoka Open	Yoshikazu Sakamoto
Novell KSB Open	Toru Suzuki
Descente Classic	Masanobu Kimura
Tsuruya Open	Peter McWhinney
Kirin Open	Yoshinori Kaneko (2)
Chunichi Crowns	Masashi Ozaki

Fuji Sankei Classic	Brian Watts
Japan PGA Championship	Masashi Ozaki (2)
Pepsi Ube Kosan Tournament	Hidemichi Tanaka
Mitsubishi Galant Tournament	Masashi Ozaki (3)
JCB Classic Sendai	Masashi Ozaki (4)
Sapporo Tokyu Open	Hajime Meshiai
Pocari Sweat Yomiuri Open	Kazuhiro Fukunaga
Mizuno Open	Yoshinori Kaneko (3)
PGA Philanthropy	Todd Hamilton
Yonex Open	Hideyuki Sato
Nikkei Cup	Hideki Kase
NST Niigata Open	Masatoshi Horikawa
Sanko Grand Summer	Kazuhiko Hosokawa
Acom International	Kazuhiko Hosokawa (2)
KBC Augusta	Masashi Ozaki (5)
Japan Match Play Championship	Nobuo Serizawa
Suntory Open	Hajime Meshiai (2)
ANA Open	Carlos Franco
Jun Classic	Masashi Ozaki (6)
Japan Open Golf Championship	Peter Teravainen
Tokai Classic	Masanobu Kimura (2)
Golf Digest Open	Yoshinori Mizumaki
Bridgestone Open	Shigeki Maruyama
Philip Morris Championship	Naomichi Ozaki
Sumitomo Visa Taiheiyo Masters	Lee Westwood (2)
Dunlop Phoenix Tournament	Masashi Ozaki (7)
Casio World Open	Paul Stankowski (4)
Japan Series Hitachi Cup	Masashi Ozaki (8)
Daikyo Open	Eduardo Herrera

OMEGA TOUR

Myanmar Open	Boonchu Ruangkit
Omega PGA Championship	Yeh Chang-Ting
Asian Match Play Championship	Jeev Milkha Singh
Sabah Masters	Thaworn Wiratchant
Singha-Thai Prasit Bangkok Open	Thammanoon Sriroj
Canlubang Classic	Craig Kamps
Tournament Players Championship	Wook-Soon Kang
Honda City Invitational	Steve Elkington
Guam Open	Joong-Kyung Mo
Volvo China Open	Prayad Marksaeng
Canon Singapore Open	John Kernohan
Kuala Lumpur Open	Wook-Soon Kang (2)
Fila Open	Oh-Chul Kwon
Philip Morris Asia Cup	Jeev Milkha Singh (2)
Lexus International	Boonchu Ruangkit (2)
Yokohama Singapore PGA Championship	Yeh Chang-Ting (2)
Dubai Creek Open	Paul Friedlander
Merlion Masters	Peter Teravainen (2)
Pakistan Steel Masters	Eric Rustand
Tugu Pratama PGA Championship	Thammanoon Sriroj (2)
Royal Classic	Richard Kaplan (2)
Omega PGA Championship	Gerry Norquist
Volvo Asian Match Play Championship	Zhang Lian-Wei (2)

AUSTRALASIAN TOUR

Heineken Classic	Ian Woosnam (2)
Ford South Australian Open	Greg Norman
Ericsson Australian Masters	Craig Parry
Canon Challenge	Peter Senior
Australian Seniors Championship	Lee Trevino

Foodlink Queensland Open	Steve Alker
Players Championship	Bradley Hughes
Alfred Dunhill Asian Masters	Bernhard Langer
MasterCard Australian PGA Championship	Phil Tataurangi (2)
Holden Australian Open	Greg Norman (4)
Greg Norman's Holden Classic	Peter Senior (2)
AMP-Air New Zealand Open	Michael Long
Schweppes Coolum Classic	Anthony Painter

AFRICAN TOURS

Philips South African Open	Ernie Els
San Lameer South African Masters	Wayne Westner
Nashua Wild Coast Sun Challenge	Wayne Westner (2)
Dimension Data Pro-Am	Mark McNulty
Alfred Dunhill South African PGA Championship	Sven Struver
FNB Players Championship	Wayne Westner (3)
Hollard Insurance Royal Swazi Classic	Richard Kaplan
Hassan II Trophy	Ignacio Garrido (2)
World Cup of Golf	South Africa/Ernie Els (5)
Nedbank Million Dollar Challenge	Colin Montgomerie (4)
Zimbabwe Open	Mark McNulty (4)
Zambia Open	Desvonde Botes

U.S. SENIOR PGA TOUR

Puerto Rico Senior Tournament of Champions	John Bland
Royal Caribbean Classic	Bob Murphy
Greater Naples IntelliNet Challenge	Al Geiberger
GTE Suncoast Classic	Jack Nicklaus
American Express Invitational	Hale Irwin
FHP Health Care Classic	Walter Morgan
Senior Slam	Raymond Floyd
Toshiba Senior Classic	Jim Colbert
Liberty Mutual Legends of Golf	Lee Trevino (2)/Mike Hill
SBC Dominion Seniors	Tom Weiskopf
The Tradition	Jack Nicklaus (2)
PGA Seniors' Championship	Hale Irwin (2)
Las Vegas Senior Classic	Jim Colbert (2)
PaineWebber Invitational	Graham Marsh
Nationwide Championship	Jim Colbert (3)
Cadillac NFL Golf Classic	Bob Murphy (2)
BellSouth Senior Classic at Opryland	Isao Aoki
Bruno's Memorial Classic	John Bland (2)
Pittsburgh Senior Classic	Tom Weiskopf (2)
du Maurier Champions	Charles Coody
Bell Atlantic Classic	Dale Douglass
Kroger Senior Classic	Isao Aoki (2)
U.S. Senior Open	Dave Stockton
Ford Senior Players Championship	Raymond Floyd (2)
Burnet Senior Classic	Vicente Fernandez
Ameritech Senior Open	Walter Morgan (2)
VFW Senior Championship	Dave Eichelberger
First of America Classic	Dave Stockton (2)
Northville Long Island Classic	John Bland (3)
Bank of Boston Senior Classic	Jim Dent
Franklin Quest Championship	Graham Marsh (2)
Boone Valley Classic	Gibby Gilbert
Bank One Classic	Mike Hill (2)
Brickyard Crossing Championship	Jimmy Powell
Vantage Championship	Jim Colbert (4)
Ralphs Senior Classic	Gil Morgan
The Transamerica	John Bland (4)

Raley's Gold Rush Classic	Jim Colbert (5)
Hyatt Regency Maui Kaanapali Classic	Bob Charles
Emerald Coast Classic	Lee Trevino (3)
Energizer Senior Tour Championship	Jay Sigel
Diners Club Matches	Jim Colbert (6)/Bob Murphy (3)

EUROPEAN SENIORS TOUR

Beko/Oger Tours Turkish Seniors Open	Bobby Verwey
De Vere Hotels Seniors Classic	Renato Campagnoli
Hippo Jersey Open	Maurice Bembridge
Castle Royle European Seniors Classic	Tommy Horton
Ryder Collingtree Seniors Classic	David Huish
Stella Senior Open	Tommy Horton (2)
Senior British Open	Brian Barnes
Lawrence Batley Seniors	Malcolm Gregson
Northern Electric Seniors	Tommy Horton (3)
Belfry PGA Seniors Championship	Terry Gale
Scottish Seniors Open	John Morgan
Motor City Seniors Classic	John Morgan (2)
The Player Championship	Tommy Horton (4)

JAPAN SENIOR TOUR

Daiichi Seimei Cup	Seiichi Kanai
TPC Starts	Haruo Yasuda
HTB Classic	Fujio Kobayashi
Komatsu Nagoya TV Cup	Masaji Kusakabe
Japan PGA Senior Championship	Koji Nakajima
Japan Senior Open Championship	Isao Aoki (3)

U.S. LPGA TOUR

Chrysler-Plymouth Tournament of Champions	Liselotte Neumann
HEALTHSOUTH Inaugural	Karrie Webb
Cup Noodles Hawaiian Ladies Open	Meg Mallon
PING/Welch's Championship	Liselotte Neumann (2)
Standard Register PING	Laura Davies
Nabisco Dinah Shore	Patty Sheehan
Twelve Bridges LPGA Classic	Kelly Robbins
Chick-fil-A Charity Championship	Barb Mucha
Sara Lee Classic	Meg Mallon (2)
Sprint Titleholders Championship	Karrie Webb (2)
McDonald's LPGA Championship	Laura Davies (3)
LPGA Corning Classic	Rosie Jones
U.S. Women's Open	Annika Sorenstam
Oldsmobile Classic	Michelle McGann
Edina Realty LPGA Classic	Liselotte Neumann (3)
Rochester International	Dottie Pepper
ShopRite LPGA Classic	Dottie Pepper (2)
Jamie Farr Kroger Classic	Joan Pitcock
Youngstown-Warren LPGA Classic	Michelle McGann (2)
Friendly's Classic	Dottie Pepper (3)
Michelob Light Heartland Classic	Vicki Fergon
du Maurier Classic	Laura Davies (5)
PING Welch's Championship	Emilee Klein
Star Bank LPGA Classic	Laura Davies (6)
State Farm Rail Classic	Michelle McGann (3)
Safeway LPGA Golf Championship	Dottie Pepper (4)
SAFECO Classic	Karrie Webb (3)
Fieldcrest Cannon Classic	Trish Johnson (2)
JAL Big Apple Classic	Caroline Pierce
CoreStates Betsy King Classic	Annika Sorenstam (3)
Samsung World Championship of Women's Golf	Annika Sorenstam (4)

ITT LPGA Tour Championship	Karrie Webb (4)
Diners Club Matches	Dottie Pepper (5)/Juli Inkster

WOMEN'S EUROPEAN TOUR

Women's Welsh Open	Lisa Hackney
Costa Azul Ladies' Open	Shani Waugh
Ford-Stimorol Danish Open	Nadene Gole
Deesse Ladies' Swiss Open	Sophie Gustafson
Evian Masters	Laura Davies (4)
Glashutte Ladies' Austrian Open	Martina Koch
Hennessy Cup	Helen Alfredsson
Guardian Irish Open	Alison Nicholas
McDonald's WPGA Championship	Tina Fischer
Weetabix Women's British Open Championship	Emilee Klein (2)
Trygg-Hansa Ladies' Open	Annika Sorenstam (2)
Compaq Open	Federica Dassu
Marks & Spencer European Open	Trish Johnson
Wilkinson Sword Ladies' English Open	Laura Davies (7)
Solheim Cup	United States
Ladies' German Open	Joanne Morley
Ladies' French Open	Trish Johnson (3)
Italian Open di Sicilia	Laura Davies (8)
Ladies' Spanish Open	Caryn Louw
Princess Lalla Meriem Cup	Lora Fairclough

WOMEN'S AUSTRALASIAN TOURS

Republic of China Open	Shoko Asano
Singapore Open	Debbie Dowling
Indonesian Open	Corinne Dibnah
Thailand Open	Shelly Rule
Malaysian JAL Open	Corinne Dibnah (2)
Holden Women's Australian Open	Catriona Matthew
Alpine Australian Ladies Masters	Jane Crafter

JAPAN LPGA TOUR

Daikin Orchid	Li Wen-Lin
Saishunkan Ladies	Young-Me Lee
Yellow Hat Tokyo Open	Aki Takamura
Kenshoen Ladies	Aiko Hashimoto
Mitsukoshi Cup	Marnie McGuire
Nasu Ogawa	Aki Nakano
Satake Classic	Laura Davies (2)
Gunze Cup World Ladies	Yukiyo Haga
Yakult Ladies	Kaori Harada
Chukyo TV Bridgestone	Mayumi Murai
Toto Motors	Shin Sora
Mitsubishi Denki	Cheng Mei-Chi
Suntory Ladies	Jae-Sook Won
Dunlop Twin Lakes	Aiko Hashimoto (2)
Japan Women's Open Championship	Aki Takamura (2)
Tohato Ladies	Toshimi Kimura
Toyo Suisan	Ok-Hee Ku
Resort Trust Ladies	Aiko Hashimoto (3)
Katokichi Queen's Cup	Suzuko Maeda
Golf 5 Ladies	Yuka Irie
Mizuno Ladies	Young-Me Lee (2)
NEC Karuizawa 72	Akiko Fukushima
Goyo Kensetsu Ladies	Chikayo Yamazaki
Fuji Sankei Classic	Ayako Okamoto
Japan LPGA Championship	Ikuyo Shiotani
Yukijirushi Ladies Tokai Classic	Suzuko Maeda (2)

Miyagi TV Cup Ladies Open	Mikino Kubo
Kosaido Ladies Golf Cup	Tseng Hsiu-Feng
Takara World Invitational	Ikuyo Shiotani (2)
Fujitsu Ladies	Akiko Fukushima (2)
Kibun Ladies Classic	Akane Ohshiro
Nichirei International	United States
Toray Japan Queens Cup	Mayumi Hirase
Itoen Ladies	Laura Davies (9)
Daio Seishi Elleair Open	Ok-Hee Ku (2)
Meiji Nyugyo Cup	Yoko Inoue

Multiple Winners of 1996

PLAYER	WINS	PLAYER	WINS
Laura Davies	9	Kazuhiko Hosokawa	2
Masashi Ozaki	8	Wook-Soon Kang	2
Jim Colbert	6	Richard Kaplan	2
Ernie Els	5	Masanobu Kimura	2
Phil Mickelson	5	Tom Kite	2
Greg Norman	5	Emilee Klein	2
Dottie Pepper	5	Arden Knoll	2
John Bland	4	Ok-Hee Ku	2
Stewart Cink	4	Young-Me Lee	2
Trevor Dodds	4	Jonathan Lomas	2
Tommy Horton	4	Suzuko Maeda	2
Tom Lehman	4	Meg Mallon	2
Mark McNulty	4	Graham Marsh	2
Colin Montgomerie	4	Pedro Martinez	2
Annika Sorenstam	4	Adam Mednick	2
Paul Stankowski	4	Hajime Meshiai	2
Karrie Webb	4	John Morgan	2
Ian Woosnam	4	Walter Morgan	2
Robert Allenby	3	Jack Nicklaus	2
Isao Aoki	3	Frank Nobilo	2
Mark Brooks	3	Mark O'Meara	2
Michael Christie	3	Loren Roberts	2
Raymond Floyd	3	Boonchu Ruangkit	2
Aiko Hashimoto	3	Peter Senior	2
Hale Irwin	3	Ikuyo Shiotani	2
Trish Johnson	3	Erol Simsek	2
Yoshinori Kaneko	3	Jeev Milkha Singh	2
Michelle McGann	3	Thammanoon Sriroj	2
Bob Murphy	3	Dave Stockton	2
Liselotte Neumann	3	Steve Stricker	2
Lee Trevino	3	Aki Takamura	2
Wayne Westner	3	Phil Tataurangi	2
John Cook	2	Peter Teravainen	2
Corinne Dibnah	2	Kalle Vainola	2
Dennis Edlund	2	Tom Weiskopf	2
Ignacio Feliu	2	Lee Westwood	2
Akiko Fukushima	2	Tiger Woods	2
Ignacio Garrido	2	Yeh Chang-Ting	2
Mike Hill	2	Zhang Lian-Wei	2
Scott Hoch	2		

World Money List

This list of the 350 leading money winners in the world of professional golf in 1996 was compiled from the results of men's (excluding seniors) tournaments carried in the Appendixes of this edition. This list includes tournaments with a minimum of 36 holes and four contestants and does not include such competitions as skins games, pro-ams and shootouts.

In the 31 years during which World Money Lists have been compiled, the earnings of the player in the 200th position have risen from a total of $3,326 in 1966 to $235,957 in 1996. The top-200 players in 1966 earned a total of $4,680,287. In 1996, the comparable total was $117,776,416.

Because of fluctuating values of money throughout the world, it was necessary to determine an average value of non-American currency to U.S. money to prepare this listing. The conversion rates used for 1996 were: British pound = US$1.55; Japanese yen = US$0.009247; Australian dollar = US$0.77; Canadian dollar = US$0.74.

POS.	PLAYER, COUNTRY	TOTAL MONEY
1	Colin Montgomerie, Scotland	$3,071,442
2	Tom Lehman, USA	2,634,804
3	Greg Norman, Australia	2,258,678
4	Scott Hoch, USA	2,155,893
5	Phil Mickelson, USA	2,115,990
6	Ernie Els, South Africa	2,089,428
7	Masashi Ozaki, Japan	1,944,034
8	Steve Stricker, USA	1,905,366
9	Mark Brooks, USA	1,850,296
10	Mark O'Meara, USA	1,654,149
11	Steve Jones, USA	1,573,108
12	Fred Couples, USA	1,556,613
13	Nick Faldo, England	1,435,670
14	Davis Love III, USA	1,430,700
15	Ian Woosnam, Wales	1,321,719
16	Brad Faxon, USA	1,198,121
17	Vijay Singh, Fiji	1,104,997
18	Yoshinori Kaneko, Japan	1,085,706
19	David Duval, USA	1,043,079
20	Frank Nobilo, New Zealand	1,033,737
21	Kenny Perry, USA	1,020,452
22	Justin Leonard, USA	1,004,640
23	Corey Pavin, USA	971,320
24	Costantino Rocca, Italy	957,397
25	Lee Westwood, England	939,104
26	Tom Watson, USA	925,046
27	John Cook, USA	921,766
28	Shigeki Maruyama, Japan	903,802
29	Paul Stankowski, USA	901,553
30	Tommy Tolles, USA	899,393
31	Tiger Woods, USA	894,060
32	Nick Price, Zimbabwe	888,882

POS.	PLAYER, COUNTRY	TOTAL MONEY
33	Robert Allenby, Australia	886,316
34	Naomichi Ozaki, Japan	869,393
35	Fred Funk, USA	856,004
36	Jim Furyk, USA	842,035
37	Mark McNulty, Zimbabwe	838,835
38	Mark Calcavecchia, USA	830,622
39	Lee Janzen, USA	828,134
40	Brian Watts, USA	825,161
41	Michael Bradley, USA	824,257
42	Jeff Maggert, USA	804,955
43	Jeff Sluman, USA	800,099
44	Loren Roberts, USA	764,231
45	Wayne Westner, South Africa	753,973
46	Hisayuki Sasaki, Japan	745,723
47	Duffy Waldorf, USA	738,882
48	Jay Haas, USA	736,936
49	Kazuhiko Hosokawa, Japan	732,249
50	Sam Torrance, Scotland	713,768
51	Payne Stewart, USA	709,112
52	Steve Elkington, Australia	707,287
53	Craig Stadler, USA	659,116
54	Craig Parry, Australia	654,448
55	Jesper Parnevik, Sweden	647,849
56	Nobuo Serizawa, Japan	647,649
57	Masanobu Kimura, Japan	643,655
58	Peter Senior, Australia	627,781
59	Andrew Coltart, Scotland	623,800
60	David Frost, South Africa	619,142
61	Todd Hamilton, USA	615,140
62	David Ishii, USA	607,318
63	David Ogrin, USA	588,598
64	Tom Kite, USA	586,732
65	Darren Clarke, Northern Ireland	583,198
66	Bob Tway, USA	577,456
67	Hajime Meshiai, Japan	565,355
68	Mark McCumber, USA	565,226
69	Frankie Minoza, Philippines	564,128
70	Woody Austin, USA	558,608
71	John Huston, USA	551,153
72	Tim Herron, USA	539,515
73	Katsuyoshi Tomori, Japan	530,515
74	Bernhard Langer, Germany	529,104
75	Miguel Angel Jimenez, Spain	520,485
76	Paul Broadhurst, England	507,351
77	Rocco Mediate, USA	495,628
78	Padraig Harrington, Ireland	494,042
79	Kirk Triplett, USA	488,793
80	Thomas Bjorn, Denmark	488,033
81	Billy Mayfair, USA	485,527
82	Scott McCarron, USA	485,446
83	Carlos Franco, Paraguay	485,277
84	Hidemichi Tanaka, Japan	484,497
85	Clarence Rose, USA	484,399
86	Paul McGinley, Ireland	477,106

POS.	PLAYER, COUNTRY	TOTAL MONEY
87	Mike Hulbert, USA	476,081
88	Tsuneyuki Nakajima, Japan	474,779
89	Billy Andrade, USA	471,418
90	Russ Cochran, USA	457,340
91	D.A. Weibring, USA	452,275
92	Stewart Cink, USA	450,363
93	Eduardo Herrera, Colombia	449,422
94	Tom Purtzer, USA	447,564
95	Paul Goydos, USA	446,936
96	Jonathan Lomas, England	445,871
97	Hideki Kase, Japan	445,324
98	Grant Waite, New Zealand	444,262
99	Peter Mitchell, England	443,631
100	Jean Van de Velde, France	439,648
101	Dudley Hart, USA	439,171
102	Raymond Russell, Scotland	435,899
103	Wayne Riley, Australia	435,424
104	Paul Lawrie, Scotland	434,616
105	Peter Teravainen, USA	423,657
106	Andrew Magee, USA	422,098
107	Stephen Ames, Trinidad & Tobago	417,515
108	Retief Goosen, South Africa	408,311
109	Hideyuki Sato, Japan	399,977
110	Fuzzy Zoeller, USA	399,579
111	Brandt Jobe, USA	395,871
112	Per-Ulrik Johansson, Sweden	389,466
113	Katsunori Kuwabara, Japan	389,120
114	Miguel Angel Martin, Spain	387,381
115	Larry Nelson, USA	382,304
116	Jerry Kelly, USA	381,531
117	Larry Mize, USA	376,035
118	Jay Don Blake, USA	374,736
119	Scott Simpson, USA	373,898
120	Lennie Clements, USA	373,516
121	Daniel Chopra, Sweden	372,698
122	Shoichi Kuwabara, Japan	366,180
123	Masahiro Kuramoto, Japan	365,283
124	Greg Turner, New Zealand	359,440
125	Willie Wood, USA	358,101
126	Toru Suzuki, Japan	349,545
127	Eduardo Romero, Argentina	343,370
128	Greg Kraft, USA	342,787
129	John Morse, USA	338,048
130	Jose Coceres, Argentina	338,037
131	John Daly, USA	337,964
132	Glen Day, USA	334,781
133	Joel Edwards, USA	332,876
134	Nolan Henke, USA	327,014
135	Tsukasa Watanabe, Japan	326,776
136	Robert Gamez, USA	325,675
137	Ignacio Garrido, Spain	321,966
138	Jim Gallagher, Jr., USA	321,490
139	Yoshinori Mizumaki, Japan	321,307
140	Kelly Gibson, USA	315,039

POS.	PLAYER, COUNTRY	TOTAL MONEY
141	Peter McWhinney, Australia	314,049
142	Rick Fehr, USA	313,187
143	Jim Payne, England	312,069
144	Bradley Hughes, Australia	311,309
145	Emlyn Aubrey, USA	309,591
146	Ryoken Kawagishi, Japan	308,668
147	Angel Cabrera, Argentina	295,296
148	Kaname Yokoo, Japan	292,755
149	Satoshi Higashi, Japan	290,172
150	Kiyoshi Maita, Japan	289,635
151	Chip Beck, USA	288,385
152	Guy Boros, USA	286,858
153	Yoshikazu Sakamoto, Japan	286,440
154	Andrew Oldcorn, Scotland	283,519
155	Patrick Burke, USA	281,246
156	Diego Borrego, Spain	279,750
157	Kazuhiro Fukunaga, Japan	278,793
158	Mike Briskey, USA	278,792
159	Rick Gibson, Canada	277,703
160	Steve Lowery, USA	276,803
161	Joey Sindelar, USA	275,531
162	Ed Fiori, USA	275,380
163	Shinichi Yokota, Japan	273,949
164	Marc Farry, France	272,545
165	Olin Browne, USA	270,403
166	Jarmo Sandelin, Sweden	269,364
167	Seiki Okuda, Japan	268,246
168	John Adams, USA	266,765
169	Chen Tze-Chung, Taiwan	265,897
170	Peter O'Malley, Australia	263,286
171	Peter Baker, England	263,102
172	Peter Hedblom, Sweden	262,203
173	Brandel Chamblee, USA	261,940
174	Alexander Cejka, Germany	261,781
175	Marco Dawson, USA	261,661
176	Russell Claydon, England	260,847
177	Hirofumi Miyase, Japan	260,429
178	Richard Green, Australia	259,369
179	Tony Johnstone, Zimbabwe	258,582
180	Brad Bryant, USA	256,813
181	Tsuyoshi Yoneyama, Japan	256,789
182	David Carter, England	256,131
183	Mark Mouland, Wales	256,085
184	Curtis Strange, USA	253,883
185	Roger Chapman, England	253,533
186	Ross McFarlane, England	253,453
187	Patrik Sjoland, Sweden	252,755
188	Len Mattiace, USA	252,227
189	Michael Christie, USA	252,046
190	Ronnie Black, USA	250,620
191	Takaaki Fukuzawa, Japan	248,931
192	Domingo Hospital, Spain	248,502
193	Peter Jacobsen, USA	246,114
194	Stewart Ginn, Australia	240,613

POS.	PLAYER, COUNTRY	TOTAL MONEY
195	Toshimitsu Izawa, Japan	239,389
196	Gary Orr, Scotland	239,126
197	Andrew Sherborne, England	238,746
198	Wook-Soon Kang, Korea	237,368
199	Taichi Teshima, Japan	236,654
200	Keiichiro Fukabori, Japan	235,957
201	Ross Drummond, Scotland	234,991
202	Jim Carter, USA	233,819
203	Carl Suneson, England	232,780
204	Paul Azinger, USA	232,041
205	Kazuhiro Takami, Japan	230,061
206	Phil Blackmar, USA	229,274
207	Brad Fabel, USA	228,667
208	David Howell, England	228,035
209	Barry Lane, England	228,001
210	Masayuki Kawamura, Japan	227,018
211	Paul Eales, England	226,560
212	Taylor Smith, USA	225,240
213	Jamie Spence, England	224,268
214	Zaw Moe, Myanmar	219,206
215	Doug Martin, USA	218,478
216	Paul Curry, England	217,272
217	Nobumitsu Yuhara, Japan	217,249
218	Wayne Levi, USA	214,779
219	Lee Rinker, USA	213,937
220	Lin Keng-Chi, Taiwan	212,343
221	Mark Davis, England	212,116
222	Neal Lancaster, USA	210,000
223	Yoshimutsu Fukuzawa, Japan	209,744
224	Richard Boxall, England	209,092
225	Tomohiro Maruyama, Japan	208,808
226	Mark Wiebe, USA	208,758
227	Scott Dunlap, USA	207,974
228	David Toms, USA	205,188
229	Pete Jordan, USA	203,744
230	Iain Pyman, England	203,068
231	David Edwards, USA	201,974
232	Wayne Grady, Australia	201,926
233	Chris Perry, USA	200,361
234	Tateo Ozaki, Japan	199,353
235	Hal Sutton, USA	198,723
236	Mathias Gronberg, Sweden	197,462
237	Blaine McCallister, USA	196,927
238	Gordon Brand, Jr., Scotland	196,909
239	Katsunari Takahashi, Japan	196,595
240	Robert Willis, Australia	195,458
241	Joakim Haeggman, Sweden	194,955
242	Hugh Royer III, USA	194,854
243	Rolf Muntz, Holland	194,571
244	Bob Gilder, USA	194,190
245	Ben Crenshaw, USA	191,790
246	David Gilford, England	191,315
247	Dan Forsman, USA	190,495
248	Gohei Sato, Japan	188,673

POS.	PLAYER, COUNTRY	TOTAL MONEY
249	Sandy Lyle, Scotland	187,637
250	Nam-Sin Park, Korea	187,493
251	David Berganio, Jr., USA	184,137
252	John Maginnes, USA	184,065
253	Sven Struver, Germany	183,631
254	Tsutomu Higa, Japan	182,348
255	Scott Gump, USA	182,332
256	John Wilson, USA	182,121
257	Rick Todd, Canada	181,181
258	Michael Campbell, New Zealand	180,052
259	Shigenori Mori, Japan	179,724
260	Eiji Mizoguchi, Japan	179,673
261	Stuart Appleby, Australia	179,672
262	Seve Ballesteros, Spain	178,705
263	Keith Fergus, USA	178,640
264	Mike Springer, USA	178,166
265	Roger Mackay, Australia	176,534
266	Dave Stockton, Jr., USA	176,056
267	Dicky Pride, USA	175,663
268	Gerry Norquist, USA	174,961
269	Trevor Dodds, Namibia	173,528
270	Santiago Luna, Spain	172,961
271	Miles Tunnicliff, England	171,928
272	Omar Uresti, USA	171,797
273	Peter Lonard, Australia	171,375
274	Stuart Cage, England	170,991
275	Brian Claar, USA	170,511
276	Fernando Roca, Spain	169,210
277	Malcolm Mackenzie, England	168,745
278	Mike Reid, USA	167,950
279	Jon Robson, England	167,706
280	Fulton Allem, South Africa	167,515
281	Jeff Wagner, Australia	166,948
282	Tom Byrum, USA	166,500
283	Harumitsu Hamano, Japan	164,715
284	Phillip Price, Wales	163,202
285	Anthony Painter, Australia	163,069
286	Ted Tryba, USA	162,944
287	Kiyoshi Murota, Japan	162,312
288	Brian Henninger, USA	162,180
289	Phil Tataurangi, New Zealand	161,865
290	Yasunobu Kuramoto, Japan	161,843
291	Toru Taniguchi, Japan	161,836
292	Ken Green, USA	161,663
293	Lanny Wadkins, USA	160,995
294	Akihito Yokoyama, Japan	160,054
295	Steven Bottomley, England	159,744
296	Joe Durant, USA	159,386
297	Robert Stephens, Australia	159,224
298	Bruce Lietzke, USA	158,191
299	Keith Clearwater, USA	157,617
300	Toru Nakamura, Japan	157,386
301	Derrick Cooper, England	157,363
302	Mark Roe, England	157,293

POS.	PLAYER, COUNTRY	TOTAL MONEY
303	Pedro Linhart, Spain	155,799
304	Thomas Gogele, Germany	154,460
305	Masatoshi Horikawa, Japan	153,926
306	Mike Cunning, USA	152,641
307	Kyung-Joo Choi, Korea	150,832
308	Koki Idoki, Japan	150,056
309	Michael Long, New Zealand	149,178
310	Bruce Fleisher, USA	148,880
311	John Kernohan, USA	146,193
312	Mitsutaka Kusakabe, Japan	145,372
313	Philip Walton, Ireland	144,944
314	Kevin Sutherland, USA	144,828
315	Yasunori Ida, Japan	142,613
316	Bobby Wadkins, USA	142,003
317	Lee Porter, USA	141,481
318	Jong-Duck Kim, Korea	140,864
319	Carl Paulson, USA	140,621
320	Ricky Willison, England	140,384
321	Frank Lickliter, USA	138,847
322	Robin Freeman, USA	138,605
323	Craig Kamps, South Africa	136,947
324	Allen Doyle, USA	136,789
325	Tom Scherrer, USA	136,323
326	Pedro Martinez, Paraguay	136,204
327	Bob Estes, USA	135,264
328	Jeev Milkha Singh, India	134,875
329	P.H. Horgan III, USA	134,348
330	Charlie Rymer, USA	132,076
331	Koichi Nogami, Japan	131,316
332	Thammanoon Sriroj, Thailand	131,197
333	Mike Sullivan, USA	131,069
334	Greg Chalmers, Australia	131,057
335	Raymond Burns, Northern Ireland	130,944
336	Gene Sauers, USA	128,654
337	Jim McGovern, USA	128,477
338	Fabrice Tarnaud, France	127,512
339	Bob Lohr, USA	127,463
340	Per Haugsrud, Norway	127,061
341	Richard Kaplan, South Africa	127,036
342	Gary Evans, England	126,558
343	Klas Eriksson, Sweden	126,229
344	Dave Rummells, USA	125,823
345	Yoshitaka Yamamoto, Japan	125,120
346	Brett Quigley, USA	123,763
347	Prayad Marksaeng, Thailand	123,572
348	Steve Jurgensen, USA	123,299
349	Martin Gates, England	123,189
350	Jack O'Keefe, USA	122,999

Career World Money List

The following is a listing of the 50 leading money winners for their careers through the 1996 season. It includes players active on both the regular and senior tours of the world. The World Money List from this and the 30 previous editions of this annual and a table prepared for a companion book, *The Wonderful World of Professional Golf* (Atheneum, 1973), form the basis for this compilation. Additional figures were taken from official records of major golf associations, although the shortcomings in records-keeping in professional golf outside the United States in the 1950s and 1960s and exclusions from U.S. records in a few cases during those years prevent these figures from being completely accurate. Conversions of foreign currency figures to U.S. dollars are based on average values during the particular years involved.

POS.	PLAYER, COUNTRY	TOTAL MONEY
1	Greg Norman, Australia	$18,671,779
2	Masashi Ozaki, Japan	15,644,708
3	Fred Couples, USA	15,485,838
4	Bernhard Langer, Germany	14,996,747
5	Nick Faldo, England	14,931,675
6	Raymond Floyd, USA	13,492,304
7	Nick Price, Zimbabwe	12,941,557
8	Lee Trevino, USA	12,865,893
9	Tom Kite, USA	12,476,193
10	David Frost, South Africa	12,198,621
11	Ian Woosnam, Wales	11,648,066
12	Seve Ballesteros, Spain	11,406,618
13	Isao Aoki, Japan	11,400,430
14	Corey Pavin, USA	11,309,128
15	Colin Montgomerie, Scotland	10,755,138
16	Payne Stewart, USA	10,721,332
17	Hale Irwin, USA	10,165,506
18	Tsuneyuki Nakajima, Japan	10,079,808
19	Davis Love III, USA	9,771,211
20	Curtis Strange, USA	9,696,201
21	Tom Watson, USA	9,523,202
22	Scott Hoch, USA	9,519,015
23	Mark O'Meara, USA	9,463,315
24	Bob Charles, New Zealand	9,307,198
25	Jack Nicklaus, USA	9,287,473
26	Mark Calcavecchia, USA	9,269,813
27	Ben Crenshaw, USA	9,233,399
28	Jim Colbert, USA	9,224,746
29	Paul Azinger, USA	8,946,978
30	Naomichi Ozaki, Japan	8,889,836
31	Jose Maria Olazabal, Spain	8,700,355
32	Gary Player, South Africa	8,556,233
33	Craig Stadler, USA	8,476,436
34	Ernie Els, South Africa	8,358,639

POS.	PLAYER, COUNTRY	TOTAL MONEY
35	George Archer, USA	8,217,617
36	Chi Chi Rodriguez, USA	7,960,028
37	Lanny Wadkins, USA	7,958,150
38	Dave Stockton, USA	7,899,973
39	Graham Marsh, Australia	7,678,576
40	Chip Beck, USA	7,289,914
41	Steve Elkington, Australia	7,248,970
42	Mike Hill, USA	7,194,060
43	Mark McNulty, Zimbabwe	7,161,163
44	Masahiro Kuramoto, Japan	7,140,177
45	Larry Mize, USA	7,065,345
46	Tom Lehman, USA	7,055,037
47	Vijay Singh, Fiji	6,994,822
48	Jay Haas, USA	6,933,132
49	Miller Barber, USA	6,894,105
50	Sandy Lyle, Scotland	6,873,161

These 50 players have won $494,979,621 in their lifetimes playing professional tournament golf.

Senior World Money List

This list includes official earnings on the U.S. PGA Tour, U.S. Senior PGA Tour, European Seniors Tour and Japan Senior Tour, along with other winnings in established unofficial events· when reliable figures could be obtained.

POS.	PLAYER, COUNTRY	TOTAL MONEY
1	Hale Irwin, USA	$1,991,569
2	Jim Colbert, USA	1,853,140
3	Raymond Floyd, USA	1,621,101
4	John Bland, South Africa	1,359,987
5	Dave Stockton, USA	1,347,685
6	Isao Aoki, Japan	1,283,999
7	Bob Murphy, USA	1,249,688
8	Jay Sigel, USA	1,169,630
9	Graham Marsh, Australia	1,066,187
10	Lee Trevino, USA	928,350
11	Walter Morgan, USA	891,053
12	J.C. Snead, USA	851,049
13	Jim Dent, USA	797,826
14	Bob Charles, New Zealand	776,677
15	Tom Wargo, USA	729,928
16	Kermit Zarley, USA	710,110

POS.	PLAYER, COUNTRY	TOTAL MONEY
17	Gary Player, South Africa	702,278
18	Jack Kiefer, USA	668,947
19	Vicente Fernandez, Argentina	665,251
20	Jimmy Powell, USA	655,029
21	Jack Nicklaus, USA	636,651
22	Mike Hill, USA	628,130
23	Tom Weiskopf, USA	589,584
24	Frank Conner, USA	561,465
25	Brian Barnes, Scotland	548,486
26	John Jacobs, USA	537,263
27	Chi Chi Rodriguez, Puerto Rico	534,234
28	John Schroeder, USA	485,789
29	Larry Gilbert, USA	482,975
30	Gibby Gilbert, USA	478,974
31	Bobby Stroble, USA	464,648
32	Bruce Summerhays, USA	453,579
33	Rick Acton, USA	445,086
34	Gil Morgan, USA	436,615
35	Simon Hobday, South Africa	424,195
36	Al Geiberger, USA	419,301
37	Bob Eastwood, USA	413,000
38	Tony Jacklin, England	411,664
39	Rocky Thompson, USA	387,719
40	Charles Coody, USA	378,554
41	Buddy Allin, USA	371,984
42	Jerry McGee, USA	350,362
43	Dave Eichelberger, USA	349,053
44	Bruce Crampton, Australia	334,224
45	Bob E. Smith, USA	334,179
46	Dale Douglass, USA	324,007
47	Terry Dill, USA	323,087
48	Tommy Aaron, USA	313,323
49	David Graham, Australia	303,415
50	John Paul Cain, USA	301,020
51	Don Bies, USA	298,688
52	Bob Dickson, USA	292,986
53	Butch Baird, USA	280,018
54	Larry Laoretti, USA	278,541
55	Larry Mowry, USA	275,778
56	Calvin Peete, USA	271,056
57	DeWitt Weaver, USA	270,597
58	Dick Rhyan, USA	253,914
59	Jim Albus, USA	244,833
60	George Archer, USA	241,793
61	Dick Hendrickson, USA	240,033
62	Larry Ziegler, USA	226,787
63	Masaru Amano, Japan	226,479
64	Tom Shaw, USA	222,408
65	Tommy Horton, England	209,382
66	Harold Henning, South Africa	209,125
67	Bunky Henry, USA	201,858
68	Mike McCullough, USA	193,960
69	Ed Sneed, USA	171,806
70	Homero Blancas, USA	169,511

POS.	PLAYER, COUNTRY	TOTAL MONEY
71	Ben Smith, USA	163,794
72	Jim Wilkinson, USA	157,428
73	Rives McBee, USA	156,078
74	Bruce Devlin, Australia	152,366
75	Arnold Palmer, USA	150,109
76	Bob Betley, USA	149,152
77	Seiichi Kanai, Japan	133,607
78	Walter Zembriski, USA	128,312
79	John Brodie, USA	124,276
80	Haruo Yasuda, Japan	122,592
81	John Morgan, England	118,223
82	Don January, USA	113,390
83	Miller Barber, USA	113,174
84	Koji Nakajima, Japan	109,799
85	Bob Wynn, USA	103,757
86	Orville Moody, USA	102,467
87	Steven Veriato, USA	94,510
88	Malcolm Gregson, England	93,140
89	Terry Gale, Australia	92,718
90	Harry Toscano, USA	90,959
91	Gay Brewer, USA	84,606
92	Robert Landers, USA	80,862
93	Noel Ratcliffe, Australia	78,858
94	David Oakley, USA	78,707
95	Gene Littler, USA	77,319
96	Antonio Garrido, Spain	75,456
97	Fujio Kobayashi, Japan	75,363
98	Hiroshi Ishii, Japan	73,067
99	Mitoshi Tomita, Japan	70,878
100	Masaji Kusakabe, Japan	68,058

Women's World Money List

This list includes official earnings on the U.S. LPGA Tour, Women's European Tour, Women's Australasian Tours and Japan LPGA Tour, along with other winnings in established unofficial events when reliable figures could be obtained.

POS.	PLAYER, COUNTRY	TOTAL MONEY
1	Laura Davies, England	$1,383,003
2	Karrie Webb, Australia	1,135,971
3	Annika Sorenstam, Sweden	868,483
4	Dottie Pepper, USA	730,698
5	Liselotte Neumann, Sweden	707,216

POS.	PLAYER, COUNTRY	TOTAL MONEY
6	Akiko Fukushima, Japan	666,303
7	Kelly Robbins, USA	629,462
8	Kaori Harada, Japan	595,682
9	Aiko Hashimoto, Japan	584,386
10	Michelle McGann, USA	566,934
11	Emilee Klein, USA	555,054
12	Ikuyo Shiotani, Japan	540,839
13	Meg Mallon, USA	513,932
14	Aki Takamura, Japan	473,054
15	Kris Tschetter, USA	456,500
16	Mayumi Murai, Japan	456,028
17	Jane Geddes, USA	454,739
18	Val Skinner, USA	437,419
19	Ok-Hee Ku, Korea	435,269
20	Suzuko Maeda, Japan	421,663
21	Ayako Okamoto, Japan	420,049
22	Akane Ohshiro, Japan	417,758
23	Kaori Higo, Japan	402,424
24	Marnie McGuire, New Zealand	398,177
25	Young-Me Lee, Korea	392,556
26	Michiko Hattori, Japan	382,800
27	Patty Sheehan, USA	381,095
28	Juli Inkster, USA	375,567
29	Brandie Burton, USA	371,548
30	Miyuki Shimabukuro, Japan	353,820
31	Natsuko Noro, Japan	352,977
32	Donna Andrews, USA	342,731
33	Barb Mucha, USA	334,237
34	Yukiyo Haga, Japan	331,940
35	Marianne Morris, USA	331,345
36	Pat Hurst, USA	316,016
37	Aki Nakano, Japan	306,368
38	Hiromi Kobayashi, Japan	295,972
39	Helen Alfredsson, Sweden	295,227
40	Mayumi Hirase, Japan	294,488
41	Penny Hammel, USA	291,170
42	Nancy Lopez, USA	287,451
43	Rosie Jones, USA	275,592
44	Pat Bradley, USA	270,789
45	Toshimi Kimura, Japan	269,902
46	Jennifer Sevil, New Zealand	266,288
47	Chieko Nishida, Japan	264,925
48	Shin Sora, Korea	260,955
49	Yoko Inoue, Japan	259,828
50	Caroline Pierce, England	259,417
51	Tracy Kerdyk, USA	258,926
52	Barb Whitehead, USA	257,602
53	Jae-Sook Won, Korea	253,966
54	Missie McGeorge, USA	251,824
55	Tseng Hsiu-Feng, Taiwan	251,019
56	Trish Johnson, England	248,407
57	Alison Nicholas, England	238,868
58	Tina Barrett, USA	234,194
59	Tammie Green, USA	229,417

POS.	PLAYER, COUNTRY	TOTAL MONEY
60	Woo-Soon Ko, Korea	225,096
61	Chris Johnson, USA	222,859
62	Catrin Nilsmark, Sweden	217,779
63	Joan Pitcock, USA	217,717
64	Julie Piers, USA	217,072
65	Ae-Sook Kim, Korea	216,986
66	Amy Fruhwirth, USA	215,541
67	Mikino Kubo, Japan	214,567
68	Akemi Yamaoka, Japan	213,601
69	Deb Richard, USA	212,468
70	Yuko Saito, Japan	203,591
71	Jane Crafter, USA	196,936
72	Keiko Arai, Japan	191,765
73	Yuka Irie, Japan	190,391
74	Kim Saiki, USA	187,266
75	Yuko Moriguchi, Japan	179,715
76	Tracy Hanson, USA	175,895
77	Beth Daniel, USA	171,403
78	Vicki Goetze, USA	171,212
79	Fuki Kido, Japan	170,078
80	Aiko Takasu, Japan	165,491
81	Junko Yasui, Japan	162,954
82	Carin Hj Koch, Sweden	161,825
83	Michie Ohba, Japan	159,864
84	Dale Eggeling, USA	159,440
85	Man-Soo Kim, Korea	156,056
86	Cheng Mei-Chi, Taiwan	154,841
87	Cathy Johnstone-Forbes, USA	150,688
88	Hiromi Takamura, Japan	150,313
89	Maggie Will, USA	147,522
90	Huang Bie-Shyun, Taiwan	145,993
91	Fumiko Muraguchi, Japan	144,917
92	Amy Benz, USA	143,748
93	Chikayo Yamazaki, Japan	140,005
94	Betsy King, USA	136,459
95	Vicki Fergon, USA	134,301
96	Li Wen-Lin, Taiwan	132,701
97	Stefania Croce, Italy	125,829
98	Dawn Coe-Jones, Canada	124,341
99	Lisa Hackney, England	123,139
100	Cindy Schreyer, USA	123,134

American Tours

Mercedes Championships

La Costa Resort & Spa, Carlsbad, California
Par 36-36–72; 7,022 yards

January 4-7
purse, $1,000,000

	SCORES				TOTAL	MONEY
Mark O'Meara	68	69	66	68	271	$180,000
Nick Faldo	70	69	68	67	274	88,000
Scott Hoch	69	69	70	66	274	88,000
Bob Tway	71	69	70	66	276	48,000
Brad Bryant	70	70	69	68	277	40,000
Davis Love III	72	71	67	68	278	36,000
Jim Gallagher, Jr.	71	67	70	71	279	30,625
Lee Janzen	71	65	72	71	279	30,625
Corey Pavin	67	71	70	71	279	30,625
Duffy Waldorf	71	70	69	69	279	30,625
Ben Crenshaw	69	71	69	71	280	26,750
Tom Lehman	71	69	72	70	282	24,750
Loren Roberts	71	71	70	70	282	24,750
Payne Stewart	74	69	71	68	282	24,750
Kenny Perry	70	74	70	69	283	22,750
Fred Funk	70	73	72	69	284	21,750
Steve Elkington	70	72	70	73	285	20,750
Greg Norman	73	73	73	67	286	20,000
Billy Mayfair	73	75	69	70	287	18,500
Hal Sutton	76	73	69	69	287	18,500
D.A. Weibring	69	75	72	71	287	18,500
Jim Furyk	74	68	72	74	288	17,000
John Morse	74	71	72	71	288	17,000
Mark Calcavecchia	73	69	72	75	289	16,000
Vijay Singh	73	71	72	73	289	16,000
Woody Austin	71	73	75	72	291	15,500
Ed Dougherty	74	73	73	73	293	15,250
Phil Mickelson	74	72	74	74	294	15,050
Ted Tryba	71	76	74	74	295	14,850
John Daly	76	75	73	75	299	14,650

Nortel Open

Tucson National Golf Resort
Par 36-36–72; 7,148 yards

January 11-14
purse, $1,250,000

Starr Pass Golf Club
Par 35-36–71; 6,942 yards
Tucson, Arizona

	SCORES				TOTAL	MONEY
Phil Mickelson	69	66	71	67	273	$225,000
Bob Tway	69	71	68	67	275	135,000
Bob Estes	69	67	71	69	276	60,000
Fred Funk	70	69	68	69	276	60,000

		SCORES			TOTAL	MONEY
Mike Hulbert	69	68	72	67	276	60,000
Lee Janzen	69	72	66	69	276	60,000
Omar Uresti	68	70	72	67	277	40,312.50
John Wilson	70	72	67	68	277	40,312.50
Ronnie Black	68	71	66	73	278	32,500
Bruce Lietzke	71	68	68	71	278	32,500
Curtis Strange	68	73	67	70	278	32,500
David Toms	69	66	69	74	278	32,500
Woody Austin	69	72	69	69	279	20,781.25
Keith Fergus	71	72	67	69	279	20,781.25
Nolan Henke	70	72	71	66	279	20,781.25
Steve Jones	73	68	70	68	279	20,781.25
Bob Lohr	70	71	66	72	279	20,781.25
Larry Nelson	65	77	68	69	279	20,781.25
Kevin Sutherland	71	70	70	68	279	20,781.25
Grant Waite	70	67	73	69	279	20,781.25
John Huston	71	71	70	68	280	14,000
Len Mattiace	74	67	70	69	280	14,000
Jesper Parnevik	70	71	73	66	280	14,000
Bart Bryant	68	74	69	70	281	11,000
Brad Bryant	71	71	70	69	281	11,000
Loren Roberts	68	72	70	71	281	11,000
Michael Bradley	69	73	68	72	282	8,320.63
Doug Martin	70	73	72	67	282	8,320.63
Mark O'Meara	68	74	67	73	282	8,320.63
Manny Zerman	67	76	69	70	282	8,320.63
Joel Edwards	67	67	72	76	282	8,320.62
Jim Gallagher, Jr.	70	66	74	72	282	8,320.62
Justin Leonard	72	70	69	71	282	8,320.62
Dillard Pruitt	66	73	68	75	282	8,320.62
John Adams	70	70	72	71	283	6,162
Phil Blackmar	69	73	71	70	283	6,162
Jim Carter	73	69	71	70	283	6,162
Steve Lowery	70	71	74	68	283	6,162
Bobby Wadkins	73	68	72	70	283	6,162
Chip Beck	72	69	69	74	284	4,380.56
Bryan Gorman	72	70	69	73	284	4,380.56
Scott Hoch	74	69	72	69	284	4,380.56
Jeff Julian	71	70	72	71	284	4,380.56
Jay Williamson	74	69	69	72	284	4,380.56
John Cook	70	70	72	72	284	4,380.55
John Morse	67	71	71	75	284	4,380.55
Steve Pate	68	69	73	74	284	4,380.55
Dicky Pride	71	69	75	69	284	4,380.55
Dan Pohl	68	75	69	73	285	3,028.58
Joe Daley	73	68	69	75	285	3,028.57
Allen Doyle	72	69	74	70	285	3,028.57
David Edwards	71	71	69	74	285	3,028.57
Jeff Maggert	73	68	67	77	285	3,028.57
Gil Morgan	68	75	71	71	285	3,028.57
Sean Murphy	68	70	73	74	285	3,028.57
Olin Browne	73	69	73	71	286	2,762.50
Patrick Burke	73	66	76	71	286	2,762.50
Brian Kamm	69	72	72	73	286	2,762.50
Billy Mayfair	72	70	73	71	286	2,762.50
Joey Sindelar	74	69	70	73	286	2,762.50
Taylor Smith	72	71	72	71	286	2,762.50
Mike Swartz	73	70	71	72	286	2,762.50
Scott Verplank	68	73	68	77	286	2,762.50

	SCORES				TOTAL	MONEY
Jerry Kelly	70	73	72	72	287	2,612.50
Tom Scherrer	73	70	71	73	287	2,612.50
Mike Standly	73	69	77	68	287	2,612.50
Steve Stricker	72	71	73	71	287	2,612.50
Curt Byrum	69	73	76	70	288	2,512.50
Jay Delsing	72	71	74	71	288	2,512.50
Todd Dempsey	73	70	75	70	288	2,512.50
David Peoples	73	70	72	73	288	2,512.50
Michael Allen	70	73	70	76	289	2,425
Chris Smith	73	70	72	74	289	2,425
Robert Wrenn	70	73	73	73	289	2,425
Steve Jurgensen	70	72	76	74	292	2,375
Brian Tennyson	73	70	75	76	294	2,350
Steve Hart	70	73	73	79	295	2,325
Andy Bean	71	72	81	81	305	2,300

Bob Hope Chrysler Classic

Indian Ridge Country Club
Par 36-36–72; 7,037 yards

January 17-21
purse, $1,300,000

Bermuda Dunes Country Club
Par 36-36–72; 6,927 yards

Indian Wells Country Club
Par 36-36–72; 6,478 yards

Tamarisk Country Club
Par 36-36–72; 6,881 yards
Palm Desert, California

	SCORES					TOTAL	MONEY
Mark Brooks	66	68	69	67	67	337	$234,000
John Huston	69	71	65	65	68	338	140,400
Scott Hoch	70	69	67	68	65	339	88,400
Brad Bryant	71	65	65	71	68	340	53,733.34
Nolan Henke	69	69	64	69	69	340	53,733.33
Payne Stewart	71	65	71	63	70	340	53,733.33
Fred Couples	72	67	67	65	70	341	39,162.50
Paul Goydos	69	64	70	69	69	341	39,162.50
Jeff Maggert	69	68	69	64	71	341	39,162.50
Kenny Perry	75	69	67	65	65	341	39,162.50
Woody Austin	74	66	69	66	67	342	31,200
Jim Furyk	72	67	67	67	69	342	31,200
Tom Kite	68	68	69	68	70	343	24,375
Bruce Lietzke	69	71	70	65	68	343	24,375
Jesper Parnevik	72	68	65	67	71	343	24,375
Omar Uresti	70	70	69	66	68	343	24,375
Jay Haas	68	72	72	67	65	344	20,150
Mike Springer	68	71	73	64	68	344	20,150
Jay Don Blake	67	72	72	66	68	345	17,550
Naomichi Ozaki	70	71	69	67	68	345	17,550
Brad Faxon	73	73	66	66	68	346	11,873.34
Brian Henninger	71	71	67	69	68	346	11,873.34
Sandy Lyle	72	69	68	69	68	346	11,873.34
David Edwards	70	71	72	68	65	346	11,873.33
Donnie Hammond	67	69	67	71	72	346	11,873.33

	SCORES					TOTAL	MONEY
Scott McCarron	74	68	71	65	68	346	11,873.33
Larry Nelson	72	70	71	68	65	346	11,873.33
Dave Stockton, Jr.	70	68	71	68	69	346	11,873.33
Mark Wiebe	70	68	65	73	70	346	11,873.33
Fulton Allem	68	68	67	70	74	347	8,450
Lee Rinker	68	70	67	71	71	347	8,450
Mike Standly	73	70	70	68	66	347	8,450
Stuart Appleby	73	69	70	70	66	348	6,581.25
Mark Calcavecchia	67	68	71	71	71	348	6,581.25
David Duval	70	72	70	64	72	348	6,581.25
Keith Fergus	74	68	71	67	68	348	6,581.25
Kelly Gibson	77	70	64	67	70	348	6,581.25
Scott Gump	69	69	71	68	71	348	6,581.25
Bob Lohr	72	68	66	70	72	348	6,581.25
Curtis Strange	71	69	68	72	68	348	6,581.25
Joe Acosta, Jr.	71	68	74	66	70	349	5,070
Lennie Clements	72	74	68	65	70	349	5,070
Jonathan Kaye	78	67	64	70	70	349	5,070
Tommy Armour III	73	69	67	72	69	350	4,040.40
Steve Jones	69	72	71	69	69	350	4,040.40
Brian Kamm	66	68	72	74	70	350	4,040.40
Neal Lancaster	76	69	69	67	69	350	4,040.40
Grant Waite	72	74	69	66	69	350	4,040.40
Allen Doyle	70	72	68	68	73	351	3,149.72
Robert Gamez	71	67	76	66	71	351	3,149.72
Steve Pate	70	73	70	67	71	351	3,149.72
Mike Donald	72	69	69	73	68	351	3,149.71
Jerry Kelly	70	71	68	73	69	351	3,149.71
Hugh Royer III	72	72	72	65	70	351	3,149.71
Ted Tryba	71	70	71	68	71	351	3,149.71
Billy Andrade	74	71	70	67	70	352	2,912
Peter Jacobsen	72	70	70	71	69	352	2,912
Gil Morgan	71	71	72	67	71	352	2,912
Mark O'Meara	75	66	70	71	70	352	2,912
Scott Simpson	71	74	70	68	69	352	2,912
John Adams	69	66	71	69	78	353	2,743
Tim Herron	73	71	72	66	71	353	2,743
John Inman	70	73	68	70	72	353	2,743
Justin Leonard	71	70	71	69	72	353	2,743
Doug Martin	73	68	70	71	71	353	2,743
Larry Mize	72	68	73	70	70	353	2,743
Ted Schulz	70	73	67	71	72	353	2,743
David Toms	71	69	71	70	72	353	2,743
Brian Claar	70	73	69	71	71	354	2,626
Jay Delsing	69	70	71	72	73	355	2,600
Bob Gilder	70	69	75	67	75	356	2,548
Gary McCord	75	71	65	69	76	356	2,548
Dillard Pruitt	73	68	70	70	75	356	2,548
Robin Freeman	71	72	70	69	75	357	2,496

Phoenix Open

TPC of Scottsdale, Scottsdale, Arizona
Par 35-36–71; 6,992 yards

January 24-27
purse, $1,300,000

	SCORES				TOTAL	MONEY
Phil Mickelson	69	67	66	67	269	$234,000
Justin Leonard	67	67	66	69	269	140,400
(Mickelson defeated Leonard on third extra hole.)						
Tom Scherrer	67	70	65	68	270	88,400
Mark Calcavecchia	72	69	68	62	271	57,200
John Wilson	67	71	67	66	271	57,200
Woody Austin	65	67	72	68	272	42,087.50
Curt Byrum	69	69	72	62	272	42,087.50
Rocco Mediate	70	67	68	67	272	42,087.50
Scott Simpson	67	71	68	66	272	42,087.50
Steve Jones	67	67	72	67	273	31,200
Sandy Lyle	68	72	67	66	273	31,200
Blaine McCallister	69	69	67	68	273	31,200
Kenny Perry	69	69	66	69	273	31,200
Andrew Magee	68	69	69	68	274	23,400
Grant Waite	70	71	73	60	274	23,400
Tom Watson	68	71	66	69	274	23,400
David Frost	69	70	69	67	275	18,850
Barry Lane	68	68	69	70	275	18,850
Dan Pohl	66	72	69	68	275	18,850
Mark Wiebe	70	71	67	67	275	18,850
Paul Azinger	69	71	70	66	276	13,520
Don Pooley	68	67	67	74	276	13,520
Vijay Singh	68	69	69	70	276	13,520
Bob Tway	66	71	69	70	276	13,520
Scott Verplank	69	66	77	64	276	13,520
Michael Bradley	69	69	71	68	277	8,847.23
Kelly Gibson	73	68	68	68	277	8,847.23
Mark Brooks	68	73	67	69	277	8,847.22
Joey Gullion	65	75	70	67	277	8,847.22
Scott Hoch	71	67	67	72	277	8,847.22
Doug Martin	68	69	70	70	277	8,847.22
Scott McCarron	71	69	70	67	277	8,847.22
Mike Standly	71	66	73	67	277	8,847.22
Ted Tryba	72	68	67	70	277	8,847.22
Joe Acosta, Jr.	67	73	68	70	278	6,272.50
Brandel Chamblee	69	71	68	70	278	6,272.50
David Duval	68	70	69	71	278	6,272.50
Billy Mayfair	73	68	68	69	278	6,272.50
Jesper Parnevik	67	66	71	74	278	6,272.50
Payne Stewart	68	71	71	68	278	6,272.50
Jay Don Blake	67	72	67	73	279	4,550
Rick Fehr	69	71	68	71	279	4,550
Fred Funk	68	70	69	72	279	4,550
Scott Gump	69	71	68	71	279	4,550
Lee Janzen	69	69	70	71	279	4,550
David Ogrin	72	70	70	67	279	4,550
Dicky Pride	71	69	72	67	279	4,550
Olin Browne	69	72	70	69	280	3,307.20
Jerry Kelly	71	71	69	69	280	3,307.20
John Morse	70	70	70	70	280	3,307.20
Charlie Rymer	69	71	67	73	280	3,307.20
Kirk Triplett	69	72	74	65	280	3,307.20
Mike Brisky	68	73	70	70	281	3,024.67

	SCORES				TOTAL	MONEY
Bruce Lietzke	69	70	71	71	281	3,024.67
Craig Stadler	68	73	70	70	281	3,024.66
Franklin Langham	64	74	72	72	282	2,938
Tom Purtzer	70	68	73	71	282	2,938
Jeff Sluman	70	70	67	75	282	2,938
John Huston	73	69	70	71	283	2,873
Steve Pate	71	70	72	70	283	2,873
Robert Gamez	73	69	68	74	284	2,782
Tom Kite	70	72	71	71	284	2,782
Gene Sauers	65	74	75	70	284	2,782
Dave Stockton, Jr.	69	71	75	69	284	2,782
Howard Twitty	66	73	70	75	284	2,782
Mike Reid	70	72	73	71	286	2,691
Chris Smith	71	67	72	76	286	2,691
Brian Henninger	70	69	75	76	290	2,639
Jim McGovern	71	70	76	73	290	2,639
Billy Andrade	67	75	77	72	291	2,600

AT&T Pebble Beach National Pro-Am

Pebble Beach Golf Links
Par 36-36–72; 6,799 yards

February 1-4
purse, $1,500,000

Spyglass Hill Golf Course
Par 36-36–72; 6,810 yards
Pebble Beach, California
(Event cancelled after second round.)

	SCORES		TOTAL	MONEY
Jeff Maggert	68	68	136	$5,000
Loren Roberts	68	69	137	5,000
Steve Jones	69	68	137	5,000
Davis Love III	71	66	137	5,000
Jay Haas	69	69	138	5,000
Tom Watson	69	69	138	5,000
Nick Faldo	69	69	138	5,000
Howard Clark	69	69	138	5,000
Jim McGovern	69	69	138	5,000
Phil Mickelson	72	66	138	5,000
Naomichi Ozaki	72	66	138	5,000
John Elliott	67	71	138	5,000
Steve Stricker	69	70	139	5,000
Tommy Tolles	69	70	139	5,000
Doug Martin	71	68	139	5,000
Craig Stadler	68	71	139	5,000
Joe Daley	72	67	139	5,000
Kenny Perry	70	69	139	5,000
Tom Purtzer	68	71	139	5,000
Mike Springer	68	71	139	5,000
Kirk Triplett	69	70	139	5,000
Omar Uresti	69	70	139	5,000
Franklin Langham	68	71	139	5,000
Billy Andrade	70	69	139	5,000
David Frost	69	70	139	5,000
Justin Leonard	67	73	140	5,000
Shigeki Maruyama	71	69	140	5,000
Guy Boros	71	69	140	5,000

	SCORES		TOTAL	MONEY
Steve Jurgensen	68	72	140	5,000
Jeff Hart	71	69	140	5,000
Jesper Parnevik	71	69	140	5,000
Steve Elkington	72	69	141	5,000
Bob Lohr	73	68	141	5,000
Mark Wiebe	70	71	141	5,000
Vijay Singh	70	71	141	5,000
Mark Brooks	71	70	141	5,000
Greg Kraft	71	70	141	5,000
Gil Morgan	73	68	141	5,000
Ernie Els	69	72	141	5,000
Fred Schulz	72	69	141	5,000
Joey Sindelar	68	73	141	5,000
Bill Porter	70	71	141	5,000
Willie Wood	70	71	141	5,000
Bob Gilder	71	71	142	5,000
Lee Rinker	68	74	142	5,000
Brian Tennyson	70	72	142	5,000
Tom Scherrer	72	70	142	5,000
Shane Bertsch	72	70	142	5,000
Donnie Hammond	69	73	142	5,000
Neal Lancaster	70	72	142	5,000
Dave Stockton, Jr.	71	71	142	5,000
Dillard Pruitt	72	70	142	5,000
Jeff Gallagher	71	71	142	5,000
Russ Cochran	70	72	142	5,000
Fred Funk	72	70	142	5,000
Brad Faxon	73	69	142	5,000
Tom Lehman	70	72	142	5,000
John Maginnes	71	71	142	5,000
Bryan Gorman	71	71	142	5,000
Howard Twitty	69	73	142	5,000
Ronnie Black	72	70	142	5,000
Fuzzy Zoeller	68	74	142	5,000
Joey Gullion	69	73	142	5,000
Mike Reid	70	73	143	5,000
Woody Austin	68	75	143	5,000
George Burns	74	69	143	5,000
Kelly Gibson	71	72	143	5,000
Chris Smith	70	73	143	5,000
Frank Lickliter	70	73	143	5,000
Mark O'Meara	74	69	143	5,000
Billy Ray Brown	74	69	143	5,000
Jim Furyk	75	68	143	5,000
John Inman	72	71	143	5,000
Andy Bean	71	72	143	5,000
Brad Fabel	71	72	143	5,000
John Wilson	71	72	143	5,000
Jack Nicklaus	71	72	143	5,000
Brian Henninger	69	74	143	5,000
Joe Acosta, Jr.	71	72	143	5,000
Tom Kite	75	68	143	5,000
Scott McCarron	74	69	143	5,000
Ben Crenshaw	70	74	144	5,000
Paul Azinger	73	71	144	5,000
Mark McCumber	71	73	144	5,000
Peter Jacobsen	72	72	144	5,000
Bill Kratzert	73	71	144	5,000
Rocco Mediate	71	73	144	5,000
Jay Delsing	70	74	144	5,000

	SCORES		TOTAL	MONEY
Ted Tryba	72	72	144	5,000
Jim Gallagher	75	69	144	5,000
Jim Carter	71	73	144	5,000
Lee Janzen	70	74	144	5,000
Mike Hulbert	72	72	144	5,000
Pete Jordan	75	69	144	5,000
John Adams	72	72	144	5,000
Fulton Allem	72	72	144	5,000
Bobby Wadkins	69	75	144	5,000
Payne Stewart	72	72	144	5,000
Jay Williamson	71	73	144	5,000
Terrence Miskell	75	69	144	5,000
Johnny Miller	75	70	145	5,000
Gary Rusnak	71	74	145	5,000
Mark Pfeil	72	73	145	5,000
Mike Standly	75	70	145	5,000
Duffy Waldorf	70	75	145	5,000
Sandy Lyle	70	75	145	5,000
Scott Gump	73	72	145	5,000
Clarence Rose	72	73	145	5,000
David Toms	73	73	146	5,000
Patrick Burke	72	74	146	5,000
Roger Maltbie	75	71	146	5,000
Arnold Palmer	74	72	146	5,000
Kiyoshi Murota	74	72	146	5,000
Scott Simpson	70	76	146	5,000
Len Mattiace	74	72	146	5,000
Mike Brisky	77	69	146	5,000
Jim Nelford	73	73	146	5,000
Sean Murphy	75	71	146	5,000
Paul Goydos	77	69	146	5,000
Bruce Fleisher	75	71	146	5,000
Hugh Royer III	71	75	146	5,000
Charlie Rymer	74	73	147	5,000
Keith Clearwater	75	72	147	5,000
Andrew Magee	72	75	147	5,000
Jeff Sluman	74	73	147	5,000
Robert Wrenn	77	70	147	5,000
Jeff Brehaut	76	71	147	5,000
Stan Utley	72	75	147	5,000
David Ogrin	75	72	147	5,000
Jarmo Sandelin	74	74	148	5,000
Brad Bryant	76	72	148	5,000
Tommy Armour III	74	74	148	5,000
Bob Estes	74	74	148	5,000
David Duval	73	75	148	5,000
Kevin Sutherland	74	74	148	5,000
Stuart Appleby	77	71	148	5,000
Brian Kamm	71	77	148	5,000
Chip Beck	72	76	148	5,000
Steve Rintoul	75	73	148	5,000
Paul Stankowski	74	74	148	5,000
Jerry Kelly	76	72	148	5,000
Jodie Mudd	76	73	149	5,000
Olin Browne	75	74	149	5,000
Shawn McEntee	72	77	149	5,000
Ron Whittaker	75	74	149	5,000
Lon Hinkle	75	74	149	5,000
Gene Sauers	73	76	149	5,000
Blaine McCallister	74	75	149	5,000

	SCORES		TOTAL	MONEY
Mike Swartz	73	76	149	5,000
Tim Herron	73	76	149	5,000
Jerry Foltz	71	78	149	5,000
Dennis Trixler	75	74	149	5,000
Robin Freeman	75	74	149	5,000
Bart Bryant	71	78	149	5,000
Michael Bradley	74	76	150	5,000
Greg Twiggs	77	73	150	5,000
Chris Perry	76	74	150	5,000
Ken Green	75	75	150	5,000
Mike McCullough	73	77	150	5,000
Charlie Gibson	73	77	150	5,000
Hisayuki Sasaki	73	77	150	5,000
Emlyn Aubrey	74	77	151	5,000
Tommy Masters	79	72	151	5,000
Grant Waite	77	74	151	5,000
Larry Nelson	73	78	151	5,000
Jeff Julian	72	79	151	5,000
Gary Hallberg	81	71	152	5,000
Taylor Smith	76	76	152	5,000
David Graham	75	77	152	5,000
Jack Nicklaus II	76	76	152	5,000
Barry Lane	73	79	152	5,000
Mark Hayes	75	78	153	5,000
Laird Small	76	77	153	5,000
Scott Medlin	78	75	153	5,000
Larry Rinker	79	75	154	5,000
Dave Fowler	79	77	156	5,000
Joel Edwards	77	80	157	5,000
Scott Dunlap	79	78	157	5,000
Carl Paulson	75	82	157	5,000
John Flannery	78	84	162	5,000

Buick Invitational

Torrey Pines Golf Course, La Jolla, California
South Course: Par 36-36–72; 7,000 yards
North Course: Par 36-36–72; 6,592 yards

February 8-11
purse, $1,200,000

	SCORES				TOTAL	MONEY
Davis Love III	66	70	69	64	269	$216,000
Phil Mickelson	68	70	66	67	271	129,600
Lennie Clements	64	65	72	71	272	54,120
Marco Dawson	66	70	70	66	272	54,120
Tom Lehman	63	70	70	69	272	54,120
Mark O'Meara	65	72	66	69	272	54,120
Scott Simpson	66	69	69	68	272	54,120
Mark Calcavecchia	68	66	70	69	273	36,000
Nick Faldo	69	70	70	64	273	36,000
Jesper Parnevik	68	67	68	71	274	31,200
Joey Sindelar	69	66	70	69	274	31,200
John Adams	68	67	68	72	275	25,200
Fred Couples	68	65	75	67	275	25,200
Jay Haas	67	72	69	67	275	25,200
Steve Elkington	68	72	66	70	276	19,200
Jim Gallagher, Jr.	68	69	68	71	276	19,200
Doug Martin	63	71	71	71	276	19,200

	SCORES				TOTAL	MONEY
Kirk Triplett	63	70	69	74	276	19,200
Duffy Waldorf	67	66	72	71	276	19,200
Paul Azinger	67	71	71	68	277	13,980
Brad Bryant	69	68	71	69	277	13,980
Kelly Gibson	66	70	68	73	277	13,980
Hisayuki Sasaki	68	69	68	72	277	13,980
Michael Bradley	64	74	68	72	278	9,285
Brad Faxon	67	72	70	69	278	9,285
Rick Fehr	68	72	70	68	278	9,285
Tim Herron	71	68	70	69	278	9,285
David Ogrin	71	68	68	71	278	9,285
Clarence Rose	66	69	70	73	278	9,285
Craig Stadler	70	69	66	73	278	9,285
Omar Uresti	67	73	66	72	278	9,285
Steve Stricker	67	67	73	72	279	7,100
Hal Sutton	68	69	73	69	279	7,100
John Wilson	65	66	73	75	279	7,100
Allen Doyle	66	73	68	73	280	5,298
Scott Dunlap	69	70	69	72	280	5,298
Pete Jordan	68	67	74	71	280	5,298
Larry Mize	71	67	71	71	280	5,298
Sean Murphy	70	70	72	68	280	5,298
Loren Roberts	70	69	70	71	280	5,298
Taylor Smith	65	71	72	72	280	5,298
Mike Springer	68	71	73	68	280	5,298
Payne Stewart	68	68	71	73	280	5,298
Mark Wiebe	69	66	69	76	280	5,298
Danny Briggs	69	71	69	72	281	3,720
David Edwards	69	68	72	72	281	3,720
Peter Jacobsen	69	71	73	68	281	3,720
Jeff Gallagher	71	67	71	73	282	2,955
Bob Lohr	68	69	74	71	282	2,955
Scott McCarron	73	67	72	70	282	2,955
Jim McGovern	74	66	71	71	282	2,955
Adam Spring	66	74	72	70	282	2,955
Kevin Sutherland	70	70	71	71	282	2,955
Brian Tennyson	70	70	73	69	282	2,955
Jay Williamson	70	69	72	71	282	2,955
Billy Ray Brown	69	70	72	72	283	2,688
Keith Fergus	66	71	73	73	283	2,688
Joey Gullion	67	67	73	76	283	2,688
Greg Twiggs	73	66	73	71	283	2,688
Scott Verplank	71	69	70	73	283	2,688
Jay Don Blake	71	69	73	71	284	2,568
Olin Browne	72	67	72	73	284	2,568
Brad Fabel	70	70	71	73	284	2,568
Dillard Pruitt	69	71	73	71	284	2,568
Lee Rinker	70	70	70	74	284	2,568
Dan Forsman	68	69	72	76	285	2,448
Bill Glasson	72	68	71	74	285	2,448
Nolan Henke	71	69	74	71	285	2,448
Jeff Julian	66	72	73	74	285	2,448
Chris Perry	70	67	75	73	285	2,448
Neal Lancaster	72	66	75	73	286	2,376
Bryan Gorman	72	68	77	70	287	2,352
Paul Goydos	70	69	74	75	288	2,316
Charlie Rymer	69	70	75	74	288	2,316
Joe Daley	70	69	78	74	291	2,280
*Charley Hoffman	69	71	77	76	293	
Wayne Levi	70	70	80	77	297	2,256

United Airlines Hawaiian Open

Waialae Country Club, Honolulu, Hawaii
Par 36-36—72; 6,975 yards

February 15-18
purse, $1,200,000

	SCORES				TOTAL	MONEY
Jim Furyk	68	71	69	69	277	$216,000
Brad Faxon	74	67	66	70	277	129,600
(Furyk defeated Faxon on third extra hole.)						
Steve Stricker	69	70	68	71	278	81,600
Tom Lehman	74	68	67	70	279	47,250
Larry Mize	71	71	67	70	279	47,250
David Ogrin	74	69	67	69	279	47,250
Scott Simpson	68	76	67	68	279	47,250
John Morse	74	73	64	69	280	34,800
Vijay Singh	72	70	71	67	280	34,800
Jeff Sluman	74	69	67	70	280	34,800
Emlyn Aubrey	72	73	65	71	281	25,440
Paul Azinger	71	70	71	69	281	25,440
Russ Cochran	73	66	70	72	281	25,440
Larry Nelson	71	74	67	69	281	25,440
Naomichi Ozaki	72	74	68	67	281	25,440
Lennie Clements	71	71	69	71	282	18,000
Joel Edwards	73	71	68	70	282	18,000
Brad Fabel	69	70	70	73	282	18,000
Brian Henninger	74	72	69	67	282	18,000
Len Mattiace	74	72	68	68	282	18,000
Mark Brooks	72	71	69	71	283	11,605.72
Allen Doyle	74	71	69	69	283	11,605.72
John Maginnes	75	68	71	69	283	11,605.72
Jeff Gallagher	76	70	67	70	283	11,605.71
Jeff Hart	71	70	69	73	283	11,605.71
David Ishii	74	73	69	67	283	11,605.71
Wayne Levi	67	73	73	70	283	11,605.71
Scott Dunlap	72	73	68	71	284	8,520
Nobuo Serizawa	76	70	66	72	284	8,520
Brian Tennyson	73	69	70	72	284	8,520
Stuart Appleby	78	69	67	71	285	6,660
Billy Ray Brown	72	75	74	64	285	6,660
Brandel Chamblee	73	67	75	70	285	6,660
Brian Claar	70	73	72	70	285	6,660
Jeff Julian	73	71	68	73	285	6,660
Neal Lancaster	73	71	72	69	285	6,660
Jesper Parnevik	75	67	72	71	285	6,660
Dan Pohl	70	72	70	73	285	6,660
Phil Blackmar	71	70	72	73	286	4,560
Jim Carter	72	71	71	72	286	4,560
Keith Clearwater	70	70	74	72	286	4,560
Nolan Henke	71	73	68	74	286	4,560
Steve Jurgensen	72	73	70	71	286	4,560
Frank Lickliter	73	70	69	74	286	4,560
Scott Medlin	70	73	72	71	286	4,560
Tray Tyner	76	69	68	73	286	4,560
Dave Barr	71	75	66	75	287	3,045
Chip Beck	74	72	71	70	287	3,045
Curt Byrum	72	74	71	70	287	3,045
Lucas Parsons	73	73	68	73	287	3,045
Dave Rummells	77	69	71	70	287	3,045
Gary Rusnak	70	72	69	76	287	3,045
Gene Sauers	73	69	72	73	287	3,045

	SCORES				TOTAL	MONEY
Lanny Wadkins	74	72	68	73	287	3,045
Jay Don Blake	69	73	71	75	288	2,676
Pete Jordan	72	73	73	70	288	2,676
Sean Murphy	76	71	72	69	288	2,676
Kenny Perry	72	69	74	73	288	2,676
Lee Rinker	73	72	71	72	288	2,676
Hisayuki Sasaki	74	71	72	71	288	2,676
Taylor Smith	75	71	70	72	288	2,676
Craig Stadler	72	72	73	71	288	2,676
Guy Boros	74	73	72	70	289	2,544
Gary Hallberg	70	71	73	75	289	2,544
John Huston	72	71	73	73	289	2,544
Steve Jones	73	73	71	73	290	2,472
Chris Perry	72	72	70	76	290	2,472
Ted Tryba	69	76	74	71	290	2,472
Robin Freeman	71	72	73	75	291	2,412
Mike Sullivan	75	68	72	76	291	2,412
Hugh Royer III	78	69	68	77	292	2,376
Bill Glasson	73	72	74	74	293	2,340
Hidemichi Tanaka	74	73	72	74	293	2,340
Mike Donald	77	70	75	72	294	2,292
Tim Herron	73	72	72	77	294	2,292
Kevin Sutherland	76	70	71	79	296	2,256
Brian Kamm	72	75	76	77	300	2,232

Nissan Open

Riviera Country Club, Pacific Palisades, California
Par 35-36–71; 6,946 yards

February 22-25
purse, $1,200,000

	SCORES				TOTAL	MONEY
Craig Stadler	67	70	73	68	278	$216,000
Mark Brooks	74	69	72	64	279	79,200
Fred Couples	69	70	71	69	279	79,200
Scott Simpson	68	70	70	71	279	79,200
Mark Wiebe	70	70	68	71	279	79,200
Kelly Gibson	70	69	71	70	280	38,850
Tom Lehman	70	70	68	72	280	38,850
Hugh Royer III	71	70	73	66	280	38,850
Lanny Wadkins	69	70	69	72	280	38,850
Steve Elkington	67	70	73	71	281	28,800
Peter Jacobsen	71	72	66	72	281	28,800
Bob Tway	71	68	69	73	281	28,800
Omar Uresti	71	72	69	69	281	28,800
Jay Don Blake	70	71	69	72	282	22,200
Sean Murphy	71	70	70	71	282	22,200
Neal Lancaster	73	68	65	77	283	20,400
John Daly	73	70	72	69	284	17,400
Billy Mayfair	73	67	72	72	284	17,400
Corey Pavin	71	71	71	71	284	17,400
Don Pooley	70	71	67	76	284	17,400
Patrick Burke	73	70	72	70	285	12,480
Brad Fabel	70	72	71	72	285	12,480
Bob Lohr	72	71	72	70	285	12,480
Gil Morgan	71	73	72	69	285	12,480
Kevin Sutherland	75	66	72	72	285	12,480
Phil Blackmar	72	69	72	73	286	8,340

	SCORES			TOTAL	MONEY
Brandel Chamblee	72	71	72	71	286	8,340
Lennie Clements	72	73	71	70	286	8,340
Rick Fehr	70	74	68	74	286	8,340
Franklin Langham	72	70	72	72	286	8,340
Scott McCarron	73	70	70	73	286	8,340
Kirk Triplett	69	70	75	72	286	8,340
Howard Twitty	72	70	72	72	286	8,340
Joel Edwards	72	69	74	72	287	6,060
Robin Freeman	70	75	69	73	287	6,060
Paul Goydos	74	70	70	73	287	6,060
Rocco Mediate	71	71	73	72	287	6,060
Mike Reid	71	69	73	74	287	6,060
Robert Wrenn	67	69	76	75	287	6,060
Chip Beck	68	71	76	73	288	4,800
Mike Brisky	70	71	72	75	288	4,800
Steve Lowery	72	68	71	77	288	4,800
Naomichi Ozaki	71	74	72	71	288	4,800
Olin Browne	73	70	72	74	289	3,468
Curt Byrum	73	71	72	73	289	3,468
Glen Day	71	70	71	77	289	3,468
Jay Haas	72	71	72	74	289	3,468
Jeff Hart	70	73	73	73	289	3,468
David Toms	68	73	74	74	289	3,468
Scott Verplank	72	73	73	71	289	3,468
Bobby Wadkins	72	71	74	72	289	3,468
Jim Carter	72	71	73	74	290	2,798.40
Kenny Perry	71	73	76	70	290	2,798.40
Tom Purtzer	72	71	71	76	290	2,798.40
Mike Riedel	73	70	73	74	290	2,798.40
Clarence Rose	72	71	71	76	290	2,798.40
Larry Mize	71	74	72	74	291	2,688
Yoshinori Mizumaki	72	72	70	77	291	2,688
Dan Pohl	70	75	74	72	291	2,688
Guy Boros	72	73	72	75	292	2,604
Keith Clearwater	72	69	73	78	292	2,604
Tim Herron	74	70	71	77	292	2,604
Tom Kite	74	69	74	75	292	2,604
Shane Bertsch	72	70	74	77	293	2,508
Mike Heinen	72	72	71	78	293	2,508
Steve Jurgensen	73	72	75	73	293	2,508
Mike Swartz	73	70	74	76	293	2,508
John Mahaffey	73	72	71	78	294	2,424
Blaine McCallister	73	72	72	77	294	2,424
Chris Smith	70	75	74	75	294	2,424
Brian Kamm	72	70	77	77	296	2,364
Hidemichi Tanaka	71	73	73	79	296	2,364
John Maginnes	72	72	78	75	297	2,328
Steve Stricker	69	73	79	77	298	2,304
Kevin Riley	74	71	79	78	302	2,280

Doral-Ryder Open

Doral Resort & Country Club, Miami, Florida
Par 36-36–72; 6,939 yards

February 29-March 3
purse, $1,800,000

	SCORES				TOTAL	MONEY
Greg Norman	67	69	67	66	269	$324,000
Michael Bradley	64	71	70	66	271	158,400
Vijay Singh	70	66	67	68	271	158,400
Fulton Allem	67	71	70	66	274	79,200
Jerry Kelly	67	71	69	67	274	79,200
Jay Haas	72	68	68	67	275	62,550
Naomichi Ozaki	69	65	71	70	275	62,550
Patrick Burke	67	73	68	69	277	46,800
Lennie Clements	71	67	68	71	277	46,800
Raymond Floyd	68	70	71	68	277	46,800
Larry Nelson	66	73	71	67	277	46,800
Jesper Parnevik	68	71	69	69	277	46,800
Jeff Sluman	66	71	72	68	277	46,800
Mike Brisky	66	73	68	71	278	30,600
Keith Clearwater	72	67	69	70	278	30,600
Glen Day	68	71	67	72	278	30,600
Wayne Levi	69	73	71	65	278	30,600
John Morse	67	73	68	70	278	30,600
Ben Crenshaw	68	71	68	72	279	25,200
Phil Blackmar	69	72	69	70	280	20,232
Steve Jones	70	72	72	66	280	20,232
Nick Price	73	69	70	68	280	20,232
Loren Roberts	69	73	68	70	280	20,232
Scott Verplank	66	74	69	71	280	20,232
Rick Fehr	68	71	70	72	281	14,700
Bob Lohr	70	70	73	68	281	14,700
Corey Pavin	66	72	71	72	281	14,700
Woody Austin	69	71	71	71	282	11,970
John Cook	72	68	70	72	282	11,970
Marco Dawson	69	71	70	72	282	11,970
Steve Elkington	71	71	72	68	282	11,970
Nick Faldo	72	68	70	72	282	11,970
Nolan Henke	68	70	74	70	282	11,970
Fred Funk	72	71	69	71	283	9,495
John Inman	71	69	72	71	283	9,495
Rocco Mediate	69	72	70	72	283	9,495
Tom Scherrer	67	73	73	70	283	9,495
Kelly Gibson	66	76	69	73	284	7,920
Tom Kite	72	70	74	68	284	7,920
Justin Leonard	69	69	73	73	284	7,920
Phil Mickelson	72	68	74	70	284	7,920
Curt Byrum	65	76	70	74	285	5,791.50
David Frost	69	72	73	71	285	5,791.50
Scott Gump	72	71	70	72	285	5,791.50
Bruce Lietzke	72	72	70	71	285	5,791.50
Andrew Magee	71	73	68	73	285	5,791.50
Mike Springer	68	76	66	75	285	5,791.50
Bob Tway	69	75	71	70	285	5,791.50
Omar Uresti	66	78	71	70	285	5,791.50
John Adams	68	75	70	73	286	4,252.50
Mark Brooks	72	72	71	71	286	4,252.50
Paul Goydos	71	73	73	69	286	4,252.50
Lee Janzen	63	76	72	75	286	4,252.50
Billy Mayfair	75	69	70	72	286	4,252.50

	SCORES				TOTAL	MONEY
Blaine McCallister	68	71	72	75	286	4,252.50
Hal Sutton	71	72	72	71	286	4,252.50
Bobby Wadkins	75	68	71	72	286	4,252.50
Fred Couples	75	68	71	73	287	3,960
Jim Furyk	70	74	72	71	287	3,960
Peter Jacobsen	71	72	73	71	287	3,960
Curtis Strange	74	70	74	69	287	3,960
Tommy Tolles	69	75	73	70	287	3,960
Chip Beck	73	70	75	70	288	3,834
Lee Rinker	70	74	71	73	288	3,834
Keith Fergus	71	73	73	72	289	3,726
Robert Gamez	72	71	76	70	289	3,726
Dicky Pride	69	74	73	73	289	3,726
Mark Wiebe	71	73	75	70	289	3,726
Stuart Appleby	71	72	74	73	290	3,600
David Edwards	70	73	74	73	290	3,600
Grant Waite	69	74	75	72	290	3,600
Brandel Chamblee	73	70	74	74	291	3,510
Mike Heinen	73	71	76	71	291	3,510
Mark Calcavecchia	71	71	78	73	293	3,438
Lanny Wadkins	71	73	75	74	293	3,438
David Toms	69	74	78	75	296	3,384
Steve Schneiter	73	71	76	80	300	3,348

Honda Classic

TPC at Eagle Trace, Coral Springs, Florida
Par 36-36–72; 7,040 yards

March 7-10
purse, $1,300,000

	SCORES				TOTAL	MONEY
Tim Herron	62	68	72	69	271	$234,000
Mark McCumber	69	68	69	69	275	140,400
Nick Price	66	72	70	68	276	67,600
Lee Rinker	64	75	68	69	276	67,600
Payne Stewart	70	70	68	68	276	67,600
Mark O'Meara	70	71	65	71	277	46,800
Michael Campbell	68	69	68	74	279	41,925
David Frost	70	69	70	70	279	41,925
Phil Blackmar	69	70	69	73	281	35,100
Nick Faldo	77	68	68	68	281	35,100
Vijay Singh	73	70	71	67	281	35,100
Emlyn Aubrey	72	67	74	69	282	25,480
Jim Gallagher, Jr.	73	69	72	68	282	25,480
Sandy Lyle	70	74	67	71	282	25,480
Doug Martin	73	70	66	73	282	25,480
Tommy Tolles	69	71	73	69	282	25,480
John Mahaffey	69	72	72	70	283	18,850
Greg Norman	70	71	70	72	283	18,850
Curtis Strange	76	69	70	68	283	18,850
David Toms	67	72	73	71	283	18,850
Olin Browne	68	68	73	75	284	13,000
Marco Dawson	69	73	69	73	284	13,000
Allen Doyle	69	74	73	68	284	13,000
Brad Fabel	69	70	71	74	284	13,000
Jeff Hart	70	72	72	70	284	13,000
Omar Uresti	72	72	70	70	284	13,000
Michael Bradley	69	68	77	71	285	9,035

	SCORES				TOTAL	MONEY
Mike Hulbert	70	73	70	72	285	9,035
Franklin Langham	67	73	71	74	285	9,035
David Peoples	71	70	71	73	285	9,035
Hisayuki Sasaki	69	74	72	70	285	9,035
Joey Sindelar	73	71	69	72	285	9,035
Patrick Burke	68	73	68	77	286	7,020
Mark Calcavecchia	67	73	72	74	286	7,020
Rick Fehr	70	73	71	72	286	7,020
Len Mattiace	71	73	74	68	286	7,020
Fuzzy Zoeller	73	71	75	67	286	7,020
John Adams	73	68	76	70	287	5,460
Keith Clearwater	74	69	74	70	287	5,460
Ed Fiori	71	72	73	71	287	5,460
Neal Lancaster	72	73	69	73	287	5,460
Gene Sauers	70	71	76	70	287	5,460
Scott Verplank	65	76	72	74	287	5,460
Brian Claar	69	76	72	71	288	3,836.86
Scott Hoch	72	69	75	72	288	3,836.86
Blaine McCallister	72	70	76	70	288	3,836.86
John Morse	71	70	71	76	288	3,836.86
Carl Paulson	71	72	74	71	288	3,836.86
Keith Fergus	69	70	73	76	288	3,836.85
Larry Nelson	70	70	79	69	288	3,836.85
Brian Henninger	68	71	75	75	289	3,128.67
Robert Wrenn	73	71	72	73	289	3,128.67
Mike Brisky	68	71	79	71	289	3,128.66
Brad Faxon	74	71	74	71	290	2,990
Wayne Levi	74	70	71	75	290	2,990
Andrew Magee	68	74	78	70	290	2,990
John Daly	71	73	74	73	291	2,925
Masahiro Kuramoto	71	72	75	73	291	2,925
Joel Edwards	71	73	76	72	292	2,821
Bob Gilder	70	75	74	73	292	2,821
Sean Murphy	71	72	74	75	292	2,821
Jesper Parnevik	72	73	72	75	292	2,821
Dave Stockton, Jr.	70	72	74	76	292	2,821
Jay Williamson	69	72	78	73	292	2,821
Stuart Appleby	73	71	77	72	293	2,691
Dave Barr	73	70	77	73	293	2,691
Frank Lickliter	73	72	78	70	293	2,691
Charlie Rymer	68	76	75	74	293	2,691
Chris DiMarco	74	71	76	73	294	2,626
Steve Rintoul	68	75	74	78	295	2,587
Brian Tennyson	68	74	79	74	295	2,587
Robin Freeman	71	73	76	76	296	2,509
Naomichi Ozaki	74	71	73	78	296	2,509
Jarmo Sandelin	75	68	80	73	296	2,509
Taylor Smith	71	74	72	79	296	2,509
John Inman	72	73	75	78	298	2,444
Gary Rusnak	71	72	82	76	301	2,418
Brian Kamm	72	73	83	76	304	2,392

Bay Hill Invitational

Bay Hill Club & Lodge, Orlando, Florida
Par 36-36–72; 7,114 yards

March 14-17
purse, $1,200,000

	SCORES				TOTAL	MONEY
Paul Goydos	67	74	67	67	275	$216,000
Jeff Maggert	72	65	70	69	276	129,600
Tom Purtzer	69	70	69	69	277	81,600
Mark Calcavecchia	70	74	66	69	279	45,240
Robert Gamez	74	67	69	69	279	45,240
Bill Glasson	71	70	68	70	279	45,240
Mark O'Meara	67	72	69	71	279	45,240
Corey Pavin	69	70	72	68	279	45,240
Glen Day	67	71	72	70	280	31,200
Steve Jones	69	70	70	71	280	31,200
Tom Lehman	69	75	68	68	280	31,200
Larry Nelson	71	70	67	72	280	31,200
Bernhard Langer	73	69	73	66	281	18,174.55
Steve Lowery	70	75	68	68	281	18,174.55
Doug Martin	71	73	69	68	281	18,174.55
Mark McCumber	71	70	72	68	281	18,174.55
Rocco Mediate	71	72	70	68	281	18,174.55
Steve Stricker	73	69	71	68	281	18,174.55
Guy Boros	73	67	66	75	281	18,174.54
Patrick Burke	71	66	69	75	281	18,174.54
Davis Love III	69	72	68	72	281	18,174.54
Vijay Singh	73	71	65	72	281	18,174.54
Kirk Triplett	73	72	67	69	281	18,174.54
Steve Elkington	71	71	68	72	282	10,560
Nick Faldo	72	68	69	73	282	10,560
Larry Mize	76	68	68	70	282	10,560
Woody Austin	70	71	70	72	283	8,700
Paul Azinger	71	70	70	72	283	8,700
Mike Brisky	73	72	70	68	283	8,700
Tom Watson	75	68	66	74	283	8,700
Robert Allenby	74	71	70	69	284	7,116
Curt Byrum	71	74	64	75	284	7,116
Masahiro Kuramoto	72	73	70	69	284	7,116
Billy Mayfair	69	73	67	75	284	7,116
Scott Simpson	74	70	70	70	284	7,116
Jim Furyk	74	71	71	69	285	5,530
Mike Hulbert	69	69	72	75	285	5,530
John Morse	73	72	68	72	285	5,530
Nick Price	72	73	71	69	285	5,530
Mike Sullivan	69	72	71	73	285	5,530
David Toms	72	73	71	69	285	5,530
Ernie Els	73	70	71	73	287	4,200
Franklin Langham	73	73	73	68	287	4,200
Bob Lohr	68	72	73	74	287	4,200
Dicky Pride	73	69	74	71	287	4,200
Hugh Royer III	71	73	68	75	287	4,200
Fulton Allem	74	69	72	73	288	3,124
Chip Beck	72	73	72	71	288	3,124
Billy Ray Brown	71	72	72	73	288	3,124
Keith Clearwater	74	72	72	70	288	3,124
Marco Dawson	71	71	72	74	288	3,124
Omar Uresti	75	69	71	73	288	3,124
Jay Haas	71	71	74	73	289	2,792
Blaine McCallister	73	71	71	74	289	2,792

	SCORES				TOTAL	MONEY
Gene Sauers	71	70	73	75	289	2,792
Andrew Magee	73	72	70	75	290	2,712
Kevin Sutherland	72	73	72	73	290	2,712
Grant Waite	76	68	72	74	290	2,712
Len Mattiace	72	73	72	74	291	2,664
Lee Janzen	76	70	72	74	292	2,616
Bruce Lietzke	74	72	73	73	292	2,616
Charlie Rymer	71	73	74	74	292	2,616
Peter Jacobsen	74	72	71	76	293	2,544
Yoshinori Mizumaki	73	69	70	81	293	2,544
Tom Scherrer	74	71	74	74	293	2,544
Nolan Henke	72	71	79	72	294	2,496
Dan Pohl	71	73	79	72	295	2,460
Joey Sindelar	74	72	72	77	295	2,460
Billy Andrade	72	74	74	77	297	2,412
Brad Bryant	71	75	74	77	297	2,412

Freeport-McDermott Classic

English Turn Golf & Country Club,
New Orleans, Louisiana
Par 36-36–72; 7,116 yards

March 21-24
purse, $1,200,000

	SCORES				TOTAL	MONEY
Scott McCarron	68	67	69	71	275	$216,000
Tom Watson	68	66	72	74	280	129,600
Tommy Tolles	70	69	66	76	281	81,600
Lennie Clements	67	66	74	76	283	43,500
Joel Edwards	72	69	70	72	283	43,500
Davis Love III	68	68	72	75	283	43,500
Steve Lowery	71	71	68	73	283	43,500
Blaine McCallister	73	64	75	71	283	43,500
Payne Stewart	74	71	67	71	283	43,500
Stuart Appleby	74	69	66	75	284	27,600
Brad Fabel	73	69	73	69	284	27,600
Jeff Gallagher	70	68	72	74	284	27,600
John Huston	69	73	71	71	284	27,600
Tom Lehman	69	71	70	74	284	27,600
Keith Clearwater	71	71	70	73	285	19,200
Franklin Langham	74	69	69	73	285	19,200
Scott Simpson	71	69	73	72	285	19,200
Hal Sutton	71	66	73	75	285	19,200
Scott Verplank	70	67	72	76	285	19,200
Bob Gilder	69	71	71	75	286	15,600
Ronnie Black	72	70	70	75	287	12,000
Ben Crenshaw	74	67	75	71	287	12,000
Paul Goydos	75	68	71	73	287	12,000
Mike Heinen	71	72	72	72	287	12,000
Scott Hoch	77	65	73	72	287	12,000
Frank Nobilo	67	73	71	76	287	12,000
John Adams	70	71	74	73	288	8,340
Olin Browne	77	64	72	75	288	8,340
Glen Day	75	66	76	71	288	8,340
Jim Furyk	66	72	76	74	288	8,340
Andrew Magee	71	72	73	72	288	8,340
Lee Rinker	70	72	73	73	288	8,340
Craig Parry	74	69	71	75	289	6,480
Chris Smith	71	71	67	80	289	6,480

	SCORES				TOTAL	MONEY
Paul Stankowski	67	72	75	75	289	6,480
Kevin Sutherland	72	69	71	77	289	6,480
Robert Wrenn	71	67	74	77	289	6,480
Jay Haas	77	68	68	77	290	5,280
Tim Herron	70	71	76	73	290	5,280
Doug Martin	69	70	75	76	290	5,280
Mike Reid	70	69	75	76	290	5,280
Chip Beck	73	71	74	73	291	4,200
Curt Byrum	71	70	73	77	291	4,200
David Edwards	72	71	72	76	291	4,200
Frank Lickliter	74	66	76	75	291	4,200
Ted Schulz	72	71	73	75	291	4,200
Phil Blackmar	72	71	72	77	292	3,172.80
Mark Brooks	73	70	75	74	292	3,172.80
Ernie Els	72	71	72	77	292	3,172.80
Steve Jones	74	71	72	75	292	3,172.80
Masahiro Kuramoto	70	69	75	78	292	3,172.80
Brian Kamm	72	65	77	79	293	2,856
John Wilson	67	73	75	78	293	2,856
Billy Ray Brown	72	72	69	81	294	2,748
Brian Claar	75	69	73	77	294	2,748
Satoshi Higashi	72	71	74	77	294	2,748
Kirk Triplett	79	65	70	80	294	2,748
John Elliott	75	70	74	76	295	2,676
Kelly Gibson	72	70	81	72	295	2,676
Sean Murphy	75	68	75	78	296	2,616
Howard Twitty	70	71	74	81	296	2,616
Jay Williamson	73	69	74	80	296	2,616
Shane Bertsch	76	65	72	84	297	2,544
Brad Bryant	74	69	72	82	297	2,544
John Inman	72	73	71	81	297	2,544
Todd Gleaton	75	70	75	78	298	2,484
Brian Tennyson	71	71	75	81	298	2,484
Jim Carter	76	68	74	81	299	2,436
Steve Jurgensen	74	71	76	78	299	2,436
Joey Gullion	71	73	79	79	302	2,376
Scott Gump	74	71	76	81	302	2,376
Dillard Pruitt	74	69	74	85	302	2,376

The Players Championship

TPC at Sawgrass, Stadium Course,
Ponte Vedra Beach, Florida
Par 36-36–72; 6,896 yards

March 28-31
purse, $3,000,000

	SCORES				TOTAL	MONEY
Fred Couples	66	72	68	64	270	$630,000
Colin Montgomerie	71	69	66	68	274	308,000
Tommy Tolles	69	64	69	72	274	308,000
David Duval	70	66	68	71	275	137,812.50
Rocco Mediate	74	69	66	66	275	137,812.50
Kenny Perry	65	71	70	69	275	137,812.50
Fuzzy Zoeller	66	70	72	67	275	137,812.50
Ernie Els	71	70	65	70	276	94,500
Jay Haas	68	68	69	71	276	94,500
Tom Lehman	70	72	67	67	276	94,500
Vijay Singh	70	68	68	70	276	94,500
Grant Waite	68	72	68	68	276	94,500

	SCORES				TOTAL	MONEY
Fred Funk	70	69	67	71	277	65,625
Jim Furyk	70	70	67	70	277	65,625
Larry Mize	70	67	71	69	277	65,625
Gil Morgan	70	69	69	69	277	65,625
Patrick Burke	72	71	69	66	278	54,250
David Frost	67	70	72	69	278	54,250
Michael Bradley	72	67	66	74	279	35,735
John Daly	68	70	69	72	279	35,735
Joel Edwards	71	67	71	70	279	35,735
Steve Elkington	68	73	68	70	279	35,735
Wayne Grady	72	69	68	70	279	35,735
Scott Gump	70	68	68	73	279	35,735
Nolan Henke	71	68	68	72	279	35,735
Tim Herron	69	73	68	69	279	35,735
Scott Hoch	71	70	70	68	279	35,735
Kirk Triplett	67	72	73	67	279	35,735
Mark Calcavecchia	67	68	75	70	280	23,275
Robert Gamez	68	73	70	69	280	23,275
Mark O'Meara	73	69	69	69	280	23,275
Masashi Ozaki	71	69	69	71	280	23,275
John Adams	71	69	71	70	281	17,718.75
Jay Don Blake	74	68	68	71	281	17,718.75
Jim Carter	70	72	66	73	281	17,718.75
Marco Dawson	72	71	69	69	281	17,718.75
Steve Jones	70	69	69	73	281	17,718.75
Phil Mickelson	71	72	64	74	281	17,718.75
Loren Roberts	73	70	70	68	281	17,718.75
Tom Watson	72	68	69	72	281	17,718.75
Blaine McCallister	72	70	66	74	282	12,950
Jeff Sluman	68	72	72	70	282	12,950
Craig Stadler	73	70	71	68	282	12,950
Payne Stewart	73	70	68	71	282	12,950
Bobby Wadkins	71	70	68	73	282	12,950
Hale Irwin	67	73	69	74	283	9,360
Lee Janzen	70	71	70	72	283	9,360
Davis Love III	69	70	72	72	283	9,360
Steve Lowery	73	70	68	72	283	9,360
Corey Pavin	67	71	76	69	283	9,360
Nick Price	70	69	73	71	283	9,360
Dillard Pruitt	71	71	71	70	283	9,360
Guy Boros	69	72	70	73	284	7,990
Neal Lancaster	73	70	69	72	284	7,990
Jeff Maggert	70	70	77	67	284	7,990
Jesper Parnevik	69	70	72	73	284	7,990
Craig Parry	66	74	72	72	284	7,990
Gene Sauers	69	72	72	71	284	7,990
Hal Sutton	72	69	73	70	284	7,990
Chip Beck	68	69	76	72	285	7,665
Frank Nobilo	68	72	72	73	285	7,665
Larry Nelson	71	69	73	73	286	7,490
Dan Pohl	72	70	73	71	286	7,490
Tom Purtzer	74	69	72	71	286	7,490
Justin Leonard	65	70	80	72	287	7,315
Mike Reid	70	73	72	72	287	7,315
Woody Austin	72	71	72	73	288	7,105
Brian Kamm	68	74	71	75	288	7,105
Doug Martin	69	71	76	72	288	7,105
Don Pooley	69	73	74	72	288	7,105
Michael Campbell	70	73	69	77	289	6,895
Mike Hulbert	73	70	73	73	289	6,895

	SCORES				TOTAL	MONEY
Ben Crenshaw	70	73	71	76	290	6,685
Jim Gallagher, Jr.	71	70	76	73	290	6,685
Ken Green	71	71	74	74	290	6,685
John Morse	68	74	74	74	290	6,685
Mark McCumber	69	74	71	79	293	6,510

BellSouth Classic

Atlanta Country Club, Marietta, Georgia
Par 36-36–72; 7,018 yards

April 4-7
purse, $1,300,000

	SCORES				TOTAL	MONEY
Paul Stankowski	68	71	70	71	280	$234,000
Brandel Chamblee	72	70	71	67	280	140,400
(Stankowski defeated Chamblee on first extra hole.)						
David Duval	68	70	68	76	282	75,400
Nick Price	68	70	73	71	282	75,400
Fred Couples	71	73	66	73	283	49,400
Tommy Tolles	69	70	69	75	283	49,400
Frank Lickliter	69	72	76	67	284	40,516.67
Corey Pavin	66	73	76	69	284	40,516.67
Neal Lancaster	67	70	75	72	284	40,516.66
Lennie Clements	69	71	72	73	285	33,800
Jerry Kelly	73	71	69	72	285	33,800
Phil Blackmar	69	71	74	72	286	25,480
Michael Bradley	68	73	73	72	286	25,480
Larry Nelson	71	75	68	72	286	25,480
Gene Sauers	69	68	76	73	286	25,480
John Wilson	66	74	73	73	286	25,480
Dan Forsman	70	73	73	71	287	17,593.34
Bob Lohr	71	73	73	70	287	17,593.34
David Frost	71	69	73	74	287	17,593.33
Jim Gallagher, Jr.	66	75	73	73	287	17,593.33
Davis Love III	71	69	71	76	287	17,593.33
Mike Reid	71	72	71	73	287	17,593.33
Russ Cochran	67	73	76	72	288	11,570
Wayne Grady	73	72	72	71	288	11,570
Colin Montgomerie	71	76	68	73	288	11,570
Kenny Perry	71	73	73	71	288	11,570
Ian Woosnam	72	75	68	73	288	11,570
Bobby Wadkins	73	68	76	72	289	9,620
Taylor Smith	74	71	72	73	290	8,265.84
Sam Torrance	74	72	74	70	290	8,265.84
Fulton Allem	69	74	73	74	290	8,265.83
Ernie Els	75	72	66	77	290	8,265.83
Jeff Hart	71	73	70	76	290	8,265.83
Joey Sindelar	75	69	72	74	290	8,265.83
Woody Austin	74	69	70	78	291	6,548.75
Jay Don Blake	72	74	67	78	291	6,548.75
Brian Claar	74	72	74	71	291	6,548.75
Gary Rusnak	73	70	70	78	291	6,548.75
Joel Edwards	73	73	73	73	292	5,200
Jeff Gallagher	76	68	75	73	292	5,200
Kelly Gibson	71	74	75	72	292	5,200
Scott Simpson	71	73	72	76	292	5,200
Dicky Thompson	71	72	73	76	292	5,200
David Toms	73	72	71	76	292	5,200

	SCORES				TOTAL	MONEY
Mark Calcavecchia	68	77	69	79	293	3,806.40
Dillard Pruitt	70	73	75	75	293	3,806.40
Steve Stricker	72	72	76	73	293	3,806.40
Kevin Sutherland	72	75	72	74	293	3,806.40
Hal Sutton	74	73	72	74	293	3,806.40
Billy Andrade	73	74	72	75	294	3,071.25
Mike Heinen	71	76	76	71	294	3,071.25
Stephen Keppler	71	76	72	75	294	3,071.25
Tom Kite	70	75	70	79	294	3,071.25
Sean Murphy	72	73	79	70	294	3,071.25
Mike Springer	74	71	72	77	294	3,071.25
Mike Swartz	75	70	73	76	294	3,071.25
Jay Williamson	74	73	72	75	294	3,071.25
Scott Medlin	73	73	74	75	295	2,899
David Ogrin	71	74	72	78	295	2,899
Lanny Wadkins	73	73	74	76	296	2,860
Joe Acosta, Jr.	71	75	75	76	297	2,769
Jim Carter	74	72	73	78	297	2,769
John Inman	69	77	73	78	297	2,769
Justin Leonard	71	71	78	77	297	2,769
Dicky Pride	71	75	76	75	297	2,769
Brian Tennyson	74	70	74	79	297	2,769
Ed Fiori	74	72	76	76	298	2,678
Donnie Hammond	72	72	76	79	299	2,652
Joey Gullion	77	70	72	81	300	2,613
Wayne Levi	71	73	81	75	300	2,613
Brett Ogle	73	72	76	81	302	2,574
Mike Sullivan	73	74	74	84	305	2,548

Masters Tournament

Augusta National Golf Club, Augusta, Georgia
Par 36-36—72; 6,925 yards

April 11-14
purse, $2,200,000

	SCORES				TOTAL	MONEY
Nick Faldo	69	67	73	67	276	$450,000
Greg Norman	63	69	71	78	281	270,000
Phil Mickelson	65	73	72	72	282	170,000
Frank Nobilo	71	71	72	69	283	120,000
Scott Hoch	67	73	73	71	284	95,000
Duffy Waldorf	72	71	69	72	284	95,000
Davis Love III	72	71	74	68	285	77,933
Jeff Maggert	71	73	72	69	285	77,933
Corey Pavin	75	66	73	71	285	77,933
David Frost	70	68	74	74	286	65,000
Scott McCarron	70	70	72	74	286	65,000
Ernie Els	71	71	72	73	287	52,500
Lee Janzen	68	71	75	73	287	52,500
Bob Tway	67	72	76	72	287	52,500
Mark Calcavecchia	71	73	71	73	288	43,750
Fred Couples	78	68	71	71	288	43,750
John Huston	71	71	71	76	289	40,000
Paul Azinger	70	74	76	70	290	32,600
David Duval	73	72	69	76	290	32,600
Tom Lehman	75	70	72	73	290	32,600
Mark O'Meara	72	71	75	72	290	32,600
Nick Price	71	75	70	74	290	32,600

	SCORES				TOTAL	MONEY
Larry Mize	75	71	77	68	291	25,000
Loren Roberts	71	73	72	75	291	25,000
Brad Faxon	69	77	72	74	292	21,000
Raymond Floyd	70	74	77	71	292	21,000
Bob Estes	71	71	79	72	293	18,900
Justin Leonard	72	74	75	72	293	18,900
John Daly	71	74	71	78	294	15,571
Jim Furyk	75	70	78	71	294	15,571
Jim Gallagher, Jr.	70	76	77	71	294	15,571
Hale Irwin	74	71	77	72	294	15,571
Scott Simpson	69	76	76	73	294	15,571
Craig Stadler	73	72	71	78	294	15,571
Ian Woosnam	72	69	73	80	294	15,571
Fred Funk	71	72	76	76	295	12,333
Bernhard Langer	75	70	72	78	295	12,333
Jay Haas	70	73	75	77	295	12,333
Colin Montgomerie	72	74	75	75	296	11,050
Vijay Singh	69	71	74	82	296	11,050
Steve Lowery	71	74	75	77	297	10,050
Jack Nicklaus	70	73	76	78	297	10,050
Seve Ballesteros	73	73	77	76	299	9,300
Alexander Cejka	73	71	78	80	302	8,800

Out of Final 36 Holes

Tommy Aaron	71	76	147
David Gilford	69	78	147
Jeff Sluman	74	73	147
Ted Tryba	72	75	147
Tom Watson	75	72	147
Fuzzy Zoeller	74	73	147
Mark Brooks	72	76	148
Bill Glasson	71	77	148
Masashi Ozaki	71	77	148
Curtis Strange	71	77	148
Hal Sutton	72	76	148
Michael Campbell	73	76	149
Sandy Lyle	75	74	149
Gary Player	73	76	149
Steve Stricker	80	69	149
Neal Lancaster	76	74	150
Arnold Palmer	74	76	150
Payne Stewart	74	76	150
*Tiger Woods	75	75	150
Ben Crenshaw	77	74	151
Ed Dougherty	76	75	151
Satoshi Higashi	76	75	151
Sam Torrance	80	71	151
Kirk Triplett	76	75	151
Gay Brewer	75	77	152
Tim Herron	76	76	152
Tom Kite	75	77	152
Kenny Perry	75	77	152
Paul Stankowski	74	78	152
Woody Austin	79	74	153
Brad Bryant	78	75	153
David Edwards	79	74	153
Costantino Rocca	78	75	153
Mark Roe	74	79	153
Billy Mayfair	77	77	154

	SCORES		TOTAL
Steve Elkington	76	79	155
Brian Henninger	76	79	155
Gordon Sherry	78	77	155
D.A. Weibring	74	81	155
Ian Baker-Finch	78	79	157
Paul Goydos	74	83	157
Chris Wollmann	79	79	158
Charles Coody	82	78	160
Jerry Courville	78	82	160
George Marucci, Jr.	79	81	160
Mark McCumber	78	82	160
Billy Casper	75	86	161
Doug Ford	81	88	169

(Professionals who did not complete 72 holes received $1,500.)

MCI Classic

Harbour Town Golf Links, Hilton Head Island,
South Carolina
Par 36-36—72; 6,912 yards

April 18-21
purse, $1,400,000

	SCORES				TOTAL	MONEY
Loren Roberts	66	69	63	67	265	$252,000
Mark O'Meara	68	69	65	66	268	151,200
Scott Hoch	71	68	65	66	270	95,200
Davis Love III	68	68	68	67	271	67,200
Nick Price	72	67	69	65	273	51,100
Vijay Singh	70	67	69	67	273	51,100
Tom Watson	67	67	72	67	273	51,100
Jeff Maggert	69	66	70	69	274	37,800
Rocco Mediate	68	68	71	67	274	37,800
Colin Montgomerie	69	66	70	69	274	37,800
Larry Nelson	67	68	69	70	274	37,800
Gene Sauers	69	72	68	65	274	37,800
Tom Lehman	68	70	67	70	275	28,000
Jeff Sluman	67	67	73	68	275	28,000
Woody Austin	72	67	67	70	276	23,800
Lee Janzen	69	70	69	68	276	23,800
Bob Tway	67	70	70	69	276	23,800
Russ Cochran	71	68	69	69	277	18,900
Bob Lohr	68	71	69	69	277	18,900
Doug Martin	67	71	69	70	277	18,900
Billy Mayfair	67	73	68	69	277	18,900
Neal Lancaster	71	70	67	70	278	12,620
Andrew Magee	68	68	72	70	278	12,620
Greg Norman	69	69	72	68	278	12,620
David Ogrin	69	71	68	70	278	12,620
Kenny Perry	70	68	72	68	278	12,620
Tom Purtzer	70	67	68	73	278	12,620
Scott Verplank	71	70	70	67	278	12,620
Glen Day	71	70	67	71	279	9,520
Nick Faldo	70	68	71	70	279	9,520
Ted Tryba	71	68	69	71	279	9,520
Jim Furyk	66	72	70	72	280	7,746.67
Scott Gump	73	68	73	66	280	7,746.67
Jay Haas	72	67	71	70	280	7,746.67
Joey Sindelar	71	70	72	67	280	7,746.67

	SCORES				TOTAL	MONEY
Paul Azinger	71	66	74	69	280	7,746.66
Bobby Wadkins	68	70	72	70	280	7,746.66
Chip Beck	69	67	73	72	281	6,160
Jim Carter	67	69	75	70	281	6,160
Bob Estes	70	72	72	67	281	6,160
Duffy Waldorf	67	72	72	70	281	6,160
Andy Bean	73	69	69	71	282	4,760
Guy Boros	66	73	74	69	282	4,760
Brad Faxon	68	71	71	72	282	4,760
Mike Hulbert	72	69	69	72	282	4,760
Justin Leonard	70	71	69	72	282	4,760
Charlie Rymer	68	70	72	72	282	4,760
Jay Don Blake	69	70	72	72	283	3,447.50
Mike Brisky	71	70	69	73	283	3,447.50
Michael Campbell	73	69	70	71	283	3,447.50
Brian Claar	71	69	73	70	283	3,447.50
Tim Dunlavey	69	71	70	73	283	3,447.50
Joel Edwards	72	69	74	68	283	3,447.50
Ken Green	66	71	74	72	283	3,447.50
Brian Kamm	73	63	72	75	283	3,447.50
John Cook	72	68	75	69	284	3,122
David Edwards	68	69	75	72	284	3,122
Robin Freeman	69	71	72	72	284	3,122
Tim Herron	72	67	74	71	284	3,122
Lee Rinker	69	71	72	72	284	3,122
John Wilson	72	68	72	72	284	3,122
Bob Boyd	71	71	72	71	285	2,982
Billy Ray Brown	71	71	68	75	285	2,982
Peter Jacobsen	71	71	71	72	285	2,982
Tommy Tolles	69	68	76	72	285	2,982
Marco Dawson	72	68	73	73	286	2,856
Sandy Lyle	71	71	75	69	286	2,856
Phil Mickelson	74	66	72	74	286	2,856
Larry Mize	72	70	74	70	286	2,856
Mike Standly	68	72	71	75	286	2,856
Michael Bradley	68	74	70	75	287	2,730
Brandel Chamblee	76	66	70	75	287	2,730
David Frost	71	71	70	75	287	2,730
Hugh Royer III	71	69	71	76	287	2,730
Fred Funk	75	66	75	73	289	2,646
Omar Uresti	72	69	70	78	289	2,646
Mark Brooks	73	69	75	74	291	2,604
Steve Stricker	76	64	76	80	296	2,576

Greater Greensboro Chrysler Classic

Forest Oaks Country Club, Greensboro, North Carolina
Par 36-36–72; 7,062 yards

April 25-28
purse, $1,800,000

	SCORES				TOTAL	MONEY
Mark O'Meara	75	68	62	69	274	$324,000
Duffy Waldorf	73	65	67	71	276	194,400
Steve Stricker	72	69	70	67	278	122,400
Emlyn Aubrey	72	67	68	72	279	86,400
Billy Andrade	68	74	67	71	280	68,400
John Huston	71	71	73	65	280	68,400
Jim Furyk	73	68	67	73	281	56,100

	SCORES				TOTAL	MONEY
Wayne Levi	74	67	71	69	281	56,100
Fuzzy Zoeller	72	70	70	69	281	56,100
Woody Austin	71	68	72	71	282	48,600
Ken Green	70	71	72	70	283	38,160
Tom Kite	68	72	70	73	283	38,160
Tom Lehman	70	71	66	76	283	38,160
David Ogrin	69	71	70	73	283	38,160
Hisayuki Sasaki	69	69	71	74	283	38,160
Marco Dawson	70	73	70	71	284	25,251.43
Joel Edwards	69	73	70	72	284	25,251.43
Brian Kamm	73	68	70	73	284	25,251.43
Corey Pavin	73	72	70	69	284	25,251.43
Joey Sindelar	72	74	67	71	284	25,251.43
Kirk Triplett	70	73	71	70	284	25,251.43
Keith Fergus	70	67	71	76	284	25,251.42
John Adams	72	73	69	71	285	13,507.50
Guy Boros	67	72	72	74	285	13,507.50
Mark Brooks	71	68	76	70	285	13,507.50
Lennie Clements	71	70	71	73	285	13,507.50
David Edwards	72	74	68	71	285	13,507.50
Rick Fehr	73	72	68	72	285	13,507.50
Ed Humenik	71	71	70	73	285	13,507.50
Lee Janzen	72	70	71	72	285	13,507.50
Craig Parry	72	72	70	71	285	13,507.50
Tom Purtzer	70	73	70	72	285	13,507.50
Clarence Rose	73	69	72	71	285	13,507.50
Taylor Smith	73	69	68	75	285	13,507.50
Ronnie Black	74	69	70	73	286	8,130
Joe Daley	70	71	76	69	286	8,130
Dan Forsman	74	71	68	73	286	8,130
Bryan Gorman	73	68	73	72	286	8,130
Frank Lickliter	70	69	71	76	286	8,130
Jim McGovern	71	74	72	69	286	8,130
Kenny Perry	71	74	69	72	286	8,130
Gene Sauers	75	70	70	71	286	8,130
Dave Stockton, Jr.	69	73	72	72	286	8,130
Kelly Gibson	72	71	70	74	287	5,760
Peter Jacobsen	72	71	70	74	287	5,760
Kevin Sutherland	72	74	72	69	287	5,760
Lanny Wadkins	72	73	76	66	287	5,760
Chip Beck	67	77	72	72	288	4,432.50
Jay Don Blake	68	75	75	70	288	4,432.50
Brad Fabel	71	72	68	77	288	4,432.50
Bob Gilder	73	70	75	70	288	4,432.50
Jeff Hart	77	67	73	71	288	4,432.50
Dillard Pruitt	75	69	74	70	288	4,432.50
Charlie Rymer	73	73	69	73	288	4,432.50
David Toms	71	73	73	71	288	4,432.50
Mark McCumber	72	71	71	75	289	4,086
Vijay Singh	70	75	72	72	289	4,086
Scott Dunlap	73	72	70	75	290	3,960
Mike Heinen	72	74	75	69	290	3,960
Bob Lohr	71	73	78	68	290	3,960
Naomichi Ozaki	68	77	74	71	290	3,960
Jeff Sluman	74	72	72	72	290	3,960
Billy Ray Brown	74	67	79	71	291	3,798
Mark Wiebe	69	76	76	70	291	3,798
John Wilson	72	72	73	74	291	3,798
Robert Wrenn	74	68	75	74	291	3,798
Stuart Appleby	72	69	73	78	292	3,618

	SCORES				TOTAL	MONEY
Robin Freeman	72	74	70	76	292	3,618
Sean Murphy	73	73	75	71	292	3,618
Larry Nelson	73	69	75	75	292	3,618
Mike Springer	75	71	74	72	292	3,618
Mike Sullivan	69	69	74	80	292	3,618
Jim Thorpe	73	72	76	72	293	3,492
John Cook	71	75	78	70	294	3,438
John Morse	74	72	75	73	294	3,438
Tim Dunlavey	69	70	76	80	295	3,384
Mike Brisky	74	72	74	76	296	3,330
Ed Fiori	74	72	72	78	296	3,330

Shell Houston Open

TPC at The Woodlands, The Woodlands, Texas
Par 36-36–72; 7,042 yards

May 2-5
purse, $1,500,000

	SCORES				TOTAL	MONEY
Mark Brooks	66	68	70	70	274	$270,000
Jeff Maggert	67	69	66	72	274	162,000
(Brooks defeated Maggert on first extra hole.)						
David Duval	66	70	67	72	275	102,000
Woody Austin	69	71	65	73	278	72,000
Greg Kraft	67	70	74	68	279	54,750
Doug Martin	67	68	72	72	279	54,750
Tommy Tolles	65	70	72	72	279	54,750
Andy Bean	69	74	69	68	280	46,500
John Cook	72	66	69	74	281	37,500
Bradley Hughes	73	68	71	69	281	37,500
Clarence Rose	68	72	68	73	281	37,500
Mike Springer	65	70	74	72	281	37,500
Payne Stewart	72	70	69	70	281	37,500
Russ Cochran	67	71	71	73	282	26,250
John Huston	69	71	71	71	282	26,250
Tom Kite	70	70	70	72	282	26,250
Len Mattiace	67	70	72	73	282	26,250
Mark Calcavecchia	72	71	68	72	283	21,000
Robert Gamez	68	73	69	73	283	21,000
Grant Waite	73	68	72	70	283	21,000
Lennie Clements	70	68	70	76	284	13,350
Ed Fiori	71	71	72	70	284	13,350
Scott Gump	71	70	68	75	284	13,350
Donnie Hammond	68	72	72	72	284	13,350
Lee Janzen	66	71	71	76	284	13,350
John Morse	73	69	71	71	284	13,350
David Ogrin	71	71	70	72	284	13,350
Craig Parry	69	71	69	75	284	13,350
Don Pooley	71	70	71	72	284	13,350
Vijay Singh	71	68	71	74	284	13,350
Bart Bryant	69	71	71	74	285	8,700
Scott Dunlap	73	71	70	71	285	8,700
Scott Hoch	71	71	68	75	285	8,700
Steve Jurgensen	69	72	72	72	285	8,700
Andrew Magee	72	71	70	72	285	8,700
D.A. Weibring	70	71	72	72	285	8,700
Brian Claar	73	71	70	72	286	6,450
Jay Delsing	68	69	78	71	286	6,450

	SCORES				TOTAL	MONEY
Rick Fehr	72	67	72	75	286	6,450
Wayne Grady	72	71	71	72	286	6,450
Dillard Pruitt	68	70	73	75	286	6,450
Charlie Rymer	71	73	71	71	286	6,450
John Wilson	69	70	72	75	286	6,450
Joel Edwards	68	75	70	74	287	4,800
Lee Rinker	71	70	74	72	287	4,800
Omar Uresti	71	70	70	76	287	4,800
Robert Wrenn	73	70	75	69	287	4,800
Phil Blackmar	74	70	70	74	288	3,693.75
Naomichi Ozaki	68	75	70	75	288	3,693.75
Carl Paulson	69	73	73	73	288	3,693.75
Hisayuki Sasaki	69	68	72	79	288	3,693.75
Mike Sullivan	74	69	70	75	288	3,693.75
Hal Sutton	72	72	74	70	288	3,693.75
Kirk Triplett	66	73	71	78	288	3,693.75
Mark Wiebe	70	72	76	70	288	3,693.75
Tom Byrum	70	72	68	79	289	3,330
Allen Doyle	72	72	74	71	289	3,330
Brian Henninger	71	69	74	75	289	3,330
Mike Hulbert	67	72	74	76	289	3,330
Jerry Kelly	69	73	74	73	289	3,330
Jim McGovern	71	72	72	74	289	3,330
Brett Ogle	70	72	70	77	289	3,330
Nolan Henke	73	68	77	72	290	3,180
Joey Sindelar	69	75	72	74	290	3,180
Jim Thorpe	76	68	73	73	290	3,180
Gary Rusnak	69	75	76	71	291	3,090
Brian Tennyson	72	71	75	73	291	3,090
Ron Whittaker	74	70	75	72	291	3,090
Ronnie Black	73	71	73	75	292	3,000
Jim Carter	69	74	77	72	292	3,000
Kevin Sutherland	74	70	76	72	292	3,000
Dave Barr	70	72	74	77	293	2,895
Ben Crenshaw	77	67	75	74	293	2,895
Joe Daley	71	70	74	78	293	2,895
Tim Herron	69	74	74	76	293	2,895
Steve Rintoul	72	67	78	77	294	2,820
Paul Azinger	73	70	82	70	295	2,775
Chip Beck	73	68	74	80	295	2,775
Marco Dawson	71	73	76	77	297	2,730
Russell Jenkines	75	67	74	82	298	2,700

GTE Byron Nelson Classic

TPC at Four Seasons, Irving, Texas
Las Colinas Course: Par 35-35–70; 6,899 yards
Cottonwood Valley Golf Course: Par 34-36–70; 6,845 yards

May 9-12
purse, $1,500,000

	SCORES				TOTAL	MONEY
Phil Mickelson	67	65	67	66	265	$270,000
Craig Parry	70	67	65	65	267	162,000
David Duval	71	64	68	65	268	102,000
Nick Price	67	66	69	67	269	66,000
Jeff Sluman	69	68	65	67	269	66,000
Mark Brooks	64	70	70	66	270	48,562.50
Gil Morgan	72	64	69	65	270	48,562.50

		SCORES			TOTAL	MONEY
Corey Pavin	67	66	67	70	270	48,562.50
Mark Wiebe	68	69	63	70	270	48,562.50
Brandel Chamblee	73	62	70	66	271	31,125
Allen Doyle	68	69	66	68	271	31,125
Steve Elkington	67	69	66	69	271	31,125
Greg Kraft	70	69	67	65	271	31,125
Jeff Maggert	67	71	66	67	271	31,125
Brett Ogle	70	68	64	69	271	31,125
Hal Sutton	69	69	66	67	271	31,125
Kirk Triplett	71	68	68	64	271	31,125
Fulton Allem	71	67	67	67	272	19,560
Jim Carter	71	65	70	66	272	19,560
Glen Day	71	67	65	69	272	19,560
Ernie Els	69	67	70	66	272	19,560
Charlie Rymer	68	71	61	72	272	19,560
Jay Don Blake	69	66	71	67	273	12,975
Dan Forsman	67	70	71	65	273	12,975
Jim Furyk	67	73	65	68	273	12,975
Jeff Gallagher	71	69	67	66	273	12,975
Jay Haas	69	68	65	71	273	12,975
Justin Leonard	68	72	69	64	273	12,975
John Maginnes	73	66	66	69	274	9,332.15
Loren Roberts	70	68	69	67	274	9,332.15
Brad Bryant	69	66	71	68	274	9,332.14
Jay Delsing	71	68	70	65	274	9,332.14
Scott McCarron	65	71	71	67	274	9,332.14
John Morse	70	65	70	69	274	9,332.14
Chris Smith	72	68	68	66	274	9,332.14
John Cook	65	70	70	70	275	7,218.75
Steve Lowery	67	69	72	67	275	7,218.75
Carl Paulson	69	68	70	68	275	7,218.75
Mike Standly	69	68	68	70	275	7,218.75
Franklin Langham	67	71	69	69	276	4,999.10
Mike Brisky	66	67	72	71	276	4,999.09
Scott Dunlap	69	68	67	72	276	4,999.09
Mike Heinen	68	70	66	72	276	4,999.09
John Mahaffey	73	66	68	69	276	4,999.09
Mike Reid	67	67	72	70	276	4,999.09
Lee Rinker	73	66	70	67	276	4,999.09
Paul Stankowski	70	68	70	68	276	4,999.09
Tommy Tolles	70	70	67	69	276	4,999.09
Bobby Wadkins	72	68	69	67	276	4,999.09
D.A. Weibring	70	69	66	71	276	4,999.09
Andy Bean	68	68	71	70	277	3,530
Billy Ray Brown	75	65	69	68	277	3,530
Mark Calcavecchia	70	70	68	69	277	3,530
Steve Jones	67	67	74	69	277	3,530
Tom Purtzer	69	70	70	68	277	3,530
Brian Tennyson	71	69	72	65	277	3,530
Ronnie Black	72	67	72	67	278	3,300
Olin Browne	68	72	72	66	278	3,300
David Edwards	69	68	68	73	278	3,300
Donnie Hammond	69	70	70	69	278	3,300
Tom Kite	72	66	68	72	278	3,300
Dicky Pride	69	71	71	67	278	3,300
Tom Watson	68	72	72	66	278	3,300
Phil Blackmar	70	68	73	68	279	3,060
Guy Boros	66	72	70	71	279	3,060
Bart Bryant	71	69	67	72	279	3,060
Curt Byrum	73	67	70	69	279	3,060

	SCORES				TOTAL	MONEY
David Feherty	69	69	71	70	279	3,060
David Frost	69	66	73	71	279	3,060
Paul Goydos	70	67	72	70	279	3,060
Scott Gump	72	65	73	69	279	3,060
Davis Love III	72	67	71	69	279	3,060
Steve Rintoul	69	70	68	73	280	2,910
Gary Rusnak	67	71	70	73	281	2,850
Kevin Sutherland	69	66	72	74	281	2,850
Scott Verplank	67	72	69	73	281	2,850
Bruce Lietzke	72	68	75	67	282	2,790
Joey Gullion	69	70	74	70	283	2,760
Anthony Rodriguez	71	67	75	74	287	2,730

MasterCard Colonial

Colonial Country Club, Ft. Worth, Texas
Par 35-35–70; 7,010 yards

May 16-19
purse, $1,500,000

	SCORES				TOTAL	MONEY
Corey Pavin	69	67	67	69	272	$270,000
Jeff Sluman	69	67	70	68	274	162,000
Rocco Mediate	68	66	68	73	275	102,000
Fred Couples	70	67	68	71	276	72,000
Davis Love III	72	70	68	67	277	60,000
Ben Crenshaw	71	71	70	66	278	48,562.50
Steve Jones	67	76	68	67	278	48,562.50
Payne Stewart	69	69	72	68	278	48,562.50
Tommy Tolles	72	64	75	67	278	48,562.50
Jeff Gallagher	66	70	71	72	279	39,000
Justin Leonard	73	69	66	71	279	39,000
David Duval	69	69	68	74	280	30,375
David Edwards	70	69	69	72	280	30,375
Naomichi Ozaki	71	70	69	70	280	30,375
Bob Tway	70	70	72	68	280	30,375
Emlyn Aubrey	67	69	71	74	281	23,250
Woody Austin	74	66	70	71	281	23,250
Scott Hoch	71	70	69	71	281	23,250
John Morse	70	69	70	72	281	23,250
Brad Faxon	72	70	72	68	282	14,683.34
Bruce Lietzke	71	71	68	72	282	14,683.34
Larry Nelson	76	67	69	70	282	14,683.34
Jim Gallagher, Jr.	70	69	72	71	282	14,683.33
Billy Mayfair	70	69	73	70	282	14,683.33
Mark McCumber	68	69	71	74	282	14,683.33
Gil Morgan	70	67	70	75	282	14,683.33
Tom Purtzer	69	69	71	73	282	14,683.33
Craig Stadler	68	68	73	73	282	14,683.33
Tom Kite	68	70	75	70	283	10,200
Vijay Singh	74	70	71	68	283	10,200
Curtis Strange	70	67	72	74	283	10,200
Peter Jacobsen	71	73	67	73	284	8,300
Franklin Langham	72	72	69	71	284	8,300
Roger Maltbie	70	70	71	73	284	8,300
Brett Ogle	68	72	67	77	284	8,300
David Ogrin	70	67	74	73	284	8,300
Craig Parry	70	69	75	70	284	8,300
Phil Blackmar	74	66	77	68	285	6,000

	SCORES				TOTAL	MONEY
Steve Elkington	70	73	71	71	285	6,000
Jim Furyk	68	73	70	74	285	6,000
Mike Heinen	69	71	69	76	285	6,000
Wayne Levi	66	68	74	77	285	6,000
Gene Sauers	70	73	73	69	285	6,000
Omar Uresti	66	69	75	75	285	6,000
Scott Verplank	70	66	73	76	285	6,000
Mark Brooks	71	67	75	73	286	3,900
Lennie Clements	73	71	71	71	286	3,900
Allen Doyle	70	74	75	67	286	3,900
Mike Hulbert	71	70	66	79	286	3,900
John Huston	69	71	70	76	286	3,900
Neal Lancaster	72	71	70	73	286	3,900
Bob Lohr	70	70	76	70	286	3,900
Doug Martin	70	72	70	74	286	3,900
Tom Watson	73	69	69	75	286	3,900
Fred Funk	72	71	70	74	287	3,450
Glen Day	73	70	76	69	288	3,345
Steve Lowery	73	70	72	73	288	3,345
Don Pooley	70	73	71	74	288	3,345
Nick Price	69	70	72	77	288	3,345
Mike Reid	73	69	72	74	288	3,345
Fuzzy Zoeller	69	75	70	74	288	3,345
Sean Murphy	76	68	67	78	289	3,225
Lanny Wadkins	70	68	73	78	289	3,225
Billy Andrade	72	69	73	76	290	3,150
Nolan Henke	68	72	78	72	290	3,150
Andrew Magee	70	68	77	75	290	3,150
Brian Claar	75	68	72	76	291	3,075
Ernie Els	75	69	71	76	291	3,075
Dave Stockton, Jr.	74	70	74	74	292	3,015
Kirk Triplett	68	74	72	78	292	3,015
Keith Clearwater	70	73	75	75	293	2,925
Marco Dawson	72	68	76	77	293	2,925
Jerry Kelly	68	74	74	77	293	2,925
Duffy Waldorf	74	69	75	75	293	2,925
Dan Pohl	72	71	73	78	294	2,850
Steve Stricker	72	71	73	79	295	2,820

Kemper Open

TPC at Avenel, Potomac, Maryland
Par 35-36–71; 7,005 yards

May 23-26
purse, $1,500,000

	SCORES				TOTAL	MONEY
Steve Stricker	69	68	65	68	270	$270,000
Brad Faxon	67	71	68	67	273	99,000
Scott Hoch	69	68	68	68	273	99,000
Mark O'Meara	67	69	70	67	273	99,000
Grant Waite	72	66	69	66	273	99,000
David Toms	71	65	66	72	274	54,000
Brad Fabel	67	70	66	72	275	50,250
Larry Mize	68	67	70	71	276	45,000
Mike Sullivan	67	69	71	69	276	45,000
John Daly	69	67	68	73	277	37,500
Corey Pavin	70	72	72	63	277	37,500
Payne Stewart	70	67	68	72	277	37,500

	SCORES				TOTAL	MONEY
Fulton Allem	71	68	67	72	278	27,300
Curt Byrum	70	72	68	68	278	27,300
Dan Forsman	71	70	69	68	278	27,300
Greg Kraft	68	71	71	68	278	27,300
Justin Leonard	71	69	73	65	278	27,300
Stuart Appleby	74	69	69	67	279	19,560
Gil Morgan	70	65	69	67	279	19,560
Chris Perry	70	66	72	71	279	19,560
Clarence Rose	71	69	70	69	279	19,560
Charlie Rymer	69	70	72	68	279	19,560
Ronnie Black	73	68	74	65	280	12,642.86
Bart Bryant	69	74	68	69	280	12,642.86
Brian Claar	70	66	73	71	280	12,642.86
Naomichi Ozaki	70	71	71	68	280	12,642.86
Gary Rusnak	72	68	70	70	280	12,642.86
Craig Parry	69	69	70	72	280	12,642.85
Jay Williamson	66	67	68	79	280	12,642.85
Jay Don Blake	71	72	68	70	281	9,315
Michael Bradley	73	68	71	69	281	9,315
Donnie Hammond	70	73	69	69	281	9,315
Scott Simpson	72	71	68	70	281	9,315
Jeff Sluman	71	70	73	67	281	9,315
Billy Ray Brown	72	71	71	68	282	6,928.13
Lennie Clements	68	74	70	70	282	6,928.13
Dillard Pruitt	73	68	74	67	282	6,928.13
Mike Springer	71	67	73	71	282	6,928.13
Jay Delsing	69	68	73	72	282	6,928.12
John Inman	72	69	67	74	282	6,928.12
Scott McCarron	66	66	74	76	282	6,928.12
Steve Rintoul	71	69	71	71	282	6,928.12
Billy Andrade	66	72	70	75	283	4,810
Olin Browne	68	69	72	74	283	4,810
Jim Carter	71	68	70	74	283	4,810
Rick Fehr	71	71	75	66	283	4,810
John Huston	71	68	74	70	283	4,810
Curtis Strange	72	69	70	72	283	4,810
Scott Gump	69	69	73	73	284	3,742.50
John Mahaffey	76	67	71	70	284	3,742.50
Phil Tataurangi	72	70	71	71	284	3,742.50
Robert Wrenn	70	72	71	71	284	3,742.50
Dave Barr	72	71	72	70	285	3,456
George Burns	71	71	70	73	285	3,456
Kelly Gibson	75	66	71	73	285	3,456
Billy Mayfair	70	73	73	69	285	3,456
Hal Sutton	73	70	71	71	285	3,456
Bob Gilder	67	71	73	75	286	3,315
Barry Jaeckel	70	68	71	77	286	3,315
Lee Janzen	72	70	70	74	286	3,315
John Maginnes	71	72	73	70	286	3,315
Hugh Royer III	72	71	72	72	287	3,240
Joel Edwards	72	71	73	72	288	3,150
Brian Henninger	71	69	70	78	288	3,150
Neal Lancaster	73	69	75	71	288	3,150
Blaine McCallister	73	67	72	76	288	3,150
Chris Smith	67	75	72	74	288	3,150
Keith Clearwater	77	66	74	72	289	3,045
Mike Hulbert	71	71	78	69	289	3,045
Bruce Fleisher	72	71	73	74	290	2,955
Robin Freeman	72	71	70	77	290	2,955
Peter Persons	72	70	77	71	290	2,955

	SCORES				TOTAL	MONEY
Brian Tennyson	74	69	73	74	290	2,955
Ken Green	71	72	76	72	291	2,880
Dicky Pride	71	70	73	78	292	2,835
Hisayuki Sasaki	69	74	77	72	292	2,835
Clark Dennis	70	73	77	73	293	2,775
Bryan Gorman	74	68	73	78	293	2,775
Frank Lickliter	72	70	80	78	300	2,730
Vijay Singh	71	72	76	82	301	2,700

Memorial Tournament

Muirfield Village Golf Club, Dublin, Ohio

Par 36-36—72; 7,104 yards

May 30-June 2

purse, $1,800,000

	SCORES				TOTAL	MONEY
Tom Watson	70	68	66	70	274	$324,000
David Duval	72	70	67	67	276	194,400
David Frost	73	68	70	67	278	104,400
Mark O'Meara	71	72	68	67	278	104,400
John Huston	74	61	71	73	279	72,000
Ernie Els	70	67	68	75	280	56,340
Brad Faxon	74	72	68	66	280	56,340
Mike Hulbert	74	68	69	69	280	56,340
Davis Love III	76	68	65	71	280	56,340
Paul Stankowski	73	66	67	74	280	56,340
Steve Lowery	67	71	71	72	281	43,200
Fuzzy Zoeller	71	69	70	71	281	43,200
Steve Stricker	72	70	70	70	282	37,800
Michael Bradley	72	70	70	71	283	31,500
Mark Calcavecchia	72	75	71	65	283	31,500
Fred Funk	70	73	68	72	283	31,500
Larry Mize	68	70	75	70	283	31,500
Woody Austin	69	69	73	73	284	25,200
Jesper Parnevik	74	70	67	73	284	25,200
Kenny Perry	70	70	71	73	284	25,200
Justin Leonard	74	72	68	71	285	18,720
Jeff Maggert	74	71	71	69	285	18,720
Rocco Mediate	73	71	70	71	285	18,720
Naomichi Ozaki	70	71	71	73	285	18,720
Payne Stewart	68	70	75	72	285	18,720
Mark Brooks	74	69	69	74	286	13,590
Craig Stadler	72	71	74	69	286	13,590
Hal Sutton	74	72	67	73	286	13,590
Tommy Tolles	73	73	72	68	286	13,590
Ben Crenshaw	74	69	70	74	287	10,240
Keith Fergus	73	68	76	70	287	10,240
Jay Haas	70	70	71	76	287	10,240
Mike Heinen	74	73	70	70	287	10,240
Tom Lehman	71	72	74	70	287	10,240
Brett Ogle	73	70	71	73	287	10,240
Tom Purtzer	73	74	67	73	287	10,240
Curtis Strange	72	71	74	70	287	10,240
Wayne Westner	68	70	71	78	287	10,240
Emlyn Aubrey	71	75	72	70	288	7,560
Joel Edwards	74	73	68	73	288	7,560
Larry Nelson	72	70	75	71	288	7,560
David Ogrin	74	71	73	70	288	7,560

	SCORES				TOTAL	MONEY
Stewart Cink	73	72	71	73	289	5,772
David Edwards	73	68	73	75	289	5,772
Mark McCumber	74	68	72	75	289	5,772
Vijay Singh	72	73	70	74	289	5,772
Bob Tway	72	74	71	72	289	5,772
Duffy Waldorf	71	74	70	74	289	5,772
Peter O'Malley	73	74	70	73	290	4,361.15
John Wilson	74	71	74	71	290	4,361.15
Paul Azinger	72	71	72	75	290	4,361.14
Andrew Coltart	75	69	72	74	290	4,361.14
Steve Elkington	73	72	72	73	290	4,361.14
Jim Furyk	69	74	72	75	290	4,361.14
Scott Hoch	71	73	73	73	290	4,361.14
John Cook	74	69	76	72	291	3,960
Allen Doyle	69	74	71	77	291	3,960
Robin Freeman	73	73	72	73	291	3,960
Wayne Grady	75	71	69	76	291	3,960
Tim Herron	73	69	75	74	291	3,960
Jerry Kelly	76	71	73	71	291	3,960
Scott McCarron	73	73	67	78	291	3,960
Jim McGovern	76	70	72	73	291	3,960
Rick Todd	71	73	72	75	291	3,960
Brad Bryant	73	73	72	74	292	3,762
Bob Lohr	73	68	73	78	292	3,762
Jay Don Blake	72	73	73	75	293	3,690
Loren Roberts	72	70	73	78	293	3,690
John Morse	75	69	74	76	294	3,618
Ted Tryba	72	72	74	76	294	3,618
Nolan Henke	76	71	72	76	295	3,546
Phil Mickelson	73	74	76	72	295	3,546
John Daly	70	74	73	79	296	3,474
Sandy Lyle	72	74	77	73	296	3,474
Scott Simpson	74	69	74	80	297	3,420
Lanny Wadkins	72	71	76	79	298	3,384
Hisayuki Sasaki	72	75	77	75	299	3,330
Gene Sauers	73	72	76	78	299	3,330

Buick Classic

Westchester Country Club, West Course, Rye, New York
Par 36-35–71; 6,779 yards

June 6-9
purse, $1,200,000

	SCORES				TOTAL	MONEY
Ernie Els	65	66	69	71	271	$216,000
Steve Elkington	66	72	70	71	279	79,200
Tom Lehman	71	71	67	70	279	79,200
Jeff Maggert	74	68	68	69	279	79,200
Craig Parry	70	66	72	71	279	79,200
Brad Faxon	70	72	67	71	280	40,200
David Frost	67	69	74	70	280	40,200
Fred Funk	72	70	67	71	280	40,200
Tim Herron	68	70	68	75	281	33,600
Corey Pavin	72	71	68	70	281	33,600
John Cook	72	70	71	69	282	25,440
Paul Goydos	70	75	69	68	282	25,440
Mike Hulbert	73	69	70	70	282	25,440
Greg Kraft	71	68	72	71	282	25,440

		SCORES			TOTAL	MONEY
Mike Reid	66	71	73	72	282	25,440
Woody Austin	70	68	73	72	283	18,600
Jeff Julian	71	69	76	67	283	18,600
Blaine McCallister	68	72	74	69	283	18,600
Greg Norman	67	70	74	72	283	18,600
Brad Bryant	70	71	72	71	284	13,980
John Maginnes	75	69	72	68	284	13,980
Vijay Singh	77	67	69	71	284	13,980
Kevin Sutherland	68	69	74	73	284	13,980
Glen Day	73	71	71	70	285	9,497.15
Hisayuki Sasaki	71	74	70	70	285	9,497.15
Chris Perry	69	76	69	71	285	9,497.14
Lee Rinker	71	73	70	71	285	9,497.14
Loren Roberts	69	72	73	71	285	9,497.14
Jeff Sluman	70	72	70	73	285	9,497.14
John Wilson	67	73	73	72	285	9,497.14
Billy Andrade	70	75	69	72	286	6,520
Brad Fabel	72	70	73	71	286	6,520
Ed Fiori	73	72	72	69	286	6,520
Joey Gullion	71	74	70	71	286	6,520
Tom Kite	72	71	72	71	286	6,520
Dicky Pride	72	71	74	69	286	6,520
Joey Sindelar	76	68	67	75	286	6,520
Taylor Smith	71	70	74	71	286	6,520
Mike Sullivan	73	69	72	72	286	6,520
Shane Bertsch	77	67	74	69	287	4,920
Brian Claar	75	69	71	72	287	4,920
Nick Faldo	71	71	73	72	287	4,920
Arjun Atwal	67	76	73	72	288	3,506.40
Emlyn Aubrey	73	69	75	71	288	3,506.40
Guy Boros	74	69	73	72	288	3,506.40
Jay Delsing	71	74	71	72	288	3,506.40
Wayne Grady	70	74	72	72	288	3,506.40
Scott Gump	70	72	77	69	288	3,506.40
Neal Lancaster	68	75	73	72	288	3,506.40
Hal Sutton	69	70	73	76	288	3,506.40
Jim Thorpe	72	73	70	73	288	3,506.40
Bruce Zabriski	73	71	70	74	288	3,506.40
Fulton Allem	70	75	73	71	289	2,714.67
Olin Browne	70	72	74	73	289	2,714.67
Jeff Gallagher	71	74	75	69	289	2,714.67
Pete Jordan	70	73	73	73	289	2,714.67
Wayne Levi	73	71	72	73	289	2,714.67
Ted Tryba	72	73	72	72	289	2,714.67
Mike Brisky	72	72	72	73	289	2,714.66
Don Pooley	71	70	74	74	289	2,714.66
Costantino Rocca	67	76	69	77	289	2,714.66
Dave Barr	72	73	75	70	290	2,520
Andy Bean	76	68	70	76	290	2,520
Jim Carter	74	70	74	72	290	2,520
Russ Cochran	74	69	72	75	290	2,520
Len Mattiace	75	70	71	74	290	2,520
Carl Paulson	70	72	72	76	290	2,520
Tom Purtzer	75	70	75	70	290	2,520
Bob Gilder	74	70	75	72	291	2,388
Ken Green	72	72	73	74	291	2,388
Rocco Mediate	72	71	75	73	291	2,388
Clarence Rose	74	69	76	72	291	2,388
Ronnie Black	69	74	78	71	292	2,268
Kelly Gibson	69	73	78	72	292	2,268

	SCORES				TOTAL	MONEY
Lee Janzen	73	71	77	71	292	2,268
Jerry Kelly	71	70	72	79	292	2,268
Mike Swartz	75	68	74	75	292	2,268
Bobby Wadkins	70	73	72	77	292	2,268
Joe Daley	73	70	76	74	293	2,172
Grant Waite	70	73	80	70	293	2,172
Chris Smith	74	70	77	73	294	2,136
Omar Uresti	71	73	77	77	298	2,112
Tim Petrovic	72	70	81	77	300	2,088

U.S. Open Championship

Oakland Hills Country Club, Bloomfield Hills, Michigan   June 13-16
Par 35-35–70; 6,990 yards   purse, $2,000,000

	SCORES				TOTAL	MONEY
Steve Jones	74	66	69	69	278	$425,000
Tom Lehman	71	72	65	71	279	204,801
Davis Love III	71	69	70	69	279	204,801
John Morse	68	74	68	70	280	111,235
Ernie Els	72	67	72	70	281	84,964.50
Jim Furyk	72	69	70	70	281	84,964.50
Ken Green	73	67	72	70	282	66,294.67
Vijay Singh	71	72	70	69	282	66,294.67
Scott Hoch	73	71	71	67	282	66,294.66
Lee Janzen	68	75	71	69	283	52,591
Colin Montgomerie	70	72	69	72	283	52,591
Greg Norman	73	66	74	70	283	52,591
Tom Watson	70	71	71	72	284	43,725.33
Dan Forsman	72	71	70	71	284	43,725.33
Frank Nobilo	69	71	70	74	284	43,725.33
David Berganio, Jr.	69	72	72	72	285	33,188.29
Nick Faldo	72	71	72	70	285	33,188.29
Mark O'Meara	72	73	68	72	285	33,188.29
Sam Torrance	71	69	71	74	285	33,188.29
Mark Brooks	76	68	69	72	285	33,188.28
Stewart Cink	69	73	70	73	285	33,188.28
John Cook	70	71	71	73	285	33,188.28
Billy Andrade	72	69	72	73	286	23,806
Woody Austin	67	72	72	75	286	23,806
Brad Bryant	73	71	74	68	286	23,806
Peter Jacobsen	71	74	70	71	286	23,806
John Daly	72	69	73	73	287	17,809.40
Pete Jordan	71	74	72	70	287	17,809.40
Jack Nicklaus	72	74	69	72	287	17,809.40
Payne Stewart	67	71	76	73	287	17,809.40
Curtis Strange	74	73	71	69	287	17,809.40
Michael Campbell	70	73	73	72	288	14,070.50
Anders Forsbrand	74	71	71	72	288	14,070.50
Steve Gotsche	72	70	74	72	288	14,070.50
Billy Mayfair	72	71	74	71	288	14,070.50
Sean Murphy	71	75	68	74	288	14,070.50
Brett Ogle	70	75	72	71	288	14,070.50
Tom Purtzer	76	71	71	70	288	14,070.50
Mike Swartz	72	72	74	70	288	14,070.50
Steve Elkington	72	70	74	73	289	9,918.20
Bob Ford	69	77	72	71	289	9,918.20

	SCORES				TOTAL	MONEY
J.L. Lewis	76	69	73	71	289	9,918.20
Lucas Parsons	75	71	73	70	289	9,918.20
Corey Pavin	73	70	72	74	289	9,918.20
Wayne Riley	73	69	74	73	289	9,918.20
Loren Roberts	72	73	69	75	289	9,918.20
Scott Simpson	70	71	76	72	289	9,918.20
Tommy Tolles	77	68	71	73	289	9,918.20
Kirk Triplett	70	73	72	74	289	9,918.20
Michael Bradley	71	74	71	74	290	6,619.10
Alexander Cejka	74	70	72	74	290	6,619.10
Kelly Gibson	71	73	71	75	290	6,619.10
Bob Gilder	73	72	75	70	290	6,619.10
Joey Gullion	73	72	73	72	290	6,619.10
Hale Irwin	72	71	73	74	290	6,619.10
Justin Leonard	71	76	67	76	290	6,619.10
Kenny Perry	73	71	75	71	290	6,619.10
Jeff Sluman	70	74	74	72	290	6,619.10
Wayne Westner	72	75	74	69	290	6,619.10
David Gilford	74	69	74	74	291	5,825
Dennis Harrington	75	71	71	74	291	5,825
Steve Lowery	73	74	73	71	291	5,825
William Murchison	76	68	74	73	291	5,825
Bill Porter	73	75	72	71	291	5,825
Steve Stricker	74	71	75	71	291	5,825
*Randy Leen	77	71	70	73	291	Medal
Paul Azinger	69	74	78	71	292	5,645
Curt Byrum	70	76	71	75	292	5,645
David Duval	75	72	75	70	292	5,645
Jim Gallagher, Jr.	71	72	73	76	292	5,645
Wayne Grady	71	75	72	74	292	5,645
Frank Lickliter	75	71	73	73	292	5,645
Andrew Morse	76	72	74	70	292	5,645
Peter O'Malley	75	73	70	74	292	5,645
David Ogrin	72	74	72	74	292	5,645
Masashi Ozaki	69	72	77	74	292	5,645
Costantino Rocca	71	74	73	74	292	5,645
Bob Tway	72	75	68	77	292	5,645
Michael Christie	72	75	72	74	293	5,505
Ian Woosnam	72	72	74	75	293	5,505
*Trip Kuehne	79	69	73	72	293	5,505
Brad Faxon	70	72	76	76	294	5,415
John Huston	73	72	76	73	294	5,415
Kent Jones	71	74	76	73	294	5,415
Skip Kendall	77	71	73	73	294	5,415
Tom Kite	76	71	72	75	294	5,415
Neal Lancaster	74	67	74	79	294	5,415
Scott McCarron	72	72	75	75	294	5,415
*Tiger Woods	76	69	77	72	294	
Jay Haas	73	72	74	76	295	5,305
Jack O'Keefe	72	71	76	76	295	5,305
Craig Parry	70	76	75	74	295	5,305
Javier Sanchez	71	76	74	74	295	5,305
Phil Mickelson	76	71	73	76	296	5,235
Tom Pernice, Jr.	74	72	74	76	296	5,235
Anthony Rodriguez	71	77	76	72	296	5,235
Jeff Maggert	75	69	81	72	297	5,165
Blaine McCallister	71	75	76	75	297	5,165
Jim Thorpe	75	71	78	73	297	5,165
Philip Walton	69	73	78	77	297	5,165
Olin Browne	73	70	76	79	298	5,105

	SCORES				TOTAL	MONEY
Omar Uresti	76	72	74	76	298	5,105
Gary Trivisonno	69	75	78	77	299	5,075
Mark Wiebe	74	74	75	77	300	5,055
Rich Yokota	79	67	76	79	301	5,035
*Steve Scott	71	73	81	76	301	
Michael Burke, Jr.	78	70	77	77	302	5,015
Shawn Kelly	73	75	79	82	309	5,000

Out of Final 36 Holes

			TOTAL
Scott Dunlap	78	71	149
Paul Goydos	71	78	149
Mike Heinen	73	76	149
Tim Herron	75	74	149
Jeff Julian	74	75	149
Darrell Kestner	77	72	149
Ty Armstrong	80	70	150
Mark Calcavecchia	77	73	150
Darren Clarke	77	73	150
Ben Crenshaw	80	70	150
Todd Demsey	77	73	150
*Wendell Hobby	74	76	150
Larry Mize	74	76	150
Francis Quinn	73	77	150
Ted Tryba	74	76	150
Duffy Waldorf	73	77	150
Kent Wiese	77	73	150
Emlyn Aubrey	78	73	151
Philip Blackmar	78	73	151
David Edwards	72	79	151
John Flannery	76	75	151
Fred Funk	74	77	151
Brandt Jobe	75	76	151
Steve Jurgensen	74	77	151
Barry Lane	75	76	151
Tom Weiskopf	76	75	151
Brian Gay	75	77	152
Scott Gump	75	77	152
Mark McCumber	76	76	152
Bryan Hughett	76	77	153
Carl Paulson	78	75	153
Kevin Sutherland	73	80	152
David Toms	76	77	153
*Reid Edstrom	77	77	154
Steve Flesch	80	74	154
Brian Henninger	78	76	154
Mark James	75	79	154
Greg Lesher	81	73	154
Peter Teravainen	75	79	154
Paul Eales	74	81	155
Ronald Ewing	80	76	156
David Frost	78	78	156
Tad Holloway	80	76	156
Darrett Brinker	78	80	158
Ian Baker-Finch	83	82	165
Charles Raulerson	83		WD
Bernhard Langer	75		DQ
Grant Waite			DQ

(Professionals who did not complete 72 holes received $1,000.)

FedEx St. Jude Classic

TPC at Southwind, Memphis, Tennessee
Par 36-35–71; 7,006 yards

June 20-23
purse, $1,350,000

	SCORES				TOTAL	MONEY
John Cook	64	62	63	69	258	$243,000
John Adams	65	64	66	70	265	145,800
Kenny Perry	67	64	67	68	266	91,800
Justin Leonard	70	64	66	67	267	59,400
Gil Morgan	70	65	68	64	267	59,400
Paul Stankowski	69	64	66	69	268	48,600
Michael Bradley	69	67	67	66	269	43,537.50
Mike Swartz	64	71	67	67	269	43,537.50
John Huston	67	68	66	69	270	36,450
Tom Purtzer	67	69	69	65	270	36,450
Kirk Triplett	68	68	64	70	270	36,450
Jay Delsing	68	68	67	68	271	31,050
Glen Day	72	68	67	65	272	26,100
Dan Forsman	69	67	67	69	272	26,100
Tim Herron	72	63	69	68	272	26,100
Stuart Appleby	65	67	73	68	273	20,250
Patrick Lee	64	67	71	71	273	20,250
Billy Mayfair	68	70	65	70	273	20,250
Peter O'Malley	68	69	66	70	273	20,250
Ted Tryba	69	66	68	70	273	20,250
Kelly Gibson	68	66	69	71	274	14,580
Dudley Hart	71	68	69	66	274	14,580
Steve Jurgensen	66	68	68	72	274	14,580
Larry Nelson	68	67	69	70	274	14,580
Bob Gilder	67	67	68	73	275	11,025
David Peoples	66	71	65	73	275	11,025
David Toms	69	67	67	72	275	11,025
Phil Blackmar	68	68	72	68	276	8,784.72
Rick Fehr	72	67	71	66	276	8,784.72
Scott Gump	70	68	69	69	276	8,784.72
Bryan Gorman	70	69	68	69	276	8,784.71
Donnie Hammond	70	69	68	69	276	8,784.71
Tom Scherrer	70	66	71	69	276	8,784.71
Dave Stockton, Jr.	70	65	70	71	276	8,784.71
Tommy Armour III	69	66	72	70	277	6,097.45
Jim McGovern	72	66	69	70	277	6,097.45
Lucas Parsons	70	69	68	70	277	6,097.45
Clarence Rose	71	66	72	68	277	6,097.45
Jim Carter	65	71	68	73	277	6,097.44
Brad Fabel	67	72	67	71	277	6,097.44
Keith Fergus	69	66	70	72	277	6,097.44
Mike Hulbert	67	69	68	73	277	6,097.44
Chris Perry	68	70	68	71	277	6,097.44
Joel Edwards	70	68	71	69	278	4,081.50
Wayne Grady	70	69	70	69	278	4,081.50
Frank Lickliter	65	74	71	68	278	4,081.50
Loren Roberts	72	67	68	71	278	4,081.50
Curtis Strange	68	72	71	67	278	4,081.50
Tray Tyner	69	68	69	72	278	4,081.50
Lennie Clements	69	70	69	71	279	3,361.50
Kevin Sutherland	67	71	70	71	279	3,361.50
Anders Forsbrand	66	70	73	71	280	3,132
Doug Martin	68	67	69	76	280	3,132
Sean Murphy	69	69	69	73	280	3,132

	SCORES				TOTAL	MONEY
Mike Reid	71	69	71	69	280	3,132
Tommy Tolles	69	71	69	71	280	3,132
Jay Williamson	67	69	68	76	280	3,132
Ronnie Black	65	72	74	70	281	2,943
Joe Daley	72	66	70	73	281	2,943
John Daly	64	71	70	76	281	2,943
Craig Parry	71	68	72	70	281	2,943
Dicky Pride	67	70	72	72	281	2,943
Charlie Rymer	72	67	71	71	281	2,943
Tim Simpson	71	68	71	71	281	2,943
Neal Lancaster	68	72	70	72	282	2,821.50
Mike Sullivan	69	68	71	74	282	2,821.50
Chip Beck	68	68	74	73	283	2,754
Joey Gullion	71	66	72	74	283	2,754
Davis Love III	72	68	74	69	283	2,754
Shane Bertsch	67	69	73	75	284	2,686.50
Steve Jones	70	69	72	73	284	2,686.50
Mark Brooks	71	68	75	73	287	2,646

Canon Greater Hartford Open

TPC at River Highlands, Cromwell, Connecticut
Par 35-35–70; 6,820 yards

June 27-30
purse, $1,500,000

	SCORES				TOTAL	MONEY
D.A. Weibring	68	65	70	67	270	$270,000
Tom Kite	72	68	66	68	274	162,000
Mark Calcavecchia	71	67	68	69	275	78,000
Dicky Pride	70	70	68	67	275	78,000
Fuzzy Zoeller	75	66	66	68	275	78,000
Mike Brisky	71	72	63	70	276	52,125
Joel Edwards	70	70	68	68	276	52,125
Brad Faxon	68	70	71	68	277	46,500
Steve Jones	72	68	71	67	278	40,500
Roger Maltbie	67	71	72	68	278	40,500
Kevin Sutherland	67	65	72	74	278	40,500
Jay Don Blake	71	71	67	70	279	28,500
Brandel Chamblee	72	68	67	72	279	28,500
Joe Daley	64	70	73	72	279	28,500
Bob Gilder	66	71	70	72	279	28,500
Tray Tyner	70	70	68	71	279	28,500
Robert Wrenn	68	71	71	69	279	28,500
Bart Bryant	73	70	71	66	280	18,257.15
Lee Janzen	73	66	72	69	280	18,257.15
Chip Beck	69	71	70	70	280	18,257.14
Patrick Burke	70	67	72	71	280	18,257.14
Robin Freeman	68	72	71	69	280	18,257.14
Robert Gamez	71	68	66	75	280	18,257.14
Wayne Levi	69	69	72	70	280	18,257.14
Olin Browne	71	69	68	73	281	11,700
Bruce Fleisher	68	70	71	72	281	11,700
Rocco Mediate	70	71	71	69	281	11,700
John Morse	71	69	69	72	281	11,700
Larry Nelson	70	70	69	72	281	11,700
Shane Bertsch	67	72	76	67	282	8,914.29
Peter Jacobsen	72	70	71	69	282	8,914.29
Lee Rinker	69	70	74	69	282	8,914.29

	SCORES				TOTAL	MONEY
Steve Stricker	73	69	76	64	282	8,914.29
Stuart Appleby	73	70	69	70	282	8,914.28
Rick Fehr	69	73	69	71	282	8,914.28
John Maginnes	71	69	69	73	282	8,914.28
John Daly	68	74	70	71	283	6,300
Bob Estes	71	70	69	73	283	6,300
Brian Henninger	70	69	69	75	283	6,300
Mike Hulbert	72	70	69	72	283	6,300
Neal Lancaster	67	72	72	72	283	6,300
Steve Lowery	67	73	72	71	283	6,300
Don Pooley	69	70	73	71	283	6,300
Steve Rintoul	70	70	71	72	283	6,300
Brian Claar	71	71	70	72	284	4,515
Steve Jurgensen	70	70	74	70	284	4,515
Jesper Parnevik	72	69	73	70	284	4,515
Joey Sindelar	74	66	72	72	284	4,515
Paul Azinger	69	74	72	70	285	3,634.29
John Inman	71	71	71	72	285	3,634.29
Andy Morse	75	67	71	72	285	3,634.29
Paul Stankowski	71	71	73	70	285	3,634.29
Glen Day	69	72	70	74	285	3,634.28
Mike Sullivan	67	71	72	75	285	3,634.28
Kirk Triplett	71	70	70	74	285	3,634.28
Woody Austin	68	74	74	70	286	3,360
Fred Funk	71	71	70	74	286	3,360
Kelly Gibson	71	71	70	74	286	3,360
Dudley Hart	68	72	72	74	286	3,360
Mark Pfeil	72	71	68	75	286	3,360
Tom Byrum	69	70	74	74	287	3,195
Dan Forsman	71	72	73	71	287	3,195
Greg Kraft	70	71	72	74	287	3,195
Frank Lickliter	73	70	68	76	287	3,195
Charlie Rymer	68	75	68	76	287	3,195
Jay Williamson	71	70	73	73	287	3,195
Andy Bean	70	72	74	73	289	3,030
Guy Boros	73	70	75	71	289	3,030
Bill Kratzert	73	68	74	74	289	3,030
Gary Rusnak	70	73	75	71	289	3,030
Dave Stockton, Jr.	69	72	74	74	289	3,030
Tommy Armour III	71	70	79	70	290	2,925
Dan Pohl	70	70	79	71	290	2,925
Scott Dunlap	72	71	70	78	291	2,850
Keith Fergus	73	70	75	73	291	2,850
David Peoples	69	73	75	74	291	2,850
Larry Rinker	71	71	75	75	292	2,775
Ted Tryba	75	68	77	72	292	2,775

Motorola Western Open

Cog Hill Golf & Country Club, Dubsdread Course,
Lemont, Illinois
Par 36-36–72; 7,073 yards

July 4-7
purse, $2,000,000

	SCORES				TOTAL	MONEY
Steve Stricker	65	69	67	69	270	$360,000
Billy Andrade	69	71	69	69	278	176,000
Jay Don Blake	67	67	73	71	278	176,000
Mike Brisky	74	67	68	70	279	78,750

		SCORES			TOTAL	MONEY
Glen Day	70	71	69	69	279	78,750
Jim Gallagher, Jr.	74	68	70	67	279	78,750
Craig Parry	69	69	70	71	279	78,750
Mark Brooks	68	70	70	72	280	54,000
Steve Elkington	70	72	67	71	280	54,000
Lee Janzen	67	68	71	74	280	54,000
Justin Leonard	69	67	72	72	280	54,000
Vijay Singh	71	70	69	70	280	54,000
Nolan Henke	67	71	71	72	281	36,400
Mark McCumber	72	68	71	70	281	36,400
Naomichi Ozaki	67	70	74	70	281	36,400
Tom Purtzer	72	71	70	68	281	36,400
Jeff Sluman	67	70	72	72	281	36,400
Chip Beck	71	71	72	68	282	23,500
Ben Crenshaw	68	73	72	69	282	23,500
Tom Lehman	73	70	68	71	282	23,500
Rocco Mediate	71	71	72	68	282	23,500
Mike Reid	70	71	69	72	282	23,500
Lee Rinker	71	71	70	70	282	23,500
Curtis Strange	70	69	72	71	282	23,500
Bob Tway	72	71	69	70	282	23,500
Grant Waite	69	74	70	70	283	13,611.12
Fred Couples	72	69	72	70	283	13,611.11
John Huston	70	68	69	76	283	13,611.11
Peter Jacobsen	68	72	70	73	283	13,611.11
Billy Mayfair	71	68	73	71	283	13,611.11
Phil Mickelson	69	71	70	73	283	13,611.11
Don Pooley	69	71	71	72	283	13,611.11
Joey Sindelar	72	69	70	72	283	13,611.11
Payne Stewart	70	70	68	75	283	13,611.11
John Cook	72	68	68	76	284	9,237.50
Paul Goydos	71	69	69	75	284	9,237.50
Scott Gump	71	69	71	73	284	9,237.50
Steve Jurgensen	71	71	66	76	284	9,237.50
Jerry Kelly	69	72	69	74	284	9,237.50
Larry Mize	67	73	71	73	284	9,237.50
Tommy Tolles	72	69	70	73	284	9,237.50
Bobby Wadkins	70	68	72	74	284	9,237.50
Stuart Appleby	73	67	70	75	285	6,800
Fred Funk	69	72	70	74	285	6,800
Tim Herron	68	71	72	74	285	6,800
Ted Tryba	71	70	69	75	285	6,800
Olin Browne	72	70	73	71	286	5,075
Jim Carter	69	72	73	72	286	5,075
Brian Claar	74	68	72	72	286	5,075
Lennie Clements	72	69	70	75	286	5,075
John Daly	70	68	76	72	286	5,075
Robin Freeman	73	69	74	70	286	5,075
Blaine McCallister	67	76	73	70	286	5,075
Gene Sauers	72	69	75	70	286	5,075
Paul Azinger	71	71	70	75	287	4,400
Brad Bryant	64	75	74	74	287	4,400
Brad Faxon	71	71	70	75	287	4,400
Keith Fergus	72	71	73	71	287	4,400
Wayne Grady	71	68	70	78	287	4,400
Neal Lancaster	71	72	71	73	287	4,400
Davis Love III	68	69	74	76	287	4,400
Jeff Maggert	70	67	73	77	287	4,400
Doug Martin	72	71	75	69	287	4,400
Jesper Parnevik	71	72	69	75	287	4,400

	SCORES				TOTAL	MONEY
Clarence Rose	68	74	69	76	287	4,400
Jim Furyk	68	75	72	73	288	4,140
Kelly Gibson	70	72	71	75	288	4,140
Ronnie Black	71	70	72	76	289	4,060
Tom Watson	72	68	74	75	289	4,060
Bob Estes	71	70	77	72	290	3,880
David Frost	72	71	72	75	290	3,880
Steve Jones	76	67	74	73	290	3,880
Franklin Langham	71	71	69	79	290	3,880
Nick Price	70	70	73	77	290	3,880
Charlie Rymer	71	70	72	77	290	3,880
Chris Smith	72	71	73	74	290	3,880
Mark Calcavecchia	69	70	72	80	291	3,720
D.A. Weibring	70	73	73	76	292	3,680
Jay Delsing	70	73	76	76	295	3,640
Joe Acosta, Jr.	68	74	77	79	298	3,600

Michelob Championship at Kingsmill

Kingsmill Golf Club, Williamsburg, Virginia
Par 35-36–71; 6,797 yards

July 11-14
purse, $1,250,000

	SCORES				TOTAL	MONEY
Scott Hoch	64	68	66	67	265	$225,000
Tom Purtzer	66	68	69	66	269	135,000
Michael Bradley	69	67	70	66	272	65,000
Fred Funk	65	69	69	69	272	65,000
Ted Tryba	70	70	65	67	272	65,000
Dicky Pride	67	68	67	71	273	45,000
Tommy Armour III	67	67	71	69	274	40,312.50
David Edwards	67	70	67	70	274	40,312.50
Olin Browne	69	69	70	67	275	33,750
Donnie Hammond	69	68	70	68	275	33,750
Mark McCumber	68	67	70	70	275	33,750
Ronnie Black	71	67	71	67	276	24,500
Keith Clearwater	67	69	70	70	276	24,500
John Maginnes	73	69	68	66	276	24,500
Blaine McCallister	71	68	68	69	276	24,500
David Ogrin	68	72	65	71	276	24,500
Tom Byrum	71	68	69	69	277	16,916.67
Rex Caldwell	70	66	68	73	277	16,916.67
Jay Haas	70	68	72	67	277	16,916.67
John Wilson	68	73	64	72	277	16,916.67
Marco Dawson	76	66	67	68	277	16,916.66
Frank Lickliter	66	69	70	72	277	16,916.66
Billy Andrade	68	71	67	72	278	10,041.67
Kelly Gibson	73	64	69	72	278	10,041.67
Clarence Rose	68	71	68	71	278	10,041.67
Taylor Smith	69	68	68	73	278	10,041.67
Kirk Triplett	69	70	73	66	278	10,041.67
Omar Uresti	67	69	71	71	278	10,041.67
Pete Jordan	71	71	66	70	278	10,041.66
Jeff Julian	66	70	71	71	278	10,041.66
Carl Paulson	73	63	69	73	278	10,041.66
Jay Don Blake	69	70	73	67	279	7,075
Steve Jurgensen	67	70	69	73	279	7,075
Steve Lowery	68	70	70	71	279	7,075

	SCORES				TOTAL	MONEY
Hisayuki Sasaki	69	72	69	69	279	7,075
Curtis Strange	65	77	68	69	279	7,075
Chip Beck	69	70	68	73	280	5,500
Bart Bryant	68	66	71	75	280	5,500
Brad Bryant	73	67	72	68	280	5,500
Mike Heinen	69	70	73	68	280	5,500
Jerry Kelly	70	68	71	71	280	5,500
Neal Lancaster	69	67	73	71	280	5,500
Jim Carter	73	68	68	72	281	3,806.25
Bob Gilder	68	69	72	72	281	3,806.25
John Inman	69	73	71	68	281	3,806.25
Len Mattiace	70	70	70	71	281	3,806.25
Jim McGovern	71	68	69	73	281	3,806.25
Gary Rusnak	70	70	68	73	281	3,806.25
Mike Springer	69	73	70	69	281	3,806.25
Tray Tyner	70	71	68	72	281	3,806.25
Joe Daley	72	69	70	71	282	2,960
Brad Fabel	70	72	72	68	282	2,960
Joey Gullion	67	72	76	67	282	2,960
Chris Perry	68	70	74	70	282	2,960
Paul Stankowski	67	73	71	71	282	2,960
Glen Day	72	70	72	69	283	2,775
Bruce Fleisher	68	71	71	73	283	2,775
Tom Gillis	70	72	71	70	283	2,775
Hugh Royer III	72	67	74	70	283	2,775
Gene Sauers	69	68	71	75	283	2,775
Ron Whittaker	69	73	73	68	283	2,775
Larry Rinker	66	71	74	72	283	2,775
Mike Hulbert	72	70	71	71	284	2,662.50
Dave Stockton, Jr.	75	67	71	71	284	2,662.50
Simon Cooke	68	69	71	77	285	2,562.50
Allen Doyle	72	69	71	73	285	2,562.50
Scott Medlin	69	70	72	74	285	2,562.50
Steve Rintoul	78	64	73	70	285	2,562.50
Kevin Sutherland	72	70	68	75	285	2,562.50
Lanny Wadkins	72	70	71	72	285	2,562.50
Jay Williamson	71	67	70	78	286	2,475
Chris Smith	68	72	75	72	287	2,437.50
Stan Utley	68	74	71	74	287	2,437.50
Mike Donald	71	70	73	76	290	2,387.50
Dudley Hart	69	72	75	74	290	2,387.50
Lee Rinker	75	67	74	76	292	2,350
Billy Ray Brown	75	67	74	77	293	2,312.50
Tom Jenkins	71	70	74	78	293	2,312.50

Deposit Guaranty Golf Classic

Annandale Golf Club, Madison, Missouri
Par 36-36—72; 6,797 yards

July 18-21
purse, $1,000,000

	SCORES				TOTAL	MONEY
Willie Wood	68	67	66	67	268	$180,000
Kirk Triplett	66	68	67	68	269	108,000
Scott Hoch	69	69	68	65	271	58,000
Greg Kraft	68	66	66	71	271	58,000
Phil Blackmar	70	68	66	68	272	35,125
David Edwards	68	67	66	71	272	35,125

	SCORES				TOTAL	MONEY
Neal Lancaster	70	67	66	69	272	35,125
David Ogrin	69	68	69	66	272	35,125
Robin Freeman	72	65	68	68	273	29,000
Steve Jurgensen	68	68	69	69	274	26,000
Bobby Wadkins	68	65	68	73	274	26,000
Glen Day	70	67	70	68	275	20,250
Brad Fabel	68	68	70	69	275	20,250
Len Mattiace	69	70	69	67	275	20,250
David Toms	68	69	68	70	275	20,250
Marco Dawson	71	69	66	70	276	15,000
Scott Gump	69	67	72	68	276	15,000
Brian Henninger	71	67	70	68	276	15,000
Clarence Rose	69	69	68	70	276	15,000
Mike Sullivan	65	70	69	72	276	15,000
Stewart Cink	70	66	68	73	277	10,400
Keith Clearwater	71	61	72	73	277	10,400
Dudley Hart	66	68	72	71	277	10,400
Hal Sutton	69	66	71	71	277	10,400
Brian Tennyson	68	70	69	70	277	10,400
Ed Fiori	69	71	68	70	278	7,100
Chris Perry	70	68	70	70	278	7,100
Mark Pfeil	68	69	71	70	278	7,100
Gary Rusnak	71	68	72	67	278	7,100
Hisayuki Sasaki	66	69	70	73	278	7,100
Mike Smith	70	68	70	70	278	7,100
Dave Stockton, Jr.	67	69	72	70	278	7,100
Billy Ray Brown	71	68	72	68	279	5,062.50
Bart Bryant	69	69	73	68	279	5,062.50
Tom Byrum	70	68	70	71	279	5,062.50
Bob Gilder	72	70	69	68	279	5,062.50
Carl Paulson	71	68	70	70	279	5,062.50
Mike Springer	69	69	70	71	279	5,062.50
Kevin Sutherland	68	67	71	73	279	5,062.50
Ron Whittaker	68	68	73	70	279	5,062.50
Lennie Clements	69	73	66	72	280	3,315.56
Russ Cochran	71	71	67	71	280	3,315.56
Donnie Hammond	69	72	72	67	280	3,315.56
Jim McGovern	72	69	69	70	280	3,315.56
Steve Rintoul	70	71	68	71	280	3,315.56
John Adams	71	65	72	72	280	3,315.55
Mark Carnevale	67	70	70	73	280	3,315.55
Mike Heinen	70	67	70	73	280	3,315.55
Ted Schulz	73	66	71	70	280	3,315.55
Stuart Appleby	71	66	71	73	281	2,412
Tommy Armour III	67	69	74	71	281	2,412
Brian Claar	71	70	68	72	281	2,412
Jeff Julian	67	67	71	76	281	2,412
Dillard Pruitt	67	73	73	68	281	2,412
Robert Gamez	66	75	70	71	282	2,270
Bob Lohr	72	70	69	71	282	2,270
Gil Morgan	72	62	72	76	282	2,270
Hugh Royer III	74	68	69	71	282	2,270
Emlyn Aubrey	70	71	69	73	283	2,160
Guy Boros	71	68	70	74	283	2,160
Jim Carter	68	72	69	74	283	2,160
Dick Mast	67	72	74	70	283	2,160
Blaine McCallister	72	69	70	72	283	2,160
Charlie Rymer	73	69	70	71	283	2,160
Tom Scherrer	70	71	71	71	283	2,160
Bill Britton	73	69	68	74	284	2,030

	SCORES				TOTAL	MONEY
Doug Dunakey	72	70	71	71	284	2,030
Kelly Gibson	70	72	70	72	284	2,030
Jeff Hart	74	67	70	73	284	2,030
David Peoples	73	68	71	72	284	2,030
Sam Randolph	73	69	69	73	284	2,030
Joel Edwards	73	69	74	69	285	1,950
Wayne Grady	71	71	71	72	285	1,950
John Elliott	70	71	73	72	286	1,860
Bryan Gorman	66	75	74	71	286	1,860
Barry Jaeckel	68	69	74	75	286	1,860
Jim Nelford	70	72	74	70	286	1,860
Peter Persons	73	69	72	72	286	1,860
Dicky Pride	68	69	73	76	286	1,860
Don Walsworth	72	70	74	70	286	1,860
John Inman	69	73	73	72	287	1,770
Leonard Thompson	70	71	76	70	287	1,770
Mike Brisky	70	72	74	73	289	1,740
Greg Powers	73	69	79	75	296	1,720

CVS Charity Classic

Pleasant Valley Country Club, Sutton, Massachusetts   July 25-28
Par 35-36–71; 7,110 yards   purse, $1,200,000

	SCORES				TOTAL	MONEY
John Cook	65	67	67	69	268	$216,000
Russ Cochran	68	64	71	68	271	129,600
Bruce Fleisher	65	67	70	72	274	81,600
Marco Dawson	68	69	68	70	275	45,240
Kenny Perry	66	71	69	69	275	45,240
Mike Reid	67	70	70	68	275	45,240
Charlie Rymer	72	66	66	71	275	45,240
Mike Standly	68	67	71	69	275	45,240
Brad Faxon	70	67	67	72	276	32,400
Dudley Hart	70	71	69	66	276	32,400
Brian Henninger	68	67	70	71	276	32,400
Paul Azinger	69	68	70	70	277	25,200
Rick Fehr	72	69	68	68	277	25,200
Robert Gamez	69	70	69	69	277	25,200
Billy Andrade	67	70	69	72	278	17,430
Patrick Burke	70	64	70	74	278	17,430
Tom Byrum	69	66	73	70	278	17,430
Mark Calcavecchia	68	72	68	70	278	17,430
Scott Gump	70	71	68	69	278	17,430
Greg Kraft	70	67	70	71	278	17,430
Doug Martin	71	69	69	69	278	17,430
Chris Perry	67	72	70	69	278	17,430
Wayne Grady	71	68	71	69	279	10,680
Wayne Levi	70	65	72	72	279	10,680
Jim McGovern	68	69	68	74	279	10,680
Sam Randolph	67	74	69	69	279	10,680
Willie Wood	71	69	67	72	279	10,680
Phil Blackmar	71	68	70	71	280	8,340
Ken Green	70	69	70	71	280	8,340
Hugh Royer III	65	71	72	72	280	8,340
Mike Springer	71	67	71	71	280	8,340
Pat Bates	71	68	74	68	281	5,713.85

		SCORES			TOTAL	MONEY
Ronnie Black	70	69	71	71	281	5,713.85
Dan Forsman	69	69	76	67	281	5,713.85
Mike Heinen	69	69	74	69	281	5,713.85
Nolan Henke	69	70	67	75	281	5,713.85
Carl Paulson	71	67	74	69	281	5,713.85
Jeff Sluman	68	71	70	72	281	5,713.85
Robert Wrenn	68	72	71	70	281	5,713.85
Olin Browne	69	68	74	70	281	5,713.84
Bart Bryant	69	71	68	73	281	5,713.84
Brian Claar	68	69	73	71	281	5,713.84
Keith Clearwater	68	69	71	73	281	5,713.84
John Inman	70	68	69	74	281	5,713.84
Allen Doyle	69	67	74	72	282	3,513.60
Steve Jurgensen	70	71	71	70	282	3,513.60
Clarence Rose	71	69	68	74	282	3,513.60
Tony Sills	71	70	72	69	282	3,513.60
Tommy Tolles	72	67	72	71	282	3,513.60
Stuart Appleby	71	69	71	72	283	2,835
Dave Barr	69	71	70	73	283	2,835
Jim Carter	68	71	73	71	283	2,835
Bob Gilder	66	72	73	72	283	2,835
Brian Kamm	72	68	69	74	283	2,835
Bob Lohr	69	72	72	70	283	2,835
Blaine McCallister	67	69	76	71	283	2,835
Tray Tyner	70	70	68	75	283	2,835
Buddy Gardner	70	71	74	69	284	2,616
Pete Jordan	71	69	70	74	284	2,616
Jerry Kelly	70	69	73	72	284	2,616
Steve Lowery	71	68	69	76	284	2,616
Fran Quinn	71	68	71	74	284	2,616
Joey Sindelar	73	68	73	70	284	2,616
Scott Trethewey	68	72	70	74	284	2,616
Jeff Gallagher	68	72	71	74	285	2,484
Barry Jaeckel	72	68	73	72	285	2,484
John Maginnes	69	70	71	75	285	2,484
Tom Scherrer	67	72	74	72	285	2,484
Emlyn Aubrey	66	69	71	80	286	2,376
Guy Boros	67	73	72	74	286	2,376
Joe Daley	70	71	75	70	286	2,376
Fred Funk	70	70	73	73	286	2,376
Kevin Sutherland	70	68	73	75	286	2,376
Bryan Gorman	72	68	72	75	287	2,292
Len Mattiace	71	70	71	75	287	2,292
Ed Fiori	66	73	74	75	288	2,220
Hubert Green	69	70	74	75	288	2,220
Franklin Langham	68	73	74	73	288	2,220
Steve Rintoul	72	69	73	74	288	2,220
David Peoples	68	71	73	80	292	2,160

Buick Open

Warwick Hills Golf & Country Club,
Grand Blanc, Michigan
Par 36-36–72; 7,105 yards

August 1-4
purse, $1,200,000

		SCORES			TOTAL	MONEY
Justin Leonard	65	64	69	68	266	$216,000
Chip Beck	69	65	70	67	271	129,600

	SCORES				TOTAL	MONEY
Woody Austin	72	65	68	68	273	57,600
Jim Carter	65	67	72	69	273	57,600
Rick Fehr	64	67	70	72	273	57,600
Dave Stockton, Jr.	69	66	66	72	273	57,600
Olin Browne	70	69	67	68	274	33,700
Fred Funk	68	72	66	68	274	33,700
Wayne Levi	68	65	71	70	274	33,700
Mark McCumber	72	67	67	68	274	33,700
Bob Tway	68	66	65	75	274	33,700
Jay Williamson	67	69	66	72	274	33,700
Russ Cochran	70	66	68	71	275	21,840
Bruce Fleisher	71	67	68	69	275	21,840
Jay Haas	67	69	72	67	275	21,840
Pete Jordan	70	70	67	68	275	21,840
Jeff Sluman	66	67	69	73	275	21,840
Joey Gullion	70	70	64	72	276	17,400
David Ogrin	70	71	66	69	276	17,400
Dan Forsman	69	70	68	70	277	15,000
Gil Morgan	70	69	69	69	277	15,000
Stuart Appleby	71	68	69	70	278	9,785.46
Scott Gump	70	69	70	69	278	9,785.46
Tom Kite	71	70	66	71	278	9,785.46
David Toms	71	71	68	68	278	9,785.46
Fuzzy Zoeller	71	70	68	69	278	9,785.46
Billy Andrade	72	66	70	70	278	9,785.45
Allen Doyle	69	65	70	74	278	9,785.45
Robin Freeman	71	67	72	68	278	9,785.45
Jeff Maggert	70	68	70	70	278	9,785.45
Mark O'Meara	68	71	70	69	278	9,785.45
Hal Sutton	73	64	73	68	278	9,785.45
John Cook	73	66	69	71	279	6,480
Kelly Gibson	72	66	70	71	279	6,480
Jeff Julian	70	69	71	69	279	6,480
Phil Mickelson	73	69	69	68	279	6,480
Ron Whittaker	69	71	68	71	279	6,480
Phil Blackmar	68	72	67	73	280	4,560
Billy Ray Brown	73	69	67	71	280	4,560
Fred Couples	69	72	71	68	280	4,560
Ernie Els	66	70	72	72	280	4,560
Jim Furyk	71	71	69	69	280	4,560
Ken Green	69	68	71	72	280	4,560
Doug Martin	70	67	70	73	280	4,560
John Morse	68	68	74	70	280	4,560
Mike Standly	71	68	68	73	280	4,560
Robert Wrenn	70	70	72	68	280	4,560
Emlyn Aubrey	70	67	73	71	281	3,016
Ronnie Black	69	70	72	70	281	3,016
Brad Fabel	73	67	67	74	281	3,016
Greg Kraft	73	67	70	71	281	3,016
Jim McGovern	70	70	68	73	281	3,016
Mike Reid	72	68	67	74	281	3,016
Andy Bean	68	73	67	74	282	2,724
Marco Dawson	69	69	68	76	282	2,724
John Maginnes	72	70	68	72	282	2,724
Paul Stankowski	72	69	69	72	282	2,724
Tommy Tolles	66	71	71	74	282	2,724
Mike Weir	71	66	72	73	282	2,724
Scott Dunlap	69	73	70	71	283	2,592
Steve Elkington	72	70	75	66	283	2,592
Clarence Rose	71	71	70	71	283	2,592

		SCORES			TOTAL	MONEY
Hisayuki Sasaki	68	71	72	72	283	2,592
Tony Sills	73	66	72	72	283	2,592
Ben Crenshaw	71	71	71	71	284	2,436
Wayne Grady	71	71	70	72	284	2,436
Jeff Hart	69	69	76	70	284	2,436
Tsuneyuki Nakajima	72	70	71	71	284	2,436
Chris Perry	70	69	73	72	284	2,436
Gene Sauers	71	70	71	72	284	2,436
Ted Tryba	71	68	70	75	284	2,436
John Wilson	70	72	69	73	284	2,436
Eric Booker	72	67	72	74	285	2,292
Donnie Hammond	71	71	71	72	285	2,292
Steve Rintoul	68	72	71	74	285	2,292
Gary Rusnak	67	73	71	74	285	2,292
Bart Bryant	68	73	72	73	286	2,172
Tom Byrum	74	68	74	70	286	2,172
Naomichi Ozaki	70	72	73	71	286	2,172
Craig Parry	69	72	70	75	286	2,172
Lucas Parsons	70	72	71	73	286	2,172
Mike Sullivan	69	69	75	73	286	2,172
Tom Purtzer	72	69	72	75	288	2,076
Andy Morse	68	72	72	76	288	2,076
Jay Don Blake	75	67	74	73	289	2,016
Steve Lowery	72	69	75	73	289	2,016
Wayne Westner	74	68	73	74	289	2,016
Joel Edwards	71	71	79	70	291	1,968

PGA Championship

Valhalla Golf Club, Louisville, Kentucky
Par 36-36–72; 7,144 yards

August 8-11
purse, $2,400,000

		SCORES			TOTAL	MONEY
Mark Brooks	68	70	69	70	277	$430,000
Kenny Perry	66	72	71	68	277	260,000
(Brooks defeated Perry on first extra hole.)						
Steve Elkington	67	74	67	70	278	140,000
Tommy Tolles	69	71	71	67	278	140,000
Justin Leonard	71	66	72	70	279	86,666.67
Jesper Parnevik	73	67	69	70	279	86,666.67
Vijay Singh	69	69	69	72	279	86,666.66
Lee Janzen	68	71	71	70	280	57,500
Per-Ulrik Johansson	73	72	66	69	280	57,500
Phil Mickelson	67	67	74	72	280	57,500
Larry Mize	71	70	69	70	280	57,500
Frank Nobilo	69	72	71	68	280	57,500
Nick Price	68	71	69	72	280	57,500
Mike Brisky	71	69	69	72	281	39,000
Tom Lehman	71	71	69	70	281	39,000
Joey Sindelar	73	72	69	67	281	39,000
Brad Faxon	72	68	73	69	282	27,285.72
Tom Watson	69	71	73	69	282	27,285.72
D.A. Weibring	71	73	71	67	282	27,285.72
Russ Cochran	68	72	65	77	282	27,285.71
David Edwards	69	71	72	70	282	27,285.71
Jim Furyk	70	70	73	69	282	27,285.71
Greg Norman	68	72	69	73	282	27,285.71

	SCORES				TOTAL	MONEY
Emlyn Aubrey	69	74	72	68	283	21,500
Miguel Angel Jimenez	71	71	71	70	283	21,500
Fred Funk	73	69	73	69	284	18,000
Mark O'Meara	71	70	74	69	284	18,000
Corey Pavin	71	74	70	69	284	18,000
Curtis Strange	73	70	68	73	284	18,000
Steve Stricker	73	72	72	67	284	18,000
Paul Azinger	70	75	71	69	285	13,000
Michael Bradley	73	72	70	70	285	13,000
Patrick Burke	71	72	69	73	285	13,000
Jay Haas	72	71	69	73	285	13,000
Tim Herron	71	73	68	73	285	13,000
Mark Calcavecchia	70	74	70	72	286	9,050
Rocco Mediate	71	72	67	76	286	9,050
David Ogrin	75	70	68	73	286	9,050
Ian Woosnam	68	72	75	71	286	9,050
Fuzzy Zoeller	76	67	72	71	286	9,050
Glen Day	72	73	70	72	287	7,375
David Duval	74	69	73	71	287	7,375
Gil Morgan	72	72	72	71	287	7,375
John Morse	74	69	72	72	287	7,375
Jeff Sluman	72	72	72	71	287	7,375
Fred Couples	74	68	74	71	287	7,375
Phil Blackmar	71	74	71	72	288	6,000
John Cook	69	75	74	70	288	6,000
Scott McCarron	69	72	74	73	288	6,000
Paul Stankowski	70	75	71	72	288	6,000
Brian Watts	70	71	71	76	288	6,000
John Adams	72	71	75	71	289	4,716.67
Bob Boyd	71	71	75	72	289	4,716.67
Alexander Cejka	71	74	72	72	289	4,716.67
Jim Gallagher, Jr.	73	70	74	72	289	4,716.67
Lee Rinker	73	71	73	72	289	4,716.67
Costantino Rocca	72	72	73	72	289	4,716.67
Neal Lancaster	71	72	73	73	289	4,716.66
Billy Mayfair	71	73	71	74	289	4,716.66
Tsuneyuki Nakajima	73	72	69	75	289	4,716.66
Ernie Els	74	68	79	69	290	4,068.75
Dan Forsman	76	69	71	74	290	4,068.75
Scott Hoch	72	72	74	72	290	4,068.75
Mark Wiebe	73	72	75	70	290	4,068.75
Nick Faldo	69	75	74	73	291	3,912.50
Wayne Grady	74	67	78	72	291	3,912.50
Craig Parry	72	73	75	71	291	3,912.50
Willie Wood	70	75	71	75	291	3,912.50
Woody Austin	70	74	75	73	292	3,812.50
Ben Crenshaw	74	71	73	74	292	3,812.50
Nolan Henke	72	70	75	75	292	3,812.50
Payne Stewart	73	70	73	76	292	3,812.50
Paul Goydos	71	73	77	72	293	3,737.50
Jeff Maggert	73	70	76	74	293	3,737.50
Marco Dawson	76	69	75	74	294	3,700
Bernhard Langer	73	72	78	72	295	3,675
Joel Edwards	68	76	75	77	296	3,650
Satoshi Higashi	72	72	80	73	297	3,612.50
Stu Ingraham	73	72	75	77	297	3,612.50
Howard Clark	73	72	75	78	298	3,562.50
John Reeves	74	71	79	74	298	3,562.50

	SCORES		TOTAL
Out of Final 36 Holes			
George Bowman	72	74	146
Brandel Chamblee	74	72	146
John Daly	72	74	146
Bob Estes	72	74	146
Mike Hulbert	78	68	146
Davis Love III	73	73	146
Mark McNulty	75	71	146
Jack Nicklaus	77	69	146
Mike Reid	74	72	146
Jeff Roth	69	77	146
Philip Walton	70	76	146
Jay Don Blake	74	73	147
Brad Bryant	74	73	147
John Huston	72	75	147
Doug Martin	73	74	147
Tom Purtzer	72	75	147
Loren Roberts	72	75	147
Scott Simpson	73	74	147
Chris Tucker	71	76	147
Billy Andrade	75	73	148
Bill Israelson	76	72	148
Mark James	73	75	148
Bob Lohr	75	73	148
Blaine McCallister	74	74	148
Jim McGovern	71	77	148
Colin Montgomerie	71	77	148
Bob Tway	75	73	148
Tom Kite	76	73	149
Craig Stadler	77	72	149
Ted Tryba	78	71	149
John Wilson	74	75	149
Robert Allenby	76	74	150
Eric Booker	78	72	150
Michael Burke, Jr.	76	74	150
Michael Campbell	75	75	150
Lennie Clements	75	75	150
David Frost	71	79	150
Sam Torrance	71	79	150
Perry Arthur	74	77	151
Steve Jones	76	75	151
Mark McCumber	75	76	151
Lonnie Nielsen	80	71	151
Naomichi Ozaki	75	76	151
Kirk Triplett	72	79	151
Grant Waite	76	75	151
Walt Chapman	77	75	152
Steve Schneiter	77	75	152
Peter Senior	76	76	152
Mike Taylor	79	73	152
Lanny Wadkins	75	77	152
Duffy Waldorf	73	79	152
Bob Ford	78	75	153
Greg Kraft	78	75	153
Ed Terasa	74	79	153
Robby Ware	80	73	153
Masashi Ozaki	75	79	154
Hal Sutton	73	81	154
Chris Anderson	75	81	156

	SCORES		TOTAL
John Bermel	81	75	156
Hubert Green	79	77	156
Ron Philo, Jr.	78	78	156
Ken Schall	75	81	156
John Deforest	78	79	157
Mike Caporale	82	78	160
Dan Bateman	81	83	164
John Nelson	82	85	167
Steve Lowery	72	77	WD
Larry Nelson	73	72	WD
Peter Jacobsen	71	84	WD

(Professionals who did not complete 72 holes received $1,200.)

Sprint International

Castle Pines Golf Club, Castle Rock, Colorado
Par 36-36–72; 7,559 yards

August 15-18
purse, $1,600,000

FINAL ROUND

	POINTS				TOTAL	MONEY
Clarence Rose	6	3	12	10	31	$288,000
Brad Faxon	6	6	12	7	31	172,800
(Rose defeated Faxon on third extra hole.)						
Bob Tway	7	2	11	10	30	92,800
Michael Bradley	9	3	11	7	30	92,800
Tom Lehman	7	4	8	8	27	60,800
Justin Leonard	6	8	4	9	27	60,800
D.A. Weibring	4	2	12	7	25	53,600
Kenny Perry	11	0	7	6	24	49,600
Nick Faldo	6	4	8	5	23	40,000
Paul Goydos	2	10	9	2	23	40,000
John Cook	10	8	3	2	23	40,000
Woody Austin	10	3	5	5	23	40,000
Billy Andrade	7	9	3	4	23	40,000
Robin Freeman	13	5	4	0	22	29,600
Andrew Magee	2	8	9	3	22	29,600
Phil Mickelson	5	9	5	2	21	27,200
Rocco Mediate	6	5	5	3	19	24,800
Jim Furyk	3	3	9	3	19	24,800
Per-Ulrik Johansson	2	6	9	1	18	21,600
Ernie Els	1	9	6	2	18	21,600
Mark Brooks	-4	10	10	0	16	18,560
Jim Gallagher, Jr.	13	-2	6	-1	16	18,560
Steve Lowery	7	12	-4	-4	11	16,640
Steve Jurgensen	8	5	3	-6	10	15,360

IN THE MONEY

				TOTAL	MONEY
Jesper Parnevik	3	0	9	15	13,066.67
Wayne Westner	2	5	8	15	13,066.67
John Inman	8	0	7	15	13,066.66
Scott Gump	1	6	6	13	10,880
Bruce Lietzke	2	7	4	13	10,880
Lee Rinker	9	8	-4	13	10,880
Kelly Gibson	5	1	7	13	10,880
Mike Reid	11	0	2	13	10,880

	POINTS			TOTAL	MONEY
Ronnie Black	6	4	2	12	9,040
Greg Norman	7	4	1	12	9,040
Bob Gilder	4	1	7	12	9,040
Bob Estes	8	-3	6	11	7,700
Joe Acosta, Jr.	4	8	-1	11	7,700
Willie Wood	5	0	6	11	7,700
Joey Sindelar	7	1	3	11	7,700
Patrick Burke	9	-3	4	10	6,560
Billy Ray Brown	9	0	1	10	6,560
Scott Hoch	10	2	-2	10	6,560
Miguel Angel Jimenez	7	1	1	9	5,130.67
Jim Carter	9	-5	5	9	5,130.67
Sandy Lyle	1	6	2	9	5,130.67
Bobby Wadkins	2	3	4	9	5,130.67
Craig Parry	5	4	0	9	5,130.66
Steve Jones	9	-4	4	9	5,130.66
Dan Forsman	0	6	2	8	3,948.80
Robert Wrenn	6	0	2	8	3,948.80
Jay Delsing	4	3	1	8	3,948.80
Gene Sauers	10	-1	-1	8	3,948.80
Jerry Kelly	2	2	4	8	3,948.80
Taylor Smith	5	3	-1	7	3,648
Bart Bryant	13	-4	-2	7	3,648
Davis Love III	5	0	2	7	3,648
Corey Pavin	4	2	1	7	3,648
Tom Watson	10	0	-3	7	3,648
Anders Forsbrand	2	5	-1	6	3,488
Scott McCarron	-3	11	-2	6	3,488
Neal Lancaster	6	-1	1	6	3,488
Tim Herron	-4	12	-2	6	3,488
Dillard Pruitt	7	1	-2	6	3,488
Hal Sutton	1	5	-1	5	3,392
Stewart Ginn	10	0	-6	4	3,360
Dicky Pride	3	2	-2	3	3,328
Peter O'Malley	7	-1	-4	2	3,296
Franklin Langham	9	0	-8	1	3,264
Jay Haas	3	2	-6	-1	3,216
Vijay Singh	0	5	-6	-1	3,216
Guy Boros	8	-1	-10	-3	3,168
John Huston	9	-3	-16	-10	3,136

NEC World Series of Golf

Firestone Country Club, South Course, Akron, Ohio   August 22-25
Par 35-35–70; 7,139 yards   purse, $2,100,000

	SCORES				TOTAL	MONEY
Phil Mickelson	70	66	68	70	274	$378,000
Billy Mayfair	66	71	70	70	277	156,800
Steve Stricker	68	72	69	68	277	156,800
Duffy Waldorf	70	70	71	66	277	156,800
Greg Norman	70	68	69	71	278	84,000
Alexander Cejka	72	71	71	66	280	72,975
Davis Love III	70	74	67	69	280	72,975
John Cook	70	69	71	71	281	65,100
Corey Pavin	73	70	70	69	282	60,900
Mark Brooks	69	69	74	71	283	50,400

	SCORES				TOTAL	MONEY
Nick Faldo	70	71	68	74	283	50,400
Fred Funk	72	70	73	68	283	50,400
Tom Lehman	72	69	74	68	283	50,400
Jim Furyk	75	69	67	73	284	35,700
Tim Herron	70	67	75	72	284	35,700
Justin Leonard	69	70	71	74	284	35,700
Mark O'Meara	73	71	69	71	284	35,700
D.A. Weibring	73	69	74	68	284	35,700
Fred Couples	73	68	72	72	285	26,525
Loren Roberts	72	73	71	69	285	26,525
Craig Stadler	73	72	67	73	285	26,525
Hal Sutton	72	69	74	70	285	26,525
Ernie Els	71	71	71	73	286	22,137.50
Paul Goydos	66	75	74	71	286	22,137.50
Steve Jones	70	69	76	71	286	22,137.50
Hidemichi Tanaka	66	75	75	70	286	22,137.50
Craig Parry	73	75	67	72	287	20,025
Costantino Rocca	74	71	75	67	287	20,025
Clarence Rose	72	71	72	72	287	20,025
Willie Wood	75	69	69	74	287	20,025
Anders Forsbrand	70	75	71	72	288	19,200
Shigeki Maruyama	75	71	70	72	288	19,200
Scott Hoch	71	68	77	73	289	18,900
Tom Watson	79	70	68	73	290	18,800
Sven Struver	72	72	72	76	292	18,700
Satoshi Higashi	75	72	74	73	294	18,550
Scott McCarron	76	70	74	74	294	18,550
Stewart Ginn	73	72	77	73	295	18,400
Seiki Okuda	81	70	72	75	298	18,200
Steve Schneiter	77	74	76	71	298	18,200
Paul Stankowski	74	75	74	75	298	18,200
Brad Bryant	73	72	77	79	301	18,000
Wayne Westner	77	68	73	74	DQ	

Greater Vancouver Open

Northview Golf & Country Club, Cloverdale,
British Columbia, Canada
Par 35-36–71; 6,900 yards

August 22-25
purse, $1,000,000

	SCORES				TOTAL	MONEY
Guy Boros	71	65	65	71	272	$180,000
Emlyn Aubrey	68	68	70	67	273	74,666.67
Lee Janzen	71	65	66	71	273	74,666.67
Taylor Smith	71	65	65	72	273	74,666.66
Shane Bertsch	70	71	68	66	275	33,900
Russ Cochran	72	67	67	69	275	33,900
Joey Gullion	71	69	67	68	275	33,900
Kenny Perry	70	70	68	67	275	33,900
Mike Weir	72	68	65	70	275	33,900
Mike Brisky	67	71	68	70	276	24,000
Tom Byrum	72	71	69	64	276	24,000
Andrew Magee	71	67	67	71	276	24,000
Craig Perry	71	72	67	66	276	24,000
John Elliott	69	71	70	67	277	17,500
Dudley Hart	70	70	68	69	277	17,500
Pete Jordan	69	70	67	71	277	17,500

	SCORES				TOTAL	MONEY
Jack Renner	71	67	73	66	277	17,500
Jeff Maggert	68	68	74	68	278	13,040
Brian Tennyson	70	68	71	69	278	13,040
David Toms	69	72	68	69	278	13,040
Mark Wurtz	72	67	70	69	278	13,040
Richard Zokol	69	73	67	69	278	13,040
Jay Delsing	73	69	69	68	279	8,900
Allen Doyle	72	69	70	68	279	8,900
Ken Duke	71	72	70	66	279	8,900
Scott Dunlap	70	68	67	74	279	8,900
Curtis Strange	70	70	66	73	279	8,900
Naomichi Ozaki	69	74	72	65	280	6,950
Carl Paulson	74	68	69	69	280	6,950
Mike Swartz	67	70	73	70	280	6,950
Denis Watson	73	70	70	67	280	6,950
Ronnie Black	68	72	70	71	281	5,660
Brian Claar	70	68	73	70	281	5,660
Sandy Lyle	73	66	72	70	281	5,660
David Ogrin	71	70	73	67	281	5,660
Bobby Wadkins	74	69	70	68	281	5,660
Joe Acosta, Jr.	70	73	66	73	282	4,100
Chip Beck	71	71	73	67	282	4,100
Bart Bryant	75	66	75	66	282	4,100
Jim Carter	74	69	68	71	282	4,100
Mike Gordon	73	69	71	69	282	4,100
Dan Halldorson	73	68	73	68	282	4,100
Larry Rinker	72	70	68	72	282	4,100
Gordon Sherry	71	71	69	71	282	4,100
Mike Smith	72	68	70	72	282	4,100
Brent Franklin	68	69	70	76	283	2,772
Bob Gilder	74	68	67	74	283	2,772
David Peoples	71	70	70	72	283	2,772
Hugh Royer III	72	69	74	68	283	2,772
Jim Thorpe	73	70	69	71	283	2,772
Bill Britton	73	68	68	75	284	2,368
Joe Daley	68	71	74	71	284	2,368
Brad Faxon	76	65	70	73	284	2,368
Lee Rinker	72	70	70	72	284	2,368
Fred Wadsworth	69	72	70	73	284	2,368
Dave Barr	73	70	69	73	285	2,240
Rex Caldwell	71	71	73	70	285	2,240
Pat Fitzsimons	72	70	70	73	285	2,240
John Inman	69	70	69	77	285	2,240
Tom Scherrer	76	67	72	71	285	2,240
Keith Clearwater	75	68	71	72	286	2,130
Robin Freeman	68	72	75	71	286	2,130
Kelly Gibson	70	72	71	73	286	2,130
Bryan Gorman	70	73	69	74	286	2,130
Ken Green	70	68	71	77	286	2,130
Sam Randolph	72	68	73	73	286	2,130
Billy Ray Brown	72	70	73	72	287	2,030
Brian Henninger	72	70	73	72	287	2,030
Steve Rintoul	70	72	73	72	287	2,030
Chris Smith	72	67	73	75	287	2,030
Kevin Sutherland	70	73	73	74	290	1,970
Tray Tyner	71	72	73	74	290	1,970
Ian Leggatt	72	70	71	78	291	1,930
Scott Medlin	72	71	73	75	291	1,930

Greater Milwaukee Open

Brown Deer Park Golf Course, Milwaukee, Wisconsin
Par 35-36–71; 6,739 yards

August 29-September 1
purse, $1,200,000

		SCORES			TOTAL	MONEY
Loren Roberts	66	65	66	68	265	$216,000
Jerry Kelly	67	66	68	64	265	129,600
(Roberts defeated Kelly on first extra hole.)						
Nolan Henke	62	66	67	71	266	57,600
Andrew Magee	68	70	65	63	266	57,600
Jesper Parnevik	65	66	63	72	266	57,600
Steve Stricker	66	67	66	67	266	57,600
Olin Browne	67	67	69	64	267	38,700
David Ogrin	68	66	66	67	267	38,700
Fred Funk	69	66	67	66	268	32,400
Steve Lowery	70	64	67	67	268	32,400
Duffy Waldorf	65	65	70	68	268	32,400
Billy Andrade	65	68	67	69	269	20,160
Stuart Appleby	69	66	64	70	269	20,160
Woody Austin	71	65	65	68	269	20,160
Brian Claar	66	68	66	69	269	20,160
Bob Estes	64	67	67	71	269	20,160
Ken Green	67	69	66	67	269	20,160
Frank Lickliter	68	68	64	69	269	20,160
John Maginnes	68	70	68	63	269	20,160
Billy Mayfair	67	68	70	64	269	20,160
Clarence Rose	70	66	67	66	269	20,160
Russ Cochran	66	67	68	69	270	11,520
Glen Day	68	69	67	66	270	11,520
Jay Haas	70	69	66	65	270	11,520
Scott Hoch	68	67	67	68	270	11,520
Richard Zokol	68	70	66	66	270	11,520
Bob Gilder	70	68	68	66	271	8,880
Mike Heinen	68	63	70	70	271	8,880
Gil Morgan	70	68	69	66	271	8,880
Shane Bertsch	67	68	70	67	272	7,620
Brad Fabel	69	68	66	69	272	7,620
Bruce Fleisher	70	67	67	68	272	7,620
Leonard Thompson	70	66	67	69	272	7,620
Jay Delsing	70	67	67	69	273	6,060
Carl Paulson	68	64	71	70	273	6,060
Chris Perry	68	67	69	69	273	6,060
Dan Pohl	69	67	68	69	273	6,060
Jeff Sluman	68	70	70	65	273	6,060
David Toms	68	71	66	68	273	6,060
Mark Calcavecchia	67	72	67	68	274	4,560
Brian Henninger	67	70	64	73	274	4,560
Greg Kraft	70	67	63	74	274	4,560
Tim Simpson	67	70	70	67	274	4,560
Mike Sullivan	66	67	71	70	274	4,560
Kevin Sutherland	69	68	69	68	274	4,560
Dave Barr	66	68	69	72	275	3,264
Ronnie Black	68	67	69	71	275	3,264
Patrick Burke	69	70	67	69	275	3,264
Tom Byrum	70	68	69	68	275	3,264
Joe Daley	71	68	69	67	275	3,264
Dillard Pruitt	69	69	70	67	275	3,264
Jay Don Blake	73	65	70	68	276	2,757
Jeff Gallagher	70	68	68	70	276	2,757

	SCORES				TOTAL	MONEY
Bryan Gorman	67	67	74	68	276	2,757
Scott Gump	70	69	68	69	276	2,757
Tom Purtzer	70	67	68	71	276	2,757
Lee Rinker	71	67	70	68	276	2,757
Brian Tennyson	68	67	70	71	276	2,757
Bobby Wadkins	69	69	70	68	276	2,757
Paul Azinger	69	70	70	68	277	2,544
Guy Boros	68	70	70	69	277	2,544
Jim Carter	71	68	68	70	277	2,544
Scott Dunlap	71	67	70	69	277	2,544
Ed Fiori	70	68	67	72	277	2,544
Mike Hulbert	67	67	73	70	277	2,544
Steve Jurgensen	67	71	72	67	277	2,544
Franklin Langham	69	70	69	69	277	2,544
Tiger Woods	67	69	73	68	277	2,544
Robin Freeman	71	67	69	71	278	2,412
Willie Wood	66	68	68	76	278	2,412
Bart Bryant	74	65	71	69	279	2,340
Jim Gallagher, Jr.	69	70	70	70	279	2,340
Tim Herron	68	71	70	70	279	2,340
Neal Lancaster	66	68	72	73	279	2,340
Bruce Lietzke	68	68	72	72	280	2,280
Payne Stewart	67	72	70	72	281	2,256

Bell Canadian Open

Glen Abbey Golf Club, Oakville, Ontario, Canada
Par 36-36–72; 7,102 yards
(Shortened to 54 holes — rain.)

September 5-8
purse, $1,500,000

	SCORES			TOTAL	MONEY
Dudley Hart	68	64	70	202	$270,000
David Duval	69	65	69	203	162,000
Tom Byrum	70	66	69	205	78,000
Scott Dunlap	64	65	76	205	78,000
Taylor Smith	68	66	71	205	78,000
Michael Bradley	70	64	72	206	54,000
Mark Calcavecchia	71	68	68	207	45,187.50
Tom Lehman	69	70	68	207	45,187.50
Jesper Parnevik	66	71	70	207	45,187.50
Joey Sindelar	70	68	69	207	45,187.50
Tiger Woods	70	70	68	208	37,500
Billy Andrade	70	68	71	209	31,500
Carl Paulson	67	72	70	209	31,500
Loren Roberts	69	71	69	209	31,500
Jim Gallagher, Jr.	71	67	72	210	24,000
Guy Hill	67	74	69	210	24,000
Bruce Lietzke	72	69	69	210	24,000
Andrew Magee	67	72	71	210	24,000
Vijay Singh	69	71	70	210	24,000
Emlyn Aubrey	69	69	73	211	16,250
Ernie Els	67	74	70	211	16,250
Frank Lickliter	67	69	75	211	16,250
Billy Mayfair	67	72	72	211	16,250
Mark O'Meara	74	65	72	211	16,250
Bob Tway	69	69	73	211	16,250
Mark Brooks	69	71	72	212	11,325

	SCORES			TOTAL	MONEY
Mike Heinen	69	72	71	212	11,325
Scott Medlin	71	68	73	212	11,325
Corey Pavin	71	69	72	212	11,325
John Adams	72	70	71	213	9,525
Chris DiMarco	68	74	71	213	9,525
Chris Perry	68	69	76	213	9,525
Mike Sullivan	69	73	71	213	9,525
Stuart Appleby	70	71	73	214	6,637.50
Trevor Dodds	69	72	73	214	6,637.50
Keith Fergus	72	69	73	214	6,637.50
Paul Goydos	70	72	72	214	6,637.50
Franklin Langham	71	72	71	214	6,637.50
Len Mattiace	69	70	75	214	6,637.50
Jim McGovern	69	73	72	214	6,637.50
Frank Nobilo	70	71	73	214	6,637.50
Lee Rinker	70	66	78	214	6,637.50
Charlie Rymer	68	74	72	214	6,637.50
Paul Stankowski	72	70	72	214	6,637.50
Grant Waite	69	72	73	214	6,637.50
David Edwards	70	71	74	215	4,500
David Morland	69	72	74	215	4,500
Dave Barr	70	70	76	216	3,870
Steve Lowery	73	69	74	216	3,870
Davidson Matyczuk	71	71	74	216	3,870
Tim Simpson	71	72	73	216	3,870
Phil Blackmar	69	70	78	217	3,498
Glen Day	70	72	75	217	3,498
Jay Delsing	70	73	74	217	3,498
Ken Green	72	71	74	217	3,498
Tim Herron	72	70	75	217	3,498
Fulton Allem	71	73	74	218	3,300
Jay Don Blake	72	72	74	218	3,300
Olin Browne	72	72	74	218	3,300
Anders Forsbrand	70	74	74	218	3,300
Arden Knoll	67	75	76	218	3,300
Dave Stockton, Jr.	70	73	75	218	3,300
Richard Zokol	71	72	75	218	3,300
Scott Gump	72	72	75	219	3,105
Justin Leonard	67	77	75	219	3,105
Bob Lohr	71	71	77	219	3,105
Kevin Sutherland	74	68	77	219	3,105
Jim Thorpe	72	70	77	219	3,105
Bobby Wadkins	69	74	76	219	3,105
Guy Boros	69	73	78	220	2,955
Keith Clearwater	70	71	79	220	2,955
Hugh Royer III	72	72	76	220	2,955
Rick Todd	70	72	78	220	2,955
John Elliott	72	72	77	221	2,850
Brian Henninger	73	69	79	221	2,850
Ian Leggatt	71	71	79	221	2,850
Greg Kraft	71	73	81	225	2,750

Quad City Classic

Oakwood Golf Club, Coal Valley, Illinois
Par 35-35–70; 6,796 yards

September 12-15
purse, $1,000,000

	SCORES				TOTAL	MONEY
Ed Fiori	66	68	67	67	268	$216,000
Andrew Magee	69	70	69	62	270	129,600
Steve Jones	68	68	67	68	271	69,600
Chris Perry	68	70	67	66	271	69,600
Phil Blackmar	69	71	65	67	272	42,150
Jeff Maggert	67	68	73	64	272	42,150
Hugh Royer III	71	68	65	68	272	42,150
Tiger Woods	69	64	67	72	272	42,150
Greg Kraft	68	70	67	69	274	30,000
Loren Roberts	69	70	69	66	274	30,000
Jeff Sluman	69	69	69	67	274	30,000
Mike Springer	69	72	65	68	274	30,000
Brian Tennyson	72	67	67	68	274	30,000
Keith Clearwater	68	72	68	67	275	20,400
Allen Doyle	70	67	69	69	275	20,400
Larry Nelson	65	74	70	66	275	20,400
Ken Schall	72	67	69	67	275	20,400
Leonard Thompson	69	71	67	68	275	20,400
Ronnie Black	72	68	71	65	276	13,050
Jim Carter	71	69	70	66	276	13,050
Russ Cochran	71	69	68	68	276	13,050
Joel Edwards	68	67	70	71	276	13,050
Brad Fabel	72	70	69	65	276	13,050
John Maginnes	68	71	69	68	276	13,050
Mark Pfeil	73	67	69	67	276	13,050
David Toms	72	69	66	69	276	13,050
Lennie Clements	70	70	68	69	277	7,820
Jay Delsing	68	68	67	74	277	7,820
Robin Freeman	68	70	71	68	277	7,820
Kelly Gibson	70	69	68	70	277	7,820
Joey Gullion	65	74	70	68	277	7,820
Dudley Hart	68	70	70	69	277	7,820
Wayne Levi	72	66	71	68	277	7,820
Jim McGovern	68	72	67	70	277	7,820
Curtis Strange	71	71	68	67	277	7,820
David Edwards	73	68	71	66	278	5,652
Bryan Gorman	74	68	69	67	278	5,652
John Inman	70	69	68	71	278	5,652
Doug Martin	70	72	70	66	278	5,652
Taylor Smith	67	69	71	71	278	5,652
John Adams	71	69	70	69	279	3,798.55
Rex Caldwell	68	72	71	68	279	3,798.55
Fred Funk	67	71	75	66	279	3,798.55
Jeff Hart	70	70	72	67	279	3,798.55
Mark Hensby	68	70	72	69	279	3,798.55
Willie Wood	73	69	69	68	279	3,798.55
Bart Bryant	71	69	70	69	279	3,798.54
Brian Henninger	71	70	68	70	279	3,798.54
Gary Rusnak	73	68	69	69	279	3,798.54
Tommy Tolles	69	72	68	70	279	3,798.54
Ron Whittaker	70	69	69	71	279	3,798.54
Dave Barr	71	70	73	66	280	2,744
Brian Claar	71	71	67	71	280	2,744
Pete Jordan	73	68	70	69	280	2,744

	SCORES				TOTAL	MONEY
Franklin Langham	69	69	70	72	280	2,744
Len Mattiace	70	70	70	70	280	2,744
Scott McCarron	67	73	70	70	280	2,744
Mike Standly	68	68	71	73	280	2,744
Denis Watson	66	76	69	69	280	2,744
D.A. Weibring	72	68	68	72	280	2,744
Brandel Chamblee	67	72	71	71	281	2,592
Sean Murphy	71	67	78	65	281	2,592
Bob Tway	71	67	72	71	281	2,592
Woody Austin	70	70	69	73	282	2,496
Michael Bradley	69	71	72	70	282	2,496
Blaine McCallister	69	73	71	69	282	2,496
Sam Randolph	70	72	69	71	282	2,496
Tony Sills	71	70	73	68	282	2,496
Jeff Julian	71	71	71	70	283	2,400
Kevin Sutherland	73	68	74	68	283	2,400
Richard Zokol	71	71	75	66	283	2,400
Bob Gilder	72	69	73	71	285	2,328
John Huston	72	69	74	70	285	2,328
Charlie Rymer	65	73	74	73	285	2,328

Presidents Cup

Robert Trent Jones Golf Club, Lake Manassas, Virginia   September 13-15
Par 36-36–72; 7,239 yards

FIRST DAY
Morning Fourballs

Fred Couples and Davis Love III (USA) defeated Greg Norman and Robert Allenby, 2 and 1
Ernie Els and Mark McNulty (Int.) defeated Scott Hoch and Mark Brooks, 2 up
Phil Mickelson and Corey Pavin (USA) defeated Vijay Singh and Masashi Ozaki, 2 and 1
Mark O'Meara and David Duval (USA) defeated Steve Elkington and Frank Nobilo, 3 and 2
Tom Lehman and Steve Stricker (USA) defeated Nick Price and Peter Senior, 4 and 2

Afternoon Foursomes

Kenny Perry and Justin Leonard (USA) defeated Price and David Frost, 3 and 2
O'Meara and Duval (USA) defeated Craig Parry and Nobilo, 2 and 1
Elkington and Singh (Int.) defeated Lehman and Stricker, 2 up
Mickelson and Pavin (USA) halved with Els and McNulty
Couples and Love (USA) defeated Norman and Allenby, 1 up

POINTS: United States 7½, International 2½

SECOND DAY
Morning Fourballs

Price and Elkington (Int.) defeated Leonard and Lehman, 2 up
Norman and Allenby (Int.) defeated Stricker and Pavin, 1 up
Perry and Hoch (USA) defeated Parry and Nobilo, 2 and 1
Ozaki and Singh (Int.) defeated Love and Couples, 2 and 1
O'Meara and Duval (USA) defeated Els and McNulty, 4 and 3

Afternoon Foursomes

Senior and Frost (Int.) defeated Pavin and Mickelson, 3 and 2
Nobilo and Allenby (Int.) defeated Love and Brooks, 3 and 2
Price and McNulty (Int.) defeated Perry and Leonard, 3 and 1
Norman and Els (Int.) defeated Lehman and Stricker, 1 up
O'Meara and Hoch (USA) defeated Elkington and Singh, 1 up

POINTS: International 7, United States 3

THIRD DAY
Singles

Parry (Int.) defeated Brooks, 5 and 4
Duval (USA) defeated Senior, 3 and 2
O'Meara (USA) defeated Price, 1 up
Frost (Int.) defeated Perry, 7 and 6
Stricker (USA) defeated Allenby, 6 and 5
Hoch (USA) defeated McNulty, 1 up
Love (USA) defeated Ozaki, 5 and 4
Elkington (Int.) defeated Leonard, 1 up
Els (Int.) defeated Mickelson, 3 and 2
Norman (Int.) defeated Pavin, 3 and 1
Nobilo (Int.) defeated Lehman, 3 and 2
Couples (USA) defeated Singh, 2 and 1

POINTS: United States 6, International 6

TOTAL POINTS: United States 16½, International 15½

B.C. Open

En-Joie Golf Club, Endicott, New York
Par 37-34–71; 6,920 yards
(Fourth round cancelled — rain.)

September 19-22
purse, $1,000,000

	SCORES			TOTAL	MONEY
Fred Funk	68	66	63	197	$180,000
Pete Jordan	67	64	66	197	108,000
(Funk defeated Jordan on first extra hole.)					
Patrick Burke	68	67	65	200	58,000
Tiger Woods	68	66	66	200	58,000
Brian Claar	66	68	68	202	40,000
Joe Daley	68	73	62	203	33,500
Hugh Royer III	70	66	67	203	33,500
Joey Sindelar	69	68	66	203	33,500
Bradley Hughes	71	68	65	204	27,000
David Ogrin	70	67	67	204	27,000
Jeff Sluman	69	67	68	204	27,000
Jay Delsing	68	70	67	205	21,000
Kelly Gibson	69	69	67	205	21,000
Craig Parry	69	67	69	205	21,000
Woody Austin	70	71	65	206	16,000
David Duval	71	71	64	206	16,000
Mike Hulbert	69	69	68	206	16,000
Jim McGovern	67	70	69	206	16,000
Carl Paulson	69	68	69	206	16,000
Gary Rusnak	69	71	67	207	10,833.34
Tommy Tolles	67	74	66	207	10,833.34

	SCORES			TOTAL	MONEY
Scott Gump	70	68	69	207	10,833.33
Greg Kraft	70	67	70	207	10,833.33
Mike Standly	69	68	70	207	10,833.33
Grant Waite	68	69	70	207	10,833.33
Brad Bryant	70	73	65	208	6,527.28
Mike Heinen	69	73	66	208	6,527.28
Len Mattiace	75	67	66	208	6,527.28
Ronnie Black	70	70	68	208	6,527.27
Mark Carnevale	71	70	67	208	6,527.27
Chris DiMarco	73	68	67	208	6,527.27
Scott Dunlap	69	72	67	208	6,527.27
Bruce Fleisher	68	70	70	208	6,527.27
Robert Gamez	72	69	67	208	6,527.27
Lee Janzen	71	67	70	208	6,527.27
Wayne Levi	67	71	70	208	6,527.27
Emlyn Aubrey	70	70	69	209	4,400
Jeff Hart	68	70	71	209	4,400
Tim Herron	71	70	68	209	4,400
Dick Mast	71	70	68	209	4,400
Mike Sullivan	70	69	70	209	4,400
Hal Sutton	72	67	70	209	4,400
Tom Byrum	71	72	67	210	3,120
Ken Green	73	68	69	210	3,120
Barry Jaeckel	71	71	68	210	3,120
Larry Rinker	67	72	71	210	3,120
Clarence Rose	71	71	68	210	3,120
Tom Scherrer	73	70	67	210	3,120
Tony Sills	71	70	69	210	3,120
Jerry Kelly	73	69	69	211	2,393.34
Chris Perry	74	69	68	211	2,393.34
Robin Freeman	74	67	70	211	2,393.33
John Morse	73	66	72	211	2,393.33
Ted Tryba	68	72	71	211	2,393.33
Tray Tyner	69	68	74	211	2,393.33
Dave Barr	70	72	70	212	2,250
Joel Edwards	69	71	72	212	2,250
Franklin Langham	71	69	72	212	2,250
Sam Randolph	71	65	76	212	2,250
John Maginnes	69	70	74	213	2,190
Taylor Smith	70	72	71	213	2,190
Brad Faxon	67	73	74	214	2,140
Dave Stockton, Jr.	72	71	71	214	2,140
Ron Whittaker	70	69	75	214	2,140
Allen Doyle	70	70	75	215	2,090
Ed Fiori	70	70	75	215	2,090
John Elliott	73	67	76	216	2,040
Brad Fabel	73	70	73	216	2,040
Jim Thorpe	70	71	75	216	2,040
Stan Utley	73	68	78	219	2,000

Buick Challenge

Callaway Gardens Resort, Pine Mountain, Georgia
Par 36-36–72; 7,057 yards
(Third and fourth rounds cancelled — rain.)

September 26-29
purse, $1,000,000

	SCORES		TOTAL	MONEY
Michael Bradley	66	68	134	$180,000
Fred Funk	69	65	134	66,000
Davis Love III	66	68	134	66,000
John Maginnes	68	66	134	66,000
Len Mattiace	66	68	134	66,000
(Bradley defeated Funk, Love, Maginnes and Mattiace on first extra hole.)				
Fred Couples	68	67	135	33,500
Marco Dawson	70	65	135	33,500
Brad Faxon	69	66	135	33,500
Brad Bryant	68	68	136	28,000
Stewart Cink	66	70	136	28,000
Hal Sutton	71	66	137	23,000
Bobby Wadkins	64	73	137	23,000
Willie Wood	69	68	137	23,000
Guy Boros	68	70	138	16,500
Olin Browne	66	72	138	16,500
Jim Furyk	69	69	138	16,500
Jerry Kelly	70	68	138	16,500
Neal Lancaster	69	69	138	16,500
Jim McGovern	65	73	138	16,500
Woody Austin	70	69	139	9,520
Paul Azinger	67	72	139	9,520
Jim Carter	69	70	139	9,520
Jeff Hart	71	68	139	9,520
Mike Hulbert	67	72	139	9,520
Peter Jacobsen	73	66	139	9,520
Carl Paulson	69	70	139	9,520
Gary Rusnak	71	68	139	9,520
Jeff Sluman	70	69	139	9,520
Mark Wiebe	70	69	139	9,520
Billy Andrade	70	70	140	5,570
Tom Byrum	69	71	140	5,570
Steve Elkington	68	72	140	5,570
Bruce Fleisher	71	69	140	5,570
Jim Gallagher, Jr.	71	69	140	5,570
Steve Lowery	71	69	140	5,570
Larry Mize	72	68	140	5,570
Craig Parry	70	70	140	5,570
Don Pooley	68	72	140	5,570
Tom Scherrer	72	68	140	5,570
Ronnie Black	70	71	141	3,080
Billy Ray Brown	67	74	141	3,080
Jeff Gallagher	69	72	141	3,080
Kelly Gibson	72	69	141	3,080
Scott Gump	68	73	141	3,080
Franklin Langham	71	70	141	3,080
Frank Lickliter	72	69	141	3,080
Blaine McCallister	70	71	141	3,080
Lee Rinker	68	73	141	3,080
Hugh Royer III	72	69	141	3,080
Gene Sauers	71	70	141	3,080
Taylor Smith	72	69	141	3,080
Mike Standly	68	73	141	3,080

	SCORES				TOTAL	MONEY
Kirk Triplett	73	68			141	3,080
Jay Williamson	70	71			141	3,080
Andy Bean	70	72			142	2,180
Mark Calcavecchia	67	75			142	2,180
Scott Dunlap	69	73			142	2,180
Brad Fabel	71	71			142	2,180
Jay Haas	74	68			142	2,180
Donnie Hammond	73	69			142	2,150
Tim Herron	73	69			142	2,180
Lee Janzen	67	75			142	2,180
Jeff Julian	69	73			142	2,180
Tom Kite	71	71			142	2,180
Scott Simpson	72	70			142	2,180
Vijay Singh	73	69			142	2,180
Mike Sullivan	72	70			142	2,180
Joe Acosta, Jr.	68	75			143	1,870
Joe Daley	71	72			143	1,870
Glen Day	73	70			143	1,870
Paul Goydos	70	73			143	1,870
Brian Henninger	71	72			143	1,870
Scott Hoch	74	69			143	1,870
Steve Jurgensen	73	70			143	1,870
John Morse	70	73			143	1,870
Sean Murphy	70	73			143	1,870
David Ogrin	72	71			143	1,870
Loren Roberts	71	72			143	1,870
Chris Smith	71	72			143	1,870
Craig Stadler	70	73			143	1,870
Kevin Sutherland	71	72			143	1,870
Jim Thorpe	71	72			143	1,870
David Toms	73	70			143	1,870
Lanny Wadkins	71	72			143	1,870
Ron Whittaker	69	74			143	1,870

Las Vegas Invitational

TPC at Summerlin
Par 36-36–72; 7,243 yards

October 2-6
purse, $1,650,000

Las Vegas Country Club
Par 36-36–72; 7,164 yards

Desert Inn Country Club
Par 36-36–72; 7,066 yards
Las Vegas, Nevada

	SCORES					TOTAL	MONEY
Tiger Woods	70	63	68	67	64	332	$297,000
Davis Love III	66	67	64	68	67	332	178,200
(Woods defeated Love on first extra hole.)							
Mark Calcavecchia	72	67	65	64	65	333	95,700
Kelly Gibson	69	69	65	65	65	333	95,700
Ronnie Black	64	65	69	66	71	335	60,225
Rick Fehr	64	62	69	73	67	335	60,225
Dave Stockton, Jr.	67	68	67	64	69	335	60,225
Paul Azinger	67	64	70	70	65	336	46,200
Fred Couples	66	67	66	67	70	336	46,200

	SCORES					TOTAL	MONEY
Paul Goydos	67	71	66	65	67	336	46,200
Phil Mickelson	68	67	68	67	66	336	46,200
Stewart Cink	70	66	67	67	67	337	31,350
Keith Fergus	62	70	67	69	69	337	31,350
Fred Funk	63	66	68	70	70	337	31,350
Dudley Hart	71	67	67	64	68	337	31,350
Dan Pohl	68	66	70	63	70	337	31,350
Tommy Tolles	69	66	68	71	63	337	31,350
Brian Henninger	66	68	72	66	66	338	24,750
John Cook	72	64	65	68	70	339	21,450
Lee Janzen	66	65	70	69	69	339	21,450
Steve Lowery	67	70	67	70	65	339	21,450
Jay Don Blake	69	70	68	66	67	340	14,478.75
Guy Boros	70	68	66	68	68	340	14,478.75
Olin Browne	66	66	73	69	66	340	14,478.75
Lennie Clements	70	68	68	68	66	340	14,478.75
Jim Furyk	66	64	71	70	69	340	14,478.75
Scott McCarron	68	66	69	67	70	340	14,478.75
Hugh Royer III	67	68	71	67	67	340	14,478.75
Jeff Sluman	68	69	70	66	67	340	14,478.75
Andy Bean	71	67	65	71	67	341	10,725
Michael Bradley	71	67	69	69	65	341	10,725
Craig Stadler	67	69	66	73	66	341	10,725
Marco Dawson	66	72	66	71	67	342	8,532.86
David Frost	65	71	71	67	68	342	8,532.86
Billy Mayfair	69	68	70	68	67	342	8,532.86
Sean Murphy	71	69	66	68	68	342	8,532.86
Robert Wrenn	69	71	66	70	66	342	8,532.86
Stuart Appleby	73	67	66	67	69	342	8,532.85
David Ogrin	69	63	67	71	72	342	8,532.85
David Edwards	68	66	69	70	70	343	6,600
Bryan Gorman	69	67	70	67	70	343	6,600
Vijay Singh	66	68	71	66	72	343	6,600
Brian Tennyson	68	70	64	71	70	343	6,600
Billy Andrade	68	67	70	67	72	344	4,988.50
Glen Day	66	67	71	70	70	344	4,988.50
Tom Purtzer	67	68	67	73	69	344	4,988.50
Mike Sullivan	64	72	66	72	70	344	4,988.50
Ted Tryba	69	67	68	71	69	344	4,988.50
Mark Wiebe	67	71	69	66	71	344	4,988.50
Joe Acosta, Jr.	67	72	67	69	70	345	3,898.13
John Adams	67	71	69	69	69	345	3,898.13
Frank Lickliter	66	67	73	73	66	345	3,898.13
Payne Stewart	63	68	73	74	67	345	3,898.13
Woody Austin	66	69	70	70	70	345	3,898.12
Mike Heinen	66	69	67	71	72	345	3,898.12
Justin Leonard	70	66	69	68	72	345	3,898.12
Clarence Rose	68	66	69	69	73	345	3,898.12
Brad Bryant	67	71	69	69	70	346	3,630
David Duval	69	68	66	68	75	346	3,630
Jeff Gallagher	72	69	64	72	69	346	3,630
Willie Wood	66	71	70	67	72	346	3,630
Omar Uresti	67	70	68	72	69	346	3,630
Jim Carter	67	72	67	68	73	347	3,481.50
Jeff Hart	69	67	69	71	71	347	3,481.50
John Maginnes	69	69	65	73	71	347	3,481.50
Don Pooley	68	66	69	70	74	347	3,481.50
Mark Brooks	68	67	68	74	71	348	3,382.50
Tom Scherrer	67	70	68	70	73	348	3,382.50
Patrick Burke	66	68	73	72	70	349	3,316.50

	SCORES				TOTAL	MONEY
Fuzzy Zoeller	69	65	71	72	72	349	3,316.50
Brian Kamm	69	68	69	73	72	351	3,234
Gary Rusnak	68	69	69	73	72	351	3,234
Duffy Waldorf	69	70	67	72	73	351	3,234
Fulton Allem	73	66	66	73	75	353	3,135
Brandel Chamblee	68	69	67	77	72	353	3,135
Wayne Levi	64	72	71	73	73	353	3,135
Craig Parry	68	67	72	74	73	354	3,052.50
Jay Williamson	70	72	65	74	73	354	3,052.50
Greg Kraft	70	66	71	74	76	357	3,003

LaCantera Texas Open

LaCantera Golf Club, San Antonio, Texas
Par 36-36–72; 6,899 yards

October 10-13
purse, $1,200,000

	SCORES				TOTAL	MONEY
David Ogrin	70	65	68	72	275	$216,000
Jay Haas	70	66	70	70	276	129,600
Tiger Woods	69	68	73	67	277	81,600
Greg Kraft	71	72	70	65	278	52,800
Len Mattiace	73	71	65	69	278	52,800
Keith Fergus	70	71	68	70	279	40,200
Tim Herron	70	70	71	68	279	40,200
John Huston	66	71	74	68	279	40,200
Scott Dunlap	70	70	71	69	280	33,600
Lee Janzen	73	67	70	70	280	33,600
Justin Leonard	71	72	71	67	281	23,828.58
Tommy Armour III	71	72	64	74	281	23,828.57
Brian Claar	69	70	71	71	281	23,828.57
Brad Fabel	71	70	69	71	281	23,828.57
Kelly Gibson	68	74	67	72	281	23,828.57
John Morse	68	71	69	73	281	23,828.57
Corey Pavin	70	70	70	71	281	23,828.57
Robert Gamez	74	68	71	69	282	16,200
J.L. Lewis	69	71	71	71	282	16,200
Dan Pohl	72	71	70	69	282	16,200
Hugh Royer III	67	74	68	73	282	16,200
Billy Ray Brown	72	70	71	70	283	11,140
Allen Doyle	73	71	70	69	283	11,140
Mike Heinen	66	75	70	72	283	11,140
Mike Hulbert	68	74	71	70	283	11,140
Steve Lowery	71	70	74	68	283	11,140
Joey Sindelar	74	71	72	66	283	11,140
Olin Browne	71	74	66	73	284	7,642.50
Mark Carnevale	73	71	67	73	284	7,642.50
Donnie Hammond	69	74	68	73	284	7,642.50
Blaine McCallister	72	70	71	71	284	7,642.50
Scott McCarron	74	68	73	69	284	7,642.50
Rocco Mediate	72	72	71	69	284	7,642.50
Sean Murphy	76	69	71	68	284	7,642.50
Bob Tway	70	67	75	72	284	7,642.50
David Frost	67	71	72	75	285	5,652
Jeff Maggert	74	67	70	74	285	5,652
Ted Tryba	70	74	68	73	285	5,652
Jay Williamson	71	69	74	71	285	5,652
Mark Brooks	76	67	71	71	285	5,652

	SCORES				TOTAL	MONEY
Tom Byrum	71	71	73	71	286	4,440
Bob Lohr	75	69	73	69	286	4,440
Dicky Pride	70	73	70	73	286	4,440
Lee Rinker	72	70	71	73	286	4,440
Ron Whittaker	73	70	75	68	286	4,440
John Adams	74	71	71	71	287	3,402
Woody Austin	68	73	75	71	287	3,402
David Berganio, Jr.	70	73	74	70	287	3,402
Jim Carter	73	72	73	69	287	3,402
Rusty Brown	75	70	74	69	288	2,872
Bob Gilder	70	68	80	70	288	2,872
Larry Mize	70	73	71	74	288	2,872
Craig Parry	71	73	69	75	288	2,872
Hisayuki Sasaki	70	69	73	76	288	2,872
Bobby Wadkins	70	73	72	73	288	2,872
Russ Cochran	71	73	72	73	289	2,700
Brian Kamm	70	75	72	72	289	2,700
Taylor Smith	72	72	71	74	289	2,700
Mike Springer	70	75	75	69	289	2,700
Andy Bean	70	71	76	73	290	2,580
Chris Perry	72	69	72	77	290	2,580
Sam Randolph	70	74	75	71	290	2,580
Tim Simpson	74	71	76	69	290	2,580
D.A. Weibring	71	71	72	75	290	2,580
John Wilson	74	71	71	74	290	2,580
Shane Bertsch	72	72	74	73	291	2,424
Phil Blackmar	75	70	74	72	291	2,424
Carl Paulson	73	71	72	75	291	2,424
Don Pooley	74	68	68	81	291	2,424
Denis Watson	75	68	72	76	291	2,424
Mark Wiebe	75	70	75	71	291	2,424
John Daly	73	68	73	77	291	2,424
Stuart Appleby	74	70	73	76	293	2,316
Rex Caldwell	72	70	76	75	293	2,316
Tray Tyner	69	74	74	72	294	2,280
Chris Smith	75	70	77	73	295	2,256

Walt Disney World/Oldsmobile Classic

Walt Disney World Resort, Lake Buena Vista, Florida
Magnolia Course: Par 36-36–72; 7,190 yards
Palm Course: Par 36-36–72; 6,957 yards
Lake Buena Vista Course: Par 36-36–72; 6,819 yards

October 17-20
purse, $1,200,000

	SCORES				TOTAL	MONEY
Tiger Woods	69	63	69	66	267	$216,000
Payne Stewart	68	63	70	67	268	129,600
Robert Gamez	66	66	70	67	269	81,600
Nolan Henke	71	64	71	64	270	57,600
Lennie Clements	67	67	66	71	271	43,800
Rick Fehr	65	65	70	71	271	43,800
Jay Haas	65	67	68	71	271	43,800
Ronnie Black	66	66	69	71	272	32,400
Jim Carter	66	65	71	70	272	32,400
Dudley Hart	68	66	69	69	272	32,400
Jerry Kelly	69	64	69	70	272	32,400
Mike Springer	69	67	70	66	272	32,400

	SCORES			TOTAL	MONEY
Glen Day	67	66	71	69	273	21,840
Scott Hoch	66	66	71	70	273	21,840
Jim McGovern	65	67	73	68	273	21,840
Larry Nelson	65	67	70	71	273	21,840
Joey Sindelar	66	71	67	69	273	21,840
Paul Azinger	72	64	71	67	274	12,774.55
Brad Fabel	67	68	71	68	274	12,774.55
Neal Lancaster	66	68	70	70	274	12,774.55
Scott McCarron	67	72	69	66	274	12,774.55
Tom Purtzer	66	70	67	71	274	12,774.55
Jeff Sluman	64	69	71	70	274	12,774.55
Brad Bryant	67	69	66	72	274	12,774.54
John Cook	69	66	69	70	274	12,774.54
Steve Jurgensen	71	67	67	69	274	12,774.54
Omar Uresti	69	69	67	69	274	12,774.54
Bobby Wadkins	68	68	68	70	274	12,774.54
Mike Sullivan	71	64	66	74	275	7,465.72
Ted Tryba	67	69	69	70	275	7,465.72
Duffy Waldorf	66	71	69	69	275	7,465.72
Fulton Allem	68	65	70	72	275	7,465.71
Greg Kraft	65	71	70	69	275	7,465.71
Jeff Maggert	70	66	71	68	275	7,465.71
Len Mattiace	69	65	73	68	275	7,465.71
Jay Don Blake	68	69	68	71	276	5,530
Joel Edwards	68	69	64	75	276	5,530
Carl Paulson	68	67	72	69	276	5,530
Don Pooley	70	67	70	69	276	5,530
Tom Scherrer	67	67	72	70	276	5,530
Stuart Appleby	69	68	69	70	276	5,530
Olin Browne	71	66	70	70	277	3,768
Patrick Burke	67	67	70	73	277	3,768
John Daly	70	68	68	71	277	3,768
Brian Kamm	66	68	74	69	277	3,768
Blaine McCallister	67	69	66	75	277	3,768
Larry Mize	69	70	69	69	277	3,768
David Ogrin	69	66	71	71	277	3,768
Gene Sauers	67	69	71	70	277	3,768
Bob Tway	66	72	68	71	277	3,768
Bart Bryant	69	69	69	71	278	2,793
Bruce Fleisher	72	67	69	70	278	2,793
Frank Lickliter	63	68	73	74	278	2,793
Steve Lowery	63	69	72	74	278	2,793
Doug Martin	66	67	73	72	278	2,793
Mike Reid	66	69	72	71	278	2,793
Loren Roberts	67	67	72	72	278	2,793
Hisayuki Sasaki	68	70	70	70	278	2,793
Phil Blackmar	73	62	71	73	279	2,592
Jim Furyk	70	70	68	71	279	2,592
Joey Gullion	64	69	72	74	279	2,592
Mike Hulbert	66	75	67	71	279	2,592
Jesper Parnevik	69	69	70	71	279	2,592
Mike Standly	71	69	64	75	279	2,592
Dave Stockton, Jr.	65	70	72	72	279	2,592
Brian Claar	69	68	70	73	280	2,448
Tim Herron	67	66	72	75	280	2,448
Peter Jacobsen	71	68	69	72	280	2,448
Corey Pavin	69	66	71	74	280	2,448
Mike Swartz	72	66	70	72	280	2,448
Joe Acosta, Jr.	73	67	68	73	281	2,352
Marco Dawson	67	72	68	74	281	2,352

	SCORES				TOTAL	MONEY
Brad Faxon	67	71	69	74	281	2,352
Russ Cochran	70	68	69	75	282	2,292
Brian Tennyson	65	69	71	77	282	2,292
John Huston	69	68	71	77	285	2,256

Tour Championship

Southern Hills Country Club, Tulsa, Oklahoma
Par 35-35–70; 6,834 yards

October 24-27
purse, $3,000,000

	SCORES				TOTAL	MONEY
Tom Lehman	66	67	64	71	268	$540,000
Brad Faxon	68	72	66	68	274	324,000
Steve Stricker	70	68	72	65	275	207,000
Kenny Perry	73	68	70	66	277	144,000
Fred Couples	68	73	68	69	278	120,000
Ernie Els	76	70	65	68	279	102,000
Justin Leonard	73	68	68	70	279	102,000
Tom Watson	70	70	69	70	279	102,000
Vijay Singh	66	71	69	74	280	87,600
Jeff Sluman	71	74	67	68	280	87,600
John Cook	70	73	70	68	281	81,000
Phil Mickelson	67	75	68	73	283	76,800
Davis Love III	72	71	71	70	284	73,200
Fred Funk	71	73	74	67	285	69,600
Mark Calcavecchia	69	71	73	73	286	63,600
David Duval	71	71	74	70	286	63,600
Jim Furyk	72	71	73	70	286	63,600
Scott Hoch	73	73	67	74	287	58,800
Steve Jones	67	73	70	77	287	58,800
Mark O'Meara	74	71	71	71	287	58,800
Corey Pavin	71	73	73	71	288	55,800
Tiger Woods	70	78	72	68	288	55,800
Michael Bradley	71	73	75	70	289	54,000
Nick Faldo	75	72	76	68	291	52,800
Tommy Tolles	73	77	74	68	292	51,600
Duffy Waldorf	74	76	72	71	293	50,400
Mark Brooks	73	75	73	74	295	49,500
Jeff Maggert	78	76	70	71	295	49,500
Greg Norman	73	72	67		WD	
Loren Roberts					WD	

Special Events

Treasure Coast Classic

Grand Harbor Golf & Beach Club, Vero Beach, Florida
Par 36-36–72; 6,564 yards

January 27-28
purse, $200,000

	SCORES		TOTAL	MONEY (Each)
Bruce Devlin/Larry Ziegler	64	60	124	$35,000
Harold Henning/Tony Jacklin	64	61	125	13,750
Harry Toscano/Richard Bassett	62	63	125	13,750
Larry Laoretti/Jack Kiefer	63	63	126	6,250
Gary Groh/Bob Menne	63	63	126	6,250
Walter Morgan/Larry Gilbert	65	62	127	2,000
Orville Moody/Brian Barnes	65	62	127	2,000
Homero Blancas/Terry Dill	65	62	127	2,000
Denise Baldwin/Karen Noble	67	60	127	2,000
Rocky Thompson/Jack Rule	62	65	127	2,000
Bobby Mitchell/Chuck Montalbano	60	67	127	2,000
Jay Sigel/Buddy Allin	59	69	128	2,000
John Paul Cain/Bruce Summerhays	65	64	129	2,000
Laurie Rinker Graham/Lauri Merten	67	62	129	2,000
Dick Hendrickson/Ben Smith	65	64	129	2,000
Lisa Kiggens/Kelly Robbins	65	64	129	2,000
Leigh Ann Mills/Sally Little	63	66	129	2,000
Marion Heck/Doug Dalziel	66	64	130	2,000
Jan Stephenson/Susie Redman	66	64	130	2,000
Sue Thomas/Mitzi Edge	62	68	130	2,000
John Jacobs/Tommy Jacobs	62	68	130	2,000
Stephanie Maynor/Michele Redman	63	68	131	2,000
Missie Berteotti/Wendy Ward	67	65	132	2,000
Katie Peterson-Parker/Nancy Bowen	66	66	132	2,000
Simon Hobday/John Bland	66	67	133	2,000
Marianne Morris/Noell Daghe	69	64	133	2,000
Barb Mucha/Laurie Brower	64	69	133	2,000
Kathy Guadagnino/Kim Williams	67	68	135	2,000
Julie Piers/Page Dunlap	67	68	135	2,000
Michelle Estill/Nancy Harvey	66	69	135	2,000
Barb Scherbak/Nancy Taylor	68	69	137	2,000
Lynn Connelly/Nicky Leroux	70	69	139	2,000

Family House Invitational

Laurel Valley Golf Club, Ligonier, Pennsylvania
Par 36-36–72; 7,066 yards

June 26-27
purse, $850,000

	SCORES		TOTAL	MONEY
Scott Hoch	64	64	128	$170,000
Steve Stricker	70	66	136	85,000
Vijay Singh	68	69	137	46,000
Kirk Triplett	69	68	137	46,000
David Duval	70	68	138	36,000

	SCORES		TOTAL	MONEY
David Frost	71	68	139	29,000
Curtis Strange	71	68	139	29,000
Jim Gallagher, Jr.	71	69	140	19,000
Billy Mayfair	71	69	140	19,000
Loren Roberts	69	71	140	19,000
Mark Calcavecchia	70	71	141	16,000
Hale Irwin	71	70	141	16,000
Lee Janzen	71	70	141	16,000
Scott Simpson	71	70	141	16,000
Ernie Els	75	67	142	16,000
Jim Furyk	70	72	142	16,000
Craig Stadler	71	71	142	16,000
Mark Brooks	72	71	143	16,000
Fred Funk	72	71	143	16,000
Tom Purtzer	71	72	143	16,000
Kenny Perry	73	71	144	16,000
Bob Tway	69	75	144	16,000
Tommy Tolles	71	74	145	16,000
D.A. Weibring	72	73	145	16,000
Justin Leonard	74	72	146	16,000
Payne Stewart	75	71	146	16,000
Jay Haas	74	73	147	16,000
Tim Herron	76	72	148	16,000
John Mazza	76	72	148	16,000
Rocco Mediate	76	72	148	16,000
Arnold Palmer	72	76	148	16,000
Jesper Parnevik	75	73	148	16,000

Ernst Championship

Inglewood Country Club, Kenmore, Washington
Par 36-35–71; 6,527 yards

July 8-9
purse, $660,000

	SCORES		TOTAL	MONEY
Phil Mickelson	68	65	133	$130,000
Fred Couples	64	69	133	65,000
(Mickelson defeated Couples on first extra hole.)				
Scott Simpson	69	65	134	32,500
Brad Faxon	69	65	134	32,500
Jay Haas	64	71	135	25,000
Gil Morgan	69	67	136	19,500
Lennie Clements	70	66	136	19,500
Blaine McCallister	71	66	137	17,500
Craig Stadler	71	66	137	17,500
John Cook	66	72	138	15,200
Nolan Henke	67	71	138	15,200
Billy Andrade	69	69	138	15,200
Steve Stricker	69	69	138	15,200
Mike Hulbert	70	68	138	15,200
Fuzzy Zoeller	71	68	139	15,000
Larry Mize	67	72	139	15,000
Gary McCord	72	68	140	15,000
Keith Clearwater	72	68	140	15,000
Mark Rohde	70	71	141	15,000
Rick Fehr	72	70	142	15,000
Kenny Perry	72	71	143	15,000
Tom Purtzer	71	72	143	15,000

	SCORES		TOTAL	MONEY
John Daly	71	73	144	15,000
Andrew Magee	74	71	145	15,000
Don Pooley	72	73	145	15,000
Billy Mayfair	73	72	145	15,000
Jeff Sluman	74	73	147	15,000
Davis Love III	69	78	147	15,000
Jeff Coston	74	77	151	15,000

Jerry Ford Invitational

Vail Golf Club
Par 35-36–71; 7,064 yards

August 19-20
purse, $300,000

Country Club of the Rockies at Arrowhead
Par 36-36–72; 7,354 yards
Vail, Colorado

	SCORES		TOTAL	MONEY
Dillard Pruitt	68	64	132	$20,000
Keith Fergus	66	67	133	10,000
Jay Don Blake	67	66	133	10,000
David Peoples	65	69	134	5,000
Andrew Magee	66	69	135	5,000
Bob Lohr	63	72	135	5,000
Jim Thorpe	63	72	135	5,000
Scott Gump	66	69	135	5,000
Gary Hallberg	69	66	135	5,000
Robin Freeman	66	70	136	5,000
Lennie Clements	66	70	136	5,000
Bill Kratzert	67	69	136	5,000
Dave Stockton	70	67	137	5,000
Mark Pfeil	66	71	137	5,000
Gary McCord	68	69	137	5,000
Chris Perry	69	68	137	5,000
Steve Jones	67	70	137	5,000
Leonard Thompson	71	68	139	5,000
Jay Delsing	69	70	139	5,000
Mark Wiebe	69	70	139	5,000
Jerry Pate	71	68	139	5,000
John Mahaffey	70	69	139	5,000
Charles Coody	65	75	140	5,000
Mike Standly	67	73	140	5,000
Dan Pohl	68	72	140	5,000
Fulton Allem	68	72	140	5,000
Donnie Hammond	69	71	140	5,000
Andy Bean	67	74	141	5,000
Mike Sullivan	69	72	141	5,000
Clarence Rose	68	73	141	5,000
Brandel Chamblee	67	74	141	5,000
Buddy Gardner	68	74	142	5,000
J.C. Snead	70	72	142	5,000
Brian Claar	71	71	142	5,000
George Burns	71	71	142	5,000
Greg Twiggs	71	71	142	5,000
Keith Clearwater	72	71	143	5,000
Tom Purtzer	72	71	143	5,000
Richard Zokol	72	71	143	5,000

	SCORES		TOTAL	MONEY
Bob Murphy	69	74	143	5,000
Barry Jaeckel	72	71	143	5,000
Jim Nelford	72	72	144	5,000
Morris Hatalsky	70	74	144	5,000
Lon Hinkle	75	69	144	5,000
Ed Fiori	73	72	145	5,000
Don Pooley	74	72	146	5,000
Jonathan Kaye	71	76	147	5,000
Steve Satterstrom	73	75	148	5,000
Hubert Green	74	74	148	5,000
Dave Eichelberger	73	77	150	5,000
Tom Apple	75	75	150	5,000
Bruce Devlin	78	73	151	5,000
Mark Lye	75	77	152	5,000
Deane Beman	76	77	153	5,000
Dow Finsterwald	79	80	159	5,000
Phil Rodgers	85	79	164	5,000
Hal Sutton	69		DQ	5,000
Jim Colbert	71		DQ	5,000
Lee Elder	80		DQ	5,000
Kirk Triplett	76		WD	5,000

Fred Meyer Challenge

Oregon Golf Club, West Linn, Oregon
Par 35-36–71; 6,815 yards

August 19-20
purse, $700,000

	SCORES		TOTAL	MONEY (Team)
Greg Norman/Brad Faxon	63	61	124	$100,000
Mark Calcavecchia/Billy Mayfair	62	63	125	80,000
Tom Lehman/Lee Janzen	63	63	126	70,000
Mark O'Meara/John Cook	61	67	128	60,000
Tom Watson/Nick Faldo	66	63	129	53,000
Brian Henninger/Fuzzy Zoeller	63	66	129	53,000
Lanny Wadkins/Jim Gallagher, Jr.	67	64	131	49,500
Steve Elkington/Craig Stadler	65	66	131	49,500
Jim Furyk/Bob Gilder	66	66	132	47,500
Jay Haas/Phil Mickelson	69	64	133	45,833
Peter Jacobsen/Arnold Palmer	66	67	133	45,833
Jack Nicklaus/Gary Nicklaus	66	67	133	45,833

Sarazen World Open Championship

Chateau Elan, Legends Course, Braselton, Georgia
Par 36-36–72; 6,967 yards

October 31-November 3
purse, $1,900,000

	SCORES				TOTAL	MONEY
Frank Nobilo	66	68	72	66	272	$342,000
Scott Hoch	68	64	70	74	276	205,000
Craig Stadler	68	69	70	71	278	99,000
Payne Stewart	69	68	71	70	278	99,000
Nick Price	68	72	70	69	279	69,000
Mark Calcavecchia	70	70	72	70	282	60,125
Davis Love III	70	67	73	72	282	60,125

	SCORES				TOTAL	MONEY
Angel Cabrera	72	70	73	68	283	53,000
Stephen Flesch	73	68	73	70	284	47,000
Todd Barranger	65	70	76	73	284	47,000
Mark McNulty	69	70	77	69	285	35,356
Mike Donald	74	73	68	70	285	35,356
P.J. Cowan	71	70	72	72	285	35,356
Gary Marks	69	72	71	73	285	35,356
Mathias Gronberg	73	69	71	73	286	26,550
Daniel Chopra	69	70	70	77	286	26,550
Miguel Angel Jimenez	72	70	74	71	287	22,750
Paul Broadhurst	69	73	72	73	287	22,750
Eduardo Romero	71	73	73	71	288	19,450
Padraig Harrington	70	72	73	73	288	19,450
Edward Fryatt	72	73	77	67	289	17,575
Philip Walton	73	71	75	70	289	17,575
Andrew Oldcorn	73	70	73	74	290	16,150
Paul McGinley	71	70	74	76	291	14,725
Anders Forsbrand	73	74	72	72	291	14,725
John Cook	68	72	77	75	292	12,206
Chris Williams	71	67	76	78	292	12,206
Fred Couples	68	79	73	72	292	12,206
Mark James	73	73	73	73	292	12,206
Barry Lane	71	72	75	75	293	10,450
Fuzzy Zoeller	72	75	72	74	293	10,450
Lucas Parsons	70	75	73	75	293	10,450
Steve Y.S. Kwon	70	75	73	75	293	10,450
Clay Devers	78	67	73	76	294	8,930
Raul Fretes	75	72	75	72	294	8,930
Chad Magee	70	73	78	73	294	8,930
Jon Robson	71	73	76	74	294	8,930
Steve Schroeder	72	75	75	73	295	7,980
Jack Nicklaus	71	75	79	71	296	7,427
John Wade	77	68	77	74	296	7,427
Alexander Cejka	74	72	75	75	296	7,427
Jaime Gomez	73	74	79	71	297	6,745
Stephen Field	72	73	79	73	297	6,745
John Daly	72	74	71	80	297	6,745
Adam Hunter	75	71	77	74	297	6,745
Ian Hutchings	75	71	77	75	298	6,270
Steve Alker	71	72	80	76	299	5,985
Elliot Boult	70	76	74	79	299	5,985
Ben Crenshaw	73	71	79	77	300	5,625
Jim Payne	77	69	73	81	300	5,625
Marcelo Santi	76	69	76	82	303	5,500
Retief Goosen	73	71	76	83	303	5,500

Lincoln-Mercury Kapalua International

Kapalua Resort, Maui, Hawaii
Plantation Course: Par 36-37–73; 7,263 yards
Bay Course: Par 35-36–71; 6,600 yards

November 7-10
purse, $1,200,000

	SCORES				TOTAL	MONEY
Paul Stankowski	69	65	67	68	269	$216,000
Fred Couples	63	71	69	67	270	130,000
Davis Love III	66	68	71	66	271	66,625
Steve Jones	64	69	69	69	271	66,625

	SCORES				TOTAL	MONEY
Bob Gilder	64	69	69	70	272	43,850
Sandy Lyle	68	68	68	69	273	38,000
Peter Jacobsen	66	69	69	70	274	33,000
Stewart Cink	69	69	70	68	276	28,875
Scott McCarron	67	68	70	71	276	28,875
Duffy Waldorf	70	71	69	67	277	24,500
Billy Mayfair	69	65	70	73	277	24,500
Justin Leonard	66	75	69	68	278	20,500
David Ogrin	69	68	70	71	278	20,500
Billy Andrade	71	74	66	68	279	17,500
Clarence Rose	67	70	73	69	279	17,500
Glen Day	67	70	69	73	279	17,500
Kirk Triplett	64	76	71	69	280	15,000
Mike Brisky	66	73	71	70	280	15,000
Dudley Hart	70	74	68	69	281	13,250
Darren Clarke	67	78	69	67	281	13,250
Mike Hulbert	64	72	73	72	281	13,250
Jim Furyk	67	74	67	73	281	13,250
Scott Simpson	70	69	72	71	282	11,750
Jim McGovern	71	73	72	66	282	11,750
Jerry Kelly	68	73	72	70	283	10,700
Olin Browne	72	68	74	69	283	10,700
Tommy Tolles	66	73	72	72	283	10,700
Woody Austin	68	68	77	71	284	9,760
Brad Faxon	67	74	73	70	284	9,760
Patrick Burke	67	73	73	71	284	9,760
Russ Cochran	66	75	72	71	284	9,760
David Peoples	69	73	72	70	284	9,760
Roger Maltbie	67	73	73	72	285	9,425
Tim Herron	67	71	73	74	285	9,425
Ben Crenshaw	67	75	72	72	286	9,308.33
Jay Don Blake	73	70	73	70	286	9,308.33
Willie Wood	71	74	71	70	286	9,308.33
Chip Beck	72	68	73	74	287	9,212.50
Grant Waite	71	72	72	72	287	9,212.50
Tom Purtzer	71	72	74	70	287	9,212.50
Emlyn Aubrey	68	78	73	68	287	9,212.50
Fred Funk	71	73	74	70	288	9,150
Nolan Henke	70	69	73	77	289	9,087.50
Ed Fiori	72	69	75	73	289	9,087.50
David Feherty	76	70	71	72	289	9,087.50
John Daly	71	75	73	70	289	9,087.50
Steve Pate	72	77	72	69	290	9,012.50
Andy Bean	71	76	75	68	290	9,012.50
Brandel Chamblee	75	73	73	70	291	8,975
John Adams	70	74	74	74	292	8,925
Steve Lowery	70	77	73	72	292	8,925
Gary McCord	69	81	70	72	292	8,925
John Morse	75	73	72	75	295	8,875
Joel Edwards	75	81	70	76	302	8,850
Paul Goydos	73	69	83	78	303	8,825
Barry Lane	73	80	79	73	305	8,800

MasterCard PGA Grand Slam

Poipu Bay Resort, Kauai, Hawaii
Par 36-36–72; 6,957 yards

November 13-14
purse, $1,000,000

	SCORES		TOTAL	MONEY
Tom Lehman	68	66	134	$400,000
Steve Jones	70	66	136	250,000
Nick Faldo	67	72	139	200,000
Mark Brooks	74	73	147	150,000

Franklin Templeton Shark Shootout

Sherwood Country Club, Thousand Oaks, California
Par 36-36–72; 7,025 yards

November 15-17
purse, $1,100,000

	SCORES			TOTAL	MONEY (Each)
Jay Haas/Tom Kite	67	60	60	187	$150,000
Craig Stadler/Lanny Wadkins	69	57	63	189	71,250
Hale Irwin/Lee Janzen	68	61	60	189	71,250
Mark O'Meara/Curtis Strange	66	64	60	190	43,000
Brad Faxon/Peter Jacobsen	68	63	59	190	43,000
Chip Beck/Scott Hoch	66	69	59	194	39,000
Raymond Floyd/Greg Norman	67	65	64	196	35,250
Jim Colbert/Bruce Lietzke	70	64	62	196	35,250
Mark Calcavecchia/Steve Elkington	69	67	61	197	32,000
John Daly/David Duval	67	66	65	198	30,000

Mexican Open

Club de Golf Mexico, Mexico City, Mexico
Par 72

November 21-24
purse, $250,000

	SCORES				TOTAL	MONEY
Stewart Cink	67	69	68	68	272	$50,000
Bob Tway	66	72	70	66	274	32,000
Kawika Cotner	71	71	70	65	277	22,500
Lee Rinker	68	69	72	68	277	22,500
Len Mattiace	69	72	70	69	280	13,250
Brian Gay	71	69	71	69	280	13,250
*Carlos Rodiles	70	70	71	69	280	13,250
Jay Don Blake	71	73	71	67	282	8,100
John Cook	68	73	72	69	282	8,100
Grant Masson	71	73	68	70	282	8,100
Lennie Clements	71	72	69	70	282	8,100
Willie Wood	67	73	71	71	282	8,100
Jeff Klein	75	71	67	70	283	5,250
Steve Parker	74	70	68	71	283	5,250
Kory Bowman	70	69	73	71	283	5,250
Steve Jurgensen	66	73	71	73	283	5,250
Scott Verplank	73	74	70	67	284	3,500
Jamie Gomez	74	70	72	68	284	3,500
Guy Boros	70	71	73	70	284	3,500
Gary Hallberg	70	71	68	76	285	2,700
*Mauricio Asbun	70	70	73	72	285	

	SCORES				TOTAL	MONEY
Oscar Serna	70	73	73	71	287	2,100
Rex Caldwell	67	78	70	72	287	2,100
Steve Holmes	73	71	70	73	287	2,100
Tommy Armour III	68	74	75	71	288	1,750
Esteban Toledo	70	76	70	72	288	1,750
Walter Hartleben	73	74	69	73	289	1,625
Steve Lamontagne	72	72	71	74	289	1,625
Eraclio Bermudez	76	73	71	70	290	1,525
*Juan Salazar	71	74	75	70	290	
Jesus Torres	74	73	68	75	290	1,525
Jorge Perez Leon	76	72	70	73	291	1,425
Keoki Cotner	72	76	70	73	291	1,425

Merrill Lynch Pebble Beach Invitational Pro-Am

Pebble Beach Golf Links, Pebble Beach, California
Par 36-36–72; 6,799 yards

November 21-24
purse, $250,000

	SCORES				TOTAL	MONEY
Kirk Triplett	68	67	66	73	274	$50,000
David Ogrin	68	69	71	69	277	26,500
Mike Springer	67	74	66	71	278	13,500
Lon Hinkle	69	75	68	67	279	6,666
Mike Reid	72	69	69	69	279	6,666
Scott McCarron	66	72	71	70	279	6,666
Bruce Fleisher	72	69	71	70	282	5,500
Gene Sauers	68	69	73	73	283	4,750
Jim Carter	67	74	69	73	283	4,750
Scott Simpson	71	73	73	67	284	4,000
Keith Fergus	68	72	72	72	284	4,000
Tim Loustalot	73	72	70	71	286	3,700
Barry Jaeckel	72	74	69	72	287	3,300
Gary McCord	69	70	75	73	287	3,300
Ronnie Black	70	68	75	74	287	3,300
Mike Weir	73	74	72	69	288	2,700
Mark Wiebe	75	74	71	68	288	2,700
Laird Small	72	71	73	72	288	2,700
Brian Mogg	72	69	75	73	289	2,135
Todd Fischer	70	71	76	72	289	2,135
Mark Pfeil	72	74	72	71	289	2,135
Tommy Masters	70	73	70	76	289	2,135
Rob Boldt	71	74	73	72	290	2,030
Patrick Burke	75	71	72	72	290	2,030
Glen Stubblefield	76	73	72	70	291	1,980
Larry Ziegler	74	69	73	75	291	1,980
Jimmy Powell	72	75	73	71	291	1,980
Bob Borowicz	74	74	71	73	292	1,920
Bruce Summerhays	70	79	71	72	292	1,920
Marion Dantzler	76	75	70	71	292	1,920
Brett Upper	71	75	74	73	293	1,850
Mick Soli	71	72	76	74	293	1,850
Shawn McEntee	73	75	72	73	293	1,850
Brent Geiberger	74	71	73	75	293	1,850
Dave Eichelberger	74	69	76	75	294	1,800
Dan Forsman	72	77	72	74	295	1,770
Andy North	75	76	68	76	295	1,770
John Morse	76	72	76	72	296	1,710
Jeff McMillian	76	73	68	79	296	1,710

	SCORES			TOTAL	MONEY
Johnny Miller	73	72	73	78	296	1,710
Shawn Kelly	75	77	67	77	296	1,710
Al Krueger	72	74	77	74	297	1,640
Woody Austin	76	77	70	74	297	1,640
Bob Ford	75	74	72	76	297	1,640
Johnny Gonzales	73	70	77	78	298	1,580
George Archer	75	74	71	78	298	1,580
Terry Dill	75	72	69	82	298	1,580
Mike Parrish	74	73	73	80	300	1,530
Gordon Johnson	72	74	76	78	300	1,530
Ted Goin	75	73	75	83	306	1,500

JCPenney Classic

Innisbrook Hilton Resort, Tarpon Springs, Florida
Par 36-36–72; 7,054 yards (men), 6,330 yards (women)
(Fourth round cancelled — rain.)

December 5-8
purse, $1,500,000

	SCORES			TOTAL	MONEY (Each)
Donna Andrews/Mike Hulbert	63	66	68	197	$187,500
Missie McGeorge/Joel Edwards	65	66	67	198	75,576
Kellie Kuehne/Tiger Woods	66	64	68	198	75,576
Pat Hurst/Scott McCarron	65	64	70	199	45,576
Laura Davies/John Daly	63	68	69	200	31,297
Dottie Pepper/Jeff Sluman	65	66	69	200	31,297
Vicki Goetze/Steve Stricker	69	64	68	201	18,527
Tina Barrett/Dan Forsman	68	65	68	201	18,527
Annika Sorenstam/Jesper Parnevik	63	69	69	201	18,527
Cathy Johnston-Forbes/Willie Wood	66	66	69	201	18,527
Catrin Nilsmark/Greg Kraft	66	69	67	202	11,079
Emilee Klein/Stewart Cink	65	69	68	202	11,079
Tammie Green/Robert Gamez	66	67	69	202	11,079
Julie Piers/Kirk Triplett	67	64	71	202	11,079
Carin Hj Koch/Doug Martin	67	69	67	203	7,811
Beth Daniel/Davis Love III	66	69	68	203	7,811
Penny Hammel/Dicky Pride	67	70	66	203	7,811
Karrie Webb/Brad Faxon	67	67	69	203	7,811
Jane Geddes/Kelly Gibson	68	64	71	203	7,811
Amy Fruhwirth/Woody Austin	68	72	63	203	7,811
Marianne Morris/Lee Rinker	68	69	67	204	5,907
Amy Benz/John Huston	67	68	69	204	5,907
Dana Dormann/Paul Stankowski	66	69	69	204	5,907
Juli Inkster/Tom Purtzer	67	65	72	204	5,907
Kris Tschetter/Billy Andrade	65	70	70	205	5,561
Maggie Will-Halpin/Jim Carter	65	70	71	206	5,373
Caroline Pierce/John Morse	68	73	71	206	5,373
Jan Stephenson/Chip Beck	66	72	68	206	5,373
Kelly Robbins/Pete Jordan	68	70	69	207	5,004
Kim Williams/Jim Dent	71	70	66	207	5,004
Tracy Kerdyk/David Ogrin	68	68	72	208	4,373
Kim Saiki/Patrick Burke	69	68	71	208	4,373
Jane Crafter/Rocco Mediate	68	70	70	208	4,373
Michelle McGann/Kenny Perry	68	70	70	208	4,373
Barb Whitehead/Emlyn Aubrey	68	70	70	208	4,373
Brandie Burton/Billy Mayfair	69	70	69	208	4,373
Chris Johnson/Steve Lowery	67	74	67	208	4,373
Dawn Coe-Jones/Dudley Hart	69	68	72	209	3,723

	SCORES			TOTAL	MONEY (Each)
Deb Richard/Peter Kostis	70	67	72	209	3,723
Nancy Scranton/Tom Wargo	68	69	72	209	3,723
Meg Mallon/Steve Pate	71	67	71	209	3,723
Melissa McNamara/Glen Day	70	68	71	209	3,723
Vicki Fergon/Taylor Smith	69	71	69	209	3,723
Dale Eggeling/Wayne Levi	70	66	74	210	3,432
Katie Peterson-Parker/Michael Bradley	68	70	72	210	3,432
Barb Mucha/Mike Brisky	67	71	72	210	3,432
Marta Figueras-Dotti/Brad Bryant	69	70	71	210	3,432
Cindy Schreyer/Hugh Royer III	69	74	68	211	3,288
Martha Nause/Jay Overton	70	73	70	213	3,231
Cindy Rarick/Gary Koch	68	74	72	214	3,173
Amy Alcott/Russ Cochran	70	74	71	215	3,115
Trish Johnson/Lawrence Farmer	74	73	75	222	3,057

Office Depot Father-Son Challenge

Windsor Club, Vero Beach, Florida
Par 36-36—72; 6,709 yards

December 7-8
purse, $800,000

	SCORES		TOTAL	MONEY (Won by professional)
Raymond and Raymond Floyd, Jr.	61	63	124	$150,000
Dave and Ron Stockton	65	61	126	100,000
Tony and Warren Jacklin	67	61	128	80,000
Tom and Eric Weiskopf	66	63	129	60,000
Larry and Drew Nelson	63	66	129	60,000
Lee and Rick Trevino	68	63	131	52,000
Jack and Gary Nicklaus	65	67	132	46,000
Gary and Wayne Player	67	66	133	42,000
Charles and Kyle Coody	67	67	134	40,000
Al and John Geiberger	65	70	135	37,000
Hale and Steve Irwin	66	69	135	37,000
Johnny and John Miller	71	65	136	34,000
David and Andrew Graham	69	69	138	32,000
Billy and Bobby Casper	72	71	143	30,000

Diners Club Matches

PGA West, La Quinta, California
Par 36-36—72; 7,112 yards

December 12-15
purse, $700,000

FIRST ROUND

Kenny Perry and Scott Hoch defeated Mark Calcavecchia and Billy Mayfair, 1 up
Steve Jones and Rick Fehr defeated Tom Lehman and Duffy Waldorf, 4 and 3
Justin Leonard and Mike Hulbert defeated Mark Brooks and Andrew Magee, 3 and 2
John Cook and Craig Stadler defeated Steve Stricker and Kirk Triplett, 19 holes

SECOND ROUND

Perry and Hoch defeated Cook and Stadler, 5 and 3
Calcavecchia and Mayfair defeated Stricker and Triplett, 1 up
Jones and Fehr defeated Brooks and Magee, 19 holes
Lehman and Waldorf defeated Leonard and Hulbert, 21 holes

(Losers after second round received $25,000 each.)

THIRD ROUND

Perry and Hoch defeated Stricker and Triplett, 1 up
Lehman and Waldorf defeated Brooks and Magee, 19 holes

(Losers after third round received $40,000 each.)

FOURTH ROUND

Lehman and Waldorf defeated Perry and Hoch, 1 up

(Lehman and Waldorf received $110,000 each; Perry and Hoch received $60,000 each.)

Lexus Challenge

La Quinta Resort & Club, Citrus Course, La Quinta, California
Par 36-36–72; 6,825 yards

December 20-21
purse, $1,000,000

	SCORES		TOTAL	MONEY (Won by professional)
Hale Irwin/Sean Connery	61	62	123	$180,000
John Brodie/Ken Griffey, Jr.	64	63	127	106,667
Chi Chi Rodriguez/Robert Wuhl	64	63	127	106,667
Lee Trevino/Kevin Costner	65	62	127	106,667
Raymond Floyd/Michael Chiklis	64	66	130	75,000
Dave Stockton/Joe Pesci	64	66	130	75,000
Gary Player/Glenn Frey	65	65	130	75,000
George Archer/Dan Jansen	67	65	132	57,500
Jim Colbert/Don Shula	63	69	132	57,500
Arnold Palmer/Chris O'Donnell	68	64	132	57,500
Jim Dent/Clint Eastwood	69	64	133	52,500
Bob Murphy/Richard Dreyfuss	74	67	141	50,000

Andersen Consulting World Championship

Grayhawk Golf Club, Talon Course, Scottsdale, Arizona
Par 36-36–72; 7,005 yards

January 4-5, 1997
purse, $3,650,000

SEMI-FINALS

Scott Hoch defeated Sam Torrance, 4 and 2
Greg Norman defeated Hisayuki Sasaki, 5 and 4

THIRD-PLACE PLAYOFF

Sasaki defeated Torrance, 2 and 1

(Sasaki received $350,000; Torrance received $300,000.)

FINAL

Norman defeated Hoch, 1 up

(Norman received $1,000,000; Hoch received $500,000.)

Japan Qualifying

Golden Palm Country Club, Kagoshima, Japan   March 30-31
Par 36-36–72; 6,970 yards

QUARTER-FINALS

Shigeki Maruyama defeated Ryoken Kawagishi, 4 and 3
Katsuyoshi Tomori defeated Hidemichi Tanaka, 3 and 2
Hideki Kase defeated Tsuneyuki Nakajima, 2 and 1
Hisayuki Sasaki defeated Masahiro Kuramoto, 1 up

(Each losing quarter-finalist received $20,000.)

SEMI-FINALS

Maruyama defeated Tomori, 5 and 4
Sasaki defeated Kase, 4 and 3

(Each losing semi-finalist received $70,000.)

FINAL

Sasaki defeated Maruyama, 3 and 2

(Maruyama received $150,000.)

United States Qualifying

Reynolds Plantation, Great Waters Course,   April 22-23
Lake Oconee, Georgia
Par 36-36–72; 7,048 yards

QUARTER-FINALS

Davis Love III defeated Corey Pavin, 2 up
Lee Janzen defeated Peter Jacobsen, 3 and 1
Scott Hoch defeated Tom Lehman, 1 up
Mark McCumber defeated Loren Roberts, 4 and 2

(Each losing quarter-finalist received $20,000.)

SEMI-FINALS

Janzen defeated Love, 1 up
Hoch defeated McCumber, 23 holes

(Each losing semi-finalist received $70,000.)

FINAL

Hoch defeated Janzen, 3 and 1

(Janzen received $150,000.)

European Qualifying

Oxfordshire Golf Club, Thame, England
Par 36-36–72; 7,187 yards

QUARTER-FINALS

Miguel Angel Jimenez defeated Barry Lane, 1 up
Sam Torrance defeated Mark James, 2 and 1
Bernhard Langer defeated Jesper Parnevik, 20 holes
Colin Montgomerie defeated Costantino Rocca, 1 up

(Each losing quarter-finalist received $20,000.)

SEMI-FINALS

Torrance defeated Jimenez, 6 and 4
Montgomerie defeated Langer, 4 and 3

(Each losing semi-finalist received $70,000.)

FINAL

Torrance defeated Montgomerie, 3 and 2

(Montgomerie received $150,000.)

International Qualifying

Blackwolf Run, River Course, Kohler, Wisconsin
Par 37-35–72; 6,991 yards

QUARTER-FINALS

Greg Norman defeated Craig Parry, 1 up
Steve Elkington defeated Vijay Singh, 3 and 2
Nick Price defeated Michael Campbell, 4 and 2
David Frost defeated Ernie Els, 1 up

(Each losing quarter-finalist received $20,000.)

SEMI-FINALS

Norman defeated Elkington, 4 and 3
Frost defeated Price, 5 and 3

(Each losing semi-finalist received $70,000.)

FINAL

Norman defeated Frost, 1 up

(Frost received $150,000.)

Nike Tour

San Jose Open

Almaden Country Club, San Jose, California
Par 36-36–72; 6,960 yards
(First round postponed — event shortened to 54 holes.)

February 22-25
purse, $200,000

	SCORES			TOTAL	MONEY
Larry Silveira	70	67	70	207	$36,000
Stewart Cink	71	67	69	207	19,600
Bobby Elliott	70	66	71	207	19,600
(Silveira defeated Cink and Elliott on second extra hole.)					
Tom Shaw	71	71	67	209	12,500
Michael Christie	71	66	73	210	9,750
Joe Cioe	72	70	68	210	9,750
Bill Porter	70	74	67	211	7,000
Greg Whisman	74	68	69	211	7,000
Mark Wurtz	71	68	72	211	7,000
Brad Ott	72	71	69	212	3,508.58
R.W. Eaks	72	70	70	212	3,508.57
Jimmy Green	70	69	73	212	3,508.57
Kevin Johnson	70	70	72	212	3,508.57
Jimmy Johnston	70	71	71	212	3,508.57
Shaun Micheel	71	68	73	212	3,508.57
Dave Rummells	73	71	68	212	3,508.57
Dave Barr	73	70	70	213	2,455
Eric Epperson	74	66	73	213	2,455
Dick Mast	71	72	70	213	2,455
Esteban Toledo	72	69	72	213	2,455
Craig Bowden	67	74	73	214	1,705.46
Bill Britton	73	70	71	214	1,705.46
Buddy Gardner	73	70	71	214	1,705.46
Tom Pernice, Jr.	72	71	71	214	1,705.46
Sonny Skinner	71	71	72	214	1,705.46
Emlyn Aubrey	74	71	69	214	1,705.45
Eric Johnson	73	68	73	214	1,705.45
Tommy Masters	71	69	74	214	1,705.45
Bill Murchison	73	72	69	214	1,705.45
Matt Peterson	71	70	73	214	1,705.45
Sam Randolph	72	73	69	214	1,705.45

Inland Empire Open

Moreno Valley Golf Club, Moreno Valley, California
Par 36-36–72; 6,801 yards

February 29-March 3
purse, $200,000

	SCORES				TOTAL	MONEY
Jim Estes	68	68	68	68	272	$36,000
Rob Moss	67	69	68	69	273	22,700
Jeff Barlow	69	68	68	69	274	16,500
Skip Kendall	69	68	69	69	275	12,500

	SCORES				TOTAL	MONEY
J.L. Lewis	66	73	70	68	277	9,750
Willie Wood	69	71	69	68	277	9,750
Eric Epperson	71	72	69	66	278	6,500
P.H. Horgan III	72	70	68	68	278	6,500
Matt Peterson	69	72	69	68	278	6,500
Greg Twiggs	70	71	69	68	278	6,500
David Berganio, Jr.	66	75	68	70	279	3,260
Stewart Cink	70	72	67	70	279	3,260
Chad Magee	66	72	70	71	279	3,260
Rob McKelvey	67	71	71	70	279	3,260
Bill Porter	68	74	69	68	279	3,260
Chris Tidland	68	71	71	69	279	3,260
Dave Barr	71	69	69	71	280	2,404
Brent Geiberger	70	67	72	71	280	2,404
Steve Jurgensen	67	70	70	73	280	2,404
Dave Rummells	73	67	71	69	280	2,404
Stan Utley	70	65	71	74	280	2,404
Emlyn Aubrey	68	73	67	73	281	1,800
Joe Durant	72	70	70	69	281	1,800
Tom Garner	73	70	71	67	281	1,800
Bob Gilder	73	69	71	68	281	1,800
Jimmy Johnston	72	66	74	69	281	1,800
Tom Shaw	70	73	72	66	281	1,800
Paul Stankowski	70	72	72	67	281	1,800
Ben Bates	69	69	75	69	282	1,240
Tim Dunlavey	70	73	70	69	282	1,240
Pat Fitzsimons	74	70	72	66	282	1,240
Tim Loustalot	70	70	70	72	282	1,240
Eric Meeks	72	67	74	69	282	1,240
Brad Ott	71	71	71	69	282	1,240

Monterrey Open

Club Campestre, Monterrey, Mexico
Par 36-36–72; 6,925 yards

March 14-17
purse, $225,000

	SCORES				TOTAL	MONEY
David Berganio, Jr.	69	68	69	66	272	$40,500
Rafael Alarcon	71	67	67	68	273	17,493.75
Todd Demsey	66	73	69	65	273	17,493.75
Jack O'Keefe	71	66	69	67	273	17,493.75
Steve Rintoul	65	70	65	73	273	17,493.75
Bob Ford	71	70	68	65	274	9,000
Tom Kalinowski	70	67	70	67	274	9,000
Willie Wood	65	68	70	71	274	9,000
Pat Bates	68	70	72	65	275	6,187.50
Anthony Rodriguez	68	68	67	72	275	6,187.50
Stewart Cink	66	70	71	69	276	3,667.50
Joe Cioe	67	72	67	70	276	3,667.50
R.W. Eaks	66	73	66	71	276	3,667.50
Danny Ellis	70	71	66	69	276	3,667.50
Skip Kendall	69	67	70	70	276	3,667.50
Stan Utley	71	67	67	71	276	3,667.50
Rick Smallridge	68	69	68	72	277	2,880
Phil Tataurangi	65	70	71	71	277	2,880
Matthew Lane	70	70	69	69	278	2,700
Paul Claxton	68	72	68	71	279	2,418.75

	SCORES				TOTAL	MONEY
Eric Johnson	68	73	64	74	279	2,418.75
Shaun Micheel	72	68	69	70	279	2,418.75
Matt Peterson	71	67	70	71	279	2,418.75
Briny Baird	72	68	72	68	280	1,856.25
Dennis Harrington	74	67	69	70	280	1,856.25
Steve Novarro	68	72	68	72	280	1,856.25
Lee Porter	71	70	72	67	280	1,856.25
Sam Randolph	70	71	71	68	280	1,856.25
Sonny Skinner	70	69	72	69	280	1,856.25
Jeff Barlow	73	68	72	68	281	1,288.13
Kawika Cotner	69	69	73	70	281	1,288.13
Ryan Howison	72	68	70	71	281	1,288.13
Dustin Phillips	68	73	71	69	281	1,288.13
Ben Bates	72	69	68	72	281	1,288.12
Steve Jurgensen	70	69	69	73	281	1,288.12
Deane Pappas	70	67	71	73	281	1,288.12
Tom Pernice, Jr.	72	69	69	71	281	1,288.12

Louisiana Open

Le Triomphe Golf & Country Club,
Broussard, Louisiana
Par 36-36–72; 6,978 yards

March 28-31
purse, $250,000

	SCORES				TOTAL	MONEY
Paul Stankowski	69	66	64	67	266	$45,000
Greg Whisman	70	66	66	68	270	28,375
Joe Durant	69	69	64	69	271	18,125
Jeff Julian	68	66	66	71	271	18,125
Matthew Lane	68	70	66	68	272	13,125
Dave Barr	72	67	65	69	273	10,000
Sean Murphy	71	64	63	75	273	10,000
Dustin Phillips	67	66	70	70	273	10,000
Pat Bates	69	71	64	70	274	6,250
Stewart Cink	73	67	66	68	274	6,250
Chris Tidland	69	68	70	67	274	6,250
Greg Petersen	70	71	63	71	275	4,375
Rafael Alarcon	72	68	67	69	276	3,768.75
J.P. Hayes	67	67	72	70	276	3,768.75
Skip Kendall	71	67	66	72	276	3,768.75
Rob McKelvey	67	65	71	73	276	3,768.75
R.W. Eaks	70	71	69	67	277	2,941.67
Lee Porter	69	70	68	70	277	2,941.67
Gary Rusnak	69	69	67	72	277	2,941.67
Karl Zoller	67	68	68	74	277	2,941.67
David Berganio, Jr.	68	66	66	77	277	2,941.66
Tim Simpson	70	68	65	74	277	2,941.66
Rick Cramer	72	67	68	71	278	2,187.50
Jerry Foltz	68	70	68	72	278	2,187.50
Chad Magee	69	69	68	72	278	2,187.50
Craig Perks	70	71	66	71	278	2,187.50
Anthony Rodriguez	69	69	72	68	278	2,187.50
Charlie Wi	66	72	68	72	278	2,187.50
Bill Murchison	72	69	67	71	279	1,650
Bob Wolcott	75	66	68	70	279	1,650
Mark Wurtz	66	75	66	72	279	1,650

Tallahassee Open

Golden Eagle Country Club, Tallahassee, Florida
Par 36-36–72; 6,965 yards

April 4-7
purse, $200,000

		SCORES			TOTAL	MONEY
P.J. Cowan	69	70	66	74	279	$36,000
P.H. Horgan III	69	70	68	72	279	22,700
(Cowan defeated Horgan on first extra hole.)						
Stewart Cink	73	71	69	68	281	16,500
Ron Philo, Jr.	70	70	65	77	282	11,500
Brett Quigley	73	69	68	72	282	11,500
Leonard Thompson	71	69	71	72	283	9,000
Jimmy Johnston	71	72	71	70	284	7,500
Pete Jordan	69	70	72	73	284	7,500
Jeff Barlow	72	72	70	71	285	4,150
Skip Kendall	72	68	72	73	285	4,150
Dick Mast	69	72	70	74	285	4,150
Tom Shaw	72	70	72	71	285	4,150
Rick Smallridge	68	73	71	73	285	4,150
Mark Wurtz	68	73	72	72	285	4,150
Bob Gilder	73	70	70	73	286	2,636
Jeff Gove	70	73	75	68	286	2,636
David Jackson	74	69	71	72	286	2,636
Bill Porter	72	72	72	70	286	2,636
Greg Twiggs	72	68	71	75	286	2,636
Steve Haskins	71	71	71	74	287	2,100
Brad Ott	70	68	76	73	287	2,100
Peter Persons	72	71	69	75	287	2,100
Charlie Wi	75	69	68	75	287	2,100
Karl Zoller	75	69	72	71	287	2,100
Tim Simpson	74	68	73	73	288	1,800
Scott Ford	71	70	72	76	289	1,422.86
Brent Geiberger	74	69	73	73	289	1,422.86
Steve Lamontagne	73	71	72	73	289	1,422.86
Shaun Micheel	72	72	73	72	289	1,422.86
Greg Whisman	71	74	70	74	289	1,422.86
Trevor Dodds	69	74	74	72	289	1,422.85
Jack Steinicke	74	68	70	77	289	1,422.85

South Carolina Classic

Country Club of South Carolina, Florence, South Carolina
Par 36-36–72; 7,159 yards

April 11-14
purse, $200,000

		SCORES			TOTAL	MONEY
Dave Rummells	69	70	69	68	276	$36,000
Scott Petersen	69	71	73	65	278	17,233.34
P.H. Horgan III	70	70	72	66	278	17,233.33
Brad Ott	68	71	69	70	278	17,233.33
Bill Porter	69	70	75	67	281	10,500
Carl Paulson	68	70	76	68	282	9,000
Steve Haskins	74	69	71	69	283	7,500
Chris Perry	72	73	72	66	283	7,500
Michael Christie	71	71	71	71	284	3,971.43
Stewart Cink	71	73	72	68	284	3,971.43
Brent Geiberger	74	70	71	69	284	3,971.43
Brett Quigley	71	72	74	67	284	3,971.43

	SCORES				TOTAL	MONEY
Clarence Rose	73	71	72	68	284	3,971.43
Larry Silveira	72	73	72	67	284	3,971.43
Peter Persons	70	69	72	73	284	3,971.42
Joe Durant	71	71	74	69	285	2,690
Tray Tyner	68	69	76	72	285	2,690
Rafael Alarcon	70	70	74	72	286	2,200
Ben Bates	72	72	73	69	286	2,200
Paul Claxton	71	74	70	71	286	2,200
Eric Epperson	71	72	71	72	286	2,200
Jimmy Johnston	68	74	72	72	286	2,200
Greg Petersen	68	75	70	73	286	2,200
Gary Rusnak	71	73	76	66	286	2,200
Tim Dunlavey	69	73	76	69	287	1,650
Larry Rinker	73	72	74	68	287	1,650
Mark Swygert	73	70	75	69	287	1,650
Greg Twiggs	67	76	76	68	287	1,650
Jeff Barlow	72	72	75	69	288	1,360
Jerry Haas	76	69	72	71	288	1,360

Alabama Classic

Cherokee Ridge Country Club, Huntsville, Alabama
Par 36-36–72; 6,934 yards
(Fourth round cancelled — rain.)

April 18-21
purse, $200,000

	SCORES			TOTAL	MONEY
P.H. Horgan III	68	67	67	202	$36,000
Jack O'Keefe	71	64	68	203	22,700
Brent Geiberger	73	65	66	204	16,500
Joe Durant	74	63	68	205	12,500
Jeff Brehaut	68	70	69	207	8,100
Michael Christie	71	70	66	207	8,100
Jerry Haas	70	67	70	207	8,100
Dennis Harrington	67	72	68	207	8,100
Bruce Vaughan	68	68	71	207	8,100
Matt Peterson	73	67	68	208	3,508.58
Greg Bruckner	69	68	71	208	3,508.57
Stewart Cink	71	67	70	208	3,508.57
Jimmy Green	71	67	70	208	3,508.57
Jimmy Johnston	69	70	69	208	3,508.57
Skip Kendall	70	67	71	208	3,508.57
Tom Pernice, Jr.	73	65	70	208	3,508.57
Paul Claxton	69	67	73	209	2,404
Kawika Cotner	72	70	67	209	2,404
Jim Estes	73	67	69	209	2,404
Bill Porter	68	71	70	209	2,404
Phil Tataurangi	69	72	68	209	2,404
Rafael Alarcon	74	68	68	210	1,750
Joe Cioe	69	68	73	210	1,750
Jerry Foltz	71	69	70	210	1,750
Len Mattiace	73	66	71	210	1,750
Rob McKelvey	69	69	72	210	1,750
Deane Pappas	73	66	71	210	1,750
Greg Parker	73	69	68	210	1,750
Brett Quigley	67	72	71	210	1,750
Bob Burns	67	71	73	211	1,186.67
Jeff Gove	70	70	71	211	1,186.67

	SCORES	TOTAL	MONEY
Tom Shaw	73 67 71	211	1,186.67
Chris Tidland	74 66 71	211	1,186.67
Patrick Lee	72 66 73	211	1,186.66
Mike Smith	71 67 73	211	1,186.66

Shreveport Open

Southern Trace Country Club, Shreveport, Louisiana
Par 36-36–72; 6,916 yards

April 25-28
purse, $200,000

	SCORES	TOTAL	MONEY
Tim Loustalot	73 70 66 68	277	$36,000
Joe Durant	66 65 74 73	278	22,700
Doug Barron	72 66 74 67	279	13,166.67
Bill Porter	70 70 70 69	279	13,166.67
Larry Silveira	70 68 72 69	279	13,166.66
Phil Tataurangi	72 68 71 69	280	9,000
Jeff Gove	72 73 68 68	281	8,000
Steve Gotsche	73 68 70 71	282	5,500
Steve Haskins	71 68 71 72	282	5,500
J.P. Hayes	76 66 68 72	282	5,500
Matt Peterson	71 72 69 70	282	5,500
Joe Cioe	75 70 66 72	283	3,030
Clark Dennis	72 72 66 73	283	3,030
Steve Larick	68 70 70 75	283	3,030
Chad Magee	73 70 69 71	283	3,030
Eric Meeks	69 74 69 71	283	3,030
Charlie Wi	70 69 70 74	283	3,030
Jeff Brehaut	71 71 71 71	284	2,250
Jaxon Brigman	68 69 74 73	284	2,250
Jack O'Keefe	71 74 71 68	284	2,250
Chris Tidland	75 68 71 70	284	2,250
Stan Utley	70 69 69 76	284	2,250
Bruce Vaughan	73 69 73 69	284	2,250
Bobby Doolittle	69 70 74 72	285	1,750
Mark Hayes	72 71 74 68	285	1,750
Tom Pernice, Jr.	71 73 69 72	285	1,750
Bob Wolcott	75 66 72 72	285	1,750
Jerry Foltz	70 70 73 73	286	1,450
Willie Wood	74 70 69 73	286	1,450
Paul Claxton	74 69 71 73	287	1,186.67
Jimmy Green	74 71 66 76	287	1,186.67
Vic Wilk	73 72 70 72	287	1,186.67
Karl Zoller	72 71 73 71	287	1,186.67
Eric Epperson	71 70 76 70	287	1,186.66
Rick Smallridge	68 70 70 79	287	1,186.66

Mississippi Gulf Coast Classic

Mississippi National Golf Club, Gautier, Mississippi
Par 36-36–72; 7,100 yards

May 9-12
purse, $200,000

	SCORES	TOTAL	MONEY
Joe Durant	67 71 65 70	273	$36,000
Brett Quigley	69 68 69 68	274	19,600

	SCORES				TOTAL	MONEY
Dave Rummells	71	69	65	69	274	19,600
Jack O'Keefe	72	71	65	67	275	12,500
Jeff Barlow	67	69	70	70	276	8,625
Bob Burns	68	69	68	71	276	8,625
Greg Twiggs	70	70	68	68	276	8,625
Greg Whisman	71	70	67	68	276	8,625
Damon Green	71	72	68	67	278	4,625
Steve Schneiter	68	69	71	70	278	4,625
Tony Sills	70	68	69	71	278	4,625
Willie Wood	70	70	67	71	278	4,625
Paul Claxton	70	70	69	70	279	2,735
Tim Dunlavey	69	67	72	71	279	2,735
R.W. Eaks	73	69	68	69	279	2,735
Scott Ford	70	73	70	66	279	2,735
Chris Hunsucker	70	72	69	68	279	2,735
Tim Loustalot	69	72	69	69	279	2,735
Steve Mulcahy	69	71	69	70	279	2,735
Dustin Phillips	72	69	70	68	279	2,735
Joe Cioe	70	70	71	69	280	1,900
Skip Kendall	68	69	71	72	280	1,900
Bill Murchison	66	72	72	70	280	1,900
Greg Petersen	72	68	69	71	280	1,900
Lee Porter	71	67	73	69	280	1,900
Ivan Smith	69	70	73	68	280	1,900
Tim Straub	70	69	68	73	280	1,900
Clark Dennis	71	71	69	70	281	1,303.34
Glen Hnatiuk	69	70	68	74	281	1,303.34
Briny Baird	72	71	67	71	281	1,303.33
Pat Bates	71	72	68	70	281	1,303.33
David Berganio, Jr.	68	70	71	72	281	1,303.33
Bob Wolcott	66	72	69	74	281	1,303.33

Carolina Classic

Prestonwood Country Club, Cary, North Carolina
Par 36-36–72; 6,879 yards

May 16-19
purse, $200,000

	SCORES			TOTAL	MONEY
Glen Hnatiuk	71	70	64	205	$36,000
Craig Perks	65	71	69	205	22,700
(Hnatiuk defeated Perks on first extra hole.)					
Phil Tataurangi	69	67	70	206	16,500
Rafael Alarcon	67	70	70	207	11,500
Bob Boyd	69	67	71	207	11,500
P.H. Horgan III	70	70	69	209	7,500
Kevin Kemp	71	69	69	209	7,500
Rob McKelvey	71	69	69	209	7,500
Lee Porter	74	67	68	209	7,500
Bob Burns	70	69	71	210	3,633.34
Ryan Howison	70	71	69	210	3,633.34
Skip Kendall	70	67	73	210	3,633.33
Jack O'Keefe	69	71	70	210	3,633.33
E.J. Pfister	69	70	71	210	3,633.33
Larry Silveira	69	72	69	210	3,633.33
Jeff Brehaut	71	71	69	211	2,411.43
Greg Bruckner	73	67	71	211	2,411.43
Paul Claxton	71	69	71	211	2,411.43

	SCORES			TOTAL	MONEY
P.J. Cowan	72	71	68	211	2,411.43
Greg Sweatt	75	68	68	211	2,411.43
Charlie Wi	72	70	69	211	2,411.43
Eric Johnson	68	73	70	211	2,411.42
Michael Christie	71	66	75	212	1,700
Joe Durant	71	68	73	212	1,700
Tim Loustalot	68	74	70	212	1,700
Dino Lucchesi	72	71	69	212	1,700
John Maginnes	72	70	70	212	1,700
Matt Peterson	70	69	73	212	1,700
Tony Sills	73	70	69	212	1,700
Michael Clark	69	72	72	213	1,230
Bobby Elliott	70	70	73	213	1,230
Dennis Harrington	73	70	70	213	1,230
Fred Wadsworth	72	69	72	213	1,230

Greater Greenville Classic

Verdae Greens Golf Club, Greenville, South Carolina
Par 36-36–72; 6,773 yards

May 23-26
purse, $200,000

	SCORES				TOTAL	MONEY
Michael Christie	68	65	69	63	265	$36,000
Danny Ellis	67	69	69	66	271	22,700
Steve Haskins	65	69	67	71	272	13,166.67
Mike Small	68	63	72	69	272	13,166.67
Joe Durant	66	66	66	74	272	13,166.66
Stewart Cink	71	69	69	64	273	9,000
Eric Johnson	69	68	69	68	274	6,000
Brad Ott	65	71	69	69	274	6,000
Matt Peterson	69	69	67	69	274	6,000
David Thore	66	69	68	71	274	6,000
Greg Twiggs	69	67	67	71	274	6,000
Rafael Alarcon	69	67	70	69	275	3,030
Paul Claxton	66	74	69	66	275	3,030
P.J. Cowan	70	70	71	64	275	3,030
Skip Kendall	71	64	70	70	275	3,030
Shaun Micheel	68	67	71	69	275	3,030
Rick Smallridge	70	66	69	70	275	3,030
Lee Porter	70	68	69	69	276	2,400
Charlie Wi	70	70	69	67	276	2,400
Mark Wurtz	69	70	69	68	276	2,400
Tom Hearn	69	70	66	72	277	2,050
Bill Porter	71	68	73	65	277	2,050
Bob Wolcott	71	69	71	66	277	2,050
Willie Wood	71	69	68	69	277	2,050
Tim Conley	70	69	70	69	278	1,650
Kawika Cotner	70	68	69	71	278	1,650
Jerry Foltz	65	66	75	72	278	1,650
Dave Rummells	71	69	70	68	278	1,650
Tim Dunlavey	68	67	72	72	279	1,360
Tom Shaw	70	69	72	68	279	1,360

Dominion Open

The Dominion Club, Glen Allen, Virginia
Par 36-36—72; 7,040 yards

May 30-June 2
purse, $200,000

	SCORES				TOTAL	MONEY
Olin Browne	67	69	73	67	276	$36,000
Michael Christie	72	67	66	72	277	15,550
Rob McKelvey	72	71	64	70	277	15,550
Carl Paulson	69	69	69	70	277	15,550
Tray Tyner	70	71	65	71	277	15,550
Brent Geiberger	70	70	68	70	278	8,500
Hugh Royer III	73	70	67	68	278	8,500
David Berganio, Jr.	72	67	68	72	279	4,800
Glen Hnatiuk	67	72	71	69	279	4,800
Jack O'Keefe	73	68	71	67	279	4,800
Dave Rummells	70	71	67	71	279	4,800
Larry Silveira	68	73	70	68	279	4,800
Willie Wood	68	71	70	70	279	4,800
Kevin Burton	70	69	70	71	280	2,920
Tim Conley	73	69	70	68	280	2,920
Kent Jones	69	71	69	71	280	2,920
Bill Murchison	69	70	74	68	281	2,302.86
Tom Pernice, Jr.	72	71	72	66	281	2,302.86
Lee Porter	71	71	68	71	281	2,302.86
Clarence Rose	70	72	69	70	281	2,302.86
Bob Wolcott	69	71	70	71	281	2,302.86
Jerry Foltz	70	69	69	73	281	2,302.85
Ron Philo, Jr.	72	71	66	72	281	2,302.85
Greg Bruckner	69	71	69	73	282	1,650
Bobby Collins	70	69	72	71	282	1,650
Kawika Cotner	71	69	68	74	282	1,650
Clark Dennis	71	68	73	70	282	1,650
Deane Pappas	66	74	68	74	282	1,650
Brett Quigley	75	66	69	72	282	1,650
Paul Claxton	72	71	71	69	283	1,186.67
Jeff Gove	74	68	70	71	283	1,186.67
Eric Johnson	68	71	76	68	283	1,186.67
Mike Sposa	71	71	70	71	283	1,186.67
Eric Epperson	68	70	71	74	283	1,186.66
Jerry Haas	68	70	72	73	283	1,186.66

Cleveland Open

Quail Hollow Resort, Concord, Ohio
Par 36-36—72; 6,712 yards

June 6-9
purse, $200,000

	SCORES				TOTAL	MONEY
Greg Twiggs	66	72	64	68	270	$36,000
Jimmy Johnston	66	67	70	68	271	22,700
Tim Loustalot	68	67	69	68	272	14,500
Jack O'Keefe	67	65	70	70	272	14,500
Stewart Cink	72	71	68	64	275	8,625
Patrick Lee	66	73	68	68	275	8,625
Sam Randolph	69	72	67	67	275	8,625
Willie Wood	69	68	69	69	275	8,625
Jeff Barlow	69	72	65	70	276	4,150
Craig Bowden	69	72	67	68	276	4,150

	SCORES				TOTAL	MONEY
Tim Dunlavey	75	68	65	68	276	4,150
Eric Johnson	68	71	68	69	276	4,150
Skip Kendall	72	68	68	68	276	4,150
Steve Parker	70	69	66	71	276	4,150
Jeff Brehaut	69	70	71	67	277	2,760
J.P. Hayes	67	73	72	65	277	2,760
Larry Silveira	69	74	66	68	277	2,760
Doug Barron	71	68	66	73	278	2,400
Barry Fabyan	71	65	68	74	278	2,400
Dean Larsson	69	70	67	72	278	2,400
Pat Bates	73	68	66	72	279	2,100
Jim Estes	71	70	67	71	279	2,100
Christian Raynor	71	68	72	68	279	2,100
Dave Rummells	67	73	70	70	280	1,850
Mike Sposa	71	68	70	71	280	1,850
Jimmy Green	72	69	70	70	281	1,600
Glen Hnatiuk	70	71	69	71	281	1,600
Lee Porter	71	70	71	69	281	1,600
Joe Cioe	71	70	70	71	282	1,264
Bobby Collins	69	71	72	70	282	1,264
P.H. Horgan III	72	68	72	70	282	1,264
Tom Pernice, Jr.	73	70	71	68	282	1,264
Mike Small	70	73	71	68	282	1,264

Knoxville Open

Three Ridges Golf Club, Knoxville, Tennessee
Par 36-36—72; 6,855 yards

June 13-16
purse, $200,000

	SCORES				TOTAL	MONEY
Eric Johnson	68	66	69	69	272	$36,000
Patrick Lee	67	66	74	67	274	19,600
Matt Peterson	68	70	68	68	274	19,600
Deane Pappas	68	73	63	71	275	11,500
Dave Rummells	68	69	70	68	275	11,500
Brent Geiberger	70	70	67	69	276	8,000
Lee Porter	67	66	74	69	276	8,000
Brett Quigley	69	67	69	71	276	8,000
Eric Epperson	69	70	68	70	277	5,000
Jimmy Johnston	68	70	70	69	277	5,000
Rob McKelvey	68	72	69	68	277	5,000
Joe Cioe	68	70	70	70	278	3,200
P.J. Cowan	70	68	72	68	278	3,200
Tim Simpson	71	69	69	69	278	3,200
Bruce Vaughan	70	69	70	69	278	3,200
Todd Barranger	69	70	69	71	279	2,360
Bobby Doolittle	69	72	68	70	279	2,360
Craig Kanada	66	70	72	71	279	2,360
Brad Lardon	69	68	70	72	279	2,360
Shaun Micheel	68	70	71	70	279	2,360
Steve Novarro	70	69	71	69	279	2,360
Chris Perry	67	72	71	69	279	2,360
Rick Smallridge	68	68	73	70	279	2,360
Tommy Armour III	67	69	74	70	280	1,418.34
Jeff Barlow	68	72	71	69	280	1,418.34
Steve Parker	68	72	71	69	280	1,418.34
Chris Tidland	74	67	70	69	280	1,418.34

	SCORES				TOTAL	MONEY
Bob Burns	71	69	70	70	280	1,418.33
Joe Durant	69	72	69	70	280	1,418.33
Tom Hearn	69	71	70	70	280	1,418.33
Greg Parker	72	69	66	73	280	1,418.33
Peter Persons	68	73	69	70	280	1,418.33
Mike Schuchart	71	69	70	70	280	1,418.33
Phil Tataurangi	69	69	71	71	280	1,418.33
Bob Wolcott	69	71	67	73	280	1,418.33

Ozarks Open

Highland Springs Country Club, Springfield, Missouri
Par 36-36—72; 7,058 yards

June 20-23
purse, $200,000

	SCORES				TOTAL	MONEY
Stewart Cink	68	67	69	68	272	$36,000
R.W. Eaks	73	66	66	67	272	22,700
(Cink defeated Eaks on third extra hole.)						
Kevin Burton	69	67	67	70	273	14,500
Skip Kendall	71	69	64	69	273	14,500
Tom Shaw	67	73	66	68	274	10,500
Mike Schuchart	69	69	70	67	275	9,000
Brent Geiberger	67	68	70	71	276	7,000
Mike Sposa	67	68	69	72	276	7,000
Willie Wood	68	72	69	67	276	7,000
Jeff Gove	69	70	71	67	277	3,508.58
Jeff Brehaut	72	70	66	69	277	3,508.57
J.P. Hayes	69	71	67	70	277	3,508.57
Matt Peterson	70	69	68	70	277	3,508.57
Sam Randolph	63	69	73	72	277	3,508.57
Gary Webb	72	66	68	71	277	3,508.57
Jerry Wood	67	69	67	74	277	3,508.57
Eric Johnson	66	71	66	75	278	2,455
Tim Loustalot	70	70	71	67	278	2,455
Rob McKelvey	70	70	69	69	278	2,455
Jack O'Keefe	71	66	76	65	278	2,455
Joe Cioe	69	67	69	74	279	2,000
Clark Dennis	67	70	69	73	279	2,000
Jimmy Green	70	70	70	69	279	2,000
Bill Murchison	71	71	70	67	279	2,000
Bruce Vaughan	71	68	68	72	279	2,000
Danny Ellis	68	73	69	70	280	1,650
Dick Mast	67	73	73	67	280	1,650
Kory Bowman	70	71	70	70	281	1,332
Greg Bruckner	71	68	70	72	281	1,332
Joe Durant	72	70	68	71	281	1,332
Marco Gortana	68	70	70	73	281	1,332
Jerry Haas	72	69	69	71	281	1,332

Dakota Dunes Open

Dakota Dunes Country Club, Dakota Dunes, South Dakota
Par 36-36–72; 7,165 yards

June 27-30
purse, $250,000

	SCORES				TOTAL	MONEY
Gary Webb	69	68	69	69	275	$45,000
Chad Magee	66	71	68	70	275	28,375
(Webb defeated Magee on second extra hole.)						
Brent Geiberger	75	68	67	66	276	20,625
Stewart Cink	68	71	70	68	277	15,625
Barry Fabyan	69	72	68	69	278	10,781.25
Matt Peterson	73	73	64	68	278	10,781.25
Larry Silveira	72	71	67	68	278	10,781.25
Karl Zoller	73	68	67	70	278	10,781.25
P.H. Horgan III	67	72	74	66	279	7,500
Charlie Wi	73	70	69	68	280	5,208.34
Brett Quigley	72	71	68	69	280	5,208.33
Willie Wood	70	73	68	69	280	5,208.33
Ben Bates	72	74	67	68	281	3,418.75
Danny Briggs	69	72	71	69	281	3,418.75
Glen Hnatiuk	71	71	71	68	281	3,418.75
Kevin Johnson	74	69	69	69	281	3,418.75
Tim Loustalot	67	74	71	69	281	3,418.75
Dave Rummells	70	72	70	69	281	3,418.75
Mike Sposa	71	72	69	69	281	3,418.75
Bruce Vaughan	74	71	70	66	281	3,418.75
R.W. Eaks	71	73	70	68	282	2,500
Chad Ginn	71	73	69	69	282	2,500
Tom Hearn	67	74	71	70	282	2,500
Dick Mast	68	71	69	74	282	2,500
Jack O'Keefe	70	73	69	70	282	2,500
Paul Claxton	72	70	70	71	283	2,000
John Flannery	75	71	67	70	283	2,000
Bill Porter	73	72	67	71	283	2,000
Rafael Alarcon	72	71	72	69	284	1,466.67
Jeff Brehaut	72	71	71	70	284	1,466.67
Greg Bruckner	71	71	72	70	284	1,466.67
Michael Christie	70	76	67	71	284	1,466.67
Joe Cioe	71	74	70	69	284	1,466.67
Steve Gotsche	69	70	73	72	284	1,466.67
Bill Murchison	74	72	66	72	284	1,466.66
E.J. Pfister	71	74	71	68	284	1,466.66
Lee Porter	70	77	69	68	284	1,466.66

Buffalo Open

Brierwood Country Club, Hamburg, New York
Par 36-36–72; 7,031 yards

July 11-14
purse, $200,000

	SCORES				TOTAL	MONEY
Jimmy Green	68	71	70	67	276	$36,000
Jeff Gove	71	65	69	71	276	22,700
(Green defeated Gove on first extra hole.)						
Patrick Lee	66	69	69	73	277	14,500
Willie Wood	71	68	68	70	277	14,500
Stewart Cink	71	67	72	68	278	10,500
David Berganio, Jr.	72	72	65	70	279	6,500

	SCORES				TOTAL	MONEY
Bob Burns	72	69	66	72	279	6,500
Tim Conley	70	68	71	70	279	6,500
Andy Dillard	68	71	70	70	279	6,500
J.P. Hayes	70	68	71	70	279	6,500
Lee Porter	72	71	68	68	279	6,500
Pat Bates	68	74	68	70	280	3,112
Paul Claxton	74	71	68	67	280	3,112
Brent Geiberger	72	71	68	69	280	3,112
Tim Straub	67	69	73	71	280	3,112
Greg Twiggs	73	68	71	68	280	3,112
David Jackson	71	70	69	71	281	2,506.67
Kevin Johnson	75	69	66	71	281	2,506.67
Rick Cramer	71	72	65	73	281	2,506.66
Larry Barber	74	69	71	68	282	2,150
Greg Ladehoff	74	69	70	69	282	2,150
Bill Porter	72	68	72	70	282	2,150
Greg Whisman	72	68	71	71	282	2,150
Jerry Haas	71	70	70	72	283	1,650
Tom Hearn	69	74	67	73	283	1,650
Rob McKelvey	70	70	70	73	283	1,650
Jack O'Keefe	73	71	72	67	283	1,650
Fran Quinn	71	72	67	73	283	1,650
Sonny Skinner	70	69	71	73	283	1,650
Glen Hnatiuk	73	70	70	71	284	1,230
Michael Long	72	70	72	70	284	1,230
Bill Murchison	70	72	72	70	284	1,230
Karl Zoller	72	72	68	72	284	1,230

Philadelphia Classic

Philmont Country Club, North Course,
Huntingdon Valley, Pennsylvania
Par 35-35–70; 6,496 yards

July 18-21
purse, $200,000

	SCORES				TOTAL	MONEY
Brett Quigley	64	67	74	68	273	$36,000
R.W. Eaks	65	71	73	66	275	19,600
Rocky Walcher	67	69	73	66	275	19,600
Greg Twiggs	69	68	70	69	276	12,500
Doug Barron	66	73	69	69	277	10,500
Michael Clark	70	66	74	68	278	8,500
Stu Ingraham	68	73	68	69	278	8,500
Larry Barber	72	66	72	69	279	5,500
Billy Downes	67	70	68	74	279	5,500
P.H. Horgan III	70	68	73	68	279	5,500
Jimmy Johnston	69	69	70	71	279	5,500
Joe Cioe	70	70	71	69	280	3,200
Edward Fryatt	70	72	69	69	280	3,200
Matt Peterson	68	73	67	72	280	3,200
Bob Wolcott	74	63	72	71	280	3,200
Pat Bates	69	70	73	69	281	2,626.67
Rob McKelvey	70	70	69	72	281	2,626.67
Tim Dunlavey	69	70	73	69	281	2,626.66
Barry Fabyan	68	71	73	70	282	2,250
Brent Geiberger	69	71	73	69	282	2,250
Greg Parker	74	68	73	67	282	2,250
Fran Quinn	70	69	69	74	282	2,250

	SCORES	TOTAL	MONEY
David Berganio, Jr.	65 73 73 72	283	1,900
Tim Straub	71 70 73 69	283	1,900
Karl Zoller	70 72 72 69	283	1,900
Craig Bowden	67 73 75 69	284	1,422.86
Rick Cramer	70 68 72 74	284	1,422.86
Steve Hawkins	69 71 73 71	284	1,422.86
Skip Kendall	71 69 72 72	284	1,422.86
Tom Shaw	69 69 73 73	284	1,422.86
Jerry Foltz	68 71 73 72	284	1,422.85
Tripp Isenhour	68 71 70 75	284	1,422.85

Miami Valley Open

Heatherwoode Golf Club, Springbrook, Ohio
Par 36-35–71; 6,730 yards

July 25-28
purse, $200,000

	SCORES	TOTAL	MONEY
J.P. Hayes	64 69 67 65	265	$36,000
Lee Porter	66 66 69 66	267	19,600
Greg Whisman	66 64 68 69	267	19,600
Brent Geiberger	68 64 70 67	269	11,500
Mike Schuchart	68 67 68 66	269	11,500
Tom Pernice, Jr.	62 69 69 70	270	8,500
Dave Rummells	66 66 70 68	270	8,500
Michael Clark	75 65 66 65	271	6,500
P.H. Horgan III	66 72 68 65	271	6,500
Joe Durant	70 66 67 69	272	4,166.67
Eric Johnson	65 70 72 65	272	4,166.67
Rocky Walcher	67 65 69 71	272	4,166.66
Jeff Brehaut	70 70 67 67	274	3,200
Skip Kendall	68 68 68 70	274	3,200
Tim Dunlavey	69 69 70 67	275	2,830
Bob Gaus	69 66 71 69	275	2,830
J.C. Anderson	71 69 69 67	276	2,455
Jack O'Keefe	69 68 72 67	276	2,455
Tim Straub	69 69 71 67	276	2,455
Gary Webb	68 73 68 67	276	2,455
Jeff Barlow	71 68 69 69	277	1,950
Doug Barron	73 67 69 68	277	1,950
David Berganio, Jr.	71 70 69 67	277	1,950
Tripp Isenhour	65 67 75 70	277	1,950
Matt Peterson	72 69 66 70	277	1,950
Chris Tidland	73 67 66 71	277	1,950
Joe Cioe	70 69 68 71	278	1,412
Tim Loustalot	68 72 70 68	278	1,412
Tony Mollica	72 68 72 66	278	1,412
Greg Parker	71 67 71 69	278	1,412
Brett Quigley	65 69 68 76	278	1,412

Gateway Classic

Lake Forest Golf & Country Club,
Lake St. Louis, Missouri
Par 36-36–72; 7,161 yards

August 1-4
purse, $200,000

	SCORES				TOTAL	MONEY
Tim Conley	68	70	71	69	278	$36,000
Javier Sanchez	69	68	70	71	278	22,700
(Conley defeated Sanchez on first extra hole.)						
Rafael Alarcon	67	70	71	71	279	16,500
Ben Bates	70	71	72	67	280	10,000
Kevin Burton	72	66	70	72	280	10,000
Michael Clark	69	69	72	70	280	10,000
Craig Kanada	70	73	69	68	280	10,000
Paul Claxton	71	65	69	76	281	6,000
Matt Gogel	71	67	71	72	281	6,000
Matthew Lane	69	69	72	71	281	6,000
Skip Kendall	69	73	68	72	282	3,750
Matt Peterson	68	66	77	71	282	3,750
Bobby Elliott	68	74	70	71	283	2,863.34
Mike Sposa	71	71	71	70	283	2,863.34
Kawika Cotner	73	71	70	69	283	2,863.33
David Jackson	71	70	69	73	283	2,863.33
Dave Rummells	71	69	72	71	283	2,863.33
Chris Stutts	70	73	70	70	283	2,863.33
Pat Bates	69	67	71	77	284	2,250
Bob Burns	71	72	70	71	284	2,250
Scott Ford	69	66	76	73	284	2,250
Eric Johnson	72	67	73	72	284	2,250
Jeff Barlow	71	72	70	72	285	1,800
Joe Durant	73	71	74	67	285	1,800
R.W. Eaks	69	72	74	70	285	1,800
Greg Whisman	74	70	67	74	285	1,800
Bob Wolcott	71	72	68	74	285	1,800
Brian Fogt	72	70	72	72	286	1,365
P.H. Horgan III	71	73	72	70	286	1,365
Bill Murchison	71	68	73	74	286	1,365
Lee Porter	71	72	69	74	286	1,365

Omaha Classic

Champions Golf Club, Omaha, Nebraska
Par 36-36–72; 7,034 yards

August 8-11
purse, $200,000

	SCORES				TOTAL	MONEY
Rocky Walcher	66	65	71	65	267	$36,000
Michael Christie	68	68	66	66	268	19,600
Steve Larick	68	68	65	67	268	19,600
Dave Rummells	68	67	69	65	269	12,500
Jeff Brehaut	67	64	70	69	270	10,500
Doug Dunakey	67	68	68	68	271	7,500
Jimmy Johnston	68	70	68	65	271	7,500
Skip Kendall	71	66	71	63	271	7,500
Lee Porter	67	69	68	67	271	7,500
Jeff Barlow	69	66	71	66	272	4,166.67
Greg Twiggs	67	69	69	67	272	4,166.67
Greg Whisman	70	65	69	68	272	4,166.66

	SCORES				TOTAL	MONEY
Joe Durant	68	66	74	65	273	3,100
Rob McKelvey	67	72	66	68	273	3,100
Gary Webb	69	70	69	65	273	3,100
Jack O'Keefe	66	72	67	69	274	2,570
Deane Pappas	66	73	69	66	274	2,570
Mike Small	71	67	68	68	274	2,570
Mike Sposa	64	66	75	69	274	2,570
Tim Loustalot	67	71	68	69	275	2,250
Alan Pate	67	68	70	70	275	2,250
Pat Bates	69	69	71	67	276	1,850
Andy Dillard	69	68	68	71	276	1,850
Bobby Doolittle	76	64	69	67	276	1,850
Steve Haskins	72	66	67	71	276	1,850
Sam Randolph	68	69	72	67	276	1,850
Mark Wurtz	70	70	68	68	276	1,850
Briny Baird	68	67	70	72	277	1,365
R.W. Eaks	69	67	70	71	277	1,365
Jimmy Green	68	70	69	70	277	1,365
Patrick Lee	68	69	71	69	277	1,365

Wichita Open

Reflection Ridge Golf Club, Wichita, Kansas
Par 36-36—72; 6,730 yards

August 15-18
purse, $200,000

	SCORES				TOTAL	MONEY
Rick Cramer	68	68	66	67	269	$36,000
J.P. Hayes	67	72	69	62	270	17,233.34
Jimmy Johnston	70	70	65	65	270	17,233.33
Craig Kanada	69	71	66	64	270	17,233.33
Stewart Cink	70	68	67	66	271	9,750
Eric Johnson	67	71	66	67	271	9,750
Craig Bowden	67	70	67	68	272	7,000
Danny Ellis	68	68	68	68	272	7,000
Tom Pernice, Jr.	63	69	68	72	272	7,000
Michael Clark	70	69	65	69	273	3,780
Clark Dennis	68	68	66	71	273	3,780
Billy Downes	73	68	65	67	273	3,780
Eric Meeks	68	65	73	67	273	3,780
Tom Shaw	70	67	67	69	273	3,780
Kawika Cotner	69	68	65	72	274	2,695
Skip Kendall	68	68	67	71	274	2,695
Matt Peterson	69	72	66	67	274	2,695
Dennis Zinkon	68	71	67	68	274	2,695
Jeff Barlow	70	68	67	70	275	2,200
Russell Beiersdorf	71	70	64	70	275	2,200
Paul Claxton	69	70	68	68	275	2,200
Doug Dunakey	70	69	67	69	275	2,200
Tim Dunlavey	66	70	69	70	275	2,200
Steve Haskins	71	67	67	71	276	1,650
Dean Larsson	66	71	71	68	276	1,650
Tim Loustalot	66	73	65	72	276	1,650
Dick Mast	73	64	68	71	276	1,650
Perry Moss	69	71	70	66	276	1,650
Mark Wurtz	70	71	66	69	276	1,650
Briny Baird	71	68	67	71	277	1,253.34
Jimmy Green	68	72	64	73	277	1,253.33
Chris Tidland	68	71	64	74	277	1,253.33

Permian Basin Open

The Club at Mission Dorado, Odessa, Texas
Par 36-36–72; 7,135 yards

August 22-25
purse, $200,000

	SCORES				TOTAL	MONEY
Michael Christie	68	71	66	65	270	$36,000
Anthony Rodriguez	69	68	65	70	272	22,700
Deane Pappas	65	69	70	69	273	16,500
Bobby Elliott	65	72	70	67	274	10,666.67
Michael Long	74	67	68	65	274	10,666.67
Pat Bates	67	69	70	68	274	10,666.66
David Berganio, Jr.	67	71	67	70	275	7,500
Perry Parker	69	69	66	71	275	7,500
Rafael Alarcon	72	68	68	68	276	5,500
Jaime Gomez	71	68	69	68	276	5,500
Michael Clark	69	71	72	65	277	3,360
Paul Claxton	71	71	68	67	277	3,360
Eric Epperson	70	70	68	69	277	3,360
Jerry Foltz	71	70	67	69	277	3,360
Larry Silveira	68	73	70	66	277	3,360
Tim Dunlavey	69	73	69	67	278	2,463.34
Mike Schuchart	71	68	70	69	278	2,463.34
Briny Baird	69	69	67	73	278	2,463.33
Rick Cramer	69	68	69	72	278	2,463.33
Mike Small	68	69	70	71	278	2,463.33
Dean Wilson	70	71	68	69	278	2,463.33
Chad Campbell	67	72	70	70	279	2,050
Jeff Gove	66	73	69	71	279	2,050
Doug Barron	67	71	69	73	280	1,750
Brent Geiberger	67	70	72	71	280	1,750
Damon Green	63	75	71	71	280	1,750
Tom Pernice, Jr.	66	75	71	68	280	1,750
Jaxon Brigman	71	68	71	71	281	1,076.25
Bobby Doolittle	69	68	69	75	281	1,076.25
Joe Durant	67	70	71	73	281	1,076.25
Bobby Gee	69	70	71	71	281	1,076.25
Steve Gotsche	68	71	72	70	281	1,076.25
Paul Gow	67	75	66	73	281	1,076.25
Jimmy Green	71	71	67	72	281	1,076.25
Dennis Harrington	68	69	72	72	281	1,076.25
Tom Hearn	72	69	70	70	281	1,076.25
Kent Jones	70	72	71	68	281	1,076.25
Steve Larick	72	67	70	72	281	1,076.25
Tom Shaw	68	72	73	68	281	1,076.25
Collin Stoops	73	68	69	71	281	1,076.25
Phil Tataurangi	68	71	68	74	281	1,076.25
Rocky Walcher	69	71	70	71	281	1,076.25
Bob Wolcott	71	70	72	68	281	1,076.25

Colorado Classic

Riverdale Dunes Golf Club, Brighton, Colorado
Par 36-35–71; 7,063 yards

September 5-8
purse, $200,000

	SCORES				TOTAL	MONEY
Stewart Cink	67	68	67	66	268	$36,000
David Berganio, Jr.	67	70	67	65	269	19,600

	SCORES				TOTAL	MONEY
Michael Christie	71	67	64	67	269	19,600
Craig Bowden	68	70	66	67	271	11,500
Bruce Vaughan	70	66	67	68	271	11,500
Craig Kanada	70	72	66	64	272	8,500
Chad Magee	71	66	64	71	272	8,500
J.P. Hayes	67	69	69	68	273	7,000
R.W. Eaks	65	67	71	71	274	4,625
Bobby Elliott	63	68	72	71	274	4,625
Damon Green	70	67	69	68	274	4,625
Matthew Lane	69	71	72	62	274	4,625
Rafael Alarcon	68	72	68	67	275	3,200
Doug Barron	68	70	66	71	275	3,200
J.C. Anderson	70	67	71	68	276	2,636
Joe Durant	66	75	71	64	276	2,636
Jerry Foltz	67	72	68	69	276	2,636
Dave Rummells	72	70	68	66	276	2,636
Mike Schuchart	69	69	69	69	276	2,636
Joe Cioe	71	71	67	68	277	2,150
P.J. Cowan	68	70	72	67	277	2,150
Jim Estes	74	68	68	67	277	2,150
Bob Gaus	68	71	69	69	277	2,150
Pat Fitzsimons	68	71	71	68	278	1,602.86
Jimmy Green	72	67	72	67	278	1,602.86
Shaun Micheel	70	71	69	68	278	1,602.86
Jack O'Keefe	70	72	67	69	278	1,602.86
Tom Shaw	69	72	71	66	278	1,602.86
Eric Meeks	69	71	67	71	278	1,602.85
Chris Tidland	70	67	69	72	278	1,602.85

Utah Classic

Riverside Country Club, Provo, Utah
Par 36-36–72; 7,001 yards

September 12-14
purse, $200,000

	SCORES			TOTAL	MONEY
Michael Christie	66	63	67	196	$36,000
R.W. Eaks	65	65	70	200	22,700
Lee Porter	67	67	68	202	14,500
Greg Twiggs	68	67	67	202	14,500
Pat Bates	70	65	68	203	9,166.67
Dennis Harrington	70	70	63	203	9,166.67
Jerry Haas	65	67	71	203	9,166.66
Patrick Lee	68	69	67	204	6,500
Dave Rummells	69	68	67	204	6,500
P.J. Cowan	66	69	70	205	4,166.67
Ryan Howison	67	66	72	205	4,166.67
Jimmy Green	69	67	69	205	4,166.66
Joe Durant	68	65	73	206	3,100
Jim Estes	70	69	67	206	3,100
Deane Pappas	68	70	68	206	3,100
Michael Clark	70	69	68	207	2,463.34
Tim Loustalot	70	68	69	207	2,463.34
Ben Bates	71	65	71	207	2,463.33
Kawika Cotner	67	70	70	207	2,463.33
Tad Holloway	72	69	66	207	2,463.33
Phil Tataurangi	69	69	69	207	2,463.33
Stewart Cink	70	66	72	208	1,900

	SCORES			TOTAL	MONEY
Rob Moss	70	68	70	208	1,900
Greg Parker	68	72	68	208	1,900
Mike Sposa	72	67	69	208	1,900
Jerry Wood	68	71	69	208	1,900
Marco Gortana	72	66	71	209	1,376.67
P.H. Horgan III	69	71	69	209	1,376.67
Matthew Lane	71	70	68	209	1,376.67
Sonny Skinner	72	68	69	209	1,376.67
Billy Downes	72	69	68	209	1,376.66
Tom Garner	67	70	72	209	1,376.66

Boise Open

Hillcrest Country Club, Boise, Idaho
Par 36-35–71; 6,773 yards

September 19-22
purse, $250,000

	SCORES				TOTAL	MONEY
Matt Gogel	67	65	67	71	270	$45,000
David Berganio, Jr.	70	64	68	69	271	21,541.67
Brett Quigley	67	70	65	69	271	21,541.67
Stewart Cink	68	62	69	72	271	21,541.66
Joe Durant	67	69	67	69	272	13,125
Rafael Alarcon	70	68	65	70	273	10,000
Pat Bates	69	65	68	71	273	10,000
Rick Cramer	63	69	64	77	273	10,000
Gary Webb	69	68	70	67	274	7,500
Doug Barron	70	67	65	73	275	4,725
Craig Bowden	70	69	68	68	275	4,725
Michael Clark	67	70	70	68	275	4,725
Tim Loustalot	66	67	67	75	275	4,725
Matt Peterson	73	65	65	72	275	4,725
Brent Geiberger	69	69	68	70	276	3,157.15
Rocky Walcher	67	70	71	68	276	3,157.15
Jeff Barlow	68	70	66	72	276	3,157.14
R.W. Eaks	66	68	68	74	276	3,157.14
Lee Porter	67	72	63	74	276	3,157.14
Mike Schuchart	67	68	69	72	276	3,157.14
Bruce Vaughan	70	66	69	71	276	3,157.14
Kent Jones	69	70	69	69	277	2,625
Clark Dennis	69	69	69	71	278	2,375
Steve Larick	67	71	70	70	278	2,375
Larry Silveira	69	67	68	74	278	2,375
Briny Baird	71	65	68	75	279	1,737.50
Russell Beiersdorf	67	72	68	72	279	1,737.50
Billy Downes	69	70	70	70	279	1,737.50
Jerry Foltz	68	68	68	75	279	1,737.50
Deane Pappas	71	68	70	70	279	1,737.50
E.J. Pfister	69	68	73	69	279	1,737.50
Mike Small	70	69	66	74	279	1,737.50
Mark Wurtz	67	70	68	74	279	1,737.50

Tri-Cities Open

Meadow Springs Country Club, Richland, Washington
Par 36-36–72; 6,926 yards

September 26-29
purse, $200,000

	SCORES				TOTAL	MONEY
Phil Tataurangi	69	67	65	66	267	$36,000
Skip Kendall	69	66	68	70	273	22,700
Marco Gortana	71	70	66	68	275	13,166.67
David Sutherland	70	67	72	66	275	13,166.67
Karl Zoller	68	68	67	72	275	13,166.66
Billy Downes	68	68	66	74	276	8,500
Jim Estes	73	67	65	71	276	8,500
Kevin Burton	68	73	68	68	277	7,000
Michael Combs	73	67	65	73	278	4,625
Jimmy Green	71	69	69	69	278	4,625
Glen Hnatiuk	72	70	67	69	278	4,625
Greg Whisman	68	73	70	67	278	4,625
Michael Christie	72	70	67	70	279	3,015
Jerry Haas	69	71	72	67	279	3,015
Tom Pernice, Jr.	71	66	70	72	279	3,015
Charlie Wi	67	74	71	67	279	3,015
David Berganio, Jr.	69	70	70	71	280	2,560
J.P. Hayes	66	67	74	73	280	2,560
Russell Beiersdorf	73	68	66	74	281	2,050
Brent Geiberger	70	67	72	72	281	2,050
Eric Johnson	69	68	72	72	281	2,050
Kevin Johnson	69	73	70	69	281	2,050
Jimmy Johnston	70	71	69	71	281	2,050
Matthew Lane	73	68	72	68	281	2,050
Deane Pappas	70	70	69	72	281	2,050
Bruce Vaughan	69	69	73	70	281	2,050
Jeff Brehaut	71	71	68	72	282	1,500
Dennis Harrington	71	66	71	74	282	1,500
Matt Peterson	70	70	70	72	282	1,500
Pat Bates	71	68	71	73	283	1,165.72
Joe Durant	69	71	73	70	283	1,165.72
Perry Moss	72	69	72	70	283	1,165.72
Kawika Cotner	69	70	68	76	283	1,165.71
Pat Fitzsimons	68	72	70	73	283	1,165.71
P.H. Horgan III	71	67	69	75	283	1,165.71
Gary Webb	72	70	69	72	283	1,165.71

Olympia Open

Indian Summer Golf & Country Club,
Olympia, Washington
Par 36-36–72; 7,216 yards

October 3-6
purse, $200,000

	SCORES				TOTAL	MONEY
Michael Clark	70	70	69	64	273	$36,000
Eric Johnson	66	75	66	70	277	22,700
Dick Mast	72	71	68	67	278	16,500
Eric Booker	68	74	68	69	279	11,500
Bob Wolcott	68	69	73	69	279	11,500
Craig Bowden	70	74	70	67	281	8,500
Kevin Johnson	72	72	68	69	281	8,500
Brent Geiberger	69	72	70	71	282	4,800

	SCORES				TOTAL	MONEY
J.P. Hayes	69	74	69	70	282	4,800
Kent Jones	68	70	71	73	282	4,800
Patrick Lee	70	70	70	72	282	4,800
Tony Sills	71	69	67	75	282	4,800
Mike Sposa	75	68	71	68	282	4,800
Joe Durant	70	71	72	70	283	2,713.34
Dave Rummells	69	70	73	71	283	2,713.34
Glen Hnatiuk	69	73	70	71	283	2,713.33
David Jackson	71	72	68	72	283	2,713.33
Larry Silveira	68	70	72	73	283	2,713.33
Mike Small	74	69	67	73	283	2,713.33
Jeff Barlow	68	71	75	70	284	2,150
Tim Conley	73	71	72	68	284	2,150
Craig Kanada	69	72	71	72	284	2,150
Lee Porter	71	69	69	75	284	2,150
J.C. Anderson	70	68	74	73	285	1,602.86
Billy Downes	73	69	70	73	285	1,602.86
Bobby Elliott	73	68	72	72	285	1,602.86
Damon Green	67	71	74	73	285	1,602.86
Dennis Harrington	72	72	69	72	285	1,602.86
Jack Steinicke	73	71	71	70	285	1,602.85
David Sutherland	72	70	69	74	285	1,602.85
David Berganio, Jr.	70	73	71	72	286	1,160
Bobby Doolittle	71	72	68	75	286	1,160
Steve Larick	68	73	75	70	286	1,160
Shaun Micheel	72	70	73	71	286	1,160
Gary Webb	66	76	74	70	286	1,160

Nike Tour Championship

Settindown Creek Country Club, Roswell, Georgia
Par 36-36–72; 7,024 yards

October 17-20
purse, $250,000

	SCORES				TOTAL	MONEY
Stewart Cink	66	71	71	73	281	$45,000
David Berganio, Jr.	66	73	72	74	285	28,375
Glen Hnatiuk	71	73	67	75	286	18,750
Lee Porter	70	71	72	73	286	18,750
Rafael Alarcon	68	74	74	71	287	12,500
Joe Durant	71	73	70	73	287	12,500
Skip Kendall	68	76	74	70	288	10,000
Brett Quigley	69	77	72	71	289	8,125
Greg Whisman	70	72	75	72	289	8,125
P.H. Horgan III	71	72	73	74	290	5,625
Eric Johnson	68	74	75	73	290	5,625
Michael Clark	73	69	70	79	291	4,250
Jeff Gove	69	76	76	70	291	4,250
Jimmy Green	72	76	73	70	291	4,250
Bobby Elliott	69	77	73	74	293	3,625
Doug Barron	72	80	74	68	294	3,362.50
Paul Claxton	73	73	74	74	294	3,362.50
Phil Tataurangi	74	70	78	73	295	3,125
Michael Christie	68	71	82	75	296	2,937.50
Rob McKelvey	75	71	80	70	296	2,937.50
R.W. Eaks	73	76	72	76	297	2,625
Brent Geiberger	70	77	78	72	297	2,625
Jimmy Johnston	72	71	77	77	297	2,625
Danny Ellis	70	82	70	76	298	2,187.50

	SCORES				TOTAL	MONEY
Jim Estes	74	74	75	75	298	2,187.50
Deane Pappas	70	75	77	76	298	2,187.50
Larry Silveira	72	78	76	72	298	2,187.50
Jeff Brehaut	69	78	76	76	299	1,800
Tim Loustalot	71	76	82	70	299	1,800
Matt Peterson	71	78	70	80	299	1,800

Canadian Tour

Payless Open

Royal Colwood Golf and Country Club,
Victoria, British Columbia
Par 35-35–70; 6,542 yards

May 30-June 2
purse, C$100,000

	SCORES				TOTAL	MONEY
Arden Knoll	64	68	68	67	267	$18,000
Davidson Matyczuk	71	66	71	63	271	10,000
Kelly Mitchum	70	64	70	69	273	5,400
Paul Devenport	69	65	69	70	273	5,400
Robert Damron	71	70	66	67	274	4,200
Trevor Dodds	71	68	68	68	275	3,012.50
Danny Mijovic	67	71	67	70	275	3,012.50
Steve Woods	75	63	70	67	275	3,012.50
Marty Schiene	67	69	73	66	275	3,012.50
Philip Jonas	69	70	69	68	276	2,200
Stuart Hendley	68	69	65	75	277	2,000
Jim Rutledge	69	73	66	70	278	1,800
Ian Hutchings	70	71	68	69	278	1,800
Mike Weir	71	69	71	67	278	1,800
Perry Parker	74	69	70	66	279	1,516.67
Ashley Chinner	74	66	67	72	279	1,516.67
Stephane Talbot	71	68	68	72	279	1,516.67
Kent Fukushima	72	71	71	66	280	1,275
Kent Wiese	70	72	66	72	280	1,275
Brad Wilson	71	69	73	67	280	1,275
Martin Price	69	70	72	69	280	1,275
Andrew Smeeth	69	68	72	71	280	1,275
Wes Martin	72	65	75	68	280	1,275
Dan Yury	70	74	71	66	281	1,043.75
David DeLong	69	73	68	71	281	1,043.75
John McMullen	73	67	72	69	281	1,043.75
Dean Claggett	71	66	73	71	281	1,043.75
Jason Samuelian	70	73	72	67	282	925
Bruce Heuchan	71	71	72	68	282	925
Scott Ford	72	68	71	71	282	925
Greg Cuthill	68	71	72	71	282	925
Jean-Louis Lamarre	70	69	74	69	282	925

BC TEL Pacific Open

Mayfair Lakes Golf & Country Club,
Richmond, British Columbia
Par 36-35–71; 6,641 yards

June 6-9
purse, C$125,000

	SCORES				TOTAL	MONEY
Guy Hill	65	67	65	67	264	$22,500
Arden Knoll	67	70	66	68	271	10,000
Scott Ford	65	68	69	69	271	10,000
Bruce Heuchan	67	66	72	68	273	6,000
Danny Mijovic	69	69	67	70	275	4,937.50
Notah Begay III	68	69	69	69	275	4,937.50
Rick Dalpos	69	70	69	68	276	4,000
Cam Emerson	72	68	68	69	277	3,218.75
Derek Gilchrist	66	70	70	71	277	3,218.75
Kelly Mitchum	65	72	70	71	278	2,750
Jason Shook	69	71	69	70	279	2,041.67
Robert Damron	68	72	68	71	279	2,041.67
Bobby Walton	69	70	70	70	279	2,041.67
Brad Lanning	70	69	74	66	279	2,041.67
Jim Rutledge	68	71	71	69	279	2,041.67
Bruce Bulina	68	69	68	74	279	2,041.67
Richard Zokol	67	69	73	70	279	2,041.67
Todd Doohan	67	69	70	73	279	2,041.67
Roy MacKenzie	65	68	74	72	279	2,041.67
Jim Nelford	71	70	69	70	280	1,593.75
Trevor Dodds	73	68	70	69	280	1,593.75
Ian Leggatt	70	70	69	72	281	1,381.25
Todd Fanning	70	70	70	71	281	1,381.25
Todd Spain	68	71	70	72	281	1,381.25
*Ted Oh	70	68	75	68	281	
Brad Sutterfield	67	70	72	72	281	1,381.25
Matt Jackson	66	69	75	71	281	1,381.25
Davidson Matyczuk	71	70	71	70	282	1,156.25
Daniel Pelczarski	72	68	75	67	282	1,156.25
Alexander Edmonds	65	74	74	69	282	1,156.25
Perry Parker	69	69	73	71	282	1,156.25
Marty Schiene	68	69	75	70	282	1,156.25
Remi Bouchard	64	72	72	74	282	1,156.25
Paul Devenport	67	68	75	72	282	1,156.25

Morningstar Classic

Morningstar International Golf Club,
Parksville, British Columbia
Par 36-36–72; 7,018 yards

June 13-16
purse, C$100,000

	SCORES				TOTAL	MONEY
Bryan DeCorso	70	65	74	68	277	$18,000
Notah Begay III	67	70	73	69	279	10,000
Oswald Drawdy	70	70	71	69	280	5,400
Clinton Whitelaw	70	69	74	67	280	5,400
Jim Rutledge	76	70	68	67	281	4,200
Derek Gilchrist	72	69	72	69	282	2,850
Kelly Mitchum	72	68	72	70	282	2,850
Bruce Bulina	71	69	71	71	282	2,850
Jean-Paul Hebert	69	69	75	69	282	2,850

		SCORES			TOTAL	MONEY
Ashley Chinner	67	69	76	70	282	2,850
Marty Schiene	71	74	74	64	283	1,950
David Morland	71	69	72	71	283	1,950
Trevor Dodds	72	71	69	72	284	1,650
Alexander Edmonds	69	70	72	73	284	1,650
Pete McCutcheon	69	69	73	73	284	1,650
Mike Weir	67	70	77	70	284	1,650
Rick Dalpos	74	72	68	71	285	1,375
Matt Jackson	73	72	69	71	285	1,375
Stephane Talbot	72	73	72	68	285	1,375
Philip Jonas	71	72	71	71	285	1,375
Brad Sutterfield	70	72	72	72	286	1,225
Trey Maples	72	69	72	73	286	1,225
Remi Bouchard	72	74	70	71	287	1,021.88
Ray Freeman	73	72	72	70	287	1,021.88
Jason Shook	71	74	70	72	287	1,021.88
Arden Knoll	72	73	68	74	287	1,021.88
Guy Hill	70	74	72	71	287	1,021.88
Perry Parker	71	71	72	73	287	1,021.88
Jack Kay	71	71	74	71	287	1,021.88
Craig Marseilles	70	69	76	72	287	1,021.88

Henry Singer Alberta Open

World Creek Golf Resort, Ponoka, Alberta
Par 36-36–72; 6,516 yards

June 20-23
purse, C$125,000

		SCORES			TOTAL	MONEY
Trevor Dodds	68	69	67	66	270	$22,500
Ian Leggatt	72	73	61	65	271	12,500
Bryan DeCorso	67	68	67	72	274	7,500
Bruce Heuchan	67	72	68	68	275	6,000
Derek Gilchrist	70	73	68	65	276	4,312.50
Todd Fanning	69	70	68	69	276	4,312.50
Clinton Whitelaw	68	68	68	72	276	4,312.50
Philip Jonas	68	67	72	69	276	4,312.50
Arden Knoll	76	69	63	69	277	2,906.25
Ray Freeman	68	74	67	68	277	2,906.25
Brad Klapprott	71	67	66	74	278	2,500
Davidson Matyczuk	73	70	69	67	279	1,984.38
Danny Mijovic	74	69	67	69	279	1,984.38
Matt Jackson	71	71	67	70	279	1,984.38
Jim Rutledge	71	70	66	72	279	1,984.38
Dan Halldorson	71	69	70	69	279	1,984.38
Mike Weir	73	67	73	66	279	1,984.38
Mike Grob	67	70	69	73	279	1,984.38
Joe Lloyd	71	65	72	71	279	1,984.38
Britt Pavelonis	72	71	68	69	280	1,562.50
Ian Hutchings	70	73	70	67	280	1,562.50
Trey Maples	71	68	68	73	280	1,562.50
Keith Whitecotton	74	70	69	68	281	1,375
Todd Spain	71	73	68	69	281	1,375
Scott Ford	70	70	72	69	281	1,375
Alexander Edmonds	72	71	68	71	282	1,218.75
Robert Ames	68	75	70	69	282	1,218.75
Kelly Mitchum	71	70	70	71	282	1,218.75
Ted Norby	70	71	69	72	282	1,218.75
Ashley Chinner	70	70	69	73	282	1,218.75

ED TEL PLAnet Open

The Ranch Golf & Country Club, Edmonton, Alberta
Par 35-35–70; 6,466 yards

June 27-30
purse, C$125,000

	SCORES				TOTAL	MONEY
Trevor Dodds	63	66	70	66	265	$22,500
Arden Knoll	63	72	65	69	269	12,500
Danny Mijovic	66	67	71	66	270	6,750
Stephane Talbot	65	65	73	67	270	6,750
Brad Sutterfield	69	68	70	64	271	5,250
Ian Hutchings	68	67	68	69	272	4,312.50
Tim Balmer	67	67	70	68	272	4,312.50
David Rueter	61	70	68	68	273	3,062.50
Mike Weir	65	69	71	68	273	3,062.50
Duane Bock	68	65	70	70	273	3,062.50
Craig Marseilles	67	69	70	69	275	2,375
Ken Duke	71	65	71	68	275	2,375
Jim Rutledge	66	69	69	71	275	2,375
Davidson Matyczuk	72	66	69	69	276	1,953.12
Bruce Bulina	69	69	70	68	276	1,953.12
Darren Griff	65	71	69	71	276	1,953.12
Ashley Chinner	68	67	71	70	276	1,953.12
Steve Woods	70	69	70	68	277	1,656.25
Paul Devenport	70	66	72	69	277	1,656.25
Kip Byrne	69	66	74	68	277	1,656.25
Ian Leggatt	68	66	74	69	277	1,656.25
Derek Gilchrist	72	68	70	68	278	1,381.25
Blair Piercy	68	69	69	72	278	1,381.25
Philip Jonas	69	67	72	70	278	1,381.25
Dan Dupuis	70	66	69	73	278	1,381.25
Brian Wright	69	66	74	69	278	1,381.25
Notah Begay III	74	66	69	70	279	1,171.88
Britt Pavelonis	70	69	71	69	279	1,171.88
Kelly Mitchum	69	70	71	69	279	1,171.88
David McKenzie	68	68	74	69	279	1,171.88
Mike Grant	71	64	73	71	279	1,171.88
Brad Wilson	66	69	73	71	279	1,171.88

Xerox Manitoba Open

Pine Ridge Golf Club, Winnipeg, Manitoba
Par 35-37–72; 6,686 yards

July 11-14
purse, C$100,000

	SCORES				TOTAL	MONEY
*Rob McMillan	70	68	71	65	274	
Mike Grob	69	70	64	75	278	$18,000
Brad Sutterfield	70	71	67	71	279	8,000
Philip Jonas	68	71	73	67	279	8,000
Notah Begay III	69	75	66	70	280	3,975
Ken Duke	72	71	66	71	280	3,975
Jason Samuelian	70	70	71	69	280	3,975
Bruce Heuchan	67	72	69	72	280	3,975
Danny Mijovic	71	72	69	69	281	2,337.50
Paul Devenport	70	72	68	71	281	2,337.50
Jay Cooper	72	70	68	71	281	2,337.50
Rich Massey	68	73	70	70	281	2,337.50
Rob Anderson	73	71	68	70	282	1,800

	SCORES			TOTAL	MONEY
Aaron Barber	68	72	68	74	282	1,800
Cam Emerson	65	71	71	75	282	1,800
Stephen Leaney	71	74	68	70	283	1,460
Kevin Baker	74	72	65	72	283	1,460
Ray Stewart	70	72	71	70	283	1,460
Duane Bock	68	74	70	71	283	1,460
Davidson Matyczuk	69	70	75	69	283	1,460
Todd Fanning	72	74	70	68	284	1,200
Ben Walter	69	75	66	74	284	1,200
Remi Bouchard	70	72	69	73	284	1,200
Jim Rutledge	70	71	72	71	284	1,200
Ian Leggatt	68	72	75	69	284	1,200
Dean Wilson	72	73	69	71	285	1,012.50
Phillip Hatchett	70	74	71	70	285	1,012.50
Brad Wilson	71	72	71	71	285	1,012.50
Jean-Paul Hebert	72	70	72	71	285	1,012.50
Jason Shook	70	75	67	74	286	912.50
Dan Dupuis	70	73	74	69	286	912.50
David Rueter	72	71	71	72	286	912.50
Jeff Mills	66	73	72	75	286	912.50

Infiniti Championship

Chestnut Hill Golf & Club, Richmond Hill, Ontario
Par 36-36—72; 7,079 yards

July 18-21
purse, C$125,000

	SCORES			TOTAL	MONEY
Trevor Dodds	67	71	73	67	278	$22,500
Arden Knoll	66	72	71	71	280	8,666.67
Stephen Leaney	63	72	74	71	280	8,666.67
Ian Leggatt	65	71	75	69	280	8,666.67
Sean Halloran	66	76	69	70	281	5,250
Jim Rutledge	71	74	72	67	284	4,312.50
Jason Shook	69	71	75	69	284	4,312.50
Chip Spratlin	72	75	66	72	285	3,375
Cam Emerson	74	71	73	68	286	2,770.83
David McKenzie	70	72	73	71	286	2,770.83
Robert Damron	67	74	72	73	286	2,770.83
Bryan DeCorso	70	73	73	71	287	2,250
Dennis Harrington	69	73	76	69	287	2,250
Remi Bouchard	68	74	75	70	287	2,250
Ashley Chinner	69	76	71	72	288	1,859.38
Martin Quinney	73	71	72	72	288	1,859.38
Ken Duke	71	70	72	75	288	1,859.38
Mike Grob	65	74	76	73	288	1,859.38
Edward Reevey	74	72	74	69	289	1,593.75
Ian Hutchings	71	72	73	73	289	1,593.75
Jean-Louis Lamarre	69	74	74	72	289	1,593.75
Kelly Mitchum	66	76	76	71	289	1,593.75
Philip Jonas	74	72	73	71	290	1,351.56
Tim Balmer	69	75	75	71	290	1,351.56
Darren Griff	71	73	72	74	290	1,351.56
Marcus Meloan	69	72	76	73	290	1,351.56
Dan Dupuis	72	73	78	68	291	1,234.38
Chris DiMarco	72	69	74	76	291	1,234.38
Stuart Hendley	71	75	74	72	292	1,156.25
Rich Massey	70	76	71	75	292	1,156.25
Oswald Drawdy	69	75	78	70	292	1,156.25

Canadian Masters

Heron Point Golf Links, Ancaster, Ontario
Par 36-36–72; 6,841 yards

July 25-28
purse, C$250,000

	SCORES				TOTAL	MONEY
Trevor Dodds	68	66	68	72	274	$45,000
Arden Knoll	67	70	69	69	275	17,333.33
Chris DiMarco	69	70	69	67	275	17,333.33
Ken Duke	68	68	69	70	275	17,333.33
Mike Weir	66	75	64	71	276	8,125
Blair Piercy	70	68	70	68	276	8,125
Stephane Talbot	70	68	69	69	276	8,125
Guy Hill	67	75	68	66	276	8,125
Daniel Pelczarski	69	69	72	66	276	8,125
Garrett Willis	73	71	68	65	277	5,250
Mike Grob	69	70	69	69	277	5,250
Ray Stewart	73	70	66	69	278	4,625
Phillip Hatchett	71	71	66	70	278	4,625
Kelly Mitchum	67	75	67	70	279	3,825
Robert Damron	72	70	66	71	279	3,825
Scott Ford	68	71	70	70	279	3,825
Stuart Hendley	70	69	70	70	279	3,825
Carlos Espinosa	73	66	70	70	279	3,825
Ian Leggatt	73	67	67	73	280	3,250
Todd Spain	70	70	70	70	280	3,250
Steve Woods	71	68	69	72	280	3,250
Darren Griff	73	70	69	69	281	2,762.50
Paul Devenport	73	70	71	67	281	2,762.50
Duane Bock	72	70	67	72	281	2,762.50
Jim Rutledge	72	69	73	67	281	2,762.50
Frank Edmonds	67	71	75	68	281	2,762.50
Marcus Meloan	76	68	72	66	282	2,437.50
Manny Zerman	73	71	69	69	282	2,437.50
Trey Maples	71	71	67	73	282	2,437.50
Mike Grant	70	72	70	71	283	2,218.75
Ian Doig	70	70	71	72	283	2,218.75
Chip Spratlin	66	72	70	75	283	2,218.75
Derek Gilchrist	69	69	73	72	283	2,218.75

Export "A" Inc. Ontario Open

St. Thomas Golf & Country Club, Union, Ontario
Par 36-35–71; 6,779 yards

August 8-11
purse, C$125,000

	SCORES				TOTAL	MONEY
Martin Price	69	69	68	68	274	$22,500
Ashley Chinner	64	71	69	70	274	12,500
(Price defeated Chinner on first extra hole.)						
Ken Duke	71	71	68	65	275	7,500
Clinton Whitelaw	68	71	70	67	276	5,625
Mike Grob	70	66	71	69	276	5,625
Brad Wilson	72	68	70	67	277	4,625
Davidson Matyczuk	70	72	69	67	278	4,000
Trevor Dodds	71	74	68	66	279	2,718.75
Gary Cowan	73	71	67	68	279	2,718.75
Mike Weir	73	70	69	67	279	2,718.75
Arden Knoll	69	71	69	70	279	2,718.75

	SCORES			TOTAL	MONEY
Darren Griff	68	71	74	66	279	2,718.75
Phillip Hatchett	68	68	75	68	279	2,718.75
Tom Gillis	70	72	67	71	280	2,062.50
Derek Gilchrist	70	69	70	71	280	2,062.50
Marty Schiene	74	71	68	68	281	1,812.50
Daniel Pelczarski	70	73	71	67	281	1,812.50
Dean Wilson	68	70	73	70	281	1,812.50
Philip Jonas	75	70	67	70	282	1,593.75
Tony Aguilar	73	72	67	70	282	1,593.75
Manny Zerman	72	71	67	72	282	1,593.75
John Robertson	70	69	70	73	282	1,593.75
Todd Spain	69	75	66	73	283	1,312.50
David Morland	71	72	68	72	283	1,312.50
Chris DiMarco	71	71	70	71	283	1,312.50
Paul Devenport	72	68	73	70	283	1,312.50
Duane Bock	71	68	72	72	283	1,312.50
Garrett Willis	68	70	73	72	283	1,312.50
David Wettlaufer	70	73	70	71	284	1,140.62
Jerry Springer	70	71	72	71	284	1,140.62
Mark Voeller	70	70	74	70	284	1,140.62
Remi Bouchard	72	67	75	70	284	1,140.62

Montclair Quebec Open

Golf Dorval, Montreal, Quebec
Par 36-35–71; 6,772 yards

August 15-18
purse, C$125,000

	SCORES			TOTAL	MONEY
Chris DiMarco	67	65	65	69	266	$22,500
Duane Bock	67	68	67	65	267	12,500
Philip Jonas	64	69	68	67	268	7,500
Perry Parker	67	66	70	66	269	6,000
Robert Meyer	68	64	68	70	270	5,250
David Rueter	68	67	68	68	271	4,000
Guy Hill	67	67	69	68	271	4,000
Clinton Whitelaw	68	66	68	69	271	4,000
Kelly Mitchum	70	70	67	65	272	2,770.83
Mike Grob	69	69	66	68	272	2,770.83
Danny Mijovic	69	67	66	70	272	2,770.83
David Morland	68	71	68	66	273	2,187.50
Ken Duke	69	70	66	68	273	2,187.50
Trevor Dodds	67	69	69	68	273	2,187.50
Notah Begay III	66	67	71	69	273	2,187.50
Bruce Heuchan	70	69	65	70	274	1,812.50
Robert Damron	68	66	70	70	274	1,812.50
Arden Knoll	68	66	69	71	274	1,812.50
Chris Anderson	69	72	67	67	275	1,562.50
Davidson Matyczuk	68	73	67	67	275	1,562.50
Derek Gilchrist	69	71	68	67	275	1,562.50
Todd Fanning	71	68	70	66	275	1,562.50
Marc Girouard	70	67	68	70	275	1,562.50
Kevi Senexal	70	70	67	69	276	1,270.83
Ashley Chinner	69	71	71	65	276	1,270.83
Dan Halldorson	72	68	68	68	276	1,270.83
Jason Samuelian	71	69	68	68	276	1,270.83
Darryl James	67	71	68	70	276	1,270.83
Brian Wright	65	70	71	70	276	1,270.83

Montclair PEI Classic

Brudnell River Golf Course, Morell, P.E.I.   August 29-September 1
Par 36-36–72; 6,542 yards   purse, C$125,000

	SCORES				TOTAL	MONEY
Frank Edmonds	71	70	69	66	276	C$22,500
Ian Leggatt	71	72	69	65	277	10,000
Mike Grob	71	70	70	66	277	10,000
Norm Jarvis	69	72	69	68	278	5,625
David Rueter	67	73	72	66	278	5,625
Guy Hill	68	71	71	69	279	4,625
Notah Begay III	68	70	70	72	280	3,687.50
Philip Jonas	68	70	74	68	280	3,687.50
Jean-Paul Hebert	77	68	73	63	281	2,770.83
David Morland	70	71	72	68	281	2,770.83
Trevor Dodds	71	69	70	71	281	2,770.83
Ashley Chinner	69	72	74	67	282	2,375
Bryan DeCorso	71	72	67	73	283	2,125
Arden Knoll	68	73	70	72	283	2,125
Bruce Bulina	67	74	73	69	283	2,125
Chris DiMarco	71	78	70	65	284	1,750
Eric Egloff	69	76	70	69	284	1,750
Jim Rutledge	72	73	71	68	284	1,750
Blair Piercy	72	69	72	71	284	1,750
David Wettlaufer	66	73	68	77	284	1,750
Todd Doohan	72	71	68	74	285	1,531.25
Paul Devenport	68	72	74	71	285	1,531.25
Bruce Heuchan	73	72	71	70	286	1,375
Britt Pavelonis	70	71	74	71	286	1,375
Kelly Mitchum	66	72	76	72	286	1,375
Manny Zerman	71	77	70	69	287	1,218.75
Jay Gunning	72	75	70	70	287	1,218.75
Keith Whitecotton	72	73	74	68	287	1,218.75
Stuart Hendley	73	72	72	70	287	1,218.75
Brian Wright	72	70	73	72	287	1,218.75

CPGA Championship

Mandarin Golf & Country Club, Markham, Ontario   September 12-15
Par 35-36–71; 6,728 yards   purse, C$100,000
(Event shortened to 54 holes — rain.)

	SCORES			TOTAL	MONEY
Ashley Chinner	67	71	67	205	C$18,000
Todd Fanning	69	69	68	206	10,000
Ray Stewart	69	68	70	207	6,000
Martin Price	70	72	67	209	4,500
Ian Leggatt	66	73	70	209	4,500
Todd Doohan	65	75	70	210	3,012.50
Chip Spratlin	69	70	71	210	3,012.50
David Miller	73	68	69	210	3,012.50
Derek Gilchrist	68	69	73	210	3,012:50
Trevor Dodds	69	71	71	211	2,100
Pete McCutcheon	73	68	70	211	2,100
Guy Hill	71	71	70	212	1,900
Danny Mijovic	70	69	74	213	1,750
Jim Rutledge	70	76	67	213	1,750

	SCORES			TOTAL	MONEY
David Banks	72	73	69	214	1,460
Duane Bock	68	74	72	214	1,460
Brian Hepler	75	67	72	214	1,460
Paul Penny	75	70	69	214	1,460
Greg Cuthill	69	75	70	214	1,460
Yvan Beauchemin	70	71	74	215	1,275
Beau Yokomoto	72	71	72	215	1,275
Jack Ray	69	73	74	216	1,105
Remi Bouchard	68	72	76	216	1,105
Jim Wahl	72	73	71	216	1,105
Steve Chapman	73	74	69	216	1,105
Scott Ford	72	74	70	216	1,105
Arden Knoll	73	71	73	217	912.50
Jeff Mills	69	76	72	217	912.50
Kevin Senecal	72	76	69	217	912.50
Adam Kase	71	71	75	217	912.50
Jason Samuelian	72	74	71	217	912.50
J.J. West	72	70	75	217	912.50
Davidson Matyczuk	73	72	72	217	912.50
David Woods	75	71	71	217	912.50

South American Tour

Colombia Open

San Andres Golf Club, Bogota, Colombia
Par 36-36–72; 7,023 yards

October 3-6
purse, US$80,000

	SCORES				TOTAL	MONEY
Arden Knoll	71	66	67	68	272	US$14,400
Angel Cabrera	69	71	66	66	272	7,600
Stephane Talbot	68	67	68	69	272	7,600
(Knoll defeated Cabrera and Talbot on second extra hole.)						
Tadahisa Inoue	68	67	71	67	273	5,120
Roberto Coceres	69	70	66	69	274	3,413.33
Ricardo Gonzalez	71	64	68	71	274	3,413.33
Jorge Benedetti	65	67	69	73	274	3,413.33
Horacio Carbonetti	68	72	70	67	277	2,160
Rodolfo Rodriguez	67	70	71	69	277	2,160
Miguel Fernandez	69	73	70	66	278	1,648
Omar Peralta	73	68	69	68	278	1,648
Jose Cantero	73	69	67	69	278	1,648
Jose Corredor	66	71	71	70	278	1,648
Gustavo Rojas	68	68	68	74	278	1,648
Nilson Cabrera	69	72	72	66	279	1,240
Pedro Martinez	68	73	68	70	279	1,240
Cesar Monasterio	70	69	70	70	279	1,240
Jesus Amaya	70	65	70	74	279	1,240

	SCORES				TOTAL	MONEY
Sebastian Fernandez	68	70	70	72	280	1,000
Armando Redondo	69	68	71	72	280	1,000
Jorge Murdoch	67	75	72	67	281	745.14
Eduardo Martinez	75	66	73	67	281	745.14
Erik Andersson	73	68	72	68	281	745.14
Eduardo Pesenti	72	69	72	68	281	745.14
Diego Serna	72	71	69	69	281	745.14
Anai Fuentes	71	69	69	72	281	745.14
Tjaart Van Der Walt	68	72	69	72	281	745.14
Ramon Franco	73	68	72	69	282	560
Acacio Jorge Pedro	68	70	74	70	282	560
Jay Hunter	68	74	69	71	282	560
Ted Gleason	67	72	71	72	282	560
Jeff Schmid	70	68	72	72	282	560
Davidson Matyczuk	70	69	68	75	282	560
Ricardo Coceres	69	68	68	77	282	560

La Sabana Open

Club Campestre La Sabana, Bogota, Colombia
Par 71; 6,345 yards

October 10-13
purse, US$80,000

	SCORES				TOTAL	MONEY
Pedro Martinez	63	69	66	67	265	US$14,400
Ruberlei Felizardo	69	66	67	67	269	7,760
Miguel Guzman	64	67	68	70	269	7,760
Erik Andersson	66	67	67	70	270	5,120
Arden Knoll	71	70	67	63	271	3,413.33
Tjaart Van Der Walt	68	68	67	68	271	3,413.33
Ariel Canete	63	67	69	72	271	3,413.33
Angel Romero	69	70	67	66	272	2,000
Rolly Hurst	66	72	66	68	272	2,000
Roy MacKenzie	69	65	69	69	272	2,000
Nilson Cabrera	67	67	68	70	272	2,000
Jose Cantero	68	71	68	66	273	1,520
Ron Wuensche	70	67	70	66	273	1,520
Angel Franco	70	69	65	69	273	1,520
Gustavo Rojas	67	71	70	66	274	1,320
Rodolfo Rodriguez	68	69	67	70	274	1,320
Stephane Talbot	71	66	69	69	275	1,120
Jesus Amaya	66	71	67	71	275	1,120
Jose Aderbal	67	66	70	72	275	1,120
Ricardo Ronderos	70	69	70	67	276	960
Jay Hunter	68	72	69	68	277	780.80
Eduardo Caballero	69	70	70	68	277	780.80
Mauricio Molina	67	68	73	69	277	780.80
Jorge Benedetti	72	67	67	71	277	780.80
Rigoberto Velasquez	69	64	70	74	277	780.80
Arnaud Langenaeken	71	67	70	70	278	672
Jorge Murdoch	71	69	73	66	279	570
Fredy Luna	68	72	73	66	279	570
Karl Brink	71	68	74	66	279	570
Cesar Monasterio	68	72	71	68	279	570
Rodolfo Gonzalez	69	72	69	69	279	570
Albert Evers	66	68	75	70	279	570

TC Ecuadorian Open

Guayaquil Country Club, Guayaquil, Ecuador
Par 36-36–72; 6,760 yards

October 17-20
purse, US$100,000

	SCORES				TOTAL	MONEY
Gustavo Rojas	71	69	65	69	274	US$18,000
Jeff Schmid	68	69	69	70	276	11,400
Blair Piercy	77	65	70	66	278	8,000
Trevor Dodds	72	70	70	67	279	5,266.67
Ricardo Gonzalez	69	73	70	67	279	5,266.67
Miguel Fernandez	71	71	67	70	279	5,266.67
Ron Wuensche	72	70	67	71	280	3,400
Roberto Coceres	71	73	69	68	281	2,700
Jorge Benedetti	67	73	72	69	281	2,700
Jose Cantero	75	68	72	67	282	2,060
Angel Franco	70	73	72	67	282	2,060
Cesar Monasterio	72	71	70	69	282	2,060
Frank Edmonds	73	71	68	70	282	2,060
Jesus Amaya	71	67	72	72	282	2,060
Omar Peralta	70	71	69	73	283	1,700
Rich Massey	72	71	73	68	284	1,500
Rodolfo Rodriguez	72	69	72	71	284	1,500
Jorge Berendt	71	69	72	72	284	1,500
Mauricio Molina	69	72	68	76	285	1,300
Miguel Guzman	70	74	74	68	286	1,106.67
Pedro Martinez	71	71	72	72	286	1,106.67
Nilson Cabrera	67	71	76	72	286	1,106.67
Priscilo Diniz	76	71	72	68	287	940
Erik Andersson	73	73	70	71	287	940
Henrik Nystrom	73	74	74	67	288	804
Guilherme Antunes	74	71	75	68	288	804
Tjaart Van Der Walt	73	72	75	68	288	804
Jay Hunter	73	70	72	73	288	804
Angel Romero	69	70	73	76	288	804
Ricardo Montenegro	71	74	73	71	289	720

Los Inkas–Peru Open

Los Inkas Golf Club, Lima, Peru
Par 36-36–72; 6,949 yards

October 24-27
purse, US$150,000

	SCORES				TOTAL	MONEY
Philip Jonas	69	67	70	70	276	US$27,000
Pedro Martinez	71	68	68	70	277	17,100
Ricardo Gonzalez	68	67	72	71	278	12,000
Eduardo Caballero	72	70	67	70	279	8,700
Scott Dunlap	72	68	68	71	279	8,700
Ruben Alvarez	71	71	69	69	280	4,875
Miguel Fernandez	68	74	69	69	280	4,875
Angel Cabrera	73	67	71	69	280	4,875
Gustavo Rojas	68	70	71	71	280	4,875
Sebastian Fernandez	74	66	72	69	281	3,450
Jorge Berendt	70	67	73	71	281	3,450
Henrik Nystrom	72	68	74	69	283	2,775
Karl Brink	72	70	71	70	283	2,775
Armando Saavedra	71	70	71	71	283	2,775
Omar Solis	72	71	68	72	283	2,775

	SCORES				TOTAL	MONEY
Davidson Matyczuk	71	70	76	67	284	2,250
Cristian Caballero	70	69	77	68	284	2,250
Raul Fretes	73	70	70	71	284	2,250
Rafael Gomez	69	69	76	71	285	1,625
Angel Franco	70	71	72	72	285	1,625
Jay Hunter	71	68	74	72	285	1,625
Rafael Barcellos	73	70	69	73	285	1,625
Erik Andersson	69	73	69	74	285	1,625
Acacio Jorge Pedro	69	69	72	75	285	1,625
Ian Leggatt	73	72	70	71	286	1,320
Jose Cardenas	74	71	71	71	287	1,122.86
Ruberlei Felizardo	73	71	72	71	287	1,122.86
Tadahisa Inoue	69	72	74	72	287	1,122.86
Luis Felipe Graf	69	70	75	73	287	1,122.86
Brian Wright	71	68	74	74	287	1,122.86
Trevor Dodds	71	68	74	74	287	1,122.86
Brad Klapprott	72	71	68	76	287	1,122.86

Litoral Open

Rosario Golf Club, Rosario, Argentina
Par 35-36–71; 6,377 yards

October 31-November 3
purse, US$100,000

	SCORES				TOTAL	MONEY
Scott Dunlap	65	70	63	69	267	US$18,000
Trevor Dodds	70	70	67	63	270	8,600
Pedro Martinez	65	71	65	69	270	8,600
Rodolfo Rodriguez	65	66	70	69	270	8,600
Miguel Fernandez	67	65	71	68	271	5,200
Jeff Schmid	71	68	69	65	273	3,800
Jorge Berendt	67	71	70	65	273	3,800
Angel Franco	75	68	64	67	274	2,700
Davidson Matyczuk	69	69	69	67	274	2,700
Sebastian Fernandez	69	67	71	68	275	2,400
Walter Miranda	70	70	68	68	276	2,100
Philip Jonas	69	70	67	70	276	2,100
Henrik Nystrom	73	68	70	66	277	1,750
Ruben Alvarez	72	68	70	67	277	1,750
Armando Saavedra	67	70	70	70	277	1,750
Ian Leggatt	71	67	68	71	277	1,750
Raul Albarrasin	67	74	69	68	278	1,500
Brad Klapprott	68	71	71	69	279	1,350
Omar Solis	68	69	69	73	279	1,350
Luis Carbonetti	74	70	69	67	280	1,070
Antonio Ortiz	74	69	69	68	280	1,070
Ariel Canete	72	72	67	69	280	1,070
Roy MacKenzie	70	71	68	71	280	1,070
Kenneth Staton	71	73	68	69	281	880
Russell Fletcher	69	72	71	69	281	880
Rodolfo Gonzalez	70	69	71	71	281	880
Gustavo Rojas	72	72	70	68	282	766.67
Roberto Coceres	69	70	73	70	282	766.67
Bruce Bulina	70	71	70	71	282	766.67
Ramon Franco	70	71	78	64	283	690
Martin Lonardi	74	70	71	68	283	690
Daniel Lobos	71	71	72	69	283	690
Eduardo Argiro	68	70	71	74	283	690

Uruguay Open

Uruguay Golf Club, Montevideo, Uruguay
Par 36-37–73; 6,458 yards

November 14-17
purse, US$80,000

	SCORES				TOTAL	MONEY
Miguel Fernandez	65	66	69	72	272	US$14,400
Jorge Berendt	66	68	76	64	274	7,760
Angel Franco	72	67	70	65	274	7,760
Pedro Martinez	68	70	67	70	275	4,640
Brad Klapprott	66	68	70	71	275	4,640
Ricardo Gonzalez	73	69	68	66	276	2,773.33
Armando Saavedra	72	68	70	66	276	2,773.33
Ken Duke	71	65	71	69	276	2,773.33
Raul Fretes	73	71	69	65	278	2,000
Erik Andersson	64	69	72	73	278	2,000
Rafael Gomez	70	68	67	74	279	1,760
Karl Brink	70	67	75	68	280	1,550
Roy MacKenzie	67	71	72	70	280	1,550
Rodolfo Gonzalez	72	72	72	66	282	1,320
Rodolfo Rodriguez	73	72	70	67	282	1,320
Jorge Benedetti	73	70	71	68	282	1,320
Tjaart Van Der Walt	70	69	73	70	282	1,320
Henrik Nystrom	72	71	71	69	283	1,120
Ruberlei Felizardo	70	73	72	69	284	1,000
Ian Leggatt	71	70	73	70	284	1,000
Gustavo Rojas	67	72	75	71	285	880
Kenneth Staton	74	71	71	70	286	739.20
Antonio Ortiz	69	75	72	70	286	739.20
Jay Hunter	74	71	70	71	286	739.20
Tony Aguilar	67	74	74	71	286	739.20
Mauricio Molina	73	68	70	75	286	739.20
Ramon Franco	72	72	72	71	287	604
Graeme Van Der Nest	72	70	74	71	287	604
Brian Wright	69	76	70	72	287	604
Cesar Monasterio	69	74	72	72	287	604

Los Leones Open

Los Leones Golf Club, Santiago, Chile
Par 36-36–72; 6,653 yards

November 21-24
purse, US$110,000

	SCORES				TOTAL	MONEY
Roberto Coceres	71	67	68	67	273	US$19,800
Gustavo Rojas	67	71	70	68	276	12,540
Acacio Jorge Pedro	70	71	70	70	281	8,800
Raul Fretes	72	74	70	66	282	6,380
Ken Duke	69	72	68	73	282	6,380
Angel Franco	69	73	70	71	283	3,813.33
Jose Cantero	71	72	68	72	283	3,813.33
Angel Cabrera	71	71	67	74	283	3,813.33
Sebastian Fernandez	69	68	75	72	284	2,750
Miguel Fernandez	75	71	65	73	284	2,750
Horacio Carbonetti	71	72	71	71	285	2,053.33
Karl Brink	70	75	68	72	285	2,053.33
Tjaart Van Der Walt	69	72	72	72	285	2,053.33
Cesar Monasterio	73	69	68	75	285	2,053.33
Mauricio Molina	71	67	72	75	285	2,053.33

	SCORES				TOTAL	MONEY
Ruben Alvarez	72	69	71	73	285	2,053.33
Armando Saavedra	73	73	72	68	286	1,292.50
Jeff Schmid	70	72	74	70	286	1,292.50
Brian Wright	75	71	69	71	286	1,292.50
Luis Felipe Graf	72	74	69	71	286	1,292.50
Jay Hunter	67	77	71	71	286	1,292.50
Rich Massey	71	71	72	72	286	1,292.50
Ricardo Montenegro	73	72	68	73	286	1,292.50
Patricio Valenzuela	71	74	68	73	286	1,292.50
Scott Dunlap	71	75	71	70	287	902
Rafael Barcellos	70	75	70	72	287	902
Neale Gandy	72	69	73	73	287	902
Francisco Valdez	71	70	72	74	287	902
Diego Ventureira	76	70	71	71	288	770
Jose Aderbal	68	75	73	72	288	770
Rafael Gomez	74	71	70	73	288	770
Angel Fernandez	71	72	72	73	288	770
Jorge Benedetti	72	72	69	75	288	770

Prince of Wales Open

Prince of Wales Country Club, Santiago, Chile
Par 36-36–72; 6,670 yards

November 28-December 1
purse, US$120,000

	SCORES				TOTAL	MONEY
Ricardo Gonzalez	68	69	67	67	271	US$21,600
Gustavo Rojas	66	65	73	69	273	12,680
Angel Cabrera	67	69	69	70	275	9,600
Ken Duke	69	67	72	68	276	7,680
Scott Dunlap	68	68	69	72	277	6,240
Cesar Monasterio	70	68	77	64	279	4,560
Raul Fretes	69	66	71	73	279	4,560
Eduardo Romero	68	69	75	68	280	3,240
Roy MacKenzie	69	69	71	71	280	3,240
Priscilo Diniz	70	69	73	69	281	2,760
Jorge Berendt	70	69	72	70	281	2,760
Miguel Fernandez	69	69	74	70	282	2,340
Luis Felipe Graf	68	70	71	73	282	2,340
Ruberlei Felizardo	72	72	70	69	283	2,040
Tjaart Van Der Walt	70	73	69	71	283	2,040
Pedro Martinez	71	71	70	71	283	2,040
Rich Massey	77	68	71	68	284	1,740
Ricardo Montenegro	69	69	71	75	284	1,740
Frank Edmonds	67	75	74	69	285	1,300
Ariel Canete	74	69	72	70	285	1,300
Jorgen Aker	70	70	75	70	285	1,300
Erik Andersson	74	71	69	71	285	1,300
Acacio Jorge Pedro	73	69	72	71	285	1,300
Eduardo Pesenti	71	69	73	72	285	1,300
Graeme Van Der Nest	75	69	73	69	286	984
Ramon Franco	73	71	71	71	286	984
Armando Saavedra	69	73	72	72	286	984
Jose Cantero	72	68	72	74	286	984
Davidson Matyczuk	77	68	73	69	287	840
Mauricio Molina	72	66	73	76	287	840
Roberto Coceres	75	71	71	70	287	840
Rafael Barcellos	72	71	70	74	287	840
Angel Franco	71	70	71	75	287	840

Argentina Open

Olivos Golf Club, Buenos Aires, Argentina
Par 71; 6,659 yards

December 5-8
purse, US$310,000

		SCORES			TOTAL	MONEY
Pedro Martinez	66	70	68	68	272	US$62,000
Tim Herron	72	70	68	64	274	36,000
Eduardo Romero	67	71	70	72	280	24,000
Jorge Berendt	73	69	70	69	281	16,500
Angel Cabrera	71	69	70	71	281	16,500
Ricardo Gonzalez	69	70	72	71	282	12,000
Craig Stadler	69	71	76	67	283	8,750
Philip Jonas	68	71	72	72	283	8,750
Rafael Barcellos	69	70	75	70	284	8,000
Ariel Canete	72	68	72	73	285	7,250
Mathias Gronberg	68	69	71	77	285	7,250
Henrik Nystrom	72	70	74	70	286	6,066.67
Ken Duke	71	74	69	72	286	6,066.67
Rafael Gomez	74	69	69	74	286	6,066.67
Tjaart Van Der Walt	70	75	72	70	287	5,100
Jorge Benedetti	73	72	71	71	287	5,100
Miguel Fernandez	69	74	71	73	287	5,100
Roy MacKenzie	76	71	72	69	288	4,350
Daniel Aguirre	71	72	75	70	288	4,350
Ruben Alvarez	72	74	74	69	289	3,700
Luis Carbonetti	75	73	69	72	289	3,700
Jay Townsend	75	72	69	73	289	3,700
Mark Calcavecchia	71	70	71	77	289	3,700
Mauricio Molina	73	72	74	71	290	2,800
Ron Wuensche	71	74	74	71	290	2,800
Sebastian Fernandez	70	71	78	71	290	2,800
Adan Domingo Sowa	73	71	73	73	290	2,800
Luis Felipe Graf	71	69	77	73	290	2,800
Erik Andersson	75	73	74	70	292	2,100
Tony Aguilar	73	73	73	73	292	2,100

Volvo Masters of Latin America

San Paulo Golf Club, Sao Paulo, Brazil
Par 71; 6,524 yards

December 12-15
purse, US$200,000

		SCORES			TOTAL	MONEY
Angel Cabrera	65	70	67	65	267	US$36,000
Eduardo Romero	72	67	70	61	270	22,800
Cesar Monasterio	67	66	70	69	272	14,400
Danny Mijovic	68	61	72	71	272	14,400
Jorge Berendt	72	70	67	66	275	9,400
Gustavo Rojas	73	68	68	66	275	9,400
Angel Franco	71	69	72	64	276	5,866.67
Ariel Canete	68	69	71	68	276	5,866.67
Pedro Martinez	70	69	67	70	276	5,866.67
Roy MacKenzie	70	70	71	66	277	4,400
Scott Dunlap	71	70	69	67	277	4,400
Philip Jonas	70	67	72	68	277	4,400
Miguel Guzman	69	71	68	70	278	3,600
Guilherme Antunes	69	69	69	71	278	3,600
Acacio Jorge Pedro	68	69	70	71	278	3,600

	SCORES				TOTAL	MONEY
Brad Klapprott	69	68	71	71	279	3,100
Eduardo Caballero	68	69	68	74	279	3,100
Karl Brink	72	70	72	66	280	2,700
Ricardo Montenegro	69	70	70	71	280	2,700
Roberto Coceres	71	68	74	68	281	1,977.14
Henrik Nystrom	71	74	67	69	281	1,977.14
Jeff Schmid	74	69	69	69	281	1,977.14
Raul Fretes	72	71	69	69	281	1,977.14
Eduardo Pesenti	70	71	70	70	281	1,977.14
Miguel Fernandez	70	73	66	72	281	1,977.14
Jay Hunter	71	68	70	72	281	1,977.14
Bruce Bulina	70	72	71	69	282	1,510
Jose Aderbal	72	69	71	70	282	1,510
Ken Duke	68	72	72	70	282	1,510
Tjaart Van Der Walt	68	73	69	72	282	1,510

European Tours

Johnnie Walker Classic

Tanah Merah Country Club, Singapore
Par 36-36–72; 7,001 yards

January 25-28
purse, £600,000

		SCORES			TOTAL	MONEY
Ian Woosnam	69	68	69	66	272	£100,000
Andrew Coltart	69	68	70	65	272	66,660
(Woosnam defeated Coltart on third extra hole.)						
Olle Karlsson	66	69	74	66	275	30,986.67
Paul Curry	68	70	69	68	275	30,986.67
Wayne Riley	70	67	67	71	275	30,986.67
Nam-Sin Park	72	67	72	65	276	15,076.67
Bradley Hughes	66	72	70	68	276	15,076.67
Craig Parry	72	68	67	69	276	15,076.67
Ernie Els	67	67	72	70	276	15,076.67
Anthony Painter	67	70	69	70	276	15,076.67
Fred Couples	68	69	69	70	276	15,076.67
Adam Hunter	69	71	68	69	277	9,970
Paul Eales	69	67	68	73	277	9,970
Darren Clarke	67	70	73	68	278	9,000
Paul McGinley	71	68	69	70	278	9,000
Doug Dunakey	71	68	70	70	279	8,280
Richard Boxall	73	70	65	71	279	8,280
Don Fardon	69	70	71	70	280	7,350
Christian Cevaer	72	70	68	70	280	7,350
John Daly	67	73	69	71	280	7,350
Sven Struver	71	70	68	71	280	7,350
Katsuyoshi Tomori	70	73	70	68	281	6,570
Anthony Gilligan	73	69	69	70	281	6,570
Howard Clark	70	68	71	72	281	6,570
Jean Van de Velde	69	71	69	72	281	6,570
*Chawalit Plaphol	72	69	70	70	281	
Shigenori Mori	74	68	72	68	282	5,940
Russell Claydon	73	67	70	72	282	5,940
Jeff Senior	71	71	68	72	282	5,940
Jeev Milkha Singh	69	73	71	70	283	4,960
Mark Mouland	73	70	71	69	283	4,960
Richard Green	73	69	70	71	283	4,960
Andrew Sherborne	68	74	70	71	283	4,960
Robert Willis	73	65	72	73	283	4,960
Sam Torrance	68	72	70	73	283	4,960
Raymond Burns	73	69	68	73	283	4,960
Isao Aoki	70	68	71	74	283	4,960
David McKenzie	68	70	71	74	283	4,960
Gary Orr	71	72	69	72	284	4,140
Bernhard Langer	68	74	71	71	284	4,140
Peter Senior	69	71	73	71	284	4,140
Jack O'Keefe	70	72	74	68	284	4,140
Terry Price	69	72	72	72	285	3,540
Periasamy Gunasagaran	71	70	72	72	285	3,540
Perry Moss	69	71	73	72	285	3,540
Mike Harwood	71	70	73	71	285	3,540
Gary Nicklaus	71	72	74	68	285	3,540

	SCORES				TOTAL	MONEY
Jay Townsend	68	74	69	74	285	3,540
Sang-Ho Choi	70	69	73	74	286	2,880
Guan-Soon Chua	75	67	71	73	286	2,880
Jim Payne	73	68	73	72	286	2,880
Greg Norman	71	72	73	70	286	2,880
Fredrik Lindgren	71	71	70	74	286	2,880
Zaw Moe	68	70	74	75	287	2,340
David Bransdon	70	71	72	74	287	2,340
Stewart Ginn	70	73	72	72	287	2,340
Robert Allenby	74	68	76	69	287	2,340
Peter Fowler	71	72	71	74	288	1,980
Peter McWhinney	72	70	75	71	288	1,980
Peter O'Malley	72	70	71	76	289	1,800
Lee Westwood	73	70	74	72	289	1,800
Mark Litton	68	75	76	70	289	1,800
Jong-Duck Kim	72	70	71	77	290	1,650
Paul Affleck	69	74	75	72	290	1,650
Michael Jonzon	71	72	76	73	292	1,530
Darren Cole	69	73	78	72	292	1,530
Stephen Ames	68	70	78	77	293	900
Hsieh Chin-Sheng	69	73	74	79	295	897
Dean Robertson	71	72	75	77	295	897

Open Catalonia

Bonmont Course, Tarragona, Spain
Par 36-36–72; 7,050 yards
(Third and fourth rounds cancelled — high winds.)

February 29-March 3
purse, £300,000

	SCORES		TOTAL	MONEY
Paul Lawrie	65	70	135	£50,000
Fernando Roca	66	70	136	33,330
Domingo Hospital	66	71	137	18,780
Emanuele Bolognesi	71	67	138	13,850
Andrew Sherborne	67	71	138	13,850
Juan Carlos Pinero	68	71	139	9,750
Jose Coceres	67	72	139	9,750
David Howell	66	74	140	7,095
Carl Suneson	74	66	140	7,095
Stephen McAllister	72	69	141	5,220
Jose Rivero	69	72	141	5,220
Eduardo Romero	71	70	141	5,220
Miguel Angel Martin	71	70	141	5,220
Richard Green	73	68	141	5,220
Rolf Muntz	72	70	142	3,851.25
David A. Russell	72	70	142	3,851.25
Eric Giraud	72	70	142	3,851.25
Peter Baker	70	72	142	3,851.25
Paul McGinley	72	70	142	3,851.25
Anders Forsbrand	74	68	142	3,851.25
Pedro Linhart	72	70	142	3,851.25
Manuel Pinero	71	71	142	3,851.25
Marcus Wills	69	74	143	3,015
Neal Briggs	72	71	143	3,015
Mats Hallberg	70	73	143	3,015
Santiago Luna	74	69	143	3,015
Mark Plummer	73	70	143	3,015

	SCORES			TOTAL	MONEY
Richard Dinsdale	70	73		143	3,015
Patrik Sjoland	72	71		143	3,015
Manuel Moreno	74	69		143	3,015
Stephen Field	70	74		144	2,313
Gary Emerson	70	74		144	2,313
Ross Drummond	73	71		144	2,313
Francisco Valera	72	72		144	2,313
Andrew Collison	72	72		144	2,313
Padraig Harrington	75	69		144	2,313
Anders Sorensen	71	73		144	2,313
Per Nyman	71	73		144	2,313
Diego Borrego	73	71		144	2,313
Fredrik Lindgren	72	72		144	2,313
Jose Manuel Carriles	74	71		145	1,620
John Bickerton	72	73		145	1,620
Michel Besanceney	72	73		145	1,620
David Williams	70	75		145	1,620
Peter Mitchell	74	71		145	1,620
Max Anglert	75	70		145	1,620
John Mellor	76	69		145	1,620
Emanuele Canonica	71	74		145	1,620
Stuart Cage	73	72		145	1,620
Raphael Jacquelin	74	71		145	1,620
Andrew Oldcorn	71	74		145	1,620
Jose Rozadilla	72	73		145	1,620
Simon Hurley	70	75		145	1,620
Oyvind Rojahn	72	74		146	940
Mike McLean	73	73		146	940
Miles Tunnicliff	72	74		146	940
Philip Walton	75	71		146	940
Juan Quiros	71	75		146	940
Ignacio Feliu	73	73		146	940
David Gilford	70	76		146	940
Derrick Cooper	74	72		146	940
Richard Boxall	76	70		146	940
Paul Way	73	73		146	940
Glenn Ralph	72	74		146	940
Scott Watson	69	77		146	940

Moroccan Open

Royal Golf Rabat, Dar-es-Salam, Morocco
Par 36-36–72; 7,362 yards

March 7-10
purse, £350,000

	SCORES				TOTAL	MONEY
Peter Hedblom	68	67	74	72	281	£58,330
Eduardo Romero	72	74	67	69	282	38,880
Wayne Westner	71	72	72	68	283	19,705
Santiago Luna	73	69	72	69	283	19,705
Costantino Rocca	70	75	69	72	286	12,526.67
Ian Woosnam	72	73	71	70	286	12,526.67
Tony Johnstone	70	73	70	73	286	12,526.67
Mathias Gronberg	75	70	72	71	288	8,750
Stephen Ames	75	70	75	69	289	6,582
Miles Tunnicliff	71	72	74	72	289	6,582
Tim Planchin	74	69	72	74	289	6,582
Peter Mitchell	71	72	71	75	289	6,582

	SCORES				TOTAL	MONEY
Raymond Russell	69	74	70	76	289	6,582
David A. Russell	74	71	70	75	290	4,742.86
Andrew Collison	72	72	74	72	290	4,742.86
John McHenry	70	73	72	75	290	4,742.86
Retief Goosen	71	72	74	73	290	4,742.86
Jose Maria Canizares	75	73	69	73	290	4,742.86
Francis Howley	72	74	74	70	290	4,742.86
Per Nyman	73	73	72	72	290	4,742.86
Jamie Spence	75	73	72	71	291	4,042.50
Russell Claydon	72	74	74	71	291	4,042.50
Mark Mouland	71	73	76	72	292	3,465
Rolf Muntz	74	74	71	73	292	3,465
Angel Cabrera	77	72	70	73	292	3,465
Alexander Cejka	70	71	78	73	292	3,465
Silvio Grappasonni	72	73	70	77	292	3,465
Anders Hansen	76	72	70	74	292	3,465
Padraig Harrington	72	71	73	76	292	3,465
Niclas Fasth	74	74	75	69	292	3,465
Ian Palmer	75	74	71	72	292	3,465
Gordon Brand, Jr.	74	75	72	72	293	2,800
Steven Richardson	73	76	70	74	293	2,800
Paul Affleck	75	69	75	74	293	2,800
Juan Carlos Pinero	75	72	72	74	293	2,800
Darren Clarke	72	73	73	75	293	2,800
Olle Karlsson	75	74	71	74	294	2,380
Mark James	75	72	76	71	294	2,380
Bob May	73	74	73	74	294	2,380
Heinz P. Thul	75	70	75	74	294	2,380
Diego Borrego	77	70	70	77	294	2,380
Thomas Gogele	74	75	73	72	294	2,380
Michel Besanceney	72	71	75	76	294	2,380
Michael Archer	75	74	74	72	295	2,100
Sam Torrance	73	73	74	76	296	1,925
Jose Coceres	70	77	75	74	296	1,925
Alberto Binaghi	76	70	80	70	296	1,925
Liam White	74	74	77	71	296	1,925
Greg Chalmers	74	74	74	75	297	1,540
Nicolas Vanhootegem	75	72	74	76	297	1,540
Anders Forsbrand	71	74	74	78	297	1,540
Philip Walton	73	74	75	75	297	1,540
David J. Russell	72	74	73	78	297	1,540
John Mellor	74	73	71	79	297	1,540
Steven Bottomley	72	72	75	78	297	1,540
Scott Watson	74	73	77	74	298	1,141
Brenden Pappas	73	74	74	77	298	1,141
Paul R. Simpson	72	75	76	75	298	1,141
Phillip Price	71	68	76	83	298	1,141
Eric Giraud	73	74	79	72	298	1,141
Per Haugsrud	73	76	78	72	299	980
Mohamed Makroune	75	73	76	75	299	980
Neal Briggs	73	75	79	72	299	980
Thomas Bjorn	76	71	73	80	300	645.50
Marcus Wills	74	75	74	77	300	645.50
Gavin Levenson	73	76	76	75	300	645.50
Robert Coles	70	76	78	76	300	645.50
Joakim Gronhagen	69	78	75	78	300	645.50
Stephen Gallagher	74	75	74	77	300	645.50
Marc Farry	69	75	79	78	301	517
Brian Marchbank	74	75	79	74	302	515
Gordon J. Brand	73	73	75	83	304	513

Dubai Desert Classic

Emirates Golf Club, Dubai, United Arab Emirates
Par 35-37–72; 7,102 yards

March 14-17
purse, £650,000

	SCORES				TOTAL	MONEY
Colin Montgomerie	67	68	67	68	270	£108,330
Miguel Angel Jimenez	63	68	70	70	271	72,210
Robert Willis	69	67	70	68	274	40,690
Fred Couples	69	69	72	65	275	32,500
Peter Baker	71	67	66	72	276	25,140
Raymond Burns	70	68	65	73	276	25,140
Carl Mason	68	73	70	66	277	15,815
Thomas Bjorn	70	71	67	69	277	15,815
Ian Woosnam	69	69	65	74	277	15,815
Jay Townsend	64	71	71	71	277	15,815
Russell Claydon	72	69	69	68	278	10,885
Mark Mouland	71	69	72	66	278	10,885
Tony Johnstone	71	66	69	72	278	10,885
Joakim Haeggman	68	72	69	69	278	10,885
Domingo Hospital	69	70	72	68	279	9,355
Stephen Ames	68	72	70	69	279	9,355
David Carter	74	68	71	67	280	8,406.67
Jamie Spence	68	68	70	74	280	8,406.67
Howard Clark	71	69	70	70	280	8,406.67
Eduardo Romero	70	70	69	72	281	7,410
Ignacio Garrido	67	75	69	70	281	7,410
Peter Mitchell	71	70	70	70	281	7,410
Mark Davis	75	65	70	71	281	7,410
Paul Lawrie	67	71	73	70	281	7,410
Niclas Fasth	70	72	72	68	282	6,052.22
Olle Karlsson	69	71	69	73	282	6,052.22
Steven Bottomley	69	73	70	70	282	6,052.22
Francisco Valera	69	71	68	74	282	6,052.22
Peter Fowler	74	67	71	70	282	6,052.22
David Gilford	68	70	71	73	282	6,052.22
Paul Broadhurst	69	69	72	72	282	6,052.22
Gary Evans	71	71	67	73	282	6,052.22
Gary Emerson	72	69	69	72	282	6,052.22
Stuart Cage	70	71	72	70	283	4,875
Gavin Levenson	72	67	71	73	283	4,875
Barry Lane	70	72	69	72	283	4,875
Wayne Riley	70	71	70	72	283	4,875
David Feherty	70	69	73	71	283	4,875
Santiago Luna	73	69	71	70	283	4,875
Paul Affleck	68	74	70	72	284	3,965
Des Smyth	71	70	73	70	284	3,965
Phillip Price	70	71	68	75	284	3,965
Dean Robertson	70	72	70	72	284	3,965
Andrew Oldcorn	68	71	72	73	284	3,965
Raymond Russell	70	70	74	70	284	3,965
David J. Russell	69	73	69	73	284	3,965
Alexander Cejka	69	73	71	71	284	3,965
Fabrice Tarnaud	69	69	79	68	285	3,185
Jonathan Lomas	72	70	72	71	285	3,185
Gordon J. Brand	73	67	72	73	285	3,185
Paul McGinley	69	72	73	71	285	3,185
Dominique Boulet	72	67	73	74	286	2,600
Eamonn Darcy	68	72	73	73	286	2,600
Stephen Field	66	73	73	74	286	2,600

	SCORES				TOTAL	MONEY
Ricky Willison	70	72	72	72	286	2,600
Costantino Rocca	70	71	66	79	286	2,600
Andrew Coltart	71	71	74	71	287	2,101.67
Paul Curry	69	70	75	73	287	2,101.67
Mark James	73	69	75	70	287	2,101.67
Hendrik Buhrmann	69	70	71	78	288	1,950
Mats Lanner	71	71	72	75	289	1,885
Martin Gates	69	72	73	76	290	1,755
Christian Cevaer	68	72	75	75	290	1,755
Robert Karlsson	72	70	78	70	290	1,755
Roger Wessels	70	68	78	75	291	1,300
Fredrik Lindgren	71	70	78	72	291	1,300
Seve Ballesteros	71	70	74	77	292	972
Simon Hurley	69	72	76	75	292	972

Portuguese Open

Aroeira, Lisbon, Portugal
Par 35-36–71; 6,661 yards

March 21-24
purse, £325,000

	SCORES				TOTAL	MONEY
Wayne Riley	65	67	69	70	271	£54,160
Mark Davis	72	68	66	67	273	28,225
Martin Gates	68	70	65	70	273	28,225
Barry Lane	70	71	71	63	275	15,007.50
Joakim Haeggman	67	72	68	68	275	15,007.50
Jose Coceres	67	68	71	70	276	11,375
Klas Eriksson	63	73	73	68	277	7,522
Jamie Spence	72	66	71	68	277	7,522
Jean Van de Velde	74	65	70	68	277	7,522
Jose Rivero	71	68	69	69	277	7,522
Miles Tunnicliff	75	66	67	69	277	7,522
Marcus Wills	73	69	69	67	278	5,410
Andrew Sherborne	72	69	69	68	278	5,410
Ricky Willison	66	73	71	69	279	4,775
Des Smyth	68	73	68	70	279	4,775
Neal Briggs	72	69	68	70	279	4,775
Paul Lawrie	72	69	70	69	280	4,126.25
Miguel Angel Jimenez	71	71	68	70	280	4,126.25
Michael Jonzon	72	72	65	71	280	4,126.25
Olle Karlsson	68	69	66	77	280	4,126.25
Steven Bottomley	71	73	69	68	281	3,550
Raymond Russell	74	69	70	68	281	3,550
Russell Claydon	66	72	73	70	281	3,550
Gary Emerson	73	70	68	70	281	3,550
Pedro Linhart	68	72	70	71	281	3,550
Diego Borrego	67	71	70	73	281	3,550
Mark Mouland	75	69	72	66	282	2,915
Peter Mitchell	71	72	69	70	282	2,915
Paul Way	72	70	69	71	282	2,915
David Feherty	70	69	71	72	282	2,915
Stuart Cage	71	70	69	72	282	2,915
Greg Chalmers	69	70	70	73	282	2,915
David Carter	71	71	65	75	282	2,915
Jarmo Sandelin	72	72	70	69	283	2,475
Mark Roe	70	70	71	72	283	2,475
Per-Ulrik Johansson	71	70	70	72	283	2,475

	SCORES				TOTAL	MONEY
Tony Johnstone	69	72	70	72	283	2,475
Alexander Cejka	72	71	67	73	283	2,475
Rolf Muntz	69	75	69	71	284	2,117.50
Paul Affleck	70	74	70	70	284	2,117.50
Gary Orr	74	69	71	70	284	2,117.50
Jim Payne	69	74	69	72	284	2,117.50
Andrew Coltart	70	72	69	73	284	2,117.50
Jay Townsend	69	68	72	75	284	2,117.50
Retief Goosen	72	72	69	72	285	1,695
Padraig Harrington	72	69	72	72	285	1,695
Christian Cevaer	70	73	71	71	285	1,695
Carl Mason	74	70	71	70	285	1,695
Per Nyman	72	68	75	70	285	1,695
Daniel Silva	67	74	71	73	285	1,695
Santiago Luna	71	72	69	73	285	1,695
Francis Howley	72	70	71	73	286	1,370
Angel Cabrera	71	72	72	71	286	1,370
Fredrik Lindgren	68	72	77	69	286	1,370
Gary Clark	73	71	71	72	287	1,116
Paul McGinley	75	69	72	71	287	1,116
Mike McLean	68	73	75	71	287	1,116
Richard Dinsdale	70	70	76	71	287	1,116
Patrik Sjoland	68	72	76	71	287	1,116
Richard Boxall	70	72	72	74	288	915
Lee Westwood	70	71	74	73	288	915
John Bickerton	72	71	73	72	288	915
Mathias Gronberg	68	73	71	76	288	915
Thomas Gogele	69	70	72	77	288	915
Per Haugsrud	67	70	76	76	289	570
Hendrik Buhrmann	71	71	72	75	289	570
Ross Drummond	71	70	76	72	289	570
Andrew Collison	72	69	76	72	289	570
Stephen Gallacher	72	70	71	77	290	479
Peter Baker	71	69	73	77	290	479
Stephen Field	73	70	71	76	290	479
Dean Robertson	70	72	72	77	291	474
Chris Hall	70	74	71	76	291	474
Fernando Roca	76	68	72	76	292	470
Stephen McAllister	71	73	74	74	292	470
Iain Pyman	71	73	75	75	294	467
Ronan Rafferty	68	76	73	78	295	465
Michel Besanceney	68	73	79	77	297	463
Gary Evans	71	73	76	WD		

Madeira Island Open

Madeira Golf Club, Madeira, Spain
Par 36-36–72; 6,606 yards

March 28-31
purse, £300,000

	SCORES				TOTAL	MONEY
Jarmo Sandelin	72	67	71	69	279	£50,000
Paul Affleck	72	69	73	66	280	33,330
David Carter	71	75	68	67	281	13,196
Des Smyth	73	71	68	69	281	13,196
Peter Mitchell	72	66	73	70	281	13,196
David J. Russell	73	69	69	70	281	13,196
Daniel Chopra	69	66	70	76	281	13,196

	SCORES				TOTAL	MONEY
Iain Pyman	71	74	71	66	282	6,427.50
Carl Suneson	71	70	70	71	282	6,427.50
Diego Borrego	74	67	70	71	282	6,427.50
Phil Golding	69	71	70	72	282	6,427.50
Peter Fowler	72	72	72	67	283	4,448.57
Jean Van de Velde	69	71	74	69	283	4,448.57
Patrik Sjoland	72	68	72	71	283	4,448.57
Thomas Gogele	70	70	71	72	283	4,448.57
Ignacio Garrido	70	70	69	74	283	4,448.57
David Howell	71	69	69	74	283	4,448.57
Andrew Oldcorn	72	65	71	75	283	4,448.57
Raymond Russell	71	74	73	66	284	3,610
Bob May	73	72	70	69	284	3,610
Stephen Ames	72	69	73	70	284	3,610
Vanslow Phillips	72	74	69	70	285	3,285
Jim Payne	70	71	73	71	285	3,285
Andrew Sherborne	72	69	71	73	285	3,285
Jose Coceres	71	73	68	73	285	3,285
Scott Watson	70	73	73	70	286	2,970
Fernando Roca	75	70	72	69	286	2,970
Stephen McAllister	73	67	70	76	286	2,970
David A. Russell	74	69	72	72	287	2,616
David Williams	70	75	70	72	287	2,616
Russell Claydon	72	70	72	73	287	2,616
Ross McFarlane	68	74	70	75	287	2,616
Mark Davis	72	68	70	77	287	2,616
Juan Carlos Pinero	72	72	72	72	288	2,280
Jose Maria Canizares	69	76	72	71	288	2,280
John Hawksworth	69	75	74	70	288	2,280
Ricky Willison	75	69	71	73	288	2,280
Paul Lawrie	71	74	70	73	288	2,280
Manuel Pinero	73	72	71	73	289	1,950
Rolf Muntz	75	71	71	72	289	1,950
Andrew Collison	76	70	75	68	289	1,950
Ove Sellberg	72	73	70	74	289	1,950
Santiago Luna	72	74	69	74	289	1,950
Pedro Linhart	74	71	69	75	289	1,950
Steven Bottomley	75	70	72	73	290	1,680
Jose Garcia	70	76	72	72	290	1,680
David Ray	73	70	70	77	290	1,680
John McHenry	70	73	73	75	291	1,470
Paul Way	71	69	77	74	291	1,470
Padraig Harrington	71	73	70	77	291	1,470
Brian Marchbank	74	71	66	80	291	1,470
Paul Lyons	68	72	76	76	292	1,260
Dean Robertson	74	70	73	75	292	1,260
Anders Haglund	70	73	77	72	292	1,260
Steen Tinning	74	71	72	76	293	1,050
Michel Besanceney	70	72	76	75	293	1,050
Michael Archer	73	69	76	75	293	1,050
Mark Pullan	73	72	75	73	293	1,050
Glenn Ralph	71	72	73	78	294	885
Fabrice Tarnaud	73	72	72	77	294	885
Antonio Sobrinho	72	74	72	76	294	885
Raphael Jacquelin	71	75	73	75	294	885
Stephen Gallacher	69	74	80	72	295	810
Rene Budde	73	72	73	78	296	765
Paul Broadhurst	73	72	75	76	296	765
Chris Hall	73	73	76	75	297	450
Peter Hedblom	75	71	72	80	298	446

	SCORES			TOTAL	MONEY
Tim Planchin	75	70 75	78	298	446
Adam Hunter	71	75 76	76	298	446
Philip Talbot	71	75 74	79	299	442
David Higgins	71	70 85	76	302	440
Christian Post	71	74 82	76	303	438

Air France Cannes Open

Royal Mougins Golf Club, Cannes, France
Par 35-36–71; 6,494 yards

April 18-21
purse, £400,000

	SCORES			TOTAL	MONEY
Raymond Russell	66	68 67	71	272	£66,660
David Carter	70	62 69	73	274	44,440
Ignacio Garrido	67	68 75	66	276	22,520
Gordon Brand, Jr.	72	73 63	68	276	22,520
Costantino Rocca	70	66 72	69	277	15,470
Jim Payne	73	69 68	67	277	15,470
Carl Suneson	73	67 68	70	278	12,000
Paul Broadhurst	70	73 70	66	279	8,232
Rolf Muntz	70	68 72	69	279	8,232
Iain Pyman	70	72 68	69	279	8,232
Padraig Harrington	68	65 72	74	279	8,232
Olivier Edmond	71	68 68	72	279	8,232
David Feherty	72	71 66	71	280	5,896
Peter Hedblom	75	64 70	71	280	5,896
Paul Affleck	71	68 68	73	280	5,896
Jean Van de Velde	72	71 66	71	280	5,896
Greg Turner	71	69 69	71	280	5,896
Ricky Willison	68	73 70	70	281	5,060
Miles Tunnicliff	67	72 67	75	281	5,060
Peter Mitchell	65	71 71	75	282	4,500
Paul McGinley	65	72 71	74	282	4,500
Fernando Roca	64	75 75	68	282	4,500
Mike McLean	72	73 68	69	282	4,500
Gary Orr	71	68 75	68	282	4,500
Paul Eales	71	70 72	69	282	4,500
Barry Lane	70	72 71	70	283	3,780
Stuart Cage	72	67 71	73	283	3,780
Stephen Gallacher	76	66 74	67	283	3,780
Marc Farry	70	69 71	73	283	3,780
Santiago Luna	75	69 72	67	283	3,780
Jon Robson	74	70 73	66	283	3,780
Mark Roe	71	72 68	73	284	3,040
Philip Walton	65	78 70	71	284	3,040
Tim Planchin	67	69 72	76	284	3,040
Silvio Grappasonni	71	70 73	70	284	3,040
Domingo Hospital	68	73 73	70	284	3,040
Darren Clarke	68	75 70	71	284	3,040
Raphael Jacquelin	71	72 68	73	284	3,040
Richard Dinsdale	70	68 74	72	284	3,040
Anssi Kankkonen	70	69 71	74	284	3,040
Michael Jonzon	69	70 72	74	285	2,560
Ignacio Feliu	71	74 70	70	285	2,560
David Gilford	73	68 72	72	285	2,560
Peter Baker	71	72 73	70	286	2,320
Per Haugsrud	74	71 69	72	286	2,320

	SCORES				TOTAL	MONEY
Chris Hall	72	69	69	76	286	2,320
Dean Robertson	71	74	68	74	287	2,000
Neal Briggs	73	69	70	75	287	2,000
Fredrik Lindgren	74	71	72	70	287	2,000
Greg Owen	73	70	68	76	287	2,000
Andrew Collison	71	73	74	69	287	2,000
Russell Claydon	73	70	69	76	288	1,560
Thomas Gogele	72	68	73	75	288	1,560
Jonathan Lomas	75	68	74	71	288	1,560
Jarmo Sandelin	70	69	69	80	288	1,560
Angel Cabrera	73	71	71	73	288	1,560
David Howell	74	69	72	73	288	1,560
Lee Westwood	71	72	77	69	289	1,240
David A. Russell	72	71	71	75	289	1,240
Anders Haglund	75	69	72	73	289	1,240
Roger Chapman	70	72	75	73	290	1,140
Gary Clark	71	68	74	77	290	1,140
Stephen McAllister	73	72	74	72	291	1,040
Wayne Riley	68	75	78	70	291	1,040
Juan Carlos Pinero	71	71	76	73	291	1,040
Fabrice Tarnaud	78	66	71	77	292	599
Quentin Dabson	72	73	74	73	292	599
Per-Ulrik Johansson	71	74	72	76	293	595
Per Nyman	71	70	76	76	293	595
Christian Post	70	74	75	75	293	592
Wayne Westner	75	69	72	79	295	590

Turespana Masters Open

El Saler, Valencia, Spain
Par 36-36–72; 6,950 yards

April 25-28
purse, £500,000

	SCORES				TOTAL	MONEY
Diego Borrego	66	67	69	69	271	£83,330
Tony Johnstone	67	69	66	69	271	55,550
(Borrego defeated Johnstone on third extra hole.)						
Peter Baker	67	70	69	69	275	31,300
Ross McFarlane	66	71	72	67	276	25,000
Fabrice Tarnaud	66	73	70	68	277	21,200
Ignacio Garrido	69	71	68	70	278	17,500
Domingo Hospital	72	71	68	68	279	12,162.50
Stuart Cage	72	71	67	69	279	12,162.50
Padraig Harrington	71	72	66	70	279	12,162.50
Greg Turner	69	68	68	74	279	12,162.50
Roger Chapman	69	73	71	67	280	8,606.67
Costantino Rocca	70	73	69	68	280	8,606.67
Francis Howley	76	64	71	69	280	8,606.67
Robert Karlsson	71	69	73	68	281	7,050
Des Smyth	71	71	70	69	281	7,050
Gary Nicklaus	72	69	70	70	281	7,050
Neal Briggs	67	73	70	71	281	7,050
Sam Torrance	73	68	67	73	281	7,050
Adam Hunter	72	71	72	67	282	5,937.50
Richard Boxall	74	69	69	70	282	5,937.50
Francisco Cea	70	69	71	72	282	5,937.50
Per Haugsrud	70	70	70	72	282	5,937.50
Jose Coceres	72	69	72	70	283	5,100

	SCORES				TOTAL	MONEY
Jim Payne	71	72	71	69	283	5,100
Jarmo Sandelin	74	69	73	67	283	5,100
Andrew Sherborne	68	72	72	71	283	5,100
Fredrik Lindgren	72	68	72	71	283	5,100
Mike McLean	72	70	70	71	283	5,100
Joakim Haeggman	71	70	70	72	283	5,100
*Jose Manuel Lara	76	67	71	69	283	
David Feherty	70	72	71	71	284	3,862.50
Eamonn Darcy	71	73	70	70	284	3,862.50
Paul Lawrie	75	69	70	70	284	3,862.50
Malcolm Mackenzie	73	71	70	70	284	3,862.50
Raymond Burns	68	71	75	70	284	3,862.50
Peter O'Malley	74	69	72	69	284	3,862.50
Mathias Gronberg	71	72	70	71	284	3,862.50
Steve Webster	74	69	70	71	284	3,862.50
Jonathan Lomas	71	71	70	72	284	3,862.50
Carl Suneson	69	71	71	73	284	3,862.50
Wayne Riley	69	67	74	74	284	3,862.50
Raymond Russell	73	70	66	75	284	3,862.50
David Howell	71	68	75	71	285	2,900
Chris Hall	68	75	72	70	285	2,900
Miguel Angel Jimenez	74	70	72	69	285	2,900
Olivier Edmond	74	70	72	69	285	2,900
Santiago Luna	74	70	69	72	285	2,900
Iain Pyman	69	70	71	75	285	2,900
Andrew Coltart	71	67	68	79	285	2,900
Ross Drummond	72	71	72	71	286	2,250
Mark Davis	71	73	73	69	286	2,250
Ronan Rafferty	72	71	75	68	286	2,250
Juan Carlos Pinero	71	69	72	74	286	2,250
David Carter	73	70	69	74	286	2,250
Steven Bottomley	71	70	69	76	286	2,250
Olle Karlsson	68	73	73	73	287	1,710
Angel Cabrera	67	76	73	71	287	1,710
Rolf Muntz	76	67	74	70	287	1,710
Robert Coles	70	73	75	69	287	1,710
Martin Gates	71	69	72	75	287	1,710
Mark Mouland	75	68	73	72	288	1,425
Wayne Westner	69	74	74	71	288	1,425
Gary Emerson	73	69	75	71	288	1,425
Per-Ulrik Johansson	73	71	74	70	288	1,425
Francisco Valera	72	70	72	75	289	1,275
Peter Hedblom	73	71	71	74	289	1,275
Mark Litton	71	69	76	74	290	748
Michel Besanceney	71	72	77	70	290	748
John McHenry	74	70	76	70	290	748
Lee Westwood	71	73	72	75	291	744
*Antonio Pastrana	70	74	78	69	291	
David A. Russell	75	68	78	71	292	742

Conte of Florence Italian Open

Bergamo Golf Club, Bergamo, Italy
Par 36-35–71; 6,609 yards

May 2-5
purse, £511,000

	SCORES				TOTAL	MONEY
Jim Payne	70	71	67	67	275	£85,166.54
Patrik Sjoland	66	71	66	73	276	56,720.92
Jonathan Lomas	72	65	71	69	277	26,401.63
Miguel Angel Jimenez	72	69	63	73	277	26,401.63
Lee Westwood	68	69	65	75	277	26,401.63
Andrew Coltart	70	68	72	68	278	17,884.97
Greg Turner	68	71	71	69	279	13,172.43
Paul Eales	71	69	69	70	279	13,172.43
Eduardo Romero	67	69	70	73	279	13,172.43
Mark Mouland	69	74	74	63	280	8,942.49
David Howell	66	70	75	69	280	8,942.49
Padraig Harrington	72	71	66	71	280	8,942.49
Mathias Gronberg	70	69	69	72	280	8,942.49
Ronan Rafferty	69	72	67	72	280	8,942.49
Mats Hallberg	73	68	73	67	281	6,915.52
David Gilford	72	69	69	71	281	6,915.52
Gary Orr	70	67	72	72	281	6,915.52
Barry Lane	69	71	68	73	281	6,915.52
Sven Struver	68	70	69	74	281	6,915.52
Paul Curry	69	73	72	68	282	5,961.66
Santiago Luna	71	70	70	71	282	5,961.66
Chris Hall	69	74	68	71	282	5,961.66
Emanuele Bolognesi	67	73	70	72	282	5,961.66
Costantino Rocca	66	71	72	73	282	5,961.66
Paul Broadhurst	71	71	71	70	283	5,280.33
Emanuele Canonica	72	70	68	73	283	5,280.33
Alberto Binaghi	68	73	68	74	283	5,280.33
Rolf Muntz	71	73	69	71	284	4,684.16
Sam Torrance	71	69	72	72	284	4,684.16
Daniel Chopra	71	71	70	72	284	4,684.16
Gary Evans	65	70	76	73	284	4,684.16
Ricky Willison	68	72	73	72	285	4,002.83
Angel Cabrera	75	67	74	69	285	4,002.83
Eric Giraud	70	71	72	72	285	4,002.83
Francisco Valera	69	72	71	73	285	4,002.83
Phillip Price	68	71	74	73	286	3,491.83
Jamie Spence	71	73	70	72	286	3,491.83
Terry Price	73	68	73	72	286	3,491.83
Wayne Westner	72	71	72	71	286	3,491.83
Mike McLean	69	70	73	74	286	3,491.83
Andrew Collison	72	71	71	73	287	3,066
Silvio Grappasonni	72	69	74	72	287	3,066
Fabrice Tarnaud	75	69	72	71	287	3,066
David Williams	73	71	69	74	287	3,066
Oyvind Rojahn	68	68	72	79	287	3,066
Thomas Levet	71	70	73	74	287	2,597.58
Dean Robertson	69	74	71	74	288	2,597.58
Tim Planchin	76	68	71	73	288	2,597.58
Andrew Sherborne	70	73	74	71	288	2,597.58
Alberto Croce	68	71	78	71	288	2,597.58
Antoine Lebouc	72	72	74	70	288	2,597.58
Anders Forsbrand	72	71	72	74	289	2,171.75
Silvio Locatelli	70	72	75	72	289	2,171.75
David A. Russell	69	75	73	72	289	2,171.75

	SCORES				TOTAL	MONEY
David Higgins	72	69	76	72	289	2,171.75
Paolo Querici	71	72	72	75	290	1,916.25
Mats Lanner	72	72	77	69	290	1,916.25
Jose Rivero	71	73	71	76	291	1,703.33
Robert Coles	69	75	71	76	291	1,703.33
Miguel Angel Martin	73	68	75	75	291	1,703.33
Juan Carlos Pinero	70	73	71	78	292	1,490.42
Massimo Scarpa	74	70	74	74	292	1,490.42
Manny Zerman	70	74	73	76	293	1,362.66
Jason Widener	71	73	72	78	294	1,277.50
Pedro Linhart	73	70	74	79	296	1,192.33
Adam Mednick	71	72	78	80	301	766

Peugeot Open de Espana

Club de Campo, Madrid, Spain
Par 36-36–72; 6,939 yards

May 9-12
purse, £550,000

	SCORES				TOTAL	MONEY
Padraig Harrington	70	64	67	71	272	£91,660
Gordon Brand, Jr.	70	67	71	68	276	61,100
Rolf Muntz	68	71	70	69	278	34,430
Eduardo Romero	70	71	72	66	279	21,637.50
Sam Torrance	70	71	70	68	279	21,637.50
Mathias Gronberg	69	70	69	71	279	21,637.50
Pedro Linhart	70	68	69	72	279	21,637.50
Robert Allenby	72	70	68	70	280	13,015
Lee Westwood	68	72	72	68	280	13,015
Fabrice Tarnaud	72	70	71	68	281	11,000
Roger Chapman	68	74	70	70	282	8,983
Retief Goosen	74	70	69	69	282	8,983
Miguel Angel Martin	71	70	68	73	282	8,983
Jose Coceres	69	70	71	72	282	8,983
Per Haugsrud	68	69	71	74	282	8,983
Peter Baker	71	71	71	70	283	7,139
Mark Roe	72	70	69	72	283	7,139
Terry Price	70	72	68	73	283	7,139
Stuart Cage	69	72	69	73	283	7,139
Peter O'Malley	67	70	71	75	283	7,139
Jon Robson	70	72	71	71	284	5,857.50
Diego Borrego	71	71	73	69	284	5,857.50
Jean Louis Guepy	73	70	69	72	284	5,857.50
Mark Mouland	73	71	71	69	284	5,857.50
Stephen Ames	71	70	70	73	284	5,857.50
Phil Golding	69	72	73	70	284	5,857.50
Domingo Hospital	72	69	71	72	284	5,857.50
David Carter	70	70	72	72	284	5,857.50
Andrew Coltart	73	69	70	73	285	4,796
Miles Tunnicliff	75	67	70	73	285	4,796
Jean Van de Velde	73	71	69	72	285	4,796
Bob May	71	68	76	70	285	4,796
Silvio Grappasonni	71	68	72	74	285	4,796
Richard Boxall	73	71	72	70	286	4,290
Emanuele Canonica	69	71	75	71	286	4,290
Eamonn Darcy	68	70	73	75	286	4,290
Stephen Gallacher	71	71	75	70	287	3,685
Marc Farry	72	71	74	70	287	3,685
Derrick Cooper	70	73	70	74	287	3,685

	SCORES				TOTAL	MONEY
Antoine Lebouc	72	71	72	72	287	3,685
Juan Carlos Pinero	72	71	75	69	287	3,685
Manuel Pinero	73	71	72	71	287	3,685
Mike Harwood	71	70	77	69	287	3,685
Glenn Ralph	71	70	73	73	287	3,685
Phillip Price	71	73	72	72	288	3,025
Ignacio Feliu	71	73	73	71	288	3,025
Andrew Sherborne	69	72	72	75	288	3,025
Miguel Angel Jimenez	73	67	75	73	288	3,025
Seve Ballesteros	72	70	76	71	289	2,475
Santiago Luna	70	72	76	71	289	2,475
Gary Evans	72	72	73	72	289	2,475
Robert Coles	73	71	71	74	289	2,475
Gary Orr	69	72	76	72	289	2,475
Marcus Wills	67	70	75	77	289	2,475
*Sergio Garcia	68	73	73	75	289	
Thomas Bjorn	69	72	75	74	290	1,881
Christian Post	71	72	77	70	290	1,881
Michael Campbell	73	71	73	73	290	1,881
Max Anglert	70	71	74	75	290	1,881
Jarmo Sandelin	70	70	76	74	290	1,881
Iain Pyman	66	77	73	75	291	1,622.50
Russell Claydon	71	70	80	70	291	1,622.50
Angel Cabrera	69	72	76	75	292	1,512.50
Ignacio Garrido	71	70	72	79	292	1,512.50
Anders Hansen	74	70	76	73	293	1,402.50
Mark Litton	71	68	75	79	293	1,402.50
Gary Clark	69	72	78	75	294	825
Paul Eales	68	74	76	77	295	823
*Jose Manuel Lara	72	69	79	76	296	
Hendrik Buhrmann	72	71	75	79	297	821
Emanuele Bolognesi	71	72	78	77	298	818
Darren Clarke	74	70	76	78	298	818

Benson and Hedges International Open

Oxfordshire Golf Club, Thame, Oxon, England
Par 36-36–72; 7,205 yards

May 16-19
purse, £700,000

	SCORES				TOTAL	MONEY
Stephen Ames	73	71	67	72	283	£116,660
Jon Robson	70	70	71	73	284	77,770
Derrick Copper	71	70	70	74	285	43,820
Andrew Coltart	77	67	68	75	287	32,320
Ross Drummond	73	69	70	75	287	32,320
Miguel Angel Jimenez	68	70	74	76	288	21,000
Wayne Riley	73	71	67	77	288	21,000
Paul Lawrie	71	71	73	73	288	21,000
Colin Montgomerie	72	68	67	84	291	14,163.33
Pierre Fulke	74	71	68	78	291	14,163.33
Stuart Cage	73	70	71	77	291	14,163.33
Richard Boxall	76	72	70	74	292	10,836
Bernhard Langer	69	71	73	79	292	10,336
Sam Torrance	71	72	72	77	292	10,836
Ian Woosnam	72	70	68	82	292	10,836
Nick Faldo	70	73	69	80	292	10,836
Joakim Haeggman	72	76	69	76	293	9,450
Eduardo Romero	75	72	71	76	294	8,456

	SCORES				TOTAL	MONEY
Retief Goosen	75	72	69	78	294	8,456
John Bickerton	74	73	72	75	294	8,456
Fabrice Tarnaud	75	71	73	75	294	8,456
Robert Allenby	74	72	70	78	294	8,456
Roger Chapman	71	76	69	79	295	7,560
Gary Orr	73	74	74	74	295	7,560
David Carter	73	73	73	76	295	7,560
Rolf Muntz	73	74	76	73	296	6,510
Peter Baker	69	74	75	78	296	6,510
Paul Moloney	72	74	69	81	296	6,510
Martin Gates	71	76	72	77	296	6,510
Wayne Westner	72	70	74	80	296	6,510
Seve Ballesteros	75	73	71	77	296	6,510
Jose Rivero	75	73	72	76	296	6,510
Paul Affleck	72	74	70	81	297	5,600
Roger Wessels	73	72	69	83	297	5,600
Mike Harwood	73	75	69	80	297	5,600
Paul Eales	74	73	70	81	298	4,970
Sandy Lyle	74	73	75	76	298	4,970
Howard Clark	69	73	75	81	298	4,970
Tim Planchin	74	74	71	79	298	4,970
Pedro Linhart	71	73	74	80	298	4,970
Marc Farry	78	68	72	80	298	4,970
Frank Nobilo	75	71	72	82	300	4,340
Barry Lane	76	72	73	79	300	4,340
Malcolm Mackenzie	72	72	75	81	300	4,340
Ignacio Garrido	71	77	73	80	301	3,850
Peter Hedblom	76	71	75	79	301	3,850
Jamie Spence	72	73	76	80	301	3,850
Fredrik Lindgren	74	72	73	82	301	3,850
Thomas Levet	77	70	73	82	302	3,290
Greg Tuner	72	75	75	80	302	3,290
Gary Evans	75	73	74	80	302	3,290
Olle Karlsson	72	72	75	83	302	3,290
Andrew Sherborne	72	76	73	82	303	2,940
Mats Lanner	75	72	74	83	304	2,590
Stephen Field	74	73	75	82	304	2,590
Jeff Hawkes	76	71	72	85	304	2,590
Emanuele Canonica	70	73	77	84	304	2,590
Ronan Rafferty	70	71	76	88	305	2,240
Mark Mouland	72	76	73	85	306	2,065
Timothy Spence	74	74	77	81	306	2,065
Klas Eriksson	73	74	75	84	306	2,065
Jean Van de Velde	69	77	71	89	306	2,065
Lee Westwood	74	73	75	85	307	1,890
Francisco Valera	72	76	74	87	309	1,820
Adam Hunter	73	73	78	88	312	1,750

Volvo PGA Championship

Wentworth Club, Surrey, England
Par 35-37–72; 6,957 yards

May 24-27
purse, £1,000,000

	SCORES				TOTAL	MONEY
Costantino Rocca	69	67	69	69	274	£166,660
Nick Faldo	67	69	72	68	276	86,850
Paul Lawrie	73	65	68	70	276	86,850
Jarmo Sandelin	70	69	72	67	278	42,466.67

	SCORES			TOTAL	MONEY
Mark McNulty	68 68 69 73			278	42,466.67
Andrew Sherborne	74 69 70 65			278	42,466.67
Gary Orr	71 67 72 69			279	25,766.67
Colin Montgomerie	73 68 69 69			279	25,766.67
Patrik Sjoland	74 67 72 66			279	25,766.67
Eduardo Romero	71 69 68 72			280	20,000
Ian Woosnam	73 70 68 70			281	17,780
Lee Westwood	73 70 69 69			281	17,780
Tony Johnstone	71 72 71 68			282	13,872.50
Stephen Ames	73 69 74 66			282	13,872.50
Eamonn Darcy	70 69 71 72			282	13,872.50
Paul Curry	68 71 69 74			282	13,872.50
Mark Litton	74 68 68 72			282	13,872.50
Mathias Gronberg	71 71 72 68			282	13,872.50
Andrew Coltart	71 72 71 68			282	13,872.50
Padraig Harrington	71 71 72 68			282	13,872.50
Jesper Parnevik	74 70 70 69			283	10,500
Alexander Cejka	71 69 71 72			283	10,500
Retief Goosen	73 71 69 70			283	10,500
Paul Eales	70 69 73 71			283	10,500
Fabrice Tarnaud	72 67 70 74			283	10,500
Paul Way	71 71 69 72			283	10,500
Miguel Ángel Jimenez	72 66 71 74			283	10,500
Steve Webster	71 73 70 69			283	10,500
Wayne Riley	75 69 70 69			283	10,500
David Gilford	71 71 70 72			284	8,242.86
Jose Maria Canizares	70 69 73 72			284	8,242.86
Mark James	72 71 73 68			284	8,242.86
Jean Van de Velde	71 70 73 70			284	8,242.86
Jose Rivero	71 70 70 73			284	8,242.86
Ross McFarlane	72 68 75 69			284	8,242.86
Niclas Fasth	70 69 74 71			284	8,242.86
Phillip Price	75 67 71 72			285	7,100
Gordon Brand, Jr.	70 72 71 72			285	7,100
Paul McGinley	73 69 69 74			285	7,100
Steven Bottomley	74 68 72 71			285	7,100
Jon Robson	71 72 74 69			286	6,200
Mark Roe	73 69 72 72			286	6,200
David Feherty	73 70 72 71			286	6,200
Roger Chapman	71 67 76 72			286	6,200
Stuart Cage	70 72 74 70			286	6,200
David Carter	71 69 71 76			287	4,900
Philip Walton	75 67 73 72			287	4,900
Paul Broadhurst	74 69 71 73			287	4,900
Greg Turner	72 69 73 73			287	4,900
Sam Torrance	71 72 71 73			287	4,900
Richard Boxall	71 72 74 70			287	4,900
Roger Wessels	73 70 72 72			287	4,900
Gary Emerson	72 69 71 75			287	4,900
Robert Allenby	69 68 75 76			288	3,800
Christy O'Connor, Jr.	74 69 75 70			288	3,800
Steen Tinning	71 73 75 69			288	3,800
Gordon Sherry	73 71 71 74			289	3,233.33
Peter O'Malley	72 71 73 73			289	3,233.33
Chris Hall	75 69 73 72			289	3,233.33
Marc Farry	74 70 72 74			290	2,750
Steven Richardson	75 69 71 75			290	2,750
Rodger Davis	70 73 76 71			290	2,750
Derrick Cooper	72 70 73 75			290	2,750
Ged Furey	76 67 75 72			290	2,750

	SCORES				TOTAL	MONEY
Raymond Burns	72	71	77	70	290	2,750
Wayne Westner	70	71	75	75	291	1,498
Olle Karlsson	71	70	76	74	291	1,498
Domingo Hospital	71	71	74	75	291	1,498
Pierre Fulke	72	72	75	73	292	1,493
Andrew Oldcorn	72	69	73	78	292	1,493
Peter Mitchell	72	72	74	75	293	1,490

Deutsche Bank Open–TPC of Europe

Gut Kaden, Hamburg, Germany
Par 36-36–72; 7,029 yards

May 30-June 2
purse, £725,000

	SCORES				TOTAL	MONEY
Frank Nobilo	65	69	72	64	270	£120,830
Colin Montgomerie	71	65	69	66	271	80,550
Darren Clarke	70	67	67	70	274	45,400
Peter Mitchell	69	70	71	65	275	30,788.33
Retief Goosen	68	67	70	70	275	30,788.33
Jamie Spence	68	69	70	68	275	30,788.33
Wayne Riley	67	71	71	67	276	16,791
Francisco Valera	68	72	70	66	276	16,791
Robert Allenby	66	70	69	71	276	16,791
Stephen Ames	68	68	71	69	276	16,791
Paul McGinley	68	71	68	69	276	16,791
Michael Jonzon	67	75	66	69	277	11,743.33
Seve Ballesteros	70	70	66	71	277	11,743.33
Carl Suneson	73	67	68	69	277	11,743.33
Per Haugsrud	71	69	67	71	278	10,213.33
Bernhard Langer	66	70	74	68	278	10,213.33
Gary Orr	70	66	69	73	278	10,213.33
Ross McFarlane	69	72	68	70	279	8,065.45
Olle Karlsson	69	69	72	69	279	8,065.45
Paul Broadhurst	69	70	72	68	279	8,065.45
Richard Boxall	66	70	71	72	279	8,065.45
Costantino Rocca	72	68	67	72	279	8,065.45
Anders Forsbrand	69	68	71	71	279	8,065.45
Jim Payne	70	71	69	69	279	8,065.45
Mike Harwood	68	69	69	73	279	8,065.45
Russell Claydon	71	70	71	67	279	8,065.45
Miguel Angel Martin	68	68	68	75	279	8,065.45
Thomas Bjorn	70	69	71	69	279	8,065.45
Mark Davis	70	68	72	70	280	6,207.50
Ian Woosnam	72	68	72	68	280	6,207.50
Miguel Angel Jimenez	68	72	67	73	280	6,207.50
Fernando Roca	68	72	72	68	280	6,207.50
Peter Baker	68	71	68	73	280	6,207.50
Stephen McAllister	70	66	73	71	280	6,207.50
Greg Turner	68	71	72	70	281	5,335
Jose Coceres	67	71	71	72	281	5,335
David Williams	72	70	68	71	281	5,335
Michael Campbell	69	69	74	69	281	5,335
Terry Price	68	73	70	70	281	5,335
Mark Mouland	69	73	71	69	282	4,682.50
Eduardo Romero	71	69	71	71	282	4,682.50
Mark McNulty	70	71	72	69	282	4,682.50
Gary Evans	69	70	71	72	282	4,682.50
Stephen Gallacher	69	73	72	69	283	3,620

	SCORES				TOTAL	MONEY
Miles Tunnicliff	72	70	71	70	283	3,620
Alexander Cejka	71	68	71	73	283	3,620
Dean Robertson	72	68	71	72	283	3,620
Daniel Chopra	67	71	76	69	283	3,620
Juan Carlos Pinero	69	69	74	71	283	3,620
Eric Giraud	67	73	72	71	283	3,620
Gary Clark	69	70	73	71	283	3,620
Gary Emerson	73	69	70	71	283	3,620
Thomas Gogele	71	68	73	71	283	3,620
Malcolm Mackenzie	67	69	74	73	283	3,620
Steen Tinning	70	69	74	71	284	2,336.67
Ross Drummond	70	72	71	71	284	2,336.67
Lee Westwood	66	75	71	72	284	2,336.67
Domingo Hospital	70	71	73	70	284	2,336.67
Greg Chalmers	68	73	71	72	284	2,336.67
Paul Moloney	72	70	71	71	284	2,336.67
Mark Roe	68	74	71	71	284	2,336.67
Christian Cevaer	72	69	73	70	284	2,336.67
Per Nyman	66	76	70	72	284	2,336.67
Simon Brown	70	72	73	70	285	1,413
Gordon Brand, Jr.	72	70	72	71	285	1,413
Ricky Willison	72	70	71	72	285	1,413
Chris Hall	68	72	71	74	285	1,413
Jarmo Sandelin	66	76	77	66	285	1,413
Adam Hunter	71	71	71	73	286	1,079
Niclas Fasth	67	75	74	70	286	1,079
Mats Hallberg	71	71	72	72	286	1,079
Stephen Field	71	71	75	70	287	1,075
Oyvind Rojahn	66	72	81	73	292	1,073
Michael Welch	69	71	78	75	293	1,071

Alamo English Open

Marriott Forest of Arden Hotel & Country Club,
Warwickshire, England
Par 36-36–72; 7,102 yards

June 6-9
purse, £650,000

	SCORES				TOTAL	MONEY
Robert Allenby	69	71	69	69	278	£108,330
Colin Montgomerie	75	68	68	68	279	56,450
Ross McFarlane	69	71	70	69	279	56,450
Peter Mitchell	70	68	73	72	283	27,593.33
Darren Clarke	71	73	69	70	283	27,593.33
Per-Ulrik Johansson	72	69	72	70	283	27,593.33
Andrew Oldcorn	66	71	73	74	284	16,753.33
Anssi Kankkonen	72	72	69	71	284	16,753.33
Miles Tunnicliff	76	69	69	70	284	16,753.33
Hendrik Buhrmann	72	70	75	68	285	12,480
Joakim Haeggman	72	72	70	71	285	12,480
Michael Welch	72	69	72	73	286	9,635.71
Greg Turner	76	68	70	72	286	9,635.71
Retief Goosen	74	69	68	75	286	9,635.71
Thomas Bjorn	72	70	69	75	286	9,635.71
Phillip Price	75	67	76	68	286	9,635.71
Mike Harwood	71	73	71	71	286	9,635.71
Robert Coles	76	69	73	68	286	9,635.71
Steve Webster	72	68	73	74	287	7,618

	SCORES				TOTAL	MONEY
Chris Hall	68	76	71	72	287	7,618
Philip Walton	73	71	73	70	287	7,618
Jim Payne	73	69	72	73	287	7,618
Niclas Fasth	71	72	69	75	287	7,618
Mark Davis	70	73	72	73	288	6,435
Domingo Hospital	70	71	72	75	288	6,435
David Gilford	73	73	73	69	288	6,435
David Carter	75	71	74	68	288	6,435
Steen Tinning	70	68	75	75	288	6,435
Gary Evans	73	70	75	70	288	6,435
Eric Giraud	71	70	76	71	288	6,435
Richard Dinsdale	76	66	71	76	289	5,557.50
Michael Campbell	71	73	72	73	289	5,557.50
Dean Robertson	73	71	76	70	290	4,940
Pierre Fulke	70	70	74	76	290	4,940
Joe Higgins	72	70	76	72	290	4,940
Stephen Ames	72	71	75	72	290	4,940
Mats Lanner	74	72	72	72	290	4,940
Michel Besanceney	70	69	76	75	290	4,940
Jose Maria Canizares	73	73	74	70	290	4,940
Mathias Gronberg	71	74	74	72	291	4,225
Malcolm Mackenzie	72	72	71	76	291	4,225
Raymond Russell	71	72	74	74	291	4,225
Paul Affleck	67	74	76	74	291	4,225
Roger Wessels	73	71	77	71	292	3,380
Mark Roe	73	73	73	73	292	3,380
Ricky Willison	69	72	72	79	292	3,380
Paul McGinley	69	73	75	75	292	3,380
Tony Johnstone	74	71	72	75	292	3,380
Raymond Burns	69	73	77	73	292	3,380
Mike McLean	74	69	72	77	292	3,380
Jon Robson	70	73	74	75	292	3,380
Phil Golding	74	72	75	71	292	3,380
Gary Emerson	76	69	77	71	293	2,535
Mark James	74	67	75	77	293	2,535
Ross Drummond	75	71	76	71	293	2,535
Angel Cabrera	75	69	75	74	293	2,535
Paul Curry	74	72	72	76	294	2,063.75
Barry Lane	73	73	71	77	294	2,063.75
Derrick Cooper	70	76	76	72	294	2,063.75
Olle Karlsson	78	67	73	76	294	2,063.75
Silvio Grappasonni	73	72	73	77	295	1,755
Andrew Sherborne	70	75	73	77	295	1,755
Russell Claydon	72	71	76	76	295	1,755
Jay Townsend	69	76	74	76	295	1,755
Miguel Angel Martin	70	76	77	72	295	1,755
Iain Pyman	70	72	75	79	296	972
David A. Russell	73	71	77	75	296	972
Fernando Roca	72	73	75	76	296	972
Fredrik Lindgren	76	70	70	80	296	972
Antoine Lebouc	74	72	80	71	297	966
Greg Chalmers	72	74	71	80	297	966
Per Haugsrud	74	72	80	72	298	960
Michael Jonzon	72	69	79	78	298	960
Thomas Gogele	69	77	79	73	298	960
Mark Mouland	73	68	82	75	298	960
Richard Boxall	74	72	75	78	299	955
Jeff Hawkes	77	69	80	75	301	953
Marc Farry	71	74	72	85	302	951

Slaley Hall Northumberland Challenge

Slaley Hall Golf Club, Hexham, England
Par 36-36–72; 7,003 yards

June 13-16
purse, £300,000

	SCORES				TOTAL	MONEY
Retief Goosen	66	69	70	72	277	£50,000
Ross Drummond	74	71	69	65	279	33,330
Robert Lee	71	71	67	72	281	18,780
Heinz P. Thul	72	69	72	70	283	11,800
Gary Evans	72	71	70	70	283	11,800
Andrew Oldcorn	71	69	71	72	283	11,800
David Howell	69	72	72	70	283	11,800
Paul Way	74	72	69	69	284	7,500
Padraig Harrington	70	71	72	72	285	6,070
Jamie Spence	73	74	69	69	285	6,070
John Bickerton	72	72	72	69	285	6,070
Ross McFarlane	77	66	72	71	286	4,644
Peter Mitchell	74	71	71	70	286	4,644
Paul McGinley	74	73	70	69	286	4,644
Rene Budde	72	75	70	69	286	4,644
John Mellor	79	68	69	70	286	4,644
Andrew Coltart	75	70	69	73	287	3,880
Angel Cabrera	75	71	66	75	287	3,880
Gary Clark	72	75	72	68	287	3,880
David A. Russell	72	76	69	71	288	3,420
Adam Hunter	69	76	72	71	288	3,420
Stephen Dodd	71	70	76	71	288	3,420
Michel Besanceney	74	70	75	69	288	3,420
Juan Carlos Pinero	68	75	71	74	288	3,420
Lee Westwood	70	71	74	74	289	3,015
Paul Broadhurst	71	75	73	70	289	3,015
Roger Chapman	77	68	73	71	289	3,015
Hendrik Buhrmann	70	70	75	74	289	3,015
Andrew Beal	76	72	71	71	290	2,655
Patrik Sjoland	72	74	71	73	290	2,655
David J. Russell	73	72	75	70	290	2,655
Magnus Persson	72	76	72	70	290	2,655
Michael Ure	70	77	72	72	291	2,400
Christian Post	75	71	71	74	291	2,400
Miles Tunnicliff	70	73	75	73	291	2,400
Jon Robson	71	73	76	72	292	2,070
Malcolm Mackenzie	71	72	78	71	292	2,070
John Hawksworth	75	71	70	76	292	2,070
Gordon J. Brand	69	72	77	74	292	2,070
Glenn Ralph	72	74	72	74	292	2,070
Richard Dinsdale	72	70	76	74	292	2,070
Mark Plummer	71	74	73	74	292	2,070
Ged Furey	73	72	73	74	292	2,070
Anders Hansen	73	73	75	72	293	1,680
David Lynn	76	72	72	73	293	1,680
Mike Clayton	76	69	76	72	293	1,680
Per Nyman	73	71	74	75	293	1,680
David R. Jones	73	73	72	75	293	1,680
Michael Archer	74	73	73	74	294	1,410
Howard Clark	76	71	76	71	294	1,410
David Higgins	73	75	72	74	294	1,410
Chris Hall	72	76	68	78	294	1,410
Anthony Painter	75	72	73	75	295	1,110
Jeremy Robinson	72	74	77	72	295	1,110

	SCORES				TOTAL	MONEY
Steven Bottomley	71	76	74	74	295	1,110
Peter Fowler	74	74	73	74	295	1,110
Max Anglert	72	72	73	78	295	1,110
Jason Widener	74	73	74	74	295	1,110
Carl Suneson	77	67	79	73	296	915
Tim Planchin	73	73	70	80	296	915
Carl Mason	74	70	78	75	297	840
George Ryall	74	72	79	72	297	840
Daniel Chopra	72	75	74	76	297	840
Anssi Kankkonen	74	72	77	75	298	660
Anders Sorensen	75	73	70	80	298	660
Derrick Cooper	74	73	77	74	298	660
Neal Briggs	74	73	81	75	303	448
Ian Spencer	78	69	77	80	304	446
*Anthony McLure	72	76	77	80	305	

BMW International Open

St. Eurach Land & Country Club, Munich, Germany
Par 37-35–72; 7,035 yards
(Third and fourth rounds cancelled — rain.)

June 20-23
purse, £525,000

	SCORES		TOTAL	MONEY
Marc Farry	65	67	132	£87,495
Richard Green	67	66	133	50,327.50
Russell Claydon	69	65	134	27,115
Padraig Harrington	68	66	134	27,115
David Higgins	64	70	134	27,115
Francisco Cea	70	65	135	15,750
Raymond Russell	69	66	135	15,750
Ignacio Garrido	67	68	135	15,750
Phil Golding	65	71	136	10,622.50
Gary Clark	72	64	136	10,622.50
Mathias Gronberg	67	69	136	10,622.50
Pierre Fulke	75	62	137	8,308.13
Fabrice Tarnaud	69	68	137	8,308.13
Francis Howley	69	68	137	8,308.13
Lee Westwood	65	72	137	8,308.13
David Howell	70	68	138	6,503.44
Mats Hallberg	70	68	138	6,503.44
David Gilford	67	71	138	6,503.44
Bernhard Langer	69	69	138	6,503.44
Mark Mouland	67	71	138	6,503.44
Marcus Wills	66	72	138	6,503.44
Alexander Cejka	70	68	138	6,503.44
Emanuele Canonica	68	70	138	6,503.44
John Bickerton	70	69	139	5,197.50
Patrik Sjoland	70	69	139	5,197.50
Mark Litton	73	66	139	5,197.50
Miles Tunnicliff	69	70	139	5,197.50
Peter Fowler	71	68	139	5,197.50
Richard Dinsdale	70	69	139	5,197.50
Stephen McAllister	69	70	139	5,197.50
Frank Nobilo	73	67	140	3,889.04
Mark McNulty	72	68	140	3,889.04
Mark James	67	73	140	3,889.04
Ignacio Feliu	71	69	140	3,889.04

	SCORES			TOTAL	MONEY
Daniel Chopra	69	71		140	3,889.04
Peter Baker	68	72		140	3,889.04
Jim Payne	71	69		140	3,889.04
Emanuele Bolognesi	69	71		140	3,889.04
Tim Planchin	67	73		140	3,889.04
Jeremy Robinson	70	70		140	3,889.04
David Williams	72	68		140	3,889.04
Chris Hall	71	69		140	3,889.04
John Mellor	70	70		140	3,889.04
Carl Suneson	70	71		141	2,782.50
Malcolm Mackenzie	69	72		141	2,782.50
David Carter	71	70		141	2,782.50
Mark Roe	69	72		141	2,782.50
Seve Ballesteros	71	70		141	2,782.50
Ronan Rafferty	69	72		141	2,782.50
Pedro Linhart	72	69		141	2,782.50
Angel Cabrera	69	72		141	2,762.50
Scott Watson	70	72		142	1,669.50
Paul Eales	70	72		142	1,669.50
Gordon Brand, Jr.	73	69		142	1,669.50
Heinz P. Thul	73	69		142	1,669.50
Christian Cevaer	74	68		142	1,669.50
Thomas Bjorn	72	70		142	1,669.50
Domingo Hospital	71	71		142	1,669.50
Darren Clarke	71	71		142	1,669.50
Robert Allenby	74	68		142	1,669.50
Raymond Burns	70	72		142	1,669.50
Antoine Lebouc	74	68		142	1,669.50
Eric Giraud	73	69		142	1,669.50
Per Haugsrud	71	71		142	1,669.50
Jeff Cranford	70	72		142	1,669.50
Sven Struver	75	67		142	1,669.50

Peugeot Open de France

National Golf Club, Paris, France
Par 36-36—72; 7,119 yards

June 27-30
purse, £600,000

	SCORES				TOTAL	MONEY
Robert Allenby	70	65	68	69	272	£100,000
Bernhard Langer	69	70	67	66	272	66,660
(Allenby defeated Langer on first extra hole.)						
Retief Goosen	66	68	72	68	274	37,560
Steven Richardson	68	63	71	73	275	27,700
Paul McGinley	70	67	75	63	275	27,700
Lee Westwood	67	68	73	68	276	21,000
Frank Nobilo	67	68	71	71	277	15,480
Greg Turner	66	70	70	71	277	15,480
Paul Broadhurst	70	64	70	73	277	15,480
Philip Walton	67	71	68	72	278	11,106.67
Peter Mitchell	70	70	69	69	278	11,106.67
Miles Tunnicliff	70	70	75	63	278	11,106.67
Gary Orr	70	65	75	69	279	9,410
Raymond Burns	67	66	75	71	279	9,410
Malcolm Mackenzie	71	65	76	68	280	7,960
Per-Ulrik Johansson	68	67	78	67	280	7,960
Gordon Brand, Jr.	67	70	72	71	280	7,960

	SCORES				TOTAL	MONEY
Ronan Rafferty	66	70	74	70	280	7,960
Mark Mouland	70	71	66	73	280	7,960
Sven Struver	69	67	76	68	280	7,960
Andre Bossert	69	72	71	69	281	6,480
Santiago Luna	69	71	72	69	281	6,480
Costantino Rocca	66	72	70	73	281	6,480
Francisco Cea	70	70	74	67	281	6,480
Ian Woosnam	69	65	78	69	281	6,480
Olle Karlsson	70	67	76	68	281	6,480
David Howell	67	70	72	72	281	6,480
Roger Chapman	68	72	74	68	282	5,106.67
Bradley Hughes	74	65	74	69	282	5,106.67
Jose Coceres	70	66	76	70	282	5,106.67
Paul Curry	69	71	72	70	282	5,106.67
Gary Clark	69	68	71	74	282	5,106.67
Sam Torrance	71	68	72	71	282	5,106.67
Wayne Riley	72	69	71	70	282	5,106.67
Miguel Angel Martin	70	70	70	72	282	5,106.67
Thomas Bjorn	66	71	76	69	282	5,106.67
Max Anglert	71	65	78	69	283	4,380
Andrew Coltart	72	66	72	73	283	4,380
Glenn Ralph	71	70	73	70	284	3,900
Richard Green	71	70	72	71	284	3,900
Sandy Lyle	70	70	72	72	284	3,900
Pierre Fulke	68	72	72	72	284	3,900
Joakim Haeggman	70	68	79	67	284	3,900
Bob May	72	68	77	67	284	3,900
Russell Claydon	72	69	70	74	285	3,120
Mark McNulty	73	67	75	70	285	3,120
Jim Payne	71	69	74	71	285	3,120
Klas Eriksson	70	66	74	75	285	3,120
Tim Planchin	71	69	71	74	285	3,120
Eric Giraud	71	68	75	71	285	3,120
Angel Cabrera	70	70	72	73	285	3,120
Daniel Chopra	67	70	72	77	286	2,400
Jay Townsend	71	66	78	71	286	2,400
Ignacio Garrido	71	67	76	72	286	2,400
Mark James	70	70	75	71	286	2,400
Francisco Valera	69	72	73	72	286	2,400
Seve Ballesteros	72	66	71	78	287	2,040
Jon Robson	70	69	75	74	288	1,860
Fredrik Lindgren	72	67	76	73	288	1,860
David Higgins	69	70	76	73	288	1,860
*Christophe Ravetto	68	73	78	69	288	
Francis Howley	73	67	79	70	289	1,710
Eduardo Romero	71	68	78	72	289	1,710
Antoine Lebouc	71	68	78	73	290	1,395
Jean Van de Velde	74	67	78	71	290	1,395
John Bickerton	71	68	80	71	290	1,395
Per Haugsrud	66	71	81	72	290	1,395
Neal Briggs	70	71	78	72	291	898
Gabriel Hjertstedt	73	68	77	74	292	896
Jeff Remesy	67	72	79	76	294	894

Murphy's Irish Open

Druids Glen Golf Club, Dublin, Ireland
Par 35-36–71; 7,025 yards

July 4-7
purse, £765,306

	SCORES				TOTAL	MONEY
Colin Montgomerie	69	69	73	68	279	£127,551.02
Andrew Oldcorn	72	68	70	70	280	66,459.19
Wayne Riley	73	68	73	66	280	66,459.19
Miguel Angel Martin	71	68	72	70	281	38,265.31
Ignacio Garrido	71	69	74	69	283	29,602.04
Raymond Russell	74	70	71	68	283	29,602.04
Phillip Price	76	70	70	68	284	17,712.24
Wayne Westner	70	70	72	72	284	17,712.24
Robert Allenby	74	69	71	70	284	17,712.24
Lee Westwood	70	71	70	73	284	17,712.24
Ricky Willison	72	69	71	72	284	17,712.24
Carl Mason	74	68	70	74	286	12,107.15
Joakim Haeggman	71	72	69	74	286	12,107.15
Ernie Els	73	70	71	72	286	12,107.15
Bernhard Langer	67	76	71	72	286	12,107.15
David Howell	73	73	73	68	287	10,785.71
Peter Mitchell	72	72	71	73	288	9,164.54
Jay Townsend	76	70	71	71	288	9,164.54
Malcolm Mackenzie	75	70	70	73	288	9,164.54
Ronan Rafferty	74	72	72	70	288	9,164.54
Sandy Lyle	75	71	68	74	288	9,164.54
Ian Woosnam	71	70	73	74	288	9,164.54
Raymond Burns	72	74	71	71	288	9,164.54
Domingo Hospital	75	70	72	71	288	9,164.54
Roger Chapman	72	73	76	68	289	7,346.94
Peter O'Malley	75	70	74	70	289	7,346.94
Frank Nobilo	71	72	72	74	289	7,346.94
Peter Baker	74	70	75	70	289	7,346.94
Andrew Coltart	72	68	76	73	289	7,346.94
Marcus Wills	73	70	74	72	289	7,346.94
Peter Hedblom	71	68	75	75	289	7,346.94
Jarmo Sandelin	74	73	72	71	290	5,969.39
Paul McGinley	73	71	70	76	290	5,969.39
Sam Torrance	71	72	76	71	290	5,969.39
Jose Coceres	71	72	75	72	290	5,969.39
Daniel Chopra	73	73	69	75	290	5,969.39
Rolf Muntz	73	70	72	75	290	5,969.39
Miles Tunnicliff	76	69	72	73	290	5,969.39
Carl Suneson	76	71	72	72	291	5,127.55
Stephen Ames	71	74	72	74	291	5,127.55
David A. Russell	71	73	76	71	291	5,127.55
John Bickerton	76	71	73	71	291	5,127.55
Russell Claydon	71	77	70	74	292	4,438.78
Michael Campbell	73	71	76	72	292	4,438.78
Darren Clarke	79	69	69	75	292	4,438.78
Mark Roe	75	71	71	75	292	4,438.78
Jim Payne	77	69	72	74	292	4,438.78
David Carter	77	71	73	72	293	3,596.94
Per-Ulrik Johansson	69	75	80	69	293	3,596.94
Roger Wessels	72	75	73	73	293	3,596.94
Bradley Hughes	74	74	74	71	293	3,596.94
Brenden Pappas	70	78	70	75	293	3,596.94
Steen Tinning	72	72	73	76	293	3,596.94
Paul Broadhurst	75	73	75	71	294	2,634.84

	SCORES				TOTAL	MONEY
Jose Rivero	76	71	75	72	294	2,634.84
Gary Murphy	70	71	81	72	294	2,634.84
Tony Johnstone	73	70	75	76	294	2,634.84
Paul Lawrie	76	72	75	71	294	2,634.84
Ross McFarlane	73	75	75	71	294	2,634.84
Eric Giraud	75	71	70	78	294	2,634.84
Fredrik Lindgren	70	74	76	75	295	2,142.86
Philip Walton	76	72	73	74	295	2,142.86
Ross Drummond	72	72	74	77	295	2,142.86
Per Haugsrud	77	71	72	76	296	1,951.54
Gary Evans	76	69	77	74	296	1,951.54
David Williams	74	73	79	71	297	1,148
Barry Lane	76	72	74	76	298	1,143
Silvio Grappasonni	74	74	72	78	298	1,143
Patrik Sjoland	75	73	75	75	298	1,143
Mats Hallberg	76	70	73	79	298	1,143
Gordon Sherry	73	74	69	83	299	1,137
Mike Clayton	76	71	74	78	299	1,137

Scottish Open

Carnoustie Golf Club, Carnoustie, Scotland
Par 36-36–72; 7,246 yards

July 10-13
purse, £480,000

	SCORES				TOTAL	MONEY
Ian Woosnam	70	74	70	75	289	£80,000
Andrew Coltart	74	76	69	74	293	53,280
Mats Hallberg	75	71	73	75	294	30,050
Diego Borrego	72	78	72	73	295	22,175
Lee Westwood	75	74	76	72	295	22,175
Malcolm Mackenzie	72	76	71	77	296	15,600
Peter Mitchell	75	74	73	74	296	15,600
Andrew Sherborne	76	75	71	75	297	10,783.33
Russell Claydon	72	72	73	80	297	10,783.33
Silvio Grappasonni	74	72	74	77	297	10,783.33
Jose Rivero	71	78	73	76	298	7,841
Bob Estes	72	76	75	75	298	7,841
Paul Lawrie	71	74	73	80	298	7,841
Sandy Lyle	79	74	68	77	298	7,841
Mathias Gronberg	76	76	72	74	298	7,841
Jay Townsend	72	72	74	81	299	5,383.67
Colin Montgomerie	70	77	71	81	299	5,383.67
Retief Goosen	75	77	78	69	299	5,383.67
Raymond Russell	76	76	73	74	299	5,383.67
Mark James	74	75	72	78	299	5,383.67
Stuart Cage	73	76	70	80	299	5,383.67
Rolf Muntz	78	70	70	81	299	5,383.67
Greg Turner	76	71	72	80	299	5,383.67
Robert Karlsson	75	74	74	76	299	5,383.67
Brian Marchbank	76	76	72	75	299	5,383.67
Jesper Parnevik	74	78	69	78	299	5,383.67
Sam Torrance	76	77	75	71	299	5,383.67
Ernie Els	76	77	71	75	299	5,383.67
Paul Broadhurst	71	76	72	80	299	5,383.67
Peter Baker	74	71	74	80	299	5,383.67
Domingo Hospital	75	74	75	76	300	3,935
Phillip Price	74	75	73	78	300	3,935

	SCORES				TOTAL	MONEY
Bradley Hughes	78	74	71	77	300	3,935
Robert Allenby	71	75	80	74	300	3,935
Pierre Fulke	77	72	77	74	300	3,935
Jim Payne	79	72	69	81	301	3,592.50
Steven Richardson	72	75	79	75	301	3,592.50
Jose Coceres	72	77	75	78	302	3,307.50
Eduardo Romero	80	71	74	77	302	3,307.50
Stephen McAllister	78	74	73	77	302	3,307.50
Peter O'Malley	73	75	74	80	302	3,307.50
Andrew Oldcorn	77	76	74	76	303	2,880
Paul Moloney	72	78	73	80	303	2,880
Carl Mason	72	74	74	83	303	2,880
Carl Suneson	75	76	72	80	303	2,880
Gordon Brand, Jr.	74	77	74	78	303	2,880
David Gilford	74	77	75	78	304	2,310
Olle Karlsson	74	79	72	79	304	2,310
Eamonn Darcy	76	77	75	76	304	2,310
Mike McLean	74	77	73	80	304	2,310
Neal Briggs	75	78	76	75	304	2,310
Dean Robertson	76	75	76	77	304	2,310
Christian Cevaer	76	76	74	78	304	2,310
Des Smyth	75	75	75	80	305	1,740
Thomas Gogele	74	76	80	75	305	1,740
Tony Johnstone	77	72	76	80	305	1,740
David J. Russell	71	81	73	80	305	1,740
Patrik Sjoland	75	78	74	78	305	1,740
Ross Drummond	73	79	73	81	306	1,475
Euan McIntosh	76	73	80	77	306	1,475
Richard Boxall	74	77	71	85	307	1,350
Martin Gates	76	75	78	78	307	1,350
Paul McGinley	75	76	79	77	307	1,350
David Curry	75	77	80	76	308	1,225
Paul Eales	78	75	77	78	308	1,225
Klas Eriksson	73	80	78	79	310	719
Ronan Rafferty	77	76	80	77	310	719
David Feherty	74	78	79	82	313	715
Marc Farry	76	76	78	83	313	715
Tommy Tolles	76	77	79	83	315	712
Andrew Collison	72	78	82	88	320	710

British Open Championship

Royal Lytham & St. Annes Golf Club,
Lytham St. Annes, England
Par 35-36–71; 6,892 yards

July 18-21
purse, £1,419,800

	SCORES				TOTAL	MONEY
Tom Lehman	67	67	64	73	271	£200,000
Mark McCumber	67	69	71	66	273	125,000
Ernie Els	68	67	71	67	273	125,000
Nick Faldo	68	68	68	70	274	75,000
Jeff Maggert	69	70	72	65	276	50,000
Mark Brooks	67	70	68	71	276	50,000
Fred Couples	67	70	69	71	277	35,000
Greg Turner	72	69	68	68	277	35,000
Greg Norman	71	68	71	67	277	35,000
Peter Hedblom	70	65	75	67	277	35,000
Vijay Singh	69	67	69	73	278	27,000

	SCORES				TOTAL	MONEY
Alexander Cejka	73	67	71	67	278	27,000
Darren Clarke	70	68	69	71	278	27,000
David Duval	76	67	66	70	279	20,250
Paul McGinley	69	65	74	71	279	20,250
Shigeki Maruyama	68	70	69	72	279	20,250
Mark McNulty	69	71	70	69	279	20,250
Padraig Harrington	68	68	73	71	280	15,500
Loren Roberts	67	69	72	72	280	15,500
Michael Welch	71	68	73	68	280	15,500
Rocco Mediate	69	70	69	72	280	15,500
Mark James	70	68	75	68	281	11,875
Jay Haas	70	72	71	68	281	11,875
Steve Stricker	71	70	66	74	281	11,875
Carl Mason	68	70	70	73	281	11,875
*Tiger Woods	75	66	70	70	281	
Tom Kite	77	66	69	70	282	9,525
Paul Broadhurst	65	72	74	71	282	9,525
Frank Nobilo	70	72	68	72	282	9,525
Ben Crenshaw	73	68	71	70	282	9,525
Corey Pavin	70	66	74	72	282	9,525
Peter Mitchell	71	68	71	72	282	9,525
David Gilford	71	67	71	74	283	7,843.75
Tommy Tolles	73	70	71	69	283	7,843.75
Hidemichi Tanaka	67	71	70	75	283	7,843.75
Brad Faxon	67	73	68	75	283	7,843.75
Mark O'Meara	67	69	72	75	283	7,843.75
Eamonn Darcy	73	69	71	70	283	7,843.75
Scott Simpson	71	69	73	70	283	7,843.75
Eduardo Romero	70	71	75	67	283	7,843.75
David Frost	70	72	71	71	284	7,150
Phil Mickelson	72	71	72	69	284	7,150
Mark Calcavecchia	72	68	76	68	284	7,150
Klas Eriksson	68	75	72	69	284	7,150
Payne Stewart	70	73	71	71	285	6,400
Bradley Hughes	70	69	75	71	285	6,400
Bill Mayfair	70	72	74	69	285	6,400
Jesper Parnevik	72	69	69	75	285	6,400
Peter Jacobsen	72	70	74	69	285	6,400
Richard Boxall	72	70	71	72	285	6,400
Jack Nicklaus	69	66	77	73	285	6,400
Jim Furyk	68	71	72	74	285	6,400
Craig Stadler	71	71	75	68	285	6,400
Nick Price	68	73	71	73	285	6,400
Todd Hamilton	71	70	74	70	285	6,400
Robert Allenby	74	68	71	73	286	5,687.50
Jim Payne	72	71	73	70	286	5,687.50
Stephen Ames	71	72	69	74	286	5,687.50
Sandy Lyle	71	69	73	73	286	5,687.50
D.A. Weibring	71	72	72	72	287	5,475
Jeff Sluman	72	70	70	75	287	5,475
Brian Barnes	73	70	69	75	287	5,475
Michael Jonzon	69	73	73	72	287	5,475
Costantino Rocca	71	70	74	73	288	5,300
Carl Suneson	73	69	74	72	288	5,300
Gordon Law	74	69	71	74	288	5,300
Brett Ogle	70	73	73	73	289	5,150
John Daly	70	73	69	77	289	5,150
David A. Russell	70	72	74	73	289	5,150
Howard Clark	72	71	76	71	290	5,050
Bob Charles	71	72	71	77	291	5,000

	SCORES				TOTAL	MONEY
Roger Chapman	72	70	70	80	292	4,875
Curtis Strange	71	72	72	77	292	4,875
Rick Todd	74	69	73	76	292	4,875
Domingo Hospital	75	68	77	72	292	4,875
Retief Goosen	72	71	74	76	293	4,750
Arnaud Langenaeken	72	71	77	78	298	4,700

Out of Final 36 Holes

Ricky Willison	72	72	144
David Feherty	77	67	144
Sam Torrance	72	72	144
Bob Estes	73	71	144
Santiago Luna	72	72	144
Barry Lane	71	73	144
Marc Farry	70	74	144
Philip Walton	72	72	144
Silvio Grappasonni	71	73	144
Jose Rivero	74	71	145
Fuzzy Zoeller	70	75	145
Tony Westwood	71	74	145
Peter O'Malley	73	72	145
Sean Murphy	76	69	145
Woody Austin	72	73	145
Steve Elkington	75	70	145
Craig Parry	74	71	145
Jose Coceres	72	73	145
Malcolm Mackenzie	71	75	146
Ross McFarlane	73	73	146
Steve Jones	73	73	146
Yoshinori Kaneko	73	73	146
Peter Senior	74	72	146
Paul Eales	73	73	146
Tony Johnstone	70	76	146
Davis Love III	72	74	146
Bill McColl	74	72	146
*Warren Bladon	73	73	146
Andrew Coltart	72	74	146
Colin Montgomerie	73	74	147
Anders Forsbrand	75	72	147
*Steve Allan	75	72	147
Mark Litton	72	75	147
Andrew Sherborne	73	74	147
Terry Price	77	70	147
Justin Leonard	79	68	147
Satoshi Higashi	75	72	147
Per-Ulrik Johansson	70	77	147
Gordon Brand, Jr.	72	75	147
Gary Player	71	76	147
Ian Woosnam	75	72	147
Steen Tinning	72	75	147
Wayne Westner	78	70	148
Stephen Field	72	76	148
Hajime Meshiai	76	72	148
Antoine Lebouc	72	76	148
Gary Emerson	76	72	148
Steven Bottomley	76	72	148
Massimo Florioli	71	77	148
David J. Russell	77	71	148
Wayne Riley	73	76	149

	SCORES				TOTAL
Joakim Haeggman	72	77			149
Diego Borrego	74	75			149
Iain Steel	72	77			149
Fabrice Tarnaud	74	75			149
Stuart Cage	74	75			149
Tim Herron	74	75			149
Jon Robson	75	74			149
Thomas Bjorn	73	76			149
*Sergio Garcia	76	73			149
Brian Watts	80	70			150
Miguel Angel Jimenez	75	75			150
Robert Lee	77	73			150
Andrew Oldcorn	77	73			150
Jay Townsend	72	78			150
Adam Mednick	75	76			151
Lee Janzen	74	77			151
Paul Azinger	74	77			151
Mats Hallberg	79	72			151
Seve Ballesteros	74	78			152
Ross Drummond	78	74			152
Bob Tway	79	73			152
Gary Brown	74	80			154
Paul Lawrie	78	77			155
Kazuhiro Fukunaga	76	81			157
Ian Baker-Finch	78	84			162
Bernhard Langer	75				WD
Des Smyth	72				DQ
Michael Campbell	75				DQ

(Professionals who did not complete 72 holes received £650.)

Sun Dutch Open

Hilversumsche Golf Club, Hilversum, Netherlands   July 25-28
Par 36-35–71; 6,636 yards   purse, £650,000

	SCORES				TOTAL	MONEY
Mark McNulty	67	65	66	68	266	£108,330
Scott Hoch	70	68	63	66	267	72,210
Raymond Russell	68	68	67	66	269	36,595
Frank Nobilo	69	68	64	68	269	36,595
John Huston	69	65	69	69	272	25,140
Jean Van de Velde	65	70	69	68	272	25,140
Phillip Price	67	72	69	65	273	19,500
Daniel Chopra	69	70	68	67	274	14,586.67
Ross McFarlane	68	68	68	70	274	14,586.67
Greg Chalmers	72	66	71	65	274	14,586.67
Lee Westwood	71	69	67	68	275	11,570
David Howell	71	65	69	70	275	11,570
Peter O'Malley	67	69	70	70	276	9,577
Mike McLean	73	67	69	67	276	9,577
Jamie Spence	71	67	69	69	276	9,577
Tony Johnstone	69	68	69	70	276	9,577
Andrew Coltart	73	68	67	68	276	9,577
Sam Torrance	70	71	67	69	277	7,642.14
Paul Lawrie	73	68	66	70	277	7,642.14
Retief Goosen	70	66	72	69	277	7,642.14
Wayne Riley	68	71	69	69	277	7,642.14

		SCORES			TOTAL	MONEY
Darren Clarke	69	70	67	71	277	7,642.14
Paul Eales	68	72	71	66	277	7,642.14
Carl Suneson	68	67	71	71	277	7,642.14
Des Smyth	64	67	75	72	278	6,435
Stephen Field	66	73	70	69	278	6,435
Roger Chapman	68	72	66	72	278	6,435
Pedro Linhart	70	69	67	72	278	6,435
Thomas Bjorn	71	66	71	70	278	6,435
Diego Borrego	72	68	68	71	279	5,655
David Gilford	68	67	72	72	279	5,655
Rodger Davis	68	70	69	72	279	5,655
Paul Broadhurst	71	69	67	73	280	5,135
Paul Curry	74	67	71	68	280	5,135
Paul Affleck	70	70	71	69	280	5,135
Mark Roe	71	69	67	73	280	5,135
Iain Pyman	69	72	67	73	281	4,420
Peter Baker	72	69	67	73	281	4,420
Rolf Muntz	71	70	69	71	281	4,420
David Carter	71	69	69	72	281	4,420
Mike Clayton	70	69	71	71	281	4,420
Philip Walton	69	68	70	74	281	4,420
Anders Haglund	68	70	69	74	281	4,420
Santiago Luna	69	69	75	69	282	3,705
Juan Carlos Pinero	71	69	72	70	282	3,705
Mark Mouland	71	68	71	72	282	3,705
Stuart Cage	67	67	73	75	282	3,705
*Maarten Lafeber	70	70	65	77	282	
Stephen Ames	71	68	70	74	283	3,185
Christian Cevaer	68	72	72	71	283	3,185
Jim Payne	70	71	67	75	283	3,185
Howard Clark	70	69	72	72	283	3,185
Per Nyman	70	71	73	70	284	2,600
Robert Coles	71	70	74	69	284	2,600
Carl Mason	69	69	71	75	284	2,600
Roger Wessels	71	69	73	71	284	2,600
Adam Hunter	70	70	70	74	284	2,600
Fabrice Tarnaud	75	66	73	71	285	2,210
Steven Richardson	68	73	75	70	286	1,982.50
Russell Claydon	66	73	77	70	286	1,982.50
Phil Golding	69	70	75	72	286	1,982.50
Gary Emerson	70	71	73	72	286	1,982.50
Chris Hall	69	71	75	73	288	1,755
David Feherty	65	71	73	79	288	1,755
David Williams	69	71	73	75	288	1,755
Miles Tunnicliff	72	68	73	76	289	1,625
Joost Steenkamer	69	69	76	76	290	975

Volvo Scandinavian Masters

Forsgardens Golf Club, Goteborg, Sweden
Par 36-36–72; 6,899 yards

August 1-4
purse, £700,000

		SCORES			TOTAL	MONEY
Lee Westwood	69	75	69	68	281	£116,660
Paul Broadhurst	72	70	71	68	281	60,795
Russell Claydon	68	71	74	68	281	60,795

(Westwood defeated Broadhurst on first extra hole and Claydon on second extra hole.)

	SCORES			TOTAL	MONEY
Santiago Luna	67	71	76	68	282	35,000
Jean Van de Velde	72	68	74	70	284	29,640
Iain Pyman	71	73	70	71	285	24,500
Thomas Bjorn	67	68	76	75	286	16,198
Carl Suneson	72	72	71	71	286	16,198
Philip Walton	77	69	70	70	286	16,198
Roger Wessels	73	72	72	69	286	16,198
Steven Bottomley	74	74	65	73	286	16,198
Miguel Angel Martin	68	72	77	70	287	10,605
Colin Montgomerie	69	76	72	70	287	10,605
Per Nyman	70	78	71	68	287	10,605
Fernando Roca	70	71	74	72	287	10,605
Silvio Grappasonni	70	70	73	74	287	10,605
Pierre Fulke	71	73	76	67	287	10,605
Mark Mouland	70	75	71	72	288	8,230
Ignacio Garrido	72	70	73	73	288	8,230
Per Haugsrud	75	71	71	71	288	8,230
Padraig Harrington	69	77	72	70	288	8,230
John Daly	71	71	76	70	288	8,230
Mark Roe	71	73	73	71	288	8,230
John Bickerton	68	73	76	71	288	8,230
Jim Payne	70	73	70	76	289	7,035
Jonathan Lomas	71	73	74	71	289	7,035
Gary Clark	73	71	73	72	289	7,035
Peter Baker	70	76	71	72	289	7,035
*Martin Erlandsson	73	75	70	71	289	
Peter Hedblom	75	72	74	69	290	6,020
Jose Rivero	71	76	73	70	290	6,020
Paul Eales	70	73	72	75	290	6,020
Per-Ulrik Johansson	70	73	73	74	290	6,020
Ian Woosnam	69	79	72	70	290	6,020
Wayne Riley	77	71	70	72	290	6,020
Peter O'Malley	71	77	70	73	291	5,390
Mats Hallberg	70	72	75	74	291	5,390
*Christoffer Hanell	72	76	73	70	291	
Glenn Ralph	75	72	74	71	292	4,620
Juan Carlos Pinero	71	74	73	74	292	4,620
Dean Robertson	73	73	74	72	292	4,620
Rolf Muntz	77	68	75	72	292	4,620
Martin Gates	69	77	73	73	292	4,620
Derrick Cooper	73	75	75	69	292	4,620
Gary Evans	72	76	74	70	292	4,620
Raymond Russell	75	72	74	71	292	4,620
Ronan Rafferty	73	74	73	72	292	4,620
Stuart Cage	71	76	73	73	293	3,710
Bernhard Langer	74	74	75	70	293	3,710
Richard Boxall	72	74	73	74	293	3,710
Robert Karlsson	75	72	74	72	293	3,710
Mark Litton	70	75	75	74	294	2,940
Pedro Linhart	72	73	78	71	294	2,940
Francis Howley	70	73	77	74	294	2,940
Stephen McAllister	74	74	73	73	294	2,940
Adam Hunter	71	76	74	73	294	2,940
Barry Lane	72	76	73	73	294	2,940
Roger Chapman	71	76	76	71	294	2,940
Gabriel Hjertstedt	70	78	77	70	295	2,073.75
Mathias Gronberg	72	75	75	73	295	2,073.75
Bob May	73	72	75	75	295	2,073.75
Sven Struver	71	75	79	70	295	2,073.75
Brian Marchbank	71	77	75	72	295	2,073.75

	SCORES				TOTAL	MONEY
Max Anglert	73	74	77	71	295	2,073.75
Gary Emerson	70	75	76	74	295	2,073.75
Mike Clayton	76	72	75	72	295	2,073.75
Ricky Willison	73	72	73	78	296	1,400
Anders Forsbrand	74	73	77	72	296	1,400
Michael Jonzon	76	72	76	73	297	1,045
Zhang Lian-Wei	70	77	75	75	297	1,045
Carl Mason	73	75	75	74	297	1,045
Paul Moloney	74	72	78	73	297	1,045
Paul Way	68	78	79	73	298	1,038
Adam Mednick	75	71	79	73	298	1,038
Eric Giraud	72	76	74	76	298	1,038
Olle Nordberg	75	73	75	76	299	1,032
David Feherty	75	73	77	74	299	1,032
Jesper Parnevik	72	74	79	74	299	1,032
David A. Russell	73	75	77	75	300	1,027
Steen Tinning	70	76	77	77	300	1,027
Steven Richardson	72	76	75	78	301	1,024
Joakim Nilsson	72	76	79	75	302	1,021
Mike McLean	73	74	79	76	302	1,021
*Viktor Gustavsson	72	74	76	81	303	

Hohe Brucke Open

Waldviertel Golf Club, Litschau, Austria
Par 36-36–72; 6,937 yards

August 8-11
purse, £250,000

	SCORES				TOTAL	MONEY
Paul McGinley	73	66	68	62	269	£41,660
David Lynn	66	68	70	66	270	21,710
Juan Carlos Pinero	65	66	68	71	270	21,710
Adam Hunter	67	74	67	64	272	11,550
Gary Clark	66	68	70	68	272	11,550
Phil Golding	67	69	70	67	273	8,125
Per Nyman	70	66	69	68	273	8,125
Max Anglert	71	68	64	71	274	6,250
Andrew Barnett	69	67	70	69	275	4,555
Rolf Muntz	67	69	74	65	275	4,555
Anders Haglund	70	71	66	68	275	4,555
Daniel Chopra	69	69	70	67	275	4,555
David Higgins	66	67	69	73	275	4,555
Stephen Dodd	67	67	71	70	275	4,555
Scott Watson	64	70	70	72	276	3,378
Bob May	70	68	68	70	276	3,378
Per Haugsrud	67	68	71	70	276	3,378
Massimo Scarpa	65	68	71	72	276	3,378
Steve Webster	66	69	71	70	276	3,378
Thomas Gogele	68	67	69	73	277	2,962.50
Andrew Sherborne	67	70	70	70	277	2,962.50
Raymond Burns	68	71	69	70	278	2,812.50
Marcus Willis	69	70	70	69	278	2,812.50
Mats Lanner	67	69	72	71	279	2,365
Matthew McGuire	70	67	69	73	279	2,365
Mikael Piltz	71	67	74	67	279	2,365
Mark Litton	69	68	68	74	279	2,365
Greg Chalmers	69	70	67	73	279	2,365
Michael Welch	71	70	69	69	279	2,365

	SCORES				TOTAL	MONEY
Ronan Rafferty	72	69	69	69	279	2,365
Roger Wessels	69	72	67	71	279	2,365
Brian Marchbank	67	71	68	73	279	2,365
Jonathan Lomas	68	66	74	71	279	2,365
Rudi Sailer	70	70	72	68	280	1,900
Barry Lane	69	66	71	74	280	1,900
Lee James	70	66	76	68	280	1,900
Silvio Grappasonni	67	70	72	71	280	1,900
Francisco Cea	70	67	75	68	280	1,900
Matthias Debove	70	71	72	68	281	1,625
Brenden Pappas	67	72	70	72	281	1,625
Anssi Kankkonen	68	71	71	71	281	1,625
Andre Bossert	67	71	74	69	281	1,625
Antoine Lebouc	70	70	68	73	281	1,625
David R. Jones	68	70	72	71	281	1,625
Simon Brown	71	68	73	70	282	1,375
Andrew Collison	73	67	67	75	282	1,375
Fredrik Larsson	70	66	73	73	282	1,375
Johan Rystrom	71	66	70	75	282	1,375
Stephen Pullan	68	72	72	71	283	1,125
Gordon J. Brand	68	72	68	75	283	1,125
Olle Nordberg	72	69	69	73	283	1,125
Heinz P. Thul	66	73	72	72	283	1,125
Roger Winchester	73	66	73	71	283	1,125
Brian Davis	71	69	74	69	283	1,125
Nic Henning	70	67	75	72	284	875
Olivier Edmond	71	70	71	72	284	875
Gabriel Hjertstedt	69	70	76	69	284	875
John Mellor	72	68	73	71	284	875
Greg Owen	67	73	73	72	285	750
Mark Stevenson	75	64	70	76	285	750
Frederic Grosset-Grange	72	69	73	71	285	750
Bill Longmuir	71	69	72	74	286	700
Tim Planchin	68	72	77	70	287	675
Robert Coles	70	71	78	69	288	650
Oyvind Rojahn	69	72	73	75	289	625
Claude Grenier	73	68	72	80	293	400

Chemapol Trophy Czech Open

Marianske Lazne Golf Club, Czech Republic
Par 34-37–71; 6,758 yards

August 15-18
purse, £750,000

	SCORES				TOTAL	MONEY
Jonathan Lomas	69	68	69	66	272	£125,000
Daniel Chopra	70	69	65	69	273	83,320
Domingo Hospital	68	70	69	67	274	36,940
Raymond Russell	69	70	71	66	276	37,500
Peter Teravainen	73	69	69	66	277	24,817.50
Jamie Spence	67	71	69	70	277	24,817.50
Lee Westwood	75	67	66	69	277	24,817.50
Peter Mitchell	70	65	70	72	277	24,817.50
Gary Orr	71	67	66	74	278	13,663.33
Gary Evans	70	68	71	69	278	13,663.33
Dean Robertson	67	68	75	68	278	13,663.33
Miles Tunnicliff	70	69	68	71	278	13,663.33
Paul Broadhurst	69	70	69	70	278	13,663.33

	SCORES				TOTAL	MONEY
Martin Gates	69	72	66	71	278	13,663.33
Mark Roe	72	68	71	68	279	10,138
Gary Clark	69	72	69	69	279	10,138
Carl Suneson	74	69	68	68	279	10,138
Richard Boxall	68	70	74	67	279	10,138
Emanuele Canonica	67	71	72	69	279	10,138
John Hawksworth	71	69	68	72	280	8,662.50
Roger Wessels	70	69	69	72	280	8,662.50
Alexander Cejka	73	68	67	72	280	8,662.50
Malcolm Mackenzie	70	71	69	70	280	8,662.50
Robert Allenby	70	71	71	69	281	7,537.50
Russell Claydon	68	68	74	71	281	7,537.50
Andrew Coltart	67	69	73	72	281	7,537.50
Patrik Sjoland	71	69	68	73	281	7,537.50
Steven Bottomley	75	67	71	68	281	7,537.50
Pedro Linhart	71	71	71	68	281	7,537.50
Phillip Price	69	69	74	70	282	6,182.14
David Higgins	68	71	73	70	282	6,182.14
Philip Walton	70	70	74	68	282	6,182.14
Paul Lawrie	72	70	66	74	282	6,182.14
Howard Clark	74	68	71	69	282	6,182.14
Angel Cabrera	73	69	71	69	282	6,182.14
Andrew Sherborne	74	68	68	72	282	6,182.14
Retief Goosen	70	68	71	74	283	5,400
Jose Rivero	72	70	71	70	283	5,400
Bob May	68	71	74	70	283	5,400
Gary Emerson	68	70	74	72	283	5,400
Nic Henning	74	68	72	70	283	5,400
Peter Baker	69	67	76	72	284	4,500
Stephen Field	72	70	73	69	284	4,500
Jim Payne	75	66	74	69	284	4,500
Jarmo Sandelin	72	70	70	72	284	4,500
Joakim Haeggman	68	68	75	73	284	4,500
David A. Russell	69	70	74	71	284	4,500
Robert Coles	69	71	74	70	284	4,500
Thomas Gogele	70	73	71	71	285	3,600
Greg Chalmers	68	73	72	72	285	3,600
Paul Affleck	68	73	75	69	285	3,600
Ross Drummond	69	73	74	70	286	3,300
Tim Planchin	69	71	70	77	287	3,150
Pierre Fulke	69	73	72	74	288	2,850
Mats Hallberg	70	73	70	75	288	2,850
Eric Giraud	72	69	72	75	288	2,850
Stuart Cage	71	72	71	75	289	2,550
David Carter	71	71	73	75	290	2,212.50
Paul McGinley	71	72	72	75	290	2,212.50
Glen Hutcheson	71	72	76	71	290	2,212.50
Mathias Gronberg	70	69	80	71	290	2,212.50
Andrew Barnett	71	71	74	74	290	2,212.50
Brian Marchbank	74	68	73	75	290	2,212.50
Neal Briggs	73	70	73	75	291	1,912.50
Thomas Levet	70	71	75	75	291	1,912.50
Anders Haglund	69	72	75	77	293	1,123
Michel Besanceney	69	71	80	73	293	1,123
Andrew Collison	74	69	74	76	293	1,123
Mike Clayton	72	71	76	75	294	1,119
Fredrik Larsson	70	72	79	74	295	1,117

Volvo German Open

Nippenburg ETC, Stuttgart, Germany
Par 36-35–71; 6,748 yards
(Fourth round cancelled — thunderstorm.)

August 22-25
purse, £700,000

	SCORES			TOTAL	MONEY
Ian Woosnam	64	64	65	193	£116,660
Iain Pyman	66	64	69	199	46,557.50
Thomas Gogele	67	65	67	199	46,557.50
Fernando Roca	66	64	69	199	46,557.50
Robert Karlsson	67	62	70	199	46,557.50
Diego Borrego	69	63	68	200	22,750
Miguel Angel Martin	66	66	68	200	22,750
Stephen Field	66	65	70	201	14,406
Paul Broadhurst	62	70	69	201	14,406
Roger Chapman	72	62	67	201	14,406
Stephen Ames	68	65	68	201	14,406
Carl Suneson	65	66	70	201	14,406
Barry Lane	68	67	67	202	9,900
Ronan Rafferty	64	72	66	202	9,900
David Carter	66	69	67	202	9,900
Michael Jonzon	67	67	68	202	9,900
Heinz P. Thul	70	67	65	202	9,900
Greg Turner	70	67	65	202	9,900
David Williams	67	67	68	202	9,900
Francisco Cea	68	66	69	203	7,455
Paul Lawrie	66	69	68	203	7,455
Gary Emerson	68	69	66	203	7,455
Des Smyth	66	69	68	203	7,455
Paul Eales	67	68	68	203	7,455
Raymond Russell	63	69	71	203	7,455
Lee Westwood	66	71	66	203	7,455
Jonathan Lomas	67	67	69	203	7,455
Peter Baker	70	66	67	203	7,455
Pedro Linhart	67	67	69	203	7,455
Michael Campbell	64	72	68	204	5,770
Paul McGinley	67	69	68	204	5,770
Mats Lanner	64	71	69	204	5,770
Steve Webster	69	66	69	204	5,770
Jose Maria Canizares	67	68	69	204	5,770
Emanuele Canonica	69	68	67	204	5,770
Robert Coles	68	66	70	204	5,770
Daniel Chopra	70	67	68	205	4,620
Antoine Lebouc	68	69	68	205	4,620
Miles Tunnicliff	66	71	68	205	4,620
Bernhard Langer	64	71	70	205	4,620
Mark James	69	67	69	205	4,620
Mark Roe	65	72	68	205	4,620
Wayne Riley	64	71	70	205	4,620
Raymond Burns	69	67	69	205	4,620
Thomas Bjorn	66	68	71	205	4,620
Domingo Hospital	70	67	69	206	3,500
Michael Welch	67	69	70	206	3,500
Ignacio Garrido	71	66	69	206	3,500
Carl Mason	69	66	71	206	3,500
Jamie Spence	67	70	69	206	3,500
Mark Mouland	67	70	69	206	3,500
Terry Price	67	68	71	206	3,500
Fabrice Tarnaud	69	68	70	207	2,426.67

	SCORES			TOTAL	MONEY
Steven Bottomley	68	69	70	207	2,426.67
Pierre Fulke	70	66	71	207	2,426.67
Frank Nobilo	71	66	70	207	2,426.67
Andrew Coltart	67	70	70	207	2,426.67
Dean Robertson	68	69	70	207	2,426.67
Santiago Luna	68	68	71	207	2,426.67
Ricky Willison	69	64	74	207	2,426.67
Peter Fowler	68	69	70	207	2,426.67
Klas Eriksson	68	69	71	208	1,890
Gary Orr	67	68	73	208	1,890
Juan Carlos Pinero	67	70	71	208	1,890
Tony Johnstone	68	69	72	209	1,187.60
Per Nyman	65	71	73	209	1,187.60
Russell Claydon	65	72	72	209	1,187.60
Per-Ulrik Johansson	71	66	72	209	1,187.60
Francis Howley	69	67	73	209	1,187.60
Eamonn Darcy	65	68	77	210	1,042
Andre Bossert	68	69	74	211	1,040
John Hawksworth	67	68	79	214	1,038

One 2 One British Masters

Collingtree Park ETC, Northampton, England
Par 36-36–72; 6,728 yards

August 28-31
purse, £700,000

	SCORES				TOTAL	MONEY
Robert Allenby	69	71	71	73	284	£116,660
Miguel Angel Martin	75	70	71	68	284	77,770
(Allenby defeated Martin on first extra hole.)						
Costantino Rocca	71	73	72	69	285	43,820
Miguel Angel Jimenez	74	72	73	67	286	35,000
Ian Woosnam	70	76	71	70	287	29,640
Jose Coceres	69	78	71	70	288	24,500
Joakim Haeggman	71	77	70	71	289	19,250
Antoine Lebouc	74	73	70	72	289	19,250
Pedro Linhart	72	73	67	78	290	12,751.67
Colin Montgomerie	68	76	77	69	290	12,751.67
Klas Eriksson	71	75	72	72	290	12,751.67
Robert Coles	74	76	71	69	290	12,751.67
Peter Mitchell	74	71	74	71	290	12,751.67
Philip Walton	71	74	74	71	290	12,751.67
Mike Clayton	69	76	73	73	291	9,464
Mark Roe	69	71	78	73	291	9,464
Phillip Price	72	76	74	69	291	9,464
Adam Hunter	70	79	73	69	291	9,464
Peter O'Malley	71	73	75	72	291	9,464
Stephen McAllister	73	76	69	74	292	8,085
David Gilford	69	74	77	72	292	8,085
Peter Hedblom	70	75	75	72	292	8,085
Iain Pyman	71	75	75	71	292	8,085
Eamonn Darcy	74	76	69	74	293	7,140
Domingo Hospital	73	77	75	68	293	7,140
Roger Chapman	71	76	74	72	293	7,140
Retief Goosen	71	74	75	73	293	7,140
Bradley Hughes	73	75	72	73	293	7,140
Gavin Levenson	66	75	76	77	294	6,020
Tony Johnstone	72	77	72	73	294	6,020

	SCORES	TOTAL	MONEY
David Howell	70 74 78 72	294	6,020
Wayne Riley	71 78 71 74	294	6,020
Daniel Chopra	74 68 79 73	294	6,020
Bob May	74 75 70 75	294	6,020
Francisco Cea	70 71 76 78	295	4,970
Steven Bottomley	71 79 72 73	295	4,970
Jean Van de Velde	73 76 72 74	295	4,970
Martin Gates	71 77 72 75	295	4,970
Paul Eales	75 71 72 77	295	4,970
Raymond Russell	69 78 74 74	295	4,970
Anders Haglund	71 77 73 74	295	4,970
Mark Mouland	71 77 73 74	295	4,970
Emanuele Canonica	69 76 76 75	296	4,200
Paul Broadhurst	73 75 74 74	296	4,200
Raymond Burns	75 75 72 74	296	4,200
Michael Jonzon	72 76 76 73	297	3,430
Stuart Cage	69 81 75 72	297	3,430
Fredrik Lindgren	74 74 73 76	297	3,430
David Carter	72 77 76 72	297	3,430
Thomas Bjorn	72 78 75 72	297	3,430
Gary Clark	75 73 76 73	297	3,430
Barry Lane	73 77 70 77	297	3,430
Paul Lawrie	72 75 72 78	297	3,430
Ove Sellberg	71 74 79 74	298	2,660
Andrew Sherborne	74 76 74 74	298	2,660
Rolf Muntz	69 81 74 74	298	2,660
Seve Ballesteros	73 75 78 73	299	2,380
George Ryall	74 75 73 78	300	2,065
Andrew Coltart	72 75 79 74	300	2,065
Paul Curry	76 71 74 79	300	2,065
Eduardo Romero	70 76 76 78	300	2,065
Ross Drummond	72 78 75 75	300	2,065
Greg Chalmers	73 77 77 73	300	2,065
Oyvind Rojahn	73 76 73 79	301	1,540
Paul Affleck	74 73 76 78	301	1,540
David Higgins	72 78 76 75	301	1,540
Eric Giraud	74 75 73 80	302	1,047
Ricky Willison	76 74 76 76	302	1,047
Mark Davis	71 73 84 75	303	1,044
Michael Welch	76 73 77 79	305	1,042

Canon European Masters

Crans-sur-Sierre Golf Club, Crans-sur-Sierre, Switzerland September 5-8
Par 36-35–71; 6,663 yards purse, £768,000

	SCORES	TOTAL	MONEY
Colin Montgomerie	65 71 61 63	260	£127,950
Sam Torrance	65 63 68 68	264	85,250
Paul Curry	66 70 65 66	267	48,070
Peter Mitchell	68 70 71 64	273	32,613.33
Seve Ballesteros	71 68 68 66	273	32,613.33
Gary Orr	66 70 68 69	273	32,613.33
Thomas Bjorn	67 72 68 67	274	19,813.33
Darren Clarke	68 68 70 68	274	19,813.33
Miguel Angel Jimenez	71 67 67 69	274	19,813.33
Mats Lanner	72 69 69 65	275	13,766.25

	SCORES				TOTAL	MONEY
Andrew Oldcorn	74	68	67	66	275	13,766.25
Paul Broadhurst	64	70	71	70	275	13,766.25
Lee Westwood	65	70	68	72	275	13,766.25
Fredrik Lindgren	71	69	70	66	276	11,060
Stephen Field	70	68	68	70	276	11,060
Ross Drummond	70	66	69	71	276	11,060
Carl Suneson	70	67	68	71	276	11,060
Padraig Harrington	69	71	71	66	277	9,280
Jarmo Sandelin	72	70	72	63	277	9,280
Miguel Angel Martin	69	70	70	68	277	9,280
Robert Coles	68	68	70	71	277	9,280
Per-Ulrik Johansson	67	73	66	71	277	9,280
Daniel Chopra	68	72	72	66	278	7,610
Christian Cevaer	73	66	73	66	278	7,610
Angel Cabrera	69	73	68	68	278	7,610
Marc Farry	70	72	68	68	278	7,610
Olle Nordberg	66	69	74	69	278	7,610
Roger Chapman	68	68	72	70	278	7,610
Bradley Hughes	66	70	71	71	278	7,610
Per Nyman	70	68	69	71	278	7,610
David Higgins	72	67	66	73	278	7,610
Patrik Sjoland	66	74	72	67	279	6,382.50
Barry Lane	67	70	71	71	279	6,382.50
Eduardo Romero	65	75	70	70	280	5,762.50
Pierre Fulke	73	69	69	69	280	5,762.50
Carl Mason	69	71	72	68	280	5,762.50
David Williams	69	71	70	70	280	5,762.50
Manuel Pinero	71	70	69	70	280	5,762.50
Domingo Hospital	69	69	67	75	280	5,762.50
Retief Goosen	72	70	68	71	281	4,522.50
Joakim Haeggman	70	71	67	73	281	4,522.50
David Gilford	69	70	71	71	281	4,522.50
Mark Roe	70	72	69	70	281	4,522.50
David Howell	70	71	70	70	281	4,522.50
Silvio Grappasonni	72	70	71	68	281	4,522.50
Stephen McAllister	71	68	74	68	281	4,522.50
Derrick Cooper	72	69	73	67	281	4,522.50
Paul Lawrie	70	70	70	71	281	4,522.50
Miles Tunnicliff	72	64	74	71	281	4,522.50
Michael Campbell	69	73	71	69	282	3,592.50
Fabrice Tarnaud	72	70	67	73	282	3,592.50
David A. Russell	72	70	69	72	283	3,205
Jean Van de Velde	71	71	69	72	283	3,205
Eric Giraud	67	69	69	78	283	3,205
Peter Fowler	72	68	72	72	284	2,662.50
Steen Tinning	69	73	71	71	284	2,662.50
Michael Welch	72	70	74	68	284	2,662.50
Malcolm Mackenzie	65	72	71	76	284	2,662.50
Sven Struver	69	72	72	72	285	2,332.50
Mathias Gronberg	69	70	74	72	285	2,332.50
Howard Clark	73	69	70	75	287	2,115
Gary Emerson	74	67	73	73	287	2,115
Gordon Sherry	72	70	73	72	287	2,115
Robert Allenby	71	71	74	71	287	2,115
Gary Clark	70	72	76	69	287	2,115
Matthew Hazelden	71	71	73	74	289	1,152
Juan Carlos Pinero	69	71	79	71	290	1,150
Massimo Florioli	68	74	75	74	291	1,146
Stephen Ames	69	72	76	74	291	1,146
Marco Scopetta	73	69	79	70	291	1,146

Trophee Lancome

St. Nom la Breteche, Paris, France
Par 35-35–70; 6,840 yards

September 12-15
purse, £650,000

		SCORES			TOTAL	MONEY
Jesper Parnevik	66	69	66	67	268	£108,330
Colin Montgomerie	66	70	66	71	273	72,210
Ross Drummond	68	68	69	69	274	40,690
David Howell	67	71	68	71	277	27,593.33
Costantino Rocca	68	69	69	71	277	27,593.33
Stuart Cage	66	74	70	67	277	27,593.33
Paul Eales	71	69	68	70	278	16,753.33
Ian Woosnam	67	68	70	73	278	16,753.33
Padraig Harrington	68	74	73	63	278	16,753.33
Jamie Spence	65	73	67	74	279	11,308
Miguel Angel Jimenez	68	71	72	68	279	11,308
Paul Broadhurst	68	71	68	72	279	11,308
Rodger Davis	70	72	69	68	279	11,308
Mark Roe	68	73	65	73	279	11,308
Silvio Grappasonni	69	67	70	75	281	8,967.50
Bernhard Langer	67	71	71	72	281	8,967.50
David Gilford	75	68	68	70	281	8,967.50
Stephen Ames	75	66	71	69	281	8,967.50
Peter Mitchell	70	73	67	72	282	7,930
Andrew Coltart	66	72	74	70	282	7,930
Per Haugsrud	71	70	72	70	283	7,312.50
Jonathan Lomas	74	69	71	69	283	7,312.50
Peter Baker	67	69	74	73	283	7,312.50
Sven Struver	72	70	70	71	283	7,312.50
Phillip Price	71	74	67	72	284	6,630
Nick Faldo	73	71	69	71	284	6,630
Martin Gates	76	67	71	70	284	6,630
Ignacio Garrido	73	69	75	68	285	5,850
Barry Lane	69	73	72	71	285	5,850
Andrew Sherborne	72	71	70	72	285	5,850
Santiago Luna	72	70	74	69	285	5,850
Andrew Oldcorn	73	69	72	71	285	5,850
Carl Mason	73	68	73	72	286	5,070
Eduardo Romero	67	75	72	72	286	5,070
Howard Clark	67	74	70	75	286	5,070
Greg Turner	73	72	73	68	286	5,070
Patrik Sjoland	74	69	75	68	286	5,070
Retief Goosen	72	71	75	69	287	4,290
Thomas Gogele	73	71	72	71	287	4,290
Seve Ballesteros	69	75	70	73	287	4,290
Ronan Rafferty	70	75	67	75	287	4,290
Richard Boxall	71	74	73	69	287	4,290
Chip Beck	70	72	72	73	287	4,290
Marc Farry	71	72	72	72	287	4,290
Richard Green	70	75	71	72	288	3,445
Darren Clarke	67	74	74	73	288	3,445
Stephen McAllister	74	70	71	73	288	3,445
Antoine Lebouc	69	70	71	78	288	3,445
Gary Orr	70	75	68	75	288	3,445
Rolf Muntz	74	66	73	75	288	3,445
Tony Johnstone	68	76	74	71	289	2,795
Sam Torrance	68	72	73	76	289	2,795
Jean Van de Velde	74	71	71	73	289	2,795
Emanuele Canonica	77	68	73	71	289	2,795

	SCORES				TOTAL	MONEY
Mark Mouland	74	71	71	74	290	2,340
Ricky Willison	72	73	73	72	290	2,340
Jose Rivero	72	72	68	78	290	2,340
Michael Campbell	72	71	74	74	291	1,982.50
Tim Planchin	71	74	70	76	291	1,982.50
Fabrice Tarnaud	71	72	72	76	291	1,982.50
Steven Richardson	71	74	71	75	291	1,982.50
Fernando Roca	71	74	69	78	292	1,787.50
Steven Bottomley	72	72	77	71	292	1,787.50
Derrick Cooper	73	72	75	74	294	1,690
Mark Davis	71	72	73	81	297	1,625

Loch Lomond World Invitational

Loch Lomond Golf Club, Glasgow, Scotland
Par 36-35–71; 7,005 yards

September 19-22
purse, £750,000

	SCORES				TOTAL	MONEY
Thomas Bjorn	70	69	68	70	277	£125,000
Jean Van de Velde	75	65	67	71	278	83,320
Robert Allenby	69	71	71	70	281	46,940
Colin Montgomerie	72	70	70	70	282	34,635
Jonathan Lomas	71	73	70	68	282	34,635
Richard Green	72	73	71	67	283	24,375
Darren Clarke	68	73	73	69	283	24,375
Miguel Angel Martin	73	73	69	69	284	16,830
Mark McNulty	73	72	70	69	284	16,830
Peter O'Malley	70	78	68	68	284	16,830
Eamonn Darcy	71	76	66	72	285	12,923.33
Greg Turner	78	70	70	67	285	12,923.33
Barry Lane	69	74	71	71	285	12,923.33
David Gilford	71	74	72	69	286	11,245
Stephen Ames	76	71	68	71	286	11,245
Lee Westwood	74	73	69	71	287	9,917.50
Glen Day	72	74	71	70	287	9,917.50
Miguel Angel Jimenez	77	70	72	68	287	9,917.50
Jose Coceres	68	77	75	67	287	9,917.50
David Howell	70	73	75	70	288	8,437.50
Ian Woosnam	73	69	75	71	288	8,437.50
Per Haugsrud	77	72	71	68	288	8,437.50
Des Smyth	75	72	70	71	288	8,437.50
Roger Chapman	71	75	69	73	288	8,437.50
Martin Gates	76	70	71	71	288	8,437.50
Jamie Spence	67	74	72	76	289	7,425
Andrew Coltart	74	71	70	74	289	7,425
Andrew Sherborne	73	72	72	72	289	7,425
Paul McGinley	72	74	69	75	290	6,281.25
Retief Goosen	72	72	75	71	290	6,281.25
Ricky Willison	72	77	71	70	290	6,281.25
Peter Baker	69	73	77	71	290	6,281.25
Costantino Rocca	72	74	72	72	290	6,281.25
Eduardo Romero	77	70	73	70	290	6,281.25
Ross Drummond	69	79	69	73	290	6,281.25
Pierre Fulke	71	72	73	74	290	6,281.25
Marc Farry	76	71	74	70	291	5,475
Nick Faldo	68	73	73	77	291	5,475
Padraig Harrington	76	74	71	71	292	5,025

	SCORES				TOTAL	MONEY
Rodger Davis	76	72	68	76	292	5,025
Pedro Linhart	69	76	72	75	292	5,025
Gordon Sherry	74	75	72	71	292	5,025
Rolf Muntz	74	75	74	70	293	4,425
Thomas Gogele	70	75	69	79	293	4,425
Iain Pyman	73	78	74	68	293	4,425
Ignacio Garrido	72	74	73	74	293	4,425
Diego Borrego	73	78	72	71	294	3,600
Andrew Oldcorn	75	73	76	70	294	3,600
Gary Clark	75	71	76	72	294	3,600
Peter Mitchell	73	77	73	71	294	3,600
Adam Hunter	77	71	75	71	294	3,600
Raymond Russell	76	74	69	75	294	3,600
Richard Boxall	75	76	70	73	294	3,600
Domingo Hospital	72	78	73	72	295	2,700
Joakim Haeggman	76	73	72	74	295	2,700
Paul Broadhurst	79	72	75	69	295	2,700
Jim Payne	73	76	73	73	295	2,700
David Carter	75	75	71	74	295	2,700
Ronan Rafferty	73	75	73	75	296	2,212.50
Fernando Roca	76	72	76	72	296	2,212.50
Derrick Cooper	74	75	74	73	296	2,212.50
Sven Struver	75	75	72	74	296	2,212.50
Brian Marchbank	75	76	73	73	297	1,987.50
Peter Hedblom	75	74	74	74	297	1,987.50
Michael Campbell	69	80	77	72	298	1,875
Tony Johnstone	80	71	72	76	299	1,124
Juan Carlos Pinero	78	72	75	74	299	1,124
Santiago Luna	76	73	75	76	300	1,120
Gary Nicklaus	75	76	73	76	300	1,120

Smurfit European Open

The K Club, Dublin, Ireland
Par 36-36–72; 7,159 yards

September 26-29
purse, £750,000

	SCORES				TOTAL	MONEY
Per-Ulrik Johansson	71	70	66	70	277	£125,000
Costantino Rocca	67	70	69	72	278	83,320
Andrew Coltart	71	68	69	71	279	42,220
Roger Chapman	72	69	69	69	279	42,220
Miguel Angel Martin	69	69	71	71	280	31,770
Paul Broadhurst	73	65	68	75	281	22,500
Jim Payne	68	69	72	72	281	22,500
Thomas Bjorn	74	69	70	68	281	22,500
Eduardo Romero	73	71	70	68	282	16,740
Per Haugsrud	71	71	73	68	283	13,442.50
Dean Robertson	70	70	74	69	283	13,442.50
Padraig Harrington	65	73	71	74	283	13,442.50
Michael Jonzon	68	74	70	71	283	13,442.50
Derrick Cooper	76	67	66	75	284	9,681
Niclas Fasth	66	76	70	72	284	9,681
Angel Cabrera	72	70	72	70	284	9,681
Malcolm Mackenzie	71	73	70	70	284	9,681
Domingo Hospital	72	73	70	69	284	9,681
Rodger Davis	69	70	73	72	284	9,681
Sandy Lyle	73	69	70	72	284	9,681

	SCORES				TOTAL	MONEY
Jamie Spence	73	70	73	68	284	9,681
Paul McGinley	70	73	71	70	284	9,681
Barry Lane	70	73	68	73	284	9,681
Richard Green	72	75	65	73	285	7,650
Colin Montgomerie	73	74	70	68	285	7,650
Lee Westwood	70	72	73	70	285	7,650
Darren Clarke	72	72	72	69	285	7,650
Raymond Russell	70	70	72	73	285	7,650
David Gilford	75	71	68	72	286	6,637.50
Sven Struver	73	70	72	71	286	6,637.50
Peter O'Malley	69	73	71	73	286	6,637.50
Gary Nicklaus	71	71	74	70	286	6,637.50
Tom Lehman	74	69	73	71	287	5,850
Raymond Burns	72	69	70	76	287	5,850
Ian Woosnam	74	72	74	67	287	5,850
Stephen Field	71	75	73	68	287	5,850
Rolf Muntz	74	68	73	72	287	5,850
Bernhard Langer	71	71	71	75	288	5,175
Jose Coceres	72	71	74	71	288	5,175
David Higgins	73	70	72	73	288	5,175
Peter Mitchell	73	70	71	74	288	5,175
Paul Eales	72	74	69	74	289	4,500
Andre Bossert	71	71	75	72	289	4,500
Peter Baker	74	70	75	70	289	4,500
Michel Besanceney	73	73	71	72	289	4,500
Mathias Gronberg	73	74	70	72	289	4,500
Gordon Brand, Jr.	69	76	70	75	290	3,975
Jimmy Heggarty	72	70	71	77	290	3,975
Michael Welch	69	72	74	76	291	3,375
Steen Tinning	71	75	69	76	291	3,375
Miguel Angel Jimenez	72	70	73	76	291	3,375
Stephen McAllister	76	71	72	72	291	3,375
Daniel Chopra	73	70	74	74	291	3,375
Emanuele Canonica	74	72	74	71	291	3,375
Eamonn Darcy	73	73	72	74	292	2,418.75
Anssi Kankkonen	76	71	74	71	292	2,418.75
Ignacio Garrido	72	73	75	72	292	2,418.75
Patrik Sjoland	75	72	74	71	292	2,418.75
Mike McLean	71	75	73	73	292	2,418.75
Adam Hunter	72	71	74	75	292	2,418.75
David Carter	74	69	72	77	292	2,418.75
Stuart Cage	72	73	79	68	292	2,418.75
Diego Borrego	69	76	74	74	293	1,743.75
Richard Boxall	71	73	75	74	293	1,743.75
Iain Pyman	73	73	75	72	293	1,743.75
Klas Eriksson	75	72	69	77	293	1,743.75
Paul Curry	76	70	76	72	294	1,122
John Bickerton	77	70	71	76	294	1,122
Jose Maria Canizares	71	73	78	73	295	1,118
Miles Tunnicliff	68	73	73	81	295	1,118
Roger Wessels	69	76	77	78	300	1,115
Christian Cevaer	73	74	77	80	304	1,113
Steven Bottomley	77	70	76	85	308	1,111

The Tour Championship enabled Tom Lehman to lead the U.S. PGA Tour money list, become Player of the Year and win the Vardon Trophy.

Allsport/Craig Jones

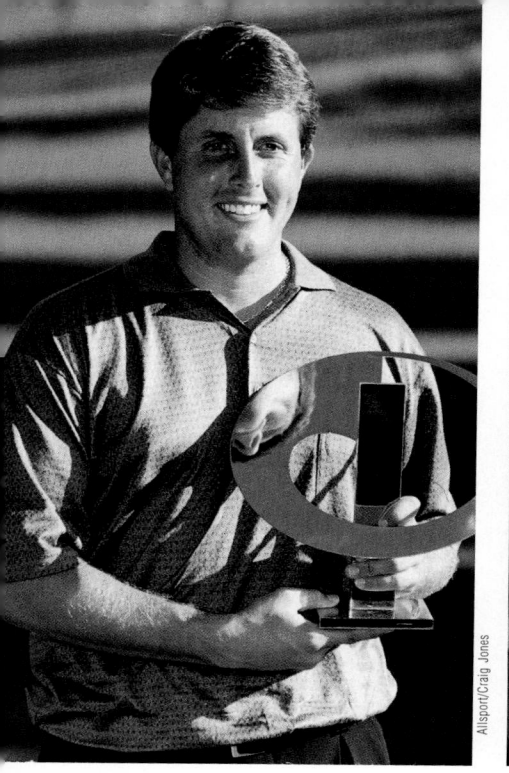

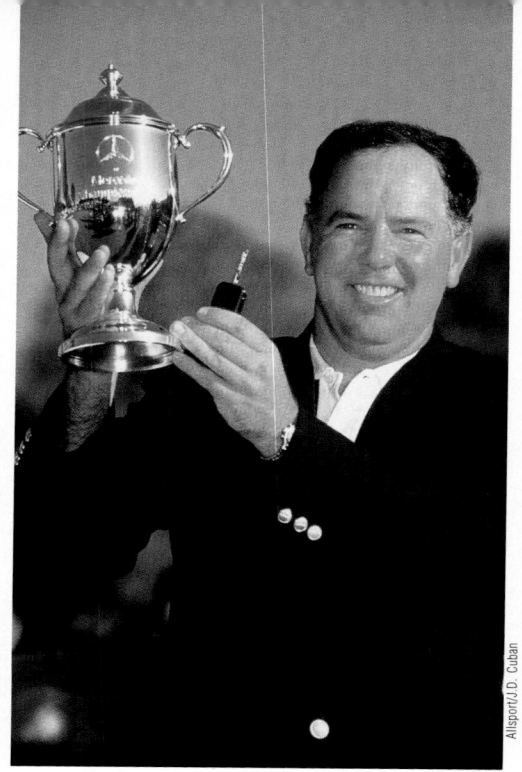

Phil Mickelson had four wins.

Allsport/J.D. Cuban

It was a great start for Mark O'Meara.

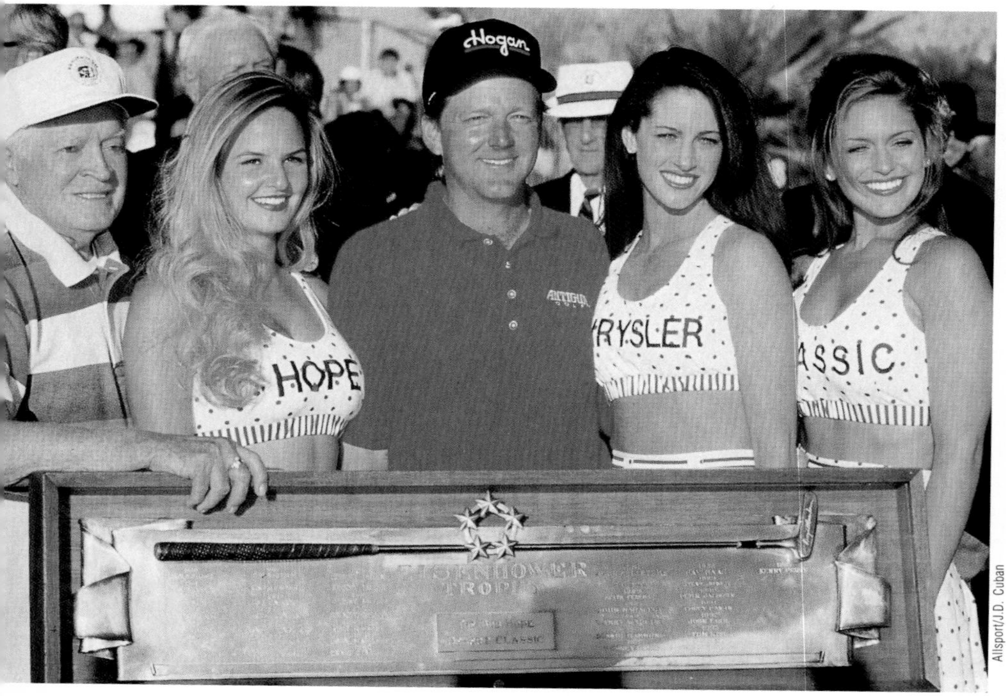

Allsport/J.D. Cuban

Bob Hope and the Chrysler girls congratulated Mark Brooks.

Steve Stricker took two titles.

Davis Love III won the Buick Invitational.

Scott Hoch grabbed the Michelob title.

Justin Leonard got his first victory.

David Duval had five top-three finishes.

Starting well, Greg Norman won at Doral.

The Buick Classic was Ernie Els' only American victory.

Vijay Singh had a good year, but no wins.

Tommy Tolles had six top-10s.

Corey Pavin won the MasterCard Colonial.

Michael C. Cohen

Michael C. Cohen

Allsport/J.D. Cuban

Allsport/J.D. Cuban

Allsport/J.D. Cuban

Loren Roberts added two titles.

John Cook shot 258 in Memphis.

Craig Stadler won in Los Angeles.

After nine years, Tom Watson won.

European Tour

Michael C. Cohen

Colin Montgomerie led the European money list for the fourth consecutive year.

Allsport/David Cannon

Ian Woosnam won four times.

Allsport/Stephen Munday

Until a September car crash, Robert Allenby was rolling.

Costantino Rocca won the Volvo PGA.

Mark McNulty posted four victories.

Lee Westwood was sixth in Europe.

Andrew Coltart ranked seventh.

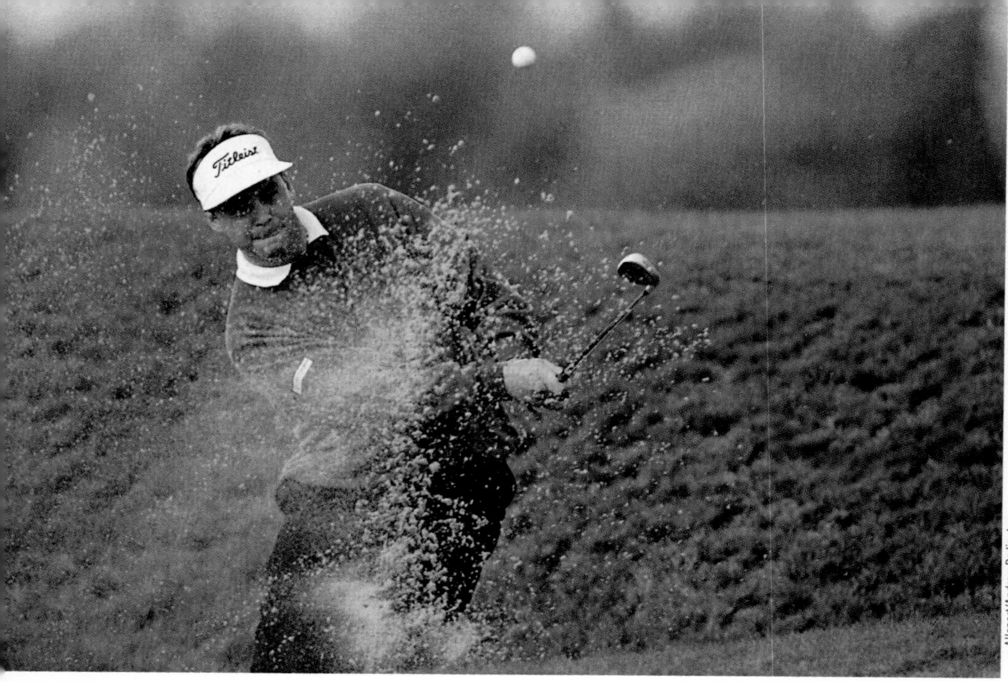

Allsport/Andrew Redington

Darren Clarke blasted to the Linde German Masters title.

Allsport/Andrew Redington

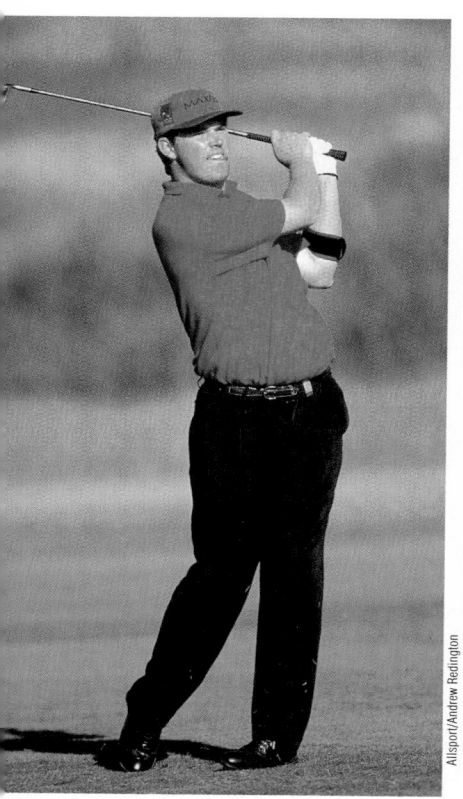

Padraig Harrington won in Spain.

Allsport/Andrew Redington

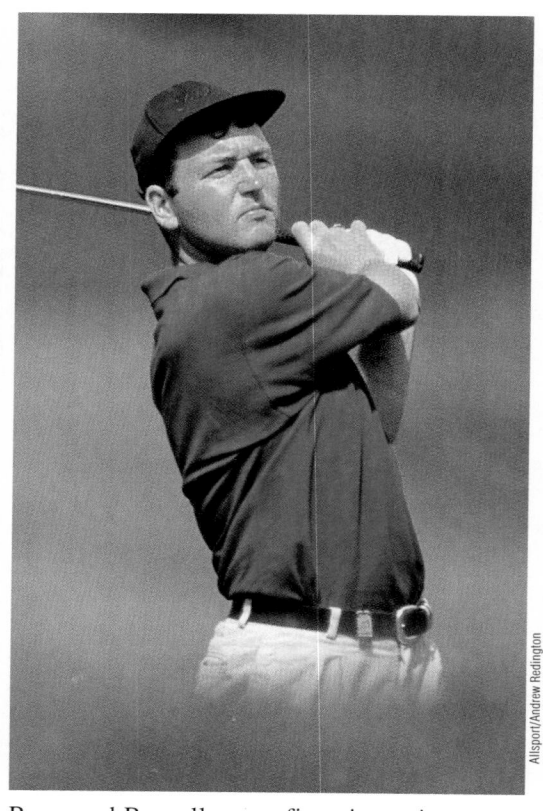

Raymond Russell was a first-time winner.

Trinidad had a winner in Stephen Ames.

Wayne Riley won in Portugal.

Frank Nobilo was victorious in Europe.

Bernhard Langer won in Hong Kong.

Jesper Parnevik took the Lancome title.

Around the World

Masashi (Jumbo) Ozaki had eight victories in Japan and won over $1.9 million.

Yoshinori Kaneko was second with three titles in Japan.

Nobuo Serizawa won the Japan Match Play championship.

Ernie Els and President Nelson Mandela celebrated the South African star's success.

Wayne Westner had three FNB Tour titles.

Sven Struver won the South African PGA, a co-sanctioned event.

Craig Parry won the Australian Masters.

Senior Tours

Jim Colbert took five Senior titles.

Hale Irwin won the PGA Seniors' title.

Isao Aoki won in America and Japan.

John Bland was a four-time winner.

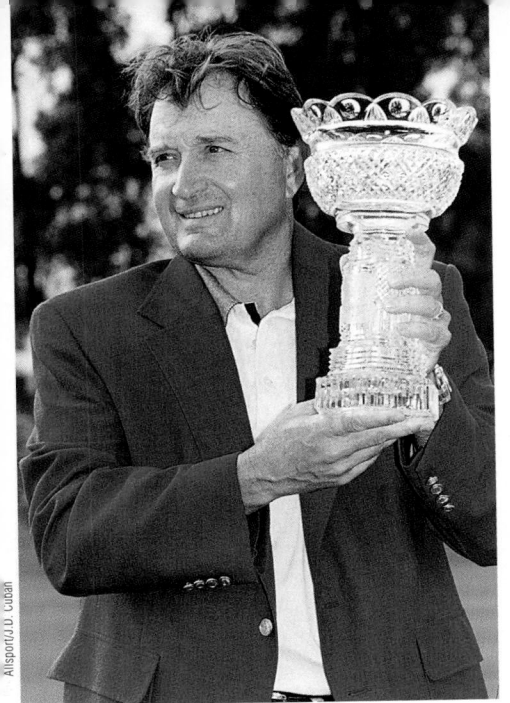

Raymond Floyd won the Senior Players.

Dave Stockton won the Senior Open.

Arnold Palmer and Jack Nicklaus drew the crowds, as they have for years.

Brian Barnes repeated in Britain.

Women's Tours

Karrie Webb became the first LPGA player to earn $1 million.

Annika Sorenstam repeated in the U.S. Women's Open.

Laura Davies took away nine trophies and won over $1.3 million.

Liselotte Neumann won three times.

Dottie Pepper had five victories.

Patty Sheehan took a splash at the Shore.

Michelle McGann was recognized for her hats — and wins.

Allsport/Stephen Munday

Emilee Klein won the Weetabix
Women's British Open title.

Michael C. Cohen

Helen Alfredsson was second in European earnings behind Davies.

The American team led by captain Judy Rankin (bottom left) won over the
Europeans in the Solheim Cup, always a highlight of women's golf.

Allsport/David Cannon

Linde German Masters

Berliner Golf and Country Club, Motzener See,
Berlin, Germany
Par 37-35–72; 6,848 yards

October 3-6
purse, £650,000

	SCORES				TOTAL	MONEY
Darren Clarke	70	64	67	63	264	£108,330
Mark Davis	69	67	67	62	265	72,210
Paul Broadhurst	71	64	65	66	266	40,690
Colin Montgomerie	70	67	65	65	267	32,500
Paul McGinley	66	67	70	65	268	23,260
Ernie Els	68	67	68	65	268	23,260
Peter Baker	66	70	64	68	268	23,260
Paul Eales	67	67	67	68	269	13,930
Padraig Harrington	68	67	66	68	269	13,930
Thomas Bjorn	71	66	69	63	269	13,930
Peter Mitchell	71	67	64	67	269	13,930
Thomas Gogele	67	75	64	64	270	11,180
Michael Campbell	67	68	69	67	271	9,983.33
Ronan Rafferty	73	68	65	65	271	9,983.33
Costantino Rocca	70	71	64	66	271	9,983.33
Jose Coceres	66	71	69	66	272	9,160
Greg Turner	68	68	66	71	273	8,775
Paul Lawrie	70	72	66	66	274	7,852
Jean Van de Velde	71	67	69	67	274	7,852
Bob May	73	68	67	66	274	7,852
Andrew Coltart	68	71	68	67	274	7,852
Mark James	69	70	67	68	274	7,852
Gordon Brand, Jr.	69	69	70	67	275	6,922.50
Marc Farry	66	70	70	69	275	6,922.50
Bernhard Langer	71	69	67	68	275	6,922.50
Mark Mouland	66	69	71	69	275	6,922.50
Joakim Haeggman	69	70	67	70	276	5,776.88
Jay Townsend	68	70	67	71	276	5,776.88
Miguel Angel Jimenez	68	70	73	65	276	5,776.88
Steen Tinning	69	68	69	70	276	5,776.88
Niclas Fasth	69	67	73	67	276	5,776.88
Per-Ulrik Johansson	71	70	67	68	276	5,776.88
Santiago Luna	72	68	67	69	276	5,776.88
Jamie Spence	73	69	67	67	276	5,776.88
Peter O'Malley	68	72	68	69	277	5,005
David Carter	69	68	74	66	277	5,005
Jarmo Sandelin	74	69	70	65	278	4,485
Richard Boxall	70	71	69	68	278	4,485
Silvio Grappasonni	71	71	69	67	278	4,485
Jim Payne	70	72	69	67	278	4,485
Lee Westwood	73	70	71	64	278	4,485
Emanuele Canonica	68	75	70	65	278	4,485
Christian Cevaer	69	71	65	74	279	3,770
Seve Ballesteros	70	72	65	72	279	3,770
Eduardo Romero	71	70	65	73	279	3,770
Mark McNulty	72	69	65	73	279	3,770
Phillip Price	70	70	69	70	279	3,770
Mark Roe	70	71	72	67	280	3,120
Steve Webster	71	72	70	67	280	3,120
Jonathan Lomas	69	68	71	72	280	3,120
Tony Johnstone	70	69	71	70	280	3,120
Paul Curry	70	71	69	70	280	3,120
Ross McFarlane	68	73	66	74	281	2,730

	SCORES				TOTAL	MONEY
Stuart Cage	70	71	69	72	282	2,470
Malcolm Mackenzie	77	66	67	72	282	2,470
Mats Lanner	70	71	66	75	282	2,470
Michael Jonzon	68	72	72	71	283	2,210
David A. Russell	67	72	75	70	284	2,015
Martin Gates	69	67	76	72	284	2,015
Peter Hedblom	72	70	72	70	284	2,015
Diego Borrego	72	69	71	73	285	1,852.50
Steven Bottomley	72	69	70	74	285	1,852.50
Steven Richardson	71	70	73	72	286	1,722.50
Sven Struver	74	68	71	73	286	1,722.50
Retief Goosen	71	71	74	71	287	1,300
Andrew Sherborne	69	72	76	70	287	1,300
Fredrik Lindgren	72	71	71	74	288	973
Heinz P. Thul	71	72	70	77	290	971
Oyvind Rojahn	70	73	75	73	291	969

Alfred Dunhill Cup

Old Course, St. Andrews, Scotland
Par 36-36—72; 6,933 yards

October 10-13
purse, £1,000,000

FIRST ROUND

ZIMBABWE DEFEATED INDIA, 2-1
Ali Sher (Ind) defeated Tony Johnstone, 72-73; Mark McNulty (Z) defeated Gaurav Ghei, 70-73; Nick Price (Z) defeated Jeev Milkha Singh, 70-71.

SWEDEN DEFEATED SCOTLAND, 2-1
Andrew Coltart (Sc) defeated Peter Hedblom, 67-70; Patrik Sjoland (Sw) defeated Raymond Russell, 68-69; Jarmo Sandelin (Sw) defeated Colin Montgomerie, 68-69.

SOUTH AFRICA DEFEATED CANADA, 2-1
Wayne Westner (SA) defeated Rick Todd, 68-77; Ernie Els (SA) defeated Rick Gibson, 65-73; Jim Rutledge (C) defeated Retief Goosen, 69-76.

IRELAND DEFEATED WALES, 2-1
Mark Mouland (W) defeated Darren Clarke, 70-71; Paul McGinley (Ire) defeated Paul Affleck, 68-70; Padraig Harrington (Ire) defeated Phillip Price, 70-74.

NEW ZEALAND DEFEATED GERMANY, 2-1
Grant Waite (NZ) defeated Heinz P. Thul, 69-69, fourth extra hole; Thomas Gogele (G) defeated Greg Turner, 71-74; Frank Nobilo (NZ) defeated Sven Struver, 66-71.

AUSTRALIA DEFEATED JAPAN, 2-1
Naomichi Ozaki (J) defeated Wayne Riley, 67-71; Steve Elkington (A) defeated Kazuhiro Takami, 68-74; Greg Norman (A) defeated Hajime Meshiai, 72-74.

UNITED STATES DEFEATED ITALY, 2-1
Mark O'Meara (US) defeated Costantino Rocca, 63-70; Emanuele Canonica (It) defeated Phil Mickelson, 72-72, second extra hole; Steve Stricker (US) defeated Silvio Grappasonni, 68-75.

ENGLAND DEFEATED SPAIN, 3-0
Lee Westwood (E) defeated Ignacio Garrido, 69-77; Jonathan Lomas (E) defeated Miguel Angel Jimenez, 70-71; Barry Lane (E) defeated Diego Borrego, 69-76.

SECOND ROUND

JAPAN DEFEATED NEW ZEALAND, 2-1
Naomichi Ozaki (J) defeated Frank Nobilo, 69-73; Grant Waite (NZ) defeated Hajime Meshiai, 72-73; Kazuhiro Takami (J) defeated Greg Turner, 70-73.

AUSTRALIA DEFEATED GERMANY, 3-0
Wayne Riley (A) defeated Heinz P. Thul, 74-76; Greg Norman (A) defeated Sven Struver, 71-73; Steve Elkington (A) defeated Thomas Gogele, 71-80.

UNITED STATES DEFEATED ENGLAND, 2-1
Barry Lane (E) defeated Mark O'Meara, 72-75; Steve Stricker (US) defeated Jonathan Lomas, 75-79; Phil Mickelson (US) defeated Lee Westwood, 72-73.

SPAIN DEFEATED ITALY, 2-1
Miguel Angel Jimenez (Sp) defeated Silvio Grappasonni, 69-79; Ignacio Garrido (Sp) defeated Emanuele Canonica, 74-79; Costantino Rocca (It) defeated Diego Borrego, 73-76.

IRELAND DEFEATED CANADA, 3-0
Darren Clarke (Ire) defeated Rick Gibson, 76-80; Padraig Harrington (Ire) defeated Rick Todd, 73-73, first extra hole; Paul McGinley (Ire) defeated Jim Rutledge, 71-77.

SOUTH AFRICA DEFEATED WALES, 2-1
Phillip Price (W) defeated Retief Goosen, 73-78; Ernie Els (SA) defeated Mark Mouland, 70-DQ; Wayne Westner (SA) defeated Paul Affleck, 72-76.

SWEDEN DEFEATED ZIMBABWE, 3-0
Patrik Sjoland (Sw) defeated Tony Johnstone, 73-76; Jarmo Sandelin (Sw) defeated Nick Price, 75-75, first extra hole; Peter Hedblom (Sw) defeated Mark McNulty, 72-73.

INDIA DEFEATED SCOTLAND, 2-1
Jeev Milkha Singh (Ind) defeated Andrew Coltart, 74-74, first extra hole; Gaurav Ghei (Ind) defeated Colin Montgomerie, 78-79; Raymond Russell (Sc) defeated Ali Sher, 71-84.

THIRD ROUND

WALES DEFEATED CANADA, 2-1
Rick Gibson (C) defeated Mark Mouland, 71-75; Phillip Price (W) defeated Jim Rutledge, 71-72; Paul Affleck (W) defeated Rick Todd, 70-72.

SOUTH AFRICA DEFEATED IRELAND, 2-1
Retief Goosen (SA) defeated Darren Clarke, 70-70, first extra hole; Paul McGinley (Ire) defeated Ernie Els, 69-71; Wayne Westner (SA) defeated Padraig Harrington, 69-70.

UNITED STATES DEFEATED SPAIN, 3-0
Mark O'Meara (US) defeated Miguel Angel Jimenez, 67-68; Steve Stricker (US) defeated Diego Borrego, 70-74; Phil Mickelson (US) defeated Ignacio Garrido, 66-77.

ITALY DEFEATED ENGLAND, 2-1
Costantino Rocca (It) defeated Lee Westwood, 72-74; Silvio Grappasonni (It) defeated Jonathan Lomas, 68-69; Barry Lane (E) defeated Emanuele Canonica, 74-76.

ZIMBABWE DEFEATED SCOTLAND, 2-1
Tony Johnstone (Z) defeated Andrew Coltart, 70-72; Mark McNulty (Z) defeated Colin Montgomerie, 69-70; Raymond Russell (Sc) defeated Nick Price, 72-76.

SWEDEN DEFEATED INDIA, 3-0
Patrik Sjoland (Sw) defeated Jeev Milkha Singh, 68-74; Peter Hedblom (Sw) defeated Gaurav Ghei, 69-72; Jarmo Sandelin (Sw) defeated Ali Sher, 72-73.

NEW ZEALAND DEFEATED AUSTRALIA, 3-0
Grant Waite (NZ) defeated Wayne Riley, 69-76; Greg Turner (NZ) defeated Steve Elkington, 69-73; Frank Nobilo (NZ) defeated Greg Norman, 66-68.

GERMANY DEFEATED JAPAN, 2-1
Sven Struver (G) defeated Naomichi Ozaki, 70-72; Thomas Gogele (G) defeated Hajime Meshiai, 71-77; Kazuhiro Takami (J) defeated Heinz P. Thul, 73-74.

SEMI-FINALS

UNITED STATES DEFEATED SWEDEN, 2-1
Mark O'Meara (US) defeated Peter Hedblom, 68-74; Steve Stricker (US) defeated Patrik Sjoland, 70-73; Jarmo Sandelin (Sw) defeated Phil Mickelson, 68-71.

NEW ZEALAND DEFEATED SOUTH AFRICA, 2-1
Grant Waite (NZ) defeated Wayne Westner, 74-74, third extra hole; Greg Turner (NZ) defeated Retief Goosen, 71-72; Ernie Els (SA) defeated Frank Nobilo, 69-72.

FINAL

UNITED STATES DEFEATED NEW ZEALAND, 2-1
Frank Nobilo (NZ) defeated Mark O'Meara, 69-72; Phil Mickelson (US) defeated Greg Turner, 69-72; Steve Stricker (US) defeated Grant Waite, 67-73.

	MATCHES WON	INDIVIDUAL GAMES WON (After Round 3)	PRIZE MONEY	
			TEAM	PLAYER
GROUP 1				
United States	3	7	£300,000	£100,000
England	1	5	45,000	15,000
Italy	1	4	25,500	8,500
Spain	1	2	19,500	6,500
GROUP 2				
Sweden	3	8	95,000	31,666
Zimbabwe	2	4	45,000	15,000
India	1	3	25,500	8,500
Scotland	0	3	19,500	6,500
GROUP 3				
South Africa	3	6	95,000	31,666
Ireland	2	6	45,000	15,000
Wales	1	4	25,500	8,500
Canada	0	2	19,500	6,500
GROUP 4				
New Zealand	2	6	150,000	50,000
Australia	2	5	45,000	15,000
Japan	1	4	25,500	8,500
Germany	1	3	19,500	6,500

Oki Pro-Am

La Moraleja Golf Club, Madrid, Spain
Par 36-36–72; 7,054 yards

October 10-13
purse, £447,000

	SCORES				TOTAL	MONEY
Tom Kite	71	68	64	70	273	£74,500.84
Angel Cabrera	71	69	62	72	274	49,662.26
Seve Ballesteros	72	66	69	69	276	27,977.55
David Gilford	69	71	66	71	277	22,350.25
Klas Eriksson	71	68	72	69	280	18,943.08
Miles Tunnicliff	74	69	69	69	281	15,645.18
Malcolm Mackenzie	69	71	72	70	282	12,292.64
Pedro Linhart	65	73	70	74	282	12,292.64
David Higgins	69	70	75	69	283	9,454.15
Gary Emerson	72	71	70	70	283	9,454.15
David Carter	72	72	71	69	284	6,551.60
Niclas Fasth	72	71	70	71	284	6,551.60
Fredrik Larsson	74	72	67	71	284	6,551.60
Anders Hansen	73	72	68	71	284	6,551.60
Juan Quiros	68	71	73	72	284	6,551.60
Joakim Haeggman	69	69	73	73	284	6,551.60
Steve Webster	70	71	70	73	284	6,551.60
Mats Lanner	75	67	68	74	284	6,551.60
Greg Chalmers	72	70	68	74	284	6,551.60
Gary Orr	72	67	69	76	284	6,551.60
Stuart Cage	69	69	76	71	285	5,095.86
Jose Maria Canizares	69	70	76	70	285	5,095.86
Juan Carlos Pinero	75	69	68	73	285	5,095.86
Thomas Bjorn	69	73	72	72	286	4,693.55
John McHenry	71	70	70	75	286	4,693.55
Andrew Sherborne	67	72	71	76	286	4,693.55
Robert Coles	75	67	72	73	287	4,157.15
Per Haugsrud	73	69	72	73	287	4,157.15
Anders Forsbrand	74	72	68	73	287	4,157.15
Mathias Gronberg	68	76	70	73	287	4,157.15
Adam Hunter	70	73	69	75	287	4,157.15
Manuel Pinero	75	69	72	72	288	3,665.44
Jon Robson	70	73	70	75	288	3,665.44
Steven Bottomley	75	69	69	75	288	3,665.44
Scott Henderson	72	71	72	74	289	3,218.44
Peter Mitchell	70	70	75	74	289	3,218.44
Brian Marchbank	72	72	72	73	289	3,218.44
Ross Drummond	70	75	72	72	289	3,218.44
Richard Boxall	70	76	71	72	289	3,218.44
Santiago Luna	68	74	72	75	289	3,218.44
Michael Campbell	74	71	68	76	289	3,218.44
Michael Jonzon	70	75	70	75	290	2,726.73
Gordon Brand, Jr.	71	73	72	74	290	2,726.73
Jose Rivero	68	75	73	74	290	2,726.73
John Hawksworth	72	70	70	78	290	2,726.73
David Lynn	72	71	72	76	291	2,369.13
Carl Suneson	73	70	74	74	291	2,369.13
David J. Russell	72	72	74	73	291	2,369.13
Roger Wessels	75	71	72	73	291	2,369.13
Neal Briggs	73	71	73	75	292	2,011.52
Miguel Angel Martin	67	76	76	73	292	2,011.52
Ricky Willison	75	71	74	72	292	2,011.52
Iain Pyman	69	73	78	72	292	2,011.52
Fabrice Tarnaud	72	74	70	77	293	1,653.92

	SCORES			TOTAL	MONEY
David A. Russell	70	74 74	75	293	1,653.92
Jose Rozadilla	72	73 73	75	293	1,653.92
Alvaro Prat	73	73 75	72	293	1,653.92
Mark Davis	76	70 73	76	295	1,430.42
Steen Tinning	74	72 77	73	296	1,385.72
Jesus Maria Arruti	73	73 73	78	297	1,318.67
Mats Hallberg	75	71 76	75	297	1,318.67
Manuel Montes	74	71 75	78	298	1,251.61
Timothy Spence	77	68 76	78	299	1,184.56
David R. Jones	71	75 77	76	299	1,184.56
Jose Sota	72	74 77	77	300	1,117.51
Dean Robertson	74	72 75	82	303	670.51

Toyota World Match Play

Wentworth Club, Surrey, England
Par 434 534 444–35; 345 434 455–37–72; 6,957 yards

October 17-20
purse, £650,000

FIRST ROUND

Steve Stricker defeated Steve Elkington, 3 and 2

Elkington	4 3 4	5 4 4	4 4 4	36	3 4 4	3 3 C	3 4 4	X X
Stricker	5 2 4	4 4 5	4 4 4	36	3 4 6	4 3 W	4 4 4	X X

Elkington leads, 2 up

Elkington	4 3 5	4 4 3	4 5 6	38	3 4 5	3 3 4	4	
Stricker	4 3 5	4 3 3	4 4 4	34	3 4 4	3 2 4	4	

Colin Montgomerie defeated Ian Woosnam, 4 and 2

Montgomerie	4 3 5	4 3 4	4 4 4	35	3 4 4	3 3 4	4 4 4	33 68
Woosnam	5 3 4	4 3 3	4 3 5	34	3 3 5	4 3 4	3 6 5	36 70

Montgomerie leads, 1 up

Montgomerie	4 3 3	4 3 3	4 4 4	32	3 4 4	4 4 4	3	
Woosnam	4 3 4	4 3 4	4 4 5	35	3 4 3	5 3 4	4	

Vijay Singh defeated Phil Mickelson, 1 up

Mickelson	5 3 5	4 4 4	4 3 4	36	3 3 4	4 3 4	4 4 3	32 68
Singh	4 2 4	4 3 4	3 4 5	33	3 3 4	4 3 4	4 5 4	34 67

Singh leads, 1 up

Mickelson	4 3 4	6 3 4	4 4 4	36	3 3 4	5 2 4	5 4 4	34 70
Singh	4 4 4	W 3 3	4 4 4	X	3 4 4	4 3 4	4 6 4	36 X

Mark O'Meara defeated Nobuo Serizawa, 7 and 5

O'Meara	5 3 4	4 3 4	4 4 4	35	3 4 4	4 5 4	4 4 4	36 71
Serizawa	5 3 4	4 3 4	5 4 4	36	3 4 4	4 4 5	5 4 4	37 73

O'Meara leads, 2 up

O'Meara	4 3 4	5 2 4	4 W 4	X	3 4 4	3		
Serizawa	4 3 5	4 3 4	4 C 4	X	4 4 5	4		

SECOND ROUND

Ernie Els defeated Steve Stricker, 1 up

Els	4 3 5	6 3 4	4 4 4	37	3 4 5	4 3 4	4 5 4	36 73
Stricker	4 3 4	W 4 4	3 4 3	X	3 4 4	3 3 4	4 4 4	33 X

Stricker leads, 6 up

Els	4 3 3	4 3 5	3 3 4	32	4 3 4	4 3 3	4 5 4	34 66
Stricker	4 3 4	5 3 5	5 4 4	37	2 4 5	4 3 4	4 5 5	36 73

Mark Brooks defeated Colin Montgomerie, 1 up

Brooks	5 3 4	C 3 3	6 5 4	X	3 3 3	4 3 4	4 5 4	33	X
Montgomerie	4 3 4	3 4 4	6 4 5	37	3 4 5	4 2 4	4 5 4	35	72

Brooks leads, 1 up

Brooks	5 4 3	5 3 5	4 3 3	35	2 4 4	4 3 3	4 4 4	32	67
Montgomerie	4 2 4	4 3 4	4 4 5	34	2 4 4	4 3 4	3 5 4	33	67

Vijay Singh defeated Steve Jones, 9 and 8

Jones	6 3 4	4 4 3	5 4 4	37	3 4 4	4 3 4	3 C 4	X	X
Singh	4 3 4	4 3 4	4 4 4	34	2 4 4	4 2 4	4 W 5	X	X

Singh leads, 3 up

Jones	4 3 5	4 3 4	4 4 4	35	4
Singh	4 3 4	3 2 3	4 4 3	30	3

Tom Lehman defeated Mark O'Meara, 6 and 5

Lehman	4 3 5	4 4 3	4 4 4	35	3 4 4	4 3 4	3 5 4	34	69
O'Meara	5 3 5	5 3 4	4 5 4	38	3 3 4	4 3 4	4 4 4	33	71

Lehman leads, 2 up

Lehman	3 2 4	4 3 4	3 4 5	32	2 4 4	3
O'Meara	4 3 4	4 3 4	4 4 4	34	3 4 4	4

SEMI-FINALS

Ernie Els defeated Mark Brooks, 10 and 8

Els	4 4 4	4 3 4	4 4 5	36	3 4 5	4 3 3	4 4 4	34	70
Brooks	4 4 4	5 3 4	5 5 5	39	3 4 5	C 3 4	4 4 5	X	X

Els leads, 6 up

Els	4 3 4	5 3 4	4 4 3	34	2
Brooks	5 4 4	5 3 4	4 4 4	37	3

Vijay Singh defeated Tom Lehman, 37 holes

Singh	4 3 3	4 3 4	4 4 4	33	3 4 4	C 3 3	4 5 4	X	X
Lehman	4 3 4	4 3 3	3 4 5	33	2 3 5	3 3 5	5 5 4	35	68

Match all-square

Singh	4 3 4	4 3 4	4 4 4	34	3 4 5	4 2 4	4 4 4	34	68
Lehman	5 3 4	4 2 4	3 4 4	33	3 5 4	4 3 4	3 4 5	35	68

Match all-square

Singh	3
Lehman	4

FINAL

Ernie Els defeated Vijay Singh, 3 and 2

Els	4 3 5	4 3 4	4 3 4	34	3 4 4	4 3 4	4 5 5	36	70
Singh	4 2 4	5 4 4	4 4 5	36	3 3 4	4 4 4	4 5 4	35	71

Els leads, 1 up

Els	5 3 4	W 3 3	4 3 3	X	3 4 5	4 3 4	4
Singh	4 3 4	C 3 4	5 4 3	X	3 3 5	4 3 4	4

THIRD-PLACE PLAYOFF

Mark Brooks defeated Tom Lehman, 1 up

Brooks	4 3 4	5 3 3	5 5 4	36	3 3 4	4 4 3	4 4 4	33	69
Lehman	5 3 4	4 3 4	5 4 4	36	3 4 4	3 3 4	3 5 5	34	70

PRIZE MONEY: Els £170,000; Singh £90,000; Brooks £60,000; Lehman £50,000; Stricker, Montgomerie, Jones, O'Meara £40,000 each; Elkington, Woosnam, Mickelson, Serizawa £30,000 each.

LEGEND: C—conceded hole to opponent; W—won hole by concession without holing out; X—no total score.

Open Novotel Perrier

Golf du Medoc, Bordeaux, France
Par 35-36–71; 6,316 yards

October 17-20
purse, £350,000

	SCORES				TOTAL	MONEY (Each)
Jonathan Lomas/Steven Bottomley	63	62	68	139	332	£35,000
Richard Boxall/Derrick Cooper	65	67	63	138	333	25,000
Wayne Westner/Malcolm Mackenzie	64	68	65	138	335	17,500
Paul Broadhurst/Ross McFarlane	65	68	65	138	336	10,750
Fredrik Lindgren/Joakim Haeggman	68	70	64	134	336	10,750
Steven Richardson/Andrew Oldcorn	66	68	64	139	337	6,500
Rodger Davis/Peter O'Malley	65	67	68	138	338	5,125
Jamie Spence/Mark Mouland	64	67	70	137	338	5,125
Jarmo Sandelin/Fabrice Tarnaud	66	69	70	135	339	4,375
Paul Curry/Andrew Sherborne	65	73	68	133	339	4,375
Wayne Riley/Carl Mason	65	69	66	140	340	3,750
Paul Eales/Russell Claydon	61	72	68	139	340	3,750
Frank Nobilo/David Frost	64	72	69	135	340	3,750
Barry Lane/Mark Roe	65	70	69	137	341	3,125
Raymond Russell/Dean Robertson	65	75	65	136	341	3,125
Philip Walton/Raymond Burns	61	68	69	145	343	2,900
Adam Hunter/Gary Orr	68	71	70	137	344	2,750
Paul Lawrie/Stephen McAllister	65	68	72	139	344	2,750
David J. Russell/Ross Drummond	66	71	67	141	345	2,600
Marc Farry/Thomas Levet	70	67	66	143	346	2,500
Christophe Pottier/Marc Pendaries	65	69	71	142	347	2,350
Santiago Luna/Jose Maria Canizares	64	71	69	143	347	2,350
Christian Cevaer/Antoine Lebouc	60	74	68	146	348	2,200
Oyvind Rojahn/Niclas Fasth	65	72	73	139	349	2,100
Jean Charles Cambon/N. Kalouguine	64	71	68	148	351	2,000
Mats Lanner/Michael Jonzon	65	73	75	140	353	1,900
Mike McLean/Neal Briggs	66	76	68	144	354	1,800
Anders Forsbrand/Jean Van de Velde	71	72	72	143	358	1,700
Eric Giraud/Tim Planchin	69	73	73	144	359	1,600
Sam Torrance/M. King	69	73	72	150	364	1,500

Volvo Masters

Valderrama, Sotogrande, Spain
Par 35-36–71; 6,819 yards

October 24-27
purse, £900,000

	SCORES				TOTAL	MONEY
Mark McNulty	72	69	67	68	276	£150,000
Jose Coceres	71	70	71	71	283	59,902.50
Sam Torrance	73	74	68	66	283	59,902.50
Wayne Westner	70	74	72	67	283	59,902.50
Lee Westwood	71	71	70	71	283	59,902.50
Andrew Oldcorn	74	66	72	72	284	31,950
Stephen Ames	67	71	77	70	285	24,750
David Carter	70	75	72	68	285	24,750
Richard Green	72	74	70	70	286	17,437.50
Frank Nobilo	71	71	70	74	286	17,437.50
Peter Mitchell	74	71	71	70	286	17,437.50
David Frost	73	75	70	68	286	17,437.50
Carl Suneson	71	69	76	71	287	13,620
Gary Orr	72	70	70	75	287	13,620

	SCORES				TOTAL	MONEY
Paul Broadhurst	73	73	70	71	287	13,620
Greg Turner	72	70	71	75	288	11,843.33
Paul Curry	68	69	81	70	288	11,843.33
Bernhard Langer	73	69	74	72	288	11,843.33
Wayne Riley	73	70	69	77	289	11,000
Raymond Russell	72	72	73	73	290	10,250
Diego Borrego	74	71	73	72	290	10,250
Roger Chapman	71	74	75	70	290	10,250
Jonathan Lomas	70	77	73	70	290	10,250
Thomas Bjorn	71	74	73	72	290	10,250
Paul Lawrie	69	74	73	75	291	9,125
Darren Clarke	72	71	76	72	291	9,125
Andrew Sherborne	74	72	75	70	291	9,125
Ian Woosnam	76	69	72	74	291	9,125
Tony Johnstone	73	77	72	70	292	8,000
Padraig Harrington	69	73	77	73	292	8,000
Colin Montgomerie	71	75	71	75	292	8,000
Russell Claydon	71	70	81	70	292	8,000
Ross McFarlane	76	73	76	67	292	8,000
David Howell	72	73	75	73	293	6,366.67
Peter Baker	75	73	74	71	293	6,366.67
Rodger Davis	75	70	77	71	293	6,366.67
Paul Eales	74	74	74	71	293	6,366.67
Miguel Angel Martin	73	75	74	71	293	6,366.67
Miguel Angel Jimenez	73	74	73	73	293	6,366.67
Andrew Coltart	73	76	70	74	293	6,366.67
Eduardo Romero	76	72	74	71	293	6,366.67
Gordon Brand, Jr.	68	78	75	72	293	6,366.67
Costantino Rocca	69	74	76	75	294	5,250
Zhang Lian-Wei	75	73	74	72	294	5,250
Per-Ulrik Johansson	71	77	74	73	295	4,766.67
Paul McGinley	78	72	72	73	295	4,766.67
Mark Davis	77	71	74	73	295	4,766.67
David Gilford	73	72	75	76	296	4,300
Marc Farry	75	77	71	73	296	4,300
Patrik Sjoland	77	77	74	68	296	4,300
Iain Pyman	71	76	76	74	297	3,750
Ross Drummond	76	74	74	73	297	3,750
Peter Hedblom	74	76	75	72	297	3,750
Retief Goosen	75	78	73	71	297	3,750
Jean Van de Velde	80	70	75	74	299	3,250
Jamie Spence	76	71	74	78	299	3,250
Ronan Rafferty	74	72	80	73	299	3,250
Domingo Hospital	76	72	77	75	300	3,060
Jim Payne	69	76	80	76	301	2,970
Ignacio Garrido	81	72	75	74	302	2,835
Alexander Cejka	78	73	74	77	302	2,835
Seve Ballesteros	74	76	76	78	304	2,700
Joakim Haeggman	76	74	79	76	305	2,610
Jarmo Sandelin	73	83	79	71	306	2,520
Daniel Chopra	81	79	78	73	311	2,430
Robert Allenby					WD	2,340

Challenge Tour

Kenya Open

Muthaiga Golf Club, Nairobi, Kenya
Par 35-36–71; 6,676 yards

February 22-25
purse, £65,000

	SCORES				TOTAL	MONEY
Mike Miller	68	66	66	72	272	£10,500
Robert Lee	69	69	66	68	272	5,495
Philip Harrison	68	70	70	64	272	5,495
(Miller defeated Lee and Harrison on first extra hole.)						
Warren Bennett	69	72	66	68	275	3,170
Mark Nichols	71	69	66	70	276	2,690
Andrew Sandywell	70	68	67	72	277	2,368
David R. Jones	70	71	66	70	277	2,368
Mikael Krantz	64	70	74	70	278	1,830
Nicolas Vanhootegem	73	68	67	70	278	1,830
Andrew Clapp	68	68	73	69	278	1,830
Francisco Cea	70	72	70	67	279	1,367
Jean-Pierre Cixous	72	70	70	67	279	1,367
Marten Olander	67	73	72	67	279	1,367
Robert Coles	71	69	70	69	279	1,367
Marc Pendaries	68	72	67	72	279	1,367
Miles Tunnicliff	72	71	69	68	280	881
Juan Ciola	70	73	70	67	280	881
Bill Longmuir	71	70	70	69	280	881
Raphael Jacquelin	69	72	66	74	281	747
Glenn Ralph	73	70	71	67	281	747
John Kiondo	69	70	72	70	281	747
Frederik Larsson	68	68	71	75	282	659
Timothy Trodd	70	70	70	72	282	659
Massimo Florioli	72	69	70	71	282	659
Simon Burnell	71	72	69	70	282	659
James Kingori	71	68	70	74	283	548
Alessando Tadini	72	69	70	72	283	548
Philip Talbot	71	70	71	71	283	548
David Lynn	70	73	72	68	283	548
David Jones	69	72	73	69	283	548
Ian Garbutt	74	69	70	70	283	548

Open de Cote D'Ivoire

Ivoire Golf Club, Abidjan, Ivory Coast
Par 36-36–72; 6,635 yards

March 7-10
purse, £70,000

	SCORES				TOTAL	MONEY
Massimo Florioli	70	72	72	70	284	£11,370.45
Michele Reale	69	74	72	73	288	7,575.75
Raphael Jacquelin	73	73	74	69	289	3,842.48
Jean-Pierre Cixous	73	72	71	73	289	3,842.48
Marc Pendaries	73	74	72	71	290	2,893.80

	SCORES				TOTAL	MONEY
Francois Lamare	76	73	72	70	291	2,450.18
Mikael Krantz	76	71	69	75	291	2,450.18
Chris Williams	71	73	76	71	291	2,450.18
Marcello Santi	72	74	76	70	292	2,074.80
Vanslow Phillips	73	73	75	72	293	1,760.85
Jean Charles Cambon	73	78	71	71	293	1,760.85
Bill Longmuir	74	72	73	74	293	1,760.85
Scott Henderson	78	73	74	69	294	1,106.63
Maurice Besse	74	74	69	77	294	1,106.63
Fredrik Jacobson	73	74	74	73	294	1,106.63
Brian Davis	76	74	75	69	294	1,106.63
Marten Olander	75	73	71	75	294	1,106.63
Amos Korblah	75	76	71	72	294	1,106.63
John Morgan	75	76	72	71	294	1,106.63
Wayne Bradley	76	71	73	75	295	773.50
James Lee	72	75	72	76	295	773.50
Daniel Westermark	75	72	74	74	295	773.50
Mikael Piltz	76	75	71	74	296	680.80
Kalle Vainola	73	73	76	74	296	680.80
Benoit Telleria	72	73	74	77	296	680.80
Carl Watts	75	73	74	74	296	680.80
Fabrice Honnorat	76	74	73	74	297	588.32
Matthias Debove	76	75	75	71	297	588.32
Andrew Clapp	76	75	76	70	297	588.32
Philip Talbot	74	75	73	75	297	588.32
Bill McColl	71	77	77	72	297	588.32

Is Molas Challenge

Is Molas Golf Club, Sardinia, Italy
Par 36-36–72; 6,980 yards

April 11-14
purse, £35,000

	SCORES				TOTAL	MONEY
Simon Burnell	73	70	75	69	287	£5,685.23
Daniel Westermark	73	71	72	72	288	2,080.94
Alberto Binaghi	74	72	71	71	288	2,080.94
Jean Francois Remesy	70	71	72	75	288	2,080.94
Massimo Florioli	74	72	69	73	288	2,080.94
Michele Reale	72	71	70	75	288	2,080.94
Stephen Pullan	73	73	75	69	290	1,173.91
Massimo Scarpa	70	72	76	72	290	1,173.91
Marten Olander	76	70	73	72	291	919.67
Mike Miller	73	71	74	73	291	919.67
Dominique Nouailhac	73	70	72	76	291	919.67
Carl Watts	72	71	70	78	291	919.67
Michael Muehr	74	75	74	69	292	534.49
Mikael Piltz	75	71	73	73	292	534.49
Nicolas Vanhootegem	70	76	73	73	292	534.49
Dennis Edlund	73	76	70	73	292	534.49
Lee James	74	72	71	75	292	534.49
Magnus Persson	72	72	72	76	292	534.49
Andrea Canessa	71	76	69	76	292	534.49
Joakim Rask	73	72	70	77	292	534.49
Joakim Nilsson	71	76	73	73	293	371.96
Kalle Vainola	73	72	72	76	293	371.96
Fredrik Jacobson	74	69	73	77	293	371.96
Ralf Berhorst	75	73	75	71	294	313.95

	SCORES				TOTAL	MONEY
Antonio Sobrinho	75	72	72	75	294	313.95
Markus Brier	73	75	71	75	294	313.95
Jean Pierre Sallat	73	72	73	76	294	313.95
Ian Garbutt	71	74	72	77	294	313.95
Scott Henderson	74	71	72	77	294	313.95
William Guy	73	70	72	79	294	313.95

Le Pavoniere Superal Challenge

Le Pavoniere Golf Club, Florence, Italy
Par 36-36–72; 7,072 yards

April 18-21
purse, £35,000

	SCORES				TOTAL	MONEY
Kalle Vainola	69	68	67	68	272	£5,685.23
Marten Olander	72	71	66	65	274	2,962.06
Ian Garbutt	67	70	68	69	274	2,962.06
Rob Edwards	71	70	68	68	277	1,493.54
Massimo Florioli	65	69	73	70	277	1,493.54
Mikael Piltz	69	68	70	70	277	1,493.54
William Guy	71	73	70	64	278	1,221.68
Michele Reale	69	74	70	66	279	1,081.77
Daniel Westermark	69	67	72	71	279	1,081.77
Markus Brier	67	73	71	69	280	955.50
Simon Burnell	72	71	71	67	281	736.42
Antonio Sobrinho	71	71	71	68	281	736.42
Joakim Rask	75	67	69	70	281	736.42
Per Jacobson	70	71	68	72	281	736.42
Marc Pendaries	69	73	67	72	281	736.42
Michael Muehr	70	72	74	66	282	433.88
Soren Kjeldsen	72	73	70	67	282	433.88
Timothy Spence	71	70	72	69	282	433.88
Fredrik Jacobson	72	68	71	71	282	433.88
Andrew Barnett	70	70	71	71	282	433.88
Carl Watts	67	73	70	72	282	433.88
Juan Ciola	67	76	64	75	282	433.88
Sebastien Delagrange	67	73	75	68	283	358.31
Brian Davis	73	70	73	68	284	334.43
Federico Bisazza	76	69	70	69	284	334.43
Alberto Binaghi	71	74	68	71	284	334.43
Heinz P. Thul	70	72	75	68	285	290.06
Andrew Clapp	71	74	72	68	285	290.06
Jean-Pierre Cixous	66	75	73	71	285	290.06
Mike Miller	73	71	70	71	285	290.06
Claude Grenier	70	72	71	72	285	290.06
Raimo Sjoberg	71	72	70	72	285	290.06

Alianca UAP Challenger

Montado Golf Club, Setubal, Portugal
Par 36-36–72; 6,565 yards

April 24-27
purse, £50,000

	SCORES				TOTAL	MONEY
Gary Marks	69	72	64	65	270	£8,121.75
Jean-Pierre Cixous	68	71	66	66	271	5,411.25
Ian Garbutt	71	68	68	68	275	3,051.75

	SCORES				TOTAL	MONEY
Joakim Rask	70	70	67	69	276	2,252.25
Mark Nichols	70	71	71	64	276	2,252.25
Greg Owen	67	69	72	69	277	1,683.10
Kalle Vainola	73	67	69	68	277	1,683.10
Fredrik Jacobson	68	72	69	68	277	1,683.10
Michael Archer	72	70	70	65	277	1,683.10
Marcello Santi	71	71	66	71	279	1,257.75
Scott Watson	73	67	69	70	279	1,257.75
Matthias Debove	68	72	70	69	279	1,257.75
Michele Reale	71	68	69	72	280	950.63
Janeirik Dahlstrom	70	70	69	71	280	950.63
John Hawksworth	71	72	69	68	280	950.63
Massimo Florioli	74	69	66	72	281	692.25
Nicolas Vanhootegem	72	70	67	72	281	692.25
Stephen Dodd	72	69	70	70	281	692.25
Per Jacobson	73	68	69	72	282	544.38
Johan Rystrom	69	71	70	72	282	544.38
Andrew Sandywell	72	70	70	70	282	544.38
Markus Brier	74	69	70	69	282	544.38
Daren Lee	72	70	71	69	282	544.38
Dominique Nouailhac	75	69	71	67	282	544.38
David Lynn	72	72	67	72	283	455.82
Craig Cassells	72	67	72	72	283	455.82
Jorgen Aker	77	65	71	70	283	455.82
Benoit Telleria	72	73	68	70	283	455.82
Robert Lee	73	67	73	71	284	400.97
Anders Hansen	74	71	69	70	284	400.97
Marten Olander	73	72	71	68	284	400.97
Alberto Binaghi	73	69	74	68	284	400.97

Canarias–Challenge Tour

Las Palmas, Gran Canaria, Canary Islands
Par 35-36–71; 6,221 yards

May 2-5
purse, £63,660

	SCORES				TOTAL	MONEY
Robert Lee	68	65	68	67	268	£10,340.61
Simon Burnell	67	66	67	73	273	5,387.55
Joakim Rask	67	70	67	69	273	5,387.55
Francisco Amatriain	67	67	66	75	275	3,103.43
John Hawksworth	70	68	68	70	276	2,422.74
Vanslow Phillips	71	67	69	69	276	2,422.74
David Lynn	68	67	70	71	276	2,422.74
Carl Watts	70	70	69	68	277	1,891.02
Jeremy Robinson	66	69	71	71	277	1,891.02
Nicolas Vanhootegem	70	64	69	74	277	1,891.02
Raphael Jacquelin	68	70	68	72	278	1,276.54
Jose Rozadilla	66	71	68	73	278	1,276.54
Alfonso Pinero	68	69	71	70	278	1,276.54
Michael Archer	67	69	71	71	278	1,276.54
Jesus Maria Arruti	69	67	67	75	278	1,276.54
Ben Tinning	65	71	71	71	278	1,276.54
Michael Muehr	67	68	69	75	279	868.96
Jose Sota	68	69	70	73	280	754.13
Magnus Persson	65	70	70	75	280	754.13
Philip Talbot	72	68	71	69	280	754.13
Stuart Little	70	70	70	70	280	754.13

	SCORES				TOTAL	MONEY
Scott Watson	68	69	71	73	281	664.14
Jose Carriles	71	70	70	70	281	664.14
Stephen Dodd	72	69	70	71	282	589.65
Joakim Gronhagen	69	72	67	74	282	589.65
Brian Davis	73	67	68	74	282	589.65
Frederik Andersson	67	70	72	73	282	589.65
Rene Budde	69	69	71	73	282	589.65
Stephen Pullan	71	68	72	72	283	524.48
John Mellor	74	66	69	74	283	524.48

Open de Dijon

Dijon Golf Club, Dijon, France
Par 36-36–72; 6,757 yards

May 16-19
purse, £43,364

	SCORES		TOTAL	MONEY
Francisco Cea	66	66	132	£7,470.73
Massimo Florioli	68	67	135	4,977.50
Vanslow Phillips	68	69	137	2,807.13
Dominique Nouailhac	70	68	138	2,242.12
Robert Lee	70	69	139	1,822.84
Benoit Telleria	68	71	139	1,822.84
Marcello Santi	71	69	140	1,319.86
Raphael Jacquelin	71	69	140	1,319.86
Nicolas Joakimides	69	71	140	1,319.86
Fredrik Jacobson	69	71	140	1,319.86
Roger Sabarros	69	71	140	1,319.86
Michele Reale	68	72	140	1,319.86
Andrew Sandywell	73	68	141	628.17
Jean Baptiste Levet	73	68	141	628.17
Jean-Pierre Cixous	72	69	141	628.17
Jonathan Hodgson	72	69	141	628.17
Kevin Carissimi	71	70	141	628.17
Michael Muehr	71	70	141	628.17
Nicolas Dupuy	70	71	141	628.17
Christophe Muniesa	70	71	141	628.17
Marten Olander	70	71	141	628.17
Sebastien Delagrange	69	72	141	628.17
Stephen Pullan	68	73	141	628.17
Antoine Lebouc	68	73	141	628.17
Dennis Edlund	71	71	142	426
John Hawksworth	71	71	142	426
Brian Davis	68	74	142	426
Greg Chalmers	73	70	143	369.95
Anders Gillner	72	71	143	369.95
Simon Brown	71	72	143	369.95
Michael Archer	71	72	143	369.95
Francisco Amatriai	71	72	143	369.95
Romain Victor	71	72	143	369.95

Club Med Open

Margara Golf Club, Margara, Italy
Par 36-36–72; 6,778 yards

May 23-26
purse, £60,871

	SCORES				TOTAL	MONEY
Ignacio Feliu	65	68	70	68	271	£9,887.61
Max Anglert	67	67	72	69	275	6,587.78
Andrew Sandywell	70	69	68	70	277	3,341.37
Greg Chalmers	68	70	71	68	277	3,341.37
Robert Lee	68	70	70	70	278	2,412.55
Alessandro Tadini	72	69	70	67	278	2,412.55
Daniel Chopra	69	72	69	69	279	2,041.62
Frederic Regard	65	72	70	72	279	2,041.62
Christophe Pottier	65	71	71	73	280	1,291.18
Carl Watts	69	69	72	70	280	1,291.18
Inigo Moral	72	69	71	68	280	1,291.18
Gianluca Baruffaldi	68	70	77	65	280	1,291.18
Andrea Canessa	69	69	71	71	280	1,291.18
Nicolas Joakimides	68	67	77	68	280	1,291.18
Massimo Scarpa	70	72	70	68	280	1,291.18
Emanuele Bolognesi	68	73	68	71	280	1,291.18
Kalle Vainola	71	68	70	71	280	1,291.18
Joakim Rask	69	69	72	71	281	737.91
Roger Winchester	68	69	73	71	281	737.91
Frederik Andersson	67	75	72	67	281	737.91
Stuart Little	70	69	69	74	282	635.04
Robert Coles	68	71	72	71	282	635.04
Dennis Edlund	70	71	69	72	282	635.04
Ian Garbutt	70	68	76	68	282	635.04
Raphael Jacquelin	70	67	72	74	283	546.01
Anders Gillner	71	70	70	72	283	546.01
Marcello Santi	70	69	71	73	283	546.01
Scott Watson	70	72	72	69	283	546.01
Daniel Westermark	71	71	70	71	283	546.01
Marc Pendaries	72	69	69	74	284	474.80
Mike Miller	71	71	67	75	284	474.80
Ben Tinning	65	73	76	70	284	474.80
Jean Francois Remesy	70	71	73	70	284	474.80

Siab Open

Soderasens Golf Club, Stockholm, Sweden
Par 71; 6,778 yards

May 30-June 2
purse, £35,000

	SCORES				TOTAL	MONEY
Kalle Vainola	67	73	70	71	281	£5,685.23
Adam Mednick	72	69	73	67	281	3,787.88
(Vainola defeated Mednick on second extra hole.)						
Kevin Carissimi	70	72	70	70	282	2,136.23
Frederik Andersson	72	74	70	67	283	1,706.25
Jorgen Aker	74	72	74	64	284	1,446.90
Dennis Edlund	71	72	70	72	285	1,274.57
Emil Madsen	68	74	75	68	285	1,274.57
Raimo Sjoberg	75	72	70	69	286	999.87
Fredrik Jacobson	73	72	71	70	286	999.87
Stephen Scahill	71	72	71	72	286	999.87
Daniel Westermark	67	73	75	71	286	999.87

	SCORES				TOTAL	MONEY
Patrik Gottfridsson	70	73	69	75	287	769.52
Ben Tinning	70	72	74	71	287	769.52
Johan Rystrom	75	71	73	69	288	543.27
Lars Tingvall	74	72	68	74	288	543.27
Magnus Persson	71	72	74	71	288	543.27
Frederik Larsson	67	75	72	74	288	543.27
Gabriel Hjertstedt	70	71	75	72	288	543.27
Mikael Piltz	72	76	70	71	289	412.92
Per Nyberg	74	72	73	70	289	412.92
Per-Ive Persson	72	77	68	73	290	371.96
Henrik Nystrom	73	73	72	72	290	371.96
Rikard Strangert	72	73	72	73	290	371.96
*Petter Edero	70	74	76	70	290	
*Jonas Torines	69	75	73	73	290	
Johan Skold	74	74	67	76	291	339.55
Rudi Sailer	72	71	71	77	291	339.55
Hans Karlsson	71	77	76	68	292	319.07
Rene Michelsen	71	73	72	76	292	319.07
Andreas Jernberg	71	78	71	73	293	293.48
Antonio Sobrinho	72	77	69	75	293	293.48
*Patric Linden	70	75	75	73	293	
Karl-Henrik Brink	65	77	77	74	293	293.48

KB Golf Challenge

Praha Karlstein, Czech Republic
Par 36-36–72; 6,966 yards

June 6-9
purse, £67,385

	SCORES				TOTAL	MONEY
Joakim Rask	67	65	68	71	271	£10,945.68
Greg Owen	64	68	74	66	272	7,292.74
Markus Brier	69	69	65	71	274	3,698.93
Mikael Krantz	69	70	67	68	274	3,698.93
Massimo Florioli	70	67	70	69	276	2,371.78
Scott Watson	72	63	72	69	276	2,371.78
Vanslow Phillips	69	68	70	69	276	2,371.78
Carlos Larrain	74	62	70	70	276	2,371.78
Daniel Westermark	68	67	69	72	276	2,371.78
Andrew Sandywell	67	72	67	71	277	1,839.61
Nicolas Vanhootegem	69	71	66	72	278	1,622.80
Jonathan Hodgson	70	70	70	68	278	1,622.80
Stephen Dodd	71	64	76	68	279	1,029.03
Marten Olander	69	72	67	71	279	1,029.03
Larry Batchelor	69	70	71	69	279	1,029.03
Simon Brown	72	65	70	72	279	1,029.03
Christophe Pottier	69	71	68	71	279	1,029.03
Francisco Cea	69	73	71	66	279	1,029.03
David Higgins	72	70	72	65	279	1,029.03
Matthias Debove	67	76	65	71	279	1,029.03
Simon Burnell	70	71	70	69	280	729.27
Carl Watts	69	73	67	71	280	729.27
Martyn Roberts	72	70	71	68	281	655.36
Per Nyberg	69	72	71	69	281	655.36
Robert Lee	70	70	71	70	281	655.36
Ian Garbutt	69	73	69	70	281	655.36
Mikael Piltz	71	70	68	73	282	558.45
Kalle Vainola	71	72	66	73	282	558.45

	SCORES			TOTAL	MONEY
Rudi Sailer	72	68	73	69	282	558.45
Steve Rey	67	68	74	73	282	558.45
Roger Sabarros	71	70	71	70	282	558.45
Dominique Nouailhac	71	72	69	70	282	558.45

Himmerland Open

Himmerland Golf Club, Himmerland, Denmark   June 7-9
Par 36-36–72; 6,889 yards   purse, £35,000

	SCORES			TOTAL	MONEY
Niklas Diethelm	69	68	68	205	£5,685.23
Knud Storgaard-Jense	67	68	70	205	3,787.88
(Diethelm defeated Storgaard-Jense on first extra hole.)					
Johan Loftby	71	68	68	207	1,763.13
Dennis Edlund	69	69	69	207	1,763.13
Andreas Jernberg	67	67	73	207	1,763.13
Joakim Nilsson	68	70	70	208	1,327.46
Patrik Gottfridsson	72	70	67	209	1,126.40
Steven Mattson	70	71	68	209	1,128.40
Karl-Henrik Brink	66	71	72	209	1,128.40
Ulrik Gustafsson	71	69	70	210	843.74
Johan Selberg	71	69	70	210	843.74
Johan Skold	70	71	69	210	843.74
Christian Post	70	70	70	210	843.74
*Peter Hansson	70	73	67	210	
Henrik Nystrom	74	68	69	211	631.32
Ben Tinning	72	73	66	211	631.32
Gabriel Hjertstedt	72	71	69	212	469.22
Rene Michelsen	70	69	73	212	469.22
Stephen Scahill	68	74	70	212	469.22
Jesper Bjorklund	68	74	70	212	469.22
Lars Tingvall	71	66	76	213	394.15
Raimo Sjoberg	69	74	70	213	394.15
Frederik Lundgren	73	68	73	214	352.34
Mats Johansson	72	67	75	214	352.34
Robert Jonsson	70	74	70	214	352.34
Erik Andersson	70	72	72	214	352.34
Johan Rystrom	75	71	69	215	294.94
Anders Hansen	73	70	72	215	294.94
Maurice Besse	71	74	70	215	294.94
Morten Backhausen	70	72	73	215	294.94
Bjorn Back	70	70	75	215	294.94
Marc Amort	68	73	74	215	294.94
Patrik Tessman	68	73	74	215	294.94

Italian Native Open

Garlenda Golf Club, Garlenda, Italy   June 12-15
Par 35-36–71; 6,532 yards   purse, £52,755

	SCORES			TOTAL	MONEY
Marcello Santi	71	68	72	66	277	£8,121.75
Michele Reale	71	69	70	67	277	5,411.25
(Santi defeated Reale on fourth extra hole.)						

	SCORES				TOTAL	MONEY
Alessandro Tadini	70	67	68	73	278	3,051.75
Silvano Locatelli	67	72	70	71	280	2,252.25
Marco Durante	69	71	70	70	280	2,252.25
Mario Tadini	70	68	71	72	281	1,750.13
Alberto Binaghi	68	69	74	70	281	1,750.13
Andrea Calcari	70	73	69	69	281	1,750.13
Gianluca Baruffaldi	69	73	75	66	283	1,482
Massimo Scarpa	69	70	76	69	284	1,311.38
Emanuele Bolognesi	66	69	73	76	284	1,311.38
Massimo Florioli	72	70	74	69	285	1,099.32
Andrea Canessa	73	68	73	71	285	1,099.32
Delio Lovato	70	72	71	73	286	950.63
Francesco Guermani	70	76	70	72	288	804.38
Amedeo Della-Valentina	71	77	68	72	288	804.38
Giuseppe Cali	71	71	72	75	289	682.50
Alessandro Rogato	71	75	72	72	290	638.63
Paolo De Salvatore	78	72	73	68	291	565.50
Giorgio Merletti	72	75	72	72	291	565.50
Geralamo Delfino	73	72	72	74	291	565.50
Giulio Girardi	73	73	78	67	291	565.50
Federico Bisazza	73	72	73	74	292	486.29
Mauro Bianco	74	72	69	77	292	486.29
Marco Luzzi	71	75	74	72	292	486.29
Giorgio Grillo	76	72	72	72	292	486.29
Alessandro Russo	69	72	74	78	293	433.88
Antonio Lionelo	74	69	75	75	293	433.88
Dan Paco Williamson	74	71	73	75	293	433.88
Alberto Limonta	74	74	74	72	294	380.26
Gianfranco Pecora	73	72	68	81	294	380.26
Diego Fiammengo	71	72	79	72	294	380.26
Baldovino Dassu	77	73	73	71	294	380.26
Roberto Zappa	74	74	73	73	294	380.26
Felice Crotti	75	70	79	70	294	380.26

Nedcar National Open

Kennemer Golf Club, Netherlands
Par 36-36–72; 6,611 yards

June 12-15
purse, £28,000

	SCORES				TOTAL	MONEY
*Neils Boysen	72	73	75	71	291	
*R. Miller	77	70	73	71	291	
*M. Van Den Berg	69	73	75	74	291	
(Boysen defeated Miller and Van Den Berg on second extra hole.)						
*M. Lafaber	72	72	74	74	292	
Stephane Lovey	73	74	73	75	295	£3,900
Ruben Wechgelaer	72	74	74	75	295	3,900
*N. Kraay	74	79	73	69	295	
Jonas Saxton	77	77	69	73	296	1,900
Tim Giles	75	80	73	69	297	1,400
Joost Steenkamer	73	74	78	72	297	1,400
*R.J. Derksen	75	73	73	76	297	
Mark Metgod	77	74	74	73	298	1,060
Hayo Bensdorp	78	72	75	73	298	1,060
Chris Van der Velde	78	75	73	73	299	920
Brian Gee	75	75	78	72	300	810
Hans Von Burg	75	75	77	73	300	810

	SCORES				TOTAL	MONEY
Raymond Stoop	75	74	74	78	301	720
Harold Moss	77	77	74	74	302	600
Andrew Allen	76	77	74	75	302	600
Allan McLean	83	72	71	76	302	600
Stuart Mathie	79	73	77	74	303	480
Eelco Bouma	75	79	74	75	303	480
Constan Smits Van Waesberghe	82	75	75	72	304	410
Roddy Watkins	78	75	78	73	304	410
Phil Helsby	80	72	78	74	304	410
Philip Horn	74	79	73	78	304	410
R. Plas	70	75	84	76	305	365
Jan Dorrestein	73	78	76	78	305	365
*J. Germes	81	74	69	81	305	365
*J.W. Moolenaar	75	78	78	75	306	
Ruud Bos	74	81	74	77	306	345
Dio Da Cruz	78	76	75	77	306	345
*V. Rodenburg	74	76	78	78	306	

Cepsa APG

Real Club de Sotogrande, Sotogrande, Spain
Par 36-36–72; 6,807 yards

June 12-15
purse, £68,966

	SCORES				TOTAL	MONEY
Ignacio Garrido	69	70	70	68	277	£8,121.75
Juan Quiros	66	69	73	70	278	5,411.25
Jose Canizares	72	72	70	67	281	3,051.75
Fernando Roca	72	73	67	70	282	2,437.50
Manuel Pinero	72	66	71	74	283	2,067
Tomas Jesus Munoz	69	72	70	73	284	1,820.82
Diego Borrego	72	73	68	71	284	1,820.82
Francisco Javier Amatriai	72	73	74	66	285	1,608.75
Pello Iguaran	69	73	71	73	286	1,313.81
Jose Rozadilla	73	72	68	73	286	1,313.81
Jesus Maria Arruti	72	70	73	71	286	1,313.81
Jose Carriles	71	71	74	70	286	1,313.81
Juan Antonio Marin	68	71	76	72	287	1,048.13
Manuel Velasco	73	73	69	73	288	776.10
Francisco Cea	70	71	78	69	288	776.10
Santiago Luna	74	69	72	73	288	776.10
Daniel Westermark	75	71	69	73	288	776.10
Francisco Tineo	74	72	73	69	288	776.10
Ricardo Jimenez	70	75	71	73	289	565.50
Sebastian Miguel	73	72	72	72	289	565.50
Manuel Moreno	71	73	71	74	289	565.50
Pedro Linhart	67	75	75	72	289	565.50
Juan Anglada	71	74	71	74	290	494
Ignacio Feliu	76	72	73	69	290	494
Bernardo Solanes	77	68	75	70	290	494
Daniel Sanchez	71	74	73	73	291	441.19
Jerome Challen	70	71	73	77	291	441.19
Inigo Moral	70	75	74	72	291	441.19
Luis Navarro	72	74	73	72	291	441.19
Juan Rosa Rueda	71	72	73	76	292	399.76
Alvaro Prat	71	74	74	73	292	399.76

France Pro

St. Omer Golf Club, St. Omer, France
Par 73; 6,904 yards

June 13-16
purse, £50,000

	SCORES				TOTAL	MONEY
Nicolas Kalouguine	71	73	67	73	284	£8,121.75
Cedric Hoffstetter	73	72	70	71	286	5,411.25
Bruno Petit	68	74	73	73	288	2,518.75
Frederic Cupillard	74	69	72	73	288	2,518.75
Jean Ignace Mouhica	67	74	74	73	288	2,518.75
Raphael Jacquelin	73	75	69	72	289	1,683.10
Jean Pierre Sallat	66	75	77	71	289	1,683.10
John Lawson	71	72	77	69	289	1,683.10
Charles Bellan	74	72	75	68	289	1,683.10
Ramuncho Artola	72	74	71	73	290	1,311.38
Jean Francois Remesy	73	73	74	70	290	1,311.38
Patrice Barquez	74	69	70	78	291	1,000.60
Matthias Debove	72	78	69	72	291	1,000.60
Nicolas Dupuy	70	74	75	72	291	1,000.60
Jean Charles Cambon	74	74	73	70	291	1,000.60
Janeirik Dahlstrom	71	72	73	76	292	719.07
Frederic Regard	76	71	71	74	292	719.07
Benoit Telleria	75	72	73	73	293	621.57
Philippe Uranga	73	77	71	72	293	621.57
Stephan Catherine	74	72	73	75	294	532.35
Paul Brown	74	74	71	75	294	532.35
Jean Marie Kula	70	72	78	74	294	532.35
Diego Dupin	73	72	75	74	294	532.35
Charles Bauer	77	71	76	70	294	532.35
Jean-Louis Schneider	72	78	68	77	295	463.13
Fabrice Honnorat	76	71	71	77	295	463.13
Jean-Michel Richard	75	73	72	75	295	463.13
Emmanuel Dussart	76	68	77	75	296	407.55
Michael Wolseley	78	72	71	75	296	407.55
Jean-Pierre Cixous	73	76	73	74	296	407.55
Marc Noel	74	75	74	73	296	407.55
Stephane Chauffour	74	75	75	72	296	407.55

Vasteras Open

Vasteras Golf Club, Vasteras, Sweden
Par 69; 5,884 yards

June 14-16
purse, £15,000

	SCORES			TOTAL	MONEY
Johan Axgren	66	67	67	200	£2,500.50
Markus Rosenlund	66	70	67	203	1,800
Adam Mednick	66	66	72	204	1,399.50
Robert Jonsson	70	71	67	208	1,075.50
Hans Karlsson	69	69	70	208	1,075.50
Bjorn Back	74	68	67	209	710.10
Kevin Carissimi	72	66	71	209	710.10
Kalle Brink	70	70	69	209	710.10
Anders Bjorklund	69	71	69	209	710.10
Claes Hovstadius	68	72	69	209	710.10

German Closed

Janus Weilrod Golf Club, Altweilnau, Germany
Par 36-36–72; 5,914 yards

June 14-16
purse, £17,520

	SCORES			TOTAL	MONEY
Simon Brown	72	71	67	210	£2,918.87
Ralf Berhorst	75	68	71	214	1,165.10
Patrick Platz	73	68	73	214	1,165.10
Howard Francis	67	74	73	214	1,165.10
Thomas Gogele	70	71	73	214	1,165.10
Stephen Chadwick	72	76	67	215	681.54
Erol Simsek	71	74	71	216	627.22
Christian Niesing	74	70	73	217	578.17
Gert-Sven Slopianka	76	74	68	218	532.61
Martin Coup	79	72	68	219	414.88
Mark Stevenson	74	74	71	219	414.88
Christian Arenz	75	73	71	219	414.88
Stuart McGregor	78	68	73	219	414.88
Alan Hogg	72	73	74	219	414.88
Mark Mattheis	79	71	70	220	274.48
Gregory Hanrahan	71	76	73	220	274.48
Marc Amort	74	73	73	220	274.48
Paul Herbert	77	75	70	222	217.83
Simon Yates	74	78	70	222	217.83
Yusuf Kaya	78	71	73	222	217.83
Oliver Eckstein	80	72	71	223	181.33
Simon Trent	72	79	72	223	181.33
Glenn Pease	76	75	72	223	181.33
Michael Hearn	79	71	73	223	181.33
Gary Locke	75	74	74	223	181.33
Christoph Killian	74	72	77	223	181.33
Lothar Jahn	78	77	69	224	155.93
Kaweh Chirband	73	79	72	224	155.93
Mike McLean	78	74	72	224	155.93
Glen Hutcheson	75	76	74	225	141.91
Ulrich Eckhardt	70	81	74	225	141.91
Michael Mitteregger	73	75	77	225	141.91

Radegast Closed Championship

Praha Karlstein, Prague, Czech Republic
Par 36-36–72; 6,966 yards

June 15-17
purse, £3,942

	SCORES			TOTAL	MONEY
Jiri Janda	73	68	71	212	£640.38
Peter Mruzek	72	71	70	213	426.67
Lumir Kainer	72	72	75	219	240.62
Karel Skopovy, Jr.	74	70	76	220	192.19
Oldrich Nechanicy	73	73	76	222	162.98
Miroslav Janda	76	73	75	224	143.57
Bohumil Syriste	73	75	76	224	143.57
Petr Strougal	71	74	80	225	126.85
Jiri Seifert	77	76	74	227	112.24
Jan Juhaniak	74	74	79	227	112.24
Ondrej Trupl	77	73	78	228	99.17
Jiri Kunsta	81	73	77	231	90.71
Adam Eisner	78	78	77	233	82.64

	SCORES			TOTAL	MONEY
Richard Pszota	79	80	77	236	74.95
Miroslav Nemec	82	76	80	238	67.27

Team Erhverv Danish Open

Simons Golf Club, Copenhagen, Denmark
Par 36-36–72; 6,780 yards

June 20-23
purse, £70,000

	SCORES				TOTAL	MONEY
Robert Jonsson	67	69	71	69	276	£11,370.45
Marten Olander	69	71	72	64	276	7,575.75
(Jonsson defeated Olander on fourth extra hole.)						
Anders Gillner	72	68	66	71	277	4,272.45
Rene Budde	72	68	70	70	280	3,412.50
*Leif Westerberg	68	70	72	70	280	
Kevin Carissimi	69	75	68	69	281	2,561.08
Andrew Sandywell	71	71	70	69	281	2,561.08
Roger Winchester	72	70	69	70	281	2,561.08
Nicolas Joakimides	70	72	68	71	281	2,561.08
Frederik Johansson	68	74	71	69	282	1,915.55
Michael Muehr	71	69	72	70	282	1,915.55
Ian Garbutt	69	71	70	72	282	1,915.55
Jesper Thuen	76	68	69	70	283	1,215.83
Johan Rystrom	71	72	72	68	283	1,215.83
Hans Karlsson	73	69	73	68	283	1,215.83
Nicolas Kalouguine	70	72	70	71	283	1,215.83
Matthew Hazelden	74	68	69	72	283	1,215.83
Frederik Lundgren	72	69	74	68	283	1,215.83
Jorgen Aker	70	70	74	69	283	1,215.83
*Morten Hagen	70	68	74	71	283	
Mike Miller	72	72	68	72	284	776.69
Kalle Vainola	75	69	68	72	284	776.69
Johan Omander	70	72	70	72	284	776.69
Patrik Gottfridsson	69	72	71	72	284	776.69
Benoit Telleria	68	72	70	74	284	776.69
Daniel Westermark	74	69	67	75	285	648.38
Morten Backhausen	71	71	75	68	285	648.38
Greg Owen	71	71	69	74	285	648.38
Joost Steenkamer	71	70	71	73	285	648.38
William Guy	72	67	73	73	285	648.38
Bill Malley	72	72	71	71	286	568.75
Jesper Kjaerbye	68	72	73	73	286	568.75
David R. Jones	70	69	76	71	286	568.75

Open dei Tessali

Golf Club Riva dei Tessali, Taranto, Italy
Par 35-36–71; 6,504 yards

June 20-23
purse, £40,581

	SCORES				TOTAL	MONEY
Stephen Scahill	73	66	69	71	279	£6,591.74
Renaud Guillard	74	63	72	71	280	4,391.86
Pauli Hughes	74	71	70	70	285	2,476.85
Federico Bisazza	70	77	70	69	286	1,978.31
Andrea Canessa	70	72	72	75	289	1,677.61

	SCORES	TOTAL	MONEY
Paul Sherman	72 70 75 73	290	1,366.03
Gianluca Baruffaldi	73 72 72 73	290	1,366.03
Jean Pierre Sallat	76 69 72 73	290	1,366.03
Alberto Binaghi	69 73 73 75	290	1,366.03
Charles Bellan	76 74 75 66	291	1,020.81
Matthias Debove	72 71 74 74	291	1,020.81
Duncan Muscroft	74 71 72 74	291	1,020.81
Mario Tadini	71 75 71 75	292	811.11
Bruno Petit	68 71 76 77	292	811.11
Frederic Grosset-Grange	74 75 74 70	293	540.36
Gianluca Pietrobono	72 78 72 71	293	540.36
Niccolo Bisazza	75 75 72 71	293	540.36
Raphael Jacquelin	72 79 70 72	293	540.36
Frederic Schmitt	77 72 69 75	293	540.36
Giorgio Merletti	73 72 72 76	293	540.36
Francisco Javier Amatriai	74 71 72 76	293	540.36
Stephane Chauffour	74 74 75 71	294	408.52
Paolo De Salvatore	74 75 73 72	294	408.52
Sebastien Delagrange	76 72 72 74	294	408.52
Diego Fiammengo	74 72 73 75	294	408.52
Jean-Pierre Cixous	75 75 72 73	295	364.01
Marco Durante	77 73 71 74	295	364.01
Filippo Barbe	75 70 74 76	295	364.01
Bryan Ingleby	75 75 75 71	296	334.34
Francesco Guermani	73 71 75 77	296	334.34

Audi Quattro Trophy

Eschenried Golf Club, Munich, Germany
Par 36-36–72; 6,658 yards

June 27-30
purse, £72,000

	SCORES	TOTAL	MONEY
Erol Simsek	70 68 63 67	268	£11,695.32
Paul Gareth Simpson	69 68 70 67	274	7,792.20
Heinz P. Thul	65 71 69 70	275	4,394.52
Fredrik Jacobson	64 69 74 69	276	3,510
Vanslow Phillips	65 71 72 69	277	2,853.63
Markus Brier	75 63 71 68	277	2,853.63
Joakim Gronhagen	69 69 71 69	278	2,321.28
Marten Olander	71 69 69 69	278	2,321.28
Andrew Sandywell	70 69 70 69	278	2,321.28
Stephen Dodd	69 72 71 67	279	1,888.38
John Mellor	68 67 74 70	279	1,888.38
David Lynn	71 68 74 67	280	1,440.86
Oliver Eckstein	71 71 67 71	280	1,440.86
Carlos Larrain	72 70 69 69	280	1,440.86
Brian Davis	69 72 68 71	280	1,440.86
Scott Watson	65 76 67 73	281	965.25
Raimo Sjoberg	71 68 70 72	281	965.25
Joakim Rask	71 69 70 71	281	965.25
Jeremy Robinson	67 70 75 69	281	965.25
Daren Lee	69 69 72 72	282	780.97
Paul Sherman	72 68 69 73	282	780.97
Dominique Nouailhac	66 71 73 72	282	780.97
Michael Muehr	71 71 70 70	282	780.97
Thomas Nielson	74 68 69 72	283	677.43
Greg Owen	70 67 72 74	283	677.43

	SCORES				TOTAL	MONEY
Gregory Hanrahan	72	70	71	70	283	677.43
Morten Backhausen	67	73	72	71	283	677.43
Claude Grenier	73	69	72	70	284	586.67
Niklas Diethelm	69	73	70	72	284	586.67
Massimo Florioli	73	69	71	71	284	586.67
Anders Hansen	70	68	75	71	284	586.67
Nicolas Joakimides	76	66	67	75	284	586.67

Memorial Olivier Barras

Crans-sur-Sierre Golf Club, Crans-sur-Sierre, Switzerland
Par 36-36–72; 7,376 yards

June 28-30
purse, £39,497

	SCORES			TOTAL	MONEY
Juan Quiros	64	68	73	205	£10,055.87
Dimitri Bieri	75	66	69	210	5,586.59
Matthew Hazelden	69	70	71	210	5,586.59
Stephen Scahill	72	70	69	211	2,141.53
Jesus Maria Arruti	70	71	70	211	2,141.53
Marcos Moreno	71	72	68	211	2,141.53
Frederik Larsson	70	71	71	212	726.26
Kalle Vainola	70	69	73	212	726.26
Jean Pierre Sallat	70	69	73	212	726.26
Zeke Martinez	70	68	75	213	547.49
Joakim Nilsson	76	68	69	213	547.49
Ignacio Feliu	73	69	71	213	547.49
Carlos Duran	67	72	74	213	547.49
Andrea Canessa	67	75	71	213	547.49
Matthew Goggin	70	73	71	214	446.93
Bernardo Solanes	73	70	71	214	446.93
Renaud Guillard	70	74	71	215	446.93
Juan Ciola	71	72	72	215	446.93
Philip Parkin	74	73	69	216	335.20
Hayo Bensdorp	67	75	75	217	335.20
Kevin Carissimi	69	70	78	217	335.20
Jeff Hall	70	71	76	217	335.20
Michele Reale	75	70	72	217	335.20
Eric Carlberg	70	77	70	217	335.20
Silvano Locatelli	73	72	72	217	335.20
Ceb Aby	71	74	73	218	279.33
Andrea Calcari	76	70	72	218	279.33
Magnus Persson	73	74	71	219	279.33
Manuel Garcia	73	72	74	219	279.33
Christophe Bovet	73	72	74	219	279.33
Tierri Corte	71	71	77	219	279.33
Laurent Lassalle	71	75	73	219	279.33

Open des Volcans

Golf des Volcans, Volcans, France
Par 36-36–72; 6,874 yards
(Fourth round cancelled — rain.)

July 4-7
purse, £59,133

	SCORES			TOTAL	MONEY
Andrew Sandywell	68	70	67	205	£9,605.22
Adam Mednick	68	72	68	208	5,004.40
Frederik Andersson	70	69	69	208	5,004.40
Laurent Lassalle	70	71	68	209	2,663.63
Greg Chalmers	69	72	68	209	2,663.63
Kevin Carissimi	72	71	67	210	2,153.39
Quentin Dabson	69	72	69	210	2,153.39
Anders Gillner	69	77	65	211	1,689.27
John Mellor	73	70	68	211	1,689.27
Pascal Edmond	71	72	68	211	1,689.27
Michele Reale	74	68	69	211	1,689.27
Fredrik Jacobson	72	71	69	212	1,360.64
Ian Garbutt	75	71	67	213	1,014.72
Vanslow Phillips	73	70	70	213	1,014.72
Anders Haglund	72	69	72	213	1,014.72
Morten Backhausen	73	67	73	213	1,014.72
Daren Lee	71	69	73	213	1,014.72
Ignacio Feliu	70	73	71	214	735.09
Stephen Scahill	70	72	72	214	735.09
Franck Aumonier	75	71	69	215	618.82
Olivier Edmond	72	72	71	215	618.82
Greg Owen	74	70	71	215	618.82
Max Anglert	73	71	71	215	618.82
Jean Charles Cambon	69	74	72	215	618.82
Mike Miller	70	72	73	215	618.82
Simon Brown	74	72	70	216	505.44
Pello Iguaran	72	74	70	216	505.44
Antoine Lebouc	73	73	70	216	505.44
Brian Davis	75	70	71	216	505.44
Christophe Pottier	69	74	73	216	505.44
Eric Carlberg	72	70	74	216	505.44

Neuchatel Open Golf Trophy

Neuchatel Golf and Country Club, Neuchatel, Switzerland
Par 35-35–70; 6,368 yards

July 5-7
purse, £37,989

	SCORES			TOTAL	MONEY
Federico Bisazza	67	68	70	205	£6,703.91
Heinz P. Thul	67	70	68	205	4,469.27
(Bisazza defeated Thul on first extra hole.)					
Oliver Eckstein	67	70	69	206	2,793.30
Marcos Moreno	70	69	70	209	2,094.97
Massimo Scarpa	68	74	67	209	2,094.97
Mark Pullan	70	70	70	210	1,675.98
Alan Lovelace	70	71	70	211	1,340.78
Markus Brier	68	71	72	211	1,340.78
Christophe Bovet	74	69	69	212	1,080.07
Stephen Pullan	67	75	70	212	1,080.07
Claes Hovstadius	69	69	74	212	1,080.07
Joakim Nilsson	74	70	69	213	789.11

	SCORES			TOTAL	MONEY
Tony Price	71	74	68	213	789.11
Jonathan Cheetham	71	70	72	213	789.11
Patrik Gottfridsson	70	74	69	213	789.11
Peter Mruzek	71	78	66	215	558.66
Hans Karlsson	73	74	68	215	558.66
Dimitri Bieri	69	76	70	215	558.66
Jorgen Aker	75	68	73	216	474.86
Lothar Jahn	71	74	72	217	430.17
Rudi Sailer	70	74	73	217	430.17
Chris Van der Velde	70	73	74	217	430.17
Bernardo Solanes	78	71	69	218	356.84
Carlos Duran	74	74	70	218	356.84
Patrick Kressig	73	74	71	218	356.84
Andrew Butterfield	75	72	71	218	356.84
John Woof	77	70	71	218	356.84
Gary Steel	71	73	74	218	356.84
Tim Huyton	70	73	75	218	356.84
Carlos Balmaseda	72	73	73	218	356.84
Lloyd Freeman	76	71	72	219	297.49
Marc Fluri	76	69	74	219	297.49
Karel Skopovy	72	77	70	219	297.49
Ulrich Eckhardt	71	77	71	219	297.49

Gosen Challenge

Warwickshire Golf Club, Warwickshire, England
Par 36-36–72; 6,860 yards

July 11-13
purse, £35,000

	SCORES				TOTAL	MONEY
Gary Owen	69	70	72	70	281	£5,685.23
John Mellor	73	69	70	69	281	3,787.88
(Owen defeated Mellor on first extra hole.)						
Timothy Spence	69	69	72	72	282	1,654.21
Ian Garbutt	71	70	73	66	282	1,654.21
Andrew Sandywell	66	71	71	74	282	1,654.21
Larry Batchelor	73	66	70	73	282	1,654.21
Anthony Wall	66	72	70	73	283	1,221.68
Marcello Santi	73	72	71	68	284	1,081.77
Gary Pooley	70	71	72	71	284	1,081.77
Matthew Stanford	75	68	71	71	285	808.08
Michael Muehr	71	70	69	75	285	808.08
Robert Coles	72	72	74	67	285	808.08
David Ray	71	72	70	72	285	808.08
Stuart Little	70	71	73	71	285	808.08
Graham Farr	70	71	70	75	286	479.46
Peter Alabaster	71	69	73	73	286	479.46
Mark Plummer	71	67	74	74	286	479.46
Vanslow Phillips	69	71	73	73	286	479.46
Roger Winchester	70	69	72	75	286	479.46
Lee James	72	69	72	73	286	479.46
Stephen Scahill	70	73	73	71	287	385.61
Simon Page	75	70	75	68	288	352.34
Greg Chalmers	69	73	73	73	288	352.34
Brian Davis	71	74	72	71	288	352.34
Bill Malley	69	73	73	73	288	352.34
Mark Foster	71	70	75	73	289	313.95
Liam Bond	74	70	73	72	289	313.95

	SCORES				TOTAL	MONEY
Carlos Balmaseda	70	70	72	77	289	313.95
Nigel Preston	73	70	74	73	290	280.68
Cameron Clark	74	70	75	71	290	280.68
Andrew Beal	71	69	72	68	290	280.68
George Ryall	74	70	73	73	290	280.68

Volvo Finnish Open

Espoo Golf Club, Espoo, Finland
Par 36-36–72; 6,720 yards

July 11-14
purse, £35,000

	SCORES				TOTAL	MONEY
Bjorn Back	72	70	69	71	282	£5,685.23
Tony Edlund	73	69	72	71	285	3,787.88
Joakim Rask	72	72	73	70	287	1,921.24
Frederik Larsson	75	68	75	69	287	1,921.24
Johan Annerfelt	72	72	73	71	288	1,446.90
Henrik Nystrom	74	71	75	69	289	1,274.57
Thomas Nielsen	70	71	76	72	289	1,274.57
Erkki Valimaa	72	73	73	72	290	1,081.77
Mikael Piltz	70	69	77	74	290	1,081.77
Per Jacobson	77	69	75	70	291	880.43
Johan Axgren	73	70	75	73	291	880.43
Johan Rystrom	73	69	72	77	291	880.43
Emil Madsen	73	73	74	73	293	631.32
Claes Hovstadius	74	71	76	72	293	631.32
Hans Karlsson	72	73	74	74	293	631.32
Patrik Gottfridsson	74	70	76	73	293	631.32
Daniel Angeflod	73	74	77	70	294	449.31
Stephen Pullan	75	72	77	70	294	449.31
Dennis Edlund	75	70	79	70	294	449.31
Terry Burgoyne	75	70	79	71	295	402.68
Erik Andersson	74	73	78	71	296	371.96
Jesper Kjaerbye	74	71	73	78	296	371.96
Peter Henriksson	68	76	82	70	296	371.96
Mark Pullan	77	71	74	75	297	339.55
Frederik Lundgren	72	76	72	77	297	339.55
Jouni Vilmunen	74	74	77	73	298	308.83
Paul Nilbrink	72	75	76	75	298	308.83
Eric Carlberg	72	74	75	77	298	308.83
Kevin Carissimi	72	72	79	75	298	308.83
Johan Kjellberg	74	73	78	74	299	279.83
*Sami Maenpaa	75	72	76	76	299	
Robert Lofqvist	73	73	77	76	299	279.83

Interlaken Open

Interlaken Golf Club, Interlaken, Switzerland
Par 36-36–72; 6,540 yards

July 26-28
purse, £55,866

	SCORES			TOTAL	MONEY
Vanslow Phillips	69	66	68	203	£9,074.58
Massimo Scarpa	69	69	66	204	4,727.93
Marten Olander	68	70	66	204	4,727.93
Stephen Dodd	71	66	68	205	2,275.45

	SCORES			TOTAL	MONEY
Heinz P. Thul	73	64	68	205	2,275.45
John Mellor	70	65	70	205	2,275.45
Fredrik Jacobson	67	67	71	205	2,275.45
Larry Batchelor	72	67	67	206	1,726.68
James Lee	70	67	69	206	1,726.68
Michele Reale	70	70	67	207	1,233.73
Matthew Goggin	70	70	67	207	1,233.73
Paolo Quirici	70	72	65	207	1,233.73
Alessandro Tadini	68	67	72	207	1,233.73
Nicolas Joakimides	68	70	69	207	1,233.73
Frederik Andersson	67	68	72	207	1,233.73
Ian Garbutt	73	69	66	208	677.46
Erol Simsek	69	71	68	208	677.46
Raphael Jacquelin	72	68	68	208	677.46
Stefano Pietrobono	69	69	70	208	677.46
Robert Jonsson	70	67	71	208	677.46
Carl Watts	68	68	72	208	677.46
Robert Lee	69	68	71	208	677.46
Gary Marks	67	69	72	208	677.46
Craig Cassells	71	69	69	209	509.29
Juan Quiros	72	66	71	209	509.29
Magnus Persson	70	70	69	209	509.29
Roger Winchester	71	69	69	209	509.29
Ben Tinning	72	68	69	209	509.29
Nicolas Vanhootegem	67	70	72	209	509.29
Joakim Gronhagen	70	72	68	210	430.31
Stephen Scahill	73	67	70	210	430.31
Daren Lee	70	70	70	210	430.31
Michael Muehr	69	73	68	210	430.31
Mike Miller	69	72	69	210	430.31

English Challenge Tour Championship

East Sussex National, Uckfield, England
Par 36-36–72; 7,081 yards

August 1-4
purse, £65,000

	SCORES				TOTAL	MONEY
Dennis Edlund	75	71	66	70	282	£10,558.28
Rob Edwards	73	71	69	70	283	7,034.63
Juan Quiros	71	74	70	71	286	3,072.11
Massimo Florioli	68	72	69	77	286	3,072.11
Kalle Vainola	72	70	70	74	286	3,072.11
Mark Nichols	71	73	65	77	286	3,072.11
Alberto Binaghi	73	72	69	73	287	2,268.83
Jimmy Heggarty	74	70	71	73	288	1,856.89
John Mellor	74	70	72	72	288	1,856.89
Gordon J. Brand	70	71	75	72	288	1,856.89
Matthew Stanford	73	66	74	75	288	1,856.89
Anthony Wall	70	75	69	75	289	1,429.11
James Lee	74	70	72	73	289	1,429.11
Mike Miller	70	74	73	73	290	1,008.93
Ignacio Feliu	67	76	74	73	290	1,008.93
Richard Walker	76	72	68	74	290	1,008.93
Francisco Cea	74	70	72	74	290	1,008.93
Massimo Scarpa	75	69	74	72	290	1,008.93
Paul Page	70	73	74	74	291	721.21
David Fisher	78	70	66	77	291	721.21

	SCORES				TOTAL	MONEY
John Vingoe	74	74	73	70	291	721.21
Jeremy Robinson	73	72	73	73	291	721.21
Roger Tuddenham	73	73	75	70	291	721.21
Simon Hurd	70	78	69	75	292	602.06
Michele Reale	75	71	70	76	292	602.06
Kevin Dickens	69	75	73	75	292	602.06
Simon Burnell	72	74	71	75	292	602.06
Frederik Andersson	70	73	71	78	292	602.06
Mikael Krantz	76	71	73	73	293	514.61
Daren Lee	74	74	75	70	293	514.61
Benoit Telleria	70	76	70	77	293	514.61
Robert Jonsson	76	71	75	71	293	514.61
Magnus Persson	75	72	73	73	293	514.61

Rolex Trophy Pro-Am

Golf Club de Geneve, Geneva, Switzerland
Par 36-36—72; 6,878 yards

August 7-10
purse, £55,866

	SCORES				TOTAL	MONEY
Dennis Edlund	66	66	68	74	274	£7,290.50
Carl Watts	72	70	69	63	274	4,553.07
(Edlund defeated Watts on first extra hole.)						
Gary Marks	69	67	62	67	275	3,519.55
Kalle Vainola	69	69	69	69	276	2,905.03
Robert Lee	68	71	72	66	277	2,513.97
Nicolas Vanhootegem	70	67	74	67	278	2,178.77
Marcello Santi	68	72	73	67	280	1,787.71
Raphael Jacquelin	73	69	67	71	280	1,787.71
Joakim Rask	68	72	73	68	281	1,396.65
Jean-Pierre Cixous	72	68	70	71	281	1,396.65
Mikael Krantz	72	68	69	72	281	1,396.65
Erol Simsek	73	69	70	70	282	1,173.18
Simon Burnell	69	70	73	71	283	1,061.45
Andrew Sandywell	71	72	71	70	284	977.65
Michele Reale	72	72	69	71	284	977.65
Vanslow Phillips	65	69	76	75	285	893.85
Frederik Andersson	69	71	74	72	286	810.06
Fredrik Jacobsen	72	70	71	73	286	810.06

Esbjerg Danish Closed

Esbjerg Golf Club, Esbjerg, Denmark
Par 35-36—71; 6,941 yards

August 9-11
purse, £23,202

	SCORES			TOTAL	MONEY
Ben Tinning	73	75	69	217	£3,712.30
Anders Sorensen	70	77	70	217	2,552.20
(Tinning defeated Sorensen on first extra hole.)					
Rene Budde	72	76	71	219	2,088.17
Soren Kjeldsen	70	75	75	220	1,740.14
Jesper Kjaerbye	71	75	76	222	1,450.12
Rene Michelsen	74	73	75	222	1,450.12
Knud Storgaard-Jense	70	77	76	223	1,276.10
Soren Rolner	71	78	75	224	1,160.09

	SCORES			TOTAL	MONEY
Morten Backhausen	73	76	76	225	1,102.09
Nigel Willett	77	78	73	228	1,044.08
Ole Eskildsen	74	81	74	229	986.08
Michael Jacobsen	75	78	77	230	928.07
Ulrik Marcher	78	77	76	231	841.07
Lars Logstrup	77	77	77	231	841.07
James Petts	75	80	77	232	522.04
Morten Gram Larsen	76	79	77	232	522.04
*Tomas Jensson	74	78	80	232	
Jesper Thuen	74	80	81	235	116.01
Vincente Danielsen	77	78	81	236	116.01
Alvah Routledge	73	82	82	237	116.01

Championnat Suisse ASG

Schonenberg Golf Club, Schonenberg, Germany
Par 36-36–72; 6,708 yards

August 9-11
purse, £22,905

	SCORES			TOTAL	MONEY
Carlos Duran	67	71	70	208	£3,910.61
Paolo Quirici	66	68	75	209	2,793.30
Dimitri Bieri	70	71	69	210	2,234.64
Marco Scopetta	76	70	69	215	1,675.98
Maurice Bembridge	73	68	75	218	1,396.65
Juan Ciola	69	76	74	219	1,117.32
Steve Rey	74	73	74	221	1,061.45
Christophe Bovet	79	71	72	222	921.79
Manolo Garcia	73	82	67	222	921.79
Yves Auberson	75	73	74	222	921.79
Tony Price	74	76	72	222	921.79
Marcos Moreno	76	73	74	223	754.19
Alisdair Malcolm	75	73	75	223	754.19
Lloyd Freeman	75	73	77	225	670.39
Bill Marx	78	75	75	228	614.53
Gianluca Patuzzo	79	73	77	229	558.66
Keith Marriott	80	78	73	231	474.86
Stefan Gort	77	76	78	231	474.86
Francis Boillat	78	77	77	232	363.13
John Wallwork	78	75	79	232	363.13

Finnish Closed Championship

Talma, Sipoo, Finland
Par 36-36–72; 6,403 yards

August 9-11
purse, £7,500

	SCORES			TOTAL	MONEY
Mikko Rantenen	71	74	71	216	£1,242.60
Juha Selin	70	69	78	217	957.84
Sami Wachter	72	74	72	218	698.96
David Brumpton	72	77	74	223	543.64
Sauli Makiluoma	76	72	76	224	440.09
Riku Soravuo	76	74	75	225	362.43
Mark Galvin	75	76	76	227	310.65
Esa Saarimaa	75	74	80	229	258.88
Jouni Vilmunen	76	74	80	230	181.21
Sampsa Jolma	75	77	78	230	181.21

Grade Premio Andersen Consulting

Quinta do Lago, Portugal
Par 36-36–72; 6,419 yards

August 9-11
purse, £7,292

	SCORES			TOTAL	MONEY
Antonio Sobrinho	68	70	69	207	£1,592
Daniel Silva	73	69	69	211	1060
Joao Pedro Carvalhosa	74	72	71	217	886
*Keith Ashdown	73	74	76	223	
Rogerio Valente	74	75	75	224	569
Nelson Cavalheiro	74	74	77	225	422
Antonio Dantas	76	77	72	225	422
Jose Dias	79	71	76	226	295
*Brian Evans	81	75	71	227	
Duarte Freitas	77	77	75	229	234
Elidio Costa	75	77	78	230	192
Sebastio Gil	75	80	75	230	192
Joao Couto	81	73	76	230	192
Jose Correia	75	76	80	231	139.50

Karsten Ping Norwegian Open

Oslo Golf Club, Oslo, Norway
Par 36-36–72; 6,639 yards

August 15-18
purse, £59,682

	SCORES				TOTAL	MONEY
Ignacio Feliu	70	69	64	70	273	£9,746.10
John Mellor	71	68	67	68	274	6,493.50
Joakim Rask	68	71	68	69	276	3,662.10
Robert Jonsson	66	72	68	72	278	2,702.70
Ian Garbutt	69	71	69	69	278	2,702.70
Stephen Pullan	70	72	69	68	279	2,100.15
Jorgen Aker	69	71	69	70	279	2,100.15
Mike Miller	72	69	70	68	279	2,100.15
Nicolas Vanhootegem	69	69	70	72	280	1,641.90
Carl Watts	72	72	67	69	280	1,641.90
Stephen Scahill	69	67	71	73	280	1,841.90
Mikael Piltz	70	69	72	70	281	1,380.60
Michael Muehr	71	69	70	72	282	1,082.25
Daren Lee	69	70	70	73	282	1,082.25
Raphael Jacquelin	69	70	73	70	282	1,082.25
Kalle Vainola	70	67	72	73	282	1,082.25
Nicolas Joakimides	68	73	69	73	283	770.25
Adam Mednick	69	74	72	68	283	770.25
Marcello Santi	69	71	73	70	283	770.25
*Henrik Bjornstad	72	72	67	72	283	
Kevin Carissimi	72	72	73	67	284	650.81
Richard Walker	74	67	72	71	284	650.81
David R. Jones	70	69	73	72	284	650.81
Matthew Stanford	71	70	72	71	284	650.81
Alberto Binaghi	71	73	71	70	285	530.16
Massimo Florioli	68	72	74	71	285	530.16
Simon Burnell	69	67	77	72	285	530.16
Marcus Wheelhouse	66	71	75	73	285	530.16
Jean Pierre Sallat	69	74	69	73	285	530.16
Joakim Gronhagen	73	67	72	73	285	530.16
Paul Gareth Simpson	72	69	70	74	285	530.16
Paul Lyons	73	71	68	73	285	530.16

Dutch Challenge

Broekpolder, Rotterdam, Netherlands
Par 36-36–72; 7,098 yards

August 22-25
purse, £60,000

	SCORES				TOTAL	MONEY
Matthew Goggin	68	69	69	68	274	£9,746.10
Nicolas Vanhootegem	72	68	68	68	276	6,493.50
Ian Garbutt	70	71	69	68	278	3,662.10
Andrew Sandywell	65	71	75	68	279	2,702.70
Per Jacobson	67	67	71	74	279	2,702.70
Raphael Jacquelin	69	70	75	67	281	2,184.98
Stephen Scahill	72	68	72	69	281	2,184.98
David Lynn	68	73	70	71	282	1,930.50
James Lee	71	72	70	71	284	1,641.90
Marcus Wheelhouse	70	74	72	68	284	1,641.90
Brian Davis	72	72	71	69	284	1,641.90
Mike Miller	68	72	74	71	285	1,200.71
Rudi Sailer	72	72	75	66	285	1,200.71
Andrew Barnett	71	73	73	68	285	1,200.71
Johan Rystrom	72	72	73	68	285	1,200.71
Andrew Butterfield	71	70	70	75	286	804.38
Benoit Telleria	66	75	73	72	286	804.38
Matthew Hazelden	71	71	68	76	286	804.38
Gary Murphy	71	70	71	74	286	804.38
Jonathan Wilshire	68	72	74	73	287	650.81
Alberto Binaghi	70	75	74	68	287	650.81
Olivier Edmond	73	69	71	74	287	650.81
Jean Francois Remesy	71	73	70	73	287	650.81
Robert Lee	70	71	73	74	288	582.08
David R. Jones	74	72	69	73	288	582.08
William Guy	74	72	68	75	289	512.85
Timothy Spence	71	71	74	73	289	512.85
Arnaud Langenaeken	72	72	73	72	289	512.85
Ruben Wechgelaer	75	71	70	73	289	512.85
Mikael Krantz	72	72	70	75	289	512.85
Warren Bennett	69	70	76	74	289	512.85

Toyota PGA Championship

Helsingor Golf Club, Helsingor, Denmark
Par 71; 6,371 yards

August 23-25
purse, £40,000

	SCORES			TOTAL	MONEY
Adam Mednick	66	67	69	202	£6,497.40
Patrik Gottfridsson	66	67	70	203	4,329
Johan Axgren	72	67	65	204	2,441.40
Frederik Andersson	66	70	69	205	1,801.80
Jose Garcia	65	72	68	205	1,801.80
Morten Backhausen	71	69	66	206	1,346.48
Paul Nilbrink	70	66	70	206	1,346.48
Mikael Lundberg	69	68	69	206	1,346.48
Eric Carlberg	68	68	70	206	1,346.48
Paul Lyons	74	65	68	207	923.52
Anders Sorensen	71	66	70	207	923.52
Daniel Westermark	69	68	70	207	923.52
Fredrik Jacobson	68	72	67	207	923.52
Mikael Piltz	68	68	71	207	923.52

	SCORES			TOTAL	MONEY
Robert Jonsson	76	64	68	208	611
Ben Tinning	72	67	69	208	611
Marten Olander	71	68	69	208	611
Hans Karlsson	70	70	69	209	464.10
Raimo Sjoberg	70	70	69	209	464.10
Peter Henriksson	69	72	68	209	464.10
Jacob Rasmussen	69	71	69	209	464.10
Jonathan Cheetham	68	68	73	209	464.10
Fredrick Mansson	70	71	69	210	371.06
Claes Hovstadius	70	68	72	210	371.06
Peter Jarnestal	69	72	69	210	371.06
Francesco Guermani	69	70	71	210	371.06
Per Nyberg	68	69	73	210	371.06
Magnus Persson	67	71	72	210	371.06
Anders Hansen	67	70	73	210	371.06
Lars Tingvall	72	68	71	211	315.90
Fredrik Eskelid	70	71	70	211	315.90
Frederik Larsson	69	69	73	211	315.90

Kentab/RGB Open

Frosaker Golf Club, Stockholm, Sweden
Par 36-36–72; 6,944 yards

August 30-September 1
purse, £40,000

	SCORES			TOTAL	MONEY
Max Anglert	69	67	66	202	£6,497.40
Dennis Edlund	66	69	68	203	4,329
Joakim Rask	70	69	71	210	2,195.70
Massimo Scarpa	69	71	70	210	2,195.70
Frederik Andersson	74	67	70	211	1,257.26
Rob Edwards	73	68	70	211	1,257.26
Brian Davis	73	64	74	211	1,257.26
Henrik Nystrom	71	73	67	211	1,257.26
Paul Lyons	71	67	73	211	1,257.26
Anthony Wall	69	74	68	211	1,257.26
Inigo Moral	69	72	70	211	1,257.26
Marcello Santi	69	70	72	211	1,257.26
Patrik Gottfridsson	73	67	72	212	799.50
Michele Reale	71	72	69	212	799.50
Johan Axgren	73	72	68	213	532.63
Marten Olander	72	72	69	213	532.63
Jorgen Aker	72	70	71	213	532.63
Per Nyberg	71	73	69	213	532.63
Soren Kjeldsen	71	71	71	213	532.63
Robert Jonsson	70	70	73	213	532.63
Anders Sorensen	68	76	69	213	532.63
Mikael Piltz	75	69	70	214	377.81
Ulrik Marcher	73	69	72	214	377.81
Gary Murphy	72	69	73	214	377.81
Gary Marks	71	74	69	214	377.81
Kalle Vainola	70	75	69	214	377.81
Lars Tingvall	70	72	72	214	377.81
Joakim Gronhagen	70	71	73	214	377.81
John Mellor	69	71	74	214	377.81
Marcus Wheelhouse	75	69	71	215	288.60
Johan Rystrom	74	71	70	215	288.60
Johan Andersson	73	72	70	215	288.60

	SCORES			TOTAL	MONEY
Paul Nilbrink	72	70	73	215	288.60
Rene Budde	72	70	73	215	288.60
Pauli Hughes	71	72	72	215	288.60
Anders Gillner	70	75	70	215	288.60
Matthew Hazelden	70	74	71	215	288.60
Matthew Goggin	70	73	72	215	288.60
Magnus Persson	68	71	76	215	288.60

Sovereign Russian Open

Moscow Country Club, Moscow, Russia
Par 36-36–72; 6,958 yards
(Fourth round cancelled — rain.)

September 5-8
purse, £64,309

	SCORES			TOTAL	MONEY
Carl Watts	70	65	68	203	£10,445.98
John Mellor	68	72	65	205	6,959.81
Markus Brier	69	70	69	208	3,925.08
Simon Brown	67	71	71	209	3,135.05
Gordon J. Brand	73	69	69	211	2,548.80
Matthew McGuire	72	70	69	211	2,548.80
Nicolas Vanhootegem	71	68	73	212	1,993.89
Michael Muehr	68	72	72	212	1,993.89
Ian Garbutt	70	70	72	212	1,993.89
Robert Lee	73	71	68	212	1,993.89
Warren Bennett	72	71	70	213	1,617.68
Matthew Goggin	73	70	71	214	1,413.91
Mike Miller	72	70	72	214	1,413.91
Mikko Rantenen	72	70	73	215	1,097.27
John Woof	71	73	71	215	1,097.27
Jean-Pierre Cixous	74	69	72	215	1,097.27
Morten Backhausen	74	72	70	216	825.56
Vanslow Phillips	71	73	72	216	825.56
Roger Winchester	72	70	74	216	825.56
Jonathan Cheetham	70	75	72	217	710.61
Kevin Carissimi	71	76	70	217	710.61
Rene Budde	75	69	73	217	710.61
Paul Gareth Simpson	74	72	72	218	635.37
Raphael Jacquelin	72	70	76	218	635.37
Joost Steenkamer	74	71	73	218	635.37
Marten Olander	74	74	71	219	586.26
Anders Sorensen	77	71	71	219	586.26
Jean Pierre Sallat	73	72	75	220	531.39
Sebastien Delagrange	75	74	71	220	531.39
Rudi Sailer	76	74	70	220	531.39
Stephen Pullan	73	75	72	220	531.39

Swedish Match Play

Hook Golf Club, Hok, Sweden
Par 36-36–72; 5,500 yards

September 5-8
purse, £50,000

FOURTH ROUND

Paul Nilbrink defeated Niclas Johnsson, 3 and 2
Massimo Scarpa defeated Carl Magnus Stromberg, 4 and 3

Adam Mednick defeated Johan Rystrom, 1 up
Pehr Magnebrant defeated Daniel Westermark, 1 up
Alberto Binaghi defeated Yngve Nilsson, 3 and 2
Johan Axgren defeated Fredrik Lundgren, 3 and 2
Fredrik Jacobson defeated Henrik Nystrom, 5 and 4
Tony Edlund defeated Bjorn Back, 4 and 3

(Each losing fourth-round player received £1,093.87.

QUARTER-FINALS

Nilbrink defeated Scarpa, 3 and 2
Mednick defeated Magnebrant, 2 and 1
Axgren defeated Binaghi, 2 and 1
Jacobson defeated Edlund, 5 and 6

(Each losing quarter-finalist received £1,806.27.

SEMI-FINALS

Mednick defeated Nilbrink, 5 and 4
Jacobsen defeated Axgren

THIRD-PLACE PLAYOFF

Nilbrink defeated Axgren, 1 up

(Nilbrink received £3,013.25, Axgren received £2,406.75.)

FINAL

Mednick defeated Jacobsen, 2 and 1

(Mednick received £8,019.29, Jacobson received £5,342.99.)

Perrier European Pro-Am

Golf Club d'Hulencourt
Par 36-36–72; 6,797 yards

Royal Waterloo Golf Club, La Marache Course
Par 36-36–72; 6,438 yards

Royal Waterloo Golf Club, Le Lion Course
Par 36-36–72; 6,368 yards
Waterloo, Belgium

September 12-15
purse, £55,000

	SCORES				TOTAL	MONEY
Kevin Carissimi	64	72	71	70	277	£8,933.92
Jesus Maria Arruti	71	70	69	67	277	5,952.38
(Carissimi defeated Arruti on fifth extra hole.)						
Greg Owen	70	71	68	70	279	2,770.63
Stephen Scahill	66	69	73	71	279	2,770.63
Daniel Westermark	66	67	76	70	279	2,770.63
Ignacio Feliu	71	72	69	69	281	1,925.14
Alberto Binaghi	70	71	69	71	281	1,925.14
Andrew Sandywell	66	75	73	67	281	1,925.14
Scott Watson	74	67	70	71	282	1,505.08
Peter Fowler	72	68	71	71	282	1,505.08

	SCORES				TOTAL	MONEY
Manuel Pinero	71	72	70	69	282	1,505.08
Matthew Goggin	70	74	70	69	283	1,154.73
Arnaud Langenaeken	73	68	71	71	283	1,154.73
Frederik Larsson	72	74	69	68	283	1,154.73
Neal Briggs	69	76	69	70	284	884.82
Tony Edlund	73	69	70	73	285	884.82
Simon Brown	71	76	68	70	285	726.62
David J. Russell	71	76	68	70	285	726.62
Rob Edwards	74	73	73	67	287	622.05
Paul Gareth Simpson	76	71	68	72	287	622.05
Carl Watts	73	76	70	68	287	622.05
Jose Canizares	73	74	74	66	287	622.05
Robert Lee	73	75	74	66	288	526.60
Federico Bisazza	74	71	72	71	288	526.60
Ian Garbutt	74	73	72	69	288	526.60
Gauthier D'Hollander	79	70	72	67	288	526.60
Nicolas Vanhootegem	75	72	71	70	288	526.60
Michele Reale	77	72	70	70	289	469.22
Amaury D'Ogimont	72	70	73	74	289	469.22
John Mellor	73	76	70	71	290	434.36
Andrew Murray	72	78	67	73	290	434.36
Anders Hansen	69	71	77	73	290	434.36

Eulen Open Galea III

RSG de Neguri, Bilbao, Spain
Par 36-36–72; 6,868 yards

September 18-21
purse, £72,000

	SCORES				TOTAL	MONEY
Jose Sota	70	71	70	68	279	£11,695.32
Fredrik Jacobson	72	71	69	71	283	4,668.30
Ignacio Feliu	73	71	68	71	283	4,668.30
Robert Lee	70	70	71	72	283	4,668.30
Stephen Scahill	74	67	69	73	283	4,668.30
Matthew Goggin	69	76	71	68	284	2,520.18
Ian Garbutt	70	71	72	71	284	2,520.18
Nicolas Kalouguine	73	67	72	72	284	2,520.18
Olivier Edmond	68	74	70	73	285	1,891.89
Inigo Moral	72	71	69	73	285	1,891.89
Andrew Sandywell	71	72	69	73	285	1,891.89
Frederik Larsson	73	72	67	73	285	1,891.89
Max Anglert	70	73	73	70	286	1,368.90
Dennis Edlund	70	74	70	72	286	1,368.90
Alberto Binaghi	68	72	72	74	286	1,368.90
Tony Edlund	71	71	74	71	287	937.87
Kalle Vainola	70	70	74	73	287	937.87
Carl Watts	69	73	71	74	287	937.87
Anders Hansen	68	71	73	75	287	937.87
Joakim Gronhagen	70	74	69	74	287	937.87
Juan Quiros	68	71	72	77	288	793.26
Jose Rozadilla	72	74	71	72	289	724.82
Roger Winchester	73	72	71	73	289	724.82
Adam Mednick	73	69	73	74	289	724.82
Matthew McGuire	73	70	70	76	289	724.82
Ben Tinning	65	77	73	75	290	656.37
Simon Brown	70	73	72	75	290	656.37
Richard Walker	71	70	80	70	291	614.25

	SCORES				TOTAL	MONEY
Magnus Persson	75	68	74	74	291	614.25
Massimo Scarpa	72	71	75	74	292	561.60
Marcus Wheelhouse	71	71	74	76	292	561.60
John Mellor	73	72	71	76	292	561.60
Eric Carlberg	74	70	70	78	292	561.60
*Juan Rosillo	70	74	71	77	292	

Telia InfoMedia Grand Prix

Ljunghusens Golf Club, Sweden
Par 36-36–72; 6,115 yards

September 25-28
purse, £75,000

	SCORES				TOTAL	MONEY
Scott Watson	72	68	69	72	281	£12,182.63
Emil Madsen	70	70	71	70	281	5,450.25
Michael Archer	70	71	70	70	281	5,450.25
Frederik Larsson	71	69	71	70	281	5,450.25
(Watson won on third extra hole.)						
Daren Lee	71	72	74	65	282	2,744.02
Colas Vanhootegem	70	72	74	66	282	2,744.02
Greg Chalmers	67	74	73	68	282	2,744.02
Adam Mednick	71	68	71	72	282	2,744.02
*Johan Girdo	68	70	73	71	282	
Hans Karlsson	69	74	72	68	283	2,052.38
Andreas Jernberg	73	68	72	70	283	2,052.38
Johan Rystrom	67	72	73	71	283	2,052.38
Johan Axgren	74	70	71	69	284	1,302.67
Massimo Florioli	73	70	73	68	284	1,302.67
Marc Pendaries	69	73	74	66	284	1,302.67
Magnus Persson	71	70	72	71	284	1,302.67
Joakim Hallberg	75	65	76	68	284	1,302.67
Fredrik Jacobson	71	67	81	65	284	1,302.67
Ben Tinning	70	68	77	69	284	1,302.67
Matthew Goggin	72	72	72	70	286	865.31
Anders Sorensen	75	68	73	70	286	865.31
Lars Tingvall	71	69	73	73	286	865.31
Tony Edlund	69	71	77	70	287	782.43
Roger Winchester	68	70	79	70	287	782.43
Raimo Sjoberg	73	71	74	70	288	716.63
Carl Magnus Stromberg	74	70	74	70	288	716.63
Brian Davis	71	69	78	70	288	716.63
Robert Jonsson	75	69	74	71	289	639.85
Jose Sota	75	68	75	71	289	639.85
Mikael Piltz	73	69	75	72	289	639.85
Carl Watts	75	67	73	74	289	639.85

First Modena Classic Open

Modena Golf Club, Modena, Italy
Par 36-36–72; 7,024 yards

September 25-28
purse, £35,000

	SCORES				TOTAL	MONEY
Lee James	69	76	68	69	282	£5,685.23
Renaud Guillard	71	73	68	70	282	3,787.88
(James defeated Guillard on first extra hole.)						

	SCORES				TOTAL	MONEY
Marcus Wheelhouse	72	72	69	70	283	2,136.23
Andrew Butterfield	72	68	73	71	284	1,576.58
Janeirik Dahlstrom	70	69	69	76	284	1,576.58
Francisco Javier Amatriai	75	73	69	68	285	1,178.17
Jean Marie Kula	73	72	69	71	285	1,178.17
Frederic Cupillard	74	72	67	72	285	1,178.17
Emanuele Bolognesi	74	71	67	73	285	1,178.17
Mario Tadini	70	75	68	73	286	955.50
Mark Pullan	73	70	73	71	287	880.43
Michael Muehr	76	72	75	65	288	666.12
Nicolas Dupuy	77	71	72	68	288	666.12
Francesco Guermani	74	71	72	71	288	666.12
Bruno Petit	74	72	71	71	288	666.12
Matthew Hazelden	68	73	71	76	288	666.12
Carlos Duran	72	74	73	70	289	427.25
Dominique Nouailhac	74	73	72	70	289	427.25
Nicolas Kalouguine	70	76	72	71	289	427.25
Federico Bisazza	73	72	72	72	289	427.25
Oliver Eckstein	74	71	70	74	289	427.25
Gianluca Baruffaldi	74	73	74	69	290	352.34
James Healey	72	74	72	72	290	352.34
Stefano Pietrobono	72	70	73	75	290	352.34
Luis Gallardo	71	71	73	75	290	352.34
Gianluca Crespi	72	74	74	71	291	319.07
Sebastien Delagrange	73	72	73	73	291	319.07
Andrea Canessa	75	74	74	69	292	298.60
Rudi Sailer	72	72	74	74	292	298.60
Markus Brier	70	72	77	74	292	298.60

Bank Pekao Polish Open

First Warsaw Golf & Country Club, Warsaw, Poland
Par 71; 6,624 yards

October 3-6
purse, £40,000

	SCORES				TOTAL	MONEY
Erol Simsek	69	67	71	75	282	£6,267.59
Dennis Edlund	70	69	72	72	283	3265.47
Christophe Pottier	73	70	68	72	283	3265.47
Greg Chalmers	71	74	71	69	285	1738.07
Frederik Larsson	71	74	74	66	285	1738.07
Simon Brown	74	67	72	73	286	1463.44
Pehr Magnebrant	72	69	72	74	287	1346.82
Marcello Santi	74	68	73	73	288	1241.48
Vanslow Phillips	70	74	73	72	289	1055.88
Marten Olander	72	71	71	75	289	1055.88
Henrik Nystrom	74	74	71	70	289	1055.88
Brian Davis	71	74	73	72	290	734.35
Ian Garbutt	77	71	71	71	290	734.35
Anthony Wall	73	76	71	70	290	734.35
Lee James	73	72	75	70	290	734.35
Marc Pendaries	67	79	71	73	290	734.35
Michele Reale	71	74	73	73	291	460.86
Stephen Scahill	76	72	70	73	291	460.86
Magnus Persson	75	68	71	77	291	460.86
Michael Muehr	70	75	74	72	291	460.86
Per Jacobson	73	75	70	73	291	460.86
Francois Lamare	76	70	72	73	291	460.86

	SCORES				TOTAL	MONEY
Mikael Krantz	74	72	73	73	292	369.43
John Mellor	76	73	72	71	292	369.43
Raimo Sjoberg	74	72	73	73	292	369.43
Stephen Pullan	75	70	75	72	292	369.43
Emil Madsen	72	76	72	72	292	369.43
Adam Tillman	73	71	77	72	293	323.54
Eric Carlberg	75	73	74	71	293	323.54
Renaud Guillard	74	75	69	75	293	323.54

UAP Grand Final

Quinta do Peru, Lisbon, Portugal
Par 36-36–72; 6,598 yards

October 17-20
purse, £65,000

	SCORES				TOTAL	MONEY
Ian Garbutt	67	71	67	67	272	£10,880
Vanslow Phillips	67	70	68	69	274	5,665
Ben Tinning	67	72	68	67	274	5,665
Brian Davis	66	71	70	68	275	3,000
Stephen Scahill	70	67	69	69	275	3,000
Fredrik Jacobson	70	69	70	68	277	2,520
Raphael Jacquelin	70	68	68	72	278	1,986
Juan Quiros	70	69	70	69	278	1,986
Ignacio Feliu	72	71	69	66	278	1,986
Heinz P. Thul	74	69	66	69	278	1,986
Nicolas Vanhootegem	74	65	71	68	278	1,986
Matthew Hazelden	69	67	72	71	279	1,405
Greg Owen	70	69	72	68	279	1,405
Frederik Andersson	67	68	76	68	279	1,405
Daniel Westermark	73	68	68	71	280	1,075
Massimo Florioli	71	69	72	68	280	1,075
Federico Bisazza	69	70	67	75	281	875
Johan Axgren	70	71	69	71	281	875
Frederik Larsson	72	70	69	71	282	763.33
Simon Burnell	70	69	67	76	282	763.33
Alberto Binaghi	71	73	70	68	282	763.33
Max Anglert	69	71	66	77	283	700
Francisco Cea	73	70	71	70	284	680
Carl Watts	70	70	72	73	285	640
John Mellor	73	70	73	69	285	640
Kevin Carissimi	75	72	68	70	285	640
Robert Lee	72	73	73	68	286	590
Scott Watson	73	70	70	73	286	590
Michele Reale	76	68	69	74	287	533.75
Erol Simsek	73	71	69	74	287	533.75
Kalle Vainola	74	69	69	75	287	533.75
Mike Miller	74	72	71	70	287	533.75

Asia/Japan Tours

Benson & Hedges Malaysian Open

Templer Park Golf Club, Kuala Lumpur, Malaysia
Par 36-36–72; 7,133 yards

January 18-21
purse, US$300,000

	SCORES				TOTAL	MONEY
Steve Flesch	66	75	71	70	282	US$50,000
Craig Jones	75	71	67	69	282	33,330
(Flesch defeated Jones on second extra hole.)						
Darren Clarke	70	72	69	72	283	18,780
Lee Porter	72	68	70	74	284	15,000
Edward Fryatt	73	70	68	74	285	12,720
Brian Wilson	75	72	70	69	286	10,500
Kevin Wentworth	71	72	76	68	287	7,740
Tony Carolan	75	70	73	69	287	7,740
Shoichi Kuwabara	70	74	73	70	287	7,740
Eric Meeks	75	72	73	68	288	5,600
Daniel Chopra	71	73	74	70	288	5,600
Christian Pena	67	75	68	78	288	5,600
Glen Joyner	70	79	73	67	289	4,192.50
Andrew Coltart	76	72	71	70	289	4,192.50
Sam Torrance	70	76	71	72	289	4,192.50
Grant Dodd	74	71	72	72	289	4,192.50
Gary Nicklaus	71	76	69	73	289	4,192.50
Ramon Brobio	70	74	72	73	289	4,192.50
Dominique Boulet	72	71	72	74	289	4,192.50
Ken Druce	71	71	73	74	289	4,192.50
Kazuo Kanayama	73	71	76	70	290	3,420
Jeff Cook	74	73	70	73	290	3,420
Matthew Goggin	71	75	71	73	290	3,420
Jim Rutledge	72	77	73	69	291	3,090
Rick Todd	73	74	73	71	291	3,090
Peter Teravainen	78	70	71	72	291	3,090
Jean Louis Guepy	74	73	71	73	291	3,090
Mohd. Ali Kadir	72	74	71	74	291	3,090
John Senden	73	73	77	69	292	2,652
Olle Nordberg	75	74	73	70	292	2,652
Ben Weir	71	78	71	72	292	2,652
Stuart Bouvier	73	75	72	72	292	2,652
Gary Webb	72	76	69	75	292	2,652

Mitsubishi Manila Southwoods Open

Manila Southwoods Golf & Country Club,
Composite Course, Manila, Philippines
Par 36-36–72; 7,132 yards

February 1-4
purse, US$250,000

	SCORES				TOTAL	MONEY
Manny Zerman	71	73	77	71	292	US$41,650
Jim Rutledge	76	69	77	70	292	21,712.50
Don Walsworth	68	73	80	71	292	21,712.50

(Zerman defeated Walsworth on first extra hole and Rutledge on second extra hole.)

	SCORES				TOTAL	MONEY
Chris Tidland	71	75	75	72	293	12,500
Carlos Larrain	71	75	71	77	294	9,675
Todd Hamilton	69	73	75	77	294	9,675
Ben Weir	71	74	75	75	295	6,450
Shaun Haberstroh	67	74	79	75	295	6,450
Lee Porter	72	73	73	77	295	6,450
Matt Gogel	71	75	80	70	296	4,537.50
Olle Nordberg	69	80	75	72	296	4,537.50
Craig McClellan	72	71	76	77	296	4,537.50
Rob Moss	66	74	79	77	296	4,537.50
Clay Devers	69	79	77	72	297	3,825
Gerry Norquist	68	75	79	75	297	3,825
George Zorkic	74	75	77	72	298	3,412.50
Kevin Wentworth	76	72	77	73	298	3,412.50
*Richard Sinfuego	70	76	76	76	298	
Steve Flesch	73	77	74	75	299	3,062.50
Bill Malley	71	78	75	75	299	3,062.50
Sang-Ho Choi	73	74	77	75	299	3,062.50
Daniel Chopra	68	69	82	80	299	3,062.50
Chang Tse-Peng	71	78	79	72	300	2,850
Mike Miles	75	74	77	75	301	2,716.67
Raul Fretes	73	75	77	76	301	2,716.67
Rodrigo Cuello	72	71	78	80	301	2,716.67
Oliver Eckstein	76	75	78	73	302	2,425
Christian Pena	72	77	79	74	302	2,425
Gavin Vearing	73	75	78	76	302	2,425
Jorge Berendt	72	73	81	76	302	2,425
Jeff Cook	75	75	75	77	302	2,425

Thai Airways International Thailand Open

Sriracha International Golf Club, Pattaya City, Thailand
Par 36-36–72; 7,019 yards

February 8-11
purse, US$300,000

	SCORES				TOTAL	MONEY
Todd Barranger	69	69	65	68	271	US$50,000
Rob Moss	70	69	68	69	276	33,330
Jim Rutledge	72	71	70	65	278	13,200
Eric Rustand	71	71	70	66	278	13,200
Carlos Larrain	70	71	71	66	278	13,200
Todd Hamilton	71	69	69	69	278	13,200
Yong-Jin Shin	70	68	68	72	278	13,200
Angel Cabrera	71	73	68	68	280	6,204
Greg Lesher	70	71	70	69	280	6,204
Kevin Wentworth	68	71	72	69	280	6,204
Larry Barber	67	72	72	69	280	6,204
Prayad Marksaeng	70	69	70	71	280	6,204
Edward Fryatt	70	70	73	68	281	4,590
Tim Straub	71	70	71	69	281	4,590
Hiroshi Ueda	71	68	73	69	281	4,590
Rick Todd	71	72	68	70	281	4,590
Don Walsworth	72	70	73	67	282	3,738
Shaun Haberstroh	73	69	72	68	282	3,738
Kazuo Kanayama	69	72	72	69	282	3,738
Daniel Chopra	76	69	67	70	282	3,738
David Sutherland	70	69	72	71	282	3,738
Jeev Milkha Singh	68	74	73	68	283	3,340

	SCORES				TOTAL	MONEY
Gary Webb	73	70	71	69	283	3,340
Lee Porter	70	72	71	70	283	3,340
Gustavo Rojas	73	69	73	69	284	2,955
Steve Flesch	72	71	71	70	284	2,955
Tony Carolan	72	70	72	70	284	2,955
Rodrigo Cuello	67	73	73	71	284	2,955
Manny Zerman	73	68	71	72	284	2,955
Christian Pena	69	70	73	72	284	2,955

Classic India Open

Royal Calcutta Golf Club, Calcutta, India
Par 36-36–72; 7,195 yards

February 15-18
purse, US$300,000

	SCORES				TOTAL	MONEY
Hidezumi Shirakata	66	72	69	70	277	US$49,980
Jyoti Randhawa	70	71	70	69	280	22,370
Basad Ali	67	70	74	69	280	22,370
Daniel Chopra	71	68	71	70	280	22,370
Don Walsworth	71	69	71	72	283	12,720
Bob May	72	73	72	68	285	7,217.14
Ron Wuensche	75	72	69	69	285	7,217.14
Arjun Atwal	74	73	68	70	285	7,217.14
Todd Barranger	68	73	73	71	285	7,217.14
Alan Bratton	68	72	72	73	285	7,217.14
Arjun Singh	71	70	70	74	285	7,217.14
Mike Tschetter	68	73	70	74	285	7,217.14
Jim Rutledge	72	72	74	68	286	4,980
Greg Lesher	72	75	70	70	287	3,943.33
Firoz Ali	66	72	78	71	287	3,943.33
Kevin Wentworth	73	70	71	73	287	3,943.33
Gustavo Rojas	72	70	72	73	287	3,943.33
Rick Todd	69	73	72	73	287	3,943.33
Jose Cantero	68	73	73	73	287	3,943.33
Bob Mattiace	69	68	76	74	287	3,943.33
Edward Fryatt	71	67	73	76	287	3,943.33
Kevin Leach	71	67	73	76	287	3,943.33
Jeev Milkha Singh	68	75	75	70	288	3,300
Jorge Berendt	74	72	70	72	288	3,300
Felix Casas	71	70	79	69	289	3,045
Angel Cabrera	72	71	74	72	289	3,045
David Sutherland	74	69	73	73	289	3,045
Jeff Cook	71	71	74	73	289	3,045
Craig McClellan	74	72	73	71	290	2,775
Ben Weir	71	74	72	73	290	2,775

Matoa International Invitational

Matoa International Golf Club, Jakarta, Indonesia
Par 36-36–72; 7,042 yards

March 6-9
purse, US$250,000

	SCORES				TOTAL	MONEY
Christian Pena	72	66	68	69	275	US$41,650
Rick Todd	69	67	68	71	275	27,775
(Pena defeated Todd on second extra hole.)						

	SCORES				TOTAL	MONEY
Dennis Paulson	71	71	70	64	276	12,916.67
Olle Nordberg	69	67	70	70	276	12,916.67
Todd Barranger	71	66	67	72	276	12,916.67
Jorge Berendt	71	68	72	66	277	7,500
Ron Wuensche	75	68	67	67	277	7,500
Larry Barber	68	69	72	68	277	7,500
Manny Zerman	69	69	69	71	278	5,600
Jong-Duk Kim	68	73	68	70	279	4,666.67
Brian Wilson	68	70	71	70	279	4,666.67
Gustavo Rojas	69	69	70	71	279	4,666.67
Anthony Painter	75	69	67	69	280	3,825
Nick Goetze	68	72	70	70	280	3,825
Eric Meeks	71	68	71	70	280	3,825
Steve Flesch	71	70	67	72	280	3,825
Raul Fretes	73	73	68	67	281	3,162.50
Madasamy Murugiah	72	69	68	72	281	3,162.50
Gary Webb	69	70	70	72	281	3,162.50
Jeff Cook	69	69	71	72	281	3,162.50
Matt Gogel	68	77	71	66	282	2,750
Pedro Martinez	68	74	70	70	282	2,750
Greg Lesher	72	66	74	70	282	2,750
Matthew Goggin	71	69	71	71	282	2,750
Jack Kay, Jr.	70	69	72	71	282	2,750
Stephen Leaney	70	71	69	72	282	2,750
Edward Fryatt	75	70	73	65	283	2,425
Shane Tait	69	74	70	70	283	2,425
Ted Gleason	69	72	72	70	283	2,425
Rob Whitlock	74	72	73	65	284	2,140
Kasiadi	75	71	71	67	284	2,140
Don Walsworth	71	70	74	69	284	2,140
Mike Cunning	76	70	68	70	284	2,140
Chris Stutts	74	69	70	71	284	2,140
*Hong Chia-Yuh	72	71	71	70	284	

Indonesia Open

Jagorawi Golf & Country Club, Jakarta, Indonesia
Par 36-36–72; 6,903 yards

March 13-16
purse, US$250,000

	SCORES				TOTAL	MONEY
Edward Fryatt	67	65	68	71	271	US$41,650
Jim Rutledge	72	70	68	64	274	21,712.50
Daniel Chopra	72	68	66	68	274	21,712.50
Anthony Painter	66	70	71	69	276	12,500
Jorge Berendt	68	69	72	68	277	9,675
Rick Todd	68	73	67	69	277	9,675
Jeff Cook	72	73	67	66	278	6,450
Joey Sadowski	70	71	69	68	278	6,450
Don Walsworth	67	74	68	69	278	6,450
Martyn Roberts	74	69	69	67	279	4,825
Nick Goetze	71	69	71	68	279	4,825
Shaun Haberstroh	71	72	69	68	280	4,350
Hidezumi Shirakata	74	70	69	68	281	3,725
Steven Conran	74	71	67	69	281	3,725
Larry Barber	69	73	69	70	281	3,725
Christian Chernock	67	75	68	71	281	3,725
Ron Wuensche	72	69	68	72	281	3,725

	SCORES				TOTAL	MONEY
Manny Zerman	70	71	70	71	282	3,108.33
Peter Teravainen	71	72	66	73	282	3,108.33
Rodrigo Cuello	68	71	70	73	282	3,108.33
Mike Miles	76	68	74	65	283	2,785
George Zorkic	72	73	69	69	283	2,785
Nasim Maan	69	71	74	69	283	2,785
Matthew Goggin	71	71	71	70	283	2,785
Tim Straub	72	71	68	72	283	2,785
Kevin Leach	73	74	69	68	284	2,247.50
Craig Jones	73	72	71	68	284	2,247.50
Mohd. Ali Kadir	76	70	69	69	284	2,247.50
Greg Lesher	68	73	74	69	284	2,247.50
Raul Fretes	76	69	69	70	284	2,247.50
Gary Webb	75	69	70	70	284	2,247.50
Ted Gleason	71	72	71	70	284	2,247.50
Pedro Martinez	70	72	72	70	284	2,247.50
Eric Meeks	70	72	71	71	284	2,247.50
Kasiadi	72	69	71	72	284	2,247.50

Rolex Masters–Singapore

Singapore Island Golf & Country Club, Singapore
Par 35-36–71; 6,749 yards
(Third round cancelled — rain.)

March 21-24
purse, US$262,500

	SCORES			TOTAL	MONEY
Mike Cunning	71	64	69	204	US$43,732.50
Don Walsworth	68	70	67	205	22,798.13
Peter Teravainen	69	67	69	205	22,798.13
Craig McClellan	67	72	67	206	11,147.50
Takao Nogami	65	72	69	206	11,147.50
Greg Lesher	67	68	71	206	11,147.50
Gerry Norquist	70	69	68	207	7,875
David Sutherland	71	70	67	208	5,897.50
Rob Whitlock	71	68	69	208	5,897.50
John Kernohan	70	68	70	208	5,897.50
Jim Rutledge	74	67	68	209	4,252.50
Edward Fryatt	73	68	68	209	4,252.50
Tim Straub	69	72	68	209	4,252.50
Manny Zerman	71	68	70	209	4,252.50
Larry Barber	70	69	70	209	4,252.50
Hsieh Yu-Shu	69	69	71	209	4,252.50
Blair Philip	70	72	68	210	3,140.16
Daniel Chopra	73	68	69	210	3,140.16
Rick Todd	70	71	69	210	3,140.16
Hidezumi Shirakata	70	71	69	210	3,140.16
Stephen Leaney	71	69	70	210	3,140.16
Gary Webb	70	70	70	210	3,140.16
Don Fardon	69	71	70	210	3,140.16
Pedro Martinez	70	68	72	210	3,140.16
*Hong Chia-Yuh	71	71	68	210	
Christian Chernock	72	70	69	211	2,585.63
Yeh Chang-Ting	72	69	70	211	2,585.63
Dominique Boulet	70	70	71	211	2,585.63
Jorge Berendt	67	72	72	211	2,585.63
Poh Eing-Cheong	71	66	74	211	2,585.63
Nico Van Rensburg	70	66	75	211	2,585.63

UBX Philippine Open

Manila Southwoods Golf & Country Club, Legends Course,
Carmona, Cavite, Philippines
Par 36-36–72; 7,132 yards

March 28-31
purse, US$300,000

	SCORES				TOTAL	MONEY
Rob Whitlock	67	72	69	70	278	US$49,980
Tim Straub	69	69	67	73	278	33,330
(Whitlock defeated Straub on third extra hole.)						
Brian Wilson	73	63	74	69	279	18,780
Frankie Minoza	70	69	71	70	280	15,000
Chris Gray	72	67	69	73	281	12,720
David Sutherland	70	72	70	70	282	10,500
Pedro Martinez	76	70	68	69	283	7,305
Matt Gogel	71	72	70	70	283	7,305
Rick Todd	74	70	68	71	283	7,305
Philip Jonas	70	68	72	73	283	7,305
Manny Zerman	74	74	69	67	284	5,580
Ken Druce	70	75	73	67	285	5,220
Andre Cruse	71	72	71	72	286	4,470
Martyn Roberts	72	73	68	73	286	4,470
John Kernohan	70	71	72	73	286	4,470
Arden Knoll	73	71	68	74	286	4,470
Hidezumi Shirakata	68	67	75	76	286	4,470
Kevin Leach	75	72	72	68	287	3,624
Larry Barber	71	73	72	71	287	3,624
Jorge Berendt	69	72	75	71	287	3,624
Joey Sadowski	70	72	73	72	287	3,624
Greg Lesher	70	69	76	72	287	3,624
Glenn Joyner	77	67	74	70	288	3,330
Edward Fryatt	71	69	78	71	289	3,180
Christian Pena	71	70	75	73	289	3,180
Oliver Eckstein	71	73	71	74	289	3,180
*Rey Pagunsan	72	74	74	70	290	
David Bartman	73	74	72	72	291	2,910
Alan Bratton	76	70	73	72	291	2,910
Clay Devers	74	75	66	76	291	2,910

Maekyung LG Fashion Open

Nam Seoul Golf & Country Club, Seoul, Korea
Par 36-36–72; 6,902 yards

April 11-14
purse, US$400,000

	SCORES				TOTAL	MONEY
Nam-Sin Park	75	75	67	68	285	US$66,640
Sung-Ho Kim	77	70	73	70	290	34,740
Rob Moss	77	73	67	73	290	34,740
Rick Todd	70	75	77	69	291	20,000
Chul-Sang Cho	72	75	70	75	292	16,960
John Kernohan	75	73	74	71	293	14,000
Kyung-Joo Choi	76	68	74	77	295	12,000
Kevin Wentworth	76	73	73	74	296	8,600
Eric Meeks	73	74	74	75	296	8,600
Mike Cunning	74	72	74	76	296	8,600
Edward Fryatt	75	72	72	77	296	8,600
Steven Conran	74	76	74	73	297	6,126.67
Jong-Duck Kim	72	80	71	74	297	6,126.67
Motomasa Aoki	76	77	69	75	297	6,126.67

		SCORES			TOTAL	MONEY
Suk-Jong Kim	73	78	71	75	297	6,126.67
Arden Knoll	72	73	76	76	297	6,126.67
Clay Devers	70	74	77	76	297	6,126.67
David Sutherland	77	74	78	69	298	4,708.57
Philip Jonas	73	77	77	71	298	4,708.57
Sung-Ha Hwang	77	77	71	73	298	4,708.57
Jin-Han Lim	78	75	72	73	298	4,708.57
Dennis Paulson	70	79	76	73	298	4,708.57
Yong-Jin Shin	73	74	78	73	298	4,708.57
Ted Gleason	78	72	74	74	298	4,708.57
*Ik-Je Chang	78	74	74	72	298	
*Jong-Myung Kim	75	73	78	72	298	
Jorge Berendt	78	71	75	75	299	4,180
Sang-Ho Choi	76	71	76	76	299	4,180
Anthony Painter	75	78	75	72	300	3,768
Hyeung-Soo Kwak	73	79	75	73	300	3,768
Hong-Sik Kim	75	79	72	74	300	3,768
Ron Wuensche	76	73	75	76	300	3,768
Pedro Martinez	81	67	75	77	300	3,768

Elord Cup–Korea Open

Han Young Country Club, Seoul, Korea
Par 36-36–72; 6,916 yards

September 12-15
purse, US$400,000

		SCORES			TOTAL	MONEY
Kyung-Joo Choi	69	73	69	68	279	US$70,000
Jong-Duck Kim	72	72	68	68	280	45,000
Jeev Milkha Singh	72	74	71	67	284	26,000
Gerry Norquist	71	69	72	73	285	22,000
Go Higaki	72	75	70	69	286	15,000
Mike Cunning	73	69	74	70	286	15,000
John Senden	70	74	68	74	286	15,000
Craig Jones	73	72	73	69	287	9,980
Sang-Ho Choi	68	74	74	71	287	9,980
Kevin Wentworth	74	73	70	71	288	7,162
Chris Williams	73	71	73	71	288	7,162
Young-Suk Kwon	68	77	71	72	288	7,162
Anthony Painter	73	70	69	76	288	7,162
Choong-Hwan Moon	71	71	74	73	289	5,903
Mitsu Nitta	71	73	70	75	289	5,903
Wook-Soon Kang	71	73	70	75	289	5,903
Richard Lee	75	71	75	69	290	5,146
Young-Il Kim	73	70	75	72	290	5,146
Shigemasa Higaki	75	70	70	75	290	5,146
*Tae-Keun Oh	75	71	67	77	290	
Do-Man Jung	75	71	73	72	291	4,457
Young-Wu Nam	72	74	73	72	291	4,457
Michael Smith	74	72	72	73	291	4,457
Jin-Han Lim	73	70	75	73	291	4,457
Yoon-Soo Choi	72	70	75	74	291	4,457
Chul-Sang Cho	69	72	76	74	291	4,457
Bu-Young Lee	68	76	73	74	291	4,457
Yong-Jin Shin	75	70	75	72	292	3,820
*Jun-Won Lee	68	75	76	73	292	
David Smail	71	73	75	73	292	3,820
Young-Tae Chae	73	74	72	73	292	3,820
No-Seok Park	72	71	73	76	292	3,820

Shinhan Donghae Open

Jaeil Country Club, Seoul, Korea
Par 36-36–72; 6,947 yards

September 19-22
purse, US$400,000

		SCO	RES		TOTAL	MONEY
Chung Joon	70	71	70	66	277	US$83,932
Jong-Duck Kim	66	70	69	73	278	47,961
Wook-Soon Kang	69	72	69	69	279	26,678
Sung-Ho Kim	66	72	70	71	279	26,678
Kwang-Soo Choi	68	70	70	72	280	17,985
*Jon-Hyun Su	69	73	72	68	282	
No-Seok Park	73	70	70	69	282	12,290
Joo-Hwan Ahn	69	72	68	73	282	12,290
Mike Tschetter	69	69	71	73	282	12,290
Hwa-Kyung Oh	66	73	69	74	282	12,290
*Hyung-Tae Kim	69	75	69	70	283	
Sang-Ho Choi	67	75	70	72	284	6,894
Richard Lee	69	72	70	73	284	6,894
Kyung-Joo Choi	67	72	72	73	284	6,894
Young-Suk Kwon	66	72	72	74	284	6,894
Yong-Jin Shin	68	67	73	76	284	6,894
Kevin Wentworth	72	69	67	76	284	6,894
Hyeung-Soo Kwak	72	69	72	72	285	4,676
Brad Andrews	71	70	71	73	285	4,676
Do-Man Jung	70	73	73	70	286	3,836
Jin-Han Lim	69	73	74	70	286	3,836
David Smail	73	71	72	70	286	3,836
Greg Lesher	68	74	73	71	286	3,836
Stuart Holmes	70	71	73	72	286	3,836
Jin-Kyu Choi	72	69	70	75	286	3,836
Rafael Ponce	71	72	75	69	287	2,877
Chul-Sang Cho	72	72	74	69	287	2,877
Wan-Tae Kim	73	72	72	70	287	2,877
Kang-Sun Lee	73	70	73	71	287	2,877
Craig Jones	70	72	74	71	287	2,877
Hong-Sik Kim	70	73	72	72	287	2,877
Choong-Hwan Moon	71	72	71	73	287	2,877
Jeff Cook	71	70	72	74	287	2,877
Motomasa Aoki	70	72	70	75	287	2,877

Chinfon Chinese Taipei Open

Tong Hwa Golf Club, Taipei, Taiwan
Par 36-36–72; 7,165 yards

October 17-20
purse, US$275,000

		SCO	RES		TOTAL	MONEY
*Hong Chia-Yuh	70	68	71	69	278	
Yu Chin-Han	76	70	71	73	290	US$38,046.25
Stuart Holmes	73	71	70	76	290	38,046.25
Chang Chin-Kuo	72	75	71	73	291	11,880
Wang Ter-Chang	75	71	71	74	291	11,880
Lin Chih-Chen	74	68	75	74	291	11,880
Andre Cruse	72	71	73	75	291	11,880
Hidezumi Shirakata	69	69	77	76	291	11,880
Eric Meeks	75	71	72	74	292	5,830
Felix Casas	70	72	73	77	292	5,830
*Su Chin-Jung	68	77	73	74	292	

	SCORES				TOTAL	MONEY
Hsieh Yu-Shu	73	73	71	76	293	5,005
Greg Bruckner	75	73	74	72	294	4,496.25
Chan Chin-Tang	75	72	75	72	294	4,496.25
Tseng Chin-Fa	72	75	75	72	294	4,496.25
Lai Ying-Juh	73	76	70	75	294	4,496.25
Chung Chun-Hsing	76	73	73	73	295	4,015
Yeh Chang-Ting	75	74	72	74	295	4,015
Jim Rutledge	71	74	74	76	295	4,015
Huang Huan-Jen	72	74	71	78	295	4,015
Hsu Tien-Lai	79	74	70	73	296	3,630
Chen Yun-Mao	75	73	74	74	296	3,630
Lu Wen-Teh	73	75	73	75	296	3,630
Tsai Chi-Huang	76	73	72	76	297	3,355
Anthony Painter	74	74	71	78	297	3,355
Huang Shih-Ho	76	75	71	76	298	3,025
Lu Wen-Der	73	76	73	76	298	3,025
Chen Yuen-Chi	75	73	74	76	298	3,025
Ray Cragun	71	75	74	78	298	3,025
Scott Gardner	69	75	80	75	299	2,640
Hsu Chie-San	74	75	74	76	299	2,640
Tsao Chien-Teng	75	72	74	78	299	2,640

Johnnie Walker Super Tour

Ta Shee Golf & Country Club, Taipei
Par 36-36–72; 6,866 yards

November 5-10
purse, US$350,000

Seoul Country Club, Seoul, Korea
Par 36-36–72; 6,374 yards

Orchard Golf & Country Club, Manila, Philippines
Par 36-36–72; 7,013 yards

Thana City Golf & Country Club, Bangkok, Thailand
Par 36-36–72; 6,905 yards

	SCORES				TOTAL	MONEY
Ernie Els	67	71	71	65	274	US$100,000
Ian Woosnam	68	70	73	63	274	65,000
(Els defeated Woosnam on first extra hole.)						
Colin Montgomerie	68	72	71	69	280	55,000
Nam-Sin Park	67	72	75	68	282	45,000
Lin Keng-Chi	67	73	72	73	285	35,000
Vijay Singh	72	71	78	68	289	25,000
Felix Casas	71	76	78	73	298	15,000
Chawalit Plaphol	75	71	77	76	299	10,000

Andersen Consulting Hong Kong Open

Hong Kong Golf Club, Composite Course,
Fanling, Hong Kong
Par 35-35–70

December 5-8
purse, US$350,000

	SCORES				TOTAL	MONEY
Rodrigo Cuello	68	70	67	70	275	US$58,345
Bill Longmuir	72	70	70	67	279	30,100

	SCORES				TOTAL	MONEY
Scott Hoch	70	72	70	67	279	30,100
Dominique Boulet	74	73	68	65	280	14,700
Brandel Chamblee	69	70	72	69	280	14,700
Don Walsworth	66	73	69	72	280	14,700
Gerry Norquist	74	67	70	70	281	9,800
Andrew Raitt	71	76	70	65	282	6,807.50
Mike Cunning	71	73	70	68	282	6,807.50
Brian Wilson	74	71	67	70	282	6,807.50
Gary Evans	72	72	68	70	282	6,807.50
Bob May	76	70	72	66	284	5,547.50
Carlos Espinosa	70	73	71	70	284	5,547.50
Oliver Eckstein	71	69	73	71	284	5,547.50
Danny Briggs	70	71	71	72	284	5,547.50
*Hong Chia-Yuh	71	74	68	71	284	
John Kernohan	69	74	72	70	285	4,970
Craig Jones	69	73	73	70	285	4,970
Fran Quinn	67	73	75	70	285	4,970
Raymond Russell	70	72	71	72	285	4,970
Charlie Wi	72	73	73	68	286	4,200
Joost Steenkamer	71	71	76	68	286	4,200
Takao Nogami	74	73	70	69	286	4,200
Felix Casas	73	71	70	72	286	4,200
Jim Rutledge	71	72	71	72	286	4,200
Warren Schutte	71	70	73	72	286	4,200
Tim Straub	72	69	70	75	286	4,200
Shaun Haberstroh	74	72	70	71	287	3,360
Clay Devers	70	75	70	72	287	3,360
Olle Nordberg	70	70	75	72	287	3,360
Colin Stoops	71	73	70	73	287	3,360
Ted Purdy	67	75	72	73	287	3,360

China Tour

Volvo Open

Shenzhen Golf Club, Shenzhen
Par 36-36—72; 7,250 yards

May 14-15
purse, US$75,000

	SCORES		TOTAL	MONEY
Glenn Joyner	70	68	138	US$13,500
John Wither	71	68	139	8,625
Aaron Meeks	71	69	140	3,806.25
Jeev Milkha Singh	70	70	140	3,806.25
Krishna Singh	69	71	140	3,806.25
Gustavo Rojas	69	71	140	3,806.25
Jerry Smith	70	71	141	2,212.50
Lu Wen-Der	70	71	141	2,212.50
Zhang Lian-Wei	69	72	141	2,212.50

	SCORES		TOTAL	MONEY
Cheng Jun	67	74	141	2,212.50
Oswald Drawdy	72	70	142	1,440
Amritinder Singh	71	71	142	1,440
Raul Fretes	70	72	142	1,440
Maan Nasim	70	72	142	1,440
Kao Yu-Huang	70	72	142	1,440
David Smail	72	71	143	956.25
Craig Kamps	72	71	143	956.25
Robert Huxtable	73	70	143	956.25
Dominique Boulet	74	69	143	956.25
Vivek Bhandari	72	71	143	956.25
Lai Ying-Juh	71	72	143	956.25
Rodney Pampling	71	72	143	956.25
Jose Cantero	70	73	143	956.25
Lu Wen-Teh	69	74	143	956.25
Richard Kan	68	75	143	956.25
Liu Guo-Jie	73	71	144	637.50
Tod Power	73	71	144	637.50
Derek Fung	73	71	144	637.50
Stephen Lindskog	74	70	144	637.50
Chen Tsang-Te	72	72	144	637.50
Yuan Ching-Chi	71	73	144	637.50
Adrian Percey	68	76	144	637.50

Coca-Cola Open

Mission Hills Golf Club, Shenzhen
Par 36-36–72; 6,970 yards

May 17-18
purse, US$75,000

	SCORES		TOTAL	MONEY
John Wither	65	69	134	US$13,500
Gregory Hanrahan	66	71	137	8,625
Christian Chernock	68	70	138	5,250
Gustavo Rojas	69	70	139	3,325
Jeev Milkha Singh	68	71	139	3,325
Vivek Bhandari	67	72	139	3,325
Lai Ying-Juh	71	69	140	2,212.50
Jose Cantero	71	69	140	2,212.50
Chang Tse-Peng	71	69	140	2,212.50
Jeff Senior	68	72	140	2,212.50
Dominique Boulet	73	68	141	1,165.38
Adrian Percey	71	70	141	1,165.38
Grant Dodd	71	70	141	1,165.38
Raul Fretes	71	70	141	1,165.38
David Smail	72	69	141	1,165.38
Aaron Meeks	72	69	141	1,165.38
Zhang Lian-Wei	72	69	141	1,165.38
Bill Fung	70	71	141	1,165.38
Robert Huxtable	70	71	141	1,165.38
Chan Chin-Tang	70	71	141	1,165.38
Chou Hung-Nan	70	71	141	1,165.38
Chen Tsang-Te	70	71	141	1,165.38
Lin Tien-Shun	69	72	141	1,165.38
Rodney Pampling	71	71	142	750
Tang Man-Kee	71	71	142	750
Cheng Jun	72	70	142	750
Lee Joon-Seok	70	72	142	750

	SCORES		TOTAL	MONEY
Chang Chin-Kuo	69	73	142	750
Stephen Lindskog	71	72	143	525
Craig Kamps	71	72	143	525
Yeh Chang-Ming	72	71	143	525
Stephen Collins	70	73	143	525
Amit Chopra	70	73	143	525
Patrick Moore	69	74	143	525
John Grieves	67	76	143	525

Blue Ribbon Open

Zhaoquing Resort & Golf Club, Zhaoquing　　　　　　　　　　　May 21-22
Par 36-37–73; 6,638 yards　　　　　　　　　　　　　　　　purse, US$75,000

	SCORES		TOTAL	MONEY
Zhang Lian-Wei	67	73	140	US$13,500
Chou Hung-Nan	72	71	143	4,103.57
Tsai Chi-Huang	71	72	143	4,103.57
Patrick Moore	71	72	143	4,103.57
Yu Chin-Han	70	73	143	4,103.57
Stephen Lindskog	70	73	143	4,103.57
Chen Tsang-Te	70	73	143	4,103.57
Jeff Senior	69	74	143	4,103.57
Lin Fu-Chin	72	72	144	1,987.50
Glenn Joyner	70	74	144	1,987.50
Marimuthu Ramayah	74	71	145	1,500
Gregory Hanrahan	71	74	145	1,500
Robert Huxtable	71	74	145	1,500
Chang Hsui-Fa	70	75	145	1,500
Lu Chien-Soon	75	71	146	1,055.36
Tang Man-Kee	74	72	146	1,055.36
Richard Kan	74	72	146	1,055.36
Li Wen-Sheng	74	72	146	1,055.36
Yuan Ching-Chi	73	73	146	1,055.36
Rafael Ponce	73	73	146	1,055.36
Jeev Milkha Singh	72	74	146	1,055.36
Lai Ying-Juh	74	73	147	806.25
Chang Tse-Peng	74	73	147	806.25
John Grieves	74	73	147	806.25
Lee Joon-Seok	74	73	147	806.25
David Smail	73	74	147	806.25
Mohd. Ali Kadir	72	75	147	806.25
Raul Fretes	76	72	148	675
Tod Power	78	71	149	462.27
Wu Xiang-Bing	74	75	149	462.27
Simon Yates	74	75	149	462.27
Gustavo Rojas	75	74	149	462.27
Jerry Smith	76	73	149	462.27
Oswald Drawdy	76	73	149	462.27
Huang Chao-Hsiang	76	73	149	462.27
Guarav Ghei	74	75	149	462.27
Zheng Wen-Gen	73	76	149	462.27
Christian Chernock	71	78	149	462.27
Krishna Singh	71	78	149	462.27

Hugo Boss Open

Guangzhou Luhu Golf Club, Guangzhou
Par 36-36–72; 6,821 yards

May 24-26
purse, US$75,000

	SCORES		TOTAL	MONEY
Mohd. Ali Kadir	66	70	136	US$13,500
Li Wen-Sheng	71	68	139	8,625
Glenn Joyner	69	71	140	5,250
Guarav Ghei	71	70	141	4,125
Paul Friedlander	72	70	142	3,075
Zhang Lian-Wei	70	73	143	2,437.50
Jerry Smith	70	73	143	2,437.50
Jeff Senior	69	74	143	2,437.50
Chou Hung-Nan	68	75	143	2,437.50
Huang Chao-Hsiang	72	72	144	1,650
Lai Ying-Juh	72	72	144	1,650
Rodney Pampling	70	74	144	1,650
Lu Chien-Soon	70	74	144	1,650
Jose Cantero	71	74	145	1,275
Dominique Boulet	74	72	146	1,162.50
Chen Tsang-Te	71	75	146	1,162.50
Richard Kan	76	71	147	937.50
Marimuthu Ramayah	75	72	147	937.50
Gregory Hanrahan	72	75	147	937.50
Adrian Percey	72	75	147	937.50
Toshihiro Tajima	73	74	147	937.50
Craig Kamps	74	73	147	937.50
Maan Nasim	71	76	147	937.50
Yu Chin-Han	70	77	147	937.50
Jeev Milkha Singh	68	79	147	937.50
Lu Wen-Der	72	76	148	562.50
Raul Fretes	72	76	148	562.50
Tsai Chi-Huang	72	76	148	562.50
Yuan Ching-Chi	73	75	148	562.50
Chang Chin-Kuo	74	74	148	562.50
Lee Joon-Seok	74	74	148	562.50
Tang Man-Kee	72	76	148	562.50
Robert Huxtable	71	77	148	562.50
Lin Fu-Chin	70	78	148	562.50
Gustavo Rojas	70	78	148	562.50
Rafael Ponce	69	79	148	562.50

Japan Tour

Token Corporation Cup

Kedoin Golf Club, Kagoshima
Par 36-36–72; 7,097 yards

March 7-10
purse, ¥100,000,000

	SCORES				TOTAL	MONEY
Yoshinori Kaneko	69	74	67	65	275	¥18,000,000
Brandt Jobe	69	70	67	70	276	10,000,000
Zaw Moe	72	68	68	70	278	6,800,000
Yoshihiko Terakawa	71	68	71	69	279	4,800,000
Mitsutaka Kusakabe	71	72	68	69	280	4,000,000
Carlos Franco	72	72	71	66	281	3,233,000
Toshimitsu Izawa	72	71	68	70	281	3,233,000
Gohei Sato	69	73	68	71	281	3,233,000
Eiji Mizoguchi	69	69	74	70	282	2,450,000
Shoichi Kuwabara	71	71	69	71	282	2,450,000
Hideki Kase	69	73	71	70	283	1,704,000
Kiyoshi Maita	69	73	70	71	283	1,704,000
Katsunori Kuwahara	70	73	69	71	283	1,704,000
Katsuyoshi Tomori	68	72	71	72	283	1,704,000
Peter Senior	72	65	74	72	283	1,704,000
Tomohiro Maruyama	69	71	74	70	284	1,213,000
Shintaro Iizuka	72	70	72	70	284	1,213,000
Hajime Meshiai	70	75	68	71	284	1,213,000
Yoshikazu Sakamoto	74	69	73	69	285	928,000
Harumitsu Hamano	70	75	69	71	285	928,000
Hirofumi Miyase	75	69	70	71	285	928,000
Kaname Yokoo	72	72	68	73	285	928,000
Masashi Ozaki	69	73	68	75	285	928,000
Toshiaki Odate	69	73	68	75	285	928,000
David Ishii	70	67	72	76	285	928,000
Koki Idoki	73	71	74	68	286	790,000
Chen Tze-Ming	70	73	75	68	286	790,000
Toru Taniguchi	69	72	74	71	286	790,000
Shoichi Yamamoto	71	72	68	75	286	790,000
Frankie Minoza	70	75	71	71	287	694,000
Isao Isozaki	72	70	73	72	287	694,000
Saburo Fujiki	72	72	68	75	287	694,000
Keiichiro Fukabori	72	69	71	75	287	694,000
Kenichi Kuboya	74	71	67	75	287	694,000
Katsumasa Miyamoto	72	70	69	76	287	694,000

Daido Drinko Shizuoka Open

Shizuoka Golf Club, Hamaoka Course, Shizuoka
Par 36-36–72; 6,902 yards
(Fourth round cancelled — rain.)

March 14-17
purse, ¥75,000,000

	SCORES			TOTAL	MONEY
Yoshikazu Sakamoto	71	72	68	211	¥13,500,000
Nobuo Serizawa	71	69	71	211	6,300,000
Carlos Franco	68	72	71	211	6,300,000

(Sakamoto defeated Serizawa and Franco on first extra hole.)

	SCORES			TOTAL	MONEY
Eduardo Herrera	70	69	73	212	3,600,000
David Ishii	74	70	69	213	3,000,000
Hideki Kase	68	72	74	214	2,700,000
Yoshinori Kaneko	73	75	67	215	2,175,000
Takaaki Fukuzawa	70	74	71	215	2,175,000
Todd Hamilton	74	75	66	215	2,175,000
Kazuo Kanayama	77	69	70	216	1,535,000
Hirofumi Miyase	75	71	70	216	1,535,000
Peter Senior	73	72	71	216	1,535,000
Hideyuki Sato	73	71	73	217	943,333
Eiichi Itai	73	76	68	217	943,333
Kiyoshi Murota	72	75	70	217	943,333
Tsukasa Watanabe	74	72	71	217	943,333
Toru Nakamura	76	73	68	217	943,333
Koki Idoki	71	74	72	217	943,333
Shoichi Kuwabara	74	72	71	217	943,333
Kazuhiko Hosokawa	75	74	68	217	943,333
Brian Watts	73	73	71	217	943,333
Shinji Ikeuchi	75	73	70	218	624,375
Saburo Fujiki	76	72	70	218	624,375
Nobumitsu Yuhara	74	74	70	218	624,375
Stewart Ginn	72	73	73	218	624,375
Katsunori Kuwabara	77	71	70	218	624,375
Ken Tanigawa	74	70	74	218	624,375
Richard Backwell	76	72	70	218	624,375
Chen Tze-Chung	70	75	73	218	624,375
Kazuhiro Takami	75	75	69	219	520,500
Seiki Okuda	72	75	72	219	520,500
Isamu Sugita	74	76	69	219	520,500
Anthony Gilligan	74	71	74	219	520,500
Ryoken Kawagishi	75	75	69	219	520,500
Kaname Yokoo	73	74	72	219	520,500

Novell KSB Open

Kinojo Country Club, Soja, Okoyama
Par 36-36–72; 6,948 yards

March 21-24
purse, ¥70,000,000

	SCORES				TOTAL	MONEY
Toru Suzuki	68	72	68	67	275	¥12,600,000
Eduardo Herrera	67	70	69	70	276	5,880,000
Brian Watts	69	68	72	67	276	5,880,000
Yoshinori Kaneko	69	73	68	69	279	3,360,000
Shinichi Yokota	67	71	69	73	280	2,660,000
Frankie Minoza	70	75	66	69	280	2,660,000
Haruo Yasuda	71	74	71	65	281	2,240,000
Masanobu Kimura	66	71	74	71	282	1,820,000
Tsutomu Higa	70	70	72	70	282	1,820,000
Brandt Jobe	71	70	71	70	282	1,820,000
Nobuo Serizawa	69	73	73	68	283	1,239,000
Haruhito Yamamoto	68	73	70	72	283	1,239,000
Keiichiro Fukabori	68	73	73	69	283	1,239,000
Peter McWhinney	66	73	73	71	283	1,239,000
Keisuke Goi	73	71	70	70	284	924,000
Shintaro Iizuka	66	71	75	72	284	924,000
Lin Keng-Chi	71	71	73	69	284	924,000
Kiyoshi Maita	71	70	70	74	285	705,600

	SCORES			TOTAL	MONEY
Stewart Ginn	65	72	77	71	285	705,600
Toru Taniguchi	72	71	69	73	285	705,600
Shinichi Akiba	68	73	70	74	285	705,600
Chen Tze-Chung	73	71	73	68	285	705,600
Seiki Okuda	67	74	73	72	286	595,000
Yoshikazu Sakamoto	73	71	70	72	286	595,000
Katsuyoshi Tomori	72	73	72	69	286	595,000
Shoichi Miyazato	68	73	77	68	286	595,000
Shoichi Kuwabara	69	73	74	71	287	560,000
Tatsuo Takasaki	69	72	73	74	288	532,000
Osamu Yamaguchi	75	69	71	73	288	532,000
Hidemichi Tanaka	70	70	77	71	288	532,000

Descente Classic

Edosaki Country Club, Ibaragi
Par 36-35–71; 6,831 yards

April 4-7
purse, ¥100,000,000

	SCORES			TOTAL	MONEY
Masanobu Kimura	69	66	69	69	273	¥16,200,000
Hideyuki Sato	67	66	71	71	275	9,000,000
Katsuyoshi Tomori	68	69	71	68	276	6,120,000
Peter McWhinney	67	72	71	67	277	3,720,000
Roger Mackay	66	69	72	70	277	3,720,000
Keiichiro Fukabori	69	65	72	71	277	3,720,000
Hirofumi Miyase	68	70	71	69	278	2,745,000
Chen Tze-Chung	65	74	69	70	278	2,745,000
Yoshinori Mizumaki	74	67	71	67	279	2,340,000
Shinji Ikeuchi	70	70	71	69	280	1,759,000
Akio Nishizawa	66	69	75	70	280	1,759,000
Hisayuki Sasaki	70	70	70	70	280	1,759,000
Kaname Yokoo	68	70	70	72	280	1,759,000
Ken Kusumoto	72	72	68	69	281	1,242,000
Seiichi Koizumi	69	69	74	69	281	1,242,000
David Ishii	71	71	69	70	281	1,242,000
Yoshimi Niizeki	69	73	68	71	281	1,242,000
Kiyoshi Maita	68	74	72	68	282	907,000
Tsuyoshi Yoneyama	70	68	75	69	282	907,000
Yasunobu Kuramoto	70	69	73	70	282	907,000
Ikuo Shirahama	71	66	73	72	282	907,000
Stewart Ginn	69	68	71	74	282	907,000
Yoshinori Kaneko	69	75	71	68	283	738,000
Yoshikazu Sakamoto	68	76	71	68	283	738,000
Kazuhiro Fukunaga	72	72	71	68	283	738,000
Toshiaki Odate	73	68	73	69	283	738,000
Hajime Meshiai	70	74	68	71	283	738,000
Katsunari Takahashi	66	74	71	72	283	738,000
Katsunori Kuwabara	68	69	72	74	283	738,000
Isamu Sugita	70	72	70	72	284	648,000
Rick Gibson	70	69	72	73	284	648,000
Toru Nakamura	71	67	72	74	284	648,000

Tsuruya Open

Sports Shinko Country Club, Yamanohara Course, Hyogo
Par 36-36—72; 6,942 yards

April 11-14
purse, ¥100,000,000

	SCORES				TOTAL	MONEY
Peter McWhinney	70	72	68	66	276	¥18,000,000
Peter Senior	67	71	72	67	277	10,000,000
Katsunari Takahashi	69	69	70	72	280	6,800,000
Yoshinori Kaneko	71	70	70	70	281	4,800,000
Ryoken Kawagishi	71	75	67	69	282	3,800,000
Stewart Ginn	71	70	70	71	282	3,800,000
Tsukasa Watanabe	72	74	71	66	283	3,200,000
Shinichi Yokota	79	69	69	67	284	2,450,000
Tsuyoshi Yoneyama	69	72	73	70	284	2,450,000
Kazuhiro Takami	71	69	74	70	284	2,450,000
Masahiro Kuramoto	74	70	69	71	284	2,450,000
Zaw Moe	73	73	72	67	285	1,693,000
Tsuneyuki Nakajima	73	71	73	68	285	1,693,000
Shigeki Maruyama	74	71	69	71	285	1,693,000
Kazuhiko Hosokawa	72	72	74	68	286	1,320,000
Tsutomu Higa	72	74	68	72	286	1,320,000
Kiyoshi Murota	72	73	69	72	286	1,320,000
David Ishii	72	74	71	70	287	1,120,000
Hsieh Chin-Sheng	75	73	70	70	288	980,000
Roger Mackay	76	73	68	71	288	980,000
Hideki Kase	73	71	72	72	288	980,000
Nobuo Serizawa	73	72	68	75	288	980,000
Hidemichi Tanaka	74	72	73	70	289	850,000
Katsuyoshi Tomori	74	72	71	72	289	850,000
Saburo Fujiki	77	70	70	72	289	850,000
Kazuhiro Fukunaga	74	68	74	73	289	850,000
Rick Gibson	73	75	73	69	290	750,000
Naoya Sugiyama	72	72	77	69	290	750,000
Koichi Suzuki	74	74	72	70	290	750,000
Koichi Takabe	73	73	72	72	290	750,000
Hideyuki Sato	76	71	69	74	290	750,000
Yoshinori Mizumaki	73	71	70	76	290	750,000

Kirin Open

Ibaragi Golf Club, Higashi Course, Ibaragi
Par 36-36—72; 7,122 yards

April 18-21
purse, ¥100,000,000

	SCORES				TOTAL	MONEY
Yoshinori Kaneko	68	71	69	70	278	¥18,000,000
Nobuo Serizawa	70	67	70	72	279	8,400,000
Tsuneyuki Nakajima	71	70	67	71	279	8,400,000
Tsukasa Watanabe	71	68	70	71	280	3,700,000
Yoshitaka Yamamoto	71	67	73	69	280	3,700,000
Hirofumi Miyase	70	69	72	69	280	3,700,000
Shigeki Maruyama	68	68	69	75	280	3,700,000
Kevin Wentworth	71	71	71	67	280	3,700,000
Seiki Okuda	68	72	75	66	281	2,450,000
David Ishii	72	68	74	67	281	2,450,000
Shigenori Mori	68	74	73	67	282	1,920,000
Peter Senior	68	70	72	72	282	1,920,000
Yoshinori Mizumaki	71	69	73	70	283	1,500,000

	SCORES				TOTAL	MONEY
Tetsu Nishikawa	76	64	71	72	283	1,500,000
Chen Tze-Chung	71	72	70	70	283	1,500,000
Jeev Milkha Singh	71	71	72	69	283	1,500,000
Kiyoshi Murota	66	70	74	74	284	1,017,142
Katsuyoshi Tomori	72	68	75	69	284	1,017,142
Shinichi Yakota	74	66	70	74	284	1,017,142
Jong-Duck Kim	72	71	73	68	284	1,017,142
Carlos Franco	69	72	72	71	284	1,017,142
Rob Moss	72	70	72	70	284	1,017,142
David Sutherland	68	71	75	70	284	1,017,142
Ikuo Shirahama	68	72	73	72	285	800,000
Takaaki Fukuzawa	72	68	74	71	285	800,000
Hajime Meshiai	72	71	74	68	285	800,000
Masahiro Kuramoto	73	68	73	71	285	800,000
Tsutomu Higa	65	72	75	73	285	800,000
Stewart Ginn	71	68	75	71	285	800,000
Daniel Chopra	68	68	76	73	285	800,000

Chunichi Crowns

Nagoya Golf Club, Wago Course, Aichi
Par 35-35–70; 6,473 yards

April 25-28
purse, ¥120,000,000

	SCORES				TOTAL	MONEY
Masashi Ozaki	64	68	69	67	268	¥21,600,000
Katsuyoshi Tomori	65	70	70	67	272	12,000,000
Yoshinori Kaneko	70	65	69	71	275	8,160,000
Tsuneyuki Nakajima	69	70	68	69	276	4,680,000
Tsuyoshi Yoneyama	67	68	68	73	276	4,680,000
Peter Senior	68	66	70	72	276	4,680,000
Craig Stadler	71	67	68	70	276	4,680,000
Tsukasa Watanabe	72	68	67	70	277	2,940,000
Seiki Okuda	68	69	70	70	277	2,940,000
Kazuhiko Hosokawa	69	73	69	66	277	2,940,000
Fred Couples	69	68	70	70	277	2,940,000
Katsunari Takahashi	67	69	73	70	279	1,956,000
Tomohiro Maruyama	72	68	69	70	279	1,956,000
Masanobu Kimura	66	69	74	70	279	1,956,000
Hirofumi Miyase	68	66	69	76	279	1,956,000
Hajime Meshiai	69	68	75	68	280	1,456,000
Tsutomu Higa	70	69	73	68	280	1,456,000
Kaname Yokoo	72	69	69	70	280	1,456,000
Kazuhiro Takami	72	70	70	69	281	1,200,000
Gohei Sato	73	70	72	66	281	1,200,000
Toru Suzuki	72	63	73	73	281	1,200,000
Masayuki Kawamura	66	68	75	73	282	1,036,800
Hsieh Chin-Sheng	70	68	70	74	282	1,036,800
Frankie Minoza	70	68	74	70	282	1,036,800
David Ishii	68	68	74	72	282	1,036,800
Todd Hamilton	65	78	70	69	282	1,036,800
Shinji Ikeuchi	68	75	68	72	283	924,000
Takaaki Fukuzawa	71	71	69	72	283	924,000
Nobumitsu Yuhara	71	70	69	73	283	924,000
John Daly	69	71	73	70	283	924,000

Fuji Sankei Classic

Kawana Hotel Golf Club, Fuji Course, Shizuoka
Par 35-36–71; 6,694 yards

May 2-5
purse, ¥120,000,000

	SCORES				TOTAL	MONEY
Brian Watts	66	67	71	68	272	¥21,600,000
Todd Hamilton	69	67	70	66	272	12,000,000
(Watts defeated Hamilton on first extra hole.)						
Tsuneyuki Nakajima	71	69	69	67	276	6,960,000
Shoichi Kuwabara	66	69	74	67	276	6,960,000
Satoshi Higashi	69	68	69	71	277	4,320,000
Masahiro Kuramoto	65	71	72	69	277	4,320,000
Hirofumi Miyase	70	71	70	66	277	4,320,000
Masashi Ozaki	69	69	67	73	278	2,940,000
Toshimitsu Izawa	64	70	73	71	278	2,940,000
Hidemichi Tanaka	69	66	75	68	278	2,940,000
Chen Tze-Chung	71	70	69	68	278	2,940,000
Tsukasa Watanabe	67	69	70	73	279	1,956,000
Koki Idoki	76	68	64	71	279	1,956,000
Shigeki Maruyama	67	72	71	79	279	1,956,000
Ken Tanigawa	69	69	71	70	279	1,956,000
Yoshitaka Yamamoto	67	73	71	69	280	1,404,000
Masayuki Kawamura	70	73	69	68	280	1,404,000
Shintaro Iizuka	68	69	69	74	280	1,404,000
Shinichi Yokota	70	71	71	68	280	1,404,000
Yoshinori Kaneko	70	68	69	74	281	1,092,000
Yoshimi Niizeki	73	68	71	69	281	1,092,000
Tatsuo Takasaki	72	71	69	69	281	1,092,000
Eduardo Herrera	71	70	68	72	281	1,092,000
Koichi Nogami	72	70	70	69	281	1,092,000
Frankie Minoza	71	68	73	69	281	1,092,000
Hideki Kase	67	67	72	76	282	960,000
Kiyoshi Maita	71	73	68	70	282	960,000
Osamu Yamaguchi	67	71	72	72	282	960,000
Ikuo Shirahama	70	71	72	70	283	854,400
Joji Furuki	72	72	70	69	283	854,400
Yoshinori Mizumaki	75	68	69	71	283	854,400
Kiyoshi Murota	69	72	72	70	283	854,400
Toru Taniguchi	72	68	69	74	283	854,400
Chen Tze-Ming	71	70	71	71	283	854,400

Japan PGA Championship

Sanyo Golf Club, Yoshii Course, Okayama
Par 36-36–72; 7,236 yards

May 9-12
purse, ¥100,000,000

	SCORES				TOTAL	MONEY
Masashi Ozaki	68	66	67	69	270	¥18,000,000
Shigeki Maruyama	70	69	65	74	278	9,000,000
Lin Chie-Hsiang	73	72	66	68	279	5,220,000
Hisayuki Sasaki	70	71	70	68	279	5,220,000
Brian Watts	70	71	69	71	281	3,420,000
Yoshinori Kaneko	69	69	71	72	281	3,420,000
Chen Tze-Chung	70	69	71	72	282	2,745,000
Masanobu Kimura	71	67	69	75	282	2,745,000
David Ishii	72	69	71	71	283	2,205,000
Kaname Yokoo	69	67	71	76	283	2,205,000

	SCORES				TOTAL	MONEY
Shintaro Iizuka	71	73	72	68	284	1,728,000
Toshimitsu Izawa	72	66	73	73	284	1,728,000
Taichi Teshima	74	72	69	70	285	1,203,000
Hirofumi Miyase	71	70	73	71	285	1,203,000
Shoichi Kuwabara	70	72	72	71	285	1,203,000
Hidemichi Tanaka	72	66	75	72	285	1,203,000
Tsuneyuki Nakajima	72	70	70	73	285	1,203,000
Nobuo Serizawa	73	68	71	73	285	1,203,000
Todd Hamilton	68	70	73	74	285	1,203,000
Haruo Yasuda	69	77	70	70	286	807,000
Hidezumi Shirakata	69	72	75	70	286	807,000
Mitsuo Harada	73	71	71	71	286	807,000
Shinichi Akiba	70	75	69	72	286	807,000
Hiroyuki Fujita	70	74	69	73	286	807,000
Peter McWhinney	74	70	67	75	286	807,000
Kazuhiko Hosokawa	69	69	73	75	286	807,000
Masayuki Kawamura	76	67	74	70	287	702,000
Katsuyoshi Tomori	71	74	69	73	287	702,000
Tatsuo Takasaki	74	72	68	73	287	702,000
Satoshi Higashi	69	73	76	70	288	657,000
Kazuo Kanayama	70	72	73	73	288	657,000

Pepsi Ube Kosan Tournament

Ube Country Club, Mannenike West Course, Yamaguchi
Par 35-36–71; 6,935 yards

May 16-19
purse, ¥80,000,000

	SCORES				TOTAL	MONEY
Hidemichi Tanaka	68	64	65	67	264	¥14,400,000
Brian Watts	68	65	68	65	266	6,048,000
Tsuneyuki Nakajima	68	69	63	66	266	6,048,000
Kazuhiko Hosokawa	69	66	67	65	267	3,456,000
Stewart Ginn	68	67	68	66	269	2,736,000
Kazuhiro Fukunaga	64	68	71	66	269	2,736,000
Brandt Jobe	71	67	65	67	270	2,304,000
Nobuo Serizawa	68	67	68	69	272	2,088,000
Hiroyuki Fujita	68	71	68	66	273	1,573,000
Koichi Nogami	71	68	67	67	273	1,573,000
Hideto Shigenobu	69	64	69	71	273	1,573,000
Eiji Mizoguchi	71	65	64	73	273	1,573,000
Tsuyoshi Yoneyama	66	69	71	68	274	998,000
Tsukasa Watanabe	68	67	70	69	274	998,000
Tomohiro Maruyama	69	67	69	69	274	998,000
Seiji Ebihara	72	68	65	69	274	998,000
Masanobu Kimura	70	67	66	71	274	998,000
Ikuo Shirahama	66	71	63	74	274	998,000
Tsutomu Higa	68	67	72	68	275	668,000
Yasunobu Kuramoto	69	68	70	68	275	668,000
Kenichi Kuboya	68	68	71	68	275	668,000
Gregory Meyer	70	68	68	69	275	668,000
Koki Idoki	70	66	69	70	275	668,000
Takaaki Fukuzawa	70	66	67	72	275	668,000
Richard Backwell	69	70	64	72	275	668,000
Hideyuki Sato	70	68	69	69	276	547,000
Tatsuo Takasaki	67	70	69	70	276	547,000
Toshiaki Odate	69	68	69	70	276	547,000
Shoichi Yamamoto	69	67	69	71	276	547,000

	SCORES				TOTAL	MONEY
Katsunari Takahashi	70	70	64	72	276	547,000
Kiyoshi Maita	67	70	66	73	276	547,000
Samson Gimson	66	68	68	74	276	547,000

Mitsubishi Galant Tournament

Oarai Golf Club, Kumamoto
Par 36-36—72; 7,190 yards

May 23-26
purse, ¥120,000,000

	SCORES				TOTAL	MONEY
Masashi Ozaki	72	70	73	64	279	¥21,600,000
Todd Hamilton	69	74	66	70	279	10,800,000
(Ozaki defeated Hamilton on first extra hole.)						
Brian Watts	71	70	66	73	280	7,344,000
Gohei Sato	73	69	68	71	281	4,752,000
Chen Tze-Ming	67	71	72	71	281	4,752,000
Shoichi Kuwabara	74	68	74	66	282	3,672,000
Tateo Ozaki	72	67	72	71	282	3,672,000
Shigeru Kawamata	70	70	73	70	283	3,132,000
Ken Tanigawa	71	70	73	70	284	2,359,000
Peter Senior	68	70	75	71	284	2,359,000
Chen Tze-Chung	69	72	72	71	284	2,359,000
Akihito Yokoyama	73	71	69	71	284	2,359,000
Taichi Teshima	72	71	72	70	285	1,749,000
Keiichiro Fukabori	71	72	70	72	285	1,749,000
Yoshinori Kaneko	73	72	71	70	286	1,246,000
Brandt Jobe	71	72	73	70	286	1,246,000
Anthony Gilligan	73	70	73	70	286	1,246,000
Yoshikazu Sakamoto	70	71	74	71	286	1,246,000
Tsutomu Higa	69	72	74	71	286	1,246,000
Shigemasa Higaki	70	75	70	71	286	1,246,000
Takaaki Fukuzawa	68	73	73	72	286	1,246,000
Toru Nakamura	72	73	73	69	287	945,000
Kazuhiko Hosokawa	74	71	72	70	287	945,000
Katsunori Kuwabara	71	73	71	72	287	945,000
Mitsutaka Kusakabe	70	72	68	77	287	945,000
Kiyoshi Maita	74	71	74	69	288	842,000
Kaname Yokoo	71	72	74	71	288	842,000
Lin Chie-Hsiang	73	72	71	72	288	842,000
Tomohiro Maruyama	78	66	71	73	288	842,000
Toru Taniguchi	72	70	71	75	288	842,000

JCB Classic Sendai

Omotezao Kokusai Golf Club, Shibata, Miyagi
Par 36-35—71; 6,646 yards

May 30-June 2
purse, ¥100,000,000

	SCORES				TOTAL	MONEY
Masashi Ozaki	69	69	67	72	277	¥18,000,000
David Ishii	70	69	70	68	277	9,000,000
(Ozaki defeated Ishii on first extra hole.)						
Nobuo Serizawa	68	68	72	70	278	5,220,000
Hidemichi Tanaka	69	72	67	70	278	5,220,000
Seiki Okuda	69	72	72	66	279	2,934,000
Tatsuo Takasaki	68	71	71	69	279	2,934,000

	SCORES				TOTAL	MONEY
Ryoken Kawagishi	69	67	71	72	279	2,934,000
Hideyuki Sato	69	69	67	74	279	2,934,000
Masayuki Okano	67	69	68	75	279	2,934,000
Shinichi Yokota	71	71	71	67	280	1,935,000
Hajime Meshiai	66	71	72	71	280	1,935,000
Katsuyoshi Tomori	72	73	68	68	281	1,656,000
Mitsutaka Kusakabe	71	71	73	67	282	1,404,000
Rick Gibson	71	72	71	68	282	1,404,000
Shigeki Maruyama	70	70	73	69	282	1,404,000
Akihito Yokoyama	74	69	74	66	283	1,053,000
Yoshinori Kaneko	69	74	72	68	283	1,053,000
Isamu Sugita	70	72	71	70	283	1,053,000
Eiichi Itai	71	71	71	70	283	1,053,000
Teruo Sugihara	71	72	73	68	284	831,000
Tomohiro Maruyama	67	72	76	69	284	831,000
Tsukasa Watanabe	72	73	68	71	284	831,000
Hiroshi Ueda	73	72	68	71	284	831,000
Kazuyoshi Yonekura	69	68	75	72	284	831,000
Kaname Yokoo	71	69	73	72	285	729,000
Yoshinori Mizumaki	69	75	68	73	285	729,000
Ken Tanigawa	71	71	70	73	285	729,000
Akiyoshi Ohmachi	72	67	73	73	285	729,000
Katsunori Kuwabara	68	75	73	70	286	648,000
Tsutomu Higa	72	72	71	71	286	648,000
Hiroshi Makino	73	70	72	71	286	648,000
Koichi Nogami	70	71	73	72	286	648,000
Shoichi Yamamoto	69	70	72	75	286	648,000

Sapporo Tokyu Open

Sapporo Kokusai Country Club, Shimamatsu Course, Hokkaido
Par 36-36–72; 6,949 yards

June 6-9
purse, ¥100,000,000

	SCORES				TOTAL	MONEY
Hajime Meshiai	70	64	72	73	279	¥18,000,000
Harumitsu Hamano	70	70	73	67	280	6,480,000
Yoshimitsu Fukuzawa	70	70	72	68	280	6,480,000
Yasunori Ida	68	73	70	69	280	6,480,000
Hisao Inoue	74	68	72	67	281	3,240,000
Masanobu Kimura	69	72	68	72	281	3,240,000
Toru Suzuki	71	69	69	72	281	3,240,000
Yoshinori Kaneko	67	75	74	66	282	2,205,000
Koichi Uehara	71	75	68	68	282	2,205,000
Kiyoshi Maita	70	67	76	69	282	2,205,000
Stewart Ginn	69	72	71	70	282	2,205,000
Katsunori Kuwabara	68	74	72	69	283	1,467,000
Nobuo Serizawa	72	70	71	70	283	1,467,000
Takaaki Fukuzawa	76	66	71	70	283	1,467,000
Satoshi Higashi	71	74	68	70	283	1,467,000
Yoshitaka Yamamoto	70	75	70	69	284	1,134,000
David Ishii	71	74	69	70	284	1,134,000
Katsuyoshi Tomori	73	67	77	68	285	927,000
Saburo Fujiki	69	72	75	70	285	927,000
Koichi Suzuki	67	72	75	71	285	927,000
Yutaka Hagawa	69	71	73	72	285	927,000
Shinichi Yokota	72	72	74	68	286	787,000

	SCORES			TOTAL	MONEY
Isamu Sugita	72	72	71	71	286	787,000
Hideyuki Sato	73	69	72	72	286	787,000
Zaw Moe	72	73	68	73	286	787,000
Hirofumi Miyase	69	73	74	71	287	711,000
Shigenori Mori	71	71	73	72	287	711,000
Rick Gibson	74	68	72	73	287	711,000
Brian Jones	72	71	70	74	287	711,000
Kazuyoshi Yonekura	71	75	75	67	288	639,000
Carlos Franco	72	74	73	69	288	639,000
Toru Nakamura	70	70	78	70	288	639,000
Kiyoshi Murota	71	70	73	74	288	639,000

Pocari Sweat Yomiuri Open

Wakasu Golf Links, Tokyo
Par 36-35–71; 6,827 yards

June 13-16
purse, ¥100,000,000

	SCORES				TOTAL	MONEY
Kazuhiro Fukunaga	68	67	64	67	266	¥18,000,000
Todd Hamilton	63	72	64	67	266	9,000,000
(Fukunaga defeated Hamilton on second extra hole.)						
Peter Senior	70	65	69	63	267	6,120,000
Roger Mackay	64	68	67	69	268	4,320,000
Hirofumi Miyase	68	69	66	66	269	3,600,000
Tomohiro Maruyama	70	69	66	65	270	2,370,000
Masahiro Kuramoto	66	69	69	66	270	2,370,000
Brian Watts	65	69	68	68	270	2,370,000
Kazuhiko Hosokawa	64	72	66	68	270	2,370,000
Hiroshi Makino	66	69	66	69	270	2,370,000
Tsukasa Watanabe	64	69	66	71	270	2,370,000
Hajime Meshiai	64	65	69	72	270	2,370,000
Katsuyoshi Tomori	71	68	68	64	271	1,296,000
Toshimitsu Izawa	70	66	71	64	271	1,296,000
Shigeki Maruyama	67	70	68	66	271	1,296,000
Kenichi Kuboya	64	72	69	66	271	1,296,000
Shinichi Yokota	67	65	70	69	271	1,296,000
Anthony Gilligan	69	70	68	65	272	888,000
Eduardo Herrera	66	69	71	66	272	888,000
Nobumitsu Yuhara	70	69	67	66	272	888,000
Toyotake Nakao	67	68	70	67	272	888,000
Shintaro Iizuka	67	69	68	68	272	888,000
David Ishii	69	70	64	69	272	888,000
Yoshinori Mizumaki	67	70	70	66	273	720,000
Toru Taniguchi	68	70	68	67	273	720,000
Rick Todd	66	71	69	67	273	720,000
Hidemichi Tanaka	68	68	69	68	273	720,000
Tateo Ozaki	67	70	68	68	273	720,000
Katsunori Kuwabara	66	69	69	69	273	720,000
Ryoken Kawagishi	65	68	70	70	273	720,000

Mizuno Open

Tokinodai Country Club, Bijodai Course, Ishikawa
Par 36-36–72; 6,814 yards

June 20-23
purse, ¥100,000,000

	SCORES				TOTAL	MONEY
Yoshinori Kaneko	66	71	65	68	270	¥18,000,000
Shinichi Yokota	69	69	66	70	274	9,000,000
Rick Gibson	75	68	71	63	277	5,220,000
Toru Taniguchi	72	67	69	69	277	5,220,000
Roger Mackay	68	74	71	65	278	2,934,000
Brian Watts	70	72	70	66	278	2,934,000
Tsuyoshi Yoneyama	69	74	68	67	278	2,934,000
Katsunori Kuwabara	70	70	70	68	278	2,934,000
Koichi Suzuki	72	69	69	68	278	2,934,000
Kazuhiro Takami	72	70	69	68	279	1,842,000
Shoichi Yamamoto	67	75	68	69	279	1,842,000
Peter McWhinney	66	74	68	71	279	1,842,000
Daisuke Serizawa	68	73	68	71	280	1,296,000
Anthony Gilligan	72	70	66	72	280	1,296,000
Shigemasa Higaki	71	68	69	72	280	1,296,000
Shigenori Mori	71	69	67	73	280	1,296,000
Ryoken Kawagishi	70	68	65	77	280	1,296,000
Tsukasa Watanabe	73	69	71	68	281	927,000
Seiki Okuda	71	70	72	68	281	927,000
Kazuhiko Hosokawa	71	71	70	69	281	927,000
Peter Senior	69	71	69	72	281	927,000
Shoichi Miyazato	70	72	70	70	282	768,000
Tsuneyuki Nakajima	67	72	72	71	282	768,000
Hideyuki Sato	69	71	71	71	282	768,000
Keiichiro Fukabori	72	69	70	71	282	768,000
David Ishii	70	71	68	73	282	768,000
Satoshi Higashi	68	75	66	73	282	768,000
Chen Tze-Chung	66	73	75	69	283	666,000
Carlos Franco	69	74	71	69	283	666,000
Teruo Nakamura	72	70	70	71	283	666,000
Toru Suzuki	69	72	71	72	283	666,000
Todd Hamilton	71	65	72	75	283	666,000

PGA Philanthropy

Oakmont Golf Club, Nara
Par 36-36–72; 7,801 yards

June 27-30
purse, ¥100,000,000

	SCORES				TOTAL	MONEY
Todd Hamilton	69	69	68	69	275	¥12,600,000
Kazuhiro Takami	71	69	68	69	277	6,300,000
Peter Senior	70	73	66	71	280	3,654,000
Tsuyoshi Yoneyama	69	64	71	76	280	3,654,000
Seiji Ebihara	68	72	70	71	281	2,520,000
Katsunori Kuwabara	70	65	73	75	283	2,268,000
Roger Mackay	73	66	76	69	284	1,732,000
Brian Watts	69	70	74	71	284	1,732,000
Ryoken Kawagishi	68	74	71	71	284	1,732,000
Kaname Yokoo	70	67	74	73	284	1,732,000
Hideyuki Sato	70	72	71	72	285	1,073,000
Katsunari Takahashi	73	71	69	72	285	1,073,000
Yoshinori Mizumaki	75	67	71	72	285	1,073,000

	SCORES				TOTAL	MONEY
Rick Gibson	72	70	68	75	285	1,073,000
Shoichi Kuwabara	72	69	68	76	285	1,073,000
Eiji Mizoguchi	73	71	72	70	286	737,000
Takaaki Fukuzawa	70	73	72	71	286	737,000
Kazuhiko Hosokawa	77	68	69	72	286	737,000
Nobuhito Sato	73	70	69	74	286	737,000
Stewart Ginn	72	72	73	70	287	592,000
Koki Idoki	72	71	71	73	287	592,000
Toshiaki Odate	70	71	71	75	287	592,000
Hsieh Chin-Sheng	66	73	71	77	287	592,000
Tsuneyuki Nakajima	69	74	73	72	288	535,000
Taichi Teshima	72	67	76	73	288	535,000
Kenichi Kuboya	72	69	73	75	289	510,000
Hirofumi Miyase	71	68	74	76	289	510,000
Toru Suzuki	72	73	73	72	290	443,000
Koji Kobayashi	71	74	73	72	290	443,000
Gohei Sato	73	70	73	74	290	443,000
Nobumitsu Yuhara	69	73	74	74	290	443,000
Seiki Okuda	70	75	70	75	290	443,000
Takuhito Nishino	72	68	74	76	290	443,000
Hideki Kase	72	72	69	77	290	443,000
Akihito Yokoyama	71	70	71	78	290	443,000
Yutaka Hagawa	72	70	70	78	290	443,000

Yonex Open

Hiroshima Country Club, Happonmatsu Course,
Hiroshima
Par 36-36–72; 6,950 yards

July 4-7
purse, ¥80,000,000

	SCORES				TOTAL	MONEY
Hideyuki Sato	67	71	69	66	273	¥14,400,000
Yoshinori Kaneko	67	72	70	68	277	7,200,000
Shoichi Kuwabara	65	72	75	66	278	4,176,000
Masanobu Kimura	68	66	71	73	278	4,176,000
Katsunori Kuwabara	68	70	70	71	279	2,880,000
Eiji Mizoguchi	70	73	70	67	280	1,810,000
Hideki Kase	67	72	72	69	280	1,810,000
Wayne Levi	68	73	70	69	280	1,810,000
Hirofumi Miyase	67	71	72	70	280	1,810,000
Tsutomu Higa	71	71	68	70	280	1,810,000
Chen Tze-Chung	68	70	71	71	280	1,810,000
Akihito Yokoyama	70	71	68	71	280	1,810,000
Brian Watts	68	72	68	72	280	1,810,000
Kazuhiko Hosokawa	69	71	73	68	281	993,000
Anthony Gilligan	75	69	69	68	281	993,000
Seiki Okuda	67	74	71	69	281	993,000
Keiichiro Fukabori	72	71	69	69	281	993,000
Richard Backwell	74	71	69	68	282	697,000
Takaaki Fukuzawa	72	71	70	69	282	697,000
Shinji Ikeuchi	70	70	73	69	282	697,000
Rick Todd	74	67	72	69	282	697,000
Masayuki Kawamura	72	70	70	70	282	697,000
Kinpachi Yoshimura	71	71	70	70	282	697,000
Seiichi Koizumi	71	71	69	71	282	697,000
Masatoshi Horikawa	69	74	71	69	283	583,000
Toru Taniguchi	67	69	77	70	283	583,000

	SCORES				TOTAL	MONEY
Kiyoshi Murota	68	74	69	72	283	583,000
Kenichi Kuboya	72	65	74	72	283	583,000
Hsieh Chin-Sheng	71	70	74	69	284	525,000
Yoshimi Niizeki	71	74	68	71	284	525,000
Samson Gimson	71	70	70	73	284	525,000
Takuhito Nishino	68	70	72	74	284	525,000

Nikkei Cup

Dejima Golf Club, Fuji Course, Ibaraki
Par 36-36–72; 6,980 yards

July 11-14
purse, ¥100,000,000

	SCORES				TOTAL	MONEY
Hideki Kase	69	71	68	63	271	¥18,000,000
Lin Keng-Chi	65	71	69	68	273	9,000,000
Mitsuhiro Watanabe	70	70	69	66	275	4,680,000
Tsuneyuki Nakajima	68	68	69	70	275	4,680,000
Toshimitsu Izawa	68	68	66	73	275	4,680,000
Yoshinori Ichioka	71	70	68	67	276	3,240,000
Hiroyuki Fujita	70	69	72	66	277	2,610,000
Katsunari Takahashi	69	70	70	68	277	2,610,000
Toshiaki Odate	71	67	67	72	277	2,610,000
Masashi Ozaki	71	69	71	67	278	1,759,000
Zaw Moe	69	68	73	68	278	1,759,000
Ryoken Kawagishi	73	67	69	69	278	1,759,000
Nobumitsu Yuhara	69	70	69	70	278	1,759,000
Shigenori Mori	71	70	72	66	279	1,152,000
Eiji Mizoguchi	71	69	72	67	279	1,152,000
Yasunori Ida	69	69	73	68	279	1,152,000
Masahiro Kuramoto	68	71	71	69	279	1,152,000
Seiji Ebihara	69	70	71	69	279	1,152,000
Chen Tze-Chung	68	69	71	71	279	1,152,000
Eiichi Itai	71	71	70	68	280	831,000
Mitsutaka Kusakabe	69	70	71	70	280	831,000
Takaaki Fukuzawa	67	69	72	72	280	831,000
Anthony Gilligan	73	68	67	72	280	831,000
Wayne Smith	69	66	70	75	280	831,000
Yoshimitsu Fukuzawa	68	73	75	65	281	720,000
Kazuhiko Hosokawa	71	68	73	69	281	720,000
Hisao Inoue	70	70	71	70	281	720,000
Saburo Fujiki	70	68	71	72	281	720,000
Keiichiro Fukabori	70	67	70	74	281	720,000
Kiyoshi Maita	70	71	71	70	282	617,000
Masatoshi Horikawa	70	70	71	71	282	617,000
Yasunobu Kuramoto	74	64	72	72	282	617,000
Shigeki Maruyama	66	72	71	73	282	617,000
Samson Gimson	67	68	74	73	282	617,000
Koki Idoki	69	72	67	74	282	617,000
Stewart Ginn	71	68	68	75	282	617,000

NST Niigata Open

Nihonkai Country Golf Club, Niigata
Par 36-36–72; 6,911 yards

July 25-28
purse, ¥60,000,000

	SCORES				TOTAL	MONEY
Masatoshi Horikawa	70	67	64	67	268	¥10,800,000
Masayuki Kawamura	66	69	65	69	269	5,400,000
Tsutomu Higa	63	68	69	70	270	3,672,000
Masayuki Okano	68	71	65	67	271	2,592,000
Gohei Sato	70	65	70	67	272	2,160,000
Toshiaki Odate	66	69	73	65	273	1,944,000
Nobuo Serizawa	69	69	69	67	274	1,647,000
Masanobu Kimura	71	67	66	70	274	1,647,000
Kazuo Kanayama	71	70	67	67	275	1,404,000
Eiichi Itai	68	69	68	71	276	1,161,000
Shigemasa Higaki	68	70	68	70	276	1,161,000
Hiroshi Ueda	71	70	68	68	277	950,400
Tsuneyuki Nakajima	68	68	70	71	277	950,400
Nobumitsu Yuhara	68	71	71	68	278	777,600
Koki Idoki	69	70	68	71	278	777,600
Katsunori Kuwabara	66	72	68	72	278	777,600
Yoshimi Niizeki	71	71	71	66	279	626,400
Gregory Meyer	68	73	68	70	279	626,400
Akihito Yokoyama	68	72	65	75	280	518,400
Naoya Sugiyama	71	68	68	73	280	518,400
Mitsunori Harakawa	71	69	70	70	280	518,400
Shinichi Akiba	70	71	69	70	280	518,400
Kaname Yokoo	68	67	73	72	280	518,400
Seiji Ebihara	70	73	68	70	281	437,400
Seiichi Kanai	69	73	71	68	281	437,400
Koji Kobayashi	70	68	74	69	281	437,400
Tatsuo Takasaki	69	71	71	70	281	437,400
Hatsuo Nakame	76	65	69	71	281	437,400
Carlos Franco	72	70	68	71	281	437,400
Harumitsu Hamano	71	71	70	70	282	361,440
Saburo Fujiki	70	70	73	69	282	361,440
Kosei Niyata	72	69	68	73	282	361,440
Seiichi Koizumi	73	68	71	70	282	361,440
Keisuke Goi	73	69	70	70	282	361,440
Yoshimitsu Fukuzawa	67	74	71	70	282	361,440
Craig Warren	70	69	75	68	282	361,440
Norio Shinozaki	70	71	69	72	282	361,440
Hiroyuki Fujita	70	73	66	73	282	361,440

Sanko Grand Summer

Sanko 72 Country Club, Gunma
Par 36-36–72; 7,066 yards

August 1-4
purse, ¥100,000,000

	SCORES				TOTAL	MONEY
Kazuhiko Hosokawa	68	66	68	70	272	¥18,000,000
Eduardo Herrera	68	67	69	73	277	9,000,000
Yasunobu Kuramoto	67	71	72	68	278	6,120,000
Katsuyoshi Tomori	71	69	69	70	279	4,320,000
Hiroshi Ishii	70	72	71	67	280	3,240,000
Brandt Jobe	69	70	69	72	280	3,240,000
Kaname Yokoo	68	70	67	75	280	3,240,000

	SCORES				TOTAL	MONEY
Frankie Minoza	69	70	73	69	281	2,340,000
Yoshimitsu Fukuzawa	69	74	67	71	281	2,340,000
Hiroyuki Fujita	68	67	74	72	281	2,340,000
Mitsuo Harada	72	73	71	66	282	1,656,000
Yasunori Ida	68	72	73	69	282	1,656,000
Masayuki Okano	67	74	70	71	282	1,656,000
Shigenori Mori	69	72	73	69	283	1,350,000
Motomasa Aoki	73	71	69	70	283	1,350,000
Kosaku Hirano	73	73	71	67	284	1,188,000
Hiroshi Ueda	71	72	70	72	285	1,080,000
Tatsuo Takasaki	72	74	69	71	286	927,000
Nobumitsu Yuhara	73	73	69	71	286	927,000
Naoya Sugiyama	69	72	72	73	286	927,000
Toyotake Nakao	71	72	69	74	286	927,000
Teruo Nakamura	71	74	73	69	287	749,000
Mitsutaka Kusakabe	69	74	74	70	287	749,000
Koichi Suzuki	73	73	71	70	287	749,000
Richard Backwell	70	75	72	70	287	749,000
Shigehiko Washio	70	73	73	71	287	749,000
Masanobu Kimura	71	74	70	72	287	749,000
Osamu Yamaguchi	72	70	73	72	287	749,000
Hideyuki Sato	71	72	71	73	287	749,000
Kiyoshi Maita	72	73	73	70	288	639,000
Hideki Kase	70	75	72	71	288	639,000
Samson Gimson	73	72	72	71	288	639,000
Carlos Franco	70	72	70	76	288	639,000

Acom International

Seve Ballesteros Golf Club, Iwaki, Ibaragi
Par 36-36–72; 6,972 yards

August 15-18
purse, ¥100,000,000

	POINTS				TOTAL	MONEY
Kazuhiko Hosokawa	8	18	14	11	51	¥18,000,000
Frankie Minoza	8	16	11	12	47	9,000,000
Payne Stewart	5	10	9	19	43	6,120,000
Masayuki Kawamura	7	8	16	8	39	3,960,000
Naoya Sugiyama	8	17	7	7	39	3,960,000
Hinoru Hatsumi	8	6	15	9	38	3,240,000
Eduardo Herrera	10	6	9	12	37	2,880,000
Yasunobu Kuramoto	9	8	7	12	36	2,475,000
Rick Gibson	14	4	13	5	36	2,475,000
Kazuhiro Takami	13	9	6	6	34	1,935,000
Tsukasa Watanabe	14	12	2	6	34	1,935,000
Hiroshi Goda	12	7	9	4	32	1,524,000
Yoshihiko Terakawa	8	8	1	15	32	1,524,000
Seiichi Koizumi	5	9	8	10	32	1,524,000
Todd Hamilton	4	15	6	5	30	1,298,000
Ryoken Kawagishi	10	5	6	8	29	1,134,000
Shinichi Akiba	2	10	12	5	29	1,134,000
Katsuyoshi Tomori	14	8	5	1	28	948,000
Anthony Gilligan	9	6	5	8	28	948,000
Roger Mackay	7	17	-1	5	28	948,000
Tomohiro Maruyama	4	8	6	9	27	802,800
Shigenori Mori	3	9	7	8	27	802,800
Norio Hirayama	15	5	5	2	27	802,800
Masatoshi Horikawa	17	1	8	1	27	802,800

	POINTS				TOTAL	MONEY
Minetaka Kanaya	11	11	1	4	27	802,800
Katsumi Kochiai	7	8	7	4	26	720,000
Peter McWhinney	-1	13	4	10	26	720,000
Hiroyuki Fujita	7	5	2	12	26	720,000
Isamu Sugita	5	9	4	7	25	666,000
Toshiaki Odate	11	6	1	7	25	666,000
Shigehiko Washio	7	8	5	5	25	666,000

KBC Augusta

Keya Golf Club, Shima, Fukuoka
Par 36-36–72; 7,154 yards

August 22-25
purse, ¥100,000,000

	SCORES				TOTAL	MONEY
Masashi Ozaki	64	70	70	69	273	¥18,000,000
Taichi Teshima	71	69	69	64	273	9,000,000
(Ozaki defeated Teshima on second extra hole.)						
Hideki Kase	68	68	70	70	276	6,120,000
Tsukasa Watanabe	68	71	71	67	277	4,320,000
Kazuhiko Hosokawa	71	70	67	70	278	3,420,000
Yoshikazu Sakamoto	69	69	69	71	278	3,420,000
Zaw Moe	72	67	72	68	279	2,124,000
Frankie Minoza	72	68	70	69	279	2,124,000
Lin Keng-Chi	68	73	69	69	279	2,124,000
Yoshimitsu Fukuzawa	66	73	70	70	279	2,124,000
Keiichiro Fukabori	68	73	67	71	279	2,124,000
Tomohiro Maruyama	72	65	71	71	279	2,124,000
Masahiro Kuramoto	68	71	67	73	279	2,124,000
Yoshinori Kaneko	71	68	71	70	280	1,350,000
Koichi Nogami	71	68	69	72	280	1,350,000
Brandt Jobe	72	70	70	69	281	1,134,000
Takaaki Fukuzawa	71	71	69	70	281	1,134,000
Katsuyoshi Tomori	72	70	72	68	282	948,000
Shoichi Kuwabara	70	72	72	68	282	948,000
Shigenori Mori	71	70	69	72	282	948,000
Richard Backwell	71	72	70	70	283	846,000
Toru Nakamura	70	69	73	71	283	846,000
Todd Hamilton	72	70	72	70	284	720,000
Katsunori Kuwabara	68	74	72	70	284	720,000
Mitsuo Harada	71	71	72	70	284	720,000
Hiroshi Ueda	70	72	72	70	284	720,000
Rick Todd	72	70	72	70	284	720,000
Eduardo Herrera	72	68	73	71	284	720,000
Nobumitsu Yuhara	70	70	73	71	284	720,000
Gregory Meyer	69	74	70	71	284	720,000
Masayuki Kawamura	71	67	73	73	284	720,000

Japan Match Play Championship

Nidom Classic Course, Hokkaido
Par 36-36–72; 6,941 yards

August 29-September 1
purse, ¥80,000,000

FIRST ROUND

Hisayuki Sasaki defeated Yoshinori Kaneko, 1 up
Masayuki Kawamura defeated Seiki Okuda, 1 up, 19 holes
Hirofumi Miyase defeated Kazuhiko Hosokawa, 3 and 2
Todd Hamilton defeated Hideyuki Sato, 1 up
Hidemichi Tanaka defeated Katsunori Kuwabara, 2 up
Nobuo Serizawa defeated Nobumitsu Yuhara, 3 and 2
Katsuyoshi Tomori defeated Eduardo Herrera, 4 and 2
Shigenori Mori defeated Toru Suzuki, 1 up, 19 holes
Shigeki Maruyama defeated Ryoken Kawagishi, 2 and 1
Masanobu Kimura defeated Stewart Ginn, 5 and 4
Peter McWhinney defeated Brian Watts, 3 and 2
Tsuneyuki Nakajima defeated Shinichi Yokota, 2 and 1
Satoshi Higashi defeated Toshimitsu Izawa, 2 and 1
Hajime Meshiai defeated Tsukasa Watanabe, 1 up
Rick Gibson defeated Hideki Kase, 4 and 2
Brandt Jobe defeated Masahiro Kuramoto, 1 up, 19 holes

(Each losing player received ¥450,000.)

SECOND ROUND

Sasaki defeated Kawamura, 2 and 1
Miyase defeated Hamilton, 1 up, 22 holes
Serizawa defeated Tanaka, 3 and 2
Mori defeated Tomori, 1 up
Maruyama defeated Kimura, 7 and 6
Nakajima defeated McWhinney, 2 and 1
Meshiai defeated Higashi, 4 and 3
Jobe defeated Gibson, 2 and 1

(Each losing player received ¥850,000.)

QUARTER-FINALS

Sasaki defeated Miyase, 2 and 1
Serizawa defeated Mori, 2 and 1
Maruyama defeated Nakajima, 6 and 4
Jobe defeated Meshiai, 4 and 3

(Each losing player received ¥1,600,000.)

SEMI-FINALS

Serizawa defeated Sasaki, 1 up, 40 holes
Jobe defeated Maruyama, 1 up

THIRD-FOURTH PLACE PLAYOFF

Maruyama defeated Sasaki, 3 and 2

(Maruyama received ¥6,000,000; Sasaki received ¥4,500,000.)

FINAL

Serizawa defeated Jobe, 1 up

(Serizawa received ¥25,000,000; Jobe received ¥12,500,000.)

Suntory Open

Narashino Country Club, Chiba
Par 36-36–72; 7,027 yards

September 5-8
purse, ¥100,000,000

	SCORES				TOTAL	MONEY
Hajime Meshiai	68	69	66	69	272	¥18,000,000
Hidemichi Tanaka	65	70	68	72	275	9,000,000
Phil Mickelson	66	69	71	70	276	6,120,000
Ryoken Kawagishi	67	70	74	66	277	3,960,000
Masahiro Kuramoto	70	71	66	70	277	3,960,000
Masashi Ozaki	70	69	69	70	278	3,060,000
Katsunori Kuwabara	68	69	70	71	278	3,060,000
Kevin Wentworth	64	75	72	68	279	2,340,000
Todd Hamilton	67	70	72	70	279	2,340,000
Naomichi Ozaki	68	69	69	73	279	2,340,000
Kazuhiro Fukunaga	71	71	69	69	280	1,728,000
Keiichiro Fukabori	73	69	65	73	280	1,728,000
Brian Watts	72	69	71	69	281	1,404,000
Tateo Ozaki	70	69	73	69	281	1,404,000
Roger Mackay	72	71	68	70	281	1,404,000
Tsukasa Watanabe	71	70	72	69	282	1,134,000
Richard Backwell	69	73	69	71	282	1,134,000
Kiyoshi Murota	72	72	71	68	283	857,000
Takaaki Fukuzawa	74	70	70	69	283	857,000
Hisayuki Sasaki	72	68	73	70	283	857,000
Tatsuo Takasaki	71	71	71	70	283	857,000
Wayne Grady	69	71	73	70	283	857,000
Toru Taniguchi	66	72	73	72	283	857,000
Eiji Mizoguchi	73	65	73	72	283	857,000
Tomohiro Maruyama	68	72	69	74	283	857,000
Akihito Yokoyama	70	72	73	69	284	738,000
Katsuyoshi Tomori	70	73	73	69	285	684,000
Kiyoshi Maita	71	71	73	70	285	684,000
Shigeki Maruyama	72	70	71	72	285	684,000
Carlos Franco	69	73	70	73	285	684,000
Joji Furuki	69	71	72	73	285	684,000

ANA Open

Sapporo Golf Club, Wattsu Course, Hokkaido
Par 36-36–72; 7,063 yards

September 12-15
purse, ¥100,000,000

	SCORES				TOTAL	MONEY
Carlos Franco	67	73	74	68	282	¥18,000,000
Masahiro Kuramoto	69	75	71	68	283	9,000,000
Ryoken Kawagishi	68	74	72	70	284	4,032,000
Hisayuki Sasaki	69	74	70	71	284	4,032,000
Koichi Nogami	72	67	74	71	284	4,032,000
Kazuhiko Hosokawa	72	70	69	73	284	4,032,000
Kiyoshi Maita	73	68	68	75	284	4,032,000
Eiji Mizoguchi	70	73	69	73	285	2,610,000
Shigenori Mori	71	76	71	68	286	1,725,000
Katsunori Kuwabara	74	71	72	69	286	1,725,000
Masayuki Kawamura	72	73	72	69	286	1,725,000
Keiichiro Fukabori	73	71	72	70	286	1,725,000
Shintaro Iizuka	69	73	73	71	286	1,725,000
Toru Suzuki	72	70	71	73	286	1,725,000

	SCORES				TOTAL	MONEY
Tateo Ozaki	72	69	71	74	286	1,725,000
Kaname Yokoo	75	69	75	68	287	1,053,000
Tomohiro Maruyama	72	71	76	68	287	1,053,000
Todd Hamilton	72	68	75	72	287	1,053,000
Kazuhiro Takami	71	69	71	76	287	1,053,000
Naomichi Ozaki	72	74	72	70	288	864,000
Nobuhito Sato	71	70	76	71	288	864,000
Hsieh Chin-Sheng	72	74	68	74	288	864,000
Tsuyoshi Yoneyama	71	75	72	71	289	774,000
Katsunari Takahashi	71	74	72	72	289	774,000
Eiichi Itai	71	72	74	72	289	774,000
Katsuyoshi Tomori	71	74	72	73	290	720,000
Toshimitsu Izawa	70	72	75	73	290	720,000
Shinji Ikeuchi	75	70	71	74	290	720,000
Shigeki Maruyama	73	73	75	70	291	666,000
Lin Keng-Chi	74	73	74	70	291	666,000
K. Nanjo	68	73	76	74	291	666,000

Jun Classic

Jun Classic Country Club, Nasu, Tochigi
Par 36-36–72; 7,358 yards

September 19-22
purse, ¥82,500,000

	SCORES			TOTAL	MONEY
Masashi Ozaki	68	64	65	197	¥14,850,000
Takaaki Fukuzawa	68	70	65	203	7,425,000
Seiki Okuda	70	69	66	205	5,049,000
Gohei Sato	71	66	69	206	3,564,000
Yoshinori Kaneko	72	69	66	207	2,821,500
Kaname Yokoo	72	68	67	207	2,821,500
Katsuyoshi Tomori	68	71	69	208	2,376,000
Kazuhiro Takami	70	67	73	210	2,041,875
Carlos Franco	73	68	69	210	2,041,875
Yoshinori Mizumaki	71	68	72	211	1,238,118
Tetsu Nishikawa	72	70	69	211	1,238,118
Yoshimitsu Fukuzawa	68	70	73	211	1,238,118
Shoichi Kuwabara	70	70	71	211	1,238,118
Samson Gimson	73	68	70	211	1,238,118
Kazuhiko Hosokawa	71	69	71	211	1,238,118
Chen Tze-Chung	68	69	74	211	1,238,118
Frankie Minoza	69	70	72	211	1,238,118
Tateo Ozaki	71	73	68	212	696,300
Hideyuki Sato	73	69	70	212	696,300
Katsuji Hasegawa	73	70	69	212	696,300
Tomohiro Maruyama	70	73	69	212	696,300
Kiyoshi Murota	71	71	70	212	696,300
Taisei Inagaki	75	69	68	212	696,300
Ryoken Kawagishi	70	71	71	212	696,300
Koichi Nogami	72	68	72	212	696,300
Hiroyuki Fujita	69	72	71	212	696,300
Shinji Ikeuchi	71	70	72	213	556,875
Kiyoshi Maita	69	72	72	213	556,875
Tsutomu Higa	69	74	70	213	556,875
Katsunori Kuwabara	69	71	73	213	556,875
Lin Keng-Chi	68	74	71	213	556,875
David Ishii	73	70	70	213	556,875

Japan Open Golf Championship

Ibaragi Country Club, Nishi Course, Ibaragi
Par 71; 7,017 yards

September 26-29
purse, ¥120,000,000

	SCORES				TOTAL	MONEY
Peter Teravainen	71	72	71	68	282	¥24,000,000
Frankie Minoza	72	66	72	74	284	13,200,000
Peter Senior	70	76	70	69	285	7,710,000
Taichi Teshima	74	73	69	69	285	7,710,000
Kaname Yokoo	73	73	72	68	286	4,560,000
Naomichi Ozaki	72	73	70	71	286	4,560,000
Masahiro Kuramoto	73	73	70	71	287	3,288,000
Hisayuki Sasaki	71	72	69	75	287	3,288,000
Toru Taniguchi	76	72	71	69	288	2,535,000
Satoshi Higashi	72	74	70	72	288	2,535,000
Kiyoshi Maita	71	74	74	70	289	1,872,000
David Ishii	78	70	69	72	289	1,872,000
Carlos Franco	68	72	76	73	289	1,872,000
Katsuyoshi Tomori	73	74	74	69	290	1,416,000
Masashi Ozaki	70	72	77	71	290	1,416,000
Kevin Wentworth	71	74	73	72	290	1,416,000
Keiichiro Fukabori	71	75	71	73	290	1,416,000
Yoshimitsu Fukuzawa	71	70	75	74	290	1,416,000
Hajime Meshiai	74	73	75	69	291	1,116,000
Brian Watts	74	74	71	72	291	1,116,000
Shigeki Maruyama	76	73	70	72	291	1,116,000
Koki Idoki	72	74	72	73	291	1,116,000
Ryoken Kawagishi	72	73	72	74	291	1,116,000
Koichi Nogami	70	75	72	74	291	1,116,000
Yoshinori Mizumaki	74	74	69	74	291	1,116,000
Katsunori Kuwabara	73	75	73	71	292	936,000
Tomohiro Maruyama	73	73	75	71	292	936,000
Hiroshi Ishii	71	75	74	72	292	936,000
Shinichi Yokota	75	73	71	73	292	936,000
Masayuki Kawamura	75	72	72	73	292	936,000
Hiroyuki Fujita	74	72	73	73	292	936,000
Takaaki Fukuzawa	73	71	74	74	292	936,000
Shoichi Yamamoto	70	75	71	76	292	936,000

Tokai Classic

Miyoshi Country Club, Nishi Course, Aichi
Par 36-36–72; 7,089 yards

October 3-6
purse, ¥110,000,000

	SCORES				TOTAL	MONEY
Masanobu Kimura	68	71	71	70	280	¥19,800,000
Shigeki Maruyama	69	72	72	68	281	7,128,000
Kazuhiko Hosokawa	72	72	68	69	281	7,128,000
Steve Jones	69	71	72	69	281	7,128,000
Kiyoshi Maita	70	72	75	65	282	3,960,000
Hisayuki Sasaki	72	71	71	70	284	3,044,250
Ken Kusumoto	71	70	73	70	284	3,044,250
Hsieh Chin-Sheng	67	75	69	73	284	3,044,250
Brian Watts	72	71	72	69	284	3,044,250
Tsukasa Watanabe	72	69	73	71	285	2,128,500
Kaname Yokoo	70	74	68	73	285	2,128,500
Katsunari Takahashi	74	70	72	70	286	1,676,400

	SCORES				TOTAL	MONEY
Isamu Sugita	75	70	70	71	286	1,676,400
Rick Todd	71	68	74	73	286	1,676,400
Shoichi Yamamoto	71	73	71	72	287	1,425,600
Seiki Okuda	72	74	72	70	288	1,158,300
Koki Idoki	75	71	68	74	288	1,158,300
Yasunori Ida	73	74	70	71	288	1,158,300
Yoshimitsu Fukuzawa	72	72	73	71	288	1,158,300
*Hideo Kawabe	73	72	74	69	288	
Nobuo Serizawa	72	73	71	73	289	930,600
Masayuki Okano	72	73	73	71	289	930,600
Shinichi Yokota	75	71	70	73	289	930,600
Naotoshi Nakamura	74	71	73	71	289	930,600
Akiyoshi Ohmachi	72	74	72	72	290	792,000
Nobumitsu Yuhara	75	67	72	76	290	792,000
Masahiro Kuramoto	68	68	79	75	290	792,000
Toru Nakamura	79	68	70	73	290	792,000
Mitsutaka Kusakabe	72	70	74	74	290	792,000
Toru Taniguchi	73	70	72	75	290	792,000
Brandt Jobe	71	76	74	69	290	792,000

Golf Digest Open

Tomei Country Club, Shizuoka
Par 35-36–71; 6,801 yards

October 10-13
purse, ¥100,000,000

	SCORES				TOTAL	MONEY
Yoshinori Mizumaki	66	67	68	72	273	¥18,000,000
Satoshi Higashi	74	67	67	66	274	7,560,000
Shoichi Kuwabara	70	68	70	66	274	7,560,000
Katsuyoshi Tomori	68	69	68	70	275	3,330,000
Toru Suzuki	72	69	67	67	275	3,330,000
David Ishii	68	69	68	70	275	3,330,000
Brian Watts	73	69	68	65	275	3,330,000
Brandt Jobe	73	66	66	70	275	3,330,000
Harumitsu Hamano	66	71	70	69	276	2,078,000
Keiichiro Fukabori	68	68	68	72	276	2,078,000
Chen Tze-Chung	71	73	66	66	276	2,078,000
Hsieh Min-Nan	69	68	69	71	277	1,524,000
Tomohiro Maruyama	66	74	70	67	277	1,524,000
Koki Idoki	69	68	73	67	277	1,524,000
Ken Tanigawa	71	68	69	70	278	1,242,000
Frankie Minoza	73	66	74	65	278	1,242,000
Seiji Ebihara	66	75	70	68	279	936,000
Hiroshi Ueda	70	69	75	65	279	936,000
Saburo Fujiki	71	71	68	69	279	936,000
Yoshihiko Terakawa	69	71	69	70	279	936,000
Yoshimitsu Izawa	70	70	70	69	279	936,000
Yoshimitsu Fukuzawa	67	72	71	69	279	936,000
Yoshimi Niizeki	71	72	68	69	280	783,000
Toru Taniguchi	66	69	71	74	280	783,000
Shinji Ikeuchi	71	72	67	71	281	684,400
Akiyoshi Ohmachi	72	71	70	68	281	684,400
Hiroshi Makino	71	67	72	71	281	684,400
Kiyoshi Murota	69	73	69	70	281	684,400
Shigenori Mori	71	72	71	67	281	684,400
Tsukasa Watanabe	68	71	72	70	281	684,400
Hsieh Chin-Sheng	68	69	74	70	281	684,400

	SCORES				TOTAL	MONEY
Shintaro Iizuka	71	67	70	73	281	684,400
Shinichi Yokota	73	67	71	70	281	684,400

Bridgestone Open

Sodegaura Country Club, Chiba
Par 36-36—72; 7,151 yards

October 17-20
purse, ¥120,000,000

	SCORES				TOTAL	MONEY
Shigeki Maruyama	67	67	67	71	272	¥21,600,000
Brian Watts	68	64	70	72	274	10,800,000
Rick Gibson	71	65	68	71	275	7,344,000
Nobumitsu Yuhara	71	68	66	71	276	4,752,000
Nick Price	67	67	72	70	276	4,752,000
Lin Keng-Chi	69	67	73	69	278	3,492,000
Kaname Yokoo	67	70	73	68	278	3,492,000
Frankie Minoza	70	69	68	71	278	3,492,000
Mark Calcavecchia	69	69	70	71	279	2,808,000
Masahiro Kuramoto	69	72	71	68	280	2,210,400
Yoshimitsu Izawa	72	70	68	70	280	2,210,400
Shinichi Yokota	65	72	73	70	280	2,210,400
Shigenori Mori	72	66	69	74	281	1,684,800
Roger Mackay	67	74	67	73	281	1,684,800
Lee Janzen	68	71	69	73	281	1,684,800
Naomichi Ozaki	71	70	68	73	282	1,310,400
Yoshinori Kaneko	74	70	70	68	282	1,310,400
Tsuneyuki Nakajima	71	70	69	72	282	1,310,400
Katsunari Takahashi	70	70	72	71	283	1,002,857
Yoshikazu Sakamoto	71	69	70	73	283	1,002,857
Tsuyoshi Yoneyama	69	72	72	70	283	1,002,857
Hsieh Chin-Sheng	72	68	71	72	283	1,002,857
Hidemichi Tanaka	74	67	72	70	283	1,002,857
Gregory Meyer	70	69	71	73	283	1,002,857
David Ishii	72	71	69	71	283	1,002,857
Yoshimitsu Fukuzawa	71	71	70	72	284	864,000
Koichi Nogami	68	72	71	73	284	864,000
Carlos Franco	69	68	74	73	284	864,000
Kiyoshi Maita	74	69	71	71	285	778,464
Tatsuo Takasaki	72	71	74	68	285	778,464
Anthony Gilligan	73	68	74	70	285	778,464
Hiroyuki Fujita	72	67	73	73	285	778,464
Kazuhiro Hosokawa	71	68	75	71	285	778,464

Philip Morris Championship

ABC Golf Club, Hyogo
Par 36-36—72; 7,176 yards

October 24-27
purse, ¥200,000,000

	SCORES				TOTAL	MONEY
Naomichi Ozaki	71	70	67	70	278	¥36,000,000
Masashi Ozaki	71	70	70	71	282	12,960,000
David Ishii	73	70	68	71	282	12,960,000
Russ Cochran	68	69	74	71	282	12,960,000
Yoshinori Kaneko	69	68	74	72	283	6,480,000
Kiyoshi Maita	69	71	75	68	283	6,480,000

	SCORES			TOTAL	MONEY
Masanobu Kimura	66	67 75 75		283	6,480,000
Nobumitsu Yuhara	73	72 72 67		284	4,680,000
Katsunori Kuwabara	69	75 69 71		284	4,680,000
Brian Watts	68	70 73 73		284	4,680,000
Tsukasa Watanabe	75	71 69 70		285	3,186,000
Takashi Umiyama	72	71 70 72		285	3,186,000
Frankie Minoza	73	73 70 69		285	3,186,000
Andrew Magee	72	74 70 69		285	3,186,000
Toru Suzuki	72	69 72 73		286	2,376,000
Shoichi Kuwabara	70	72 72 72		286	2,376,000
Carlos Franco	70	71 74 71		286	2,376,000
Hisayuki Sasaki	70	69 75 73		287	2,016,000
Tateo Ozaki	74	68 74 72		288	1,698,000
Nobuo Serizawa	71	73 74 70		288	1,698,000
Kazuhiro Takami	73	73 70 72		288	1,698,000
Satoshi Higashi	73	74 71 70		288	1,698,000
Katsuyoshi Tomori	70	73 69 76		288	1,698,000
Chen Tze-Chung	70	70 74 74		288	1,698,000
Tetsu Nishikawa	69	76 73 71		289	1,476,000
Hidemichi Tanaka	77	66 75 71		289	1,476,000
Todd Hamilton	72	71 73 73		289	1,476,000
Hideyuki Sato	72	71 74 73		290	1,332,000
Takaaki Fukuzawa	72	70 77 71		290	1,332,000
Tsuyoshi Yoneyama	71	73 73 73		290	1,332,000
Keiichiro Fukabori	76	68 73 73		290	1,332,000
Bob Gilder	72	70 74 74		290	1,332,000

Sumitomo Visa Taiheiyo Masters

Taiheiyo Club, Gotemba Course, Shizuoka
Par 36-36–72; 7,072 yards
(Third round cancelled — fog.)

November 7-10
purse, ¥112,500,000

	SCORES		TOTAL	MONEY
Lee Westwood	68	70 68	206	¥20,250,000
Jeff Sluman	69	69 68	206	8,505,000
Costantino Rocca	69	69 68	206	8,505,000
(Westwood defeated Sluman on first extra hole and Rocca on fourth extra hole.)				
Hisayuki Sasaki	67	68 72	207	4,840,000
Yoshinori Kaneko	71	70 67	208	3,645,000
Hideyuki Sato	68	70 70	208	3,645,000
Larry Mize	71	67 70	208	3,645,000
Naomichi Ozaki	74	67 68	209	2,784,375
Frankie Minoza	69	73 67	209	2,784,375
Yoshinori Mizumaki	69	72 69	210	2,072,250
Masanobu Kimura	73	66 71	210	2,072,250
Peter Senior	70	73 67	210	2,072,250
Hideki Kase	70	70 71	211	1,458,000
Seiki Okuda	75	67 69	211	1,458,000
Shigeki Maruyama	68	72 71	211	1,458,000
Seve Ballesteros	72	70 69	211	1,458,000
Brandt Jobe	73	70 68	211	1,458,000
Kiyoshi Murota	71	69 72	212	1,093,500
Katsuyoshi Tomori	72	71 69	212	1,093,500
Koki Idoki	73	67 73	213	951,750
Katsunori Kuwabara	71	75 67	213	951,750
Peter McWhinney	69	77 67	213	951,750

	SCORES	TOTAL	MONEY
Craig Parry	68 73 72	213	951,750
Akiyoshi Ohmachi	73 74 67	214	820,125
Katsunari Takahashi	73 71 70	214	820,125
Takaaki Fukuzawa	74 70 70	214	820,125
Nobumitsu Yuhara	68 74 72	214	820,125
Masahiro Kuramoto	75 70 69	214	820,125
Mark Brooks	71 70 73	214	820,125
*Tastuhiko Takahashi	73 71 70	214	

Dunlop Phoenix Tournament

Phoenix Country Club, Miyazaki
Par 35-36–71; 6,803 yards

November 14-17
purse, ¥200,000,000

	SCORES	TOTAL	MONEY
Masashi Ozaki	68 67 69 73	277	¥36,000,000
Naomichi Ozaki	67 71 69 73	280	15,120,000
Tom Watson	66 70 71 73	280	15,120,000
Yoshinori Kaneko	69 70 70 72	281	7,920,000
Frankie Minoza	74 70 68 69	281	7,920,000
Costantino Rocca	73 72 69 68	282	6,120,000
Lee Westwood	67 68 77 70	282	6,120,000
Hajime Meshiai	69 69 74 71	283	5,220,000
Robert Gamez	72 69 74 69	284	4,880,000
Toshimitsu Izawa	71 72 74 68	285	3,870,000
Jim Furyk	76 69 70 70	285	3,870,000
Harumitsu Hamano	74 73 70 69	286	3,048,000
Seiki Okuda	71 71 74 70	286	3,048,000
Brandt Jobe	74 70 70 72	286	3,048,000
Tsuneyuki Nakajima	71 71 73 72	287	2,376,000
Carlos Franco	72 70 75 70	287	2,376,000
Miguel Angel Jimenez	72 71 73 71	287	2,376,000
Jeff Sluman	73 72 73 70	288	2,016,000
Masayuki Kawamura	73 68 72 76	289	1,836,000
Fred Funk	70 72 75 72	289	1,836,000
Tateo Ozaki	73 70 75 72	290	1,656,000
Nobumitsu Yuhara	73 73 69 75	290	1,656,000
Masahiro Kuramoto	71 75 74 70	290	1,656,000
Hisayuki Sasaki	71 72 74 74	291	1,440,000
Chen Tze-Chung	77 71 72 71	291	1,440,000
Rick Gibson	73 71 74 73	291	1,440,000
Craig Parry	70 74 75 72	291	1,440,000
David Ishii	72 69 73 77	291	1,440,000
Larry Nelson	71 72 74 74	291	1,440,000
Brian Watts	73 76 70 72	291	1,440,000

Casio World Open

Ibusuki Golf Club, Kaimon, Kagoshima
Par 36-36–72; 7,028 yards

November 21-24
purse, ¥150,000,000

	SCORES	TOTAL	MONEY
Paul Stankowski	69 69 71 68	277	¥27,000,000
David Ishii	69 70 72 66	277	13,500,000

(Stankowski defeated Ishii on second extra hole.)

	SCORES				TOTAL	MONEY
Masashi Ozaki	74	67	68	69	278	7,830,000
Tateo Ozaki	70	69	70	69	278	7,830,000
Carlos Franco	73	67	68	71	279	5,400,000
Yoshikazu Sakamoto	72	70	70	68	280	4,590,000
Hisayuki Sasaki	74	69	66	71	280	4,590,000
Yutaka Hagawa	69	72	70	70	281	3,510,000
Tsukasa Watanabe	70	74	66	71	281	3,510,000
Peter Teravainen	70	70	69	72	281	3,510,000
Brian Watts	71	72	71	68	282	2,592,000
Robert Gamez	69	73	72	68	282	2,592,000
Saburo Fujiki	74	70	70	70	284	2,025,000
Kiyoshi Murota	69	73	73	69	284	2,025,000
Mitsutaka Kusakabe	70	70	74	70	284	2,025,000
Shigeki Maruyama	72	69	70	73	284	2,025,000
Tomohiro Maruyama	71	70	70	74	285	1,471,500
Tsuyoshi Yoneyama	70	74	68	73	285	1,471,500
Shoichi Kuwabara	70	73	71	71	285	1,471,500
Kazuhiko Hosokawa	71	70	75	69	285	1,471,500
Ryoken Kawagishi	73	71	73	69	286	1,221,750
Yasunobu Kuramoto	72	71	71	72	286	1,221,750
Zaw Moe	69	77	68	72	286	1,221,750
Mark Brooks	71	71	73	71	286	1,221,750
Hideyuki Sato	69	75	71	72	287	1,053,000
Harumitsu Hamano	71	74	72	70	287	1,053,000
Toshimitsu Izawa	71	74	70	72	287	1,053,000
Yoshimitsu Fukuzawa	74	71	72	70	287	1,053,000
Hidemichi Tanaka	71	75	70	71	287	1,053,000
Jeff Sluman	70	76	71	70	287	1,053,000
Jim Furyk	72	77	68	70	287	1,053,000

Japan Series Hitachi Cup

Tokyo Yomiuri Country Club, Tokyo
Par 36-36—72; 7,022 yards

November 28-December 1
purse, ¥100,000,000

	SCORES				TOTAL	MONEY
Masashi Ozaki	62	68	65	67	262	¥30,000,000
Shigeki Maruyama	68	67	65	66	266	13,200,000
Naomichi Ozaki	69	69	63	70	271	7,200,000
Hidemichi Tanaka	69	66	67	70	272	4,363,333
Frankie Minoza	65	65	70	72	272	4,363,333
Carlos Franco	68	68	66	70	272	4,363,333
Kazuhiko Hosokawa	74	71	68	63	276	3,000,000
Toru Suzuki	73	66	69	69	277	2,650,000
Peter McWhinney	72	64	68	74	278	2,300,000
Todd Hamilton	71	67	68	74	280	1,875,000
Brandt Jobe	74	70	70	66	280	1,875,000
Hideyuki Sato	67	70	71	73	281	1,550,000
Nobuo Serizawa	70	70	71	70	281	1,550,000
Brian Watts	72	70	71	68	281	1,550,000
Tsuneyuki Nakajima	71	70	70	71	282	1,300,000
Hajime Meshiai	71	71	69	71	282	1,300,000
Masanobu Kimura	73	67	70	73	283	1,115,000
David Ishii	71	69	70	73	283	1,115,000
Yoshinori Kaneko	72	71	70	71	284	980,000
Peter Teravainen	68	72	73	71	284	980,000
Yoshikazu Sakamoto	73	71	71	70	285	900,000

	SCORES				TOTAL	MONEY
Yoshinori Mizumaki	70	73	70	75	288	860,000
Kazuhiro Fukunaga	67	69	76	77	289	820,000
Masatoshi Horikawa	74	73	71	75	293	790,000

Daikyo Open

Daikyo Country Club, Onna, Okinawa
Par 36-35–71; 6,308 yards

December 5-8
purse, ¥120,000,000

	SCORES				TOTAL	MONEY
Eduardo Herrera	67	69	68	68	272	¥21,600,000
Katsunori Kuwabara	70	73	66	68	277	10,800,000
Akihito Yokoyama	74	65	70	69	278	6,264,000
Toru Nakamura	66	72	71	69	278	6,264,000
David Ishii	67	72	74	66	279	4,104,000
Brian Watts	72	67	72	68	279	4,104,000
Satoshi Higashi	71	70	73	66	280	3,132,000
Tsuyoshi Yoneyama	71	73	68	68	280	3,132,000
Toru Suzuki	65	72	77	66	280	3,132,000
Saburo Fujiki	73	68	72	68	281	2,210,400
Eiji Mizoguchi	68	73	73	67	281	2,210,400
Ken Kusumoto	71	72	69	69	281	2,210,400
Seiki Okuda	71	73	69	69	282	1,749,600
Isamu Sugita	69	72	73	68	282	1,749,600
Shinji Ikeuchi	71	73	70	69	283	1,490,400
Yasunobu Kuramoto	70	71	70	72	283	1,490,400
Koichi Suzuki	70	74	70	70	284	1,123,200
Nobuo Serizawa	72	72	68	72	284	1,123,200
Yutaka Hagawa	71	74	71	68	284	1,123,200
Hiroshi Makino	70	73	71	70	284	1,123,200
Katsuyoshi Tomori	72	70	75	67	284	1,123,200
Ken Tanigawa	69	71	73	71	284	1,123,200
Seiichi Kanai	69	72	72	72	285	885,600
Hajime Meshiai	72	69	76	68	285	885,600
Masanobu Kimura	73	71	72	69	285	885,600
Mitsutaka Kusakabe	69	72	70	74	285	885,600
Lin Chie-Hsiang	67	76	73	69	285	885,600
Kazuhiko Hosokawa	73	72	70	70	285	885,600
Frankie Minoza	71	74	71	69	285	885,600
Tomohiro Maruyama	70	72	73	71	286	740,571
Gohei Sato	76	68	71	71	286	740,571
Masayuki Kawamura	73	73	73	67	286	740,571
Yasunori Ida	72	72	73	69	286	740,571
Hirofumi Miyase	74	71	75	66	286	740,571
Shoichi Kuwabara	69	72	74	71	286	740,571
Shigeki Maruyama	71	71	77	67	286	740,571

Omega Tour

Myanmar Open

Yangon Golf Club, Yangon, Myanmar
Par 36-36–72; 7,011 yards

January 4-7
purse, US$150,000

		SCORES			TOTAL	MONEY
Boonchu Ruangkit	68	72	76	77	293	US$24,225
Jeff Senior	71	73	73	76	293	16,695
(Ruangkit defeated Senior on first extra hole.)						
Myint Thaung	78	70	73	73	294	9,945
Danny Zarate	75	74	74	74	297	6,750
Tony Maloney	76	74	75	72	297	6,750
Thaworn Wiratchant	73	76	71	78	298	4,500
Thammanoon Sriroj	77	74	73	74	298	4,500
Mardan Mamat	77	76	72	73	298	4,500
Craig Kamps	75	72	74	78	299	3,173
*Soe Soe	76	76	75	72	299	
Chang Chin-Kuo	76	76	76	71	299	3,173
Jin-Kyu Choi	72	76	77	75	300	2,393
Dominique Boulet	79	70	77	74	300	2,393
Jamnian Chitprasong	83	75	69	73	300	2,393
Zaw Moe	76	75	77	72	300	2,393
Supacheep Meesom	76	75	77	72	300	2,393
Lin Keng-Chi	77	76	75	72	300	2,393
Madasamy Murugiah	76	77	73	75	301	1,980
Jeev Milkha Singh	74	74	78	75	301	1,980
Yasuo Sone	73	79	73	77	302	1,805
Win Soe	74	75	80	73	302	1,805
Greg Hanrahan	73	76	79	74	302	1,805
Simon Yates	77	80	73	72	302	1,805
Preecha Senaprom	77	76	74	76	303	1,665
Prayad Marksaeng	73	80	75	75	303	1,665
Suphavaarangoon Veerawut	80	77	75	71	303	1,665
Takehito Daijo	77	75	74	78	304	1,463
Arjun Atwal	77	79	71	77	304	1,463
Chang Hsiu-Fa	77	76	75	76	304	1,463
Derek Fung	80	74	76	74	304	1,463
Kyi-Hla Han	75	76	80	73	304	1,463
Supoj Meesawad	80	77	73	74	304	1,463

Omega PGA Championship

Clearwater Bay Golf & Country Club, Hong Kong
Par 35-35–70; 6,032 yards

January 11-14
purse, US$500,000

		SCORES			TOTAL	MONEY
Yeh Chang-Ting	67	68	69	67	271	US$80,750
Mark Mouland	70	71	67	68	276	55,650
Richard Kaplan	71	70	71	65	277	31,000
Mike Cunning	69	69	71	70	279	25,000
Jeev Milkha Singh	75	68	70	67	280	20,000

	SCORES				TOTAL	MONEY
Chung Chun-Hsing	69	71	70	71	281	12,554
John Kernohan	69	76	70	66	281	12,554
Scott Taylor	70	70	69	72	281	12,554
Robert Willis	71	72	71	67	281	12,554
Boonchu Ruangkit	73	69	71	68	281	12,554
Chen Tze-Chung	76	67	71	67	281	12,554
Yuan Ching-Chi	70	75	65	72	282	7,906
Amandeep Johl	71	71	71	69	282	7,906
Bill Fung	74	69	72	67	282	7,906
Simon Owen	68	74	72	68	282	7,906
Sang-Ho Choi	77	70	67	69	283	6,490
Hsieh Yu-Shu	76	72	69	66	283	6,490
Nico Van Rensburg	70	73	73	67	283	6,490
Dominique Boulet	71	72	68	72	283	6,490
Hsieh Chin-Sheng	73	70	71	69	283	6,490
Don Fardon	72	71	68	73	284	5,700
Jong-Duck Kim	69	74	68	73	284	5,700
Simon Yates	75	71	72	66	284	5,700
Rodrigo Cuello	74	74	68	69	285	5,175
Young-Suk Kwon	74	67	73	71	285	5,175
Aaron Meeks	72	73	74	66	285	5,175
Tony Mills	70	71	74	70	285	5,175
Zaw Moe	73	75	71	67	286	4,725
Nam-Sin Park	78	68	69	71	286	4,725
Brad Andrews	80	69	70	68	287	4,230
Lin Keng-Chi	77	71	71	68	287	4,230
Jin-Kyu Choi	71	71	72	73	287	4,230
Chen Tze-Ming	72	75	73	67	287	4,230
Lin Chie-Hsiang	70	72	72	73	287	4,230

Asian Match Play Championship

Sta. Elena Golf Club, Laguna, Manila, Philippines
Par 36-36–72; 7,114 yards

January 18-21
purse, US$200,000

FIRST ROUND

Lu Wen-Teh defeated Lin Keng-Chi, 1 up
Yeh Chang-Ting defeated Jong-Duck Kim, 1 up
Nico Van Rensburg defeated Jamnian Chitprasong, 5 and 3
Jeev Milkha Singh defeated Scott Taylor, 1 up
John Kernohan defeated Robert Willis, 2 up
Mike Cunning defeated Nam-Sin Park, 6 and 4
Zaw Moe defeated Carlos Espinosa, 2 up
Boonchu Ruangkit defeated Young-Suk Kwon, 4 and 3

(Losers in first round received $7,000 each.)

SECOND ROUND

Yeh defeated Lu, 4 and 2
Singh defeated Van Rensburg, 4 and 3
Cunning defeated Kernohan, 19 holes
Ruangkit defeated Moe, 1 up

(Losers in second round received $11,000 each.)

THIRD ROUND

Singh defeated Yeh, 6 and 5
Ruangkit defeated Cunning, 8 and 7

THIRD-FOURTH PLACE PLAYOFF

Cunning defeated Yeh, 4 and 2

(Cunning received $22,000; Yeh received $15,000.)

FINAL

Singh defeated Ruangkit, 3 and 1

(Singh received $45,000; Ruangkit received $30,000.)

Sabah Masters

Sabah Golf & Country Club, Kota Kinabalu, Malaysia
Par 36-36–72; 6,970 yards

March 14-17
purse, US$200,000

	SCORES				TOTAL	MONEY
Thaworn Wiratchant	72	71	70	69	282	US$32,300
Jeff Wagner	73	66	71	74	284	17,330
Lin Chih-Chen	70	72	74	68	284	17,330
Norikazu Kawakami	74	71	73	68	286	10,000
David Bransdon	73	70	72	72	287	8,000
Mike Cunning	71	75	68	74	288	5,615
Andrew Bonhomme	74	70	74	70	288	5,615
Nam-Sin Park	72	75	72	69	288	5,615
Leith Wastle	76	70	71	71	288	5,615
Chen Liang-Hsi	77	69	70	74	290	3,835
Marciano Pucay	71	74	74	71	290	3,835
George Olaybar	77	71	70	73	291	3,162.50
Nico Van Rensburg	73	72	77	69	291	3,162.50
Gerry Norquist	77	72	72	70	291	3,162.50
Madasamy Murugiah	76	72	72	71	291	3,162.50
Mardan Mamat	76	71	71	74	292	2,700
Tim Elliott	76	73	71	72	292	2,700
Lu Wen-Teh	75	73	74	70	292	2,700
Rohtas Singh	73	74	71	75	293	2,282.86
Eddie Bagtas	73	70	75	75	293	2,282.86
Tsao Chien-Teng	74	71	74	74	293	2,282.86
Hsieh Yu-Shu	75	71	74	73	293	2,282.86
Brad Andrews	75	74	71	73	293	2,282.86
Jeff Senior	75	71	74	73	293	2,282.86
Yeh Chang-Ting	76	71	76	70	293	2,282.86
Jyoti Randhawa	70	75	73	76	294	1,890
Young-Wu Nam	75	73	72	74	294	1,890
Prayad Marksaeng	73	72	75	74	294	1,890
Paul Foley	74	72	75	73	294	1,890
Danny Zarate	73	77	72	72	294	1,890
Makoto Komura	73	74	77	70	294	1,890

Singha-Thai Prasit Bangkok Open

Royal Gems Golf & Country Club, Bangkok, Thailand
Par 36-36–72; 6,964 yards

March 28-31
purse, US$175,000

	SCORES				TOTAL	MONEY
Thammanoon Sriroj	67	71	68	68	274	US$28,262.50
Stephen Scahill	71	67	68	69	275	19,477.50

		SCORES			TOTAL	MONEY
Thaworn Wiratchant	66	71	69	72	278	9,800
Gerry Norquist	72	68	70	68	278	9,800
Preecha Senaprom	68	73	71	67	279	7,000
Wang Ter-Chang	68	70	73	69	280	5,687.50
Jeff Wagner	68	70	71	71	280	5,687.50
Rangsan Raksomjit	68	69	71	73	281	3,747.18
Chen Liang-Hsi	71	71	73	66	281	3,747.18
Tanet Saengsui	71	70	71	69	281	3,747.18
Zaw Moe	72	71	69	69	281	3,747.18
Nobuhito Sato	70	72	68	72	282	2,767.18
Saneh Saengsui	71	69	72	70	282	2,767.18
Nico Van Rensburg	71	70	70	71	282	2,767.18
Dan Cruz	70	72	70	70	282	2,767.18
Marcus Wheelhouse	70	72	73	68	283	2,632.50
Andrew Bonhomme	70	69	73	71	283	2,632.50
Jeff Senior	71	71	70	71	283	2,632.50
Scott Taylor	69	68	73	74	284	1,997.50
Chung Chun-Hsing	71	71	68	74	284	1,997.50
Tim Elliott	70	70	72	72	284	1,997.50
Stuart Bouvier	71	71	73	69	284	1,997.50
Paul Friedlander	76	68	71	69	284	1,997.50
Aaron Meeks	68	69	76	71	284	1,997.50
Mohd. Khalid Yusof	70	71	72	71	284	1,997.50
Hsieh Yu-Shu	74	69	69	73	285	1,653.75
Yeh Chang-Ting	70	71	71	73	285	1,653.75
Rohtas Singh	68	71	73	73	285	1,653.75
Jamnian Chitprasong	69	72	75	69	285	1,653.75
Masayoshi Yamazoe	70	72	74	69	285	1,653.75
Don Fardon	70	72	72	71	285	1,653.75

Canlubang Classic

Canlubang Golf Club, Laguna, Manila, Philippines
Par 36-36–72; 6,737 yards

April 18-21
purse, US$175,000

		SCORES			TOTAL	MONEY
Craig Kamps	74	66	73	68	281	US$28,263
Wook-Soon Kang	71	73	67	70	281	19,478
(Kamps defeated Kang on first extra hole.)						
Simon Owen	69	69	71	73	282	9,800
Rodrigo Cuello	68	70	71	73	282	9,800
David Bransdon	70	67	68	78	283	5,688
Patrick Moore	70	67	74	72	283	5,688
Nico Van Rensburg	71	74	66	72	283	5,688
Mardan Mamat	70	71	70	72	283	5,688
Chawalit Plaphol	74	68	68	74	284	3,405
Sang-Ho Choi	76	71	65	72	284	3,405
Kenny Walker	70	71	71	72	284	3,405
Clay Devers	74	67	72	71	284	3,405
Andrew Bonhomme	75	70	72	68	285	2,633
Robert Huxtable	72	73	71	69	285	2,633
Brad Andrews	74	71	70	70	285	2,633
Young-Wu Nam	71	72	71	71	285	2,633
Stuart Bouvier	70	68	75	73	286	2,310
Yoshiaki Daijo	72	73	72	69	286	2,310
Robert Stephens	70	70	72	75	287	2,051
Young-Suk Kwon	72	69	73	73	287	2,051

	SCORES	TOTAL	MONEY
Wang Ter-Chang	73 69 72 73	287	2,051
Roger Antonio	75 71 72 69	287	2,051
Chul-Sang Cho	73 74 70 70	287	2,051
Aaron Meeks	72 72 69 75	288	1,733
Yurio Akitomi	71 71 71 75	288	1,733
Vivek Bhandari	70 70 74 74	288	1,733
Robert Willis	71 72 73 72	288	1,733
Chung Chun-Hsing	74 74 70 70	288	1,733
Tsao Chien-Teng	72 76 70 70	288	1,733
Kwang-Soo Choi	75 72 70 71	288	1,733

Tournament Players Championship

Tanjong Puteri Golf Resort, Johor Bahru, Malaysia
Par 36-36–72; 7,009 yards

April 25-28
purse, US$175,000

	SCORES	TOTAL	MONEY
Wook-Soon Kang	70 68 67 70	275	US$28,263
Go Higaki	70 72 67 66	275	19,478
(Kang defeated Higaki on first extra hole.)			
John Senden	69 69 72 66	276	9,800
Jeev Milkha Singh	66 72 68 70	276	9,800
Gerry Norquist	69 69 68 71	277	7,000
Simon Owen	70 68 70 70	278	5,250
Clay Devers	70 68 69 71	278	5,250
Robert Willis	72 67 67 72	278	5,250
George Olaybar	73 64 75 67	279	3,405
Scott Taylor	65 70 76 68	279	3,405
Hsieh Yu-Shu	73 67 71 68	279	3,405
John Kernohan	69 69 72 69	279	3,405
Jerry Smith	69 70 72 69	280	2,746
Eric Rustand	71 70 67 72	280	2,746
Craig Kamps	69 72 71 69	281	2,520
Andrew Bonhomme	69 69 71 72	281	2,520
Nico Van Rensburg	73 69 71 69	282	2,188
Thammanoon Sriroj	69 69 73 71	282	2,188
Jun Kikuchi	72 67 72 71	282	2,188
Dan Cruz	68 71 72 71	282	2,188
Joon-Suk Lee	68 71 71 72	282	2,188
Simon Yates	70 72 73 68	283	1,943
Lin Chih-Chen	70 71 72 70	283	1,943
Dominique Boulet	70 70 70 73	283	1,943
Chawalit Plaphol	71 74 72 67	284	1,785
Mohd. Ali Kadir	74 71 71 68	284	1,785
Vivek Bhandari	67 74 71 72	284	1,785
Tom Concon	75 69 74 67	285	1,552
Zhang Lian-Wei	71 74 72 68	285	1,552
Danny Zarate	73 71 70 71	285	1,552
Hiroyuki Tsutsui	72 71 71 71	285	1,552
Joong-Kyung Mo	71 71 70 73	285	1,552
Mardan Mamat	70 68 73 74	285	1,552

Honda City Invitational

Blue Canyon Country Club, Phuket, Thailand
Par 36-36—72; 7,023 yards

May 2-5
purse, US$300,000

	SCORES				TOTAL	MONEY
Steve Elkington	71	73	68	69	281	US$48,450
Felix Casas	70	71	69	72	282	33,390
Peter Fowler	69	73	72	69	283	16,800
Robert Willis	72	73	69	69	283	16,800
Lin Chih-Chen	73	75	71	66	285	10,500
Li Wen-Sheng	70	72	74	69	285	10,500
Andrew Bonhomme	70	70	72	73	285	10,500
Danny Zarate	73	77	69	67	286	6,424
Colin Montgomerie	75	73	68	70	286	6,424
Jeff Senior	73	73	70	70	286	6,424
Jamnian Chitprasong	76	73	65	72	286	6,424
Larry Barber	71	73	73	70	287	4,855
Gerry Norquist	73	72	72	70	287	4,855
Kenny Walker	72	69	75	71	287	4,855
Thammanoon Sriroj	73	74	73	68	288	4,230
Bernhard Langer	72	72	74	70	288	4,230
Mike Cunning	72	72	73	71	288	4,230
Simon Owen	69	76	74	70	289	3,675
Clay Devers	75	70	73	71	289	3,675
Shigemasa Higaki	69	77	70	73	289	3,675
Masayoshi Yamazoe	69	75	71	74	289	3,675
Peter Teravainen	73	76	73	68	290	3,285
Jeev Milkha Singh	69	75	75	71	290	3,285
Nobuhito Sato	77	73	68	72	290	3,285
Scott Taylor	71	72	72	75	290	3,285
Wang Ter-Chang	76	74	70	71	291	2,970
Yurio Akitomi	73	75	71	72	291	2,970
Patrick Moore	71	72	71	77	291	2,970
Nico Van Rensburg	78	72	74	68	292	2,655
Amnuay Homcham	71	73	74	74	292	2,655
Grant Dodd	75	73	69	75	292	2,655
Tsai Chi-Huang	69	75	73	75	292	2,655

Guam Open

Leo Palace Resort, Manenggon Hills, Guam
Par 36-36—72; 6,757 yards

May 9-12
purse, US$175,000

	SCORES				TOTAL	MONEY
Joong-Kyung Mo	77	73	70	67	287	US$28,263
Jeff Wagner	77	72	72	69	290	13,026
Aaron Meeks	74	79	67	70	290	13,026
Don Fardon	74	73	72	71	290	13,026
Chen Liang-Hsi	73	75	76	68	292	6,125
Jerry Smith	73	72	75	72	292	6,125
Tom Concon	81	72	67	72	292	6,125
Chang Tse-Peng	76	75	75	67	293	4,139
Leith Wastle	76	74	70	73	293	4,139
Hsieh Yu-Shu	79	77	69	69	294	3,239
Scott Taylor	72	72	78	72	294	3,239
Jeff Senior	70	73	72	79	294	3,239
Masakazu Noritake	71	75	73	76	295	2,814

	SCORES				TOTAL	MONEY
Yeh Chang-Ting	76	75	72	73	296	2,625
Rafael Ponce	75	74	73	74	296	2,625
John Senden	80	78	73	66	297	2,468
Peter Fowler	75	77	75	71	298	2,310
Yuji Senoguchi	78	72	71	77	298	2,310
Nobuhito Sato	78	80	73	68	299	2,106
Carlos Espinosa	77	76	77	69	299	2,106
Arjun Atwal	75	77	74	73	299	2,106
Beorn Tiger Lee	74	77	73	76	300	1,969
Kenji Iwamoto	77	72	73	78	300	1,969
John Kernohan	82	81	67	71	301	1,838
Ramon Brobio	77	79	72	73	301	1,838
Norio Matsuki	78	75	72	76	301	1,838
Tsai Chi-Huang	78	79	73	72	302	1,706
Marcus Wheelhouse	80	72	74	76	302	1,706
Stuart Bouvier	77	79	78	69	303	1,601
Nozomi Kawahara	74	80	73	76	303	1,601

Volvo China Open

Beijing International Golf Club, Beijing, China
Par 36-36–72; 6,956 yards

May 30-June 2
purse, US$400,000

	SCORES				TOTAL	MONEY
Prayad Marksaeng	70	66	67	66	269	US$72,000
Hsieh Yu-Shu	71	66	70	71	278	42,000
Wook-Soon Kang	71	68	72	68	279	24,400
Christian Pena	73	65	72	69	279	24,400
Nam-Sin Park	73	72	69	66	280	16,200
Yuan Ching-Chi	69	69	70	72	280	16,200
Maan Nasim	72	69	72	68	281	11,560
Thammanoon Sriroj	68	71	74	68	281	11,560
Chou Hong-Nan	73	65	73	70	281	11,560
Jeff Wagner	67	72	71	71	281	11,560
Mike Cunning	68	71	69	73	281	11,560
Nobuhito Sato	66	74	75	67	282	6,575
Chul-Sang Cho	71	73	70	68	282	6,575
Yeh Chang-Ting	68	74	71	69	282	6,575
Robert Willis	70	71	71	70	282	6,575
Edward Fryatt	70	67	74	71	282	6,575
Felix Casas	66	72	72	72	282	6,575
Rodney Pampling	69	70	69	74	282	6,575
Jong-Duck Kim	68	71	68	75	282	6,575
Lu Wen-Teh	73	69	73	68	283	4,400
Aaron Meeks	69	73	73	68	283	4,400
Masayoshi Yamazoe	72	71	71	69	283	4,400
Chawalit Plaphol	72	72	70	69	283	4,400
Gerry Norquist	71	72	67	73	283	4,400
No-Seok Park	72	72	70	70	284	3,590
Thaworn Wiratchant	72	69	72	71	284	3,590
Steve Conran	70	69	74	71	284	3,590
Raul Fretes	74	69	70	71	284	3,590
Chen Liang-Hsi	73	70	72	70	285	2,933
Brad Andrews	71	70	74	70	285	2,933
Christian Chernock	71	73	70	71	285	2,933
Dominique Boulet	72	69	73	71	285	2,933
Paul Friedlander	70	69	74	72	285	2,933
Wu Xiang-Bing	67	76	68	74	285	2,933

Canon Singapore Open

Laguna National Golf and Country Club, Singapore
Par 36-36–72; 7,134 yards

August 8-11
purse, US$500,000

	SCORES				TOTAL	MONEY
John Kernohan	73	70	73	69	285	US$80,750
Craig Kamps	72	69	76	69	286	29,830
Bradley King	74	68	74	70	286	29,830
Peter Lonard	70	70	75	71	286	29,830
Darren Cole	72	71	72	71	286	29,830
Robert Willis	75	67	70	74	286	29,830
Peter Teravainen	69	71	76	71	287	13,750
Yoshiaki Daijo	70	69	72	76	287	13,750
Masayoshi Yamazoe	70	75	72	71	288	10,575
Hsieh Yu-Shu	72	71	71	74	288	10,575
Rafael Ponce	73	72	71	73	289	8,880
Chen Liang-Hsi	70	70	75	74	289	8,880
Go Higaki	75	70	74	71	290	8,040
Takao Nogami	74	73	75	69	291	6,662.50
Young-Suk Kwon	71	77	74	69	291	6,662.50
Mike Cunning	75	70	76	70	291	6,662.50
Zaw Moe	73	73	73	72	291	6,662.50
Prayad Marksaeng	74	75	70	72	291	6,662.50
Udom Duangdecha	73	72	73	73	291	6,662.50
Lin Keng-Chi	71	68	76	76	291	6,662.50
Felix Casas	68	73	72	78	291	6,662.50
Mike Harwood	74	72	76	70	292	5,400
Mardan Mamat	72	75	73	72	292	5,400
Wook-Soon Kang	73	76	69	74	292	5,400
Paul Foley	73	74	71	74	292	5,400
Nico Van Rensburg	71	72	74	75	292	5,400
Chung Chun-Hsing	73	71	78	71	293	4,725
Jeff Wagner	74	72	75	72	293	4,725
Jim Rutledge	74	72	73	74	293	4,725
Simon Owen	72	72	71	78	293	4,725

Kuala Lumpur Open

Staffield Golf Resort, Kuala Lumpur, Malaysia
Par 36-36–72; 7,020 yards

August 15-18
purse, US$200,000

	SCORES				TOTAL	MONEY
Wook-Soon Kang	69	68	68	70	275	US$32,300
Kenny Walker	71	65	70	70	276	17,330
Brad Andrews	70	65	70	71	276	17,330
Shigemasa Higaki	73	69	68	67	277	9,000
Zhang Lian-Wei	68	67	72	70	277	9,000
Simon Owen	74	70	66	68	278	7,000
Eric Rustand	72	71	70	66	279	5,500
Stuart Bouvier	72	67	72	68	279	5,500
Mardan Mamat	69	71	73	67	280	3,891
Jerry Smith	68	71	71	70	280	3,891
Robert Stephens	70	68	70	72	280	3,891
Nobuhito Sato	69	68	68	75	280	3,891
Paul Foley	73	69	73	66	281	2,947.20
Robert Pactolerin	68	72	71	70	281	2,947.20
Jeff Senior	69	72	69	71	281	2,947.20

	SCORES				TOTAL	MONEY
Robert Huxtable	73	68	69	71	281	2,947.20
Paul Friedlander	70	71	67	73	281	2,947.20
Clay Devers	71	74	70	67	282	2,416
Poh Eing-Cheong	72	72	70	68	282	2,416
Jeev Milkha Singh	68	71	73	70	282	2,416
Richard Kaplan	70	71	70	71	282	2,416
Joon-Suk Lee	70	72	67	73	282	2,416
Tim Elliott	69	74	72	68	283	2,100
Hendrik Buhrmann	73	73	67	70	283	2,100
Gaurav Ghei	74	69	69	71	283	2,100
Greg Hanrahan	67	72	71	73	283	2,100
Jeff Wagner	71	67	71	74	283	2,100
Tony Christie	68	74	74	68	284	1,830
Arjun Singh	70	74	70	70	284	1,830
Norio Matsuki	68	70	72	74	284	1,830
Mike Cunning	72	69	68	75	284	1,830

Fila Open

Kwan Ak Golf & Country Club, Seoul, Korea
Par 36-36—72; 7,415 yards

August 22-25
purse, US$300,000

	SCORES				TOTAL	MONEY
Oh-Chul Kwon	71	68	74	66	279	US$48,450
Kyung-Joo Choi	69	73	70	68	280	33,390
Young-Il Kim	73	71	69	68	281	18,600
Sang-Ho Choi	73	67	73	69	282	15,000
Jeev Milkha Singh	69	71	74	70	284	12,000
Greg Hanrahan	71	74	72	68	285	7,938
Robert Willis	71	71	73	70	285	7,938
Nobuhito Sato	71	68	75	71	285	7,938
Wook-Soon Kang	69	73	72	71	285	7,938
Kwang-Soo Choi	68	75	70	72	285	7,938
Joon-Suk Lee	76	68	73	69	286	5,160
Hyung-Soo Lim	72	72	71	71	286	5,160
Yong-Jin Shin	69	74	69	74	286	5,160
Jong-Duck Kim	69	74	75	69	287	4,320
Robert Stephens	73	73	72	69	287	4,320
Wan-Tae Kim	72	69	73	73	287	4,320
Clay Devers	69	70	74	74	287	4,320
Robert Huxtable	70	73	76	69	288	3,527.14
Ali Sher	68	76	76	70	288	3,527.14
John Senden	73	73	72	70	288	3,527.14
Joong-Kyung Mo	76	70	72	70	288	3,527.14
Choong-Hwan Moon	69	77	72	70	288	3,527.14
Simon Owen	69	73	72	74	288	3,527.14
Jong-Il Kim	69	70	74	75	288	3,527.14
Gerry Norquist	72	73	74	70	289	2,925
Jeff Wagner	71	73	74	71	289	2,925
Carlos Espinosa	72	72	72	73	289	2,925
Choon-Bok Moon	71	73	71	74	289	2,925
Yeh Chang-Ting	74	69	72	74	289	2,925
Yong-Nam Yang	72	70	73	74	289	2,925

Philip Morris Asia Cup

Cheung-Gu Country Club, Korea
Par 36-36–72; 6,796 yards

August 29-September 1
purse, US$300,000

	SCORES				TOTAL	MONEY
Jeev Milkha Singh	66	66	65	65	262	US$50,000
Wook-Soon Kang	66	67	65	70	268	30,400
Jong-Duck Kim	66	65	66	73	270	19,000
Yong-Jin Shin	63	72	69	68	272	14,000
Clay Devers	70	66	70	67	273	10,833.33
Sung-Ho Kim	68	69	71	65	273	10,833.33
Jeff Wagner	69	67	72	65	273	10,833.33
Chul-Sang Cho	69	70	67	69	275	8,750
Thammanoon Sriroj	70	70	66	69	275	8,750
Gaurav Ghei	68	72	68	68	276	7,237.50
Gerry Norquist	66	75	66	69	276	7,237.50
Hsieh Yu-Shu	69	66	72	69	276	7,237.50
Kyung-Joo Choi	65	69	71	71	276	7,237.50
Nam-Sin Park	66	68	71	72	277	6,425
Kwang-Soo Choi	69	69	69	70	277	6,425
Lin Chih-Chen	69	68	75	66	278	5,675
Hyeung-Soo Kwak	70	67	73	68	278	5,675
John-Joon Kong	65	73	72	68	278	5,675
Boonchu Ruangkit	69	72	70	67	278	5,675
Nico Van Rensburg	71	67	72	69	279	4,816.66
Robert Willis	71	68	70	70	279	4,816.66
Yoon-Soo Choi	73	68	66	72	279	4,816.66
Kang-Sun Lee	67	71	73	69	280	4,300
Young-Wu Nam	69	71	72	68	280	4,300
Andrew Bonhomme	70	70	72	69	281	3,400
Sang-Ho Choi	69	70	72	70	281	3,400
Young-Suk Kwon	72	66	67	76	281	3,400
Aaron Meeks	72	71	67	71	281	3,400
Jin-Han Lim	67	71	71	72	281	3,400
Carlos Espinosa	69	69	73	70	281	3,400
Joong-Kyung Mo	69	69	72	71	281	3,400

Lexus International

Bangpoo Country Club, Bangkok, Thailand
Par 36-36–72; 7,048 yards

September 26-29
purse, US$200,000

	SCORES				TOTAL	MONEY
Boonchu Ruangkit	75	69	67	65	276	US$32,300
Mike Cunning	69	68	69	70	276	22,260
(Ruangkit defeated Cunning on first extra hole.)						
Felix Casas	72	70	70	65	277	11,200
Nico Van Rensburg	70	68	69	70	277	11,200
Eric Rustand	67	70	72	69	278	6,500
Jerry Smith	70	68	70	70	278	6,500
Hiromichi Namiki	66	70	72	70	278	6,500
Craig Kamps	70	71	66	71	278	6,500
Robert Willis	71	73	69	66	279	4,043.33
Joong-Kyung Mo	68	74	68	69	279	4,043.33
Masayoshi Yamazoe	71	70	67	71	279	4,043.33
Lu Chien-Soon	73	71	65	71	280	3,434
Robert Pactolerin	74	70	68	69	281	3,138

	SCORES				TOTAL	MONEY
Prayad Marksaeng	69	69	72	71	281	3,138
Andrew Bonhomme	67	73	74	68	282	2,704
Marciano Pucay	71	72	69	70	282	2,704
Stuart Bouvier	73	71	68	70	282	2,704
Paul Friedlander	72	68	70	72	282	2,704
Dominique Boulet	71	68	70	73	282	2,704
Gerry Norquist	69	71	75	68	283	2,190
Madasamy Murugiah	72	69	73	69	283	2,190
Fran Quinn	70	71	72	70	283	2,190
John Senden	72	70	71	70	283	2,190
Eddie Bagtas	70	72	70	71	283	2,190
Carlos Espinosa	67	74	71	71	283	2,190
Saneh Saengsui	67	73	72	71	283	2,190
Clay Devers	68	72	72	71	283	2,190
Kenny Walker	72	69	75	68	284	1,773.33
Prateep Kaewvises	70	71	74	69	284	1,773.33
Paul Foley	68	74	71	71	284	1,773.33
Mohd. Ali Kadir	70	74	69	71	284	1,773.33
Robert Stephens	69	69	73	73	284	1,773.33
Chawalit Plaphol	70	69	70	75	284	1,773.33

Yokohama Singapore PGA Championship

Jurong Country Club, Singapore
Par 36-36—72; 6,568 yards

October 3-6
purse, US$200,000

	SCORES				TOTAL	MONEY
Yeh Chang-Ting	66	69	71	69	275	US$32,300
Fran Quinn	71	67	67	71	276	22,260
Nico Van Rensburg	71	68	68	70	277	12,400
Chang Tse-Peng	74	71	67	66	278	8,333.33
Lin Chih-Chen	70	73	67	68	278	8,333.33
Andrew Bonhomme	63	70	70	75	278	8,333.33
Chua Guan-Soon	68	74	72	65	279	5,153.33
Chawalit Plaphol	68	70	72	69	279	5,153.33
Preecha Senaprom	71	67	68	73	279	5,153.33
Arjun Singh	70	72	71	68	281	3,580
Danny Zarate	71	72	68	70	281	3,580
Eric Rustand	71	68	71	71	281	3,580
Shigemasa Higaki	67	72	70	72	281	3,580
Arjun Atwal	66	72	73	71	282	2,820
Carlos Espinosa	69	72	70	71	282	2,820
Felix Casas	69	71	70	72	282	2,820
Mardan Mamat	69	72	67	74	282	2,820
Kyi-Hla Han	70	66	72	74	282	2,820
Rafael Ponce	70	69	73	71	283	2,440
Grant Dodd	72	70	69	72	283	2,440
Masakazu Noritake	70	75	72	67	284	2,100
Kenny Walker	70	73	72	69	284	2,100
Prayad Marksaeng	69	74	72	69	284	2,100
Krishna Singh	72	70	73	69	284	2,100
Jerry Smith	69	72	73	70	284	2,100
Mike Cunning	72	70	71	71	284	2,100
Mohd. Ali Kadir	71	72	70	71	284	2,100
Peter Teravainen	70	71	71	72	284	2,100
Udom Duangdecha	67	73	70	74	284	2,100
Joon-Suk Lee	72	72	71	70	285	1,770
Poh Eing-Cheong	72	69	72	72	285	1,770

Dubai Creek Open

Dubai Creek Golf & Yacht Club, Dubai
Par 36-36–72; 6,781 yards

October 15-18
purse, US$350,000

	SCORES				TOTAL	MONEY
Paul Friedlander	69	70	69	72	280	US$56,525
Craig Kamps	68	75	71	70	284	30,327.50
Kyi-Hla Han	68	72	71	73	284	30,327.50
Robert Stephens	73	70	71	71	285	14,583.33
Young-Woo Nam	72	72	70	71	285	14,583.33
Kyung-Joo Choi	70	69	67	79	285	14,583.33
Jeev Milkha Singh	71	68	75	72	286	9,625
Joong-Kyung Mo	71	73	68	74	286	9,625
Joon-Suk Lee	76	71	69	71	287	7,805
Peter Teravainen	75	71	70	72	288	6,711
Gaurav Ghei	69	74	72	73	288	6,711
Scott Taylor	76	72	69	72	289	5,534.25
Clay Devers	76	69	70	74	289	5,534.25
Jyoti Randhawa	72	72	70	75	289	5,534.25
Gerry Norquist	73	69	72	75	289	5,534.25
Udom Duangdecha	73	72	73	72	290	4,725
Thaworn Wiratchant	70	74	70	76	290	4,725
John Kernohan	71	70	73	76	290	4,725
Robert Willis	76	72	71	72	291	4,048.33
Arjun Atwal	77	67	74	73	291	4,048.33
Kenny Walker	76	72	69	74	291	4,048.33
Thammanoon Sriroj	77	68	71	75	291	4,048.33
Robert Huxtable	74	70	71	76	291	4,048.33
Wan-Tae Kim	69	72	73	77	291	4,048.33
Arjun Singh	76	72	73	71	292	3,517.50
Hendrik Buhrmann	69	74	77	72	292	3,517.50
Jeff Wagner	73	76	69	74	292	3,517.50
Lee Petters	70	73	70	79	292	3,517.50
Jamnian Chitprasong	74	75	74	70	293	3,052
Philip Parkin	73	75	69	76	293	3,052
Shigemasa Higaki	76	70	69	78	293	3,052
Carlos Espinosa	71	72	72	78	293	3,052
Marciano Pucay	73	70	71	79	293	3,052

Merlion Masters

SAFRA Resort & Country Club, Singapore
Par 36-36–72; 6,873 yards

November 7-10
purse, US$175,000

	SCORES				TOTAL	MONEY
Peter Teravainen	70	70	70	68	278	US$28,262.50
Zaw Moe	71	71	72	64	278	19,477.50
(Teravainen defeated Moe on first extra hole.)						
Hendrik Buhrmann	71	70	72	67	280	8,868.67
Leith Wastle	70	70	73	67	280	8,868.67
Nico Van Rensburg	67	75	70	68	280	8,868.67
Jerry Smith	68	71	74	68	281	4,393.96
Richard Kaplan	72	69	71	69	281	4,393.96
Robert Huxtable	72	67	73	69	281	4,393.96
Thaworn Wiratchant	73	72	67	69	281	4,393.96
Samson Gimson	70	71	71	69	281	4,393.96
Robert Pactolerin	72	72	67	70	281	4,393.96

	SCORES				TOTAL	MONEY
Tony Christie	72	71	70	69	282	2,909.38
Lin Chien-Bing	67	71	74	70	282	2,909.38
Kenny Walker	71	70	74	68	283	2,825
Paul Foley	73	70	70	70	283	2,825
Preecha Senaprom	74	72	73	65	284	2,271.50
Tsai Chi-Huang	74	71	70	69	284	2,271.50
Chang Tse-Peng	74	70	71	69	284	2,271.50
Derek Fung	70	72	72	70	284	2,271.50
Lin Chih-Chen	71	74	68	71	284	2,271.50
Arjun Atwal	72	70	76	67	285	1,942.50
Joong-Kyung Mo	73	73	70	69	285	1,942.50
Mardan Mamat	72	74	70	69	285	1,942.50
Lu Wen-Teh	71	75	69	70	285	1,942.50
Jong-Duck Kim	67	71	76	71	285	1,942.50
Craig Kamps	74	71	74	67	286	1,627.50
Go Higaki	71	73	72	70	286	1,627.50
Aaron Meeks	71	69	75	71	286	1,627.50
Soe-Kway Naing	71	73	70	72	286	1,627.50
Chua Guan-Soon	72	71	71	72	286	1,627.50
Marimuthu Ramayah	69	74	70	73	286	1,627.50
Mohd. Ali Kadir	69	69	73	75	286	1,627.50

Pakistan Steel Masters

Karachi Golf Club, Karachi, Pakistan
Par 36-36—72; 7,010 yards

November 14-17
purse, US$225,000

	SCORES				TOTAL	MONEY
Eric Rustand	70	69	65	72	276	US$36,337.50
Thammanoon Sriroj	68	73	70	71	282	25,042.50
Muhammed Sajid	70	72	71	70	283	13,950
Young-Suk Kwon	71	69	72	73	285	10,125
Jerry Smith	70	70	71	74	285	10,125
Nico Van Rensburg	72	76	70	68	286	6,316.88
Shakeel Hussain	70	76	70	70	286	6,316.88
Thaworn Wiratchant	73	74	69	70	286	6,316.88
Paul Foley	70	72	71	73	286	6,316.88
Imdad Hussain	72	70	72	73	287	4,314.38
Young-Wu Nam	68	71	73	75	287	4,314.38
Arjun Singh	72	74	71	71	288	3,557.81
Mardan Mamat	75	71	70	72	288	3,557.81
Tony Christie	71	71	74	72	288	3,557.81
Mark Brown	71	73	69	75	288	3,557.81
Dominique Boulet	72	75	73	69	289	3,037.50
Nadeem Inayaat	69	76	70	74	289	3,037.50
Yoshiaki Daijo	70	71	70	78	289	3,037.50
Waheed Balooch	72	74	76	68	290	2,707.50
Gaurav Ghei	71	73	74	72	290	2,707.50
Zaw Moe	75	69	73	73	290	2,707.50
Ghulam Nabi	74	75	73	69	291	2,463.75
Tony Mills	73	70	76	72	291	2,463.75
Tony Maloney	73	72	74	72	291	2,463.75
Robert Huxtable	70	76	73	72	291	2,463.75
Greg Hanrahan	71	76	74	72	293	2,160
Simon Yates	72	71	76	74	293	2,160
Supacheep Meesom	69	77	72	75	293	2,160
Beorn Tiger Lee	75	70	73	75	293	2,160
Gary Harris	71	73	74	75	293	2,160

Tugu Pratama PGA Championship

Damai Indah Golf and Country Club,
Jakarta, Indonesia
Par 36-36–72

November 28-December 1
purse, US$250,000

	SCORES				TOTAL	MONEY
Thammanoon Sriroj	67	66	74	67	274	US$40,375
Chua Guan-Soon	71	68	69	67	275	27,825
Paul Foley	71	67	70	69	277	15,500
Hendrik Buhrmann	72	67	69	70	278	12,600
George Olaybar	71	62	69	67	279	8,750
Daniel Chopra	67	67	75	70	279	8,750
Yong-Jin Shin	69	68	71	71	279	8,750
Mardan Mamat	72	69	69	70	280	5,141
Charlie Wi	68	70	71	71	280	5,141
Clay Devers	68	71	69	72	280	5,141
Eric Rustand	69	69	68	74	280	5,141
Joon-Suk Lee	68	71	66	75	280	5,141
Nico Van Rensburg	67	72	74	68	281	3,840
Greg Hanrahan	69	70	68	71	281	3,840
Madasamy Murugiah	67	69	72	73	281	3,840
Arjun Atwal	72	68	69	73	282	3,525
Brad Andrews	71	70	73	69	283	3,035.71
Simon Yates	71	73	70	69	283	3,035.71
Danny Zarate	72	73	68	70	283	3,035.71
Jeff Senior	70	70	72	71	283	3,035.71
Mike Cunning	72	69	70	72	283	3,035.71
Kenny Walker	74	66	68	76	283	3,035.71
John Kernohan	68	67	69	79	283	3,035.71
Felix Casas	71	76	68	69	284	2,687.60
Ramon Brobio	73	72	69	70	284	2,687.60
Jeev Milkha Singh	70	68	73	73	284	2,687.60
Jerry Smith	70	71	69	74	284	2,687.60
Prayad Marksaeng	69	70	76	70	285	2,325
Gerry Norquist	73	72	68	72	285	2,325
Carlos Espinosa	70	73	70	72	285	2,325

Royal Classic

Burapha Golf Club, Pattaya, Thailand
Par 36-36–72

December 5-8
purse, US$325,000

	SCORES				TOTAL	MONEY
Richard Kaplan	65	70	69	67	271	US$52,487.50
Nico Van Rensburg	69	66	70	66	271	36,172.50
(Kaplan defeated Van Rensburg on first extra hole.)						
Nam-Sin Park	70	67	69	67	273	20,150
Boonchu Ruangkit	69	68	70	68	275	16,250
Paul Foley	65	70	72	70	277	12,187.50
Danny Zarate	69	68	70	70	277	12,187.50
Robert Huxtable	71	71	68	68	278	9,750
Jerry Smith	67	67	75	70	279	7,686
Kyi-Hla Han	67	72	68	72	279	7,686
Prayad Marksaeng	72	71	73	64	280	6,231.88
Jong-Duck Kim	69	72	70	69	280	6,231.88
Leith Wastle	71	68	72	70	281	5,580.25
John Senden	70	74	68	70	282	4,689.75

	SCORES				TOTAL	MONEY
Kwang-Soo Choi	72	71	69	70	282	4,689.75
Eric Rustand	69	70	73	70	282	4,689.75
Oh-Chul Kwon	69	72	70	71	282	4,689.75
Nobuhito Sato	73	68	69	72	282	4,689.75
Rafael Ponce	68	72	69	73	282	4,689.75
Jin-Han Lim	68	73	70	72	283	3,859.38
Gary Harris	67	70	74	72	283	3,859.38
Hsieh Yu-Shu	70	69	72	72	283	3,859.38
Joong-Kyung Mo	69	66	73	75	283	3,859.38
Mohd. Ali Kadir	71	68	75	70	284	3,363.75
Wook-Soon Kang	70	69	75	70	284	3,363.75
Jeff Wagner	67	72	75	70	284	3,363.75
Kyung-Joo Choi	69	71	74	70	284	3,363.75
Yurio Akitomi	68	72	74	70	284	3,363.75
Wang Ter-Chang	71	71	70	72	284	3,363.75
Udom Duangdecha	72	72	75	67	286	2,876.25
Lin Chih-Chen	71	72	72	71	286	2,876.25
Thammanoon Sriroj	71	69	74	72	286	2,876.25
Samson Gimson	72	67	73	74	286	2,876.25

Omega PGA Championship

Clearwater Bay Golf & Country Club,
Sai Kung, Hong Kong
Par 35-35–70

December 12-15
purse, US$500,000

	SCORES				TOTAL	MONEY
Gerry Norquist	63	66	68	71	268	US$80,750
John Senden	68	72	66	63	269	43,325
Jeff Wagner	66	69	69	65	269	43,325
Daniel Chopra	64	67	72	67	270	20,833.33
Brad Andrews	66	65	69	70	270	20,833.33
Clay Devers	68	66	66	70	270	20,833.33
Mark Mouland	68	66	70	67	271	12,162.50
Lu Wen-Teh	70	68	66	67	271	12,162.50
Joon-Suk Lee	66	69	67	69	271	12,162.50
Rob Willis	67	65	69	70	271	12,162.50
Prayad Marksaeng	68	65	71	68	272	9,175
Jong-Duck Kim	67	70	70	67	274	8,091.67
Richard Kaplan	65	69	69	71	274	8,091.67
Paul Foley	69	65	67	73	274	8,091.67
Mike Cunning	67	65	73	70	275	7,200
Yuan Ching-Chi	66	70	69	70	275	7,200
Hendrik Buhrmann	64	71	72	70	277	6,466.67
Nam-Sin Park	66	72	69	70	277	6,466.67
Wook-Soon Kang	66	72	67	72	277	6,466.67
Chang Tse-Peng	69	67	73	69	278	5,550
Hiromichi Namiki	70	67	72	69	278	5,550
Zhang Lian-Wei	69	69	68	72	278	5,550
Preecha Senaprom	68	67	70	73	278	5,550
Robert Stephens	63	66	76	73	278	5,550
Eric Rustand	67	69	68	74	278	5,550
Dominique Boulet	65	69	70	74	278	5,550
Kenny Walker	68	70	74	68	280	4,800
Mohd. Khalid Yusof	70	67	69	74	280	4,800
Boonchu Ruangkit	71	64	70	75	280	4,800
Jeff Senior	71	70	73	67	281	4,175

	SCORES				TOTAL	MONEY
Wan-Tae Kim	66	70	72	73	281	4,175
Mardan Mamat	68	70	69	74	281	4,175
Rodrigo Cuello	66	66	74	75	281	4,175
Zaw Moe	70	67	68	76	281	4,175
Jeev Milkha Singh	68	66	69	78	281	4,175

Volvo Asian Match Play Championship

Emeralda Golf & Country Club, Jakarta, Indonesia
Par 36-36–72; 7,090 yards

December 20-22
purse, US$200,000

FIRST ROUND

Richard Kaplan defeated Craig Kamps, 6 and 4
Boonchu Ruangkit defeated Paul Friedlander, 1 up
Thaworn Wiratchant defeated Felix Casas, 3 and 2
Nico Van Rensburg defeated Paul Foley, 1 up
Kenny Walker defeated Eric Rustand, 4 and 3
Jin-Kyu Choi defeated Thammanoon Sriroj, 21 holes
Jeff Wagner defeated Oh-Chul Kwon, 5 and 3
John Kernohan defeated Glenn Joyner, 4 and 3

(Each winning player received $3,100; each losing player received $2,025.)

QUARTER-FINALS

Zhang Lian-Wei defeated Jeev Milkha Singh, 4 and 2
Thaworn Wiratchant defeated Maan Nasim, 5 and 3
Prayad Marksaeng defeated John Wither, 2 and 1
Wook-Soon Kang defeated Robert Stephens, 2 and 1

(Each losing player received $6,500.)

SEMI-FINALS

Zhang Lian-Wei defeated Thaworn Wiratchant, 4 and 3
Wook-Soon Kang defeated Prayad Marksaeng, 1 up

(Each losing player received $11,000.)

FINAL

Zhang Lian-Wei defeated Wook-Soon Kang, 1 up

(Zhang received $40,000; Kang received $21,000.)

Australasian Tour

Heineken Classic

The Vines Resort, Perth, Western Australia
Par 36-36–72; 7,001 yards

February 1-4
purse, A$1,000,000

		SCO	RES		TOTAL	MONEY
Ian Woosnam	69	71	65	72	277	A$180,000
Paul McGinley	69	68	69	72	278	84,750
Jean Van de Velde	72	67	67	72	278	84,750
Stewart Ginn	72	72	66	70	280	48,000
Anthony Painter	70	73	72	66	281	36,000
Richard Green	70	74	70	67	281	36,000
John Daly	71	67	67	76	281	36,000
Dean Robertson	70	67	76	69	282	24,600
Bradley Hughes	69	70	74	69	282	24,600
Martyn Roberts	70	72	69	71	282	24,600
Don Fardon	69	72	69	72	282	24,600
Wayne Smith	66	68	75	73	282	24,600
Craig Parry	72	69	74	68	283	16,350
Andrew Sherborne	70	72	70	71	283	16,350
Rodney Pampling	69	69	72	73	283	16,350
Rick Gibson	67	73	69	74	283	16,350
Greg Norman	73	68	75	68	284	10,906.25
Scott Laycock	69	73	73	69	284	10,906.25
Steven Richardson	70	69	75	70	284	10,906.25
Greg Turner	66	74	74	70	284	10,906.25
Darren Clarke	73	71	69	71	284	10,906.25
Matthew Goggin	70	71	72	71	284	10,906.25
Grant Dodd	74	68	69	73	284	10,906.25
Richard Boxall	70	73	67	74	284	10,906.25
David Smail	70	74	72	69	285	7,585.71
Anthony Gilligan	75	69	71	70	285	7,585.71
Paul Devenport	75	66	73	71	285	7,585.71
Adam Hunter	68	72	73	72	285	7,585.71
Eiji Mizoguchi	69	72	71	73	285	7,585.71
Roger Chapman	72	71	69	73	285	7,585.71
Roger Wessels	73	66	70	76	285	7,585.71

Ford South Australian Open

Kooyonga Golf Club, Adelaide, South Australia
Par 37-35–72; 6,717 yards

February 8-11
purse, A$300,000

		SCO	RES		TOTAL	MONEY
Greg Norman	74	72	69	69	284	A$54,000
Jean Louis Guepy	72	71	71	71	285	30,600
Peter O'Malley	73	77	68	68	286	17,325
Glenn Joyner	67	70	77	72	286	17,325
Phillip Tataurangi	77	69	71	70	287	12,000
Craig Parry	73	75	71	70	289	9,700
Greg Chalmers	69	72	74	74	289	9,700

	SCORES				TOTAL	MONEY
Bradley Hughes	67	73	74	75	289	9,700
Lyndsay Stephen	72	75	74	69	290	7,050
Grant Moorhead	74	75	70	71	290	7,050
Doug Dunakey	72	73	72	73	290	7,050
Peter McWhinney	77	69	70	74	290	7,050
Leith Wastle	70	75	73	73	291	5,250
David Iwasaki-Smith	71	75	72	73	291	5,250
David Smail	75	76	72	69	292	3,999
John Clifford	73	73	74	72	292	3,999
Jeff Wagner	72	73	73	74	292	3,999
Shane Tait	72	75	71	74	292	3,999
Wayne Grady	72	76	68	76	292	3,999
Stephen Collins	76	75	73	69	293	3,140
Stephen Leaney	76	69	73	75	293	3,140
Stuart Bouvier	71	76	71	75	293	3,140
Perry Moss	75	72	78	69	294	2,423.33
Gavin Coles	74	74	74	72	294	2,423.33
Peter Fowler	75	72	77	70	294	2,423.33
Jack O'Keefe	78	70	74	72	294	2,423.33
Ben Jackson	76	75	72	71	294	2,423.33
Jeff Senior	73	72	76	73	294	2,423.33
Grant Kenny	76	72	73	73	294	2,423.33
David McKenzie	72	74	73	75	294	2,423.33
Brett Ogle	73	70	74	77	294	2,423.33

Ericsson Australian Masters

Huntingdale Golf Club, Melbourne, Victoria
Par 37-36–73; 6,994 yards

February 15-18
purse, A$750,000

	SCORES				TOTAL	MONEY
Craig Parry	71	66	71	71	279	A$135,000
Bradley Hughes	69	68	71	73	281	76,500
Jeff Wagner	67	74	70	71	282	50,625
Robert Allenby	68	72	72	71	283	31,000
Jon Evans	72	69	71	71	283	31,000
Rick Gibson	70	69	68	76	283	31,000
Darren Cole	72	69	72	71	284	24,000
Peter Lonard	70	69	74	72	285	21,750
*Jarrod Moseley	72	69	77	69	287	
Brett Ogle	70	74	71	72	287	18,500
Peter Senior	72	69	72	74	287	18,500
Jack O'Keefe	72	68	72	75	287	18,500
Wayne Smith	71	72	74	71	288	12,300
John Daly	77	68	70	73	288	12,300
Anthony Painter	70	74	70	74	288	12,300
David Smail	75	70	69	74	288	12,300
Andre Stolz	72	67	74	75	288	12,300
Craig Jones	71	70	71	76	288	12,300
Marcus Wheelhouse	73	71	72	73	289	8,718.75
Matthew Goggin	69	75	70	75	289	8,718.75
Peter Teravainen	71	76	74	69	290	7,500
Elliot Boult	74	71	75	70	290	7,500
Mark Allen	75	73	71	71	290	7,500
Peter O'Malley	75	72	71	72	290	7,500
Jamie Taylor	74	69	74	73	290	7,500
Michael Campbell	71	74	71	74	290	7,500

	SCORES				TOTAL	MONEY
Grant Kenny	73	72	74	72	291	5,175
Lyndsay Stephen	73	72	73	73	291	5,175
Shane Tait	74	72	72	73	291	5,175
Stephen Leaney	76	72	70	73	291	5,175
Peter McWhinney	72	76	69	74	291	5,175
Scott Laycock	67	75	73	76	291	5,175
Katsuyoshi Tomori	74	73	68	76	291	5,175
Clark Dennis	72	72	70	77	291	5,175
Richard Green	67	73	73	78	291	5,175

Canon Challenge

Terrey Hills Golf Club, Sydney, New South Wales
Par 36-36–72; 7,019 yards

February 22-25
purse, A$400,000

	SCORES				TOTAL	MONEY
Peter Senior	70	72	67	69	278	A$72,000
Robert Willis	74	69	71	66	280	29,000
Robert Allenby	72	69	70	69	280	29,000
Bradley King	69	70	67	74	280	29,000
Phillip Tataurangi	72	74	71	64	281	14,400
Peter Lonard	69	72	71	69	281	14,400
Peter O'Malley	70	69	72	70	281	14,400
Craig Jones	69	73	70	70	282	11,200
John Senden	67	70	72	73	282	11,200
Darren Cole	72	71	71	69	283	9,400
Craig Parry	70	70	72	71	283	9,400
Mark Allen	69	77	69	69	284	6,560
Grant Kenny	69	73	73	69	284	6,560
Mike Clayton	69	71	75	69	284	6,560
Stephen Leaney	72	76	69	67	284	6,560
Stephen Scahill	69	74	70	71	284	6,560
Jamie Taylor	72	66	73	73	284	6,560
Bradley Forrester	69	74	71	72	286	4,445
Robert Stephens	69	73	75	69	286	4,445
Steve Alker	75	70	68	73	286	4,445
Scott Laycock	71	71	74	70	286	4,445
Shane Tait	69	74	75	69	287	3,880
Anthony Gilligan	77	67	70	73	287	3,880
Jack O'Keefe	71	75	71	70	287	3,880
Richard Green	73	74	69	71	287	3,880
Toru Suzuki	72	75	77	64	288	3,160
Steve Conran	71	73	74	70	288	3,160
Richard Backwell	72	72	74	70	288	3,160
Terry Price	73	71	75	70	289	2,660
Michael Long	71	69	77	72	289	2,660
Doug Dunakey	71	76	70	72	289	2,660
Taichi Teshima	67	75	70	77	289	2,660

Australian Seniors Championship

Gold Creek Country Club, Canberra, ACT
Par 36-36–72; 7,117 yards

March 7-10
purse, A$50,000

	SCORES				TOTAL	MONEY
Lee Trevino	72	69	70	71	282	A$9,000
Terry Gale	70	72	73	72	287	5,375
Noel Ratcliffe	73	75	71	73	292	3,650
Bill Dunk	77	73	71	74	295	2,625
Michael Wilsdon	76	75	74	72	297	2,300
Randall Vines	77	73	75	73	298	2,125
Bob Shaw	74	75	73	77	299	1,875
Kenichi Tsurumoto	73	69	74	84	300	1,475
Bruce Devlin	75	74	74	77	300	1,475
Peter Headland	72	76	75	78	301	1,400
Elliott Booth	74	74	78	77	303	1,300
Paul Hart	79	75	74	76	304	1,200
Takahiko Hori	80	74	77	75	306	1,100
Hiroshi Tahara	76	78	75	78	307	1,000
Alan Heil	78	75	78	77	308	816.67
Ian Brander	74	79	78	77	308	816.67
George Bell	77	79	78	74	308	816.67
Donald Reiter	79	78	72	80	309	600
Colin Johnston	76	78	76	79	309	600
Walter Godfrey	78	75	77	79	309	600
Paul Connell	80	74	76	79	309	600
Graeme Abbott	79	77	77	76	309	600
Tom Linskey	76	78	78	78	310	462.50
Frank Conallin	78	76	77	79	310	462.50
John Klatt	81	75	77	78	311	425
Neville Bell	76	79	79	77	311	425
Peter Tutt	83	78	76	75	312	387.50
Dennis Ingram	78	76	78	80	312	387.50
Michael Kelly	84	76	75	78	313	365
Peter Lancaster	79	80	77	78	314	342.50
Tom Barber	78	78	81	77	314	342.50

Foodlink Queensland Open

Windaroo Golf & Country Club, Beenleigh, Queensland
Par 36-36–72; 6,851 yards

October 17-20
purse, A$400,000

	SCORES				TOTAL	MONEY
Steve Alker	67	69	67	72	275	A$36,000
Greg Chalmers	65	67	72	72	276	20,400
Stephen Leaney	71	69	70	68	278	11,550
Bradley Hughes	68	70	71	69	278	11,550
Peter Lonard	69	70	67	73	279	8,000
Shane Tait	74	69	64	73	280	6,800
Michael Long	67	70	69	74	280	6,800
Peter Senior	71	71	70	69	281	5,600
Steve Conran	70	69	71	71	281	5,600
*Wayne Perske	70	73	70	70	283	
Paul Gow	72	69	71	71	283	4,466.66
Leith Wastle	69	68	74	72	283	4,466.66
Glenn Joyner	72	69	68	74	283	4,466.66
Matthew Ecob	74	72	67	71	284	3,136

	SCORES				TOTAL	MONEY
Chris Taylor	68	74	70	72	284	3,136
Matthew Goggin	70	71	70	73	284	3,136
Marcus Cain	66	75	68	75	284	3,136
Andrew Bonhomme	68	73	65	78	284	3,136
Anthony Edwards	77	66	73	69	285	2,121.42
Darin Anderson	76	68	69	72	285	2,121.42
Tim Elliott	70	70	72	73	285	2,121.42
Peter Harrington	70	70	71	74	285	2,121.42
David Smail	70	69	72	74	285	2,121.42
Jeff Senior	70	71	70	74	285	2,121.42
Craig Warren	72	70	68	75	285	2,121.42
Justin Cooper	70	73	74	69	286	1,635
David McKenzie	72	72	71	71	286	1,635
Richard Lee	71	73	69	73	286	1,635
Elliot Boult	70	72	70	74	286	1,635
Scott Laycock	73	71	73	70	287	1,360
Rodney Pampling	75	71	69	72	287	1,360
J.J. West	68	72	72	75	287	1,360

Players Championship

Robina Woods Golf Club, Gold Coast, Queensland
Par 35-36–71; 6,647 yards

October 24-27
purse, A$500,000

	SCORES				TOTAL	MONEY
Bradley Hughes	70	65	66	69	270	A$90,000
Peter Lonard	72	73	67	70	282	42,375
Robert Stephens	74	66	69	73	282	42,375
J.J. West	65	70	77	72	284	20,666.66
Peter Teravainen	70	74	68	72	284	20,666.66
Scott Laycock	67	71	72	74	284	20,666.66
Justin Cooper	67	64	79	75	285	16,000
Darren Cole	72	70	74	70	286	14,500
Greg Chalmers	71	71	74	71	287	11,200
Gavin Coles	71	72	72	72	287	11,200
Tony Christie	69	75	71	72	287	11,200
Craig Spence	65	74	74	74	287	11,200
Stephen Leaney	69	72	72	74	287	11,200
David McKenzie	72	72	73	71	288	8,250
Paul Gow	74	69	71	74	288	8,250
Dominique Boulet	69	74	79	67	289	5,987.50
Craig Kamps	73	68	77	71	289	5,987.50
Paul Devenport	72	70	74	73	289	5,987.50
Wayne Grady	73	70	72	74	289	5,987.50
Darren Barnes	72	70	73	74	289	5,987.50
Anthony Painter	70	69	75	75	289	5,987.50
Lyndsay Stephen	73	73	72	72	290	4,591.66
Tony Carolan	76	69	72	73	290	4,591.66
Adam Henwood	72	73	72	73	290	4,591.66
David Smail	74	69	73	74	290	4,591.66
Jean Louis Guepy	71	71	73	75	290	4,591.66
Hendrik Buhrmann	72	72	72	74	290	4,591.66
Rodney Pampling	70	73	74	74	291	3,550
Matthew Goggin	77	69	71	74	291	3,550
Gavin Vearing	71	73	71	76	291	3,550

Alfred Dunhill Asian Masters

Hong Kong Golf Club, Hong Kong
Par 35-36–71; 6,671 yards

October 31-November 3
purse, A$705,412

	SCORES				TOTAL	MONEY
Bernhard Langer	66	67	69	65	267	A$113,923.98
Wook-Soon Kang	64	70	69	66	269	64,556.92
Scott Laycock	66	68	65	71	270	42,721.49
Boonchu Ruangkit	67	67	67	70	271	30,379.72
Stephen Leaney	70	64	68	71	273	25,316.44
Ernie Els	71	69	66	68	274	21,518.97
Scott Taylor	67	69	68	70	274	21,518.97
Greg Chalmers	70	66	71	68	275	17,088.59
Richard Kaplan	72	66	66	71	275	17,088.59
Hsieh Yu-Shu	67	66	68	74	275	17,088.59
Dominique Boulet	71	71	67	67	276	12,183.53
Craig Kamps	71	65	71	69	276	12,183.53
Chris Gray	71	68	66	71	276	12,183.53
Justin Cooper	69	67	68	72	276	12,183.53
Peter McWhinney	71	67	70	69	277	9,156.11
Aaron Meeks	66	68	73	70	277	9,156.11
Shane Tait	69	69	69	70	277	9,156.11
Darren Cole	67	70	69	72	278	7,594.93
Matthew Goggin	70	72	69	68	279	6,748.41
Bradley Hughes	66	71	71	71	279	6,748.41
Wayne Grady	71	65	69	74	279	6,748.41
Paul Devenport	63	70	72	74	279	6,748.41
Thaworn Wiratchant	70	72	68	70	280	6,033.75
Rodney Pampling	69	69	69	73	280	6,033.75
Seve Ballesteros	71	70	66	73	280	6,033.75
Lucien Tinkler	73	69	72	67	281	4,454.11
David Ecob	70	69	72	70	281	4,454.11
Jong-Duck Kim	73	69	72	67	281	4,454.11
Michael Long	70	69	72	70	281	4,454.11
No-Seok Park	66	67	75	73	281	4,454.11
Matthew Ecob	70	72	66	73	281	4,454.11
Young-Wu Nam	71	69	68	73	281	4,454.11
Felix Casas	68	70	69	74	281	4,454.11

MasterCard Australian PGA Championship

New South Wales Golf Club, Sydney, New South Wales
Par 36-36–72; 6,850 yards

November 14-17
purse, A$400,000

	SCORES				TOTAL	MONEY
Phillip Tataurangi	71	72	69	67	279	A$72,000
Rodger Davis	71	73	69	67	280	33,900
Peter Lonard	69	69	72	70	280	33,900
Wayne Smith	66	77	70	69	282	16,533.33
Anthony Painter	71	69	71	71	282	16,533.33
Chris Gray	68	70	66	78	282	16,533.33
Terry Price	72	72	68	71	283	12,800
Jeff Wagner	70	74	70	71	285	11,600
Shane Tait	70	74	75	67	286	9,400
Richard Green	73	71	72	70	286	9,400
Michael Long	70	75	69	72	286	9,400
Paul Gow	76	68	69	73	286	9,400

	SCORES				TOTAL	MONEY
Robin Byrd	68	72	79	68	287	5,808.57
Wayne Grady	72	74	71	70	287	5,808.57
David Howell	73	70	74	70	287	5,808.57
Stuart Appleby	74	73	69	71	287	5,808.57
Steve Alker	71	71	73	72	287	5,808.57
Justin Cooper	70	68	73	76	287	5,808.57
Jerry Kelly	73	66	71	77	287	5,808.57
Byron Clarkson	74	72	75	67	288	4,140
Adam le Vesconte	75	71	71	71	288	4,140
Stuart Bouvier	74	69	73	72	288	4,140
Paul McGinley	71	75	69	73	288	4,140
Darren Clarke	69	77	75	68	289	2,934.54
Ashley Andrews	74	73	73	69	289	2,934.54
Euan Walters	73	72	74	70	289	2,934.54
Stephen Allan	74	70	72	73	289	2,934.54
David Ecob	71	73	74	71	289	2,934.54
Martin Walsh	75	70	72	72	289	2,934.54
Jamie Taylor	69	76	71	73	289	2,934.54
Bryan Roach	66	75	75	73	289	2,934.54
Robert Stephens	72	70	73	74	289	2,934.54
Craig Jones	72	75	68	74	289	2,934.54
Ben Oxley	71	75	68	75	289	2,934.54

Holden Australian Open

Australian Golf Club, Sydney, New South Wales
Par 36-36—72; 7,046 yards

November 21-24
purse, A$1,000,000

	SCORES				TOTAL	MONEY
Greg Norman	67	73	71	69	280	A$180,000
Wayne Grady	70	77	72	69	288	102,000
David Smail	72	73	72	73	290	67,500
Klas Eriksson	68	71	76	76	291	48,000
Peter O'Malley	78	74	71	69	292	34,250
Tiger Woods	79	72	71	70	292	34,250
Paul McGinley	76	74	72	70	292	34,250
Grant Waite	72	75	74	71	292	34,250
Peter Lonard	78	73	74	68	293	26,000
Anthony Painter	72	75	71	75	293	26,000
Jon Evans	75	74	75	70	294	20,000
Terry Price	73	73	76	72	294	20,000
Jean Louis Guepy	72	74	75	73	294	20,000
Richard Green	70	75	77	73	295	14,480
Steve Alker	72	78	73	72	295	14,480
Robert Stephens	69	79	74	73	295	14,480
Lyndsay Stephen	75	73	74	73	295	14,480
Rolf Muntz	71	71	79	74	295	14,480
Peter Senior	77	75	73	71	296	10,178.57
Michael Long	75	75	76	70	296	10,178.57
Adrian Percey	72	79	74	71	296	10,178.57
Martyn Roberts	75	74	75	72	296	10,178.57
Rodger Davis	71	72	79	74	296	10,178.57
David Howell	70	75	76	75	296	10,178.57
Stephen Leaney	73	73	72	78	296	10,178.57
*David Gleeson	73	77	77	70	297	
Richard Boxall	76	77	71	73	297	7,900
Craig Warren	73	73	76	75	297	7,900

	SCORES				TOTAL	MONEY
Robert Allenby	77	74	71	75	297	7,900
*Paul Marshall	72	74	81	71	298	
David Ecob	75	73	78	72	298	6,400
Tim Elliott	74	76	76	72	298	6,400
Michael Campbell	76	76	72	74	298	6,400
John Senden	77	72	75	74	298	6,400
Marcus Cain	78	73	71	76	298	6,400
Justin Cooper	72	74	75	77	298	6,400

Greg Norman's Holden Classic

Royal Melbourne Golf Club, Composite Course,
Sydney, Australia
Par 35-37–72; 6,994 yards

November 28-December 1
purse, A$700,000

	SCORES				TOTAL	MONEY
Peter Senior	69	73	69	70	281	A$126,000
Greg Norman	69	75	69	69	282	71,400
Michael Long	70	71	70	72	283	47,350
Jerry Kelly	70	69	72	74	285	33,600
Robert Stephens	70	75	70	71	286	26,600
Wayne Smith	72	71	70	73	286	26,600
Peter Fowler	70	72	75	70	287	19,775
Grant Waite	74	73	69	71	287	19,775
Shane Tait	72	74	69	72	287	19,775
Jean Van de Velde	73	71	71	72	287	19,775
John Senden	73	72	74	69	288	14,000
Elliot Boult	69	70	78	71	288	14,000
Rolf Muntz	67	72	76	73	288	14,000
Scott Laycock	73	72	75	69	289	11,550
*Jarrod Moseley	74	72	71	72	289	
Richard Green	71	72	72	74	289	11,550
Darren Cole	71	72	77	70	290	9,193.33
Michael Campbell	71	73	73	73	290	9,193.33
Peter Lonard	77	68	72	73	290	9,193.33
Paul Gow	71	73	76	71	291	7,125
Jim Furyk	72	75	73	71	291	7,125
Anthony Edwards	76	71	72	72	291	7,125
Stephen Leaney	68	75	73	75	291	7,125
Lucas Parsons	67	72	77	75	291	7,125
Marcus Wheelhouse	71	73	72	75	291	7,125
Craig Parry	69	73	72	77	291	7,125
Andrew Bonhomme	73	74	75	70	292	4,830
Richard Boxall	75	73	72	72	292	4,830
Wayne Riley	71	73	75	73	292	4,830
Mike Harwood	72	74	73	73	292	4,830
David Diaz	73	74	72	73	292	4,830
Rob Willis	70	78	71	73	292	4,830
Peter O'Malley	73	75	71	73	292	4,830
Bradley Forrester	72	71	75	74	292	4,830
David Bransdon	72	74	72	74	292	4,830

AMP-Air New Zealand Open

Paraparaumu Golf Club, Wellington, New Zealand
Par 35-36–71; 6,473 yards

December 5-8
purse, A$437,484

	SCORES				TOTAL	MONEY
Michael Long	65	71	72	67	275	A$78,747.12
Peter O'Malley	68	75	70	66	279	44,623.36
Shane Tait	66	71	73	70	280	29,530.17
Greg Turner	67	76	72	66	281	17,061.87
Peter Senior	71	68	73	69	281	17,061.87
Paul Barnsley	70	70	70	71	281	17,061.87
Peter Lonard	67	68	72	74	281	17,061.87
Greg Chalmers	70	70	75	67	282	11,812.06
Marcus Wheelhouse	68	74	72	68	282	11,812.06
Mark Allen	64	69	76	73	282	11,812.06
Rodney Pampling	67	71	71	74	283	9,624.64
Peter Fowler	72	72	69	71	284	8,312.19
Grant Waite	69	71	71	73	284	8,312.19
Darren Cole	68	76	73	68	285	6,099.25
Steve Alker	72	72	71	70	285	6,099.25
David Smail	71	71	72	71	285	6,099.25
Andrew Bonhomme	71	72	71	71	285	6,099.25
Stephen Scahill	66	73	73	73	285	6,099.25
Elliot Boult	71	71	70	73	285	6,099.25
Ben Jackson	72	71	76	67	286	4,527.95
Rodger Davis	70	76	72	68	286	4,527.95
Rob Willis	70	75	71	70	286	4,527.95
Daniel Motusenko	70	72	72	72	286	4,527.95
Simon Owen	73	72	73	69	287	3,817.04
Simon Tooman	70	71	74	72	287	3,817.04
Stephen Leaney	70	72	71	74	287	3,817.04
Adam Henwood	71	71	70	75	287	3,817.04
Matthew Lane	71	71	75	71	288	2,974.89
Mark Brown	69	75	73	71	288	2,974.89
Chris Gray	72	70	75	71	288	2,974.89
Neil Kerry	71	73	71	73	288	2,974.89
Anthony Edwards	70	72	72	74	288	2,974.89

Schweppes Coolum Classic

Hyatt Regency Resort, Coolum, Queensland
Par 36-36–72; 6,918 yards

December 12-15
purse, A$200,000

	SCORES				TOTAL	MONEY
Anthony Painter	71	68	68	73	280	A$36,000
Matthew Ecob	75	72	70	65	282	20,400
Mike Clayton	70	73	71	69	283	8,940
Gary Evans	70	74	71	68	283	8,940
Greg Chalmers	71	66	75	71	283	8,940
Michael Long	72	67	71	73	283	8,940
Rodney Pampling	69	67	73	74	283	8,940
Stephen Leaney	72	67	73	72	284	5,400
Peter Lonard	67	71	73	73	284	5,400
Stuart Bouvier	69	73	69	73	284	5,400
Wayne Grady	66	73	72	74	285	4,400
Darren Barnes	75	69	72	70	286	3,416
David Ecob	70	74	72	70	286	3,416

	SCORES				TOTAL	MONEY
Stuart Appleby	68	69	78	71	286	3,416
Martyn Roberts	71	68	76	71	286	3,416
Phillip Chapman	67	74	71	74	286	3,416
Paul Devenport	73	70	73	71	287	2,600
Jeff Woodland	71	76	72	69	288	2,222.50
Chris Gray	73	70	74	71	288	2,222.50
Lucas Parsons	72	73	72	71	288	2,222.50
Craig Jones	70	72	73	73	288	2,222.50
Craig Warren	70	78	70	71	289	1,986.66
Brad King	69	73	74	73	289	1,986.66
Bob Shearer	74	70	71	74	289	1,986.66
Gavin Stratfold	72	75	71	72	290	1,592
Darren Cole	72	71	74	73	290	1,592
Mark Allen	75	69	73	73	290	1,592
Tim Elliott	71	72	73	74	290	1,592
Shane Robinson	70	72	72	76	290	1,592
Richard Green	71	73	74	73	291	1,275
Craig Parry	67	76	73	75	291	1,275
Robin Byrd	73	73	70	75	291	1,275
Elliot Boult	71	69	75	76	291	1,275

African Tours

Philips South African Open

Royal Cape Golf Club, Cape Town, South Africa
Par 36-36–72; 7,050 yards

January 18-21
purse, R750,000

	SCORES				TOTAL	MONEY
Ernie Els	65	70	74	66	275	R118,500
Brenden Pappas	72	68	70	66	276	86,250
Mark McNulty	71	71	68	67	277	51,900
David Howell	66	74	70	69	279	36,826
Retief Goosen	71	72	68	70	281	24,525
Justin Hobday	74	68	72	67	281	24,525
Warren Schutte	72	72	71	66	281	24,525
Kevin Stone	67	70	73	71	281	24,525
Chris Davison	69	71	73	69	282	14,775
Andrew Pitts	72	69	72	69	282	14,775
Michael Scholz	69	70	72	71	282	14,775
Pat Horgan	72	69	70	72	283	11,493.75
James Kingston	73	73	70	67	283	11,493.75
Brad Ott	72	69	70	72	283	11,493.75
Greg Reid	74	72	68	69	283	11,493.75
Michael Archer	71	72	69	72	284	9,425
Trevor Dodds	70	76	68	70	284	9,425
Ian Leggatt	66	76	75	67	284	9,425
Gavin Levenson	73	68	70	73	284	9,425
Schalk van der Merwe	71	73	70	70	284	9,425
Bruce Vaughan	73	71	72	68	284	9,425
Hugh Baiocchi	75	73	71	66	285	7,987.50
Oswald Drawdy	75	71	71	68	285	7,987.50
Ian Hutchings	75	72	70	68	285	7,987.50
Derek James	70	70	74	71	285	7,987.50
Steve Ford	73	73	71	69	286	6,732.14
Paul Friedlander	72	74	72	68	286	6,732.14
Richard Kaplan	70	74	71	71	286	6,732.14
Bobby Lincoln	73	71	69	73	286	6,732.14
Patrick Moore	76	72	66	72	286	6,732.14
Sean Pappas	74	70	73	69	286	6,732.14
Dean van Staden	71	73	71	71	286	6,732.14

San Lameer South African Masters

San Lameer Country Club, Margate, South Africa
Par 36-36–72; 6,104 yards

January 25-28
purse, R750,000

	SCORES				TOTAL	MONEY
Wayne Westner	69	68	70	73	280	R118,500
Patrick Moore	69	72	71	71	283	58,325
Warren Schutte	70	72	70	71	283	58,325
Chris Williams	71	69	69	74	283	58,325
Mike Christie	67	76	69	72	284	28,762.50
Trevor Dodds	71	73	70	70	284	28,762.50
Ian Hutchings	70	73	74	68	285	20,287.50

	SCORES				TOTAL	MONEY
Mark McNulty	68	69	72	76	285	20,287.50
Fran Quinn	73	69	72	72	286	15,450
Greg Reid	72	70	73	71	286	15,450
Brad Ott	72	74	70	71	287	13,425
Ronnie McCann	74	71	72	71	288	12,525
Bobby Lincoln	73	72	73	71	289	10,562.50
Ian Palmer	70	70	71	78	289	10,562.50
Rudi Sailer	68	76	68	77	289	10,562.50
Michael Scholz	71	75	74	69	289	10,562.50
Des Terblanche	69	77	71	72	289	10,562.50
Schalk van der Merwe	72	70	73	74	289	10,562.50
Hugh Baiocchi	69	74	71	76	290	8,487.50
Chris Davison	70	73	70	77	290	8,487.50
Marco Gortana	72	74	68	76	290	8,487.50
Nic Henning	69	76	71	74	290	8,487.50
David Higgins	68	72	74	76	290	8,487.50
John Mashego	72	72	70	76	290	8,487.50
Alex Baillie	71	76	74	70	291	7,087.50
Lee James	71	72	75	73	291	7,087.50
Craig Kamps	71	72	71	77	291	7,087.50
Richard Kaplan	74	72	67	78	291	7,087.50
Hennie Swart	72	73	74	72	291	7,087.50
Steve van Vuuren	76	69	72	74	291	7,087.50

Nashua Wild Coast Sun Challenge

Wild Coast Sun County Club, Port Edward, South Africa
Par 35-35–70; 6,353 yards

February 1-4
purse, R750,000

	SCORES				TOTAL	MONEY
Wayne Westner	66	68	69	65	268	R118,500
Mike Christie	68	66	72	66	272	69,075
Greg Petersen	66	68	70	68	272	69,075
Retief Goosen	71	69	67	66	273	31,450
Ian Palmer	67	69	70	67	273	31,450
Chris Williams	68	70	68	67	273	31,450
Michael Archer	67	67	73	67	274	22,125
Trevor Dodds	67	69	74	65	275	15,693.75
Richard Kaplan	70	67	73	65	275	15,693.75
Mark McNulty	67	69	74	65	275	15,693.75
Bruce Vaughan	67	73	70	65	275	15,693.75
Mike Board	72	71	66	67	276	11,775
Bobby Lincoln	72	69	66	69	276	11,775
Kevin Stone	65	70	71	70	276	11,775
Wayne Bradley	67	70	70	70	277	10,325
Paul Friedlander	67	70	72	68	277	10,325
Sean Pappas	69	64	71	73	277	10,325
Hugh Baiocchi	67	66	80	65	278	9,225
Hendrik Buhrmann	71	70	69	68	278	9,225
Andrew Park	74	68	69	67	278	9,225
Cameron Beckman	72	69	74	64	279	8,325
Steve Ford	68	70	75	66	279	8,325
Lee James	68	68	75	68	279	8,325
Sammy Daniels	72	71	70	67	280	7,425
Ronnie McCann	67	72	73	68	280	7,425
Adam Mednick	70	67	72	71	280	7,425
Robbie Stewart	73	63	75	69	280	7,425

	SCORES				TOTAL	MONEY
Timothy Trodd	69	68	70	73	280	7,425
Rudi Sailer	68	70	71	72	281	6,750
John McHenry	71	71	76	64	282	6,375
Patrick Moore	65	70	75	72	282	6,375
Nico Van Rensburg	67	72	72	71	282	6,375

Dimension Data Pro-Am

Gary Player Country Club, Sun City, South Africa
Player Course: Par 36-36—72; 7,484 yards
Lost City Course: Par 36-36—72; 7,236 yards

February 8-11
purse, R2,400,000

	SCORES				TOTAL	MONEY
Mark McNulty	69	67	73	73	282	R351,204
Brenden Pappas	69	77	64	76	286	172,938
Nick Price	68	72	74	72	286	172,938
Ricky Willison	73	73	72	68	286	172,938
Andre Cruse	73	67	73	74	287	91,908
Mike Christie	71	73	72	72	288	78,810
Trevor Dodds	74	72	72	71	289	56,240
Marco Gortana	71	73	69	76	289	56,240
Patrick Moore	72	73	71	73	289	56,240
Gary Evans	72	72	69	77	290	39,016.50
John McHenry	72	71	73	74	290	39,016.50
Des Smyth	73	73	73	71	290	39,016.50
Marcus Wills	77	67	73	73	290	39,016.50
Thomas Bjorn	72	73	69	77	291	28,884.66
Eamonn Darcy	73	73	72	73	291	28,884.66
Mats Hallberg	71	72	77	71	291	28,884.66
Pat Horgan	72	73	75	71	291	28,884.66
Bobby Lincoln	75	72	73	71	291	28,884.66
Deane Pappas	72	69	78	72	291	28,884.66
Paulo Quirici	73	70	75	73	291	28,884.66
Steve van Vuuren	76	70	75	70	291	28,884.66
Ian Woosnam	74	72	74	71	291	28,884.66
Raymond Burns	75	69	74	74	292	23,043.60
Michael du Toit	74	71	73	74	292	23,043.60
Thomas Gogele	72	70	75	75	292	23,043.60
Sven Struver	68	75	74	75	292	23,043.60
Greg Turner	72	72	75	73	292	23,043.60
Chris Davison	71	74	76	72	293	19,891.20
Justin Hobday	74	69	72	78	293	19,891.20
Ian Hutchings	73	73	72	75	293	19,891.20
David J. Russell	73	71	76	73	293	19,891.20
Des Terblanche	71	74	71	77	293	19,891.20

Alfred Dunhill South African PGA Championship

Houghton Golf Club, Johannesburg, South Africa
Par 36-36—72; 7,035 yards
(First round cancelled — rain.)

February 15-18
purse, R2,000,000

	SCORES			TOTAL	MONEY
Sven Struver	66	73	63	202	R266,725
Ernie Els	64	68	73	205	155,533.50

	SCORES			TOTAL	MONEY
David Feherty	65	69	71	205	155,533.50
Richard Boxall	69	68	69	206	76,375.50
Iain Pyman	69	67	70	206	76,375.50
Brett Liddle	70	66	71	207	54,879.50
Carl Mason	70	67	70	207	54,879.50
Paul Broadhurst	68	74	66	208	29,954.55
Andrew Coltart	69	67	72	208	29,954.55
Trevor Dodds	70	69	69	208	29,954.55
David Howell	66	71	71	208	29,954.55
Tony Johnstone	70	71	67	208	29,954.55
Frank Nobilo	72	66	70	208	29,954.55
Ian Palmer	71	69	68	208	29,954.55
Costantino Rocca	68	72	68	208	29,954.55
Bruce Vaughan	67	70	71	208	29,954.55
Adilson da Silva	70	71	68	209	19,838.66
Chris Davison	67	74	68	209	19,838.66
David Frost	70	68	71	209	19,838.66
Alan McLean	71	67	71	209	19,838.66
Gary Orr	72	64	73	209	19,838.66
Michael Scholz	65	71	73	209	19,838.66
Des Smyth	72	66	71	209	19,838.66
Greg Turner	69	71	69	209	19,838.66
Wayne Westner	70	70	69	209	19,838.66
Cameron Beckman	69	69	72	210	15,192.77
Mike Christie	71	68	71	210	15,192.77
Eamonn Darcy	70	67	73	210	15,192.77
Silvio Grappasonni	70	71	69	210	15,192.77
Bobby Lincoln	73	69	68	210	15,192.77
Mark Mouland	69	70	71	210	15,192.77
Rolf Muntz	71	68	71	210	15,192.77
Ronan Rafferty	74	69	67	210	15,192.77
Oyvind Rojahn	69	70	71	210	15,192.77

FNB Players Championship

Durban Country Club, Durban, South Africa
Par 36-36–72; 6,642 yards

February 22-25
purse, R2,400,000

	SCORES				TOTAL	MONEY
Wayne Westner	66	67	67	70	270	R379,680
Jose Coceres	66	71	69	65	271	276,480
Paul Eales	69	70	65	70	274	166,320
David Feherty	69	70	69	67	275	100,880
Ross McFarlane	67	74	67	67	275	100,880
Costantino Rocca	69	69	71	66	275	100,880
David Frost	72	67	69	68	276	71,040
Andrew Coltart	71	69	67	70	277	55,680
Mark McNulty	72	69	69	67	277	55,680
Ernie Els	69	71	67	71	278	39,800
Ignacio Garrido	69	72	69	68	278	39,800
Tony Johnstone	70	69	70	69	278	39,800
Deane Pappas	72	68	71	67	278	39,800
Andrew Sherborne	70	70	68	70	278	39,800
Carl Suneson	68	72	67	71	278	39,800
Steve Woods	71	70	68	70	279	33,600
Stuart Hendley	73	69	69	69	280	30,600
Ronan Rafferty	72	72	68	68	280	30,600

	SCORES			TOTAL	MONEY
Jay Townsend	71	69 68 72		280	30,600
Bruce Vaughan	68	75 71 66		280	30,600
Paul McGinley	69	74 68 70		281	27,120
Mark Mouland	70	68 69 74		281	27,120
Steven Richardson	72	67 70 72		281	27,120
Paul Broadhurst	70	75 69 68		282	23,840
Christian Cevaer	72	71 70 69		282	23,840
Marco Gortana	71	72 71 68		282	23,840
Gavin Levenson	71	71 71 69		282	23,840
Mike McLean	69	69 74 70		282	23,840
Des Terblanche	69	71 71 71		282	23,840
Gary Orr	67	78 70 68		283	21,120
Warren Schutte	67	73 73 70		283	21,120

Hollard Insurance Royal Swazi Classic

Royal Swazi Sun Golf Club, Mbabane, Swaziland
Par 36-36–72; 6,455 yards

February 29-March 3
purse, R500,000

	SCORES			TOTAL	MONEY
Richard Kaplan	66	67 70 68		271	R79,000
Wayne Westner	69	65 67 70		271	57,500
(Kaplan defeated Westner on first extra hole.)					
Chris Davison	69	66 71 67		272	29,575
Des Terblanche	70	67 68 67		272	29,575
Bradford Vaughan	66	69 69 70		274	20,650
Ian Hutchings	70	72 68 67		277	17,770
Wallie Coetsee	68	69 70 71		278	11,320
Brett Liddle	70	70 69 69		278	11,320
Bobby Lincoln	68	70 70 70		278	11,320
Sean Pappas	68	69 70 71		278	11,320
Clinton Whitelaw	70	69 69 70		278	11,320
Mike Board	71	68 70 70		279	7,093.75
Kyle Coody	68	73 66 72		279	7,093.75
Marco Gortana	69	69 67 74		279	7,093.75
Vaughn Greenwald	72	71 66 70		279	7,093.75
John Nelson	69	71 69 70		279	7,093.75
Andrew Pitts	70	71 69 69		279	7,093.75
Kevin Stone	69	67 72 71		279	7,093.75
Schalk van der Merwe	72	70 68 69		279	7,093.75
Darren Fichardt	71	70 70 69		280	5,716.66
Jimmy Johnson	72	69 71 68		280	5,716.66
Steve van Vuuren	66	70 69 75		280	5,716.66
Paul Friedlander	73	71 69 68		281	5,175
Gavin Levenson	72	70 72 67		281	5,175
Greg Petersen	68	71 72 70		281	5,175
Ashley Roestoff	68	71 72 70		281	5,175
Andre Cruse	71	73 69 69		282	4,510
Adilson da Silva	73	70 67 72		282	4,510
Nic Henning	68	73 69 72		282	4,510
Mawonga Nomwa	67	70 73 72		282	4,510
Steve Woods	68	69 74 71		282	4,510

Hassan II Trophy

Royal Golf Dar-es-Salam, Red Course, Rabat, Morocco
Par 36-37–73; 7,350 yards

November 7-10
purse, US$393,100

	SCORES				TOTAL	MONEY
Ignacio Garrido	69	68	72	70	279	US$90,000
Nick Price	69	71	67	74	281	38,500
Wayne Westner	71	72	69	69	281	38,500
Marc Farry	72	72	71	68	283	23,000
Lennie Clements	72	73	73	68	286	15,750
Mark Roe	72	68	74	72	286	15,750
Craig Stadler	71	71	68	76	286	15,750
Carl Suneson	72	70	72	72	286	15,750
Mathias Gronberg	71	66	79	71	287	11,500
Roger Chapman	71	73	68	75	287	11,500
Sam Torrance	75	69	73	72	289	9,750
Jesper Parnevik	74	74	73	68	289	9,750
Jonathan Kaye	78	71	71	71	291	9,000
Jim Thorpe	70	75	75	75	295	8,500
Mark McCumber	71	75	73	77	296	8,000
Padraig Harrington	75	74	73	75	297	7,500
Michael Campbell	74	74	71	80	299	7,450
Bobby Casper	75	75	72	77	299	7,450
Arnaud Langenaeken	76	76	74	75	301	6,900
Carlo Blanchard	80	76	77	75	308	6,600
Mohamed Makroune	76	77	78	77	308	6,600
Ross McFarlane	77	80	77	76	310	6,300
John Mahaffey	77	77	80	77	311	6,200
Fatmi Moussa	77	75	81	80	313	6,100
Nicolas Taudenhaupt	87	80	77	74	318	6,000
Ismail Bendiab	80	81	81	80	322	5,000
Billy Casper	79	77			DQ	

World Cup of Golf

Erinvale Golf Club, Cape Town, South Africa
Par 36-36–72; 7,002 yards

November 21-24
purse, US$1,500,000

	INDIVIDUAL SCORES				TOTAL
SOUTH AFRICA (547)—$200,000					
Ernie Els	68	72	65	67	272
Wayne Westner	68	72	65	70	275
UNITED STATES (565)—$100,000					
Tom Lehman	73	70	70	70	283
Steve Jones	73	70	70	69	282
SCOTLAND (566)—$62,500					
Andrew Coltart	70	72	72	71	285
Paul Lawrie	69	70	70	72	281
GERMANY (571)—$50,000					
Bernhard Langer	71	68	72	69	280
Alexander Cejka	74	76	68	73	291

	INDIVIDUAL SCORES				TOTAL

FRANCE (572)—$40,000
Jean Van de Velde	73	68	70	75	286
Marc Farry	71	73	74	68	286

DENMARK (579)—$26,250
Thomas Bjorn	67	74	76	68	285
Rene Budde	71	73	76	74	294

ARGENTINA (579)—$26,250
Ricardo Gonzalez	71	73	68	72	284
Jorge Berendt	71	74	72	78	295

ITALY (580)—$14,000
Manuel Zerman	72	78	75	72	297
Costantino Rocca	71	71	72	69	283

NAMIBIA (580)—$14,000
Trevor Dodds	70	70	74	72	286
Schalk van der Merwe	76	76	69	73	294

WALES (580)—$14,000
Ian Woosnam	70	73	67	71	281
Mark Mouland	73	76	76	74	299

ZIMBABWE(581)—$9,250
Mark McNulty	72	71	72	72	287
Tony Johnstone	79	76	72	67	294

CANADA (581)—$9,250
Rick Gibson	70	73	69	75	287
Rick Todd	75	69	77	73	294

SWEDEN (583)—$7,500
Jarmo Sandelin	74	71	73	74	292
Patrik Sjoland	75	69	73	74	291

SPAIN (584)—$5,667
Diego Borrego	71	76	78	72	297
Ignacio Garrido	74	75	70	68	287

AUSTRALIA (584)—$5,667
Bradley Hughes	75	74	77	73	299
Stuart Appleby	74	71	70	70	285

MEXICO (584)—$5,667
Rafael Alarcon	75	68	72	72	287
Cesar Perez	73	75	77	72	297

SWITZERLAND (585)—$4,450
Andre Bossert	70	76	79	72	297
Paolo Quirici	75	70	71	72	288

COLOMBIA (585)—$4,450
Albert Evers	71	74	76	76	297
Rigoberto Velasque	72	73	69	74	288

IRELAND (586)—$4,300
Darren Clarke	71	75	76	64	286
Padraig Harrington	74	75	73	78	300

	INDIVIDUAL SCORES				TOTAL
JAPAN (587)—$4,150					
Tsuneyuki Nakajima	78	75	72	69	294
Katsunori Kuwabara	74	74	74	71	293
CHINA (587)—$4,150					
Cheng Jun	69	75	74	81	299
Zhang Lian-Wei	73	70	78	67	288
ENGLAND (588)—$4,000					
Jim Payne	71	76	74	74	295
Peter Mitchell	78	75	69	71	293
CHINESE TAIPEI (594)—$3,900					
Chen Liang-Hsi	73	76	77	71	297
Chang Tse-Peng	73	76	74	74	297
NEW ZEALAND (597)—$3,800					
Phillip Tataurangi	74	74	73	81	302
Paul Devenport	73	77	73	72	295
SRI LANKA (605)—$3,650					
Tissa Chandradasa	83	79	76	77	315
Nandesena Perera	76	71	74	69	290
JAMAICA (605)—$3,650					
Delroy Cambridge	72	78	73	72	295
Seymour Rose	82	74	79	75	310
PUERTO RICO (606)—$3,500					
Miguel Suarez	74	77	74	76	301
Wilfredo Morales	76	79	78	72	305
PARAGUAY (608)—$3,400					
Ramon Franco	75	74	77	82	308
Nelson Cabrera	74	74	75	77	300
CZECH REPUBLIC (612)—$3,300					
Jiri Janda	71	81	74	75	301
Peter Mruzek	78	76	82	75	311
HONG KONG (623)—$3,200					
Derek Fung	80	75	75	78	308
Man-Kee Tang	74	82	79	80	315
VENEZUELA (627)—$3,100					
Henrique Lavie	78	81	72	79	310
Frederico Sauce	79	83	76	79	317
CHILE (716)—$3,000					
Roy MacKenzie	73	75	99	99	346
Guillermo Encina	73	99	99	99	370

INTERNATIONAL TROPHY

WINNER: Els - 272 - $100,000. RUNNER-UP: Westner - 275 - $50,000. ORDER OF FINISH: Langer - 280 - $25,000; Woosnam, Lawrie - 281 - $12,500 each.

Nedbank Million Dollar Challenge

Gary Player Country Club, Sun City, South Africa
Par 36-36–72; 7,691 yards

November 28-December 1
purse, US$2,510,000

	SCORES				TOTAL	MONEY
Colin Montgomerie	65	71	70	68	274	$1,000,000
Ernie Els	67	70	71	66	274	250,000
(Montgomerie defeated Els on third extra hole.)						
Steve Jones	67	71	67	70	275	187,500
Nick Price	71	67	66	71	275	187,500
Steve Stricker	68	70	69	70	277	137,500
Ian Woosnam	68	69	67	73	277	137,500
Bernhard Langer	69	70	69	71	279	110,000
Mark O'Meara	69	70	70	72	281	100,000
Mark Brooks	68	70	72	73	283	100,000
Tom Lehman	71	71	68	73	283	100,000
Nick Faldo	73	68	69	73	283	100,000
Corey Pavin	68	71	76	69	284	100,000

Zimbabwe Open

Chapman Golf Club, Harare, Zimbabwe
Par 36-36–72

December 5-8
purse, R400,000

	SCORES				TOTAL	MONEY
Mark McNulty	72	61	68	69	270	R63,200
Justin Hobday	71	65	71	67	274	36,840
Nick Price	68	68	70	68	274	36,840
Des Terblanche	65	67	73	72	277	19,640
Clinton Whitelaw	70	70	67	73	280	16,520
*Marc Cayeux	69	69	69	74	281	
Mark Murless	71	67	73	70	281	12,980
Hugh Baiocchi	73	67	71	71	282	8,370
Trevor Dodds	72	69	71	70	282	8,370
Andrew Pitts	69	67	76	70	282	8,370
Steve van Vuuren	65	69	75	73	282	8,370
Brett Liddle	75	65	70	74	284	6,280
Andrew Park	72	67	75	70	284	6,280
Hennie Swart	75	64	73	72	284	6,280
Adilson da Silva	72	69	75	69	285	5,600
Steven Waltman	72	70	72	71	285	5,600
Sammy Daniels	73	68	74	71	286	4,846.66
Sean Farrell	77	68	68	73	286	4,846.66
Dion Fourie	69	73	71	73	286	4,846.66
Nic Henning	73	70	70	73	286	4,846.66
Ian Palmer	73	74	68	71	286	4,846.66
Greg Reid	72	68	71	75	286	4,846.66
Ian Dougan	73	69	74	71	287	4,320
*Glen Cayeux	75	68	70	75	288	
Jannie le Grange	74	72	73	69	288	4,080
Bradford Vaughan	72	71	71	74	288	4,080
Desvonde Botes	72	68	74	75	289	3,560
Chris Davison	76	68	75	70	289	3,560
Darren Fichardt	77	70	71	71	289	3,560
Ian Hutchings	70	74	71	74	289	3,560
Colin Sorour	75	68	74	72	289	3,560
Schalk van der Merwe	67	73	72	77	289	3,560

Zambia Open

Ndola Golf Club, Ndola, Zambia
Par 36-36–72

December 13-15
purse, R150,000

	SCORES			TOTAL	MONEY
Desvonde Botes	68	70	70	208	R22,500
Neil Homann	66	71	72	209	16,500
Glen Hutcheson	70	70	71	211	10,500
Alan Michell	68	71	72	211	10,500
John Nelson	72	70	70	212	7,500
Andrew Pitts	71	69	72	212	7,500
Agriaan van Pletzen	68	70	74	212	7,500
Vaughn Greenwald	72	69	72	213	5,700
Paul Blaikie	71	71	72	214	4,800
Wimpie Botha	74	71	70	215	2,707.50
Don Gammon	73	70	72	215	2,707.50
Nasho Kamungeremu	75	67	73	215	2,707.50
Chad Ransby	74	70	71	215	2,707.50
Chris Williams	72	72	71	215	2,707.50
Robert Wragg	68	75	72	215	2,707.50
Keith Horne	73	73	70	216	1,855
Brett Liddle	71	75	70	216	1,855
Alan McLean	71	75	70	216	1,855
Roy Mugglestone	67	78	71	216	1,855
Steve van Vuuren	69	72	75	216	1,855
Douglas Wood	72	71	73	216	1,855
Derek Crawford	71	74	72	217	1,635
James Berry	71	74	73	218	1,477.50
Wallie Coetsee	76	71	71	218	1,477.50
Johan Krugel	72	75	71	218	1,477.50
Paul Marks	74	73	71	218	1,477.50
Jason O'Connell	72	71	75	218	1,477.50
Hennie Swart	72	77	69	218	1,477.50
Sean Farrell	72	74	73	219	1,267.50
Colin Sorour	75	70	74	219	1,267.50
Steven Waltman	75	71	73	219	1,267.50
Mike Williams	73	74	72	219	1,267.50

Senior Tours

Puerto Rico Senior Tournament of Champions

Hyatt Dorado Beach Resort, East Course,
Dorado Beach, Puerto Rico
Par 36-36–72; 6,740 yards

January 19-21
purse, $800,000

	SCORES			TOTAL	MONEY
John Bland	69	68	70	207	$151,000
Jim Colbert	67	70	71	208	89,000
Raymond Floyd	69	70	70	209	60,833.34
Graham Marsh	68	70	71	209	60,833.33
Lee Trevino	69	69	71	209	60,833.33
Bob Charles	72	68	70	210	36,500
Hale Irwin	71	71	68	210	36,500
Jack Nicklaus	70	72	68	210	36,500
Mike Hill	71	70	70	211	26,166.67
Dave Stockton	69	73	69	211	26,166.67
Bob Murphy	68	70	73	211	26,166.66
J.C. Snead	73	69	70	212	22,000
Jim Albus	73	69	72	214	19,500
George Archer	69	71	74	214	19,500
Simon Hobday	73	69	73	215	17,500
Tony Jacklin	68	70	77	215	17,500
Jim Dent	75	71	70	216	15,500
Jimmy Powell	71	75	70	216	15,500
Walter Morgan	75	72	70	217	14,000
Don Bies	72	74	72	218	13,200
Tom Weiskopf	73	74	72	219	12,400
Tom Wargo	77	72	71	220	11,700
Bruce Devlin	73	76	72	221	11,200

Royal Caribbean Classic

The Links at Key Biscayne, Key Biscayne, Florida
Par 35-36–71; 6,754 yards

February 2-4
purse, $850,000

	SCORES			TOTAL	MONEY
Bob Murphy	69	67	67	203	$127,500
Hale Irwin	65	71	71	207	74,800
Rick Acton	68	67	73	208	61,200
Raymond Floyd	69	68	72	209	45,900
Mike Hill	72	66	71	209	45,900
John Bland	72	69	71	212	28,900
Bob Charles	68	71	73	212	28,900
John Jacobs	72	67	73	212	28,900
Graham Marsh	71	72	69	212	28,900
Jim Dent	70	70	73	213	20,400
Simon Hobday	71	66	76	213	20,400
John Schroeder	71	67	75	213	20,400
Lee Trevino	73	67	74	214	17,000
Bruce Devlin	73	69	73	215	15,300

	SCORES			TOTAL	MONEY
Gary Player	73	71	71	215	15,300
Jimmy Powell	72	67	76	215	15,300
Butch Baird	72	71	73	216	13,175
Rives McBee	70	71	75	216	13,175
Jim Colbert	71	70	76	217	10,901.25
Frank Conner	74	70	73	217	10,901.25
Bruce Crampton	69	73	75	217	10,901.25
Larry Ziegler	75	70	72	217	10,901.25
Jim Albus	71	68	79	218	9,350
Tommy Aaron	75	72	72	219	8,308.75
Homero Blancas	71	69	79	219	8,308.75
John Paul Cain	72	72	75	219	8,308.75
Terry Dill	69	74	76	219	8,308.75
Dale Douglass	76	70	74	220	6,885
Jim Ferree	70	74	76	220	6,885
Walter Morgan	74	72	74	220	6,885
Dick Rhyan	67	72	81	220	6,885
Masaru Amano	73	70	78	221	5,865
Chi Chi Rodriguez	74	71	76	221	5,865
Rocky Thompson	76	71	74	221	5,865
Wally Armstrong	74	73	75	222	4,896
Tony Jacklin	70	74	78	222	4,896
Jerry McGee	76	73	73	222	4,896
J.C. Snead	76	72	74	222	4,896
Tom Wargo	75	72	75	222	4,896
George Archer	77	71	75	223	3,995
Harold Henning	75	70	78	223	3,995
Jack Kiefer	76	69	78	223	3,995
Bob E. Smith	71	73	79	223	3,995
Bruce Summerhays	77	69	77	223	3,995

Greater Naples IntelliNet Challenge

The Classics at Lely Resort, Naples, Florida
Par 36-36—72; 6,805 yards

February 9-11
purse, $600,000

	SCORES			TOTAL	MONEY
Al Geiberger	68	63	71	202	$90,000
Isao Aoki	68	68	67	203	52,800
Simon Hobday	68	67	69	204	43,200
Raymond Floyd	67	67	71	205	32,400
Jimmy Powell	67	68	70	205	32,400
Rick Acton	72	66	68	206	21,600
Jay Sigel	67	73	66	206	21,600
Bobby Stroble	69	68	69	206	21,600
Bob Murphy	70	67	70	207	15,600
Gary Player	69	70	68	207	15,600
Dick Rhyan	71	68	68	207	15,600
Brian Barnes	72	67	69	208	11,850
Jim Dent	66	72	70	208	11,850
Dale Douglass	71	66	71	208	11,850
Graham Marsh	69	70	69	208	11,850
Bob Charles	69	69	71	209	7,652.73
Frank Conner	68	70	71	209	7,652.73
Marion Heck	71	70	68	209	7,652.73
Mike Hill	73	69	67	209	7,652.73
Dick McClean	71	68	70	209	7,652.73

	SCORES			TOTAL	MONEY
Tom Shaw	69	72	68	209	7,652.73
Bruce Summerhays	69	71	69	209	7,652.73
Rocky Thompson	68	73	68	209	7,652.73
Bruce Crampton	66	70	73	209	7,652.72
Jerry McGee	68	67	74	209	7,652.72
DeWitt Weaver	71	66	72	209	7,652.72
Jim Albus	72	70	68	210	4,980
Larry Gilbert	69	71	70	210	4,980
John Jacobs	70	68	72	210	4,980
J.C. Snead	71	68	71	210	4,980
Dave Stockton	68	71	71	210	4,980
John Bland	70	69	72	211	4,050
Bruce Devlin	71	73	67	211	4,050
Bob Irving	70	74	67	211	4,050
Jack Kiefer	68	70	73	211	4,050
Orville Moody	71	72	69	212	3,440
Calvin Peete	73	70	69	212	3,440
Bob E. Smith	68	72	72	212	3,440
Tommy Aaron	67	71	75	213	2,760
Masaru Amano	71	72	70	213	2,760
Bob Dickson	75	66	72	213	2,760
Tony Jacklin	71	73	69	213	2,760
Joe Jimenez	70	72	71	213	2,760
Harry Toscano	70	72	71	213	2,760
Jim Wilkinson	70	72	71	213	2,760
Larry Ziegler	76	71	66	213	2,760

GTE Suncoast Classic

TPC of Tampa Bay, Lutz, Florida
Par 35-36–71; 6,638 yards

February 16-18
purse, $750,000

	SCORES			TOTAL	MONEY
Jack Nicklaus	76	68	67	211	$112,500
J.C. Snead	74	73	65	212	66,000
Bob Murphy	76	68	69	213	54,000
Simon Hobday	74	71	69	214	45,000
Mike McCullough	73	71	71	215	31,000
Calvin Peete	72	72	71	215	31,000
Bob E. Smith	75	70	70	215	31,000
Isao Aoki	73	66	77	216	20,625
Raymond Floyd	80	68	68	216	20,625
Hale Irwin	77	71	68	216	20,625
Dave Stockton	74	71	71	216	20,625
Bob Charles	77	73	67	217	15,750
Bruce Summerhays	74	74	69	217	15,750
Rick Acton	74	71	73	218	12,387.50
George Archer	74	74	70	218	12,387.50
Terry Dill	73	71	74	218	12,387.50
Walter Morgan	76	73	69	218	12,387.50
Jay Sigel	75	72	71	218	12,387.50
Tom Weiskopf	74	72	72	218	12,387.50
John Bland	81	69	69	219	9,037.50
Dale Douglass	76	73	70	219	9,037.50
Al Geiberger	71	73	75	219	9,037.50
Mike Joyce	73	73	73	219	9,037.50
Butch Baird	74	73	73	220	7,331.25

	SCORES			TOTAL	MONEY
Mike Hill	80	71	69	220	7,331.25
Tom Shaw	79	69	72	220	7,331.25
Rocky Thompson	75	75	70	220	7,331.25
Bud Allin	72	79	70	221	5,940
Masaru Amano	77	73	71	221	5,940
Don Bies	75	74	72	221	5,940
Homero Blancas	74	76	71	221	5,940
Bruce Devlin	73	76	72	221	5,940
Tommy Aaron	79	77	66	222	4,725
Jerry McGee	76	70	76	222	4,725
Larry Mowry	76	73	73	222	4,725
Ed Sneed	76	73	73	222	4,725
Lee Trevino	75	73	74	222	4,725
John Paul Cain	86	66	71	223	3,900
Larry Gilbert	78	73	72	223	3,900
Arnold Palmer	75	76	72	223	3,900
Jimmy Powell	73	75	75	223	3,900

American Express Invitational

TPC at Prestancia, Sarasota, Florida
Par 36-36–72; 6,927 yards

February 23-25
purse, $900,000

	SCORES			TOTAL	MONEY
Hale Irwin	66	67	64	197	$135,000
Bob Murphy	69	65	68	202	79,200
Terry Dill	68	68	67	203	59,400
Graham Marsh	66	67	70	203	59,400
Frank Conner	69	65	70	204	39,600
Raymond Floyd	70	67	67	204	39,600
Dick Rhyan	72	65	69	206	27,450
Dave Stockton	65	68	73	206	27,450
Lee Trevino	68	69	69	206	27,450
Tom Weiskopf	68	66	72	206	27,450
John Paul Cain	69	69	69	207	21,600
Isao Aoki	66	68	74	208	17,775
John Bland	69	70	69	208	17,775
Jim Colbert	67	70	71	208	17,775
Mike Hill	67	71	70	208	17,775
Tony Jacklin	68	69	72	209	13,554
John Jacobs	70	70	69	209	13,554
Jay Sigel	68	68	73	209	13,554
Bob E. Smith	69	70	70	209	13,554
Jim Wilkinson	68	72	69	209	13,554
Rick Acton	70	71	69	210	10,500
Homero Blancas	69	70	71	210	10,500
Simon Hobday	73	67	70	210	10,500
George Archer	70	68	73	211	8,415
Bruce Crampton	71	69	71	211	8,415
Jack Kiefer	69	71	71	211	8,415
Walter Morgan	70	70	71	211	8,415
Calvin Peete	72	69	70	211	8,415
Gary Player	71	70	70	211	8,415
Bud Allin	72	72	68	212	6,498
Brian Barnes	69	68	75	212	6,498
Jerry McGee	69	74	69	212	6,498
Jimmy Powell	74	69	69	212	6,498

	SCORES	TOTAL	MONEY
Larry Ziegler	70 69 73	212	6,498
Tommy Aaron	70 68 75	213	4,800
Butch Baird	69 68 76	213	4,800
Miller Barber	68 71 74	213	4,800
Gary Cowan	76 70 67	213	4,800
Jim Dent	72 70 71	213	4,800
Bob Eastwood	69 75 69	213	4,800
Larry Laoretti	70 72 71	213	4,800
Gary Schroeder	68 74 71	213	4,800
John Schroeder	68 67 78	213	4,800

FHP Health Care Classic

Ojai Valley Inn & Country Club, Ojai, California
Par 35-35–70; 6,190 yards

March 1-3
purse, $800,000

	SCORES	TOTAL	MONEY
Walter Morgan	62 71 66	199	$120,000
Gary Player	64 67 68	199	70,400
(Morgan defeated Player on first extra hole.)			
Jack Kiefer	64 68 69	201	57,600
John Schroeder	70 65 67	202	43,200
Dave Stockton	69 67 66	202	43,200
Rick Acton	72 67 64	203	28,800
George Archer	65 71 67	203	28,800
Tom Shaw	66 66 71	203	28,800
Isao Aoki	68 69 67	204	17,942.86
Dale Douglass	68 68 68	204	17,942.86
Bob Eastwood	67 70 67	204	17,942.86
Jerry McGee	68 69 67	204	17,942.86
Jay Sigel	65 71 68	204	17,942.86
Bud Allin	68 68 68	204	17,942.85
Rocky Thompson	68 67 69	204	17,942.85
Jim Colbert	65 72 68	205	13,600
John Bland	69 70 67	206	11,660
Frank Conner	66 73 67	206	11,660
Al Geiberger	72 69 65	206	11,660
Tom Wargo	65 70 71	206	11,660
Butch Baird	72 67 68	207	8,880
Simon Hobday	70 69 68	207	8,880
John Jacobs	69 67 71	207	8,880
Mike McCullough	68 71 68	207	8,880
Jim Wilkinson	71 67 69	207	8,880
Bobby Stroble	70 67 71	208	7,280
Harry Toscano	69 71 68	208	7,280
Walter Zembriski	70 73 65	208	7,280
Masaru Amano	66 72 71	209	6,180
Bob Betley	73 64 72	209	6,180
Bob Brue	73 69 67	209	6,180
Joe Jimenez	67 69 73	209	6,180
Bruce Devlin	75 69 66	210	5,160
Gene Littler	70 69 71	210	5,160
Ben Smith	66 71 73	210	5,160
Bruce Summerhays	73 73 64	210	5,160
Jim Albus	72 70 69	211	4,160
Dick Hendrickson	71 69 71	211	4,160
Tony Jacklin	70 69 72	211	4,160

	SCORES			TOTAL	MONEY
Larry Laoretti	68	66	77	211	4,160
Dick Rhyan	72	69	70	211	4,160
DeWitt Weaver	68	67	76	211	4,160

Senior Slam

Cabo Real Golf Club, Los Cabos, Mexico
Par 36-36–72; 6,945 yards

March 4-5
purse, $500,000

	SCORES		TOTAL	MONEY
Raymond Floyd	75	65	140	$250,000
Jack Nicklaus	72	71	143	125,000
Tom Weiskopf	70	74	144	75,000
J.C. Snead	71	75	146	50,000

Toshiba Senior Classic

Newport Beach Country Club,
Newport Beach, California
Par 36-35–71; 6,516 yards

March 15-17
purse, $1,000,000

	SCORES			TOTAL	MONEY
Jim Colbert	68	65	68	201	$150,000
Bob Eastwood	71	68	64	203	88,000
Hale Irwin	72	67	66	205	72,000
Jack Kiefer	70	69	68	207	54,000
Lee Trevino	68	70	69	207	54,000
Bud Allin	72	67	69	208	34,000
George Archer	70	68	70	208	34,000
Calvin Peete	70	70	68	208	34,000
Rocky Thompson	69	70	69	208	34,000
Bob Charles	71	70	68	209	26,000
Frank Conner	69	72	69	210	18,875
Jim Dent	69	74	67	210	18,875
Al Geiberger	69	70	71	210	18,875
Walter Morgan	70	70	70	210	18,875
Gary Player	71	72	67	210	18,875
John Schroeder	68	71	71	210	18,875
DeWitt Weaver	70	70	70	210	18,875
Larry Ziegler	69	74	67	210	18,875
Isao Aoki	71	71	69	211	12,825
Homero Blancas	68	75	68	211	12,825
Larry Laoretti	69	73	69	211	12,825
Bruce Summerhays	71	73	67	211	12,825
Rick Acton	77	70	65	212	10,500
John Paul Cain	69	71	72	212	10,500
Gene Littler	73	71	68	212	10,500
Larry Gilbert	75	66	72	213	9,100
Tony Jacklin	72	72	69	213	9,100
Dave Stockton	70	71	72	213	9,100
Deane Beman	76	69	69	214	6,654.55
Bruce Crampton	75	71	68	214	6,654.55
Dick Hendrickson	73	70	71	214	6,654.55
Dave Hill	73	71	70	214	6,654.55
Dick Rhyan	74	70	70	214	6,654.55

	SCORES			TOTAL	MONEY
Bob E. Smith	72	73	69	214	6,654.55
Gay Brewer	70	75	69	214	6,654.54
Bob Murphy	68	72	74	214	6,654.54
Jimmy Powell	72	73	69	214	6,654.54
Tom Shaw	72	70	72	214	6,654.54
Jay Sigel	70	74	70	214	6,654.54
Tommy Aaron	72	75	68	215	4,800
Jim Albus	70	72	73	215	4,800
Mike Hill	72	77	66	215	4,800
Bobby Stroble	71	70	74	215	4,800

Liberty Mutual Legends of Golf

PGA West, Stadium Course, La Quinta, California
Par 36-36–72; 6,843 yards

March 22-24
purse, $1,100,000

	SCORES			TOTAL	MONEY (Team)
Lee Trevino/Mike Hill	68	67	63	198	$200,000
Jimmy Powell/Orville Moody	65	66	69	200	73,333.33
Jack Nicklaus/Gary Player	65	69	66	200	73,333.33
Chi Chi Rodriguez/Harold Henning	69	67	64	200	73,333.33
Simon Hobday/George Archer	67	65	69	201	45,000
Jim Colbert/Bob Murphy	71	69	62	202	35,000
Larry Laoretti/Walter Morgan	71	69	63	203	31,500
Gene Littler/Don January	69	67	67	203	31,500
Dave Hill/Bob Wynn	73	64	67	204	26,000
Jay Sigel/Graham Marsh	71	67	66	204	26,000
Bruce Crampton/Ben Smith	70	71	64	205	24,000
Miller Barber/Jim Ferree	70	73	63	206	20,000
Dave Stockton/Al Geiberger	72	65	69	206	20,000
Jim Dent/Dave Eichelberger	73	69	65	207	15,333.33
J.C. Snead/Gibby Gilbert	70	70	67	207	15,333.33
Tony Jacklin/Bob Charles	68	70	69	207	15,333.33
Homero Blancas/Tom Shaw	68	71	69	208	13,000
Arnold Palmer/Tom Wargo	70	70	70	210	11,000
Butch Baird/Larry Mowry	69	73	68	210	11,000
Charles Coody/Dale Douglass	68	71	71	210	11,000
Don Bies/Bruce Devlin	69	73	72	214	8,500
Bud Allin/Bob Lunn	72	72	70	214	8,500
Frank Beard/John Brodie	72	72	72	216	6,500
Joe Jimenez/Charles Sifford	72	73	71	216	6,500
Mike Fetchick/Bob Toski	73	74	71	218	6,000
Gay Brewer/Billy Casper	74	74	70	218	6,000
Calvin Peete/Lee Elder	72	76	72	220	6,000
Mike Souchak/Paul Harney	72	75	73	220	6,000
Ken Still/Lionel Hebert	75	74	76	225	5,000
Don Massengale/Lou Graham	73	73	79	225	5,000
Dow Finsterwald/Tommy Jacobs	75	74	77	226	5,000
Bob Goalby/Billy Maxwell	75	76	75	226	5,000
Mason Rudolph/Johnny Pott	80	78	74	232	5,000

SBC Dominion Seniors

Dominion Country Club, San Antonio, Texas
Par 36-36–72; 6,814 yards

March 29-31
purse, $650,000

	SCORES			TOTAL	MONEY
Tom Weiskopf	69	69	69	207	$97,500
Bob Dickson	70	68	71	209	47,666.67
Gary Player	67	74	68	209	47,666.67
Graham Marsh	69	69	71	209	47,666.66
Tom Shaw	72	74	65	211	31,200
Homero Blancas	74	69	69	212	23,400
Raymond Floyd	66	76	70	212	23,400
Jimmy Powell	69	70	73	212	23,400
Charlie Epps	66	73	74	213	16,900
Jerry McGee	73	72	68	213	16,900
Chi Chi Rodriguez	68	72	73	213	16,900
Bob Betley	72	75	67	214	13,216.67
Tony Jacklin	71	71	72	214	13,216.67
Jay Sigel	70	72	72	214	13,216.66
George Archer	73	69	73	215	11,050
Frank Conner	70	71	74	215	11,050
Bob Eastwood	68	76	71	215	11,050
Charles Coody	72	71	73	216	8,888.75
Gibby Gilbert	70	77	69	216	8,888.75
Ben Smith	71	74	71	216	8,888.75
Lee Trevino	70	71	75	216	8,888.75
Butch Baird	73	74	70	217	5,985.91
Brian Barnes	72	75	70	217	5,985.91
John Bland	70	74	73	217	5,985.91
Jim Dent	69	76	72	217	5,985.91
John Jacobs	71	71	75	217	5,985.91
Joe Jimenez	70	71	76	217	5,985.91
Gene Littler	70	72	75	217	5,985.91
Orville Moody	71	77	69	217	5,985.91
J.C. Snead	72	73	72	217	5,985.91
Dave Stockton	69	74	74	217	5,985.91
Larry Mowry	69	69	79	217	5,985.90
Terry Dill	72	74	72	218	4,290
Bobby Stroble	75	74	69	218	4,290
Tom Wargo	70	74	74	218	4,290
Tommy Aaron	72	72	75	219	3,588
Dick Hendrickson	70	72	77	219	3,588
Don Massengale	72	76	71	219	3,588
Jim Wilkinson	74	75	70	219	3,588
Larry Ziegler	72	73	74	219	3,588

The Tradition

Golf Club at Desert Mountain, Cochise Course,
Scottsdale, Arizona
Par 36-36–72; 6,869 yards

April 4-7
purse, $1,000,000

	SCORES				TOTAL	MONEY
Jack Nicklaus	68	74	65	65	272	$150,000
Hale Irwin	65	76	65	69	275	88,000
Raymond Floyd	67	72	69	73	281	72,000
Bob Murphy	71	70	69	72	282	60,000

	SCORES				TOTAL	MONEY
Al Geiberger	73	71	69	70	283	44,000
Walter Morgan	71	72	72	68	283	44,000
George Archer	72	74	69	69	284	34,000
John Bland	72	76	66	70	284	34,000
Gary Player	70	73	73	69	285	27,000
J.C. Snead	69	69	75	72	285	27,000
Jay Sigel	72	70	71	73	286	24,000
Isao Aoki	69	73	69	76	287	19,200
Butch Baird	68	72	73	74	287	19,200
Dick Hendrickson	70	76	69	72	287	19,200
Chi Chi Rodriguez	72	73	70	72	287	19,200
Tom Weiskopf	72	68	72	75	287	19,200
Jimmy Powell	74	72	71	71	288	15,500
Rocky Thompson	75	76	73	64	288	15,500
Bob Charles	73	75	66	75	289	12,825
Simon Hobday	72	77	70	70	289	12,825
Graham Marsh	72	73	70	74	289	12,825
Dave Stockton	71	77	71	70	289	12,825
Dale Douglass	74	76	70	70	290	10,250
Jack Kiefer	70	76	72	72	290	10,250
Bruce Summerhays	76	76	68	70	290	10,250
DeWitt Weaver	71	69	74	76	290	10,250
Bruce Crampton	74	76	70	71	291	8,500
Larry Gilbert	70	71	75	75	291	8,500
Calvin Peete	73	75	73	70	291	8,500
Kermit Zarley	79	73	69	70	291	8,500
Jim Colbert	66	76	73	77	292	6,750
Frank Conner	72	74	73	73	292	6,750
Charles Coody	76	72	71	73	292	6,750
Bob Dickson	68	73	76	75	292	6,750
Terry Dill	75	72	75	70	292	6,750
John Jacobs	71	78	72	71	292	6,750
John Paul Cain	71	75	76	71	293	5,200
Bob Eastwood	72	77	73	71	293	5,200
Ben Smith	76	74	72	71	293	5,200
Bob E. Smith	72	73	75	73	293	5,200
Lee Trevino	74	78	67	74	293	5,200
Tom Wargo	76	71	69	77	293	5,200

PGA Seniors' Championship

PGA National Golf Club, Palm Beach Gardens, Florida
Par 36-36—72; 6,869 yards

April 18-21
purse, $1,100,000

	SCORES				TOTAL	MONEY
Hale Irwin	66	74	69	71	280	$198,000
Isao Aoki	69	71	71	71	282	105,000
Vicente Fernandez	68	76	67	73	284	75,000
Brian Barnes	72	71	69	75	287	51,666.67
Chi Chi Rodriguez	71	73	71	72	287	51,666.67
Bud Allin	72	67	75	73	287	51,666.66
Larry Gilbert	67	74	74	73	288	32,500
Bob Murphy	74	72	74	68	288	32,500
John Schroeder	69	75	71	73	288	32,500
Tom Weiskopf	72	74	72	70	288	32,500
Chuck Montalbano	71	75	73	70	289	17,500
Walter Morgan	75	74	72	68	289	17,500

	SCORES				TOTAL	MONEY
Jay Sigel	72	74	71	72	289	17,500
Ed Sneed	78	69	71	71	289	17,500
Bob Charles	72	69	72	77	290	14,750
Graham Marsh	71	70	74	75	290	14,750
Tom Wargo	74	73	71	72	290	14,750
Larry Ziegler	72	77	72	69	290	14,750
Raymond Floyd	74	74	73	70	291	13,500
J.C. Snead	72	72	75	73	292	12,750
Rocky Thompson	73	71	74	74	292	12,750
Bob Dickson	71	76	72	74	293	11,500
Jack Nicklaus	77	72	74	70	293	11,500
Lee Trevino	75	76	70	72	293	11,500
Tommy Aaron	69	75	77	73	294	9,500
John Bland	73	73	74	74	294	9,500
Frank Conner	77	72	73	72	294	9,500
Jack Kiefer	71	71	75	77	294	9,500
Mike McCullough	72	77	75	70	294	9,500
Steve Spray	75	76	75	69	295	8,000
Homero Blancas	72	76	70	78	296	6,250
Antonio Garrido	74	76	70	76	296	6,250
Marion Heck	73	74	72	77	296	6,250
John Jacobs	71	76	76	73	296	6,250
Joe Jimenez	73	74	77	72	296	6,250
Gary Player	73	70	79	74	296	6,250
Larry Laoretti	73	77	75	72	297	3,937.50
Bruce Lehnhard	74	76	71	76	297	3,937.50
Bruce Summerhays	70	75	76	76	297	3,937.50
DeWitt Weaver	75	75	76	71	297	3,937.50

Las Vegas Senior Classic

TPC at Summerlin, Las Vegas, Nevada
Par 36-36–72; 6,963 yards

April 26-28
purse, $1,000,000

	SCORES			TOTAL	MONEY
Jim Colbert	63	74	70	207	$150,000
Bob Charles	65	70	72	207	81,000
Dave Stockton	69	70	68	207	81,000
(Colbert defeated Charles on first extra hole and Stockton on fourth extra hole.)					
Hale Irwin	68	68	72	208	60,800
Tommy Aaron	65	70	74	209	44,800
J.C. Snead	68	71	70	209	44,800
Raymond Floyd	69	70	71	210	36,800
Isao Aoki	70	72	69	211	30,900
Jim Dent	69	72	70	211	30,900
Chi Chi Rodriguez	67	75	70	212	27,000
Al Geiberger	68	72	73	213	23,000
Larry Gilbert	69	71	73	213	23,000
Jay Sigel	72	71	70	213	23,000
Walter Morgan	72	72	70	214	20,000
Bob Murphy	72	70	73	215	18,500
Bruce Summerhays	71	73	71	215	18,500
Don Bies	75	70	71	216	14,500
Gibby Gilbert	68	73	75	216	14,500
Jimmy Powell	71	74	71	216	14,500
Ed Sneed	72	71	73	216	14,500
Tom Weiskopf	71	74	71	216	14,500

	SCORES			TOTAL	MONEY
Larry Ziegler	74	69	73	216	14,500
John Bland	69	79	69	217	10,016.67
Larry Laoretti	69	75	73	217	10,016.67
Calvin Peete	70	73	74	217	10,016.67
Lee Trevino	72	73	72	217	10,016.67
Butch Baird	72	71	74	217	10,016.66
Jack Kiefer	67	75	75	217	10,016.66
Bud Allin	70	76	72	218	8,100
John Paul Cain	72	76	70	218	8,100
John Schroeder	74	69	75	218	8,100
Charles Coody	78	73	68	219	6,950
Bruce Crampton	69	76	74	219	6,950
DeWitt Weaver	72	76	71	219	6,950
Kermit Zarley	67	75	77	219	6,950
Tony Jacklin	72	76	72	220	5,825
Graham Marsh	72	73	75	220	5,825
Tom Shaw	70	73	77	220	5,825
Rocky Thompson	68	82	70	220	5,825
Harold Henning	75	75	71	221	5,300

PaineWebber Invitational

TPC at Piper Glen, Charlotte, North Carolina
Par 36-36–72; 6,774 yards

May 3-5
purse, $800,000

	SCORES			TOTAL	MONEY
Graham Marsh	66	71	69	206	$120,000
Brian Barnes	66	74	67	207	64,000
Tom Wargo	68	73	70	207	64,000
Jack Kiefer	70	68	70	208	48,000
Larry Gilbert	67	70	72	209	35,200
Walter Morgan	70	70	69	209	35,200
Bob Murphy	74	67	69	210	27,200
Jimmy Powell	70	70	70	210	27,200
J.C. Snead	71	70	70	211	22,400
Isao Aoki	70	71	71	212	20,000
Vicente Fernandez	72	71	69	212	20,000
Don Bies	72	72	69	213	14,933.34
Frank Conner	71	73	69	213	14,933.34
John Paul Cain	70	72	71	213	14,933.33
Larry Laoretti	71	68	74	213	14,933.33
Dick Rhyan	70	71	72	213	14,933.33
Rocky Thompson	68	72	73	213	14,933.33
Homero Blancas	70	71	73	214	10,608
Dick Hendrickson	71	67	76	214	10,608
John Jacobs	68	72	74	214	10,608
Bruce Summerhays	72	70	72	214	10,608
Kermit Zarley	71	71	72	214	10,608
Miller Barber	77	68	70	215	8,200
John Bland	73	70	72	215	8,200
Jim Dent	70	74	71	215	8,200
Gibby Gilbert	73	69	73	215	8,200
Bob Betley	71	71	74	216	6,960
Arnold Palmer	70	70	76	216	6,960
Chi Chi Rodriguez	70	73	73	216	6,960
Butch Baird	70	74	73	217	5,900
Jim Colbert	72	73	72	217	5,900

	SCORES			TOTAL	MONEY
Tom Shaw	77	72	68	217	5,900
Bobby Stroble	71	72	74	217	5,900
Terry Dill	74	74	70	218	4,760
Mike McCullough	76	72	70	218	4,760
Jerry McGee	74	74	70	218	4,760
Chuck Montalbano	75	73	70	218	4,760
Larry Mowry	73	75	70	218	4,760
Larry Ziegler	76	71	71	218	4,760
Bob Dickson	71	75	73	219	3,920
Charlie Epps	71	78	70	219	3,920
Ben Smith	76	72	71	219	3,920
Bob E. Smith	75	71	73	219	3,920

Nationwide Championship

The Golf Club of Georgia, Alpharetta, Georgia
Par 36-36–72; 6,777 yards

May 10-12
purse, $1,200,000

	SCORES			TOTAL	MONEY
Jim Colbert	71	66	69	206	$180,000
Isao Aoki	71	68	70	209	105,600
Hale Irwin	69	73	68	210	86,400
John Bland	69	73	69	211	59,200
Bob Charles	65	71	75	211	59,200
Harold Henning	70	69	72	211	59,200
Don Bies	68	72	72	212	36,600
Bruce Crampton	68	68	72	212	36,600
Bob Eastwood	71	71	70	212	36,600
Bob Murphy	68	70	74	212	36,600
Bob Dickson	71	70	72	213	26,400
Jay Sigel	69	72	72	213	26,400
Tom Wargo	70	75	68	213	26,400
Brian Barnes	74	71	69	214	22,200
Chi Chi Rodriguez	73	71	70	214	22,200
Bud Allin	73	70	72	215	18,072
Larry Gilbert	69	71	75	215	18,072
Graham Marsh	68	71	76	215	18,072
Walter Zembriski	72	74	69	215	18,072
Larry Ziegler	71	72	72	215	18,072
Terry Dill	72	69	75	216	13,000
Dave Eichelberger	71	73	72	216	13,000
Walter Morgan	71	73	72	216	13,000
Dick Rhyan	73	71	72	216	13,000
J.C. Snead	72	73	71	216	13,000
Bobby Stroble	69	68	79	216	13,000
Tom Shaw	73	73	71	217	8,749.10
Tommy Aaron	71	71	75	217	8,749.09
Gay Brewer	74	72	71	217	8,749.09
Frank Conner	70	74	73	217	8,749.09
Dale Douglass	70	71	76	217	8,749.09
Simon Hobday	70	71	76	217	8,749.09
John Jacobs	68	73	76	217	8,749.09
Bob E. Smith	73	71	73	217	8,749.09
Dave Stockton	70	75	72	217	8,749.09
Rocky Thompson	71	74	72	217	8,749.09
Tom Weiskopf	72	69	76	217	8,749.09
Jimmy Blanks	71	73	74	218	6,120

	SCORES			TOTAL	MONEY
Al Geiberger	73	72	73	218	6,120
Jerry McGee	69	78	71	218	6,120
Orville Moody	74	72	72	218	6,120
Jimmy Powell	71	75	72	218	6,120

Cadillac NFL Golf Classic

Upper Montclair Country Club, Clifton, New Jersey
Par 36-36–72; 6,774 yards

May 17-19
purse, $950,000

	SCORES			TOTAL	MONEY
Bob Murphy	62	71	69	202	$142,500
Jay Sigel	69	64	71	204	83,600
Tommy Aaron	67	69	70	206	68,400
Masaru Amano	70	69	69	208	43,700
Larry Gilbert	71	70	67	208	43,700
Dave Stockton	72	62	74	208	43,700
Bobby Stroble	73	64	71	208	43,700
Tom Wargo	68	71	71	210	30,400
Vicente Fernandez	73	67	71	211	24,700
Walter Morgan	72	73	66	211	24,700
Lee Trevino	67	72	72	211	24,700
Kermit Zarley	73	73	66	212	17,733.34
Larry Ziegler	73	72	67	212	17,733.34
Jim Colbert	73	67	72	212	17,733.33
Bruce Crampton	72	70	70	212	17,733.33
Raymond Floyd	70	72	70	212	17,733.33
Jack Kiefer	68	72	72	212	17,733.33
J.C. Snead	75	69	69	213	14,250
John Bland	75	69	70	214	12,571.67
Larry Mowry	70	73	71	214	12,571.67
Simon Hobday	71	70	73	214	12,571.66
Dick Rhyan	75	68	72	215	10,481.67
Ben Smith	72	72	71	215	10,481.67
Bob Charles	72	71	72	215	10,481.66
Rick Acton	77	67	72	216	8,098.75
Butch Baird	73	74	69	216	8,098.75
Deane Beman	76	72	68	216	8,098.75
Frank Conner	73	76	67	216	8,098.75
Bob Eastwood	72	71	73	216	8,098.75
Jimmy Powell	71	73	72	216	8,098.75
John Schroeder	76	67	73	216	8,098.75
DeWitt Weaver	74	70	72	216	8,098.75
Jim Dent	70	71	76	217	5,985
Bob Dickson	70	73	74	217	5,985
Dale Douglass	74	71	72	217	5,985
John Jacobs	74	67	76	217	5,985
Bob E. Smith	73	73	71	217	5,985
Billy Casper	76	72	70	218	5,035
Robert Landers	76	70	72	218	5,035
Bruce Summerhays	73	75	70	218	5,035

BellSouth Senior Classic at Opryland

Springhouse Golf Club, Nashville, Tennessee
Par 36-36—72; 6,783 yards

May 24-26
purse, $1,200,000

	SCORES			TOTAL	MONEY
Isao Aoki	64	68	70	202	$180,000
Graham Marsh	68	68	67	203	96,000
Jay Sigel	66	69	68	203	96,000
Bruce Summerhays	69	70	65	204	72,000
Simon Hobday	68	67	70	205	49,600
Hale Irwin	67	66	72	205	49,600
Dick Rhyan	66	71	68	205	49,600
John Jacobs	68	66	72	206	38,400
Bob Murphy	69	66	72	207	33,600
Bud Allin	70	70	68	208	28,800
Dave Stockton	71	69	68	208	28,800
Lee Trevino	67	68	73	208	28,800
John Schroeder	71	70	68	209	23,400
Bob E. Smith	69	73	67	209	23,400
Brian Barnes	73	69	68	210	17,106.67
John Bland	71	67	72	210	17,106.67
Jim Dent	73	68	69	210	17,106.67
Larry Laoretti	70	73	67	210	17,106.67
Jerry McGee	68	71	71	210	17,106.67
Robert Zimmerman	70	70	70	210	17,106.67
Gary Player	68	67	75	210	17,106.66
Tom Wargo	67	72	71	210	17,106.66
Kermit Zarley	68	72	70	210	17,106.66
Miller Barber	68	70	73	211	11,730
Bob Eastwood	68	70	73	211	11,730
Mike Joyce	70	73	68	211	11,730
Rocky Thompson	72	68	71	211	11,730
John Paul Cain	72	70	70	212	9,504
Bob Dickson	69	68	75	212	9,504
Tony Jacklin	69	71	72	212	9,504
Walter Morgan	71	71	70	212	9,504
Calvin Peete	68	71	73	212	9,504
Raymond Floyd	69	71	73	213	7,560
Al Geiberger	73	70	70	213	7,560
Larry Mowry	72	71	70	213	7,560
DeWitt Weaver	72	70	71	213	7,560
Walter Zembriski	71	68	74	213	7,560
Rick Acton	71	72	71	214	6,120
Butch Baird	69	71	74	214	6,120
Homero Blancas	74	71	69	214	6,120
Mike Hill	73	70	71	214	6,120
Orville Moody	72	69	73	214	6,120

Bruno's Memorial Classic

Greystone Golf Club, Birmingham, Alabama
Par 36-36—72; 7,012 yards

May 31-June 2
purse, $1,050,000

	SCORES			TOTAL	MONEY
John Bland	67	70	71	208	$157,500
John Paul Cain	69	70	69	208	84,000
Kermit Zarley	72	68	68	208	84,000

(Brand defeated Zarley on second extra hole and Cain on third extra hole.)

	SCORES			TOTAL	MONEY
Isao Aoki	70	69	70	209	63,000
Hale Irwin	72	70	69	211	46,200
Graham Marsh	70	69	72	211	46,200
J.C. Snead	69	74	69	212	37,500
Raymond Floyd	73	69	71	213	28,875
Bob Murphy	69	73	71	213	28,875
Calvin Peete	77	67	69	213	28,875
Bruce Summerhays	67	69	77	213	28,875
Tommy Aaron	72	72	70	214	17,503.50
Jim Colbert	71	72	71	214	17,503.50
Al Geiberger	70	72	72	214	17,503.50
John Jacobs	72	69	73	214	17,503.50
Jack Kiefer	71	72	71	214	17,503.50
John Schroeder	74	70	70	214	17,503.50
Bob E. Smith	69	73	72	214	17,503.50
Dave Stockton	71	73	70	214	17,503.50
DeWitt Weaver	73	71	70	214	17,503.50
Tom Weiskopf	75	71	68	214	17,503.50
Miller Barber	72	70	73	215	11,046
Bob Charles	74	72	69	215	11,046
Tony Jacklin	72	70	73	215	11,046
Tom Wargo	70	74	71	215	11,046
Larry Ziegler	72	75	68	215	11,046
Don Bies	72	73	71	216	8,925
Larry Laoretti	71	73	72	216	8,925
Tom Shaw	73	70	73	216	8,925
Rocky Thompson	70	73	73	216	8,925
Jay Sigel	73	72	72	217	7,717.50
Lee Trevino	74	72	71	217	7,717.50
Butch Baird	76	73	69	218	6,772.50
Jim Dent	74	76	68	218	6,772.50
Dale Douglass	69	74	75	218	6,772.50
Dave Eichelberger	71	75	72	218	6,772.50
Rick Acton	75	73	71	219	5,145
Bruce Devlin	73	73	73	219	5,145
Gibby Gilbert	71	76	72	219	5,145
Larry Gilbert	76	71	72	219	5,145
Arnold Palmer	75	74	70	219	5,145
Gary Player	76	71	72	219	5,145
Jimmy Powell	76	68	75	219	5,145
Bobby Stroble	73	75	71	219	5,145
Bob Wynn	70	71	78	219	5,145

Pittsburgh Senior Classic

Quicksilver Golf Club, Midway, Pennsylvania
Par 36-36–72; 6,896 yards

June 7-9
purse, $1,100,000

	SCORES			TOTAL	MONEY
Tom Weiskopf	68	67	70	205	$165,000
Brian Barnes	70	72	66	208	88,000
J.C. Snead	70	71	67	208	88,000
Bob Eastwood	69	69	71	209	66,000
Hale Irwin	71	68	72	211	52,800
Jim Dent	73	71	68	212	41,800
Dave Eichelberger	70	69	73	212	41,800
Isao Aoki	72	72	70	214	29,040

	SCORES			TOTAL	MONEY
John Paul Cain	73	68	73	214	29,040
Frank Conner	74	70	70	214	29,040
Larry Laoretti	74	68	72	214	29,040
Dave Stockton	73	71	70	214	29,040
Graham Marsh	74	67	74	215	20,900
Jay Sigel	75	70	70	215	20,900
Ben Smith	74	69	72	215	20,900
Rocky Thompson	73	69	74	216	17,600
DeWitt Weaver	71	73	72	216	17,600
Kermit Zarley	72	68	76	216	17,600
Bruce Crampton	72	72	73	217	13,346.67
Terry Dill	72	75	70	217	13,346.67
Joe Jimenez	73	70	74	217	13,346.67
Chi Chi Rodriguez	74	74	69	217	13,346.67
Vicente Fernandez	72	69	76	217	13,346.66
Arnold Palmer	69	74	74	217	13,346.66
Jim Colbert	77	71	70	218	9,585.72
Dick Rhyan	73	74	71	218	9,585.72
John Schroeder	75	74	69	218	9,585.72
Bob Carson	74	71	73	218	9,585.71
Jerry McGee	73	70	75	218	9,585.71
Bruce Summerhays	73	72	73	218	9,585.71
Tom Wargo	72	72	74	218	9,585.71
Bunky Henry	72	77	70	219	7,590
Gene Littler	73	71	75	219	7,590
Gary Player	73	69	77	219	7,590
Tony Jacklin	71	74	75	220	6,765
Jim Wilkinson	74	70	76	220	6,765
Bud Allin	79	70	72	221	6,050
Tom Shaw	74	74	73	221	6,050
Tom Ulozas	77	71	73	221	6,050
Don Bies	72	72	78	222	5,390
Jack Kiefer	74	72	76	222	5,390
Bobby Mitchell	76	73	73	222	5,390

du Maurier Champions

Hamilton Golf & Country Club, Ancaster, Ontario
Par 35-35–70; 6,667 yards

June 13-16
purse, $1,100,000

	SCORES				TOTAL	MONEY
Charles Coody	69	70	67	65	271	$165,000
Larry Mowry	66	67	69	70	272	96,800
Don Bies	68	67	69	69	273	66,000
John Bland	68	65	72	68	273	66,000
Jack Kiefer	69	66	69	69	273	66,000
Bob Dickson	67	69	70	68	274	41,800
Jimmy Powell	73	67	67	67	274	41,800
Kermit Zarley	70	66	67	72	275	35,200
Bob Charles	70	68	69	69	276	29,700
Lee Trevino	70	68	66	72	276	29,700
Tony Jacklin	68	70	68	71	277	26,400
Frank Conner	72	68	69	69	278	22,366.67
Graham Marsh	68	70	73	67	278	22,366.67
Jim Colbert	69	67	72	70	278	22,366.66
Larry Gilbert	71	73	65	70	279	18,150
Larry Laoretti	73	69	67	70	279	18,150

	SCORES				TOTAL	MONEY
Walter Morgan	71	70	68	70	279	18,150
Tom Wargo	67	68	72	72	279	18,150
Dale Douglass	68	75	68	69	280	13,706
John Jacobs	69	71	71	69	280	13,706
Mike McCullough	68	72	71	69	280	13,706
Bob E. Smith	73	70	70	67	280	13,706
Ed Sneed	69	74	67	70	280	13,706
Jim Albus	68	72	72	69	281	11,000
Butch Baird	68	73	72	68	281	11,000
Bobby Stroble	69	73	68	71	281	11,000
Tommy Aaron	69	69	74	70	282	9,350
John Paul Cain	68	74	65	75	282	9,350
David Graham	72	70	70	70	282	9,350
Calvin Peete	68	69	70	75	282	9,350
Gary Player	69	68	71	75	283	7,920
Greg Powers	71	71	70	71	283	7,920
Bruce Summerhays	75	72	68	68	283	7,920
Dick Hendrickson	74	70	69	71	284	6,930
Robert Landers	68	73	70	73	284	6,930
Steven Veriato	68	71	73	72	284	6,930
Rick Acton	69	66	74	76	285	5,940
Bud Allin	69	76	74	66	285	5,940
Bruce Crampton	71	69	71	74	285	5,940
Dick Rhyan	73	68	71	73	285	5,940

Bell Atlantic Classic

Chester Valley Golf Club, Malvern, Pennsylvania
Par 35-35–70; 6,777 yards

June 21-23
purse, $900,000

	SCORES			TOTAL	MONEY
Dale Douglass	69	69	68	206	$135,000
John Schroeder	68	67	71	206	72,000
Tom Wargo	67	69	70	206	72,000
(Douglass defeated Schroeder and Wargo on third extra hole.)					
Jim Colbert	69	70	69	208	48,600
Walter Morgan	69	70	69	208	48,600
Bobby Stroble	67	70	72	209	36,000
Bob Charles	72	68	70	210	30,600
Bob Murphy	70	70	70	210	30,600
Jim Dent	73	69	69	211	23,400
Vicente Fernandez	68	73	70	211	23,400
Jay Sigel	69	66	76	211	23,400
Isao Aoki	71	71	70	212	18,300
John Bland	70	70	72	212	18,300
Frank Conner	73	71	68	212	18,300
Bud Allin	70	73	70	213	13,995
Jack Kiefer	72	69	72	213	13,995
Gary Player	68	73	72	213	13,995
Chi Chi Rodriguez	70	72	71	213	13,995
Terry Dill	70	74	69	213	13,995
J.C. Snead	72	72	69	213	13,995
Dick Rhyan	71	70	73	214	11,160
Gay Brewer	74	69	72	215	8,660
Bob Dickson	71	72	72	215	8,660
Al Geiberger	74	70	71	215	8,660
Dick Hendrickson	70	73	72	215	8,660

	SCORES			TOTAL	MONEY
Larry Laoretti	73	69	73	215	8,660
Bob E. Smith	71	71	73	215	8,660
Dave Eichelberger	73	71	71	215	8,660
Bobby Mitchell	73	73	69	215	8,660
Walter Zembriski	74	70	71	215	8,660
Charles Coody	73	69	74	216	6,210
Bruce Summerhays	71	70	75	216	6,210
Butch Baird	70	74	72	216	6,210
Bob Eastwood	73	72	71	216	6,210
Robert Gaona	71	73	72	216	6,210
Raymond Floyd	74	68	75	217	4,968
John Jacobs	68	75	74	217	4,968
Jerry McGee	70	72	75	217	4,968
Ed Sneed	71	72	74	217	4,968
Gene Littler	72	73	72	217	4,968

Kroger Senior Classic

Golf Center at Kings Island, Grizzly Course,
Mason, Ohio
Par 36-35–71; 6,628 yards

June 28-30
purse, $900,000

	SCORES			TOTAL	MONEY
Isao Aoki	63	69	66	198	$135,000
Mike Hill	67	66	70	203	72,000
Rocky Thompson	69	68	66	203	72,000
Jay Sigel	65	71	68	204	48,600
J.C. Snead	62	73	69	204	48,600
Terry Dill	67	68	70	205	36,000
Bob E. Smith	69	64	73	206	32,400
Bob Charles	70	69	68	207	22,800
Jim Dent	70	68	69	207	22,800
Bob Dickson	71	71	65	207	22,800
Dick Hendrickson	71	70	66	207	22,800
Bob Murphy	71	67	69	207	22,800
Jimmy Powell	68	73	66	207	22,800
Robert Landers	69	69	70	208	15,750
Walter Morgan	68	71	69	208	15,750
John Schroeder	70	69	69	208	15,750
Ed Sneed	69	68	71	208	15,750
Brian Barnes	69	65	75	209	13,095
Gibby Gilbert	67	70	72	209	13,095
Rick Acton	72	69	70	211	10,305
Al Geiberger	70	68	73	211	10,305
Bunky Henry	72	67	72	211	10,305
John Jacobs	71	70	70	211	10,305
Graham Marsh	71	71	69	211	10,305
Rives McBee	71	72	68	211	10,305
Masaru Amano	72	69	71	212	7,323.75
John Bland	71	73	68	212	7,323.75
Charles Coody	68	72	72	212	7,323.75
Bruce Crampton	68	72	72	212	7,323.75
Dave Eichelberger	68	71	73	212	7,323.75
Tony Jacklin	70	70	72	212	7,323.75
Gene Littler	72	70	70	212	7,323.75
Don Massengale	70	72	70	212	7,323.75
Bud Allin	67	71	75	213	5,310

	SCORES			TOTAL	MONEY
Butch Baird	69	73	71	213	5,310
Joe Jimenez	71	70	72	213	5,310
Jack Kiefer	74	73	66	213	5,310
Calvin Peete	68	73	72	213	5,310
Bobby Stroble	67	70	76	213	5,310
Jim Albus	70	75	69	214	4,050
Homero Blancas	71	74	69	214	4,050
Bob Boss	68	71	75	214	4,050
Dale Douglass	71	68	75	214	4,050
Bob Eastwood	75	66	73	214	4,050
Harold Henning	65	76	73	214	4,050
Jerry McGee	70	72	72	214	4,050

U.S. Senior Open

Canterbury Golf Club, Beachwood, Ohio
Par 36-36—72; 6,765 yards

July 4-7
purse, $1,200,000

	SCORES				TOTAL	MONEY
Dave Stockton	70	67	67	73	277	$212,500
Hale Irwin	72	71	69	67	279	125,000
Raymond Floyd	70	73	69	68	280	79,801
Graham Marsh	69	74	70	69	282	55,618
Tony Jacklin	74	68	70	72	284	42,482.50
Jay Sigel	72	69	71	72	284	42,482.50
Bob Charles	66	72	73	74	285	35,863
John Bland	74	67	72	73	286	30,539.33
Walter Morgan	73	71	72	70	286	30,539.33
Bruce Summerhays	73	69	74	70	286	30,539.33
Isao Aoki	74	71	72	70	287	26,286
Jim Colbert	73	71	74	70	288	23,860.50
Frank Conner	73	73	75	67	288	23,860.50
Jimmy Powell	71	74	73	71	289	21,215.50
Bill Tindall	70	72	75	72	289	21,215.50
Jack Nicklaus	77	72	68	73	290	19,536
Butch Baird	74	72	71	74	291	16,548.80
Brian Barnes	73	71	76	71	291	16,548.80
John Jacobs	74	71	76	70	291	16,548.80
Chi Chi Rodriguez	71	72	70	78	291	16,548.80
DeWitt Weaver	74	74	73	70	291	16,548.80
Charles Coody	75	74	70	73	292	12,298.80
Jim Dent	74	73	73	72	292	12,298.80
Dale Douglass	77	73	73	69	292	12,298.80
David Graham	72	75	73	72	292	12,298.80
Mike McCullough	75	74	69	74	292	12,298.80
Jim Albus	73	75	75	70	293	8,904.40
Larry Gilbert	76	73	72	72	293	8,904.40
Larry Mowry	74	74	75	70	293	8,904.40
Bob Murphy	75	72	71	75	293	8,904.40
Steven Veriato	72	78	74	69	293	8,904.40
Marion Heck	74	73	72	75	294	7,615
Larry Laoretti	74	75	72	73	294	7,615
John D. Morgan	74	71	75	74	294	7,615
Joe Carr	79	66	74	76	295	6,687.20
Dave Eichelberger	71	79	73	72	295	6,687.20
Vicente Fernandez	75	74	68	78	295	6,687.20
Tom Wargo	74	71	76	74	295	6,687.20

		SCORES			TOTAL	MONEY
Tom Weiskopf	75	75	70	75	295	6,687.20
Jimmy Blanks	76	73	73	74	296	5,764.67
Bob Diamond	75	73	73	75	296	5,764.67
Jimmie Jones	76	74	72	74	296	5,764.67

Ford Senior Players Championship

TPC of Michigan, Dearborn, Michigan
Par 36-36—72; 6,876 yards

July 11-14
purse, $1,500,000

		SCORES			TOTAL	MONEY
Raymond Floyd	71	66	65	73	275	$225,000
Hale Irwin	70	67	69	71	277	132,000
Brian Barnes	74	70	67	69	280	108,000
Jack Kiefer	72	74	67	68	281	81,000
Jerry McGee	70	68	69	74	281	81,000
Bob Charles	67	72	70	73	282	57,000
Gibby Gilbert	68	72	72	70	282	57,000
Larry Gilbert	71	71	69	72	283	39,600
Calvin Peete	72	68	71	72	283	39,600
Dave Stockton	74	68	69	72	283	39,600
Rocky Thompson	74	70	71	68	283	39,600
Lee Trevino	67	71	71	74	283	39,600
Jim Dent	75	72	68	69	284	28,500
Chi Chi Rodriguez	70	74	70	70	284	28,500
J.C. Snead	72	67	70	75	284	28,500
Mike Hill	72	70	75	68	285	21,278.58
Bob Betley	70	72	71	72	285	21,278.57
John Bland	68	69	78	70	285	21,278.57
Jim Colbert	72	73	71	69	285	21,278.57
Vicente Fernandez	73	74	66	72	285	21,278.57
Jay Sigel	71	73	68	73	285	21,278.57
Tom Wargo	73	70	72	70	285	21,278.57
Al Geiberger	73	73	69	71	286	16,500
Tommy Aaron	71	70	72	74	287	14,025
Simon Hobday	70	70	72	75	287	14,025
Walter Morgan	75	68	72	72	287	14,025
Jack Nicklaus	74	70	72	71	287	14,025
John Schroeder	79	72	68	68	287	14,025
Bruce Summerhays	68	70	72	77	287	14,025
Isao Aoki	72	75	74	67	288	11,300
Don Bies	74	71	71	72	288	11,300
Bob E. Smith	72	71	72	73	288	11,300
Rick Acton	72	73	73	72	290	8,887.50
Tony Jacklin	75	75	71	69	290	8,887.50
John Jacobs	76	72	70	72	290	8,887.50
Bob Murphy	78	71	68	73	290	8,887.50
Ed Sneed	78	71	69	72	290	8,887.50
DeWitt Weaver	72	71	74	73	290	8,887.50
Kermit Zarley	73	69	73	75	290	8,887.50
Walter Zembriski	71	73	67	79	290	8,887.50

Burnet Senior Classic

Bunker Hills Golf Club, Coon Rapids, Minnesota
Par 36-36–72; 6,894 yards

July 19-21
purse, $1,250,000

	SCORES			TOTAL	MONEY
Vicente Fernandez	69	68	68	205	$187,500
Bruce Crampton	69	69	68	206	100,000
J.C. Snead	66	71	69	206	100,000
Raymond Floyd	68	74	65	207	75,000
Jim Colbert	73	65	70	208	48,750
John Jacobs	69	70	69	208	48,750
Dave Stockton	69	70	69	208	48,750
Tom Wargo	68	69	71	208	48,750
John Bland	69	72	68	209	28,035.72
Terry Dill	69	72	68	209	28,035.72
Walter Morgan	72	71	66	209	28,035.72
Al Geiberger	69	68	72	209	28,035.71
Jimmy Powell	65	74	70	209	28,035.71
John Schroeder	69	70	70	209	28,035.71
DeWitt Weaver	71	70	68	209	28,035.71
Jack Kiefer	72	69	69	210	18,270.84
Kermit Zarley	72	72	66	210	18,270.84
Frank Conner	71	69	70	210	18,270.83
Jim Dent	68	68	74	210	18,270.83
Larry Gilbert	68	70	72	210	18,270.83
Bob Wynn	74	66	70	210	18,270.83
Simon Hobday	71	70	70	211	13,468.75
Hale Irwin	69	69	73	211	13,468.75
Larry Laoretti	71	70	70	211	13,468.75
Jim Wilkinson	74	68	69	211	13,468.75
Bob Dickson	73	70	69	212	11,375
Bob Eastwood	72	71	69	212	11,375
Lee Trevino	68	75	69	212	11,375
Jim Albus	72	68	73	213	9,875
Dave Eichelberger	72	71	70	213	9,875
Steven Veriato	70	70	73	213	9,875
Tommy Aaron	68	79	67	214	7,437.50
Butch Baird	72	70	72	214	7,437.50
Don Bies	71	74	69	214	7,437.50
Dale Douglass	70	73	71	214	7,437.50
David Graham	69	74	71	214	7,437.50
Dick Hendrickson	72	70	72	214	7,437.50
Don Massengale	73	70	71	214	7,437.50
Jay Sigel	70	70	74	214	7,437.50
Bob E. Smith	71	70	73	214	7,437.50
Rocky Thompson	73	71	70	214	7,437.50

Ameritech Senior Open

Kemper Lakes Country Club, Long Grove, Illinois
Par 36-36–72; 6,830 yards

July 26-28
purse, $1,100,000

	SCORES			TOTAL	MONEY
Walter Morgan	63	70	72	205	$165,000
John Bland	70	69	68	207	96,800
Bob Murphy	68	73	67	208	79,200
Raymond Floyd	69	65	75	209	59,400

	SCORES			TOTAL	MONEY
David Graham	69	69	71	209	59,400
Rives McBee	68	72	70	210	44,000
Graham Marsh	69	69	73	211	39,600
Jimmy Powell	69	72	72	213	30,250
Chi Chi Rodriguez	72	66	75	213	30,250
John Schroeder	72	68	73	213	30,250
Jay Sigel	72	70	71	213	30,250
Frank Conner	72	71	71	214	21,725
Jack Kiefer	71	69	74	214	21,725
Dave Stockton	72	74	68	214	21,725
Kermit Zarley	70	69	75	214	21,725
Jim Albus	73	68	74	215	17,077.50
Bud Allin	70	73	72	215	17,077.50
Jim Dent	72	72	71	215	17,077.50
Al Geiberger	74	69	72	215	17,077.50
Terry Dill	72	73	71	216	14,520
Rick Acton	69	71	77	217	13,200
Hale Irwin	71	74	72	217	13,200
Mike Hill	73	72	73	218	11,550
Calvin Peete	71	72	75	218	11,550
Bob E. Smith	70	73	75	218	11,550
Jim Colbert	71	73	75	219	8,580
Dave Eichelberger	71	73	75	219	8,580
Bunky Henry	73	76	70	219	8,580
Tony Jacklin	72	75	72	219	8,580
Larry Laoretti	76	70	73	219	8,580
Jerry McGee	72	74	73	219	8,580
Tom Shaw	71	77	71	219	8,580
J.C. Snead	72	73	74	219	8,580
Bruce Summerhays	69	78	72	219	8,580
DeWitt Weaver	77	69	73	219	8,580
Joe Jimenez	76	70	74	220	6,435
Dick Rhyan	73	71	76	220	6,435
Homero Blancas	73	75	73	221	5,610
Bruce Crampton	72	74	75	221	5,610
Bob Eastwood	77	71	73	221	5,610
Vicente Fernandez	76	77	68	221	5,610
Dick Hendrickson	72	73	76	221	5,610

VFW Senior Championship

Loch Lloyd Country Club, Belton, Missouri
Par 35-35–70; 6,539 yards

August 2-4
purse, $900,000

	SCORES			TOTAL	MONEY
Dave Eichelberger	64	68	68	200	$135,000
Jim Colbert	65	69	68	202	79,200
Dave Stockton	66	70	68	204	59,400
Lee Trevino	68	70	66	204	59,400
Bob Murphy	73	65	67	205	43,200
Rick Acton	73	65	69	207	27,900
Gibby Gilbert	68	69	70	207	27,900
Larry Gilbert	69	69	69	207	27,900
Simon Hobday	71	69	67	207	27,900
Walter Morgan	67	68	72	207	27,900
Bobby Stroble	70	71	66	207	27,900
Frank Conner	65	65	78	208	18,300

	SCORES			TOTAL	MONEY
J.C. Snead	70	65	73	208	18,300
Bruce Summerhays	70	66	72	208	18,300
Jerry McGee	66	73	70	209	14,418
Dick Rhyan	70	74	65	209	14,418
Steven Veriato	70	71	68	209	14,418
Kermit Zarley	71	67	71	209	14,418
Robert Zimmerman	70	72	67	209	14,418
Gay Brewer	70	70	70	210	10,845
Larry Laoretti	71	69	70	210	10,845
Calvin Peete	69	71	70	210	10,845
Tom Wargo	68	70	72	210	10,845
Rives McBee	73	70	68	211	9,225
Ben Smith	71	67	73	211	9,225
Jim Albus	70	70	72	212	7,650
Homero Blancas	77	70	65	212	7,650
Jim Dent	68	73	71	212	7,650
Don January	71	72	69	212	7,650
Robert Landers	73	69	70	212	7,650
Mike McCullough	70	70	72	212	7,650
Butch Baird	72	69	72	213	6,075
Bob Dickson	69	74	70	213	6,075
Dale Douglass	72	72	69	213	6,075
Bob Eastwood	68	73	72	213	6,075
Bud Allin	72	70	72	214	4,691.25
Bob Betley	72	72	70	214	4,691.25
Bruce Crampton	70	76	68	214	4,691.25
Jimmy Powell	68	73	73	214	4,691.25
Tom Shaw	68	72	74	214	4691.25
Bob E. Smith	71	71	72	214	4,691.25
Rocky Thompson	73	71	70	214	4,691.25
Jim Wilkinson	72	71	71	214	4,691.25

First of America Classic

Egypt Valley Country Club, Ada, Michigan
Par 36-36–72; 6,913 yards

August 9-11
purse, $850,000

	SCORES			TOTAL	MONEY
Dave Stockton	68	69	69	206	$127,500
Bob Murphy	73	66	68	207	74,800
Jimmy Powell	69	68	71	208	56,100
Tom Wargo	67	74	67	208	56,100
Frank Conner	74	66	69	209	37,400
Bobby Stroble	68	65	76	209	37,400
Tommy Aaron	66	74	70	210	24,820
Jim Albus	69	71	70	210	24,820
Walter Morgan	70	70	70	210	24,820
Harry Toscano	74	64	72	210	24,820
Kermit Zarley	71	71	68	210	24,820
Bruce Summerhays	67	69	75	211	18,700
Rick Acton	72	70	70	212	15,725
Jim Dent	73	73	66	212	15,725
Larry Gilbert	70	70	72	212	15,725
Ben Smith	71	74	67	212	15,725
John Bland	68	72	73	213	13,175
Simon Hobday	71	72	70	213	13,175
Bob Wynn	72	72	70	214	11,248.34

	SCORES			TOTAL	MONEY
Butch Baird	72	70	72	214	11,248.33
Walter Zembriski	70	72	72	214	11,248.33
Bruce Devlin	72	73	70	215	8,942
Mike Hill	71	72	72	215	8,942
Rives McBee	71	75	69	215	8,942
Mike McCullough	72	71	72	215	8,942
Dick Rhyan	70	73	72	215	8,942
Homero Blancas	71	72	73	216	7,565
Bob Carson	73	75	68	216	7,565
Bob Eastwood	71	76	70	217	6,566.25
Dick Hendrickson	73	74	70	217	6,566.25
Bunky Henry	77	70	70	217	6,566.25
Tony Jacklin	75	68	74	217	6,566.25
Terry Carlson	73	72	73	218	5,737.50
David Graham	71	74	73	218	5,737.50
Bob Betley	75	73	71	219	4,711.43
Lee Elder	74	76	69	219	4,711.43
Larry Laoretti	75	73	71	219	4,711.43
Bob Lunn	74	74	71	219	4,711.43
Larry Mowry	77	70	72	219	4,711.43
Ed Sneed	75	68	76	219	4,711.43
Masaru Amano	73	74	72	219	4,711.42

Northville Long Island Classic

Meadow Brook Club, Jericho, New York
Par 36-36—72; 6,775 yards

August 16-18
purse, $800,000

	SCORES			TOTAL	MONEY
John Bland	70	66	66	202	$120,000
Jim Colbert	67	67	71	205	70,400
Raymond Floyd	66	67	73	206	57,600
Masaru Amano	69	68	70	207	43,200
Jay Sigel	67	67	73	207	43,200
Jim Dent	69	71	68	208	30,400
Graham Marsh	70	72	66	208	30,400
Isao Aoki	71	69	69	209	22,000
Bob Betley	69	68	72	209	22,000
Larry Gilbert	66	72	71	209	22,000
Bob E. Smith	69	72	68	209	22,000
Jack Nicklaus	69	70	71	210	16,800
Dick Rhyan	68	72	70	210	16,800
Rick Acton	72	71	68	211	14,400
Mike McCullough	66	72	73	211	14,400
Bruce Summerhays	71	71	69	211	14,400
Jim Albus	68	73	71	212	10,380
Brian Barnes	68	72	72	212	10,380
John Paul Cain	70	71	71	212	10,380
Bob Charles	71	71	70	212	10,380
Frank Conner	71	70	71	212	10,380
Jerry McGee	70	68	74	212	10,380
Walter Morgan	68	69	75	212	10,380
J.C. Snead	71	68	73	212	10,380
Vicente Fernandez	71	69	73	213	7,626.67
Gibby Gilbert	70	70	73	213	7,626.67
Miller Barber	67	71	75	213	7,626.66
Bob Dickson	74	68	72	214	6,640

	SCORES			TOTAL	MONEY
Tommy Jacobs	72	67	75	214	6,640
Chi Chi Rodriguez	71	68	75	214	6,640
Butch Baird	70	75	70	215	5,520
Charles Coody	70	71	74	215	5,520
Terry Dill	68	75	72	215	5,520
John Schroeder	73	70	72	215	5,520
Lee Trevino	69	73	73	215	5,520
Tommy Aaron	74	72	70	216	4,500
Bud Allin	71	72	73	216	4,500
Bruce Devlin	73	72	71	216	4,500
Jack Kiefer	68	74	74	216	4,500
Don Bies	72	71	74	217	3,520
Homero Blancas	75	74	68	217	3,520
Gay Brewer	73	70	74	217	3,520
Bob Carson	74	73	70	217	3,520
Mike Fetchick	75	69	73	217	3,520
Bunky Henry	72	70	75	217	3,520
Rives McBee	75	72	70	217	3,520
Tom Wargo	72	70	75	217	3,520

Bank of Boston Senior Classic

Nashawtuc Country Club, Concord, Massachusetts
Par 36-36–72; 6,730 yards

August 23-25
purse, $800,000

	SCORES			TOTAL	MONEY
Jim Dent	69	68	67	204	$120,000
Jay Sigel	71	66	68	205	64,000
Tom Wargo	68	67	70	205	64,000
Isao Aoki	67	72	67	206	48,000
Bob E. Smith	69	72	66	207	35,200
Bobby Stroble	73	69	65	207	35,200
Vicente Fernandez	70	69	70	209	27,200
Raymond Floyd	68	68	73	209	27,200
Larry Gilbert	71	70	69	210	21,600
Hale Irwin	72	69	69	210	21,600
Jim Albus	70	69	72	211	17,000
Graham Marsh	71	70	70	211	17,000
John Schroeder	69	72	70	211	17,000
J.C. Snead	70	69	72	211	17,000
David Graham	69	71	72	212	13,200
Tony Jacklin	71	72	69	212	13,200
Kermit Zarley	69	70	73	212	13,200
Larry Ziegler	67	72	73	212	13,200
Bob Charles	70	71	72	213	9,706.67
Frank Conner	68	73	72	213	9,706.67
Jack Kiefer	70	72	71	213	9,706.67
Jerry McGee	69	74	70	213	9,706.67
Terry Dill	69	68	76	213	9,706.66
Mike McCullough	70	71	72	213	9,706.66
Butch Baird	72	72	70	214	7,133.34
Bunky Henry	71	73	70	214	7,133.34
Bob Betley	75	72	67	214	7,133.33
Dick Hendrickson	70	71	73	214	7,133.33
Ben Smith	68	76	70	214	7,133.33
Ed Sneed	72	75	67	214	7,133.33
Brian Barnes	70	73	72	215	5,760

	SCORES			TOTAL	MONEY
Don Bies	71	73	71	215	5,760
Jim Wilkinson	69	74	72	215	5,760
Lee Trevino	72	72	72	216	4,628.58
Rick Acton	73	73	70	216	4,628.57
Homero Blancas	75	67	74	216	4,628.57
Dave Eichelberger	72	72	72	216	4,628.57
Bruce Summerhays	72	69	75	216	4,628.57
Tom Ulozas	70	74	72	216	4,628.57
DeWitt Weaver	71	72	73	216	4,628.57

Franklin Quest Championship

Park Meadows Golf Club, Park City, Utah
Par 36-36–72; 7,026 yards

August 30-September 1
purse, $800,000

	SCORES			TOTAL	MONEY
Graham Marsh	70	65	67	202	$120,000
Kermit Zarley	70	66	68	204	70,400
Jack Kiefer	68	67	70	205	57,600
Brian Barnes	71	65	70	206	43,200
Vicente Fernandez	69	67	70	206	43,200
Bob Charles	70	70	67	207	27,200
Mike McCullough	67	69	71	207	27,200
Bob Murphy	70	71	66	207	27,200
Gary Player	64	74	69	207	27,200
John Bland	71	70	67	208	19,200
Tony Jacklin	74	64	70	208	19,200
Lee Trevino	69	68	71	208	19,200
Rick Acton	75	66	68	209	19,200
Ed Sneed	66	72	71	209	19,200
Bob Wynn	70	71	68	209	19,200
Homero Blancas	70	72	68	210	12,048
David Graham	71	67	72	210	12,048
John Jacobs	65	69	76	210	12,048
Jay Sigel	70	69	71	210	12,048
Dave Stockton	70	69	71	210	12,048
Bob Carson	72	69	70	211	9,333.34
Butch Baird	73	68	70	211	9,333.33
John Schroeder	70	67	74	211	9,333.33
Dave Eichelberger	67	71	74	212	7,648
Robert Gaona	73	71	68	212	7,648
Bob E. Smith	71	71	70	212	7,648
Bobby Stroble	67	71	74	212	7,648
DeWitt Weaver	73	65	74	212	7,648
Bob Betley	73	68	72	213	5,546.67
Frank Conner	72	70	71	213	5,546.67
Harold Henning	71	72	70	213	5,546.67
Rives McBee	71	71	71	213	5,546.67
Jerry McGee	71	74	68	213	5,546.67
Jimmy Powell	72	71	70	213	5,546.67
Bob Dickson	69	71	73	213	5,546.66
Steven Veriato	70	69	74	213	5,546.66
Larry Ziegler	72	66	75	213	5,546.66
Jim Albus	74	66	74	214	4,160
Charles Coody	72	69	73	214	4,160
Dennis Coscina	71	68	75	214	4,160
Terry Dill	73	66	75	214	4,160

Boone Valley Classic

Boone Valley Golf Club, Augusta, Missouri
Par 36-35–71; 7,052 yards

September 6-8
purse, $1,200,000

	SCORES			TOTAL	MONEY
Gibby Gilbert	68	66	69	203	$180,000
Hale Irwin	70	63	70	203	105,600
(Gilbert defeated Irwin on first extra hole.)					
Isao Aoki	69	67	68	204	79,200
Bunky Henry	66	65	73	204	79,200
Frank Conner	69	68	68	205	52,800
Gary Player	69	69	70	205	52,800
Jack Kiefer	70	70	66	206	38,400
Graham Marsh	67	70	69	206	38,400
Tom Wargo	67	70	69	206	38,400
Jim Dent	67	69	71	207	26,640
Vicente Fernandez	65	70	72	207	26,640
John Schroeder	69	71	67	207	26,640
Jay Sigel	70	68	69	207	26,640
Bruce Summerhays	65	72	70	207	26,640
Rick Acton	68	71	69	208	19,800
Tony Jacklin	70	68	70	208	19,800
Bob Murphy	68	69	71	208	19,800
Tom Shaw	69	67	72	208	19,800
John Bland	69	73	67	209	15,880
Al Geiberger	70	69	70	209	15,880
Mike Hill	72	71	66	209	15,880
Kermit Zarley	69	72	69	210	15,880
Bob Betley	73	66	72	211	12,300
Don Bies	71	74	66	211	12,300
Dave Eichelberger	72	71	68	211	12,300
Jerry McGee	71	67	73	211	12,300
Tommy Aaron	70	68	74	212	10,440
Jim Albus	69	70	73	212	10,440
David Graham	74	68	70	212	10,440
Bob Charles	74	69	70	213	9,240
Jim Colbert	68	69	76	213	9,240
Bruce Crampton	72	72	70	214	7,577.14
Bob Eastwood	73	71	70	214	7,577.14
Charles Coody	67	74	73	214	7,577.14
Larry Gilbert	72	70	72	214	7,577.14
Bruce Lehnhard	67	73	74	214	7,577.14
Ed Sneed	71	67	76	214	7,577.14
Dave Stockton	73	70	71	214	7,577.14
Rives McBee	71	71	73	215	6,360
Bob Carson	71	74	71	216	5,760
Simon Hobday	69	75	72	216	5,760
Steve Spray	73	69	74	216	5,760
Larry Ziegler	72	75	69	216	5,760

Bank One Classic

Kearney Hill Links, Lexington, Kentucky
Par 36-36–72; 6,760 yards

September 13-15
purse, $600,000

	SCORES			TOTAL	MONEY
Mike Hill	70	69	68	207	$90,000
Isao Aoki	67	75	66	208	48,000

	SCORES			TOTAL	MONEY
Gibby Gilbert	69	71	68	208	48,000
Dick Hendrickson	70	73	66	209	29,600
J.C. Snead	71	72	66	209	29,600
Jim Wilkinson	66	73	70	209	29,600
Rick Acton	71	72	67	210	16,114.29
John Bland	73	73	64	210	16,114.29
Al Geiberger	70	75	65	210	16,114.29
John Jacobs	73	71	66	210	16,114.29
Jim Albus	70	72	68	210	16,114.28
Bobby Stroble	69	70	71	210	16,114.28
Bruce Summerhays	72	70	68	210	16,114.28
Larry Laoretti	73	69	69	211	10,500
Mike McCullough	70	69	72	211	10,500
John Schroeder	71	73	67	211	10,500
Ben Smith	70	71	70	211	10,500
Masaru Amano	74	71	67	212	8,460
Butch Baird	72	72	68	212	8,460
Terry Dill	74	69	69	212	8,460
Larry Gilbert	70	71	72	213	7,200
DeWitt Weaver	71	76	66	213	7,200
Tommy Aaron	70	74	70	214	6,300
Bob Betley	71	74	69	214	6,300
David Graham	71	73	70	214	6,300
Bud Allin	72	70	73	215	5,580
Dennis Coscina	74	73	68	215	5,580
John Paul Cain	74	73	69	216	4,752
Bob Carson	72	76	68	216	4,752
Jim Dent	74	70	72	216	4,752
Gary Player	74	70	72	216	4,752
Ed Sneed	70	78	68	216	4,752
Charles Coody	74	73	70	217	3,625.72
Chi Chi Rodriguez	73	73	71	217	3,625.72
Walter Zembriski	74	73	70	217	3,625.72
Jimmy Adams	74	71	72	217	3,625.71
Tony Jacklin	70	73	74	217	3,625.71
Walter Morgan	72	73	72	217	3,625.71
Steve Robbins	72	73	72	217	3,625.71
Bruce Crampton	74	72	72	218	2,940
Jim Ferree	73	74	71	218	2,940
Bob E. Smith	70	77	71	218	2,940

Brickyard Crossing Championship

Brickyard Crossing Golf Club, Indianapolis, Indiana
Par 36-36—72; 6,678 yards
(Third round cancelled — rain.)

September 20-22
purse, $750,000

	SCORES		TOTAL	MONEY
Jimmy Powell	68	66	134	$112,500
John Jacobs	69	66	135	66,000
Bud Allin	67	69	136	54,000
Rick Acton	68	70	138	37,000
Bobby Stroble	67	71	138	37,000
Tom Wargo	66	72	138	37,000
John Bland	69	70	139	25,500
Bob Wynn	69	70	139	25,500
Masaru Amano	69	71	140	18,750

	SCORES			TOTAL	MONEY
Bunky Henry	72	68		140	18,750
Tony Jacklin	68	72		140	18,750
Jay Sigel	69	71		140	18,750
Jim Colbert	71	70		141	12,058.34
David Graham	72	69		141	12,058.34
Ed Sneed	72	69		141	12,058.34
Isao Aoki	69	72		141	12,058.33
Jim Dent	71	70		141	12,058.33
Bob Dickson	70	71		141	12,058.33
Mike Hill	70	71		141	12,058.33
Lee Trevino	69	72		141	12,058.33
Kermit Zarley	68	73		141	12,058.33
Terry Dill	72	70		142	8,081.25
Simon Hobday	65	77		142	8,081.25
Jerry McGee	72	70		142	8,081.25
Walter Morgan	71	71		142	8,081.25
Frank Conner	70	73		143	6,375
Robert Landers	71	72		143	6,375
Larry Laoretti	72	71		143	6,375
Bruce Summerhays	70	73		143	6,375
Jim Wilkinson	73	70		143	6,375
Walter Zembriski	71	72		143	6,375
Vicente Fernandez	73	71		144	5,400
Butch Baird	70	75		145	4,725
Bob Betley	66	79		145	4,725
Gay Brewer	72	73		145	4,725
Bob Murphy	70	75		145	4,725
Ben Smith	70	75		145	4,725
Bruce Crampton	71	75		146	3,750
Bruce Devlin	70	76		146	3,750
Gibby Gilbert	76	70		146	3,750
Graham Marsh	72	74		146	3,750
Pat O'Brien	70	76		146	3,750
Harry Toscano	72	74		146	3,750

Vantage Championship

Tanglewood Country Club, Clemmons, North Carolina
Par 36-36–72; 6,670 yards

September 27-29
purse, $1,500,000

	SCORES			TOTAL	MONEY
Jim Colbert	65	70	69	204	$225,000
Hale Irwin	69	67	69	205	110,000
Gary Player	70	65	70	205	110,000
Kermit Zarley	66	71	68	205	110,000
John Bland	67	70	69	206	62,000
Mike Hill	68	70	68	206	62,000
J.C. Snead	66	68	72	206	62,000
Don January	66	71	70	207	45,000
DeWitt Weaver	66	71	70	207	45,000
Jim Dent	73	68	67	208	36,000
Larry Gilbert	68	70	70	208	36,000
Simon Hobday	69	68	71	208	36,000
Rick Acton	66	71	72	209	28,500
Raymond Floyd	69	67	73	209	28,500
Calvin Peete	68	71	70	209	28,500
Brian Barnes	71	73	66	210	21,278.58

	SCORES			TOTAL	MONEY
Frank Conner	70	69	71	210	21,278.57
Graham Marsh	67	74	69	210	21,278.57
Jerry McGee	73	67	70	210	21,278.57
Gil Morgan	69	70	71	210	21,278.57
Larry Mowry	68	72	70	210	21,278.57
Rocky Thompson	70	73	67	210	21,278.57
Walter Morgan	72	72	67	211	14,378.58
Bud Allin	71	69	71	211	14,378.57
Isao Aoki	74	66	71	211	14,378.57
Terry Dill	68	74	69	211	14,378.57
Al Geiberger	72	68	71	211	14,378.57
Gibby Gilbert	71	67	73	211	14,378.57
Bobby Stroble	72	68	71	211	14,378.57
Tommy Aaron	69	71	72	212	10,371.43
Butch Baird	71	70	71	212	10,371.43
Dale Douglass	68	73	71	212	10,371.43
Vicente Fernandez	72	69	71	212	10,371.43
Bunky Henry	70	75	67	212	10,371.43
Tony Jacklin	69	72	71	212	10,371.43
Don Bies	71	69	72	212	10,371.43
Bob Charles	70	70	73	213	7,950
Bruce Devlin	66	75	72	213	7,950
Jay Sigel	71	73	69	213	7,950
Bob E. Smith	70	74	69	213	7,950
Dave Stockton	71	68	74	213	7,950

Ralphs Senior Classic

Wilshire Country Club, Los Angeles, California
Par 35-36–71; 6,575 yards

October 4-6
purse, $800,000

	SCORES			TOTAL	MONEY
Gil Morgan	68	68	66	202	$120,000
Jim Colbert	66	68	69	203	64,000
Chi Chi Rodriguez	67	66	70	203	64,000
Raymond Floyd	66	70	68	204	48,000
Bob Charles	69	68	69	206	31,200
John Jacobs	73	67	66	206	31,200
Graham Marsh	67	68	71	206	31,200
Dave Stockton	70	65	71	206	31,200
Jim Albus	70	71	66	207	20,000
Don Bies	71	68	68	207	20,000
Larry Gilbert	67	71	69	207	20,000
Walter Morgan	68	69	70	207	20,000
Dale Douglass	69	67	72	208	16,000
Bud Allin	68	72	69	209	13,600
Bob Dickson	69	72	68	209	13,600
Dick Hendrickson	71	68	70	209	13,600
Jerry McGee	69	71	69	209	13,600
Tom Wargo	71	73	65	209	13,600
John Bland	70	71	69	210	10,586.67
Bob E. Smith	71	71	68	210	10,586.67
Bruce Summerhays	74	67	69	210	10,586.66
Brian Barnes	69	71	71	211	8,226.67
Bob Eastwood	72	66	73	211	8,226.67
Larry Mowry	69	73	69	211	8,226.67
Jimmy Powell	69	73	69	211	8,226.67

	SCORES			TOTAL	MONEY
Bunky Henry	66	72	73	211	8,226.66
John Schroeder	68	68	75	211	8,226.66
Charles Coody	68	71	73	212	5,940
Vicente Fernandez	72	71	69	212	5,940
Harold Henning	66	74	72	212	5,940
Calvin Peete	71	70	71	212	5,940
Dick Rhyan	67	72	73	212	5,940
Tom Shaw	71	69	72	212	5,940
Ben Smith	70	70	72	212	5,940
Harry Toscano	71	72	69	212	5,940
Rick Acton	69	76	68	213	4,251.43
Homero Blancas	74	68	71	213	4,251.43
Dennis Coscina	75	69	69	213	4,251.43
Orville Moody	75	67	71	213	4,251.43
Bobby Stroble	72	71	70	213	4,251.43
Rocky Thompson	67	74	72	213	4,251.43
John Paul Cain	68	72	73	213	4,251.42

The Transamerica

Silverado Country Club, South Course,
Napa, California
Par 35-37–72; 6,632 yards

October 11-13
purse, $700,000

	SCORES			TOTAL	MONEY
John Bland	69	69	66	204	$105,000
Jim Colbert	71	68	66	205	61,600
Bobby Stroble	68	67	71	206	50,400
John Jacobs	70	71	66	207	42,000
Vicente Fernandez	72	66	70	208	33,600
Tom Wargo	68	72	69	209	28,000
Charles Coody	70	72	68	210	21,350
Bob Dickson	71	72	67	210	21,350
Chi Chi Rodriguez	69	71	70	210	21,350
Lee Trevino	71	64	75	210	21,350
Bob Eastwood	67	74	70	211	13,600
Dick Hendrickson	73	68	70	211	13,600
Bob Murphy	70	71	70	211	13,600
Jay Sigel	68	70	73	211	13,600
J.C. Snead	73	68	70	211	13,600
Tom Weiskopf	71	67	73	211	13,600
Kermit Zarley	70	70	71	211	13,600
Jim Albus	74	66	72	212	10,185
Harold Henning	70	71	71	212	10,185
Al Geiberger	70	72	71	213	8,680
David Graham	72	69	72	213	8,680
Simon Hobday	72	69	72	213	8,680
Brian Barnes	68	74	72	214	7,014
Bruce Crampton	68	75	71	214	7,014
Terry Dill	72	68	74	214	7,014
Dave Eichelberger	71	68	75	214	7,014
Ed Sneed	72	74	68	214	7,014
Tommy Aaron	67	69	79	215	5,810
Rick Acton	69	71	75	215	5,810
Dave Stockton	70	67	78	215	5,810
Larry Gilbert	73	70	73	216	4,433.34
Bunky Henry	69	73	74	216	4,433.34

	SCORES			TOTAL	MONEY
Bob E. Smith	73	71	72	216	4,433.34
Don Bies	74	71	71	216	4,433.33
Tony Jacklin	74	73	69	216	4,433.33
Jack Kiefer	75	70	71	216	4,433.33
Tom Shaw	74	72	70	216	4,433.33
Jim Wilkinson	73	76	67	216	4,433.33
Walter Zembriski	72	69	75	216	4,433.33
Bud Allin	67	74	76	217	3,360
Masaru Amano	71	77	69	217	3,360
Calvin Peete	74	72	71	217	3,360
John Schroeder	74	69	74	217	3,360

Raley's Gold Rush Classic

Serrano Country Club, El Dorado Hills, California
Par 36-36–72; 6,772 yards

October 18-20
purse, $800,000

	SCORES			TOTAL	MONEY
Jim Colbert	67	68	67	202	$120,000
Dave Stockton	70	69	68	207	70,400
Butch Baird	73	64	71	208	52,800
Jack Kiefer	66	73	69	208	52,800
Hale Irwin	69	69	71	209	38,400
Dick Hendrickson	70	69	72	211	28,800
Harold Henning	67	73	71	211	28,800
Jay Sigel	70	72	69	211	28,800
Tommy Aaron	73	68	71	212	21,600
David Graham	71	69	72	212	21,600
John Bland	71	74	68	213	17,000
Charles Coody	71	69	73	213	17,000
Walter Morgan	73	74	66	213	17,000
Chi Chi Rodriguez	71	70	72	213	17,000
John Paul Cain	72	73	69	214	11,730
Bruce Crampton	73	67	74	214	11,730
Terry Dill	74	70	70	214	11,730
Bob Duval	76	69	69	214	11,730
Bob Eastwood	70	75	69	214	11,730
Dave Eichelberger	72	70	72	214	11,730
Jerry McGee	76	66	72	214	11,730
John Schroeder	75	71	68	214	11,730
Jim Ferree	70	72	73	215	7,840
Jimmy Powell	77	69	69	215	7,840
Bob E. Smith	72	70	73	215	7,840
J.C. Snead	73	69	73	215	7,840
Bruce Summerhays	68	72	75	215	7,840
DeWitt Weaver	70	70	75	215	7,840
Jim Dent	71	74	71	216	6,180
Tom Shaw	73	71	72	216	6,180
Bobby Stroble	71	73	72	216	6,180
Kermit Zarley	75	70	71	216	6,180
Gary Brewer	79	70	68	217	4,834.29
Bob Charles	74	73	70	217	4,834.29
Simon Hobday	75	73	69	217	4,834.29
Tony Jacklin	74	73	70	217	4,834.29
Bruce Devlin	69	73	75	217	4,834.28
Al Geiberger	70	75	72	217	4,834.28
Rocky Thompson	71	67	79	217	4,834.28

	SCORES			TOTAL	MONEY
Brian Barnes	74	69	75	218	3,760
Don Bies	73	73	72	218	3,760
Rives McBee	74	71	73	218	3,760
Ben Smith	69	75	74	218	3,760
Tom Wargo	74	72	72	218	3,760

Hyatt Regency Maui Kaanapali Classic

Kaanapali Resort, North Course,
Kaanapali, Hawaii
Par 35-36–71; 6,590 yards

October 25-27
purse, $650,000

	SCORES			TOTAL	MONEY
Bob Charles	64	65	69	198	$97,500
Hale Irwin	63	66	70	199	57,200
Steven Veriato	69	65	66	200	46,800
Don Bies	68	67	68	203	39,000
Deane Beman	68	70	66	204	31,200
Bud Allin	67	67	71	205	22,100
John Jacobs	68	66	71	205	22,100
Don January	70	69	66	205	22,100
Graham Marsh	67	68	70	205	22,100
Charles Coody	67	69	70	206	16,250
Dave Stockton	69	70	67	206	16,250
Jim Albus	73	67	67	207	13,216.67
Bobby Stroble	68	69	70	207	13,216.67
Jerry McGee	69	67	71	207	13,216.66
Dave Hill	69	71	68	208	11,050
Bob Murphy	68	69	71	208	11,050
DeWitt Weaver	73	69	66	208	11,050
Bob Betley	69	73	67	209	8,619
Dale Douglass	69	68	72	209	8,619
Mike McCullough	71	66	72	209	8,619
Larry Mowry	70	72	67	209	8,619
Tom Shaw	70	70	69	209	8,619
Masaru Amano	66	75	69	210	6,662.50
Terry Carlson	72	68	70	210	6,662.50
Tommy Jacobs	70	70	70	210	6,662.50
Rocky Thompson	74	67	69	210	6,662.50
Rick Acton	71	70	70	211	5,395
Jim Colbert	77	68	66	211	5,395
Bob Dickson	71	70	70	211	5,395
Robert Landers	71	72	68	211	5,395
Bob E. Smith	70	71	70	211	5,395
Frank Conner	73	72	67	212	4,192.50
Jim Ferree	68	72	72	212	4,192.50
Bill Holstead	65	71	76	212	4,192.50
Steve Robbins	73	67	72	212	4,192.50
Bruce Summerhays	73	69	70	212	4,192.50
Bob Wynn	69	72	71	212	4,192.50
Butch Baird	69	71	73	213	2,925
Homero Blancas	69	71	73	213	2,925
Terry Dill	73	68	72	213	2,925
Dick Hendrickson	71	71	71	213	2,925
Harold Henning	72	67	74	213	2,925
Larry Laoretti	74	70	69	213	2,925
Rives McBee	73	68	72	213	2,925

	SCORES			TOTAL	MONEY
Bobby Mitchell	73	69	71	213	2,925
Orville Moody	73	72	68	213	2,925
Harry Toscano	71	74	68	213	2,925
Jim Wilkinson	70	75	68	213	2,925

Emerald Coast Classic

The Moors Golf Club, Milton, Florida
Par 36-35–71; 6,843 yards

November 1-3
purse, $1,050,000

	SCORES			TOTAL	MONEY
Lee Trevino	69	79	68	207	$157,500
Bob Eastwood	69	71	67	207	70,350
David Graham	72	66	69	207	70,350
Mike Hill	68	71	68	207	70,350
Dave Stockton	66	71	70	207	70,350
(Trevino won on first extra hole.)					
Jim Dent	67	73	68	208	35,700
Hale Irwin	70	69	69	208	35,700
Jay Sigel	66	71	71	208	35,700
Rocky Thompson	67	71	70	208	35,700
John Bland	67	75	67	209	24,150
Frank Conner	69	72	68	209	24,150
Graham Marsh	66	73	70	209	24,150
Walter Morgan	65	75	69	209	24,150
Masaru Amano	69	72	69	210	17,850
Isao Aoki	69	72	69	210	17,850
Bruce Crampton	67	71	72	210	17,850
Dave Eichelberger	66	70	74	210	17,850
Kermit Zarley	71	69	70	210	17,850
Larry Gilbert	66	70	75	211	14,332.50
Bruce Summerhays	69	72	70	211	14,332.50
John Paul Cain	71	73	68	212	12,250
Vicente Fernandez	70	69	73	212	12,250
Gil Morgan	67	74	71	212	12,250
Jim Colbert	68	78	67	213	10,500
Gary Player	74	70	69	213	10,500
Tom Shaw	69	77	67	213	10,500
Dale Douglass	68	75	71	214	8,925
Bob Murphy	71	73	70	214	8,925
John Schroeder	71	72	71	214	8,925
Jim Wilkinson	72	69	72	214	8,925
Brian Barnes	77	72	71	215	6,930
Bruce Devlin	68	78	69	215	6,930
Terry Dill	69	76	70	215	6,930
John Jacobs	69	71	75	215	6,930
Jerry McGee	72	72	71	215	6,930
Jimmy Powell	65	77	73	215	6,930
Tom Wargo	73	70	72	215	6,930
Bob Charles	70	74	72	216	5,355
Charles Coody	72	72	72	216	5,355
Raymond Floyd	69	72	75	216	5,355
Mike McCullough	71	69	76	216	5,355
J.C. Snead	71	71	74	216	5,355

Energizer Senior Tour Championship

The Dunes Golf & Beach Club, Myrtle Beach,
South Carolina
Par 36-36–72; 6,815 yards

November 7-10
purse, $1,600,000

	SCORES				TOTAL	MONEY
Jay Sigel	69	69	69	72	279	$280,000
Kermit Zarley	72	71	69	69	281	160,000
John Bland	70	71	72	70	283	121,000
Jim Colbert	70	70	74	69	283	121,000
Jim Dent	72	71	70	71	284	89,000
Bob Charles	68	71	71	76	286	70,000
Frank Conner	71	67	76	72	286	70,000
Isao Aoki	71	74	69	73	287	55,500
Vicente Fernandez	68	70	75	74	287	55,500
Mike Hill	69	70	74	75	288	42,875
Hale Irwin	67	75	76	70	288	42,875
Graham Marsh	74	69	73	72	288	42,875
Tom Wargo	72	74	74	68	288	42,875
Raymond Floyd	72	70	72	75	289	33,000
John Jacobs	72	71	71	75	289	33,000
Jimmy Powell	71	72	75	71	289	33,000
J.C. Snead	72	75	70	73	290	29,000
Dave Stockton	73	73	74	71	291	27,500
Lee Trevino	70	73	78	71	292	26,000
John Schroeder	74	73	74	73	294	23,750
Bobby Stroble	71	75	74	74	294	23,750
Gibby Gilbert	71	73	80	71	295	21,500
Brian Barnes	74	71	77	74	296	20,000
Jack Kiefer	72	74	71	79	296	20,000
Bruce Summerhays	75	75	76	71	297	18,500
Bob Murphy	72	74	73	79	298	17,250
Gary Player	74	68	78	78	298	17,250
Larry Gilbert	70	75	77	79	301	16,250
Walter Morgan	77	72	77	75	301	16,250
Rick Acton	71	77	72	84	304	15,500
Tom Weiskopf	77	72	77	79	305	15,000

Diners Club Matches

PGA West, La Quinta, California
Par 36-36–72; 6,870 yards

December 12-15
purse, $700,000

FIRST ROUND

Jim Colbert and Bob Murphy defeated J.C. Snead and Gibby Gilbert, 4 and 3
Tom Wargo and John Jacobs defeated Jimmy Powell and Larry Mowry, 4 and 3
Hale Irwin and Dave Stockton defeated Jim Dent and Gary Player, 3 and 1
Jay Sigel and Vicente Fernandez defeated Walter Morgan and Larry Laoretti, 22 holes

SECOND ROUND

Colbert and Murphy defeated Wargo and Jacobs, 1 up
Snead and Gilbert defeated Powell and Mowry, 3 and 1
Irwin and Stockton defeated Morgan and Larry Laoretti, 1 up
Sigel and Fernandez defeated Dent and Player, 3 and 2

(Losers after second round received $25,000 each.)

THIRD ROUND

Colbert and Murphy defeated Powell and Mowry, 3 and 2
Sigel and Fernandez defeated Irwin and Stockton, 4 and 3

(Losers after third round received $40,000 each.)

FOURTH ROUND

Colbert and Murphy defeated Sigel and Fernandez, 3 and 1

(Colbert and Murphy received $110,000 each; Sigel and Fernandez received $60,000 each.)

European Seniors Tour

Beko/Oger Tours Turkish Seniors Open

National Golf Club, Antalya, Turkey
Par 36-36—72; 6,562 yards

May 10-12
purse, £100,000

	SCORES			TOTAL	MONEY
Bobby Verwey	74	74	70	218	£16,556.29
Tommy Horton	75	75	71	221	11,019.87
Noel Ratcliffe	73	73	76	222	5,539.74
Chick Evans	72	75	75	222	5,539.74
Brian Huggett	74	75	74	223	4,264.90
Antonio Garrido	74	74	76	224	3,682.12
Harry Flatman	74	74	76	224	3,682.12
David Creamer	74	81	69	224	3,682.12
Jim Rhodes	72	78	75	225	3,099.34
Francisco Abreu	74	75	77	226	2,807.95
Walt Sauer	72	80	75	227	2,339.96
Malcolm Gregson	74	75	78	227	2,339.96
Randall Vines	75	75	77	227	2,339.96
Hugh Boyle	76	77	75	228	1,721.85
John Morgan	75	75	78	228	1,721.85
Snell Lancaster	73	72	83	228	1,721.85
Frank Hill	75	74	80	229	1,214.13
Howell Fraser	81	73	75	229	1,214.13
Terry Squires	77	79	73	229	1,214.13
Brian Waites	72	81	76	229	1,214.13
Hugh Inggs	78	75	76	229	1,214.13
Alberto Croce	81	75	73	229	1,214.13
Doug Daziel	77	77	76	230	1,000
Roger Fidler	79	75	76	230	1,000
Andrew Gauld	74	82	75	231	854.31
Renato Campagnoli	77	77	77	231	854.31
Bob Menne	77	77	77	231	854.31
Manuel Alvarez	77	76	78	231	854.31

	SCORES			TOTAL	MONEY
Gordon Gray	79	74	78	231	854.31
Jay Dolan	76	79	76	231	854.31

De Vere Hotels Seniors Classic

Belton Woods Golf Club, Grantham, England
Par 36-36–72; 6,774 yards

May 31-June 2
purse, £75,000

	SCORES			TOTAL	MONEY
Renato Campagnoli	70	69	66	207	£12,500
Antonio Garrido	74	70	68	212	6,497.50
Tommy Horton	74	71	67	212	6,497.50
Roberto Bernardini	72	71	71	214	3,690
Doug Dalziel	76	70	70	216	3,110
Neil Coles	74	70	72	216	3,110
Liam Higgins	76	73	66	217	2,670
Tienie Britz	75	68	74	217	2,670
David Oakley	72	71	75	218	2,133.33
John Hudson	73	73	72	218	2,133.33
John Morgan	75	75	68	218	2,133.33
Harry Flatman	76	71	72	219	1,680
Bill Hardwick	69	72	78	219	1,680
Hugh Inggs	73	72	75	220	1,370
Jim Rhodes	74	73	73	220	1,370
Brian Huggett	74	73	74	221	1,120
Chick Evans	77	72	72	221	1,120
Randall Vines	76	76	71	223	930
Gaylord Burrows	75	74	74	223	930
Malcolm Gregson	76	76	71	223	930
Noel Ratcliffe	78	70	76	224	830
Brian Waites	75	76	74	225	785
Arnold O'Connor	78	75	72	225	785
Francisco Abreu	78	72	76	226	725
George Will	76	76	74	226	725
Gordon Gray	74	78	75	227	665
Walt Sauer	76	77	74	227	665
Maurice Bembridge	78	76	74	228	596
Alec Bickerdike	81	73	74	228	596
Tony Grubb	76	74	78	228	596
David Huish	77	77	74	228	596
Vincent Tshabalala	79	75	74	228	596

Hippo Jersey Open

La Moye Golf Club, Jersey
Par 36-36–72; 6,664 yards

June 7-9
purse, £100,000

	SCORES			TOTAL	MONEY
Maurice Bembridge	68	67	67	202	£15,000
Roberto Bernardini	70	69	70	209	6,075
Alberto Croce	67	69	73	209	6,075
Vincent Tshabalala	65	73	71	209	6,075
David Huish	68	70	71	209	6,075
David Butler	69	71	70	210	3,408.33
Renato Campagnoli	68	70	72	210	3,408.33

	SCORES			TOTAL	MONEY
Brian Watts	71	70	69	210	3,408.33
Malcolm Gregson	69	72	71	212	2,675
Paul Leonard	74	67	71	212	2,675
Liam Higgins	72	70	71	213	2,200
John Morgan	67	75	71	213	2,200
Tommy Horton	68	73	73	214	1,800
Brian Huggett	71	74	69	214	1,800
David Creamer	73	67	75	215	1,310
Bobby Verwey	72	70	73	215	1,310
Antonio Garrido	73	72	70	215	1,310
DeRay Simon	73	70	72	215	1,310
Hugh Inggs	68	74	73	215	1,310
Neil Coles	74	72	70	216	1,075
Bernard Hunt	69	74	73	216	1,075
Bobby Browne	72	70	75	217	980
Harry Flatman	72	76	69	217	980
Doug Dalziel	70	76	73	219	920
Snell Lancaster	70	75	75	220	860
Roy Whitehead	75	69	76	220	860
David Snell	71	78	72	221	780
Tony Grubb	73	72	76	221	780
Jim Rhodes	71	76	74	221	780
Helmuth Schumacher	75	74	73	222	730
John Hudson	74	73	75	222	730

Castle Royle European Seniors Classic

Castle Royle Golf Club, Maidenhead,
Berkshire, England
Par 36-36–72; 6,828 yards

June 14-16
purse, £75,000

	SCORES			TOTAL	MONEY
Tommy Horton	68	68	69	205	£12,500
Brian Huggett	69	69	67	205	8,320
(Horton defeated Huggett on first extra hole.)					
John Morgan	66	68	72	206	4,675
David Huish	67	67	73	207	3,455
Bobby Verwey	70	67	70	207	3,455
David Oakley	71	67	71	209	3,000
Maurice Bembridge	69	70	72	211	2,780
Liam Higgins	71	72	69	212	2,450
Jim Rhodes	71	74	67	212	2,450
Vincent Tshabalala	71	69	73	213	1,772
Antonio Garrido	72	70	71	213	1,772
Brian Waites	68	75	70	213	1,772
Noel Ratcliffe	70	73	70	213	1,772
Renato Campagnoli	73	71	69	213	1,772
Francisco Abreu	70	71	73	214	1,230
Harry Flatman	69	73	72	214	1,230
Helmuth Schumacher	67	69	79	215	857.78
David Creamer	70	71	74	215	857.78
Malcolm Gregson	75	68	72	215	857.78
Howell Fraser	74	69	72	215	857.78
Doug Dalziel	73	70	72	215	857.78
Alberto Croce	71	73	71	215	857.78
Ross Whitehead	72	74	69	215	857.78
Hugh Inggs	71	75	69	215	857.78

	SCORES			TOTAL	MONEY
DeRay Simon	77	69	69	215	857.78
Lloyd Monroe	68	72	76	216	623.33
Roberto Bernardini	71	72	73	216	623.33
John Huston	71	73	72	216	623.33
Jose Cabo	72	73	71	216	623.33
David Talbot	72	73	71	216	623.33
Neil Coles	73	73	70	216	623.33

Ryder Collingtree Seniors Classic

Collingtree Park ETC, Northampton, England
Par 36-36—72; 6,570 yards

June 28-30
purse, £60,000

	SCORES			TOTAL	MONEY
David Huish	73	73	73	219	£9,700
Malcolm Gregson	71	74	74	219	5,025
Noel Ratcliffe	71	79	69	219	5,025
(Huish defeated Gregson and Ratcliffe on first extra hole.)					
Antonio Garrido	73	76	71	220	2,700
Alberto Croce	76	71	73	220	2,700
Liam Higgins	72	73	76	221	2,175
Neil Coles	70	81	70	221	2,175
Francisco Abreu	75	75	72	222	1,753.33
John Morgan	70	76	76	222	1,753.33
DeRay Simon	76	73	73	222	1,753.33
Tienie Britz	74	77	72	223	1,430
Renato Campagnoli	74	69	80	223	1,430
Tommy Horton	75	74	75	224	1,290
Hugh Boyle	73	76	76	225	1,158.33
Brian Waites	71	73	81	225	1,158.33
Chick Evans	70	76	79	225	1,158.33
Doug Dalziel	73	78	76	227	925.83
Jim Rhodes	78	77	72	227	925.83
Roberto Bernardini	75	74	78	227	925.83
Paul Leonard	72	72	83	227	925.83
Randall Vines	76	72	79	227	925.83
Peter Butler	73	80	74	227	925.83
David Creamer	76	76	76	228	737.50
Maurice Bembridge	79	78	71	228	737.50
Tony Grubb	76	82	71	229	670
Howell Fraser	74	79	77	230	625
David Snell	77	78	76	231	576.67
Harry Flatman	76	79	76	231	576.67
Bryan Carter	82	77	72	231	576.67
David Butler	76	77	79	232	537
Vincent Tshabalala	77	78	77	232	537
Ross Whitehead	73	81	78	232	537
Helmuth Schumacher	79	75	78	232	537

Stella Senior Open

Idstein Golf Club, Frankfurt, Germany
Par 36-36–72; 6,742 yards

July 12-14
purse, £100,000

	SCORES			TOTAL	MONEY
Tommy Horton	66	67	68	201	£16,660
Noel Ratcliffe	70	67	66	203	11,100
Brian Huggett	71	65	70	206	6,260
Renato Campagnoli	70	67	70	207	5,000
John Morgan	71	69	66	208	4,065
Malcolm Gregson	68	72	68	208	4,065
Antonio Garrido	71	70	68	209	3,580
Randall Vines	73	72	65	210	2,930
Maurice Bembridge	68	69	73	210	2,930
Harry Flatman	72	71	67	210	2,930
Neil Coles	70	70	70	210	2,930
David Butler	70	72	70	212	2,153.33
David Huish	70	67	75	212	2,153.33
Bobby Verwey	69	71	72	212	2,153.33
Brian Waites	70	73	70	213	1,450
Bill Hardwick	75	68	70	213	1,450
Liam Higgins	71	70	72	213	1,450
DeRay Simon	67	75	71	213	1,450
Joe Carr	71	70	72	213	1,450
Lloyd Monroe	72	71	71	214	1,180
Snell Lancaster	74	70	71	215	1,090
John Fourie	72	75	68	215	1,090
Mike Hoyle	71	76	68	215	1,090
Chester Jervis	77	71	68	216	920
Jim Rhodes	71	73	72	216	920
Howell Fraser	73	66	77	216	920
Alberto Croce	70	74	72	216	920
Peter Butler	69	75	72	216	920
Sooky Maharaj	70	74	72	216	920
David Oakley	76	71	69	216	920

Senior British Open

Royal Portrush Golf Club, Portrush, Northern Ireland
Par 36-36–72; 6,672 yards

July 25-28
purse, £350,000

	SCORES				TOTAL	MONEY
Brian Barnes	72	65	66	74	277	£58,330
Bob Charles	68	69	69	74	280	30,380
David Oakley	71	68	69	72	280	30,380
Tommy Horton	68	74	69	70	281	17,500
John Morgan	70	71	72	70	283	14,840
Malcolm Gregson	67	74	69	75	285	12,250
Tom Wargo	68	70	76	72	286	9,625
Antonio Garrido	72	69	72	73	286	9,625
*Vinny Giles III	71	71	73	71	286	
Neil Coles	67	70	74	76	287	7,840
Chick Evans	70	70	76	72	288	7,000
Snell Lancaster	69	74	75	72	290	6,440
Harry Flatman	76	70	73	72	291	5,830
David Creamer	72	72	71	76	291	5,830
Mike Nutter	77	71	72	72	292	5,040

	SCORES				TOTAL	MONEY
Art Silvestrone	73	75	75	69	292	5,040
Noel Ratcliffe	74	75	70	73	292	5,040
Gary Player	70	76	69	77	292	5,040
Brian Huggett	75	73	71	75	294	4,288.75
Jim Rhodes	73	72	73	76	294	4,288.75
Matt McCrorie	69	74	75	76	294	4,288.75
Maurice Bembridge	74	74	75	71	294	4,288.75
Liam Higgins	73	73	73	76	295	3,850
Wally Armstrong	77	70	72	76	295	3,850
Randall Vines	70	75	77	73	295	3,850
Peter Green	69	74	76	76	295	3,850
*Kenny Stevenson	74	76	73	72	295	
David Butler	75	72	74	76	297	3,550
Bobby Browne	76	70	77	74	297	3,550
*Roy Smethurst	67	76	77	77	297	
Roland Stafford	74	76	73	75	298	3,250
Alberto Croce	75	72	76	75	298	3,250
Brian Waites	72	75	76	75	298	3,250
Tienie Britz	76	72	74	76	298	3,250
*William Shean, Jr.	73	71	75	79	298	

Lawrence Batley Seniors

Fixby Golf Club, Huddersfield,
West Yorkshire, England
Par 35-36–71; 6,432 yards

August 1-3
purse, £75,000

	SCORES			TOTAL	MONEY
Malcolm Gregson	69	75	65	209	£11,850
Neil Coles	73	70	68	211	6,125
Alberto Croce	73	69	69	211	6,125
Maurice Bembridge	71	73	68	212	3,500
David Creamer	73	71	69	213	2,538
Paul Leonard	72	71	70	213	2,538
Tienie Britz	70	71	72	213	2,538
Tommy Horton	71	69	73	213	2,538
Antonio Garrido	72	72	69	213	2,538
DeRay Simon	74	69	71	214	1,860
Harry Flatman	71	75	66	214	1,860
Terry Gale	76	67	72	215	1,595
John Morgan	72	73	70	215	1,595
Doug Dalziel	72	74	70	216	1,380
Noel Ratcliffe	73	73	70	216	1,380
Chick Evans	75	66	75	216	1,380
Randall Vines	75	73	69	217	1,170
Mike Ingham	70	74	73	217	1,170
Brian Waites	75	73	69	217	1,170
Renato Campagnoli	73	72	73	218	1,020
Tony Grubb	71	73	74	218	1,020
Rafe Botts	74	73	72	219	880
Roberto Bernardini	73	70	76	219	880
Bryan Carter	76	66	77	219	880
David Oakley	75	72	73	220	755
Francisco Abreu	74	74	72	220	755
Hugh Inggs	75	72	74	221	688
Peter Butler	77	77	67	221	688
David Butler	74	76	72	222	652
Michael Murphy	74	75	73	222	652

Northern Electric Seniors

Slaley Hall Golf & Country Club,
Northumberland, England
Par 36-36–72; 6,627 yards

August 16-18
purse, £60,000

	SCORES			TOTAL	MONEY
Tommy Horton	67	67	75	209	£9,700
Noel Ratcliffe	70	69	74	213	5,025
Antonio Garrido	68	74	71	213	5,025
Bobby Verwey	72	69	73	214	2,900
Roger Fidler	75	68	72	215	2,500
Doug Dalziel	76	66	74	216	2,083.33
Chick Evans	73	68	75	216	2,083.33
Malcolm Gregson	74	69	73	216	2,083.33
Brian Waites	73	72	73	218	1,680
Terry Gale	72	74	72	218	1,680
Vincent Tshabalala	74	69	76	219	1,430
Howell Fraser	71	76	72	219	1,430
David Creamer	73	71	76	220	1,290
Hugh Inggs	77	75	68	221	1,158.33
John Morgan	68	79	74	221	1,158.33
Jim Rhodes	73	73	75	221	1,158.33
Maurice Bembridge	77	70	75	222	1,025
Tony Grubb	73	73	76	222	1,025
John Fourie	75	71	78	224	950
Randall Vines	72	80	73	225	851.67
David Butler	73	77	75	225	851.67
Alberto Croce	79	70	76	225	851.67
Hugh Boyle	74	76	76	226	760
David Huish	74	77	76	227	670
Mike Ingham	76	72	79	227	670
Hedley Muscroft	76	77	74	227	670
Roberto Bernardini	77	75	76	228	588
DeRay Simon	77	73	78	228	588
Harry Flatman	78	76	75	229	554
Frank Hill	76	75	79	230	543
Tienie Britz	75	76	79	230	543

Belfry PGA Seniors Championship

The Belfry, West Midlands, England
Par 36-36–72; 6,763 yards

August 22-25
purse, £150,000

	SCORES				TOTAL	MONEY
Terry Gale	72	70	72	70	284	£25,000
Tommy Horton	71	68	74	72	285	16,640
Hugh Baiocchi	76	72	71	70	289	9,350
Chick Evans	73	75	68	74	291	6,910
Maurice Bembridge	76	72	69	74	291	6,910
Hugh Inggs	69	80	72	73	294	5,780
Gordon Parkhill	75	72	72	75	294	5,780
Wally Armstrong	70	73	73	79	295	4,106.67
Malcolm Gregson	71	75	77	72	295	4,106.67
Noel Ratcliffe	74	72	77	72	295	4,106.67
Antonio Garrido	75	70	75	75	295	4,106.67
Brian Waites	76	71	74	74	295	4,106.67
Randall Vines	79	70	75	71	295	4,106.67

	SCORES				TOTAL	MONEY
David Creamer	74	74	73	75	296	2,490
Francisco Abreu	76	73	77	70	296	2,490
Snell Lancaster	76	72	69	79	296	2,490
David Oakley	78	74	72	72	296	2,490
Brian Huggett	72	76	75	74	297	1,930
Vincent Tshabalala	76	78	70	73	297	1,930
Renato Campagnoli	75	77	73	73	298	1,690
Jim Rhodes	77	70	77	74	298	1,690
Alberto Croce	73	76	75	75	299	1,570
Siegfried Vollrath	75	77	75	72	299	1,570
John Morgan	72	76	78	74	300	1,420
Helmuth Schumacher	75	74	74	77	300	1,420
Harry Flatman	77	75	72	76	300	1,420
Jose Cabo	73	78	75	76	302	1,240
Bobby Verwey	74	75	77	76	302	1,240
Liam Higgins	75	74	78	75	302	1,240
Tony Grubb	80	71	80	71	302	1,240

Scottish Seniors Open

Newmachar Golf Club, Aberdeen, Scotland
Par 36-36–72; 6,529 yards

September 6-8
purse, £100,000

	SCORES			TOTAL	MONEY
John Morgan	71	68	70	209	£16,660
Tommy Horton	71	68	74	213	11,100
David Snell	68	71	75	214	4,847.50
Jim Mitchell	72	71	71	214	4,847.50
Bobby Verwey	73	69	72	214	4,847.50
Hugh Baiocchi	71	69	74	214	4,847.50
Arnold O'Connor	71	71	73	215	3,306.67
Brian Barnes	68	73	74	215	3,306.67
David Oakley	75	71	69	215	3,306.67
Bill Hardwick	71	70	75	216	2,580
Malcolm Gregson	72	70	74	216	2,580
David Huish	68	73	75	216	2,580
Brian Waites	72	76	69	217	2,050
Roger Fidler	70	73	74	217	2,050
Alberto Croce	73	74	71	218	1,566.67
Noel Ratcliffe	72	74	72	218	1,566.67
DeRay Simon	72	70	76	218	1,566.67
Snell Lancaster	75	70	74	219	1,190
Brian Huggett	72	72	75	219	1,190
Hugh Inggs	74	71	74	219	1,190
Maurice Bembridge	69	74	76	219	1,190
John Fourie	71	73	75	219	1,190
Randall Vines	72	74	74	220	1,013.33
Vincent Tshabalala	72	71	77	220	1,013.33
Harry Flatman	74	71	75	220	1,013.33
Neil Coles	70	74	77	221	876.67
Renato Campagnoli	74	73	74	221	876.67
Agim Bardha	71	76	74	221	876.67
Wally Armstrong	74	74	73	221	876.67
Gordon Parkhill	73	72	76	221	876.67
David Butler	74	72	75	221	876.67

Motor City Seniors Classic

Warwickshire Golf Club, West Midlands, England
Par 36-36–72; 6,787 yards

October 4-6
purse, £80,000

	SCORES			TOTAL	MONEY
John Morgan	72	69	72	213	£13,350
Randall Vines	75	71	69	215	5,950
Tommy Horton	74	71	70	215	5,950
Bill Hardwick	71	75	69	215	5,950
Neil Coles	75	71	70	216	3,087.50
Frank Hill	76	70	70	216	3,087.50
Liam Higgins	75	71	70	216	3,087.50
Tienie Britz	73	70	73	216	3,087.50
Siegfried Vollrath	72	70	75	217	2,490
Francisco Abreu	76	72	70	218	2,165
Paul Leonard	75	69	74	218	2,165
Alberto Croce	74	72	73	219	1,622.50
Don McCart	75	73	71	219	1,622.50
Wally Armstrong	74	73	72	219	1,622.50
Matt McCrorie	74	72	73	219	1,622.50
Noel Ratcliffe	75	71	74	220	1,112.50
Antonio Garrido	73	74	73	220	1,112.50
Bobby Verwey	73	76	71	220	1,112.50
Volker Krajewski	72	70	78	220	1,112.50
Stewart Adwick	74	72	75	221	927.50
Malcolm Gregson	72	74	75	221	927.50
David Creamer	72	74	76	222	806.25
John Fourie	73	72	77	222	806.25
Jim Rhodes	73	73	76	222	806.25
David Huish	75	74	73	222	806.25
Bryan Carter	75	75	73	223	679
Jan Dorrestein	76	74	73	223	679
Chick Evans	75	74	74	223	679
Bernard Hunt	73	78	72	223	679
Jose Cabo	70	76	77	223	679

The Player Championship

Buckinghamshire Golf Club, Buckinghamshire, England
Par 36-36–72; 6,880 yards

October 18-20
purse, £120,000

	SCORES			TOTAL	MONEY
Tommy Horton	68	69	69	206	£20,000
Malcolm Gregson	67	70	71	208	10,400
Gary Player	68	70	70	208	10,400
Noel Ratcliffe	70	71	69	210	6,000
Jim Rhodes	72	75	65	212	5,300
Neil Coles	72	70	71	213	4,650
Wally Armstrong	68	70	75	213	4,650
Brian Huggett	74	70	70	214	3,775
Maurice Bembridge	72	69	73	214	3,775
David Oakley	72	69	73	214	3,775
John Morgan	70	69	75	214	3,775
Liam Higgins	72	68	75	215	3,200
Harry Flatman	71	75	70	216	2,700
David Huish	71	70	75	216	2,700
Hugh Baiocchi	71	72	73	216	2,700

	SCORES			TOTAL	MONEY
Antonio Garrido	70	74	72	216	2,700
David Butler	75	71	71	217	2,175
Vincent Tshabalala	72	69	76	217	2,175
Peter Townsend	76	72	70	218	1,721.43
Francisco Abreu	74	74	70	218	1,721.43
Roberto Bernardini	72	75	71	218	1,721.43
Brian Waites	72	74	72	218	1,721.43
Alberto Croce	72	69	77	218	1,721.43
David Creamer	70	74	74	218	1,721.43
Bill Hardwick	68	70	80	218	1,721.43
Bobby Verwey	75	73	71	219	1370
Renato Campagnoli	73	71	75	219	1370
Hugh Inggs	72	70	77	219	1370
Randall Vines	75	72	73	220	1245
Paul Leonard	74	71	75	220	1245

Japan Senior Tour

Daiichi Seimei Cup

Tomigato Golf Club, Chiba
Par 36-36–72; 6,428 yards

May 17-19
purse, ¥50,000,000

	SCORES			TOTAL	MONEY
Seiichi Kanai	72	69	69	210	¥7,500,000
Ryosuke Ota	71	69	73	213	3,125,000
Mitoshi Tomita	70	72	71	213	3,125,000
Ichiro Ino	68	75	71	214	1,520,000
Hsieh Min-Nan	75	72	67	214	1,520,000
Hiroshi Ishii	70	78	66	214	1,520,000
Norihiko Matsumoto	72	72	70	214	1,520,000
Kuo Chie-Hsiung	72	71	71	214	1,520,000
Takahiro Takeyasu	73	73	71	217	867,000
Hideo Jibiki	75	67	75	217	867,000
Koji Nakajima	73	74	70	217	867,000
Toshiki Matsui	74	68	75	217	867,000
Osamu Watanabe	74	71	72	217	867,000
Seiji Ogawa	73	76	69	218	750,000
Ichiro Teramoto	70	74	74	218	750,000
Toshikazu Izumi	72	75	71	218	750,000
Sadao Ogawa	72	74	73	219	667,500
Shoji Kikuchi	72	75	72	219	667,500
Fujio Kobayashi	76	73	70	219	667,500
Katsuji Hasegawa	73	73	73	219	667,500
Tetsuhiro Ueda	79	71	69	219	667,500
Seiji Katayama	74	76	69	219	667,500
Hsu Chie-San	71	73	75	219	667,500
Kenichi Tsurumoto	73	71	75	219	667,500

	SCORES			TOTAL	MONEY
Fumio Tanaka	74	73	73	220	595,000
Teruo Sugihara	74	72	74	220	595,000
Masayuki Imai	75	73	73	221	570,000
Wataru Horiguchi	73	73	75	221	570,000
Kenji Ueda	73	71	77	221	570,000
Shichiro Enomoto	76	74	72	222	535,000
Shigeru Uchida	73	74	75	222	535,000
Syunji Kanazawa	74	70	78	222	535,000
Mitsuhiro Kitsuta	78	72	72	222	535,000

TPC Starts

Narita Golf Club, Ibaragi
Par 36-36–72; 6,800 yards

May 30-June 2
purse, ¥50,000,000

	SCORES				TOTAL	MONEY
Haruo Yasuda	72	67	69	72	280	¥7,500,000
Seiichi Kanai	69	70	74	70	283	3,500,000
Hiroshi Ishii	66	75	72	73	286	2,750,000
Hsieh Min-Nan	70	77	71	71	289	2,000,000
Kuo Chie-Hsiung	75	69	71	75	290	1,587,500
Sukree Ohchan	71	73	74	72	290	1,587,500
Koji Nakajima	76	70	74	71	291	1,075,000
Wataru Horiguchi	73	75	72	71	291	1,075,000
Kenichi Tsurumoto	71	76	72	73	292	850,000
Mitsuo Iwata	71	73	75	73	292	850,000
Katsuji Hasegawa	71	74	75	73	293	761,666
Takuo Terashima	74	75	71	73	293	761,666
Norihiko Matsumoto	71	71	77	74	293	761,666
Takahiro Takeyasu	72	69	75	78	294	707,500
Fumio Tanaka	72	74	75	73	294	707,500
Teruo Suzumura	72	72	78	73	295	685,000
Seiji Ogawa	72	75	77	72	296	632,500
Fujio Kobayashi	75	72	75	74	296	632,500
Mitsuhiro Kitta	72	73	76	75	296	632,500
Ichiro Teramoto	74	74	75	73	296	632,500
Katsumi Hara	74	74	75	73	296	632,500
Toshikazu Izumi	76	74	73	73	296	632,500
Fukuji Kikuchi	73	69	79	76	297	558,750
Masao Kikuchi	76	71	75	75	297	558,750
Chen Chen-Chung	77	74	75	71	297	558,750
Osamu Watanabe	76	73	74	74	297	558,750
Toshiki Matsui	73	73	77	75	298	530,000
Masayuki Imai	74	75	78	72	299	495,000
Shoji Kikuchi	75	73	78	73	299	495,000
Hisao Kinoshita	74	72	73	80	299	495,000
Hiroshi Tahara	73	74	78	74	299	495,000
Toji Yokoi	73	75	74	77	299	495,000
Ichiro Togawa	74	72	77	76	299	495,000

HTB Classic

Mitsui Kanko Golf Club, Hokkaido
Par 36-36–72; 6,442 yards

July 5-7
purse, ¥30,000,000

	SCORES			TOTAL	MONEY
Fujio Kobayashi	72	70	71	213	¥4,500,000
Hsieh Min-Nan	68	74	73	215	1,875,000
Ichiro Teramoto	72	73	70	215	1,875,000
Izuru Taka	71	78	67	216	1,200,000
Sadao Ogawa	70	71	76	217	975,000
Shigeru Uchida	71	76	70	217	975,000
Takahiro Takeyasu	73	75	70	218	610,800
Ichiro Togawa	74	71	73	218	610,800
Katsumi Hara	70	73	75	218	610,800
Kuo Chie-Hsiung	72	73	73	218	610,800
Kenichi Tsurumoto	69	79	70	218	610,800
Akira Yabe	72	76	71	219	486,000
Seiji Ogawa	71	77	72	220	460,000
Tetsuhiro Ueda	72	75	73	220	460,000
Mitoshi Tomita	71	76	73	220	460,000
Koji Nakajima	69	77	75	221	432,000
Katsuji Hasegawa	72	77	72	221	432,000
Teruo Suzumura	75	75	71	221	432,000
Kesahiko Uchida	74	73	75	222	391,500
Hisashi Suzumura	73	76	73	222	391,500
Takuo Terashima	74	75	73	222	391,500
Toshiki Matsui	72	76	74	222	391,500
Norihiko Matsumoto	77	72	73	222	391,500
Osamu Watanabe	73	70	79	222	391,500
Ichiro Ino	74	73	76	223	357,000
Hiroshi Ishii	76	73	74	223	357,000
Fumio Tanaka	70	76	78	224	342,000
Hiroshi Tahara	73	75	76	224	342,000
Ryosuke Ota	72	80	72	224	342,000
Hideo Jibiki	75	76	74	225	318,000
Chen Chen-Chung	73	75	77	225	318,000
Jun Nobechi	73	78	74	225	318,000
Kanae Nobechi	74	78	73	225	318,000
Tsutomu Kakuta	74	79	72	225	318,000

Komatsu Nagoya TV Cup

Hananoki Golf Club, Aichi
Par 36-36–72; 6,742 yards

September 13-15
purse, ¥40,000,000

	SCORES			TOTAL	MONEY
Masaji Kusakabe	70	68	69	207	¥6,000,000
Haruo Yasuda	67	70	71	208	2,800,000
Mitoshi Tomita	69	69	71	209	2,200,000
Fujio Kobayashi	72	70	69	211	1,500,000
Izuru Taka	73	68	70	211	1,500,000
Katsuji Hasegawa	71	68	73	212	1,100,000
Terry Gale	71	68	73	212	1,100,000
Shoji Kikuchi	70	70	73	213	800,000
Takuo Terashima	69	72	72	213	800,000
Norihiko Matsumoto	70	73	70	213	800,000
*Osamu Kasugai	71	71	71	213	

	SCORES			TOTAL	MONEY
*Koichi Ohime	71	70	72	213	
Fumio Tanaka	74	72	68	214	624,666
Wataru Horiguchi	73	71	70	214	624,666
Ryosuke Ota	71	70	73	214	624,666
Katsumi Hara	73	73	68	214	624,666
Kuo Chie-Hsiung	73	71	70	214	624,666
Kenichi Tsurumoto	75	70	69	214	624,666
Tetsuhiro Ueda	73	70	72	215	564,000
Ichiro Teramoto	70	70	75	215	564,000
Osamu Watanabe	73	70	72	215	564,000
Akira Yabe	72	74	70	216	528,000
Hiroshi Ishii	75	72	69	216	528,000
Hisashi Suzumura	71	73	72	216	528,000
Hsieh Min-Nan	70	73	74	217	498,000
Hideo Hashimoto	72	72	73	217	498,000
Seiichi Kanai	70	68	80	218	452,000
Fukuji Kikuchi	71	74	73	218	452,000
Masao Kikuchi	72	73	73	218	452,000
Mitsutaka Kono	75	72	71	218	452,000
Takahiro Takeyasu	72	73	73	218	452,000
Hiroshi Tahara	75	73	70	218	452,000
Seiji Katayama	73	72	73	218	452,000
Syunji Kanazawa	71	71	76	218	452,000

Japan PGA Senior Championship

Shimoakima Country Club, Aichi
Par 36-36–72; 6,742 yards

October 3-6
purse, ¥50,000,000

	SCORES				TOTAL	MONEY
Koji Nakajima	76	73	67	71	287	¥7,500,000
Terry Gale	73	72	67	76	288	3,500,000
Seiichi Kanai	70	70	76	73	289	2,166,666
Wataru Horiguchi	70	72	73	74	289	2,166,666
Hiroshi Ishii	76	73	71	69	289	2,166,666
Katsuji Hasegawa	72	73	73	74	292	1,287,500
Teruo Suzumura	70	73	73	76	292	1,287,500
Haruo Yasuda	69	76	72	76	293	1,000,000
Shoji Kikuchi	80	70	73	71	294	850,000
Fujio Kobayashi	76	71	74	73	294	850,000
Ichiro Ino	70	76	75	75	296	750,000
Masaji Kusakabe	72	75	76	73	296	750,000
Akira Yabe	75	74	72	75	296	750,000
Teruo Sugihara	75	74	71	76	296	750,000
Hsieh Min-Nan	76	76	70	75	297	685,000
Namio Takasu	72	75	73	77	297	685,000
Osamu Watanabe	70	76	72	79	297	685,000
Kikuo Arai	72	76	74	77	299	640,000
Seiji Ogawa	75	75	75	74	299	640,000
Hsu Chie-San	75	75	74	75	299	640,000
Noriji Asai	75	73	75	77	300	595,000
Masaharu Ohshima	74	78	72	76	300	595,000
Mitoshi Tomita	78	76	70	76	300	595,000
Sadao Ogawa	73	74	72	83	302	557,500
Hisashi Suzumura	74	77	76	75	302	557,500
Shichiro Enomoto	74	77	75	77	303	510,000
Fumio Tanaka	76	76	74	77	303	510,000

	SCORES				TOTAL	MONEY
Isao Matsui	76	74	78	75	303	510,000
Mitsuhiro Kitta	78	74	73	78	303	510,000
Yoshihiro Takada	75	74	75	79	303	510,000
Ichiro Togawa	73	75	81	74	303	510,000
Kenichi Tsurumoto	71	75	78	79	303	510,000

Japan Senior Open Championship

Fuji County Club, Shyuga Course, Fuji
Par 36-36–72; 6,853 yards

November 21-24
purse, ¥50,000,000

	SCORES				TOTAL	MONEY
Isao Aoki	70	67	67	71	275	¥7,500,000
Graham Marsh	68	71	73	68	280	3,125,000
Gary Player	66	70	71	73	280	3,125,000
Koji Nakajima	70	70	70	72	282	2,000,000
Haruo Yasuda	71	70	71	71	283	1,587,500
Toshikazu Izumi	69	75	70	69	283	1,587,500
Kikuo Arai	73	72	70	70	285	1,150,000
Katsuji Hasegawa	69	75	73	69	286	1,000,000
Seiichi Kanai	71	74	71	71	287	830,000
Mitoshi Tomita	69	76	73	69	287	830,000
Toshiki Matsui	71	72	73	71	287	830,000
*Michiyuki Kurokawa	70	70	74	73	287	
Ryosuke Ota	71	70	73	74	288	747,500
Yutaka Suzuki	73	71	71	73	288	747,500
Akira Yabe	75	69	70	75	289	692,500
Tetsuhiro Ueda	72	69	78	70	289	692,500
Teruo Sugihara	72	73	75	69	289	692,500
Norihiko Matsumoto	72	72	73	72	289	692,500
Hsieh Min-Nan	75	67	73	75	290	640,000
Wataru Horiguchi	76	75	72	67	290	640,000
Osamu Watanabe	72	72	73	73	290	640,000
Masaji Kusakabe	70	74	74	73	291	610,000
Sadao Ogawa	73	73	71	75	292	580,000
Hiroshi Ishii	75	74	72	71	292	580,000
Ichiro Teramoto	75	74	73	70	292	580,000
*Yahei Goto	73	74	69	76	292	
Ichiro Ino	71	75	75	72	293	540,000
Jun Nobechi	76	75	71	71	293	540,000
Teruo Suzumura	72	76	73	72	293	540,000
Hideyo Sugimoto	72	75	74	73	294	515,000
Mitsuo Yoshida	69	73	73	79	294	515,000
*Hayatoshi Ando	73	71	79	71	294	

Women's Tours

Chrysler-Plymouth Tournament of Champions

Grand Cypress Golf Club, Orlando, Florida
Par 36-36–72; 6,382 yards

January 11-14
purse, $725,000

		SCORES			TOTAL	MONEY
Liselotte Neumann	67	66	72	70	275	$117,500
Karrie Webb	71	73	74	68	286	73,500
Laura Davies	72	72	71	72	287	47,750
Missie McGeorge	69	74	70	74	287	47,750
Pat Bradley	73	74	78	66	291	28,166
Kelly Robbins	73	73	77	68	291	28,166
Chris Johnson	72	73	74	72	291	28,166
Barb Mucha	74	78	72	68	292	17,655
Tammie Green	72	76	74	70	292	17,655
Beth Daniel	75	71	75	71	292	17,655
Betsy King	69	80	70	73	292	17,655
Dottie Pepper	76	73	72	72	293	13,016
Woo-Soon Ko	76	70	75	72	293	13,016
Martha Nause	68	74	75	76	293	13,016
Jenny Lidback	73	76	73	72	294	11,007
Lisa Kiggens	71	74	75	74	294	11,007
Jane Geddes	74	74	73	74	295	10,120
Helen Alfredsson	77	76	75	68	296	8,953
Nancy Lopez	75	73	77	71	296	8,953
Dale Eggeling	72	80	72	72	296	8,953
Val Skinner	73	76	75	72	296	8,953
Alison Nicholas	72	77	74	73	296	8,953
Patty Sheehan	70	77	72	77	296	8,953
Michelle McGann	74	74	77	72	297	7,574
Gail Graham	76	71	76	74	297	7,574
Dawn Coe-Jones	74	77	69	77	297	7,574
Sherri Steinhauer	73	78	75	72	298	6,758
JoAnne Carner	76	73	75	74	298	6,758
Barb Thomas	70	78	74	76	298	6,758
Becky Iverson	75	70	77	76	298	6,758

HEALTHSOUTH Inaugural

Disney's Lake Buena Vista Club, Orlando, Florida
Par 36-36–72; 6,336 yards

January 19-21
purse, $450,000

		SCORES		TOTAL	MONEY
Karrie Webb	70	70	69	209	$67,500
Martha Nause	73	68	68	209	36,230
Jane Geddes	72	67	70	209	36,230
(Webb defeated Nause on first extra hole and Geddes on fourth extra hole.)					
Michelle McGann	73	71	66	210	21,511
Patty Sheehan	66	71	73	210	21,511
Mayumi Hirase	73	69	69	211	14,605
Helen Alfredsson	70	70	71	211	14,605
Laura Davies	72	70	70	212	11,208

	SCORES			TOTAL	MONEY
Caroline Pierce	67	73	72	212	11,208
Vicki Fergon	72	72	69	213	8,679
Nancy Harvey	71	72	70	213	8,679
Alice Miller	73	68	72	213	8,679
Laurie Brower	72	74	68	214	6,170
Val Skinner	74	70	70	214	6,170
Shirley Furlong	72	72	70	214	6,170
Missie McGeorge	71	72	71	214	6,170
Tracy Hanson	71	72	71	214	6,170
Liselotte Neumann	73	69	72	214	6,170
Luciana Bemvenuti	73	69	72	214	6,170
Jill McGill	71	70	73	214	6,170
Tina Barrett	73	73	69	215	4,434
Nancy Lopez	70	76	69	215	4,434
Beth Daniel	73	72	70	215	4,434
Kim Williams	71	73	71	215	4,434
Betsy King	72	70	73	215	4,434
Julie Piers	70	72	73	215	4,434
Alicia Dibos	72	69	74	215	4,434
Meg Mallon	74	72	70	216	3,343
Ellie Gibson	72	74	70	216	3,343
Amy Alcott	72	74	70	216	3,343
Kris Tschetter	73	72	71	216	3,343
Cindy Schreyer	73	72	71	216	3,343
Kathryn Marshall	73	72	71	216	3,343
Michelle Bell	73	71	72	216	3,343
Dana Dormann	68	74	74	216	3,343
Kristi Albers	72	67	77	216	3,343

Cup Noodles Hawaiian Ladies Open

Kapolei Golf Course, Kapolei, Oahu, Hawaii
Par 36-36—72; 6,069 yards

February 22-24
purse, $600,000

	SCORES			TOTAL	MONEY
Meg Mallon	74	70	68	212	$90,000
Karrie Webb	75	69	69	213	55,855
Jane Geddes	71	71	72	214	40,759
Tracy Kerdyk	70	74	72	216	31,702
Mitzi Edge	76	72	69	217	21,536
Carin Hj Koch	73	73	71	217	21,536
Sherrin Smyers	69	73	75	217	21,536
Marianne Morris	71	74	73	218	15,700
Carolyn Hill	76	76	67	219	11,774
Tracy Hanson	76	73	70	219	11,774
Michelle Estill	75	74	70	219	11,774
Wendy Ward	77	71	71	219	11,774
Marnie McGuire	75	73	71	219	11,774
Kelly Robbins	76	74	70	220	8,528
Sherri Turner	75	73	72	220	8,528
Kaori Higo	74	72	74	220	8,528
Janice Gibson	75	69	76	220	8,528
Missie McGeorge	72	79	70	221	7,095
Nancy Ramsbottom	76	72	73	221	7,095
Patty Sheehan	76	69	76	221	7,095
Laurie Brower	72	73	76	221	7,095
Judy Dickinson	76	77	69	222	5,791

	SCORES			TOTAL	MONEY
Ikuyo Shiotani	74	76	72	222	5,791
Sue Thomas	78	70	74	222	5,791
Deb Richard	74	73	75	222	5,791
Karen Davies	74	73	75	222	5,791
Caroline Pierce	73	74	75	222	5,791
Susie Redman	77	73	73	223	4,614
Vicki Fergon	77	72	74	223	4,614
Woo-Soon Ko	71	78	74	223	4,614
Chris Johnson	75	72	76	223	4,614
Luciana Bemvenuti	74	73	76	223	4,614
Dale Eggeling	73	73	77	223	4,614
Beth Daniel	73	72	78	223	4,614

PING/Welch's Championship

Randolf Park North Golf Course, Tucson, Arizona
Par 35-37–72; 6,222 yards

March 14-17
purse, $450,000

	SCORES				TOTAL	MONEY
Liselotte Neumann	68	71	69	68	276	$67,500
Cathy Johnston-Forbes	71	70	65	71	277	41,891
Karen Weiss	72	69	71	67	279	24,530
Michelle McGann	69	68	74	68	279	24,530
Dale Eggeling	69	70	69	71	279	24,530
Annika Sorenstam	75	66	70	69	280	15,850
Tracy Kerdyk	72	72	68	69	281	11,321
Karrie Webb	70	72	69	70	281	11,321
Mardi Lunn	71	71	68	71	281	11,321
Patty Sheehan	71	66	71	73	281	11,321
Catrin Nilsmark	73	72	70	67	282	8,604
Elaine Crosby	72	71	73	67	283	6,663
Alice Miller	73	71	70	69	283	6,663
Jane Geddes	71	71	71	70	283	6,663
Val Skinner	70	73	69	71	283	6,663
Cindy Figg-Currier	70	71	71	71	283	6,663
Hiromi Kobayashi	73	69	69	72	283	6,663
Kris Tschetter	71	70	69	73	283	6,663
Lauri Merten	73	70	70	71	284	4,631
Tracy Hanson	73	70	70	71	284	4,631
Helen Alfredsson	72	70	71	71	284	4,631
Deb Richard	71	71	71	71	284	4,631
Martha Nause	69	72	72	71	284	4,631
Dana Dormann	71	69	73	71	284	4,631
Kathryn Marshall	70	72	70	72	284	4,631
Joan Pitcock	75	66	71	72	284	4,631
Sherri Turner	73	68	70	73	284	4,631
Mayumi Hirase	70	73	73	69	285	3,169
Nancy Harvey	73	69	73	70	285	3,169
Juli Inkster	70	70	75	70	285	3,169
Ellie Gibson	73	71	70	71	285	3,169
Alison Nicholas	72	71	71	71	285	3,169
Robin Walton	76	66	72	71	285	3,169
Pat Bradley	68	72	74	71	285	3,169
Catriona Matthew	72	67	75	71	285	3,169
Alicia Dibos	70	69	75	71	285	3,169
Karen Davies	73	71	69	72	285	3,169
Dottie Pepper	69	72	71	73	285	3,169
Danielle Ammaccapane	72	66	66	81	285	3,169

Standard Register PING

Moon Valley Country Club, Phoenix, Arizona
Par 36-37–73; 6,445 yards

March 21-24
purse, $700,000

	SCORES				TOTAL	MONEY
Laura Davies	71	73	69	71	284	$105,000
Kristal Parker-Gregory	69	72	69	75	285	65,165
Kelly Robbins	73	70	72	71	286	47,553
Karrie Webb	70	73	77	68	288	33,462
Sherri Steinhauer	69	73	76	70	288	33,462
Annika Sorenstam	74	68	76	71	289	21,251
Liselotte Neumann	71	74	71	73	289	21,251
Dottie Pepper	74	67	75	73	289	21,251
Deb Richard	76	71	76	67	290	14,265
Kris Tschetter	74	70	75	71	290	14,265
Nancy Lopez	71	72	74	73	290	14,265
Patty Sheehan	71	71	74	74	290	14,265
Judy Dickinson	76	72	73	70	291	9,812
Brandie Burton	70	70	79	72	291	9,812
Dawn Coe-Jones	69	74	75	73	291	9,812
Pat Bradley	72	72	72	75	291	9,812
Hiromi Kobayashi	72	71	73	75	291	9,812
Val Skinner	70	70	75	76	291	9,812
Barb Mucha	68	73	73	77	291	9,812
Vicki Goetze	74	73	74	71	292	7,581
Susie Redman	70	75	76	71	292	7,581
Meg Mallon	74	73	72	73	292	7,581
Marianne Morris	68	72	76	76	292	7,581
Beth Daniel	72	74	81	66	293	6,199
Joan Pitcock	75	70	82	66	293	6,199
Michelle McGann	75	73	76	69	293	6,199
Mardi Lunn	75	72	77	69	293	6,199
Lisa Kiggens	71	73	79	70	293	6,199
Cindy Schreyer	75	70	73	75	293	6,199
Trish Johnson	72	73	73	75	293	6,199

Nabisco Dinah Shore

Mission Hills Country Club, Rancho Mirage, California
Par 36-36–72; 6,460 yards

March 28-31
purse, $900,000

	SCORES				TOTAL	MONEY
Patty Sheehan	71	72	67	71	281	$135,000
Kelly Robbins	71	72	71	68	282	64,158
Meg Mallon	71	70	71	70	282	64,158
Annika Sorenstam	67	72	73	70	282	64,158
Amy Fruhwirth	71	73	68	71	283	32,305
Karrie Webb	72	70	70	71	283	32,305
Brandie Burton	75	67	68	73	283	32,305
Hollis Stacy	69	71	74	70	284	23,550
Kris Tschetter	71	74	70	70	285	21,285
Deb Richard	73	71	73	69	286	16,212
Liselotte Neumann	73	69	75	69	286	16,212
Val Skinner	74	71	71	70	286	16,212
Rosie Jones	72	67	75	72	286	16,212
Tracy Hanson	69	69	74	74	286	16,212
Nancy Lopez	73	72	73	69	287	12,114

	SCORES				TOTAL	MONEY
Missie McGeorge	74	70	74	69	287	12,114
Joan Pitcock	71	74	71	71	287	12,114
Laura Davies	72	70	70	75	287	12,114
Marianne Morris	76	71	71	70	288	10,189
Stephanie Farwig	71	73	73	71	288	10,189
Tracy Kerdyk	67	72	77	72	288	10,189
Juli Inkster	70	70	74	74	288	10,189
Pat Bradley	73	76	71	69	289	8,111
Jane Geddes	74	72	74	69	289	8,111
Donna Andrews	74	70	76	69	289	8,111
Akiko Fukushima	74	68	78	69	289	8,111
Amy Alcott	68	78	71	72	289	8,111
Penny Hammel	75	69	73	72	289	8,111
Dottie Pepper	71	71	75	72	289	8,111
Nanci Bowen	76	70	70	73	289	8,111

Twelve Bridges LPGA Classic

Twelve Bridges Golf Club, Lincoln, California
Par 37-34–71; 6,040 yards

April 4-7
purse, $500,000

	SCORES				TOTAL	MONEY
Kelly Robbins	73	68	68	64	273	$75,000
Val Skinner	69	68	71	65	273	46,546
(Robbins defeated Skinner on fifth extra hole.)						
Emilee Klein	65	71	73	68	277	27,256
Meg Mallon	73	68	67	69	277	27,256
Barb Mucha	68	70	69	70	277	27,256
Donna Andrews	73	71	68	66	278	14,341
Robin Walton	70	71	69	68	278	14,341
Cindy Schreyer	70	69	68	71	278	14,341
Annika Sorenstam	69	66	72	71	278	14,341
Rosie Jones	72	71	67	69	279	10,064
Deb Richard	72	68	70	69	279	10,064
Amy Fruhwirth	76	67	73	64	280	8,806
Juli Inkster	72	70	71	68	281	7,799
Tracy Hanson	75	65	71	70	281	7,799
Tracy Kerdyk	69	71	68	73	281	7,799
Dana Dormann	74	69	70	69	282	6,541
Laura Davies	70	74	68	70	282	6,541
Wendy Ward	74	68	67	73	282	6,541
Karrie Webb	73	73	69	68	283	5,786
Michelle McGann	70	72	73	68	283	5,786
Brandie Burton	74	67	68	74	283	5,786
Leta Lindley	75	73	68	68	284	4,826
Jane Geddes	70	77	66	71	284	4,826
Nanci Bowen	73	70	70	71	284	4,826
Marianne Morris	71	71	71	71	284	4,826
Martha Nause	72	69	72	71	284	4,826
Mardi Lunn	71	70	71	72	284	4,826
Penny Hammel	76	70	69	70	285	4,126
Liselotte Neumann	75	70	68	72	285	4,126
Catrin Nilsmark	73	70	69	73	285	4,126

Chick-fil-A Charity Championship

Eagle's Landing Country Club, Stockbridge, Georgia
Par 36-36–72; 6,187 yards

April 19-21
purse, $550,000

	SCORES			TOTAL	MONEY
Barb Mucha	68	70	70	208	$82,500
Liselotte Neumann	74	68	68	210	44,282
Dottie Pepper	70	69	71	210	44,282
Marianne Morris	74	69	68	211	23,985
Michelle McGann	74	68	69	211	23,985
Rosie Jones	73	69	69	211	23,985
Deb Richard	71	71	70	212	14,575
Hiromi Kobayashi	70	70	72	212	14,575
Page Dunlap	70	70	72	212	14,575
Gail Graham	73	72	69	214	9,931
Alison Nicholas	76	68	70	214	9,931
Mayumi Hirase	73	71	70	214	9,931
Tina Barrett	69	74	71	214	9,931
Michele Redman	70	71	73	214	9,931
Brandie Burton	74	72	69	215	7,431
Stefania Croce	71	75	69	215	7,431
Pat Hurst	73	72	70	215	7,431
Vicki Fergon	70	71	74	215	7,431
Danielle Ammaccapane	74	72	70	216	6,121
Terry-Jo Myers	73	71	72	216	6,121
Kathryn Marshall	72	72	72	216	6,121
Trish Johnson	73	70	73	216	6,121
Karen Lunn	71	72	73	216	6,121
Katie Peterson-Parker	75	70	72	217	5,147
Helen Alfredsson	73	72	72	217	5,147
Michelle Estill	72	72	73	217	5,147
Karen Weiss	66	75	76	217	5,147
Kris Tschetter	77	71	70	218	4,258
Sherri Turner	74	74	70	218	4,258
Mardi Lunn	76	71	71	218	4,258
Luciana Bemvenuti	70	77	71	218	4,258
Val Skinner	68	79	71	218	4,258
Laurie Brower	73	73	72	218	4,258
Stephanie Farwig	72	74	72	218	4,258

Sara Lee Classic

Hermitage Golf Course, Old Hickory, Tennessee
Par 36-36–72; 6,290 yards

April 26-28
purse, $600,000

	SCORES			TOTAL	MONEY
Meg Mallon	70	71	69	210	$90,000
Stephanie Farwig	72	69	71	212	48,307
Pam Wright	71	70	71	212	48,307
Tracy Hanson	72	74	67	213	28,682
Emilee Klein	75	69	69	213	28,682
Mayumi Hirase	74	73	67	214	15,498
Hiromi Kobayashi	75	70	69	214	15,498
Terry-Jo Myers	74	69	71	214	15,498
Jane Crafter	72	71	71	214	15,498
Karen Davies	72	70	72	214	15,498
Marianne Morris	68	73	73	214	15,498

	SCORES			TOTAL	MONEY
Pat Bradley	75	71	69	215	9,359
Brandie Burton	75	70	70	215	9,359
Lisa Kiggens	74	71	70	215	9,359
Kelly Robbins	73	69	73	215	9,359
Kristi Albers	72	70	73	215	9,359
Barb Mucha	79	69	68	216	6,948
Stefania Croce	73	75	68	216	6,948
Tracy Kerdyk	75	72	69	216	6,948
Missie McGeorge	74	72	70	216	6,948
Jill McGill	73	73	70	216	6,948
Mary Beth Zimmerman	76	68	72	216	6,948
Helen Alfredsson	70	72	74	216	6,948
Jennifer Wyatt	74	72	71	217	5,313
Suzanne Strudwick	74	72	71	217	5,313
Helen Dobson	76	69	72	217	5,313
Juli Inkster	73	70	74	217	5,313
Amy Benz	70	73	74	217	5,313
Stephanie Maynor	71	70	76	217	5,313
Caroline Pierce	71	69	77	217	5,313

Sprint Titleholders Championship

LPGA International, Daytona Beach, Florida
Par 36-36—72; 6,393 yards

May 2-5
purse, $1,200,000

	SCORES				TOTAL	MONEY
Karrie Webb	71	65	70	66	272	$180,000
Kelly Robbins	70	68	69	66	273	111,711
Val Skinner	67	67	70	70	274	81,519
Tina Barrett	70	69	70	66	275	52,332
Laura Davies	70	69	67	69	275	52,332
Catrin Nilsmark	69	66	68	72	275	52,332
Pat Bradley	73	67	68	68	276	35,626
Annika Sorenstam	69	72	70	66	277	31,400
Juli Inkster	73	68	71	66	278	24,510
Emilee Klein	71	71	68	68	278	24,510
Stefania Croce	73	68	68	69	278	24,510
Dawn Coe-Jones	68	70	68	72	278	24,510
Chris Johnson	70	68	72	69	279	20,036
Vicki Goetze	70	74	68	68	280	17,620
Nanci Bowen	69	73	69	69	280	17,620
Mayumi Hirase	68	72	67	73	280	17,620
Michelle Dobek	76	68	68	69	281	14,902
Liselotte Neumann	70	73	69	69	281	14,902
Marianne Morris	70	72	70	69	281	14,902
Kris Tschetter	72	67	73	69	281	14,902
Martha Nause	74	70	69	69	282	12,135
Stephanie Farwig	72	72	68	70	282	12,135
Alicia Dibos	71	71	70	70	282	12,135
Tammie Green	73	70	68	71	282	12,135
Leta Lindley	73	70	67	72	282	12,135
Michelle McGann	71	67	70	74	282	12,135
Tracy Kerdyk	74	70	70	69	283	9,840
Brandie Burton	71	72	71	69	283	9,840
Kim Williams	72	71	68	72	283	9,840
Jennifer Wyatt	71	70	70	72	283	9,840
Colleen Walker	73	69	67	74	283	9,840
Michelle Estill	69	70	69	75	283	9,840

McDonald's LPGA Championship

Du Pont Country Club, Wilmington, Delaware
Par 35-36–71; 6,386 yards

May 10-12
purse, $1,200,000

	SCORES			TOTAL	MONEY
Laura Davies	72	71	70	213	$180,000
Julie Piers	72	72	70	214	111,711
Penny Hammel	73	72	70	215	72,461
Jane Crafter	75	68	72	215	72,461
Judy Dickinson	71	74	71	216	37,800
Juli Inkster	70	73	73	216	37,800
Shirley Furlong	70	73	73	216	37,800
Val Skinner	73	69	74	216	37,800
Hiromi Kobayashi	71	70	75	216	37,800
Michelle Dobek	72	75	70	217	22,342
Patty Sheehan	72	74	71	217	22,342
Meg Mallon	69	75	73	217	22,342
Kristi Albers	72	71	74	217	22,342
Lisa Kiggens	75	70	73	218	17,058
Betsy King	72	72	74	218	17,058
Jill Briles-Hinton	73	69	76	218	17,058
Annika Sorenstam	69	73	76	218	17,058
Carin Hj Koch	73	74	72	219	13,080
Kris Tschetter	75	71	73	219	13,080
Kathryn Marshall	73	73	73	219	13,080
Sherri Steinhauer	74	71	74	219	13,080
Deb Richard	74	70	75	219	13,080
Amy Benz	73	71	75	219	13,080
Nancy Lopez	70	73	76	219	13,080
Kelly Robbins	69	71	79	219	13,080
Jill McGill	76	70	74	220	9,744
Susie Redman	74	72	74	220	9,744
Dottie Pepper	70	76	74	220	9,744
Terry-Jo Myers	74	71	75	220	9,744
Jane Geddes	71	74	75	220	9,744
Caroline Pierce	75	69	76	220	9,744
Missie McGeorge	74	70	76	220	9,744
Beth Daniel	72	72	76	220	9,744

LPGA Corning Classic

Corning Country Club, Corning, New York
Par 36-36–72; 6,062 yards

May 23-26
purse, $600,000

	SCORES				TOTAL	MONEY
Rosie Jones	67	69	71	69	276	$90,000
Val Skinner	67	75	66	70	278	55,855
Joan Pitcock	69	72	70	68	279	36,230
Nancy Ramsbottom	71	71	68	69	279	36,230
Cindy Schreyer	73	70	69	68	280	23,398
Jane Geddes	71	70	69	70	280	23,398
Chris Johnson	68	71	73	69	281	17,813
Dale Eggeling	73	73	69	67	282	13,511
Sherri Turner	69	75	68	70	282	13,511
Patty Sheehan	71	68	73	70	282	13,511
Patti Liscio	70	71	68	73	282	13,511
Lauri Merten	72	72	73	66	283	10,567

	SCORES				TOTAL	MONEY
Laurie Rinker-Graham	72	72	72	68	284	9,057
Brandie Burton	72	73	67	72	284	9,057
Caroline Pierce	71	72	69	72	284	9,057
Cindy Rarick	71	70	71	72	284	9,057
Nancy Lopez	74	70	71	70	285	7,396
Kristal Parker-Gregory	71	70	74	70	285	7,396
Pat Bradley	72	69	73	71	285	7,396
Michelle Estill	72	68	69	76	285	7,396
Dana Dormann	68	77	72	69	286	6,116
Barb Mucha	68	71	77	70	286	6,116
Alison Nicholas	70	70	75	71	286	6,116
Tammie Green	74	72	67	73	286	6,116
Liselotte Neumann	67	72	72	75	286	6,116
Jill McGill	69	77	72	69	287	5,313
Sherri Steinhauer	72	73	72	70	287	5,313
Danielle Ammaccapane	68	76	68	75	287	5,313
Janet Anderson	72	75	72	69	288	4,607
Tracy Hanson	70	74	75	69	288	4,607
Jody Anschutz	69	73	76	70	288	4,607
Janice Gibson	71	76	69	72	288	4,607
Kris Monaghan	71	72	73	72	288	4,607

U.S. Women's Open

Pine Needles Lodge & Golf Club, Southern Pines,
North Carolina
Par 35-35–70; 6,207 yards

May 30-June 2
purse, $1,200,000

	SCORES				TOTAL	MONEY
Annika Sorenstam	70	67	69	66	272	$212,500
Kris Tschetter	70	74	68	66	278	125,000
Pat Bradley	74	70	67	69	280	60,372
Jane Geddes	71	69	70	70	280	60,372
Brandie Burton	70	70	69	71	280	60,372
Laura Davies	74	68	70	69	281	40,077
Catrin Nilsmark	72	73	68	69	282	35,995
Cindy Rarick	73	70	72	68	283	29,584
Liselotte Neumann	74	69	70	70	283	29,584
Val Skinner	74	68	71	70	283	29,584
Tammie Green	72	70	69	72	283	29,584
Jenny Lidback	70	76	68	70	284	24,654
Alison Nicholas	74	70	74	67	285	23,243
Patty Sheehan	74	71	72	69	286	19,664
Stefania Croce	72	70	74	70	286	19,664
Cindy Schreyer	74	70	70	72	286	19,664
Maggie Will	71	72	70	73	286	19,664
Michele Redman	70	73	69	74	286	19,664
Cathy Johnston-Forbes	72	75	71	69	287	14,374
Meg Mallon	77	68	72	70	287	14,374
Karrie Webb	74	73	68	72	287	14,374
Beth Daniel	69	78	68	72	287	14,374
Wendy Ward	76	68	71	72	287	14,374
Mayumi Hirase	74	69	69	75	287	14,374
Michiko Hattori	74	71	74	69	288	10,482
Kim Williams	69	78	69	72	288	10,482
Becky Iverson	73	71	71	73	288	10,482
Nancy Harvey	72	71	69	76	288	10,482
Karen Weiss	74	72	73	70	289	8,134

	SCORES	TOTAL	MONEY
Susie Redman	73 73 71 72	289	8,134
Rosie Jones	71 70 76 72	289	8,134
Tracy Kerdyk	73 72 69 75	289	8,134
Emilee Klein	71 69 73 76	289	8,134

Oldsmobile Classic

Walnut Hills Country Club, East Lansing, Michigan
Par 36-36–72; 6,191 yards

June 6-9
purse, $600,000

	SCORES	TOTAL	MONEY
Michelle McGann	71 66 70 65	272	$90,000
Liselotte Neumann	69 71 67 65	272	55,855
(McGann defeated Neumann on third extra hole.)			
Meg Mallon	71 67 72 63	273	40,759
Tracy Hanson	68 73 63 70	274	31,702
Donna Andrews	68 69 72 66	275	25,663
Kris Tschetter	71 68 70 68	277	19,473
Laura Davies	73 65 71 68	277	19,473
Cathy Johnston-Forbes	74 66 68 70	278	13,524
Kelly Robbins	69 68 71 70	278	13,524
Dana Dormann	66 70 72 70	278	13,524
Pat Bradley	68 67 71 72	278	13,524
Alison Nicholas	67 69 71 72	279	10,320
Emilee Klein	68 66 73 72	279	10,320
Marianne Morris	72 72 69 67	280	8,034
Susie Redman	70 71 72 67	280	8,034
Brandie Burton	74 69 68 69	280	8,034
Sally Little	70 70 71 69	280	8,034
Annika Sorenstam	71 68 72 69	280	8,034
Jenny Lidback	69 71 70 70	280	8,034
Jan Stephenson	71 72 66 71	280	8,034
Dale Eggeling	66 74 72 69	281	6,281
Caroline Pierce	71 70 68 72	281	6,281
Robin Hood	69 71 69 72	281	6,281
Beth Daniel	68 70 70 73	281	6,281
Deb Richard	74 67 73 68	282	5,640
Hiromi Kobayashi	71 72 69 70	282	5,640
Wendy Ward	73 70 75 65	283	5,368
Barb Whitehead	74 69 71 70	284	4,915
Carin Hj Koch	70 73 71 70	284	4,915
Kim Saiki	68 76 68 72	284	4,915
Chris Johnson	70 71 71 72	284	4,915

Edina Realty LPGA Classic

Edinburgh USA, Brooklyn Park, Minnesota
Par 36-36–72; 6,141 yards

June 14-16
purse, $550,000

	SCORES	TOTAL	MONEY
Liselotte Neumann	67 73 67	207	$82,500
Brandie Burton	72 68 67	207	39,208
Suzanne Strudwick	69 68 70	207	39,208
Carin Hj Koch	72 63 72	207	39,208
(Neumann defeated Burton, Strudwick and Koch on third extra hole.)			

	SCORES			TOTAL	MONEY
Dawn Coe-Jones	69	74	65	208	19,741
Jane Geddes	68	72	68	208	19,741
Emilee Klein	69	68	71	208	19,741
Jane Crafter	72	69	68	209	12,385
Michelle Estill	71	69	69	209	12,385
Amy Benz	71	67	71	209	12,385
Laurel Kean	72	65	72	209	12,385
Renee Heiken	71	71	68	210	8,579
Dina Ammaccapane	71	71	68	210	8,579
Tracy Kerdyk	70	71	69	210	8,579
Kris Tschetter	69	68	73	210	8,579
Nancy Lopez	69	67	74	210	8,579
Allison Finney	71	70	70	211	6,918
Pat Hurst	70	67	74	211	6,918
Donna Andrews	65	72	74	211	6,918
Kris Monaghan	70	73	69	212	5,839
Barb Whitehead	73	66	73	212	5,839
Vicki Goetze	71	68	73	212	5,839
Cindy Rarick	70	69	73	212	5,839
Val Skinner	69	70	73	212	5,839
Betsy King	75	69	69	213	4,953
Cindy Figg-Currier	75	68	70	213	4,953
Penny Hammel	70	73	70	213	4,953
Jill McGill	72	68	73	213	4,953
Stephanie Farwig	75	71	68	214	3,868
Michelle McGann	72	74	68	214	3,868
LaRee Pearl Sugg	71	75	68	214	3,868
Janet Anderson	70	75	69	214	3,868
Denise Killeen	73	71	70	214	3,868
Carolyn Hill	72	72	70	214	3,868
Sherri Steinhauer	70	74	70	214	3,868
Wendy Doolan	72	71	71	214	3,868
Stephanie Maynor	68	74	72	214	3,868
Michele Redman	69	70	75	214	3,868

Rochester International

Locust Hill Country Club, Pittsford, New York
Par 35-37–72; 6,162 yards
(First round cancelled — rain.)

June 20-23
purse, $600,000

	SCORES			TOTAL	MONEY
Dottie Pepper	69	66	71	206	$90,000
Annika Sorenstam	72	67	69	208	55,855
Amy Fruhwirth	68	71	72	211	40,759
Barb Whitehead	76	68	69	213	26,166
Allison Finney	73	71	69	213	26,166
Michelle Estill	69	70	74	213	26,166
Jane Crafter	73	70	71	214	14,380
Nancy Lopez	73	69	72	214	14,380
Ellie Gibson	69	72	73	214	14,380
Alicia Dibos	70	70	74	214	14,380
Lori West	69	71	74	214	14,380
Kim Cathrein	72	74	70	216	9,401
Donna Andrews	73	71	72	216	9,401
Jill McGill	74	69	73	216	9,401
Betsy King	73	70	73	216	9,401

	SCORES			TOTAL	MONEY
Karen Weiss	72	71	73	216	9,401
Kris Monaghan	75	73	69	217	6,277
Sherri Steinhauer	74	73	70	217	6,277
Kelly Robbins	74	73	70	217	6,277
Meg Mallon	75	71	71	217	6,277
Kristal Parker-Gregory	74	72	71	217	6,277
Noelle Daghe	73	72	72	217	6,277
Gail Graham	71	74	72	217	6,277
Leta Lindley	72	72	73	217	6,277
Cindy Schreyer	72	71	74	217	6,277
Tina Barrett	72	71	74	217	6,277
Dana Dormann	71	72	74	217	6,277
Sue Thomas	72	69	76	217	6,277
Dina Ammaccapane	71	70	76	217	6,277
Dale Eggeling	74	73	71	218	4,409
Patty Sheehan	72	75	71	218	4,409
Tammie Green	74	72	72	218	4,409
Catriona Matthew	74	71	73	218	4,409
Rosie Jones	71	73	74	218	4,409
Tracy Hanson	72	70	76	218	4,409

ShopRite LPGA Classic

Greate Bay Resort & Country Club,
Somers Point, New Jersey
Par 36-35–71; 6,235 yards

June 28-30
purse, $750,000

	SCORES			TOTAL	MONEY
Dottie Pepper	67	66	69	202	$112,500
Amy Benz	64	66	76	206	69,819
Annika Sorenstam	67	72	68	207	40,885
Michelle McGann	70	67	70	207	40,885
Marianne Morris	68	68	71	207	40,885
Amy Fruhwirth	71	69	68	208	24,342
Denise Killeen	70	67	71	208	24,342
Sally Little	67	74	68	209	17,738
Meg Mallon	71	67	71	209	17,738
Jane Geddes	66	72	71	209	17,738
Patty Sheehan	69	72	69	210	12,554
Val Skinner	69	70	71	210	12,554
Dale Eggeling	68	70	72	210	12,554
Pat Bradley	69	68	73	210	12,554
Amy Alcott	69	68	73	210	12,554
Kelly Robbins	73	67	71	211	9,459
Laurie Rinker-Graham	71	69	71	211	9,459
Caroline Pierce	65	75	71	211	9,459
Jill McGill	71	66	74	211	9,459
Wendy Doolan	66	70	75	211	9,459
Susie Redman	72	70	70	212	7,174
Robin Hood	70	72	70	212	7,174
Cathy Johnston-Forbes	69	73	70	212	7,174
Kay Cockerill	72	69	71	212	7,174
Beth Daniel	69	72	71	212	7,174
Mayumi Hirase	69	72	71	212	7,174
Suzanne Strudwick	69	71	72	212	7,174
Emilee Klein	69	70	73	212	7,174
Tracy Hanson	67	69	76	212	7,174

	SCORES			TOTAL	MONEY
Juli Inkster	72	71	70	213	5,580
Gail Graham	69	72	72	213	5,580
Kris Tschetter	69	70	74	213	5,580
Liselotte Neumann	69	70	74	213	5,580
Tina Barrett	68	70	75	213	5,580

Jamie Farr Kroger Classic

Highland Meadows Golf Club, Sylvania, Ohio
Par 34-37–71; 6,319 yards

July 5-7
purse, $575,000

	SCORES			TOTAL	MONEY
Joan Pitcock	68	66	70	204	$86,250
Marianne Morris	69	68	68	205	53,528
Catrin Nilsmark	66	74	66	206	31,345
Mitzi Edge	69	70	67	206	31,345
Nanci Bowen	67	71	68	206	31,345
Kris Monaghan	75	67	66	208	18,662
Beth Daniel	69	68	71	208	18,662
Dottie Pepper	71	71	67	209	14,322
Tracy Hanson	73	64	72	209	14,322
Dana Dormann	71	73	66	210	9,439
Rosie Jones	71	71	68	210	9,439
Gail Graham	73	68	69	210	9,439
Pat Bradley	71	70	69	210	9,439
Cathy Johnson-Forbes	72	68	70	210	9,439
Mayumi Hirase	69	70	71	210	9,439
Terry-Jo Myers	70	68	72	210	9,439
Alicia Dibos	67	70	73	210	9,439
Karrie Webb	71	73	67	211	6,267
Maggie Will	72	71	68	211	6,267
Penny Hammel	72	71	68	211	6,267
Vicki Goetze	72	70	69	211	6,267
Ellie Gibson	71	71	69	211	6,267
Jill McGill	74	66	71	211	6,267
Danielle Ammaccapane	70	70	71	211	6,267
Kelly Robbins	70	69	72	211	6,267
Brandie Burton	75	70	67	212	4,668
Kim Bauer	70	75	67	212	4,668
Dale Eggeling	71	73	68	212	4,668
Susan Veasey	69	73	70	212	4,668
Jane Geddes	71	70	71	212	4,668
Kim Saiki	72	68	72	212	4,668
Juli Inkster	68	70	74	212	4,668
Cindy Figg-Currier	68	69	75	212	4,668

Youngstown-Warren LPGA Classic

Avalon Lakes Golf Course, Warren, Ohio
Par 36-36–72; 6,308 yards

July 12-14
purse, $600,000

	SCORES			TOTAL	MONEY
Michelle McGann	71	64	65	200	$90,000
Kim Saiki	68	67	68	203	55,855
Kelly Robbins	67	70	68	205	40,759

	SCORES			TOTAL	MONEY
Laurie Brower	71	70	65	206	31,702
Janet Anderson	74	65	68	207	20,077
Tammie Green	68	71	68	207	20,077
Vicki Goetze	70	68	69	207	20,077
Deb Richard	69	65	73	207	20,077
Pat Hurst	69	73	66	208	13,435
Lori West	69	69	70	208	13,435
Tracy Hanson	69	72	68	209	11,473
Dottie Pepper	69	71	70	210	9,963
Meg Mallon	69	70	71	210	9,963
Karrie Webb	71	65	74	210	9,963
Mayumi Hirase	71	69	71	211	8,252
Donna Andrews	72	67	72	211	8,252
Missie McGeorge	69	70	72	211	8,252
Lorie Kane	71	69	72	212	7,397
Barb Mucha	67	72	73	212	7,397
Dale Eggeling	73	71	69	213	6,254
Karen Lunn	72	69	72	213	6,254
Penny Hammel	69	71	73	213	6,254
Amy Fruhwirth	67	72	74	213	6,254
Jean Bartholomew	71	67	75	213	6,254
Cathy Johnston-Forbes	70	68	75	213	6,254
Julie Piers	70	75	69	214	5,041
Noelle Daghe	73	70	71	214	5,041
Barb Bunkowsky Scherbak	70	73	71	214	5,041
Tracy Kerdyk	71	71	72	214	5,041
Laurel Kean	69	70	75	214	5,041
Hiromi Kobayashi	70	68	76	214	5,041

Friendly's Classic

Crestview Country Club, Agawam, Massachusetts
Par 36-36–72; 6,381 yards

July 18-21
purse, $500,000

	SCORES				TOTAL	MONEY
Dottie Pepper	68	69	73	69	279	$75,000
Brandie Burton	67	72	66	75	280	46,546
Mardi Lunn	67	69	70	75	281	33,966
Annika Sorenstam	69	72	72	73	286	26,418
Pat Hurst	75	71	72	69	287	21,386
Beth Daniel	72	70	75	72	289	14,341
Marianne Morris	68	74	75	72	289	14,341
Kim Saiki	70	73	72	74	289	14,341
Barb Whitehead	72	68	74	75	289	14,341
Kristi Albers	73	73	73	71	290	9,336
Shelley Hamlin	69	77	72	72	290	9,336
Karen Davies	74	70	74	72	290	9,336
Connie Chillemi	70	69	74	77	290	9,336
Dina Ammaccapane	71	73	76	71	291	7,142
Amy Benz	74	69	75	73	291	7,142
Trish Johnson	73	73	71	74	291	7,142
Carolyn Hill	74	71	72	74	291	7,142
Gail Graham	77	72	75	68	292	5,821
Lenore Rittenhouse	74	70	76	72	292	5,821
Cindy Rarick	76	72	70	74	292	5,821
Martha Nause	74	70	73	75	292	5,821
Kris Tschetter	72	72	73	75	292	5,821
Sue Thomas	74	74	77	68	293	5,004

	SCORES				TOTAL	MONEY
Stephanie Maynor	74	72	75	72	293	5,004
Anne Marie Palli	73	74	73	74	294	4,614
Susie Redman	71	75	74	74	294	4,614
Stefania Croce	73	71	76	74	294	4,614
Pat Bradley	73	71	78	73	295	4,161
Michelle Dobek	73	72	73	77	295	4,161
Margaret Platt	68	75	72	80	295	4,161

Michelob Light Heartland Classic

Forest Hills Country Club, St. Louis, Missouri
Par 36-36–72; 6,337 yards

July 25-28
purse, $550,000

	SCORES				TOTAL	MONEY
Vicki Fergon	71	63	68	74	276	$82,500
Patti Liscio	73	71	69	67	280	44,282
Pat Hurst	70	72	66	72	280	44,282
Juli Inkster	70	72	69	71	282	29,060
Betsy King	71	73	68	71	283	23,524
Karrie Webb	71	74	71	68	284	17,850
Catrin Nilsmark	71	72	70	71	284	17,850
Heather Drew	72	70	75	68	285	12,385
Nancy Taylor	74	70	70	71	285	12,385
Carin Hj Koch	69	73	70	73	285	12,385
Penny Hammel	68	73	69	75	285	12,385
Michelle Bell	74	73	70	69	286	7,289
Wendy Doolan	75	70	72	69	286	7,289
Dale Eggeling	74	71	72	69	286	7,289
Sue Thomas	69	76	72	69	286	7,289
Barb Whitehead	72	76	67	71	286	7,289
Robin Walton	74	68	73	71	286	7,289
Pearl Sinn	73	71	70	72	286	7,289
Tina Barrett	73	71	70	72	286	7,289
Barb Mucha	69	74	71	72	286	7,289
Melissa McNamara	71	69	74	72	286	7,289
Vicki Goetze	71	73	69	73	286	7,289
Danielle Ammaccapane	67	74	72	73	286	7,289
Mitzi Edge	71	74	70	72	287	5,202
Jan Stephenson	75	69	71	72	287	5,202
Caroline Pierce	69	72	72	74	287	5,202
Brandie Burton	75	73	70	70	288	4,621
Nanci Bowen	74	73	71	70	288	4,621
Stefania Croce	71	72	73	72	288	4,621
Nancy Lopez	70	74	71	73	288	4,621

du Maurier Classic

Edmonton Country Club, Edmonton, Alberta, Canada
Par 35-37–72; 6,324 yards

August 1-4
purse, $1,000,000

	SCORES				TOTAL	MONEY
Laura Davies	71	70	70	66	277	$150,000
Nancy Lopez	68	71	69	71	279	80,513
Karrie Webb	65	68	74	72	279	80,513
Meg Mallon	72	65	69	74	280	52,837

	SCORES				TOTAL	MONEY
Pat Hurst	69	70	68	74	281	42,772
Liselotte Neumann	69	74	67	73	283	32,456
Annika Sorenstam	71	70	69	73	283	32,456
Kathy Postlewait	72	68	70	74	284	24,909
Dana Dormann	69	70	71	74	284	24,909
Amy Fruhwirth	70	71	71	73	285	20,128
Rosie Jones	70	71	68	76	285	20,128
Catriona Matthew	71	73	72	70	286	14,808
Chris Greatrex	74	69	71	72	286	14,808
Juli Inkster	73	72	68	73	286	14,808
Emilee Klein	71	73	69	73	286	14,808
Barb Mucha	68	74	71	73	286	14,808
Marta Figueras-Dotti	70	71	72	73	286	14,808
Val Skinner	71	72	69	74	286	14,808
Judy Dickinson	73	70	73	71	287	11,574
Jan Stephenson	73	71	70	73	287	11,574
Joan Pitcock	73	67	71	76	287	11,574
Melissa McNamara	69	74	71	74	288	10,567
Michele Redman	71	74	72	72	289	8,861
Hiromi Kobayashi	73	71	73	72	289	8,861
Lori West	72	71	74	72	289	8,861
Jane Crafter	71	72	74	72	289	8,861
Laurie Brower	71	74	71	73	289	8,861
Alice Ritzman	71	72	72	74	289	8,861
Kathryn Marshall	69	72	74	74	289	8,861
Michelle Estill	75	69	69	76	289	8,861
Nanci Bowen	70	72	69	78	289	8,861

PING Welch's Championship

Blue Hill Country Club, Canton, Massachusetts
Par 36-36—72; 6,137 yards

August 8-11
purse, $500,000

	SCORES				TOTAL	MONEY
Emilee Klein	71	69	68	65	273	$75,000
Karrie Webb	65	73	68	69	275	46,546
Meg Mallon	72	68	69	67	276	33,966
Gail Graham	69	70	70	68	277	26,418
Danielle Ammaccapane	68	71	71	68	278	21,386
Liselotte Neumann	72	67	70	70	279	17,612
Barb Whitehead	71	70	70	69	280	14,844
Pat Bradley	70	72	73	66	281	11,825
Rosie Jones	69	72	71	69	281	11,825
Lorie Kane	70	70	70	71	281	11,825
Marianne Morris	72	72	71	67	282	9,209
Alice Ritzman	70	70	69	73	282	9,209
Tammie Green	70	74	68	71	283	8,329
Juli Inkster	68	71	74	71	284	7,573
Pearl Sinn	71	71	70	72	284	7,573
Amy Fruhwirth	70	73	73	69	285	6,567
Vicki Fergon	67	74	75	69	285	6,567
Michele Redman	73	69	73	70	285	6,567
Stephanie Maynor	73	74	70	69	286	5,356
Val Skinner	71	73	72	70	286	5,356
Kris Monaghan	71	73	72	70	286	5,356
Penny Hammel	72	71	72	71	286	5,356
Wendy Ward	72	71	72	71	286	5,356

	SCORES				TOTAL	MONEY
Deb Richard	72	69	74	71	286	5,356
Missie Berteotti	71	69	72	74	286	5,356
Denise Killeen	73	74	72	68	287	3,950
Betsy King	73	70	75	69	287	3,950
Amy Benz	72	74	71	70	287	3,950
Leta Lindley	75	69	73	70	287	3,950
Vicki Goetze	72	72	72	71	287	3,950
Terry-Jo Myers	75	71	69	72	287	3,950
Tracy Hanson	69	70	76	72	287	3,950
Melissa McNamara	69	73	72	73	287	3,950
Janet Anderson	67	70	76	74	287	3,950
Nanci Bowen	71	70	71	75	287	3,950

Star Bank LPGA Classic

Country Club of the North, Dayton, Ohio
Par 36-36–72; 6,331 yards

August 23-25
purse, $550,000

	SCORES			TOTAL	MONEY
Laura Davies	68	66	70	204	$82,500
Maggie Will	70	69	68	207	44,282
Pat Hurst	67	71	69	207	44,282
Juli Inkster	70	70	68	208	29,060
Donna Andrews	69	75	65	209	17,324
Dottie Pepper	71	68	70	209	17,324
Nancy Lopez	68	71	70	209	17,324
Elaine Crosby	68	71	70	209	17,324
Kelly Robbins	68	70	71	209	17,324
Rosie Jones	73	70	67	210	10,277
Tracy Kerdyk	73	69	68	210	10,277
Brandie Burton	71	66	73	210	10,277
Beth Daniel	69	68	73	210	10,217
Jill McGill	73	72	66	211	7,688
Betsy King	69	73	69	211	7,688
Missie McGeorge	72	68	71	211	7,688
Marianne Morris	68	72	71	211	7,688
Susan Veasey	70	68	73	211	7,688
Michelle McGann	72	72	68	212	6,023
Michelle Mackall	71	73	68	212	6,023
Shelley Hamlin	69	73	70	212	6,023
Amy Benz	71	70	71	212	6,023
Penny Hammel	69	72	71	212	6,023
Kris Tschetter	72	67	73	212	6,023
Kris Monaghan	75	69	69	213	4,837
Laurel Kean	73	71	69	213	4,837
Laurie Rinker-Graham	73	70	70	213	4,837
Tammie Green	72	70	71	213	4,837
Wendy Ward	69	73	71	213	4,837
Julie Piers	70	71	72	213	4,837

State Farm Rail Classic

Rail Golf Course, Springfield, Illinois
Par 36-36–72; 6,403 yards

August 31-September 2
purse, $575,000

	SCORES			TOTAL	MONEY
Michelle McGann	69	65	68	202	$86,250
Laura Davies	68	68	66	202	46,294
Barb Whitehead	68	66	68	202	46,294
(McGann defeated Davies and Whitehead on third extra hole.)					
Tracy Kerdyk	66	68	69	203	30,381
Catriona Matthew	67	70	67	204	20,639
Chris Johnson	67	69	68	204	20,639
Betsy King	67	67	70	204	20,639
Hiromi Kobayashi	66	70	69	205	12,948
Laurel Kean	68	67	70	205	12,948
Pat Bradley	67	68	70	205	12,948
Mayumi Hirase	66	68	71	205	12,948
Barb Mucha	67	69	70	206	10,126
Shani Waugh	70	71	66	207	8,960
Shelley Hamlin	67	71	69	207	8,960
Kris Tschetter	63	75	69	207	8,960
Dina Ammaccapane	69	71	68	208	7,088
Pamela Wright	71	68	69	208	7,088
Allison Finney	68	71	69	208	7,088
Sue Thomas	71	67	70	208	7,088
LaRee Pearl Sugg	68	70	70	208	7,088
Karen Weiss	71	65	72	208	7,088
Alicia Dibos	72	69	68	209	5,370
Ellie Gibson	71	70	68	209	5,370
Donna Andrews	68	71	70	209	5,370
Marianne Morris	69	68	72	209	5,370
Sherri Turner	68	69	72	209	5,370
Cindy Haley	68	69	72	209	5,370
Emilee Klein	67	70	72	209	5,370
Alice Miller	69	65	75	209	5,370
Trish Johnson	70	72	68	210	4,112
Wendy Doolan	70	71	69	210	4,112
Dale Eggeling	70	70	70	210	4,112
Jean Bartholomew	72	67	71	210	4,112
Alice Ritzman	71	68	71	210	4,112
Penny Hammel	68	71	71	210	4,112
Pearl Sinn	68	71	71	210	4,112

Safeway LPGA Golf Championship

Columbia Edgewater Country Club, Portland, Oregon
Par 36-36–72; 6,294 yards

September 6-8
purse, $550,000

	SCORES			TOTAL	MONEY
Dottie Pepper	65	70	67	202	$82,500
Chris Johnson	69	65	70	204	51,201
Karrie Webb	70	69	69	208	33,211
Stefania Croce	69	68	71	208	33,211
Kelly Robbins	69	73	67	209	21,448
Juli Inkster	71	69	69	209	21,448
Alison Nicholas	69	71	70	210	16,328
Maggie Will	71	74	66	211	12,392

	SCORES			TOTAL	MONEY
Donna Andrews	70	68	73	211	12,392
Annika Sorenstam	68	70	73	211	12,392
Cathy Johnston-Forbes	69	68	74	211	12,392
Leta Lindley	74	69	69	212	9,438
Nancy Lopez	70	70	72	212	9,438
Rosie Jones	75	70	68	213	7,039
Brandie Burton	72	71	70	213	7,039
Hiromi Kobayashi	69	74	70	213	7,039
Mary Beth Zimmerman	72	70	71	213	7,039
Catrin Nilsmark	68	73	72	213	7,039
Michelle Estill	69	71	73	213	7,039
Emilee Klein	69	71	73	213	7,039
Dawn Coe-Jones	68	72	73	213	7,039
Tammie Green	70	67	76	213	7,039
Jan Stephenson	72	73	69	214	5,152
Jane Crafter	69	76	69	214	5,152
Patty Sheehan	73	71	70	214	5,152
Deb Richard	72	72	70	214	5,152
Betsy King	74	67	73	214	5,152
Moira Dunn	69	72	73	214	5,152
Tracy Kerdyk	70	76	69	215	4,179
Mayumi Hirase	71	73	71	215	4,179
Kim Saiki	71	72	72	215	4,179
Wendy Doolan	75	66	74	215	4,179
Cindy Rarick	71	70	74	215	4,179
Jane Geddes	71	70	74	215	4,179

SAFECO Classic

Meridian Valley Country Club, Kent, Washington
Par 36-36–72; 6,241 yards

September 12-15
purse, $550,000

	SCORES				TOTAL	MONEY
Karrie Webb	66	71	71	69	277	$82,500
Patty Sheehan	65	72	70	72	279	51,201
Barb Mucha	72	70	68	70	280	33,211
Tammie Green	71	64	69	76	280	33,211
Val Skinner	69	68	70	74	281	23,524
Pat Hurst	71	71	70	70	282	16,697
Amy Fruhwirth	70	70	71	71	282	16,697
Kate Hughes	69	71	71	71	282	16,697
Wendy Ward	74	71	69	69	283	12,316
Deb Richard	70	72	68	73	283	12,316
Mitzi Edge	71	71	71	71	284	9,797
Dana Dormann	71	70	72	71	284	9,797
Liselotte Neumann	71	71	69	73	284	9,797
Hiromi Kobayashi	68	72	73	72	285	7,837
Tina Barrett	67	74	71	73	285	7,837
Annika Sorenstam	77	66	68	74	285	7,837
Kelly Robbins	71	68	72	74	285	7,837
Rosie Jones	74	71	72	70	287	6,384
Betsy King	73	71	70	73	287	6,384
Jill McGill	71	72	70	74	287	6,384
Tracy Kerdyk	75	67	70	75	287	6,384
Jan Stephenson	70	72	69	76	287	6,384
Julie Piers	74	72	72	70	288	5,058
Sue Thomas	72	70	74	72	288	5,058

	SCORES				TOTAL	MONEY
Vicki Fergon	70	71	75	72	288	5,058
Nanci Bowen	72	71	71	74	288	5,058
Donna Andrews	70	71	72	75	288	5,058
Catrin Nilsmark	71	69	73	75	288	5,058
Dina Ammaccapane	69	70	71	78	288	5,058
Dale Eggeling	73	73	72	71	289	3,742
Alison Munt	73	72	72	72	289	3,742
Marianne Morris	73	71	72	73	289	3,742
Leta Lindley	73	73	69	74	289	3,742
Brandie Burton	71	74	70	74	289	3,742
Pamela Kometani	73	71	71	74	289	3,742
Gail Graham	69	73	73	74	289	3,742
Emilee Klein	69	72	73	75	289	3,742
Kim Saiki	68	72	71	78	289	3,742
Caroline Pierce	68	71	72	78	289	3,742

Fieldcrest Cannon Classic

Peninsula Country Club, Charlotte, North Carolina
Par 36-36–72; 6,318 yards

September 26-29
purse, $500,000

	SCORES				TOTAL	MONEY
Trish Johnson	67	71	68	64	270	$75,000
Kim Saiki	68	67	70	68	273	46,546
Dottie Pepper	68	67	68	71	274	33,966
Tracy Kerdyk	68	69	71	68	276	23,902
Dale Eggeling	68	69	68	71	276	23,902
Cindy Schreyer	68	69	74	66	277	16,228
Helen Alfredsson	67	72	71	67	277	16,228
Barb Mucha	70	68	69	71	278	11,825
Donna Andrews	68	69	70	71	278	11,825
Gail Graham	67	67	71	73	278	11,825
Carin Hj Koch	68	71	72	68	279	9,183
Judy Dickinson	73	70	67	69	279	9,183
Michelle McGann	70	73	68	69	280	7,547
Laura Davis	72	68	71	69	280	7,547
Pat Hurst	68	71	70	71	280	7,547
Robin Hood	65	71	71	73	280	7,547
Martha Nause	70	71	74	66	281	6,038
Missie McGeorge	68	73	72	68	281	6,038
Beth Daniel	70	69	72	70	281	6,038
Chris Johnson	70	69	71	71	281	6,038
Cindy Haley	70	69	68	74	281	6,038
Cindy Rarick	71	72	71	68	282	4,747
Hollis Stacy	72	69	73	68	282	4,747
Kim Bauer	71	71	71	69	282	4,747
Sally Little	70	69	73	70	282	4,747
Lori West	72	68	71	71	282	4,747
Susan Veasey	72	68	68	74	282	4,747
Kris Tschetter	68	73	66	75	282	4,747
Wendy Doolan	68	75	71	69	283	3,773
Kris Monaghan	71	68	75	69	283	3,773
Hiromi Kobayashi	67	71	74	71	283	3,773
Maggie Will	68	73	70	72	283	3,773
Dina Ammaccapane	71	69	70	73	283	3,773
Emilee Klein	70	70	70	73	283	3,773

JAL Big Apple Classic

Wykagyl Country Club, New Rochelle, New York
Par 35-36–71; 6,176 yards

October 3-5
purse, $725,000

	SCORES			TOTAL	MONEY
Caroline Pierce	72	67	72	211	$108,750
Tina Barrett	77	72	67	216	58,371
Karrie Webb	72	71	73	216	58,371
Missie McGeorge	75	70	72	217	38,306
Deb Richard	74	75	69	218	24,260
Amy Fruhwirth	74	72	72	218	24,260
Laurie Brower	73	70	75	218	24,260
Dottie Pepper	71	71	76	218	24,260
Jane Geddes	76	75	68	219	15,443
Vicki Goetze	71	74	74	219	15,443
Michelle McGann	75	67	77	219	15,443
Emilee Klein	76	72	72	220	12,403
Leigh Ann Mills	74	72	74	220	12,403
Carin Hj Koch	72	77	72	221	10,944
Cindy Rarick	77	70	74	221	10,944
Jan Stephenson	76	74	72	222	9,120
Kim Saiki	74	75	73	222	9,120
Jenny Lidback	74	74	74	222	9,120
Marianne Morris	73	75	74	222	9,120
Kristi Albers	74	72	76	222	9,120
Maggie Will	74	79	70	223	6,910
Sally Little	74	77	72	223	6,910
Michele Redman	78	72	73	223	6,910
Michelle Estill	77	73	73	223	6,910
Beth Daniel	73	77	73	223	6,910
Barb Whitehead	78	71	74	223	6,910
Nanci Bowen	75	74	74	223	6,910
Luciana Bemvenuti	74	75	74	223	6,910
Penny Hammel	75	73	75	223	6,910
Alicia Dibos	76	77	71	224	5,277
Margaret Platt	76	75	73	224	5,277
Val Skinner	75	76	73	224	5,277
Kelly Robbins	77	71	76	224	5,277
Annika Sorenstam	76	72	76	224	5,277
Robin Hood	72	75	77	224	5,277

CoreStates Betsy King Classic

Berkleigh Country Club, Kutztown, Pennsylvania
Par 35-37–72; 6,075 yards

October 10-13
purse, $600,000

	SCORES				TOTAL	MONEY
Annika Sorenstam	66	69	67	68	270	$90,000
Laura Davies	69	65	71	73	278	55,855
Dawn Coe-Jones	73	72	72	66	283	36,230
Liselotte Neumann	70	75	70	68	283	36,230
Caroline Pierce	70	74	71	70	285	23,398
Beth Daniel	73	70	71	71	285	23,398
Mayumi Hirase	74	72	71	69	286	15,901
Jane Geddes	74	71	72	69	286	15,901
Tina Barrett	71	71	72	72	286	15,901
Barb Whitehead	72	72	73	70	287	9,594
Amy Read	75	72	68	72	287	9,594

	SCORES				TOTAL	MONEY
Brandie Burton	73	72	70	72	287	9,594
Kristi Albers	72	67	76	72	287	9,594
Kim Williams	70	74	70	73	287	9,594
Dottie Pepper	73	70	71	73	287	9,594
Kelly Robbins	74	70	69	74	287	9,594
Cindy Schreyer	69	73	71	74	287	9,594
Juli Inkster	70	69	72	76	287	9,594
Kris Tschetter	73	75	70	70	288	6,793
Jan Stephenson	72	76	70	70	288	6,793
Joan Pitcock	74	70	72	72	288	6,793
Dale Eggeling	70	73	71	74	288	6,793
Penny Hammel	75	71	73	70	289	5,773
·Susan Veasey	74	73	71	71	289	5,773
Meg Mallon	70	69	78	72	289	5,773
Deb Richard	75	70	71	73	289	5,773
Kathryn Marshall	75	68	79	68	290	5,041
Margaret Platt	73	75	71	71	290	5,041
Gail Graham	78	67	73	72	290	5,041
Kim Saiki	70	74	71	75	290	5,041

Samsung World Championship of Women's Golf

Ildong Lakes Golf Club, Seoul, Korea
Par 36-36–72; 6,377 yards

October 17-20
purse, $500,000

	SCORES				TOTAL	MONEY
Annika Sorenstam	66	69	69	70	274	$125,000
Helen Alfredsson	71	68	70	66	275	70,000
Seri Park	68	67	70	72	277	45,000
Kris Tschetter	71	69	71	68	279	28,500
Jane Geddes	69	69	73	68	279	28,500
Liselotte Neumann	74	66	74	68	282	20,000
Karrie Webb	70	70	70	72	282	20,000
Val Skinner	67	71	72	72	282	20,000
Brandie Burton	73	73	69	68	283	16,000
Aiko Hashimoto	71	73	72	68	284	14,750
Emilee Klein	66	74	71	73	284	14,750
Rosie Jones	73	68	74	72	287	13,750
Marianne Morris	69	71	72	75	287	13,750
Barb Mucha	73	71	71	75	290	13,000
Michelle McGann	73	73	73	72	291	12,500
Pat Bradley	74	72	74	72	292	12,000

ITT LPGA Tour Championship

Desert Inn Golf Club, Las Vegas, Nevada
Par 36-36–72; 6,324 yards

November 21-24
purse, $700,000

	SCORES				TOTAL	MONEY
Karrie Webb	69	70	68	65	272	$150,000
Kelly Robbins	70	70	71	65	276	60,000
Nancy Lopez	73	68	69	66	276	60,000
Emilee Klein	69	68	70	69	276	60,000
Brandie Burton	72	69	69	67	277	30,000
Laura Davies	69	70	71	67	277	30,000
Juli Inkster	68	70	72	67	277	30,000

		SCORES			TOTAL	MONEY
Pat Hurst	71	75	65	68	279	20,000
Michelle McGann	68	71	71	69	279	20,000
Annika Sorenstam	73	68	73	67	281	16,000
Penny Hammel	68	71	74	68	281	16,000
Caroline Pierce	71	72	70	69	282	13,500
Jane Geddes	68	74	71	71	284	12,500
Deb Richard	74	70	72	69	285	11,500
Val Skinner	69	74	71	72	286	11,000
Mayumi Hirase	67	79	73	68	287	9,500
Patty Sheehan	76	73	69	69	287	9,500
Tracy Kerdyk	73	71	71	72	287	9,500
Rosie Jones	75	69	70	73	287	9,500
Dottie Pepper	71	72	71	73	287	9,500
Barb Mucha	75	71	72	70	288	7,750
Kris Tschetter	73	73	69	73	288	7,750
Barb Whitehead	72	75	72	70	289	7,000
Liselotte Neumann	70	73	73	73	289	7,000
Meg Mallon	70	73	72	74	289	7,000
Tina Barrett	73	73	73	72	291	6,500
Marianne Morris	71	74	75	72	292	6,250
Pat Bradley	76	71	78	68	293	5,875
Amy Fruhwirth	77	74	70	72	293	5,875
Hiromi Kobayashi	74	79	70	74	297	5,500

Diners Club Matches

PGA West, La Quinta, California
Par 36-36—72; 6,214 yards

December 12-15
purse, $700,000

FIRST ROUND

Karrie Webb and Michelle McGann defeated Patty Sheehan and Nancy Lopez, 2 and 1
Dottie Pepper and Juli Inkster defeated Annika Sorenstam and Catrin Nilsmark, 3 and 1
Emilee Klein and Kris Tschetter defeated Laura Davies and Karen Lunn, 2 and 1
Kelly Robbins and Tammie Green defeated Liselotte Neumann and Jane Geddes,
5 and 4

SECOND ROUND

Sorenstam and Nilsmark defeated Sheehan and Lopez, 3 and 1
Pepper and Inkster defeated Webb and McGann, 3 and 2
Neumann and Geddes defeated Klein and Tschetter, 4 and 3
Robbins and Green defeated Davies and Lunn, 4 and 2

(Losers after second round received $25,000 each.)

THIRD ROUND

Robbins and Green defeated Klein and Tschetter, 4 and 2
Pepper and Inkster defeated Webb and McGann, 19 holes

(Losers after third round received $40,000 each.)

FOURTH ROUND

Pepper and Inkster defeated Robbins and Green, 1 up

(Pepper and Inkster received $110,000 each; Robbins and Green received $60,000 each.)

Women's European Tour

Women's Welsh Open

St. Pierre Hotel & Country Club, Chepstow, Wales
Par 36-37–73; 6,207 yards

May 2-5
purse, £75,000

	SCORES				TOTAL	MONEY
Lisa Hackney	73	75	69	72	289	£11,250
Laura Navarro	77	73	71	69	290	7,612.50
Kristel Mourgue D'Algue	79	74	72	67	292	5,250
Patricia Meunier Lebouc	76	73	70	75	294	4,050
Federica Dassu	78	75	73	70	296	2,322
Corinne Dibnah	77	75	70	74	296	2,322
Caroline Hall	72	76	75	73	296	2,322
Julie Forbes	77	71	73	75	296	2,322
Lora Fairclough	72	76	76	72	296	2,322
Shani Waugh	74	76	76	71	297	1,440
Sarah Bennett	79	74	72	72	297	1,440
Debbie Dowling	73	78	75	72	298	1,196.25
Amaia Arruti	78	76	70	74	298	1,196.25
Stephanie Dallongeville	72	76	71	79	298	1,196.25
Joanne Morley	74	75	76	73	298	1,196.25
Dale Reid	77	74	76	72	299	1,065
Charlotta Sorenstam	79	75	73	72	299	1,065
Helen Wadsworth	77	77	72	73	299	1,065
Karina Orum	77	74	77	72	300	990
Marina Arruti	74	76	74	76	300	990
Penny Grice-Whittaker	78	74	75	74	301	907.50
Wendy Dicks	78	76	72	75	301	907.50
Lara Tadiotto	80	72	75	74	301	907.50
Loraine Lambert	77	76	76	72	301	907.50
Pernilla Sterner	77	75	74	75	301	907.50
Diane Barnard	74	81	72	75	302	828.75
Sophie Gustafson	78	76	73	75	302	828.75
Raquel Carriedo-Tomas	80	76	74	73	303	761.25
Debbie Doniger	78	73	76	76	303	761.25
Valerie Michaud	78	74	76	75	303	761.25
Charlotta Eliasson Wharton	78	73	77	75	303	761.25

Costa Azul Ladies' Open

Troia Golf Club
Par 36-36–72; 5,707 yards

May 9-11
purse, £60,000

Aroeira Golf Club
Par 36-36–72; 5,982 yards
Lisbon, Portugal

	SCORES			TOTAL	MONEY
Shani Waugh	71	72	71	214	£9,000
Marie Laure de Lorenzi	76	73	67	216	4,018.50
Helene Koch	69	75	72	216	4,018.50

	SCORES			TOTAL	MONEY
Mary Grace Estuesta	72	71	73	216	4,018.50
Aideen Rogers	73	72	71	216	4,018.50
Julie Forbes	74	71	72	217	1,800
Joanne Morley	73	74	70	217	1,800
Anne-Marie Knight	76	71	70	217	1,800
Corinne Dibnah	76	69	73	218	1,272
Lara Tadiotto	68	78	72	218	1,272
Claire Duffy	71	70	78	219	1,034
Loraine Lambert	72	73	74	219	1,034
Rachel Hetherington	76	71	72	219	1,034
Lisa Jensen	69	77	74	220	915
Asa Gottmo	69	76	75	220	915
Charlotta Sorenstam	72	73	76	221	840
Caroline Hall	70	75	76	221	840
Patricia Meunier Lebouc	72	73	76	221	840
Lisa Hackney	73	78	70	221	840
Dale Reid	70	73	79	222	744
Tracy Loveys	77	71	74	222	744
Sarah Bennett	72	76	74	222	744
Valerie Michaud	76	74	72	222	744
Iben Tinning	77	71	74	222	744
Diane Barnard	74	75	74	223	663
Regine Lautens	72	75	76	223	663
Amaia Arruti	77	73	73	223	663
Marina Arruti	71	82	70	223	663
Federica Dassu	70	79	75	224	582
Anna-Carin Jonasson	69	78	77	224	582
Stephanie Dallongeville	76	74	74	224	582
Tina Fischer	72	78	74	224	582
Helen Wadsworth	75	74	75	224	582

Ford-Stimorol Danish Open

Vejle Golf Club, Vejle, Denmark
Par 36-36—72; 5,659 yards

June 7-9
purse, £80,000

	SCORES			TOTAL	MONEY
Nadene Gole	71	65	73	209	£12,000
Gillian Stewart	67	73	71	211	6,013.33
Rachel Hetherington	72	69	70	211	6,013.33
Anne-Marie Knight	68	70	73	211	6,013.33
Marie Laure de Lorenzi	73	69	70	212	2,864
Wendy Dicks	73	70	69	212	2,864
Lisa Hackney	73	70	69	212	2,864
Loraine Lambert	67	69	77	213	1,896
Martina Koch	69	71	73	213	1,896
Stephanie Dallongeville	72	71	71	214	1,482.66
Nicola Moult	75	67	72	214	1,482.66
Pernilla Sterner	72	70	72	214	1,482.66
Maria Hjorth	72	69	74	215	1,206.40
Anna-Carin Jonasson	74	72	69	215	1,206.40
Charlotta Sorenstam	70	74	71	215	1,206.40
Sophie Gustafson	75	73	67	215	1,206.40
Irene Yeoh	68	78	69	215	1,206.40
Debbie Dowling	70	72	74	216	1,019.42
Helene Koch	69	71	76	216	1,019.42
Barbara Pestana	70	71	75	216	1,019.42

	SCORES			TOTAL	MONEY
Raquel Carriedo-Tomas	70	74	72	216	1,019.42
Petra Rigby-Jinglov	74	71	71	216	1,019.42
Kristel Mourgue d'Algue	77	66	73	216	1,019.42
Iben Tinning	72	74	70	216	1,019.42
Federica Dassu	77	71	69	217	884
Laurette Maritz	75	68	74	217	884
Xonia Wunsch-Ruiz	70	75	72	217	884
Lynnette Brooky	71	72	74	217	884
Dale Reid	73	73	72	218	752
Isabella Maconi	74	72	72	218	752
Joanne Mills	73	72	73	218	752
Julie Forbes	74	74	70	218	752
Lora Fairclough	71	73	74	218	752
Evelyn Orley	69	76	73	218	752
Charlotta Eliasson Wharton	73	72	73	218	752

Deesse Ladies' Swiss Open

Golf & Country Club de Maison Blanche,
Geneva, Switzerland
Par 37-36–73; 6,102 yards

June 13-16
purse, £80,000

	SCORES				TOTAL	MONEY
Sophie Gustafson	69	69	73	69	280	£12,000
Lisa Hackney	73	73	66	69	281	8,120
Patricia Meunier Lebouc	68	72	71	72	283	4,960
Charlotta Eliasson Wharton	71	70	70	72	283	4,960
Laura Navarro	72	71	70	71	284	3,392
Xonia Wunsch-Ruiz	72	72	70	71	285	2,600
Julie Forbes	73	70	68	74	285	2,600
Dale Reid	73	71	72	70	286	1,896
Lara Tadiotto	72	69	73	72	286	1,896
Marie Laure de Lorenzi	69	70	78	70	287	1,362.66
Charlotta Sorenstam	76	71	69	71	287	1,362.66
Raquel Carriedo-Tomas	72	71	74	70	287	1,362.66
Loraine Lambert	73	73	70	71	287	1,362.66
Joanne Morley	72	75	71	69	287	1,362.66
Helen Wadsworth	73	70	75	69	287	1,362.66
Federica Dassu	75	68	74	71	288	1,120
Stephanie Dallongeville	73	70	76	69	288	1,120
Tina Fischer	76	70	70	72	288	1,120
Lora Fairclough	73	76	70	69	288	1,120
Gillian Stewart	74	73	72	70	289	1,016
Joanne Mills	72	73	72	72	289	1,016
Morag Wright	75	74	71	69	289	1,016
Diane Barnard	76	73	73	68	290	932
Nadene Gole	68	73	75	74	290	932
Tracy Loveys	76	71	71	72	290	932
Anne-Marie Knight	72	75	73	70	290	932
Susan Moon	73	75	74	69	291	848
Malin Burstrom	76	68	76	71	291	848
Barbara Pestana	75	73	73	70	291	848
Janet Soulsby	72	72	73	75	292	740
Caryn Louw	75	71	72	74	292	740
Petra Rigby-Jinglov	75	71	74	72	292	740
Pernilla Sterner	80	69	73	70	292	740
Kristel Mourgue d'Algue	72	73	76	71	292	740
Sara Forster	71	75	73	73	292	740

Evian Masters

Royal Golf Club Evian, Evians-les-Bains, France
Par 36-36–72; 5,908 yards

June 19-22
purse, £375,000

	SCORES				TOTAL	MONEY
Laura Davies	72	69	65	68	274	£56,250
Carin Hj Koch	73	68	67	70	278	38,000
Helen Alfredsson	70	72	68	69	279	26,250
Mardi Lunn	76	69	66	70	281	18,031.25
Amy Alcott	72	70	68	71	281	18,031.25
Alison Nicholas	70	70	71	71	282	13,125
Karrie Webb	71	73	68	71	283	11,250
Marie Laure de Lorenzi	73	71	70	71	285	8,416.66
Lisa Hackney	66	74	75	70	285	8,416.66
Caroline Peek	70	70	72	73	285	8,416.66
Charlotta Sorenstam	73	69	70	74	286	6,668.75
Patricia Meunier Lebouc	69	72	72	73	286	6,668.75
Katie Peterson-Parker	72	72	72	71	287	6,025
Natascha Fink	70	76	70	72	288	5,818.75
Martina Koch	74	72	68	74	288	5,818.75
Trish Johnson	70	72	69	78	289	5,406.25
Amaia Arruti	75	71	71	72	289	5,406.25
Rachel Hetherington	72	72	71	74	289	5,406.25
Lora Fairclough	70	74	71	74	289	5,406.25
Federica Dassu	72	75	72	71	290	4,925
Regine Lautens	70	75	74	71	290	4,925
Gillian Stewart	72	71	72	76	291	4,382.50
Sally Prosser	70	72	75	74	291	4,382.50
Mary Grace Estuesta	70	70	75	76	291	4,382.50
Stephanie Dallongeville	72	73	75	71	291	4,382.50
Loraine Lambert	72	71	75	73	291	4,382.50
Diane Barnard	70	70	77	75	292	3,812.50
Penny Grice-Whittaker	74	72	73	73	292	3,812.50
Catrin Nilsmark	70	74	70	78	292	3,812.50
Wendy Dicks	73	73	70	76	292	3,812.50

Glashutte Ladies' Austrian Open

Colony Club Gutenhof, Himberg, Austria
Par 36-37–73; 6,267 yards

June 28-30
purse, £60,000

	SCORES			TOTAL	MONEY
Martina Koch	74	68	71	213	£9,000
Lynnette Brooky	71	72	72	215	6,090
Joanne Morley	72	69	75	216	4,200
Karina Orum	71	75	71	217	2,892
Mary Grace Estuesta	72	71	74	217	2,892
Mandy Sutton	74	73	71	218	1,800
Raquel Carriedo-Tomas	74	73	71	218	1,800
Cathy Schmitt	75	65	78	218	1,800
Mardi Lunn	75	66	78	219	1,216
Loraine Lambert	70	73	76	219	1,216
Anne-Marie Knight	74	74	71	219	1,216
Debbie Dowling	75	71	74	220	957
Shani Waugh	70	75	75	220	957
Stephanie Dallongeville	74	70	76	220	957
Rachel Hetherington	71	70	79	220	957

	SCORES			TOTAL	MONEY
Dale Reid	75	73	73	221	876
Janet Soulsby	76	74	72	222	766
Xonia Wunsch-Ruiz	74	71	77	222	766
Irene Yeoh	71	75	76	222	766
Sofie Eriksson	77	71	74	222	766
Petra Rigby-Jinglov	74	73	75	222	766
Helen Dobson	75	74	73	222	766
Kirsty Speak	74	74	74	222	766
Fiona Pike	76	73	73	222	766
Shannon Hanley	74	71	77	222	766
Diane Barnard	75	71	77	223	618
Elisabeth Aron	72	72	79	223	618
Lara Tadiotto	71	72	80	223	618
Nicola Moult	70	73	80	223	618
Valerie Michaud	73	76	74	223	618
Lisa Hackney	73	76	74	223	618
Marina Arruti	73	76	74	223	618

Hennessy Cup

Golf und Land-Club Koln, Koln, Germany
Par 36-36–72; 6,261 yards

July 4-7
purse, £300,000

	SCORES				TOTAL	MONEY
Helen Alfredsson	68	70	71	71	280	£45,000
Trish Johnson	71	71	70	68	280	25,700
Liselotte Neumann	68	70	75	67	280	25,700
(Alfredsson defeated Neumann on first extra hole and Johnson on second extra hole.)						
Annika Sorenstam	71	70	74	68	283	16,150
Carin Hj Koch	71	73	73	68	285	10,733.33
Karina Orum	68	73	71	73	285	10,733.33
Joanne Morley	70	77	71	67	285	10,733.33
Laura Davies	76	69	74	67	286	7,500
Dale Reid	74	75	73	66	288	6,700
Stephanie Dallongeville	72	77	72	68	289	6,000
Marie Laure de Lorenzi	75	73	70	72	290	5,335
Stefania Croce	77	71	70	72	290	5,335
Asa Gottmo	74	71	73	73	291	4,710
Tina Fischer	73	72	74	72	291	4,710
Lora Fairclough	75	72	74	70	291	4,710
Lisa Hackney	70	70	75	77	292	4,490
Sofia Gronberg	71	74	77	71	293	4,215
Xonia Wunsch-Ruiz	78	69	79	67	293	4,215
Mardi Lunn	73	76	74	70	293	4,215
Charlotta Sorenstam	75	75	72	71	293	4,215
Suzanne Strudwick	70	76	76	72	294	3,830
Loraine Lambert	74	74	74	72	294	3,830
Sandrine Mendiburu	75	76	75	68	294	3,830
Alison Nicholas	75	73	75	72	295	3,503.33
Sally Prosser	76	73	75	71	295	3,503.33
Mary Grace Estuesta	75	76	71	73	295	3,503.33
Federica Dassu	76	74	76	70	296	3,150
Laura Navarro	73	74	77	72	296	3,150
Valerie Michaud	70	76	75	75	296	3,150
Anne-Marie Knight	74	72	75	75	296	3,150

Guardian Irish Open

Citywest Country House Hotel & Golf,
Saggart, County Dublin, Ireland
Par 36-36–72; 6,106 yards

July 25-28
purse, £110,000

	SCORES				TOTAL	MONEY
Alison Nicholas	69	73	65	70	277	£16,500
Trish Johnson	70	73	71	71	285	11,165
Laura Davies	71	73	69	73	286	6,820
Natascha Fink	73	72	70	71	286	6,820
Sophie Gustafson	73	73	69	72	287	4,664
Penny Grice-Whittaker	71	71	71	75	288	3,850
Allison Shapcott	70	74	75	70	289	2,838
Lisa Jensen	71	76	70	72	289	2,838
Lisa Hackney	76	73	67	73	289	2,838
Marie Laure de Lorenzi	72	77	70	71	290	2,112
Rachel Hetherington	75	73	70	72	290	2,112
Diane Barnard	71	78	69	73	291	1,724.80
Gillian Stewart	71	74	72	74	291	1,724.80
Marika Preti	72	71	72	76	291	1,724.80
Patricia Meunier Lebouc	73	75	66	77	291	1,724.80
Joanne Morley	76	72	73	70	291	1,724.80
Federica Dassu	72	73	72	75	292	1,540
Tracey Craik	75	74	72	71	292	1,540
Sofia Gronberg	75	74	71	73	293	1,399.20
Janet Soulsby	77	71	74	71	293	1,399.20
Sarah Nicklin	75	71	71	76	293	1,399.20
Tina Fischer	72	76	70	75	293	1,399.20
Myra McKinlay	76	68	72	77	293	1,399.20
Emma-Jane Smith	74	74	74	72	294	1,281.50
Pernilla Sterner	77	72	75	70	294	1,281.50
Karina Orum	76	73	73	73	295	1,166
Laura Navarro	73	77	72	73	295	1,166
Martina Koch	74	74	75	72	295	1,166
Valerie Michaud	73	74	72	76	295	1,166
Anne-Marie Knight	73	72	75	75	295	1,166

McDonald's WPGA Championship

The Gleneagles Hotel, King's Course,
Perthshire, Scotland
Par 37-35–72; 5,830 yards

August 8-11
purse, £150,000

	SCORES				TOTAL	MONEY
Tina Fischer	68	69	72	69	278	£22,500
Trish Johnson	72	70	68	69	279	10,046.25
Charlotta Sorenstam	70	69	71	69	279	10,046.25
Loraine Lambert	70	71	71	67	279	10,046.25
Helen Wadsworth	69	68	71	71	279	10,046.25
Marie Laure de Lorenzi	70	67	71	72	280	4,215
Alison Nicholas	75	72	65	68	280	4,215
Karen Pearce	70	70	68	72	280	4,215
Rachel Hetherington	73	70	68	69	280	4,215
Federica Dassu	74	66	73	68	281	2,890
Corinne Dibnah	73	67	68	73	281	2,330
Sophie Gustafson	73	72	71	66	282	2,497.50
Lisa Hackney	72	70	70	70	282	2,497.50
Jane Crafter	74	72	70	67	283	2,325

	SCORES				TOTAL	MONEY
*Mhairi McKay	73	66	76	68	283	
Pamela Wright	75	69	70	70	284	2,160
Joanne Mills	71	72	72	69	284	2,160
Kathryn Marshall	72	73	72	67	284	2,160
Joanne Morley	71	69	74	70	284	2,160
Laurette Maritz	74	70	73	68	285	1,908
Dale Reid	74	70	72	69	285	1,908
Maria Hjorth	73	69	73	70	285	1,908
Natascha Fink	74	71	71	69	285	1,908
Patricia Meunier Lebouc	69	76	72	68	285	1,908
Laura Navarro	72	66	77	71	286	1,747.50
Catriona Matthew	68	74	71	73	286	1,747.50
Laura Davies	73	74	73	67	287	1,635
Wendy Dicks	73	68	71	75	287	1,635
Julie Forbes	73	72	72	70	287	1,635
Sally Prosser	76	69	75	68	288	1,522.50
Iben Tinning	78	69	75	67	288	1,522.50

Weetabix Women's British Open Championship

Woburn Golf & Country Club, Duke's Course,
Milton Keynes, England
Par 35-38–73; 6,309 yards

August 15-18
purse, £500,000

	SCORES				TOTAL	MONEY
Emilee Klein	68	66	71	72	277	£80,000
Amy Alcott	72	70	70	72	284	42,500
Penny Hammel	71	70	72	71	284	42,500
Alison Nicholas	68	71	74	72	285	20,416.66
Jane Geddes	72	73	70	70	285	20,416.66
Lisa Hackney	71	69	73	72	285	20,416.66
Marie Laure de Lorenzi	74	72	68	72	286	9,571.42
Rosie Jones	69	71	73	73	286	9,571.42
Chris Johnson	72	69	73	72	286	9,571.42
Pat Bradley	70	75	69	72	286	9,571.42
Tracy Kerdyk	70	70	72	74	286	9,571.42
Deb Richard	71	73	71	71	286	9,571.42
Barb Whitehead	76	70	71	69	286	9,571.42
Catrin Nilsmark	72	76	68	71	287	6,600
Annika Sorenstam	69	70	73	75	287	6,600
Karrie Webb	69	70	74	74	287	6,600
Dale Eggeling	69	77	71	70	287	6,600
Barb Mucha	73	71	74	69	287	6,600
Laura Davies	72	75	71	70	288	5,675
Dale Reid	68	74	74	72	288	5,675
Jenny Lidback	68	73	73	74	288	5,675
Helen Alfredsson	69	76	69	74	288	5,675
Donna Andrews	80	65	74	69	288	5,675
Kiyoe Yamazaki	71	70	74	73	288	5,675
Tania Abitbol	70	75	70	74	289	4,850
Maria Hjorth	70	70	71	78	289	4,850
Kathryn Marshall	71	72	73	73	289	4,850
Joanne Morley	72	71	74	72	289	4,850
Tina Barrett	71	74	69	75	289	4,850
Sofia Gronberg	75	73	71	71	290	4,100
Julie Piers	68	73	72	77	290	4,100
Akiko Fukushima	74	74	69	73	290	4,100
Charlotta Sorenstam	76	70	71	73	290	4,100
Vicki Goetze	74	70	72	74	290	4,100

Trygg-Hansa Ladies' Open

Haninge Golf Club, Stockholm, Sweden
Par 36-37–73; 6,188 yards

August 22-25
purse, £125,000

	SCORES				TOTAL	MONEY
Annika Sorenstam	70	70	70	69	279	£18,750
Alison Nicholas	69	71	68	72	280	10,718.75
Joanne Morley	70	69	67	74	280	10,718.75
Liselotte Neumann	68	65	72	76	281	6,750
Marie Laure de Lorenzi	72	69	72	71	284	5,300
Patricia Meunier Lebouc	69	73	71	72	285	4,062.50
Kathryn Marshall	70	73	71	71	285	4,062.50
Maria Bertilskold	70	74	70	72	286	3,125
Catrin Nilsmark	69	73	69	76	287	2,800
Joanne Mills	72	71	73	72	288	2,500
Karina Orum	73	72	68	76	289	2,154.16
Helen Alfredsson	74	71	71	73	289	2,154.16
Jane Leary	71	75	70	73	289	2,154.16
Suzanne Strudwick	69	76	71	75	291	1,937.50
Pamela Wright	73	74	73	72	292	1,850
Lora Fairclough	72	76	72	72	292	1,850
Sofia Gronberg	78	69	74	72	293	1,635.71
Xonia Wunsch-Ruiz	75	69	76	73	293	1,635.71
Maria Hjorth	76	73	72	72	293	1,635.71
Charlotta Sorenstam	71	73	75	74	293	1,635.71
Raquel Carriedo-Tomas	74	71	71	77	293	1,635.71
Pernilla Sterner	76	74	71	72	293	1,635.71
Charlotta Eliasson Wharton	74	73	75	71	293	1,635.71
Maureen Madill	77	72	78	67	294	1,400
Nadene Gole	74	74	73	73	294	1,400
Linda Ericsson	73	77	73	71	294	1,400
Aideen Rogers	73	75	72	74	294	1,400
Tina Fischer	71	77	72	74	294	1,400
Sophie Gustafson	73	75	75	72	295	1,231.25
Valerie Michaud	72	74	79	70	295	1,231.25
Valerie Van Ryckeghem	72	75	77	71	295	1,231.25
Kristel Mourgue d'Algue	68	78	77	72	295	1,231.25

Compaq Open

Orebro Golf Club, Orebro, Sweden
Par 37-35–72; 6,085 yards

August 29-September 1
purse, £100,000

	SCORES				TOTAL	MONEY
Federica Dassu	70	69	70	71	280	£15,000
Kathryn Marshall	69	71	70	70	280	8,575
Helen Alfredsson	70	75	67	68	280	8,575
(Dassu defeated Alfredsson on third extra hole and Marshall on fourth extra hole.)						
Marie Laure de Lorenzi	72	69	71	69	281	5,400
Joanne Mills	72	73	70	67	282	4,240
Mette Hageman	75	68	72	68	283	3,500
Corinne Dibnah	75	71	69	69	284	2,750
Joanne Morley	70	70	72	72	284	2,750
Karina Orum	74	70	74	67	285	2,240
Susan Moon	74	73	68	72	287	1,853.33
Laura Navarro	73	71	71	72	287	1,853.33
Myra McKinlay	77	69	71	70	287	1,853.33

	SCORES				TOTAL	MONEY
Charlotta Sorenstam	73	70	71	74	288	1,465.71
Patricia Meunier Lebouc	74	72	74	68	288	1,465.71
Loraine Lambert	74	71	70	73	288	1,465.71
Valerie Michaud	77	68	73	70	288	1,455.71
Valerie Van Ryckeghem	73	72	70	73	288	1,465.71
Kirsty Speak	72	71	71	74	288	1,465.71
Fiona Pike	73	72	71	72	288	1,465.71
Mandy Sutton	71	74	72	72	289	1,285
Julie Forbes	73	73	69	74	289	1,285
Xonia Wunsch-Ruiz	70	72	73	75	290	1,180
Sophie Gustafson	75	70	70	75	290	1,180
Tina Fischer	74	72	70	74	290	1,180
Pernilla Sterner	72	76	73	69	290	1,180
Charlotta Eliasson Wharton	74	70	73	73	290	1,180
Debbie Dowling	76	72	73	70	291	1,045
Sofia Gronberg	71	73	73	74	291	1,045
Liselotte Neumann	72	73	72	74	291	1,045
Raquel Carriedo-Tomas	68	76	77	70	291	1,045

Marks & Spencer European Open

Marriott Hanbury Manor Golf & Country Club, Ware, Hertfordshire, England
Par 36-36—72; 5,954 yards

September 5-8
purse, £100,000

	SCORES				TOTAL	MONEY
Trish Johnson	74	66	64	70	274	£15,000
Pernilla Sterner	69	71	71	68	279	8,575
Anne-Marie Knight	73	70	66	70	279	8,575
Federica Dassu	72	68	68	72	280	5,400
Dale Reid	70	70	71	70	281	4,240
Corinne Dibnah	66	70	74	72	282	3,500
Laura Davies	70	63	76	75	284	3,000
Lora Fairclough	71	69	71	74	285	2,500
Karina Orum	73	68	70	75	286	1,950
Sophie Gustafson	73	70	66	77	286	1,950
Laura Navarro	71	73	73	69	286	1,950
Fiona Pike	72	72	69	73	286	1,950
Stephanie Dallongeville	67	70	76	75	288	1,580
Iben Tinning	72	72	68	76	288	1,580
Laurette Maritz	72	69	76	72	289	1,460
Mary Grace Estuesta	74	69	71	75	289	1,460
Loraine Lambert	73	72	68	76	289	1,460
Raquel Carriedo-Tomas	72	73	75	70	290	1,380
Helen Dobson	78	69	70	74	291	1,340
Marjan De Boer	72	72	73	75	292	1,210
Janet Soulsby	76	71	71	74	292	1,210
Tracey Craik	71	75	68	78	292	1,210
Sally Prosser	76	69	74	73	292	1,210
Cathy Schmitt	71	75	69	77	292	1,210
Alison Brighouse	72	75	72	73	292	1,210
Sarah Bennett	76	71	68	77	292	1,210
Debbie Dowling	72	75	74	72	293	1,060
Mette Hageman	73	70	75	75	293	1,060
Kirsty Speak	78	69	72	74	293	1,060
Marina Arruti	76	70	77	71	294	1,000

Wilkinson Sword Ladies' English Open

Oxfordshire Golf Club, Thame, Oxfordshire, England
Par 36-36–72; 6,062 yards

September 12-15
purse, £100,000

		SCO	RES		TOTAL	MONEY
Laura Davies	72	66	68	67	273	£15,000
Helen Alfredsson	67	70	71	69	277	10,150
Laura Navarro	68	70	73	70	281	7,000
Corinne Dibnah	69	74	70	69	282	4,820
Stephanie Dallongeville	70	71	70	71	282	4,820
Marie Laure de Lorenzi	71	64	80	69	284	2,513.33
Dale Reid	74	73	68	69	284	2,513.33
Shani Waugh	71	74	68	71	284	2,513.33
Anna-Carin Jonasson	73	72	71	68	284	2,513.33
Kathryn Marshall	71	70	72	71	284	2,513.33
Anne-Marie Knight	74	69	68	73	284	2,513.33
Trish Johnson	76	71	69	71	287	1,568
Janet Soulsby	71	72	71	73	287	1,568
Wendy Dicks	72	71	73	71	287	1,568
Maria Hjorth	70	77	70	70	287	1,568
Pernilla Sterner	74	73	71	69	287	1,568
Alison Nicholas	72	75	71	70	288	1,400
Karina Orum	78	75	69	66	288	1,400
Barbara Pestana	73	75	71	70	289	1,303.33
Sofie Eriksson	73	72	74	70	289	1,303.33
Patricia Meunier Lebouc	70	71	75	73	289	1,303.33
Valerie Van Ryckeghem	75	69	70	76	290	1,240
Laurette Maritz	75	74	73	69	291	1,195
Tracey Craik	78	70	70	73	291	1,195
Susan Moon	74	78	70	70	292	1,105
Sally Prosser	75	75	70	72	292	1,105
Mary Grace Estuesta	74	76	72	70	292	1,105
Kirsty Speak	76	72	72	72	292	1,105
Janice Arnold	76	72	72	73	293	970
Regine Lautens	71	76	73	73	293	970
Sophie Gustafson	75	76	72	70	293	970
Sarah Burnell	75	71	78	69	293	970
Sarah Bennett	71	73	75	74	293	970

Solheim Cup

St. Pierre Hotel Golf & Country Club, Chepstow, Wales
Par 36-36–72; 6,386 yards

September 20-22

FIRST DAY
Foursomes

Kelly Robbins and Michelle McGann (USA) halved with Annika Sorenstam and Catrin Nilsmark.

Patty Sheehan and Rosie Jones (USA) defeated Laura Davies and Alison Nicholas, 1 up.

Beth Daniel and Val Skinner (USA) defeated Marie Laure de Lorenzi and Dale Reid, 1 up.

Dottie Pepper and Brandie Burton (USA) defeated Helen Alfredsson and Liselotte Neumann, 2 and 1.

POINTS: United States 3½, Europe ½

Fourballs

Davies and Trish Johnson (Europe) defeated Robbins and Pat Bradley, 6 and 5.
Sorenstam and Kathryn Marshall (Europe) defeated Skinner and Jane Geddes, 1 up.
Pepper and Betsy King (USA) defeated Neumann and Nilsmark, 1 up.
Meg Mallon and Daniel (USA) halved with Alfredsson and Nicholas.

POINTS: United States 1½, Europe 2½

SECOND DAY
Foursomes

Davies and Johnson (Europe) defeated Sheehan and Jones, 4 and 3.
Sorenstam and Nilsmark (Europe) defeated Pepper and Burton, 1 up.
Mallon and Geddes (USA) halved with Neumann and Marshall.
Alfredsson and de Lorenzi (Europe) defeated Robbins and McGann, 4 and 3.

POINTS: United States ½, Europe 3½

Fourballs

Davies and Lisa Hackney (Europe) defeated Daniel and Skinner, 6 and 5.
McGann and Mallon (USA) halved with Sorenstam and Johnson.
Robbins and King (USA), defeated de Lorenzi and Joanne Morley, 2 and 1.
Nilsmark and Neumann (Europe) defeated Sheehan and Geddes, 3 and 1.

POINTS: United States 1½, Europe 2½

THIRD DAY
Singles

Sorenstam (Europe) defeated Bradley, 2 and 1.
Skinner (USA) defeated Marshall, 2 and 1.
McGann (USA) defeated Davies, 3 and 2.
Daniel (USA) halved with Neumann.
Burton (USA) defeated Hackney, 1 up.
Pepper (USA) defeated Johnson, 3 and 2.
Robbins (USA) halved with Nicholas.
King (USA) defeated de Lorenzi, 5 and 4.
Jones (USA) defeated Morley, 5 and 4.
Geddes (USA) defeated Reid, 2 up.
Sheehan (USA) defeated Nilsmark, 2 and 1.
Mallon (USA) defeated Alfredsson, 4 and 2.

POINTS: United States 10, Europe 2

TOTAL POINTS: United States 17, Europe 11

Ladies' German Open

Hotel Treudelberg Golf & Country Club,
Hamburg, Germany
Par 36-37–73; 6,157 yards

September 26-29
purse, £75,000

	SCORES				TOTAL	MONEY
Joanne Morley	69	72	72	68	281	£11,250
Maria Hjorth	67	73	71	74	285	7,612.50
Lisa Hackney	69	75	70	72	286	5,250
Helen Wadsworth	71	70	72	74	287	4,050

		SCORES			TOTAL	MONEY
Lynnette Brooky	70	72	72	74	288	2,902.50
Evelyn Orley	72	70	71	75	288	2,902.50
Laura Navarro	72	75	70	72	289	2,062.50
Rachel Hetherington	69	70	75	75	289	2,062.50
Marie Laure de Lorenzi	69	70	74	78	291	1,590
Charlotta Sorenstam	71	75	72	73	291	1,590
Asa Gottmo	71	72	75	74	292	1,380
Wendy Dicks	69	79	69	76	293	1,220
Patricia Meunier Lebouc	68	75	75	75	293	1,220
Sandrine Mendiburu	69	69	73	82	293	1,220
Sally Prosser	71	74	75	74	294	1,095
Joanne Mills	72	73	73	76	294	1,095
Pernilla Sterner	75	72	71	76	294	1,095
Diane Barnard	72	71	75	77	295	967.50
Mette Hageman	72	76	73	74	295	967.50
Anna-Carin Jonasson	70	75	76	74	295	967.50
Stephanie Dallongeville	73	71	74	77	295	967.50
Raquel Carriedo-Tomas	74	76	73	72	295	967.50
Kristel Mourgue d'Algue	71	76	70	78	295	967.50
Tina Fischer	72	74	73	77	296	885
Gillian Stewart	74	72	75	76	297	828.75
Sophie Gustafson	76	73	69	79	297	828.75
Valerie Michaud	69	75	72	81	297	828.75
Jane Leary	71	73	75	78	297	828.75
Maureen Madill	72	74	75	77	298	705
Sofia Gronberg	73	71	74	80	298	705
Laurette Maritz	76	73	72	77	298	705
Karina Orum	71	73	77	77	298	705
Sara Melin	70	75	75	78	298	705
Sarah Bennett	68	75	80	75	298	705
Valerie Van Ryckeghem	71	76	75	76	298	705

Ladies' French Open

Le Golf d'Arras, Anzin Saint Aubin, Arras, France
Par 36-37–73; 5,800 yards

October 11-13
purse, £60,000

	SCORES			TOTAL	MONEY
Trish Johnson	62	68	70	200	£9,000
Raquel Carriedo-Tomas	68	72	70	210	6,090
Marie Laure de Lorenzi	70	69	73	212	3,328
Gillian Stewart	69	70	73	212	3,328
Mette Hageman	72	71	69	212	3,328
Lisa Hackney	72	71	70	213	1,950
Myra McKinlay	70	72	71	213	1,950
Janet Soulsby	74	70	70	214	1,287
Lisa Jensen	69	75	70	214	1,287
Sophie Gustafson	71	73	70	214	1,287
Fiona Pike	72	71	71	214	1,287
Susan Moon	71	70	74	215	957
Sally Prosser	68	73	74	215	957
Asa Gottmo	76	70	69	215	957
Kristel Mourgue d'Algue	70	73	72	215	957
Tracey Craik	74	72	70	216	817
Caryn Louw	70	71	75	216	817
Patricia Meunier Lebouc	71	77	68	216	817
Joanne Morley	71	73	72	216	817

	SCORES			TOTAL	MONEY
Sarah Bennett	73	71	72	216	817
Iben Tinning	71	71	74	216	817
Maureen Madill	74	71	72	217	708
Odile Roux	73	73	71	217	708
Charlotta Sorenstam	74	74	69	217	708
Natascha Fink	70	76	71	217	708
Sandrine Mendiburu	71	77	69	217	708
*Caroline Laurens	72	73	72	217	
Wendy Dicks	69	75	74	218	582
Barbara Pestana	73	75	70	218	582
Chantale Orth	71	72	75	218	582
Tracy Eakin	72	71	75	218	582
Aideen Rogers	72	74	72	218	582
Loraine Lambert	73	73	72	218	582
Julie Forbes	74	70	74	218	582
Pernilla Sterner	69	75	74	218	582
Valerie Michaud	75	68	75	218	582

Italian Open di Sicilia

Il Picciolo Golf Club, Castiglione di Sicilia, Italy
Par 36-37–73; 5,615 yards

October 17-20
purse, £100,000

	SCORES				TOTAL	MONEY
Laura Davies	68	70	68	76	282	£15,000
Tina Fischer	68	76	70	71	285	8,575
Fiona Pike	69	74	76	66	285	8,575
Marjan De Boer	71	75	67	76	289	4,820
Gillian Stewart	72	71	72	74	289	4,820
Kristel Mourgue d'Algue	69	75	73	73	290	3,500
Valerie Van Ryckeghem	73	79	68	72	292	3,000
Raquel Carriedo-Tomas	71	73	74	75	293	2,246.66
Kirsty Speak	71	74	75	73	293	2,246.66
Marina Arruti	73	75	74	71	293	2,246.66
Maureen Madill	71	76	72	75	294	1,723.33
Karen Pearce	76	71	76	71	294	1,723.33
Martina Koch	72	68	79	75	294	1,723.33
Loraine Lambert	74	73	75	73	295	1,550
Karina Orum	75	75	73	73	296	1,480
Anna-Carin Jonasson	72	76	78	70	296	1,480
*Sofia Sandolo	80	71	72	73	296	
Janet Soulsby	75	76	71	75	297	1,400
Myra McKinlay	70	76	75	76	297	1,400
Stefania Croce	75	74	77	72	298	1,226.25
Maria Hjorth	73	70	76	79	298	1,226.25
Sophie Gustafson	72	74	80	72	298	1,226.25
Mandy Sutton	69	79	71	79	298	1,226.25
Laura Navarro	69	77	73	79	298	1,226.25
Sarah Bennett	74	75	75	74	298	1,226.25
Helen Wadsworth	72	80	74	72	298	1,226.25
Mandy Adamson	69	77	76	76	298	1,226.25
*Giulia Sergas	79	74	74	71	298	
Regine Lautens	71	77	74	77	299	1,090
Patricia Gonzalez	71	78	76	75	300	1,030
Sofie Eriksson	72	73	77	78	300	1,030
Pernilla Sterner	69	80	72	79	300	1,030

Ladies' Spanish Open

Hyatt La Manga Club, South Course,
Cartagena, Spain
Par 36-36–72; 6,114 yards

October 31-November 2
purse, £60,000

	SCORES			TOTAL	MONEY
Caryn Louw	69	70	67	206	£9,000
Amaia Arruti	74	70	66	210	6,090
Lora Fairclough	70	74	67	211	4,200
Marjan De Boer	72	70	72	214	3,240
Trish Johnson	72	71	73	216	2,148
Anna-Carin Jonasson	74	74	68	216	2,148
Isabella Maconi	73	72	71	216	2,148
Susan Moon	72	71	74	217	1,422
Raquel Carriedo-Tomas	73	71	73	217	1,422
Debbie Dowling	72	74	72	218	1,075.50
Laura Navarro	71	74	73	218	1,075.50
Pernilla Sterner	70	74	74	218	1,075.50
Kristel Mourgue d'Algue	74	74	70	218	1,075.50
Sofia Gronberg	70	76	74	220	865
Janet Soulsby	70	77	73	220	865
Xonia Wunsch-Ruiz	76	72	72	220	865
Barbara Pestana	74	69	77	220	865
Sara Melin	71	75	74	220	865
Valerie Van Ryckeghem	70	74	76	220	865
Regine Lautens	76	73	72	221	762
Mette Hageman	73	76	72	221	762
Sophie Gustafson	74	75	72	221	762
Penny Grice-Whittaker	73	77	72	222	663
Wendy Dicks	72	74	76	222	663
Malin Burstrom	75	75	72	222	663
Natascha Fink	72	76	74	222	663
Sandy Lambert	76	77	69	222	663
Sarah Bennett	71	75	76	222	663
Anna Radford	76	74	72	222	663
Vibeke Stensrud	75	75	72	222	663

Princess Lalla Meriem Cup

Royal Golf Dar-es-Salam, Blue Course, Rabat, Morocco
Par 73; 6,400 yards

November 7-10
purse, £65,000

	SCORES				TOTAL	MONEY
Lora Fairclough	69	68	77	70	284	US$13,000
Sally Prosser	70	71	73	74	288	9,100
Sofia Gronberg	71	70	73	75	289	5,915
Patricia Meunier Lebouc	71	73	74	71	289	5,915
Amaia Arruti	71	74	74	71	290	3,900
Kristel Mourgue d'Algue	73	77	76	68	294	3,120
Gillian Stewart	75	70	76	75	296	2,925
Valerie Michaud	77	77	72	70	296	2,925
Sandrine Mendiburu	75	74	74	75	298	2,600
Xonia Wunsch-Ruiz	76	71	81	70	298	2,600
Regine Lautens	76	73	76	75	300	2,600
Federica Dassu	76	78	75	75	304	2,600
Susan Moon	77	79	75	78	309	2,600
Nancy Scranton	81	76	85	77	319	2,600
Veronique Palli	82	82	82	84	330	2,600

Women's Australasian Tours

Republic of China Open

Chang Gung Golf Club, Taipei, Taiwan
Par 36-36–72; 6,420 yards

January 31-February 3
purse, US$120,000

	SCORES			TOTAL	MONEY
Shoko Asano	72	73	73	218	US$16,500
Huang Bie-Shyun	74	75	71	220	6,840
Tseng Hsiu-Feng	75	74	71	220	6,840
Li Wen-Lin	73	73	74	220	6,840
Sophie Gustafson	69	75	76	220	6,840
Huang Yu-Chen	70	74	76	220	6,840
Debbie Dowling	73	78	70	221	3,410
Lisa Depaulo	70	77	75	222	2,750
Lisa Grimes	71	76	75	222	2,750
Jennifer Steiner	69	77	76	222	2,750
Wu Ming-Yeh	73	77	73	223	1,970
Momoyo Kawakubo	76	77	70	223	1,970
Young-Me Lee	75	72	76	223	1,970
Ai-Yu Tu	70	74	79	223	1,970
Tsai Li-Hsiang	70	78	76	224	1,750
Evelyn Orley	71	76	77	224	1,750
Janet Soulsby	70	75	79	224	1,750
Sarah Bennett	73	72	79	224	1,750
Joanne Morley	78	71	76	225	1,620
*Lu Hsiao-Chuan	72	73	81	226	
Tai Yu-Chuan	73	75	78	226	1,540
Huang Hui-Fan	75	73	78	226	1,540
Rachel Hetherington	75	75	77	227	1,400
Liz Earley	74	78	75	227	1,400
Caroline Hall	72	73	82	227	1,400
Lee Chiou-Yann	76	76	76	228	1,150
Chen Li-Ying	79	71	78	228	1,150
Mitsuyo Hirata	73	76	79	228	1,150
Yuko Yabe	74	79	75	228	1,150
Cheng Mei-Chi	72	81	75	228	1,150
Karen Weiss	76	79	73	228	1,150

Singapore Open

Tanah Merah Country Club, Garden Course, Singapore
Par 36-36–72; 6,111 yards

February 8-10
purse, US$80,000

	SCORES			TOTAL	MONEY
Debbie Dowling	73	71	71	215	US$11,250
Young-Me Lee	73	72	70	215	7,500
(Dowling defeated Lee on fourth extra hole.)					
Tai Yu-Chuan	73	74	69	216	6,625
Lisa Depaulo	73	71	73	217	3,825
Rachel Hetherington	68	74	75	217	3,825
Jackie Smith	68	79	71	218	2,550

	SCORES			TOTAL	MONEY
Anna Jonasson	73	74	72	219	1,786
Tseng Hsiu-Feng	71	76	72	219	1,786
Corinne Dibnah	71	75	73	219	1,786
Irene Yeoh	71	74	74	219	1,786
Sophie Gustafson	69	75	75	219	1,786
Martina Koch	70	71	78	219	1,786
Cheng Mei-Chi	73	73	74	220	1,289
Shelly Rule	76	70	74	220	1,289
Dale Reid	70	75	75	220	1,289
Natascha Fink	73	76	72	221	1,102
Caroline Hall	72	75	74	221	1,102
Masako Ishihara	75	75	71	221	1,102
Patricia Ehrhart	73	73	75	221	1,102
Christy Erb	72	72	77	221	1,102
Loraine Lambert	73	71	77	221	1,102
Lori Tatum	74	74	74	222	952
Iben Tinning	73	77	72	222	952
Shoko Asano	73	71	78	222	952
Asayo Ito	72	77	74	223	821
Kayo Segawa	73	75	75	223	821
Mary Estuesta	73	74	76	223	821
Karen Weiss	73	70	80	223	821
*Jennifer Rosales	72	79	73	224	
Janet Soulsby	75	75	74	224	653
Kiernan Prechtl	72	75	77	224	653
Sally Prosser	70	76	78	224	653
Xonia Wunsch-Ruiz	73	72	79	224	653
Regine Lautens	72	79	73	224	653
Aki Noto	76	76	72	224	653

Indonesian Open

Finna Golf & Country Club, Surabaya,
Java, Indonesia
Par 36-36—72; 6,165 yards

February 15-17
purse, US$100,000

	SCORES			TOTAL	MONEY
Corinne Dibnah	73	70	73	216	US$13,500
Lisa Hackney	72	70	74	216	9,000
(Dibnah defeated Hackney on fourth extra hole.)					
Anna Jonasson	72	71	74	217	6,750
Caroline Hall	73	72	73	218	5,400
Jackie Smith	75	75	70	220	3,210
Kiyoe Yamazaki	72	73	75	220	3,210
Sophie Gustafson	73	72	75	220	3,210
*Wei Yun-Jye	73	73	75	221	
Young-Me Lee	77	74	70	221	2,385
Joanne Morley	75	74	72	221	2,385
Loraine Lambert	76	74	72	222	1,723
Smriti Mehra	72	77	73	222	1,723
Lee Chiou-Yann	71	77	74	222	1,723
Eui-Young Shim	75	73	74	222	1,723
Mary Estuesta	76	76	71	223	1,548
Kelly Crawford	74	75	75	224	1,503
Debbie Dowling	75	77	73	225	1,435
Camie Hoshino	74	74	77	225	1,435
*Dorothy Delasin	79	74	73	226	

	SCORES			TOTAL	MONEY
Dale Reid	72	78	76	226	1,300
Nicola Moult	79	73	74	226	1,300
Mi-Sook Kang	76	74	76	226	1,300
Martina Koch	73	79	74	226	1,300
Tina Fischer	81	71	75	227	1,030
Hiromi Kaneda	73	78	76	227	1,030
Christy Erb	77	74	76	227	1,030
Jennifer Steiner	78	74	75	227	1,030
Lori Tatum	74	78	75	227	1,030
Janet Soulsby	78	76	73	227	1,030
Maureen Madill	70	73	84	227	1,030
Mette Hageman	76	79	72	227	1,030

Thailand Open

President Country Club, Bangkok, Thailand
Par 36-36–72; 5,980 yards

February 22-24
purse, US$110,000

	SCORES			TOTAL	MONEY
Shelly Rule	76	70	70	216	US$15,000
Corinne Dibnah	73	71	72	216	10,000
(Rule defeated Dibnah on first extra hole.)					
Jennifer Steiner	70	75	72	217	6,750
Loraine Lambert	76	71	70	217	6,750
Camie Hoshino	71	76	71	218	3,033
Lisa Depaulo	75	72	71	218	3,033
Susan Farron	72	70	76	218	3,033
Debbie Dowling	72	72	74	218	3,033
Sophie Gustafson	68	72	78	218	3,033
Rachel Hetherington	70	72	76	218	3,033
Iben Tinning	71	77	71	219	1,770
Caroline Hall	74	73	72	219	1,770
Kimberly Kell	75	70	74	219	1,770
Joanne Morley	71	73	75	219	1,770
Sarah Bennett	68	73	78	219	1,770
*Wei Yun-Jye	75	75	70	220	
Kelly Crawford	74	76	70	220	1,570
Dale Reid	75	74	71	220	1,570
Lori Tatum	75	73	72	220	1,570
Mary Estuesta	78	74	69	221	1,470
Elizabeth Makings	81	69	72	222	1,320
Lisa Hackney	72	79	71	222	1,320
Fusako Nagata	76	72	74	222	1,320
Valerie Michaud	74	75	73	222	1,320
Shoko Yamamoto	75	73	74	222	1,320
Nicola Moult	78	71	74	223	1,145
Xonia Wunsch-Ruiz	73	73	77	223	1,145
Kiyoe Yamazaki	75	75	74	224	1,045
Martina Koch	76	73	75	224	1,045
Natascha Fink	76	74	75	225	905
Kyoko Ono	77	72	76	225	905
Jackie Smith	80	72	73	225	905
Karen Weiss	77	77	71	225	905

Malaysian JAL Open

Tuanku Jaafar Golf Club, Kuala Lumpur, Malaysia
Par 36-36–72; 6,300 yards

February 29-March 2
purse, US$90,000

	SCORES			TOTAL	MONEY
Corinne Dibnah	67	70	80	217	US$12,750
Caroline Hall	69	76	74	219	8,500
Debbie Dowling	76	73	74	223	5,015
Lori Tatum	74	73	76	223	5,015
Lisa Hackney	73	73	77	223	5,015
Hideko Maeda	76	71	78	225	2,890
Eui-Young Shim	76	73	77	226	2,635
Jackie Smith	72	78	77	227	2,380
Susan Farron	76	75	77	228	1,861
Loraine Lambert	71	78	79	228	1,861
Juli Christopher	76	72	81	228	1,861
Iben Tinning	74	74	81	229	1,547
Sarah Nicklin	77	74	79	230	1,461
Dale Reid	69	80	81	230	1,461
Martina Koch	75	69	86	230	1,461
*Jennifer Rosales	73	78	79	230	
Patricia Ehrhart	76	78	77	231	1,291
Wendy Dicks	71	80	80	231	1,291
Elizabeth Makings	78	77	76	231	1,291
Kimberly Kell	74	76	81	231	1,291
Sarah Bennett	73	75	83	231	1,291
Janet Soulsby	76	78	78	232	1,079
Jennifer Steiner	74	80	78	232	1,079
Kelly Crawford	79	76	77	232	1,079
Joanne Morley	74	73	85	232	1,079
Natascha Fink	77	81	74	232	1,079
*Wei Yun-Jye	79	76	77	232	
Valerie Michaud	78	74	81	233	952
Anna Jonasson	79	75	80	234	866
Shelly Rule	75	76	83	234	866
Sophie Gustafson	74	75	85	234	866

Holden Women's Australian Open

Yarra Yarra Golf Club, Melbourne, Victoria
Par 37-36–73; 5,958 yards

November 7-10
purse, A$300,000

	SCORES				TOTAL	MONEY
Catriona Matthew	72	74	68	69	283	A$45,000
Karrie Webb	72	72	72	70	286	30,000
Liselotte Neumann	72	72	71	72	287	18,000
Corinne Dibnah	68	71	71	80	290	15,000
Debbi Koyama	71	70	76	74	291	11,700
Kathryn Marshall	71	73	70	77	291	11,700
Wendy Doolan	78	71	73	70	292	8,550
Carin Hj Koch	77	72	72	71	292	8,550
Karen Weiss	74	72	74	72	292	8,550
Amy Read	72	68	78	74	292	8,550
Mardi Lunn	68	71	77	77	293	5,700
Katherine Golden	71	74	69	79	293	5,700
Rachel Hetherington	76	73	72	75	296	4,620
Maria Hjorth	72	75	72	77	296	4,620

	SCORES				TOTAL	MONEY
Jane Crafter	73	71	73	80	297	4,200
Karina Orum	74	73	79	72	298	3,780
Jan Stephenson	72	74	76	76	298	3,780
Susan Farron	71	71	78	78	298	3,780
Anne-Marie Knight	75	75	74	75	299	3,300
Shani Waugh	76	75	72	76	299	3,300
Nadene Gole	75	75	70	79	299	3,300
*Adele Bannerman	73	78	75	74	300	
Cindy Rarick	73	74	77	76	300	3,000
Helen Wadsworth	75	74	72	79	300	3,000
Joanne Morley	79	74	73	75	301	2,760
Kristal Parker-Gregory	75	74	75	77	301	2,760
Sherri Turner	74	75	75	78	302	2,580
Loraine Lambert	73	77	76	77	303	2,232
Jane Geddes	74	75	76	78	303	2,232
Alison Munt	74	75	73	81	303	2,232
Dale Reid	72	77	71	83	303	2,232
Stephanie Martin-Cobb	71	75	73	84	303	2,232

Alpine Australian Ladies Masters

Royal Pines Resort, Gold Coast, Queensland
Par 37-36–73; 6,153 yards

November 14-17
purse, A$350,000

	SCORES				TOTAL	MONEY
Jane Crafter	69	65	71	68	273	A$52,500
Jane Geddes	69	69	69	67	274	28,000
Laura Davies	67	70	68	69	274	28,000
Liselotte Neumann	69	72	66	68	275	17,500
Wendy Doolan	68	69	73	67	277	14,000
Karrie Webb	73	69	69	68	279	13,300
Carin Hj Koch	70	69	75	66	280	11,200
Corinne Dibnah	67	70	72	71	280	11,200
Shani Waugh	70	69	72	70	281	9,450
Kristal Parker-Gregory	71	70	72	69	282	7,525
Catriona Matthew	65	71	74	72	282	7,525
Maria Hjorth	71	70	73	69	283	5,495
Robin Walton	70	72	71	70	283	5,495
Sherri Turner	69	72	72	70	283	5,495
Ellie Gibson	67	71	71	74	283	5,495
Joanne Morley	72	72	72	68	284	4,410
Rachel Hetherington	70	72	71	71	284	4,410
Dale Reid	73	69	69	73	284	4,410
Mardi Lunn	68	74	74	69	285	3,920
Cristie Kerr	71	72	70	72	285	3,920
Katherine Golden	72	73	72	69	286	3,360
Loraine Lambert	70	72	73	71	286	3,360
Libby Wilson	72	71	72	71	286	3,360
Jan Stephenson	69	73	72	72	286	3,360
Fiona Pike	74	71	69	72	286	3,360
Jennifer Sevil	74	71	69	72	286	3,360
Cindy Rarick	72	71	74	70	287	2,800
Joanne Mills	66	75	73	73	287	2,800
Fayette Purser	73	73	73	69	288	2,590
Kathryn Marshall	74	75	71	69	289	2,415
Debbi Koyama	73	74	73	69	289	2,415
*Tanya Holl	76	70	68	75	289	

Japan LPGA Tour

Daikin Orchid

Ryukyu Golf Club, Okinawa
Par 36-36—72; 6,276 yards

March 1-3
purse, ¥60,000,000

	SCORES			TOTAL	MONEY
Li Wen-Lin	73	72	67	212	¥10,800,000
Miyuki Shimabukuro	74	70	70	214	4,740,000
Yuko Moriguchi	71	71	72	214	4,740,000
Suzuko Maeda	74	73	68	215	3,300,000
Aiko Hashimoto	70	76	69	215	3,300,000
Ayako Okamoto	74	72	70	216	2,250,000
Mikino Kubo	68	74	74	216	2,250,000
Mieko Nomura	72	74	71	217	1,650,000
Kaori Higo	74	70	73	217	1,650,000
Huang Hui-Fan	77	71	70	218	1,110,000
Hiromi Takamura	75	72	71	218	1,110,000
Chieko Nishida	71	75	72	218	1,110,000
Huang Bie-Shyun	72	68	78	218	1,110,000
Keiko Arai	79	69	71	219	900,000
Aki Takamura	72	76	71	219	900,000
Chikako Matsuzawa	75	72	72	219	900,000
Keiko Ono	76	73	71	220	690,000
Yuri Kawanami	73	75	72	220	690,000
Hiroko Inoue	74	73	73	220	690,000
Patty Sheehan	74	72	74	220	690,000
Huang Yueh-Chyn	73	76	72	221	570,000
Kikuko Shibata	75	73	73	221	570,000
Michiko Hattori	74	74	73	221	570,000
Akiko Fukushima	72	72	77	221	570,000
Jennifer Sevil	74	76	72	222	504,000
Shoko Asano	75	75	72	222	504,000
Woo-Soon Ko	74	75	73	222	504,000
Takayo Bandoh	78	71	73	222	504,000
Ikuyo Shiotani	74	74	74	222	504,000
Akane Ohshiro	74	74	74	222	504,000
Shin Sora	73	75	74	222	504,000

Saishunkan Ladies

Kumamoto Kuko Country Club, Kumamoto
Par 36-36—72; 6,470 yards
(First round cancelled; third round shortened to 27 holes — rain.)

March 15-17
purse, ¥45,000,000

	SCORES		TOTAL	MONEY
Young-Me Lee	69	39	108	¥8,100,000
Chie Yoshida	71	37	108	3,960,000
(Lee defeated Yoshida on first extra hole.)				
Miyuki Shimabukuro	74	35	109	1,992,000
Kyoe Fumihira	74	35	109	1,992,000

	SCORES		TOTAL	MONEY
Ikuyo Shiotani	73	36	109	1,992,000
Yoko Inoue	73	36	109	1,992,000
Ok-Hee Ku	71	38	109	1,992,000
Fuki Kido	71	38	109	1,992,000
Keiko Arai	70	39	109	1,992,000
Michiko Hattori	76	34	110	749,000
Natsuko Noro	74	36	110	749,000
Jae-Sook Won	73	37	110	749,000
Chikayo Yamazaki	72	38	110	749,000
Ray Bell	71	39	110	749,000
Shin Sora	69	41	110	749,000
Toshimi Kimura	69	41	110	749,000
Mayumi Murai	75	36	111	522,000
Akiko Fukushima	74	37	111	522,000
Yuri Kawanami	72	39	111	522,000
Aiko Hashimoto	75	37	112	400,000
Man-Soo Kim	75	37	112	400,000
Ae-Sook Kim	75	37	112	400,000
Mayumi Yamada	75	37	112	400,000
Hiromi Takamura	74	38	112	400,000
Tomoyo Taguchi	74	38	112	400,000
Shoko Asano	73	39	112	400,000
Ai-Yu Tu	73	39	112	400,000
Kaori Harada	77	36	113	333,000
Huang Bie-Shyun	75	38	113	333,000
Nayoko Yoshikawa	74	39	113	333,000
Aki Takamura	73	40	113	333,000
Reiko Kashiwado	73	40	113	333,000
Kumiko Fuchi	73	40	113	333,000
Takayo Bandoh	72	41	113	333,000

Yellow Hat Tokyo Open

Wakasa Golf Links, Wakasa
Par 36-36–72; 6,355 yards

March 29-31
purse, ¥50,000,000

	SCORES			TOTAL	MONEY
Aki Takamura	67	76	64	207	¥9,000,000
Toshimi Kimura	74	75	67	216	3,950,000
Ae-Sook Kim	73	70	73	216	3,950,000
Kaori Higo	73	74	70	217	3,000,000
Marnie McGuire	71	78	70	219	2,250,000
Miyuki Shimabukuro	71	74	74	219	2,250,000
Kaori Harada	74	76	70	220	1,500,000
Takayo Bandoh	72	75	73	220	1,500,000
Chieko Nishida	70	75	75	220	1,500,000
Suzuko Maeda	70	80	71	221	967,000
Yuka Shiroto	74	75	72	221	967,000
Jae-Sook Won	71	81	70	222	664,000
Yukiyo Haga	73	79	70	222	664,000
Huang Bie-Shyun	74	77	71	222	664,000
Fumiko Muraguchi	75	76	71	222	664,000
Kayo Fukumoto	75	75	72	222	664,000
Michiko Hattori	73	76	73	222	664,000
Woo-Soon Ko	72	77	73	222	664,000
Mieko Suzuki	70	79	73	222	664,000
Junko Yasui	70	78	74	222	664,000

	SCORES			TOTAL	MONEY
Hiroko Inoue	70	77	75	222	664,000
Wu Ming-Yeh	73	79	71	223	425,000
Young-Me Lee	76	75	72	223	425,000
Natsuko Noro	71	80	72	223	425,000
Tai Yu-Chuan	75	76	72	223	425,000
Mitsuyo Hirata	73	78	72	223	425,000
Aiko Hashimoto	74	76	73	223	425,000
Ai-Yu Tu	74	76	73	223	425,000
Rie Fujiwara	72	78	73	223	425,000
Kumiko Hiyoshi	73	76	74	223	425,000

Kenshoen Ladies

Dohgo Golf Club, Ehime
Par 36-36–72; 6,277 yards

April 5-7
purse, ¥50,000,000

	SCORES			TOTAL	MONEY
Aiko Hashimoto	72	70	70	212	¥9,000,000
Kaori Higo	71	72	70	213	4,400,000
Michiko Hattori	71	70	73	214	3,500,000
Ae-Sook Kim	72	71	72	215	3,000,000
Ai-Yu Tu	77	70	69	216	2,083,000
Suzuko Maeda	70	76	70	216	2,083,000
Ok-Hee Ku	70	70	76	216	2,083,000
Aki Takamura	71	74	72	217	1,375,000
Miki Oda	74	71	72	217	1,375,000
Mikino Kubo	72	75	71	218	1,000,000
Chieko Nishida	71	78	70	219	895,000
Hisako Takeda	75	74	70	219	895,000
Aiko Takasu	72	74	73	219	895,000
Natsuko Noro	75	73	72	220	745,000
Huang Bie-Shyun	73	74	73	220	745,000
Junko Yasui	74	71	75	220	745,000
Yumi Kokubo	77	72	72	221	620,000
Rie Mitsuhashi	78	71	72	221	620,000
Miyuki Shimabukuro	73	77	72	222	508,000
Nayoko Yoshikawa	75	75	72	222	508,000
Kaori Harada	74	72	76	222	508,000
Tai Yu-Chuan	72	79	72	223	450,000
Takayo Bandoh	73	76	74	223	450,000
Kikuko Shibata	75	74	74	223	450,000
Kasumi Fujii	78	71	74	223	450,000
Masako Ichiguchi	73	76	74	223	450,000
Hiromi Takamura	74	74	75	223	450,000
Jennifer Sevil	74	77	73	224	365,000
Reiko Kashiwado	75	76	73	224	365,000
Hiroko Inoue	73	77	74	224	365,000
Chikako Matsuzawa	79	71	74	224	365,000
Wu Ming-Yeh	72	78	74	224	365,000
Michie Ohba	75	75	74	224	365,000
Mitsuyo Hirata	76	73	75	224	365,000
Mariko Watanabe	75	74	75	224	365,000
Kasumi Adachi	73	76	75	224	365,000
Akemi Yamaoka	72	76	76	224	365,000
Yukiko Ito	73	75	76	224	365,000

Mitsukoshi Cup

Segovia Golf Club, Ibaraki
Par 36-36–72; 6,109 yards

April 11-14
purse, ¥60,000,000

	SCORES				TOTAL	MONEY
Marnie McGuire	73	72	74	74	293	¥10,800,000
Kaori Harada	70	77	73	74	294	5,280,000
Aki Takamura	75	76	71	73	295	4,200,000
Ikuyo Shiotani	72	73	79	72	296	3,000,000
Junko Yasui	77	74	70	75	296	3,000,000
Akiko Fukushima	75	73	72	76	296	3,000,000
Natsuko Noro	73	76	74	74	297	1,800,000
Jennifer Sevil	72	75	76	74	297	1,800,000
Tseng Hsiu-Feng	71	75	74	77	297	1,800,000
Kaori Higo	73	72	75	78	298	1,200,000
Suzuko Maeda	74	78	74	75	301	1,140,000
Hiromi Takamura	75	77	74	76	302	990,000
Jean Bartholomew	73	77	74	78	302	990,000
Hiroe Tani	75	78	71	78	302	990,000
Yoko Inoue	71	78	72	81	302	990,000
Ok-Hee Ku	73	80	77	74	304	810,000
Tai Yu-Chuan	76	78	74	76	304	810,000
Woo-Soon Ko	74	76	80	75	305	608,000
Atsuko Kikuchi	77	77	75	76	305	608,000
Toshimi Kimura	75	78	74	78	305	608,000
Akane Ohshiro	77	75	75	78	305	608,000
Kikuko Shibata	72	78	75	80	305	608,000
Chieko Nishida	76	73	75	81	305	608,000
Aiko Hashimoto	74	78	71	82	305	608,000
Yuko Saito	74	78	78	76	306	534,000
Michiko Hattori	72	79	78	77	306	534,000
Shin Sora	73	79	76	79	307	510,000
Yuko Motoyama	70	81	74	82	307	510,000
*Yoko Nakano	74	80	79	75	308	
Wu Ming-Yeh	73	81	76	78	308	480,000
Fumiko Muraguchi	77	75	77	79	308	480,000
Takayo Bandoh	71	78	76	83	308	480,000

Nasu Ogawa

Nasu Ogawa Golf Club, Tochigi
Par 36-36–72; 6,255 yards

April 19-21
purse, ¥50,000,000

	SCORES			TOTAL	MONEY
Aki Nakano	73	73	70	216	¥9,000,000
Aiko Hashimoto	73	74	72	219	4,400,000
Keiko Arai	75	74	71	220	3,000,000
Ok-Hee Ku	74	72	74	220	3,000,000
Mitsuyo Hirata	71	75	74	220	3,000,000
Tseng Hsiu-Feng	75	70	76	221	1,875,000
Miyuki Shimabukuro	72	71	78	221	1,875,000
Hiromi Takamura	75	76	71	222	1,500,000
Marnie McGuire	76	74	73	223	1,055,000
Akemi Yamaoka	70	77	76	223	1,055,000
Woo-Soon Ko	69	76	78	223	1,055,000
Mayumi Murai	78	75	71	224	740,000
Natsuko Noro	70	81	73	224	740,000

	SCORES			TOTAL	MONEY
Yukiyo Haga	77	73	74	224	740,000
Nobuko Kizawa	70	78	76	224	740,000
Ray Bell	73	74	77	224	740,000
Ai-Yu Tu	74	72	78	224	740,000
Yuri Kawanami	76	78	71	225	458,000
Chie Yoshida	75	76	74	225	458,000
Jennifer Sevil	71	80	74	225	458,000
Hisako Higuchi	73	76	76	225	458,000
Miki Oda	72	76	77	225	458,000
Kikuko Shibata	72	76	77	225	458,000
Man-Soo Kim	73	75	77	225	458,000
Kiyoe Yamazaki	71	77	77	225	458,000
Tai Yu-Chuan	73	74	78	225	458,000
Yuko Moriguchi	71	80	75	226	375,000
Jae-Sook Won	74	77	75	226	375,000
Shin Sora	73	76	77	226	375,000
Wu Ming-Yeh	75	74	77	226	375,000
Jeanne Kei	72	76	68	226	375,000

Satake Classic

Hiroshima Country Club, Hiroshima
Par 36-36–72; 6,196 yards

April 26-28
purse, ¥50,000,000

	SCORES			TOTAL	MONEY
Laura Davies	72	66	72	210	¥9,000,000
Suzuko Maeda	72	70	68	210	4,400,000
(Davies defeated Maeda on first extra hole.)					
Aki Takamura	76	69	67	212	3,500,000
Akiko Fukushima	73	69	71	213	3,000,000
Ikuyo Shiotani	70	76	68	214	1,800,000
Kaori Harada	73	72	69	214	1,800,000
Annika Sorenstam	75	70	69	214	1,800,000
Junko Yasui	71	72	71	214	1,800,000
Hiromi Takamura	71	69	74	214	1,800,000
Chieko Nishida	72	73	70	215	1,000,000
Toshimi Kimura	72	74	70	216	865,000
Yuko Moriguchi	69	74	73	216	865,000
Shin Sora	72	70	74	216	865,000
Chie Yoshida	70	77	70	217	740,000
Kaori Higo	70	75	72	217	740,000
Woo-Soon Ko	71	76	71	218	640,000
Natsuko Noro	70	72	76	218	640,000
Liselotte Neumann	75	74	70	219	472,000
Yuka Irie	71	75	73	219	472,000
Mikako Kanamori	75	71	73	219	472,000
Jennifer Sevil	74	71	74	219	472,000
Michie Ohba	72	73	74	219	472,000
Tseng Hsiu-Feng	78	66	75	219	472,000
Yoko Inoue	72	69	78	219	472,000
Yukiyo Haga	75	73	72	220	400,000
Fuki Kido	72	75	73	220	400,000
Reiko Kashiwado	75	72	73	220	400,000
Toshiko Fujisaki	72	75	73	220	400,000
Michiko Hattori	77	73	71	221	340,000
Takayo Bandoh	75	75	71	221	340,000
Mayumi Murai	79	71	71	221	340,000

	SCORES			TOTAL	MONEY
Hisako Takeda	71	79	71	221	340,000
Keiko Arai	72	76	73	221	340,000
Kikuko Shibata	71	75	75	221	340,000
Hiromi Hirakata	72	74	75	221	340,000
Aiko Takasu	72	73	76	221	340,000

Gunze Cup World Ladies

Tokyo Yomiuri Golf Club, Tokyo
Par 36-36—72; 6,409 yards

May 2-5
purse, ¥60,000,000

	SCORES				TOTAL	MONEY
Yukiyo Haga	73	75	69	71	288	¥10,800,000
Mayumi Murai	68	76	70	75	289	5,280,000
Man-Soo Kim	74	71	68	77	290	4,200,000
Chieko Nishida	73	75	73	70	291	2,775,000
Keiko Arai	71	74	73	73	291	2,775,000
Megumi Matsuo	76	69	72	74	291	2,775,000
Michiko Hattori	72	73	70	76	291	2,775,000
Ikuyo Shiotani	75	73	71	73	292	1,500,000
Kayo Yamada	75	69	74	74	292	1,500,000
Young-Me Lee	76	68	72	76	292	1,500,000
Suzuko Maeda	75	74	72	72	293	1,032,000
Akiko Fukushima	76	73	69	75	293	1,032,000
Aiko Takasu	73	74	71	75	293	1,032,000
Carin Hj Koch	72	72	72	77	293	1,032,000
Misayo Fujisawa	76	74	71	73	294	792,000
Patty Sheehan	70	72	77	75	294	792,000
Wu Ming-Yeh	74	71	73	76	294	792,000
Fumiko Muraguchi	76	69	72	77	294	792,000
Huang Yueh-Chyn	78	71	74	72	295	612,000
Ok-Hee Ku	71	75	73	76	295	612,000
Aiko Hashimoto	70	75	75	76	296	564,000
Miyuki Shimabukuro	75	73	71	77	296	564,000
Akemi Yamaoka	74	74	73	76	297	528,000
Akane Ohshiro	78	72	71	76	297	528,000
Mikino Kubo	71	76	73	77	297	528,000
Shin Sora	72	73	75	77	297	528,000
Marie Laure de Lorenzi	72	72	78	76	298	486,000
Tai Yu-Chuan	72	75	74	77	298	486,000
Kasumi Fujii	78	72	70	78	298	486,000
*Midori Yoneyama	75	75	77	72	299	
Jennifer Sevil	75	74	73	77	299	444,000
Takayo Bandoh	73	77	72	77	299	444,000
Natsuko Noro	76	72	72	79	299	444,000
Huang Bie-Shyun	75	72	73	79	299	444,000

Yakult Ladies

Fukuoka Kokusai Country Club, Fukuoka
Par 36-36—72; 6,317 yards

May 10-12
purse, ¥60,000,000

	SCORES			TOTAL	MONEY
Kaori Harada	73	70	67	210	¥10,800,000
Mayumi Murai	73	69	73	215	5,280,000

	SCORES			TOTAL	MONEY
Ok-Hee Ku	72	74	70	216	3,600,000
Chieko Nishida	74	69	73	216	3,600,000
Aki Takamura	70	71	75	216	3,600,000
Miyuki Shimabukuro	71	74	72	217	2,100,000
Ikuyo Shiotani	72	73	72	217	2,100,000
Woo-Soon Ko	70	74	73	217	2,100,000
Akane Ohshiro	67	77	74	218	1,500,000
Akemi Yamaoka	74	75	70	219	1,200,000
Aiko Hashimoto	70	76	74	220	1,038,000
Tseng Hsiu-Feng	71	75	74	220	1,038,000
Yukiyo Haga	71	74	75	220	1,038,000
Fuki Kido	73	72	75	220	1,038,000
Fumiko Muraguchi	77	72	72	221	738,000
Hiromi Takamura	73	75	73	221	738,000
Kikuko Shibata	74	74	73	221	738,000
Yuko Saito	72	76	73	221	738,000
Yuko Motoyama	73	75	73	221	738,000
Huang Bie-Shyun	73	73	75	221	738,000
Marnie McGuire	77	74	71	222	546,000
Kumiko Hiyoshi	74	77	71	222	546,000
Kaori Higo	73	77	72	222	546,000
Chikako Matsuzawa	74	76	72	222	546,000
Yumiko Akagi	76	72	74	222	546,000
Tomoko Ueda	75	71	76	222	546,000
Aiko Takasu	75	75	73	223	480,000
Suzuko Maeda	73	76	74	223	480,000
Yuka Shiroto	74	73	76	223	480,000
Kiyoe Yamazaki	73	74	76	223	480,000
Kasumi Adachi	72	74	77	223	480,000

Chukyo TV Bridgestone

Kasugai Country Club, Aichi
Par 36-36–72; 6,304 yards

May 17-19
purse, ¥50,000,000

	SCORES			TOTAL	MONEY
Mayumi Murai	67	71	73	211	¥9,000,000
Kumiko Hiyoshi	68	69	75	212	4,400,000
Hiromi Takamura	74	70	71	215	3,000,000
Karrie Webb	70	73	72	215	3,000,000
Aki Takamura	70	72	73	215	3,000,000
Miyuki Shimabukuro	71	73	72	216	1,750,000
Kaori Higo	73	70	73	216	1,750,000
Emilee Klein	74	69	73	216	1,750,000
Marnie McGuire	71	73	73	217	1,250,000
Ikuyo Shiotani	70	77	71	218	876,000
Michiko Hattori	69	78	71	218	876,000
Fuki Kido	72	73	73	218	876,000
Kiyoe Yamazaki	72	72	74	218	876,000
Aiko Hashimoto	69	74	75	218	876,000
Akane Ohshiro	76	74	69	219	620,000
Cheng Mei-Chi	74	74	71	219	620,000
Junko Yasui	71	76	72	219	620,000
Chieko Nishida	71	74	74	219	620,000
Akemi Yamaoka	73	72	74	219	620,000
Kaori Harada	70	79	71	220	465,000
Yuko Moriguchi	78	69	73	220	465,000

	SCORES			TOTAL	MONEY
Yoko Inoue	74	76	71	221	425,000
Wu Ming-Yeh	72	78	71	221	425,000
Yuka Irie	80	70	71	221	425,000
Yuri Kawanami	74	73	74	221	425,000
Oh-Soon Lee	73	74	74	221	425,000
Kayo Yamada	70	76	75	221	425,000
Chikako Matsuzawa	75	76	71	222	360,000
Mayumi Ishii	75	76	71	222	360,000
Yuko Motoyama	73	77	72	222	360,000
Aiko Takasu	73	75	74	222	360,000
Kyoe Fumihira	73	74	75	222	360,000
Man-Soo Kim	74	72	76	222	360,000
Kyoko Ono	70	76	76	222	360,000

Toto Motors

Toto Hanno Country Club, Saitama
Par 36-36–72; 6,206 yards

May 24-26
purse, ¥50,000,000

	SCORES			TOTAL	MONEY
Shin Sora	71	71	67	209	¥9,000,000
Miyuki Shimabukuro	71	68	71	210	3,950,000
Ayako Okamoto	69	70	71	210	3,950,000
Akane Ohshiro	73	67	71	211	2,750,000
Huang Bie-Shyun	66	72	73	211	2,750,000
Takayo Bandoh	72	74	66	212	1,875,000
Tai Yu-Chuan	71	72	69	212	1,875,000
Kayo Yamada	73	73	67	213	1,024,000
Yukiyo Haga	69	75	69	213	1,024,000
Chieko Nishida	71	73	69	213	1,024,000
Suzuko Maeda	71	72	70	213	1,024,000
Reiko Kashiwado	69	74	70	213	1,024,000
Tatsuko Morimoto	74	69	70	213	1,024,000
Cheng Mei-Chi	72	69	72	213	1,024,000
Hiromi Takamura	71	73	70	214	630,000
Norimi Terasawa	71	73	70	214	630,000
Chikayo Yamazaki	69	73	72	214	630,000
Young-Me Lee	72	69	73	214	630,000
Michiko Hattori	68	73	73	214	630,000
Mayumi Murai	71	75	69	215	465,000
Marnie McGuire	73	71	71	215	465,000
Misayo Fujisawa	70	74	71	215	465,000
Kikuko Shibata	69	71	75	215	465,000
Aki Nakano	71	73	72	216	425,000
Ae-Sook Kim	71	72	73	216	425,000
Wu Ming-Yeh	70	73	73	216	425,000
Michie Ohba	69	74	73	216	425,000
Mikino Kubo	74	71	72	217	380,000
Yuko Motoyama	75	70	72	217	380,000
Satoko Sawada	73	72	72	217	380,000
Kayo Fukumoto	71	73	73	217	380,000
Akemi Yamaoka	72	71	74	217	380,000

Mitsubishi Denki

Kitarokkoh Country Club, Hyogo
Par 36-37–73; 6,263 yards

May 31-June 2
purse, ¥50,000,000

	SCORES			TOTAL	MONEY
Cheng Mei-Chi	72	70	73	215	¥9,000,000
Norimi Terasawa	69	70	76	215	4,400,000
(Cheng defeated Terasawa on second extra hole.)					
Mayumi Murai	71	72	74	217	3,500,000
Miyuki Shimabukuro	71	75	72	218	2,750,000
Yuka Shiroto	71	71	76	218	2,750,000
Aki Takamura	75	72	72	219	1,875,000
Chikako Matsuzawa	71	74	74	219	1,875,000
Michie Ohba	75	74	71	220	1,171,000
Shin Sora	76	72	72	220	1,171,000
Man-Soo Kim	73	75	72	220	1,171,000
Jennifer Sevil	74	73	73	220	1,171,000
Aiko Takasu	76	73	72	221	810,000
Aki Nakano	71	76	74	221	810,000
Fuki Kido	73	74	74	221	810,000
Natsuko Noro	72	74	75	221	810,000
Mitsuyo Hirata	74	77	71	222	585,000
Huang Bie-Shyun	74	73	75	222	585,000
Ok-Hee Ku	74	72	76	222	585,000
Ae-Sook Kim	74	72	76	222	585,000
Akiko Fukushima	69	74	79	222	585,000
Yukiyo Haga	75	75	73	223	450,000
Tai Yu-Chuan	75	74	74	223	450,000
Oh-Soon Lee	74	75	74	223	450,000
Kayo Fukumoto	73	75	75	223	450,000
Huang Yueh-Chyn	72	76	75	223	450,000
Kaori Higo	71	75	77	223	450,000
Aiko Hashimoto	74	75	75	224	375,000
Yuko Saito	75	74	75	224	375,000
Tai Yu-Hsia	74	75	75	224	375,000
Akane Ohshiro	74	74	76	224	375,000
Ai-Yu Tu	75	73	76	224	375,000
Toshimi Kimura	72	75	77	224	375,000
Kayo Yamada	73	74	77	224	375,000
Kiyoe Yamazaki	73	74	77	224	375,000
Reiko Kashiwado	71	76	77	224	375,000

Suntory Ladies

Japan Memorial Golf Club, Hyogo
Par 36-36–72; 6,342 yards

June 6-9
purse, ¥50,000,000

	SCORES				TOTAL	MONEY
Jae-Sook Won	68	71	64	72	275	¥9,000,000
Kaori Harada	70	71	64	75	280	4,400,000
Fuki Kido	71	68	71	71	281	3,500,000
Mayumi Murai	69	70	69	75	283	3,000,000
Mikino Kubo	71	73	69	71	284	2,083,000
Ae-Sook Kim	70	68	74	72	284	2,083,000
Jennifer Sevil	72	68	72	72	284	2,083,000
Akemi Yamaoka	71	72	69	73	285	1,375,000
Nobuko Kizawa	69	71	71	74	285	1,375,000

	SCORES				TOTAL	MONEY
Nayoko Yoshikawa	76	72	66	72	286	891,000
Yuko Motoyama	68	71	73	74	286	891,000
Tomoko Ueda	75	70	66	75	286	891,000
Makiko Hasegawa	71	70	70	75	286	891,000
Akane Ohshiro	72	72	69	74	287	730,000
Yukiyo Haga	69	71	72	75	287	730,000
Hisako Takeda	72	76	72	68	288	580,000
Akiko Fukushima	75	69	72	72	288	580,000
Aki Takamura	73	73	68	74	288	580,000
Kaori Higo	71	72	68	77	288	580,000
Norimi Terasawa	77	70	70	72	289	445,000
Michiko Okada	71	74	70	74	289	445,000
Natsuko Noro	74	72	68	75	289	445,000
Yumi Kokubo	74	70	71	75	290	420,000
Ray Bell	73	70	71	76	290	420,000
Ok-Hee Ku	71	77	74	69	291	380,000
Tatsuko Morimoto	74	74	72	71	291	380,000
Shin Sora	71	76	70	74	291	380,000
Cheng Mei-Chi	72	73	72	74	291	380,000
Reiko Kashiwado	74	71	72	74	291	380,000
Aki Nakano	73	69	73	76	291	380,000

Dunlop Twin Lakes

Twin Lakes Country Club, Gunma
Par 36-36–72; 6,254 yards

June 13-16
purse, ¥50,000,000

	SCORES				TOTAL	MONEY
Aiko Hashimoto	71	69	69	72	281	¥9,000,000
Mayumi Murai	73	71	71	68	283	3,350,000
Aki Nakano	68	73	74	68	283	3,350,000
Kaori Harada	72	72	69	70	283	3,350,000
Tseng Hsiu-Feng	73	71	68	71	283	3,350,000
Kumiko Hiyoshi	70	73	71	70	284	2,000,000
Kyoko Ono	72	71	72	71	286	1,625,000
Toshimi Kimura	69	77	68	72	286	1,625,000
Jennifer Sevil	73	73	70	71	287	1,250,000
Wu Ming-Yeh	73	75	70	70	288	950,000
Marnie McGuire	75	73	67	73	288	950,000
Ayako Okamoto	72	76	73	68	289	800,000
Junko Yasui	72	74	70	73	289	800,000
Nayoko Yoshikawa	69	73	73	74	289	800,000
Michiko Okada	70	78	73	69	290	650,000
Kaori Higo	76	71	71	72	290	650,000
Man-Soo Kim	70	73	72	75	290	650,000
Kiyoe Yamazaki	75	73	74	69	291	500,000
Tai Yu-Hsia	76	72	70	73	291	500,000
Shin Sora	72	72	69	78	291	500,000
Aiko Takasu	74	73	73	72	292	435,000
Misayo Fujisawa	72	72	74	74	292	435,000
Takayo Bandoh	75	73	72	73	293	400,000
Hiroko Inoue	70	76	74	73	293	400,000
Fuki Kido	73	72	74	74	293	400,000
Michie Ohba	72	75	72	74	293	400,000
Fumiko Muraguchi	76	71	70	76	293	400,000
Hisako Higuchi	73	74	73	74	294	350,000
Woo-Soon Ko	73	72	74	75	294	350,000

	SCORES				TOTAL	MONEY
Mariko Ohtani	76	70	73	75	294	350,000
Mikiko Furuya	75	73	71	75	294	350,000
Aiko Fukushima	75	71	70	78	294	350,000

Japan Women's Open Championship

Ryugasaki Country Club, Ibaraki
Par 36-36–72; 6,383 yards

June 20-23
purse, ¥70,000,000

	SCORES				TOTAL	MONEY
Aki Takamura	75	73	72	71	291	¥14,000,000
Kaori Harada	74	75	71	72	292	7,700,000
Aiko Hashimoto	73	73	77	72	295	5,425,000
Man-Soo Kim	82	71	74	69	296	3,255,000
Ayako Okamoto	75	72	76	73	296	3,255,000
*Mayumi Nakajima	79	74	71	73	297	
Hiromi Kobayashi	76	78	72	72	298	2,227,000
Jae-Sook Won	73	73	77	75	298	2,227,000
Marnie McGuire	75	74	75	75	299	1,734,000
Akemi Yamaoka	75	71	78	75	299	1,734,000
Hisako Takeda	81	74	73	72	300	1,454,000
*Han-Lee Won	74	76	72	78	300	
Yuko Saito	76	74	79	72	301	1,150,000
Toshimi Kimura	78	77	73	73	301	1,150,000
Nayoko Yoshikawa	80	75	71	75	301	1,150,000
Kiyoe Yamazaki	77	76	76	73	302	929,000
Cheng Mei-Chi	77	77	72	76	302	929,000
Akiko Fukushima	74	79	76	74	303	801,000
Miyuki Shimabukuro	73	78	74	78	303	801,000
Michiko Hattori	79	77	76	72	304	652,000
Young-Me Lee	77	77	75	75	304	652,000
Chikako Matsuzawa	77	75	77	75	304	652,000
Hisako Higuchi	82	74	73	75	304	652,000
Keiko Arai	76	78	74	76	304	652,000
Aiko Takasu	74	73	77	80	304	652,000
Michie Ohba	74	69	81	80	304	652,000
Wu Ming-Yeh	82	74	76	73	305	561,000
Jennifer Sevil	80	72	76	77	305	561,000
Huang Bie-Shyun	76	75	76	78	305	561,000
Natsuko Noro	73	76	77	79	305	561,000

Tohato Ladies

Oak Village Golf Club, Ichihara
Par 36-36–72; 6,326 yards

June 28-30
purse, ¥50,000,000

	SCORES			TOTAL	MONEY
Toshimi Kimura	74	74	75	223	¥9,000,000
Fumiko Muraguchi	73	74	78	225	4,400,000
Jennifer Sevil	73	79	75	227	2,550,000
Ikuyo Shiotani	75	76	76	227	2,550,000
Kaori Harada	81	69	77	227	2,550,000
Natsuko Noro	72	78	77	227	2,550,000
Yumi Kokubo	75	74	78	227	2,550,000
Yuko Saito	76	76	76	228	1,250,000

	SCORES			TOTAL	MONEY
Michie Ohba	75	75	78	228	1,250,000
Shin Sora	73	75	80	228	1,250,000
Aiko Hashimoto	79	73	77	229	820,000
Man-Soo Kim	78	74	77	229	820,000
Keiko Arai	78	74	77	229	820,000
Aki Nakano	73	78	78	229	820,000
Ray Bell	71	79	79	229	820,000
Fuki Kido	79	70	80	229	820,000
Tseng Hsiu-Feng	82	72	76	230	595,000
Hisako Takeda	74	77	79	230	595,000
Reiko Kashiwado	76	73	81	230	595,000
Atsuko Kikuchi	78	75	78	231	490,000
Huang Bie-Shyun	74	78	79	231	490,000
Chikako Matsuzawa	75	79	78	232	465,000
Chikayo Yamazaki	79	75	78	232	465,000
Chieko Nishida	75	73	84	232	465,000
Miho Koyama	83	72	78	233	440,000
Michiko Hattori	75	75	83	233	440,000
Jae-Sook Won	76	78	80	234	410,000
Mikako Kanamori	79	75	80	234	410,000
Nobuko Kizawa	76	76	82	234	410,000
Mayumi Ishii	78	73	83	234	410,000

Toyo Suisan

Kosaido Sapporo Country Club, Hokkaido
Par 36-36–72; 6,412 yards

July 5-7
purse, ¥50,000,000

	SCORES			TOTAL	MONEY
Ok-Hee Ku	64	73	73	210	¥9,000,000
Akiko Fukushima	68	77	67	212	3,350,000
Aki Nakano	69	74	69	212	3,350,000
Akane Ohshiro	70	72	70	212	3,350,000
Ikuyo Shiotani	71	69	72	212	3,350,000
Man-Soo Kim	67	71	75	213	2,000,000
Huang Bie-Shyun	71	76	67	214	1,625,000
Miyuki Shimabukuro	68	74	72	214	1,625,000
Yukiyo Haga	66	79	70	215	1,250,000
Shin Sora	69	75	72	216	943,000
Kaori Harada	70	73	73	216	943,000
Aki Takamura	72	70	74	216	943,000
Kikuko Shibata	70	77	70	217	765,000
Yuka Irie	70	76	71	217	765,000
Miho Koyama	71	73	73	217	765,000
Mikino Kubo	71	72	74	217	765,000
Rie Fujiwara	69	78	71	218	548,000
Akemi Yamaoka	73	73	72	218	548,000
Chieko Nishida	71	74	73	218	548,000
Fuki Kido	71	74	73	218	548,000
Kumiko Hiyoshi	71	74	73	218	548,000
Hisako Takeda	71	76	72	219	445,000
Yoko Kobayashi	70	77	72	219	445,000
Kiyoe Yamazaki	72	74	73	219	445,000
Kayo Yamada	71	75	73	219	445,000
Hisako Higuchi	70	76	73	219	445,000
Mayumi Murai	71	74	74	219	445,000
Yumi Kokubo	72	77	71	220	385,000

	SCORES			TOTAL	MONEY
Jae-Sook Won	74	74	72	220	385,000
Yumiko Akagi	72	76	72	220	385,000
Suzuko Maeda	71	76	73	220	385,000
Keiko Okano	72	75	73	220	385,000
Tseng Hsiu-Feng	73	72	75	220	385,000

Resort Trust Ladies

Maple Point Country Club, Uenohara
Par 36-36–72; 6,401 yards

July 12-14
purse, ¥50,000,000

	SCORES			TOTAL	MONEY
Aiko Hashimoto	70	68	71	209	¥9,000,000
Akiko Fukushima	74	68	67	209	4,400,000
(Hashimoto defeated Fukushima on first extra hole.)					
Ae-Sook Kim	71	72	70	213	3,250,000
Yoko Inoue	70	69	74	213	3,250,000
Yuka Irie	75	68	71	214	2,500,000
Fuki Kido	71	72	72	215	1,750,000
Yuko Moriguchi	71	72	72	215	1,750,000
Woo-Soon Ko	72	70	73	215	1,750,000
Jennifer Sevil	71	72	73	216	1,125,000
Akemi Yamaoka	70	72	74	216	1,125,000
Oh-Soon Lee	75	71	71	217	880,000
Man-Soo Kim	73	70	74	217	880,000
Misayo Fujisawa	72	76	70	218	755,000
Cheng Mei-Chi	73	72	73	218	755,000
Shin Sora	71	73	74	218	755,000
Chieko Nishida	74	73	72	219	555,000
Kiyoe Yamazaki	71	76	72	219	555,000
Hisako Higuchi	70	76	73	219	555,000
Aiko Takasu	73	72	74	219	555,000
Kikuko Shibata	73	72	74	219	555,000
Toshimi Kimura	73	75	72	220	420,000
Natsuko Noro	77	71	72	220	420,000
Yuri Kawanami	78	70	72	220	420,000
Nobuko Kizawa	74	73	73	220	420,000
Junko Yasui	75	70	75	220	420,000
Reiko Kashiwado	73	72	75	220	420,000
Akiko Ogawa	75	74	72	221	370,000
Hisako Takeda	74	74	73	221	370,000
Miyuki Shimabukuro	73	71	77	221	370,000
Aki Takamura	72	71	78	221	370,000

Katokichi Queen's Cup

Hokkaido Naie Country Club, Hokkaido
Par 36-36–72; 6,400 yards

July 19-21
purse, ¥50,000,000

	SCORES			TOTAL	MONEY
Suzuko Maeda	66	68	76	210	¥9,000,000
Akiko Fukushima	69	71	71	211	4,400,000
Michie Ohba	71	71	70	212	3,500,000
Chieko Nishida	70	74	69	213	2,500,000
Yoko Inoue	69	72	72	213	2,500,000

	SCORES			TOTAL	MONEY
Yumiko Akagi	71	70	72	213	2,500,000
Hisako Takeda	71	72	71	214	1,625,000
Yuri Kawanami	69	72	73	214	1,625,000
Aki Nakano	67	75	73	215	1,250,000
Woo-Soon Ko	76	67	73	216	930,000
Natsuko Noro	69	73	74	216	930,000
Kiyoe Yamazaki	71	70	75	216	930,000
Mikiko Furuya	75	71	71	217	745,000
Oh-Soon Lee	74	71	72	217	745,000
Norimi Terasawa	73	71	73	217	745,000
Shoko Asano	70	72	75	217	745,000
Fuki Kido	72	71	75	218	620,000
Fumiko Muraguchi	71	76	72	219	477,000
Jae-Sook Won	73	72	74	219	477,000
Jennifer Sevil	72	73	74	219	477,000
Akemi Yamaoka	73	72	74	219	477,000
Wu Ming-Yeh	70	75	74	219	477,000
Kayo Fukumoto	71	74	74	219	477,000
Kyoko Isoda	70	72	77	219	477,000
Ai-Yu Tu	75	74	71	220	385,000
Yuko Nakamura	75	73	72	220	385,000
Junko Yoshida	73	75	72	220	385,000
Junko Yasui	73	75	72	220	385,000
Toshimi Kimura	72	72	76	220	385,000
Aiko Takasu	71	73	76	220	385,000
Tseng Hsiu-Feng	69	73	78	220	385,000
Tomiko Ikebuchi	70	72	78	220	385,000

Golf 5 Ladies

Mizunami Country Club, Gifu
Par 36-36–72; 6,441 yards

July 26-28
purse, ¥50,000,000

	SCORES			TOTAL	MONEY
Yuka Irie	67	71	73	211	¥9,000,000
Marnie McGuire	71	72	68	211	4,400,000
(Irie defeated McGuire on first extra hole.)					
Woo-Soon Ko	71	72	69	212	3,500,000
Aiko Takasu	72	69	72	213	2,312,000
Oh-Soon Lee	72	69	72	213	2,312,000
Michie Ohba	72	68	73	213	2,312,000
Yuko Motoyama	72	68	73	213	2,312,000
Miyuki Shimabukuro	72	72	70	214	1,250,000
Cheng Mei-Chi	72	72	70	214	1,250,000
Ikuyo Shiotani	72	70	72	214	1,250,000
Yuko Saito	73	73	69	215	920,000
Young-Me Lee	70	74	71	215	920,000
Tseng Hsiu-Feng	70	74	72	216	795,000
Natsuko Noro	73	71	72	216	795,000
Yoko Kobayashi	70	74	72	216	795,000
Mitsuko Hamada	73	73	71	217	595,000
Jae-Sook Won	72	72	73	217	595,000
Kozue Azuma	72	72	73	217	595,000
Toshimi Kimura	74	69	74	217	595,000
Junko Yoshida	70	70	77	217	595,000
Mayumi Murai	77	70	71	218	465,000
Suzuko Maeda	73	74	71	218	465,000

	SCORES			TOTAL	MONEY
Tomoko Ueda	72	74	72	218	465,000
Kyoko Isoda	71	75	72	218	465,000
Akiko Ogawa	71	70	77	218	465,000
Huang Bie-Shyun	76	71	72	219	390,000
Hisako Takeda	74	73	72	219	390,000
Nayoko Yoshikawa	76	71	72	219	390,000
Kaori Harada	73	73	73	219	390,000
Kyoko Ono	71	75	73	219	390,000
Mariko Watanabe	72	74	73	219	390,000
Junko Yasui	71	74	74	219	390,000
Jennifer Sevil	70	74	75	219	390,000
Yuri Kawanami	72	72	75	219	390,000
Chieko Nishida	71	69	79	219	390,000

Mizuno Ladies

Asahi Kokusai Hamamura Onsen Golf Club, Tottori
Par 36-36—72; 6,330 yards

August 2-4
purse, ¥60,000,000

	SCORES			TOTAL	MONEY
Young-Me Lee	68	74	70	212	¥10,800,000
Natsuko Noro	74	69	70	213	4,020,000
Akane Ohshiro	71	69	73	213	4,020,000
Yuko Saito	67	73	73	213	4,020,000
Ayako Okamoto	65	71	77	213	4,020,000
Jae-Sook Won	73	72	69	214	2,250,000
Michiko Hattori	71	71	72	214	2,250,000
Yuko Motoyama	73	73	69	215	1,341,000
Kaori Higo	75	69	71	215	1,341,000
Jennifer Sevil	69	75	71	215	1,341,000
Kayo Yamada	72	71	72	215	1,341,000
Ok-Hee Ku	70	71	74	215	1,341,000
Ikuyo Shiotani	70	70	76	216	1,014,000
Chieko Nishida	73	75	69	217	894,000
Kaori Harada	74	73	70	217	894,000
Yukiyo Haga	73	73	71	217	894,000
Kiyoe Yamazaki	71	76	71	218	684,000
Miyuki Shimabukuro	73	73	72	218	684,000
Oh-Soon Lee	74	70	74	218	684,000
Aiko Takasu	74	68	76	218	684,000
Tseng Hsiu-Feng	76	71	72	219	558,000
Marnie McGuire	73	73	73	219	558,000
Yoko Inoue	68	77	74	219	558,000
Shoko Asano	72	73	74	219	558,000
Tai Yu-Chuan	73	71	75	219	558,000
Huang Bie-Shyun	77	72	71	220	486,000
Fumiko Muraguchi	73	76	71	220	486,000
Mikino Kubo	70	79	71	220	486,000
Tomiko Ikebuchi	76	73	71	220	486,000
Hisako Takeda	72	76	72	220	486,000
Fusako Nagata	74	73	73	220	486,000
Aki Nakano	71	75	74	220	486,000

NEC Karuizawa 72

Karuizawa 72 Country Club, Nagano
Par 36-36–72; 6,440 yards

August 9-11
purse, ¥60,000,000

	SCORES			TOTAL	MONEY
Akiko Fukushima	71	63	72	206	¥10,800,000
Ayako Okamoto	73	67	71	211	5,280,000
Yuka Irie	71	72	69	212	3,600,000
Kaori Higo	69	71	72	212	3,600,000
Natsuko Noro	68	70	74	212	3,600,000
Junko Yasui	69	71	74	214	2,250,000
Yumiko Akagi	72	70	72	214	2,250,000
Kyoko Ono	76	69	70	215	1,650,000
Akane Ohshiro	72	70	73	215	1,650,000
Ikuyo Shiotani	72	71	73	216	1,136,000
Toshimi Kimura	71	72	73	216	1,136,000
Woo-Soon Ko	69	73	74	216	1,136,000
Michiko Okada	76	70	71	217	924,000
Michiko Hattori	71	74	72	217	924,000
Reiko Kashiwado	70	74	73	217	924,000
Miki Oda	70	73	74	217	924,000
Shin Sora	70	79	69	218	664,000
Yoko Inoue	75	72	71	218	664,000
Keiko Arai	73	71	74	218	664,000
Mutsuko Maekawa	72	72	74	218	664,000
Masako Ichiguchi	72	71	75	218	664,000
Yuko Saito	71	78	70	219	564,000
Akemi Yamaoka	72	74	73	219	564,000
Mayumi Murai	71	76	73	220	522,000
Yuko Moriguchi	70	77	73	220	522,000
Tomoko Ueda	72	74	74	220	522,000
Kozue Azuma	71	75	74	220	522,000
Akiko Ogawa	71	72	77	220	522,000
Kasumi Fujii	74	74	73	221	468,000
Miyuki Shimabukuro	72	75	74	221	468,000
Fusako Nagata	73	73	75	221	468,000
Yuri Kawanami	74	72	75	221	468,000

Goyo Kensetsu Ladies

Tomisato Golf Club, Chiba
Par 36-36–72; 6,192 yards

August 23-25
purse, ¥60,000,000

	SCORES			TOTAL	MONEY
Chikayo Yamazaki	73	70	73	216	¥10,800,000
Yukiyo Haga	73	73	71	217	4,360,000
Kaori Higo	70	75	72	217	4,360,000
Yuko Saito	70	73	74	217	4,360,000
Jennifer Sevil	71	76	71	218	3,000,000
Fuki Kido	78	68	73	219	2,100,000
Mieko Nomura	72	74	73	219	2,100,000
Natsuko Noro	68	72	79	219	2,100,000
Michiko Hattori	74	71	75	220	1,206,000
Akane Ohshiro	68	76	76	220	1,206,000
Keiko Arai	68	76	76	220	1,206,000
Chie Yoshida	71	72	77	220	1,206,000
Akemi Yamaoka	74	75	72	221	882,000

	SCORES			TOTAL	MONEY
Yuko Moriguchi	77	72	72	221	882,000
Kaori Harada	75	73	73	221	882,000
Tatsuko Morimoto	71	72	78	221	882,000
Suzuko Maeda	79	72	71	222	702,000
Woo-Soon Ko	71	76	75	222	702,000
Ayako Shibata	75	76	72	223	549,000
Michie Ohba	73	77	73	223	549,000
Sachiko Oshima	72	77	74	223	549,000
Yoko Kobayashi	72	75	76	223	549,000
Yoko Inoue	71	73	79	223	549,000
Aiko Hashimoto	76	75	73	224	474,000
Marnie McGuire	76	74	74	224	474,000
Mikiko Furuya	75	74	75	224	474,000
Toshimi Kimura	70	78	76	224	474,000
Mitsuyo Hirata	71	77	76	224	474,000
Yuko Motoyama	74	72	78	224	474,000
Wu Ming-Yeh	75	75	75	225	432,000

Fuji Sankei Classic

Fujizakura Country Club, Yamanashi
Par 36-36—72; 6,409 yards

August 30-September 1
purse, ¥60,000,000

	SCORES			TOTAL	MONEY
Ayako Okamoto	72	67	71	210	¥10,800,000
Akane Ohshiro	70	71	70	211	5,280,000
Marnie McGuire	71	69	72	212	4,200,000
Natsuko Noro	73	72	68	213	3,300,000
Aiko Hashimoto	72	70	71	213	3,300,000
Huang Hui-Fan	73	72	70	215	2,400,000
Fumiko Muraguchi	74	70	72	216	2,100,000
Ikuyo Shiotani	72	71	74	217	1,650,000
Misayo Fujisawa	71	72	74	217	1,650,000
Michiko Okada	72	76	71	219	1,020,000
Ae-Sook Kim	74	73	72	219	1,020,000
Kayo Yamada	74	73	72	219	1,020,000
Jennifer Sevil	75	71	73	219	1,020,000
Akiko Fukushima	74	71	74	219	1,020,000
Keiko Arai	72	70	77	219	1,020,000
Nadene Gole	73	69	77	219	1,020,000
Akemi Yamaoka	74	75	71	220	690,000
Mayumi Murai	75	73	72	220	690,000
Takayo Bandoh	73	75	72	220	690,000
Li Wen-Lin	73	73	74	220	690,000
Kaori Harada	73	75	73	221	540,000
Yoko Inoue	72	76	73	221	540,000
Kumiko Hiyoshi	74	74	73	221	540,000
Fusako Nagata	74	74	73	221	540,000
Aki Nakano	73	74	74	221	540,000
Chieko Nishida	72	75	74	221	540,000
Kaori Higo	73	73	75	221	540,000
Yukiyo Haga	76	70	75	221	540,000
Toshiko Fujisaki	73	71	77	221	540,000
Yuko Motoyama	69	79	74	222	450,000
Woo-Soon Ko	75	72	75	222	450,000
Mieko Nomura	75	72	75	222	450,000
Tomoko Ueda	74	73	75	222	450,000

	SCORES			TOTAL	MONEY
Shin Sora	71	75	76	222	450,000
Michiko Hattori	71	75	76	222	450,000

Japan LPGA Championship

Nagaoka Country Club, Niigata
Par 36-36–72; 6,427 yards

September 5-8
purse, ¥65,000,000

	SCORES				TOTAL	MONEY
Ikuyo Shiotani	74	70	71	68	283	¥11,700,000
Kaori Higo	74	67	74	69	284	5,720,000
Michiko Hattori	73	67	73	72	285	4,550,000
Keiko Arai	74	70	69	74	287	3,575,000
Akiko Fukushima	70	71	69	77	287	3,575,000
Kaori Harada	73	71	71	73	288	2,600,000
Aiko Hashimoto	73	75	70	72	290	2,112,000
Suzuko Maeda	69	75	74	72	290	2,112,000
Takayo Bandoh	73	73	75	70	291	1,360,000
Yukiyo Haga	72	73	74	72	291	1,360,000
Toshimi Kimura	71	72	73	75	291	1,360,000
Chieko Nishida	71	73	75	73	292	1,059,000
Natsuko Noro	73	72	73	74	292	1,059,000
Akane Ohshiro	72	75	72	74	293	962,000
Shin Sora	75	70	73	77	295	864,000
Ayako Okamoto	71	71	75	78	295	864,000
Ae-Sook Kim	76	74	72	74	296	669,000
Tatsuko Morimoto	74	75	73	74	296	669,000
Nayoko Yoshikawa	75	72	74	75	296	669,000
Yoko Inoue	72	76	72	76	296	669,000
Woo-Soon Ko	75	74	75	73	297	533,000
Marnie McGuire	74	74	74	75	297	533,000
Aki Takamura	75	71	75	76	297	533,000
Wu Ming-Yeh	74	76	69	78	297	533,000
Sachiko Oshima	72	74	72	79	297	533,000
Mikiko Furuya	79	72	71	76	298	487,000
Aki Nakano	72	72	77	77	298	487,000
Akemi Yamaoka	76	75	74	74	299	435,000
Yuko Moriguchi	76	73	76	74	299	435,000
Huang Bie-Shyun	77	73	73	76	299	435,000
Kayo Yamada	72	77	74	76	299	435,000
Michiko Okada	74	73	76	76	299	435,000
Mayumi Murai	75	74	72	78	299	435,000

Yukijirushi Ladies Tokai Classic

Ryosen Golf Club, Mie
Par 36-36–72; 6,351 yards

September 13-15
purse, ¥60,000,000

	SCORES			TOTAL	MONEY
Suzuko Maeda	73	71	66	210	¥10,800,000
Aiko Hashimoto	72	69	70	211	5,280,000
Akiko Fukushima	73	68	71	212	4,200,000
Aki Nakano	74	70	69	213	3,300,000
Kaori Harada	70	72	71	213	3,300,000
Miyuki Shimabukuro	76	70	68	214	2,250,000

	SCORES			TOTAL	MONEY
Ayako Okamoto	69	69	76	214	2,250,000
Yuko Moriguchi	74	74	67	215	1,327,000
Kaori Higo	72	74	69	215	1,327,000
Yuko Saito	73	72	70	215	1,327,000
Woo-Soon Ko	72	72	71	215	1,327,000
Ikuyo Shiotani	70	72	73	215	1,327,000
Jennifer Sevil	72	73	71	216	948,000
Michiko Okada	71	72	73	216	948,000
Chieko Nishida	72	75	70	217	708,000
Fusako Nagata	75	72	70	217	708,000
Michiko Hattori	73	72	72	217	708,000
Toshiko Fujisaki	75	70	72	217	708,000
Junko Yasui	70	74	73	217	708,000
Shin Sora	68	75	74	217	708,000
Aiko Takasu	72	73	73	218	546,000
Young-Me Lee	74	75	70	219	498,000
Tseng Hsiu-Feng	70	78	71	219	498,000
Hisako Takeda	76	72	71	219	498,000
Masako Ichiguchi	71	76	72	219	498,000
Fumiko Muraguchi	73	72	74	219	498,000
Ok-Hee Ku	73	71	75	219	498,000
Yukiyo Haga	73	70	76	219	498,000
Kozue Azuma	75	73	72	220	432,000
Natsuko Noro	71	76	73	220	432,000
Jae-Sook Won	68	79	73	220	432,000
Kayo Yamada	70	76	74	220	432,000

Miyagi TV Cup Ladies Open

Yashiro Golf Club, Miyagi
Par 36-36–72; 6,263 yards

September 20-22
purse, ¥50,000,000

	SCORES			TOTAL	MONEY
Mikino Kubo	68	75	71	214	¥9,000,000
Michie Ohba	73	69	73	215	3,950,000
Michiko Hattori	72	69	74	215	3,950,000
Shin Sora	72	71	73	216	2,750,000
Kaori Higo	70	67	79	216	2,750,000
Yukiyo Haga	73	73	71	217	1,750,000
Kayo Yamada	74	70	73	217	1,750,000
Nayoko Yoshikawa	71	69	77	217	1,750,000
Jennifer Sevil	71	75	72	218	1,058,000
Ok-Hee Ku	72	72	74	218	1,058,000
Chieko Nishida	73	71	74	218	1,058,000
Tseng Hsiu-Feng	75	73	71	219	825,000
Ikuyo Shiotani	72	75	72	219	825,000
Yumiko Akagi	71	72	76	219	825,000
Miki Oda	74	73	73	220	725,000
Kyoko Ono	73	75	73	221	575,000
Toshiko Fujisaki	74	74	73	221	575,000
Aiko Hashimoto	74	73	74	221	575,000
Akemi Yamaoka	72	74	75	221	575,000
Aiko Takasu	72	70	79	221	575,000
Aki Nakano	74	74	74	222	450,000
Fusako Nagata	73	75	74	222	450,000
Mayumi Murai	71	76	75	222	450,000
Suzuko Maeda	70	73	79	222	450,000

	SCORES			TOTAL	MONEY
Yuko Motoyama	75	73	75	223	405,000
Yuri Kawanami	76	72	75	223	405,000
Tomoko Ueda	73	75	75	223	405,000
Huang Hui-Fan	73	75	75	223	405,000
Akiko Fukushima	71	74	78	223	405,000
Takayo Bandoh	74	75	75	224	350,000
Fukumi Tani	77	71	76	224	350,000
Yukiko Koyama	77	71	76	224	350,000
Yuko Inoue	70	77	77	224	350,000
Akane Ohshiro	73	71	80	224	350,000
Oh-Soon Lee	72	72	80	224	350,000

Kosaido Ladies Golf Cup

Chiba Kosaido Country Club, Chiba
Par 36-36–72; 6,240 yards

September 27-29
purse, ¥60,000,000

	SCORES			TOTAL	MONEY
Tseng Hsiu-Feng	70	71	72	213	¥10,800,000
Kaori Harada	72	74	69	215	4,740,000
Young-Me Lee	72	69	74	215	4,740,000
Hiromi Takamura	76	73	68	217	2,775,000
Yukiyo Haga	72	75	70	217	2,775,000
Rie Fujiwara	75	72	70	217	2,775,000
Ai-Yu Tu	73	73	72	217	2,775,000
Miyuki Shimabukuro	74	73	71	218	1,402,000
Mariko Ohtani	69	78	71	218	1,402,000
Mitsuyo Hirata	71	75	72	218	1,402,000
Yuko Inoue	70	75	73	218	1,402,000
Chieko Nishida	75	73	71	219	930,000
Huang Hui-Fan	73	75	71	219	930,000
Ae-Sook Kim	74	73	72	219	930,000
Tomoko Ueda	73	73	73	219	930,000
Hisako Higuchi	73	70	76	219	930,000
Marnie McGuire	75	75	70	220	624,000
Ikuyo Shiotani	75	73	72	220	624,000
Aki Takamura	75	72	73	220	624,000
Kikuko Shibata	74	73	73	220	624,000
Yuko Saito	72	74	74	220	624,000
Yuko Motoyama	73	71	76	220	624,000
Shin Sora	75	76	70	221	510,000
Fumiko Omata	74	74	73	221	510,000
Ok-Hee Ku	75	72	74	221	510,000
Masako Ichiguchi	73	73	75	221	510,000
Kazumi Takada	71	75	75	221	510,000
Nayoko Yoshikawa	73	77	72	222	456,000
Akemi Yamaoka	72	76	74	222	456,000
Huang Hui-Fan	73	75	74	222	456,000
Aiko Hashimoto	72	73	77	222	456,000

Takara World Invitational

Caledonian Golf Club, Chiba
Par 36-36—72; 6,204 yards

October 3-6
purse, ¥80,000,000

	SCORES				TOTAL	MONEY
Ikuyo Shiotani	71	71	69	71	282	¥14,400,000
Kris Tschetter	73	70	72	69	284	7,040,000
Mayumi Murai	74	70	72	70	286	5,200,000
Ayako Okamoto	71	71	70	74	286	5,200,000
Ae-Sook Kim	73	70	72	72	287	3,600,000
Young-Me Lee	72	72	71	72	287	3,600,000
Michiko Hattori	73	70	73	72	288	2,400,000
Nayoko Yoshikawa	73	74	68	73	288	2,400,000
Laura Davies	70	70	74	74	288	2,400,000
Akane Ohshiro	73	71	75	70	289	1,524,000
Yuko Motoyama	72	76	70	71	289	1,524,000
Kayo Yamada	74	74	73	69	290	1,328,000
Kyoko Ono	71	75	69	75	290	1,328,000
Rachel Hetherington	77	66	73	75	291	1,208,000
Marnie McGuire	74	70	76	72	292	1,048,000
Chieko Nishida	74	74	70	74	292	1,048,000
Aiko Takasu	73	69	76	74	292	1,048,000
Woo-Soon Ko	72	75	72	74	293	888,000
Aki Nakano	72	76	76	70	294	736,000
Kozue Azuma	71	76	76	71	294	736,000
Jennifer Sevil	71	75	76	72	294	736,000
Akemi Yamaoka	75	70	75	74	294	736,000
Natsuko Noro	70	77	77	71	295	672,000
Fumiko Omata	69	74	74	78	295	672,000
Tseng Hsiu-Feng	73	74	77	72	296	632,000
Mikino Kubo	75	73	75	73	296	632,000
Natsuko Inoue	72	76	73	75	296	632,000
Kiyoe Yamazaki	77	71	76	73	297	600,000
Jae-Sook Won	76	74	73	75	298	568,000
Keiko Arai	74	75	73	76	298	568,000
Miyuki Shimabukuro	77	72	72	77	298	568,000

Fujitsu Ladies

Hamano Golf Club, Chiba
Par 36-36—72; 6,386 yards

October 11-13
purse, ¥60,000,000

	SCORES			TOTAL	MONEY
Akiko Fukushima	69	68	68	205	¥10,800,000
Jae-Sook Won	68	69	68	205	5,280,000
(Fukushima defeated Won on third extra hole.)					
Fusako Nagata	72	71	68	211	3,900,000
Aiko Takasu	72	69	70	211	3,900,000
Akemi Yamaoka	72	71	69	212	3,000,000
Miyuki Shimabukuro	70	74	69	213	2,100,000
Jennifer Sevil	72	72	69	213	2,100,000
Mikiko Furuya	72	71	70	213	2,100,000
Mikino Kubo	72	73	69	214	1,350,000
Marnie McGuire	73	70	71	214	1,350,000
Nayoko Yoshikawa	73	73	69	215	1,008,000
Mayumi Murai	72	73	70	215	1,008,000
Mitsuko Hamada	70	74	71	215	1,008,000

	SCORES			TOTAL	MONEY
Toshimi Kimura	75	70	70	215	1,008,000
Yoko Inoue	76	68	71	215	1,008,000
Keiko Arai	74	73	69	216	654,000
Yukiyo Haga	72	74	70	216	654,000
Yuko Moriguchi	75	71	70	216	654,000
Kumiko Hiyoshi	70	75	71	216	654,000
Aki Takamura	72	73	71	216	654,000
Shin Sora	72	73	71	216	654,000
Ikuyo Shiotani	73	71	72	216	654,000
Ayako Okamoto	72	71	73	216	654,000
Huang Yu-Chen	77	70	70	217	504,000
Huang Yueh-Chyn	73	74	70	217	504,000
Kikuko Shibata	74	72	71	217	504,000
Young-Me Lee	70	75	72	217	504,000
Junko Yasui	71	74	72	217	504,000
Rie Fujiwara	73	72	72	217	504,000
Michiko Okada	72	71	74	217	504,000

Kibun Ladies Classic

Arashiyama Country Club, Saitama
Par 73; 6,453 yards

October 18-20
purse, ¥50,000,000

	SCORES			TOTAL	MONEY
Akane Ohshiro	70	70	75	215	¥9,000,000
Young-Me Lee	71	70	75	216	4,400,000
Mikino Kubo	72	76	69	217	2,750,000
Akiko Fukushima	74	71	72	217	2,750,000
Hiromi Kobayashi	69	74	74	217	2,750,000
Woo-Soon Ko	72	70	75	217	2,750,000
Kaori Higo	73	72	73	218	1,625,000
Kyoko Ono	75	68	75	218	1,625,000
Chieko Nishida	71	72	76	219	1,022,000
Yuko Saito	71	71	77	219	1,022,000
Jae-Sook Won	71	70	78	219	1,022,000
Toshiko Fujisaki	71	70	78	219	1,022,000
Michiko Hattori	74	72	74	220	795,000
Yuko Moriguchi	71	73	76	220	795,000
Ok-Hee Ku	72	69	79	220	795,000
Tomoko Ueda	74	75	72	221	620,000
Yukiyo Haga	75	72	74	221	620,000
Mitsuyo Hirata	73	72	76	221	620,000
Natsuko Noro	73	71	77	221	620,000
Reiko Kashiwado	72	77	73	222	480,000
Kozue Azuma	74	75	73	222	480,000
Hiromi Takamura	70	77	75	222	480,000
Fumiko Omata	74	71	77	222	480,000
Fumiko Muraguchi	78	69	76	223	445,000
Yuko Motoyama	70	74	79	223	445,000
Akemi Yamaoka	68	75	80	223	445,000
Li Wen-Lin	74	73	77	224	420,000
Tai Yu-Chuan	72	74	78	224	420,000
Wu Ming-Yeh	76	74	75	225	370,000
Michiko Okada	74	76	75	225	370,000
Ayako Shibata	75	75	75	225	370,000
Mayumi Yamada	73	77	75	225	370,000
Kayoko Ikoma	76	74	75	225	370,000

	SCORES			TOTAL	MONEY
Mayumi Murai	72	76	77	225	370,000
Marnie McGuire	73	74	78	225	370,000
Shin Sora	75	71	79	225	370,000

Nichirei International

Ami Golf Club, Ibaragi-ken
Par 36-36–72; 6,337 yards

October 25-27
purse, US$675,000

FIRST DAY
Better Ball

Pat Hurst and Barb Mucha (USA) defeated Miyuki Shimabukuro and Mayumi Murai, 64-66.
Ok-Hee Ku and Natsuko Noro (Japan) defeated Emilee Klein and Kris Tschetter, 64-68.
Karrie Webb and Michelle McGann (USA) defeated Aki Nakano and Kaori Higo, 65-67.
Akane Ohshiro and Toshimi Kimura (Japan) defeated Joan Pitcock and Barb Whitehead, 67-69.
Marianne Morris and Penny Hammel (USA) tied Ayako Okamoto and Akiko Fukushima, 68-68.
Suzuko Maeda and Yukiyo Haga (Japan) defeated Julie Piers and Hiromi Kobayashi, 65-68.
Chris Johnson and Tracy Kerdyk (USA) defeated Ikuyo Shiotani and Aki Takamura, 65-70.
Kaori Harada and Michiko Hattori (Japan) defeated Val Skinner and Brandie Burton, 68-70.
Jane Geddes and Liselotte Neumann (USA) defeated Marnie McGuire and Aiko Hashimoto, 64-67.

POINTS: United States 4½, Japan 4½

SECOND DAY
Better Ball

Whitehead and McGann (USA) defeated Shiotani and Takamura, 64-68.
Johnson and Kerdyk (USA) defeated McGuire and Hashimoto, 65-69.
Nakano and Higo (Japan) defeated Klein and Tschetter, 65-66.
Webb and Pitcock (USA) defeated Ohshiro and Kimura, 64-66.
Piers and Kobayashi (USA) defeated Shimabukuro and Murai, 65-66.
Ku and Noro (Japan) defeated Morris and Hammel, 64-68.
Mucha and Hurst (USA) defeated Maeda and Hattori, 65-68.
Geddes and Neumann (USA) defeated Okamoto and Fukushima, 64-65.

POINTS: United States 7, Japan 2

THIRD DAY
Singles

Mucha (USA) defeated Kimura, 71-75.
Pitcock (USA) defeated McGuire, 71-74.
Hurst (USA) tied Nakano, 74-74.
Burton (USA) defeated Haga, 68-75.
Piers (USA) defeated Maeda, 73-74.
Morris (USA) tied Shimabukuro, 76-76.
Whitehead (USA) defeated Murai, 72-76.
Skinner (USA) defeated Ohshiro, 74-81.
Klein (USA) tied Shiotani, 71-71.

Takamura (Japan) defeated Neumann, 71-72.
Hattori (Japan) defeated Hammel, 71-73.
Higo (Japan) defeated Tschetter, 71-72.
Johnson (USA) tied Noro, 73-73.
Hashimoto (Japan) defeated Geddes, 68-73.
Kerdyk (USA) defeated Harada, 74-75.
Fukushima (Japan) defeated Kobayashi, 71-72.
Ku (Japan) defeated McGann, 71-77.
Webb (USA) defeated Okamoto, 68-73.

TOTAL POINTS: United States 21½, Japan 14½

(Each member of USA team received $24,000; each member of Japanese team received $13,500.)

Toray Japan Queens Cup

Tone Golf Club, Ibaragi-ken
Par 36-36–72; 6,064 yards

November 1-3
purse, US$750,000

	SCORES			TOTAL	MONEY
Mayumi Hirase	70	70	72	212	US$112,500
Laura Davies	71	73	68	212	69,819
(Hirase defeated Davies on third extra hole.)					
Hiromi Kobayashi	67	74	72	213	50,949
Barb Whitehead	70	74	70	214	39,627
Susie Redman	70	74	71	215	29,248
Maggie Will	69	71	75	215	29,248
Jennifer Sevil	74	74	68	216	19,876
Marianne Morris	74	72	70	216	19,876
Liselotte Neumann	74	71	71	216	19,876
Tina Barrett	75	76	66	217	13,530
Marnie McGuire	72	73	72	217	13,530
Young-Me Lee	72	73	72	217	13,530
Sherri Steinhauer	71	74	72	217	13,530
Penny Hammel	71	74	72	217	13,530
Deb Richard	70	76	72	218	10,340
Ikuyo Shiotani	69	77	72	218	10,340
Akane Ohshiro	74	71	73	218	10,340
Carin Hj Koch	75	76	68	219	8,200
Brandie Burton	76	74	69	219	8,200
Chieko Nishida	71	79	69	219	8,200
Yoko Inoue	72	76	71	219	8,200
Kim Saiki	71	77	71	219	8,200
Kristal Parker-Gregory	75	72	72	219	8,200
Yuka Irie	71	74	74	219	8,200
Jane Geddes	73	71	75	219	8,200
Julie Piers	73	78	69	220	6,666
Junko Yasui	72	75	73	220	6,666
Akiko Fukushima	72	74	74	220	6,666
Caroline Pierce	77	74	70	221	5,685
Natsuko Noro	72	78	71	221	5,685
Chris Johnson	75	73	73	221	5,685
Aiko Takasu	73	73	75	221	5,685
Miyuki Shimabukuro	72	72	77	221	5,685
Michie Ohba	70	73	78	221	5,685

Itoen Ladies

Great Island Club, Chiba
Par 36-36–72; 6,459 yards

November 8-10
purse, ¥60,000,000

	SCORES			TOTAL	MONEY
Laura Davies	68	65	66	199	¥10,800,000
Kaori Harada	72	72	70	214	4,740,000
Akiko Fukushima	71	71	72	214	4,740,000
Natsuko Noro	73	71	71	215	3,300,000
Kaori Higo	73	69	73	215	3,300,000
Mieko Nomura	70	77	69	216	2,100,000
Michiko Hattori	72	72	72	216	2,100,000
Mayumi Murai	69	73	74	216	2,100,000
Ok-Hee Ku	73	71	73	217	1,278,000
Fuki Kido	69	74	74	217	1,278,000
Akane Ohshiro	72	70	75	217	1,278,000
Kyoko Isoda	74	73	71	218	984,000
Mayumi Hirase	72	73	73	218	984,000
Young-Me Lee	72	73	73	218	984,000
Yuko Motoyama	69	75	74	218	984,000
Aki Takamura	74	76	69	219	774,000
Vicki Goetze	74	75	70	219	774,000
Yuko Moriguchi	72	72	75	219	774,000
Keiko Arai	76	75	70	221	600,000
Kayo Yamada	76	75	70	221	600,000
Li Wen-Lin	73	75	73	221	600,000
Shin Sora	73	74	74	221	600,000
Junko Yasui	73	78	71	222	528,000
Ayako Okamoto	71	77	74	222	528,000
Woo-Soon Ko	71	75	76	222	528,000
Mariko Ohtani	71	73	78	222	528,000
Akemi Yamaoka	73	71	78	222	528,000
Yuko Saito	71	72	79	222	528,000
Yuri Kawanami	75	76	72	223	450,000
Fumiko Muraguchi	74	76	73	223	450,000
Chieko Nishida	73	75	75	223	450,000
Cheng Mei-Chi	72	76	75	223	450,000
Suzuko Maeda	76	72	75	223	450,000
Tomoko Ueda	73	74	76	223	450,000
Mikiko Furuya	71	76	76	223	450,000

Daio Seishi Elleair Open

Elleair Golf Club, Matsuyama, Kagawa
Par 36-36–72; 6,326 yards

November 15-17
purse, ¥65,000,000

	SCORES			TOTAL	MONEY
Ok-Hee Ku	71	69	66	206	¥11,700,000
Michiko Hattori	69	71	71	211	5,720,000
Yuko Moriguchi	70	73	70	213	4,550,000
Marnie McGuire	73	71	70	214	3,250,000
Vicki Goetze	69	73	72	214	3,250,000
Akemi Yamaoka	71	72	71	214	3,250,000
Yoko Inoue	69	76	70	215	1,950,000
Kaori Harada	72	72	71	215	1,950,000
Akiko Fukushima	72	69	74	215	1,950,000
Akane Ohshiro	75	70	71	216	1,300,000

	SCORES			TOTAL	MONEY
Rie Mitsuhashi	72	74	71	217	1,040,000
Ayako Okamoto	74	71	72	217	1,040,000
Woo-Soon Ko	73	72	72	217	1,040,000
Wu Ming-Yeh	71	73	73	217	1,040,000
Mayumi Hirase	73	71	73	217	1,040,000
Shin Sora	72	69	76	217	1,040,000
Ai-Yu Tu	70	70	77	217	1,040,000
Jae-Sook Won	72	74	72	218	715,000
Ritsu Imahori	75	71	72	218	715,000
Michiko Okada	72	72	74	218	715,000
Young-Me Lee	73	75	71	219	637,000
Aiko Hashimoto	73	75	72	220	598,000
Yuka Irie	78	70	72	220	598,000
Yuko Nakamura	77	72	71	220	598,000
Miyuki Shimabukuro	70	78	73	221	539,500
Tomiko Ikebuchi	75	72	74	221	539,500
Chikayo Yamazaki	72	74	75	221	539,500
Cheng Mei-Chi	74	72	75	221	539,500

Meiji Nyugyo Cup

Aoshima Golf Club, Miyazaki
Par 36-36—72; 6,346 yards

November 21-24
purse, ¥60,000,000

	SCORES				TOTAL	MONEY
Yoko Inoue	71	69	72	69	281	¥10,800,000
Akiko Fukushima	68	77	72	65	282	5,400,000
Natsuko Noro	72	69	73	69	283	3,300,000
Ok-Hee Ku	71	70	70	72	283	3,300,000
Akane Ohshiro	72	74	70	68	284	2,040,000
Aki Nakano	75	69	72	68	284	2,040,000
Woo-Soon Ko	72	70	75	69	286	1,680,000
Marnie McGuire	71	69	75	71	286	1,680,000
Ikuyo Shiotani	71	72	71	72	286	1,680,000
Kaori Harada	72	68	71	75	286	1,680,000
Yukiyo Haga	73	73	71	70	287	1,440,000
Jennifer Sevil	72	70	76	70	288	1,380,000
Michiko Hattori	75	73	74	67	289	1,200,000
Junko Yasui	73	74	73	69	289	1,200,000
Kaori Higo	72	73	73	71	289	1,200,000
Yuko Saito	71	70	76	72	289	1,200,000
Kumiko Hiyoshi	74	75	69	71	289	1,200,000
Aki Takamura	73	73	74	70	290	990,000
Mayumi Murai	76	70	73	71	290	990,000
Chieko Nishida	72	71	69	79	291	900,000
Akemi Yamaoka	77	74	73	68	292	870,000
Suzuko Maeda	72	75	74	72	293	825,000
Hisako Takeda	72	73	73	75	293	825,000
Kyoko Ono	73	75	76	70	294	766,000
Fumiko Muraguchi	72	74	75	73	294	766,000
Aiko Hashimoto	73	76	76	70	295	720,000
Shin Sora	75	73	77	72	297	645,000
Wu Ming-Yeh	75	72	74	76	297	645,000
Michiko Okada	70	76	75	76	297	645,000
Keiko Arai	75	74	71	77	297	645,000